W9-CSA-235

Philosophy of Religion

Philosophy of Religion

An Anthology

SEVENTH EDITION

MICHAEL REA

University of Notre Dame

LOUIS P. POJMAN

Late of the United States Military Academy, West Point

CENGAGE
Learning·

Australia • Brazil • Mexico • Singapore • United Kingdom • United States

CENGAGE
Learning®

**Philosophy of Religion: An Anthology,
Seventh Edition**
Michael Rea and Louis P. Pojman

Product Director: Suzanne Jeans

Product Manager: Debra Matteson

Content Developer: Ian Lague

Content Coordinator: Joshua Duncan

Media Developer: Phil Lanza

Associate Marketing Manager: Shanna Shelton

Content Project Manager: Alison Eigel Zade

Art Director: Kristina Mose-Libon, PMG

Manufacturing Planner: Sandee Milewski

Rights Acquisition Specialist: Roberta Broyer

Production Service & Compositor: Cenveo®
Publisher Services

Cover Designer: PreMediaGlobal

Cover Image: © Danita Delimont/Gallo
Images/Getty Images

© 2015, 2012, 2008 Cengage Learning

ALL RIGHTS RESERVED. No part of this work covered by the copyright herein may be reproduced, transmitted, stored, or used in any form or by any means graphic, electronic, or mechanical, including but not limited to photocopying, recording, scanning, digitizing, taping, web distribution, information networks, or information storage and retrieval systems, except as permitted under Section 107 or 108 of the 1976 United States Copyright Act, without the prior written permission of the publisher.

For product information and technology assistance, contact us at
Cengage Learning Customer & Sales Support, 1-800-354-9706

For permission to use material from this text or product, submit all requests online at **www.cengage.com/permissions**.
Further permissions questions can be emailed to
permissionrequest@cengage.com.

Library of Congress Control Number: 2013949046

ISBN-13: 978-1-285-19732-6

ISBN-10: 1-285-19732-1

Cengage Learning
200 First Stamford Place, 4th Floor
Stamford, CT 06902
USA

Cengage Learning is a leading provider of customized learning solutions with office locations around the globe, including Singapore, the United Kingdom, Australia, Mexico, Brazil and Japan. Locate your local office at **international.cengage.com/region**.

Cengage Learning products are represented in Canada by Nelson Education, Ltd.

For your course and learning solutions, visit **www.cengage.com**.

Purchase any of our products at your local college store or at our preferred online store **www.cengagebrain.com**.

Instructors: Please visit **login.cengage.com** and log in to access instructor-specific resources.

Printed in the United States of America
1 2 3 4 5 6 7 17 16 15 14 13

Dedicated to the memory of Louis A. and Helen Pojman and to the memory of Robert E. Rea

Contents

Preface

Welcome to the seventh edition of *Philosophy of Religion: An Anthology*. This volume, originally edited by the late Louis Pojman, has been in print for more than twenty-five years, and it has enjoyed wide use throughout the profession. The purpose of the volume is to provide an accessible and engaging introduction to some of the most important ideas, topics, and figures in contemporary philosophy of religion. It is exciting to have once again the opportunity to revise and update the text, breathing fresh air into several sections of the work while at the same time retaining what has consistently proven useful to a wide variety of instructors and students over the life of the anthology.

The present edition takes further steps in the direction of diversifying the perspectives represented in the volume. The first subsection, entitled "Concepts of God and the Ultimate," has been expanded with two new selections that focus on concepts central to the Hindu and Mahayana Buddhist religious traditions. Two new readings by Grace Jantzen help to bring a feminist perspective to the sections on the problem of evil and religious experience. There is a brand new subsection entitled "The Nature of Faith," with readings by Richard Swinburne, Lara Buchak, and Daniel Howard-Snyder. The section on the problem of evil has also been expanded. In addition to Grace Jantzen's essay, I have added a classic science-fiction story by Ursula K. LeGuin to the "Historical and Literary Perspectives" subsection, essays by J. L. Schellenberg and Michael J. Murray to provide greater coverage of the problem of divine hiddenness, and an essay by Daniel Howard-Snyder on the so-called skeptical theist response to the problem of evil. There are also new readings by Evan Fales, Linda Zagzebski, and Lynne Rudder Baker in the sections on religious experience, faith and reason, and death and immortality (respectively).

Those familiar with earlier editions will also notice that the volume has been substantially reorganized, reflecting a shift in pedagogy. Whereas earlier editions treated religion and science, religious experience, and miracles as independent topics, the present edition, in recognition of the strong interconnections among these topics, treats them together under the heading "Religion and Experience." The new subheadings in this section make explicit the fact that mystical experience and perception of God are the primary focus of the readings usually grouped under the generic label "religious experience," and that the epistemology of *testimony* is centrally at issue in the subsection on miracles. Also, as previously mentioned, the section on faith and reason now includes a subsection on the nature of faith; and the section on the problem of evil now explicitly covers the topic of divine hiddenness as well. Finally, there have been several minor alterations to most of the sections—a few older papers have been either removed or replaced by newer or more "classic" material.

Despite the changes, much has remained the same. The same format of general introductions followed by individual classic and contemporary readings has been continued, and the same topics are still treated: traditional arguments for the existence of God, religious experience, the problem of evil, the attributes of God, death and immortality, faith and reason, religion and science, and religious pluralism. In some cases, more difficult readings have been replaced by simpler ones. There are also individual introductions to each reading. Some of the general introductions have been modified or updated, but here too I have tried to preserve as much as possible of what was already good and useful, making, for the most part, only very modest changes for the sake of clarity or accuracy.

This book has been used successfully in both undergraduate and graduate courses. It functions well as a stand-alone text, or may be profitably accompanied by a single-author introductory textbook, such as my own *Introduction to the Philosophy of Religion*, co-authored with Michael Murray and published by Cambridge University Press (2008).

I am grateful to the anonymous reviewers who offered advice that led to the various changes in the present edition of the text, and to Joann Kozyrev and Ian Lague at Cengage Learning for helpful advice and support at each of the various stages of this project. I am also grateful to Bob Hartman, who proofread portions of the manuscript for me, and to Kathryn Pogin and Meg Schmitt for valuable assistance in finding some of the readings that have been incorporated in the present edition. Thanks are also due to Stacey Dong and Meg Schmitt for help in clearing the permissions.

I have left Lou Pojman's original dedication of the volume intact, but also added one of my own, in honor of the memory of my father. Finally, I want to close with words of gratitude to my friends Darci (Cadis) Bradbury, Megan (Cadis) Hudzinski, Robert Timm, Tracy Peck, Kevin McClure, Mark Rodriguez, and Marc Bellaart; to my sister, Cheryl Marzano; to my children, Aaron, Kristina, Gretchen, Matthias, and Penelope Rea; and to my wife, Chris. All of these people have, in one way or another, influenced my thinking about the issues treated in this book, inspired me to want to learn how to make those issues more accessible to others, or both.

Michael C. Rea
University of Notre Dame
South Bend, Indiana

PART I

The Concept of God

XENOPHANES (c. 570–c. 478 B.C.E.) SAID THAT "men create the gods in their own image." He said this in no small part because the gods worshipped by his ancient Greek contemporaries were remarkably humanlike. They took human form, entered into human relationships, suffered from human vices and other imperfections, had very human desires, and so on. Similarly, Sigmund Freud (1858–1939) thought that we (Western monotheists) create God in the image of our fathers. In his view, belief in God was the result of projecting upon the heavens our need for a father figure who will serve as our protector and guarantor of justice, just as our earthly fathers did in our childhoods. On his view, the Western monotheistic concept of God is primarily just a reflection of our own ideals about fatherhood.

Views like these do not sit well with religious believers. We prefer to think that our concept of deity comes from divine revelation or from sober philosophical reflection. It should not just be a reflection of our ideals and anthropocentric biases. But the experiences and texts that human beings treat as divine revelation differ widely in their representations of God or the gods. Philosophical intuitions vary widely as well. It is a challenge to sort through the competing voices, and the challenge is made all the more difficult by the fact that, in sorting them out, we know that we must take care to avoid falling into the trap of crafting the divine in our own image and likeness.

One way—maybe the best way—to avoid falling into that trap is to devote some effort to thinking through some of the different "models" for thinking about the divine that are suggested by the sacred texts and religious traditions of the world and by our own philosophical intuitions. We probably cannot avoid relying on some driving model (thinking of God as our heavenly father, say) in our theorizing about God, but at least we can make ourselves aware that we are doing so, and we can recognize some of the limits and alternatives to the model(s) we have chosen. In Part I.A., we consider a few different models of deity with just this aim in mind.

In Part I.B., we turn to a discussion of specific divine attributes. Although there are various models with which we might fruitfully work in our thinking about divinity, contemporary philosophy of religion has mostly been occupied with the *perfect-being* model of God. As we shall see in Part I.A., working with this model means taking as our starting point the idea that God is perfect and allowing that idea to play the dominant role in shaping our decisions about which attributes to ascribe to God. Philosophers working with this model generally agree that God, if God exists, is at least omniscient (all-knowing), omnipotent (all-powerful), and omnibenevolent (perfectly good). Indeed, *theism* is typically defined as the view that there exists a being with those three attributes. *Classical theism*, however, goes a few steps further, adding to theism the claim that God is immutable (not subject to change), impassible (not subject to passion), simple (lacking parts), timeless (not subject to the flow of time), and in no way dependent on other things. Because theism and classical theism have taken center stage in contemporary philosophy of religion, our treatment of divine attributes focuses on controversies associated with attributes drawn from these lists.

I.A. CONCEPTS OF GOD AND THE ULTIMATE

Introduction

IN THE JEWISH AND CHRISTIAN SCRIPTURES, we are given a variety of models for structuring our thinking about God. Some are clearly metaphorical or analogical, others not. God is represented as a shepherd, as our heavenly father, and as the stern employer of the parable of the talents. God is a farmer sowing seed or tending to a vineyard, a mighty warrior going before his nation in battle, and our companion in paradise. God is a winged protector under whose pinions we can take shelter, and a perfect being for whom nothing is impossible and compared with whom nobody is good. God is a righteous judge who will dutifully, even if grudgingly, respond to the persistent pestering of a neighbor, and the "Ancient of Days," seated on a throne of fire. The Upanishads identify God as the invisible "Spirit behind the eyes and ears" who fills the (demi)gods with wonder. Philosophical reflection has identified God as the uncaused cause, the ground of all being, and the ordering principle of the universe.

Theorizing about God in a systematic way involves decisions about which of these models to prioritize and which to de-emphasize, especially when conflicts arise. Would a loving father *really* behave like a stern employer toward his beloved child? Perhaps, yes; but there are lines to be drawn, and questions to be raised about whether God would be *more* like the loving father in some particular instance or more like the stern employer. We must also make decisions about which aspects of our models to take seriously and which not. Does God really have wings or any sort of body at all? Is God really a spirit somehow located "behind" our eyes and ears? Of course not, we think; but then what shall we make of the long tradition in the West that associates *maleness* with God? Is there something more correct about referring to God as "father" rather than "mother"? We must furthermore make decisions about how to interpret our models. Suppose we endorse the claim that God is, for us, a loving heavenly parent. What exactly does it *mean* to be a loving parent? Could one be a loving parent and withhold one's presence from one's child? Suppose we say that God is perfect. What exactly does perfection involve? Can one be perfect and be subject to the flow of time? Can a perfect being be subject to passion or change? All of these decisions will be contentious; all are fodder for philosophical debate.

We begin here with selections from several ancient Greek philosophers: Xenophanes (mentioned at the beginning of this introduction), Aristotle (384–322 B.C.E.), the Stoic philosopher Cleanthes of Assos (c. 330–c. 230 B.C.E.), and Diogenes Laertius (third century, C.E.), who is reporting on the thought of Zeno of Citium (334–262 B.C.E.), the founder of Stoicism. Together, these thinkers lay out some of the most important ancient Greek philosophical conceptions of deity. For Xenophanes, as we have seen, the gods are merely human constructs. For Aristotle, God plays an explanatory role: the first cause of all things, the "unmoved mover" whose motion serves as the ultimate explanation of the motion of everything else. For the Stoics, God is best thought of as the "soul" of the world. On their view, the soul of a *body* is its ordering principle: The activity of the soul is the ultimate explanation for the ordered and coordinated behavior of all of the body's parts. As the Stoics see it, the divine *logos*, or "reason," plays precisely the same role in the universe. The "Hymn of Cleanthes," which is included among the selections from ancient Greek philosophers, reflects some of these ideas.

The ancient Greek views just mentioned came to underlie some of the most important developments in medieval philosophical theology. But since the time of Anselm of Canterbury (1033–1109), a different but related idea about God has dominated Western philosophical theology (in the Christian tradition, anyway). That idea is the *perfect-being* model of God. *Perfect-being theology*, described more fully in this section's essay by Thomas V. Morris, is a method of theorizing about God wherein one takes as a starting point the idea that God is perfect and then relies on intuitions about perfection to reach conclusions about what God is like. Of course, there is nothing in the enterprise of perfect-being theology that would preclude using (say) scripture to arrive at truths about God. So the method is not *purely* philosophical. But part of what it means to allow our idea of perfection to structure our thinking about God is to allow it to color our interpretation of scripture, even as we also allow scripture to inform our understanding of the nature of perfection.

Earlier, we noted that the medieval philosopher-theologians endorsed what is now called *classical theism*—a view according to which God is not subject to change, passion, time, decomposition, or dependence. Classical theism is perhaps best seen as what one gets when one does perfect-being theology under the influence of ancient Greek philosophical notions about perfection. Indeed, when people speak of the "God of the philosophers," it is often the God of classical theism that they have in mind. One important question, however, is whether the so-called God of the philosophers has any real claim to being *the God of Abraham, Isaac, and Jacob*, or *God, the Father of Jesus*, or *God, the object of our ultimate concern*.

Some critics of classical theism are more or less content to work within the framework of perfect-being theology but argue that scriptural representations of

God need to be given a lot more weight than (Greek-influenced) philosophical intuitions in informing our understanding of perfection. The proponents of *open theism* are among those who support this way of thinking. As Clark Pinnock notes in the third reading of this section, the God of open theism is temporal, subject to change and passion, responsive to creation, and endowed with less than fully detailed foreknowledge of what will happen as events in time unfold. There is no suggestion that this view involves thinking of God as less than perfect, however; rather, the idea is simply that classical theism embodies inadequate assumptions about what it would mean for God to be a perfect person.

Not everyone, however, is content to theorize about God in the way that the perfect-being theologians do. For some philosophers and (surprisingly) many theologians, humans simply are not equipped to build true theories about what God is like. Although there are many perspectives from which one might raise this concern, one common idea is that the main obstacle to our theoretical efforts is *divine transcendence*. To say that God is transcendent is to say that God is so different from us as to be largely—maybe even almost entirely—beyond human categories of thought. Thus, in the eyes of many contemporary theologians, although we can perhaps structure our thinking about God with various metaphors and models, we need to abandon the illusion that some particular model will help us to "get everything right" about God.

For Sallie McFague, writing in this section's fourth essay, this is a freeing thought: We are free to explore the usefulness for our time and circumstances of a variety of different models for thinking about God, some of which are themselves ways of "imagining and expressing divine transcendence and immanence." (The term *immanence* refers to the idea that God is somehow *in* the world.) One such model—harking back to the ancient Stoics—involves the idea of the world as God's body.

Paul Tillich is another theologian who maintains that divine transcendence pushes much of our thought about God into the realm of "mere" metaphor and modeling. As Tillich argues in this section's fifth essay, God is, first and foremost, our "ultimate concern." As such, God is beyond *everything* in the world—even beyond the category of existence. This might seem to suggest that, on Tillich's view, God simply does not exist. But to say that would be misleading. Tillich writes in a tradition that is deeply skeptical of the idea that God can be non-metaphorically classified in terms of human categories. Most people share this concern with respect to overtly anthropomorphic categories—like *father* or *mighty warrior*. But some, including Tillich, insist that even the classification *being* is one that God must be seen as transcending. For Tillich, God is the "ground of being" or, indeed, "being-itself." What exactly this might mean is, of course, a serious and difficult question. But, according to Tillich, one consequence of it is that, apart from the bare "unsymbolic" claim that God is "being-itself," nothing more can be said about God that is not symbolic or metaphorical.

There may be real virtue in trying to avoid both anthropomorphism and undue reliance on philosophical intuition in developing our conception of deity. Still, one concern that might be raised against views like Tillich's is that the concept of God that one arrives at by way of his methods still looks very much like just another "God of the philosophers", rather than a God before whom we might dance and sing and fall to our knees in worship (to echo some memorable imagery from the twentieth-century German philosopher, Martin Heidegger). On a related note, one might worry that Tillich's way of understanding God undermines much of what is important in religious *practice*—perhaps most centrally, the *love of God*. Although Martin Buber's essay in this section was published eight years before the appearance of Tillich's *Systematic Theology*, Buber raises a similar concern about understandings of God that, like Tillich's, emphasize divine transcendence. Focusing on the work of the German-Jewish philosopher Hermann Cohen, Buber notes the tension within Cohen's thought between thinking of God as, on the one hand, "beyond existence" (as Tillich does) and, on the other hand, as one whom we can love.

With the final two essays in this section we turn our attention toward two Eastern religious traditions—Hinduism and (Mahayana) Buddhism. In "The Vedic-Upanisadic Conception of God," Sushanta Sen examines whether the conception of deity in the Vedas, the sacred scriptures of Hinduism, more closely resembles Western monotheism or some form of polytheism. Sen makes the case that in the Upanishadic portion of the Vedas, in any case, the relevant conception of deity is monotheistic. In the course of doing so, Sen explains Upanishadic ideas about the attributes of God and about the status of "minor" divinities. The article also explores God's transcendence and God's relationship to creation.

In contrast to the other essays in this section, Christopher Ives's "Emptiness: Soteriology and Ethics in Mahayana Buddhism" does not articulate a conception of any sort of god, but presents for our consideration instead the Buddhist conception of a nondivine "Ultimate." Mahayana Buddhism is the greater of the two main traditions within Buddhism (the lesser being Theravada Buddhism). As Ives traces out the history, the Buddha himself rejected the idea of an eternal, independent self (which, as Sen notes, is effectively identified with God in Hinduism). But Nagarjuna, one of the most important philosophers within the Mahayana tradition, urged taking the further step of denying the independent reality of the so-called *dharmas*, the various mental and physical factors that give rise to the ever-changing processes that we (mistakenly) identify with the self. As Ives understands it, this doctrine effectively implies that *nothing* has a "self" (where "having a self" presumably means having some independent reality), and so everything is *empty* in just the sense that nothing has independent existence in and of itself.

Ives emphasizes that Emptiness "is not a religious ultimate in the sense of a transcendent Being or eternal Oneness." But in reading Ives's account of Emptiness together with Tillich's essay, it is interesting to note that much of what Ives says about Emptiness directly mirrors what Tillich says about God. Emptiness is beyond all distinctions; it is beyond even the distinction between being and non-being; it gives rise to all things; and it is the ground of all being. There are differences too, of course; but the similarities are indeed striking.

I.A.1

Selections from Ancient Greek Philosophers

XENOPHANES (Fragments)

[1] Homer and Hesiod ascribed to the gods whatever is infamy and reproach among men: theft and adultery and deceiving each other.

[2] Mortals suppose that the gods are born and have clothes and voices and shapes like their own.

[3] But if oxen, horses, and lions had hands or could paint with their hands and fashion works as men do, horses would paint horse-like images of gods and oxen ox-like ones, and each would fashion bodies like their own.

[4] The Ethiopians consider the gods flat-nosed and black; the Thracians blue-eyed and red-haired.

[5] There is one god, among gods and men the greatest, not at all like mortals in body or mind.

[6] He sees as a whole, thinks as a whole, and hears as a whole.

[7] But without toil he moves everything by the thought of his mind.

[8] He always remains in the same place, not moving at all, nor is it fitting for him to change his position at different times.

[9] Everything comes from earth and returns to earth in the end.

[10] No man knows or ever will know the truth about the gods and about everything I speak of: for even if one chanced to say the complete truth, yet oneself knows it not; but seeming is wrought over all things.

[11] Not from the beginning have the gods revealed all things to mortals, but by long seeking men find what is better.

ARISTOTLE (SELECTIONS FROM *METAPHYSICS* 12.3, 6–7, AND 9)

3. [...]

There are three kinds of substances, (a) One kind is matter, which is a *this* in appearance, for what exists by contact and not by organic unity is matter and an underlying subject; (b) another is nature, which is a *this*, and it is that to which something changes, and a possession; and (c) a third is the composite of the two, which is an individual, as for example Socrates or Callias.

In some cases, that which is a *this* does not exist apart from the composite substance.

[...]

6. Since three kinds of substances were named, two of them physical and one immovable, we should discuss the latter, in view of the fact that there must be some eternal substance which is immovable. For substances are the first of all things, and if they are all destructible, all things are destructible. But it is impossible for motion either to be generated or to be destroyed; for it always existed. The same applies to time; for if there is no time, neither

Xenophanes fragments reprinted from Forest Baird and Walter Kaufmann, eds., *Philosophic Classics: Vol. I: Ancient Philosophy*, 2nd Edition, © 1997, p. 16. Reprinted by permission of Pearson Education, Inc., Upper Saddle River, NJ. Aristotle selections reprinted from *Aristotle's Metaphysics*, translated with glossary and introduction by Hippocrates G. Apostle (Peripatetic Press 1979). Reprinted by permission of Peripatetic Press. The Hymn of Cleanthes is reprinted from James Adams, *The Vitality of Platonism* (Cambridge: Cambridge University Press, 1911). Selections from Diogenes *Lives* are reprinted from Diogenes Laertius, *Lives and Opinions of Eminent Philosophers*, trans. C. D. Younge (London: Bohn, 1853).

can there be a *before* and an *after* in time. And so motion, too, is continuous in the same manner as time is; for either motion and time are the same, or time is an *attribute* of motion. But motion cannot be continuous except with respect to place, and of this motion, only the one which is circular.

Moreover, if there is a thing which can move other things or can act upon them but which will not *actually* do so, then there will be no motion; for that which has a potency may not be *actualizing* it. So there is no gain even if we posit eternal substances, like those who posit the Forms, unless there is in them a principle which can cause a change. But even such a principle is not enough (nor is any substance other than the Forms), for, if this principle will not be in activity, there will be no motion. Moreover, if the substance of such a principle is a potency, still this is not enough even if this principle is in activity, for motion will not be eternal; for that which exists potentially may not be existing [*actually*]. Hence, there must be a principle of such a kind that its *substance* is *actuality*. Moreover, such substances must be without matter; for they must be eternal, if indeed something else is also eternal. They must exist, then, as *actualities*.

Yet there is a *difficulty*; for it seems that whatever exists in *actuality* also has the potency for it, but that whatever has a potency need not *actualize* it, and so potency seems to be prior to *actuality*. But if this is so, nothing will exist; for something may have the potency to be and still not be. And indeed, the same impossibility follows from the statements of the theologians who generate the universe from Night, or of the physicists who say that all things were together. For how will anything be moved if no cause exists in *actuality*? Matter itself will certainly not move itself, but carpentry will move it; and neither the menses nor the earth will move themselves, but the seeds will act on the earth and the semen on the menses.

This is why some thinkers, like Leucippus and Plato, posit eternal activity; for they say that motion is eternal. But they do not state why this exists nor which it is, nor yet its manner or the cause of it. For nothing is moved at random, but there must always be something, just as it is at present with

physical bodies which are moved in one way by nature but in another by force or by the intellect or by something else. Then again, which of them is first? For this makes a great difference. Plato cannot even state what it is that he sometimes considers to be the principle, that is, that which moves itself; for, as he himself says, the soul came after, and it is generated at the same time as the universe.

Now to regard potency as prior to *actuality* is in one sense right and in another sense not right; and we have already stated how this is so. That *actuality* is prior is confirmed by Anaxagoras (for *Intelligence* according to him exists in *actuality*), by Empedocles (who posits *Friendship* and *Strife*), and by others, such as Leucippus, who say that motion always exists. If so, then *Chaos* or *Night* did not exist for an infinite time, but the same things existed always, whether passing through cycles or in some other way, if indeed *actuality* is prior to potency. So if the same things always take place in cycles, there must be something, say A, which always remains and is in activity in the same way. But if there is to be generation and destruction, there must be something else, say B, which is always in activity now in one way and now in another. So it is necessary for it to be active in one way according to itself and in another according to something else; then the latter is either still another thing, say C, or the first thing. Surely, it must be the first thing; for otherwise C would still be its own cause and the cause of B. So it is better to say that it is the first, for it is this that is the cause of being in activity always in the same way, and it is something else that is the cause of being in activity in another way; and so it is evident that that which is always active in distinct ways requires two causes. And, in fact, it is in this way that motions take place. So why should we seek other principles?

7. Since the account given in this manner is possible, and if it were not, the universe would have been generated from *Night* or from the *togetherness of all things* or from nonbeing, the *difficulties* may be regarded as solved, and so there is something which is always moved with an unceasing motion, which is circular; and this is clear not only by arguments but also from the facts. So, the first heaven must be eternal; and further, there is also

something which this moves. And since that which is moved and is a mover is thus an intermediate, there is something which causes motion without being moved, and this is eternal, a substance, and an *actuality*. And this is the way in which the object of desire or the intelligible object moves, namely, without itself being moved. Of these, the primary objects are the same; for the object of *desire* is that which *appears* to be noble, and the primary object of wish is that which *is* noble. We desire because it seems rather than it seems because we desire; and thinking is the starting-point. Now the intellect is moved by the intelligible, and things which are intelligible in virtue of themselves are in one of the two columns of opposites; and of these, substances are primary, and of substances, that which is simple and in *actuality* is primary. Oneness is not the same as the simple; for "one" signifies a measure, but "simple" signifies the manner in which something exists. Moreover, both the noble and that which is chosen for its own sake are in the same column of opposites; and that which is primary is always the best, or by analogy so.

That the final cause exists in immovable things is clear by distinguishing the two meanings of "final cause." For the final cause may be (a) for some thing or (b) that for the sake of which, and of these the one may exist but the other may not; and it [the final cause] causes motion as something which is loved, and that which is moved moves the others. If, then, something is moved, it can be otherwise than as it is; so even if the primary locomotion exists as an *actuality,* still that which is moved qua being moved can be otherwise with respect to place, even if not with respect to its *substance*. And since there is some mover which causes motion but is itself immovable and exists as *actuality*, this can in no way be otherwise than as it is. Now of all changes locomotion is primary, and of locomotions the circular is primary; and it is this motion which the immovable mover causes. This mover, then, exists of necessity; and if so, then nobly, and as such, it is a first principle. For "necessity" has the following senses: (a) by force, which is contrary to a thing's tendency, (b) that without which the good is impossible, and (c) that

which cannot be otherwise but exists without qualification.

Such, then, is the principle upon which depends the heaven and nature. And its *activity* is like the best which we can have but for a little while. For it exists in this manner eternally (which is impossible for us), since its *actuality* is also pleasure. And it is because of this [activity] that being awake, sensing, and thinking are most pleasant, and hopes and memories are pleasant because of these. Now thinking according to itself is of the best according to itself, and thinking in the highest degree is of that which is best in the highest degree. Thus, in partaking of the intelligible, it is of Himself that the Intellect is thinking; for by apprehending and thinking it is He Himself who becomes intelligible, and so the Intellect and its intelligible object are the same. For that which is capable of receiving the intelligible object and the *substance* is the intellect, and the latter is in *actuality* by possessing the intelligible object; so that the possession of the intelligible is more divine than the potency of receiving it, and the contemplation of it is the most pleasant and the best. If, then, the manner of God's existence is as good as ours sometimes is, but eternally, then this is marvelous, and if it is better, this is still more marvelous; and it is the latter. And life belongs to God, for the *actuality* of the intellect is life, and He is *actuality*; and His *actuality* is in virtue of itself a life which is the best and is eternal. We say that God is a living being which is eternal and the best; so life and continuous duration and eternity belong to God, for this is God.

Those who believe, as the Pythagoreans and Speusippus do, that the most noble and the best are not in the principle, because the principles of plants and of animals are also causes but nobility and completeness are in what comes from them, do not think rightly. For the seed comes from other things which are prior and complete, and that which is first is not the seed but the complete thing. One might say, for example, that prior to the seed is the man, not the man who comes from this seed but the man from whom this seed comes.

It is evident from what has been said that there exists a substance which is eternal and immovable and separate from sensible things. It has also been shown that this substance cannot have any magnitude but is without parts and indivisible. For it causes motion for an infinite time, but no finite thing has infinite potency. Since every magnitude is either infinite or finite, this substance cannot have a finite magnitude because of what we said, and it cannot be infinite in view of the fact that there exists no infinite magnitude at all. Moreover, it cannot be affected or altered; for all the other motions are posterior to locomotion. It is clear, then, why these facts are so.

[. . .]

9. Certain problems arise with regard to The Intellect [God]; for He seems to be the most divine of things manifest to us, yet there are certain difficulties as to how He can exist as such. For if He is not thinking of anything, why the veneration of Him? He is like a man who sleeps. And if He is thinking, but what decides this thinking is something else (for the *substance* of that which decides thinking is not thinking, but a potency), then He cannot be the best substance. For it is because of [the act of] thinking that honor belongs to Him. Moreover, whether His *substance* is intellect or thinking, of what does He think? Either He thinks of Himself or of something else; and if something else, then either always of the same thing or sometimes of one thing and sometimes of another. But does it make any difference or not whether He is thinking of that which is noble rather than of any chance thing? Would it not be absurd to be *thinking* of certain things? Clearly, then, He is thinking of that which is most divine and most honorable, and He is not changing; for change would be for the worse, and this change would then be a motion.

First, then, if He were not thinking but a potency, it is reasonable that the continuity of His thinking would be fatiguing Him. Moreover, it is clear that something else would be more honorable than The Intellect, namely, the object of thought; for to think or thinking may belong even to that which thinks of the worst objects, so that if this is to be avoided (for there are even things which it is better not to see than to see), Thinking would not be the best of things. It is of Himself, then, that The

Intellect is thinking, if He is the most excellent of things, and so Thinking is the thinking of Thinking.

But it appears that *knowledge* and sensation and opinion and *thought* are always of other objects, and only incidentally of themselves. Moreover, if thinking and being thought are distinct, in virtue of which of these does goodness belong to The Intellect? For to be thinking and to be an object of thought are not the same. Or is it not that in some cases *knowledge* and its object are the same? In the productive sciences, this object is the *substance* or the essence but without the matter, in the theoretical sciences it is the formula and the thought. Accordingly, since the intellect and the object of thought are not distinct in things which have no matter, the two will be the same, and so both thought and the object of thought will be one.

Further, there remains the problem whether the object of Thinking is composite; for if so, Thinking would be changing in passing from one part of the whole to another part. Is it not the case that what has no matter is indivisible, like the human intellect, or even that which is thinking of a composite object in an interval of time? For it does not possess goodness in this part or in that part but possesses the highest good in the whole, though it is distinct from it. It is in this manner that Thinking is the thinking of Himself through all eternity.

CLEANTHES OF ASSOS (HYMN TO ZEUS)

O God most glorious, called by many a
    name,
Nature's great King, through endless years
    the same;
Omnipotence, who by thy just decree
Controllest all, hail, Zeus, for unto thee
Behooves thy creatures in all lands to call.
We are thy children, we alone, of all
On earth's broad ways that wander to and
    fro,
Bearing thine image whereso'er we go.

Wherefore with songs of praise thy power
  I will forth show
Lo! yonder Heaven, that round the earth
  is wheeled,
Follows thy guidance, still to thee doth
  yield
Glad homage; thine unconquerable hand
Such flaming minister, the levin brand,
Wieldeth, a sword two-edged, whose
  deathless might
Pulsates through all that Nature brings to
  light;
Vehicle of the universal Word, that flows
Through all, and in the light celestial
  glows
Of stars both great and small. A King of
  Kings
Through ceaseless ages, God, whose
  purpose brings
To birth, whate'er on land or in the sea
Is wrought, or in high heaven's
  immensity;
Save what the sinner works infatuate.
Nay, but thou knowest to make crooked
  straight:
Chaos to thee in order: in thine eyes
The unloved is lovely, who didst
  harmonize
Things evil with things good, that there
  should be
One Word through all things
  everlastingly.
One Word—whose voice alas! the wicked
  spurn;
Insatiate for the good their spirits yearn:
Yet seeing see not, neither hearing hear
God's universal law, which those revere,
By reason guided, happiness who win.
The rest, unreasoning, diverse shapes of sin
Self-prompted follow: for an idle name
Vainly they wrestle in the lists of fame:
Others inordinately riches woo,
Or dissolute, the joys of flesh pursue.
Now here, now there they wander,
  fruitless still,
Forever seeking good and finding ill.

Zeus the all-bountiful, whom darkness
  shrouds,
Whose lightning lightens in the
  thunderclouds;
Thy children save from error's deadly
  away:
Turn thou the darkness from their souls
  sway:
Vouchsafe that unto knowledge they
  attain;
For thou by knowledge art made strong to
  reign
O'er all, and all things rulest righteously.
So by thee honoured, we will honour
  thee,
Praising thy works continually with songs,
As mortals should; nor higher meed
  belongs
E'en to the gods, than justly to adore
The universal law for evermore.

ZENO OF CITIUM (SELECTIONS FROM DIOGENES LAERTIUS'S *LIVES AND OPINIONS OF EMINENT PHILOSOPHERS*)

They think that there are two general principles in the universe, the active and the passive. That the passive is matter, an existence without any distinctive quality. That the active is the reason which exists in the passive, that is to say, God.... [T]hat he, being eternal, and existing throughout all matter, makes everything.... But they say that principles and elements differ from one another. And Zeno, the Cittiaean, lays down this doctrine in his treatise on Essence.... [T]hat the one had no generation or beginning, and will have no end; but that the elements may be destroyed by the operation of fire. Also that the elements are bodies, but principles have no bodies and no forms, and elements too have forms.

[...]

They also teach that God is unity, and that he is called Mind, and Fate, and Jupiter, and by many other names besides. And that, as he was in the beginning by himself, he turned into water the whole substance which pervaded the air; and as the seed is contained in the produce, so too, he being the seminal principle of the world, remained behind in moisture, making matter fit to be employed by himself in the production of those things which were to come after; and then, first of all, he made the four elements, fire, water, air, and earth. And Zeno speaks of these in his treatise on the Universe....

Now an element is that out of which at first all things which are are produced, and into which all things are resolved at last. And the four elements are all equally an essence without any distinctive quality, namely, matter; but fire is the hot, water the moist, air the cold, and earth the dry—though this last quality is also common to the air. The fire is the highest, and that is called aether, in which first of all the sphere was generated in which the fixed stars are set, then that in which the planets resolve; after that the air, then the water; and the sediment as it were of all is the earth, which is placed in the centre of the rest.

They also speak of the world in a threefold sense; at one time meaning God himself, whom they call a being of a certain quality, having for his peculiar manifestation universal substance, a being imperishable, and who never had any generation, being the maker of the arrangement and order that we see; and who, after certain periods of time, absorbs all substance in himself, and then re-produces it from himself. And this arrangement of the stars they call the world, and so the third sense is one composed of both the preceding ones. And the world is a thing which is peculiarly of such and such a quality consisting of universal substance ... being a system compounded of heaven and earth, and all the creatures which exist in them; or it may be called a system compounded of Gods and men, and of the things created on their account. And the heaven is the most remote circumference of the world, in which all the Divine Nature is situated.

Again, the world is inhabited and regulated according to intellect and providence ... since mind penetrates into every part of the world, just as the soul pervades us; but it is in a greater degree in some parts, and in a less degree in others. For instance, it penetrates as a habit, as, for instance, into the bones and sinews; and into some it penetrates as the mind does, for instance, into the dominant principle. And thus the whole world, being a living thing, endowed with a soul and with reason, has the aether as its dominant principle....

[...]

They also say that God is an animal immortal, rational, perfect, and intellectual in his happiness, unsusceptible of any kind of evil, having a foreknowledge of the world and of all that is in the world; however, that he has not the figure of a man; and that he is the creator of the universe, and as it were, the Father of all things in common, and that a portion of him pervades everything, which is called by different names according to its powers; for they call him Δία [Dia] as being the person (ὁί ὄν) everything is, and Ζῆνα [Zaena], inasmuch as he is the cause of life, (τοῦ Ζῆν), or because he pervades life. And Ἀθηνα [Athena], with reference to the extension of his dominant power over the aether (εἰς αἰθέρα). And Ἥρα [Hera], on account of his extension through the air (εἰς ἀέρα). And Ἥφαιστος [Hephaestos], on account of his pervading fire, which is the chief instrument of art; and Ποσειδων, [Poseidon], as pervading moisture, and Δημήτηρ [Demeter], as pervading the earth (Γῆ). And in the same way, regarding some other of his peculiar attributes, they have given him other names.

The substance of God is asserted by Zeno to be the universal world, and the heaven....

I.A.2

The Concept of God

THOMAS V. MORRIS

Thomas V. Morris (1952–) was professor of philosophy at the University of Notre Dame until the late 1990s, when he left to found the Morris Institute for Human Values. He is best known for his work in philosophical theology. In the present chapter, excerpted from his book Our Idea of God, *Morris explains and defends the method of* perfect-being theology.

In the fifth century B.C., the Greek poet Pindar posed the question "What is God?" and presented the answer "Everything." Whatever its intellectual merits, given the time and place of its utterance, this answer considered by Pindar was clearly not a very discriminating response. Nor was it a claim that would be accepted by many traditional religious believers.

The view which seems to have been expressed so succinctly by Pindar, the belief that God is everything or, as it is more typically stated, the belief that everything is God, is usually called *pantheism*. Most religious people, at least most people within the more advanced religious traditions of the world, have used the word 'God' and its correlates in other languages not to refer in this way to everything in general, but rather to refer only to something in particular, something quite ultimate, a being on whom we and our world depend. This is the religious view known as *theism*, the belief in a God distinct from all other things. Any belief that there are two or more such beings independent of one another, and each properly considered divine, is a brand of *polytheism*. The belief that there is only one ultimate divine being, the conviction proclaimed in one way or another by Judaism, Christianity and Islam, is called *monotheism*.

Throughout human history, there have been many different conceptions of the divine. And this fact in itself poses us a problem. The problem is not just how we can arrive at our own idea of God. The problem is how we can arrive at the best idea of God, a conception worthy of our greatest energies, intellectual and otherwise.

THE PROBLEM OF METHOD

When we reflect on ultimate religious issues, what precise concept of deity will we be employing? And how can this be decided? With this latter question, we confront the premier problem of method in philosophical theology. Is there some single method for arriving at an idea of God? And if so, then why are there so many differences among people as to how we should describe the divine? Are there rather many different rival methods for arriving at a basic conception of deity? And if there are, which method is to be preferred? How is this issue to be decided? Is there a way of rationally choosing a best method for thinking about God? Before we can hope to make any real progress in our attempt to think about God, we must confront this barrage of questions and seek to

Reprinted from Thomas V. Morris, *Our Idea of God* (University of Notre Dame Press edition, 1991). Used with permission of the author.

determine whether they can be answered with any significant degree of confidence.

In every science, the issue of method is of great importance. For without a reliable method of discovery or testing, we can never be confident of our ability to attain reliable beliefs, and thus knowledge, in any such area, where we are moving beyond the bounds of immediate experience. Individual sciences have begun to flourish only as their practitioners have come to agree on the appropriateness and basic trustworthiness of particular methods for dealing with their most fundamental problems. And in so far as theology, in its own unique way, purports to be, in effect, a science of God and things divine, it too must face and grapple with the issue of method if it is to flourish.

Intelligent and rational disagreement of any kind presupposes some level of agreement or shared understanding. A disagreement, for instance, over who is currently the best tennis player in the world will typically presuppose at least some basic agreement over what the game of tennis is, and thus over what sort of people are to count as tennis players. Theists and atheists disagree over whether there is a God. Christians and non-Christians often disagree over whether the story of Jesus is a true story of God living among us as a human being. In order for these disagreements to be intelligent and rational, the theist and the atheist must both have in mind some single idea of God, and so must the Christian and his non-Christian interlocutor. Otherwise, one party would not be denying what the other party is affirming. If they were not operating, at least at some level, with the same idea of God, however rough-edged or vague, their specific disagreements could not even be formulated We can think of the theist as believing that some particular idea of God is successfully reality-depicting. Along the same lines, we can think of the atheist who is in disagreement with him as believing that *the same idea of God* fails to be truly reality-depicting.

When a Christian and a non-Christian disagree over whether the story of Jesus presents God to us in a true and particularly distinctive way, their disagreement can occur over the basic issue of whether there is a God at all. Or it can occur as a disagreement between theists—the one believing that God once took human form and came to dwell among us as Jesus, the other asserting that the God who exists did no such thing. This disagreement over Jesus could not take place as an intelligent conflict of belief without some shared understanding of the basic idea of God. And where is this idea to come from? Exactly what idea is it to be?

The theist proposes; his opponent denies. The Christian proposes; his opponent denies. As a general rule, he who proposes must explain. It is his responsibility to articulate clearly what exactly the proposal is. It is thus up to the theist, and up to the Christian, to explain what exactly is meant by the word "God." But of course it is presumably in the interests of all parties to such religious disputes that the best idea of God which can be formulated be the one which is introduced for discussion. And so we need to ask what procedure or method for articulating an idea of God will best provide for this sort of result.

The problem of method in philosophical theology is posed by the fact that there are, in principle, many possible methods for arriving at, or articulating, an idea of God. One possible way of proceeding, for example, would be to attempt to consult all the purported revelations claimed by different religious traditions throughout human history, and draw from them a composite portrait of the divine. This possible method for arriving at a determinate conception of God can be referred to as the method of *universal revelational theology*. It is a procedure which has seemed attractive to many sincere inquiring people, and even to some ecumenically minded Christians, but it is a method with at least one fundamental flaw. Many of the purported revelations of God to be found throughout human history conflict. They offer incompatible accounts of the divine. How are we supposed to separate the sheep from the goats, the wheat from the chaff? The simple, apparently openminded method of *universal revelational theology* does not itself provide us with a criterion of selection. It is not sufficiently discriminating, however ecumenically attractive it initially might appear to some people.

What is needed is a touchstone for theological acceptability, a standard, a measuring stick, a reliable guide for constructing our idea of God, a criterion which will help us avoid inconsistency. And of course, Christians have traditionally taken the Bible to provide exactly this.[1] Some Christian theologians have gone on to insist that the Bible provides us with our only fully reliable source of knowledge about God. In line with this, they sometimes go on to the extreme of recommending a distinct method for articulating a basic conception of deity which we can call, quite simply, *purely biblical theology*.[2] The guiding principle of this method is that we should go to the Bible, and only to the Bible, for our idea of God.

One problem for purely biblical theology is that, despite some theologians' claims to follow its strictures, it is not clear that anyone can manage to do so if they are seeking a philosophically adequate conception of the divine. The rule definitive of this method, as I understand it here, is that we should think or say about God only what is explicitly said about him in the Bible, or in addition what is strictly, logically implied by what the Bible manifestly contains. The reason why no philosopher or theologian seeking a philosophically adequate conception of God can manage finally to adhere to this rule is that, in our capacity of asking philosophical questions about the nature of God, we inevitably ask questions the biblical documents were not designed to answer.

The Bible is not a textbook of philosophical theology. Its texts on God are thus neither as complete nor as specific as the philosophical theologian needs in order to be able to answer fully his conceptual, or philosophical, questions.

Are these philosophical questions then illegitimate from a biblical standpoint? I see no reason to think so at all. From the fact that the biblical documents, written as they were to deal with burning practical questions of the greatest personal significance, do not address all the possible philosophical questions which can also, in their own way, be of the greatest intellectual significance, it does not follow at all that these more theoretical questions are illegitimate, or that they are unimportant. They can

be quite important for the constructing of any comprehensive Christian world-view, and answers to them can help us to understand more deeply the biblical answers to more immediately practical questions. It can even be argued that it is incumbent upon any intelligent person who finds himself asking philosophical questions about matters of religious belief to do whatever it is in his power to do in order to find answers to them. Otherwise, such a person may be blocked from responding to God as a believer in the full integrity of his personality. It is never incumbent upon a Christian to eschew the quest for understanding, even when it leads him beyond the letter of the commitments of the Bible.

The challenge for the Christian philosopher or theologian should not be that of confining what he says about God to what the Bible has already said, but rather it should be that of constructing a philosophical theology which is thoroughly consonant with the biblical portrayal of God. What should be sought are not just philosophical ideas which happen to be logically consistent, or minimally compatible, with the biblical materials, but rather ideas which are deeply attuned to the biblical revelation, and thus consonant with the whole tenor of the Bible.

But if we are to build on the ideas of the Bible, we need a further method. We need a biblically based theology which is not as restrictive as the method of purely biblical theology. We need a method for drawing from, elaborating upon, and augmenting the content of the biblical materials in a way that will allow us to address any important philosophical issues concerning the nature of God which were not given fully developed answers by the biblical authors.

Some philosophers have suggested that the central idea of the Bible is its presentation of God as our creator, and as the creator of our world. It has also been said that the most central characterization of God in the Bible is its portrayal of him as the creator of all. In connection with these claims, we need to consider a method for thinking about deity which we can call *creation theology*. This method for articulating a conception of God centers around the claim that God is to be understood as the ultimate creator of every reality which exists distinct from himself. The precise method to be employed in connection with this claim is then explanatory in nature.

In this method for articulating a concept of God, it is said that, in order to explain the existence and nature of our universe, we must postulate the existence of a cause whose nature and activity would be sufficient for the production of such an astounding effect as the entire physical cosmos, with all its denizens, must be considered to be. Thus, according to the method of creation theology, the concept of God is properly taken to be the concept of a being who can serve the theoretical role of such an explanation.

As a way of thinking about God, creation theology has much to recommend it. First, as we have suggested, it has strong revelational backing. And second, it has seemed to many people to be an eminently rational method of thought. Indeed, it seems to consist in a procedure of postulational reasoning which, as used in the natural sciences, has proved its value time and again as a method of intellectual discovery: to explain the existence, occurrence or behavior of A we postulate the existence, occurrence or behavior of B; we postulate only what is strictly required for explaining A, and by so doing we quite often arrive at what is later confirmed as the truth. This method of thinking thus often appeals to people who consider themselves to be of a tough-minded, hard-nosed, scientific mindset. Even philosophers dubious of any claims to revelation, and thus disinclined to grant any special philosophical significance to the Bible as a source of ideas can find themselves strongly attracted to this basic method for articulating a concept of divinity. It seems to be a procedure which rationally can stand on its own.

But as a sole, independent method for articulating a conception of God, creation theology looks frustratingly incomplete. The idea of God arising exclusively out of this sort of explanatory reasoning inevitably has a rather minimal content which is both religiously and philosophically unsatisfying. Any being whose creative activity could explain adequately the existence of our universe would presumably have to be extraordinarily powerful and knowledgeable. But exactly how much power and knowledge should we think of him as enjoying? Creation theology will direct us to conceive of God as having enough power to create this cosmos. It will license us to ascribe to God at least this much power. But the problem is that a great many theists have wanted to ascribe to God the power to have created other sorts of universes instead, universes with more objects or with different kinds of objects. The belief is that he did not exhaust his power in his creation of this universe. Can creation theology authorize such a belief? It is hard to see how. And even if it could, it seems beyond the range of its method to specify exactly how much superabundant power God has.

And what of God's character? Is there enough evidence in the existence and nature of the universe to warrant fully the postulation of the idea of God as a morally perfect creator? In view of all the evil in the world—the pain, suffering and injustice—it would seem not. At least, it would be extremely difficult if possible at all to arrive at such an idea from nothing more than an explanatory extrapolation from our world. And yet this is something most theists would endorse as a central component in their idea of God.

There are two simple ways to augment creation theology in order to attempt to alleviate these inadequacies. First, for those who are suspicious of claims to revelation and who thus want to employ this sort of method on its own, it is possible to see creation theology as only the initial impetus to, and a mere partial application of, a broader *comprehensive explanatory theology*, a method which would take as its data to be explained not only the existence and basic nature of our universe, but also all those occurrences in human history deemed to be of religious significance: apparent miracles, signs of providential intent, and various sorts of religious experience. An explanatory method which casts its net more broadly in this way can be expected to arrive at a correspondingly more finely specified final explanation or explanatory postulation.

Although this broadening of method would probably result in some improvement, it is a bit difficult to see how it would help in resolving the specific questions which have been raised. Some idea of divine character in relation to humans could be hypothesized, but the result would probably still fall far short of the extreme claims theists, and in particular Christian theists, have thought it important to make for God. And there is no evident way at all that this broadening could deal with the problem of specifying the full degree of power enjoyed by God. So a good deal of incompleteness would still remain.

We should not forget, however, that we introduced the method of creation theology as a biblically based idea. As the psalmist wrote, "The heavens declare the glory of God, and the firmament proclaims his handiwork" (Ps 19:1). If it, or even its broader relative, is thought of as a method for augmenting the descriptions of God already to be found in the Bible, it matters somewhat less what this method, operating under its own steam, can produce. Its results are automatically viewed as augmented by what the Bible already contains, and when it comes to questions about the character of God, that augmentation is considerable. For the God of the Bible is "righteous and upright" (Deut 32:4), "gracious and compassionate, slow to anger, abounding in lovingkindness" (Joel 2:13); "all his works are truth, and his ways justice" (Dan 4:37); "great is the LORD, and greatly to be praised" (Ps 48:1).

But questions still remain unanswered. Even a biblically based creation theology, or a broader, biblically based comprehensive explanatory theology, seem to leave certain central and relevant philosophical questions about the nature of God unanswered. How do we specify the precise scope of God's power and knowledge, the full strength of his character, the mode of his being or the nature of his reality? The Bible clearly points us in a certain direction, toward an exalted, ultimate conception of God. It just does not address all our relevant philosophical questions. Both creation theology and comprehensive explanatory theology offer us help in that regard. But they too, for all their value, seem to stop short of providing sufficient guidance for dealing with all our legitimate questions about the grandeur of deity. So the issue naturally arises:

Is there a method which is both revelational and rational, compatible with both the insights of the Bible and sound explanatory methods, which will offer, in principle, a complete philosophical perspective on God, and thus will result in the best conception of God we can attain? An idea stated quite succinctly by Saint Anselm, archbishop of Canterbury (A.D. 1033–1109), can be taken to have provided us with at least the elements of just that sort of method, if properly understood and developed.

PERFECT BEING THEOLOGY

According to Anselm, God is to be thought of most fundamentally as "that than which no greater can be conceived."[3] Most contemporary philosophers have taken Anselm's basic idea here to be best interpreted to mean that God is to be thought of as *the greatest possible being*, an individual exhibiting *maximal perfection*. This core conception of deity is both very general and at the same time highly focused. It does not explicitly give us many specifics concerning God, hence its generality. But it provides a single focus for all our reflections about divinity, one point of light to guide all our thinking about the nature of God. The idea of God as the greatest possible being is not itself a full-blown conception of deity; rather, it is more like the main element in a recipe for cooking up our idea of God in detail. This core idea, along with an accompanying method for its development, will be what constitutes Anselm's most distinctive contribution to religious thinking, the philosophical procedure known as *perfect being theology*.

The ideas to be found in perfect being theology are not altogether original with Anselm. The conception of God as unsurpassably great is clearly itself a central biblical idea. But what Anselm provided was a precise philosophical statement of that idea and an examination of some of its implications. It was thus Anselm who pioneered the clarification and use of this biblically based and philosophically attuned method of thinking about God.

We can characterize the core of perfect being theology as the thesis that:

(G) God is a being with the greatest possible array of compossible great-making properties.

Clearly, the terms in this thesis require some elucidation. A *great-making property* is any property, or attribute, or characteristic, or quality which it is intrinsically good to have, any property which endows its bearer with some measure of value, or greatness, or metaphysical stature, regardless of external circumstances. The key idea here is of course that of *intrinsic goodness*. By contrast, *extrinsic goodness* has to do with value determined by external relations or outward circumstances. For example, if there is a sniper on the roof of my office building prepared to shoot anyone who leaves during the next hour, then the property of staying inside this building for more than an hour is a good property or attribute for me to have. But its value clearly depends entirely on external circumstances.

Very often, when we say of something that it is good, what we mean is that it is extrinsically good. Some nutritionists and physicians tell us nowadays that the habit of eating oatmeal for breakfast almost every morning is a good thing. But this surely has nothing to do with the intrinsic experience or event of eating oatmeal. Eating oatmeal regularly is *good* only because it is *good for* maintaining low blood cholesterol. And maintaining low blood cholesterol is in turn a good thing because it is good for avoiding heart trouble and maintaining general good health. It will help us to get a precise philosophical grasp of extrinsic goodness and its relation to intrinsic goodness if we symbolize the conditions under which claims to goodness hold true.

When it is said of some object, or property, A, that A is extrinsically good, what is really meant is that having A or standing in some particular relation to A is good for standing in some distinct relation R to some object or state of affairs B, something extrinsic or external to A. To say that A is *good for* this is to say that standing in the right relation to A is conducive to, or productive of, this further relation. But then we will in this way think of A as good or a good only if we also think of standing in R to B as itself a good thing. And if we here again have in mind extrinsic goodness, then standing in R to B must in turn be good for standing in some further relation $R1$ to some object C. That's just what extrinsic goodness requires, as we have seen. Let "P" name the property of standing in relation R to object B, and "$P1$" name the property of standing in $R1$ to C. In the realm of extrinsic goodness, P will be thought of as good in so far as, and only in so far as, it leads to $P1$. But this will make no sense unless $P1$ is itself judged a good thing. And if this judgment is again one of extrinsic goodness, then $P1$ must be good in virtue of leading to some further relation $R2$ to some object C, the property of standing in which we can denote as "$P2$."

What we are now in position to see is something very interesting. Some modern philosophers with world views very different from Anselm's have thought that all goodness is extrinsic, and thus that there is nothing which is intrinsically good. If this were true, then perfect being theology could not even get off the ground, for there would be no great-making properties to attribute to God. But could all goodness be extrinsic goodness? It seems highly problematic to think so, for supposing this to be true lands us in a perplexing dilemma. If all goodness is extrinsic goodness, then P cannot be good unless it leads to $P1$, which cannot be good unless it in turn leads to some value-endowing $P2$, which itself cannot be good or a source of value unless it leads to some value-endowing $P3$, and so forth. At some point, either we arrive at a value-endowing Pn which is identical with some earlier $Pn\text{-}m$, in which case we are faced with a perplexing circularity of explanation, or else there never arises such an identity, in which case we are faced with what philosophers call an "infinite regress" of explanations. But to be posed with the prospect that all ascriptions of goodness are either circular or infinitely complex is to be posed with an unsatisfying dilemma.

The other possibility, the alternative envisioned by Anselm and many theists, is that some things are intrinsically good, good in themselves, and thus are proper ultimate stopping points in explanations of goodness. That is to say, the recognition of something as an intrinsic good can be an appropriate terminus, or endpoint, to any explanation of value. Thus, a conception of value which countenances intrinsic as well as extrinsic values would seem to be more intellectually or rationally satisfying than one endorsing only extrinsic value. And it is just such a broader conception of value which Anselm's understanding of God requires.

So a great-making property is to be thought of as a property it is intrinsically good to have. And the core thesis of perfect being theology, proposition (G), ascribes to God the greatest possible array of *compossible* great-making properties. An array or collection of properties is compossible just in case it is possible that they all be had by the same individual at the same time, or all together. A simple example of a pair of noncompossible properties would be the property of being married and the property of being a bachelor. Knowledge and benevolence, on the other hand, are compossible properties. If God is thought of as having the greatest possible array of compossible great-making properties, we are thinking of God's nature as consisting in a cluster of properties intrinsically good to have, properties which can all be exemplified together, and which are such that their additive value, as a group, is unsurpassable by any other possible array of great-making properties. And if God is being thought of singularly as *the* greatest possible being, he is thought to be the sole possessor of such an array of properties. He is being thought of as being so great that no other, independent being could possibly rival him in greatness. With this, we arrive at the supreme conception of perfection, and moreover at the greatest possible idea that a human being could ever entertain. For what idea could possibly be greater than the idea of a unique, greatest possible being, necessarily without peer?

But we are still at a level of high abstraction and generality here. We are in need of more specifics. We have at this point only the core of a detailed conception of deity. To begin to fill out this conception of the divine, to employ the full method of perfect being theology, we need to begin to consult our value intuitions. What properties can we intuitively recognize as great-making properties, and what clusters of properties can be seen likewise to correspond to a high value, or an exalted metaphysical stature? It is part of the method of perfect being theology for us to consult our intuitions on these matters. It is one of the assumptions of this method that there will be at least widespread agreement among people who are rightly positioned and well disposed concerning at least many such intuitions.

Now, it should be pointed out that by the word "intuition" we do not necessarily mean to denote here some mysterious faculty for information gathering. Nor do we refer to anything which is an infallible guide to truth. Intuition is much more commonplace than that. Someone intuitively judges a proposition or claim to be true just in case, on merely considering the proposition, or the content of the claim, it appears true to him, and that appearance does not derive entirely from either perceptual belief-forming mechanisms (such as sight, hearing or smell) or from mere definitional conventions (from our human decisions) to use a word to have a certain meaning, as could be the case in the proposition: *The sentence "A triangle is a closed plane figure with three straight sides" expresses a truth.* Simply put, an intuitively formed belief seems to be a sort of naturally formed belief, a belief whose acceptance does not derive entirely from linguistic definition, evidence, testimony, memory, inference or sense experience. Our intuitions are among our most basic judgments about the world around us. We intuitively judge that $2 + 2 = 4$, that nothing could be colored without being extended, that the basic properties of matter are the same in different regions of the universe, that there are some fundamental principles of logical reasoning which are reliable, and that it is wrong to torture innocent people for no reason. And these are just a few examples. We could not even begin to use logic, mathematics or scientific method without an intuitive judgment that their most basic assumptions, propositions and principles are true. Some critics ask why we should trust such intuitions, or any intuitions at all. But to ask why anyone should ever rely on intuition is like asking why anyone should ever believe what seems to him to be true.

The point, however, should be made that not all intuitions are equal. It seems that there are degrees of intuitive support a proposition can have—some intuitions are just stronger than others. And some are reliable, whereas others are not. Most practitioners of perfect being theology take our intuitions about matters of value, as they do most other intuitions, to be innocent until proven guilty, or reliable until proven deceptive. The alternative is a form of skepticism with few attractions.

In order to elaborate an Anselmian idea of God, all practitioners of perfect being theology consult their value intuitions about what basic properties are great-making properties. Beginning with one of the least controversial candidates for the status of great-making property, we can represent schematically the development of a conception of a perfect being which I think would accord in one way or another with the intuitions of most of those who employ this method. In one representative example of an ascending order of discovery concerning the various aspects of his greatness in metaphysical stature, God can be conceived of in this way as:

(1) conscious (a minded being capable of and engaged in states of thought and awareness),

(2) a conscious free agent (a being capable of free action),

(3) a thoroughly benevolent, conscious agent,

(4) a thoroughly benevolent conscious agent with significant knowledge,

(5) a thoroughly benevolent conscious agent with significant knowledge and power,

(6) a thoroughly benevolent conscious agent with unlimited knowledge and power, who is the creative source of all else,

(7) a thoroughly benevolent conscious agent with unlimited knowledge and power who is the necessarily existent, ontologically independent creative source of all else.

And with this, we have arrived at what, with all its implications, is the highest conception of all, the conception of a unique, maximally perfect, or greatest possible, being. It is some such cumulative development of intuitions concerning intrinsic goodness, great-making properties, and the comparative greatness of different arrays of such properties that every practitioner of perfect being theology must undertake.

This representative list of seven stages of development in the elaboration of an Anselmian conception of God was constructed quite simply. First, it is agreed by many people that a being capable of conscious awareness is of greater intrinsic value or metaphysical stature than a thing with no such capacity, a rock for example. But then, it would be even greater not to be just a passive perceiver of things, or a conscious being confined to its own thoughts, but rather to be a conscious being capable of acting out its values and intentions into the world. And if to be an agent is good in itself, then to be an agent whose agency is thoroughly characterized by morally good or benevolent intentions is even better. Likewise, it is better for such an agent to have significant knowledge and power than to be extremely limited in these respects; and, finally, it would seem to be greater still to suffer no limits in these areas. Ultimately, a being unlimited in power and knowledge who was the source of all other beings would seem to be superior to one who, for all his excellence, was just one among other independent beings. And, at the limit of our conceptions, it would seem to be the greatest possible status to be such a being, exalted in all other respects, whose foothold in reality was so firm that it is impossible that the being not exist. Each level in our schematic ascent thus represents a development in our conception of greatness appropriate for the greatest possible being, which is God.

QUESTIONS AND REFINEMENTS: THE ULTIMATE METHOD

Do all practitioners of perfect being theology agree at every point concerning what God is like? Any look at the history of philosophical theology, or at the current literature on our idea of God, will show that the answer is no.[4] No method for thinking about God is a fully mechanical procedure, capable of turning out precisely the same results regardless of who employs it. There is plenty of room for disagreement among those who conceptualize God in Anselm's way, as we shall have occasion to see in later chapters.

Some philosophers think of God as timelessly eternal, an individual existing outside the bounds of time as well as space. Others conceive of God as an everlasting individual, existing throughout the entirety of time. Their disagreement can sometimes be seen to be a dispute over which of these alternate relations to time would be a more perfect form of existence. Value intuitions here and elsewhere can differ, as can intuitions over what is or is not possible. Our intuitions thus have *defeasible epistemic status*. The epistemic status of a belief or judgment is its status with respect to the goal of knowledge (in Greek, *episteme*). A belief has positive epistemic status, we can say, in case the person with the belief is justified in holding it, given the goal of attaining knowledge. But the status of a belief is defeasible in case it is possible that it be undermined or overturned. To say that our intuitions are defeasible is thus to say that, whatever positive degree of warrant or support they supply for a judgment or belief, they are in principle, and often in practice, correctable. They are not, to emphasize the point made earlier, infallible.

Our construction of an Anselmian conception of God is fueled by our value intuitions and by our modal intuitions—our intuitions concerning what is possible and impossible. But because intuitions are correctable, and because our intuitions are typically not comprehensive, that is to say, because we do not typically have intuitions clearly leading us on every issue relevant to attaining a full conception of deity which might arise, the method of perfect being theology is not in principle cut off from creative interaction with other methods for conceiving of God. And, in fact, I think it is best seen as the primary method for integrating all other plausible methods for thinking of God.

Let us first consider for a moment the fact that we do not have any reason to believe that we

human beings have a comprehensive capacity for generating all the intuitions which might be needed for recognizing all the great-making properties that ought to enter into our idea of God. We thus might miss some important divine attributes if we rely upon perfect being theology and our value intuitions alone for our idea of deity. Now, some such attributes could conceivably be supplied by the method of creation theology, or the broader comprehensive explanatory theology. Consider for example the property of being powerful. Some people claim to have no value intuitions that support the judgment that this is a great-making property. They may feel that the property of being powerful is in itself, or intrinsically, value-neutral and that it can take on extrinsic value only as a function of what kind of being has the property, and how the power in question is used. If people with these judgments about power were to think about God using only the method of perfect being theology, they would have difficulty arriving at any satisfactory judgment concerning the resources and scope for divine agency. But it is a basic postulation of creation theology that God is to be thought of as having great power. The only difficulty for creation theology might be in specifying the precise extent of that power, as we have seen. But at this point, once we have granted that God has great power, the perspective of perfect being theology can kick in and specify that God's power will have no limits that imply imperfection or inferiority. His power will be viewed as being as exalted as possible. In some such way, it could be possible for perfect being theology to be supplemented by creation theology, which would then in turn be supplemented by Anselmian thinking. In this way a dynamic interaction of the two methods could be possible.

But it is also possible that our intuitions fail to settle some question about the nature of God, and the property in question is not such that it would have to be postulated as a characteristic of the divine by either creation theology or comprehensive explanatory theology. It is quite plausible to think that if there were any such divine attributes that would be important for us to know of, and yet which are such as to slip through the net of our intuitions and of our explanatory needs, God would reveal them to us. The goodness of God conceptualized by perfect being theology would seem to guarantee that. Thus, it behooves us to be open to consulting the apparent data of revelation available to us.

But even more importantly, the intuitions we do have, and the explanatory postulations we do make might not all be trustworthy. They might thus need to be corrected at the bar of special revelation. Consider as an example one particular case having to do with value intuitions. In recent years, Nicholas Wolterstorff has pointed out that many Christians, unduly influenced by ancient Stoic thought, have supposed it to be a perfection to be absolutely undisturbed by any passion or emotion whatsoever. Accordingly, they have characterized God as *impassible*, incapable of perturbation by any emotion or passion. Wolterstorff argues that this is out of step with the biblical portrayal of God as a suffering God.[5] The upshot of his argument is that some classical theological intuitions about impassibility must be corrected by the content of the biblical revelation. As the nature of Wolterstorff's case makes clear, it is possible for our value intuitions to be skewed or distorted by a dominant or powerful philosophical tradition. Any well-attested data from revelation should be allowed to overturn, or correct, contrary value intuitions such as these.

So the method of perfect being theology needs a revelational control. But it's also true that perfect being theology itself can act as an interpretive constraint on how we read the Bible. For example, from earliest times biblical commentators have assured us that when in the Old Testament the Bible speaks of "the hand of God" or "the mouth of God," we are not to suppose that God has, literally, bodily parts such as hands and a mouth. Why? Because it is more perfect not to be by nature limited to such a form of indirect agency as that of having to work by means of hands and speak by means of a mouth. The dynamic of interactions among the plausible methods for thinking about God is thus a complex matter. Each method can provide its own input data for our conception of God, and can offer constraints on the data to be gained from the other methods. For Christians, creation theology, comprehensive explanatory theology, and perfect being theology are to be endorsed in so far as they capture leading ideas or directions of thought to be found in the Bible, and provide for a philosophical extension of these ideas. Perfect being theology, capturing as it does the most majestic conception of God imaginable, rightly provides a leading method for our thinking and a touchstone for our employment and integration of the procedures of all the other plausible methods for thinking about the nature of God. In its intuitive and integrative force, I think, it is without parallel and thus properly establishes for us priorities in our conceiving of God. God is to be thought of as a being without any limitations that imply imperfection or inferiority. God is to be thought of as the greatest possible being. And he is to be conceived as the greatest possible creative source of being.

Creation theology and perfect being theology pick up on different strands of biblical thinking, strands of thought that are deeply intertwined throughout the whole history of Judeo-Christian thought. They can also be thought of as echoes of Platonism, in the case of perfect being theology, with its stress on value, and Aristotelianism, in the case of creation theology, with its emphasis on causation. Both the concern with value and the concern with causation are enduring and legitimate preoccupations within the enterprises of general philosophical reflection and theology inquiry. It is my suggestion that not only do these concerns complement one another in our thinking about God, but that, properly understood, the methods to which they give rise not only interact in a natural way, but finally coincide in their ultimate results. It can be argued that anyone who begins with creation theology and endorses a few simple and independently plausible metaphysical theses, widely endorsed by theists of all kinds throughout the centuries, will find himself with the conclusion that stands as the core of perfect being theology.[6] Simply put, if God is conceived of as, necessarily, the ultimate cause of every other being, and we endorse some principle to the effect that no effect can equal or exceed its ultimate cause in plenitude of being, or metaphysical stature, or intrinsic value, then it will follow that this creator God is the greatest possible being. That is to say, starting with creation theology can plausibly be thought to result in the endorsement of the fundamental tenet of perfect being theology, the full explication of which will require the use of its attendant method. And I think it is also quite plausible to hold that a reasonable development of perfect being theology will result in an endorsement of the core thesis of creation theology, the claim that God is the creator of anything which might exist distinct from himself. For as we have already seen while working through a representative seven-step development of the Anselmian idea of God, if we imagined any existing universe as existing wholly independent of God, as depending in no way on God for its existence and activity, it would seem that the conception of God with which we were operating was not that of a greatest possible being after all. For, surely, a being would have greater value, or greater metaphysical stature, if it was an absolute source of existence, such that nothing else could exist without deriving its reality from this being. Thus, in order for God truly to be thought of as the greatest possible being, he would also have to be thought of

as what we can call an "absolute creator." Such, I think, is the link from perfect being theology to creation theology.

And once the practitioner of perfect being theology has arrived at this point, it stands to reason that he will find the method of creation theology to be important for filling out that conception of God as absolute creator. Thus, when it comes to the two distinctively philosophical methods for conceiving of God used by Christians and others through the centuries more than any other procedure, it seems reasonable to think that, regardless of which one might seem initially most attractive as a procedure, a theist will end up also endorsing the core claim and employing the procedures distinctive of the other method as well. There is something intellectually satisfying about this. For perfect being theology focuses on the intrinsic properties of God, whereas creation theology emphasizes the actual and potential relations holding between God and all else possible. They both seek, in their own ways, to explicate one important facet or another of metaphysical ultimacy, the intent they both have in common. Thus, they both can function in our attempt to articulate a philosophically adequate, as well as a biblically responsible, concept of God.

NOTES

1. For an argument supporting the appropriateness of this, see William Charlton, *Philosophy and Christian Belief* (London: Sheed and Ward, 1988).

2. This sort of suggestion can be found in the work of the evangelical theologian J. I. Packer. See, for example, "What Do You Mean When You Say God?" *Christianity Today*, September 19, 1986, pp. 27–31.

3. See S. N. Deane, trans., *St. Anselm: Basic Writings*, 2d ed. (LaSalle, Ill.: Open Court Publishing Company, 1968). More recently available is M. J. Charlesworth, trans., *St. Anselm's Proslogion* (Notre Dame: University of Notre Dame Press, 1979). Objections that can be raised against the Anselmian perspective are discussed at some length in Thomas V. Morris, *Anselmian Explorations* (Notre

Dame: University of Notre Dame Press, 1987), especially in chapter one. This perspective is further developed and defended in George Schlesinger, *New Perspectives on Old-Time Religion* (Oxford: Oxford University Press, 1988).

4. For more on this, see the editorial introduction to Thomas V. Morris, ed., *The Concept of God* (Oxford: Oxford University Press, 1987).

5. Nicholas Wolterstorff, "Suffering Love," in *Philosophy and the Christian Faith,* ed. Thomas V. Morris (Notre Dame: University of Notre Dame Press, 1988), pp. 196–237.

6. For an argument to this effect, see Thomas V. Morris, "A Theistic Proof of Perfection," *Sophia* 26 (July 1987): 31–35.

I.A.3

The Openness of God—Systematic Theology

CLARK H. PINNOCK

Clark H. Pinnock (1937–2010) was professor emeritus of systematic theology at McMaster Divinity School in Canada. His most important recent work focused on the development and advocacy of open theism, a view that stands in contrast to classical theism and maintains that God is, among other things, temporal, subject to change and passion, and limited in his knowledge of the future. In this selection, Pinnock presents a variety of systematic theological considerations that speak in favor of this way of thinking about God.

The concept of God is the most important topic in theology—and the most mysterious. Dealing with it makes one aware of the limitations of our finite understanding. We are not starting from scratch, though, or operating only from the light of human wisdom, but are reflecting on those perfections that must be ascribed to the divine Being on the basis of God's own self-disclosure in Jesus Christ. On the basis of revelation we strive for a biblically and conceptually sound understanding of God and of the package of divine properties that contribute to a coherent understanding. Each attribute needs to be explained coherently and the attributes together shown to be compatible with one another and with the vision of God as a whole. I believe that unless the portrait of God is compelling, the credibility of belief in God is bound to decline.

In Christian theology we are not dealing with just any old concept of God, but with the surprising God and Father of our Lord Jesus. This is a God who does not remain at a safe distance, worrying about his own honor, but one who bares his holy arm and rescues humankind through sharing their distress and affliction. We are not dealing with

an unapproachable deity but with God who has a human face and who is not indifferent to us but is deeply involved with us in our need.

Doctrines are important because they express the truth-claims of religion both for insiders and outsiders. They try faithfully to state what we believe and to describe the realities that underlie these commitments in a timely way. Doctrines explore the cognitive substance of the Christian message. A doctrine of God seeks to distill in conceptual form what we know about God through revelation, truth that bears ultimate significance for humanity.

No doctrine can be more important than the doctrine of God. It is the principal doctrine in any theology, because apart from it the vision of faith cannot be stated. The whole creation is grounded in God, and the flow of history is the sphere of the outworking of his purposes. The doctrine is of more than academic interest; it is also of great missiological and practical importance. How can we commend belief unless we have formed a convincing conception of God for ourselves? Modern atheism has resulted in part from distortions that were

From *The Openness of God: A Biblical Challenge to the Traditional Understanding of God*, by Clark H. Pinnock, Richard Rice, et al. Copyright ©1994 Clark H. Pinnock, Richard Rice, John Sanders, William Hasker, and David Basinger. Used by permission of InterVarsity Press, PO Box 1400, Downers Grove, IL 60515. www.ivpress.com. Most endnotes omitted.

allowed to enter the doctrine of God from the direction of philosophy. We cannot believe if we have conceptualized God in existentially repugnant ways. It makes a difference whether God is portrayed as genuinely related to human life or as standing aloof from it and indifferent to human needs. On the other hand, formulating this doctrine in a way that shows the relevance of belief in God has great apologetic value as people learn that God shares in their sorrows and is touched by the feelings of their infirmities.

Humility is essential when thinking about such lofty matters. What the apostle said about our knowing "only in part" is very apt and his exclamation rings true: "O the depth of the riches and wisdom and knowledge of God! How unsearchable are his judgments and how inscrutable his ways!" (Rom 11:33 NRSV). In theology, as in the Christian life generally, we are pilgrims traveling en route to God's kingdom. Some things are too high for us, and we can always learn more in conversation with others. Nevertheless, we hope to get a little closer to the truth by our efforts; if we reach a dead end, we will not be too proud to retrace our steps and try a different path. We insist on distinguishing between the Bible and our attempts to interpret it, and we believe that God always has more light to shed on his Word than we have received.

BASIC MODELS

Interpretation is a human activity in which we distinguish between the primary biblical data and any presuppositions and interests we bring to the task. In theology, as in science, we also make use of models. Models help us to deal with complex subjects like Christology, ecclesiology, salvation and so forth. We face a great variety of data needing interpretation and are compelled to choose an angle of approach to them. In the case of the doctrine of God, we all have a basic portrait of God's identity in our minds when we search the Scriptures, and this model influences our exposition. What a great difference it makes, for example, whether we think of God as a stern judge, a loving parent or an indulgent grandfather. In theology we experiment with plausible angles of vision and try them out.

Two models of God in particular are the most influential that people commonly carry around in their minds. We may think of God primarily as an aloof monarch, removed from the contingencies of the world, un-changeable in every aspect of being, as an all-determining and irresistible power, aware of everything that will ever happen and never taking risks. Or we may understand God as a caring parent with qualities of love and responsiveness, generosity and sensitivity, openness and vulnerability, a person (rather than a metaphysical principle) who experiences the world, responds to what happens, relates to us and interacts dynamically with humans. These correspond to … differences … between the God of Greek philosophy and the God of the Bible. God is sovereign in both models, but the mode of his sovereignty differs.

In [*The Openness of God*] we are advancing the second, or the open, view of God. Our understanding of the Scriptures leads us to depict God, the sovereign Creator, as voluntarily bringing into existence a world with significantly free personal agents in it, agents who can respond positively to God or reject his plans for them. In line with the decision to make this kind of world, God rules in such a way as to uphold the created structures and, because he gives liberty to his creatures, is happy to accept the future as open, not closed, and a relationship with the world that is dynamic, not static. We believe that the Bible presents an open view of God as living and active, involved in history, relating to us and changing in relation to us. We see the universe as a context in which there are real choices, alternatives and surprises. God's openness means that God is open to the changing realities of history, that God cares about us and lets what we do impact him. Our lives make a difference to God—they are truly significant. God is delighted when we trust him and saddened when we rebel against him. God made us significant creatures and treats us as such. We are significant to God and the apple of his eye (Ps 17:8).

We hope to persuade people both inside and outside the church to regard God in this fashion, because we believe it is more biblical and meaningful to do so. Some critics may speak of "a battle of the gods," as if we were advocating a God other than the God of historic Christianity. What we are really doing is conducting a competition between models of God. We are trying to understand the God of Christian revelation better. I realize that reconsidering one's model of God may be a delicate issue for some readers. It may feel as if, when a familiar way of thinking about God is questioned, God himself is lost or has become distant. But the experience of reconceptualizing can be positive. After the initial anxiety of rethinking, one will find God again in a fresh way around the next bend in the reflective road. Rather than worry about *our* discomfort, perhaps we should be concerned about *God's* reputation. Does it not concern us that God's name is often dishonored because of poor theologies of God? How can we expect Christians to delight in God or outsiders to seek God if we portray God in biblically flawed, rationally suspect and existentially repugnant ways? We cannot expect it.

SYSTEMATIC THEOLOGY

Many contemporary Christians will not be surprised by the model we call the openness of God or free will theism. They already enjoy a vital personal relationship with God and experience God as dynamically responding to them. Few doubt that what they do in life has an impact on God and calls forth appropriate responses from God. The problem actually lies more in systematic theology than it does in religious experience. For some reason, when we do theology we lose sight of the openness of God that we experience. There is resistance to conceptualizing it, even though it is existentially familiar.

This is because of tradition. The history of doctrine has seen a tilt toward divine transcendence over against God's immanence. Theology emphasized one set of divine properties to the neglect of another and disturbed the delicate balance between them. Though God is both transcendent and immanent, theology has tended to be one-sided. In

Isaiah we hear the balance as God says: "I dwell in the high and holy place, *and* also with him who is of a contrite and humble spirit" (Is 57:15 RSV). Though acknowledging the truth of divine immanence, theologians usually place the preponderance of their emphasis on God's transcendence. They prefer to speak more of God's power than of weakness, more of God's eternity than of temporality, and more of God's immutability than of loving changeableness in relation to us. This represents a theological distortion that must be corrected, without being overcorrected. I hope the reader will not see my position as an overreaction; it is not my intention.

It is important to recognize that God (according to the Bible) is both transcendent (that is, self-sufficient, the Creator of the world, ontologically other than creation, sovereign and eternal) and at the same time immanent (that is, present to the world, active within history, involved, relational and temporal). Combining the two, we say that God is so transcendent that he creates room for others to exist and maintains a relationship with them, that God is so powerful as to be able to stoop down and humble himself, that God is so stable and secure as to be able to risk suffering and change. Theology must strive to do greater justice to the two truths and hold them in proper balance. God must not be situated in our thinking so far away that he becomes irrelevant to human life or so near that he becomes dependent on the world, not by volition but necessarily.

Traditional theology has been biased in the direction of transcendence as the result of undue philosophical influences. Greek thinking located the ultimate and the perfect in the realm of the immutable and absolutely transcendent. This led early theologians (given that the biblical God is also transcendent) to experiment with equating the God of revelation with the Greek ideal of deity. However, a price had to be paid in terms of faithfulness to Scripture and relevance to human life. A striking example of this is the way they distorted the divine self-ascription "I AM WHO I AM" (Ex 3:14). This text, which points to the living God of the exodus, was transmuted into a principle of metaphysical immutability, as the dynamic "I AM" of the Hebrew text became the impersonal "being who is" of the Greek Septuagint (LXX), enabling theologians like Philo and Origen to link a changeless Greek deity with the God who acts in history. What God is saying to Moses in this verse is not "I exist" or even "I will be present." God is saying that he will be a faithful God for his people. This is an example of the way in which the image of God as defined on the horizon of Greek thinking threatened to replace the image of the living God of the biblical revelation in theology. The God of promise who acts in history tended to be replaced by a metaphysical statement about abstract being.

No one should criticize the fathers for trying to integrate current philosophical beliefs and biblical insights. If God is the God of the universe and if truth is one, theologians should try to integrate all of the truth that they know from any quarter. But it is essential to integrate the various insights in such a way that the biblical message is not negated or compromised. In the integration the insights of revelation must be normative and not swept aside.

Fortunately the tilt toward transcendence in traditional dogmatics was not always extreme. Christians did not consistently lose sight of the dynamic portrait of God in the Scriptures. It was present in hymns, sermons and liturgies, which tend to be more conservative in relation to biblical language. It was even present in theology, particularly in dealing with a subject like the incarnation. When contemplating this mystery, the same theologians would often admit that in becoming flesh the logos underwent change, because of God's desire to be gracious to humanity. The doctrine of the incarnation requires nuanced thinking about God's immutability, and this was not lost upon the fathers. Nevertheless, the one-sided stress on God's transcendence (on God turned away from us, not toward us) would continue to distort Catholic and Protestant theology to the present time.

My task here is to correct this imbalance in the handling of the transcendence and immanence of God. This requires allowing Scripture to challenge tradition and not permitting theology to be Hellenic where that would be unbiblical. While open

to everything that is good in Greek thinking, we must discard what is not good. We cannot allow undue loyalty to traditional paradigms and esteemed theologians to prevent needed revision of the doctrine of God for today.

Modern culture can actually assist us in this task because the contemporary horizon is more congenial to dynamic thinking about God than is the Greek portrait. Today it is easier to invite people to find fulfillment in a dynamic, personal God than it would be to ask them to find it in a deity who is immutable and self-enclosed. Modern thinking has more room for a God who is personal (even tripersonal) than it does for a God as absolute substance. We ought to be grateful for those features of modern culture which make it easier to recover the biblical witness.

Let me attempt now to correct the imbalance in theology's handling of transcendence and immanence by expounding on the relevant divine perfections. In doing so, I will take care not to engage in overcorrection or to reverse the tilt, this time in the direction of immanence, as liberal theology has customarily done. Let us seek a way to revise classical theism in a dynamic direction without falling into process theology.

THE TRINITY

The doctrine of the Trinity is the centerpiece of Christian theism. The church has always confessed that the God who created all things is one and many (not an undifferentiated simple unity) and embodies a relational fullness and richness of being in himself. Given the fact that Father and Son are persons and that the Spirit is spoken of in personal terms in the Scriptures, it is appropriate to speak of God as a community of persons rather than as modes of being.

This doctrine is relevant to the openness of God because the social trinity is an open and dynamic structure. It does not portray God as a solitary, domineering individual but as the essence of loving community. When presented as a solitary potentate, God appears as the enemy of human freedom and atheism flourishes, but when seen as social trinity, God is the ultimate in community, mutuality and sharing. The doctrine enables us to break with substantialist assumptions about God being a "thing" and puts the idea of three relationally interconnected persons in its place. The Trinity points to a relational ontology in which God is more like a dynamic event than a simple substance and is essentially relational, ecstatic and alive. God exists as diverse persons united in a communion of love and freedom. God is the perfection of love and communion, the very antithesis of self-sufficiency.

The Trinity lets us say simultaneously two very important things about God—that God is (on the one hand) self-sufficient in fullness and (on the other hand) open to the world in overflowing love. It sheds light on God's genuine delight in creatures as social beings themselves and on why he would invite them to share the richness of the divine fellowship as his friends. His love for us is not the benevolence of a distant king but like the tender love of a nursing mother (Is 49:15).

The trinitarian model seems superior to process theism in this matter of the divine openness. It lets us criticize classical theism without moving in that direction. Process thinking does not have a patent on the dynamic, relational and temporal nature of God. The triune God (unlike God in process theism) does not need the world to make up for a love and mutuality lacking in his nature. The Trinity allows the church to confess that God is both self-sufficient and loving at the same time. The problem in process theology seems to be the fact that it requires us to view the world as necessary to God, with the implication that God is not free in creation but necessarily tied to a world. The Trinity, being an event of relationship, can be open to the world by choice and can work toward the mutuality in history already present in God's being.

The Trinity depicts a relational God who is ontologically other and a dynamic world that has real value. As internally social and self-sufficient, God does not need the world but creates it out of the abundance of his rich inner life. This makes God free to create and respond to the world, free

to be gracious and take the initiative where necessary. Gregory Boyd writes:

> Only if God is antecedently actual, relational, and self-sufficient in relation to the world can God be free enough to do what scripture proclaims that God did in fact do in Jesus Christ. Only a God who is internally social within Godself can perform the more than necessary feat of opening up this sociality to what is fundamentally other than Godself. Only a God who is socially and self-sufficiently triune as lover, beloved, and loving can take the radical and completely unprovoked initiative to take on within this One's self the full nature of a non-divine self in order to effect wholeness in the whole of the non-divine creation.

THE CREATION

The triune God is the Creator of the world out of nothing. This means that God does not simply influence preexisting matter but that everything depends on God for its existence. Belief in creation captures an essential dimension of the theistic worldview because it posits the world as the creation of God, as having its origin in God. Each being owes its existence to God, whose own being is independent of any world, making any relationship with the world voluntary, not necessitated. It also implies that God has the power to intervene in the world, interrupting (if need be) the normal causal sequences.

However, contrary to the opinions of some, this act of creation does not entail that God controls and determines everything. God is free to make such creatures as he wills and has chosen to make some with the capacity for choice. God has given them a relative and derived autonomy. As H. P. Owen puts it, "God can create such beings as he wills; and has chosen to make some creatures with the capacity for free choice."

Being socially triune, God has made a world with freedom, in which loving relationships can flourish. It is an ecosystem capable of echoing back the triune life of God. We may think of humanity as the created image of God's social nature, enacting on the finite level the relational movements that occur eternally in God. This must be why in the beginning God said the creation was "good"—because it brings such pleasure to God in this respect As triune, God would be self-sufficient without creating any world, but as triune, God delights in a world in which he can interact with creatures for whom his love can overflow. God does not need a world in the sense of having a deficiency in his nature but wants one that delights his heart and pleases him.

This helps to explain why God made human beings—because they are able to respond to God and to hear his Word. Their lives, like God's own life, are dynamic and oriented toward fulfillment in the coming kingdom. God wanted a world where personal relations and loving communion could occur. It would be a world not wholly determined but one peopled with creaturely free agents. Without having to do so metaphysically, God seeks fellowship with us, out of grace and overflowing love. Sovereign and free, God chooses to be involved with us.[1] He does not remain in splendid isolation but enters into relationship with his creatures. In the incarnation God stoops down, shares our lives and involves himself in our joys and sorrows. God chooses to express his deity not in the mode of aloofness, independency and total control but in creating free beings on the finite level and entering lovingly into their lives.[2]

Thus God has created a world that in a creaturely way reflects the goodness that characterizes God's own experience as triune. At great cost, God is leading the world forward to the place where it will reflect more perfectly the goodness that God himself enjoys. God does all this without having to do it, without being compelled by anything outside of himself. God's bliss cannot be increased, but it can express itself in the world. The creation is an occasion for the expression of God's experience outside of God. In the spirit of the ancient image of the ecstatic dance of the triune God, we can say that the purpose of creation is to express this same delightful movement on the level of the creature, ever summoning new partners to the dance. Beyond metaphysical necessity, God creates a nondivine world with real significance and accepts the risks of entering into a relationship with it. The aim was to create an echo in space and time of the communion that God experiences in eternity, a reflection on the creaturely level of the loving movement within God. The decision gave God the possibility of reflecting on himself in the created other and of enjoying the delight of real interaction. It should be plain why the creation is so dear to God's heart.

TRANSCENDENCE AND IMMANENCE

In relation to the world, God the Creator is both transcendent and immanent. There are many polarities in theology: one and many, three persons and one essence, one person and two natures, and so forth. In a dialectical way, God both transcends the world and participates in it, is both high and lifted up and at the same time very close to it. God transcends and surpasses the world as its Maker but also indwells it and is active within it. Though transcendent, God is committed to us and wills to be in relation with us. As Isaiah says, God the Holy One is in our midst (Is 12:6). Though sovereign and free, God decides not to dwell alone but to establish communion with us. He has chosen to be God for us, even God for us in a human form.

A partial analogy is that of the artist, one who transcends her work and shapes it outside of herself and yet also imparts something of herself to it. The analogy cannot capture the intimacy and penetration of God's indwelling the world, though, for in a much greater way God, though ontologically distinct from created forms, creates a world external to himself and chooses to be present and immanent within it. On the one hand, God is sovereign and free and does not need the world; on the other hand, God has decided not to be alone but uses his freedom to establish communion with creatures and to exist in openness to the unfolding world.

By divine immanence I mean that God is everywhere present in all that exists. The world and God are not radically separated realities—God is present within every created being. As Paul said, quoting a Greek poet, "In him we live and move and have our being" (Acts 17:28). Today we understand the world as an interconnected ecosystem, a dynamic and developing whole, which has made this idea of God's immanence even more meaningful. It has become easier for us to imagine God the Spirit everywhere working as creativity in the whole cosmic situation. God is not detached from the world. Creation is not an event that happened and is done with. It is an ongoing process in which every particle, every atom, every molecule is held in existence by the Creator. Divine creativity has been taking place from the beginning until now, respecting what has already been made and calling forth new possibilities for the future. The whole world in which we dwell expresses God's continuous activity.

Process theology denies ontological independence, maintaining that God needs the world as much as the world needs God. This drops out the crucial distinction between God and the world so central to the scriptural portrayal. It makes God too passive, able only to experience the world and to organize the elements that present themselves to him. The Bible describes God as more present to the world than that, as a deity working out salvation in history and moving all things forward to a new creation.

The relation of God and creation is asymmetrical. The Creator gives life and freedom to the creature and voluntarily limits the exercise of his power in relation to it, God's openness to the world is freely chosen, not compelled. Process theism deserves commendation for opposing a static concept of God and for seeking a dynamic model, but not just any dynamic model will do. It is important to have a dynamic model that is biblically and theologically sound. Social trinitarian metaphysics (a relational ontology) gives us a God who is ontologically other but at the same time is ceaselessly relating and responsive.

In the second verse of Genesis we read about God's Spirit soaring over the creation. God not only created out of nothing—God also sustains the world, calls forth life and renews the face of the ground. God is on the inside of creation, in the processes not in the gaps. God is immanent throughout the universe in all of its changeableness and contingency and active in the whole long process of its development. The Creator has a mysterious relationship with every bit of matter and with every person. We need to recover the immanence of God, which helps us to relate to the new creation story being supplied by modern science.

THE POWER OF GOD

As Creator, God is unquestionably the superior power. His is the power to exist and the power to control all things. God depends on nothing else in order to be and is therefore free at the most fundamental level. But almightiness is not the whole story. In a world reflecting a triune community, God does not monopolize the power. Were he to do so, there could be no created order, certainly not a dynamic one with free agents, and not one producing love and communion. To achieve that kind of creation, God needs to deploy his power in more subtle ways. Though no power can stand against him, God wills the existence of creatures with the power of self-determination. This means that God is a superior power who does not cling to his right to dominate and control but who voluntarily gives creatures room to flourish. By inviting them to have dominion over the world (for example), God willingly surrenders power and makes possible a partnership with the creature.

Condescension is involved in God's decision to make this kind of a world. By willing the existence of significant beings with independent status alongside of himself, God accepts limitations not imposed from without. In other words, in ruling over the world God is not all-determining but may will to achieve his goals through other agents, accepting the limitations of this decision. Yet this does not make God "weak," for it requires more power to rule over an undetermined world than it would over a determined one. Creating free creatures and working with them does not contradict God's omnipotence but requires it. Only omnipotence has the requisite degree and quality of power to undertake such a project. God has the power and ability to be (in Harry Boer's words) an "ad hoc" God, one who responds and adapts to surprises and to the unexpected. God sets goals for creation and redemption and realizes them ad hoc in history. If Plan A fails, God is ready with Plan B.[3]

Divine condescension is apparent in the realm of redemption, where God manifests his power paradoxically in the cross of Christ. What an astounding way for God to deploy power, in the form of servanthood and self-sacrifice. This was the mode of power God knew in his wisdom to be appropriate for bringing about reconciliation, and it reveals that love rather than almighty power is the primary perfection of God. When love says that power will not work in a situation, power is allowed to withdraw in favor of powerlessness. God does not overcome his enemies (for example) by forcing but by loving them. God works, not in order to subject our wills but to transform our hearts. Love and not sheer power overcomes evil— God does not go in for power tactics.[4]

We could also say that love is the mode in which God's power is exercised. God neither surrenders power in order to love nor denies love in the need to rule, but combines love and power perfectly. This power creates life and then awakens and stimulates it in others. The question is not whether but in what manner God exercises power. The model cannot be domination but is one of nurturing and empowering.[5]

We must not define omnipotence as the power to determine everything but rather as the power that enables God to deal with any situation that arises. Plainly God is not at the moment all in all— this has yet to happen when the kingdom comes (1 Cor 15:28). God's power presently is more subtle, much greater in fact than the coercive power of a puppeteer. Monopoly power is easy to manage—more difficult is a power that makes free agents and governs a universe where creatures can disobey. Omnipotence does not mean that nothing can go contrary to God's will (our sins go against it)

but that God is able to deal with any circumstance that may arise. The idea that it means a divine decree and total control is an alarming concept and contrary to the Scriptures. Total control is not a higher view of God's power but a diminution of it. The biblical narrative plainly reveals that God has rivals and has to struggle with them.

In an attempt to preserve the notion of God's power as total control, some advocate what they call biblical compatibilism, the idea that one can uphold genuine freedom and divine determinism at the same time. This is sleight of hand and does not work. Just the fact of our rebellion as sinners against God's will testifies it is not so. The fall into sin was against the will of God and proves by itself that God does not exercise total control over all events in this world. Evils happen that are not supposed to happen, that grieve and anger God. Free will theism is the best way to account for this fact. To say that God hates sin while secretly willing it, to say that God warns us not to fall away though it is impossible, to say that God loves the world while excluding most people from an opportunity of salvation, to say that God warmly invites sinners to come knowing all the while that they cannot possibly do so—such things do not deserve to be called mysteries when that is just a euphemism for nonsense.

The all-powerful God delegates power to the creature, making himself vulnerable. In giving us dominion over the earth, God shares power with the creature. The fact of sin in history reveals the adverse effect that disobedience has on God's purpose. God allows the world to be affected by the power of the creature and takes risks accompanying any genuine relatedness. There is a paradox of strength and vulnerability of God according to the Scriptures. Though ontologically strong, God can be vulnerable because of the decision to make a world like this. The Lord of the universe has chosen to limit his power by delegating some to the creature. God gives room to creatures and invites them to be covenant partners, opening up the possibility of loving fellowship but also of some initiative being taken away from God and creatures coming into conflict with his plans. God gives us room to rebel against him, and when that happens patiently waits for the prodigal to return.

The theme of God's kingdom helps us to understand divine sovereignty from another angle. Jesus announces that God's rule is near but not yet in full effect. At present, God's will is resisted by powers of darkness, but the day will come when his will shall triumph. At present, evil is mounting a challenge to God's rule with considerable effect. The powers of darkness put up stiff resistance and to a degree block God's plans; that is, they can restrict God's ability to respond to a given crisis. Hence Paul says that the Spirit groans and waits with us for the final redemption (Rom 8:23). God's ability to turn things around is circumscribed in ways we cannot understand, yet this is more than countered by the hope of the coming kingdom. Evil may have its day, but it will not finally triumph.[6] By his decision to create a world like ours, God showed his willingness to take risks and to work with a history whose outcome he does not wholly decide. Theology does not work with an abstract idea of power that confuses sovereignty with tyranny.[7]

Divine sovereignty involves a flexible outworking of God's purposes in history. It refers to his ability, as the only wise God, to manage things, despite resistance to his will. Owing to the emphasis in theology on almightiness, we have tended to neglect the form of power called persuasion. It is not the only kind of power God has at his disposal, but it is a noble form that has been neglected in the tradition, where power tends to be associated, even equated, with coercion. The power of God's love (for example) does not command but woos and transforms us. This power can deliver us from evil and transform the wicked heart. Yet to reduce God's power to persuasion would make God too passive—it would be an overreaction against almightiness.

At the same time, however, the power of persuasion is an admirable power. Is God's power not as wonderfully displayed in his condescension to our weakness as in the starry heavens? It is so clear from Scripture, illustrated in God's dealings with Moses, that God does not overpower his servants, even though he could easily do so, but rather works with mortals and all of their hesitations and uncertainties. God honors Moses' dignity to the extent that when he cannot persuade him to accept the call, he resorts to an alternate plan, calling Aaron into the picture. God aims for the best in every situation and is even willing to work with options that are less than the best. God accepts what people decide to do with the powers they have been given. The future is determined by God not alone but in partnership with human agents. God gives us a role in shaping what the future will be. He is flexible and does not insist on doing things his way. God will adjust his own plans because he is sensitive to what humans think and do.

Understanding God's power gives us some help with the vexed problem of evil. If this is a world in which evil is possible but not inevitable, then it can be seen as stemming primarily from the misuse of freedom. The full display of God's sovereignty would not be a present reality but something to come at the end of history, when his glory is revealed, rather than at the present time, when the Spirit suffers with us and the universe groans.

We can call this model of divine openness free will theism. Upholding God's power, it understands God to be voluntarily self-limited, making room for creaturely freedom. Without making God finite, this definition appreciates God's delighting in a universe which he does not totally control.

THE IMMUTABLITY OF GOD

The Trinity is unchangeably what it is from everlasting to everlasting—and nothing can change that. Furthermore, we can always rely on God to be faithful to his promises; he is not in any way fickle or capricious. Immutability ought to focus on the faithfulness of God as a relational, personal being.

But the tradition has taken immutability far in the direction of immobility and inertness. Some have claimed that God is wholly actual and not at all potential and thus cannot change in any way. They have equated the biblical idea of faithfulness with the Greek idea that requires any changes related to God to occur only on the human side. This is the error that tempted some of the early theologians to explain the incarnation without admitting that God changed, and to explain away dozens of biblical references to God's repenting and changing.

This is a mistake from a biblical standpoint. The God of the Bible is a God of action, not inaction. God is immutable in essence and in his trustworthiness over time, but in other respects God changes. For example, God changes in his response to events in history. The Bible states that when God saw the extent of human wickedness on the earth, he was sorry that he had made humankind (Gen 6:5). The book of Jonah says that when God saw the conversion of Nineveh, he repented of the evil he said he would do to it (Jon 3:10). This latter passage is very revealing because it tells us that God experiences temporal passage, learns new facts when they occur and changes plans in response to what humans do.

God is unchanging in nature and essence but not in experience, knowledge and action. In nature, God is consistently reliable and loving and can be depended on completely. God's character is faithful and reliable—he is a steadfast friend who binds himself to us and does not forsake us. His concern for the creature is constant and unaffected by anything. From the point of view of experience, however, God responds to the changing needs of his children and changes direction when necessary. God is changeless in nature, but his nature is that of a creative person who interacts. God's immutability does not rule out God's responsiveness, the quality that enables God to deal with every new happening and to bend it toward his objectives without violating its integrity.

When I say that God is subject to change, I am referring to a uniquely divine kind of changeability. I do not mean that God is subject to change involuntarily, which would make God a contingent being, but that God allows the world to touch him, while being transcendent over it.

THE IMPASSIBILITY OF GOD

Impassibility is the most dubious of the divine attributes discussed in classical theism, because it suggests that God does not experience sorrow, sadness or pain. It appears to deny that God is touched by the feelings of our infirmities, despite what the Bible eloquently says about his love and his sorrow. How can God be loving and not pained by evil? How can God be impassible when the incarnate Son experienced suffering and death?[8]

The suffering or pathos of God is a strong biblical theme—God's love, wrath, jealousy and suffering are all prominent. God suffers when there is a broken relationship between humanity and himself. In this context, God agonizes over his people and says: "My heart recoils within me, my compassion grows warm and tender" (Hosea 11:8 RSV). God is not cool and collected but is deeply involved and can be wounded. The idea of God's impassibility arises more from Plato than from the Bible.

The theme of suffering strongly brings out God's openness to the world. Not aloof and impassive, God does not just imagine what it would be like to suffer, he actually suffers because of his decision to love. God has chosen to be open to the world and to share in its suffering because of his love. God's transcendence over the world does not prevent him from interacting with the world or from being affected by the world.

What does it mean to say that God suffers? This is a mystery of God's inner life. Plato was not altogether wrong to say that God must be free of certain kinds of passion and emotion. After all, God is not a creature; therefore, he does not suffer in exactly the ways that we do. Responding to pain, for example, must in some ways be an imaginative response to the suffering of a creature. How could God experience physical pain, if he is not physical? How could he suffer the pain of loneliness, if he is triune? Or the pain of fear when he is securely God? What we should say is that God sympathizes in his relationship with us. God risked suffering when he opened himself up to the world, when he made it possible for the creature to have an impact on him. God risked suffering when he decided to love and be loved by the creature. A lover's existence is inescapably affected by the other, especially when the loved one acts in ways that grieve and disappoint. Listen to the suffering in God's yearning for his wayward son: "Is Ephraim my dear son? Is he my darling child? For as often as I speak against him, I do remember him still. Therefore my heart yearns for him; I will surely have mercy on him" (Jer 31:20 RSV). Obviously God feels the pain of broken relationships.

At the same time, impassibility is a subtle idea with a grain of truth. We have to distinguish ways in which God can suffer from ways in which God cannot suffer. God is beyond certain modes of suffering, just as he is beyond certain modes of change. We could say that God is impassible in nature but passible in his experience of the world. Change occurs in the world and affects God when he becomes aware of it. When that change involves innocent suffering (for example), God responds tenderly to it.

GOD'S ETERNITY

Should we say that God is temporally everlasting or timelessly eternal? Classical theism has made the strong claim that God is timeless, in the sense of existing outside of time and sequence. This view strongly emphasizes God's transcendence over the world. And since a timeless being would be totally actualized, it implies strong immutability and impassibility as well.

However, timelessness presents many difficulties from a theological standpoint. First, it is hard to form any idea of what timelessness might mean, since all of our thinking is temporally conditioned. A timeless being could not make plans and carry them out. Second, it creates problems for biblical history, which portrays God as One who projects plans, experiences the flow of temporal passage and faces the future as not completely settled. How can a timeless God be the Creator of a temporal world? Why is God described as being involved in temporal realities? Third, it seems to undermine our worship of God. Do we not praise God, not because he is beyond time and change but because he works redemptively in time and brings about salvation? Fourth, if God did not experience events as they transpire, he would not experience or know the world as it actually is. If God's eternity were timeless, God could not be related to our temporal world. In actual fact, though, the biblical symbols do not speak of divine timelessness but of God's faithfulness over time. Though we wither and die, God abides and is not threatened or undone by time. We need an understanding of God's eternity that does not cancel or annihilate time but stands in a positive relation to it, which is for us not against us.

Experiencing temporal passage, God confronts a future that is open. The distinction between what is possible and what is actual is valid for God as well as for us. The past is actual, the present is becoming, and the future is possible. The everlasting One is active and dynamic through all of this flow, envisaging future possibilities and working to realize them. Transcendent to temporal passage, God is in the process without being involuntarily subject to it.

When I say that God is eternal, I mean that God transcends our experience of time, is immune from the ravages of time, is free from our inability to remember, and so forth. I affirm that God is with us in time, experiencing the succession of events with us. Past, present and future are real to God. This underlies the biblical claim that God is an agent who works in history, who makes plans and carries them out, who remembers the past and gives promises about the future. God's eternity embraces time and takes temporal events into the divine life.

The God of the Bible is not timeless. His eternity means that there has never been and never will be a time when God does not exist. Timelessness limits God. If he were timeless, God would be unable to work salvation in history, would be cut off from the world, have no real relationship with people and would be completely static. God is not temporal as creatures are, however, but can enter into time and relate to sequence and history. When I say that God is in time, I do not mean that God is exhaustively in time. Even in human experience, we partially transcend time through memory, imagination and reason. God's transcendence over time is vastly more perfect than is ours. Putting it positively, the Creator of time and space is at the same time the One who most perfectly experiences time. God loves time and enters into the experience of time, not only in the incarnation but always. The Bible sees God as present to the flow of history, facing the future as partly an unsettled matter. I say partly because much of the future is settled by what has already happened and by what God plans to do.[9]

DIVINE KNOWLEDGE

Obviously God must know all things that can be known and know them truly. To be able to know all that can be known is a dimension of God's power. Ignorance, or not to know something God needs to know in order to govern the universe and pursue his will, would be a serious limitation. However, omniscience need not mean exhaustive foreknowledge of all future events. If that were its meaning, the future would be fixed and determined, much as is the past. Total knowledge of the future would imply a fixity of events. Nothing in the future would need to be decided. It also would imply that human freedom is an illusion, that we make no difference and are not responsible.

What does the Bible say about God's knowledge? Many believe that the Bible says that God has exhaustive foreknowledge, but it does not. It says, for example, that God tested Abraham to see what he would do and after the test says through the angel: "Now I know that you fear God" (Gen 22:12). This was a piece of information that God was eager to secure. In another place Moses said that God was testing the people in order to know whether they actually love him or not (Deut 13:3). Total foreknowledge would jeopardize the genuineness of the divine-human relationship. What kind of dialogue is it where one party already knows what the other will say and do? I would not call this a personal relationship. Commenting on Israel's wickedness, God expresses frustration: "nor did it enter my mind that they should do this abomination" (Jer 32:35 NRSV). God had not anticipated it. In the book of Jonah, God threatens Nineveh with destruction and then calls it off (much to Jonah's chagrin) when the people repent (Jon 3:10). Their repenting was not something God knew in advance would happen. He was planning to destroy them but changed his mind when they converted.

Often God says things like this in the Bible: "Perhaps they will understand" or "It may be that they will listen." From such phrases we must deduce that God has different options depending on people's responses that are still outstanding (see Jer 26:3; Ezek 12:3; etc.). In saying "perhaps," God also indicates that he does not possess complete knowledge of the future. The dozens of examples like this throughout Scripture establish that the Bible thinks of an open future that is not completely certain. The popular belief in God's total omniscience is not so much a biblical idea as an old tradition.

The few verses that seem to go further do not require exhaustive foreknowledge. God's knowledge is wonderful and far-reaching (Ps 139:1–6) but need not be limitless with respect to the future. Isaiah records prophecies about things to come (Is 44:23–28), but these chiefly establish what God promises to do and do not prove limitless foreknowledge. Prophecies are generally open-ended and dependent in some way on the human response to them.

We should not think of God's omniscience as a vast encyclopedia of past, present and future facts. The Bible does not see it this way, nor is it a helpful way to think of it. When God gave creatures freedom, he gave them an open future, a future in a degree to be shaped by their decisions, not a future already determined in its every detail. We do not limit God by saying that he can be surprised by what his creatures do. It would be a serious limitation if God could not experience surprise and delight. The world would be a boring place without anything unexpected ever happening.

Those who are unsure of this should ask themselves if they think God *could* create a world where he would not be in total control of everything, where he would experience risk and where he would not foreknow all decisions of his creatures in advance. Surely this must be possible if God is all-powerful.

Then is this world not just like that? Has God not already made just such a world? Does the Bible not assume it—do we not experience it as such?

Philosophically speaking, if choices are real and freedom significant, future decisions cannot be exhaustively foreknown. This is because the future is not determinate but shaped in part by human choices. The future is not fixed like the past, which can be known completely. The future does not yet exist and therefore cannot be infallibly anticipated, even by God. Future decisions cannot in every way be foreknown, because they have not yet been made. God knows everything that can be known— but God's foreknowledge does not include the undecided.

It would seriously undermine the reality of our decisions if they were known in advance, spelled out in a heavenly register and absolutely certain to happen. It would make the future fixed and certain and render illusory the sense of our making choices between real options. We might think of this with the analogy of parents and children. As a parent, God knows what he needs to know to deal with any contingency that might arise but does not know or need to know every detail of the future. God is a person and deals with us as persons. This means that God understands us, has intuition into every situation we face and is able to deal appropriately with every situation.

This implies that God learns things and (I would add) enjoys learning them. It does not mean that God is anybody's pupil or that he has to overcome ignorance and learn things of which he should have been aware. It means that God created a dynamic and changing world and enjoys getting to know it. It is a world of freedom, capable of genuine novelty, inexhaustible creativity and real surprises. I believe that God takes delight in the spontaneity of the universe and enjoys continuing to get to know it in a love that never changes, just as we love to get to know our children as they grow up. God is the best learner of all because he is completely open to all the input of an unfolding world, whereas we are finite and slow to react, reluctant to learn and inclined to distort reality in our own interest. Rather than supposing God

cannot learn, we should try to learn as God learns. If this matter of God's learning surprises anyone, be reminded that simple foreknowledge also implies that God learns from what creatures do. I am not speaking in a temporal sense now but in the sense that part of what God knows depends on what creatures do.

Thus, God does not foreknow every future choice or the outcome of every human decision. God is all-knowing in the sense that he knows all that it is possible to know and powerful enough to do whatever is needed. Under these circumstances, more power and wisdom are required for God to bring his will to pass in a world that he does not control than in one that he did control. As Gregory Boyd remarks, "It takes far more self-confidence, far more wisdom, far more love and sensitivity to govern that which is personal and free than it does to govern that over which one has absolute control."[10] As a political aside, what would we think of those who contend that total control is praiseworthy as a mode of governance?

CONCLUSION

The God whom we love and worship is the living God who is metaphysically social and desires relationship with us. God is One whose ways are marked by flexibility and dynamism, who acts and reacts on behalf of his people, who does not exist in splendid isolation from a world of change, but relates to his creatures and shares life with them. God not only directs but interacts. No unmoved mover, God responds sensitively to what happens on earth and relates to us. God is the omnipotent Creator but exercises his power subtly and carefully in the world. By bringing other free agents into being and entering into their lives in love, God is open.

We are seeking to correct the tradition without overcorrecting the error. God is high above all yet fills all things. God is unchanging yet relates to us in a changing world. God cannot be perplexed but suffers with his people. God's power is limitless but is deployed in ways that may appear weak. God is not subject to change or decay but can relate to temporal passage. God knows everything but is still learning what the world is becoming.

The open view of God stresses qualities of generosity, sensitivity and vulnerability more than power and control. It allows us to think of God as taking risks. Instead of locating God above and beyond history, it stresses God's activity in history, responding to events as they happen, in order to accomplish his purposes. Rather than deciding the future all by himself, God made creatures with the capacity to surprise and delight him. Like a loving parent, he rejoices with them when they are happy and suffers with them when they are in pain. In and through everything, God is committed to their welfare and continually works to achieve what is best for them.

The picture of God that I receive from the Bible is of One who takes risks and jeopardizes his own sovereignty in order to engage in historical interactions with created reality. The triune God pursues this path out of the love that is fundamental to his very being. This does not make history the author of God. It portrays God as the author of history who delights in meaningful interaction with creatures as his purposes for the world are realized.[11]

NOTES

1. Karl Barth, *Church Dogmatics* 2/1 (Edinburgh: T&T Clark, 1957), pp. 272–321.

2. Otto Weber, *Foundations of Dogmatics* (Grand Rapids, Mich.: Eerdmans, 1981), 1:440–47.

3. Harry R. Boer, *An Ember Still Glowing: Humankind in the Image of God* (Grand Rapids, Mich.: Eerdmans, 1990), chap. 8. As an Arminian I can only wish for more Calvinists like this. For a rendition of divine providence after this fashion by an Arminian, see Jack Cottrell, *God the Ruler* (Joplin, Mo.: College Press, 1984).

4. Douglas J. Hall, *God and Human Suffering* (Minneapolis: Augsburg, 1986), chap. 4.

5. Elizabeth A. Johnson, *She Who Is: The Mystery of God in Feminist Theological Discourse* (New York: Crossroad, 1992), pp. 369–70. This book parallels my thesis about the openness of God despite the fact that Johnson identifies her position with panentheism (pp. 230–31). In reality she denies that the world exists necessarily and that God needs the world ontologically. She uses the word *Asymmetrical* to describe the relation between God and the world and therefore should not be using the term *panentheism*. Not to be overbold, I would say that Johnson needs a term like *the openness of God* to describe her view.

6. Walter Wink, "Prayer and the Powers," chap. 16 in *Engaging the Powers* (Minneapolis: Fortress, 1992).

7. Wolfhart Pannenberg, *Systematic Theology*, vol 1 (Grand Rapids, Mich.: Eerdmans, 1991), 416.

8. Terence E. Fretheim, *The Suffering of God: An Old Testament Perspective* (Philadelphia: Fortress, 1984), and Paul S. Fiddes, *The Creative Suffering of God* (Oxford: Clarendon, 1988).

9. Nelson Pike, *God and Timelessness* (New York: Schocken Books, 1970), and Hasker, *God, Time and Knowledge*.

10. Gregory A. Boyd, *Trinity and Process, A Critical Evaluation and Reconstruction of Hartshorne's Di-polar Theism Towards a Trinitarian Metaphysics* (New York: Peter Lang, 1992), p. 336.

11. Anticipating the criticism that the open view of God is a form of process theology, let me reiterate two chief ways in which it differs. First, God is ontologically other than the world, which is not necessary to God—the world exists only because God wills it. Therefore, God is not dependent on the world out of necessity but willingly, because he chose to create a world in which there would be mutuality and relational interdependence. Second, God not only sustains the world as the ground of its being but also acts in history to bring about salvation. God was particularly active in that stream of human history which culminated in the life, death and resurrection of Jesus, and involved himself in marvelous actions that go beyond his undergirding of the world process. God is also active in the entire history of the world by the Spirit, which sustains and directs all things.

I.A.4

God and the World

SALLIE McFAGUE

Sallie McFague (1933–) is a well-known feminist theologian whose work on metaphor in theology has been highly influential. Among her best-known books are Metaphorical Theology: Models of God in Religious Language *and* The Body of God: An Ecological Theology, *from which the present selection is taken. Here, McFague explores the idea that the world is God's body and contrasts this model for thinking about God with other models that have been prominent within the Jewish and Christian traditions. She denies that her model is* pantheistic. (Pantheism *is the view that the world is God. By contrast,* panentheism—*the sort of view that McFague seems to recommend—is the view that the world is, or is very much like, a part of God.)*

A MEDITATION ON EXODUS 33:23B: ''AND YOU SHALL SEE MY BACK; BUT MY FACE SHALL NOT BE SEEN''

When Moses in an audacious moment asks of God, "Show me your glory," God replies that "no one can see me and live," but he does allow Moses a glimpse of the divine body—not the face, but the back (Exodus 33:20–23). The passage is a wonderful mix of the outrageous (God has a *backside*?!) and the awesome (the display of divine glory too dazzling for human eyes). The passage unites guts and glory, flesh and spirit, the human and the divine, and all those other apparent dualisms with a reckless flamboyance that points to something at the heart of the Hebrew and Christian traditions: God is not afraid of the flesh. We intend to take this incarnationalism seriously and see what it does, could, mean in terms of the picture of reality from postmodern science. Were we to imagine "the Word

made flesh" as not limited to Jesus of Nazareth but as the body of the universe, all bodies, might we not have a homey but awesome metaphor for both divine nearness *and* divine glory? Like Moses, when we ask, "Show me your glory," we might see the humble bodies of our own planet as visible signs of the invisible grandeur. Not the face, not the depths of divine radiance, but enough, more than enough. We might begin to see (for the first time, perhaps) the marvels at our feet and at our fingertips: the intricate splendor of an Alpine forget-me-not or a child's hand. We might begin to realize the extraordinariness of the ordinary. We would begin to delight in creation, not as the work of an external deity, but as a sacrament of the living God. We would see creation as bodies alive with the breath of God. We might realize what this tradition has told us, although often shied away from embracing unreservedly: we live and move and have our being *in* God. We might see ourselves and everything else as the living body of God.

We would, then, have an entire planet that reflects the glory, the very being—although not the

Reprinted from *The Body of God: An Ecological Theology* (Augsburg Fortress, 1993). Used by permission of Augsburg Fortress Publishers. Most endnotes omitted.

face—of God. We would have a concrete panorama for meditation on divine glory and transcendence: wherever we looked, whether at the sky with its billions of galaxies (only a few visible to us) or the earth (every square inch of which is alive with millions of creatures) or into the eyes of another human being, we would have an image of divine grandeur. The more we meditated on these bits of the divine body, the more intricate, different, and special each would become. Such meditation is a suitable way for limited, physical creatures with lively imaginations such as ourselves to contemplate the divine being. It is enriching for it does not occur only at one place but everywhere and not just in one form but in an infinite myriad of forms. It is neither otherworldly nor abstract, but is a this-worldly, concrete form of contemplating divine magnificence. It is a way for limited, physical beings like ourselves to meditate on divine transcendence in an immanent way. And it is based on the assumption, central to the Christian tradition, that God not only is not afraid of the flesh but loves it, *becomes* it.

If we are allowed, indeed, invited as Moses was to see God's glory in the divine back, then we experience not only awe as we meditate on the wonders of our planet but also compassion for all bodies in pain. If God is available to us in bodies, then bodies become special. The metaphor of the world as God's body knits together the awe we feel for the magnificent intricacy and splendor of all the diverse kinds of bodies *and* the pain we feel for a suffering human or animal body. We cannot in good conscience marvel with aesthetic delight at the one and not identify with the pain of the other: bodies are beautiful and vulnerable. If God is physical, then the aesthetic and the ethical unite: praising God in and through the beauty of bodies entails caring for the most basic needs of all bodies on the planet. If God is physical, then the divine becomes part of the everyday, part of the pain and pleasure of bodily existence.

We begin to see a new way of imagining and expressing divine transcendence and immanence. It is not a model of transcendence in which God is king and the world is the realm of a distant,

external ruler who has all power and expects unquestioned obedience from his subjects, human beings. Nor is it a model of immanence in which God the king once entered the world by becoming a servant in the form of one human being. Rather, it is a radicalization of both divine transcendence and immanence. The model of the universe as God's body radicalizes transcendence for *all* of the entire fifteen-billion-year history and the billions of galaxies is the creation, the outward being, of the One who is the source and breath of all existence. In the universe as a whole as well as in each and every bit and fragment of it, God's transcendence is embodied. The important word here is "embodied": the transcendence of God is not available to us except as embodied. We do not see God's face, but only the back. But we *do* see the back.

The world (universe) as God's body is also, then, a radicalization of divine immanence, for God is not present to us in just one place (Jesus of Nazareth, although also and especially, paradigmatically there), but in and through all bodies, the bodies of the sun and moon, trees and rivers, animals, and people. The scandal of the gospel is that the Word became flesh; the radicalization of incarnation sees Jesus not as a surd, an enigma, but as a paradigm or culmination of the divine way of enfleshment.

We are suggesting, then, that the model of the universe as God's body is a way of expressing both radical transcendence *and* immanence, but in a fashion that limits our perception and knowledge to the back of God. In other words, we are dealing here with a model or metaphor, not a description: the universe as God's body is a rich, suggestive way to radicalize the glory, the awesomeness, the beyond-all-imagining power and mystery of God in a way that at the same time radicalizes the nearness, the availability, the physicality of divine immanence. In this one image of the world as God's body, we are invited to see the creator *in* the creation, the source of all existence in and through what is bodied forth from that source. And yet, as we contemplate divine transcendence immanently in the bodies of all things and creatures, we know what we see is the back, not the face, of God. The very recognition and acceptance of that limit gives us permission, as the Hebrew psalmists also felt, to revel in the many embodiments divine transcendence takes: the clouds and winds, thunder and water, deer and young lambs, midwives and mothers, kings and shepherds. Everything can be a metaphor for God, because no *one* thing *is* God. The body of God is not the human body nor any other body; rather, all bodies are reflections of God, all bodies are the backside of divine glory.

Radicalizing the incarnation, therefore, by using the model of the universe as God's body is neither idolatry nor pantheism: the world, creation, is not identified or confused with God. Yet it is the place where God is present to us. Christianity's most distinctive belief is that divine reality is always mediated through the world, a belief traditionally expressed in the Chalcedonian formula that Christ was "fully God, fully man." For our time when we understand human existence in continuity with all other forms of life and hence must think of our relation to God in an ecological context, that mediation is appropriately radicalized and expanded to include the entire cosmos. In both instances, the Word is made flesh, God is available to us only through the mediation of embodiment. We are offered not the face of God, but the back. God is neither enclosed in nor exhausted by the body shown to us, but it is a body that is given.

It is enough and it is a body. "It is enough" acknowledges that for those who are persuaded to live within this model, it provides guidance and significance to life, a way of being in the world. Those who wager on this construct believe it tells them something about the way things are; in other words, that it gives them intimations of how God and the world are related. That intimation is suggested by the metaphor of body. "It is a body" suggests content, substance, for what it means to live within this particular construct. It places a premium on the physical, the lowly, the mundane, the specific, the vulnerable, the visible, the other, the needy, for all these words describe aspects of bodies of various kinds. No body, no material form, is absolute, eternal, general, abstract, otherworldly, self-sufficient, invincible, or invisible. Bodies in the universe, in all their differences, share some characteristics that suggest a focus, an area of concern, for those who would live within the construct of the body of God. At one level our model—the universe as God's body—moves us in the direction of contemplating the glory and grandeur of divine creation, an aesthetic awe at unending galactic wonders, while at another level it moves us in the direction of compassionate identification with and service to the fragile, suffering, oppressed bodies that surround us. The model embraces both the guts and the glory, both the mud and the mystery—or, more precisely, suggests that the peculiar form of divine glory available to us, if we live within this model, is *only* through the guts, the mud. Incarnationalism, radicalized, means that we do not, ever, at least in this life, see God face to face, but only through the mediation of the bodies we pay attention to, listen to, and learn to love and care for.

We have used Exodus 33:20–23b as a meditation to help us reflect on some of the most important dimensions of the model of the universe as God's body within a Christian context. In the rest of this chapter and the next, we will analyze the model in more formal terms. First, we will look at five major models within the Christian tradition for understanding the relationship of God and the world: the deistic, the dialogic, the monarchical, the agential, and the organic. We will conclude that combining the organic (the world as the body of God) and the agential (God as the spirit of the body) results in a personal and ecological way of reimagining the tradition's Lord of creation in terms compatible with contemporary science. In the next chapter [of *The Body of God*] we will turn to the Christic paradigm as the place where, within that tradition, we gain some guidance on the "shape" of the body, the forms or patterns with which to understand divine immanence. This paradigm suggests a trajectory or direction for creation. It is not one that we find in evolutionary history, but from our wager of faith in the liberating, healing, and inclusive teachings, life, and death of Jesus of Nazareth, we *can* read it back into natural, historical, and cultural evolution as a way to express its goal. We will suggest that the model of the body of God, when seen within a Christic framework, can serve as a unifying metaphor, encompassing in scope both creation and salvation—the liberation, healing, and fulfillment of all bodies. We will also ask in what ways the model of God as spirit of the body is a continuation and a revision of the tradition's understanding of divine transcendence and immanence as expressed in its trinitarian formula.

MAJOR MODELS OF GOD AND THE WORLD

The First Vatican Council (1890) expressed a view of the relation of God and the world that is, with some variations, a common one in major creeds of various Christian churches since the Reformation:

> The Holy, Catholic, Apostolic, Roman Church believes and confesses that there is one true and living God, Creator and Lord of Heaven and earth, almighty, eternal, immense, incomprehensible, infinite in intelligence, in will, and in all perfection, who, as being one, sole, absolutely simple and immutable spiritual substance, is to be declared really and essentially distinct from the world, of supreme beatitude in and from himself, and ineffably exalted above all things beside himself which exist or are conceivable.[1]

What drives this statement is the passion to remove God from any real connection with the world—"really and essentially distinct from the world" sums it up. In fact, it is difficult to imagine how a God so described could have a genuine, significant relationship with anything outside the divine reality. And yet the Christian tradition has insisted that God not only created the world but admired it and loved at least its human creatures sufficiently so that when they "fell," God became one of them, suffering and dying to redeem them from their sins. The two images of God—one as the distant, all-powerful, perfect, immutable Lord existing in lonely isolation, and the other as the One who enters human flesh as a baby to eventually assume the alienation and oppression of all peoples in the world—do not fit together. Jesus as the immanent, loving image of God is a surd, an enigma, against the background of the distant, exalted, incomprehensible deity. In its credal statements on God and Jesus the tradition attempts to express this view of radical transcendence and radical immanence: the totally distant, "other" God, exalted and perfect, entered into human flesh in Jesus of Nazareth, so that this one man is fully divine and fully human. In the worldview current in first-century Mediterranean times and operable through the Middle Ages, that way of radicalizing and relating transcendence and immanence had some credibility; but it does not in our time. This view seems neither sufficiently radical (God is transcendent only over our world and especially human beings and immanent only in one human being) nor believable (it assumes a dualistic view of reality with God dwelling somewhere external to and exalted above the world and yet entering it at one particular point).

What other options are there for relating God and the world? The principal criteria guiding our analysis and critique of various options will be the radicalization of divine transcendence and immanence as well as those mentioned earlier (embodied experience, usefulness, and compatibility with Christian faith and the contemporary picture of reality). We will suggest that the model of God the spirit, the giver and renewer of her body, the universe, is one that is compatible with readings of both Christianity and postmodern science. A couple of brief comments about this proposal are necessary before setting it in the context of other traditional and contemporary models. First, it is a personal model of God, assuming that we will inevitably imagine God in our image, but to do so with the notion of spirit rather than self, soul, or mind suggests that divine agency is concerned not only with human beings but with all forms of life: God's spirit is the breath of life in all lifeforms. Second, recalling our discussion of the face and back of God, the model of God as spirit of his body, the universe, implies that both terms, *spirit* and *body*, are backside terms: they are both metaphors. Spirit is not really God, while body is a metaphor, nor is spirit closer to divine reality; rather, they are both forms of God's visible being, ways of expressing immanent transcendence and transcendent immanence suitable for creatures like us who are inspirited bodies. The depth and mystery of God are not available to us in this or any other model: the glory of God is only reflected in the world and then in a dim and distorted mirror. It is this dim, distorted mirror that we attempt to model.

We will have much more to say about our model, but with this sketch in mind let us look briefly at some alternatives in order to place the model within a broader context. First, the deistic model, the simplest and least satisfying one, arose during the sixteenth-century scientific revolution. It imagines God as a clockmaker who winds up the clock of the world by creating its laws and then leaves it to run by itself. The model has the advantage of freeing science to investigate the world apart from divine control but essentially banishes God from the world. It is, sadly, the view of many contemporary scientists as well as Christians, with the qualification that some Christians allow periodic, personal interventions of God in times of crisis such as natural disasters, accidents, and death. The view encourages an irresponsible, idolatrous attitude in the scientific community, allowing it to claim for itself sole rights both to interpret and to dispose of the world. On the part of Christians it encourages an interventionist, God-of-the-gaps view of divine activity.

The second view of God and the world, the dialogic one, has deep roots in both Hebrew and Christian traditions: God speaks and we respond. It has been a central view within Protestantism and was highlighted in twentieth-century existentialism. In its contemporary form the relation between God and the world is narrowed to God and the individual: the I-Thou relation between God and a human being. As seen, for instance, in the writings of Søren Kierkegaard or Rudolf Bultmann, this position focuses on sin, guilt, and forgiveness and has the advantage of allowing for a continuous relationship with God, but does so at the expense of indifference to the natural and social worlds. The dialogic position assumes two tracks, religion versus culture (the latter including scientific knowledge and all social institutions such as government, the economy, the family), with each left to run its own affairs. God and the human being meet, not in the world, whether of nature or culture, but only in the inner, internal joy and pain of human experiences. Liberation theologies have protested the focus on individual (usually white, male, Western, affluent) alienation and despair, insisting that God's relation to the world must include the political and social dimensions as well.

The monarchical model, the relation of God and the world in which the divine, all-powerful king controls his subjects and they in turn offer him loyal obedience, is the oldest and still the most prevalent one. It is both a personal and a political model, correcting the impersonalism of the deistic model and the individualism of the dialogic. It also underscores the "godness" of God, for the monarchical imagery calls forth awe and reverence, as well as vocational meaningfulness, since membership in the kingdom entails service to the divine Lord. But since all power is controlled by the king, issues of human freedom and theodicy are highly problematic. Moreover, and most critical for our concerns, the king is both distant from the natural world and indifferent to it, for as a political model it is limited to human beings. The continuing power of this model in liturgical use is curious, since contemporary members of royalty scarcely call up responses of awe, reverence, and obedience, but its nostalgic appeal, as evidenced in the gusto with which we all sing Christmas carols that are rife with this imagery, cannot be underestimated. Any model that would attempt to criticize or partially subvert it ought to look carefully at the main reason for its attraction: it is the only model that attempts to dramatize divine transcendence. Nonetheless, the model of God as king is domesticated transcendence, for a king rules only over human beings, a minute fraction of created reality. The king/realm model is neither genuinely transcendent (God is king over one species recently arrived on a minor planet in an ordinary galaxy) nor genuinely immanent (God as king is an external superperson, not the source, power, and goal of the entire universe).

A fourth model, the agential, also has strong backing in the Hebrew and Christian traditions. Here God is assumed to be an agent whose intentions and purposes are realized in history, especially human history. It has been revived during this century as a way of talking about divine purpose throughout the entire span of cosmic history. The analogy that is often used in this model to explain divine action in the world is the human self realizing its purposes through its body: God is related to the world and realizes the divine intentions and purposes in the world, in a way similar to how we use our bodies to carry out our purposes. This view of divine action has the advantage of internalizing divine action within cosmic processes; however, since these actions are one with the processes, it is difficult if not impossible to differentiate divine action from evolutionary history. Moreover, since the human being is the prototype for divine action, the human body emerges implicitly as the model for God's body, suggesting anthropomorphism: God is understood as a superperson with a high degree of control over the world in a way similar to our control over the actions of our bodies. Finally, at least in its contemporary form, the model has been advanced largely to satisfy intellectual puzzles: How might we imagine divine action in an internal rather than an external, supernatural fashion? The classic agential model, which is at heart personal (God as father, mother, lord, lover, king, friend), God as actor and doer, creating and redeeming the world, has profound ethical and liturgical dimensions, while the contemporary version does not. But if the model were God as spirit (breath, life) of the body (the world, universe) rather than the mind or self that directs and controls creation, the ethical and liturgical dimensions might reemerge.

The agential model should, I believe, be joined with the fifth and final major model, the organic, for either alone is lacking in light of our criteria but together they suggest a more adequate model. The organic model is the one on which this essay is focused: the world or universe as God's body. However, alone, that is, apart from the agential model, which suggests a center of being not exhausted by or completely identified with the world or universe, the organic model is pantheistic. The world is, becomes, divine. Christian thinking, with its ancient commitment to a transcendent deity who created a world distinct from himself has had, as we have seen, a highly ambivalent relationship to the organic model.

Two recent instances of serious reconsideration of it, both under pressure from the view of reality in postmodern science and both combining agency and organism, are process theology and the work of Teilhard de Chardin. Process thought moves toward a social view of agency (every entity or actual occasion is an agent, including God), while Teilhard suggests a more traditional view of God as the supreme agent guiding the evolutionary process toward more and more complex, unified agents. The process version of organicism emphasizes the interdependence and reciprocity of all agents, with God as one among many, though the preeminent one, while Teilhard's version gives a greater role to divine purpose and direction. These are both exciting, provocative proposals with profound implications for an ecological sensibility. Process ontology, with its insistence on the agency or subjectivity of all entities, provides a basis for the intrinsic value of every created being, living and nonliving. Teilhard's view also underscores the value of each and every aspect of evolutionary reality, although in a more traditional sacramental mode. All things are being transformed through their processes of natural growth toward the divine source and goal of their existence. Both of these variations on the organic model are pan*en*theistic, not pantheistic; in both, divine transcendence and immanence are radicalized, with Teilhard expressing the radicalization mythologically and process theology conceptually. In differing degrees both are credible, persuasive readings of postmodern science and Christianity.

My essay is a continuation and development of these projects at the metaphorical level. While Teilhard certainly did work poetically and mythologically, as I have suggested, his images were rather esoteric (Omega Point, noogenesis), referring to parts of the process of evolutionary teleology. Process theologians, although conceptually oriented, have also suggested some powerful metaphors, notably A. N. Whitehead's notion of God as the Great Companion. They have also revived a limited use for the model of the world as God's body.[2] Both process theology and Teilhard are radical revisionings of the relation of God and the world; however, neither suggests an overall *model* for reimaging that relation.

SPIRIT AND BODY

My essay undertakes such a task, although with a profound debt to the organic and agential models of Teilhard and process theology. The agential model preserves transcendence, while the organic model underscores immanence. Alone, the agential model overemphasizes the transcendent power and freedom of God at the expense of the world. Alone, the organic model tends to collapse God and the world, denying the freedom and individuality of both. But if the model were that God is related to the world as spirit is to body, perhaps the values of both the agential and organic models could be preserved.

Two related issues, however, face us immediately. The first is the suitability of *any* personal language for God as being compatible with contemporary science. The second, assuming that we can provide reasons for retaining agential language, is the *kind* of personal imagery that is most appropriate. The dilemma set by these issues is an acute one: the Hebrew and Christian traditions are profoundly and, 1 would argue, indelibly agential; yet postmodern science, as we have seen, does not appear to permit any purpose or agency apart from local causation. This dilemma has caused some theologians to retreat from personal language for God except in worship. The implication is that personal language does not really refer to God but is necessary for liturgical purposes, while the proper way to

speak of God in the context of postmodern science is impersonally. One unfortunate result of this position is a willingness to continue to use traditional metaphors for God such as God as lord and father (since they are "only" liturgical images), without working toward more appropriate ones.

This approach permits, I believe, too strong a control of science over theology. If it can be shown that *all* personal metaphors are incompatible with postmodern science, the case becomes stronger. But since little reconstructive work on such models has been attempted, the images in question are traditional ones, not necessarily all personal ones. I agree that the monarchical, triumphalistic, patriarchal imagery for God is impossible to square with an evolutionary, ecological, cosmological framework. Even some of the more intimate models—God as mother (and father), lover, and friend—need to be balanced by other, less anthropocentric ones. But are all personal models worthless, discordant, incongruous from the perspective of contemporary science? Moreover, if we do discard them all and speak of God only or principally in impersonal terms, can we any longer pretend that we still belong within the Western religious paradigm? Finally, is not the refusal to imagine God in personal terms a gesture in the direction of disembodiment: *we* are embodied agents, and is it not therefore natural and appropriate, as the outermost contemporary evolutionary phylum, to imagine our creator "in our image"?

The major model we are investigating in depth is the combined agential-organic one of the universe (world) as God's body, a body enlivened and empowered by the divine spirit. We have dealt in some detail with the organic aspect of the model, the universe as God's body, but what of the agential or personal aspect, the spirit? To begin framing an answer to this question, we need to start with ourselves as the concrete, embodied beings we are. We are embodied personal agents, and if we are not to be surds or outcasts in the world, we need to imagine God's relationship to the world in a way that includes us, that makes us feel at home. Mechanistic, impersonal models exclude us; personal, organic ones include us. If the history of the universe and especially the evolutionary history of our planet makes it clear that we do, in fact, belong here and that evolution has resulted in self-conscious beings, then does it not make sense to imagine the relationship between God and the world in a manner that is continuous with that evolutionary history, especially if, as we shall suggest, there is a way of modeling personal agency that also touches one of the deepest traditions of Christian thought?

That tradition is of God as spirit—not Holy Ghost, which suggests the unearthly and the disembodied, nor initially the Holy Spirit, which has been focused largely on human beings and especially the followers of Christ, but the spirit of God, the divine wind that "swept over the face of the waters" prior to creation, the life-giving breath given to all creatures, and the dynamic movement that creates, recreates, and transcreates throughout the universe. Spirit, as wind, breath, life is the most basic and most inclusive way to express centered embodiment. All living creatures, not just human ones, depend upon breath. Breath also knits together the life of animals and plants, for they are linked by the exchange of oxygen and carbon dioxide in each breath inhaled and exhaled. Breath is a more immediate and radically dependent way to speak of life than even food or water, for we literally live from breath to breath and can survive only a few minutes without breathing. Our lives are enclosed by two breaths—our first when we emerge from our mother's womb and our last when we "give up the ghost" (spirit).

Spirit is a wide-ranging, multidimensional term with many meanings built upon its physical base as the breath of life. We speak of a person's spirit, their vigor, courage, or strength; of team spirit, the collective energy of people at play; of the spirit of '76 or the spirit of Tienanmen Square, the vitality, grit, and resolution of a people banding together in a common cause to oppose oppression; of a spirited horse or the spirit of a sacred grove—animals, trees, and mountains can also have spirit. All these connotations are possible because of the primary meaning of spirit as the breath of life: "Then the Lord God formed man [sic] from the dust of the ground and breathed into his nostrils the breath of life"

(Gen. 2:7). Bracketing the sexism of the Genesis 2 creation story, it nonetheless suggests the prime analogy of this essay: the dust of the universe enlivened by the breath of God. Each of us, and each and every other part of the body as well, owes our existence, breath by breath as we inhale and exhale, to God. We "live and move and have our being" in God (Acts 17:28). Indeed we do. That is, perhaps, the most basic confession that can be made: I owe my existence at its most fundamental level— the gift of my next breath—to God. God is my creator and recreator, the One who gives and renews my life, moment by moment, at its most basic, physical level. And so does everything else in creation also live, moment by moment, by the breath of God, says our model.

We are suggesting, then, that we think of God metaphorically as the spirit that is the breath, the life, of the universe, a universe that comes from God and could be seen as the body of God. Both of these terms, *spirit* and *body*, are metaphors: both refer properly to ourselves and other creatures and entities in our experience of the world. Neither describes God, for both are *back*, not *face*, terms. Nonetheless, even with these qualifications, questions abound. Let us look at a few of them. Why choose *spirit* rather than other personal, agential terms such as *self, mind, heart, will, soul*, and the like? Does spirit language for God make sense in terms of postmodern science and the Christian tradition? Does contemporary science substantiate such language, or does it accommodate or allow it? Can Christians use the model of God as embodied spirit, and, more pointedly, in a transcendent sky-God tradition, is it pantheistic? Does it collapse God and the world?

One reason for suggesting spirit as the way to speak of divine agency is that it undercuts anthropocentrism and promotes cosmocentrism. Only a human being has a mind or self, whereas spirit, while able to include mind and self, has a much broader range. Most attempts to use the body metaphor in regard to God rely on the analogy of mind/body: God relates to the world as the mind (self) relates to the body. Not only does this form of the analogy involve difficult, often dualistic, arguments concerning the mind/body correlation, but, just as important for our considerations, it implies that divine activity in relation to the world is primarily intellectual and controlling: God is Mind or Will. This is an old, deep tradition in the Hebrew and Christian traditions as manifest in Wisdom and Logos theologies: God creates the universe as its orderer, as the One who gives it direction, limits, and purpose. The emphasis is on the work of the mind, the work of intelligence and control. It is precisely this concern that surfaces in the ancient enterprise of natural theology: the need to answer the questions of why and how. But a spirit theology suggests another possibility: that God is not primarily the orderer and controller of the universe but its source and empowerment, the breath that enlivens and energizes it. The spirit perspective takes seriously the fecundity, diversity, range, and complexity of life and of life-supporting systems. It does not claim that the divine mind is the cause of what evolutionary theory tells us can have only local causes; rather, it suggests that we think of these local causes as enlivened and empowered by the breath of God. A spirit theology focuses attention not on how and why creation occurred either in the beginning or over the evolutionary aeons of time, but on the rich variety of living forms that have been and are *now* present on our planet. The breath of God enlivening each and every entity in the body of the universe turns our attention to a theology of nature, a theology concerned with the relationship of God and our living, breathing planet. The principal reason, then, for preferring spirit to alternative possibilities is that it underscores the connection between God and the world as not primarily the Mind that orders, controls, and directs the universe, but as the Breath that is the source of its life and vitality. The connection is one of *relationship* at the deepest possible level, the level of life, rather than *control* at the level of ordering and directing nature. And since, as we recall, our tendency is not only to model God in our image but to model ourselves on the models with which we imagine God, the metaphor of breath rather than mind might help us to support, rather than control, life in all its forms. Thus, in a spirit theology, we might see ourselves as united with all other living creatures through the breath that moves through all parts of the body, rather than as the demilords who order and control nature.

But is this model commensurate with twentieth-century science? If one understands the spirit of God as the source of the dynamic vitality of the universe and especially as the breath of all lifeforms, then our focus is not on the purpose or direction of divine activity but on our dependence on God as the present and continuing creator. Our concern is not primarily intellectual but aesthetic and ethical: wonder and awe at the immensity, richness, and diversity of creation as well as gratitude and care for all its forms of life. Our response to this model is as grateful recipients of life rather than puzzlers over its mysteries. Contemporary science does not mandate or even imply such a model, but it is commensurate with an organic interpretation of its story. Since we and all other creatures and entities are in some sense inspirited bodies (even trees and oceans move with the winds), then if we were to think of God as in some sense continuous with this evolutionary history, one way to do so would be as the spirit of the entire body of the universe. This is not, of course, a scientific description nor is it a theological one; rather, it is a way of thinking about God and the world that makes sense in terms of postmodern science. It allows us to understand ourselves who have evolved into spiritual, embodied creatures as neither freaks nor surds in our world. It also allows us to think of God as the source of our being, the source of all being, not as the one who intervenes from the outside to initiate creation, patch it up, or direct it, but as the one who supplies us with the breath for all the incredible rich, teeming fecundity and variety of life.

It is a model of God and the world that focuses on "the wonderful life" that has emerged from evolutionary history, rather than on the divine ordering of the process. It does not attempt to enter into scientific discussions on the how and why of that history, but suggests that if one is *already* a person of faith (which cannot be arrived at or substantiated by postmodern science), then the picture of reality as an organic whole, a body, dependent on and sustained by the spirit of God, is one that fits with, is appropriate to, evolutionary history. This theology of nature is not a natural theology: it does not say that the scientific story gives evidence (even the tiniest bit) for belief in this or any other model of God and the world. All it says is that this way of conceiving of God and the world makes more sense in terms of the scientific picture than alternatives such as the deistic, dialogic, and monarchical models. But this is enough. A theology of nature does not ask for scientific proof, only for a picture to help us think and act holistically about God, ourselves, and our world.

Where does this model stand in regard to the Christian tradition? We can answer that question on one level simply and forth-rightly by recalling the theme of the 1991 World Council of Churches assembly in Canberra, Australia: "Come, Holy Spirit—Renew the Whole Creation," or the affirmation from the Nicene Creed: "I believe in the Holy Spirit, the Lord and Giver of Life." While the spirit of God, now the Holy Spirit, has often played a lackluster role in relation to the Father and the Son in Christian trinitarian thought, its credentials in both the Hebrew Scriptures and in the New Testament are more than solid. The motif that runs throughout is the spirit as the source of life and the renewer of life: a theology of the spirit focuses on God as the creator and redeemer of life. The trajectory begins with the spirit of God hovering over the waters of chaos and breathing life into living beings; the spirit renews creation in the gift of baptism, the second birth; and fulfills it in the eschatological vision of all creation in harmonious union. One of the great assets of the model is precisely its amorphous character in contrast to the highly human, personal, and androcentric nature of Father and Son: spirit is not necessarily human, personal (though it is relational), or male. In fact, it often has been designated female; but it may be best that, for once in Christian reflection, we let God be "it." "It" (the divine spirit) roams where it will, not focused on the like-minded (the fathers and the sons—or even the mothers and daughters), but permeating, suffusing, and energizing the innermost being of each and every entity in creation in ways

unknown and unknowable in our human, personal categories.

The joining of the spirit that gives life to every creature with the Holy Spirit that renews all creation suggests a connection between Christian theology and the two forms of evolution—biological and biocultural. Creation, the gift of the spirit, could be seen as the action of God in the aeons of evolutionary development, which has resulted in the wonderful life we see about us as well as in ourselves. (This is a retrospective reading of creation in evolutionary terms.) In the model of the universe as God's body, divine incarnation is not limited to redemption but is everywhere evident in the bodies that live through the breath of the spirit. Within this model of the universe as God's body, God's presence and action are evident as the breath of life that gives all bodies, all forms of matter, the energy or power to become themselves. This understanding of divine action in light of evolutionary development focuses on *empowerment*, not direction. It does not claim that God is guiding the process in general or in particular; rather, it suggests that *all* life, regardless of which individuals or species prosper, is dependent upon God. God's creative action is not intermittent or occasional; on the contrary, it is continuous and universal, for without the sustaining breath of God, all the wonderful life, including our own, would fade and die. The "purpose" of creation from this perspective, however, is not human beings (or any other species), but the fecundity, richness, and diversity of *all* that is bodied forth from God and sustained in life by the breath of God. Needless to say, creation in this picture involves enormous waste, suffering, and death for all kinds of bodies—to suggest anything less or different is sentimental and false to the contemporary scientific picture of reality.

In Christian theology, however, the spirit of God is also the Holy Spirit, the spirit shaped and made known in the Hebrew Scriptures as well as in the life, teachings, and death of Jesus of Nazareth and the community that formed around him. Moreover, evolution is not only biological; with self-conscious creatures it enters a historical, cultural phase. At this point divine purpose can be spoken of within the evolutionary process in a new and special way. It is not only empowerment of but also a *direction* for all that teeming life, a direction expressed by Christians in the stories, images, and ideas of the Hebrew people, its paradigmatic founder Jesus, and all the lives and understandings of disciples over the centuries. The guide for interpreting that direction is called the Holy Spirit, and it works *through* human beings: we become the mind and heart as well as the hands and feet of the body of God on our planet. Christians claim that God has been in the natural process as its creator and sustainer (the spirit of the body) since the beginning, but now that process has been given a particular direction (a "new creation") characterized by inclusive love, especially for the vulnerable and oppressed. For Christians, the spirit has been qualified or given shape and scope by the Holy Spirit and is a direction or purpose for life that depends on our cooperation as God's partners.

Hence, we can say that God's action as the spirit of the body is twofold. The spirit is the source of life, the breath of creation; at the same time, the Holy Spirit is the source of the renewal of life, the direction or purpose for all the bodies of the world—a goal characterized by inclusive love.

One central issue remains in regard to our model of God as the spirit of life bodied forth in the universe: Is it pantheistic? This is a complex issue in Christian theology with intricate historical dimensions we cannot settle here. Nonetheless, the criteria for models of God and the world operative in this essay—commensurability with postmodern science as well as our own embodied experience and the well-being of our planet—cause us to lean toward an interpretation of Christian faith that accommodates this model. Since the model is commensurate with contemporary science, mirrors our own experience as embodied spirits, and connects us at the basic level of life-giving breath with all other lifeforms on our planet, we are encouraged to look to those traditions within Christianity that emphasize the spirit in similar ways. These traditions can be characterized as neither theist nor pantheist, but pan*entheist*: "God is not exhausted by finite beings, not even all finite beings, yet God is

in all finite creatures and apart from God there is nothing; nor is God 'apart' from anything."[3] This description of a panentheistic view of the relation of God and the world is compatible with our model of God as the spirit that is the source, the life, the breath of all reality. Everything that is is *in* God and God is *in* all things and yet God is not identical with the universe, for the universe is dependent on God in a way that God is not dependent on the universe. We joined the agential and organic models in order to express the asymmetrical and yet profoundly interrelational character of the panentheistic model of God and the world: while we, as members of the body, are radically dependent upon the life-giving breath from the spirit, God, as the spirit, is not so dependent upon the universe. Pantheism says that God is embodied, necessarily and totally; traditional theism claims that God is disembodied, necessarily and totally; panentheism suggests that God is embodied but not necessarily or totally. Rather, God is sacramentally embodied: God is mediated, expressed, in and through embodiment, but not necessarily or totally. It is, as we recall, the back and not the face of God that we are allowed to see.

Panentheism is, I would suggest, a strong motif in both Hebrew and Christian traditions that take seriously the mediation of God to the world. These traditions deny, on the one hand, a picture of God as an external superperson (or Unmoved Mover) distant from and alien to the world and, on the other hand, a view of God as immediately available to the mind of human beings or as identified with natural processes. Rather, the panentheistic tradition is found in all those passages in the Hebrew Scriptures that mediate the divine presence through human words and acts as well as natural phenomena and in the New Testament in its central declaration that "the Word was made flesh" in Jesus of Nazareth. In all these instances, mediation and incarnation are central and, therefore, are open to, or ought to be open to, the embodiment of God, especially in its panentheistic form of the world (universe) as God's body and God as its spirit.

To sum up: we have suggested that God as the embodied spirit of the universe is a personal/

organic model that is compatible with interpretations of both Christian faith and contemporary science, although not demanded by either. It is a way of speaking of God's relation to all matter, all creation, that "makes sense" in terms of an incarnational understanding of Christianity and an organic interpretation of postmodern science. It helps us to be *whole* people within our faith and within our contemporary world. Moreover, the model does not reduce God to the world nor relegate God to another world; on the contrary, it radicalizes both divine immanence (God is the breath of each and every creature) and divine transcendence (God is the energy empowering the entire universe). Finally, it underscores our bodiliness, our concrete physical existence and experience that we share with all other creatures: it is a model on the side of the well-being of the planet, for it raises the issue of ethical regard toward *all* bodies as all are interrelated and interdependent.

NOTES

1. Vincent McNabb, ed., *The Decrees of the Vatican Council* (London, 1907) as quoted by Grace Jantzen, *God's World, God's Body* (Philadelphia: Westminster Press, 1984), 102.

2. A. N. Whitehead, *Process and Reality: An Essay in Cosmology* (New York: Macmillan, 1929), 16f. The classic process theology essay on the model of the world as God's body is by Charles Hartshorne, "The Theological Analogies and the Cosmic Organism," *Man's Vision of God and the Logic of Theism* (New York: Willett, Clark, and Co., 1941), 171–211. While Hartshorne uses the human body as the base of his organic model, he does so with a fine eye to sociality and diversity by focusing on the complex cellular constitution of the body.

3. Raymond Keith Williamson, *Introduction to Hegel's Philosophy of Religion* (Albany, NY: SUNY Press, 1984), 254.

I.A.5

The Reality of God

PAUL TILLICH

Paul Tillich (1886–1965) was one of the most influential theologians of the twentieth century and taught at some of the most important American and German divinity schools, including the University of Chicago, Harvard Divinity School, and Union Theological Seminary. The following selection is taken from Volume 1 of his Systematic Theology. *Tillich argues that "God" refers to our "ultimate concern," and that the only nonsymbolic characterization of God that we can offer is one according to which God is "being-itself."*

From Paul Tillich, *Systematic Theology,* vol. 1. (Chicago, IL: University of Chicago Press). © 1951 by the University of Chicago. All rights reserved. Reprinted by permission of University of Chicago Press.

A. THE MEANING OF ''GOD''

1. A Phenomenological Description

a) God and man's ultimate concern.—''God'' is the answer to the question implied in man's finitude; he is the name for that which concerns man ultimately. This does not mean that first there is a being called God and then the demand that man should be ultimately concerned about him. It means that whatever concerns a man ultimately becomes god for him, and, conversely, it means that a man can be concerned ultimately only about that which is god for him. The phrase "being ultimately concerned" points to a tension in human experience. On the one hand, it is impossible to be concerned about something which cannot be encountered concretely, be it in the realm of reality or in the realm of imagination. Universals can become matters of ultimate concern only through their power of representing concrete experiences. The more concrete a thing is, the more the possible concern about it. The completely concrete being, the individual person, is the object of the most radical concern—the concern of love. On the other hand, ultimate concern must transcend every preliminary finite and concrete concern. It must transcend the whole realm of finitude in order to be the answer to the question implied in finitude. But in transcending the finite the religious concern loses the concreteness of a being-to-being relationship. It tends to become not only absolute but also abstract, provoking reactions from the concrete element. This is the inescapable inner tension in the idea of God. The conflict between the concreteness and the ultimacy of the religious concern is actual wherever God is experienced and this experience is expressed, from primitive prayer to the most elaborate theological system. It is the key to understanding the dynamics of the history of religion, and it is the basic problem of every doctrine of God, from the earliest priestly wisdom to the most refined discussions of the trinitarian dogma.

A phenomenological description of the meaning of "God" in every religion, including the Christian, offers the following definition of the meaning of the term "god." Gods are beings who transcend the realm of ordinary experience in power and meaning, with whom men have relations which surpass ordinary relations in intensity and significance. A discussion of each element of this basic description will give a full phenomenological picture of the meaning of "god," and this will be the tool with which an interpretation of the nature and the development of the phenomena which are called "religious" may be fashioned.

Gods are "beings." They are experienced, named, and defined in concrete intuitive (*anschaulich*) terms through the exhaustive use of all the ontological elements and categories of finitude. Gods are substances, caused and causing, active and passive, remembering and anticipating, arising and disappearing in time and space. Even though they are called "highest beings," they are limited in power and significance. They are limited by other gods or by the resistance of other beings and principles, for example, matter and fate. The values they represent limit and sometimes annihilate each other. The gods are open to error, compassion, anger, hostility, anxiety. They are images of human nature or subhuman powers raised to a superhuman realm. This fact, which theologians must face in all its implications, is the basis of all theories of "projection" which say that the gods are simply imaginary projections of elements of finitude, natural and human elements. What these theories disregard is that projection always is projection *on* something—a wall, a screen, another being, another realm. Obviously, it is absurd to class that on which the projection is realized with the projection itself. A screen is not projected; it receives the projection. The realm against which the divine images are projected is not itself a projection. It is the experienced ultimacy of being and meaning. It is the realm of ultimate concern.

Therefore, not only do the images of the gods bear all the characteristics of finitude—this makes them images and gives them concreteness—but they also have characteristics in which categorical finitude is radically transcended. Their identity as finite substances is negated by all kinds of substantial transmutations and expansions, in spite of the sameness of their names. Their temporal limitations are overcome; they are called "immortals" in spite of the fact that their appearance and disappearance are presupposed. Their spatial definiteness is negated when they act as multi- or omnipresent, yet they have a special dwelling place with which they are intimately connected. Their subordination to the chain of causes and effects is denied, for overwhelming or absolute power is attributed to them in spite of their dependence on other divine powers and on the influence finite beings have on them. In concrete cases they demonstrate omniscience and perfection in spite of the struggles and betrayals going on among the gods themselves. They transcend their own finitude in power of being and in the embodiment of meaning. The tendency toward ultimacy continuously fights against the tendency toward concreteness.

The history of religion is full of human attempts to participate in divine power and to use it for human purposes. This is the point at which the magic world view enters religious practice and offers technical tools for an effective use of divine power. Magic itself is a theory and practice concerning the relation of finite beings to each other; it assumes that there are direct, physically unmediated sympathies and influences between beings on the "psychic" level, that is, on the level which comprises the vital, the subconscious, and the emotional. In so far as the gods are beings, magic relations in both directions are possible—from man to the gods and from the gods to man—and they are the basis for human participation in divine power.

Nonmagical, personalistic world views lead to a person-to-person relationship to divine power, which is appropriated through prayer, that is, through an appeal to the personal center of the divine being. The god answers in a free decision. He might or he might not use his power to fulfil the content of the prayer. In any case, he remains free, and attempts to force him to act in a particular way are considered magic. Seen in this context, every prayer of supplication illustrates the tension between the concrete element and the ultimate element in the idea of God. Theologians have suggested that this type of prayer should be replaced by thanksgiving in order to avoid magic connotations (Ritschl). But actual religious life reacts violently against such

a demand. Men continue to use the power of their god by asking his favors. They demand a concrete god, a god with whom man can deal.

A third way of trying to use the divine power is through a mystical participation in it which is neither magical nor personalistic. Its main characteristic is the devaluation of the divine beings and their power over against the ultimate power, the abyss of being-itself. The Hindu doctrine that the gods tremble when a saint exercises radical asceticism is another illustration of the tension between the gods as beings with a higher, though limited, power and the ultimate power which they express and conceal at the same time. The conflict between the Brahma power and the god Brahman as an object of a concrete relation with man points to the same tension within the structure of man's ultimate concern which was noted above.

The gods are superior not only in power but also in meaning. They embody the true and the good. They embody concrete values, and as gods they claim absoluteness for them. The imperialism of the gods which follows from this situation is the basis of all other imperialisms. Imperialism is never the expression of will to power as such. It always is a struggle for the absolute victory of a special value or system of values, represented by a special god or hierarchy of gods. The ultimacy of the religious concern drives toward universality in value and in meaning; the concreteness of the religious concern drives toward particular meanings and values. The tension is insoluble. The co-ordination of all concrete values removes the ultimacy of the religious concern. The subordination of concrete values to any one of them produces antiimperialistic reactions on the part of the others. The drowning of all concrete values is an abyss of meaning and value evokes antimystical reactions on the part of the concrete element in man's ultimate concern. The conflict between these elements is present in every act of creedal confession, in every missionary task, in every claim to possess final revelation. It is the nature of the gods which creates these conflicts, and it is man's ultimate concern which is mirrored in the nature of the gods.

We have discussed the meaning of "god" in terms of man's relation to the divine, and we have taken this relationship into the phenomenological description of the nature of the gods. This underlines the fact that the gods are not objects within the context of the universe. They are expressions of the ultimate concern which transcends the cleavage between subjectivity and objectivity. It remains to be emphasized that an ultimate concern is not "subjective." Ultimacy stands against everything which can be derived from mere subjectivity, nor can the unconditional be found within the entire catalogue of finite objects which are conditioned by each other.

If the word "existential" points to a participation which transcends both subjectivity and objectivity, then man's relation to the gods is rightly called "existential." Man cannot speak of the gods in detachment. The moment he tries to do so, he has lost the god and has established just one more object within the world of objects. Man can speak of the gods only on the basis of his relation to them. This relation oscillates between the concreteness of a give-and-take attitude, in which the divine beings easily become objects and tools for human purposes, and the absoluteness or a total surrender on the side of a man. The absolute element of man's ultimate concern demands absolute intensity, infinite passion (Kierkegaard), in the religious relation. The concrete element drives men toward an unlimited amount of relative action and emotion in the cult in which the ultimate concern is embodied and actualized, and also outside it. The Catholic system of relativities represents the concrete element most fully, while Protestant radicalism predominantly emphasizes the absolute element. The tension in the nature of the gods, which is the tension in the structure of man's ultimate concern (and which, in the last analysis, is the tension in the human situation), determines the religions of mankind in all their major aspects.

[...]

3. God as Being

a) *God as being and finite being.*—The being of God is being-itself. The being of God cannot be understood as the existence of a being alongside others or above others. If God is *a* being, he is subject to the categories of finitude, especially to space and substance. Even if he is called the "highest being" in the sense of the "most perfect" and the "most powerful" being, this situation is not changed. When applied to God, superlatives become diminutives. They place him on the level of other beings while elevating him above all of them. Many theologians who have used the term "highest being" have known better. Actually they have described the highest as the absolute, as that which is on a level qualitatively different from the level of any being—even the highest-being. Whenever infinite or unconditional power and meaning are attributed to the highest being, it has ceased to be *a* being and has become being-itself. Many confusions in the doctrine of God and many apologetic weaknesses could be avoided if God were understood first of all as being-itself or as the ground of being. The power of being is another way of expressing the same thing in a circumscribing phrase. Ever since the time of Plato it has been known—although it often has been disregarded, especially by the nominalists and their modern followers—that the concept of being as being, or being-itself, points to the power inherent in everything, the power of resisting nonbeing. Therefore, instead of saying that God is first of all being-itself, it is possible to say that he is the power of being in everything and above everything, the infinite power of being. A theology which does not dare to identify God and the power of being as the first step toward a doctrine of God relapses into monarchic monotheism, for if God is not being-itself, he is subordinate to it, just as Zeus is subordinate to fate in Greek religion. The structure of being-itself is his fate, as it is the fate of all other beings. But God is his own fate; he is "by himself"; he possesses "aseity." This can be said of him only if he is the power of being, if he is being-itself.

As being-itself God is beyond the contrast of essential and existential being. We have spoken of the transition of being into existence, which involves the possibility that being will contradict and lose itself. This transition is excluded from being-itself (except in terms of the christological paradox), for being-itself does not participate in nonbeing. In this it stands in contrast to every being. As classical theology has emphasized, God is beyond essence and existence. Logically, being-itself is "before," "prior to," the split which characterizes finite being.

For this reason it is as wrong to speak of God as the universal essence as it is to speak of him as existing. If God is understood as universal essence, as the form of all forms, he is identified with the unity and totality of finite potentialities; but he has ceased to be the power of the ground in all of them, and therefore he has ceased to transcend them. He has poured all his creative power into a system of forms, and he is bound to these forms. This is what pantheism means.

On the other hand, grave difficulties attend the attempt to speak of God as existing. In order to maintain the truth that God is beyond essence and existence while simultaneously arguing for the existence of God, Thomas Aquinas is forced to distinguish between two kinds of divine existence: that which is identical with essence and that which is not. But an existence of God which is not united with its essence is a contradiction in terms. It makes God a being whose existence does not fulfil his essential potentialities; being and not-yet-being are "mixed" in him, as they are in everything finite. God ceases to be God, the ground of being and meaning. What really has happened is that Thomas has had to unite two different traditions: the Augustinian, in which the divine existence is included in his essence, and the Aristotelian, which derives the existence of God from the existence of the world and which then asserts, in a second step, that his existence is identical with his essence. Thus the question of the existence of God can be neither asked nor answered. If asked, it is a question about that which by its very nature is above existence, and therefore the answer—whether negative or affirmative—implicitly denies the nature of God. It is as atheistic to affirm the existence of God as it is to deny it. God is being-itself, not *a* being. On this basis a first step can be taken toward the solution of the problem which usually is discussed as the immanence and the transcendence of God. As the

power of being, God transcends every being and also the totality of beings—the world. Being-itself is beyond finitude and infinity; otherwise it would be conditioned by something other than itself, and the real power of being would lie beyond both it and that which conditioned it. Being-itself infinitely transcends every finite being. There is no proportion or gradation between the finite and the infinite. There is an absolute break, an infinite "jump." On the other hand, everything finite participates in being-itself and in its infinity. Otherwise it would not have the power of being. It would be swallowed by nonbeing, or it never would have emerged out of nonbeing. This double relation of all beings to being-itself gives being-itself a double characteristic. In calling it creative, we point to the fact that everything participates in the infinite power of being. In calling it abysmal, we point to the fact that everything participates in the power of being in a finite way, that all beings are infinitely transcended by their creative ground.

Man is bound to the categories of finitude. He uses the two categories of relation—causality and substance—to express the relation of being-itself to finite beings. The "ground" can be interpreted in both ways, as the cause of finite beings and as their substance. The former has been elaborated by Leibniz in the line of the Thomistic tradition, and the latter has been elaborated by Spinoza in the line of the mystical tradition. Both ways are impossible. Spinoza establishes a naturalistic pantheism, in contrast to the idealistic type which identifies God with the universal essence of being, which denies finite freedom and in so doing denies the freedom of God. By necessity God is merged into the finite beings, and their being is his being. Here again it must be emphasized that pantheism does not say that God is everything. It says that God is the substance of everything and that there is no substantial independence and freedom in anything finite.

Therefore, Christianity, which asserts finite freedom in man and spontaneity in the nonhuman realm, has rejected the category of substance in favor of the category of causality in attempting to express the relation of the power of being to the beings who participate in it. Causality seems to make the world dependent on God, and, at the same time, to separate God from the world in the way a cause is separated from its effect. But the category of causality cannot "fill the bill," for cause and effect are not separate; they include each other and form a series which is endless in both directions. What is cause at one point in this series is effect at another point and conversely. God as cause is drawn into this series, which drives even him beyond himself. In order to disengage the divine cause from the series of causes and effects, it is called the first cause, the absolute beginning. What this means is that the category of causality is being denied while it is being used. In other words, causality is being used not as a category but as a symbol. And if this is done and is understood, the difference between substance and causality disappears, for if God is the cause of the entire series of causes and effects, he is the substance underlying the whole process of becoming. But this "underlying" does not have the character of a substance which underlies its accidents and which is completely expressed by them. It is an underlying in which substance and accidents preserve their freedom. In other words, it is substance not as a category but as a symbol. And, if taken symbolically, there is no difference between *prima causa* and *ultima substantia*. Both mean, what can be called in a more directly symbolic term, "the creative and abysmal ground of being." In this term both naturalistic pantheism, based on the category of substance, and rationalistic theism, based on the category of causality, are overcome.

Since God is the ground of being, he is the ground of the structure of being. He is not subject to this structure; the structure is grounded in him. He *is* this structure, and it is impossible to speak about him except in terms of this structure. God must be approached cognitively through the structural elements of being-itself. These elements make him a living God, a God who can be man's concrete concern. They enable us to use symbols which we are certain point to the ground of reality.

b) God as being and the knowledge of God.—The statement that God is being-itself is a nonsymbolic statement. It does not point beyond itself. It means

what it says directly and properly; if we speak of the actuality of God, we first assert that he is not God if he is not being-itself. Other assertions about God can be made theologically only on this basis. Of course, religious assertions do not require such a foundation for what they say about God; the foundation is implicit in every religious thought concerning God. Theologians must make explicit what is implicit in religious thought and expression; and, in order to do this, they must begin with the most abstract and completely unsymbolic statement which is possible, namely, that God is being-itself or the absolute.

However, after this has been said, nothing else can be said about God as God which is not symbolic. As we already have seen, God as being-itself is the ground of the ontological structure of being without being subject to this structure himself. He *is* the structure; that is, he has the power of determining the structure of everything that has being. Therefore, if anything beyond this bare assertion is said about God, it no longer is a direct and proper statement, no longer a concept. It is indirect, and it points to something beyond itself. In a word, it is symbolic.

The general character of the symbol has been described. Special emphasis must be laid on the insight that symbol and sign are different; that, while the sign bears no necessary relation to that to which it points, the symbol participates in the reality of that for which it stands. The sign can be changed arbitrarily according to the demands of expediency, but the symbol grows and dies according to the correlation between that which is symbolized and the persons who receive it as a symbol. Therefore, the religious symbol, the symbol which points to the divine, can be a true symbol only if it participates in the power of the divine to which it points.

There can be no doubt that any concrete assertion about God must be symbolic, for a concrete assertion is one which uses a segment of finite experience in order to say something about him. It transcends the content of this segment, although it also includes it. The segment of finite reality which becomes the vehicle of a concrete assertion about

God is affirmed and negated at the same time. It becomes a symbol, for a symbolic expression is one whose proper meaning is negated by that to which it points. And yet it also is affirmed by it, and this affirmation gives the symbolic expression an adequate basis for pointing beyond itself.

The crucial question must now be faced. Can a segment of finite reality become the basis for an assertion about that which is infinite? The answer is that it can, because that which is infinite is being-itself and because everything participates in being-itself. The *analogia entis* is not the property of a questionable natural theology which attempts to gain knowledge of God by drawing conclusions about the infinite from the finite. The *analogia entis* gives us our only justification of speaking at all about God. It is based on the fact that God must be understood as being-itself.

The truth of a religious symbol has nothing to do with the truth of the empirical assertions involved in it, be they physical, psychological, or historical. A religious symbol possesses some truth if it adequately expresses the correlation of revelation in which some person stands. A religious symbol *is* true if it adequately expresses the correlation of some person with final revelation. A religious symbol can die only if the correlation of which it is an adequate expression dies. This occurs whenever the revelatory situation changes and former symbols become obsolete. The history of religion, right up to our own time, is full of dead symbols which have been killed not by a scientific criticism of assumed superstitions but by a religious criticism of religion. The judgment that a religious symbol *is* true is identical with the judgment that the revelation of which it is the adequate expression is true. This double meaning of the truth of a symbol must be kept in mind. A symbol *has* truth: it is adequate to the revelation it expresses. A symbol *is* true: it is the expression of a true revelation.

Theology as such has neither the duty nor the power to confirm or to negate religious symbols. Its task is to interpret them according to theological principles and methods. In the process of interpretation, however, two things may happen: theology may discover contradictions between symbols within the theological circle and theology may speak not only as theology but also as religion. In the first case, theology can point out the religious dangers and the theological errors which follow from the use of certain symbols; in the second case, theology can become prophecy, and in this role it may contribute to a change in the revelatory situation.

Religious symbols are double-edged. They are directed toward the infinite which they symbolize *and* toward the finite through which they symbolize it. They force the infinite down to finitude and the finite up to infinity. They open the divine for the human and the human for the divine. For instance, if God is symbolized as "Father," he is brought down to the human relationship of father and child. But at the same time this human relationship is consecrated into a pattern of the divine-human relationship. If "Father" is employed as a symbol for God, fatherhood is seen in its theonomous, sacramental depth. One cannot arbitrarily "make" a religious symbol out of a segment of secular reality. Not even the collective unconscious, the great symbol-creating source, can do this. If a segment of reality is used as a symbol for God, the realm of reality from which it is taken is, so to speak, elevated into the realm of the holy. It no longer is secular. It is theonomous. If God is called the "king," something is said not only about God but also about the holy character of kinghood. If God's work is called "making whole" or "healing," this not only says something about God but also emphasizes the theonomous character of all healing. If God's self-manifestation is called "the word," this not only symbolizes God's relation to man but also emphasizes the holiness of all words as an expression of the spirit. The list could be continued. Therefore, it is not surprising that in a secular culture both the symbols for God and the theonomous character of the material from which the symbols are taken disappear.

A final word of warning must be added in view of the fact that for many people the very term "symbolic" carries the connotation of nonreal. This is partially the result of confusion between sign and symbol and partially due to the identification of reality with empirical reality, with the entire realm of objective things and events. Both reasons have been undercut explicitly and implicitly in the fore-going chapters [of *Systematic Theology*, vol. 1]. But one reason remains, namely, the fact that some theological movements, such as Protestant Hegelianism and Catholic modernism, have interpreted religious language symbolically in order to dissolve its realistic meaning and to weaken its seriousness, its power, and its spiritual impact. This was not the purpose of the classical essays on the "divine names," in which the symbolic character of all affirmations about God

was strongly emphasized and explained in religious terms, nor was it a consequence of these essays. Their intention and their result was to give to God and to all his relations to man more reality and power than a nonsymbolic and therefore easily superstitious interpretation could give them. In this sense symbolic interpretation is proper and necessary; it enhances rather than diminishes the reality and power of religious language, and in so doing it performs an important function.

I.A.6

The Love of God and the Idea of Deity

MARTIN BUBER

Martin Buber (1878–1965) was an extremely influential Jewish philosopher and theologian. He is best known for his book I and Thou. *The present selection is an essay written in 1943 and reprinted, among other places, in his* The Eclipse of God. *Here he explores the tension in Hermann Cohen's thought between the idea of a transcendent God and the love of God that is so important to the religious life.*

1

In those scribbled lines affecting us as cries of the very soul, which Pascal wrote after two ecstatic hours, and which he carried about with him until his death, sewn into the lining of his doublet, we find under the heading *Fire* the note: "God of Abraham, God of Isaac, God of Jacob—not of the philosophers and scholars."

These words represent Pascal's change of heart. He turned, not from a state of being where there is no God to one where there is a God, but from the God of the philosophers to the God of Abraham.

Overwhelmed by faith, he no longer knew what to do with the God of the philosophers; that is, with the God who occupies a definite position in a definite system of thought. The God of Abraham, the God in whom Abraham had believed and whom Abraham had loved ("The entire religion of the Jews," remarks Pascal, "consisted only of the love of God"), is not susceptible of introduction into a system of thought precisely because He is God. He is beyond each and every one of those systems, absolutely and by virtue of His nature. What the philosophers describe by the name of God cannot be more than an idea. But God, "the God of

Translated by I. M. Lask, and reprinted from Martin Buber, *Israel and the World: Essays in a Time of Crisis* (Farrar, Straus, and Young, Inc., 1948). Used with permission.

Abraham," is not an idea; all ideas are absorbed in Him. Nor is that all. If I think even of a state of being in which all ideas are absorbed, and think some philosophic thought about it as an idea—then I am no longer referring to the God of Abraham. The "passion" peculiar to philosophers is, according to a hint dropped by Pascal, pride. They offer humanity their own system in place of God.

"What!" cries Pascal, "the philosophers recognized God and desired not merely that men should love him, but that they should reach their level and then stop!" It is precisely because the philosophers replace him by the image of images, the idea, that they remove themselves and remove the rest of us furthest from him. There is no alternative. One must choose. Pascal chose, during one of those all-overthrowing moments, when he felt his sick-bed prayer was answered: "To be apart from the world, divested of all things, lonely in your Presence, in order to respond to your justice with all the motions of my heart."

Pascal himself, to be sure, was not a philosopher but a mathematician, and it is easier for a mathematician to turn his back on the God of the philosophers than for a philosopher. For the philosopher, if he were really to wish to turn his back on that God, would be compelled to renounce the attempt to include God in his system in any conceptual form. Instead of including God as one theme among others, that is, as the highest theme of all, his philosophy both wholly and in part would be compelled to point toward God, without actually dealing with him. This means that the philosopher would be compelled to recognize and admit the fact that his idea of the Absolute was dissolving at the point where the Absolute *lives*; that it was dissolving at the point where the Absolute is loved; because at that point the Absolute is no longer the "Absolute" about which one may philosophize, but God.

2

Those who wish clearly to grasp the nature of the endless and hopeless struggle which lay in wait for the philosopher of the critical period should read the very long notes in Kant's unfinished posthumous work, written over a period of seven years during his old age. They reveal a scene of incomparable existential tragedy. Kant calls the principle constituting the transition to the completion of the transcendental philosophy by the name of the "Principle of Transcendental Theology"; here his concern is with the questions, "What is God?" and "Is there a God?"

Kant explains: "The function of transcendental philosophy is still unresolved: Is there a God?" As long as there was no reply to that question, the task of his philosophy was still unfulfilled; at the end of his days, when his spiritual powers were waning, it was "still unresolved." He toiled on at this problem, constantly increasing his efforts, from time to time weaving the answer, yet time and again unraveling the woof. He reached an extreme formulation: "To think Him and to believe in Him is an identical act." Furthermore, "the thought of Him is at one and the same time the belief in Him and his personality." But this faith does not result in God's becoming existent for the philosophy of the philosopher. "God is not an entity outside of me, but merely a thought within me." Or, as Kant says on another occasion, "merely a moral relation within me."

Nevertheless, He possesses a certain kind of "reality." "God is only an idea of reason, but one possessing the greatest practical internal and external reality." Yet it is obvious that this kind of reality is not adequate to make the thought about God identical with the "belief in Him and His personality." Transcendental philosophy, whose task was to ascertain whether there is a God, finally found itself compelled to state: "It is preposterous to ask whether there is a God."

The contradiction goes even deeper when Kant treats belief from this point of view. He incidentally outlines a fundamental distinction between "to believe God" and "to believe in God." "To believe God" obviously means God's being the ideational content of one's faith. This is a deduction from the fact that "to believe in God" means in the terminology of Kant, as he himself expressly states, to believe in a living God. To believe in God means, therefore, to stand in a personal relationship to that God; a relationship in which it is possible to stand only toward a living entity.

This distinction becomes still clearer through Kant's addendum: to believe "not in an entity which is only an idol and is not a personality." It follows that a God who is not a living personality is an idol. Kant comes that close at this point to the *reality* of faith. But he does not permit its validity to stand. His system compels him decisively to restrict what he has said. The same page of manuscript contains the following passage: "The idea of God as a living God is nothing but the inescapable fate of man." But if the idea of God is only that, then it is totally impossible to "believe in God" legitimately; that is, it is impossible to stand in a personal relationship with him. Man, declares the philosopher, is compelled to believe in him the moment he thinks God. But the philosopher is compelled to withdraw the character of truth from this faith, and together with it the character of reality (any reality, that is, which is more than merely psychological). Here, apparently of necessity, that which was decisive for Pascal, as it was for Abraham, is missing; namely, the love of God.

3

But a philosopher who has been overwhelmed by faith *must* speak of love.

Hermann Cohen, the last in the series of great disciples of Kant, is a shining example of a philosopher who has been overwhelmed by faith.

Belief in God was an important point in Cohen's system of thought as early as in his youth, when it interested him as a psychological phenomenon. His explanations of "the origin of the mythology of gods" and of the "poetic act" involved in "god-creating fantasy," contained in his study on "Mythological Conceptions concerning God and Soul" which appeared in 1868 in Steinthal's periodical, *Zeitschrift fuer Voelkerpsychologie,* was an expression of this interest. Faith was there treated as relative to psychological distinction; but in the course of the development of Cohen's philosophical system faith's status as an independent concept, distinct from knowledge, was to become questionable.

In his "Ethics of Pure Will" (1904), Cohen writes: "God must not become the content of belief, if that belief is to mean something distinct from knowledge." Of the two kinds of belief which Kant distinguishes in his posthumous work, namely, "to believe God" (that is, to introduce the idea of God into a system of knowledge), and "to believe in a living God" (that is, to have a vital relationship to him as a living entity), Cohen rejects the second even more strongly than Kant. In this way he means to overcome the "great equivocality" of the word "belief." Whereas Kant saw in the idea of God only the "fate" of the human species, Cohen wishes to "separate the concept of life from the concept of God." He finds support for his argument in Maimonides (though he limited the extent of that support three years later, saying that Maimonides had been careful to distinguish between the concept of life when applied to God and the same concept when applied to man; a distinction on the part of Maimonides which entirely differs from Cohen's distinction).

God is an idea for Cohen, as he was for Kant. "We call God an idea," says Cohen, "meaning the center of all ideas, the idea of truth." God is not a personality; as such He only appears "within the confines of myth." And He is no existence at all, neither a natural existence nor a spiritual, "just as in general the idea cannot be linked with the concept of existence." The concept of God is introduced into the structure of ethical thought, because, as the idea of truth, it is instrumental in establishing the unity of nature and morality. This view of God as an idea Cohen regards as "the true religiosity," which can evolve only when every relation involving belief in a living God is shown to be problematical, and nullified. God's only place is within a system of thought. The system defends itself with stupendous vigour against the living God who is bound to make questionable its perfection, and even its absolute authority. Cohen, the thinker, defends himself against the belief which, rising out of an ancient heritage, threatens to overwhelm him. He defends himself with success; the success of the system-creator. Cohen has constructed the last home for the God of the philosophers.

And yet Cohen has been overwhelmed by faith in more exemplary fashion than any other of the contemporary philosophers, although his labours to incorporate God into a system were in no way hindered. On the contrary: from that moment his labours turned into an admirable wrestle with his own experience.

Cohen objectified the results of his succumbing to faith by merging it in his system of concepts. Nowhere in his writings does he directly state it; but the evidence is striking. When was it that the decisive change occurred?

4

The answer lies in the change that crept into Cohen's way of thinking about the love of God. It was only at a late period that Cohen, who concurrently with the development of his system was dealing in a series of essays with the heritage of the Jewish faith, gave an adequate place to the cornerstone of that faith, the love of God, the essential means by which the Jewish faith realized its full and unique value. Only three years after the "Ethics," in his important research into "Religion and Morality," whose formulations, even keener than those of the "Ethics," interdict "interest in the so-called person of God and the so-called living God," declaring that the prophets of Israel "combatted" the direct relation between man and God, do we find a new note about the love of God. "The more that the knowledge of God is simultaneously felt to be love of God, the more passionate becomes the battle for faith, the struggle for the knowledge of God and for the love of God." It is evident that at this point Cohen is beginning to approach the *vital* character of faith. Yet the love of God still remains something abstract and not given to investigation.

Once again, three years later, Cohen's short essay on "The Love of Religion" begins with the curious sentence, "The love of God is the love of religion," and its first section ends with the no less curious sentence, "The love of God is therefore the knowledge of morality." If we carefully consider the two uses of the word "is," we are able to distinguish a purpose: which is to classify something as yet unclassified but nevertheless obtruding as central; to classify it by a process of identification with something else already comprehended, and thus put it in its place; but that

identification does not prove successful. All that is necessary to see this clearly is to compare the above-cited sentences with any one of the Biblical verses which enjoin or praise the love of God, which are the origin of that concept. What Cohen is enjoining and praising at this point is something essentially and qualitatively different from the love of religion and the knowledge of morality, although it includes both. Yet in Cohen's revision of his Berlin lectures of 1913–14, published in 1915 under the title, "The Concept of Religion in the System of Philosophy," he gives expression to a love which does away once and for all with that curious "is."

"If I love God," says Cohen (and this use of his of "I" touches the heart of the reader, like every genuine "I" in the work of every genuine philosopher), "then I no longer think Him . . ." (and that "no longer" is almost direct testimony) ". . . only the sponsor of earthly morals. . . ." But what? But the avenger of the poor in world history. "It is that avenger of the poor whom I love." And later, to the same effect: "I love in God the father of man." At this point "father" means the "shield and aid of the poor," for, "Man is revealed to me in the poor man."

How long a way have we come from the "love of religion"! Yet the new element in Cohen is expressed with even greater clarity and energy: "Therefore shall the love of God exceed all knowledge. . . . A man's consciousness is completely filled when he loves God. Therefore, this knowledge, which absorbs all others, is no longer merely knowledge, but love." And it is extremely logical that the Biblical commandment to love God is cited and interpreted at this point in the same connection: "I cannot love God without devoting my whole heart as living for the sake of my fellowmen, without devoting my entire soul as responsive to all the spiritual trends in the world around me, without devoting all my force to this God in His correlation with man."

At this point I wish to introduce an objection related, admittedly, not to these sentences of Cohen's, but to another that has a connection with them. Cohen speaks of the paradox "that I have to love man." "Worm that I am," he continues, "consumed by passions, cast as bait for egoism, I must nevertheless love man. If I am able to do so, and so far as I am able to do so, I shall be able to love God." Strong words these, yet the lives of many important persons controvert the last sentence. The teaching of the Bible overcomes the paradox in a precisely contrary fashion. The Bible knows that it is impossible to command the love of man. I am incapable of feeling love toward every man, though God himself commands me. The Bible does not directly enjoin the love of man, but by using the dative puts it rather in the form of an *act* of love (Lev. 19:18, 34). I must act lovingly toward my *rea*, my "companion" (usually translated "my neighbour"), that is toward every man with whom I deal in the course of my life, including the *ger*, the "stranger" or "sojourner"; I must bestow the favours of love on him, I must treat him with love as one who is "like unto me." (I must love "to him"; a construction only found in these two verses in the Bible.) Of course I must love him not merely with superficial gestures but with an essential relationship. It lies within my power to will it, and so I can accept the commandment. It is not my will which gives me the emotion of love toward my "neighbour" aroused within me by my behaviour.

On the other hand, the Torah commands one to love God (Deut. 6:5; 10:12; 11:1); only in that connection does it enjoin heartfelt love of the sojourner who is one's "neighbour" (Deut. 10:19)—because God loves the sojourner. If I love God, in the course of loving Him I come to love the one whom God loves, too. I can love God as God from the moment I know Him; and Israel, to whom the commandment is addressed, does know Him. Thus I can accept the injunction to love my fellow-man.

Cohen is, to be sure, actually referring to something else. For now he raises the question whether he should take offense at God's being "only an idea." "Why should I not be able," he replies, "to love ideas? What is man after all but a social idea, and yet I can love him as an individual only through and by virtue of that fact. Therefore, strictly considered, I can only love the social idea of man."

To me, it seems otherwise. Only if and because I love this or that specific man can I elevate my relation to the social idea of man into that emotional relationship involving my whole being which I am

entitled to call by the name of love. And what of God? Franz Rosenzweig warned us that Cohen's idea of God should not be taken to mean that God is "only an idea" in Cohen's eyes. The warning is pertinent: Rosenzweig is right to emphasize that an idea for Cohen is not "only an idea." Yet, at the same time, we must not ignore that other "only," whose meaning is quite different indeed in Cohen's phrase, "a God who is only an idea." Let us, if we will, describe our relation to the idea of the beautiful and the idea of the good by the name of love—though in my opinion all this has content and value for the soul only in being rendered concrete and made real. But to love God differs from that relationship in essential quality. He who loves God loves Him precisely insofar as He is not "only an idea," and can love Him *because* He is not "only an idea." And I permit myself to say that though Cohen indeed thought of God as an idea, Cohen too loved Him as—God.

5

In the great work prepared after "The Concept of Religion" and posthumously published under the title of "Religion of Reason, from the Sources of Judaism," Cohen returns to this problem with even greater prominence: "How can one love an idea?"—and replies, "How can one love anything save an idea?" He substantiates his reply by saying, "For even in the love of the senses one loves only the idealized person, only the idea of the person." Yet even if it were correct that in the love of "the senses" (or more correctly, in the love which comprehends sensuality) one loves only the idealized person, that does not at all mean that nothing more than the idea of the person is loved; even the idealized person remains a person, and has not been transformed into an idea. It is only because the person whom I idealize actually exists that I can love the idealized one. Even though for Dante it was *la gloriosa donna della mia mente*, yet the decisive fact is that first he saw the real Beatrice, who set the "spirit of life" trembling in him. But does not the motive force which enables and empowers us to idealize a beloved person arise from the deepest substance of that beloved person? Is not the true idealization in the deepest sense a *discovery* of the essential self meant by God in creating the person whom I love?

"The love of men for God," says Cohen, "is the love of the moral ideal. I can love only the ideal, and I can comprehend the ideal in no other way save by loving it." Even on this level, the very highest for the philosopher who is overwhelmed by faith, he declares what the love of God is, and not what it includes. But man's love for God *is not* love of the moral ideal; it only includes that love. He who loves God only as the moral ideal is bound soon to reach the point of despair at the conduct of the world where, hour after hour, all the principles of his moral idealism are apparently contradicted. Job despairs because God and the moral ideal seem diverse to him. But He who answered Job out of the tempest is more exalted even than the ideal sphere. He is not the archetype of the ideal, but he contains the archetype. He issues forth the ideal, but does not exhaust himself in the issuing. The unity of God is not the Good; it is the Super-good. God desires that men should follow His revelation, yet at the same time He wishes to be accepted and loved in His deepest concealment. He who loves God loves the ideal and loves God more than the ideal. He knows himself to be loved by God, not by the ideal, not by an idea, but even by Him whom ideality cannot grasp, namely, by that *absolute personality* we call God. Can this be taken to mean that God "is" a personality? The absolute character of His personality, that paradox of paradoxes, prohibits any such statement. It only means that God loves as a personality and that He wishes to be loved like a personality. And if He was not a person in Himself, He, so to speak, became one in creating Man, in order to love man and be loved by him—in order to love me and be loved by me. For, even supposing that ideas can also be loved, the fact remains that persons are the only ones who love. Even the philosopher who has been overwhelmed by faith, though he afterward continue to hug his system even more closely than before, and to interpret the love between God and man as the love between an idea and a person— even he, nevertheless, testifies to the existence of a love between God and man that is basically recip-

rocal. That philosophy too, which, in order to preserve the Being (*esse; Sein*) of God, deprives Him of existence (*existentia; Dasein*), indicates however unintentionally the bridge standing indestructibly on the two pillars, one imperishable and the other ever crumbling, God and man.

6

Cohen once said of Kant, "What is characteristic of his theology is the non-personal *in the usual sense,* the truly spiritual principle: the sublimation of God into an idea." And he adds, "And nothing less than this is the deepest basis of the Jewish idea of God." As far as Kant is concerned, Cohen was correct in this judgment. But throughout Kant's posthumous work we can see emerging every now and then resistance to this sublimation of God into an idea; a sublimation which later even more prominently prevents in Cohen the linking of the idea with the concept of existence.

"Under the concept of God," writes Kant, "Transcendental Philosophy refers to a substance possessing the greatest existence," but he also qualifies God as "the ideal of a substance which we create ourselves." What we have in these notes, which sometimes appear chaotic, are the records of a suit at law, the last phase which the thought of the idea of God assumes for its thinker, of a suit between the two elements, "idea" and "God," which are contained in the idea of God; a suit which time and again reverts to the same point, until death cuts it short. Cohen set out to put the idea into a sequence so logical as to make it impossible for any impulse to opposition to develop. Even when overwhelmed by faith, Cohen continued the struggle to preserve this sequence. In so doing, he was of the opinion that "the deepest basis of the Jewish idea of God" was on his side. But even the deepest basis of the Jewish idea of God can be achieved only by plunging into that word by which God revealed Himself to Moses, "I shall be there." It gives exact expression to the personal "existence" of God (not to His abstract "being"), and expression even to His living presence, which most directly of all His attributes touches the man to whom He manifests Himself.

The speaker's self-designation as the God of Abraham, God of Isaac, and God of Jacob (Exod. 3:15) is indissolubly united with that manifestation of "I shall be there,"★ and He cannot be reduced to a God of the philosophers.

But the man who says, "I love in God the father of man" has essentially already renounced the God of the philosophers in his innermost heart, even though he may not confess it to himself. Cohen did not consciously choose between the God of the philosophers and the God of Abraham, rather believing to the last that he could succeed in identifying the two. Yet his inmost heart, that force from which thought too derives its vitality, had chosen and decided for him. The identification had failed, and of necessity had to fail. For the idea of God, that masterpiece of man's construction, is only the image of images, the most lofty of all the images by which man imagines the imageless God. It is essentially repugnant to man to recognize this fact, and remain satisfied. For when man learns to love God, he senses an actuality which rises above the idea. Even if he makes the philosopher's great effort to sustain the object of his love as an object of his philosophic thought, the love itself bears witness to the existence of the Beloved.

NOTE

★Exod. 3:14, part of the phrase commonly translated: "I am that I am."

I.A.7

The Vedic-Upanisadic Concept of Brahman (The Highest God)

SUSHANTA SEN

Sushanta Sen taught in the Philosophy Department at Visva-Bharati University in India. In this essay, Sen explores the conception of deity found in the Upanisadic portion of the Vedas, the sacred scriptures of Hinduism. Although Hinduism is often regarded as polytheistic, Sen argues that the conception of deity found in the Upanisads more closely resembles monotheism.

INTRODUCTORY REMARKS

In India, unlike the West, the line of demarcation between philosophy and religion is so very thin that the one often flows into the other, making her philosophy as much religious as her religion philosophical. This is particularly true of Hinduism and is evident from the fact that the Vedas, the foundational scriptures of the Hindu religion, stand as the unquestionable authority for all the six orthodox

Reprinted from *Concepts of the Ultimate*, edited by Linda J. Tessier, published 1989 by St. Martin's Press. Reproduced with permission of Palgrave MacMillan.

systems of Hindu philosophy (*āstika darsana*). In these systems the Vedas are often invoked as the final court of appeal in matters of philosophical controversy, or a well reasoned conclusion arrived at by a valid logical argument is sought to be corroborated by some textual citations from the Vedas as a plea for its acceptance. Indeed, the very definition of Hindu orthodoxy (*āstikya*) which distinguishes it from other non-Hindu heterodox (*ñastika*) systems of Indian religions, like Buddhism and Jainism, affirms its unqualified faith in the truth of the Vedas. This is borne out by the fact that though Hinduism in the course of time branched off into a bewildering variety of conflicting sects, none of them quarrels over the authority of the Vedas; and the Vedas are claimed to command such infallible authority because their contents are believed to be the records of direct revelation of Truth received by the pure-hearted saints and seers of remote antiquity. This persistent allegiance to the essential teachings of the Vedas explains why Hinduism is justifiably called *vaidika dharma* or the religion of the Vedas. Hence the Hindu concept of God primarily means the Vedic concept of God.

THE VEDIC-UPANISADIC TEACHINGS ON GOD: THE IDEA OF SELF-GOD (ATMAN-BRAHMAN) IDENTITY

But it is not a very easy task to distill the essence of the Vedic teachings on God out of their huge bulk and their rich diversity of metaphors and allegories. The thematic division of the Vedas into three different parts—the Saṁhitās, Brāhmanas and the Upanisads[1]—makes the matter more difficult, because the theme of the one part seems to contradict the theme of the other. Thus, to a casual reader cursorily glancing over the pages of the Vedas, the polytheistic overtone of the Saṁhitās and the Brāhmanas in admitting a number of gods (*devas*) and offering sacrificial oblation to them appears to be flatly incongruous with the strictly monotheistic

conception of God that permeates the whole corpus of the Upanisadic literature. The countless passages of the Upanisads seek to elaborate one fundamental theme in a variety of ways: "There is but one Being, not a second" (*Ekam eva advitiyam*).[2] This one universal Being has been variously termed in the Upanisads as *Brahman, Isvara, Paramātman,* and so on, for all of which the blanket English term "God" may be used, though each one of them has a characteristic shade of meaning distinct from the others. Now, this sort of thematic discrepancy of the one part of the Vedas with the others makes it rather difficult to ascertain which one of these two parts is to be accepted as truly representing the Vedic idea of God—the polytheism of the Saṁhitās and the Brāhmanas or the monotheism of the Upanisads. This is a problem which we shall discuss in detail in the next section. But for the present purpose let us see if the Samhitā portion of the Vedas, where polytheism is most prominently displayed, can suggest any intelligible hint toward its solution.

We have it on the authority of the Vedas themselves as well as on the evidence of other Sanskrit writings that the "Gāyatri" verse of the Vedas,[3] through the impartation of which a Hindu of the upper three castes is initiated for the first time into spiritual life, contains the quintessence of the entire mass of Vedic literature. In the *Atharva-Veda,* the Gāyatri has been described as the "mother of the Vedas" (Veda-mātā)[4] containing their essential spirit. This particular cryptic verse of the Rg-Veda, therefore, should be taken as the main trunk of the great Vedic tree of which the other elements are its dispensible ramifications. In this Gāyatri verse it has been said that there is one Universal Being who is self-luminous and manifests himself in this and many other worlds; and this Being dwells in our heart as our Inner Ruler. It has been translated into English as follows:

> We meditate on the most resplendent and adorable light of the self-luminous Spirit who dwells in the heart as its inner ruler and manifests Himself as the earth, and sky and the heavens; may He guide our thoughts along the right path.[5]

This Gāyatri conception of a self-luminous Universal Spirit and of His residence in the human heart was later crystallized in the Upanisads, the concluding part of the Vedas, into the doctrine of an all-pervading *Brāhman* (God) and His identity with the individual Self (*Ātman*). The individual self, however limited and imperfect it may appear, is in its final depths Divine in nature, because "the most resplendent and adorable light of the self-luminous spirit" dwells in it. This doctrine of the essential identity of the self (*Ātman*) with God (*Brāhman*)—first suggested in the Gāyatri verse but fully developed in the Upanisads—is, therefore, the central creed of the Vedas, and indeed of Hinduism in general. The four "great sayings" (mahāvākyas) of the Upanisads, like "that thou art" (*tat tvam asi*),[6] I am Brahman (*aham Brahmāsmi*), and so on, as well as countless other passages, point to this central doctrine. Since the Self and God are ultimately identical, enquiry into the nature of God resolves itself into an enquiry into the nature of the Self. This explains why the concept of *Ātman* or the Self is the pivot around which all the doctrines of the Upanisads revolve. "What is that, Venerable Sir, which being known everything else is known?"—an eager seeker asked Angirā, the great sage of the Upanisadic period.[7] The Upanisads found the answer to this question in the knowledge of the true nature of the Self.

The Self (*Ātman*) is, according to the Upanisads, the inner essence of humanity—a permanent substance which remains fixed and constant amidst all sorts of change of the body, sense-organs and the mind. The body of a person may change beyond recognition, the sense-organs may be mutilated and the mind may be (and in fact is) in a state of incessant flux—its sensations, emotions, ideas, images and such like, are continuously gliding away one after another. But the fact that one never loses one's self-identity to oneself proves that somewhere within this ceaseless phantasmagoria there exists an abiding reality which simply witnesses these changes but does not become affected by them. This permanent immutable substance in humanity is called the *Ātman* or Self. This *Ātman,* however, is thought to be not only the *inner essence* of humanity

but also the outer essence of the Universe. The Upanisads do not make any distinction between within and without. We read in the *Kathopanisad:* "What is within us is also without. What is without is also within. He who sees difference between what is within and what is without goes evermore from death to death."[8] When viewed as the ultimate metaphysical principle of the outer Universe, the *Ātman* is termed *Brahman.* There is endless change without in the shape of movement, growth, decay and death, and at the heart of these changes there is an abiding reality called *Brahman.* Again, at the heart of endless changes within our body-mind complex there is an abiding reality called *Ātman,* and these two principles are treated as one and the same. *Ayam Ātmā Brahman*—"this Self is the Brahman"—is one of the "great sayings" (mahāvākyas) in which the Upanisads sum up this teaching.

But a crucial question can be raised here: if an immutable changeless *Ātman* is the sole reality of humanity and the Universe, then how are we to view the phenomena of change and becoming which characterize the world of our everyday experience? The reply of Upanisadic Hinduism to this question would be that whatever undergoes change and is unstable, fleeting and evanescent cannot have any intrinsic value and reality of its own. Hence, change or becoming is to be regarded as more or less unreal and as the source of all pain and suffering of our life. It is the *Ātman* only that lies beyond any possibility of change and suffering. But though itself devoid of any suffering and change, the *Ātman,* under the spell of a cosmic nescience (*avidyā*), forgets its real nature and wrongly identifies itself with the changing phenomena of its body and mind. These latter are not parts of the Self itself but are its *Kosas,* or the sheaths within which it is wrapped. This mistaken identification of the *Ātman* with what it is not, that is, its bodily and mental sheaths, is held to be responsible for all the sorrows and sufferings of human life, because the Self wrongly imagines that various affections and afflictions which really belong to the body-mind complex are aspects of its own nature. Only when the *Ātman* is able to abstract itself from these sheaths by a long and rigorous spiritual training under the guidance of a Guru or spiritual guide does it shine forth in its pristine divine glory as the same with God (*Brahman*). But so long as this does not happen the Self suffers from the illusion that it is subject to all the evils, imperfections and limitations of its external sheaths and thus makes itself a miserable victim of the distressing sense of finitude, suffering and death.

But at the same time the fact that each conscious individual instinctively desires to escape suffering and resist death proves that this miserable and wretched existence is neither one's essential nature nor final destiny. For if some foreign element enters our body, such as a particle of dust in the eye or a thorn in the flesh, the body immediately reacts to it and tries to rid itself of it; likewise, every person wants to get rid of the sorrows and sufferings of human life, which therefore shows that these do not belong to the essence of the Self but are foreign elements which have become imposed on it. This suggests again that the natural condition of the Self is a state of perfect and unalloyed peace or bliss (*ānanda*) absolutely free from all sufferings and imperfections. This painless perfect state of the Self has been variously termed in the Upaniṣads *mukti, moksa, kaivalya, apavarga,* and so on, and the attainment of this state is described as the supreme end of human life (*carana purusārtha*).

But how is one to attain this ideal state? Only by tearing off the veil of cosmic nescience (*avidyā*) and thus realizing the essential identity of one's inner Self with Brahman: this is the invariable answer of the Upaniṣads. When one realizes this identity one knows the truth that "the Self is free from evil, free from old age, free from death, free from grief, hunger and thirst . . .,"[9] that is free from all temporality, affections and afflictions of body and mind. That is why humans are described in the Upaniṣads as the "sons of Immortality" (*amrtasya putrāh*).

This doctrine of the essential identity of the human Self (*Ātman*) with God (*Brahman*) represents the central spiritual insight of the Vedic-Upaniṣadic seers and gives Hinduism its distinctive character. It is interesting to note here that this ancient Upaniṣadic doctrine of *Ātman-Brahman* identity finds a parallel expression in the medieval Christian mystic Eckhart: "To gauge the Soul we must gauge it

with God, for the Ground of God and the Ground of the Soul are one and the same."[10] To know the Self, therefore, is to know God: and to know God is to know everything, because everything in the Universe is pervaded by God, "all this is enveloped by God."[11] Thus the strange question—what is that which, being known, everything else becomes known?—finds its answer in the human Self: *Ātmānam Viddhi:* "know your own Self." It is for this reason that all the Upaniṣadic writings together go by the name, *ātmavidyā,* a study of the nature of the Self.

THE STATUS OF MINOR GODS (DEVAS) IN HINDUISM

As the Upaniṣads are called *ātmavidyā,* so the Saṁhitās, the first and oldest part of the Vedas, may aptly be designated as *devavidyā,* a study of the nature of gods, because these are collections of hymns and prayers addressed to different gods, or the *devas* as they are called. A particular Ṛg-Vedic verse (VIII.28.1) and the traditional commentaries on the Vedas allude to 33 such *devas,* viz. Indra, Varuna, Usha, Agni, and so on. These gods are said to be the supernatural and luminous[12] personalities through whose active agency and guidance different objects of nature and phenomena are able to function. Understood in this sense Indra is the god of rain, thunder and storm, Varuna the god of sky, Usha the goddess of dawn, Agni the deity of fire, and so on. Though the relation of these Vedic gods with nature is very intimately conceived, they are not mere natural forces *personified,* as often interpreted by Western scholars. It would be truer to understand them as *personalities* presiding over different phenomena of nature (*abhimāna-devatās*) and guiding and controlling them. Prayers for favour could be addressed to them, for they were deities more powerful than ourselves and had control over nature, and as personalities they could be gracious.

But a very crucial question which we have already raised immediately crops up here: how can the existence of many gods (*devas*), as we find it in the Saṁhitā portion of the Vedas, be reconciled with the basic Upaniṣadic doctrine that God (*Brahman*) is one and only one and that the individual Self (*Ātman*) is essentially identical with God? Unless this question is satisfactorily answered, a critic of Hinduism might argue, the entire bulk of Vedic literature on which Hinduism is based remains a senseless mumbo-jumbo of irreconcilable contradictions.

To an objection of this kind a typical Hindu reply would be that there is no pure and unmixed polytheism in Hinduism. What appears to be polytheism in the verses of the Saṁhitās is really monotheism, only clothed in polytheistic guise. This leads us to a more basic enquiry into the nature of the existence of these Vedic deities (*devas*) and their metaphysical status.

If we take the pre-Christian pagan religion of the classical Greeks and the Romans to be typical examples of pure polytheism, it is not difficult to see why Hinduism cannot be subsumed under this category. In Graeco-Roman paganism the main difference between gods and humans is that the former are immortal while the latter are not, and a mortal can never attain to the status of a god. But in Hinduism humans and gods share a common fate in that both are created by an omnipotent creator God and as creatures both are subject to birth and death. Like human beings, the destiny of these gods is determined by the karmic law of cause and effect, and this law sets a beginning and an end to their status as gods. In accordance with the law of *karma,* a pervasive assumption in Indian religio-philosophical thought, the joys and sufferings of human life are strictly conditioned by and proportionate to the merits (*punyas*) and demerits (*pāpas*) of actions (*karmas*) performed by the individual: virtuous actions are rewarded by appropriate happiness and evil deeds are punished by befitting misery. Now if the merits of actions earned by someone are of such immense magnitude that all earthly pleasures are too paltry to provide rewards proportionate to these merits, then after physical death he or she is reborn as a god (*deva*) in heaven to enjoy uninterrupted heavenly bliss, and remains there as an extraordinarily powerful being to govern certain courses of nature. Unmixed pleasure and superhuman power characterize the lives of these heavenly gods. Again, when someone dies who has acquired the highest merit by performing some special kinds of penance and Vedic sacrifice (*yajña*), that person is reborn again not only as a god but as the king of gods, Indra, whose commands the lesser gods obey. But the lives of all these gods including Indra come to a definite end when their accumulated merits become exhausted by the enjoyment of heavenly pleasures and privileges; and after that they have to die from heaven as gods and be reborn again on earth as ordinary human beings within the process of repeated reincarnations known as *samsāra*. This cycle of births and deaths, either as humans or gods, goes on until they realize their essential identity with *Brahman*.

It is interesting to note here that these Vedic gods are declared to be cosmic officials holding certain positions (*padas*) and having certain duties. Thus the term "Indra," the king of gods, is not the name of a person but designates an office or a post (*Indra-pada*). Anyone who has rendered oneself worthy of it by virtue of meritorious deeds becomes entitled to this post and occupies it. But when the merits of these good *karmas* are exhausted, one has to abdicate this office and another Indra at once steps into one's place. Thus, though these godly offices (*padas*) are constant, the individual beings that carry out the duties of Indra, Agni and the rest change.

Now considering these two peculiarities of the Vedic gods—their mortality and the ability of humans to rise to the status of gods—it is not permissible to equate the so-called Vedic polytheism with the pure polytheism of the ancient Greeks and Romans. But the most important feature to be noticed about these Vedic gods is that, though they are powerful enough to control the forces of nature and to some extent the destiny of worldly individuals, they are never described as creators of humanity and nature. Creatorship in Hinduism is an exclusive property of an Omnipotent God (*Īśvara*) who is one and uncreated. The gods (*devas*) of the Hindu pantheon correspond rather to the angels and saints and share the feature of not having possessed their high status from all eternity. The angels were created by God at the time of creation; saints attained to sainthood only after their lives on earth. The difference, however, is that unlike angels and saints these Vedic deities (*devas*) lose their status again at a later stage, whereas the former retain it by divine decree for all time. Technically, the angels and saints are sempiternal creatures, that is, they have a beginning but (apart from divine annihilation) no end. And just as the introduction of a variety of these sempiternal beings does not affect the fundamental monotheism of Christianity, so the existence of different gods (*devas*) does not in any way deprive the "One God" theory of the Upanisads of its basic monotheistic character.

But this is not the whole story concerning the Vedic gods, and Hinduism has gone much deeper than this in its treatment of them. Among the great variety of gods it has discovered a fundamental unity, a unity which has prevented it from degenerating into a crude form of polytheism. This point has been made abundantly clear by Swami Vivekananda, a saint and savant of Hinduism, in a comparative study of other non-Hindu polytheistic mythologies.[13] In these mythologies, says Vivekananda, it is usually found that one particular god competes with other gods, becoming prominent and assuming the supreme position over others, while the other gods gradually die out. Thus, in the Jewish mythology, Jehovah becomes supreme of all the Molochs, and the other Molochs are forgotten or lost forever; Jehovah becomes the God of gods. In the same way, in Greek mythology, Zeus comes to the forefront and assumes a great magnitude, becoming the God of the Universe, and all the other gods are degraded into minor angels. This seems to be a worldwide process. But in the Hindu polytheistic mythology we find an exception. Among the Vedic gods any one is raised to the status of the Omnipotent God for the time being when that god is praised and worshipped by the Vedic sages. Thus, when Indra is worshipped it is said that he is the all-powerful and all-knowing Supreme Lord, and the other gods, like Baruna, Ushā, Agni and so forth, only obey his commands. But in the next book of the same Veda, or sometimes in the same book, when hymns are addressed to Varuna it is said that he is the Almighty and Omniscient God, and Indra and others only obey his command. In this way all other gods occupy the position of the Supreme Lord of all in turns. Observing this peculiarity of the Vedic pantheon, Professor Max Müller, instead of characterizing the Vedic faith as polytheism, coined a new name for it and called it "henotheism." But to give a new name to a new situation does not explain the situation itself. Hence Max Müller's use of the new term "henotheism" instead of polytheism does not really explain why the different Vedic gods are elevated one after another to assume the status of Almighty and Omniscient God of the Universe. The explanation, however, is there in the Vedic texts themselves. It has been expressly stated in one of the hymns of the Vedas: *Ekam sat viprā vahudhā vadanti*[14]—"That which exists is one: sages call It by various names." Hence only the names or concepts of gods are different, but the Reality underlying these concepts is one and the same. Multiple ways of conceiving Reality are not incompatible with the unity of the Reality conceived. Varying degrees of intellectual capacity of different individuals in apprehending one and the same Reality result in the formation of various concepts of gods. But at the heart of all these variations the same Reality reigns: "That which exists is one: sages call it by various names." And this is obviously not polytheism. What appears to be polytheism in the Samhitā portion of the Vedas is really monotheism, only dressed in polytheistic language. And though the language of polytheism clamours to draw our attention in these Samhitā verses, whispering notes of monotheism are not altogether absent in them, as is evident from the Gāyatri verse of the Rg-Veda already quoted. This undercurrent of monotheism in the first and oldest part of the Vedas, that is, the Samhitās, becomes dominant in the Upanisads of a later period when the Upanisadic sage declares in unequivocal terms: *Ekam eva advitīyam*—"There is but One Being, not a second." This "One-God" theory, therefore, is the uncompromising creed of the Vedas, and the Hindu concept of God should be divined in terms of it. Hinduism has never been a pure polytheistic religion.

THE IMMANENT AND TRANSCENDENT ASPECTS OF GOD

Though God is one and only one in Hinduism, God's nature has been conceived in the Vedas in two different aspects—immanent and transcendent. In the immanent aspect God is said to be creator, preserver and destroyer of the world (*srsti-sthiti pralaya karta*). The notion of a Creator God constitutes a fundamental category in almost all the major religious traditions of the world, and Hinduism is no exception. But one distinctive feature of the Hindu conception of the Creator God lies in that, after creating the world, God does not stand outside but remains within it. The concept of a God residing in Heaven above the universe and occasionally interfering with the affairs of the world at moments of crisis is quite alien to the Hindu mind. God, according to Hinduism, remains in the very bosom of the Universe, pervades and permeates the whole of it, and controls it while remaining within it.[15] Hence God has been described in the Hindu scriptures as the inherent creator and inner controller of the world, or the *Antaryamin*. To appreciate properly why God is said to be inherently embedded in the Universe we need to understand the Hindu theory of creation, a detailed discussion of which is reserved for the next section. However, for the present purpose it is sufficient to note that God in the immanent aspect is no other than the Personal God of religion who, in the later Bhakti cult of Hinduism, has been invested with six attributes, viz., majesty (*aisvarya*), omnipotence (*virya*), glory (*yasa*), beauty (*sri*), knowledge (*jñana*), and dispassion (*vairagya*). This immanent God with attributes (*saguna Brahman*), who can be worshipped and prayed to, is specifically termed *Isvara* in the Upanisadic literature.

But though God resides within the world and pervades the whole of it, God's being is not wholly exhausted in it; God is also beyond the world. God is both immanent and transcendent in relation to the world. This is suggested by a famous hymn of the Rg-Veda known as Purusa-sukta: "God pervades the whole world by a quarter of His being, while the three fourth of Him stands over as immortal in the sky."[16] The language of this hymn is of course metaphorical: we shall see later that God in the transcendental aspect defies all human measurement—both in terms of quality and quantity. But what it really suggests is that God's being cannot be unresidually equated with the world, that God is not merely the totality of the objects of the world but something more: God is also beyond the world. This "beyond-aspect" of God is called *Brahman* just as God's immanent aspect is known as *Isvara* in the Upanisads. Not only in the Rg-Veda but in other Hindu scriptures also the concept of God as "beyond" is repeatedly emphasized.[17]

Now, from God's transcendence follows God's necessary inaccessibility to the human mind and to linguistic description. To quote from an Upanisad: *Brahman* is that "from where mind and speech recoil, baffled in their quest."[18] Since *Brahman* transcends the limits of all phenomenality, the concepts of our discursive reason and the words of our language through the instrumentality of which we interpret the phenomenal world do not have any legitimate application: and any attempt to apply these to *Brahman* will distort and falsify the nature of *Brahman*. Hence conceptual thought cannot grasp the real nature of *Brahman,* nor can language describe *Brahman* by any positive terms. *Brahman* can only be described negatively as "not this, not this" (*neti neti*).[19]

But a long process of spiritual practice (*Yoga*) is able to free our minds from these concepts and transform our discursive reason into a direct state of transcendental intuition. This transformed, deconceptualized state of our minds is known as *samadhi* in the *Yoga-Sutra* of Patanjali, and it is said that the knowledge of the true nature of *Brahman* dawns in this state. In the light of such intuitive transcendental experience (*samadhi*), the Upanisads describe the essential nature of *Brahman* as pure existence, consciousness and bliss (*sat-cit-ananda*). Yet all these references of the scriptures do not and cannot describe the real nature of *Brahman*. These are at best suggestive hints of the great Transcendent Reality. All that we may gather from these is that *Brahman* is not void or blank (*sunya*), nor an insentient something, but that *Brahman* is the source and support of every object and experience in nature; One without a second.

This *Brahman* when conceived as the creative energy (*śakti*) of the Universe is called Īśvara, and there is no substantial difference between the two. In fact Īśvara is the highest possible reading of the *Brahman* by the finite human mind; but beyond that mental measurement God stands as the highest, transcendental and impersonal Absolute which, however, is too much an abstraction to be loved and worshipped. So a religious devotee chooses the immanent aspect of God in order to establish a personal relationship. Thus, from the religious point of view, the concept of *Īśvara* is more important than the concept of *Brahman*. In the concluding section of this chapter let us concentrate on this and see in what sense Īśvara is said to be the creator and destroyer of the world.

GOD (ĪŚVARA) AND CREATION

The Vedic-Upanisadic theory of creation rests on the explicit rejection of two other rival theories—creation *ex nihilo* and creation out of the pre-existing materials of the Universe. According to the former theory, nothing but God existed before creation and God created the universe out of nothing by sheer creative will. We find this theory of creation being mentioned and rejected in one of the principal Upanisads, and the argument on the strength of which it is rejected is that an existent entity can never be produced out of nothing (*kathamasatah sajjāyeteti*).[20] This argument rests on a particular view of causation known as *sat-kārya-vāda* in the Samkhya system of Hindu philosophy.[21] According to it the effect (*kārya*) must exist (*sat*) in its material cause in an extremely rarefied form before it is actually produced. One gets oil from seeds, because oil is somehow contained within the seeds before these are squeezed and crushed. A thousand efforts on the part of the agent will not produce a single drop of oil from the crushing of sand, because sand does not already contain oil. Hence what is called production or creation really means the evolution of a thing which was already

involved in its material cause. What was involved becomes evolved; what was enveloped becomes developed; what was latent becomes patent; and this is all that creation means in Hinduism. Hence a thing cannot be created or produced out of sheer "nothing" in which it was not involved before. To say, therefore that God created the world *ex-nihilo* is to flout this fundamental principle of creation.

As an antidote to this theory, another theory of creation is put forward by some cosmologists and philosophers which may be designated as the "Design" theory of the world. According to this theory, God created the universe not out of sheer nothing but out of pre-existing materials like atoms (*paramānus*), space (*dik*), time (*kāli*) and so on, which are co-eval entities with God. These materials were already present before and outside God, and God as a conscious efficient agent merely shaped or designed the world out of them. On this theory God is not so much a creator as a designer or architect of the Universe. But Hinduism rejects this theory, finding it as faulty as the theory of creation *ex nihilo*. The chief defect of this theory is that it reduces God to a dependent, limited and finite being. An architect has to depend on the materials available and can only do what these materials make possible. In this way God becomes restricted by the materials of creation, and God's omnipotence is lost. Thus, though the Design theory avoids the defects of the *ex-nihilo* theory of creation, it does so at the cost of an omnipotent God. Hence it cannot be accepted as a satisfactory solution to the problem of creation.

Having rejected these two extreme views, Upanisadic Hinduism puts forward its own theory of creation in positive terms. According to it, God created the world not out of sheer nothingness, nor out of pre-existing materials lying outside God, but from within God. God is both the material cause and the efficient cause of the world (*abhinnanimittopadāna*). In ordinary empirical cases of production, the material cause (*upādana kārana*) and the efficient cause (*nimitta kārana*) are two different things, and the material cause lies outside the efficient cause. In the case of the production of a clay pot, the clay out of which the pot is made is its material cause and the potter who consciously makes the pot is its efficient cause. After the pot is produced it continues to have an independent existence apart from and outside the potter. But this is not so with the creation of the world. Here God (Īsvara) is said to be both the efficient cause and the material cause of the world. God creates the world out of God's own inner nature. God is both the creator and the stuff of the world at the same time. Hence after creating the world, God does not stand outside it but is involved in every bit of it. God pervades and permeates the whole Universe, because it is God that has become the Universe; the Universe is an extension of God's own being, a projection of God's inner nature (prakṛti). To quote from an Upaniṣad: "Just as a spider throws out the web from within itself and again draws it in . . . so also does God (akṣara) create the Universe."[22]

Another interesting feature of the Hindu theory of creation is that created Nature is said to be eternal, without any absolute beginning and absolute end. No point in time is imaginable at which God existed but not yet a world. The world has a beginning and an end only in a relative sense, to be explained shortly. It is not that the Universe was created a few thousand years ago for the first time and that it will be destroyed forever a few thousand years hence. It is not that at a particular point of time God created the world, and since then God has been resting in peace except for occasional interference in its affairs. The creative energy is still going on; God is eternally creating and is never at rest. In the Gītā, Śrikrsna, who is believed by a sect of the Hindus to be the incarnation (avatāra) of God, declares: "If I remain inactive for a single moment, the entire universe will fall into pieces."[23]

But how can the idea of eternal creation without beginning and end be reconciled with the notion of cyclical dissolution of the world, or the pralaya as it is called in different Hindu scriptures? The answer is as follows. According to Hindu metaphysics the created universe is a mass of vibrations remaining at a certain level of frequency. But there are periods when this whole mass of vibrations becomes extremely rarefied, starts receding and finally gets reabsorbed into God from where it was projected forth. This unmoved mass of vibrations of the Universe within God is known as pralaya or the cosmic dissolution. But it should not be taken to mean the absolute destruction of the Universe. The Universe during pralaya does not explode into absolute non-being forever. Having reached the lowest level of frequency it merely exists as an unmanifested condition within God. What was evolved from God becomes again involved within God. But after a period of such temporary involution the whole world again evolves forward at the beginning of a new cycle. This process of involution and evolution of the world goes on backward and forward like ocean-waves through all eternity. Again this sort of pralaya does not take place simultaneously in all parts of the Universe. A particular solar system like ours may be disintegrating but thousands of others will continue to exist in their manifested condition. Thus creation taken as a whole is eternal in the sense that it has neither an absolute beginning nor an absolute end. Whenever in the Hindu scriptures the words "beginning" and "end" of the world are used, they should be taken to mean the beginning and end of one particular cycle, and no more than that.

NOTES AND REFERENCES

1. Traditionally the Vedas are divided into four parts—Saṁhitās, Brāhmanas, Aranyakas, and Upanisads. But since the āranyakas intend to be the philosophical interpretations of Brāhmanic ritualism, these may be treated as parts of the Brāhmanas and not as a separate branch of the Vedas.

2. Chāndogya Upaniṣad, VI.2.1.

3. Ṛg-Veda, III.62.10.

4. Atharva Veda, XIX.7.12.

5. S. K. Chatterjee, The Fundamentals of Hinduism (University of Calcutta, 1970) p. 6.

6. Chāndogya Upaniṣad, VI.8.7.

7. *Muṇḍaka Upaniṣad*, I.1.3.

8. *Kathopaniḍad*, II.1.10.

9. *Chāndogya Upaniṣad*, VIII.7.1.

10. Quoted in Aldous Huxley, *Perennial Philosophy* (London: Chatto & Windus, 1974) p. 19.

11. *Isopaniṣad*, 1.

12. In fact the word "deva" is derived from the Sanskrit root *div* which means "to shine." Thus derived, the word *devas* (gods) would etymologically mean the bright ones who shine in their glory.

13. See Swami Vivekananda, *Hinduism* (Sri Ramakrishna Math, Mylapore, Madras-4, India, 1968) pp. 23–4.

14. *Ṛg-Veda*, I.164-6.

15. *Bhagavad Gītā*, XV.13.

16. *Ṛg-Veda*, I.90.3.

17. *Bṛhadāranyaka Upaniṣad*, III.9.26; *Bhagavad-Gītā*, X.42 and XV.16-17.

18. *Taittiriya Upaniṣad*, II.9.1.

19. *Bṛhadāranyaka Upaniṣad*, III.9.26.

20. *Chāndogya Upaniṣad*, VI.2.1-2.

21. In the Saṁkhya system elaborate arguments are given in support of this theory of causation. For an excellent summary of these arguments see S. Radhakrishan, *Indian Philosophy* (London: Allen & Unwin, 1962) Vol. II, pp. 256–8.

22. *Muṇḍaka Upaniṣad*, I.1.7.

23. *Bhagavad-Gītā*, III.24.

I.A.8

Emptiness: Soteriology and Ethics in Mahayana Buddhism[1]

CHRISTOPHER IVES

Christopher Ives (1954 -) is professor of religious studies at Stonehill College, and specializes in Asian religions. His publications include Zen Awakening and Society *(1992),* The Emptying God *(co-edited with John B. Cobb, Jr., 1990), and* Divine Emptiness and Historical Fullness *(1995). In this essay, Ives examines the role of Emptiness in Mahayana Buddhism, the greater of the two main traditions within Buddhism.*

"Emptiness" has its true connotations in the process of salvation, and it would be a mistake to regard it as a purely intellectual concept, or to make it into a thing, and give it an ontological meaning. The relative nothing ("this is absent in that") cannot be hypostatized into an absolute nothing, into the non-existence of everything, or the denial of all reality and of all being.[2]

Reprinted from *Concepts of the Ultimate*, edited by Linda J. Tessier, published 1989 by St. Martin's Press. Reproduced with permission of Palgrave MacMillan.

The search for the "ultimate" in Mahayana Buddhism leads inevitably to emptiness (*śūnyatā*). Emptiness first emerges as a key Buddhist concept in the *Prajñāparamitā Sūtras* (Perfection of Wisdom Sutras), Mahayana Sanskrit writings of the 1st century BCE. On the basis of this group of sutras, the great Indian philosopher Nagarjuna (2nd century CE) gives emptiness a systematic philosophical expression. In his writings, especially the *Mūlamadhyamika-kārikās* (Stanzas on the Middle Way), Nagarjuna sets forth emptiness as a thoroughgoing negation of independent self-existence and a refutation of substantialist conceptual approaches to reality, with the intention of dissolving human attachment and consequent suffering. Later Mahayana thinkers develop these aspects of emptiness as an ontologically descriptive term and, more importantly, a soteriological device, a skillful means (*upāya*) of leading people beyond ignorance to liberation. It is primarily in the latter sense that emptiness functions as the "ultimate" in Mahayana Buddhism.

The Sanskrit term *śūnyatā* derives from the root *śvi*, which means to swell. That which is swollen appears full when viewed from the outside, but is often empty within.[3] Such emptiness is not necessarily negative, however, for it can function constructively, as does the hollowness that enables a temple bell to ring or a gourd to function as a water vessel. (As we will see, emptiness also refers to the metal of the bell and the walls of the gourd.) In conjunction with this connotation of the term, *śūnyatā* is also the Sanskrit word for zero, the "empty" number in mathematics. As mathematicians well know, "in the total (holistic) system of digits, the zero is a necessary starting point as well as conclusion...."[4]

Nagarjuna draws on these connotations of *śūnyatā* in responding to *Abhidharma* Buddhist thought, especially as conveyed in the *Abhidharma Pitaka,* the "basket" of the Pali Canon that elaborates on the ethical, psychological and ontological concepts in Gautama Buddha's talks. *Abhidharma* thinkers follow the historical Buddha in his negation of an eternal, independent self (*ātman*). They assert that the "self" is an everchanging process, not a thing, and arises through the dependent co-origination (*pratîtya-samutpāda*) of numerous *dharmas,* the physical and mental factors constituting reality. The traditional formula of dependent co-origination is, in the Buddha's words,

> When this is present, that comes to be; from the arising of this, that arises.
>
> When this is absent, that does not come to be; on the cessation of this, that ceases.[5]

To clarify the constitution of subjectivity and the emergence of ignorance and suffering, *Abhidharma* Buddhists analyze and classify the various *dharmas,* which can be "this" or "that" in the above formula. At times, *dharmas* are discussed as independent, atomistic entities. The *Sarvastivada* ("everything exists") school of *Abhidharma* thought argues that space and Nirvana are unconditioned *dharmas.*

Nagarjuna criticizes this hypostatization of the elementary factors or *dharmas,* labelling it a metaphysical error, a form of ignorance (*avidyā*) which conduces to attachment and further suffering. He contends that not only composite entities but also their compositional elements come into being through the interaction of various conditions in a constantly changing field of interaction. In other words, *all* things lack own-being (*svabhāva*)[6]; they are empty (*śūnya*), devoid of independent self-existence. Nagarjuna is not arguing that nothing exists or that we live in an illusory nihilistic void, but that there are no independent, unchanging, permanent essences. As he writes, "Since there is no *dharma* whatever originating independently, no *dharma* whatever exists which is not empty."[7] Simply put, Nagarjuna proceeds a step beyond the earlier Buddhist notion of "personal selflessness" and expounds the "selflessness of dharmas." Of course, in the process he reconceptualizes the Theravadin notion of dependent co-origination, for "in the context of emptiness (*śūnyatā*), co-originating dependently loses its meaning as the link between two "things"; rather it becomes the form for expressing the phenomenal "becoming" as the lack of any self-sufficient, independent reality."[8] Thus Nagarjuna states, "The 'originating dependently' we call 'emptiness.'"[9]

Emptiness as the negation of independent self-existence pertains not only to the human self, the array of things in our world, and the compositional factors, but to the religious ideal of *nirvāna* as well. Unlike *Sarvastivadin Abhidharma* thought, Nagarjuna does not regard *nirvāna* as an independent, unconditioned state. Convinced of universal relatedness, he considers such an independent reality a mental fabrication and argues that true *nirvāna* is not found apart from living-dying (*samsāra*), but realized in its midst:

> There is nothing whatever which differentiates the existence-in-flux (*samsāra*) from *nirvāna;*
> And there is nothing which differentiates *nirvāna* from existence-in-flux.[10]

From the standpoint of unawakened, conventional knowledge, *samsāra* and *nirvāna* are seen as thoroughly opposite, whereas in absolute knowledge they are grasped as non-dual. Further, in the realization of emptiness, one is not attached to either of the realms conceptualized in conventional knowledge: *samsāra* or *nirvāna,* the secular or the sacred. This non-attachment constitutes religious freedom. "In the realization of emptiness through complete detachment from both the secular and the sacred worlds one can freely move back and forth between the two worlds without hindrance."[11]

Nagarjuna even argues that emptiness itself is empty. "Emptiness" does not refer to a transcendent, substantial Reality. As one scholar remarks, "when emptiness is described as inexpressible, inconceivable, and devoid of designation, it does not imply that there is such a thing having these as characteristics"[12] Again, emptiness is synonymous with dependent co-origination, with the continuous changing system of relationships called "becoming." It is not apart from actuality, as indicated by the famous line in the Heart Sutra, "Form is emptiness and emptiness is form."

Emptiness, then, is not a religious ultimate in the sense of a transcendent Being or eternal Oneness. In fact, emptiness negates the reification of *anything* as an ultimate. This point is of crucial soteriological significance. "Only by realizing that the *dharma* [the historical Buddha's teaching], the Path, and the Buddha were not ultimate entities to

be grasped by intellectual or meditative techniques could one be free from the attempt to possess an Ultimate as well as be free from the sorrow resulting from not attaining that illusory 'Ultimate.'"[13] Nagarjuna's articulation of emptiness thus serves to dissolve ignorant structures of experience and lead us toward a realization of liberating wisdom (*prajñā*). "Epistemologically, emptiness is *prajñā,* an unattached insight that truth is absolutely true."[14] But what is the nature of attachment and suffering?

As the historical Buddha discussed in his talks on the Four Holy Truths, human suffering is caused primarily by desire or craving (*trsna*). Through ignorance (*avidyā*) of dependent co-origination and impermanence, a person takes the objectified self and other experiential objects to be independent, enduring entities, and through this mode of experience grows attached to them positively (desire and love) or negatively (aversion and hatred). This ignorance of the conditioned nature of the self and its world derives in large part from hypostatizing that which we experience and giving it a convenient designation, such as "me," "you," "us," "them," "career," "fame," or "wealth"). To the degree subjectivity positions itself as some thing or self, identifies with that position and whatever bolsters it, becomes negatively attached—through aversion, fear and hatred—to entities threatening it, and works to protect and maintain its position relative to the non-self, subjectivity becomes alienated from its world, the very context and source of its be-ing. Moreover, in objectifying itself through self-consciousness, subjectivity becomes split into a reflective subject and reflected-upon object, and thus becomes estranged even from itself.[15]

To loosen attachment to the boundaries created by the "thinking-thinging"[16] process, Nagarjuna explicates the relational character of reality. In the *Mūlamadhyamika-kārikās,* he sets forth emptiness to negate the reification of the convenient constructions (*prajñapti*) of language and the projection of them onto reality. He

> asserts that the so-called essence is nothing but a hypostatization of word-meaning. The word, he says, is not of such a nature

that it indicates a real object. Instead of being a sure guarantee of the existence of an ontological essence, every word is itself a mere baseless mental construction whose meaning is determined by the relation in which it stands to other words. Thus the meaning of a word immediately changes as soon as the whole network of which it is but a member changes even slightly.[17]

Essentially, "emptiness is a non-referring word about referring words."[18] That is to say, "Emptiness is not a term outside the expressional system, but is simply the key term within it.... Like all other expressions, it is empty, but it has a peculiar relation within the system of designations. It symbolizes non-system, a surd within the system of constructs."[19]

Further, through a dialectical analysis of various philosophical viewpoints, Nagarjuna demonstrates the inherent contradictions of any doctrinal standpoint that attempts to grasp reality conceptually. This analytical method is called *prasanga,* a type of *reductio ad absurdum.* One form this dialectical method takes is the negation of a tetralemma. Nagarjuna argues that a *dharma* is

neither 1. existent
nor 2. non-existent
nor 3. both existent and non-existent
nor 4. neither existent nor non-existent.

This is echoed in Nagarjuna's eightfold negation:

I salute the Buddha,
The foremost of all teachers;
He has taught
The doctrine of dependent co-arising,
[The reality of all things is marked by]
No origination, no extinction;
No permanence, no impermanence;
No identity, no difference;
No arrival, no departure.[20]

In this way, Nagarjuna negates (empties) the ontological categories of being and non-being, and rejects both naive realism and nihilism. Reality eludes discursive, discriminating thought and its dualistic categories of being and non-being, subject and object, identity and difference, cause and effect. It cannot be objectified or articulated by any word, theory or thought process; any attempt to grasp it conceptually is doomed to failure and, more crucially, suffering. Again, this does not imply that there is an independent, substantial "thing" eluding us. Rather, reality is beyond all distinctions of thing and no-thing, being and non-being, immanent and transcendent, or eternal and temporal. As the open, dynamic context of becoming, "it" gives rise to all things, though never apart from them. Emptiness hence signifies that (1) nothing in the world has any self-existence, and (2) no concept or theory, nor the cognitive process that creates and uses it, can grasp the nature of reality.

A mere intellectual understanding of these two senses of emptiness is not sufficient to bring about a cessation of suffering, for ignorance colours not only the intellectual but also the emotional and volitional aspects of human existence. To understand emptiness non-objectively in its full religious significance, ignorant subjectivity must be sloughed off. This emptying requires more than a mere philosophical dialectic, so Nagarjuna's logic must be linked with an engaged religious quest. Through meditation and other religious practices, or through despair of the ego-self and a realization of the human predicament, one arrives at what Zen refers to as Great Doubt and Great Death, in which dualistic ego-consciousness is broken through. More specifically, subjectivity entangled in the ignorant reification and attachment process reaches an impasse and ultimately drops away, an event the Japanese Zen master Dogen (1200-1253) calls "the dropping off of mind and body." Simultaneously, unattached liberated subjectivity awakens. This subjectivity is not attached to or identified with any particular self-definition or form, and hence has been termed the "Formless Self" by a modern Zen master, Shin'ichi Hisamatsu. And since emptiness understood as absolute subjectivity is beyond the grasp of language and conceptual thought, it is said to be "unattainable" (*anupalambha*), or unobjectifiable. This aspect of emptiness generates such metaphors as a sword unable to cut itself or an eye unable to see itself while functioning effectively in actuality.

The goal of Nagarjuna's dialectic and the accompanying quest, then, is a transcendence of subjectivity that reifies things or states of affairs and becomes attached to that which has been reified. In Nagarjuna's writings and before him "in the *Prajñaparamita,* supreme enlightenment is identified with the attainment of *śūnyatā.* In other words, the object of the Buddhist life is to find an unattached abode in this realization. This abode is called *apratishthita,* not-abiding."[21] In Mahayana Buddhism, non-abiding, liberated subjectivity is equipped with the wisdom (*prajñā*) that "sees" the arising of all things in emptiness (dependent co-origination). Such wisdom does not indicate a retreat from actuality into annihilation or a void, but a dynamic realization that emptiness is none other than form, that is, the world of events. This dynamic regrasping of actuality in terms of open, processive emptiness is empowered by the energy formerly blocked in the attempt to maintain a delineated self and its boundaries. "To maintain this integrated self, enormous *binding force,* or *clinging,* is required. Setting loose the binding force of ego-clinging thus releases the tremendous potential energy within, and this constitutes what Buddhism calls Enlightenment and liberation."[22]

In conjunction with this transformation, subjectivity has shifted epistemologically from conventional, practical knowledge and truth (*samvrti-satya*) in which the person was entangled, to liberated religious knowledge and truth (*paramārtha-satya*), the insight into universal emptiness. On the basis of the latter, the person is able to make use of conventional knowledge in the everyday practical realm without causing suffering by reifying the convenient concepts used in such knowledge. Epistemologically, "all dualism or conceptual distinction is reconstructed in the realization of Emptiness without any possibility of clinging to distinction."[23] And in making the shift to the second truth, the anxiety, pain and disease previously experienced disappear as subjectivity stops clinging and opens up to empty, dependent co-arising. Paradoxically

(at least when seen from our ordinary perspective), salvation is achieved not by realizing an eternal, unchanging reality outside of becoming, but by overcoming the subjectivity that seeks permanence apart from actuality and thus entering fully into becoming Here and Now. In this way, the problem of the search for permanent being outside of becoming is dissolved, rather than "solved" through the discovery of a permanent Reality, the way normal subjectivity imagines the problem to be solvable. One's whole being shifts from substantialist, dualistic thought, to non-substantial thought, or, in the words of one Buddhist scholar, from the "*Svabhava*" way of thinking to the "*Nihsvabhava*" ("no-own-being," empty) way of thinking, as delineated in the following:

The *Svabhava* Way	The *Nihsvabhava* Way
independent	interdependent
unitary	structural
entity and substance	events and actions
static	dynamic
fixed	fluid
bound	free
definitely restricted	infinite possibilities
clinging and attachment	release and detachment
thatness	thusness[24]

It must be noted here, however, that the empty (*Nihsvabhava*) way of thinking or experiencing is not a theory advanced in opposition to theories based on substantialist *svabhavic* thought. Rather, it cuts through all cognition, all theoretical standpoints that attempt to objectify reality and grasp its nature conceptually. (Emptiness serves to circumvent such thought, not to give it a correct object to ponder.) Nagarjuna asks us to empty ourselves of such objectification, discrimination, and conceptualization— and then experience in terms of *prajñā.*

In addition to the critical, soteriological and epistemological aspects of the term, emptiness also plays a positive "ontological" role in Nagarjuna's thought. To Nagarjuna, emptiness is not merely a negation of own-being (*svabhāva*), for it is only by virtue of emptiness that things can "be." As discussed earlier, to be is to co-originate with other things through mutual conditioning. And to be open to the various conditions, the relational entity must be *empty* of any independent, self-contained status. Thus, as one Buddhist scholar tells us, "things exist by virtue of their true emptiness.... If things were not empty of a substance or essence, they could not exist even for a second; conversely, without things, there can be no emptiness. This is not hard to understand if it is remembered that emptiness refers only to the mode of being of existents."[25] In Nagarjuna's words,

> When emptiness "works," then everything in existence "works." If emptiness does not "work," then all existence does not "work."[26]

Since universal interrelating provides the necessary condition for things to "be," all apparently enduring entities (me, you, the piece of paper before us) are constantly "open" to constitutive factors; accordingly, an independent entity with own-being cannot even begin to exist. It is not that things exist *even though* they are empty, but that things exist *precisely because* they are empty. On this basis we express schematically the meaning of the aforementioned couplet from the Heart Sutra, "Form is emptiness, emptiness is form":

form is emptiness	no own-being (*svabhāva*); "things" arise only through dependent co-origination
emptiness is form	the dependent co-origination by virtue of which "things" arise is not apart from them

Thus it is not the case that emptiness or dependent co-origination exists temporally or ontologically prior to actuality; rather, emptiness as dependent co-origination is the actual dynamics of reality in its very becoming.

In awakening to emptiness as the dynamics of becoming, as the mode of be-ing, we realize the convergence of ontology, epistemology and ethics. Ontologically, the emptied self ceases to posit itself as an enduring, bounded entity standing in opposition to the objects of its experience (including itself

as objectified in dualistic knowing). It experiences the world as a system of dynamic, processive interrelationships (temporal) and mutual constitution (atemporal and structural in the now). More exactly, the emptied self *is* its experience. That is to say, it is not that we *have* an experience of something, but that we *are* our experience. In the immediacy of direct experience prior to later reflection, the experiencer, experiencing and experienced are not separate. Epistemologically, this openness and direct experience is *prajñā,* defined here as experiencing in the mode of emptiness, that is, nihsvabhavically. Psychologically, "the dawning of *prajñā,* by which one sees the emptiness of things, is an act of absolute encompassing whereby one's boundaries expand to include everything. To see emptiness is to become emptiness, or, ... to become empty is to see emptiness."[27] To use the terminology of one Zen philosopher, this openness is the "boundless expanse of Awakening" (*Kaku-no-hirogari*).[28] This can be understood only when the reflective, hypostatizing ("thinging") ego-self is emptied and formless subjectivity (Awakening) opens up. In Nagarjuna's parlance, this is the shift from *samvrti-satya* to *paramārtha-satya.*

Given that the "self" is precisely the dynamism of experiencing, human knowing and being converge. More exactly put, emptiness indicates the level at which knowing and being (and doing) are still undivided. Understood in this way, "emptiness" functions as the ground of Mahayana Buddhist ethics. When we conceive of *śūnyatā* as "emptying," that which is emptied is the self-centred, defensive, boundary-forming ego-self. Emptying is a liberating expansion, in which emptied subjectivity becomes a context for fullness. It is not unlike the sky, the other meaning of the Chinese ideograph for *śūnyatá.* As one Zen master states, "We should always live in the dark, empty sky. The sky is always the sky. Even though clouds and lightning come, the sky is not disturbed."[29]

Through this emptying of the ego-self, the artificial distinctions and discriminations made with regard to others are emptied as well. The other is now seen for what he or she is. In Buddhist terminology, the person is seen in his or her suchness, or "as-it-is-ness." And at a deeper level, our sense of self expands to include others. One contemporary Zen master writes,

> The practice of "being with them" [realizing mutual constitution] converts the third person, *they, it, she, he,* into the first person *I,* and *we.* For Dogen Zenji, the others who are "none other than myself" include mountains, rivers, and the great earth....
>
> This is compassion, suffering with others. "Dwell nowhere, and bring forth that mind" [Diamond Sutra]. "Nowhere" is the zero of purest experience, known inwardly as fundamental peace and rest. To "come forth" is to stand firmly and contain the myriad things.[30]

In conjunction with the realization of such subjectivity, we are emptied of rigid attachment to personal notions of truth and falsehood, right and wrong. We realize that all views, including our own, are tentative and partial. Here the road to tolerance, inclusiveness and participation opens before us, and we begin to serve each other as we interact and inter-create in the open context of emptiness. We shift from a svabhavic, self-centred outlook to a holistic, organic view of actuality. No longer frightened and defensive, we can act freely and creatively in the web of interrelationship. "Not holding on to a notion of self, we are invited to engage ourselves courageously in the world, to see the nature of suffering clearly, and with discriminating awareness to undertake the task of liberating all sentient beings."[31]

As indicated by this statement, such clear seeing (*prajñā*) is inseparable from compassion (*karunā*) and the functioning of a Bodhisattva. Emptied of the psychologically isolated and self-centred ego-self, we realize the interaction between all entities; and in this expansion of subjectivity and openness to actuality we empathically experience suffering. Entering the world of suffering, the Bodhisattva functions through various skillful means (*upāyā*) to awaken others to emptiness, to liberated, unattached, boundless subjectivity. The compassionate activity realized in conjunction with liberated experiencing-being (*prajñā*) constitutes what might be called a creative expression of emptiness.

Understood as self-emptying, wisdom and compassion, emptiness points to such values as unselfishness and non-possession. By realizing inter-relatedness and thereby emptying ourselves of attachment to distinctions between "me" and "you" or "us" and "them," we can begin fully to share or give of ourselves. This shift away from selfish clinging and attachment has ramifications for relationships between the Western and Eastern blocs, wealthy and impoverished nations, higher and lower socio-economic classes, the powerful and the disenfranchised, and the human and natural realms. The characteristics of unselfishness and non-possession stand in contrast to the oft-encountered emphasis on competition, control and dominance emerging from the view of people as independent selves with certain claims and possessions.

On the basis of emptiness, we can also regrasp power as a reciprocal, mutually-enabling force, not a one-way or hierarchical form of coercion. In an interview, one Buddhologist states,

> In the patriarchal, hierarchical construction of reality, you have a one-way linear causality. We've been conditioned by that notion since Aristotle, and it has dominated both religion and science. Consequently power is seen as emanating from the top down. It is essentially power-*over,* and equated with domination, having one's way, pushing things around, being invulnerable to change. Such a notion of power requires defenses, whether of the ego or the nation state.
>
> But in dependent co-arising, causality is not linear. Power is a two-way street. It is not power-over, but power-with, where beings mutually affect and mutually enhance each other. The old linear notion is essentially that of a zero-sum game: the more you have the less I have; "you win, I lose." But it is breaking down now, as more and more folks are talking about playing a "win-win game." That idea is very close to

synergy, which literally means power-with, and which requires no defenses because it operates through openness. This is the kind of power we find at play in an ecosystem or neural net, where open interaction is essential to skillful functioning and the arising of intelligence and beauty.[32]

Emptiness also allows for an expansion of ethics beyond the human realm to all aspects of the cosmos. Through *prajñā,* non-human sentient beings, non-conscious life forms, and inorganic natural processes in the world are experienced in their uniqueness and realized as contributory to the being of oneself. This gives rise to reverent, non-violent attitudes toward the natural domain and a commitment to maintaining a healthy environment for all life forms. In this sense, awakening to emptiness grounds one in a cosmocentric rather than an anthropocentric standpoint,[33] a standpoint with extensive implications for ecology and economics.

The realization of emptiness, then, does not lead to a static annihilation or void apart from daily living. Buddhist detachment is from the self-centred ego, not from the world. Further, it is emptiness that makes change, freedom and creative action possible, for it breaks beyond selfishness, rigidity, intransigency and the myriad boundaries set up by human ignorance, and indicates a dynamic process of becoming in which transformation can occur. As we saw above, it is on the basis of this transformational freedom that a Bodhisattva functions to lead others beyond ignorance. Nevertheless, for Buddhism to fully enter into the modern age as a system of transformation in the deepest sense, it must undertake the task of clarifying how a Bodhisattva's engaged salvific activity relates to social, political and economic liberation. That is to say, Buddhists must set forth how various conditions in actuality express large-scale ignorance, how such conditions affect individual and group attempts to realize political and spiritual liberation, and how Buddhism provides a basis for—and can motivate people to engage themselves in—constructive social action and liberation in all senses of the term. Approaching this task on the basis of emptiness, Mahayana Buddhists can play a greater role in the ongoing struggle for spiritual and social liberation in the modern world, and thereby express the true significance of emptiness as a religious ultimate.

NOTES

1. I wish to thank Professors Masao Abe and Steve Smith for their valuable suggestions at various stages of the writing of this essay.

2. Edward Conze, *Buddhist Thought in India* (Ann Arbor: University of Michigan Press, 1967) p. 61.

3. Edward Conze, *Buddhism: Its Essence and Development* (New York: Harper & Row, 1975) p. 130.

4. Kenneth K. Inada, "The America Involvement with Sunyata," in *Buddhism and American Thinkers,* eds Kenneth K. Inada and Nolan Jacobson (Albany: State University of New York Press, 1984) p. 82.

5. David J. Kalupahana, *Buddhist Philosophy, A Historical Analysis* (Honolulu: University Press of Hawaii, 1976) p. 28.

6. According to Richard Robinson and Willard L. Johnson, *svabhāva* indicates "something (1) existing through its own power rather than that of another, (2) possessing an invariant and inalienable mark, and (3) having an immutable essence." *The Buddhist Religion, An Introduction,* 3rd edn (Belmont, CA: Wadsworth, 1982) p. 69.

7. *Mūlamadhyamika-kārikās,* XXIV, 19, tr., Frederick Streng, in *Emptiness, A Study in Religious Meaning* (Nashville: Abingdon, 1967) p. 213.

8. Frederick Streng, *Emptiness, A Study in Religious Meaning,* p. 63.

9. *Mūlamadhyamika-kārikās,* XXIV, 18, in Streng, p. 213.

10. Ibid., XXV, 19, in Streng, p. 217.

11. Masao Abe, "Substance, Process, and Emptiness," *Japanese Religions,* Vol. 11 (September 1980) Nos. 2 and 3, p. 26.

12. Op. cit., Streng, p. 80.

13. Ibid., p. 158.

14. Hsueh-li Cheng, *Nagarjuna's "Twelve Gate Treatise"* (Dordrecht, Holland: D. Reidel, 1982) p. 14.

15. See Richard DeMartino, "The Human Situation and Zen Buddhism," in *Zen Buddhism and Psychoanalysis,* ed. Erich Fromm (New York: Harper & Row, 1970) pp. 142–77 for a detailed treatment of the bifurcation of the self.

16. Ken Wilber, *No Boundary* (Boulder, CO: Shambhala, 1981) p. 41.

17. Toshihiko Izutsu, *Toward a Philosophy of Zen Buddhism* (Boulder, CO: Prajna, 1982) pp. 105–6.

18. Douglas D. Daye, "Major Schools of the Mahayana: Madhyamika," in *Buddhism, A Modern Perspective,* ed. Charles S. Prebish (University Park, PA: Pennsylvania State University Press, 1978) p. 92.

19. Richard H. Robinson, *Early Madhyamika in India and China* (New York: Samuel Weiser, 1978) p. 49.

20. Translated by Hsueh-li Cheng, *Nagarjuna's "Twelve Gate Treatise,"* pp. 15–6.

21. Daisetz Teitaro Suzuki, *Studies in the Lankavatara Sutra* (London: Routledge & Kegan Paul, 1975) p. 94.

22. Garma C. C. Chang, *The Buddhist Teaching of Totality: The Philosophy of Hwa Yen Buddhism* (University Park, PA: Pennsylvania State University Press, 1971) pp. 78–9.

23. Masao Abe, "God, Emptiness, and Ethics" (unpublished) p. 5.

24. Op. cit., Chang, p. 85, partially adapted here.

25. Francis H. Cook, *Hua-yen Buddhism, The Jewel Net of Indra* (University Park, PA: Pennsylvania State University Press, 1977) p. 102.

26. *Mūlamadhyamika-kārikās,* XXIV, 14, in Streng, p. 213.

27. Op. cit., Cook, p. 107.

28. Masao Abe coined this term to express the open, inclusive nature of Awakening.

29. Shunryu Suzuki, *Zen Mind, Beginner's Mind* (New York: John Weatherhill, 1973) p. 86.

30. Robert Aitken, *A Mind of Clover* (San Francisco: North Point, 1984) p. 173.

31. Fred Eppsteiner, "In the Crucible: The Tiep Hien Precepts," in *The Path of Compassion, Contemporary Writings on Engaged Buddhism* (hereafter *PC*), eds Fred Eppsteiner and Dennis Maloney (Buffalo: White Pine, 1985) p. 101.

32. Joanna Macy, "In Indra's Net: A Conversation with Joanna Macy," in *PC,* p. 106.

33. See Masao Abe, "Dogen on Buddha Nature," *The Eastern Buddhist,* New Series, Vol. IV (May 1971) No. 1.

I.B. CLASSICAL THEISTIC ATTRIBUTES

Introduction

CLASSICAL THEISM, AS WE HAVE ALREADY NOTED, attributes to God properties like omnibenevolence (being perfectly good), timelessness (being outside the flow of time), immutability (changelessness), omnipotence (being all-powerful), and omniscience (being all-knowing). Each of these attributes, however, raises difficult philosophical puzzles—puzzles that have sometimes been used to challenge the very coherence of the traditional Judeo-Christian concept of God. In this section of our text, we explore some of the best known and most widely discussed of these puzzles. We focus on four main issues: (1) God's relationship to time, (2) the nature of divine omnipotence, (3) the tension between divine moral perfection and divine freedom, and (4) the tension between divine omniscience and human freedom.

1. God and Time

Virtually all theists would agree that God's life is immune to the ravages of time—God lasts forever—and that God somehow transcends time and space. But what do these claims mean? Does God last forever by being wholly outside of time, or by having a temporal life that goes on forever? Is God's life wholly unmarked by temporal succession? Or does the claim that God transcends time and space mean only that God exists outside of our physical space-time, even if his own life still unfolds sequentially? Some philosophers use the terms *eternal* and *everlasting* to mark the distinction between timeless and temporally infinite existence (respectively); others—as in our first two readings in this section—simply distinguish between atemporal eternity and temporal eternity. In either case, the central question about God's relationship to time is whether, to use the oft-quoted words of Boethius, God enjoys "the complete possession of illimitable life all at once," or whether instead God experiences his life in sequence like every other person with whom we are acquainted.[1]

The notion of timeless eternity first appears in Parmenides's poem "The Way of Truth," in which he says of the One, "It neither was at any time nor will be since it is now all at once a single whole." Parmenides and his disciple, Zeno, denied the reality of time. The concept of the timeless eternal was further developed by Plato in the dialogue *Timaeus*, in which it is glorified as infinitely superior to the temporal. The *Timaeus* deeply influenced the early Church, and through Augustine and Boethius the doctrine of eternity (as timelessness) made its way into Christian thought, becoming the dominant position in mainstream Christianity. In the Middle Ages and the Reformation period, it was embraced by Anselm, Aquinas, Luther, Calvin, and the vast majority of theologians, but challenged by Duns Scotus and William of Ockham. In recent times, Anthony Kenny, Nelson Pike, and Nicholas Wolterstorff, among others, have argued that the notion of timelessness is unbiblical and incoherent, and that God should instead be viewed as everlasting.

In our readings, Hugh McCann defends the traditional timeless notion of God's eternity, whereas Stephen T. Davis defends the notion of temporal eternity. In the first reading, Davis offers three arguments in favor of temporal eternity: (1) The concept of God's creative activity makes far more sense if we accept the notion that he exists in time. For if God creates a given temporal thing, his act of creation itself must be temporal. (2) A timeless being cannot be the personal, caring, involved God of the Bible. (3) The idea that God's timeless eternity is somehow simultaneous with this-worldly events seems to result in absurd consequences—e.g., that events in 3021 B.C.E. are no earlier than the events of 1986 for God, then time must be illusory. But there is no good reason to deem time illusory. Hence the notion of timeless eternity seems incoherent. Davis answers several objections to his view, concluding that the concept of temporal eternity is more coherent than the notion of timeless eternity.

---

[1] E. K. Rand, ed. In H. F. Stewart, E. K. Rand, and S. J. Tester, *Boethius: The Theological Tractates and the Consolation of Philosophy* (London: Heinemann; Cambridge, MA: Harvard 1973). Quoted in, among other places, Eleonore Stump and Norman Kretzmann's "Eternity," *Journal of Philosophy* 78 (1981): 429–58.

In his contribution, "The God Beyond Time," McCann argues just the opposite. He examines objections to the atemporal notion of God and tries to answer them, beginning with Davis's first argument, that the concept of God's creative *activity* makes far more sense if we accept the notion that he exists in time. McCann argues that although things may be said to be brought about at some *time*, this does not entail that God must *exist at some time* in order to bring them about. He contends that it is coherent to talk about temporal differences from our point of view but not from God's. Hence, the idea of timelessness is coherent. The whole of Creation is one eternal fiat. Furthermore, McCann argues, the notion of an atemporal God makes better sense of God's sovereignty and omniscience without creating problems for human freedom.

2. Omnipotence

Theists maintain that God is omnipotent—all-powerful. But what is omnipotence? Is it the ability to do just anything at all? Some philosophers, following Descartes, hold that it is, and that it even includes the ability to violate logical truths. But this is a hard view even to grasp, much less believe, because all rational thought and discourse seem to presuppose the truths of logic. Hence, the overwhelming majority of philosophers and theologians, at least since Aquinas, have not thought that omnipotence includes the ability to do the logically impossible. Following their lead, we may roughly define omnipotence as the ability to do whatever is not logically impossible. God can create a universe, but (for example) he cannot make outright contradictions true.

Still, there are problems with this definition. On the surface, at least, it does not seem contradictory to say that God could make a stone heavier than he could lift or that he could sin if he wanted to (though his being perfectly good keeps him from exercising this power). Consider the paradox of the stone, as formulated by Wade Savage:[2]

1. Either x can create a stone that x cannot lift, or x cannot create a stone that x cannot lift.

2. If x can create a stone that x cannot lift, then, necessarily, there is at least one task that x cannot perform (namely, lift the stone in question).

3. If x cannot create a stone that x cannot lift, then, necessarily, there is at least one act that x cannot perform (namely, create the stone in question).

4. Hence, there is at least one task that x cannot perform.

5. If x is an omnipotent being, then x can perform any task.

6. Therefore, x is not omnipotent.

Because x could be any being whatsoever, the paradox apparently proves that the notion of omnipotence is incoherent.

In our readings, George Mavrodes argues that because God is *essentially* omnipotent, the act of creating a stone heavier than he can lift is a logical impossibility. Thus, he cannot do it; but, because omnipotence requires only the ability to do the logically possible, the fact that he cannot do it does not count against his omnipotence. This solution has been criticized by Wade Savage as a case of question begging, supposing as it does that the statement "God is omnipotent" is necessarily true. A second line of thought is taken by Harry Frankfurt, who argues that if God is able to do one impossible thing, make a stone heavier than he can lift, he can also do a second impossible thing and lift that stone. So the paradox of the stone does not show that the notion of omnipotence is incoherent. Other philosophers have developed still further responses to this puzzle.

Similar to the paradox of the stone but more crucial to our idea of God is the question of whether God's omnipotence gives him the power to sin. Again, Aquinas and many medieval theologians argue that such power would be pseudo-power, in fact, impotence. Others, following William of Ockham, have argued that God necessarily cannot sin because sin is defined as simply being that which is opposed to God's will and God cannot oppose his own will at one and the same time. Still others argue that an omniscient and perfectly free being cannot sin because sin necessarily involves a failure in reason or freedom.

3. Omniscience and Human Freedom

An omniscient being knows everything. More exactly, an omniscient being knows every truth and has no false beliefs. But the concept of omniscience raises some challenging questions. One of the more important questions—the one that is the focus of our sixth, seventh, and eighth readings in this section—asks what happens to human freedom if God has exhaustive knowledge of the future. Suppose you are now considering a marriage proposal. Either it is true now that you will accept, or it is true now that you won't—there seems to be no other option. Suppose it is true that you will accept. Then God has believed from time immemorial that you will accept this marriage proposal. How then can you possibly refuse? It seems that in order to refuse, you would have to bring it about either that God never believed that you would accept, or that God has a false belief. But you cannot do either of those things. So, it seems, you cannot refuse. But if you cannot refuse, then it seems that your accepting will not be free because there is no alternative available to you.

Our sixth reading in this section is Augustine's classic discussion of the problem of divine freedom and foreknowledge. Following that is one of the most widely discussed contemporary formulations of the problem: Nelson Pike argues forcefully for the conclusion that divine foreknowledge is incompatible with human freedom. Finally, in our eighth reading, Alvin Plantinga responds to Pike's argument, arguing that it is a mistake to think that if God knows the future, then human freedom would require the ability to change the past or to make God have a false belief.

4. Omnibenevolence and Divine Freedom

Our final pair of readings in this section explores a tension between God's moral perfection and God's *own* freedom. Traditionally, theists have maintained that God is morally unsurpassable: it is a necessary truth that nobody is or can be morally better than God. Suppose that this is what is involved in being morally perfect. Now consider this dilemma: Either there is a best creatable world, or there isn't. If there is, then God would have to create it. For suppose he were to create less than the best. Then, so the reasoning goes, God would have been morally surpassable. For he would have been such that he could have done better; and if God could have done better, so it is argued, then God could have been (morally) better. On the other hand, suppose there is no best creatable world: Suppose the space of worlds God could have created is such that, for any world you pick, there is a better one that God could have created. Then it seems that for anything God might have done, God might have done something better—in which case, by the same reasoning we have just given, God would have been morally surpassable. Thus, if this line of reasoning is sound, either there is a best creatable world and God is not free to refrain from creating it, or there is no best creatable world and so the world could not have been the creation of a morally perfect God. In our ninth reading, William Rowe presses this line of reasoning and defends it against a variety of objections. In our tenth reading, Edward Wierenga responds, defending the conclusion that a morally unsurpassable God can be free after all.

I.B.1

Temporal Eternity

STEPHEN T. DAVIS

Stephen T. Davis is professor of philosophy at Claremont McKenna College. He is the author of several books and numerous articles in the philosophy of religion. Among his works are Christian Philosophical Theology *(2006) and* The Debate about the Bible: Inerrancy versus Infallibility *(1977). In the present selection, he defends the view that God is temporally eternal against the classical view that God is atemporal.*

One divine property that we will deal with early in the book is God's eternality. It will be best if we discuss it here because one's opinion on this subject is likely to affect opinions one has about several other divine properties, especially omnipotence, omniscience and immutability. Thus we must now raise the thorny question of God's relation to time.

It is part of the Judeo-Christian tradition that God is eternal.

> *Lord, thou has been our dwelling place in all generations.*
> *Before the mountains were brought forth, or ever thou hadst formed the earth and the world, from everlasting to everlasting thou art God.*

Stephen T. Davis, *Logic and the Nature of God*, published 1983 (MacMillan Press, LTD: London & Basingstoke). Reproduced with permission of Palgrave MacMillan.

Thou turnest man back to the dust, and sayeth, "Turn back, O children of man!"
For a thousand years in thy sight are but as yesterday when it is past, or as a watch in the night. (Ps. 90:1–4)
Of old thou didst lay the foundation of the earth, and the heavens are the work of thy hands.
They will perish, but thou dost endure; they will all wear out like a garment.
Thou changest them like raiment, and they pass away; but thou art the same and thy years have no end. (Ps. 102:25–7)
I am the Alpha and the Omega, the first and the last, the beginning and the end. (Rev. 22:13)

But what does it mean to say that God is eternal? Jews and Christians agree that God's eternality entails that he has always existed and always will exist, that he has no beginning and no end. But from this central point there are two routes that might be taken. One is to say that God is *timelessly eternal* and the other is to say that he is *temporally eternal*.

Let us first consider the view that God is timelessly eternal or "outside of time." There are a variety of reasons a Christian might be tempted by this thesis. One might be to emphasize God's transcendence over his creation as much as possible. Another might be to reconcile divine foreknowledge and human freedom. (Boethius and others have argued that human beings can be free despite God's knowledge of what they will do in their future because God's knowledge is timeless.) Another might be to retain consistency with other things one says about God, for example that he is immutable. (And it certainly does seem true that a timeless being—to be defined below—must be immutable.)

Whatever the reasons, a variety of Christian theologians and philosophers have claimed that God is timeless. For example, Anselm graphically depicts God's relation to time as follows:

Thou wast not, then, yesterday, nor wilt thou be tomorrow; but yesterday and today and tomorrow thou art; or, rather, neither yesterday; nor today nor tomorrow thou art; but, simply, thou art, outside all time. For yesterday and today and tomorrow have no existence, except in time; but thou, although nothing exists without thee nevertheless dost not exist in space or time, but all things exist in thee.[1]

That God is timeless was also claimed by Augustine and Boethius before Anselm, and was also held after him, notably by Aquinas and Schleiermacher. In a famous definition, Boethius called eternity "the complete possession all at once of illimitable life"; it is a kind of "now that stands still." (Notice that Boethius is using "eternal" as a synonym for "timeless," which I am not.) Since God is eternal, he lives in what might be called an "everlasting present"; he has an infinity of movable time—past, present and future—all at once everlastingly present to him. Boethius is perhaps most clear on this point when he speaks of divine foreknowledge:

Wherefore since ... God hath always an everlasting and present state, his knowledge also surpassing all motions of time, remaineth in the simplicity of his presence, and comprehending the infinite spaces of that which is past and to come, considereth all things in his simple knowledge, as though they were now in doing. So that, if thou wilt weigh his foreknowledge with which he discerneth all things, thou wilt more rightly esteem it to be the knowledge of a never fading instant than a foreknowledge as of a thing to come.[2]

Following Boethius, Aquinas stressed that for God there is no past, present and future, and no before and after, that all is "simultaneously whole" for him.[3]

These statements are not easy to understand. What precisely is meant by the term "timeless" or "timeless being"? Following Nelson Pike, let us say that a given being is timeless if and only if it:

(1) lacks temporal location
    and
(2) lacks temporal extension.[4]

A being lacks temporal location if it does not make sense to say of it, for example, that it existed before the French Revolution or that it will exist on Jimmy Carter's seventieth birthday. Thus, if God is timeless, statements like these cannot meaningfully be made about him. A being lacks temporal extension if it has no duration, i.e. if it makes no sense to say of it, for example, that it has lived for eighty years or that it was alive during the entire period of the Truman administration.

It is not easy to feel that one has fully grasped the notion of a timeless being. Perhaps this is in part because it is difficult to see precisely what criteria (1) and (2) imply. Very possibly they imply another characteristic of a timeless being, one which is also difficult to state and explicate precisely:

(3) Temporal terms have no significant application to him.

What is a "temporal term"? Without wishing to suggest that my list is exhaustive, let me stipulate that a temporal term is one like those included in the following list: "past," "present," "future," "before," "after," and other similar terms like "simultaneous," "always," "later," "next year," "forever," "at 6:00 P.M.," etc. Now there appears to be a sense in which temporal terms cannot meaningfully be predicated of a being that lacks temporal location and temporal extension. Neither the timeless being itself, nor its properties, actions or relations with other beings can be significantly modified by temporal terms. Thus if God is a timeless being, the following sentences are either meaningless or necessarily false:

- God existed before Moses.
- God's power will soon triumph over evil.
- Last week God wrought a miracle.
- God will always be wiser than human beings.

Does this imply that time as we understand it is unreal, a kind of illusion? If the timeless being in question is God, the ultimate reality of the universe, the creator of the heavens and the earth, one might well push the argument in this way: if from God's point of view there is no past, present and future, and no before and after, then—it might well be argued—there is no ultimately real past, present and future, and no ultimately real relationship of before and after. Thus time as we experience it is unreal.

But the argument need not be pushed in this direction. Even if God is a timeless being, it can be argued that time is real and that our temporal distinctions are apt just because God created time (for us to live "in"). Perhaps an analogy from space will help. Just because God is spaceless (he has no spatial location or extension) no one wants to say that space is unreal. It is just that God does not exist in space as we do. Similarly, he does not exist "in" time, but time is still real, both for us and for God. Well then—one might want to ask at this point—if God is timeless is it or is it not meaningful to say that "God existed before Moses" or that "God will always be wiser than human beings"? The answer is that it depends on who you are: for us these statements are meaningful and true; for God they are meaningless or at least necessarily false.

Is the doctrine of divine timelessness coherent? I do not know. I suspect it is possible for a philosopher to lay out a concept of divine timelessness which I am unable to refute, i.e. prove incoherent. I will discuss one such attempt later in this chapter. However, throughout [*Logic and the Nature of God*], for reasons I will presently explain, I do not propose to assume that God is timeless. In fact, I plan to make and argue for the assumption that God is "temporally eternal." In my view, this is a far simpler procedure, with far fewer theological dangers, as I will explain. For the fact is that every notion of divine timelessness with which I am familiar is subject to difficulties which, at the very least, seem serious.

I will argue against the doctrine of divine timelessness on two counts: first, that a timeless being cannot be the Christian God; and second, that the notion of a timeless being is probably incoherent. The first point has been convincingly argued by both Nelson Pike and Richard Swinburne.[5] I will not mention all of the traditional attributes of God they claim timelessness rules out; I will instead concentrate on just two: the claim that God is the creator of the universe, and the claim that God is a personal being who acts in human history, speaking, punishing, warning, forgiving, etc. Both notions are obviously crucial to Christianity; if timelessness really does rule them out this will constitute a very good reason for a Christian to reject the doctrine.

Notice the following argument:

(5) God creates x.

(6) x first exists at T.

(7) Therefore, God creates x at T.

If this argument is valid, it seems to rule out the possibility of a timeless God creating anything at all, the universe or anything in it, for "x" here is a variable ranging over anything at all about which it is logically possible that it be created. The reason the argument rules out the doctrine that God is creator is that (7) cannot be true if God lacks temporal location. For we saw earlier that no temporal term like "at T" can meaningfully be applied to a being or to the actions of a being that lacks temporal location and temporal extension. God is not the creator Christians have traditionally believed in if he is not the creator of things like me and the eucalyptus tree outside my office. But no timeless being can be the creator of such things since they came into existence at various points in time. Thus timelessness is inconsistent with the Christian view of God as creator.

But cannot God, so to speak, timelessly create something temporal? Aquinas, at least, argued that he can. God may create something at a certain point in time (say, create me in the year 1940), but it does not follow from this, Aquinas would say, that God's act of creating occurred at that point in time (or indeed at any point in time); his creating may well be based on changeless and eternal aspects of his will. Thus Aquinas says:

> God's act of understanding and willing is, necessarily, His act of making. Now, an effect follows from the intellect and the will according to the determination of the intellect and the command of the will. Moreover, just as the intellect determines every other condition of the thing made, so does it prescribe the time of its making; for art determines not only that this thing is to be such and such, but that it is to be at this particular time, even as a physician determines that a dose of medicine is to be drunk at such

a particular time. So that, if his act of will were of itself sufficient to produce the effect, the effect would follow anew from his previous decision, without any new action on his part. Nothing, therefore, prevents our saying that God's action existed from all eternity, whereas its effect was not present from eternity, but existed at that time when, from all eternity, He ordained it.[6]

Thus—so Aquinas would say—(5) and (6) in the above argument do not entail (7) after all.

Is Aquinas correct? It depends on what he means by "eternity" in the above lines. If he means temporal eternity I believe he is correct. It may well be true that God can, so to speak, "from all eternity create x at T." I have no wish to deny this, at any rate. A temporally eternal being apparently can eternally (that is, at all points in time) will that a given temporal being come to exist at a certain point in time. Of course, this case is not precisely parallel to the case of Aquinas's physician at a given point in time willing that a dosage be taken at a later point in time. But nevertheless, as concerns temporal eternality, Aquinas appears to be correct: as it stands, the (5)–(7) argument is invalid.

But Aquinas's argument, which in my opinion successfully applies to temporally eternal things, does not apply to timeless things. (Notice that the physician in his example is not timeless.) Even if it is true that I was created in 1940 not because of a choice God made in 1940 (or at some other time) but because of a temporally eternal divine choice, this does not make the choice *timeless* in the sense of lacking temporal location and extension. Temporally eternal things certainly do have temporal extension. It would still make sense and quite possibly be true to say, "God willed in 1940 that Davis exist" (although it would also be meaningful and perhaps equally true to make the same statement with 3469 B.C. or A.D. 2610 or any other date substituted for 1940). Equally, if all God's decisions and actions are temporally eternal they are *simultaneous* with each other; and statements like "x's desire to create a and x's decision to do b are simultaneous" cannot, as we saw, meaningfully be made about a timeless being.[7] This too is to apply a temporal term—"simultaneous"—to it.

Of course, nothing prevents a defender of timelessness from simply insisting that an action (e.g. the causing of something to exist) can be timeless and the effect (e.g. its coming into existence) temporal. Such a person can ask why the temporality of the effect requires that the cause be temporal. But to anticipate a point I will make in more detail later, the answer to this is that we have on hand no acceptable concept of atemporal causation, i.e. of what it is for a timeless cause to produce a temporal effect. Surely, as Nelson Pike argues, in all the cases of causation with which we are familiar, a temporal relationship obtains between an action and its effect. We are in no position to deny that this need always be the case unless we are armed with a usable concept of atemporal causation, which we are not.

Let us return to the argument mentioned above:

(5) God creates x.

(6) x first exists at T.

(7) Therefore, God creates x at T.

What we need to notice is that (7) is ambiguous between (7a) and (7b):

(7a) God, at T, creates x.

(7b) God creates x, and x first exists at T.

Now (7a) clearly cannot be true of God if God is timeless—a being that performs some action at a certain point in time is temporal. So (7b) is the interpretation of (7) that will be preferred by the defender of divine timelessness. Notice that (7b) is simply the conjunction of (5) and (6), and accordingly is indeed entailed by (5) and (6). But can (7b) be true of God if God is timeless? Only if we have available a usable concept of atemporal causation, which, as I say, we do not have. Therefore, we are within our rights in concluding that (5) and (6) entail that God is temporal, i.e. that a timeless being cannot be the creator of the universe.

Accordingly, it is not clear how a timelessly eternal being can be the creator of this temporal universe. If God creates a given temporal thing, then God's act of creation is itself temporal (though it may be temporally eternal). If God is timelessly eternal in the sense defined earlier, he cannot create temporal things.

Second, a timeless being cannot be the personal, caring, involved God we read about in the Bible. The God of the Bible is, above all, a God who cares deeply about what happens in history and who acts to bring about his will. He makes plans. He responds to what human beings do, e.g. their evil deeds or their acts of repentance. He seems to have temporal location and extension. The Bible does not hesitate to speak of God's years and days (see Psalm 102:24, 27; Hebrews 1:12). And God seems to act in temporal sequences—first he rescues the children of Israel from Egypt and later he gives them the Law; first he sends his son to be born of a virgin and later he raises him from the dead. These are generalizations meant to be understood as covering the whole Bible rather than specific passages; nevertheless here are two texts where such points seem to be made:

> If you obey the commandments of the Lord your God ... by loving the Lord your God, by walking in his ways, and by keeping his commandments and his statutes and his ordinances, then you shall live and multiply, and the Lord your God will bless you.... But if your heart turns away, and you will not hear, but are drawn away to worship other gods and serve them, I declare to you this day, that you shall perish. (Deut. 30:16–18)

> In many and various ways God spoke of old to our fathers by the prophets; but in these last days he has spoken to us by a Son. (Heb. 1:1–2)

But the obvious problem here is to understand how a timeless being can plan or anticipate or remember or respond or punish or warn or forgive. All such acts seem undeniably temporal.[8] To make plans is to formulate intentions about the future. To anticipate is to look forward to what is future. To remember is to have beliefs or knowledge about what is past. To respond is to be affected by events that have occurred in the past. To punish is to cause someone to suffer because of something done in the past. To warn is to caution someone about dangers that might lie in the future. To forgive someone is to restore a past relationship that was damaged by an offense.

On both counts, then, it is difficult to see how a timeless being can be the God in which Christians have traditionally believed. It does not seem that there is any clear sense in which a timeless being can be the creator of the universe or a being who acts in time.

The other and perhaps more important argument against divine timelessness is that both the notion of a timeless being per se and the notion of a timeless being who is also omniscient are probably incoherent. The incoherence of the notion per se can be seen by considering carefully the Boethius-Anselm-Aquinas claim that for God all times are simultaneously present. Events occurring at 3021 B.C., at 1982, and at A.D. 7643, they want to say, are all "simultaneously present" to God. If this just means that at any point in time God knows in full and complete detail what happens at any other point in time, I can (and do) accept it. But it clearly means something different and much stronger than this, and in this stronger sense (whatever precisely it comes to) the claim does not seem possibly true.[9]

That is, if the doctrine of timelessness requires us to say that the years 3021 B.C. and A.D. 7643 are simultaneous, then the doctrine is false, for the two are not simultaneous. They may of course be simultaneous in some sense if time is illusory. But since I see no good reason to affirm that time is illusory and every reason to deny that it is illusory, I am within my rights in insisting that the two indicated years are not simultaneous and that the doctrine of divine timelessness is accordingly probably false.

Suppose an event that occurred yesterday is the cause of an event that will occur tomorrow, e.g. suppose your having thrown a banana peel on the pavement yesterday will cause me to trip and break a bone tomorrow. How can the throwing of the banana peel and the breaking of the bone be simultaneous? Surely if the first caused the second the first must be temporally prior to the second; and if

so, they are not simultaneous. (Perhaps some causes are simultaneous with their effects, but not causes of events of this sort.)

But the following objection might be raised: "Any argument for the conclusion that timeless beings cannot exist must be mistaken for the simple reason that timeless beings do exist." It has been seriously suggested, for example, that numbers are timeless beings. Thus William Kneale says:

> An assertion such as "There is a prime number between five and ten" can never be countered sensibly by the remark "You are out of date: things have altered recently." And this is the reason why the entities discussed in mathematics can properly be said to have a timeless existence. To say only that they have a sempiternal or omnitemporal existence (i.e., an existence at all times) would be unsatisfactory because this way of talking might suggest that it is at least conceivable that they should at some time cease to exist, and that is an absurdity we want to exclude.[10]

Is the number seven, for example, timeless? I do not think so. (I agree that it is eternal and that it would be absurd to suggest that it might not exist; it is, in short, a sort of "necessary being.") But if the number seven is not just eternal but timeless, then on our earlier definition of "timeless," the following statements cannot meaningfully be made:

- The number seven existed on 27 July 1883.
- The number seven was greater than the number six during the whole of the Punic wars.
- The number seven existed yesterday and will exist tomorrow.

But the number seven is not a timeless being; all three of these sentences, in my opinion, are not only meaningful but true. (The fact that the first might be taken by someone to suggest that the number seven might not exist at some time other than 27 July 1883 is only an interesting psychological fact about the person who misreads it in this way. The statement implies nothing of the sort.)

But defenders of divine timelessness can raise an objection to this argument that their notion is incoherent. They can say something like this:

Of course talk about "eternal present," "simultaneously whole," etc. seems incoherent to us. This is because such talk is at best a stumbling way of understanding a mystery—the mystery of God's transcendence over time—that we cannot really understand. Statements like "my nineteenth birthday occurred before my twentieth" only seem indubitable to us because, unlike God, our minds are limited. If we had God's intellectual prowess, if we understood temporal reality as he does, we would see that this statement is false or inadequate or misleading. We would then see time correctly.

There may be some sense in which the claims being made here are true. I will not deny them, at any rate.... God's consciousness of time may indeed so far transcend ours that the best way we have of expressing it is by making apparently incoherent statements. But whether or not these claims are true, I am quite sure that we have no good reason to believe them. Like it or not, we are stuck with these limited minds of ours; if we want to be rational we have no choice but to reject what we judge to be incoherent. It may be true, in some sense, that some statements we presently consider true (like "my nineteenth birthday occurred before my twentieth") are really false or inadequate or misleading when understood in some way which we cannot now understand. But it is irrational for us now to affirm that this is true....

We have been discussing the notion of timelessness as an attempt to understand the Christian tradition that God is eternal. It can now be seen why I find the notion inadequate and why I much prefer the other alternative, which is to say that God is temporally eternal. Let us say that a temporally eternal being is (1) eternal in the sense that there never was or will be a moment when it does not exist, (2) temporal in the sense that it has both temporal location and temporal extension, and (3) temporal in the sense that the distinctions among past, present and future, and between before and after, can meaningfully be applied to it. If God is such a temporally eternal being, there are still several ways of understanding his relation to time.

Perhaps the simplest way is to say that time has always existed alongside God. This is difficult to state coherently—"Time has always existed" reduces to the tautology "There is no moment of time in which time does not exist." Perhaps it is better to state this view as the simple claim that time is not a contingent, created thing like the universe.

A second possibility is espoused by Augustine. He says that time was created by God, exists, and then will cease to exist. Before the creation of the universe and after the universe ceases to exist there exists not time but timeless eternity. Thus God has control over time—he created it and can presumably destroy it whenever he wants. While this view has some attractions—time or at least our consciousness of it does seem in some sense dependent on the existence of mutable things—a possible problem is that the notion of timeless eternity before the creation of the universe and after it ceases to exist may be just as difficult to understand as the doctrine of timeless eternity itself. This problem may well be solvable, however. In timeless eternity there will presumably be no appearance of temporal succession, i.e. of events occurring before or after each other, which is at least one of the fundamental problems connected with regarding God as timeless at the same time that we live in a world of apparent temporal succession.

A third possibility was suggested by the eighth century church father John of Damascus. Time has always existed, John appears to say, yet is only measurable when things like the sun and moon exist. Thus before the creation there existed nonmeasurable time, and after the end of the heavens and the earth non-measurable time will again exist. Measurable time is what exists from the point of creation of the world to the point of its destruction.

Since it is probably the simplest, and since I see no danger in it for Christianity (as I will argue below), I will adopt the first alternative: time was not created; it necessarily exists (like numbers); it depends for its existence on nothing else. Time, perhaps, is an eternal aspect of God's nature rather than a reality independent of God. But the point is that God, on this view, is a temporal being. Past, present and future are real to him; he has simultaneity and succession in his states, acts and knowledge. He knows statements like "Today is 24 April" and "My nineteenth birthday occurred before my twentieth." He has temporal location. It makes good sense to say: "God exists today" and "God was omniscient on Napoleon's birthday." And he has temporal extension. It makes good sense to say "God existed during the entire period of the Punic wars" and to ask, "How long has God existed?" The answer to the latter is: forever.

The three main motives for the theory of timeless eternity, I suggested, were to reconcile human freedom and divine foreknowledge, to retain consistency with other things one says about God, and to exalt God's transcendence as much as possible. As to the first, I believe foreknowledge and freedom can be reconciled without appealing to any doctrine of timelessness.... As to the second, I do not believe that anything I say about God in this book (or indeed anything said about God in the Bible) logically requires that he be timeless. And as to the third, I feel no need to exalt God's transcendence in every possible way. What Christians must do, I believe, is emphasize God's transcendence over his creation in the ways that scripture does and in ways that seem essential to Christian theism. And I do not believe that the Bible teaches, implies or presupposes that God is timeless. Nor do I feel any theological or philosophical need to embrace timelessness.

Nor is there any reason to doubt that a temporal God who is "in" time just as we are is everything the Judeo-Christian God is traditionally supposed to be. He can still be an eternal being, i.e. a being without beginning or end. He can still be the creator of the universe. He can still be immutable in the sense of remaining ever true to his promises and purposes and eternally retaining his essential nature. (But he cannot be immutable in other stronger senses.) He can still have complete knowledge of all past, present and future events. (If he "transcends time," it is only in the sense that he has this power—a power no other being has.) He can still be the loving, omnipotent redeemer Christians worship.

Some might still wish to object to this as follows: "Surely God must be free of all temporal limitations if he is truly God. But a temporal God is not so free. Thus God must be timeless." The answer to this is that a temporally eternally God such as I have described is free of certain temporal limitations, e.g. he is free of our inability to remember things that happened hundreds of years ago. Furthermore, not even a timelessly eternal God is free of all temporal limitations, for he is actually unable to experience "before" or "after." His nature limits him; he is unable to experience such things, for if he did experience them he would be temporal. There is temporal limitation whichever view we take. It appears that however we look at it, the doctrine of divine temporal eternity is greatly preferable to timeless eternity. So it is the former that I will embrace.

NOTES

1. Anselm, *St Anselm: Basic Writings* (LaSalle, Illinois: Open Court Publishing Company, 1958), p. 25.

2. Boethius, *The Theological Treatises and the Consolation of Philosophy* (Loeb Classical Library, London: William Heinemann, 1918), pp. 403–5; cf. also pp. 21–3, 401–5.

3. The *Summa Theologica of St. Thomas Aquinas* (London: Burns, Oates and Washbourne, 1920), Pt. I, Q. X, Arts. 2 and 4.

4. These points are taken from Nelson Pike's *God and Timelessness* (New York: Schocken Books, 1970), p. 7. Pike's work is an outstanding study of this subject and has influenced me at several points.

5. Ibid., pp. 97–118, 125–8; Richard Swinburne, *The Coherence of Theism* (Oxford University Press, 1977), pp. 221–2.

6. Thomas Aquinas, *Summa Contra Gentiles*, trans A. C. Pegis (Notre Dame, Indiana: University of Notre Dame Press, 1975), II, 35.

7. This has been argued by Nicholas Woltersdorff in his "God Everlasting." See *God and the Good*, ed. Clifton J. Orlebeke and Lewis B. Smedes (Grand Rapids, Michigan: William B. Eerdmans, 1975), pp. 181–203.

8. See Pike, *God and Timelessness*, pp. 128–9; Swinburne, *The Coherence of Theism*, pp. 220–1.

9. See Swinburne, *The Coherence of Theism*, pp. 220–1.

10. William Kneale, "Time and Eternity in Theology," *Proceedings of the Aristotelian Society*, vol. 61 (1961), p. 98.

I.B.2

The God Beyond Time

HUGH J. McCANN

Hugh J. McCann (1942–) is emeritus professor of philosophy at Texas A&M University and works primarily in the areas of metaphysics, philosophy of action, and philosophy of religion. In this essay, he opposes the position of the last essay (Stephen Davis's "Temporal Eternity") and defends the classical doctrine that God is atemporal.

By both tradition and common agreement, God is supposed to be eternal. But the agreement is today more apparent than real, for there is profound conflict over how this claim is to be understood. Traditional theologians, for the most part, took it to mean that God is completely outside of time, and is in fact the Creator of it. Only such a God, they reasoned, could justly be called the Creator of heaven and earth, could have full knowledge of what for us is the future, and could have the sovereignty and immutability appropriate to the divine essence. More recently, however, all of this has come into dispute. It is argued that only a God who is in time could create anything at all, and that only a temporal God could be the loving father Scripture describes, who periodically intervenes in nature and history for our sake. Furthermore, a timeless God's

knowledge would be woefully inadequate: Being outside of time, he would be unable to know what is true now, and hence unable to know *any* tensed proposition, not just certain ones about the future. Hence, it is claimed, God's eternity must be understood as *sempiternity*. He is an everlasting God, one who always was and will be, but who is otherwise subject to temporal passage just like you and me. Such a God may not match the ideal of eternalists, but he has as much sovereignty as a God can have, and knows all that a God can know. And if he is not unchanging in knowledge and action, he can still be unchanging in character and temperament.

In what follows I want to defend the first of the above conceptions. I shall argue that there is no reason to think a timelessly eternal God cannot create, or act so as to alter the course of events in the

Hugh McCann, "The God Beyond Time." Reprinted with permission of the author.

world, and that only a timeless creator can exercise rational and complete sovereignty over creation. As for knowledge, I will claim it is, if anything, a time-bound God whose knowledge of tensed propositions must be limited, whereas a timeless God's knowledge of them is complete. I want to begin by getting clear on the two notions of eternity at stake in the dispute, and giving some reasons why God was traditionally understood as timelessly eternal.

I. SEMPITERNITY VERSUS TIMELESSNESS

The more familiar of these two concepts is that of sempiternity or everlastingness. Under this conception God is a temporally persistent or enduring entity just like you and me.[1] He is located within time, and subject to the restrictions of tense and temporal passage. So like us, he has a history and a future; he remembers and anticipates, presumably observes the course of the universe, and acts at his pleasure to produce change in the world he has created. The difference is that God's career extends through all of time, which on this sort of view is usually taken to be without beginning or end. He always was, is now, and always will be. On this conception of eternity, it makes sense to say of God that he always knew you would be reading this sentence at this moment, that he knows now that you are doing so, and that he will always know hereafter that you did. In short, but for its being unbounded at either end, the life and experience of an everlasting God need not in principle be much different from yours and mine.

The conception of God as timelessly eternal is less familiar, and radically different. On this view God, unlike you and I, is not located within time, and tense and related temporal conceptions have no application to him whatever. Strictly speaking, therefore, it is false to say of God that he ever has existed, that he exists now, or that he ever will exist. At best, such claims are a clumsy way of indicating what we who are within time can always truthfully *assert*. And that is simply this: that God exists—

where the verb, though in the grammatical present, signifies nothing of temporal presentness, but rather a reality that stands completely outside of time, untouched by becoming or transition of any kind. God exists timelessly on this account, and his life and experience, while they may concern the world of change, are themselves unchanging. So it would also be wrong to say God ever has known or will know about your reading this or any other sentence. Yet, it would be true that he knows, timelessly, that you are reading this sentence—even, if he is omniscient, that you are reading it now. God knows this, and everything else as well, in a single, timeless act of awareness that encompasses all of heaven and earth, in its complete history. His action as Creator is from the same vantage point. There is no time at which he creates the universe, for time itself is an aspect of the world of change and that is what God creates. In a single *fiat* he produces the entire universe, in all of its history, all of it with equal directness and absolute control. This does not prevent its being the case that from our perspective within time, not everything does, or even could, occur at once. But that is tensed talk, which does not apply to God. From his perspective, the production of all that, as we would say, ever was or will be, occurs in a single, unified act, in timeless eternity.

Timeless eternity is, to say the least, not familiar to us, and the conception of it is not easy to grasp. One may wonder, therefore, how it gained ascendancy in accounts of God's nature. Scripture, it is fair to say, leans heavily in the opposite direction. The God of the Bible creates the world over a six-day period, and then desists from his labors on the seventh (Gen. 1:1–2:2). At intervals, he speaks to Moses and the prophets, and he intervenes repeatedly in his people's history to save them from disaster. Above all, he is portrayed as *reacting* to the behavior of humankind; he adjusts his behavior to our own, as when he desists from his plan to destroy Nineveh (Jon. 3:10). Obviously, this is not a God who is remote from the world. His involvement in it is deep, and his actions as a loving father are attuned to the needs of each situation.

There is no denying that such an interactive God is more easily understood as temporal. As always with the reading of Scripture, however, one must be cautious, for too much literalism leads straight into trouble. Indeed, the very first phrase of the entire Bible tells us that the God about to be described as creating the world in six days did so "in the beginning." How could this be if time had no beginning? Furthermore, this same God is presented as a spatial being: as having a head, hands and feet, as dwelling in cities and tabernacles, as moving from place to place. If it is fair to take this kind of talk as metaphorical, then surely passages that portray God as temporal can in principle be so taken as well. Finally, the Bible contains clear hints of a much more sophisticated conception. The name God gives himself from the burning bush, "I am" (Exod. 3:14), becomes entirely unimpressive when taken to mean only that he existed at that moment. Or consider the sudden shift to the grammatical present in such passages as, "Before the mountains were born, or thou didst give birth to the earth and the world, even from everlasting to everlasting, thou art God" (Ps. 90:2), or, "I say to you, before Abraham was born, I am" (John 8:58). It is not unreasonable to think passages like this aim at an atemporal conception. Finally, despite his seeming change of mind about the Ninevites, the Bible is at points fairly decisive in claiming that in God there is no change, not even a shadow of it (Mal. 3:6, James 1:17).

This kind of conflict is familiar. It has been said that the Bible is a book not of theology but of life, and so cannot be expected to offer a unified and seamlessly consistent theory of the divine nature. That is the work of philosophers and theologians, who have usually aimed at an account that respects the rigors of metaphysics as well as the content of faith. And from a metaphysical perspective, it is not surprising that some theories would call for a timeless God. The view that ultimate reality is timeless is as old as Parmenides, and its association with theories of the divine nature was probably inevitable. But there are reasons for the alliance. Both in Scripture and in cosmological proofs for the existence of God, he is portrayed as the Creator of everything but himself and as ruling the universe with complete power and authority. But if God is in time, his

sovereignty is restricted: There is something other than himself that he did not create—namely, time itself—and his experience and action are made subject to the limitations of opportunity. Better, then, if possible, to have a God who in creating the world creates time, but whose own being lies beyond it. A second consideration, of which we will see more below, has to do with human freedom. If it is true that God gives us wills that escape the reach of causal determination, then to treat him as temporal is to threaten his omniscience. How could he know today what I will do tomorrow if I have not yet decided? A timelessly eternal God, by contrast, should be able to know as much about tomorrow as he does about today: everything, presumably.

But perhaps the deepest running argument for a timelessly eternal God is that the divine essence, as well as we are able to understand it, seems incompatible with any sort of change. A thing changes either by coming to have a characteristic it previously lacked, or by losing a characteristic it previously had. Thus an apple might change colors by ceasing to be green and becoming red; or it may fall to the earth, thereby exchanging its position at the end of a branch for one on the ground. Now the characteristics with respect to which a thing changes must be accidental rather than essential ones, at least if the thing is to continue existing, for the essential properties of a thing are by definition characteristics without which it cannot continue in being. An apple may change its color or position, but it cannot cease to be colored or positioned at all and remain in existence, for color and position are essential to apples. The same considerations apply to God. If he is to undergo change without ceasing to be, it must be by gaining or losing accidental features. Perhaps he comes to have a thought he previously did not, or to act in a new way. It turns out, however, that unlike created beings, God cannot have accidental features.

The reason for this is that if God does have accidental properties, his authority over the universe has to be limited. It is fair to demand that any accidental properties God has will have a sufficient explanation. Otherwise, his having them would be arbitrary and not in accordance with the concept of a perfect being. But unfortunately, the explanation for the presence of an accidental property in a thing can never arise entirely from the thing's own nature. If it did, the property would be entailed by the entity's essence, and so be essential rather than accidental. But if it is essential, then it is not a property with respect to which the thing could change after all. So the accidental properties of a thing must always be explained at least in part from without: The color of the apple will depend in part on its environment, and its location will hinge on the forces to which it is subject. And the same applies to God. If his thought and activity change from time to time, there will have to be an explanation, and the explanation will have to invoke things other than the divine nature. Perhaps what he is thinking will be explained by the events of the moment, or his activity by the opportunity they present. But whatever the explanation is, it will have to invoke something extrinsic to the divine nature, and it cannot do so without introducing dependence and passivity into God. His experience will depend on the stage of world history, and he will have to await his chances to redirect it. For traditional theology at least, that is not what one expects of the Sovereign Lord of heaven and earth.

A perfectly sovereign God cannot, then, have accidental properties; and of course a being that cannot even have accidental properties cannot change with respect to them. On the traditional conception, therefore, God must be completely immutable, completely beyond the reach of becoming. It does not even make sense to put him in time, since he would then have shifting relations of simultaneity with the events of the world, which is not possible. It is unlikely, however, that proponents of the temporal conception of eternity would be persuaded by this argument. For one thing, they may have misgivings about the very idea of there being timelessly eternal entities and states of affairs. Secondly, they might claim the conception of the divine nature called for by atemporalists is simply too demanding. Perhaps it *is* wrong, strictly speaking, to think of there being any change in a being whose essence is to be, and who enjoys complete sovereignty over the world. But, the temporalist might point out, the

fact is that we do this with God all the time: we speak of him as learning about things as they occur, and as causing different events at different times. And although we may try to observe protocol by insisting that all of God's knowledge and activity occurs in a single, eternal act, it is not clear that this advances our understanding very much. Indeed, the temporalist may go further. He may argue that causation and knowing, or at least some knowing, are in themselves *intrinsically* temporal operations, so that if we apply these concepts to God at all, we must conceive of him as a temporal being. I want to address these concerns in order, beginning with the one about there being timelessly eternal things.

II. ATEMPORAL STATES OF AFFAIRS

A number of reasons might be given for doubting that there is a realm of timeless entities or timeless facts about them. Some are based on misunderstandings. It may be thought, for example, that if for God there is no time, then time must somehow be unreal—an illusion, perhaps, that accompanies our own creaturely perceptions, but not a genuine aspect of the real world. And it might well be argued that this is too much to swallow; time is too central, too inexpungible from our experience to be plausibly considered an illusion. There is no reason, however, why defenders of timeless eternity need be committed to such a view. After all, no one takes the fact that God is not a spatial entity to imply that space is an illusion, so why take such a position with respect to time? Furthermore, atemporalism is not committed to the view that for God there is no time. It holds, to be precise, that God is not *in* time, that his life and experience transcend change and temporal passage. It does not follow from this that time is unreal or even that God is unfamiliar with it. Indeed, if he is both omniscient and the Creator of time, precisely the opposite would have to be the case. The only restriction is that his activity and awareness must not involve change, even though the world that is their object does. It may, of course, be argued that this is not possible, and we shall shortly be examining such arguments. But the important thing to see at this point is that an argument is needed; it is in no way obvious that the atemporalist position here is untenable.

A second reason for doubting that there are timeless states of affairs stems from the way in which defenders of timeless eternity have been prone to express their view. Boethius described timeless eternity as "the complete possession, all at once, of illimitable life," and held that the God who possesses this life comprehends "the infinite spaces of that which is past and to come ... as though they were now in doing."[2] Following this precedent, it is not uncommon for timeless eternity to be described in terms that are at least partly temporal rather than timeless. God's experience is held to be of an "eternal present," for example, or we may be told that in eternity all of the world's history is "simultaneously present" to God. As a stepping stone to understanding timeless eternity such language is probably to be expected, and it is useful in some ways. It conveys the point that God's experience of the world is single and unchanging, that it involves no serial presentation of events or alteration of content. It also suggests something else to which the defender of timeless eternity should be committed: that the *content* of God's experience of the world includes its temporal features, that he is aware of things in their temporality as well as in all other aspects of their being.

But to say that all of history is eternally or simultaneously *present* to God leads to implications that are not intended, and that we should not accept. It suggests, first, that besides having temporal content, God's act of experiencing the world is itself a temporal thing, that it occurs in a kind of unchanging present moment, notwithstanding the fact that it is supposed to be completely outside time. This in itself is a contradiction, to which defenders of timeless eternity need not be committed. A lot more contradictions threaten if we add that God's experience must be of all of history, which now must be conceived as *simultaneously* present to God. This makes all of history present "at once" to God's now retemporalized act of

awareness, and the effect is that all of history must be held to be simultaneous. So we would have to say that the American Civil War is simultaneous with the Protestant Reformation, that yesterday's events are simultaneous with tomorrow's, etc.[3] Obviously, however, these things are false.

One way of dealing with these problems is to seek to define notions of presentness and simultaneity that would be appropriate to the timeless order and would not carry unacceptable implications.[4] But I think it is better, at least for present purposes, simply to drop the idea that history is "present" to God, in any sense other than being given to him timelessly in experience or awareness. This is not to say the events of which God is aware are not temporal, but it is to say his awareness of them is not. God creates and is aware of all of history neither simultaneously nor at different times, but eternally. His activity as Creator and Knower is unified and unchanging, but it does not occur at any present moment, not even a supposed eternal one. It simply is. To proceed in this way deprives us of some handy ways for describing timeless eternity, but it also forces us to describe the realities it involves in ways that do not threaten immediate contradiction.[5]

But are there any timeless realities? After all, the sempiternalist might urge, apart from its supposed indispensability for describing how things are with God, we would have no need of the notion of timeless reality at all. Nothing in our earthly experience, it seems, is usefully described in terms of timelessness; and since heavenly experience is not now available to us, it may well be that the timeless realities eternalists suppose pertain to it are not really there, but instead are just figments of our inability to comprehend. To this atemporalists have replied that we are in fact familiar with timeless entities, namely, those of the conceptual and mathematical realms. Such entities as propositions and numbers, they have held, are incapable of intrinsic change, and truths about them represent timelessly eternal states of affairs. Consider the fact that the number 2 is even. This, obviously, is not something we expect to change, for we do not view the number 2 as capable of change. And when we say that 2 is even, we mean to assert more than just a fact we take to hold at that particular moment. That 2 is incapable of change, according to the atemporalist, makes the number 2 as timeless a reality as any. And the fact that it is even, along with all other mathematical and conceptual facts, counts as a timelessly eternal state of affairs.[6]

The temporalist rejoinder here is that this view of things goes too far. Granted, mathematical entities and facts do not change. But, it is insisted, all this means is that these are sempiternal, or everlasting, realities, not that they are atemporal. And while "2 is even" does have import beyond the present moment, it need not be taken as reporting a timeless fact. Instead, it can be taken as *omnitemporal*—that is, as speaking about all times. We can understand "2 is even" as saying that 2 always was even, is even now, and always will be even. To do this is to understand 2 as sempiternal rather than timeless, and it accommodates the unchanging character of the fact that 2 is even. What need is there to go further than this, and commit ourselves to an ontology of timeless states of affairs? And of course the same applies to truths about Euclidean triangles, trigonometric functions, or any other conceptual entity you like. In short, there is just no need to invoke the concept of timeless eternity to deal with conceptual realities. Any entity we might view as timelessly eternal can equally well be treated as sempiternal, and any statement we might think describes something timeless can be effectively replaced with one that is omnitemporal—which describes unchanging, but nevertheless temporal, realities.

Unfortunately, however, the replacement does not always work—a fact that emerges when we consider how the sempiternalist would have to formulate the very issues over which he and the atemporalist disagree. Presumably, the sempiternalist would endorse the following two statements:

(a) There are no timelessly eternal states of affairs.

(b) There is no timelessly eternal God.

The atemporalist, by contrast, would be expected to reject (a) and (b), since he holds that there *are* timelessly eternal facts and a timeless God. But in fact the atemporalist *cannot* reject (a) and (b), if they

are understood in the way sempiternalists must understand them—that is, as meaning:

(c) There never have been, are not now, and never will be any timelessly eternal states of affairs.

(d) There never has been, is not now, and never will be a timelessly eternal God.

On the contrary, defenders of timeless eternity must agree with (c) and (d), since they deny that temporal existence pertains to any timeless entity, God or otherwise. But then (c) and (d) cannot express what (a) and (b) mean. In order to capture what the disagreement is about, (a) and (b) have to be taken as atemporal statements, and cannot be replaced by omnitemporal ones. The only way the sempiternalist can express his disagreement with the atemporalist, then, is to accept the idea of there being timeless states of affairs, at least of a negative variety. And once that is done the notion of timeless states of affairs can no longer be considered suspect.

Indeed, it is a mistake to think it is even permissible to treat entities like numbers, propositions, and the like—that is, entities that are incapable of intrinsic change—as temporal. It is tempting to think of time as a matter of there being some cosmic clock "out there," beyond any specific type of change, but nevertheless ticking away inexorably the destiny of anything we can find an expression to refer to. But there is no such thing, and if there were, it would have nothing to do with the temporality of the world as we know it. In that world, things are not made subject to change by being temporal; rather, they are made temporal by being subject to change. It makes sense to treat atoms, or the heavens, or you and me as temporal beings because all of these things are subject to intrinsic changes, and because some of these changes can be used to measure others. Outside of this, the idea of becoming loses its empirical hold, and with it goes any useful notion of time.

Once this is realized, it becomes pointless to treat entities not subject to change as temporal—especially if, as we have just seen, timeless states of affairs have to be accepted anyway. Nothing about abstract entities can usefully be held to be simultaneous with anything in the world of becoming. There is nothing about any supposed career of the number 2, for example, that we are justified in claiming to be simultaneous with my writing this sentence. To be sure, relations between the number and other things can come to be and pass away, as when I think about the number during my writing. But as far as the number 2 is concerned this is only a relational, not an intrinsic change. The intrinsic change is only in me: I begin to have a thought, and later cease to have it. And, of course, that change could occur whether 2 is in time or not. Only if there are intrinsic changes in the number itself would it be correct to say 2 undergoes an alteration simultaneous with my writing this sentence or with any other genuine event. There are, however, no such changes. Hence, there is nothing about the number 2 that is simultaneous with anything that goes on in the world of genuine becoming. But if this is so, what justification could there be for claiming 2 is an entity "in time"? None, I submit, short of a conception of time that borders on outright mythology. And if that is correct, then 2 and all other abstract entities are eternal, and intrinsic facts about them must be counted as timelessly eternal states of affairs. Does it follow, as Stephen Davis has complained, that we can no longer meaningfully assert, say, that the number 7 was greater than the number 6 during the whole of the Punic Wars?[7] Of course not. Such statements are perfectly meaningful, just as it is meaningful to assert that the interior angles of a triangle total 360 degrees. It is just that they are false: numbers, and triangles, are simply not that sort of thing.

III. ETERNITY AND CREATION

The God of tradition is causally involved with the universe in what appear to be two ways. First, he is responsible for its existence. Popular accounts of this are usually quasi-deistic: God is held to have created the universe "in the beginning," in a series of phases, and then ceased activity. Thus, the universe had a beginning in time and presumably has since continued to exist on its own. But even if it is denied that the universe had a beginning in time, standard theology still makes God responsible for its existence. He must, it is claimed, have been responsible for the existence of the historical whole, since even the existence of a sempiternal universe demands an explanation. God's second causal role is as a worker of wonders. Periodically, he intervenes in history's course to produce unusual and sometimes titanic events for the sake of our well-being. Now both as Creator and as Providential Intervener, God causes specific events to occur at specific times. And it may be argued that no one can cause an event to occur at a given time without being active at that time. So if the parting of the Red Sea occurred in, say, 1500 B.C., then God would have to have been active in 1500 B.C. to cause it, and similarly for any other change he produces. If this is true, then a God who is not in time cannot create or cause anything.[8]

Why should it be, however, that in order to produce a change which occurs at t, the agent of the change must be active at t? One possibility is that causation itself is an intrinsically temporal concept, signifying an operation that must occur in time. This appears to be the position of Stephen Davis, who holds that God's activity as Creator can only be understood to occur in time, on the ground that we do not have what he calls a "usable concept of atemporal causation."[9] In fact, however, causation is not an intrinsically temporal concept at all. It could not possibly be, for one simple reason: Causation is not a process. When a cue ball strikes an object ball, thereby causing it to accelerate, there is not, between the impact and the acceleration, a third event tucked in, which is the former's causing the latter. Indeed, if there were such an event we would most likely have to invent a second sort of causation to explain its relation to the other two. But as things are there is no need, for causation is not in itself a kind of change. Rather, it signifies a relation of explanation, wherein one thing is held to account for the occurrence of another. There is nothing intrinsically either temporal or atemporal about the notion of explanation, hence to know that a causal relation exists tells us nothing whatever about whether the cause is operative in time or outside it.

If the concept of causation, taken by itself, is neutral on the issue of temporality, then whether a particular causal operation is temporal or not has to depend on how the effect is produced, and whether the agent must change in order to produce it. And where our own activity as agents is concerned, that certainly is necessary. It is worth noting here that we do not require human agents to be active at the very moment an effect is produced. There can be wide temporal gaps—as when by planting bulbs in my garden in the fall, I cause it to have daffodils in the spring. But such gaps are permissible only when my activity as agent occurs before the effect in question, and is connected to it by a continuous process. The reason for this is important: When we, as agents, cause changes in the world beyond ourselves, we have to do so indirectly, by taking advantage of natural processes that begin in us. Natural processes are, of course, temporal, and they do not permit gaps between cause and effect. So for me to cause changes in this way, there has to be a continuous natural process that begins with some doing of mine, and issues in the effect. The process need not, of course, be lengthy: When I ring a doorbell, it is so brief that my activity of pressing the button may well overlap with the sound it causes. Always, however, I have to be active at or before the time of the effect to which my action leads when I produce effects in this way.

Now, of course, it cannot be that every effect I produce as an agent is produced indirectly. If it were, each means I employ would require another, and I would never get anything done. So the doing on my part that initiates a sequence of natural change must be a *direct* product of my agency. This is a controversial topic, but we can see that at least two things would have to be true of such an activity. First, whatever makes it a manifestation of my agency would have to be intrinsic to it.[10] I would have to be active *in* the doing, rather than producing it by some further means, or by some fictitious process of "causing." Second, if this activity is supposed to initiate a process by which I produce further changes, then it is going to have to be found *in me*, since I do not have the capacity to affect the external world directly. But, of course, I am a being

in time, and what that means is that even when my agency is directly exercised, I am going to have to be active in time for the exercise to occur. That is, I am going to have to change. As to what the fundamental activity through which I effect changes in the world is, that is part of the controversy. The most plausible candidate is probably my willing the sorts of physical exertion by which I perform voluntary bodily movements. And obviously, willing involves change. I cannot will all of my movements at once, and if I could, it would accomplish nothing. Rather, I must engage in the appropriate exertion at the appropriate time, taking advantage of the opportunities the world presents as they arise. And the same would be true no matter what events we took as direct manifestations of human agency. We would have to change in their production, and so could give rise to them only by being active in time.

We have good reasons for thinking, then, that where human agency is concerned, one can produce an effect at *t* only by being active at or before *t*. But do such reasons apply to God? The answer is that they do not. Obviously, God cannot create the world by exploiting any natural process, for there are no natural processes independent of the very world he creates. Moreover, it would be a violation of God's sovereignty to suppose his creative power was limited by available means or in any way hostage to principles external to it. Rather, God's creative activity must be viewed as direct: The results he produces are *ex nihilo*. They are not the outgrowth of changes in anything else or of any manufacturing process, but instead are direct manifestations of his agency. Yet, unlike direct manifestations of human agency, the results of God's creative activity are not changes in him. Rather, the world whose being is owing to God exists as a being in its own right. It cannot be identified with God; for although its existence requires an explanation his does not. And unlike God, who is simple and immaterial, the world is a material entity, composed of parts. It turns out, then, that the reasons why a human agent can produce a change at *t* only by acting at or before *t* do not apply to God. Creation cannot involve the exploitation of natural processes, and although the results produced through it are in time, they are not modifications of God.

Are there any other reasons for thinking a being who produces a temporal result must be acting in time? I can think of none, and if that is correct, then there is no reason to suppose a timelessly eternal God is precluded from being the Creator of heaven and earth. Such a being could create the entire universe in a single, unchanging, timeless act. Moreover, in the single act of creating the universe, he would be responsible for its entire existence, through all of its history. It is important to recognize this, for a lot of our tendency to believe that God, as agent, has to be temporal is owing to the fact that, from our position within the bounds of time, God often seems to be more involved in some events than in others. This is reinforced by the biblical story of Creation, which seems to make God directly responsible only for the first existence of things, and by popular conceptions of miracles as involving God occasionally bestirring himself to alter the course of history. Now, in fact, there is nothing about being timelessly eternal that would prevent God from being more directly involved in some of history than the rest. Nevertheless, this model of God's involvement in the universe is adequate neither to the needs of creation nor to divine providence. On the first point, God cannot just cause the world to exist "at *t*." Indeed, if the atemporalist view is correct, then independent of God's creating the world of change, there is no "*t*" at which he could cause it to exist. Furthermore, we have no reason to suppose a world that requires a God to create it could somehow keep itself existing once it appears, nor can we imagine any mechanism it might use to do so. On the contrary, God must sustain the world in existence: He must be just as responsible for its surviving another instant as he is for it being here at all. Second, as for providence, a perfectly loving father, one who knows the fall of every sparrow, has to be fully and intimately involved in each aspect of the world's career. This does not prevent there being extraordinary events. If the concept of a miracle requires that there be events that are discontinuous with others as far as natural explanations go, well and good. But we should not let that lead us to believe the occurrence of the others is somehow less a manifestation of God's power. Were it not for his creative activity, nothing would be going on at all,

and the most mundane events fall as much within the purview of providence as the most spectacular. Even from our own, timebound perspective, then, God's creative involvement and concern with the world must be understood as complete and all-embracing. And this should help us to see that the Creator of heaven and earth can after all be timelessly eternal.[11]

But he cannot be temporally eternal, for several reasons. First, if, contrary to what is suggested above, there really is an absolute time "out there," uncreated by God but restrictive of his behavior, then God is not the Creator of heaven and earth, and that is that. There is a pervasive aspect of the universe he has not put there. And if we try to fix this by making him the Creator of time after all, then we give up the claim that God is essentially temporal. God could not create time unless his own being transcends it, and his act of creating it could not be temporal. Second, if time exists independently of the world then God would have had to decide when to produce the world, when to begin his activity as Creator. But what reason could there have been for creating it at one time rather than another? Nor can we avoid this problem by making the created world everlasting too, for even then God would have had to decide whether to have things occur at the times they do, or to move everything forward or backward by, say, twenty-four hours. Again, however, there could not possibly be a reason for such a choice. This is not to say, of course, that God might not have plunged ahead. After all, he might have had good reason for creating a universe at sometime or other, rather than never doing so. All the same, a God who creates in this way could not be fully rational. He would have justification for creating the world, but not for creating it "at *t*."[12]

But the strongest reason for rejecting a temporal creator is what this notion does to God's sovereignty. An all-powerful God should be not just the producer of the universe but its complete master, the absolute ruler of everything that is not himself. To make him subject to the limitations of time flies in the face of this conception. Once launched on the enterprise of creation, at least, such a creator must busy himself with whatever tasks are at hand. If he has goals to achieve by his action, then like us he must await his opportunities, which are now limited by the stern taskmaster of becoming. And like us, his experience of his creation must be hemmed in by time: limited, in the case of the past, to memories that, however vivid, must be of events that can never be retrieved; limited, in the case of the future, to anticipations each of whose fulfillment takes literally forever to come, only to vanish like smoke. Such a God may be the master of much, but of time he is a slave. And that is a high price to pay for accepting the groundless supposition that only a temporal being can produce temporal effects.

IV. ETERNITY AND OMNISCIENCE

An omniscient God should know of every true proposition that it is true, and of every false proposition that it is false. And it is probably fair to say that when it comes to omniscience, proponents of timeless eternity have traditionally thought they had the upper hand. Suppose John mows his lawn next Saturday. If so then it would have been correct to assert now that he will. That is, the statement "John will mow his lawn next Saturday" is true. But suppose also that John's action is free, in the sense that until he decides one way or the other, there are no conditions in place that determine which way he will act. If so, then it does not appear that a temporal being could *know*, prior to the event, what John will do. One could, of course, make a lucky guess: I might venture a prediction that John will mow his lawn next Saturday, believe it is true, and turn out to be right. But it does not follow that I *knew* what John would do; my prediction, though correct, appears to have lacked sufficient grounds.

Needless to say, the same argument applies to God if he is temporal. If the behavior of rational agents is free in the sense described—and it is often claimed that moral responsibility requires this—then no conditions obtain in advance that would enable God to predict such behavior with certainty. It seems the only way he could avoid mistakes would be by an incredible series of lucky guesses or by simply not entertaining beliefs about future free actions. In neither case would he be omniscient. So unless another way can be found for God to know about

future free actions, defenders of temporal eternity must make do with a restricted notion of divine omniscience. Contrast this with the situation of a timelessly eternal God. Such a God does not know about events either before or after their occurrence, or even simultaneously with it. Rather, he knows them timelessly, in a single act of awareness whose content comprises all of history. But then free actions on our part impose no deficit of knowledge on him. A timeless God cannot be in the dark about what for us is the future, since he is directly aware of all of it. He knows, therefore, about John's mowing his lawn next Saturday because he is eternally aware of that very action. And, of course, this does not compromise John's freedom, any more than it would if next Saturday had already arrived, and you and I were watching him mow his lawn.[13]

Initially, then, it would appear defenders of timeless eternity are able to offer a more robust and satisfying account of divine omniscience. Recently, however, sempiternalists have mounted a counterattack, claiming that in fact the limitations on God's omniscience are far worse if he is timelessly eternal than if he is temporal. For suppose in fact John is mowing his lawn right now, and that I report his activity to you by asserting:

(e) John is mowing his lawn.

It would be a mistake to interpret (e) as reporting some timeless state of affairs. That is, (e) says more than that there is (timelessly) some act of lawn mowing on John's part, or even that such an act is (timelessly) located at the point in history which happens to be today. These readings fail to respect the tense of (e), which does not reduce to any timeless reality. Rather, the full force of (e) is that John's act of mowing his lawn is occurring *now*, that it is actually *present*. The situation with the other tenses is similar: If I predict John will mow his lawn again next Saturday, I am saying that act will occur after the present; and if I say he mowed it last Saturday, I am saying the act in question occurred before the present.

Always, then, tensed statements are indexed to a certain temporal location *as present*. But then, it may be argued, knowing which tensed statements are true requires knowing what the present moment is. And, it is claimed, that is something a timelessly eternal God cannot know. Being outside of time, he cannot, as we would say, know what time it is. That is, he cannot know which moment in time is the present one, and hence cannot know which ones are past and which future. But then it must be that a timelessly eternal God cannot know *any* tensed proposition. He cannot know what John will do next week, what he is doing now, or what he has ever done, and the same for any other tensed state of affairs. Not an enviable position for a supposedly omniscient God, and a far worse one than simply being unable to tell about John's future free actions.[14]

A hint that there is something wrong here can be gotten from the fact that an exactly analogous argument could have been given for propositions that are spatially indexed.[15] Suppose I assert that it is raining *here*. My assertion has to mean more than that there is a rainstorm, or that rain is falling outside my study. Neither of the latter statements respects the element of perspective the word "here" introduces, an element that does not reduce to other spatial relations. And surely if God is omniscient and it is raining here, he must know that. Yet no one argues on these grounds that God must be located in space or in any way subject to its limitations. So some sort of mistake appears to have been made. But to have a hint that something is wrong and to be able to say what it is are two different things, and the sources of the present error are not easy to locate. One possible source can, I think, be dismissed pretty quickly. It cannot be the case that when I assert (e), I am in part asserting something about myself—such as that I am in the same temporal location as John's act of lawn mowing, or that I am experiencing that act now. Any temptation to think this is the problem can be overcome simply by realizing that if in fact (e) is true—if John is now mowing his lawn—then this would have been true even if I had never lived. That would be impossible if (e) contained information about me, since it would then be rendered incorrect simply by my failing to exist. Tensed propositions involve a perspective on the world of change, just as spatially indexed propositions involve one on space; but they say nothing about anyone occupying that perspective.

But if this is not the source of the error, then what is? Here is one way in which it can begin: It might be thought that tensed propositions change their truth value, depending on whether the events they report are actually occurring. One might think, for example, that proposition (e) was false before John began mowing his lawn, is true only while he mows it, and thereafter will become false again. And one might think that only a God in time could detect changing truth values. Now, in fact, this last claim is in no way obvious. Atemporalists might well insist that here as elsewhere, there is no reason to think awareness of change requires a changing awareness, and that a God outside of time could be as much aware of truth value changes as of any others. But there is a more fundamental error here, for the fact is that tensed propositions do not change in truth value. What misleads us about this, I think, is a belief that when we employ the same *sentence* assertively on different occasions, we must be asserting the same proposition—so that if twenty-four hours ago I had also uttered the sentence "John is mowing his lawn" assertively, I would then have been asserting exactly the same proposition—namely, (e)—that I assert using the sentence now. But that is mistaken. We might express (e) more carefully as:

John is (this moment) mowing his lawn.

This is to be distinguished from the proposition I would have asserted had I said yesterday that John was mowing his lawn. For even if I had used exactly the same words, the phrase "this moment" would yesterday have referred to a different time. This means the proposition I would have asserted yesterday—let us call it (f)—would have been indexed to a different "now," and that gives the two propositions different truth conditions. What happened yesterday is decisive for the truth of (f) but irrelevant to that of (e); and what happens today has everything to do with the truth of (e) and nothing to do with that of (f). In short, (e) and (f) count as entirely different pieces of information, and so are different propositions.

This is borne out by our attitudes when we make tensed statements. If I had asserted yesterday that John was mowing his lawn, I would have meant he was mowing it *then*. Were I wrong, I would not have claimed vindication when he began mowing it today, holding that what I said yesterday had now become true. Rather, I need to make a new statement, (e), to cover the present case. Or, suppose John also mowed his lawn two weeks ago, and that I said so at the time. When, upon seeing him mowing it today, I assert (e), you would not accuse me of repeating myself, of stating the same fact I asserted two weeks ago. That fact was an entirely different one. The situation is similar with other tenses. If today I assert that Lincoln will be assassinated, I am not saying something that used to be true. Rather, my statement is false: Lincoln is not going to be assassinated; he already was. If, on the other hand, I report that Lincoln was assassinated, I am not asserting a proposition that used to be false. My assertion is true, because it is indexed to the present, and only what holds from the perspective of the present counts for its truth or falsity.

Each time I use a tensed sentence to make an assertion, then, I am asserting a *different* proposition, even if the sentences are indistinguishable. [16] Each proposition is tied to the perspective of a particular temporal moment, and different conditions determine its truth or falsity. With this in mind, consider again the idea that propositions can change truth values. It is, of course, a suspect idea from the outset. Propositions are abstract entities, which we have seen are incapable of intrinsic change. And propositions that describe timeless states of affairs, like "2 is even," could not change truth values anyway. The state of affairs they describe will either obtain (timelessly) or not, and that is the end of the matter. So change in truth value would have to be confined to tensed propositions, and it would have to be owing to some change outside the proposition itself. But now it turns out that tensed propositions depend for their truth only on what obtains from the perspective in time to which they are indexed. It follows that tensed propositions cannot change in truth value either. Their truth conditions are defined by a perspective that is localized to a single instant. And any conditions thus defined must simply either be satisfied or not. They cannot change within the bounds of a single point in time, and nothing that occurs at any other time matters. How could it? If when I assert (e) my statement does not even concern yesterday or tomorrow, how could conditions

yesterday or tomorrow have anything to do with its truth? Obviously, they could not. So even tensed propositions do not change truth values. Indeed, for all that is capable of "happening" to the truth or falsity of a proposition, there is no good reason even for taking the predicates "is true" and "is false" to be tensed predicates. On the contrary, there is every reason to think the truth or falsity of propositions, even tensed ones, is in itself a timelessly eternal state of affairs, one that is not even capable of change.

Where does this leave us on the issue of whether a God beyond time can know tensed propositions? If the above argument is correct, the truth or falsity of a tensed proposition is not an elusive thing at all. It is, rather, a timeless and unchanging state of affairs, just like the truth or falsity of a statement in mathematics. But then surely it should not be a difficult assignment for a timeless God to know a tensed proposition. What would be required, presumably, is the same thing such knowledge requires in our own case—namely, direct experience of the world of change. We have seen no reason to deny such experience to a timeless God, who traditionally has been held to have direct and unchanging awareness of the entire sweep of history. So it looks like God can know tensed propositions after all. Yet it might be thought that something is still missing. What of the point about what time it is? If tensed propositions are indexed to times, wouldn't God have to know what time it is in order to know that it is (e) rather than, say, (f) that actually describes what John is presently doing? And doesn't this require more than simply having John's action presented to him in awareness? Wouldn't God also have to know that, as opposed to all the other stages of history of which he is aware, the one in which John's act is embedded is the one that is really going on right now? And how could he know this further fact from outside of time?

The answer is that there is no such fact to be known, for there is never anything to "what time it is" beyond the events whose simultaneous occurrence constitutes any given stage of the world's history. The belief that there is more arises from a pervasive but misleading way of representing our experience of change, which underlies the above objection. It begins with our analogizing time to space: We think of the events that make up the world's history as being lined up "out there" in order of their occurrence, rather like a row of barges floating on a river. Then, to account for the fact that our experience is a changing one, we put the river in motion. We think of time itself as flowing past us, sweeping along with it a history all of which is equally real, but only some of which is present. The question what time it "really" is is then just the question, What part of history is really before us? But the question is bogus, as is this picture of temporal transition. It may be useful for some purposes to analogize time to space. But once I do, I have used time up. There is no second time to accommodate or measure any supposed flow of the first or of the events within it. Yet a second time is precisely what we demand if we insist that the truth of statement (e) requires, in addition to the event of John mowing his lawn, a further event of the mowing being present. There is no such event, and the demand for it is just one more manifestation of the myth that there is a time "out there," independent of change. The truth is quite the opposite: The presence of John's mowing his lawn is to be found in the event itself. When it is not present, it does not exist at all. As for the elusive sense of "passage" that characterizes our experience of the world, it is simply a manifestation of the fact that we belong to that world: that our experience of it is not just an experience of change but also a changing experience. Admittedly, this is a difficult thing to describe, and in trying to do so we may feel almost compelled to fall back on the idea of time as a kind of quasi-space that we traverse in living out our lives. But that is a deception. Becoming is a reality; but it consists neither in our marching through time nor in time marching past us.

There is, perhaps, more that could be said about temporal transition and our awareness of it. But the above considerations are enough to show that it is not a matter of an additional change that accrues to events which are somehow already there. Rather, temporal transition lies in the phenomenon of change itself, in the fact that there are entities that undergo alteration of their characteristics. Because this is so, to be aware of the temporal features of events cannot require any more than that one be aware of the events themselves. It is a mistake, therefore, to think that in order to know which tensed proposition describes John's behavior God must, in addition to being directly aware of that behavior, know that it is "really" happening. There is no other way to be directly aware of an event than to be aware of it as really happening. The most we could require in addition is that God know the *setting* of John's behavior: which events are simultaneous with it, which come before, and which after. This, presumably, would be necessary in order to know the other tensed propositions that hold from the perspective of that setting. And to be sure, a timeless God cannot learn about relations of before and after in the way we do, by experiencing different events seriatim. But there is no more reason to think a God beyond time must be ignorant of the distribution of events within it than there is to think a God outside space cannot know the relative positions of physical objects. If he is timelessly aware of all events, then surely he is aware of how they are positioned with respect to each other.

If this is correct, then the God who is beyond time knows all there is to know about what time it is. More important, he knows each and every tensed proposition that is true, from each and every temporal perspective the entire history of the universe has to offer. Furthermore, his position in this respect is far superior to that of a temporal God. For consider again proposition (f), which we said was the proposition I would have asserted yesterday had I then claimed "John is mowing his lawn." And let us suppose (f) is (timelessly, of course) true. John, we may imagine, has a large lawn that takes two days to mow. Now we seem to have a pretty clear idea what proposition (f) is; and certainly we can know *that* (f) is true, since we can know John was mowing his lawn yesterday. Yet it may be questioned whether I could ever *assert* (f) from my present temporal vantage point. It looks as though I am confined in my assertions of tensed propositions to those which are temporally indexed to the point in time at which the assertion is made. If that is so, then even though I can always know that (f) is true, the time is forever gone when (f) could have been a *vehicle* of knowledge for me. As a temporal being, I can only grasp the world from one temporal perspective at a time, and that has to be reflected in the way my knowledge is formulated. In a way, then, I lack access to (f), even though I know it is true. And of course the same limitation would apply to a temporal God. It may not be a serious limitation in terms of the usual definition of omniscience, for it does not prevent him from knowing of each true proposition *that* it is true, and of each false one that it is false. Nevertheless, it reflects the confinement we place upon God when we make him temporally eternal. He, like us, can only see things a certain way. And if that means there are other ways which are closed to him, the result can only be a limitation on his knowing.

V. CONCLUSION

The case for thinking God is timelessly eternal is, then, far stronger than the case for thinking he is temporal. Timeless eternity is more in keeping with God's nature as traditionally defined, and there is no persuasive reason to think it impairs either his creative power or his ability to know. Admittedly, it is the more difficult conception. To say that God can produce and comprehend the universe in all its history in a single timeless act is to attribute to him powers far beyond our own. And even if the attribution is justified, we have far less feel for what it would be like to be such a God than we do for the God of sempiternalism, who is by contrast rather comforting. His experience and abilities are very like our own, even if vastly greater, and we may find it far easier to see in a temporal God the loving father of religious tradition. Nevertheless, I think the timeless conception is to be preferred. The acceptability of a theory of God's nature cannot, after all, be a function of its anthropomorphism. Rather, we must try to understand God's nature in terms that maximize his perfection, both in himself and in his hegemony over creation. Where eternity is concerned, I think it is the timeless conception that does that. And although the task may be more difficult, there is no real reason for pessimism about finding in such a God the personal traits traditionally ascribed to him. It may be that all we need is a higher conception of those as well, a conception commensurate with a God whose ways are as far above our own as the heavens are above the earth.[17]

NOTES

1. The terminology of *enduring* or *persistence* is to be preferred over that which treats God as temporally "extended." The latter suggests God is spread out in time as a physical object is in space, which is an unacceptable analogy. One consequence of it is that just as a physical object cannot exist in its entirety at a single spatial point, so God would be unable to exist at any point in time. But then he could not exist now or at any other time, which is precisely the opposite of what defenders of sempiternity wish to claim.

2. Boethius, *The Consolation of Philosophy*, Bk. V, sec. 6.

3. Cf. Richard Swinburne, *The Coherence of Theism* (New York: Oxford University Press, 1977), pp. 220–21.

4. For this approach, see Eleonore Stump and Norman Kretzmann, "Eternity," *The Journal of Philosophy* 78 (1981): 429–58.

5. For further discussion see Paul Helm, *Eternal God* (New York: Oxford University Press, 1988), chap. 2.

6. William Kneale, "Time and Eternity in Theology," *Proceedings of the Aristotelian Society* 61 (1960–61): 87–108.

7. Stephen T. Davis, *Logic and the Nature of God* (Grand Rapids, Mich.: Eerdmans, 1983). [Reprinted in this anthology. See previous reading.]

8. Arguments of this kind are given by Stephen Davis, op. cit., Nelson Pike, *God and Timelessness* (New York: Schocken Books, 1970), pp. 104–107; and Swinburne, op. cit., p. 221.

9. Stephen Davis, *Logic and the Nature of God*, op. cit.

10. This assumes that human agency does not reduce to a causal relation between passive states like desire and biological events such as the motion of a limb. I have defended this claim in a number of places. See, for example, "Intrinsic Intentionality," *Theory and Decision* 20 (1986): 247–73.

11. These themes are further elaborated by Jonathan Kvanvig and myself in "Divine Conservation and the Persistence of the World," in *Divine and Human Action*, ed. T. V. Morris (Ithaca, N.Y.: Cornell University Press, 1988), pp. 13–19; and in "The Occasionalist Proselytizer: A Modified Catechism," in *Philosophical Perspectives* 5 (1991), ed.

J. E. Tomberlin (Atascadero, Calif.: Ridgeview Publishing Company), pp. 587–615.

12. This argument stems from Leibniz. *The Leibniz-Clarke Correspondence*, ed., H. G. Alexander (New York: Barnes & Noble, 1956), pp. 26–27.

13. The problem of divine foreknowledge and human freedom is a difficult one, and recent discussions of it have become complicated indeed. For an excellent summary see John Martin Fischer, "Recent Work on God and Freedom," *American Philosophical Quarterly* 29 (1992): 91–109.

14. Arguments like this stem from A. N. Prior, "The Formalities of Omniscience," *Philosophy* 37 (1962): 114–29. See also Norman Kretzmann, "Omniscience and Immutability," *The Journal of Philosophy* 63 (1966): 409–21.

15. Helm, op. cit., pp. 43–44.

16. Similar treatments of tensed sentences can be found in Richard Swinburne, "Tensed Facts," *American Philosophical Quarterly* 27 (1990): 117–30; and in E. J. Lowe, "The Indexical Fallacy in McTaggart's Proof of the Unreality of Time," *Mind* 96 (1987): 62–70.

17. I am grateful to my colleague Jonathan Kvanvig, and to Philip Quinn, Eleonore Stump, and Louis Pojman for helpful discussions of earlier versions of this paper.

I.B.3

Is God's Power Limited?

ST. THOMAS AQUINAS

Thomas Aquinas (1225–1274), one of the greatest theologians in the Western tradition, argues that although it is difficult to explain what God's omnipotence is, it requires only the ability to do those things that are logically possible. Because God possesses all perfections and sinning is an imperfection, the ability to sin is not part of his omnipotence.

We proceed thus to the Third Article:

Objection 1. It seems that God is not omnipotent. For movement and passiveness belong to everything. But this is impossible for God, since He is immovable, as was said above. Therefore He is not omnipotent.

Obj. 2. Further, sin is an act of some kind. But God cannot sin, nor *deny Himself*, as it is said *2 Tim.* ii. 13. Therefore He is not omnipotent.

Obj. 3. Further, it is said of God that He manifests His omnipotence *especially by sparing and having mercy*. Therefore the greatest act possible to the divine power is to spare and have mercy. There are things much greater, however, than sparing and having mercy; for example, to create another world, and the like. Therefore God is not omnipotent.

Obj. 4. Further, upon the text, *God hath made foolish the wisdom of this world* (*I Cor.* i. 20), the *Gloss* says: *God hath made the wisdom of this world foolish* by showing those things to be possible which it judges to be impossible. Whence it seems that nothing is to be judged possible or impossible in reference to inferior causes, as the wisdom of this world judges them; but in reference to the divine power. If God, then,

From *Summa Theologica*, part 1. In *The Basic Writings of St. Thomas Aquinas*, vol. 1, edited by Anton C. Pegis (New York: Random House, 1945), pp. 262–64, by permission of the Anton Pegis Estate.

were omnipotent, all things would be possible; nothing, therefore, impossible. But if we take away the impossible, then we destroy also the necessary; for what necessarily exists cannot possibly not exist. Therefore, there would be nothing at all that is necessary in things if God were omnipotent. But this is an impossibility. Therefore God is not omnipotent.

On the contrary, It is said: *No word shall be impossible with God (Luke* i:37).

I answer that, All confess that God is omnipotent; but it seems difficult to explain in what His omnipotence precisely consists. For there may be a doubt as to the precise meaning of the word "all" when we say that God can do all things. If, however, we consider the matter aright, since power is said in reference to possible things, this phrase, *God can do all things*, is rightly understood to mean that God can do all things that are possible; and for this reason He is said to be omnipotent. Now according to the Philosopher a thing is said to be possible in two ways. First, in relation to some power; thus whatever is subject to human power is said to be possible to man. Now God cannot be said to be omnipotent through being able to do all things that are possible to created nature; for the divine power extends farther than that. If, however, we were to say that God is omnipotent because He can do all things that are possible to His power, there would be a vicious circle in explaining the nature of His power. For this would be saying nothing else but that God is omnipotent because He can do all that He is able to do.

It remains, therefore, that God is called omnipotent because he can do all things that are possible absolutely; which is the second way of saying a thing is possible. For a thing is said to be possible or impossible absolutely, according to the relation in which the very terms stand to one another: possible, if the predicate is not incompatible with the subject, as that Socrates sits; and absolutely impossible when the predicate is altogether incompatible with the subject, as, for instance, that a man is an ass.

It must, however, be remembered that since every agent produces an effect like itself, to each active power there corresponds a thing possible as its proper object according to the nature of that act on which its active power is founded; for instance, the power of giving warmth is related, as to its proper object, to the

being capable of being warmed. The divine being, however, upon which the nature of power in God is founded, is infinite; it is not limited to any class of being, but possesses within itself the perfection of all being. Whence, whatsoever has or can have the nature of being is numbered among the absolute possibles, in respect of which God is called omnipotent.

Now nothing is opposed to the notion of being except non-being. Therefore, that which at the same time implies being and non-being is repugnant to the notion of an absolute possible, which is subject to the divine omnipotence. For such cannot come under the divine omnipotence; not indeed because of any defect in the power of God, but because it has not the nature of a feasible or possible thing. Therefore, everything that does not imply a contradiction in terms is numbered among those possibles in respect of which God is called omnipotent; whereas whatever implies contradiction does not come within the scope of divine omnipotence, because it cannot have the aspect of possibility. Hence it is more appropriate to say that such things cannot be done, than that God cannot do them. Nor is this contrary to the word of the angel, saying: *No word shall be impossible with God (Luke* i. 37). For whatever implies a contradiction cannot be a word, because no intellect can possibly conceive such a thing.

Reply Obj. **1.** God is said to be omnipotent in respect to active power, not to passive power, as was shown above. Whence the fact that He is immovable or impassible is not repugnant to His omnipotence.

Reply Obj. **2.** To sin is to fall short of a perfect action; hence to be able to sin is to be able to fall short in action, which is repugnant to omnipotence. Therefore it is that God cannot sin, because of His omnipotence. Now it is true that the Philosopher says that *God can deliberately do what is evil.* But this must be understood either on a condition, the antecedent of which is impossible—as, for instance, if we were to say that God can do evil things if He will. For there is no reason why a conditional proposition should not be true, though both the antecedent and consequent are impossible: as if one were to say: *If man is an ass, he has four feet.* Or he may be understood to mean that God can do some things which now seem to be evil: which, however, if He did them, would then be good. Or he is, perhaps, speaking after the common manner of the pagans, who thought that men became gods, like Jupiter or Mercury.

Reply Obj. **3.** God's omnipotence is particularly shown in sharing and having mercy, because in this it is made manifest that God has supreme power, namely, that He freely forgives sins. For it is not for one who is bound by laws of a superior to forgive sins of his own free choice. Or, it is thus shown because by sparing and having mercy upon men, He leads them to the participation of an infinite good; which is the ultimate effect of the divine power. Or it is thus shown because, as was said above, the effect of the divine mercy is the foundation of all the divine works. For nothing is due anyone, except because of something already given him gratuitously by God. In this way the divine omnipotence is particularly made manifest, because to it pertains the first foundation of all good things.

Reply Obj. **4.** The absolute possible is not so called in reference either to higher causes, or to inferior causes, but in reference to itself. But that which is called possible in reference to some power is named possible in reference to its proximate cause. Hence those things which it belongs to God alone to do immediately—as, for example, to create, to justify, and the like—are said to be possible in reference to a higher cause. Those things, however, which are such as to be done by inferior causes, are said to be possible in reference to those inferior causes. For it is according to the condition of the proximate cause that the effect has contingency or necessity, as was shown above. Thus it is that the wisdom of the world is deemed foolish, because what is impossible to nature it judges to be impossible to God. So it is clear that the omnipotence of God does not take away from things their impossibility and necessity.

I.B.4

Some Puzzles Concerning Omnipotence

GEORGE MAVRODES

George Mavrodes (1926–) is emeritus professor of philosophy at the University of Michigan. In this reading, he applies the Thomistic view of God's omnipotence to the paradox of the stone (see the previous selection). Mavrodes argues that, since creating a stone too heavy for God to lift involves doing something that is logically impossible, God's inability to do this does not count against his omnipotence.

The doctrine of God's omnipotence appears to claim that God can do anything. Consequently, there have been attempts to refute the doctrine by giving examples of things which God cannot do; for example, He cannot draw a square circle.

Responding to objections of this type, St. Thomas pointed out that "anything" should be here construed to refer only to objects, actions, or states of affairs whose descriptions are not self-contradictory.[1] For it is only such things whose nonexistence might

George Mavrodes, "Some Puzzles Concerning Omnipotence," in *The Philosophical Review*. Volume 72, no. 2, pp. 221–223.
© 1963, Cornell University Press. All rights reserved. Used by permission of the current publisher, Duke University Press.

plausibly be attributed to a lack of power in some agent. My failure to draw a circle on the exam may indicate my lack of geometrical skill, but my failure to draw a square circle does not indicate any such lack. Therefore, the fact that it is false (or perhaps meaningless) to say that God could draw one does no damage to the doctrine of His omnipotence.

A more involved problem, however, is posed by this type of question: can God create a stone too heavy for Him to lift? This appears to be stronger than the first problem, for it poses a dilemma. If we say that God can create a stone, then it seems that there might be such a stone. And if there might be a stone too heavy for Him to lift, then He is evidently not omnipotent. But if we deny that God can create such a stone, we seem to have given up His omnipotence already. Both answers lead us to the same conclusion.

Further, this problem does not seem obviously open to St. Thomas' solution. The form "x is able to draw a square circle" seems plainly to involve a contradiction, while "x is able to make a thing too heavy for x to lift" does not. For it may easily be true that I am able to make a boat too heavy for me to lift. So why should it not be possible for God to make a stone too heavy for Him to lift?

Despite this apparent difference, this second puzzle *is* open to essentially the same answer as the first. The dilemma fails because it consists of asking whether God can do a self-contradictory thing. And the reply that He cannot does no damage to the doctrine of omnipotence.

The specious nature of the problem may be seen in this way. God is either omnipotent or not.[2] Let us assume first that He is not. In that case the phrase "a stone too heavy for God to lift" may not be self-contradictory. And then, of course, if we assert either that God is able or that He is not able to create such a stone, we may conclude that He is not omnipotent. But this is no more than the assumption with which we began, meeting us again after our roundabout journey. If this were all that the dilemma could establish it would be trivial. To be significant it must derive this same conclusion *from the assumption that God is omnipotent*; that is, it must show that the assumption of the omnipotence of God leads to a *reductio*. But does it?

On the assumption that God is omnipotent, the phrase "a stone too heavy for God to lift" becomes self-contradictory. For it becomes "a stone which cannot be lifted by Him whose power is sufficient for lifting anything." But the "thing" described by a self-contradictory phrase is absolutely impossible and hence has nothing to do with the doctrine of omnipotence. Not being an object of power at all, its failure to exist cannot be the result of some lack in the power of God. And, interestingly, it is the very omnipotence of God which makes the existence of such a stone absolutely impossible, while it is the fact that I am finite in power which makes it possible for me to make a boat too heavy for me to lift.

But suppose that some die-hard objector takes the bit in his teeth and denies that the phrase "a stone too heavy for God to lift" is self-contradictory, even on the assumption that God is omnipotent. In other words, he contends that the description "a stone too heavy for an omnipotent God to lift" is self-coherent and therefore describes an absolutely possible object. Must I then attempt to prove the contradiction which I assume above as intuitively obvious? Not necessarily. Let me reply simply that if the objector is right in this contention, then the answer to the original question is "Yes, God can create such a stone." It may seem that this reply will force us into the original dilemma. But it does not. For now the objector can draw no damaging conclusion from this answer. And the reason is that he has just now contended that such a stone is compatible with the omnipotence of God. Therefore, from the possibility of God's creating such a stone it cannot be concluded that God is not omnipotent. The objector cannot have it both ways. The conclusion which he himself wishes to draw from an affirmative answer to the original question is itself the required proof that the descriptive phrase which appears there is self-contradictory. And "it is more appropriate to say that such things cannot be done, than that God cannot do them."[3]

The specious nature of this problem may also be seen in a somewhat different way.[4] Suppose that some theologian is convinced by this dilemma that he must give up the doctrine of omnipotence. But he resolves to give up as little as possible, just enough to meet the argument. One way he can do so is by retaining the infinite power of God with regard to lifting, while placing a restriction on the sort of stone He is able to create. The only restriction required here, however, is that God must not be able to create a stone too heavy for Him to lift. Beyond that the dilemma has not even suggested any necessary restriction. Our theologian has, in effect, answered the original question in the negative; and he now regretfully supposes that this has required him to give up the full doctrine of omnipotence. He is now retaining what he supposes to be the more modest remnants which he has salvaged from that doctrine.

We must ask, however, what it is which he has in fact given up. Is it the unlimited power of God to create stones? No doubt. But what stone is it which God is now precluded from creating? The stone too heavy for Him to lift, of course. But we must remember that nothing in the argument required the theologian to admit any limit on God's power with regard to the lifting of stones.

He still holds that to be unlimited. And if God's power to lift is infinite, then His power to create may run to infinity also without outstripping that first power. The supposed limitation turns out to be no limitation at all, since it is specified only by reference to another power which is itself infinite. Our theologian need have no regrets, for he has given up nothing. The doctrine of the power of God remains just what it was before.

Nothing I have said above, of course, goes to prove that God is, in fact, omnipotent. All I have intended to show is that certain arguments intended to prove that He is not omnipotent fail. They fail because they propose, as tests of God's power, putative tasks whose descriptions are self-contradictory. Such pseudo-tasks, not falling within the realm of possibility, are not objects of power at all. Hence the fact that they cannot be performed implies no limit on the power of God, and hence no defect in the doctrine of omnipotence.

NOTES

1. St. Thomas Aquinas, *Summa Theologiae*, Ia, q. 25, a. 3.
2. I assume, of course, the existence of God, since that is not being brought in question here.
3. St. Thomas, *loc. cit.*
4. But this method rests finally on the same logical relations as the preceding one.

I.B.5

The Logic of Omnipotence

HARRY G. FRANKFURT

Harry G. Frankfurt (1929–) is emeritus professor of philosophy at Princeton University and the author of many important works in philosophy, including an influential study of René Descartes. In this essay he argues that even if Mavrodes's solution to the paradox of the stone (see previous selection)

From *The Philosophical Review* 73 (1964): 262–63.

is incorrect, the critic of omnipotence is not helped. For if God can do the impossible and create a stone heavier than he can lift, he can also do another impossible thing and lift that stone.

George Mavrodes has recently presented an analysis designed to show that, despite some appearances to the contrary, a certain well-known puzzle actually raises no serious difficulties in the notion of divine omnipotence.[1] The puzzle suggests a test of God's power—can He create a stone too heavy for Him to lift?—which, it seems, cannot fail to reveal that His power is limited. For He must, it would appear, either show His limitations by being unable to create such a stone or by being unable to lift it once He had created it.

In dealing with this puzzle, Mavrodes points out that it involves the setting of a task whose description is self-contradictory—the task of creating a stone too heavy for an omnipotent being to lift. He calls such tasks "pseudo-tasks" and he says of them: "Such pseudo-tasks, not falling within the realm of possibility, are not objects of power at all. Hence the fact that they cannot be performed implies no limit on the power of God, and hence no defect in the doctrine of omnipotence."[2] Thus his way of dealing with the puzzle relies upon the principle that an omnipotent being need not be supposed capable of performing tasks whose descriptions are self-contradictory.

Now this principle is one which Mavrodes apparently regards as self-evident, since he offers no support for it whatever except some references which indicate that it was also accepted by Saint Thomas Aquinas. I do not wish to suggest that the principle is false. Indeed, for all I know it may even be self-evident. But it happens to be a principle which has been rejected by some important philosophers.[3] Accordingly, it might be preferable to have an analysis of the puzzle in question which does not require the use of this principle. And in fact, such an analysis is easy to provide.

Suppose, then, that God's omnipotence enables Him to do even what is logically impossible and that He actually creates a stone too heavy for Him to lift. The critic of the notion of divine omnipotence is quite mistaken if he thinks that this supposition plays into his hands. What the critic wishes to claim, of course, is that when God has created a stone which He cannot lift He is then faced with a task beyond His ability and is therefore seen to be limited in power. But this claim is not justified.

For why should God not be able to perform the task in question? To be sure, it is a task—the task of lifting a stone which He cannot lift—whose description is self-contradictory. But if God is supposed capable of performing one task whose description is self-contradictory—that of creating the problematic stone in the first place—why should He not be supposed capable of performing another—that of lifting the stone? After all, is there any greater trick in performing two logically impossible tasks than there is in performing one?

If an omnipotent being can do what is logically impossible, then He can not only create situations which He cannot handle but also, since He is not bound by the limits of consistency, He can handle situations which He cannot handle.

NOTES

1. George Mavrodes, "Some Puzzles Concerning Omnipotence," *The Philosophical Review* 72 (1963), 221–23.

2. Ibid., p. 223.

3. Descartes, for instance, who in fact thought it blasphemous to maintain that God can do only what can be described in a logically coherent way: "The truths of mathematics . . . were established by God and entirely depend on Him, as much as do all the rest of His creatures. Actually, it would be to speak of God as a Jupiter or Saturn and to subject Him to the Styx and to the Fates, to say that these

truths are independent of Him. . . . You will be told that if God established these truths He would be able to change them, as a king does his laws; to which it is necessary to reply that this is correct. . . . In general we can be quite certain that God can do whatever we are able to understand, but not that He cannot do what we are unable to understand. For it would be presumptuous to think that our imagination extends as far as His power" (letter to Mersenne, 15 April 1630). "God was as free to make it false that all the radii of a circle are equal as to refrain from creating the world" (letter to Mersenne, 27 May 1630). "I would not even dare to say that God cannot arrange that a mountain should exist without a valley, or that one and two should not make three; but I only say that He has given me a mind of such a nature that I cannot conceive a mountain without a valley or a sum of one and two which would not be three, and so on, and that such things imply contradictions in my conception" (letter to Arnauld, 29 July 1648). "As for the difficulty in conceiving how it was a matter of freedom and indifference to God to make it true that the three angles of a triangle should equal two right angles, or generally that contradictions should not be able to be together, one can easily remove it by considering that the power of God can have no limit. . . . God cannot have been determined to make it true that contradictions cannot be together, and consequently He could have been determined to make it true that contradictions cannot be together, and consequently he could have done the contrary" (letter to Mesland, 2 May 1644).

I.B.6

Divine Foreknowledge and Human Free Will

ST. AUGUSTINE

St. Augustine (354–430) was Bishop of Hippo in North Africa and one of the greatest thinkers in the history of the Christian Church. Among his most well-known works are The City of God, Confessions, On Christian Doctrine, *and* On the Trinity. *In the present selection he argues that God's foreknowledge of human actions does not necessitate those actions. Specifically, human sin was not committed because God knew that it would happen, but God knew that it would happen because he knows how humans will choose. We enter the dialogue with a question by Augustine's disciple, Evodius.*

EVODIUS: . . . Since these things are true, I very much wonder how God can have foreknowledge of everything in the future, and yet we do not sin by necessity. It would be an irreligious and completely insane attack on God's foreknowledge to say that something could happen otherwise than as God foreknew. So suppose that God foreknew that the first human being was going to sin. Anyone who admits, as I do, that God foreknows everything in the future will have to grant me that. Now

From *On the Free Choice of the Will*, trans. with introduction and notes by Thomas Williams (Indianapolis, IN: Hackett Publishing Company, 1993). ©1993 by Thomas Williams. Reprinted by permission of Hackett Publishing Company, Inc. All rights reserved.

I won't say that God would not have made him— for God made him good, and no sin of his can harm God, who not only made him good but showed His own goodness by creating him, as He also shows His justice by punishing him and His mercy by redeeming him—but I will say this: *since God foreknew that he was going to sin, his sin necessarily had to happen. How, then, is the will free when such inescapable necessity is found in it?*

AUGUSTINE: . . . Surely this is the problem that is disturbing and puzzling you. How is it that these two propositions are not contradictory and inconsistent: (1) God has foreknowledge of everything in the future; and (2) We sin by the will, not by necessity? For, you say, if God foreknows that someone is going to sin, then it is necessary that he sin. But if it is necessary, the will has no choice about whether to sin; there is an inescapable and fixed necessity. And so you fear that this argument forces us into one of two positions: either we draw the heretical conclusion that God does not foreknow everything in the future; or, if we cannot accept this conclusion, we must admit that sin happens by necessity and not by will. Isn't that what is bothering you?

EVODIUS: That's it exactly.

AUGUSTINE: So you think that anything that God foreknows happens by necessity and not by will.

EVODIUS: Precisely.

AUGUSTINE: Now pay close attention. Look inside yourself for a little while, and tell me, if you can, what sort of will you are going to have tomorrow: a will to do right or a will to sin?

EVODIUS: I don't know.

AUGUSTINE: Do you think that God doesn't know either?

EVODIUS: Not at all—God certainly does know.

AUGUSTINE: Well then, if God knows what you are going to will tomorrow, and foresees the future wills of every human being, both those who exist now and those who will exist in the future, he surely foresees how he is going to treat the just and the irreligious.

EVODIUS: Clearly, if I say that God foreknows all of my actions, I can much more confidently say that he foreknows his own actions and foresees with absolute certainty what he is going to do.

AUGUSTINE: Then aren't you worried that someone might object that God himself will act out of necessity rather than by his will in everything that he is going to do? After all, you said that whatever God foreknows happens by necessity, not by will.

EVODIUS: When I said that, I was thinking only of what happens in his creation and not of what happens within himself. For those things do not come into being; they are eternal.

AUGUSTINE: So God does nothing in his creation.

EVODIUS: He has already established, once for all, the ways in which the universe that he created is to be governed; he does not administer anything by a new act of will.

AUGUSTINE: Doesn't he make anyone happy?

EVODIUS: Of course he does.

AUGUSTINE: And he does this when that person is made happy.

EVODIUS: Right.

AUGUSTINE: Then suppose, for example, that you are going to be happy a year from now. That means that a year from now God is going to make you happy.

EVODIUS: That's right too.

AUGUSTINE: And God knows today what he is going to do a year from now.

EVODIUS: He has always foreknown this, so I admit that he foreknows it now, if indeed it is really going to happen.

AUGUSTINE: Then surely you are not God's creature, or else your happiness does not take place in you.

EVODIUS: But I am God's creature, and my happiness does take place in me.

AUGUSTINE: Then the happiness that God gives you takes place by necessity and not by will.

EVODIUS: His will *is* my necessity.

AUGUSTINE: And so you will be happy against your will.

EVODIUS: If I had the power to be happy I would be happy right now. Even now I will to be happy, but I'm not, since it is God who makes me happy. I cannot do it for myself.

AUGUSTINE: How clearly the truth speaks through you! You could not help thinking that the only thing that is within our power is that which we do when we will it. Therefore, nothing is so much within our power as the will itself, for it is near at hand the very moment that we will. So we can rightly say, "We grow old by necessity, not by will"; or "We become feeble by necessity, not by will"; or "We die by necessity, not by will," and other such things. But who would be crazy enough to say "We do not will by the will"? Therefore, although God foreknows what we are going to will in the future, it does not follow that we do not will by the will.

When you said that you cannot make yourself happy, you said it as if I had denied it. Not at all; I am merely saying that when you do become happy, it will be in accordance with your will, not against your will. Simply because God foreknows your future happiness—and nothing can happen except as God foreknows it, since otherwise it would not be foreknowledge—it does not follow that you will be happy against your will. That would be completely absurd and far from the truth. So God's foreknowledge, which is certain even today of your future happiness, does not take away your will for happiness once you have begun to be happy; and in the same way, your blameworthy will (if indeed you are going to have such a will) does not cease to be a will simply because God foreknows that you are going to have it.

Just notice how imperceptive someone would have to be to argue thus: "If God has foreknown my future will, it is necessary that I will what he has foreknown, since nothing can happen otherwise than as he has foreknown it. But if it is necessary, then one must concede that I will it by necessity and not by will." What extraordinary foolishness! If God foreknew a future will that turned out not to be a will at all, things would indeed happen otherwise than as God foreknew them. And I will overlook this objector's equally monstrous statement that "it is necessary that I will," for by assuming necessity he tries to abolish will. For if his willing is necessary, how does he will, since there is no will?

Suppose he expressed it in another way and said that, since his willing is necessary, his will is not in his own power. This would run up against the same problem that you had when I asked whether you were going to be happy against your will. You replied that you would already be happy if you had the power; you said that you have the will but not the power. I answered that the truth had spoken through you. For we can deny that something is in our power only if it is not present even when we will it; but if we will, and yet the will remains absent, then we are not really willing at all. Now if it is impossible for us not to will when we are willing, then the will is present to those who will; and if something is present when we will it, then it is in our power. So our will would not be a will if it were not in our power. And since it is in our power, we are free with respect to it. But we are not free with respect to anything that we do not have in our power, and anything that we have cannot be nothing.

Thus, we believe both that God has foreknowledge of everything in the future and that nonetheless we will whatever we will. Since God foreknows our will, the very will that he foreknows will be what comes about. Therefore, it will be a will, since it is a will that he foreknows. And it could not be a will unless it were in our power. Therefore, he also foreknows this power. It follows, then, that his foreknowledge does not take away my power; in fact, it is all the more certain that I will have that power, since he whose foreknowledge never errs foreknows that I will have it.

EVODIUS: I agree now that it is necessary that whatever God has foreknown will happen, and that he foreknows our sins in such a way that our wills remain free and are within our power. . . .

I.B.7

God's Foreknowledge and Human Free Will Are Incompatible

NELSON PIKE

Nelson Pike (1930 – 2010) was emeritus professor of philosophy at the University of California at Irvine and one of the leading figures in the philosophy of religion. In this article he argues that given commonly held theological assumptions about God's nature, no human action is free.

In Part V, Section III of his *Consolatio Philosophiae*, Boethius entertained (though he later rejected) the claim that if God is omniscient, no human action is voluntary. This claim seems intuitively false. Surely, given only a doctrine describing God's *knowledge*, nothing about the voluntary status of human actions will follow. Perhaps such a conclusion would follow from a doctrine of divine omnipotence or divine providence, but what connection could there be between the claim that God is *omniscient* and the claim that human actions are determined? Yet Boethius thought he saw a problem here. He thought that if one collected together just the right assumptions and principles regarding God's knowledge, one could derive the conclusion that if God exists, no human action is voluntary. Of course, Boethius did not think that all the assumptions and principles required to reach this conclusion are true (quite the contrary), but he thought it important to draw attention to them nonetheless. If a theologian is to construct a doctrine of God's knowledge which does not commit him to determinism, he must first understand that there is a way of thinking about God's knowledge which would so commit him.

In this paper, I shall argue that although his claim has a sharp counterintuitive ring, Boethius was right in thinking that there is a selection from among the various doctrines and principles clustering about the notions of knowledge, omniscience, and God which, when brought together, demand the conclusion that if God exists, no human action is voluntary. Boethius, I think, did not succeed in making explicit all of the ingredients in the problem. His suspicions were sound, but his discussion was incomplete. His argument needs to be developed. This is the task I shall undertake in the pages to follow. I should like to make clear at the outset that my purpose in rearguing this thesis is not to show that determinism is true, nor to show that God does not exist, nor to show that either determinism is true or God does not exist. Following Boethius, I shall not claim that the items needed to generate the problem are either philosophically or theologically adequate. I want to concentrate attention on the implications of a certain set of assumptions. Whether the assumptions are themselves acceptable is a question I shall not consider.

I

A. Many philosophers have held that if a statement of the form "*A* knows *X*" is true, then "*A* believes

Reprinted from Nelson Pike, "Divine Omniscience and Voluntary Action," *The Philosophical Review* 74 (1965): 27–46.

X" is true and "*X*" is true. As a first assumption, I shall take this partial analysis of "*A* knows *X*" to be correct. And I shall suppose that since this analysis holds for all knowledge claims, it will hold when speaking of God's knowledge. "God knows *X*" entails "God believes *X*" and "'*X*' is true."

Secondly, Boethius said that with respect to the matter of knowledge, God "cannot in anything be mistaken."[1] I shall understand this doctrine as follows. Omniscient beings hold no false beliefs. Part of what is meant when we say that a person is omniscient is that the person in question believes nothing that is false. But, further, it is part of the "essence" of God to be omniscient. This is to say that any person who is not omniscient could not be the person we usually mean to be referring to when using the name "God." To put this last point a little differently: if the person we usually mean to be referring to when using the name "God" were suddenly to lose the quality of omniscience (suppose, for example, He came to believe something false), the resulting person would no longer be God. Although we might call this second person "God" (I might call my cat "God"), the absence of the quality of omniscience would be sufficient to guarantee that the person referred to was not the same as the person formerly called by that name. From this last doctrine it follows that the statement "if a given person is God, that person is omniscient" is an a priori truth. From this we may conclude that the statement "If a given person is God, that person holds no false beliefs" is also an a priori truth. It would be conceptually impossible for God to hold a false belief. "'*X* is true" follows from "God believes *X*." These are all ways of expressing the same principle—the principle expressed by Boethius in the formula "God cannot in anything be mistaken."

A second principle usually associated with the notion of divine omniscience has to do with the scope or range of God's intellectual gaze. To say that a being is omniscient is to say that he knows everything. "Everything" in this statement is usually taken to cover future, as well as present and past, events and circumstances. In fact, God is usually said to have had foreknowledge of everything that has ever happened. With respect to anything that was, is, or will be the case, God knew, *from eternity*, that it would be the case.

The doctrine of God's knowing everything from eternity is very obscure. One particularly difficult question concerning this doctrine is whether it entails that with respect to everything that was, is, or will be the case, God knew *in advance* that it would be the case. In some traditional theological texts, we are told that God is *eternal* in the sense that He exists "outside of time," that is, in the sense that He bears no temporal relations to the events or circumstances of the natural world.[2] In a theology of this sort, God could not be said to have known that a given natural event was going to happen before it happened. If God knew that a given natural event was going to occur *before* it occurred, at least one of God's cognitions would then have occurred before some natural event. This, surely, would violate the idea that God bears no temporal relations to natural events.[3] On the other hand, in a considerable number of theological sources, we are told that God *has always* existed—that He existed long *before* the occurrence of any natural event. In a theology of this sort, to say that God is eternal is not to say that God exists "outside of time" (bears no temporal relations to natural events), it is to say, instead, God has existed (and will continue to exist) at each moment.[4] The doctrine of omniscience which goes with this second understanding of the notion of eternity is one in which it is affirmed that God *has always* known what was going to happen in the natural world. John Calvin wrote as follows:

> When we attribute foreknowledge to God, we mean that all things have ever been and perpetually remain before, his eyes, so that to his knowledge nothing is future or past, but all things are present; and present in such manner, that he does not merely conceive of them from ideas formed in his mind, as things remembered by us appear to our minds, but really he holds and sees them as if (*tanquam*) actually placed before him.[5]

All things are "present" to God in the sense that He "sees" them as if (*tanquam*) they were actually before Him. Further, with respect to any given natural event, not only is that event "present" to God in the sense indicated, it has *ever been and has perpetually remained* "present" to Him in that sense. This latter is the point of special interest. Whatever one thinks of the idea that God "sees" things as if "actually placed before him," Calvin would appear to be committed to the idea that God has *always known* what was going to happen in the natural world. Choose an event (E) and a time (T_2) at which E occurred. For any time (T_1) prior to T_2 (say, five thousand, six hundred, or eighty years prior to T_2), God knew at T_1 that E would occur at T_2. It will follow from this doctrine, of course, that with respect to any human action, God knew well in advance of its performance that the action would be performed. Calvin says, "when God created man, He foresaw what would happen concerning him." He adds, "little more than five thousand years have elapsed since the creation of the world."[6] Calvin seems to have thought that God foresaw the outcome of every human action well over five thousand years ago.

In the discussion to follow, I shall work only with this second interpretation of God's knowing everything *from eternity*. I shall assume that if a person is omniscient, that person has always known what was going to happen in the natural world—and, in particular, has always known what human actions were going to be performed. Thus, as above, assuming that the attribute of omniscience is part of the "essence" of God, the statement "For any natural event (including human actions), if a given person is God, that person would always have known that that event was going to occur at the time it occurred" must be treated as an a priori truth. This is just another way of stating a point admirably put by St. Augustine when he said: "For to confess that God exists and at the same time to deny that He has foreknowledge of future things is the most manifest folly.... One who is not prescient of all future things is not God."[7]

B. Last Saturday afternoon, Jones mowed his lawn. Assuming that God exists and is (essentially) omniscient in the sense outlined above, it follows that (let us say) eighty years prior to last Saturday afternoon, God knew (and thus believed) that Jones would mow his lawn at that time. But from this it follows, I think, that at the time of action (last Saturday afternoon) Jones was not able—that is, it was not *within Jones's power*—to refrain from mowing his lawn.[8] If at the time of action, Jones had been able to refrain from mowing his lawn, then (the most obvious conclusion would seem to be) at the time of action, Jones was able to do something which would have brought it about that God held a false belief eighty years earlier. But God cannot in anything be mistaken. It is not possible that some belief of His was false. Thus, last Saturday afternoon, Jones was not able to do something which would have brought it about that God held a false belief eighty years ago. To suppose that it was would be to suppose that, at the time of action, Jones was able to do something having a conceptually incoherent description, namely something that would have brought it about that one of God's beliefs was false. Hence, given that God believed eighty years ago that Jones would mow his lawn on Saturday, if we are to assign Jones the power on Saturday to refrain from mowing his lawn, this power must not be described as the power to do something that would have rendered one of God's beliefs false. How then should we describe it vis-à-vis God and His belief? So far as I can see, there are only two other alternatives. First, we might try describing it as the power to do something that would have brought it about that God believed otherwise than He did eighty years ago; or, secondly, we might try describing it as the power to do something that would have brought it about that God (who, by hypothesis, existed eighty years earlier) did not exist eighty years earlier—that is, as the power to do something that would have brought it about that any person who believed eighty years ago that Jones would mow his lawn on Saturday (one of whom was, by hypothesis, God) held a false belief, and thus was not God. But again, neither of these latter can be accepted. Last Saturday afternoon, Jones was not able to do something that would have brought it about that God believed otherwise than He did eighty years ago. Even if we suppose (as was suggested by Calvin) that eighty years ago God knew Jones would mow his lawn on Saturday in the sense that He "saw" Jones mowing his lawn as if this action were occurring before Him, the fact remains that God knew (and thus believed) eighty years prior to Saturday that Jones would mow his lawn. And if God held such a belief eighty years prior to Saturday, Jones did not have the power on Saturday to do something that would have made it the case that God did not hold this belief eighty years earlier. No action performed at a given time can alter the fact that a given person held a certain belief at a time prior to the time in question. This last seems to be an a priori truth. For similar reasons, the last of the above alternatives must also be rejected. On the assumption that God existed eighty years prior to Saturday, Jones on Saturday was not able to do something that would have brought it about that God did not exist eighty years prior to that time. No action performed at a given time can alter the fact that a certain person existed at a time prior to the time in question. This, too, seems to me to be an a priori truth. But if these observations are correct, then, given that Jones mowed his lawn on Saturday, and given that God exists and is (essentially) omniscient, it seems to follow that at the time of action, Jones did not have the power to refrain from mowing his lawn. The upshot of these reflections would appear to be that Jones's mowing his lawn last Saturday cannot be counted as a voluntary action. Although I do not have an analysis of what it is for action to be *voluntary*, it seems to me that a situation in which it would be wrong to assign Jones the *ability* or *power* to do *other* than he did would be a situation in which it would also be wrong to speak of his action as voluntary. As a general remark, if God exists and is (essentially) omniscient in the sense specified above, no human action is voluntary.[9]

As the argument just presented is somewhat complex, perhaps the following schematic representation of it will be of some use.

1. "God existed at T_1" entails "If Jones did X at T_2, God believed at T_1 that Jones would do X at T_2."

2. "God believes X" entails "X is true."

3. It is not within one's power at a given time to do something having a description that is logically contradictory.

4. It is not within one's power at a given time to do something that would bring it about that someone who held a certain belief at a time prior to the time in question did not hold that belief at the time prior to the time in question.

5. It is not within one's power at a given time to do something that would bring it about that a person who existed at an earlier time did not exist at that earlier time.

6. If God existed at T_1 and if God believed at T_1 that Jones would do X at T_2, then if it was within Jones's power at T_2 to refrain from doing X, then (1) it was within Jones's power at T_2 to do something that would have brought it about that God held a false belief at T_1, or (2) it was within Jones's power at T_2 to do something which would have brought it about that God did not hold the belief He held at T_1, or (3) it was within Jones's power at T_2 to do something that would have brought it about that any person who believed at T_1 that Jones would do X at T_2 (one of whom was, by hypothesis, God) held a false belief and thus was not God—that is, that God (who by hypothesis existed at T_1) did not exist at T_1.

7. Alternative 1 in the consequent of item 6 is false (from 2 and 3).

8. Alternative 2 in the consequent of item 6 is false (from 4).

9. Alternative 3 in the consequent of item 6 is false (from 5).

10. Therefore, if God existed at T_1, and if God believed at T_1 that Jones would do X at T_2, then it was not within Jones's power at T_2 to refrain from doing X (from 6 through 9).

11. Therefore, if God existed at T_1 and if Jones did X at T_2, it was not within Jones's power at T_2 to refrain from doing X (from 1 and 10).

In this argument, items 1 and 2 make explicit the doctrine of God's (essential) omniscience with which I am working. Items 3, 4, and 5 express what I take to be part of the logic of the concept of ability or power as it applies to human beings. Item 6 is offered as an analytic truth. If one assigns Jones the power to refrain from doing X at T_2 (given that God believed at T_1 that he would do X at T_2), so far as I can see, one would have to describe this power in one of the three ways listed in the consequent of item 6. I do not know how to argue that these are the only alternatives, but I have been unable to find another. Item 11, when generalized for all agents and actions, and when taken together with what seems to me to be a minimal condition for the application of "voluntary action," yields the conclusion that if God exists (and is essentially omniscient in the way I have described) no human action is voluntary.

C. It is important to notice that the argument given in the preceding paragraphs avoids use of two concepts that are often prominent in discussions of determinism.

In the first place, the argument makes no mention of the *causes* of Jones's action. Say (for example, with St. Thomas)[10] that God's foreknowledge of Jones's action was, itself, the cause of the action (though I am really not sure what this means). Say, instead, that natural events or circumstances caused Jones to act. Even say that Jones's action had no cause at all. The argument outlined above remains unaffected. If eighty years prior to Saturday, God believed that Jones would mow his lawn at that time, it was not within Jones's power at the time of action to refrain from mowing his lawn. The reasoning that justifies this assertion makes no mention of a causal series preceding Jones's action.

Secondly, consider the following line of thinking. Suppose Jones mowed his lawn last Saturday. It was then *true* eighty years ago that Jones would mow his lawn at that time. Hence, on Saturday, Jones was not able to refrain from mowing his lawn. To suppose that he was would be to suppose that he was able on Saturday to do something that would have made false a proposition that was *already true* eighty years earlier. This general kind of argument for determinism is usually associated with Leibniz, although it was anticipated in Chapter IX of Aristotle's *De Interpretatione*. It has been used since, with some modification, in Richard Taylor's article, "Fatalism."[11] This argument, like the one I have offered above, makes no use of the notion of causation. It turns, instead, on the notion of its being *true eighty years ago* that Jones would mow his lawn on Saturday.

I must confess that I share the misgivings of those contemporary philosophers who have wondered what (if any) sense can be attached to a statement of the form "it was true at T_1 that E would occur at T_2."[12] Does this statement mean that had someone believed, guessed, or asserted at T_1 that E would occur at T_2, he would have been right?[13] (I shall have something to say about this form of determinism later in this paper.) Perhaps it means that at T_1 there was sufficient evidence upon which to predict that E would occur at T_2.[14] Maybe it means neither of these. Maybe it means nothing at all.[15] The argument presented above presupposes that it makes straightforward sense to suppose that God (or just anyone) held a true belief eighty years prior to Saturday. But this is not to suppose that *what* God believed *was true eighty years prior to Saturday*. Whether (or in what sense) it was true eighty years ago that Jones would mow his lawn on Saturday is a question I shall not discuss. As far as I can see, the argument in which I am interested requires nothing in the way of a decision on this issue.

II

I now want to consider three comments on the problem of divine foreknowledge which seem to be instructively incorrect.

A. Leibniz analyzed the problem as follows:

> They say that what is foreseen cannot fail to exist and they say so truly; but it follows not that what is foreseen is necessary. For necessary truth is that whereof the contrary is

impossible or implies a contradiction. Now the truth which states that I shall write tomorrow is not of that nature, it is not necessary. Yet, supposing that God foresees it, it is necessary that it come to pass, that is, the consequence is necessary, namely that it exist, since it has been foreseen; for God is infallible. This is what is termed a *hypothetical necessity*. But our concern is not this necessity; it is an abso*lute* necessity that is required, to be able to say that an action is necessary, that it is not contingent, that it is not the effect of free choice.[16]

The statement "God believed at T_1 that Jones would do X at T_2" (where the interval between T_1 and T_2 is, for example, eighty years) does not entail "'Jones did X at T_2' is necessary." Leibniz is surely right about this. All that will follow from the first of these statements concerning "Jones did X at T_2" is that the latter is true, not that it is necessarily true. But this observation has no real bearing on the issue at hand. The following passage from St. Augustine's formulation of the problem may help to make this point clear.

> Your trouble is this. You wonder how it can be that these two propositions are not contradictory and incompatible, namely that God has foreknowledge of all future events, and that we sin voluntarily and not by necessity. For if, you say, God foreknows that a man will sin, he must necessarily sin. But if there is necessity there is no voluntary choice of sinning, but rather fixed and unavoidable necessity.[17]

In this passage, the term "necessity" (or the phrase "by necessity") is not used to express a modal-logical concept. The term "necessity" is here used in contrast with the term "voluntary," not (as in Leibniz) in contrast with the term "contingent." If one's action is necessary (or by necessity), this is to say that one's action is not voluntary. Augustine says that if God has foreknowledge of human actions, the actions are necessary. But the form of this conditional is "P implies Q," not "P implies $N(Q)$."

"Q" in the consequent of this conditional is the claim that human actions are not voluntary—that is, the one is not able, or does not have the power, to do other than he does.

Perhaps I can make this point clearer by reformulating the original problem in such a way as to make explicit the modal operators working within it. Let it be *contingently* true that Jones did X at T_2. Since God holds a belief about the outcome of each human action well in advance of its performance, it is then *contingently true* that God believed at T_1 that Jones would do X at T_2. But it follows from this that it is *contingently* true that at T_2 Jones was not able to refrain from doing X. Had he been (contingently) able to refrain from doing X at T_2, then either he was (contingently) able to do something at T_2 that would have brought it about that God held a false belief at T_1, or he was (contingently) able to do something at T_2 that would have brought it about that God believed otherwise than He did at T_1, or he was (contingently) able to do something at T_2 that would have brought it about that God did not exist at T_1. None of these latter is an acceptable alternative.

B. In *Concordia Liberi Arbitrii*, Luis de Molina wrote as follows:

> It was not that since He foreknew what would happen from those things which depend on the created will that it would happen; but, on the contrary, it was because such things would happen through the freedom of the will, that He foreknew it; and that He would foreknow the opposite if the opposite was to happen.[18]

Remarks similar to this one can be found in a great many traditional and contemporary theological texts. In fact, Molina assures us that the view expressed in this passage has always been "above controversy"—a matter of "common opinion" and "unanimous consent"—not only among the Church fathers, but also, as he says, "among all catholic men."

One claim made in the above passage seems to me to be truly "above controversy." With respect to any given action foreknown by God, God would have foreknown the opposite if the opposite was to happen. If we assume the notion of omniscience outlined in the first section of this paper, and if we agree that omniscience is part of the "essence" of God, this statement is a conceptual truth. I doubt if anyone would be inclined to dispute it. Also involved in this passage, however, is at least the suggestion of a doctrine that cannot be taken as an item of "common opinion" among *all* catholic men. Molina says it is not because God foreknows what He foreknows that men act as they do: it is because men act as they do that God foreknows what He foreknows. Some theologians have rejected this claim. It seems to entail that men's actions determine God's cognitions. And this latter, I think, has been taken by some theologians to be a violation of the notion of God as self-sufficient and incapable of being affected by events of the natural world.[19] But I shall not develop this point further. Where the view put forward in the above passage seems to me to go wrong in an interesting and important way is in Molina's claim that God can have foreknowledge of things that will happen "through the freedom of the will." It is this claim that I here want to examine with care.

What exactly are we saying when we say that God can know in advance what will happen *through the freedom of the will*? I think that what Molina has in mind is this. God can know in advance that a given man is going to choose to perform a certain action sometime in the future. With respect to the case of Jones mowing his lawn, God knew at T_1 that Jones would *freely* decide to mow his lawn at T_2. Not only did God know at T_1 that Jones would mow his lawn at T_2. He also knew at T_1 that this action would be performed freely. In the words of Emil Brunner, "God knows that which will take place in freedom in the future as something which happens in freedom."[20] What God knew at T_1 is that Jones would *freely* mow his lawn at T_2.

I think that this doctrine is incoherent. If God knew (and thus believed) at T_1 that Jones would do X at T_2,[21] I think it follows that Jones was not able to do other than X at T_2 (for reasons already given). Thus, if God knew (and thus believed) at

T_1 that Jones would do X at T_2, it would follow that Jones did X at T_2, but not freely. It does not seem to be possible that God could have believed at T_1 that Jones would freely do X at T_2. If God believed at T_1 that Jones would do X at T_2, Jones's action at T_2 was not free; and if God also believed at T_1 that Jones would freely act at T_2, it follows that God held a false belief at T_1—which is absurd.

C. Frederich Schleiermacher commented on the problem of divine foreknowledge as follows:

> In the same way, we estimate the intimacy between two persons by the foreknowledge one has of the actions of the other, without supposing that in either case, the one or the other's freedom is thereby endangered. So even the divine foreknowledge cannot endanger freedom.[22]

St. Augustine made this same point in *De Libero Arbitrio*. He said:

> Unless I am mistaken, you would not directly compel the man to sin, though you knew beforehand that he was going to sin. Nor does your prescience in itself compel him to sin even though he was certainly going to sin, as we must assume if you have real prescience. So there is no contradiction here. Simply you know beforehand what another is going to do with his own will. Similarly God compels no man to sin, though he sees beforehand those who are going to sin by their own will.[23]

If we suppose (with Schleiermacher and Augustine) that the case of an intimate friend having foreknowledge of another's action has the same implications for determinism as the case of God's foreknowledge of human actions, I can imagine two positions which might then be taken. First, one might hold (with Schleiermacher and Augustine) that God's foreknowledge of human actions cannot entail determinism—since it is clear that an intimate friend can have foreknowledge of another's voluntary actions. Or, secondly, one might hold that an intimate friend cannot have foreknowledge of another's voluntary actions—since it is clear that God cannot have foreknowledge of such actions. This second position could take either of two forms. One might hold that since an intimate friend *can* have foreknowledge of another's actions, the actions in question cannot be voluntary. Or, alternatively, one might hold that since the other's actions *are* voluntary, the intimate friend cannot have foreknowledge of them.[24] But what I propose to argue in the remaining pages of this paper is that Schleiermacher and Augustine were mistaken in supposing that the case of an intimate friend having foreknowledge of other's actions has the same implications for determinism as the case of God's foreknowledge of human actions. What I want to suggest is that the argument I used above to show that God cannot have foreknowledge of voluntary actions cannot be used to show that an intimate friend cannot have foreknowledge of another's actions. Even if one holds that an intimate friend *can* have foreknowledge of another's voluntary actions, one ought not to think that the case is the same when dealing with the problem of divine foreknowledge.

Let Smith be an ordinary man and an intimate friend of Jones. Now, let us start by supposing that Smith believed at T_1 that Jones would do X at T_2. We make no assumption concerning the truth or falsity of Smith's belief, but assume only that Smith held it. Given only this much, there appears to be no difficulty in supposing that at T_2 Jones was able to do X and that at T_2 Jones was able to do not-X. So far as the above description of the case is concerned, it might well have been within Jones's power at T_2 to do something (namely, X) which would have brought it about that Smith held a true belief at T_1, and it might well have been within Jones's power at T_2 to do something (namely, not-X) which would have brought it about that Smith held a false belief at T_1. So much seems apparent.

Now let us suppose Smith *knew* at T_1 that Jones would do X at T_2. This is to suppose that Smith correctly believed (with evidence) at T_1 that Jones would do X at T_2. It follows, to be sure, that Jones did X at T_2. But now let us inquire about what Jones was *able* to do at T_2. I submit that

there is nothing in the description of this case that requires the conclusion that it was not within Jones's power at T_2 to refrain from doing X. By hypothesis, the belief held by Smith at T_1 was true. Thus, by hypothesis, Jones did X at T_2. But even if we assume that the belief held by Smith at T_1 was *in fact* true, we can add that the belief held by Smith at T_1 *might* have turned out to be false.[25] Thus, even if we say that Jones *in fact* did X at T_2, we can add that Jones *might not* have done X at T_2—meaning by this that it was within Jones's power at T_2 to refrain from doing X. Smith held a true belief which might have turned out to be false, and, correspondingly, Jones performed an action which he was able to refrain from performing. Given that Smith correctly believed at T_1 that Jones would do X at T_2, we can still assign Jones the *power* at T_2 to refrain from doing X. All we need add is that the power in question is one which Jones *did not exercise*.

These last reflections have no application, however, when dealing with God's foreknowledge. Assume that God (being essentially omniscient) existed at T_1, and assume that He believed at T_1 that Jones would do X at T_2. It follows, again, that Jones did X at T_2. God's beliefs are true. But now, as above, let us inquire into what Jones was *able* to do at T_2. We cannot claim now, as in the Smith case, that the belief held by God at T_1 was *in fact* true but *might* have turned out to be false. No sense of "might have" has application here. It is a conceptual truth that God's beliefs are true. Thus, we cannot claim, as in the Smith case, that Jones *in fact* acted in accordance with God's beliefs but had the *ability* to refrain from so doing. The ability to refrain from acting in accordance with one of God's beliefs would be the ability to do something that would bring it about that one of God's beliefs was false. And no one could have an ability of this description. Thus, in the case of God's foreknowledge of Jones's action at T_2, if we are to assign Jones the ability at T_2 to refrain from doing X, we must understand this ability in some way other than the way we understood it when dealing with Smith's foreknowledge. In this case, either we must say that it was the ability at T_2 to bring it about that

God believed otherwise than He did at T_1; or we must say that it was the ability at T_2 to bring it about that any person who believed at T_1 that Jones would do X at T_2 (one of whom was, by hypothesis, God) held a false belief and thus was not God. But, as pointed out earlier, neither of these last alternatives can be accepted.

The important thing to be learned from the study of Smith's foreknowledge of Jones's action is that the problem of divine foreknowledge has as one of its pillars the claim the truth is *analytically* connected with God's *beliefs*. No problem of determinism arises when dealing with human knowledge of future actions. This is because truth is not analytically connected with human belief even when (as in the case of human knowledge) truth is contingently conjoined to belief. If we suppose that Smith knows at T_1 that Jones will do X at T_2, what we are supposing is that Smith believes at T_1 that Jones will do X at T_2 and (as an additional, contingent, fact) that the belief in question is true. Thus having supposed that Smith knows at T_1 that Jones will do X at T_2, when we turn to a consideration of the situation of T_2 we can infer (1) that Jones *will* do X at T_2 (since Smith's belief is true), and (2) that Jones does not have the power at T_2 to do something that would bring it about that Jones did not *believe* as he did at T_1. But paradoxical though it may seem (and it seems paradoxical only at first sight), Jones can have the power at T_2 to do something that would bring it about that Smith did not have *knowledge* at T_1. This is simply to say that Jones can have the *power* at T_2 to do something that would bring it about that the belief held by Smith at T_1 (which was, in fact, true) was (instead) false. We are required only to add that since Smith's belief was in fact true (that is, was knowledge) Jones *did not* (in fact) *exercise* that power. But when we turn to a consideration of God's foreknowledge of Jones's action at T_2 the elbowroom between belief and truth disappears and, with it, the possibility of assigning Jones even the *power* of doing other than he does at T_2. We begin by supposing that God *knows* at T_1 that Jones will do X at T_2. As above, this is to suppose that God believes at T_1 that Jones will do X at T_2, and it is to suppose that this belief

is true. But it is *not* an additional, contingent fact that the belief held by God is true. "God believes X" entails "X is true." Thus, having supposed that God knows (and thus believes) at T_1 that Jones will do X at T_2, we can infer (1) that Jones *will do* X at T_2 (since God's belief is true); (2) that Jones does not have the power at T_2 to do something that would bring it about that God did not hold the belief He held at T_1, and (3) that Jones does not have the power at T_2 to do something that would bring it about that the belief held by God at T_1 was false. This last is what we could *not* infer when truth and belief were only factually connected—as in the case of Smith's knowledge. To be sure, "Smith knows at T_1 that Jones will do X at T_2" and "God knows at T_1 that Jones will do X at T_2" both entail "Jones will do X at T_2" ("A knows X" entails "X is true"). But this similarity between "Smith knows X" and "God knows X" is not a point of any special interest in the present discussion. As Schleiermacher and Augustine rightly insisted (and as we discovered in our study of Smith's foreknowledge) the mere fact that someone knows in advance how another will act in the future is not enough to yield a problem of the sort we have been discussing. We begin to get a glimmer of the knot involved in the problem of divine foreknowledge when we shift attention away from the *similarities* between "Smith knows X" and "God knows X" (in particular, that they both entail "'X' is true") and concentrate instead on the logical *differences* which obtain between Smith's knowledge and God's knowledge. We get to the difference which makes the difference when, after analyzing the notion of knowledge as true belief (supported by evidence) we discover the radically dissimilar relations between truth and belief in the two cases. When truth is only factually connected with belief (as in Smith's knowledge) one can have the power (though, by hypothesis, one will not exercise it) to do something that would make the belief false. But when truth is analytically connected with belief (as in God's belief) no one can have the power to do something which would render the belief false.

To conclude: I have assumed that any statement of form "A knows X" entails a statement of the form "*A* believes *X*" as well as a statement of the form "'*X*' is true." I have then supposed (as an analytic truth) that if a given person is omniscient, that person (1) holds no false beliefs, and (2) holds beliefs about the outcome of human actions in advance of their performance. In addition, I have assumed that the statement "if a given person is God that person is omniscient" is an a priori statement. (This last I have labeled the doctrine of God's essential omniscience.) Given these items (plus some premises concerning what is and what is not within one's power), I have argued that if God exists, it is not within one's power to do other than he does. I have inferred from this that if God exists, no human action is voluntary.

As emphasized earlier, I do not want to claim that the assumptions underpinning the argument are acceptable. In fact, it seems to me that a theologian interested in claiming both that God is omniscient and that men have free will could deny any one (or more) of them. For example, a theologian might deny that a statement of the form "*A* knows *X*" entails a statement of the form "*A* believes *X*" (some contemporary philosophers have denied this) or, alternatively, he might claim that this entailment holds in the case of human knowledge but fails in the case of God's knowledge. This latter would be to claim that when knowledge is attributed to God, the term "knowledge" bears a sense other than the one it has when knowledge is attributed to human beings. Then again, a theologian might object to the analysis of "omniscience" with which I have been working. Although I doubt if any Christian theologian would allow that an omniscient being could believe something false, he might claim that a given person could be omniscient

although he did not hold beliefs about the outcome of human actions *in advance* of their performance. (This latter is the way Boethius escaped the problem.) Still again, a theologian might deny the doctrine of God's essential omniscience. He might admit that if a given person is God that person is omniscient, but he might deny that this statement formulates an a priori truth. This would be to say that although God is omniscient, He is not *essentially* omniscient. So far as I can see, within the conceptual framework of theology employing any one of these adjustments, the problem of divine foreknowledge outlined in this paper could not be formulated. There thus appears to be a rather wide range of alternatives open to the theologian at this point. It would be a mistake to think that commitment to determinism is an unavoidable implication of the Christian concept of divine omniscience.

But having arrived at this understanding, the importance of the preceding deliberations ought not to be overlooked. There is a pitfall in the doctrine of divine omniscience. That knowing involves believing (truly) is surely a tempting philosophical view (witness the many contemporary philosophers who have affirmed it). And the idea that God's attributes (including omniscience) are essentially connected to His nature, together with the idea that an omniscient being would hold no false beliefs and would hold beliefs about the outcome of human actions in advance of their performance, might be taken by some theologians as obvious candidates for inclusion in a finished Christian theology. Yet the theologian must approach these items critically. If they are embraced together, then if one affirms the existence of God, one is committed to the view that no human action is voluntary.

NOTES

1. *Consolatio Philosophiae*, Bk. V, sec. 3, par. 6.

2. This position is particularly well formulated in St. Anselm's *Proslogium*, ch. xix and *Monologium*, chs. xxi–xxii; and in Frederich Schleiermacher's *The Christian Faith*, Pt. 1, sec. 2, par. 51. It is also

explicit in Boethius, op. cit., secs. 4–6, and in St. Thomas' *Summa Theologica*, Pt. 1, Q. 10.

3. This point is explicit in Boethius, op. cit., secs. 4–6.

4. This position is particularly well expressed in William Paley's *Natural Theology*, ch. xxiv. It is also

involved in John Calvin's discussion of predestination, *Institutes of the Christian Religion*, Bk. III, ch. xxi; and in some formulations of the first cause argument for existence of God, e.g., John Locke's *Essay Concerning Human Understanding*, Bk. IV, ch. x.

5. *Institutes of the Christian Religion*, Bk. III, ch. xxi; this passage trans. by John Allen (Philadelphia, 1813), II, 145.

6. Ibid., p. 144.

7. *City of God*, Bk. V, sec. 9.

8. The notion of someone being *able* to do something and the notion of something being within one's power are essentially the same. Traditional formulations of the problem of divine foreknowledge (e.g., those of Boethius and Augustine) made use of the notion of what is (and what is not) *within one's power*. But the problem is the same when framed in terms of what one is (and one is not) *able* to do. Thus, I shall treat the statements "Jones was able to do *X*," "Jones had the ability to do *X*," and "It was within Jones's power to do *X*" as equivalent. Richard Taylor, in "I Can," *Philosophical Review*, LXIX (1960), 78–89, has argued that the notion of ability or power involved in these last three statements is incapable of philosophical analysis. Be this as it may, I shall not here attempt such an analysis. In what follows I shall, however, be careful to affirm only those statements about what is (or is not) within one's power that would have to be preserved on any analysis of this notion having even the most distant claim to adequacy.

9. In Bk. II, ch. xxi, secs. 8–11 of the *Essay*, John Locke says that an agent is not *free* with respect to a given action (i.e., that an action is done "under necessity") when it is not within the agent's power to do otherwise. Locke allows a special kind of case, however, in which an action may be *voluntary* though done under necessity. If a man chooses to do something without knowing that it is not within his power to do otherwise (e.g., if a man chooses to stay in a room without knowing that the *room* is locked), his action may be voluntary though he is not free to forbear it. If Locke is right in this (and I shall not argue the point one way or the other), replace "voluntary" with (let us say) "free" in the above paragraph and throughout the remainder of this paper.

10. *Summa Theologica*, Pt. 1, Q. 14, a. 8.

11. *Philosophical Review*, LXXI (1962), 56–66. Taylor argues that if an event *E* fails to occur at T_2, then at T_1 it was true that *E* would fail to occur at T_2. Thus, at T_1, a necessary condition of anyone's performing an action sufficient for the occurrence of *E* at T_2 is missing. Thus at T_1, no one could have the power to perform an action that would be sufficient for the occurrence of *E* at T_2. Hence, no one has the power at T_1 to do something sufficient for the occurrence of an event at T_2 that is not going to happen. The parallel between this argument and the one recited above can be seen very clearly if one reformulates Taylor's argument, pushing back the time at which it was true that *E* would not occur at T_2.

12. For a helpful discussion of difficulties involved here, see Rogers Albritton's "Present Truth and Future Contingency," a reply to Richard Taylor's "The Problem of Future Contingency," both in the *Philosophical Review*, LXVI (1957), 1–28.

13. Gilbert Ryle interprets it this way. See "It Was to Be," *Dilemmas* (Cambridge, 1954).

14. Richard Gale suggests this interpretation in "Endorsing Predictions," *Philosophical Review*, LXX (1961), 378–385.

15. This view is held by John Turk Saunders in "Sea Fight Tomorrow?" *Philosophical Review*, LXVII (1958), 367–378.

16. *Theodicée*, Pt. 1, sec. 37. This passage trans. by E. M. Huggard (New Haven, 1952), p. 144.

17. *De Libero Arbitrio*, Bk. III. This passage trans. by J. H. S. Burleigh, *Augustine's Earlier Writings* (Philadelphia, 1955).

18. This passage trans. by John Mourant, *Readings in the Philosophy of Religion* (New York, 1954), p. 426.

19. Cf. Boethius' *Consolatio*, Bk. V, sec. 3, par. 2.

20. *The Christian Doctrine of God*, trans. by Olive Wyon (Philadelphia, 1964), p. 262.

21. Note: no comment here about freely doing *X*.

22. *The Christian Faith*, Pt. 1, sec. 2, par. 55. This passage trans. by W. R. Matthew (Edinburgh, 1928), p. 228.

23. Loc. cit.

24. This last seems to be the position defended by Richard Taylor in "Deliberation and

Foreknowledge," *American Philosophical Quarterly*, 1 (1964).

25. The phrase "might have" as it occurs in this sentence does not express mere *logical* possibility. I am not sure how to analyze the notion of possibility involved here, but I think it is roughly the same notion as is involved when we say, "Jones might have been killed in the accident (had it not been for the fact that at the last minute he decided not to go)."

I.B.8

God's Foreknowledge and Human Free Will Are Compatible

ALVIN PLANTINGA

Alvin Plantinga (1932–) was, until his retirement, professor of philosophy at the University of Notre Dame and is one of the most important figures in the fields of metaphysics, epistemology, and the philosophy of religion. His works include God and Other Minds *(1957),* The Nature of Necessity *(1974), and* God, Freedom, and Evil *(1974). In this article, Plantinga appeals to the notion of possible worlds in order to show that Pike's logic misfires and that there really is no incompatibility between divine foreknowledge and human free will.*

The last argument I wish to discuss is perhaps only mildly atheological. This is the claim that God's omniscience is incompatible with *human freedom.* Many people are inclined to think that if God is omniscient, then human beings are never free. Why? Because the idea that God is omniscient implies that at any given time God knows not only what *has* taken place and what is taking place, but also what *will* take place. He knows the future as well as the past. But now suppose He knows that Paul will perform some trivial action tomorrow— having an orange for lunch, let's say. If God knows in advance that Paul will have an orange for lunch tomorrow, then it must be the case that he'll have an orange tomorrow; and if it *must* be the case that Paul will have an orange tomorrow, then it isn't possible that Paul will *refrain* from so doing—in which case he won't be free to refrain, and hence won't be free with respect to the action of taking the orange. So if God knows in advance that a person will perform a certain action A, then that person isn't free with respect to that action. But if God is omniscient, then for any person and any action he performs, God knew in advance that he'd perform that action. So if God is omniscient, no one ever performs any free actions.

Reprinted from Alvin Plantinga, *God, Freedom and Evil* (New York: Harper & Row, 1974), pp. 66–72, by permission of the author.

This argument may initially sound plausible, but the fact is it is based upon confusion. The central portion can be stated as follows:

(49) If God knows in advance that X will do A, then it must be the case that X will do A

and

(50) If it must be the case that X will do A, then X is not free to refrain from A.

From (49) and (50) it follows that if God knows in advance that someone will take a certain action, then that person isn't free with respect to that action. But (49) bears further inspection. Why should we think it's *true*? Because, we shall be told, if God knows that X will do A, it *logically follows* that X will do A: it's necessary that if God knows that p, then p is true. But this defense of (49) suggests that the latter is *ambiguous*; it may mean either

(49a) Necessarily, if God knows in advance that X will do A, then indeed X will do A

or

(49b) If God knows in advance that X will do A, then it is necessary that X will do A.

The atheological argument requires the truth of (49b); but the above defense of (49) supports only (49a), not (49b). It is indeed necessarily true that if God (or anyone else) knows that a proposition P is true, then P is true; but it simply doesn't follow that if God knows P, then P is necessarily true. *If I know that Henry is a bachelor, then Henry is a bachelor* is a necessary truth; it does not follow that if I know that Henry is a bachelor, then it is necessarily true that he is. I know that Henry is a bachelor: what follows is only that *Henry is married* is false; it doesn't follow that it is necessarily false.

So the claim that divine omniscience is incompatible with human freedom seems to be based upon confusion. Nelson Pike has suggested[1] an interesting revision of this old claim: he holds, not that human freedom is incompatible with God's being omniscient, but with God's being *essentially* omniscient. Recall ... that an object X has a property P essentially if X has P in every world in which X exists—if, that is, it is impossible that X should have existed but lacked P. Now many theologians and philosophers have held that at least some of God's important properties are essential to him in this sense. It is plausible to hold, for example, that God is essentially omnipotent. Things could have gone differently in various ways; but if there had been no omnipotent being, then God would not have existed. *He* couldn't have been powerless or limited in power. But the same may be said for God's *omniscience*. If God is omniscient, then He is unlimited in knowledge; He knows every true proposition and believes none that are false. If He is *essentially* omniscient, furthermore, then He not only *is not* limited in knowledge; He *couldn't* have been. There is no possible world in which He exists but fails to know some truth or believes some falsehood. And Pike's claim is that this belief—the belief that God is essentially omnipotent—is inconsistent with human freedom.

To argue his case Pike considers the case of Jones who mowed his lawn at T_2—last Saturday, let's say. Now suppose that God is essentially omniscient. Then at any earlier time T_1—80 years ago, for example—God believed that Jones would mow his lawn at T_2. Since He is *essentially* omniscient, furthermore, it isn't possible that God falsely believes something; hence His having believed at T_1 that Jones would mow his lawn at T_2 entails that Jones does indeed mow his lawn at T_2. Pike's argument (in his own words) then goes as follows:

1. "God existed at T_1" entails "if Jones did X at T_2, God believed at T_1 that Jones would do X at T_2."
2. "God believes X" entails "X is true."
3. It is not within one's power at a given time to do something having a description that is logically contradictory.
4. It is not within one's power at a given time to do something that would bring it about that someone who held a certain belief at a time prior to the time in question did not hold that belief at the time prior to the time in question.

5. It is not within one's power at a given time to do something that would bring it about that a person who existed at an earlier time did not exist at that earlier time.

6. If God existed at T_1 and if God believed at T_1 that Jones would do X at T_2, then if it was within Jones' power at T_2 to refrain from doing X, then (1) it was within Jones' power at T_2 to do something that would have brought it about that God held a false belief at T_1, or (2) it was within Jones' power at T_2 to do something which would have brought it about that God did not hold the belief He held at T_1, or (3) it was within Jones' power at T_2 to do something that would have brought it about that any person who believed at T_1 that Jones would do X at T_2 (one of whom was, by hypothesis, God) held a false belief and thus was not God—that is, that God (who by hypothesis existed at T_1) did not exist at T_1.

7. Alternative 1 in the consequent of item 6 is false (from 2 and 3).

8. Alternative 2 in the consequent of item 6 is false (from 4).

9. Alternative 3 in the consequent of item 6 is false (from 5).

10. Therefore, if God existed at T_1 and if God believed at T_1 that Jones would do X at T_2, then it was not within Jones' power at T_2 to refrain from doing X (from 1 and 10).[2]

What about this argument? The first two premises simply make explicit part of what is involved in the idea that God is essentially omniscient; so there is no quarreling with them. Premises 3–5 also seem correct. But that complicated premise (6) warrants a closer look. What exactly does it say? I think we can understand Pike here as follows. Consider

(51) God existed at T_1, and God believed at T_1 that Jones would do X at T_2, and it was within Jones' power to refrain from doing X at T_2.

What Pike means to say, I believe, is that either (51) entails

(52) It was within Jones' power at T_2 to do something that would have brought it about that God held a false belief at T_1

or (51) entails

(53) It was with Jones' power at T_2 to do something that would have brought it about that God did not hold the belief He did hold at T_1

or it entails

(54) It was within Jones' power at T_2 to do something that would have brought it about that anyone who believed at T_1 that Jones would do X at T_2 (one of whom was by hypothesis God) held a false belief and thus was not God—that is, that God (who by hypothesis existed at T_1) did not exist at T_1.

[The remainder of Pike's reasoning consists in arguing that each of (52), (53), and (54) is necessarily false, if God is essentially omniscient; hence (51) is necessarily false, if God is essentially omniscient, which means that God's being essentially omniscient is incompatible with human freedom.] Now suppose we look at these one at a time. Does (51) entail (52)? No. (52) says that it was within Jones' power to do something—namely, refrain from doing X—such that if he had done that thing, then God *would* have held a false belief at T_1. But this does not follow from (51). If Jones had refrained from X, then a proposition that God *did in fact* believe would have been false; but if Jones had refrained from X at T_2, then God (since He is omniscient) *would not have believed at* T_1 *that Jones will do X at* T_2. What follows from (51) is not (52) but only (52'):

(52') It was within Jones' power to do something such that if he had done it, then a belief that God *did hold at* T_1 *would have been false.*

But (52') is not at all paradoxical and in particular does not imply that it was within Jones' power to do something that would have brought it about that God held a false belief.

Perhaps we can see this more clearly if we look at it from the vantage point of possible worlds. We are told by (51) both that in the actual world God believes that Jones does X at T_2 and also that it is within Jones' power to *refrain* from doing X at T_2. Now consider any world W in which Jones *does* refrain from doing X. In *that* world, a belief that God holds in the actual world—in Kronos—is false. That is, if W had been actual, then a belief that God *does in fact* hold would have been false. But it does not follow that in W God holds a false belief. For it doesn't follow that if W had been actual, God would have believed that Jones would do X at T_2. Indeed, if God is essentially omniscient (omniscient in every world in which He exists) what follows is that in W God did not believe at T_1 that Jones will do X at T_2; He believed instead that Jones will *refrain* from X. So (51) by no means implies that it was within Jones' power to bring it about that God held a false belief at T_1.

What about

(53) It was within Jones' power at T_2 to do something that would have brought it about that God did not hold the belief He did hold at T_1?

Here the first problem is one of understanding. How are we to take this proposition? One way is this. What (53) says is that it was within Jones' power, at T_2, to do something such that if he had done it, then at T_1 God would have held a certain belief and also not held that belief. That is, (53) so understood attributes to Jones the power to bring about a contradictory state of affairs [call this interpretation (53a)]. (53a) is obviously and resoundingly false; but there is no reason whatever to think that (51) entails it. What (51) entails is rather

(53b) It was within Jones' power at T_2 to do something such that if he had done it, then God would not have held a belief that in fact he did hold.

This follows from (51) but is perfectly innocent. For suppose again that (51) is true, and consider a world W in which Jones refrains from doing X. If

God is essentially omniscient, then in this world W He is omniscient and hence does not believe at T_1 that Jones will do X at T_2. So what follows from (51) is the harmless assertion that it was within Jones' power to do something such that if he had done it, then God would not have held a belief that in fact (in the actual world) He did hold. But by no stretch of the imagination does it follow that if Jones had done it, then it would have been true that God *did* hold a belief He didn't hold. Taken one way (53) is obviously false but not a consequence of (51); taken the other it is a consequence of (51) but by no means obviously false.

(54) fares no better. What it says is that it was within Jones' power at T_2 to do something such that if he had done it, then God would not have been omniscient and thus would not have been God. But this simply doesn't follow from (51). The latter does, of course, entail

(54′) It was within Jones' power to do something such that if he'd done it, then anyone who believed at T_1 that Jones would do X at T_2 would have held a false belief.

For suppose again that (51) is in fact true, and now consider one of those worlds W in which Jones refrains from doing X. In that world

(55) Anyone who believed at T_1 that Jones will do X at T_2 held a false belief

is true. That is, if W had been actual, (55) would have been true. But again in W God does not believe that Jones will do X at T_2; (55) is true in W but isn't relevant to God there. If Jones had refrained from X, then (55) would have been true. It does not follow that God would not have been omniscient; for in those worlds in which Jones does not do X at T_2, God does not believe at T_1 that He does.

Perhaps the following is a possible source of confusion here. If God is *essentially* omniscient, then He is omniscient in every possible world in which He exists. Accordingly there is no possible world in which He holds a false belief. Now consider any belief that God does in fact hold. It might be tempting to suppose that if He is essentially omniscient, then He holds that belief in every world in which He exists. But of course this doesn't follow. It is not essential to Him to hold the beliefs He does hold; what is essential to Him is the quite different property of holding only true beliefs. So if a belief is true in Kronos but false in some world *W*, then in Kronos God holds that belief and in *W* He does not.

Much more should be said about Pike's piece, and there remain many fascinating details. I shall leave them to you, however. And by way of concluding our study of natural atheology: none of the arguments we've examined has prospects for success; all are unacceptable. There are arguments we haven't considered, of course; but so far the indicated conclusion is that natural atheology doesn't work.

NOTES

1. Nelson Pike, "Divine Omniscience and Voluntary Action," *Philosophical Review* 74 (January 1965): 27.

2. Ibid., pp. 33–34.

I.B.9

Can God Be Free?

WILLIAM ROWE

William Rowe (1931–) is emeritus professor of philosophy at Purdue University and the author of numerous books and articles in the philosophy of religion, including Can God Be Free?, *a book which develops at greater length the argument of the present selection. In this article, Rowe argues for the conclusion that if there is a best creatable world, then a morally perfect God would have to create that world; and if there is no best creatable world, then either there is no morally perfect God or God is not the creator.*

The question, Can God Be Free?, is an important philosophical question. But before endeavoring to answer this question, there are two preliminary points that must be discussed. The first, and most important, is this: What conception of God is being presupposed when we ask whether or not God can be free? The conception of God presupposed here is the idea of God that has been dominant in the major religions of the West—Judaism, Christianity, and Islam. The dominant idea of God in these religious traditions is of a being who necessarily exists and is necessarily all-powerful, all-knowing, and perfectly good. Thus when we ask whether God exists, we here mean to be asking whether there is a being who necessarily exists and is necessarily all-powerful, all-knowing, and perfectly good.

Reprinted from *Faith and Philosophy* 19 (2002): 405–424. Used with permission.

Of course, it is no easy matter to say in any precise way just what it is for a being to be all-powerful, all-knowing, and perfectly good. Nevertheless, we will presuppose here that some plausible account can be given of these attributes. Second, when we ask whether God can be free, we need to first ask: "free with respect to what?" Clearly, in an important sense God is not free with respect to doing evil, for if he were free with respect to doing evil he would be free to cease to be perfectly good. But if there is such a being as God he is no more free to cease to be perfectly good than he is free to cease to exist, to cease to be all-powerful, or to cease to be all-knowing. God is necessarily perfectly good, all-powerful, and all-knowing. He is, therefore, not free to cease to possess these perfections. Hence, in our question "Can God be Free?" we are not asking whether God can be free with respect to his essential attributes. For the answer to that question is clearly negative. What then are we asking about when we ask whether God can be free? We are asking whether God is free with respect to *creating a world*. And one persistent theme in the great religious traditions of the West is that God does enjoy freedom with respect to creating a world. This freedom is thought to be twofold:

1. God was free to refrain from creating any world at all;

   and,

2. God was free to create other worlds instead of the world he did in fact create.

So, supposing there is such a being as God, the question we shall explore here is whether God was free not to create at all, and free to have created other worlds than the one he has created. If we assume with Leibniz that among possible worlds there is one that is best, it is difficult to see how the best possible being (God) would be free to create some world other than the best. But before we pursue the question of whether God must create the best possible world, it will be helpful here to pause in our discussion and try to get clearer about the notion of a possible world and some related concepts.

Often we think that although things are a certain way they didn't have to be that way, they could have been different. Suppose we were late getting to class today. We believe, however, that things could have turned out differently. Had we not stopped on the way to chat with a friend, for example, we almost certainly would have been on time. So, what we may call the *actual* state of affairs, our being late for class, need not have been actual at all. Here then we make a distinction between two possible states of affairs—ways things might be—and note that although one is actual (our being late for class today), the other (our being on time for class) was possible, it could have been actual instead. The link between possible states of affairs that are not actual and our common ways of thinking about the world lies in our frequent belief that things could have been otherwise. Whenever we correctly think that things could have gone in a way different from the way they actually went, we are distinguishing between some possible state of affairs that is actual (the way things did go) and some possible state of affairs that didn't become actual (the way things could have gone but didn't). Every state of affairs that is actual is clearly a *possible* state of affairs, one that, logically speaking, could be actual. But, as we've seen in the example of our not being late for class, possible states of affairs may fail to be actualized. Perhaps, then, we should think of a possible state of affairs as one that could be actual and could fail to be actual. But this view overlooks a useful distinction philosophers draw between a state of affairs that is *possible* and a state of affairs that is *contingent*. A contingent state of affairs is a possible state of affairs that may be actual or fail to be actual. Since a possible state of affairs is one that could be actual, if it is also such that it could fail to be actual (like, for example, our being on time for class today), then it is a *contingent* state of affairs. It can be actual and can fail to be actual. But some states of affairs are such that although they are possible, and therefore can be actual, they cannot fail to be actual, they *must be* actual. These possible states of affairs are necessary, not contingent. Consider the state of affairs consisting in the number three's being larger than the number two.

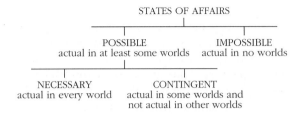

STATES OF AFFAIRS

POSSIBLE
actual in at least some worlds

IMPOSSIBLE
actual in no worlds

NECESSARY
actual in every world

CONTINGENT
actual in some worlds and
not actual in other worlds

Certainly, this state of affairs is possible—it's not like there being an object that is both square and round, an impossible state of affairs. So, it is a possible state of affairs. But is it contingent? Could it have failed to be actual. No. The number three's being larger than the number two is not just possible, it is also necessary, it obtains in every possible world. So, while many possible states of affairs are contingent in that they obtain in some worlds but not in others,[1] many possible states of affairs are necessary, they obtain in every possible world. The Diagram above shows the way philosophers often distinguish among states of affairs.

In order to grasp the idea of a *possible world* it is helpful to consider two important relations among states of affairs: *inclusion* and *preclusion*. A state of affairs S *includes* a state of affairs S* just in case it is impossible that S should obtain and S* not obtain. (For example, *Gordie Howe's being the greatest hockey player of the 20th century* includes *someone's being the greatest hockey player of the 20th century*.) S precludes S* just in case it is impossible that S obtain and S* obtain. (So, *Gordie Howe's being the greatest hockey player of the 20th century* precludes *Wayne Gretsky's being the greatest hockey player of the 20th century*.) Following Alvin Plantinga, we can now say what it is for a state of affairs to be *maximal* and, therefore, a *possible world*. "A State of affairs S is . . . *maximal* if for every state of affairs S', S includes S' or S precludes S'. And a possible world is simply a possible state of affairs that is maximal."[2]

Having seen that a possible world is a maximal state of affairs, we can now consider what it is for a possible world to be better than some other possible world. Some states of affairs may be said to be intrinsically better than other states of affairs. For example, following Samuel Clarke we may say that *there being innocent beings who do not suffer eternally* is

necessarily better than *there being innocent beings who do suffer eternally*. Of the second of these two states of affairs we would say that it is a bad state of affairs, something that ought not to be. But the first state of affairs is not a bad state of affairs. The basic idea here is that some states of affairs possess intrinsic value. That is, they may be intrinsically good, intrinsically bad, or intrinsically neutral (neither good nor bad). They are intrinsically good by virtue of containing intrinsically good qualities such as happiness, love, enjoyment, beauty, good intentions, or the exercise of virtue.[3] And states of affairs are intrinsically bad by virtue of containing intrinsically bad qualities such as unhappiness, hate, dissatisfaction, ugliness, bad intentions, or the exercise of vice. Still other states of affairs, may contain little or no intrinsic value. *There being stones*, for example, is a state of affairs that contains little if any intrinsic value. Such states of affairs are, we might say, intrinsically neutral. But *someone's being happy*, for example, is an intrinsically good state of affairs, while *someone's being unhappy* is an intrinsically bad state of affairs.

One might infer from the preceding paragraph that if God exists, the world he creates would not include any bad states of affairs.[4] However, supposing it would be in God's power to create such a world, there are at least two reasons to question this inference. First, as theodicists have argued since the time of Augustine, freedom of the will, if not itself a great intrinsic good, appears to be indispensable for some of the very important goods we know of—freely given love, freely sacrificing for the well-being of others, freely chosen acts of charity, etc. Indeed, from the point of view of the creator it might well be uninteresting to create beings who are programmed from the start to worship God, to honor him, to do good to others. From the perspective of the creator it may well be better to have beings who can freely choose to love and worship or not to love and worship, for love and worship that is freely given is of much greater value than love and worship that is compelled. But if God does choose to create a world with creatures free to do good or evil, the world may include evil as a result of some of their free choices.[5] Second, there is a principle, *the Principle of Organic Unities*,[6] held by a number of philosophers from Leibniz to the present day. According to this principle, the intrinsic value of a whole may not be equal to the sum of the intrinsic value of each of its parts. Compare, for example, *Jones's feeling happy upon contemplating torturing an innocent human being* with *Jones's feeling unhappy upon contemplating torturing an innocent human being*. The difference between these two states of affairs is that the first contains an intrinsically good state (Jones's feeling happy) as a part, whereas the second contains an intrinsically bad state (Jones feeling unhappy) as a part. But surely the first state as a whole is a much worse state of affairs than the second. So, while a given part of a whole may be intrinsically good (Jones's feeling happy), the whole of which it is a part may be worse for the presence of the good part than it would be were a certain bad part (Jones's feeling unhappy) to be in its place. So, for all we know, the best world may include some intrinsically bad states of affairs. It hardly follows from this consideration that there may be tears in heaven, but it does suggest that we should hesitate to conclude too much from the mere presence of some tears on earth. For, as we've seen, a state of affairs that constitutes an *organic unity* may be better for the presence of a bad part than it would be were the bad part replaced by a good part. So, again, we must note that a possible world with some bad parts may be better than a possible world with no bad parts.

We've seen that the good-making qualities (happiness, love, enjoyment, beauty, good intentions, an exercise of virtue, etc.) figure in states of affairs (e.g., someone's being happy, someone's loving another, etc.) that are intrinsically good; whereas the bad-making qualities (unhappiness, hate, dissatisfaction, ugliness, bad intentions, or the exercise of vice) figure in states of affairs (e.g., someone's being unhappy, someone's hating another, etc.) that are intrinsically bad. It is important, however, to distinguish the *intrinsic* value of someone's being unhappy from the *extrinsic* value of someone's being unhappy. The intrinsic value of a state of affairs is inherent in that state of affairs—it necessarily belongs to that state of affairs no matter

what that state of affairs is a part of or what the circumstances are in which it occurs. But the extrinsic value of a state of affairs may change from one set of circumstances to another. Sometimes, for example, a person's being unhappy is productive of good, in which case it may be a good thing (i.e., it may be extrinsically good) for that person to be unhappy. But that doesn't affect the matter of the intrinsic value of someone's being unhappy. For it is a good thing that the person was unhappy only in the sense of what that person's unhappiness leads to, or is a necessary part of, not in terms of its own intrinsic value. Unhappiness, in itself, is always bad. In addition, we should not confuse the intrinsic value of a state of affairs with the intrinsic value of a state of affairs of which it is a part. As we've noted someone's being unhappy on contemplating the undeserved suffering of others is a better state of affairs than someone's being happy on contemplating the undeserved suffering of others. But that truth is entirely compatible with someone's being happy necessarily being *intrinsically better than* someone's being unhappy. For the intrinsic value of the part, someone's being unhappy, must not be confused with the intrinsic value of the whole (someone's being unhappy on contemplating the undeserved suffering of others) of which it is a part.

Since a possible world just is a *maximal* state of affairs, its value will reflect the values of the states of affairs contained in it. So, possible worlds themselves will be intrinsically good, intrinsically bad, or intrinsically neutral. In addition one possible world will be intrinsically better than, equal to, or worse than another possible world. And, as Leibniz noted, it is by knowing the intrinsic values of the possible worlds that God is guided in his choice of a world to create.

We are now in a position to consider seriously our question: Is God free with respect to creating a world? Assuming that God exists, this question falls into two parts: (1) Was God free to refrain from creating any world at all?; (2) Was God free to create other worlds instead of the world he did in fact create? Let's begin with our second question. We earlier noted that possible worlds can be ranked according to their value all the way from bad worlds, to neutral worlds, and then to good worlds. Suppose then that God chooses to display his goodness and power in creating a world. We can imagine God, as it were, surveying all these worlds and deciding which one to create. He considers all the bad worlds, the neutral worlds (neither good nor bad) and all the good worlds. Let's suppose, along with Leibniz and Samuel Clarke, that the series of increasingly good worlds culminates in the best possible world, a world than which no possible world is as good or better. Similarly, we can suppose that the series of increasingly bad worlds culminates in a world than which no possible world is as bad or worse.[7] Faced with choosing from among these two series of worlds the world he shall create, it is obvious that an infinitely good being would not, indeed *could not*, create one of the bad worlds. Which good world would he then create? Again, it seems obvious that he would create the very best world, the best of all possible worlds. As Leibniz points out since "to do less good than one could is to be lacking in wisdom or in goodness," the most perfect understanding "*cannot fail* to act in the most perfect way, and consequently to choose the best."[8] In a well-known essay[9] Robert Adams has argued on the basis of the doctrine of divine grace that God would not be morally obligated to create the best world that he can. But even if his argument is successful, it still may be necessary for God to create the best world he can. It just won't be his moral duty.[10] In short, his creating the best world may be a supererogatory act, the morally best act he can do, even if his failure to do it would not be a violation of his moral duty. And it appears to be inconceivable that a supremely perfect being would act to bring about less good than he can. On the assumption that God (the supremely perfect being) exists and that there is a best, creatable world, we've reached the conclusion that God is neither free not to create a world nor free to create a world less than the best creatable world. Indeed, God would of necessity create the best of the creatable worlds, leaving us with no basis for thanking him, or praising him for creating the world he does. For given that God exists and that there is a best creatable world, God's nature as an omnipotent, omniscient,

perfectly good being would require him to create that best world. Doing less than the best he can do—create the best creatable world—would be inconsistent with his being the perfect being he is.

But what if there is no best world? What if, as Aquinas thought to be true, for each creatable world there is a better world that God can create instead?[11] In short, there is no best world. Here, I believe, in supposing that God exists and creates a world when for every creatable world there is a better creatable world, we are supposing a state of affairs that is simply impossible. I'm not suggesting here that there is an impossibility in the idea that God exists. Nor am I suggesting that there is an impossibility in the idea that for every creatable world there is a better creatable world. I am suggesting that there is an impossibility in the idea both that God exists and creates a world and that for every creatable world there is a better creatable world. For whatever world God would create he would be doing less good than he can do. And it is impossible for God to do less good than he can. The underlying principle yielding the conclusion that there is an impossibility in the idea both that God creates a world and that for every creatable world there is a better creatable world is the following:

> If an omniscient being creates a world when there is a better world it could create, then it would be possible for there be a being morally better than it.

Since God is a being than which it is not possible for there to be a morally better being, it is clear, given both the principle just cited and the no best world hypothesis, that God could not exist and be the creator of a world. For any being that exists and creates a world when there is a better world it could have created instead is, according to the principle cited above, a being than which a morally better being is possible, and, therefore, not the best possible being. So the issue now before us is whether this principle (if an omniscient being creates a world when there is a better world it could create, then it would be possible for there to be a being morally better than it) is indeed true. My own view is that the principle in question will appear to many to be plausible, if not self-evident. For if an omniscient being creates a world when it could have created a better world, then that being has done something less good than it could do (create a better world). But any being who knowingly does something (all things considered) less good than it could do falls short of being the best possible being. So, unless we find some reason to reject the principle stated above or a reason to reject the line of argument supporting it, we are at the very least within our rights to accept it and use it as a principle in our reasoning. But the result of using this principle in our reasoning about God and the world is just this: if the actual world is not the best world that an omnipotent, omniscient being could create, God does not exist. God does not exist because were he to exist and create a world when there is a better world he could have created instead, then he would be a being than which a better being is possible. For he himself would have been a better being had he created a better world. But since it is not possible for any being (including God) to be better than God (the best possible being) in fact is, the world God has created must be the very best world he could have created. Therefore, if God does exist and creates a world W, W is the very best among the worlds that God could have created. W is the best creatable world. Hence, we see the problem of no best creatable world. For if for every creatable world there is a better creatable world and our principle is true, God does not exist. What then can be said against the principle: if an omniscient being creates a world when there is a better world it could create, then it would be possible for there to be a being morally better than it?

We may begin by considering the view set forth by Norman Kretzmann in his perceptive study of Aquinas's view of creation. In the course of his discussion of Aquinas, Kretzmann concludes with Aquinas that for any world God might create there is a better world he could create. (His disagreement with Aquinas concerns only whether God is free not to create at all.) Kretzmann's second conclusion—the one presently of interest to us—is that it is a *mistake* to think (as I do) that if God exists and cannot avoid choosing something less

good than he could choose, then God cannot be essentially perfectly good. And he proceeds to explain why he thinks it is a mistake.

> Like Aquinas, I think that the logical truth that God's actions conform to the principle of noncontradiction entails no limit on his power. And if it would be a violation of the principle of non-contradiction for God to create a world better than any other world he could create, then a fortiori that logical truth which does not diminish his power also leaves his *goodness* undiminished. God's being that than which nothing better can be conceived of cannot entail his producing a world than which none better can be conceived of. No matter which possible world he actualizes, there must be infinitely many possible worlds better than the actual world in some respect or other.[12]

Kretzmann relies on what he takes to be an analogy or parallel between power and goodness. His idea is this. Since we agree that failure to bring about what is logically impossible does not imply any limit on God's power, we should also agree that failure to bring about what is logically impossible does not diminish God's goodness. Given that there is no best possible world, Kretzmann points out that it is logically impossible for God to create a world better than any other world he could create. So, the fact that God does not create such a world diminishes neither his power nor his goodness. And that being so, Kretzmann sees no difficulty in God's being perfectly good and creating a world less good than other creatable worlds.

Perhaps we can view Kretzmann as appealing to the following principle:

A. If S is a logically impossible state of affairs, then the fact that a being does not bring about S does not entail that the being in question lacks power or perfect goodness.

This principle strikes me as self-evidently true. The fact that God fails to do what *logically cannot be done* is a bad reason to think that God is morally imperfect or lacking in power. On Aquinas's view it is logically impossible for God to create the best possible world. And since he cannot do that, the fact that he doesn't do it, as Kretzmann notes, implies no imperfection in God. I entirely agree with Kretzmann's point on this. But the fact that there is a bad reason to conclude that God is not perfectly good does not mean that there is no good reason to conclude that God is not perfectly good. And the fact that God fails to do what *logically can be done* may be a good reason to conclude that God is not perfectly good.[13] The principle that provides this good reason is the principle we've already introduced and will now refer to as "Principle B."

> B. If an omniscient being creates a world when there is a better world that it could have created, then it is possible that there exists a being morally better than it.[14]

If B is true, as I think it is, and if it is also true that

> C. If a being is essentially perfectly good then it is not possible that there exist a being morally better than it,

then if it is true that for any creatable world there is another creatable world better than it, it is also true that *no* omnipotent, omniscient being who creates a world is essentially perfectly good. Moreover, if we add to this Kretzmann's first conclusion that a perfectly good, omnipotent, omniscient being *must* create, it will follow that there is no omnipotent, omniscient, perfectly good being.

Suppose Aquinas and Kretzmann are right in believing that for any creatable world there is another creatable world that is better than it. Our second objection emerges when we consider what the theistic God is to do in this situation. If some creatable world is better than any world God alone inhabits, then, on my principle B (slightly extended) it appears that God must create some world. On the other hand, as we've just seen, on my principle B it also follows that he cannot create a world if some other creatable world is better. "So," the objector now concludes, "on your principle B it follows that God must create a world and also must not create a

world. Surely, then, since your principle leads to a contradiction, however plausible principle B sounds, we must reject it."

My response to this objection is that on the supposition that for every creatable world there is another world that is better than it, principle B does not lead to a contradiction. What principle B leads to is the conclusion that there is no essentially omnipotent, omniscient, perfectly good being.

But is principle B true? Daniel and Frances Howard-Snyder have endeavored to refute principle B by inviting us to consider three hypothetical world creators: Jove, Juno and Thor.[15] They suppose Jove to be an omnipotent, omniscient being who is confronted with an infinite number of increasingly better possible worlds from which to select one to create. Jove, they suggest, decides to create one of these good worlds by using a randomizing device. Being good, Jove has no interest in creating a world that isn't good.[16] Each of the infinite number of good worlds is assigned a positive natural number beginning with "1" for the least good world, "2" for a slightly better world, and so on. Jove uses the randomizing device to pick one of these good worlds, and, as a result, world no. 777 is created. Now, of course, Jove could have created a better world. But the Howard-Snyders think that it does not follow from this fact that Jove is *morally surpassable*. That is, from the fact that Jove could have created a better world than the world he did create (no. 777), they think that it does not follow that it is *logically possible* for there to have existed a being with a degree of moral goodness in excess of Jove's.[17]

In a response to their article[18] I suggested the following:

> In support of their view the Howard-Snyders, invite us to consider other possible omnipotent, omniscient[19] world creators, Juno and Thor, and argue that although they produce morally better worlds than Jove, they are not morally better creators. Juno does just what Jove did but her randomizing machine happens to select a better world, no. 999. Thor

doesn't use a randomizing machine but selects world no. 888 over Jove's world no. 777 because he sees that it is better and prefers creating no. 888 to creating any lesser world. Even though Juno ends up producing a better world than Jove, the Howard-Snyders are clearly right in viewing Jove and Juno as morally equivalent. For had her randomizing machine hit on world 777, rather than world 999, Juno would have created world 777. So, it was blind luck, not a higher standard of selection, that resulted in Juno's selection of world 999. But what of Thor? From their discussion it would seem that Thor is morally superior to Jove and Juno, for it looks as though Thor's degree of moral goodness is such that he is not prepared to settle for world no. 777 *unless* he is unable to create a better world. But the fact that Jove intentionally included worlds numbered 1–777 as possibilities for selection by his randomizing machine shows that Jove is morally prepared to settle for any of the worlds from 1–777 *even though* he is able to create a better world.[20] So, it does appear that, other things being equal, Thor is a morally better being than Jove.[21]

In a subsequent article[22] against principle B, the Howard-Snyders question my account of Thor, suggesting that it is incoherent. They wonder what principle or reason Thor acts on. They say:

> For example, suppose Thor's reason is this: worlds numbered 888 and higher are better than worlds numbered 887 and lower. (This seems to be the reason that Rowe has Thor act on. See the quotation above.) This reason relies on the general principle that if world w is better than world w-1, then w-1 is unacceptable for creation. Any being who accepted an instance of this principle when it involved the world no. 888 but did not accept other instances of it would be irrational, and hence not essentially omniscient. Any being who accepted

the principle in its full generality would be led never to create, given (as we are supposing) that for each world there is a better.[23]

This leads them to suggest that my account of Thor is *incoherent*. But I believe it is clear from my article that I do not have Thor act on the principle "don't create if there is a better creatable world," for such a principle, given that for any world there is a better, can only result in Thor's not creating any world at all. Since Thor is *omniscient* and does in fact create world 888, it logically follows that he cannot act on the principle that they suggest I have him act on. Of course, while Thor, given his infinite intelligence, cannot act on such a principle, it doesn't follow that with finite intelligence I cannot make the mistake of attributing to Thor such a principle of action when he creates world 888. So, what principle do I have Thor act on? I believe that the principle on which Thor acts is very much like the principle on which Jove acts. Let's look again at Jove. Some worlds he sees as not good enough to be acceptable as candidates for creation. The worlds that are acceptable to him in terms of his own degree of goodness are then ordered in terms of increasing goodness, and one of them, world 777, is randomly selected for creation. Thor, as I have described him, does pretty much the same thing. The difference is that worlds 1–800 are insufficiently good to be acceptable to him as candidates for creation, given that there are better worlds he can create. The worlds that are acceptable to him in terms of his own degree of goodness are then ordered in terms of increasing goodness and one of them, world 888, is randomly selected for creation. I conclude that the description the Howard-Snyders give of Jove is logically consistent with there being a being who is better than Jove. And the story we have told about Thor is consistent and, if true, gives us reason to believe that Thor is a better being than Jove.

Can we state the principles on which both Jove and Thor act, and explain how it is that although they act on the same principles, they produce worlds that differ in their degree of goodness?

I suggest that Jove and Thor may act on the following principles:

P1. Do not create any world that is not a good world.

P2. Do not create any good world whose goodness is less than what one judges as *acceptable*, given that one can create a better world.

Clearly, both Thor and Jove act in accordance with P1 and P2. Neither is prepared to create a less than good world. And neither is prepared to create a good world whose degree of goodness is less than what he judges as acceptable in a world, given that he can create a better world. The difference between them is this. Jove's standard of goodness in world creating is such that he is prepared to settle for *any* good world even if there is a better that he can create. Thor, however, has a higher standard. He is not prepared to create any of the good worlds from W1 to W800 *provided* there is a better world that he can create. Of course, Thor's allegiance to P2 does not preclude him absolutely from creating, say, W777. It prevents him only on the condition that there is a better world he can create. Gala apples taste much better than Jonathan apples. I know that, and my standard of apple selection is never to come home with Jonathan apples when Gala are available. But that doesn't mean I won't or can't select Jonathan apples when Gala apples are not available. A good apple, even if it's a Jonathan, is better than no apple at all.

In their article the Howard-Snyders suppose that it cannot be that Thor and Jove act on the *same* principle. They suppose that if my story about Thor being better than Jove is correct then Thor must be acting on a *higher principle* than the principle on which Jove acts. And, since there will be worlds better than the world Thor creates, they then conclude that "there is another principle which treats as unacceptable some of the worlds which were treated as acceptable by Thor's principle, and that other principle is such that there is a third principle which treats as unacceptable some of the worlds which were treated as acceptable by the second, and so on, *ad infinitum*." Lacking a proof of the impossibility of such an infinite array of world-creating principles, they say,

> It seems odd to say the least that there should be infinitely many such general principles. At least we see no reason to accept that there are.[24]

As I've tried to make clear above, the story I tell is quite consistent even if there is no such infinite progression of world-creating principles. Principles P1 and P2 will suffice so long as for any being in the position of Jove or Thor there is another being whose degree of goodness is such that its application of P1 and P2 results in the selection of a better world to create. And if we allow, as the Howard-Snyders do, an infinite number of possible worlds beginning with Jove's good world W1, why not allow the possibility of an infinite series of good world creators each being better than the preceding one. Indeed, why not allow, if needed, an infinite number of different but related world-creating principles. But, as I've suggested, I don't see the necessity of supposing that my story is coherent only if there is an infinite number of distinct world-creating principles. But suppose an infinite number of such principles is required. Perhaps it is odd at that there should be infinitely many world-creating principles. But even if it is odd, we should note that oddness and impossibility are far different matters. Many extremely odd things are logically possible. And if it is logically possible that there is an absolutely infinite number of increasingly better worlds, why should it be impossible that there be an infinite number of principles of world creation? In any case, however, I see no reason to think that there need be an infinite number of such principles in order for the story of Thor and Jove to be coherent. Indeed, I have suggested that Jove and Thor can act on the very same principles. Moreover, since it is possible that there be world creators whose degrees of goodness increasingly exceed Thor's, it is possible that the very same principles would result in increasingly better beings creating increasingly better worlds than Thor's world.

The fundamental question at issue in the discussion concerning Jove and Thor is this: Is it logically possible both that for any creatable world there is a better creatable world and that there exists an omnipotent, omniscient, perfectly good being who creates one of these creatable worlds? My position is that it is not possible that both should be true.

Why do I hold this position? I hold it because, as I've stated earlier, I think the following [Principle B] is necessarily true.

B. If an omniscient being creates a world when it could have created a better world, then it is possible that there be a being morally better than it.[25]

By telling their story about Jove, the Howard-Snyders hoped to cast doubt on Principle B. I believe that my alternative story about Thor undermines their attempt. Where does this leave us? I assert that B is necessarily true. Many theists assert the following [Principle A] to be true.

A. It is logically possible both that for any creatable world there is a better creatable world and that there exists an omnipotent, omniscient, perfectly good being who creates one of these worlds.

Both of us cannot be right. But how can we hope to settle the question of who has the more plausible position? Are we simply at a stalemate, a situation where neither can show the other's position to be implausible without employing as a premise one of the principles that is at issue in the debate? I believe that the Howard-Snyders have endeavored to advance the debate in a way that does not beg the question. They suppose both that Jove is an omnipotent, omniscient creator of a good world (# 777) and that for every creatable world there is a better, but leave as an open question whether Jove's goodness can be unsurpassable. The question then is whether we have some good reason to think that an omnipotent, omniscient creator of a better world than # 777 may be better than Jove. As we've seen, the answer depends on the *reason* such a being has for creating a better

world than # 777. If such a being (their Juno), given her degree of goodness, judges as acceptable for creation the *same* worlds as Jove, then the fact that her randomizer selects world # 999 for creation gives us no reason at all to think that Juno is a better being than Jove, even though she ends up creating a better world than does Jove. But if, like Thor, the being's degree of goodness is such that he judges that worlds of lesser value than # 800 are unacceptable candidates for creation, then the fact that its randomizer selects world # 800 or higher gives us reason to think that Thor is a better being than Jove. Of course, if we had simply concluded that Jove's goodness is surpassable because Jove could have created a world better than # 777, this would have been to beg the question at issue. For we would have been appealing to Principle B to rule out Jove being an unsurpassably good being. But no such appeal was made in reasoning to the conclusion that Thor is a better being than Jove.

Principle B, if true, does not refute theism. But if both Principle B and theism are true, then the world we live in is an unsurpassably good world—no possible world that an omnipotent being could have created would be better than the actual world. I suspect that part of the motivation for the theist to accept the view that there is no best creatable world is that the alternative seems (1) to limit severely God's freedom in creating, and (2) to leave the theist with the burden of defending the Leibnizian thesis that this world, with all its evil, is a world than which a better creatable world is not even a logical possibility.

Thomas Morris, like the Howard-Snyders and Kretzmann, thinks that among the worlds creatable by God there is no best world. He notes two difficulties in the Liebnizian idea that there is a best possible world. First, he points out that some philosophers are doubtful that there is a single scale on which all creaturely values can be weighted so as to determine what world possesses the maximum amount of value. "Some world A might be better than rival world B in some respects, but with B surpassing A in others, and the relevant values not such that they could be summed over and compared overall."[26] In short, if some valuable states of affairs are incommensurable with other valuable states of affairs, it may be impossible to rank the states of affairs in terms of one being better than, worse than, or equal to the other. And if that should be so, we could have two worlds such that neither is better than the other, worse than the other, or equal in value with the other. Second, Morris notes that a number of philosophers have thought that for any world containing "a certain number of goods, n, there is always conceivable a greater world with $n + 1$ goods, or good creatures. So, on the simplest grounds of additive value alone, it seems impossible there could be a single best possible world. And without this, of course, the Leibnizian demand collapses."[27] But Morris's main concern lies elsewhere. Like the Howard-Snyders and Kretzmann, Morris wants to show that there is no incoherence in the idea of a *perfectly good* creator creating a world when there is *no best world* for that being to create.

> For just as it seems initially very natural to suppose that a superlatively good, wise, and powerful being will produce only an unsurpassable perfect creation, so likewise it can seem every bit as natural to suppose that an incoherence or impossibility discovered in the latter notion indicates an incoherence or impossibility buried within the former.[28]

Since it is just that incoherence we have been arguing for, it is important to note Morris's efforts to show that the incoherence in question is imagined, and not real. Noting that Quinn holds that in the no best world scenario a creator of a world is such that "it is possible that there is an agent morally better than he is, namely an omnipotent moral agent who actualizes one of those morally better worlds," and Rowe holds "if a being were to create a world when there is a morally better world it could create, then it would be possible for there to be a being morally better than it," Morris states that these views are "absolutely unacceptable to traditional theists, for whom both perfection and creation are important ideas."[29]

In developing his objection to the views expressed by Quinn and Rowe, Morris introduces

a useful thesis—*the Expression Thesis: The goodness of an agent's actions is expressive of the agent's goodness.* I'm inclined to take something like this thesis as underlying the claim expressed in Principle B: If an omniscient being creates a world when it could have created a better world, then it is possible that there be a being morally better than it. Of course, the expression thesis depends on what Morris may well have supposed: that the agent's motive for performing the good action is to bring about a good state of affairs. Without supposing that motive we have no reason to think that the goodness of an agent's action—measured in terms of the quality of its result—is expressive of the agent's goodness. But what are we to say of a being who performs an action that he knows will bring about less good, all things considered, than he could have brought about by performing a slightly different action? In this case, applying the expression thesis, we should conclude that the agent's degree of goodness is something less that it could be. For the agent has acted to bring about less good than he knew would have been brought about by his performing a slightly different action. But clearly, if an agent knowingly acts to bring about less good overall than he could have brought about by performing a slightly different action that was in his power to perform, that agent's degree of moral goodness is somewhat less than it could be. And it is precisely this point that underlies the judgment that in the no best world scenario it is impossible for the creator to be perfectly good. For, as we saw in the discussion of the Howard-Snyders story about Jove, Juno, and Thor, when a being creates a world that is less good than another world it could have created, the world it creates will satisfy its standard of world-creating, even given that it could create a better world. But then it is possible that there should be a being whose degree of goodness is such that it will not create that less good world given that it is able to create a better world. So, again I conclude that if a being creates a world when it could have created a better world, then it is possible that there should be a being morally better than it. And from this it follows that if for every creatable world there is a better creatable world, there is no absolutely perfect being who creates a world. And since it is better to create a good world rather than not create any world at all, on the no best creatable world scenario there is no maximally perfect being.

Morris's basic mistake, I believe, is his view, shared by Kretzmann, that to hold, as I do, that if there is no best world for a being to create then no being can create a world and be a being than which a better creator is impossible, just is to hold God accountable for not doing what is logically impossible to be done—creating the best world. Thus Morris writes:

> If you and I do less well than we're capable of doing, then those around us may conclude, and may sometimes justifiably conclude, that we are not at the level of goodness that could be exemplified. But failing to do the best you can is a flaw or manifests an incompleteness in moral character in this way only if doing the best you can is at least a logical possibility. If doing the best he can in creating a world is for God an impossibility, ... then not doing his best in creating cannot be seen as a flaw or as manifesting an incompleteness in the character of God. The notion of a perfect expression of an unsurpassable character would then itself be an incoherence.[30]

Of course, if it is logically impossible for there to be a best world, then God's not creating the best possible world does not count against his perfect goodness. Nowhere do I suggest that it does. What counts against God's perfect goodness (specifically, his moral perfection) is his creating a world when he could have created a world better than it. The charge is not that a being who fails to do what is impossible to be done (create the best world when there is no best world to be created) is lacking in perfect goodness. The charge is that a being who creates a world when it could have created a better world is less than supremely perfect. And the plain fact is that if there is no best creatable world then God, if he creates a world, will create a world than which he could have created a better world.[31] Morris simply fails to address the issue at stake here.

It is important to distinguish three different principles:

a. Failing to do the best one can is a defect only if doing the best one can is possible for one to do.

b. Failing to do better than one did is a defect only if doing better than one did is possible for one to do.

c. Failing to do better than one did is a defect only if doing the best one can is possible for one to do.

Both (a) and (b) are true. But (c) is not true. And it is (c) that Morris needs to make his argument work.

Suppose, for the moment, that you are an omnipotent, omniscient being and are contemplating the infinite series of numbers: 1, 2, 3, 4, etc., etc. You are also contemplating the infinite series of creatable worlds containing creatures that are overall good worlds, as opposed both to bad worlds and neutral worlds—worlds that are neither good nor bad. You let each of the numbers represent the overall degree of good that a possible world possesses, where "1" represents the least good world—a world with no pain perhaps, and just one momentary experience of pleasure on the part of some lower animal. "2" represents the possible world that is one degree better than the world 1, "3" represents the possible world that is one degree better than the world 2, etc., etc. Being omniscient you see that there is no best possible world for you to create. Just as the series of natural numbers increases infinitely so does the series of increasingly better worlds from which you will select one to create. Seeing that there is no best possible world to create, you realize that no matter how good a world you create there will be better worlds you could have chosen to create instead of it. Glancing at world 1, and comparing it with world 1000, you see that world 1000 is significantly better than world 1, just as you see that world 1,000,000 is significantly better than world 1000. Nevertheless, in spite of noticing the enormous disparity between the least good world and the goodness of some worlds numerically much greater, you decide that you will create the *least good* world and proceed to actualize world 1. Isn't it obvious that in deliberately choosing to create the *least good* of the infinite series of increasingly better possible, creatable worlds you display a degree of goodness in world-creating that is inconsistent with *perfect goodness*?

> "Wait!" you will say. "You judge me unfairly. I see that if I could have created a maximally good world I might be subject to some criticism here for creating a world so limited in value as world 1. But there is no maximally good world. So clearly I'm *perfectly justified* in creating the *poorest* in the infinite series of increasingly better worlds. You should not have any doubts at all about my being *perfectly good*!"

Surely this defense of one's "perfect goodness" is woefully inadequate. A perfectly good being cannot, consistent with its perfect goodness, consciously elect to create the least good world when there is an infinite number of increasingly better worlds as available for creation as the least good world. But it is just this conclusion that Morris's position would require us to accept. Since the conclusion is clearly false, if not absurd, we should reject it. Instead, we should say that the degree of goodness an omniscient being possesses is reflected in the degree of goodness in the world it creates. And what this reasoning leads us to is the conclusion Leibniz reached: An unsurpassably good, omnipotent, omniscient creator will create an unsurpassably good world. Indeed, unsurpassable goodness in an omnipotent, omniscient world-creator is consistent only with the creation of an unsurpassably good world. For there is an impossibility in the idea both that there exists an infinite series of increasingly better creatable worlds and that there also exists an unsurpassably good, omnipotent, omniscient being who creates one of these worlds.

The conclusion we've just reached points to an incompatibility between the necessary existence of the theistic God and the *possibility* Morris embraces: that the series of increasingly better creatable worlds goes on to infinity. But how could a mere possibility be inconsistent with the existence of the theistic

God? After all, isn't it one thing to conclude that God's infinite perfection precludes his actualizing a bad possible world, and quite another thing to conclude that God's infinite perfection precludes there even being such a thing as a bad possible world? And if God's existence doesn't rule out bad possible worlds, why should it rule out an infinite series of increasingly better possible worlds? The answer to these questions consists in seeing that if God necessarily exists and is necessarily such that whatever world is actual can be so only by virtue of his creating it, then since it is impossible for God (an absolutely perfect being) to create a bad world, there cannot be any bad worlds. In short, given God's necessary perfections and necessary existence, the only possible, non-actual worlds are worlds God *can create*. And once we see that given God's necessary existence and necessary perfections no world creatable by God can be a bad world, we are well on our way to seeing that it is likewise impossible that there should be an unending series of increasingly better creatable worlds.

Morris nicely captures the essence of the view I've just described by noting that such a God "is a delimiter of possibilities."

> If there is a being who exists necessarily, and is necessarily omnipotent, omniscient, and good, then many states of affairs which otherwise would represent genuine possibilities, and by all non-theistic tests of logic and semantics do represent possibilities, are strictly impossible in the strongest sense. In particular, worlds containing certain sorts or amounts of disvalue or evil are metaphysically ruled out by the nature of God, divinely precluded from the realm of real possibility.[32]

Return now to our earlier contention that possible worlds include very good worlds, neutral worlds, and very bad worlds. In addition we suggested that just as for every good world there is a better possible world, so too for every bad world there is a possible world whose degree of badness is greater. Morris will allow that such worlds are "conceivable." But since he holds that God is a *delimiter of possibilities* and that it is impossible for God to create a world that is a bad world, the bad worlds we conceive of are not, at least for the theist, *genuinely possible*. For the only way such worlds could be genuinely possible is for it to be possible for God to create them. But God's perfect nature necessarily precludes him from creating such worlds. Therefore, such worlds aren't really possible all things considered.

Morris's general point here strikes me as sound. If p is necessarily true and q is inconsistent with p, then, even though we can conceive of q and q seems to us to be a paradigm case of a genuine possibility, q isn't really possible at all. So, if there is a necessarily perfect being who necessarily exists, then even though we can *conceive* of a bad world, that bad world is really not a *possible world* provided that for a world to be actual it must be actualized by the necessarily perfect being. Consider, for example, a world in which nearly all the sentient beings have lives so full of suffering that it would be better had they never existed. Such a world is a bad world. Is this world, so understood, a possible world? It certainly seems to be. But given that a possible world can be actual only if it is created by a necessarily perfect being, and such a being necessarily exists, then that world really isn't a possible world, it only seems to be possible. Of course, what is sauce for the goose (Morris) is sauce for the gander (Rowe). If this bad world, which certainly seems to be possible, really is a possible world, then it is simply *impossible* that there is a necessarily perfect being who is necessarily the creator of any world that is actual. Which then are we more sure of: that some bad world is genuinely possible or that there necessarily exists a being who is necessarily omnipotent, omniscient, and perfectly good? The former is a "delimiter of necessities" just as the latter is a "delimiter of possibilities." Just as what is necessary precludes certain "possibilities," so does what is possible preclude certain "necessities." The theist begins with the necessary existence of a being who is essentially perfect and concludes that a bad world isn't even a possibility. The non-theist begins with the possibility of there being a bad world and concludes that there is no essentially perfect being who necessarily exists.

Suppose we accept Morris's view about God as a delimiter of possibilities. Suppose, that is, that we agree with him that if there is a being who exists necessarily, and is necessarily omnipotent, omniscient, and good, then many states of affairs which otherwise would have been possible are strictly impossible. If so, then if there is such a being we should agree that there are no possible worlds that are overall bad worlds. For such a world is possible only if it is possible for God to actualize that world. But God's necessary perfections preclude him from actualizing it. Therefore, such a world is not really a possible world.

Having adopted Morris's view that God is a delimiter of possibilities, suppose we now return to the stalemate between the view I've argued for:

> *It is impossible for God to exist and create an inferior world when he could have created a better world;*

and the view my opponent maintains:

> *God is free to create some good world even though there is an unlimited number of better worlds any one of which he could have created instead.*

My opponent may well agree with me that given God's absolute perfection God could not create a world less than the best world. In short, *if* there is a best world all things considered, we may both agree with Leibniz and Clarke that God will necessarily create that world. (Of course, there remains the problem of explaining the precise sense in which God could be *free* in creating the best possible world.) It is only when we come to the no best world scenario that our views clash so profoundly. But Morris, perhaps unwittingly, has shown us a way to resolve the problem. God is the ultimate *delimiter of possibilities*. Thus, if God exists the series of increasingly good possible worlds has a limit—the best possible world. A creator that is necessarily good could not possibly create a less than good world. So, given that this being is a delimiter of possibilities, there are no possible worlds that are not good worlds. Furthermore, a necessarily perfect being could not possibly create a world that is less good than some other world it could create. So, given that this being creates a world and is a delimiter of possibilities, the world he creates cannot be one than which there is a better creatable world. Thus, following the path that Morris has pointed out, we conclude that God's necessary existence and necessary perfections would rule out two seeming possibilities: (1) there being possible worlds that are bad; (2) there being no best possible world. If God exists, his necessary existence and necessary perfections rule out the apparent existence of possible worlds that are bad as well as the apparent possibility that for any world God can create there is

a better world he could create. What then should we conclude about the *actual* world? We should conclude that if the theistic God does exist, the actual world is the best possible world.[33] And therein lies the seeds of another argument against the existence of the God of traditional theism. For however much we may succeed in trying to fit the terrible evils in our world into some rational plan, few are prepared to think with Leibniz that this world is as good as any world could possibly be.

NOTES

1. In saying that a state of affairs *obtains* (or is *actual*) in a given possible world we mean that that state of affairs would be actual were that world the actual world.

2. Alvin Plantinga, *The Nature of Necessity* (Oxford: Oxford University Press, 1974), p. 45.

3. See Roderick M. Chisholm, "The Defeat of Good and Evil," in *The Problem of Evil*, ed. by Marilyn McCord Adams and Robert Merrihew Adams, (Oxford: Oxford University Press, 1990).

4. Actually, since possible worlds necessarily exist, God doesn't create them. But from the fact that a possible world exists, it doesn't follow that it is *actual*. Only one world can be the actual world. And what God does is create particular things—stones, human beings, etc.—and enable them to be arranged in such a way that a particular possible world is actualized. So, it is not in the literal sense of "creates" that God creates a world. With this understood, we will continue to refer to some possible world as being "created" by God.

5. But surely there would be possible worlds in which creatures are free to do good or evil and, as it happens, always use their freedom to do good. Wouldn't God create one of those worlds? For an impressive argument as to why it might not be in God's power to create such a world see Alvin Plantinga, *The Nature of Necessity* (Oxford University Press, 1974), Ch. IX.

6. See G. E. Moore, *Principia Ethica* (Cambridge: Cambridge University Press, 1903), pp. 187ff.

7. In the service of simplicity we will set aside the neutral worlds.

8. See Leibniz's *Theodicy*, trans. E. M. Huggard, ed. Austin Farrer (LaSalle, Ill: Open Court 1985), section 201. (Emphasis mine)

9. "Must God Create the Best?" *Philosophical Review* 81 (July 1972): 317–32.

10. I advance this point in "The Problem of Divine Perfection and Freedom," *Reasoned Faith*, ed. Eleonore Stump, Cornell University Press, 1993, 223–33.

11. Aquinas didn't understand a world to be a maximal state of affairs. But were he to have thought of a world in this way he would have asserted that there is no best world.

12. "A Particular Problem of Creation," 238.

13. In this discussion of Kretzmann I suppose, for effect, that it is possible for God to be less than perfectly good. What is true is that any being that fails to do what is the best it can do is not perfectly good and, therefore, not God.

14. As we noted earlier, a being may be perfectly morally correct in the sense of never failing in its obligations and still be such that it could be morally better by virtue of the performance of some supererogatory act.

15. Daniel and Frances Howard-Snyder, "How an Unsurpassable Being Can Create a Surpassable World," *Faith and Philosophy*, April, 1994.

16. In order not to beg the question at issue, the Howard-Snyders do not assume that Jove is morally unsurpassable.

17. In the context of this discussion, a being is morally unsurpassable only if it is logically impossible for there to be a morally better being.

18. "The Problem of No Best World," *Faith and Philosophy*, April, 1994.

19. For some reason the Howard-Snyders neglect to attribute omniscience to Juno and Thor. I assume this to be a slip. Clearly, if we want to compare their goodness to Jove's, we should attribute to them the infinite power and knowledge that was attributed to Jove. I'll return to this point in discussing Thor's degree of goodness.

20. And the same is true of Juno, even though she accidentally ends up with world no. 999.

21. It is important to note that to say one being is morally better than another is not to imply that the second being has done anything morally wrong or violated any moral obligation.

22. "The *Real* Problem of No Best World," *Faith and Philosophy*, July 1996.

23. Ibid., p. 423.

24. Ibid., p. 424.

25. Indeed, it is possible for that very being to have been better than it in fact is.

26. "Perfection and Creation," *Reasoned Faith*, ed. Eleonore Stump, Cornell University Press, 1993, 223–33.

27. Ibid, p. 237.

28. Ibid.

29. Ibid., p. 239.

30. Ibid., p. 244.

31. This is technically incorrect. For if there is no best world, but several worlds equally good and none better, then a being could freely chose one of these worlds to create. The reader is to understand that in supposing that there is no best world we are thinking only of the circumstance in which for every world there is a better world.

32. *Anselmian Explorations* (University of Notre Dame Press, 1987), p. 48.

33. If we countenance libertarian freedom among the creatures in the best possible world, it could be that the best possible world is not creatable by God. For if the creatures are free to do right or not do right, then it won't be entirely up to God whether the best world he can create is the best possible world. I ignore these complications here. But clearly they are important to a thorough discussion of the problem of divine freedom.

I.B.10

The Freedom of God

EDWARD WIERENGA

Edward Wierenga (1947–) is professor of philosophy at the University of Rochester. He is the author of The Nature of God, *and many other works in the philosophy of religion. In this article, Wierenga responds to William Rowe's argument for the conclusion that God cannot be free. After considering and rejecting several other responses to Rowe's argument, Wierenga defends the claim that God can be free with respect to an action, even when a logically sufficient condition of God's performing the action obtains.*

Reprinted from *Faith and Philosophy* 19 (2002): 425–436. Used with permission.

Discussions of God and freedom typically focus on the relation of God's knowledge to human freedom. Of course, if there really is a conflict between divine foreknowledge and human free action, there might be the same conflict between divine foreknowledge and God's own free action. Thus, when Evodius confessed that "if I say that God foreknows all of *my* actions, I can much more confidently say that he foreknows *his own* actions and foresees with absolute certainty what he is going to do," Augustine responded, "Then aren't you worried that someone might object that God himself will act out of necessity rather than by his will in everything that he is going to do? After all, you said that whatever God foreknows happens by necessity, not by will."[1] In this paper, however, I want to investigate a different problem for God's own freedom, one that he would not share with other agents whose future actions he foreknows. Instead, it is a problem that arises precisely because, on classical theism, God is so different from his creatures. In particular, God is essentially omniscient, omnipotent, and perfectly good, whereas presumably no creature has those attributes, not even accidentally. It would seem to follow, therefore, that whenever God is in circumstances C in which a certain action A is the best action, he would know that A is the best action, he would want to do A, and he would be able to do A. That is, from

(1) In C, A is the best action for God to do,

it seems to follow, given God's essential possession of these divine attributes, that

(2) In C God knows that A is the best action, wants to do A, and is able to do A.

But it also seems to be true that

(3) If in C God knows that A is the best action, wants to do A, and is able to do A, then God does A in C.

Indeed, (3) would seem to be a necessary truth—how could an omnibenevolent, omnipotent, and omniscient God fail to do what he knew to be best, wanted to do, and was able to do?[2] But then in virtue of God's essential perfections, whenever he is in circumstances in which a certain action

is the best, a logically sufficient condition obtains for his performing that action. But now a problem looms: if God is ever in such circumstances, it would seem that he is unable in those circumstances to refrain from performing the action in question. He could not refrain from performing the action in those circumstances, since it is impossible that he be in those circumstances and not perform it. As Thomas Flint puts it, characterizing this as a libertarian view of freedom, "an agent is truly free with respect to an action only if the situation in which he is placed is logically and causally compatible with both his performing and his not performing the action."[3] In this paper I will investigate the problem of divine freedom for an essentially perfect being, on the assumption that libertarianism is the correct view about freedom. In the following section I will consider a solution that holds that God need not do what is best. Next, I will consider the response that God at least sometimes finds himself in circumstances in which there is no unique best action, so there is at least a range of cases in which he is free. Finally, I shall offer my own solution that challenges some standard assumptions about what libertarianism requires.

I. MUST GOD CREATE THE BEST?

One way of avoiding this problem of divine freedom is to deny that God must do what is best. Robert Adams has defended this approach, holding that "*even if* there is a best among possible worlds, God could create another instead of it, and still be perfectly good."[4] Adams denies, in effect, the inference from (1) to (2). Now if God were in circumstances in which an action A is his best action, then it would be hard to reconcile his omniscience with his not knowing that A is best. And I take it that, as a more detailed presentation of the problem would have put it, if an action is the best action for an agent it is one of the agent's *alternatives*, that is, one of the actions *open to the agent*. So it would also be difficult to deny that God would be able to perform the best action, even apart from his omnipotence. But Adams' view holds that it does not follow from

God's perfect goodness that he would *want* to perform that action. This is suggested by Adams' remark quoted above, that God could fail to actualize the best possible world "and still be perfectly good." Moreover, Adams' defense of his position involves considering and rejecting reasons why God's failing to perform the best action would be wrong.

Adams concedes that "by utilitarian standards it is a moral obligation to bring about the best state of affairs that one can," but he rejects those standards in favor of ones he takes to be "more typical of Judeo-Christian religious ethics."[5] Accordingly, he casts about for other reasons why God's failing to actualize the best world would be wrong. He first considers the possibility that failing to actualize such a world would violate someone's rights, or involve treating someone unkindly, or harm someone. Adams has an ingenious response to this suggestion. He argues that if God were to harm anyone in his choice of a world, it would have to be someone he created. But by not actualizing the best possible world God would not harm the creatures existing in it *if* he failed to create them, since he could only have obligations to existing creatures. Next Adams claims that God could actualize a world having these features:

(i) None of the individual creatures in it would exist in the best of all possible worlds.

(ii) None of the creatures in it has a life which is so miserable on the whole that it would be better for that creature if it had never existed.

(iii) Every individual creature in the world is at least as happy on the whole as it would have been in any other possible world in which it could have existed.[6]

He then claims that if God does actualize a world having these features he does not wrong any of the creatures existing in it, "for none of them would have been benefitted by his creating any other world instead."[7] Hence if God does actualize a world satisfying these conditions, none of the creatures who would then exist would be harmed by God creating that world rather than a far better one. So if God could actualize a world satisfying

these three traits, it looks as though Adams is correct in holding that God need not harm anyone or violate any creature's rights if he were to do less than the best that is open to him. That still leaves it open that there might be another reason why a perfectly good being might want to do what is best, but it would not be for wanting to refrain from harming anyone.

Adams' second attempt to find a reason why a perfectly good being would want to do what is best is somewhat more complicated. Adams begins by inquiring whether choosing to make a world less good than he could have made would reveal a defect in God's *character*.[8] He notes that an ideal of Judeo-Christian moral theory is *grace*, which he defines as "a disposition to love which is not dependent on the merit of the person loved."[9] Adams then claims that "a God who is gracious with respect to creating might well choose to create and love less excellent creatures than he could have chosen."[10] Now if this is merely to identify *some* virtue God has that is compatible with doing less than his best, it would not *establish* that doing so is compatible with his moral goodness, for he might have *other virtues* not thus compatible. And it is not surprising that some virtues would be compatible with doing less than one's best. Adams in fact identifies as virtues being noble, being high-minded, and being free from envy,[11] all of which would seem to be compatible with doing less than what was best. So either Adams' defense is incomplete or else God's exercise of grace plays some positive role or makes some contribution to the value of his action (or to a world he actualizes) which enables it to provide a moral justification of God's doing less than his best.

However, Adams says something that initially suggests that he would deny that the exercise of grace makes such a contribution. After claiming that "a God who is gracious with respect to creating might well choose to create and love less excellent creatures than he could have chosen," he adds

> This is not to suggest that grace in creation consists in a preference for imperfection as such. God could have chosen to create the best of all possible creatures, and still have

been gracious in choosing them. God's graciousness in creation does not imply that the creatures he has chosen to create must be less excellent than the best possible. It implies, rather, that even if they are the best possible creatures, that is not the ground for his choosing them. And it implies that there is nothing in God's nature or character which would require him to act on the principle of choosing the best possible creatures to be the object of his creative powers.[12]

If God is gracious both in the best of all possible worlds (temporarily assuming with Adams that there is one) as well as in some lesser worlds, it is hard to see how his graciousness can make more of a difference in the value of one world rather than another.

There is a way of thinking of these things, however, that suggests that divine grace might actually make a difference to the value of a world. Perhaps in worlds with less perfect creatures God exercises *more* graciousness, or perhaps his graciousness is *more magnificent* for going so far beyond what is deserved. The former idea is suggested by a familiar question raised in Romans, "Should we continue in sin in order that grace may abound?" (Rom. 6:1b). Paul's answer, of course, is that eliciting additional grace is not a good reason to sin; but he does not deny the principles that added sin results in extra grace and that extra grace is a good thing. A related idea is that of *felix culpa*, as found in the *Exsultet: O felix culpa, quae talem ac tantum meruit habere Redemptorem*! ("Oh happy sin that merited so great a redeemer").[13] A way of understanding this thought is that God's gracious gift of redemption through the incarnation of his son makes such a contribution to the value of the world that its value exceeds that of a world in which no one sins. Indeed, in his discussion of the incarnation, Aquinas cites both of these passages in support of his contention that "there is no reason why human nature should not have been raised to something greater after sin. For God allows evils to happen in order to bring a greater good therefrom" (*S. T.* III, 3, *ad* 3).

In other words, the addition of God's graciousness, especially in the form of the incarnation, results in a greater good (a world of higher value) than a world with no sin and less grace.[14]

If human nature is "raised to something greater" by God's gracious provision of transformation and sanctification through the incarnation, then God's graciousness *could* make a world better and it *would* give him a reason to prefer some worlds to others. Adams might be right that "nothing in God's nature or character ... would require him to ... choos[e] the best possible creatures" but that is because it might compel him instead to create a world with creatures who could be *made* better. In other words, it might give him a reason to actualize a world containing corruptible creatures who need fixing rather than a world with creatures who are perfect in the first place.

Is divine incarnation so great a good that any world that contains it is *infinitely* valuable? Would all worlds with a divine incarnation therefore be tied for best? These are difficult questions, and to attempt answers without a fuller account of what gives worlds their value, of how to value the incarnation and the changes it makes, and how to compare values if they are *infinite* is rash.[15] Fortunately, we do not need to answer these questions to see that Adams' attempt to show that a good God might not want to do what is best is incomplete. Perhaps, as Adams argues, God has some traits of character, not wanting to cause harm, or, possibly, being gracious, that are compatible with not wanting to do what is best. But this leaves it open that a perfectly good God has *other* traits of character that do make him want to do what is best. And it may be that the second of the traits Adams identifies, namely, graciousness, can make enough of a difference to the value of worlds actually to give God a reason to want to do what is best.

II. A RANGE OF CHOICES

Adams denies, in effect, that

(2) In *C* God knows that *A* is the best action, wants to do *A*, and is able to do *A*.

follows from

(1) In C, A is the best action for God to do,

In contrast, Richard Swinburne and Thomas Flint seem to accept not only this inference, but the principle,

(3) If in C God knows that A is the best action, wants to do A, and is able to do A, then God does A in C,

as well. They agree, as Swinburne puts it, that "God's perfect goodness … constrains him to act in certain ways,"[16] that "God's goodness thus limits his capacity for choice."[17]

Accordingly, Swinburne and Flint attempt to describe cases in which God is presented with a range of choices, so that he will count as free at least in those circumstances in which he is faced with such an array. Swinburne begins by endorsing the claim that "if there is a best action, [God] will do it," but he adds that "if there are alternative equal best actions, he will do one of them."[18] So the first case in which God's goodness leaves him room to make a free choice is the case in which there are equally good alternatives from which to choose.

The second case is that of an infinite range of choices of a certain sort. Swinburne introduces this case as follows,

> often the range of actions open to God is an infinite range of actions, each of which is inferior to some other action. Thus, for any world of conscious agents which God could create *ex nihilo*, there is plausibly a better one—for instance, one obtained by adding one more conscious agent (sufficiently distant from the others not to crowd them). And so among the actions of creating conscious agents *ex nihilo* there is no best.[19]

It is important to note, as Swinburne does, that just as when more than one alternative is tied for best, God's goodness constrains him to choose from the set of those tied for best, so, when there is an infinite range of possibilities, each one inferior to

some other, if it is better to choose one of those alternatives rather than none, then God's goodness constrains him to choose from that range. In Swinburne's example, if it is better to have a world with conscious agents created *ex nihilo* than not to, then God's goodness constrains him to pick from the infinite range of worlds like that. But the particular choice of alternative, both in the case of ties for best and in the case of infinite series with no best, is up to God. As Swinburne puts it, "Insofar as he acts within that framework, his perfect goodness does not dictate what he will do; and any acts within that framework we may call acts of will."[20]

Thomas Flint's position is structurally similar. He imagines God to face a "galaxy" of worlds open to him to actualize. Some of these galaxies are "oligarchic": there is a maximal level of goodness that the available worlds can have, and more than one world has it. Other galaxies are "anarchic": for any world in it, there is a better.[21] In the former case, God has a range of choices tied for best, and in the latter case, God has an infinite range to choose from. Flint concludes that "neither an anarchic nor an oligarchic galaxy endangers God's freedom."[22]

So both Swinburne and Flint think that God is free in at least certain situations, namely, when he faces a tie for best alternative or when there is an infinite series of increasingly better alternatives with no best.[23] A potential problem, looms, however. Some philosophers hold that a perfectly good being (or at least one who is either omnipotent or omniscient) cannot be in a situation in which there are infinitely many better and better alternatives. On the face of it, this is a startling claim. Why should whether a being is perfectly good limit the *structure* of what situations it can face?[24] Philip Quinn gives the following reason, which is intended to apply to *omnipotent* moral agents. He takes it to be "a fairly obvious truth" that

(4) Necessarily, for all w, w' and x, if w is an actualizable world and w' is an actualizable world and w is a morally better world than w', then if x is an omnipotent moral agent and x actualizes w', then x is such that there is some possible world in which there is a y such that y is a

better moral agent in that world than he [that is, x] is in $w{\neq}$.[25]

Quinn's idea, although (4) does not exactly state this, is that if x were to actualize a world w, when there is a better world w available, then it is possible that someone actualize w and thereby be a morally better agent than x is. But if it is possible for someone to be morally better than x, then x is not morally *perfect*. This assumes that the value of the work redounds precisely to the moral status of the agent. This assumption seems to me far from obvious, but perhaps we can see that by considering another version of the objection.

In William Rowe's version, it is God's omniscience which added to moral perfection prevents him from being in a situation in which he faces an infinite series of increasingly better alternatives. Rowe claims

(5) If an omniscient being creates a world when there is a better world it could create, then it would be possible for there to be a being morally better than it.[26]

In support of this thesis, which he takes to be "plausible, if not self-evident," Rowe adds, "if an omniscient being creates a world when it could have created a better world, then that being has done something less good than it could do (create a better world). But any being who knowingly does something . . . less good than it could do falls short of being the best possible being."[27] Whatever plausibility this principle might have in the case of choices among a finite number of alternatives seems to me to disappear when the choice in question is from among an infinite number of choices where it is better to pick one rather than none. But Rowe has more to say in its defense: he claims that some cases devised by Daniel and Frances Howard-Snyder, intended to show that beings who choose differently among an infinite set of increasingly better alternatives can be morally equivalent, actually show the opposite. The Howard-Snyders first suppose that worlds can be divided into what I shall call permissible and impermissible worlds.[28–30] Permissible worlds are those in which no individuals

have lives not worth living and no evils are unjustified by a compensating good. Impermissible worlds are those in which some individuals have lives that are not worth living, or some evils have no compensating good. They then suppose that the permissible worlds can be ordered according to value, and they propose three scenarios in which a deity chooses one of the permissible worlds. In the original case, their deity, Jove, employs a randomizing device which selects world 777. The Howard-Snyders men propose two alternative scenarios. In the first, a second deity, Juno, uses the same randomizing device and as a result chooses world 999. They claim that Jove and Juno are morally equivalent. Next they consider a third deity, Thor, who, eschewing the randomizer, nevertheless aims at creating a better world than Jove and so chooses world 888. The Howard-Snyders contend that Thor is not morally better than Jove, either. It is at this point that Rowe disagrees. He claims that Jove and Thor might have different *standards* in virtue of which Thor would count as morally superior. He writes, "Jove's standard of goodness in world creating is such that he is prepared to settle for *any* good [permissible] world even if there is a better one he can create. Thor, however, has a higher standard. He is not prepared to create any of the good worlds from W1 to W800 *provided* there is a better one he can create." Rowe concludes that his assessment of Thor undermines the attempt of the Howard-Snyders to discredit (5).

A modest revision of these stories shows, I think, that there is no difference between these deities, after all. As they develop their account, the Howard-Snyders assume that there is a minimal permissible world. (Their numbering begins with 1.) But why should we think that an infinite array of permissible worlds such that for every world there is a better must have a least valuable member? Perhaps those features that make a world permissible have no lower bound. Swinburne identifies among the things that contribute to the value of a world, in addition to the presence of conscious agents, "the kinds of knowledge and powers [God] gives to things and . . . the lengths of days he keeps them in being." We might add to this list the amount of pleasure these agents experience or the kind of compensation there is for the evils they endure. It is plausible to suppose that having conscious agents with knowledge and power, who live acceptably long lives, relatively free of pain and compensated in appropriate ways for the evils they endure contributes to the value of a world. And, of course, there will be no limit to how many such agents there could be, no limit to how long they could live, and no limit to how sufficiently they can be compensated for the evil they endure. That is why it seemed plausible to suppose that there could be an infinite series of ever more valuable permissible worlds. But it seems equally plausible that there might be no lowest acceptable level of knowledge and power, no shortest acceptable lifespan, no minimal acceptable amount of pleasure or compensation for evil for a world to be permissible. In other words, just as there might be no best of all possible worlds, there might also be no least acceptable world. So when God chooses a world, or when the deities in the Howard-Snyders example choose a world, it might not only be the case that for any world chosen there is a better; it might also be the case that for any world chosen there is an acceptable world that is not as good. In that case, it is hard to see how Thor in the example could be acting on a nobler principle or higher standard than Jove. Each picks a world to which infinitely many worlds are superior and which is itself superior to infinitely many other worlds. Thor does not have a principle according to which he rejects as unsuitable more worlds than Jove rejects. There can be no basis for Thor's rejection of worlds lower than 800, if there are infinitely many in that category; both make an arbitrary choice. These deities can create worlds of differing value without thereby differing themselves in goodness.

I have been arguing in support of the proposal of Swinburne and Flint that God might be presented with an infinite series of worlds from which to choose with no feature of any of those worlds compelling him, in virtue of his perfect goodness, to create *it*. They had suggested that, as well as the possibility that God might be presented with ties for best action, as part of an attempt to provide room for God to act freely, unconstrained by his

perfect nature. But it is time to return to the question of whether this proposal is an adequate defense of God's freedom. I think that it is not, for it amounts to saying that God is free only *when it does not matter what he does*. In any situation in which there is a best action open to God, Swinburne and Flint agree that his nature compels him to do it. They only find room for God's freedom in circumstances in which any choice he makes is on a par with any other, where he might as well choose blindly or randomly, and that is not a significant amount of freedom.

III. GOD'S FREEDOM

We began by noticing that it seems to follow from

(1) In *C, A* is the best action for God to do,

that

(2) In *C* God knows that *A* is the best action, wants to do *A*, and is able to do *A*.

Moreover,

(3) If in *C* God knows that *A* is the best action, wants to do *A*, and is able to do *A*, then God does *A* in *C*

appears to be necessarily true. Then we asked how God could ever be free, if, whenever an action was his best alternative, a necessary condition of his performing it, namely, (2), obtains. Adams attempted, unsuccessfully I claimed, to deny the inference of (2) from (1). Swinburne and Flint accept the conclusion that God is not free whenever he has a best alternative, and they try to delineate what I claimed to be an unacceptably limited role for his freedom, namely, when what he chooses does not matter. We should, I think, look more closely at the assumption that if a necessary condition for God's performing an action obtains, then he does not perform that action freely. Thomas Flint claims, as we saw, that "an agent is truly free with respect to an action only if the situation in which he is placed is logically and causally compatible with both his performing and his not performing the action."[31] No doubt libertarians will agree that an agent is free with respect to performing an action only if there are no antecedent causally sufficient conditions for the agent's performing the action. But why should we, even if we are libertarians, extend this to antecedent *logically* sufficient conditions? After all, at least some libertarians are prepared to countenance the *prior truth* that an agent will (freely) perform an action, despite its being a logically sufficient condition of the agent's perforating the action. So why should we think that the truth of

(2) In *C* God knows that *A* is the best action, wants to do *A*, and is able to do *A*

is incompatible with God's doing *A* freely in *C*?

Here I think an appeal to compatibilist accounts of free will, of all things, is instructive. Compatibilists hold that an action can be free even though antecedent causal conditions for its performance exist. But canny compatibilists[32] insist that not just any antecedent causal conditions are so compatible—they have to be the right ones, arising in the right matter. Often the right ones are taken to be the agent's beliefs and desires. And the right manner is the customary way in which people come to have beliefs and desires, not through drugs or hypnosis or nefarious neurosurgeons manipulating their brains. The compatibilist then defends the claim that an action caused by an agent's beliefs and desires arising in the right way is nevertheless free by emphasizing that the beliefs and desires are the agent's *own*, that they are internal to the agent.

Those who reject the compatibilist account are often persuaded by arguments, like those of Peter van Inwagen,[33] that purport to show that, if determinism is true, an agent's beliefs and desires themselves have antecedent causes stretching back to before the agent even existed. The relevant causal conditions are thus not really internal to the agent.[34] The insight, to repeat, of the compatibilist is that the right antecedent conditions, internal to the agent, are compatible with the agent acting freely; on this interpretation, the compatibilist's mistake is in taking the proffered conditions to be internal in this way.

Let us apply the compatibilist's insight to the case of God. Even if in some circumstances *C* God's knowing that *A* is the best action, his wanting to do *A*, and his being able to do *A* is a logically sufficient condition of his doing *A* in *C*, it is nevertheless in virtue of *his own nature* that he knows that *A* is the best action, wants to do *A*, and is able to do *A*.[35] There is no long chain stretching back to things separate from him that give him this constellation of knowledge, desire, and ability; it is due to his *own* knowledge and power and goodness. I see no reason not to say, accordingly, that God is free, even when he does what is best.[36]

NOTES

1. Augustine, *De libero arbitrio,* III, 3., translated by Thomas Williams in *On Free Choice of the Will* (Indianapolis: Hackett, 1993), p. 75. Emphasis added.

2. Theodore Guleserian apparently thinks that doing what is best (optimal, in his term) is a *nonmoral* act, and he claims, in effect, but without extended argument, that traditional theism denies (3). See his "Can God Be Trusted?" *Philosophical Studies* 106 (2001): 293–303, esp. pp. 298–99.

3. Thomas P. Flint, "The Problem of Divine Freedom," *American Philosophical Quarterly* 20 (1983): 255–264, p. 255. Flint describes the view that God exists necessarily and has his perfections essentially as "Anselmian," and he connects that assumption with endorsement of the Ontological Argument. Flint also notes that libertarian freedom is an assumption of the Free Will Defense against evil. Flint thus develops the problem of divine freedom as a conflict arising from two positions many contemporary Christian philosophers accept. Flint's own response focuses on the question of which *possible worlds* God is able to actualize.

4. Robert M. Adams, "Must God Create the Best?" in his *The Virtue of Faith and Other Essays in Philosophical Theology* (New York: Oxford

University Press, 1987), pp. 51–64. The essay originally appeared in *Philosophical Review* 81 (1972): 317–332. Adams does not himself endorse the claim that there is a best of all possible worlds.

5. Ibid., p. 52.

6. Ibid., p. 53.

7. Ibid., p. 54. Philip L. Quinn provides a penetrating discussion of some of Adams' claims in "God, Moral Perfection, and Possible Worlds," in Frederick Sontag and M. Darrol Bryant, eds., *God: The Contemporary Discussion* (New York: Rose of Sharon Press, 1982), pp. 197–215.

8. Ibid., p. 56. In a new endnote added to the reprinted version of his paper, Adams indicates that he now prefers to state his claim by reference to an imperfection in character rather than a defect, agreeing with a criticism by Philip Quinn that someone could have no defects while yet not being "superlatively good."

9. Ibid., p. 56. Grace for Adams thus resembles Anders Nygren's account of agapic love. Cf. Anders Nygren, *Agape and Eros; A Study of the Christian Idea of Love*, trans. A. G. Hebert (New York: The Macmillan Co., 1932–39).

10. Ibid., p.56.

11. Ibid., p. 56.

12. Ibid., pp. 56–57.

13. This hymn was formerly thought to derive from Augustine. It is now attributed to his mentor, Ambrose. See *The Penguin Book of Latin Verse*, Frederick Brittain, ed. (Baltimore: Penguin Books, 1962), p. 94. It is traditionally sung on Easter Eve during the lighting of the Pascal candle.

14. Assuming that something like God's grace (and the resultant change in human nature) can contribute to the value of a world is to assume, what seems plausible, that it is not merely creaturely happiness, as in Adams' account, that contributes to the value of a world. Quinn (*op. cit.*) criticizes Adams for his exclusive interest in "felicity."

15. An interesting discussion of the problem of infinite utility is Jamie Dreier, "Boundless Good" (unpublished).

16. Richard Swinburne, *The Christian God* (Oxford: Oxford University Press, 1994), p. 134.

17. Ibid., p. l35.

18. Ibid.

19. Ibid.

20. Ibid.

21. Thomas Flint, "The Problem of Divine Freedom," p. 258. I am suppressing the details of Flint's meticulous and ingenious account of how worlds are collected into galaxies as well as his arguments about other types of galaxies.

22. Ibid. p. 259.

23. I have not presented Flint's account fully enough to show that this is indeed his view. Given what we have seen in the text, we are only entitled to attribute to him the claim that it is *possible* that God is free.

24. Perhaps a perfectly good being will never face a situation in which an alternative is to make reparations for a past moral wrong, but this is different from what I am calling the structure of a set of alternatives.

25. Philip L. Quinn, "God, Moral Perfection, and Possible Worlds," p. 213.

26. William L. Rowe, "Can God Be Free?" selection I. B.9. See also his "The Problem of Divine Perfection and Freedom," in Eleonore Stump, ed. *Reasoned Faith* (Ithaca: Cornell University Press, 1993), pp. 223–33.

27. "Can God Be Free?".

28. Daniel and Frances Howard Snyder, "How an Unsurpassable Being Can Create a Surpassable World," *Faith and Philosophy* 11 (1994): 260–68. Rowe replied in "The Problem of No Best World," *Faith and Philosophy* 11 (1994): 269–71, as well as in "Can God Be Free?".

29. "Can God Be Free?".

30. *The Christian God*, p. 135.

31. "The Problem of Divine Freedom," p. 255.

32. I believe this term is due to Daniel Dennett, but I have not been able to find the source.

33. Peter van Inwagen, *An Essay on Free Will* (Oxford: Clarendon Press, 1983).

34. I do not pretend to be summarizing van Inwagen's arguments here, which are considerably more involved and ingenious than we need to see now.

35. Thomas Talbott defends a similar view in "On the Divine Nature and the Nature of Divine

Freedom," *Faith and Philosophy* 5 (1988): 3–24. Talbott quotes the following instructive passage from C. S. Lewis:

"Whatever human freedom means, Divine freedom cannot mean indeterminacy between alternatives and choice of one of them Perfect goodness can never debate about the end to be obtained, and perfect wisdom cannot debate about the means most suited to achieve it. The freedom of God consists in the fact that no cause other than Himself produces His acts and no external obstacle impedes them—that His own goodness is the root from which they all grow and His own omnipotence the air in which they all flower." *The Problem of Pain* (New York: Macmillan, 1962), p. 35.

36. I am grateful to Richard Feldman and John Bennett for helpful discussion of the issues of this paper and to William Rowe for allowing me to see an advance copy of "Can God Be Free?".

PART II

Traditional Arguments for the Existence of God

CAN THE EXISTENCE OF GOD be demonstrated or made probable by argument? The debate between those who believe that reason can demonstrate that God exists and those who do not has an ancient lineage, going back to Protagoras (c. 450 B.C.E.) and Plato (427–347 B.C.E.). The Roman Catholic Church has traditionally held that the existence of God is demonstrable by human reason. The strong statement of the First Vatican Council (1870) indicates that human reason is adequate to arrive at a state of knowledge:

> If anyone says that the one and true God, our creator and Lord, cannot be known with certainty with the natural light of human reason by means of the things that have been made: let him be anathema.

Many others, including philosophers within the Catholic tradition and other theistic traditions, have denied that human reason is adequate to arrive at knowledge or demonstrate the existence of God.

Arguments for the existence of God divide into two main groups: a priori and a posteriori arguments. An *a priori argument* is one whose premises one can justifiably believe without having experiences of the world beyond what is needed to acquire the concepts involved in the premises. An *a posteriori argument*, on the other hand, is an argument with at least one premise that can be justifiably believed only on the basis of experience. In this work we consider one a priori argument for the existence of God and two a posteriori arguments. The a priori argument is the ontological argument. The a posteriori arguments are the cosmological argument and the teleological argument.

The question before us in this part of our work is, What do the arguments for the existence of God establish? Do any of them demonstrate beyond reasonable doubt the existence of a supreme being or deity? Do any of them make it probable (given the evidence at hand) that such a being exists?

II.A. THE ONTOLOGICAL ARGUMENT FOR THE EXISTENCE OF GOD

Introduction

THE ONTOLOGICAL ARGUMENT for the existence of God is perhaps the most intriguing of all the arguments for theism. First devised by St. Anselm (1033–1109), Archbishop of Canterbury in the eleventh century, the argument has continued to puzzle and fascinate philosophers ever since. Let the testimony of the agnostic philosopher Bertrand Russell serve as a typical example here:

> I remember the precise moment, one day in 1894, as I was walking along Trinity Lane [at Cambridge University where Russell was a student], when I saw in a flash (or thought I saw) that the ontological argument is valid. I had gone out to buy a tin of tobacco; on my way back, I suddenly threw it up in the air, and exclaimed as I caught it: "Great Scott, the ontological argument is sound!"[*]

The argument is important not only because it claims to be an a priori proof for the existence of God but also because it is the primary locus of such philosophical problems as whether existence is a property and whether the notion of necessary existence is intelligible. Furthermore, it has special religious significance because it is the only one of the traditional arguments that clearly reaches the conclusion that there exists a being with the traditional necessary attributes of God—that is, omnipotence, omniscience, omnibenevolence, and other great-making properties.

The first reading in this section begins with a selection from Anselm's *Proslogion*, wherein we find his famous argument, followed by an objection raised by Gaunilo, a monk who was a contemporary of Anselm's. Also included is Anselm's reply to Gaunilo.

Anselm's inquiry begins from a position of *faith* that God exists. His goal is to supplement his faith with *understanding*. Thus, he begins with a prayer: "Therefore, Lord, you who grant understanding to faith, grant that, insofar as you know it is useful for me, I may understand that you exist as we believe you exist, and that you are what we believe you to be." Following this prayer, he embarks on his argument: "Now we believe that you are something than which nothing greater can be thought. So can it be that no such nature exists, since 'The fool has said in his heart, "There is no God."'?"

The argument that Anselm goes on to present may be thought of as a *reductio ad absurdum*. It begins with a supposition (*S*: suppose that the greatest conceivable being exists in the mind alone) that is contradictory to what Anselm desires to prove. The argument then goes on to show that (*S*), together with other certain or self-evident assumptions, yields a contradiction, thus reducing (*S*) to absurdity. Since (*S*) leads to a contradiction, it follows that the contradictory of (*S*) must be true: it is not the case that the greatest conceivable being exists in the mind alone; rather, this being must exist in reality.

---

[*]*Autobiography of Bertrand Russell* (New York: Little, Brown & Co., 1967).

A key premise in Anselm's argument is the thesis that it is better to exist in reality than to exist in the mind alone. Anselm's idea, in short, is that, because of this, a being that exists in the mind alone could not be the greatest conceivable being; for we could conceive a being just like that one who existed not only in the mind but also in reality, and *this* being—the one who exists in reality—would be better than the one who exists in the mind alone.

In objecting to the argument, Gaunilo argues, in effect, that we might just as easily derive the existence of a greatest conceivable island. Because it is better that an otherwise perfect island exist in reality than simply in the mind alone, it would seem to follow by the same reasoning that a greatest conceivable island exists in reality. Anselm, unsurprisingly, thinks that Gaunilo's analogy fails. However, just as there is controversy over how exactly Anselm's argument ought to be formulated (and over whether Gaunilo managed to understand it correctly), so too there is controversy over just how to interpret Anselm's response.

Our second reading is the critique by Immanuel Kant (1724–1804), who accused the proponent of the argument of defining God into existence. Kant claims that Anselm makes the mistake of treating "exists" as a first-order predicate like "blue" or "great." When we say that the castle is blue, we are adding a property (viz., blueness) to the idea of a castle, but when we say that the castle exists, we are not adding anything to the concept of a castle. We are saying only that the concept is exemplified or instantiated. In Anselm's argument, "exists" is treated as a first-order predicate, which adds something to the concept of an entity and makes it *greater*. This, according to Kant, is the fatal flaw in the argument.

There are many considerations involved in the ontological argument that are not dealt with in our readings. For a clear discussion of the wider issues involved in this argument, see William Rowe's introductory work, *Philosophy of Religion* (Chapter 3, "The Ontological Argument").

II.A.1

The Ontological Argument

ST. ANSELM

St. Anselm (1033–1109), Abbot of Bec and later Archbishop of Canterbury, is the originator of one of the most intriguing arguments ever devised by the human mind, the ontological argument for the

From *Monologion and Proslogion, with the replies of Gaunilo and Anselm*, trans. with introduction and notes by Thomas Williams.
Reprinted by permission of Hackett Publishing Company, Inc. All rights reserved.

existence of a supremely perfect being. After the short selection from Anselm's Proslogion, *there follows a brief selection from Gaunilo's reply,* In Behalf of the Fool, *and a counterresponse by Anselm.*

(ST. ANSELM'S PRESENTATION)

Therefore, Lord, you who grant understanding to faith, grant that, insofar as you know it is useful for me, I may understand that you exist as we believe you exist, and that you are what we believe you to be. Now we believe that you are something than which nothing greater can be thought. So can it be that no such nature exists, since "The fool has said in his heart, 'There is no God'" (Psalm 14:1; 53:1)? But when this same fool hears me say "something than which nothing greater can be thought," he surely understands what he hears; and what he understands exists in his understanding,[1] even if he does not understand that it exists [in reality]. For it is one thing for an object to exist in the understanding and quite another to understand that the object exists [in reality]. When a painter, for example, thinks out in advance what he is going to paint, he has it in his understanding, but he does not yet understand that it exists, since he has not yet painted it. But once he has painted it, he both has it in his understanding and understands that it exists because he has now painted it. So even the fool must admit that something than which nothing greater can be thought exists at least in his understanding, since he understands this when he hears it, and whatever is understood exists in the understanding. And surely that than which a greater cannot be thought cannot exist only in the understanding. For if it exists only in the understanding, it can be thought to exist in reality as well, which is greater. So if that than which a greater cannot be thought exists only in the understanding, then that than which a greater *cannot* be thought is that than which a greater *can* be thought. But that is clearly impossible. Therefore, there is no doubt that something than which a greater cannot be thought exists both in the understanding and in reality....

This [being] exists so truly that it cannot be thought not to exist. For it is possible to think that something exists that cannot be thought not to exist, and such a being is greater than one that can be thought not to exist. Therefore, if that than which a greater cannot be thought can be thought not to exist, then that than which a greater cannot be thought is *not* that than which a greater cannot be thought; and this is a contradiction. So that than which a greater cannot be thought exists so truly that it cannot be thought not to exist.

And this is you, O Lord our God. You exist so truly, O Lord my God, that you cannot be thought not to exist. And rightly so, for if some mind could think something better than you, a creature would rise above the Creator and sit in judgment upon him, which is completely absurd. Indeed, everything that exists, except for you alone, can be thought not to exist. So you alone among all things have existence most truly, and therefore most greatly. Whatever else exists has existence less truly, and therefore less greatly. So then why did "the fool say in his heart, 'There is no God,'" when it is so evident to the rational mind that you among all beings exist most greatly? Why indeed, except because he is stupid and a fool? . . .

But how has he said in his heart what he could not think? Or how could he not think what he said in his heart, since to say in one's heart is the same as to think? But if he really—or rather, *since* he really—thought this, because he said it in his heart, and did not say it in his heart, because he could not think it, there must be more than one way in which something is "said in one's heart" or "thought." In one sense of the word, to think a thing is to think the word that signifies that thing. But in another sense, it is to understand what exactly the thing is. God can be thought not to exist in the first sense, but not at all in the second sense. No one who understands what God is can think that God does not exist, although he may say these words in his heart with no signification at all, or with some peculiar signification. For God is that than which a greater cannot be thought. Whoever understands this properly, understands that this being exists in such a way that he cannot, even in thought, fail to exist. So whoever understands that God exists in this way cannot think that he does not exist.

Thanks be to you, my good Lord, thanks be to you. For what I once believed through your grace, I now understand through your illumination, so that even if I did not want to *believe* that you exist, I could not fail to *understand* that you exist. . . .

(GAUNILO'S CRITICISM)

"For example, there are those who say that somewhere in the ocean is an island, which, because of the difficulty—or rather, impossibility—of finding what does not exist, some call 'the Lost Island.' This island (so the story goes) is more plentifully endowed than even the Isles of the Blessed with an indescribable abundance of all sorts of riches and delights. And because it has neither owner nor inhabitant, it is everywhere superior in its abundant riches to all the other lands that human beings inhabit.

"Suppose someone tells me all this. The story is easily told and involves no difficulty, and so I understand it. But if this person went on to draw a conclusion, and say, 'You cannot any longer doubt that this island, more excellent than all others on earth, truly exists somewhere in reality. For you do not doubt that this island exists in your understanding, and since it is more excellent to exist not merely in the understanding, but also in reality, this island must also exist in reality. For if it did not, any land that exists in reality would be greater than it. And so this more excellent thing that you have understood would not in fact be more excellent.'– If, I say, he should try to convince me by, this argument that I should no longer doubt whether the island truly exists, either I would think he was joking, or I would not know whom I ought to think more foolish: myself, if I grant him his conclusion, or him, if he thinks he has established the existence of that island with any degree of certainty, without first showing that its excellence exists in my understanding as a thing that truly and undoubtedly exists and not in any way like something false or uncertain.". . .

(ST. ANSELM'S REJOINDER)

But, you say, this is just the same as if someone were to claim that it cannot be doubted that a certain island in the ocean, surpassing all other lands in its fertility (which, from the difficulty—or rather, impossibility—of finding what does not exist, is called "the Lost Island"), truly exists in reality, because someone can easily understand it when it is described to him in words. I say quite confidently that if anyone can find for me something existing either in reality or only in thought to which he can apply this inference in my argument, besides that than which a greater cannot be thought, I will find and give to him that Lost Island, never to be lost again. In fact, however, it has already become quite clear that that than which a greater cannot be thought cannot be thought not to exist, since its existence is a matter of such certain truth. For otherwise it would not exist at all.

Finally, if someone says that he thinks it does not exist, I say that when he thinks this, either he is thinking something than which a greater cannot be thought, or he is not. If he is not, then he is not thinking that it does not exist, since he is not thinking it at all. But if he is, he is surely thinking something that cannot be thought not to exist. For if it could be thought not to exist, it could be thought to have a beginning and an end, which is impossible. Therefore, someone who is thinking it, is thinking something that cannot be thought not to exist. And of course someone who is thinking this does not think that that very thing does not exist. Otherwise he would be thinking something that cannot be thought. Therefore, that than which a greater cannot be thought cannot be thought not to exist. . . .

NOTE

1. The word here translated "understanding" is "*intellectus.*" The text would perhaps read better if I translated it as "intellect," but this would obscure the fact that it is from the same root as the verb "*intelligere,*" "to understand." Some of what Anselm says makes a bit more sense if this fact is constantly borne in mind.

II.A.2

A Critique of the Ontological Argument

IMMANUEL KANT

The German philosopher Immanuel Kant (1724–1804) in his famous work Critique of Pure Reason *(1781), from which our selection is taken, set forth a highly influential critique of the ontological argument. Essentially, the objection is that "existence is not a predicate," whereas the opposite is assumed to be true in the various forms of the ontological argument. So, for example, when you say that Mary is my mother, you are noting some property that describes or adds to who Mary is. But when you say, "Mary, my mother, exists," you are not telling us anything new about Mary; you are simply affirming that the concepts in question are exemplified. "Existence" is a second-order predicate or property, not to be treated as other first-order, normal predicates or properties are.*

THE IMPOSSIBILITY OF AN ONTOLOGICAL PROOF OF THE EXISTENCE OF GOD

It is evident from what has been said, that the conception of an absolutely necessary being is a mere idea, the objective reality of which is far from being established by the mere fact that it is a need of reason. On the contrary, this idea serves merely to indicate a certain unattainable perfection, and rather limits the operations than, by the presentation of new objects, extends the sphere of the understanding. But a strange anomaly meets us at the very threshold; for the inference from a given existence in general to an absolutely necessary existence, seems to be correct and unavoidable, while the conditions of the *understanding* refuse to aid us in forming any conception of such a being.

Philosophers have always talked of an absolutely necessary being, and have nevertheless declined to take the trouble of conceiving whether—and how—a being of this nature is even cogitable, not to mention that its existence is actually demonstrable. A verbal definition of the conception is certainly easy enough; it is something, the non-existence of which is impossible. But does this definition throw any light upon the conditions which render it impossible to cogitate the non-existence of a thing—conditions which

From Kant's *Critique of Pure Reason*, translated by J. M. D. Meiklejohn (New York: Colonial Press, 1900). Translation revised by Louis Pojman.

we wish to ascertain, that we may discover whether we think anything in the conception of such a being or not? For the mere fact that I throw away, by means of the word *Unconditioned*, all the conditions which the understanding habitually requires in order to regard anything as necessary, is very far from making clear whether by means of the conception of the unconditionally necessary I think of something, or really of nothing at all.

Nay, more, this chance-conception, now become so current, many have endeavored to explain by examples, which seemed to render any inquiries regarding its intelligibility quite needless. Every geometrical proposition—a triangle has three angles—it was said, is absolutely necessary; and thus people talked of an object which lay out of the sphere of our understanding as if it were perfectly plain what the conception of such a being meant.

All the examples adduced have been drawn, without exception, from *judgments*, and not from *things*. But the unconditioned necessity of a judgment does not form the absolute necessity of a thing. On the contrary, the absolute necessity of a judgment is only a conditioned necessity of a thing, or of the predicate in a judgment. The proposition above-mentioned, does not enounce that three angles necessarily exist, but, upon condition that a triangle exists, three angles must necessarily exist—in it. And thus this logical necessity has been the source of the greatest delusions. Having formed an *a priori* conception of a thing, the content of which was made to embrace existence, we believed ourselves safe in concluding that, because existence belongs necessarily to the object of the conception (that is, under the condition of my positing this thing as given), the existence of the thing is also posited necessarily, and that it is therefore absolutely necessary—merely because its existence has been cogitated in the conception.

If, in an identical judgment, I annihilate the predicate in thought, and retain the subject, a contradiction is the result; and hence I say, the former belongs necessarily to the latter. But if I suppress both subject and predicate in thought, no contradiction arises; for there is *nothing* at all, and therefore no means of forming a contradiction. To suppose the existence of a triangle and not that of its three angles, is self-contradictory; but to suppose the non-existence of both triangle and angles is perfectly admissible. And so is it with the conception of an absolutely necessary being. Annihilate its existence in thought, and you annihilate the thing itself with all its predicates; how then can there be any room for contradiction? Externally, there is nothing to give rise to a contradiction, for a thing cannot be necessary externally; nor internally, for, by the annihilation or suppression of the thing itself, its internal properties are also annihilated. God is omnipotent—that is a necessary judgment. His omnipotence cannot be denied, if the existence of a Deity is posited—the existence, that is, of an infinite being, the two conceptions being identical. But when you say, *God does not exist*, neither omnipotence nor any other predicate is affirmed; they must all disappear with the subject, and in this judgment there cannot exist the least self-contradiction.

You have thus seen, that when the predicate of a judgment is annihilated in thought along with the subject, no internal contradiction can arise, be the predicate what it may. There is no possibility of evading the conclusion—you find yourselves compelled to declare: There are certain subjects which cannot be annihilated in thought. But this is nothing more than saying: There exist subjects which are absolutely necessary—the very hypothesis which you are called upon to establish. For I find myself unable to form the slightest conception of a thing which, when annihilated in thought with all its predicates, leaves behind a contradiction; and contradiction is the only criterion of impossibility, in the sphere of pure *a priori* conceptions.

Against these general considerations, the justice of which no one can dispute, one argument is adduced, which is regarded as furnishing a satisfactory demonstration from the fact. It is affirmed, that there is one and only one conception, in which the non-being or annihilation of the object is self-contradictory, and this is the conception of an *ens realissimum*.[*] It possesses, you say, all reality, and you feel yourselves justified in admitting the possibility

_____

[*]Latin: "most real being."

of such a thing. (This I am willing to grant for the present, although the existence of a conception which is not self-contradictory, is far from being sufficient to prove the possibility of an object.[1]) Now the notion of all reality embraces in it that of existence; the notion of existence lies, therefore, in the conception of this possible thing. If this thing is annihilated in thought, the internal possibility of the thing is also annihilated, which is self-contradictory.

I answer: It is absurd to introduce—under whatever term disguised—into the conception of a thing, which is to be cogitated solely in reference to its possibility, the conception of its existence. If this is admitted, you will have apparently gained the day, but in reality have enounced nothing but a mere tautology. I ask, is the proposition, *this or that thing* (which I am admitting to be possible) exists, an analytical or a synthetical proposition? If the former, there is no addition made to the subject of your thought by the affirmation of its existence; but then the conception in your minds is identical with the thing itself, or you have supposed the existence of a thing to be possible, and then inferred its existence from its internal possibility—which is but a miserable tautology. The word *reality* in the conception of the thing, and the word *existence* in the conception of the predicate, will not help you out of the difficulty. For, supposing you were to term all positing of a thing, reality, you have thereby posited the thing with all its predicates in the conception of the subject and assumed its actual existence, and this you merely repeat in the predicate. But if you confess, as every reasonable person must, that every existential proposition is synthetical, how can it be maintained that the predicate of existence cannot be denied without contradiction—a property which is the characteristic of analytical propositions, alone.

I should have a reasonable hope of putting an end forever to this sophistical mode of argumentation, by a strict definition of the conception of existence, did not my own experience teach me that the illusion arising from our confounding a logical with a real predicate (a predicate which aids in the determination of a thing) resists almost all the endeavors of explanation and illustration. A *logical predicate* may be what you please, even the subject

may be predicated of itself; for logic pays no regard to the content of a judgment. But the determination of a conception is a predicate, which adds to and enlarges the conception. It must not, therefore, be contained in the conception.

Being is evidently not a real predicate, that is, a conception of something which is added to the conception of some other thing. It is merely the positing of a thing, or of certain determinations in it. Logically, it is merely the copula of a judgment. The proposition, *God is omnipotent*, contains two conceptions, which have a certain object or content; the word *is*, is no additional predicate—it merely indicates the relation of the predicate to the subject. Now, if I take the subject (God) with all its predicates (omnipotence being one), and say, *God is*, or *There is a God*, I add no new predicate to the conception of God, I merely posit or affirm the existence of the subject with all its predicates—I posit the *object* in relation to my *conception*. The content of both is the same; and there is no addition made to the conception, which expresses merely the possibility of the object, by my cogitating the object—in the expression, it *is*—as absolutely given or existing. Thus the real contains no more than the possible. A hundred real dollars contain no more than a hundred possible dollars. For, as the latter indicate the conception, and the former the object, on the supposition that the content of the former was greater than that of the latter, my conception would not be an expression of the whole object, and would consequently be an inadequate conception of it. But in reckoning my wealth there may be said to be more in a hundred real dollars, than in a hundred possible dollars—that is, in the mere conception of them. For the real object—the dollars—is not analytically contained in my conception, but forms a synthetical addition to my conception (which is merely a determination of my mental state), although this objective reality—this existence—apart from my conception, does not in the least degree increase the aforesaid hundred dollars.

It does not matter which predicates or how many of them we may think a thing possesses, I do not make the least addition to it when we further declare that this thing exists. Otherwise, it would not be the exact same thing that exists, but something more than we had thought in the idea or concept; and hence, we could not say that the exact object of my thought exists. On the contrary, it exists with the same defect with which I have thought it, since otherwise what exists would be something different from what I thought. So when I think of a being as the highest reality, without any imperfection, the question still remains whether or not this being exists. For although, in my idea, nothing may be lacking in the possible real content of a thing in general, something is still lacking in its relation to my mental state; that is, I am ignorant of whether the object is also possible *a posteriori*. It is here we discover the core of our problem. If the question regarded an object of sense merely, it would be impossible for me to confuse the idea of a thing with its existence. For the concept of the object merely enables me to think of it according to universal conditions of experience; while the existence of the object permits me to think of it within the context of actual experience. However, in being connected with the content of experience as a whole, the concept of the object is not enlarged. All that has happened is that our thought has thereby acquired another possible perception. So it is not surprising that, if we attempt to think existence through the pure categories alone, we cannot specify a single mark distinguishing it from mere possibility.

Whatever be the content of our conception of an object, it is necessary to go beyond it, if we wish to predicate existence of an object. In the case of sensuous objects, this is attained by their connection according to empirical laws with some one of my perceptions; but when it comes to objects of pure thought, there is no means whatever of knowing of their existence, since it would have to be known in a completely *a priori* manner. But all our knowledge of existence (be it immediately by perception or by inferences connecting some object with a perception) belongs entirely to the sphere of experience—which is in perfect unity with itself—and although an existence out of this sphere cannot be absolutely declared to be impossible, it is a hypothesis the truth of which we have no means of discovering.

The idea of a supreme being is in many ways a very useful idea; but for the very reason that it is an idea, it is incapable of enlarging our knowledge with regard to the existence of things. It is not even sufficient to instruct us as to the possibility of a being which we do not know to exist. The analytical criterion of possibility, which consists in the absence of contradiction in propositions, cannot be denied it. But the connection of real properties in a thing is a synthesis of the possibility of which an *a priori* judgment cannot be formed, because these realities are not presented to us specifically; and even if this were to happen, a judgment would still be impossible, because the criterion of possibility of synthetical cognitions must be sought for in the world of experience, to which the object of an idea cannot belong. And thus the celebrated Leibniz has utterly failed in his attempt to establish upon *à priori* grounds the possibility of this sublime ideal being.

The celebrated ontological or Cartesian argument for the existence of a supreme being is therefore insufficient; and we may as well hope to increase our stock of knowledge by the aid of mere ideas, as the merchant to increase his wealth by adding a few zeros to his bank account.

NOTE

1. A conception is always possible, if it is not self-contradictory. This is the logical criterion of possibility, distinguishing the object of such a conception from *the nihil negativum*. But it may be, notwithstanding, an empty conception, unless the objective reality of this synthesis, by which it is generated, is demonstrated; and a proof of this kind must be based upon principles of possible experience, and not upon the principle of analysis or contradiction. This remark may be serviceable as a warning against concluding, from the possibility of a conception—which is logical, the possibility of a thing—which is real.

II.B. THE COSMOLOGICAL ARGUMENT FOR THE EXISTENCE OF GOD

Introduction

ASKING PEOPLE WHY THEY BELIEVE in God is likely to evoke something like the following response: "Well, things didn't just pop up out of nothing. Someone, a pretty powerful Someone, had to cause the universe to come into existence. You just can't have causes going back forever. God must have made the world. Nothing else makes sense."

All versions of the cosmological argument begin with the a posteriori premises that the universe exists and that something outside the universe is required to explain its existence. That is, the universe is *contingent*, depending on something outside of itself for its existence. That "something else" is logically prior to the birth of the universe. It constitutes the reason for the existence of the universe. Such a being is God.

One version of the cosmological argument is called the "first-cause argument." From the fact that some things are caused, we may reason to the existence of a first cause. The Dominican friar St. Thomas Aquinas (1225–1274) gives a version of this argument in our first reading. His "second way" is based on the idea of causation:

> We find that among sensible things there is an ordering of efficient causes, and yet we do not find—nor is it possible to find—anything that is an efficient cause of its own self. For if something were an efficient cause of itself, then it would be prior to itself—which is impossible.
>
> But it is impossible to go on to infinity among efficient causes. For in every case of ordered efficient causes, the first is a cause of the intermediate and the intermediate is a cause of the last—and this regardless of whether the intermediate is constituted by many causes or by just one. But when a cause is removed, its effect is removed. Therefore, if there were no first among the efficient causes, then neither would there be a last or an intermediate. But if the efficient causes went on to infinity, there would not be a first efficient cause, and so there would not be a last effect or any intermediate efficient causes, either—which is obviously false. Therefore, one must posit some first efficient cause—which everyone calls God.

In general outline, the argument goes something like this:

1. There exist things that are caused.
2. Nothing can be the cause of itself.
3. There cannot be an infinite regress of causes.
4. Therefore, there exists an uncaused first cause.
5. If there is an uncaused first cause, then the uncaused first cause is God.
6. Therefore, God exists.

What can we say of this argument? Certainly the first premise is true—some things have causes. Indeed, it is natural to believe that every event has a cause that explains why the event happened. The second premise also seems correct, for how could something that didn't exist cause anything, let alone its own existence? (Note that being *self-caused,* which premise 2 takes to be impossible, is different from being *uncaused.* There is nothing obviously implausible about the idea that something or someone existed from eternity and so is uncaused, whereas it is very hard to imagine how a nonexistent thing might cause itself to come into being.)

One difficulty with the argument, however, concerns premise 3, which states that there cannot be an infinite regress of causes. There is an infinite regress of numbers; so why couldn't there be an infinite regress of causes? One response to this question is that there is a significant difference between numbers and causes. Numbers are abstract entities that exist necessarily, whereas causes are concrete, temporal entities—events, substances, persons, and so on—which are the sorts of things that need to be brought into existence. Numbers exist at all times and in all possible worlds. Napoleon, Mt. Everest, the gunfight at the O.K. Corral, and so on are not eternal but need causal explanations.

The child asks, "Mommy, who made me?" and the mother responds, "You came from my womb." The child persists, "Mommy, who made you and your womb?" The mother responds that she came from a fertilized egg in her mother's womb. But the child persists, until finally the mother is forced to admit that she does not know the answer, or perhaps says that God is the ultimate source of everything. The question, however, is whether one can explain where everything came from without appealing to God. In other words, does the argument from first cause, *even if it is valid,* give us reason to think that *God* is the first cause?

In our second reading, the eighteenth-century philosopher Samuel Clarke sets forth a different version of the cosmological argument, the argument from contingency (Aquinas's third way). Clarke, like Aquinas before him, identifies the independent and necessary being with God. We are dependent, or contingent, beings. Reducing the argument to the bare bones, the argument from contingency is this:

1. Every being that exists is either contingent or necessary.

2. Not every being can be contingent.

3. Therefore, there exists a necessary being upon which the contingent beings depend.

4. A necessary being on which all contingent beings exist is what we mean by *God.*

5. Therefore, God exists.

A necessary being is independent, and has the explanation of its existence in itself, whereas contingent beings do not have the reason for their existence in themselves but depend on other beings and, ultimately, depend on a necessary being.

In our third reading, William Rowe examines the cosmological argument, and especially versions like the argument from contingency based on the *principle of sufficient reason* (PSR)—the thesis that everything must have an explanation to account for it. He points out problems connected with this principle.

In our fourth reading, William Lane Craig and J. P. Moreland defend the *kalām* cosmological argument, an argument first set forth by Arab Islamic scholars, al-Kindi and al-Ghazali, in the Middle Ages.

In our final reading, Paul Draper analyzes the *kalām* argument and claims that Craig's defense of the cosmological argument fails, both because it fails to establish that the universe had a beginning and because it rests on an equivocation of the phrase "begins to exist."

II.B.1

The Five Ways

ST. THOMAS AQUINAS

The Dominican friar St. Thomas Aquinas (1225–1274) is considered by many to be the greatest theologian in Western religion. The five ways of showing the existence of God given in this selection are versions of the cosmological argument. The first way concerns the fact that there is change (or motion) and argues that there must be an Unmoved Mover that originates all change but itself is not moved. The second way is from the idea of causation and argues that there must be a first, uncaused cause to explain the existence of all other causes. The third way is from the idea of contingency. It argues that because there are dependent beings (e.g., humans), there must be an independent or necessary being on whom the dependent beings rely for their subsistence. The fourth way is from excellence, and it argues that because there are degrees of excellence, there must be a perfect being from whence all excellences come. The final way is from the harmony of things. There is a harmony of nature, which calls for an explanation. The only sufficient explanation is that there is a divine designer who planned this harmony.

ARTICLE 3: DOES GOD EXIST?

It seems that God does not exist:

Objection 1: If one of a pair of contraries were infinite, it would totally destroy the other contrary. But by the name "God" one means a certain infinite good. Therefore, if God existed, there would be nothing evil. But there is evil in the world. Therefore, God does not exist.

Objection 2: What can be accomplished with fewer principles is not done through more principles. But it seems that everything that happens in the world could have been accomplished through other principles, even if God did not exist; for things that are natural are traced back to nature as a principle, whereas things that are purposeful are traced back to human reason or will as a principle. Therefore, there is no need to claim that God exists.

But contrary to this: Exodus 1:14 says under the personage of God, "I am Who am."

I respond: There are five ways to prove that God exists.

Printed with the permission of the translator, Alfred J. Freddoso. This translation is being published by Saint Augustine's Press.

The *first* and clearest way is that taken from motion:

It is certain, and obvious to the senses, that in this world some things are moved.

But everything that is moved is moved by another. For nothing is moved except insofar as it is in potentiality with respect to that actuality toward which it is moved, whereas something effects motion insofar as it is in actuality in a relevant respect. After all, to effect motion is just to lead something from potentiality into actuality. But a thing cannot be led from potentiality into actuality except through some being that is in actuality in a relevant respect; for example, something that is hot in actuality—say, a fire—makes a piece of wood, which is hot in potentiality, to be hot in actuality, and it thereby moves and alters the piece of wood. But it is impossible for something to be simultaneously in potentiality and in actuality with respect to same thing; rather, it can be in potentiality and in actuality only with respect to different things. For what is hot in actuality cannot simultaneously be hot in potentiality; rather, it is cold in potentiality. Therefore, it is impossible that something should be both mover and moved in the same way and with respect to the same thing, or, in other words, that something should move itself. Therefore, everything that is moved must be moved by another.

If, then, that by which something is moved is itself moved, then it, too, must be moved by another, and that other by still another. But this does not go on to infinity. For if it did, then there would not be any first mover and, as a result, none of the others would effect motion, either. For secondary movers effect motion only because they are being moved by a first mover, just as a stick does not effect motion except because it is being moved by a hand. Therefore, one has to arrive at some first mover that is not being moved by anything. And this is what everyone takes to be God.

The *second* way is based on the notion of an efficient cause:

We find that among sensible things there is an ordering of efficient causes, and yet we do not find—nor is it possible to find—anything that is an efficient cause of its own self. For if something were an efficient cause of itself, then it would be prior to itself—which is impossible.

But it is impossible to go on to infinity among efficient causes. For in every case of ordered efficient causes, the first is a cause of the intermediate and the intermediate is a cause of the last—and this regardless of whether the intermediate is constituted by many causes or by just one. But when a cause is removed, its effect is removed. Therefore, if there were no first among the efficient causes, then neither would there be a last or an intermediate. But if the efficient causes went on to infinity, there would not be a first efficient cause, and so there would not be a last effect or any intermediate efficient causes, either—which is obviously false. Therefore, one must posit some first efficient cause—which everyone calls God.

The *third* way is taken from the possible and the necessary, and it goes like this:

Certain of the things we find in the world are able to exist and able not to exist; for some things are found to be generated and corrupted and, as a result, they are able to exist and able not to exist.

But it is impossible that everything should be like this; for that which is able not to exist is such that at some time it does not exist. Therefore, if everything is such that it is able not to exist, then at some time nothing existed in the world. But if this were true, then nothing would exist even now. For what does not exist begins to exist only through something that does exist; therefore, if there were no beings, then it was impossible that anything should have begun to exist, and so nothing would exist now—which is obviously false. Therefore, not all beings are able to exist [and able not to exist]; rather, it must be that there is something necessary in the world.

Now every necessary being either has a cause of its necessity from outside itself or it does not. But it is impossible to go on to infinity among necessary beings that have a cause of their necessity—in the same way, as was proved above, that it is impossible to go on to infinity among efficient causes. Therefore, one must posit something that is necessary *per se*, which does not have a cause of its necessity from outside itself but is instead a cause of necessity for the other [necessary] things. But this everyone calls God.

The *fourth* way is taken from the gradations that are found in the world:

In the world some things are found to be more and less good, more and less true, more and less noble, etc. But *more* and *less* are predicated of diverse things insofar as they approach in diverse ways that which is maximal in a given respect. For instance, the hotter something is, the closer it approaches that which is maximally hot. Therefore, there is something that is maximally true, maximally good, and maximally noble, and, as a result, is a maximal being; for according to the Philosopher in *Metaphysics* 2, things that are maximally true are maximally beings.

But, as is claimed in the same book, that which is maximal in a given genus is a cause of all the things that belong to that genus; for instance, fire, which is maximally hot, is a cause of all hot things. Therefore, there is something that is a cause for all beings of their *esse*, their goodness, and each of their perfections—and this we call God.

The *fifth* way is taken from the governance of things:

We see that some things lacking cognition, viz., natural bodies, act for the sake of an end. This is apparent from the fact that they always or very frequently act in the same way in order to bring about that which is best, and from this it is clear that it is not by chance, but by design, that they attain the end.

But things lacking cognition tend toward an end only if they are directed by something that has cognition and intelligence, in the way that an arrow is directed by an archer. Therefore, there is something intelligent by which all natural things are ordered to an end—and this we call God.

Reply to objection 1: As Augustine says in the *Enchiridion*, "Since God is maximally good, He would not allow any evil to exist in His works if He were not powerful enough and good enough to draw good even from evil." Therefore, it is part of God's infinite goodness that He should permit evils and elicit goods from them.

Reply to objection 2: Since it is by the direction of a higher agent that nature acts for the sake of a determinate end, those things that are done by nature must also be traced back to God as a first cause. Similarly, even things that are done by design must be traced back to a higher cause and not to human reason and will. For human reason and will are changeable and subject to failure, but, as was shown above, all things that can change and fail must be traced back to a first principle that is unmoved and necessary *per se*.

II.B.2

The Argument from Contingency

SAMUEL CLARKE

Samuel Clarke (1675–1729), an English philosopher and Anglican minister, one of the first to appreciate the work of Isaac Newton, here sets forth a version of the argument from contingency. It is based on the idea that if some beings are dependent, or contingent, there must of necessity be an independent being upon which all other beings are dependent.

Reprinted from *A Discourse Concerning Natural Religion* (1705).

There has existed from eternity some one unchangeable and independent being. For since something must needs have been from eternity; as hath been already proved, and is granted on all hands: either there has always existed one unchangeable and *independent* Being, from which all other beings that are or ever were in the universe, have received their original; or else there has been an infinite succession of changeable and *dependent* beings, produced one from another in an endless progression, without any original cause at all: which latter supposition is so very absurd, that tho' all atheism must in its account of most things (as shall be shown hereafter) terminate in it, yet I think very few atheists ever were so weak as openly and directly to defend it. For it is plainly impossible and contradictory to itself. I shall not argue against it from the supposed impossibility of infinite succession, *barely and absolutely considered in itself;* for a reason which shall be mentioned hereafter: but, if we consider such an infinite progression, as *one* entire endless *series of dependent* beings; 'tis plain this whole series of beings can have no cause *from without*, of its existence; because in it are supposed to be included *all things* that are or ever were in the universe: and 'tis plain it can have no reason *within itself*, of its existence; because no one being in this infinite succession is supposed to be self-existent or necessary (which is the only ground or reason of existence of any thing, that can be imagined *within the thing itself*, as will presently more fully appear), but every one *dependent* on the foregoing: and where *no part* is necessary, 'tis manifest *the whole* cannot be necessary; absolute necessity of existence, not being an outward, relative, and accidental determination; but an inward and essential property of the nature of the thing which so exists. An infinite succession therefore of merely *dependent beings*, without any original independent cause; is a *series* of beings, that has neither necessity nor cause, nor any reason *at all* of its existence, neither *within itself* nor *from without*: that is, 'tis an express contradiction and impossibility; 'tis a supposing *something to be caused*, (because it's granted in every one of its stages of succession, not to be necessary and from itself); and yet that in the whole it is caused *absolutely by nothing*: Which every man knows is a contradiction to be done *in time*; and because duration in this case makes no difference, 'tis equally a contradiction to suppose it done from eternity: And consequently there must *on the contrary*, of necessity have existed from eternity, *some one* immutable and *independent* Being: Which, what it is, remains in the next place to be inquired.

II.B.3

An Examination of the Cosmological Argument

WILLIAM ROWE

Brief biographical remarks about William Rowe appear before selection I.B.9. In the present selection, taken from the second edition of his Philosophy of Religion: An Introduction *(1993), Rowe begins by distinguishing between a priori and a posteriori arguments and setting the cosmological*

From Rowe, *Philosophy of Religion*, 2nd edition. © 1993 Cengage Learning.

argument in historical perspective. Next, he divides the argument into two parts: that which seeks to prove the existence of a self-existent being and that which seeks to prove that this self-existent being is the God of theism. He introduces the principle of sufficient reason—"There must be an explanation (a) of the existence of any being and (b) of any positive fact whatever"—and shows its role in the cosmological argument. In the light of this principle, he examines the argument itself and four objections to it.

STATING THE ARGUMENT

Arguments for the existence of God are commonly divided into *a posteriori* arguments and *a priori* arguments. An *a posteriori* argument depends on a principle or premise that can be known only by means of our experience of the world. An *a priori* argument, on the other hand, purports to rest on principles all of which can be known independently of our experience of the world, by just reflecting on and understanding them. Of the three major arguments for the existence of God—the Cosmological, the Teleological, and the Ontological—only the last of these is entirely *a priori*. In the Cosmological Argument one starts from some simple fact about the world, such as that it contains things which are caused to exist by other things. In the Teleological Argument a somewhat more complicated fact about the world serves as a starting point, the fact that the world exhibits order and design. In the Ontological Argument, however, one begins simply with a concept of God....

Before we state the Cosmological Argument itself, we shall consider some rather general points about the argument. Historically, it can be traced to the writings of the Greek philosophers, Plato and Aristotle, but the major developments in the argument took place in the thirteenth and in the eighteenth centuries. In the thirteenth century Aquinas put forth five distinct arguments for the existence of God, and of these, the first three are versions of the Cosmological Argument.[1] In the first of these he started from the fact that there are things in the world undergoing change and reasoned to the conclusion that there must be some ultimate cause of change that is itself unchanging. In the second he started from the fact that there are things in the world that clearly are caused to exist by other things and reasoned to the conclusion that there must be

some ultimate cause of existence whose own existence is itself uncaused. And in the third argument he started from the fact that there are things in the world which need not have existed at all, things which do exist but which we can easily imagine might not, and reasoned to the conclusion that there must be some being that had to be, that exists and could not have failed to exist. Now it might be objected that even if Aquinas' arguments do prove beyond doubt the existence of an unchanging changer, an uncaused cause, and a being that could not have failed to exist, the arguments fail to prove the existence of the theistic God. For the theistic God, as we saw, is supremely good, omnipotent, omniscient, and creator of but separate from and independent of the world. How do we know, for example, that the unchanging changer isn't evil or slightly ignorant? The answer to this objection is that the Cosmological Argument has two parts. In the first part the effort is to prove the existence of a special sort of being, for example, a being that could not have failed to exist, or a being that causes change in other things but is itself unchanging. In the second part of the argument the effort is to prove that the special sort of being whose existence has been established in the first part has, and must have, the features—perfect goodness, omnipotence, omniscience, and so on—which go together to make up the theistic idea of God. What this means, then, is that Aquinas' three arguments are different versions of only the first part of the Cosmological Argument. Indeed, in later sections of his *Summa Theological* Aquinas undertakes to show that the unchanging changer, the uncaused cause of existence, and the being which had to exist are one and the same being and that this single being has all of the attributes of the theistic God.

We noted above that a second major development in the Cosmological Argument took place in the eighteenth century, a development reflected in the writings of the German philosopher, Gottfried Leibniz (1646–1716), and especially in the writings of the English theologian and philosopher, Samuel Clarke (1675–1729). In 1704 Clarke gave a series of lectures, later published under the title *A Demonstration of the Being and Attributes of God*. These lectures constitute, perhaps, the most complete, forceful, and cogent presentation of the Cosmological Argument we possess. The lectures were read by the major skeptical philosopher of the century, David Hume (1711–1776), and in his brilliant attack on the attempt to justify religion in the court of reason, his *Dialogues Concerning Natural Religion*, Hume advanced several penetrating criticisms of Clarke's arguments, criticisms which have persuaded many philosophers in the modern period to reject the Cosmological Argument. In our study of the argument we shall concentrate our attention largely on its eighteenth-century form and try to assess its strengths and weaknesses in the light of the criticisms which Hume and others have advanced against it.

The first part of the eighteenth-century form of the Cosmological Argument seeks to establish the existence of a self-existent being. The second part of the argument attempts to prove that the self-existent being is the theistic God, that is, has the features which we have noted to be basic elements in the theistic idea of God. We shall consider mainly the first part of the argument, for it is against the first part that philosophers from Hume to Russell have advanced very important objections.

In stating the first part of the Cosmological Argument we shall make use of two important concepts, the concept of a *dependent being* and the concept of a *self-existent being*. By a *dependent being* we mean *a being whose existence is accounted for by the causal activity of other things*. Recalling Anselm's division into the three cases: "explained by another," "explained by nothing," and "explained by itself," it's clear that a dependent being is a being whose existence is explained by another. By a *self-existent being* we mean *a being whose existence is accounted for by its own nature*. This idea ... is an essential element in the theistic concept of God. Again, in terms of

Anselm's three cases, a self-existent being is a being whose existence is explained by itself. Armed with these two concepts, the concept of a dependent being and the concept of a self-existent being, we can now state the first part of the Cosmological Argument.

1. Every being (that exists or ever did exist) is either a dependent being or a self-existent being.

2. Not every being can be a dependent being.

Therefore,

3. There exists a self-existent being.

DEDUCTIVE VALIDITY

Before we look critically at each of the premises of this argument, we should note that this argument is, to use an expression from the logician's vocabulary, *deductively valid*. To find out whether an argument is deductively valid, we need only ask the question: If its premises were true, would its conclusion have to be true? If the answer is yes, the argument is deductively valid. If the answer is no, the argument is deductively invalid. Notice that the question of the validity of an argument is entirely different from the question of whether its premises are in fact true. The following argument is made up entirely of false statements, but it is deductively valid.

1. Babe Ruth is the President of the United States.

2. The President of the United States is from Indiana.

Therefore,

3. Babe Ruth is from Indiana.

The argument is deductively valid because even though its premises are false, if they were true its conclusion would have to be true. Even God, Aquinas would say, cannot bring it about that the premises of this argument are true and yet its conclusion is false, for God's power extends only to what is possible, and it is an absolute impossibility that Babe

Ruth be the President, the President be from Indiana, and yet Babe Ruth not be from Indiana.

The Cosmological Argument (that is, its first part) is a deductively valid argument. If its premises are or were true, its conclusion would have to be true. It's clear from our example about Babe Ruth, however, that the fact that an argument is deductively valid is insufficient to establish the truth of its conclusion. What else is required? Clearly that we know or have rational grounds for believing that the premises are true. If we know that the Cosmological Argument is deductively valid, and can establish that its premises are true, we shall thereby have proved that its conclusion is true. Are, then, the premises of the Cosmological Argument true? To this more difficult question we must now turn.

PSR AND THE FIRST PREMISE

At first glance the first premise might appear to be an obvious or even trivial truth. But it is neither obvious nor trivial. And if it appears to be obvious or trivial, we must be confusing the idea of a self-existent being with the idea of a being that is not a dependent being. Clearly, it is true that any being is either a dependent being (explained by other things) or it is not a dependent being (not explained by other things). But what our premise says is that any being is either a dependent being (explained by other things) or it is a self-existent being (explained by itself). Consider again Anselm's three cases.

a. explained by another

b. explained by nothing

c. explained by itself

What our first premise asserts is that each being that exists (or ever did exist) is either of sort *a* or of sort *c*. It denies that any being is of sort *b*. And it is this denial that makes the first premise both significant and controversial. The obvious truth we must not confuse it with is the truth that any being is either of sort *a* or not of sort *a*. While this is true it is neither very significant nor controversial.

Earlier we saw that Anselm accepted as a basic principle that whatever exists has an explanation of its existence. Since this basic principle denies that any thing of sort *b* exists or ever did exist, it's clear that Anselm would believe the first premise of our Cosmological Argument. The eighteenth-century proponents of the argument also were convinced of the truth of the basic principle we attributed to Anselm. And because they were convinced of its truth, they readily accepted the first premise of the Cosmological Argument. But by the eighteenth century, Anselm's basic principle had been more fully elaborated and had received a name, the *Principle of Sufficient Reason*. Since this principle (PSR, as we shall call it) plays such an important role in justifying the premises of the Cosmological Argument, it will help us to consider it for a moment before we continue our enquiry into the truth or falsity of the premises of the Cosmological Argument.

The Principle of Sufficient Reason, as it was expressed by both Leibniz and Samuel Clarke, is a very general principle and is best understood as having two parts. In its first part it is simply a restatement of Anselm's principle that there must be an explanation of the existence of any being whatever. Thus if we come upon a man in a room, PSR implies that there must be an explanation of the fact that that particular man exists. A moment's reflection, however, reveals that there are many facts about the man other than the mere fact that he exists. There is the fact that the man in question is in the room he's in, rather than somewhere else, the fact that he is in good health, and the fact that he is at the moment thinking of Paris, rather than, say, London. Now, the purpose of the second part of PSR is to require an explanation of these facts, as well. We may state PSR, therefore, as the principle that *there must be an explanation (a) of the existence of any being, and (b) of any positive fact whatever*. We are now in a position to study the role this very important principle plays in the Cosmological Argument.

Since the proponent of the Cosmological Argument accepts PSR in both its parts, it is clear that he will appeal to its first part, PSRa, as justification for the first premise of the Cosmological Argument. Of course, we can and should enquire into the deeper question of whether the proponent of the argument is rationally justified in accepting PSR itself. But we shall put this question aside for the moment. What we need to see first is whether he is correct in thinking that *if* PSR is true then both of the premises of the Cosmological Argument are true. And what we have just seen is that if only the first part of PSR, that is, PSRa, is true, the first premise of the Cosmological Argument will be true. But what of the second premise of the argument? For what reasons does the proponent think that it must be true?

THE SECOND PREMISE

According to the second premise, not every being that exists can be a dependent being, that is, can have the explanation of its existence in some other being or beings. Presumably, the proponent of the argument thinks there is something fundamentally wrong with the idea that every being that exists is dependent, that each existing being was caused by some other being which in turn was caused by some other being, and so on. But just what does he think is wrong with it? To help us in understanding his thinking, let's simplify things by supposing that there exists only one thing now, A_1, a living thing perhaps, that was brought into existence by something else, A_2, which perished shortly after it brought A_1 into existence. Suppose further that A_2 was brought into existence in similar fashion some time ago by A_3, and A_3 by A_4, and so forth back into the past. Each of these beings is a *dependent* being, it owes its existence to the preceding thing in the series. Now if nothing else ever existed but these beings, then what the second premise says would not be true. For if every being that exists or ever did exist is an A and was produced by a preceding A, then every being that exists or ever did exist would be dependent and, accordingly, premise two of the Cosmological Argument would be false. If the proponent of the Cosmological Argument is correct there must, then, be something wrong with the idea that every being that exists or did exist is an A and that they

form a causal series: A_1 caused by A_2, A_2 caused by A_3, A_3 caused by A_4, ... A_n caused by A_{n+1}. How does the proponent of the Cosmological Argument propose to show us that there is something wrong with this view?

A popular but mistaken idea of how the proponent tries to show that something is wrong with the view, that every being might be dependent, is that he uses the following argument to reject it.

1. There must be a *first* being to start any causal series.

2. If every being were dependent there would be no *first* being to start the causal series.

Therefore,

3. Not every being can be a dependent being.

Although this argument is deductively valid, and its second premise is true, its first premise overlooks the distinct possibility that a causal series might be *infinite*, with no first member at all. Thus if we go back to our series of A beings, where each A is dependent, having been produced by the preceding A in the causal series, it's clear that if the series existed it would have no first member, for every A in the series there would be a preceding A which produced it, *ad infinitum*. The first premise of the argument just given assumes that a causal series must stop with a first member somewhere in the distant past. But there seems to be no good reason for making that assumption.

The eighteenth-century proponents of the Cosmological Argument recognized that the causal series of dependent beings could be infinite, without a first member to start the series. They rejected the idea that every being that is or ever was is dependent not because there would then be no first member to the series of dependent beings, but because there would then be no explanation for the fact that there are and have always been dependent beings. To see their reasoning let's return to our simplification of the supposition that the only things that exist or ever did exist are dependent beings. In our simplification of that supposition only one of the dependent beings exists at a time, each one perishing as it produces the next in the series. Perhaps the first thing to note about this supposition is that there is no individual A in the causal series of dependent beings whose existence is unexplained—A_1 is explained by A_2, A_2 by A_3, and A_n by A_{n+1}. So the first part of PSR, PSRa, appears to be satisfied. There is no particular being whose existence lacks an explanation. What, then, is it that lacks an explanation, if every particular A in the causal series of dependent beings has an explanation? It is the *series itself* that lacks an explanation, or, as I've chosen to express it, *the fact that there are and have always been dependent beings*. For suppose we ask why it is that there are and have always been As in existence. It won't do to say that As have always been producing other As—we can't explain why there have always been As by saying there always have been As. Nor, on the supposition that only As have ever existed, can we explain the fact that there have always been As by appealing to something other than an A—for no such thing would have existed. Thus the supposition that the only things that exist or ever existed are dependent things leaves us with a fact for which there can be no explanation; namely, the fact that there are and have always been dependent beings.

QUESTIONING THE JUSTIFICATION OF THE SECOND PREMISE

Critics of the Cosmological Argument have raised several important objections against the claim that if every being is dependent the series or collection of those beings would have no explanation. Our understanding of the Cosmological Argument, as well as of its strengths and weaknesses, will be deepened by a careful consideration of these criticisms.

The first criticism is that the proponent of the Cosmological Argument makes the mistake of treating the collection or series of dependent beings as though it were itself a dependent being, and, therefore, requires an explanation of its existence. But, so the objection goes, the collection of dependent beings is not itself a dependent being any more than a collection of stamps is itself a stamp.

A second criticism is that the proponent makes the mistake of inferring that because each member of the collection of dependent beings has a cause, the collection itself must have a cause. But, as Bertrand Russell noted, such reasoning is as fallacious as to infer that the human race (that is, the collection of human beings) must have a mother because each member of the collection (each human being) has a mother.

A third criticism is that the proponent of the argument fails to realize that for there to be an explanation of a collection of things is nothing more than for there to be an explanation of each of the things making up the collection. Since in the infinite collection (or series) of dependent beings, each being in the collection does have an explanation—by virtue of having been caused by some preceding member of the collection—the explanation of the collection, so the criticism goes, has already been given. As David Hume remarked, "Did I show you the particular causes of each individual in a collection of twenty particles of matter, I should think it very unreasonable, should you afterwards ask me, what was the cause of the whole twenty. This is sufficiently explained in explaining the cause of the parts."[2]

Finally, even if the proponent of the Cosmological Argument can satisfactorily answer these objections, he must face one last objection to his ingenious attempt to justify premise two of the Cosmological Argument. For someone may agree that if nothing exists but an infinite collection of dependent beings, the infinite collection will have no explanation of its existence, and still refuse to conclude from this that there is something wrong with the idea that every being is a dependent being. Why, he might ask, should we think that everything has to have an explanation? What's wrong with admitting that the fact that there are and have always been dependent beings is a *brute fact*, a fact having no explanation whatever? Why does everything have to have an explanation anyway? We must now see what can be said in response to these several objections.

Responses to Criticism

It is certainly a mistake to think that a collection of stamps is itself a stamp, and very likely a mistake to think that the collection of dependent beings is itself a dependent being. But the mere fact that the proponent of the argument thinks that there must be an explanation not only for each member of the collection of dependent beings but for the collection itself is not sufficient grounds for concluding that he must view the collection as itself a dependent being. The collection of human beings, for example, is certainly not itself a human being. Admitting this, however, we might still seek an explanation of why there is a collection of human beings, of why there are such things as human beings at all. So the mere fact that an explanation is demanded for the collection of dependent beings is no proof that the person who demands the explanation must be supposing that the collection itself is just another dependent being.

The second criticism attributes to the proponent of the Cosmological Argument the following bit of reasoning.

1. Every member of the collection of dependent beings has a cause or explanation.

Therefore,

2. The collection of dependent beings has a cause or explanation.

As we noted in setting forth this criticism, arguments of this sort are often unreliable. It would be a mistake to conclude that a collection of objects is light in weight simply because each object in the collection is light in weight, for if there were many objects in the collection it might be quite heavy. On the other hand, if we know that each marble weighs more than one ounce, we could infer validly that the collection of marbles weighs more than an ounce. Fortunately, however, we don't need to decide whether the inference from 1 to 2 is valid or invalid. We need not decide this question because

the proponent of the Cosmological Argument need not use this inference to establish that there must be an explanation of the collection of dependent beings. He need not use this inference because he has in PSR a principle from which it follows immediately that the collection of dependent beings has a cause or explanation. For according to PSR, every positive fact must have an explanation. If it is a fact that there exists a collection of dependent beings then, according to PSR, that fact too must have an explanation. So it is PSR that the proponent of the Cosmological Argument appeals to in concluding that there must be an explanation of the collection of dependent beings, and not some dubious inference from the premise that each member of the collection has an explanation. It seems, then, that neither of the first two criticisms is strong enough to do any serious damage to the reasoning used to support the second premise of the Cosmological Argument.

The third objection contends that to explain the existence of a collection of things is the same thing as to explain the existence of each of its members. If we consider a collection of dependent beings where each being in the collection is explained by the preceding member which caused it, it's clear that no member of the collection will lack an explanation of its existence. But, so the criticism goes, if we've explained the existence of every member of a collection, we've explained the existence of the collection—there's nothing left over to be explained. This forceful criticism, originally advanced by David Hume, has gained considerable support in the modern period. But the criticism rests on an assumption that the proponent of the Cosmological Argument would not accept. The assumption is that to explain the existence of a collection of things it is *sufficient* to explain the existence of every member in the collection. To see what is wrong with this assumption is to understand the basic issue in the reasoning by which the proponent of the Cosmological Argument seeks to establish that not every being can be a dependent being.

In order for there to be an explanation of the existence of the collection of dependent beings, it's clear that the eighteenth-century proponents would require that the following two conditions be satisfied:

C1. There is an explanation of the existence of each of the members of the collection of dependent beings.
C2. There is an explanation of why there are any dependent beings.

According to the proponents of the Cosmological Argument, if every being that exists or ever did exist is a dependent being—that is, if the whole of reality consists of nothing more than a collection of dependent beings—C1 will be satisfied, but C2 will not be satisfied. And since C2 won't be satisfied, there will be no explanation of the collection of dependent beings. The third criticism, therefore, says in effect that if C1 is satisfied, C2 will be satisfied, and, since in a collection of dependent beings each member will have an explanation in whatever it was that produced it, C1 will be satisfied, So, therefore, C2 will be satisfied and the collection of dependent beings will have an explanation.

Although the issue is a complicated one, I think it is possible to see that the third criticism rests on a mistake: the mistake of thinking that if C1 is satisfied C2 must also be satisfied. The mistake is a natural one to make for it is easy to imagine circumstances in which if C1 is satisfied C2 also will be satisfied. Suppose, for example that the whole of reality includes not just a collection of dependent beings but also a self-existent being. Suppose further that instead of each dependent being having been produced by some other dependent being, every dependent being was produced by the self-existent being. Finally, let us consider both the possibility that the collection of dependent beings is finite in time and has a first member, and the possibility that the collection of dependent beings is infinite in past time, having no first member. Using G for the self-existent being, the first possibility may be diagramed as follows:

G, we shall say, has always existed and always will. We can think of d_1 as some presently existing dependent being, d_2, d_3, and so forth as dependent beings that existed at some time in the past, and d_n as the first dependent being to exist. The second possibility may be portrayed as follows:

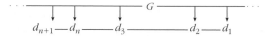

On this diagram there is no first member of the collection of dependent beings. Each member of the infinite collection, however, is explained by reference to the self-existent being G which produced it. Now the interesting point about both these cases is that the explanation that has been provided for the members of the collection of dependent beings carries with it, at least in part, an answer to the question of why there are any dependent beings at all. In both cases we may explain why there are dependent beings by pointing out that there exists a self-existent being that has been engaged in producing them. So once we have learned that the existence of each member of the collection of dependent beings has its existence explained by the fact that G produced it, we have already learned why there are dependent beings.

Someone might object that we haven't really learned why there are dependent beings until we also learn *why* G has been producing them. But, of course, we could also say that we haven't really explained the existence of a particular dependent being, say d_3, until we also learn not just that G produced it but *why* G produced it. The point we need to grasp, however, is that once we admit that every dependent being's existence is explained by G, we must admit that the fact that there are dependent beings has also been explained. So it is not unnatural that someone should think that to explain the existence of the collection of dependent beings is nothing more than to explain the existence of its members. For, as we've seen, to explain the collection's existence is to explain each member's existence and to explain why there are any dependent beings at all. And in the examples we've considered, in doing the one (explaining why each dependent being exists) we've already done the other (explained why there are any dependent beings at all). We must now see, however, that on the supposition that the whole of reality consists *only* of a collection of dependent beings, to give an explanation of each member's existence is not to provide an explanation of why there are dependent beings.

In the examples we've considered, we have gone outside of the collection of dependent beings in order to explain the members' existence. But if the only beings that exist or ever existed are dependent beings then each dependent being will be explained by some other dependent being, ad infinitum. This does not mean that there will be some particular dependent being whose existence is unaccounted for. Each dependent being has an explanation of its existence; namely, in the dependent being which preceded it and produced it. So C1 is satisfied: there is an explanation of the existence of each member of the collection of dependent beings. Turning to C2, however, we can see that it will not be satisfied. We cannot explain why there are (or have ever been) dependent beings by appealing to all the members of the infinite collection of dependent beings. For if the question to be answered is why there are (or have ever been) any dependent beings at all, we cannot answer that question by noting that there always have been dependent beings, each one accounting for the existence of some other dependent being. Thus on the supposition that every being is dependent, it seems there will be no explanation of why there are dependent beings. C2 will not be satisfied. Therefore, on the supposition that every being is dependent there will be no explanation of the existence of the collection of dependent beings.

THE TRUTH OF PSR

We come now to the final criticism of the reasoning supporting the second premise of the Cosmological Argument. According to the criticism, it is admitted that the supposition that every being is dependent implies that there will be a *brute fact* in the universe, a fact, that is, for which there can be no explanation whatever. For there will be no explanation of the fact that dependent beings exist and have always been in existence. It is this brute fact that the proponents of the argument were describing when they pointed out that if every being is dependent, the series or collection of dependent beings would lack an explanation of *its* existence. The final criticism asks what is wrong with admitting that the universe contains such a brute, unintelligible fact. In asking this question the critic challenges the fundamental principle, PSR, on which the Cosmological Argument rests. For, as we've seen, the first premise of the argument denies that there exists a being whose existence has no explanation. In support of this premise the proponent appeals to the first part of PSR. The second premise of the argument claims that not every being can be dependent. In support of this premise the proponent appeals to the second part of PSR, the part which states that there must be an explanation of any positive fact whatever.

The proponent reasons that if every being were a dependent being, then although the first part of PSR would be satisfied—every being would have an explanation—the second part would be violated; there would be no explanation for the positive fact that there are and have always been dependent beings. For first, since every being is supposed to be dependent, there would be nothing outside of the collection of dependent beings to explain the collection's existence. Second, the fact that each member of the collection has an explanation in some other dependent being is insufficient to explain why there are and have always been dependent beings. And, finally, there is nothing about the collection of dependent beings that would suggest that it is a self-existent collection. Consequently, if every being were dependent, the fact that there are and have always been dependent beings would have no explanation. But this violates the second part of PSR. So the second premise of the Cosmological Argument must be true: Not every being can be a dependent being. This conclusion, however, is no better than the principle, PSR, on which it rests. And it is the point of the final criticism to question the truth of PSR. Why, after all, should we accept the idea that every being and every positive fact must have an explanation? Why, in short, should we believe PSR? These are important questions, and any final judgment of the Cosmological Argument depends on how they are answered.

Most of the theologians and philosophers who accept PSR have tried to defend it in either of two ways. Some have held that PSR is (or can be) known *intuitively* to be true. By this they mean that if we fully understand and reflect on what is said by PSR we can see that it must be true. Now, undoubtedly, there are statements which are known intuitively to be true. "Every triangle has exactly three angles" or "No physical object can be in two different places in space at one and the same time" are examples of statements whose truth we can apprehend just by understanding and reflecting on them. The difficulty with the claim that PSR is intuitively true, however, is that a number of very able philosophers fail to apprehend its truth, and some even claim that the principle is false. It is doubtful, therefore, that many of us, if any, know intuitively that PSR is true.

The second way philosophers and theologians who accept PSR have sought to defend it is by claiming that although it is not known to be true, it is, nevertheless, a presupposition of reason, a basic assumption that rational people make, whether or not they reflect sufficiently to become aware of the assumption. It's probably true that there are some assumptions we all make about our world, assumptions which are so basic that most of us are unaware of them. And, I suppose, it might be true that PSR is such an assumption. What bearing would this view of PSR have on the Cosmological Argument? Perhaps the main point to note is that even if PSR is a presupposition we all share, the premises of the Cosmological Argument could still be false. For PSR itself could still be false. The fact, if it is a fact, that all of us *presuppose* that every existing being and every positive fact has an explanation does not imply

that no being exists, and no positive fact obtains, without an explanation. Nature is not bound to satisfy our presuppositions. As the American philosopher William James once remarked in another connection, "In the great boarding house of nature, the cakes and the butter and the syrup seldom come out so even and leave the plates so clear."

Our study of the first part of the Cosmological Argument has led us to the fundamental principle on which its premises rest, the Principle of Sufficient Reason. Since we do not seem to know that PSR is true, we cannot reasonably claim to know that the premises of the Cosmological Argument are true. They might be true. But unless we do know them to be true they cannot *establish* for us the conclusion that there exists a being that has the explanation of its existence within its own nature. If it were shown, however, that even though we do not *know* that PSR is true we all, nevertheless, *presuppose* PSR to be true, then, whether PSR is true or not, to be consistent we should accept the Cosmological Argument. For, as we've seen, its premises imply its conclusion and its premises do seem to follow from PSR. But no one has succeeded in *showing* that PSR is an assumption that most or all of us share. So our final conclusion must be that although the Cosmological Argument might be a *sound* argument (valid with true premises), it does not provide us with good rational grounds for believing that among these beings that exist there is one whose existence is accounted for by its own nature. Having come to this conclusion, we may safely put aside the second part of the argument. For even if it succeeded in showing that a self-existent being would have the other attributes of the theistic God, the Cosmological Argument would still not provide us with good rational grounds for belief in God, having failed in its first part to provide us with good rational grounds for believing that there is a self-existent being.

NOTES

1. See St. Thomas Aquinas, *Summa Theologica, Ila.* 2, 3.

2. David Hume, *Dialogues Concerning Natural Religion*, Part IX, ed. H. D. Aiken (New York: Hafner Publishing Company, 1948), pp. 59–60.

II.B.4

The *Kalām* Cosmological Argument

WILLIAM LANE CRAIG AND J. P. MORELAND

William Lane Craig (1949–) is professor of philosophy at Biola University in Los Angeles. He received his PhD in philosophy from the University of Birmingham (England) and a ThD from the University of Munich (Germany). J. P. Moreland (1948–) is also professor of philosophy at Biola University. He received his PhD in philosophy from the University of Southern California. Professors Craig and Moreland are the authors of numerous works in philosophy of religion, including Philosophical Foundations for a Christian Worldview *(2003), from which the following selection is taken. The* kalām *argument is a version of the cosmological argument developed by the Arab Islamic scholars al-Kindi and al-Ghazali in the Middle Ages. In this article Craig and Moreland develop two versions of the* kalām *argument, both aiming to prove that the universe must have a cause of its existence.*

The cosmological argument is a family of arguments that seek to demonstrate the existence of a Sufficient Reason or First Cause of the existence of the cosmos. The roll of the defenders of this argument reads like a *Who's Who* of western philosophy: Plato, Aristotle, ibn Sina, Al Ghazali, Maimonides, Anselm, Aquinas, Scotus, Descartes, Spinoza, Leibniz and Locke, to name but some. The arguments can be grouped into three basic types: the *kalām* cosmological argument for a First Cause of the beginning of the universe, the Thomist cosmological argument for a sustaining Ground of Being of the world, and the Leibnizian cosmological argument for a Sufficient Reason why something exists rather than nothing.

The *kalām* cosmological argument derives its name from the Arabic word designating medieval Islamic scholasticism, the intellectual movement largely responsible for developing the argument. It aims to show that the universe had a beginning at some moment in the finite past and, since something cannot come out of nothing, must therefore have a transcendent cause, which brought the universe into being. Classical proponents of the argument sought to demonstrate that the universe began to exist on the basis of philosophical arguments against the existence of an infinite, temporal regress of past events. Contemporary interest in the argument arises largely out of the startling empirical evidence of astrophysical cosmology for a beginning of space and time. Today the controlling paradigm of cosmology is the standard big bang model, according to which the space-time universe originated *ex nihilo* about fifteen billion years ago. Such an origin *ex nihilo* seems to many to cry out for a transcendent cause.

By contrast the Thomist cosmological argument, named for the medieval philosophical theologian Thomas Aquinas, seeks a cause that is first, not in the temporal sense, but in the sense of rank.

Taken from *Philosophical Foundations for a Christian Worldview* by J. P. Moreland and William Lane Craig. Copyright © 2003 by J. P. Moreland and William Lane Craig. Used by permission of InterVarsity Press PO Box 1400 Downers Grove, IL 60515. www.ivpress.com

Aquinas agreed that "if the world and motion have a first beginning, some cause must clearly be posited for this origin of the world and of motion" (*Summa contra gentiles* 1.13.30). But since he did not regard the *kalām* arguments for the past's finitude as demonstrative, he argued for God's existence on the more difficult assumption of the eternity of the world. On Aquinas's Aristotelian-inspired metaphysic, every existing finite thing is composed of essence and existence and is therefore radically contingent. A thing's essence is an individual nature which serves to define what that thing is. Now if an essence is to exist, there must be conjoined with that essence an act of being. This act of being involves a continual bestowal of being, or the thing would be annihilated. Essence is in potentiality to the act of being, and therefore without the bestowal of being the essence would not exist. For the same reason no substance can actualize itself; for in order to bestow being on itself it would have to be already actual. A pure potentiality cannot actualize itself but requires some external cause. Now although Aquinas argued that there cannot be an infinite regress of causes of being (because in such a series all the causes would be merely instrumental and so no being would be produced, just as no motion would be produced in a watch without a spring even if it had an infinite number of gears) and that therefore there must exist a First Uncaused Cause of being, his actual view was that there can be no intermediate causes of being at all, that any finite substance is sustained in existence immediately by the Ground of Being. This must be a being that is not composed of essence and existence and, hence, requires no sustaining cause. We cannot say that this being's essence includes existence as one of its properties, for existence is not a property, but an act, the instantiating of an essence. Therefore, we must conclude that this being's essence just *is* existence. In a sense, this being has no essence; rather, it is the pure act of being, unconstrained by any essence. It is, as Thomas says, *ipsum esse subsistens*, the act of being itself subsisting. Thomas identifies this being with the God whose name was revealed to Moses as "I am" (Ex 3:14).

The German polymath Gottfried Wilhelm Leibniz, for whom the third form of the argument is named, sought to develop a version of the cosmological argument from contingency without the Aristotelian metaphysical underpinnings of the Thomist argument. In his essay "The Principles of Nature and of Grace, Based on Reason," Leibniz wrote, "The first question which should rightly be asked is this: why is there something rather than nothing?" Leibniz meant this question to be truly universal, not merely to apply to finite things. On the basis of his principle of sufficient reason, as stated in his treatise *The Monadology*, that "no fact can be real or existent, no statement true, unless there be a sufficient reason why it is so and not otherwise," Leibniz held that his question must have an answer. It will not do to say that the universe (or even God) just exists as a brute fact, a simple fact that cannot be explained. There must be an explanation why it exists. He went on to argue that the sufficient reason cannot be found in any individual thing in the universe, nor in the collection of such things which comprise the universe, nor in earlier states of the universe, even if these regress infinitely. Therefore, there must exist an ultramundane being that is metaphysically necessary in its existence, that is to say, its nonexistence is impossible. It is the sufficient reason for its own existence as well as for the existence of every contingent thing.

In evaluating these arguments, let us consider them in reverse order. A simple statement of a Leibnizian cosmological argument runs as follows:

1. Every existing thing has an explanation of its existence, either in the necessity of its own nature or in an external cause.

2. If the universe has an explanation of its existence, that explanation is God.

3. The universe is an existing thing.

4. Therefore the explanation of the existence of the universe is God.

Is this a good argument? One of the principal objections to Leibniz's own formulation of the argument is that the principle of sufficient reason as stated in *The Monadology* seems evidently false. There cannot be an explanation of why there are any contingent states of affairs at all, for if such an explanation is contingent, then it too must have a further explanation, whereas if it is necessary, then the states of affairs explained by it must also be necessary. Some theists have responded to this objection by agreeing that one must ultimately come to some explanatory stopping point that is simply a brute fact, a being whose existence is unexplained. For example, Richard Swinburne claims that in answering the question "Why is there something rather than nothing?" we must finally come to the brute existence of some contingent being. This being will not serve to explain its own existence (and, hence, Leibniz's question goes unanswered), but it will explain the existence of everything else. Swinburne argues that God is the best explanation of why everything other than the brute Ultimate exists because as a unique and infinite being God is simpler than the variegated and finite universe.

But the above formulation of the Leibnizian argument avoids the objection without retreating to the dubious position that God is a contingent being. Premise (1) merely requires any existing *thing* to have an explanation of its existence, either in the necessity of its own nature or in some external cause. This premise is compatible with there being brute *facts* about the world. What it precludes is that there could exist things—substances exemplifying properties—that just exist inexplicably. This principle seems quite plausible, at least more so than its contradictory, which is all that is required for a successful argument. On this analysis, there are two kinds of being: necessary beings, which exist of their own nature and so have no external cause of their existence, and contingent beings, whose existence is accounted for by causal factors outside themselves.

Premise (2) is, in effect, the contrapositive of the typical atheist response to Leibniz that on the atheistic worldview the universe simply exists as a brute contingent thing. Atheists typically assert that, there being no God, it is false that everything has an explanation of its existence, for the universe, in this case, just exists inexplicably. In so saying, the atheist implicitly recognizes that if the universe has an explanation, then God exists as its explanatory ground. Since, as premise (3) states, the universe is obviously an existing thing (especially evident in its very early stages when its density was so extreme), it follows that God exists.

It is open to the atheist to retort that while the universe has an explanation of its existence, that explanation lies not in an external ground but in the necessity of its own nature. In other words, (2) is false; the universe is a metaphysically necessary being. This was the suggestion of David Hume, who demanded, "Why may not the material universe be the necessarily existent being?" Indeed, "How can anything, that exists from eternity, have a cause, since that relation implies a priority in time and a beginning of existence?" (*Dialogues Concerning Natural Religion*, Part 9).

This is an extremely bold suggestion on the part of the atheist. We have, we think we can safely say, a strong intuition of the universe's contingency. A possible world in which no concrete objects exist certainly seems conceivable. We generally trust our modal intuitions on other matters; if we are to do otherwise with respect to the universe's contingency, then atheists need to provide some reason for such skepticism other than their desire to avoid theism. But they have yet to do so.

Still, it would be desirable to have some stronger argument for the universe's contingency than our modal intuitions alone. Could the Thomist cosmological argument help us here? If successful, it would show that the universe is a contingent being causally dependent on a necessary being for its continued existence. The difficulty with appeal to the Thomist argument, however, is that it is very difficult to show that things are, in fact, contingent in the special sense required by the argument. Certainly things are naturally contingent in that their continued existence is dependent on a myriad of factors including particle masses and fundamental forces, temperature, pressure, entropy level and so forth, but this natural contingency does not suffice to establish things' metaphysical contingency in the sense that being must continually be added to their essences lest they be spontaneously annihilated.

Indeed, if Thomas's argument does ultimately lead to an absolutely simple being whose essence is existence, then one might well be led to deny that beings are metaphysically composed of essence and existence if the idea of such an absolutely simple being proves to be unintelligible. . . .

But what about the *kalām* cosmological argument? An essential property of a metaphysically necessary and ultimate being is that it be eternal, that is to say, without beginning or end. If the universe is not eternal, then it could not be, as Hume suggested, a metaphysically necessary being. But it is precisely the aim of the *kalām* cosmological argument to show that the universe is not eternal but had a beginning. It would follow that the universe must therefore be contingent in its existence. Not only so, the *kalām* argument shows the universe to be contingent in a very special way: it came into existence out of nothing. The atheist who would answer Leibniz by holding that the existence of the universe is a brute fact, an exception to the principle of sufficient reason, is thus thrust into the very awkward position of maintaining not merely that the universe exists eternally without explanation, but rather that for no reason at all it magically popped into being out of nothing, a position which might make theism look like a welcome alternative. Thus the *kalām* argument not only constitutes an independent argument for a transcendent Creator but also serves as a valuable supplement to the Leibnizian argument.

The *kalām* cosmological argument may be formulated as follows:

1. Whatever begins to exist has a cause.

2. The universe began to exist.

3. Therefore, the universe has a cause.

Conceptual analysis of what it means to be a cause of the universe then aims to establish some of the theologically significant properties of this being.

Premise (1) seems obviously true—at the least, more so than its negation. It is rooted in the metaphysical intuition that something cannot come into being from nothing. Moreover, this premise is constantly confirmed in our experience. Nevertheless,

a number of atheists, in order to avoid the argument's conclusion, have denied the first premise. Sometimes it is said that quantum physics furnishes an exception to premise (1), since on the subatomic level events are said to be uncaused (according to the so-called Copenhagen interpretation). In the same way, certain theories of cosmic origins are interpreted as showing that the whole universe could have sprung into being out of the subatomic vacuum. Thus the universe is said to be the proverbial free lunch.

This objection, however, is based on misunderstandings. In the first place, not all scientists agree that subatomic events are uncaused. A great many physicists today are quite dissatisfied with the Copenhagen interpretation of subatomic physics and are exploring deterministic theories like that of David Bohm. Thus subatomic physics is not a proven exception to premise (1). Second, even on the traditional, indeterministic interpretation, particles do not come into being out of nothing. They arise as spontaneous fluctuations of the energy contained in the subatomic vacuum, which constitutes an indeterministic cause of their origination. Third, the same point can be made about theories of the origin of the universe out of a primordial vacuum. Popular magazine articles touting such theories as getting "something from nothing" simply do not understand that the vacuum is not nothing but rather a sea of fluctuating energy endowed with a rich structure and subject to physical laws. Thus there is no basis for the claim that quantum physics proves that things can begin to exist without a cause, much less that the universe could have sprung into being uncaused from literally nothing.

Other critics have said that premise (1) is true only for things *in* the universe, but it is not true *of* the universe itself. But the argument's defender may reply that this objection misconstrues the nature of the premise. Premise (1) does not state merely a physical law like the law of gravity or the laws of thermodynamics, which are valid for things within the universe. Premise (1) is not a physical principle. Rather, premise (1) is a metaphysical principle: being cannot come from nonbeing; something cannot come into existence uncaused from nothing. The principle therefore applies to all of reality, and it is thus metaphysically absurd that the universe should pop into being uncaused out of nothing. This response seems quite reasonable: for on the atheistic view, there was not even the *potentiality* of the universe's existence prior to the big bang, since nothing is prior to the big bang. But then how could the universe become actual if there was not even the potentiality of its existence? It makes much more sense to say that the potentiality of the universe lay in the power of God to create it.

Recently some critics of the *kalām* cosmological argument have denied that in beginning to exist the universe *became actual* or *came into being*. They thereby focus attention on the theory of time underlying the *kalām* argument.... On a static or so-called B-theory of time (according to which all moments of time are equally existent) the universe does not in fact come into being or become actual at the big bang; it just exists tenselessly as a four-dimensional space-time block that is finitely extended in the *earlier than* direction. If time is tenseless, then the critics are right that the universe never really comes into being, and therefore the quest for a cause of its coming into being is misconceived. Although Leibniz's question, "Why is there (tenselessly) something rather than nothing?" should still rightly be asked, there would be no reason to look for a cause of the universe's beginning to exist, since on tenseless theories of time the universe did not truly begin to exist by virtue of its having a first event, any more than a meter stick begins to exist by virtue of its having a first centimeter. In affirming that things which begin to exist need a cause, the proponent of the *kalām* cosmological argument assumes the following understanding of that notion, where x ranges over any entity and t ranges over times, whether instants or moments of nonzero finite duration:

A. x begins to exist at t if and only if x comes into being at t.

B. x comes into being at t if and only if (i) x exists at t, and the actual world includes no state of affairs in which x exists timelessly, (ii) t is either the first time at which x exists or is separated from any $t' < t$ at which x existed by an interval during which x does not exist, and (iii) x's existing at t is a tensed fact.

The key clause in (B) is (iii). By presupposing a dynamic or so-called A-theory of time, according to which temporal becoming is real, the proponent of the *kalām* cosmological argument justifiably assumes that the universe's existing at a first moment of time represents the moment at which the universe came into being. Thus the real issue separating the proponent of the *kalām* cosmological argument and critics of the first premise is the objectivity of tense and temporal becoming.

Premise (2), *The universe began to exist*, has been supported by both deductive philosophical arguments and inductive scientific arguments. The first of four arguments for this premise that we will consider is the argument based on *the impossibility of the existence of an actual infinite*. It may be formulated as follows:

1. An actual infinite cannot exist.

2. An infinite temporal regress of physical events is an actual infinite.

3. Therefore an infinite temporal regress of physical events cannot exist.

In order to assess this argument, it will be helpful to define some terms. By an actual infinite, the argument's defender means any collection having at a time t a number of definite and discrete members that is greater than any natural number $\{0, 1, 2, 3, \ldots\}$. This notion is to be contrasted with a potential infinite, which is any collection having at any time t a number of definite and discrete members that is equal to some natural number but which over time increases endlessly toward infinity as a limit. By *exist* proponents of the argument mean "have extra-mental existence," or "be instantiated in the real world." By a "physical event," they mean any change occurring within the space-time universe. Since any change takes time, there are no instantaneous events. Neither could there be an infinitely slow event, since such an "event" would in reality be a changeless state. Therefore, any event will have a finite, nonzero duration. In order that all the events comprising the temporal regress of past events be of equal duration, one arbitrarily stipulates some event as our standard and, taking as our point of departure the present standard event, we consider any series of such standard events ordered according to the relation *earlier than*. The question is whether this series of events is comprised of an actually infinite number of events or not. If not, then since the universe is not distinct from the series of past physical events, the universe must have had a beginning, in the sense of a first standard event. It is therefore not relevant whether the temporal series had a beginning *point* (a first temporal instant). The question is whether there was in the past an event occupying a nonzero, finite temporal interval that was absolutely first, that is, not preceded by any equal interval.

Premise (1) asserts, then, that an actual infinite cannot exist in the real, spatiotemporal world. It is usually alleged that this sort of argument has been invalidated by Georg Cantor's work on the actual infinite and by subsequent developments in set theory. But this allegation misconstrues the nature of both Cantor's system and modern set theory, for the argument does not in fact contradict a single tenet of either. The reason is this: Cantor's system and set theory are simply a universe of discourse, a mathematical system based on certain adopted axioms and conventions. The argument's defender may hold that while the actual infinite may be a fruitful and consistent concept within the postulated universe of discourse, it cannot be transposed into the spatiotemporal world, for this would involve counterintuitive absurdities. This can be shown by concrete examples that illustrate the various absurdities that would result if an actual infinite were to be instantiated in the real world.

Take, for example, Hilbert's Hotel, a product of the mind of the great German mathematician David Hilbert. As a warm-up, let us first imagine a hotel with a finite number of rooms. Suppose, furthermore, that all the rooms are full. When a new guest arrives asking for a room, the proprietor apologizes, "Sorry, all the rooms are full," and that is the end of the story. But now let us imagine a hotel with an infinite number of rooms and suppose once

more that *all the rooms are full*. There is not a single vacant room throughout the entire infinite hotel. Now suppose a new guest shows up, asking for a room. "But of course!" says the proprietor, and he immediately shifts the person in room #1 into room #2, the person in room #2 into room #3, the person in room #3 into room #4 and so on, out to infinity. As a result of these room changes, room #1 now becomes vacant, and the new guest gratefully checks in. But remember, before he arrived, all the rooms were full! Equally curious, according to the mathematicians, there are now no more persons in the hotel than there were before: the number is just infinite. But how can this be? The proprietor just added the new guest's name to the register and gave him his keys—how can there not be one more person in the hotel than before?

But the situation becomes even stranger. For suppose an infinity of new guests show up at the desk, asking for a room. "Of course, of course!" says the proprietor, and he proceeds to shift the person in room #1 into room #2, the person in room #2 into room #4, the person in room #3 into room #6 and so on out to infinity, always putting each former occupant into the room number twice his own. Because any natural number multiplied by two always equals an even number, all the guests wind up in even-numbered rooms. As a result, all the odd-numbered rooms become vacant, and the infinity of new guests is easily accommodated. And yet, before they came, all the rooms were full! And again, strangely enough, the number of guests in the hotel is the same after the infinity of new guests check in as before, even though there were as many new guests as old guests. In fact, the proprietor could repeat this process *infinitely many times*, and yet there would never be one single person more in the hotel than before.

But Hilbert's Hotel is even stranger than the German mathematician made it out to be. For suppose some of the guests start to check out. Suppose the guest in room #1 departs. Is there not now one fewer person in the hotel? Not according to the mathematicians! Suppose the guests in rooms #1, 3, 5, . . . check out. In this case an infinite number of people have left the hotel, but according to the mathematicians, there are no fewer people in the hotel! In fact, we could have every other guest check out of the hotel and repeat this process infinitely many times, and yet there would never be any fewer people in the hotel. Now suppose the proprietor doesn't like having a half-empty hotel (it looks bad for business). No matter! By shifting occupants as before, but in reverse order, he transforms his half-vacant hotel into one that is jammed to the gills. You might think that by these maneuvers the proprietor could always keep this strange hotel fully occupied. But you would be wrong. For suppose that the persons in rooms #4, 5, 6, ... checked out. At a single stroke the hotel would be virtually emptied, the guest register would be reduced to three names, and the infinite would be converted to finitude. And yet it would remain true that the same number of guests checked out this time as when the guests in rooms #1, 3, 5, ... checked out! Can anyone believe that such a hotel could exist in reality?

Hilbert's Hotel certainly seems absurd. Since nothing hangs on the illustration's involving a hotel, the argument, if successful, would show in general that it is impossible for an actually infinite number of things to exist in spatiotemporal reality. Students sometimes react to such illustrations as Hilbert's Hotel by saying that we really do not understand the nature of infinity and, hence, these absurdities result. But this attitude is simply mistaken. Infinite set theory is a highly developed and well-understood branch of mathematics, and these absurdities can be seen to result precisely because we *do* understand the notion of a collection with an actually infinite number of members.

Sometimes it is said that we can find counterexamples to the claim that an actually infinite number of things cannot exist, so that premise (1) must be false. For instance, is not every finite distance capable of being divided into 1/2, 1/4, 1/8, ..., on to infinity? Does that not prove that there are in any finite distance an actually infinite number of parts? The defender of the argument may reply that this objection confuses a potential infinite with an actual infinite. He will point out that while you can continue to divide any distance for as long as

you want, such a series is merely potentially infinite, in that infinity serves as a limit that you endlessly approach but never reach. If you assume that any distance is *already* composed out of an actually infinite number of parts, then you are begging the question. You are assuming what the objector is supposed to prove, namely that there is a clear counterexample to the claim that an actually infinite number of things cannot exist.

Again, it is worth reiterating that nothing in the argument need be construed as an attempt to undermine the theoretical system bequeathed by Cantor to modern mathematics. Indeed, some of the most eager enthusiasts of the system of transfinite mathematics are only too ready to agree that these theories have no relation to the real world. Thus Hilbert, who exuberantly extolled Cantor's greatness, nevertheless held that the Cantorian paradise exists only in the ideal world invented by the mathematician and is nowhere to be found in reality. The case against the existence of the actual infinite need say nothing about the use of the idea of the infinite in conceptual mathematical systems.

The second premise states that *an infinite temporal regress of events is an actual infinite.* The second premise asserts that if the series or sequence of changes in time is infinite, then these events considered collectively constitute an actual infinite. The point seems obvious enough, for if there has been a sequence composed of an infinite number of events stretching back into the past, then an actually infinite number of events have occurred. If the series of past events were an actual infinite, then all the absurdities attending the real existence of an actual infinite would apply to it.

In summary: if an actual infinite cannot exist in the real, spatiotemporal world and an infinite temporal regress of events is such an actual infinite, we can conclude that an infinite temporal regress of events cannot exist, that is to say, the temporal series of past physical events had a beginning. And this implies the second premise of the original syllogism of the *kalām* cosmological argument.

The second argument against the possibility of an infinite past that we will consider is the argument based on *the impossibility of forming an actual infinite by successive addition.* It may be formulated as follows:

1. The temporal series of physical events is a collection formed by successive addition.

2. A collection formed by successive addition cannot be an actual infinite.

3. Therefore, the temporal series of physical events cannot be an actual infinite.

Here one does not assume that an actual infinite cannot exist. Even if an actual infinite can exist, it is argued that the temporal series of events cannot be such, since an actual infinite cannot be formed by successive addition, as the temporal series of events is.

Premise (1) presupposes once again an A-theory of time. On such a theory the collection of all past events prior to any given event is not a collection whose members all tenselessly coexist. Rather, it is a collection that is instantiated sequentially or successively in time, one event coming to pass on the heels of another. Since temporal becoming is an objective feature of the physical world, the series of past events is not a tenselessly existing continuum, all of whose members are equally real. Rather, the members of the series come to be and pass away one after another.

Premise (2) asserts that a collection formed by successive addition cannot be an actual infinite. Sometimes this is described as the impossibility of traversing the infinite. In order for us to have "arrived" at today, temporal existence has, so to speak, traversed an infinite number of prior events. But before the present event could arrive, the event immediately prior to it would have to arrive, and before that event could arrive, the event immediately prior to it would have to arrive, and so on ad infinitum. No event could ever arrive, since before it could elapse there will always be one more event that had to have happened first. Thus, if the series of past events were beginningless, the present event could not have arrived, which is absurd.

This argument brings to mind Betrand Russell's account of Tristram Shandy, who, in the novel by Sterne, writes his autobiography so slowly

that it takes him a whole year to record the events of a single day. Were he mortal, he would never finish, asserts Russell, but if he were immortal, then the entire book could be completed, since to each day there would correspond a year, and both are infinite. Russell's assertion is untenable on an A-theory of time, however, since the future is in reality a potential infinite only. Though he write forever, Tristram Shandy would only get farther and farther behind, so that instead of finishing his autobiography, he will progressively approach a state in which he would be *infinitely* far behind. But he would never reach such a state because the years and hence the days of his life would always be finite in number though indefinitely increasing.

But let us turn the story about: Suppose Tristram Shandy has been writing from eternity past at the rate of one day per year. Should not Tristram Shandy now be infinitely far behind? For if he has lived for an infinite number of years, Tristram Shandy has recorded an equally infinite number of past days. Given the thoroughness of his autobiography, these days are all consecutive days. At any point in the past or present, therefore, Tristram Shandy has recorded a beginningless, infinite series of consecutive days. But now the question inevitably arises: *Which* days are these? Where in the temporal series of events are the days recorded by Tristram Shandy at any given point? The answer can only be that *they are days infinitely distant from the present.* For there is no day on which Tristram Shandy is writing that is finitely distant from the last recorded day.

If Tristram Shandy has been writing for one year's time, then the most recent day he could have recorded is one year ago. But if he has been writing two years, then that same day could not have been recorded by him. For since his intention is to record *consecutive* days of his life, the most recent day he could have recorded is the day immediately after a day at least two years ago. This is because it takes a year to record a day, so that to record two days he must have two years. Similarly, if he has been writing three years, then the most recent day recorded could be no more recent than three years ago plus two days. In fact, the recession into the past of the most recent recordable day can be plotted according to the formula: (present date − n years of writing) $+$ ($n − 1$) days. In other words, the longer he has written the further behind he has fallen. But what happens if Tristram Shandy has, *ex hypothesi*, been writing for an infinite number of years? The first day of his autobiography recedes to infinity, that is to say, to a day infinitely distant from the present. Nowhere in the past at a finite distance from the present can we find a recorded day, for by now Tristram Shandy is infinitely far behind. The beginningless, infinite series of days which he has recorded are days which lie at an infinite temporal distance from the present. What therefore follows from the Tristram Shandy story is that an infinite series of past events is absurd, for there is no way to traverse the distance from an infinitely distant event to the present, or, more technically, for an event that was once present to recede to an infinite temporal distance.

But now a deeper absurdity bursts into view. For if the series of past events is an actual infinite, then we may ask, why did Tristram Shandy not finish his autobiography yesterday or the day before, since by then an infinite series of moments had already elapsed? Given that in infinite time he would finish the book, then at any point in the infinite past he should already have finished. No matter how far along the series of past events one regresses, Tristram Shandy would have already completed his autobiography. Therefore, at no point in the infinite series of past events could he be finishing the book. We could never look over Tristram Shandy's shoulder to see if he were now writing the last page. For at any point an actually infinite sequence of events would have transpired and the book would have already been completed. Thus at no time in eternity will we find Tristram Shandy writing, which is absurd, since we supposed him to be writing from eternity. And at no point will he finish the book, which is equally absurd, because for the book to be completed, he must at some point have finished. What the Tristram Shandy story really tells us is that an actually infinite temporal regress is absurd.

Sometimes critics indict this argument as a sleight-of-hand trick like Zeno's paradoxes of motion. Zeno argued that before Achilles could cross the stadium, he would have to cross halfway; but before he could cross halfway, he would have to cross a quarter of the way; but before he could cross a quarter of the way, he would have to cross an eighth of the way, and so on to infinity. It is evident that Achilles could not even move! Therefore, Zeno concluded, motion is impossible. Now even though Zeno's argument is very difficult to refute, nobody really believes that motion is impossible. Even if Achilles must pass through an infinite number of halfway points in order to cross the stadium, somehow he manages to do so! The argument against the impossibility of traversing an infinite past, some critics allege, must commit the same fallacy as Zeno's paradox.

But such an objection fails to reckon with two crucial disanalogies of an infinite past to Zeno's paradoxes: whereas in Zeno's thought experiments the intervals traversed are *potential* and *unequal*, in the case of an infinite past the intervals are *actual* and *equal*. The claim that Achilles must pass through an infinite number of halfway points in order to cross the stadium is question-begging, for it already assumes that the whole interval is a composition of an infinite number of points, whereas Zeno's opponents, like Aristotle, take the line as a whole to be conceptually prior to any divisions which we might make in it. Moreover, Zeno's intervals, being unequal, sum to a merely finite distance, whereas the intervals in an infinite past sum to an infinite distance. Thus his thought experiments are crucially disanalogous to the task of traversing an infinite number of equal, actual intervals to arrive at our present location.

It is frequently objected that this sort of argument illicitly presupposes an infinitely distant starting point in the past and then pronounces it impossible to travel from that point to today. But if the past is infinite, then there would be no starting point whatever, not even an infinitely distant one. Nevertheless, from any given point in the past, there is only a finite distance to the present, which is easily "traversed." But in fact no proponent of the *kalām* argument of whom we are aware has assumed that there was an infinitely distant starting point in the past. (Even the Tristram Shandy paradox does not assert that there was an infinitely distant first day, but merely that there were days infinitely distant in the past.) The fact that there is *no beginning* at all, not even an infinitely distant one, seems only to make the problem worse, not better. To say that the infinite past could have been formed by successive addition is like saying that someone has just succeeded in writing down all the negative numbers, ending at −1. And, we may ask, how is the claim that from any given moment in the past there is only a finite distance to the present even relevant to the issue? The defender of the *kalām* argument could agree to this happily. For the issue is how the *whole* series can be formed, not a finite portion of it. Does the objector think that because every *finite* segment of the series can be formed by successive addition that the whole *infinite* series can be so formed? That is as logically fallacious as saying because every part of an elephant is light in weight, the whole elephant is light in weight. The claim is therefore irrelevant.

In summary: If a collection formed by successive addition cannot be an actual infinite, then since the temporal series of events is a collection formed by successive addition, it follows that the temporal series of past physical events is not beginningless.

The third argument for the universe's beginning advanced by contemporary proponents of the *kalām* cosmological argument is an inductive argument based on the expansion of the universe. In 1917, Albert Einstein made a cosmological application of his newly discovered gravitational theory, the general theory of relativity (GTR). In so doing he assumed that the universe exists in a steady state, with a constant mean mass density and a constant curvature of space. To his chagrin, however, he found that GTR would not permit such a model of the universe unless he introduced into his gravitational field equations a certain "fudge factor" in order to counterbalance the gravitational effect of matter and so ensure a static universe. Unfortunately, Einstein's static universe was balanced on a razor's edge, and the least perturbation would cause the universe either to implode or to expand. By taking this feature of Einstein's model seriously, the

Russian mathematician Alexander Friedman and the Belgian astronomer Georges Lemaître were able to formulate independently in the 1920s solutions to the field equations which predicted an expanding universe.

In 1929 the astronomer Edwin Hubble showed that the red-shift in the optical spectra of light from distant galaxies was a common feature of all measured galaxies and was proportional to their distance from us. This red-shift was taken to be a Doppler effect indicative of the recessional motion of the light source in the line of sight. Incredibly, what Hubble had discovered was the isotropic expansion of the universe predicted by Friedman and Lemaître on the basis of Einstein's GTR.

According to the Friedman-Lemaître model, as time proceeds, the distances separating galactic masses become greater. It is important to understand that as a GTR-based theory, the model does not describe the expansion of the material content of the universe into a preexisting, empty space, but rather the expansion of space itself. The ideal particles of the cosmological fluid constituted by the galactic masses are conceived to be at rest with respect to space but to recede progressively from one another as space itself expands or stretches, just as buttons glued to the surface of a balloon would recede from one another as the balloon inflates. As the universe expands, it becomes less and less dense. This has the astonishing implication that as one reverses the expansion and extrapolates back in time, the universe becomes progressively denser until one arrives at a state of "infinite density"[1] at some point in the finite past. This state represents a singularity at which space-time curvature, along with temperature, pressure and density, becomes infinite. It therefore constitutes an edge or boundary to space-time itself. The term "big bang" is thus potentially misleading, since the expansion cannot be visualized from the outside (there being no "outside," just as there is no "before" with respect to the big bang).

The standard big bang model, as the Friedman-Lemaître model came to be called, thus describes a universe that is not eternal in the past but that came into being a finite time ago. Moreover—and this deserves underscoring—the origin it posits is an absolute origin *ex nihilo*. For not only all matter and energy, but space and time themselves come into being at the initial cosmological singularity. There can be no natural, physical cause of the big bang event, since, in Quentin Smith's words, "it belongs analytically to the concept of the cosmological singularity that it is not the effect of prior physical events. The definition of a singularity... entails that it is *impossible to extend the spacetime manifold beyond the singularity*.... This rules out the idea that the singularity is an effect of some prior natural process."[2] Sir Arthur Eddington, contemplating the beginning of the universe, opined that the expansion of the universe was so preposterous and incredible that "I feel almost an indignation that anyone should believe in it—except myself."[3] He finally felt forced to conclude, "The beginning seems to present insuperable difficulties unless we agree to look on it as frankly supernatural."[4]

Sometimes objectors appeal to scenarios other than the standard model of the expanding universe in an attempt to avert the absolute beginning predicted by the standard model. But while such theories are possible, it has been the overwhelming verdict of the scientific community that none of them is more probable than the big bang theory. The devil is in the details, and once you get down to specifics you find that there is no mathematically consistent model that has been so successful in its predictions or as corroborated by the evidence as the traditional big bang theory. For example, some theories, like the oscillating universe (which expands and recontracts forever) or the chaotic inflationary universe (which continually spawns new universes), do have a potentially infinite future but turn out to have only a finite past. Vacuum fluctuation universe theories (which postulate an eternal vacuum out of which our universe is born) cannot explain why, if the vacuum was eternal, we do not observe an infinitely old universe. The quantum gravity universe theory propounded by the famous physicist Stephen Hawking, if interpreted realistically, still involves an absolute origin of the universe even if the universe does not begin in a so-called singularity, as it does in the standard big bang theory. The recent speculative cyclic ekpyrotic scenario championed by Paul Steinhardt not only leaves unresolved the difficulties facing the old oscillating universe but has also been shown to require a singular beginning in the past. In sum, according to Hawking, "Almost everyone now believes that the universe, and *time itself*, had a beginning at the Big Bang."[5]

The fourth argument for the finitude of the past is also an inductive argument, this time on the basis of the thermodynamic properties of the universe. According to the second law of thermodynamics, processes taking place in a closed system always tend toward a state of equilibrium. Now our interest in the law concerns what happens when it is applied to the universe as a whole. The universe is, on a naturalistic view, a gigantic closed system, since it is everything there is and there is nothing outside it. This seems to imply that, given enough time, the universe and all its processes will run down, and the entire universe will come to equilibrium. This is known as the heat death of the universe. Once the universe reaches this state, no further change is possible. The universe is dead.

There are two possible types of heat death for the universe. If the universe will eventually recontract, it will die a "hot" death. As it contracts, the stars gain energy, causing them to burn more rapidly so that they finally explode or evaporate. As everything in the universe grows closer together, the black holes begin to gobble up everything around them, and eventually begin themselves to coalesce. In time, all the black holes finally coalesce into one large black hole that is coextensive with the universe, from which the universe will never reemerge.

On the other hand if, as is more likely, the universe will expand forever, then its death will be cold, as the galaxies turn their gas into stars, and the stars burn out. At 10^{30} years the universe will consist of 90% dead stars, 9% supermassive black holes formed by the collapse of galaxies, and 1% atomic matter, mainly hydrogen. Elementary particle physics suggests that thereafter protons will decay into electrons and positrons so that space will be filled with a rarefied gas so thin that the distance between an electron and a positron will be about the size of the present galaxy. Eventually all black holes will completely evaporate and all the matter in the ever-expanding universe will be reduced to a thin gas of elementary particles and radiation. Equilibrium will prevail throughout, and the entire universe will be in its final state, from which no change will occur.

Now the question that needs to be asked is this: if given enough time the universe will reach heat death, then why is it not in a state of heat death now, if it has existed forever, from eternity? If the universe did not begin to exist, then it should now be in a state of equilibrium. Like a ticking clock, it should by now have run down. Since it has not yet run down, this implies, in the words of one baffled scientist, "In some way the universe must have been *wound up*."[6]

Some people have tried to escape this conclusion by adopting an oscillating model of the universe which never reaches a final state of equilibrium. But even apart from the physical and observational problems plaguing such a model, the thermodynamic properties of this model imply the very beginning of the universe that its proponents sought to avoid. Because entropy increases from cycle to cycle in such a model, it has the effect of generating larger and longer oscillations with each successive cycle. Thus, as one traces the oscillations back in time, they become progressively smaller until one reaches a first and smallest oscillation. Hence, the oscillating model has an infinite future, but only a finite past. In fact, it is estimated on the basis of current entropy levels that the universe cannot have gone through more than 100 previous oscillations.

Even if this difficulty were avoided, a universe oscillating from eternity past would require an infinitely precise tuning of initial conditions in order to last through an infinite number of successive bounces. A universe rebounding from a single, infinitely long contraction is, if entropy increases during the contracting phase, thermodynamically untenable and incompatible with the initial low-entropy condition of our expanding phase. Postulating an entropy decrease during the contracting phase in order to escape this problem would require us to postulate inexplicably special low-entropy

conditions at the time of the bounce in the life of an infinitely evolving universe. Such a low-entropy condition at the beginning of the expansion is more plausibly accounted for by the presence of a singularity or some sort of quantum creation event.

So whether one adopts a recontracting model, an ever-expanding model or an oscillating model, thermodynamics suggests that the universe had a beginning. The universe appears to have been created a finite time ago, and its energy was somehow simply put in at the creation as an initial condition.

On the basis of these four arguments for the finitude of the past, the proponent of the *kalām* argument seems to have good grounds for affirming the second premise of the *kalām* cosmological argument: that the universe began to exist. It therefore follows that the universe has a cause. Conceptual analysis enables us to recover a number of striking properties that must be possessed by such an ultra-mundane being. For as the cause of space and time, this entity must transcend space and time and therefore exist atemporally and nonspatially, at least without the universe. This transcendent cause must therefore be changeless and immaterial, since timelessness entails changelessness, and changelessness implies immateriality. Such a cause must be beginningless and uncaused, at least in the sense of lacking any antecedent causal conditions. Ockham's razor will shave away further causes, since we should not multiply causes beyond necessity. This entity must be unimaginably powerful, since it created the universe without any material cause.

Finally, and most remarkably, such a transcendent cause is plausibly taken to be personal. Three reasons can be given for this conclusion. First, there are two types of causal explanation: scientific explanations in terms of laws and initial conditions and personal explanations in terms of agents and their volitions. A first state of the universe *cannot* have a scientific explanation, since there is nothing before it, and therefore it can be accounted for only in terms of a personal explanation. Second, the personhood of the cause of the universe is implied by its timelessness and immateriality, since the only entities we know of that can possess such properties are either minds or abstract objects, and abstract objects do not stand in causal relations. Therefore, the transcendent cause of the origin of the universe must be of the order of mind. Third, this same conclusion is also implied by the fact that we have in this case the origin of a temporal effect from a timeless cause. If the cause of the origin of the universe were an impersonal set of necessary and sufficient conditions, it would be impossible for the cause to exist without its effect. For if the necessary and sufficient conditions of the effect are timelessly given, then their effect must be given as well. The only way for the cause to be timeless and changeless but for its effect to originate anew a finite time ago is for the cause to be a personal agent who freely chooses to bring about an effect without antecedent determining conditions. Thus we are brought, not merely to a transcendent cause of the universe, but to its Personal Creator. He is, as Leibniz maintained, the Sufficient Reason why anything exists rather than nothing.

NOTES

1. This should not be taken to mean that the density of the universe takes on a value of H_0 but rather that the density of the universe is expressed by a ratio of mass to volume in which the volume is zero; since division by zero is impermissible, the density is said to be infinite in this sense.

2. Quentin Smith, "The Uncaused Beginning of the Universe," in *Theism, Atheism and Big Bang Cosmology*, by William Lane Craig and Quentin Smith (Oxford: Clarendon, 1993), p. 120.

3. Arthur Eddington, *The Expanding Universe* (New York: Macmillan, 1933), p. 124.

4. Ibid., p. 178.

5. Stephen Hawking and Roger Penrose, *The Nature of Space and Time*, The Isaac Newton Institute Series of Lectures (Princeton, N.J.: Princeton University Press, 1996), p. 20.

6. Richard Schlegel, "Time and Thermodynamics," in *The Voices of Time*, ed. J. T. Fraser (London: Penguin, 1948), p. 511.

II.B.5

A Critique of the *Kalām* Cosmological Argument

PAUL DRAPER

Paul Draper (1957–) is professor of philosophy at Purdue University and the author of several important essays in the philosophy of religion. In this article he analyzes William Lane Craig's philosophical defense of the kalām *cosmological argument. Draper contends that Craig's defense fails, both because it fails to establish that the universe had a beginning and because it rests on an equivocation of the phrase "begins to exist."*

Copyright © Paul Draper 1997. Used by permission of the author.

Epistemology begins in doubt, ethics in conflict, and metaphysics in wonder.

In a recent book,[1] William Lane Craig offers a philosophical and scientific defense of a very old and very wonderful argument: the *kalām* cosmological argument. Unlike other cosmological arguments, the *kalām* argument bases its conclusion that the universe has a cause of its existence on the premise that the universe began to exist a finite time ago. Craig calls it the "*kalām*" cosmological argument because "*kalām*" is the name of a theological movement within Islam that used reason, including this argument, to defend the Muslim faith against philosophical objections. After being fully developed by Arab thinkers like al-Kindi and al-Ghazali, the argument eventually made its way to the West, where it was rejected by St. Thomas Aquinas and defended by St. Bonaventure.[2] My focus in this paper will be on Craig's philosophical defense of the argument. I will try to show that this defense fails, both because it fails to establish that the universe had a beginning and because it commits the fallacy of equivocation.

Compare the following two cosmological arguments, each of which concludes that the universe has a cause of its existence:

1. Every contingent thing (including things that are infinitely old) has a cause of its existence.

2. The universe is contingent.

3. Therefore, the universe has a cause of its existence.

1. Everything that begins to exist has a cause of its existence.

2. The universe began to exist.

3. Therefore, the universe has a cause of its existence.

The first of these arguments is sometimes called the argument from contingency. It was suggested by Aristotle, clearly formulated by Arabic philosophers like ibn Sina, and later championed in the West by St. Thomas Aquinas. I find it completely unpersuasive. For although the second premise is clearly true (so long as "contingent" means "logically contingent"),

I do not find the first premise appealing at all. If something is infinitely old, then it has always existed, and it's hard to see why something that has always existed requires a cause of its existence, even if it is logically possible that it not have existed. (Indeed, it's not even clear that something that has always existed *could* have a cause of its existence.)

The second of these arguments is the *kalām* cosmological argument. This argument avoids the weakness of the argument from contingency by denying that the universe is infinitely old and maintaining that the universe needs a cause, not because it is contingent, but rather because it had a beginning. In other words, it replaces the weak premise that every contingent thing needs a cause of its existence with the compelling premise that everything that begins to exist needs a cause of its existence. Of course, a price must be paid for strengthening the first premise: the second premise—that the universe began to exist—is not by a long shot as unquestionably true as the claim that the universe is contingent.

Craig, however, provides a spirited and plausible defense of this premise. He offers four arguments in support of it, two of which are philosophical (armchair cosmology at its best) and two of which are scientific (but still interesting). Both philosophical arguments depend on a distinction between a potential infinite and an actual infinite. A potential infinite is a series or collection that can increase forever without limit but is always finite (e.g., the set of events that have occurred since the birth of my daughter or the set of completed years after 1000 BCE). An actual infinite is a set of distinct things (real or not) whose number is actually infinite (e.g., the set of natural numbers). The first philosophical argument claims that there can't be an infinite regress of events, because actual infinites cannot exist in reality. According to the second argument, an infinite regress of events is impossible because, even if actual infinites could exist in reality, they could not be formed by successive addition.

The first scientific argument is based on the evidence for the Big Bang theory, which seems to many scientists to support the view that the universe had a beginning. The second scientific argument appeals to the Second Law of Thermodynamics.

According to this law, the amount of energy available to do mechanical work always decreases in a closed system. Thus, since the universe as a whole is a closed system with a finite amount of such energy, an infinitely old universe is incompatible with the fact that we have not yet run out of such energy—the universe has not yet reached its "equilibrium end state." Since I'm no scientist, I will focus my attention on Craig's philosophical arguments, beginning with the second one.

As Craig himself points out, his second philosophical argument is very similar to the argument that Immanuel Kant uses to support the thesis of his first antinomy:

> If we assume that the world has no beginning in time, then up to every given moment an eternity has elapsed and there has passed away in the world an infinite series of successive states of things. Now the infinity of a series consists in the fact that it can never be completed through successive synthesis. It thus follows that it is impossible for an infinite world-series to have passed away, and that a beginning of the world is therefore a necessary condition of the world's existence.[3]

Craig formulates the argument as follows:

(i)   The temporal series of events is a collection formed by successive addition.

(ii) A collection formed by successive addition cannot be an actual infinite.

(iii) Thus, the temporal series of events cannot be an actual infinite. (from i and ii)

(iv) Therefore, the temporal regress of events is finite. (from iii)[4]

This argument is closely related to Zeno's paradoxes, which depend on the claim that one cannot complete an infinite series of tasks one at a time since that would imply an infinitieth member of the series. As it stands, the argument is unconvincing. For while it is true that one cannot start with a finite collection and then by adding one new member at a time turn it into an infinite collection (no matter how much time one has available), nothing

of the sort is required in order for the past to be infinite. For if the temporal regress of events is infinite, then the universe has never had a finite number of past events. Rather, it has always been the case that the collection of past events is infinite. Thus, if the temporal regress of events is infinite, then the temporal series of events is not an infinite collection formed by successively adding to a finite collection. Rather, it is a collection formed by successively adding to an infinite collection. And surely it is not impossible to form an infinite collection by successively adding to an already infinite collection.

One might object that, if the temporal regress of events is infinite, then there must be some event E separated from the birth of my daughter by an infinite number of intermediate events, in which case the collection containing E and all those intermediate events would have to be an actually infinite collection formed by successively adding to a finite collection of events, namely the collection containing E as its only member. This objection fails because it is simply not true that, if the temporal regress of events is infinite, then there must be two events separated by an infinite number of intermediate events. For consider the set of natural numbers. It is actually infinite, yet every member of it is such that there is a finite number of members between it and its first member.[5]

Craig's first philosophical argument is, I believe, much more promising than his second. It bases its conclusion that the temporal regress of physical events must be finite—there must have been a first physical event—on the premises that an actual infinite cannot exist in reality and an infinite temporal regress of events is an actual infinite.[6] From this and the further claim that a first physical event could not have been preceded by an eternal absolutely quiescent physical universe, the conclusion is drawn that the physical universe had a beginning. The first stage of this argument can be formulated as follows:

a.   No set of real things is actually infinite.

b.   If there was no first event, then the set of all real events occurring prior to the birth of my daughter is actually infinite.

c.   Therefore, there was a first event.

Craig defends premise (a) of this argument by pointing out that the assumption that a set of real things is actually infinite has paradoxical implications.[7] For example, it implies that we could have a library consisting of infinitely many black books (each might be assigned an even number). We could then add infinitely many red books (each might be assigned an odd number) and yet not increase the number of books in the library by a single volume. Indeed, we could add infinitely many different colors of books with infinitely many books of each color (the red books could be assigned rational numbers between 0 and 1, the black books rational numbers between 1 and 2, and so on) and not increase our collection by a single volume.

These paradoxes arise because the following three statements constitute an inconsistent triad:

S1. A set has more members than any of its proper subsets.

S2. If the members of two sets can be placed in one-to-one correspondence, then neither set has more members than the other.

S3. There are actually infinite sets.

For example, since the set of even numbers has one-to-one correspondence with the set of natural numbers and even with the set of rational numbers, S2 implies that one could add infinitely many red books or infinitely many books of each of infinitely many different colors to the library without increasing the size of that library's collection. (One need only make sure that the additions are *denumerably* infinite.) But of course S1 implies that any such addition would increase the size of the collection since the set of even numbers is a proper subset both of the set of natural numbers and of the set of rational numbers. Thus, two intuitively appealing principles together imply a contradiction on the assumption that there can be an actually infinite collection of books. One way to avoid this contradiction is to reject the assumption that there can be an actually infinite collection of books. So the underlying argument in defense of the claim that no collection of real things is actually infinite is simply that, since S1 and S2 are both true of collections of real things, it

follows that S3 is not true of such collections—no collections of real things are actually infinite.

Craig claims that Georg Cantor's theory of transfinite numbers is consistent because it rejects the first member of the triad. But this member is not rejected because it can be proven false about actually infinite sets, nor is the second member accepted because it can be proven that if a one-to-one correspondence between the elements of two actually infinite sets can be established then the sets are equivalent. Rather, equivalent sets are simply defined as sets having one-to-one correspondence. Thus, while Cantor's theory is a consistent mathematical system, there is, according to Craig, no reason to think that it has any interesting ontological implications. In particular, it does not provide any reason to think that S1 is false about actually infinite sets and hence provides no justification for thinking that actual infinites can exist in reality.[8]

Notice that, if Craig is right that past events are real but future events are not, then his argument for a first event does not commit him to the position that there is a last event. For consider the following parallel argument for the conclusion that there will be a last event:

(a) No set of real things is actually infinite.

(b) If there will be no last event, then the set of all real events occurring after the birth of my daughter is actually infinite.

(c) Therefore, there will be a last event.

Since future events are not real, the second premise of this argument is false. If there is no last event, then the set of all real events occurring after the birth of my daughter is merely potentially infinite— not actually infinite. This collection can increase in size indefinitely, but it will always be finite. Past events, on the other hand, are all real. So if there is no first past event, then the set of all real past events is actually infinite, not potentially infinite. Craig concludes that, although there may be no last event, there must be a first event, and hence, since matter cannot exist without events occurring, it follows that the universe has not always existed—it began to exist.

Although this fascinating argument for the second premise of the *kalām* argument may be sound, Craig has not given us adequate reason to believe it is. The problem concerns the inconsistent triad mentioned above. What Craig needs to do is to show that, when it comes to collections of real things, we should reject the third member of the triad instead of S1 or S2. But he has not shown this. S1 and S2 are certainly true for finite collections. But it's far from clear that they are true for all collections. Allow me to explain why.

Consider S1, which says that a set has more members than any of its proper subsets. If "more" means "a greater number," then the claim that S1 is true for actually infinite sets requires us to make sense of claiming that actually infinite sets have a *number* of members. But an actually infinite set doesn't have a natural number of members or a rational number of members or a real number of members, so one such set can't have a greater natural or rational or real number of members than another. Of course, an actually infinite set does have a transfinite number of members. But transfinite numbers are what Cantor defines them to be. And given his definition, it simply isn't true that actually infinite sets have a greater transfinite number of members than all of their proper subsets. We could say that an actually infinite set has a greater "infinite number" of members than all of its proper subsets, but Craig gives us no theory of infinite numbers that would justify that claim.

Of course, Craig might claim that no such theory is necessary, that we don't even need to make use of the word *number* here; for it's just obvious that, in some sense of the word *more*, any set that has every member that another set has and some members it doesn't have has more members than the other set. I agree this is obvious, but in the case of infinite sets, this is obvious only because "more" can just mean "has every member the other set has and some members it doesn't have." If, however, we grant Craig that S1 is true on these grounds, then why accept S2? Why not claim instead that actually infinite collections of real objects are possible, but the fact that two of them have one-to-one correspondence is not a good reason to believe that neither has "more"

members than the other? Why, for example, is it more reasonable to believe that actually infinite libraries are impossible than to believe that, although they are possible, one such library can have "more" books than a second despite the fact that the books in the first can be placed in one-to-one correspondence with the books in the second? Craig provides no good answer to these questions. Obviously he cannot all of a sudden appeal to Cantor's theory to justify accepting S2. For that would commit him to rejecting S1. And since, when infinite sets are compared, the word *more* cannot mean what it does when finite sets are compared, the fact that S2 is true for finite sets is not by itself a good reason to believe that it is true for all sets.

So Craig fails to show that S1 and S2 are both true of all collections of real objects, and hence he fails to show that actually infinite collections of real objects are impossible. Therefore, his first philosophical argument, like his second, fails to establish that an infinite regress of events is impossible and so fails to establish that the universe began to exist. This leaves us with Craig's scientific arguments. Since I lack the expertise to evaluate these arguments, let's assume, for the sake of argument, that they succeed and hence that the universe did begin to exist. Must we then conclude that the *kalām* argument succeeds? This would be a profound result. Granted, this argument doesn't get all the way to God's existence. But accepting its conclusion does require rejecting naturalism—since nothing can be a cause of its own existence, a cause outside the natural world would be required.

As wonderful as this conclusion is, I do not believe that Craig's defense of the *kalām* argument justifies accepting it, even assuming that his scientific arguments are sound. This is because Craig commits the fallacy of equivocation. The verb "to begin" has a narrow or strict sense and a broad or loose sense. In the narrow sense, "to begin" means "to begin within time." When used in this way, "x begins to exist" implies that there was a time at which x did not exist and then a later time at which x exists. But "to begin" can also mean "to begin either within or with time." When used in this way, "x begins to exist" does not imply that there was a time at which x did not exist, because the past may itself be finite in which case something that begins to exist at the first moment in time is such that there never was a time at which it did not exist—it begins with time rather than within time. Now consider the two premises of the *kalām* argument in the light of this distinction.

The second premise is that the universe began to exist. All of Craig's arguments in favor of this premise, including his scientific ones, would be unsound if one interpreted "began to exist" in the second premise as meaning "began to exist within time." For nothing in these arguments counts against a relational view of time. And on a relational view of time, a first temporal event is simultaneous with a first moment in time. This would mean that, if the temporal series of past events is finite, then the universe began to exist with time. Indeed, if anything, the arguments in favor of the second premise support a beginning with time. For if an infinite regress of events is an actual infinite and for that reason impossible, then it would seem that an infinite past would be an actual infinite and for that reason impossible. Moreover, one of Craig's scientific arguments appeals to an interpretation of the Big Bang Theory according to which time did not exist "before" the big bang. So the most that Craig has established is that the universe began to exist either within or with time.

The first premise is that anything that begins to exist has a cause of its existence. What does "begins to exist" mean here? Craig defends this premise by claiming that it is an "empirical generalisation enjoying the strongest support experience affords."[9] But experience only supports the claim that anything that begins to exist within time has a cause of its existence. For we have no experience whatsoever of things beginning to exist with time.[10] Such things

would require timeless causes. And even if it is conceptually possible for a temporal event to have a timeless cause, we certainly have no experience of this. Of course, Craig also claims that premise (1) is intuitively obvious—that it needs no defense at all. But it is far from obvious that a universe that begins to exist with time needs a cause of its existence. Like an infinitely old universe, a universe that begins to exist with time has always existed—for any time t, the universe existed at t. And once again, it's far from obvious that something that has always existed requires a cause for its existence. It's not even clear that such a thing *could* have a cause of its existence.

So in order to be justified in believing both of the premises of the argument—justified, that is, solely on the basis of Craig's defense of those premises—we would need to equivocate on the meaning of "begins to exist." We would need to use this term in the narrow sense in the first premise and in the broad sense in the second premise. But then the conclusion of the argument would not follow from its premises. Thus, Craig commits the fallacy of equivocation.[11]

Do my objections to Craig's defense of the *kalām* argument prove that it is doomed? I don't think so. The argument remains promising. Perhaps, for example, it could be shown that an absolute theory of time is correct, and that such a theory, together with scientific or new philosophical evidence against an infinitely old universe, implies a beginning of the universe within time. Or perhaps it could be shown that the universe began to exist with time and that even something that begins to exist with time requires a cause of its existence. So my conclusion is not that the *kalām* argument should be dismissed. It is just that it has not yet been adequately defended. I still *wonder* whether the argument is a good one.

NOTES

1. William Lane Craig, *The Kalām Cosmological Argument* (New York: Harper & Row Publishers), 1979.

2. For a brief but interesting history of the argument, see Craig, Part I.

3. Immanuel Kant, *Critique of Pure Reason,* trans. Norman Kemp Smith (London: Macmillan & Co., 1929), p. 396. Quoted by Craig on p. 189.

4. Craig, p. 103.

5. Cf. Quentin Smith, "*Infinity and the Past*," in *Theism, Atheism, and Big Bang Cosmology*, ed. William Lane Craig and Quentin Smith (Oxford: Clarendon Press, 1993), pp. 78–83; Antony Flew, "The Case for God Challenged," in *Does God Exist?: The Great Debate*, ed. J. P. Moreland and Kai Nielsen (Nashville: Thomas Nelson Publishers, 1990), p. 164; and Keith Parsons, "Is There a Case for Christian Theism?" in *Does God Exist?: The Great Debate*, p. 187.

6. Craig, p. 69.

7. Craig, pp. 82–87.

8. Craig, pp. 94–95.

9. Craig, p. 145. Craig also suggests here that premise (1) could be defended by appealing to an a priori category of causality. Such Kantian maneuvering does not seem very promising in this context. For in order to reconcile it with the realism presupposed by the *kalām* argument, one would need to claim that the causal principle must, as a necessary precondition of thought, hold without exception in the noumenal world!

10. Cf. Quentin Smith, "The Uncaused Beginning of the Universe," in *Theism, Atheism, and Big Bang Cosmology*, p. 123.

11. In "The Caused Beginning of the Universe" (in *Theism, Atheism, and Big Bang Cosmology*) Craig denies that his inference is equivocal on the grounds that "our conviction of the truth of the causal principle is not based upon an inductive survey of existents in space-time, but rather upon the metaphysical intuition that something cannot come out of nothing" (p. 147). Of course, he did appeal to such a survey in his book, but Craig claims that this was just "a last-ditch defence of the principle designed to appeal to the hard-headed empiricist who resists the metaphysical intuition that properly grounds our conviction of the principle" (p. 147, note 13). This response to the charge of equivocation is not at all convincing. For metaphysical intuitions about contingent matters are notoriously unreliable—that's why so many contemporary philosophers are, quite justifiably, "hard-headed empiricists." Further, at the risk of committing the genetic fallacy, it is worth pointing out that it is probably our experience of things beginning to exist within time that causes some of us to have the metaphysical intuition that something cannot come out of nothing.

II.C. THE TELEOLOGICAL ARGUMENT FOR THE EXISTENCE OF GOD

Introduction

THE TELEOLOGICAL ARGUMENT for the existence of God begins with the premise that the world exhibits intelligent purpose, order, or other marks of design, and it proceeds to the conclusion that there must be or probably is a divine intelligence, a supreme designer, to account for the observed or perceived intelligent purpose or order. Although core ideas of the argument can be found in Plato, in the Bible (Rom. 1), and in Cicero, the most well-known treatment of it is found in William Paley's *Natural Theology* (1802). In his opening chapter, included here as our first selection, he offers his famous "watch" argument, which begins as follows:

> In crossing a heath, suppose I pitched my foot against a stone, and were asked how the stone came to be there, I might possibly answer, that for anything I knew to the contrary, it had lain there for ever; nor would it, perhaps, be very easy to show the absurdity of this answer. But suppose I found a watch upon the ground, and it should be inquired how the watch happened to be in that place, I should hardly think of the answer

which I had before given—that, for anything I knew, the watch might have always been there. Yet why should not this answer serve for the watch as well as for the stone? Why is it not as admissible in the second case, as in the first?

Paley argues that just as we infer the existence of an intelligent designer to account for the purpose-revealing watch, we must analogously infer the existence of an intelligent grand designer to account for the purpose-revealing world.

"Every indication of contrivance, every manifestation of design, which existed in the watch, exists in the works of nature; with the difference, on the side of nature, of being greater and more, and that in a degree which exceeds all computation." The skeleton of the argument looks like this:

1. Human artifacts are products of intelligent design (purpose).
2. The works of nature resemble these human artifacts, particularly in having parts that are functionally organized.
3. Therefore, the works of nature are (probably) products of intelligent design (purpose).
4. But these works are vastly more complex and far greater in number than human artifacts.
5. Therefore, there probably is a powerful and vastly intelligent designer who designed the works of nature.

Ironically, Paley's argument was attacked even before Paley had set it down, for David Hume (1711–1776) had long before written his famous *Dialogues Concerning Natural Religion* (published posthumously in 1779), the classic critique of the teleological argument. Paley seems to have been unaware of it. A selection from the *Dialogues* is included as our second reading. In it, the natural theologian, Cleanthes, debates the orthodox believer, Demea, and the skeptic or critic, Philo, who does most of the serious arguing.

Hume, through Philo, attacks the argument from several different angles. He argues first of all that the universe—which might itself be viewed as one of Paley's "works of nature"—is not sufficiently like the productions of human design to support the argument. Philo puts it as follows:

> But can you think, Cleanthes, that your usual phlegm and philosophy
> have been preserved in so wide a step as you have taken, when you
> compare to the universe, houses, ships, furniture, machines and from their
> similarity in some circumstances infer a similarity in their causes? . . . But
> can a conclusion, with any propriety, be transferred from the parts to the
> whole? Does not the great disproportion bar all comparison and
> inferences? From observing the growth of a hair, can we learn anything
> concerning the generation of a man?

In other words, one cannot argue from the parts to the whole.

Philo's second objection is that the analogy from artifact to divine designer fails because we have no other universe with which to compare this one. We would need to make such a comparison to decide if it were the kind of universe that was designed or simply the kind that developed on its own. As C. S. Peirce put it, "Universes are not as plentiful as blackberries." Because there is only one of them, we have no standard of comparison by which to judge it. Paley's answer to this would be that if we could find one clear instance of purposefulness in nature (e.g., the eye), it would be sufficient to enable us to conclude that there is probably an intelligent designer. Hume makes several other points against the design argument as well. Those are left to the reader to find in the text.

A modern objection to the argument, one that was anticipated by Hume, is that based on Darwinian evolution, which has cast doubt on the notion of teleological explanation altogether. In his *Origin of Species* (1859) Darwin claimed that the process of development from simpler organisms to more complex ones took place gradually over millions of years through an apparently nonpurposeful process of trial and error, of natural selection, and of survival of the fittest. As Julian Huxley put it, the evolutionary process

> results immediately and automatically from the basic property of living matter—that of self-copying, but with occasional errors. Self-copying leads to multiplication and competition; the errors in self-copying are what we call mutations, and mutations will inevitably confer different degrees of biological advantage or disadvantage on their possessors. The consequence will be differential reproduction down the generations—in other words, natural selection.[*]

As important as Darwin's contribution is in offering us an alternative model of biological development, it doesn't altogether destroy the argument from design. The theist might argue (for example) that evolution by natural selection is simply the *way* in which a divine designer has chosen to work out his or her purpose for the world, and the inference to the existence of a designer can then still be construed as an inference to the best explanation. The idea here is that, although life has its origins in the ordinary operation of the laws of nature, those laws themselves, as well as the initial conditions of the universe, are to be explained by the activity of a divine designer. Relatedly, a proponent of the design argument might turn her attention away from biological structures altogether and look for marks of design elsewhere in the universe—for example, in the apparent "fine-tuning" of the natural laws and physical constants. She might then argue that, regardless of whether a design inference is warranted as an explanation for biological purpose, such an inference is, at any rate, warranted as an explanation for these other features of the universe.

This basic strategy is sketched by Richard Swinburne in the third reading in this section, titled "Arguments from Design." Swinburne identifies two different kinds of design argument: an argument from temporal order and an argument from spatial order. The former starts from the premise that the universe unfolds over time in a way that is governed by laws that can neither explain themselves nor be explained by the natural sciences. The latter starts from the familiar

---

[*]*Evolution as Process* (New York: Harper & Row, 1953), 4.

observation that things in the world—biological structures, for example—display a kind of order and complexity that can only arise naturally in a universe with very particular (fine-tuned) laws, physical constants, and initial conditions which, again, can neither explain themselves nor be explained scientifically. Swinburne argues that for both kinds of order, *personal explanations*—explanations that appeal to a cosmic designer—seem to be the best, most rational explanations that we have available to us.

In our fourth and final reading in this section, "A Scientific Argument for the Existence of God," Robin Collins examines in much greater detail the idea that the fine-tuning of the natural laws and fundamental physical constants provides the resources for a convincing version of the argument from design. Collins defends the conclusion that theism is more probable than atheism given the evidence of fine-tuning. To take just a few examples of the kind of evidence in focus here, Collins notes that if gravity had been stronger or weaker by one part in 10^{40}, or if the neutron were not about 1.001 times the mass of the proton, or if the electromagnetic force had been slightly stronger or weaker, life would have been impossible. The likelihood of the laws and fundamental constants being so well coordinated as to allow for the possibility of life is staggeringly low; thus, Collins argues, the fact that the laws and constants *are* so well coordinated constitutes evidence that their values are not the result of chance but rather are due to the creative activity of an intelligent designer.

II.C.1

The Watch and the Watchmaker

WILLIAM PALEY

William Paley (1743–1805), Archdeacon of Carlisle, was a leading evangelical apologist. His most important work is Natural Theology, or Evidences of the Existence and Attributes of the Deity Collected from the Appearances of Nature *(1802), the first chapter of which is reprinted here. Paley argues that just as we infer the existence of an intelligent designer to explain the presence of a subtle and complex artifact like a watch, so too we must infer the existence of an intelligent Grand Designer to explain the existence of the works of nature, which are far more subtle, complex, and cleverly contrived than any human artifact.*

From William Paley, *Natural Theology, or Evidences of the Existence and Attributes of the Deity Collected from the Appearances of Nature* (1802).

STATEMENT OF THE
ARGUMENT

In crossing a heath, suppose I pitched my foot against a stone, and were asked how the stone came to be there, I might possibly answer, that, for anything I knew to the contrary, it had lain there for ever; nor would it, perhaps, be very easy to show the absurdity of this answer. But suppose I found a watch upon the ground, and it should be inquired how the watch happened to be in that place, I should hardly think of the answer which I had given—that, for anything I knew, the watch might have always been there. Yet why should not this answer serve for the watch as well as for the stone? Why is it not as admissible in the second case as in the first? For this reason, and for no other; viz., that, when we come to inspect the watch, we perceive (what we could not discover in the stone) that its several parts are framed and put together for a purpose, e.g. that they are so formed and adjusted as to produce motion, and that motion so regulated as to point out the hour of the day; that, if the different parts had been differently shaped from what they are, if a different size from what they are, or placed after any other manner, or in any other order than that in which they are placed, either no motion at all would have been carried on in the machine, or none which would have answered the use that is now served by it. To reckon up a few of the plainest of these parts, and of their offices, all tending to one result:—We see a cylindrical box containing a coiled elastic spring, which, by its endeavor to relax itself, turns round the box. We next observe a flexible chain (artificially wrought for the sake of flexure) communicating the action of the spring from the box to the fusee. We then find a series of wheels, the teeth of which catch in, and apply to, each other, conducting the motion from the fusee to the balance, and from the balance to the pointer, and, at the same time, by the size and shape of those wheels, so regulating that motion as to terminate in causing an index, by an equable and measured progression, to pass over a given space in a given time. We take notice that the wheels are made of brass, in order to keep them from rust; the springs of steel, no other metal being so elastic; that over the face of the watch there is placed a glass, a material employed in no other part of the work, but in the room of which, if there had been any other than a transparent substance, the hour could not be seen without opening the case. This mechanism being observed, (it requires indeed an examination of the instrument, and perhaps some previous knowledge of the subject, to perceive and understand it; but being once, as we have said, observed and understood,) the inference, we think, is inevitable, that the watch must have had a maker; that there must have existed, at some time, and at some place or other, an artificer or artificers who formed it for the purpose which we find it actually to answer; who comprehended its construction, and designed its use.

I. Nor would it, I apprehend, weaken the conclusion, that we had never seen a watch made; that we had never known an artist capable of making one; that we were altogether incapable of executing such a piece of workmanship ourselves, or of understanding in what manner it was performed; all this being no more than what is true of some exquisite remains of ancient art, of some lost and to the generality of mankind, of the more curious productions of modern manufacture. Does one man in a million know how oval frames are turned? Ignorance of this kind exalts our opinion of the unseen and unknown artist's skill, if he be unseen and unknown, but raises no doubt in our minds of the existence and agency of such an artist, at some former time, and in some place or other. Nor can I perceive that it varies at all the inference, whether the question arise concerning a human agent, or concerning an agent of a different species, or an agent possessing, in some respect, a different nature.

II. Neither, secondly, would it invalidate our conclusion, that the watch sometimes went wrong, or that it seldom went exactly right. The purpose of the machinery, the design, and the designer, might be evident, and, in the case supposed, would be evident, in whatever way we accounted for the irregularity of the movement, or whether we could account for it or not. It is not necessary that a machine be perfect, in order to show with what design it was made; still less necessary, where the only question is, whether it were made with any design at all.

III. Nor, thirdly, would it bring any uncertainty into the argument, if there were a few parts of the watch, concerning which we could not discover, or had not yet discovered, in what manner they conduced to the general effect; or even some parts, concerning which we could not ascertain whether they conduced to that effect in any manner whatever. For, as to the first branch of the case, if by the loss, or disorder, or decay of the parts in question, the movement of the watch were found in fact to be stopped, or disturbed, or retarded, no doubt would remain in our minds as to the utility or intention of these parts, although we should be unable to investigate the manner according to which, or the connection by which, the ultimate effect depended upon their action or assistance; and the more complex is the machine, the more likely is this obscurity to arise. Then, as to the second thing supposed, namely, that there were parts which might be spared without prejudice to the movement of the watch, and that he had proved this by experiment, these superfluous parts, even if we were completely assured that they were such, would not vacate the reasoning which we had instituted concerning other parts. The indication of contrivance remained, with respect to them, nearly as it was before.

IV. Nor, fourthly, would any man in his senses think the existence of the watch, with its various machinery, accounted for, by being told that it was one out of possible combinations of material forms; that whatever he had found in the place where he found the watch, must have contained some internal configuration or other; and that this configuration might be the structure now exhibited, viz., of the works of a watch, as well as a different structure.

V. Nor, fifthly, would it yield his inquiry more satisfaction, to be answered, that there existed in things a principle of order, which had disposed the parts of the watch into their present form and situation. He never knew a watch made by the principle of order; nor can he even form to himself an idea of what is meant by a principle of order, distinct from the intelligence of the watchmaker.

VI. Sixthly, he would be surprised to hear that the mechanism of the watch was no proof of contrivance, only a motive to induce the mind to think so.

VII. And not less surprised to be informed, that the watch in his hand was nothing more than the result of the laws of *metallic* nature. It is a perversion of language to assign any law as the efficient, operative cause of anything. A law presupposes an agent; for it is only the mode according to which an agent proceeds; it implies a power; for it is the order according to which that power acts. Without this agent, without this power, which are both distinct from itself, the *law* does nothing, is nothing. The expression, "the law of metallic nature," may sound strange and harsh to a philosophic ear; but it seems quite as justifiable as some others which are more familiar to him such as "the law of vegetable nature," "the law of animal nature," or, indeed, as "the law of nature" in general, when assigned as the cause of phenomena in exclusion of agency and power, or when it is substituted into the place of these.

VIII. Neither, lastly, would our observer be driven out of his conclusion, or from his confidence in its truth, by being told that he knew nothing at all about the matter. He knows enough for his argument: he knows the utility of the end: he knows the subserviency and adaptation of the means to the end. These points being known, his ignorance of other points, his doubts concerning other points, affect not the certainty of his reasoning. The consciousness of knowing little need not beget a distrust of that which he does know....

APPLICATION OF THE ARGUMENT

Every indication of contrivance, every manifestation of design, which existed in the watch, exists in the works of nature; with the difference, on the side of nature, of being greater and more, and that in a degree which exceeds all computation. I mean that the contrivances of nature surpass the contrivances of art, in the complexity, subtilty, and curiosity of the mechanism; and still more, if possible, do they go beyond them in number and variety; yet in a multitude of cases, are not less evidently mechanical, not less evidently contrivances, not less evidently accommodated to their end, or suited to their office, than are the most perfect productions of human ingenuity.

II.C.2

A Critique of the Design Argument

DAVID HUME

The Scottish empiricist and skeptic David Hume (1711–1776) is one of the most important philosophers who ever lived. Among his most important works are A Treatise on Human Nature, An Enquiry Concerning Human Understanding, *and* Dialogues Concerning Natural Religion *(published posthumously in 1779), from which the present selection is taken. The* Dialogues *contain the classic critique of the argument from design. Our reading is from Parts 2 and 5 of this dialogue. Cleanthes, who opens our selection, is a natural theologian, the Paley of his time, who opposes both the orthodox believer, Demea, and the skeptic, Philo. It is Philo who puts forth the major criticisms against the argument from design.*

Cleanthes: Look round the world: Contemplate the whole and every part of it: You will find it to be nothing but one great machine, subdivided into an infinite number of lesser machines, which again admit of subdivisions to a degree beyond what human senses and faculties can trace and explain. All these various machines, and even their most minute parts, are adjusted to each other with an accuracy which ravishes into admiration all men who have ever contemplated them. The curious adapting of means to ends, throughout all nature, resembles exactly, though it much exceeds, the productions of human contrivance; of human design, thought, wisdom, and intelligence. Since therefore the effects resemble each other, we are led to infer, by all the rules of analogy, that the causes also resemble, and that the Author of Nature is somewhat similar to the mind of man, though possessed of much larger faculties, proportioned to the grandeur of the work which he has executed. By this argument *a posteriori*, and by this argument alone, do we prove at once the existence of a Deity and his similarity to human mind and intelligence.

Demea: I shall be so free, *Cleanthes,* said *Demea,* as to tell you that from the beginning I could not approve of your conclusion concerning the similarity of the Deity to men; still less can I approve of the mediums by which you endeavor to establish it. What! No demonstration of the Being of God! No abstract arguments! No proofs *a priori!* Are these which have hitherto been so much insisted on by philosophers all fallacy, all sophism? Can we reach no farther in this subject than experience and probability? I will say not that this is betraying the cause of a Deity; but surely, by this affected candor, you give advantages to atheists which they never could obtain by the mere dint of argument and reasoning.

Philo: What I chiefly scruple in this subject, said *Philo,* is not so much that all religious arguments are by *Cleanthes* reduced to experience, as that they appear not to be even the most certain and irrefragable of that inferior kind. That a stone will fall, that fire will burn, that the earth has solidity, we have observed a thousand and a thousand times; and when any new instance of this nature is presented, we draw without hesitation the accustomed inference. The

From David Hume, *Dialogue Concerning National Religion* (1779) London: Longman Green, 1878.

exact similarity of the cases gives us a perfect assurance of a similar event, and a stronger evidence is never desired nor sought after. But wherever you depart, in the least, from the similarity of the cases, you diminish proportionably the evidence; and may at last bring it to a very weak *analogy,* which is confessedly liable to error and uncertainty. After having experienced the circulation of the blood in human creatures, we make no doubt that it takes place in *Titius* and *Maevius;* but from its circulation in frogs and fishes it is only a presumption, though a strong one, from analogy that it takes place in men and other animals. The analogical reasoning is much weaker when we infer the circulation of the sap in vegetables from our experience that the blood circulates in animals; and those who hastily followed that imperfect analogy are found, by more accurate experiments, to have been mistaken.

If we see a house, *Cleanthes,* we conclude, with the greatest certainty, that it had an architect or builder because this is precisely that species of effect which we have experienced to proceed from that species of cause. But surely you will not affirm that the universe bears such a resemblance to a house that we can with the same certainty infer a similar cause, or that the analogy is here entire and perfect. The dissimilitude is so striking that the utmost you can here pretend to is a guess, a conjecture, a presumption concerning a similar cause; and how that pretension will be received in the world, I leave you to consider.

Cleanthes: It would surely be very ill received, replied *Cleanthes;* and I should be deservedly blamed and detested did I allow that the proofs of a Deity amounted to no more than a guess or conjecture. But is the whole adjustment of means to ends in a house and in the universe so slight a resemblance? The economy of final causes? The order, proportion, and arrangement of every part? Steps of a stair are plainly contrived that human legs may use them in mounting; and this inference is certain and infallible. Human legs are also contrived for walking and mounting; and this inference, I allow, is not altogether so certain because of the dissimilarity which you remark; but does it, therefore, deserve the name only of presumption or conjecture?

Demea: Good God! cried *Demea,* interrupting him, where are we? Zealous defenders of religion allow that the proofs of a Deity fall short of perfect evidence! And you, *Philo,* on whose assistance I depended in proving the adorable mysteriousness of the Divine Nature, do you assent to all these extravagant opinions of *Cleanthes?* For what other name can I give them? or, why spare my censure when such principles are advanced, supported by such an authority, before so young a man as *Pamphilus?*

Philo: You seem not to apprehend, replied *Philo,* that I argue with *Cleanthes* in his own way, and, by showing him the dangerous consequences of his tenets, hope at last to reduce him to our opinion. But what sticks most with you, I observe, is the representation which *Cleanthes* has made of the argument *a posteriori;* and, finding that that argument is likely to escape your hold and vanish into air, you think it so disguised that you can scarcely believe it to be set in its true light. Now, however much I may dissent, in other respects, from the dangerous principle of *Cleanthes,* I must allow that he has fairly represented that argument, and I shall endeavor so to state the matter to you that you will entertain no further scruples with regard to it.

Were a man to abstract from everything which he knows or has seen, he would be altogether incapable, merely from his own ideas, to determine what kind of scene the universe must be, or to give the preference to one state or situation of things above another. For as nothing which he clearly conceives could be esteemed impossible or implying a contradiction, every chimera of his fancy would be upon an equal footing; nor could he assign any just reason why he adheres to one idea or system, and rejects the others which are equally possible.

Again, after he opens his eyes and contemplates the world as it really is, it would be impossible for him at first to assign the cause of any one event, much less of the whole of things, or of the universe. He might set his fancy a rambling, and she might bring him in an infinite variety of reports and representations. These would all be possible; but, being all equally possible, he would never of himself give a satisfactory account for his preferring one of them to the rest. Experience alone can point out to him the true cause of any phenomenon.

Now, according to this method of reasoning, *Demea,* it follows (and is, indeed, tacitly allowed by *Cleanthes* himself) that order, arrangement, or the adjustment of final causes, is not of itself any proof of design, but only so far as it has been experienced to proceed from that principle. For aught we can know *a priori,* matter may contain the source or spring of order originally within itself, as well as mind does; and there is no more difficulty in conceiving that the several elements, from an internal unknown cause, may fall into the most exquisite arrangement, than to conceive that their ideas, in the great universal mind, from a like internal unknown cause, fall into that arrangement. The equal possibility of both these suppositions is allowed. But, by experience, we find, according to *Cleanthes,* that there is a difference between them. Throw several pieces of steel together, without shape or form; they will never arrange themselves so as to compose a watch. Stone and mortar and wood, without an architect, never erect a house. But the ideas in a human mind, we see, by an unknown, inexplicable economy, arrange themselves so as to form the plan of a watch or house. Experience, therefore, proves that there is an original principle of order in mind, not in matter. From similar effects we infer similar causes. The adjustment of means to ends is alike in the universe, as in a machine of human contrivance. The causes, therefore, must be resembling.

I was from the beginning scandalized, I must own, with this resemblance which is asserted between the Deity and human creatures, and must conceive it to imply such a degradation of the Supreme Being as no sound theist could endure. With your assistance, therefore, *Demea,* I shall endeavor to defend what you justly call the adorable mysteriousness of the Divine Nature, and shall refute this reasoning of *Cleanthes,* provided he allows that I have made a fair representation of it.

When *Cleanthes* had assented, *Philo,* after a short pause, proceeded in the following manner.

That all inferences, *Cleanthes,* concerning fact are founded on experience, and that all experimental reasonings are founded on the supposition that similar causes prove similar effects, and similar effects similar causes, I shall not at present much dispute with you. But observe, I entreat you, with what extreme caution all just reasoners proceed in the transferring of experiments to similar cases. Unless the cases be exactly similar, they repose no perfect confidence in applying their past observation to any particular phenomenon. Every alteration of circumstances occasions a doubt concerning the event; and it requires new experiments to prove certainly that the new circumstances are of no moment or importance. A change in bulk, situation, arrangement, age, disposition of the air, or surrounding bodies; any of these particulars may be attended with the most unexpected consequences. And unless the objects be quite familiar to us, it is the highest temerity to expect with assurance, after any of these changes, an event similar to that which before fell under our observation. The slow and deliberate steps of philosophers here, if anywhere, are distinguished from the precipitate march of the vulgar, who, hurried on by the smallest similitude, are incapable of all discernment or consideration.

But can you think, *Cleanthes,* that your usual phlegm and philosophy have been preserved in so wide a step as you have taken when you compared to the universe houses, ships, furniture, machines; and, from their similarity in some circumstances, inferred a similarity in their causes? Thought, design, intelligence, such as we discover in men and other animals, is no more than one of the springs and principles of the universe, as well as heat or cold, attraction or repulsion, and a hundred others which fall under daily observation. It is an active cause by which some particular parts of nature, we find, produce alterations on other parts. But can a conclusion, with any propriety, be transferred from parts to the whole? Does not the great disproportion bar all comparison and inference? From observing the growth of a hair, can we learn anything concerning the generation of a man? Would the manner of a leaf's blowing, even though perfectly known, afford us any instruction concerning the vegetation of a tree?

But allowing that we were to take the *operations* of one part of nature upon another for the foundation of our judgment concerning the *origin* of the whole (which never can be admitted), yet why select so minute, so weak, so bounded a principle as the reason and design of animals is found to be upon this planet? What peculiar privilege has this little agitation of the brain which we call "thought," that we must thus make it the model of the whole universe? Our partiality in our own favor does indeed present it on all occasions, but sound philosophy ought carefully to guard against so natural an illusion.

So far from admitting, continued *Philo,* that the operations of a part can afford us any just conclusion concerning the origin of the whole, I will not allow any one part to form a rule for another part if the latter be very remote from the former, is there any reasonable ground to conclude that the inhabitants of other planets possess thought, intelligence, reason, or anything similar to these faculties in men? When nature has so extremely diversified her manner of operation in this small globe, can we imagine that she incessantly copies herself throughout so immense a universe? And if thought, as we may well suppose, be confined merely to this narrow corner, and has even there so limited a sphere of action, with what propriety can we assign it for the original cause of all things? The narrow view of a peasant who makes his domestic economy the rule for the government of kingdoms is in comparison a pardonable sophism.

But were we ever so much assured that a thought and reason resembling the human were to be found throughout the whole universe, and were its activity elsewhere vastly greater and more commanding than it appears in this globe; yet I cannot see why the operations of a world constituted, arranged, adjusted, can with any propriety be extended to a world which is in its embryo state, and is advancing towards that constitution and arrangement. By observation we know somewhat of the economy, action, and nourishment of a finished animal; but we must transfer with great caution that observation to the growth of a fetus in the womb, and still more to the formation of an animalcule in the loins of its male parent. Nature, we find, even from our limited experience, possesses an infinite number of springs and principles which incessantly discover themselves on every change of her position and situation. And what new and unknown principles would actuate her in so new and unknown a situation as that of the formation of a universe, we cannot, without the utmost temerity, pretend to determine.

A very small part of this great system, during a very short time, is very imperfectly discovered to us; and do we thence pronounce decisively concerning the origin of the whole?

Admirable conclusion! Stone, wood, brick, iron, brass, have not, at this time, in this minute globe of earth, an order or arrangement without human art and contrivance; therefore, the universe could not originally attain its order and arrangement without something similar to human art. But is a part of nature a rule for another part very wide of the former? Is it a rule for the whole? Is a very small part a rule for the universe? Is nature in one situation a certain rule for nature in another situation vastly different from the former?

And can you blame me, *Cleanthes,* if I here imitate the prudent reserve of *Simonides,* who, according to the noted story, being asked by *Hiero, What God was?* desired a day to think of it, and then two days more; and after that manner continually prolonged the term, without ever bringing in his definition or description? Could you even blame me if I had answered, at first, *that I did not know,* and was sensible that this subject lay vastly beyond the reach of my faculties? You might cry out skeptic and raillier, as much as you pleased; but, having found in so many other subjects much more familiar the imperfections and even contradictions of human reason, I never should expect any success from its feeble conjectures in a subject so sublime and so remote from the sphere of our observation. When two species of objects have always been observed to be conjoined together, I can infer, by custom, the existence of one wherever I see the existence of the other; and this I call an argument from experience. But how this argument can have place where the objects, as in the present case, are single, individual, without parallel or specific resemblance, may be difficult to explain. And will any man tell me with a serious countenance that an orderly universe must arise from some thought and art like the human because we have experience of it? To ascertain this reasoning it were requisite that we had experience of the origin of worlds; and it is not sufficient, surely, that we have seen ships and cities arise from human art and contrivance. . . .

Philo: But to show you still more inconveniences, continued *Philo,* in your anthropomorphism, please to take a new survey of your principles. *Like effects prove like causes.* This is the experimental argument; and this, you say too, is the sole theological argument. Now it is certain that the liker the effects are which are seen and the liker the causes which are inferred, the stronger is the argument. Every departure on either side diminishes the probability and renders the experiment less conclusive. You cannot doubt of the principle; neither ought you to reject its consequences.

All the new discoveries in astronomy which prove the immense grandeur and magnificence of the works of nature are so many additional arguments for a Deity, according to the true system of theism; but, according to your hypothesis of experimental theism, they become so many objections, by removing the effect still farther from all resemblance to the effects of human art and contrivance. For if *Lucretius,* even following the old system of the world, could exclaim:

> Who is strong enough to rule the sum, who to hold in hand and control the mighty bridle of the unfathomable deep? who to turn about all the heavens at one time, and warm the fruitful worlds with ethereal fires, or to be present in all places and at all times.[1]

If Tully[2] esteemed this reasoning so natural as to put it into the mouth of his Epicurean:

> What power of mental vision enabled your master Plato to descry the vast and elaborate architectural process which, as he makes out, the deity adopted in building the structure of the universe? What method of engineering was employed? What tools and levers and derricks? What agents carried out so vast an understanding?

And how were air, fire, water, and earth enabled to obey and execute the will of the architect?

If this argument, I say, had any force in former ages, how much greater must it have at present when the bounds of nature are so infinitely enlarged and such a magnificent scene is opened to us? It is still more unreasonable to form our idea of so unlimited a cause from our experience of the narrow productions of human design and invention.

The discoveries by microscopes, as they open a new universe in miniature, are still objections, according to you; arguments, according to me. The farther we push our researches of this kind, we are still led to infer the universal cause of all to be vastly different from mankind, or from any object of human experience and observation.

And what say you to the discoveries in anatomy, chemistry, botany? . . .

Cleanthes: These surely are no objections, replied *Cleanthes;* they only discover new instances of art and contrivance. It is still the image of mind reflected on us from innumerable objects. Philo: Add a mind like the human, said Philo. I know of no other, replied *Cleanthes. Philo:* And the liker, the better, insisted Philo. To be sure, said *Cleanthes.*

Philo: Now, *Cleanthes,* said *Philo,* with an air of alacrity and triumph, mark the consequences. First, by this method of reasoning you renounce all claim to infinity in any of the attributes of the Deity. For, as the cause ought only to be proportioned to the effect, and the effect, so far as it falls under our cognizance, is not infinite: What pretensions have we, upon your suppositions, to ascribe that attribute to the Divine Being? You will still insist that, by removing him so much from all similarity to human creatures, we give in to the most arbitrary hypothesis, and at the same time weaken all proofs of his existence.

Secondly, you have no reason, on your theory, for ascribing perfection to the Deity, even in his finite capacity; or for supposing him free from every error, mistake, or incoherence, in his undertakings. There are many inexplicable difficulties in the works of Nature which, if we allow a perfect author to be proved *a priori*, are easily solved, and become only seeming difficulties from the narrow capacity of man, who cannot trace infinite relations. But according to your method of reasoning, these difficulties become all real; and, perhaps, will be insisted on as new instances of likeness to human art and contrivance. At least, you must acknowledge that it is impossible for us to tell, from our limited views, whether this system contains any great faults or deserves any considerable praise if compared to other possible and even real systems. Could a peasant, if the *Aeneid* were read to him, pronounce that poem to be absolutely faultless, or even assign to it its proper rank among the productions of human wit, he who had never seen any other production?

But were this world ever so perfect a production, it must still remain uncertain whether all the excellences of the work can justly be ascribed to the workman. If we survey a ship, what an exalted idea must we form of the ingenuity of the carpenter who framed so complicated, useful, and beautiful a machine? And what surprise must we feel when we find him a stupid mechanic who imitated others, and copied an art which, through a long succession of ages, after multiplied trials, mistakes, corrections, deliberations, and controversies, had been gradually improving? Many worlds might have been botched and bungled, throughout an eternity, ere this system was struck out; much labor lost; many fruitless trials made; and a slow but continued improvement carried on during infinite ages in the art of world-making. In such subjects, who can determine where the truth, nay, who can conjecture where the probability lies, amidst a great number of hypotheses which may be proposed, and a still greater which may be imagined?

And what shadow of an argument, continued Philo, can you produce from your hypothesis to prove the unity of the Deity? A great number of men join in building a house or ship, in rearing a city, in framing a commonwealth; why may not several deities combine in contriving and framing a world? This is only so much greater similarity to human affairs. By sharing the work among several, we may so much further limit the attributes of each, and get rid of that extensive power and knowledge which must be supposed in one deity, and which, according to you, can only serve to weaken the proof of his existence. And if such foolish, such vicious creatures as man can yet often unite in framing and executing one plan, how much more those deities or demons, whom we may suppose several degrees more perfect?

To multiply causes without necessity is indeed contrary to true philosophy, but this principle applies not to the present case. Were one deity antecedently proved by your theory who were possessed of every attribute requisite to the production of the universe, it would be needless, I own (though not absurd), to suppose any other deity existent. But while it is still a question whether all these attributes are united in one subject or dispersed among several independent beings; by what phenomena in nature can we pretend to decide the controversy? Where we see a body raised in a scale, we are sure that there is in the opposite scale, however concealed from sight, some counterpoising weight equal to it; but it is still allowed to doubt whether that weight be an aggregate of several distinct bodies or one uniform united mass. And if the weight requisite very much exceeds anything which we have ever seen conjoined in any single body, the former supposition becomes still more probable and natural. An intelligent being of such vast power and capacity as is necessary to produce the universe, or, to speak in the language of ancient philosophy, so prodigious an animal, exceeds all analogy and even comprehension.

But further, *Cleanthes,* men are mortal, and renew their species by generation; and this is common to all living creatures. The two great sexes of male and female, says *Milton,* animate the world. Why must this circumstance, so universal, so essential, be excluded from those numerous and limited deities? Behold, then, the theogony of ancient times brought back upon us.

And why not become a perfect anthropomorphite? Why not assert the deity or deities to be corporeal, and to have eyes, a nose, mouth, ears, etc.? *Epicurus* maintained that no man had ever seen reason but in a human figure; therefore, the gods must have a human figure. And this argument, which is deservedly so much ridiculed by *Cicero*, becomes, according to you, solid and philosophical.

In a word, *Cleanthes,* a man who follows your hypothesis is able, perhaps, to assert or conjecture that the universe sometime arose from something like design: But beyond that position he cannot ascertain one single circumstance, and is left afterwards to fix every point of his theology by the utmost license of fancy and hypothesis. This world, for aught he knows, is very faulty and imperfect, compared to a superior standard; and was only the first rude essay of some infant deity who afterwards abandoned it, ashamed of his lame performance: It is the work only of some dependent, inferior deity, and is the object of derision to his superiors: It is the production of old age and dotage in some superannuated deity; and ever since his death has run on at adventures, from the first impulse and active force which it received from him.... You justly give signs of horror, *Demea,* at these strange suppositions; but these, and a thousand more of the same kind, are *Cleanthes'* suppositions, not mine. From the moment the attributes of the Deity are supposed finite, all these have place. And I cannot, for my part, think that so wild and unsettled a system of theology is, in any respect, preferable to none at all.

Cleanthes: These suppositions I absolutely disown, cried *Cleanthes:* They strike me, however, with no horror, especially when proposed in that rambling way in which they drop from you. On the contrary, they give me pleasure when I see that, by the utmost indulgence of your imagination, you never get rid of the hypothesis of design in the universe, but are obliged at every turn to have recourse to it. To this concession I adhere steadily; and this I regard as a sufficient foundation for religion.

NOTES

1. *On the Nature of Things*, II, 1096–1099 (trans. by W. D. Rouse).
2. Tully was a common name for the Roman lawyer and philosopher, Marcus Tullius Cicero, 106–43 BC.

The excerpt is from *The Nature of the Gods*, i, viii, 19 (trans. By H. Rackham).

II.C.3

Arguments from Design

RICHARD SWINBURNE

Richard Swinburne (1934–) was, until his retirement, the Nolloth Professor of the Philosophy of the Christian Religion at Oxford University. He has written extensively in philosophy of religion, and his body of work includes several pieces on the traditional arguments for the existence of God. In the present article, written for the journal Think: Philosophy for Everyone, *Swinburne*

Reprinted from *Think* 1 (2002): 49–54, by permission of Cambridge University Press.

identifies two forms of the argument from design—the argument from temporal order and the argument from spatial order. Both arguments identify features of the natural world that, so Swinburne argues, cannot be explained scientifically and cannot plausibly be taken as "brute facts" about the universe. The best explanation, he argues, will be a personal *explanation—one which appeals to the designing activity of a supernatural personal agent.*

Reasons for believing that there is a God have been around as long as there have been people holding this belief; and philosophers have tried to knock these reasons into "arguments" of more rigorous form as long as there have been philosophers. My view is that when these arguments are articulated in the right way (i.e. in a form similar to arguments in science or history) and taken together, they make a powerful cumulative case for the existence of God.

Among the strongest arguments for the existence of God, it seems to me, are two forms of the "argument from design"—which I shall call the argument from temporal order and the argument from spatial order. The argument from temporal order begins by drawing our attention to the fact that throughout all of possibly infinite time and space material objects behave in the simple way codified by scientific laws. What exactly are the most fundamental laws of nature we may not yet know—maybe they are the field equations of the General Theory of Relativity, or maybe the laws of a Grand Unified Theory or of a still grander theory yet to be formulated. To say that such laws govern matter is just to say that every bit of matter, every neutron and proton and electron throughout endless space and time behaves in exactly the same way (i.e. in accord with exactly the same fundamental laws). How extraordinary that is!

Clearly this could not ever be explained scientifically—for scientific explanation of the operation of a natural law consists in showing it to be a consequence of some more fundamental laws—we explain the operation of Galileo's law of fall on Earth by showing it to be a consequence, for the particular circumstances of Earth, of Newton's laws of motion; and we may be able to explain the operation of Einstein's laws by those of Grand Unified Theory. But my concern is with the operation of the most fundamental laws of all. Either it is a brute inexplicable fact that there are such laws at all, or it is to be explained by a pattern of explanation slightly different from the scientific.

The second form of argument—the argument from spatial order—draws our attention to the intricate construction of plants, animals, and humans. They are so organized as to be able to catch the food for which their digestive apparatus is suited, escape from the predators most keen to catch them, breed and reproduce—they are like very, very complicated machines. Now, of course, there is a well-known explanation of all this in terms of evolution by Natural Selection. Once upon a time, the story goes, there were very simple organisms, and they had offspring which varied from the parents in various ways (some of them being taller, some shorter, some simpler and some more complex than their parents). Those best fitted to survive (and often complexity of organization provides a selective advantage) did so and they in turn produced offspring with characteristics differing slightly from their own in random directions; and so it was that complex plants, animals, and humans evolved. This story is surely basically correct. But why were there simple organisms in the first place? Presumably because the matter-energy at the time of the "Big Bang" when the Universe (or at any rate our present state of it) began 15 billion years ago had just the quantity, density, and initial velocity as to lead in the course of time to the evolution of organisms. And why are there laws of evolution? That is, laws which bring it about that animal genes mutate randomly, that animals produce many offspring, etc.? Presumably because these laws follow from the fundamental laws of nature. Only a certain sort of critical arrangement of matter and certain kinds of laws of nature will give rise to organisms. And recent scientific work on the "fine tuning" of the Universe has shown that the initial matter and the laws of nature had to have very, very special features indeed if organisms were to evolve. For example, the Big Bang had to be of exactly the right size—if it had been a very slightly bigger bang, the quanta of energy would have receded from each other too fast for matter to condense into galaxies, stars and planets and so allow organisms to evolve. If the Bang had been very slightly smaller, the Universe would have collapsed before it was cool enough for the chemical elements to form and so to allow organisms to evolve. Also, if the laws of nature still had the same form but the physical constants in them had slightly different values from their actual ones (or if they had had any of most other different forms), there would have been no evolution. So how extraordinary it is that the initial conditions and laws were so "fine-tuned" as to produce plants, animals and humans! This again not merely is not, but, because of the very nature of science, *could* not, ever be something scientifically explicable. Science could not explain why the basic laws of nature are as they are, nor why the matter at the time of the Big Bang (or everlastingly, if there was no beginning) had the features it did. All this is where science starts from, what it explains other things in terms *of*. So again, either these are brute inexplicable facts, or they are to be explained by a pattern of explanation slightly different from the scientific.

Fortunately there is just such a pattern which we use all the time in explaining mundane phenomena. I call it personal explanation. When we explain the book being on the table, or the words of these sentences being on my writing-paper, we explain them in terms of the action of a person with capacities for making a difference to things and a purpose which he seeks to achieve thereby. The words being on the paper are to be explained as brought about by a person (me) with a capacity to move my body in certain ways (i.e. write), and a purpose (to have an article to send to the editor). Scientific explanations often postulate unobservables (e.g. protons and electrons) in order to explain the observable data; and the grounds for supposing they do is that the explanatory hypothesis is simple and leads us with some probability to expect the data which we would not otherwise expect. Personal explanations in terms of unobservable persons

are to be accepted on similar grounds. The simplicity of a hypothesis is a matter of it postulating few entities with few simple properties.

The data inexplicable by science to which I have drawn attention—the uniform behaviour of objects in accord with laws of nature, and the special character of those laws and of the initial (or boundary) conditions of the Universe—are readily explicable in terms of the action of a God, omnipotent (all-powerful), omniscient (all-knowing) and perfectly free. He is constantly active, moving the stars and atoms in a regular way (as we may move our bodies in a regular way in the patterns of a dance), and in just such ways as, together with the primeval matter which he makes, to bring forth animals and humans. Being omnipotent, he can do this. Being omniscient, he will see good reason for doing it. A regularly evolving world is beautiful, and the humans who will eventually emerge can learn how the world works—which they can do only if there are simple laws of nature for them to understand—and then they can themselves choose to some extent how to form the world for good or ill. It is good that there be humans playing a role in the creation process. God, being perfectly free, will not be prevented by irrational forces from bringing about what he perceives to be good.

It is sometimes said that the laws of nature being as they are, and the initial conditions being as they were in our Universe, would be explained if there were a trillion other universes with various different laws and initial conditions. Then it would be very probable that there would be one universe in which these factors were just right for the evolution of animals and humans. But it would be the height of irrationality to postulate a trillion universes (as opposed to one God) in order to explain our Universe, unless there were particular features of our Universe best explained by a super-theory which had the trillion-universe consequence. But even so that super-theory would have to postulate very special boundary conditions for the super-Universe of universes and very special super-laws of nature which had the consequence that there would evolve such a variety of universes that it was very probable that at least one would be life-evolving. Most super-theories (as well as being very complicated) will not have that consequence. So we have the problem of just why the super-Universe had laws of nature and boundary conditions of just that kind. And so again, whether of one universe or of one super-universe, either its order and "fine-tuned" character are brute inexplicable facts or they are to be explained by a pattern of explanation slightly different from the scientific.

The hypothesis of theism is a very simple hypothesis. It postulates one personal being, not many. Persons are beings with powers to make differences to the world, knowledge of how to do so, and some degree of freedom in how to do so. God is postulated as a very simple kind of person—having infinite degrees of power, knowledge, and freedom; or, put negatively, zero limits to his power, knowledge and freedom. Scientists always postulate infinite (or zero) degrees of properties if they can do so consistently with the data, as the simplest hypothesis. They

postulate that photons have zero rest mass rather than some very, very small rest mass which would predict the data equally well; and they used to postulate that the gravitational force had infinite velocity until other considerations forced a different hypothesis upon them. To postulate God is to postulate one being of a very simple kind, and this hypothesis makes it not improbable that we will find the data to which I have drawn attention.

To suppose these data to be just brute inexplicable facts seems, however, highly irrational. To suppose that it is simply a vast coincidence that every bit of matter everywhere in the Universe behaves in exactly the same way is irrational to the point of absurdity—and even more so when there is a simple rival hypothesis which leads us to expect those data, as well as the further datum of the world being fine-tuned to produce animals and humans. Reason leads us inescapably from Nature up to Nature's God.

II.C.4

A Scientific Argument for the Existence of God

ROBIN COLLINS

Robin Collins (1961–) is professor of philosophy at Messiah College, and he has written several articles on the argument from design. The article included here presents a simplified version of an argument that he has developed in much more technical detail elsewhere. He begins by noting that life would have been impossible had certain laws of nature and fundamental physical constants (such as the gravitational constant) been even slightly different. He then argues that since this apparent "fine-tuning" of the laws and constants is significantly more probable on the assumption that the universe was designed to be hospitable for life than on the assumption that it was not designed at all, such apparent fine-tuning counts as evidence in favor of the existence of a designer.

From *Reason for the Hope Within*, Michael J. Murray, ed., © 1999, Wm. B. Eerdmans, Grand Rapids, MI. Used with permission.

I. INTRODUCTION

The Evidence of Fine-Tuning

Suppose we went on a mission to Mars, and found a domed structure in which everything was set up just right for life to exist. The temperature, for example, was set around 70° F and the humidity was at 50 percent; moreover, there was an oxygen recycling system, an energy gathering system, and a whole system for the production of food. Put simply, the domed structure appeared to be a fully functioning biosphere. What conclusion would we draw from finding this structure? Would we draw the conclusion that it just happened to form by chance? Certainly not. Instead, we would unanimously conclude that it was designed by some intelligent being. Why would we draw this conclusion? Because an intelligent designer appears to be the only plausible explanation for the existence of the structure. That is, the only alternative explanation we can think of—that the structure was formed by some natural process—seems extremely unlikely. Of course, it is *possible* that, for example, through some volcanic eruption various metals and other compounds could have formed, and then separated out in just the right way to produce the "biosphere," but such a scenario strikes us as extraordinarily unlikely, thus making this alternative explanation unbelievable.

The universe is analogous to such a "biosphere," according to recent findings in physics. Almost everything about the basic structure of the universe—for example, the fundamental laws and parameters of physics and the initial distribution of matter and energy—is balanced on a razor's edge for life to occur. As the eminent Princeton physicist Freeman Dyson notes, "There are many ... lucky accidents in physics. Without such accidents, water could not exist as liquid, chains of carbon atoms could not form complex organic molecules, and hydrogen atoms could not form breakable bridges between molecules"[1]—in short, life as we know it would be impossible.

Scientists call this extraordinary balancing of the parameters of physics and the initial conditions of the universe the "fine-tuning of the cosmos." It has been extensively discussed by philosophers, theologians, and scientists, especially since the early 1970s, with hundreds of articles and dozens of books written on the topic. Today, it is widely regarded as offering by far the most persuasive current argument for the existence of God. For example, theoretical physicist and popular science writer Paul Davies—whose early writings were not particularly sympathetic to theism—claims that with regard to the basic structure of the universe, "the impression of design is overwhelming."[2] Similarly, in response to the life-permitting fine-tuning of the nuclear resonances responsible for the oxygen and carbon synthesis in stars, the famous astrophysicist Sir Fred Hoyle declares that

> I do not believe that any scientists who examined the evidence would fail to draw the inference that the laws of nuclear physics have been deliberately designed with regard to the consequences they produce inside stars. If this is so, then my apparently random quirks have become part of a deep-laid scheme. If not then we are back again at a monstrous sequence of accidents.[3]

A few examples of this fine-tuning are listed below:

1. If the initial explosion of the big bang had differed in strength by as little as one part in 10^{60}, the universe would have either quickly collapsed back on itself, or expanded too rapidly for stars to form. In either case, life would be impossible. (As John Jefferson Davis points out, an accuracy of one part in 10^{60} can be compared to firing a bullet at a one-inch target on the other side of the observable universe, twenty billion light years away, and hitting the target.)[4]

2. Calculations indicate that if the strong nuclear force, the force that binds protons and neutrons together in an atom, had been stronger or weaker by as little as five percent, life would be impossible.[5]

3. Calculations by Brandon Carter show that if gravity had been stronger or weaker by one

part in 10^{40}, then life-sustaining stars like the sun could not exist. This would most likely make life impossible.[6]

4. If the neutron were not about 1.001 times the mass of the proton, all protons would have decayed into neutrons or all neutrons would have decayed into protons, and thus life would not be possible.[7]

5. If the electromagnetic force were slightly stronger or weaker, life would be impossible, for a variety of different reasons.[8]

Imaginatively, one could think of each instance of fine-tuning as a radio dial: unless all the dials are set exactly right, life would be impossible. Or, one could think of the initial conditions of the universe and the fundamental parameters of physics as a dart board that fills the whole galaxy, and the conditions necessary for life to exist as a small one-foot-wide target: unless the dart hits the target, life would be impossible. The fact that the dials are perfectly set, or that the dart has hit the target, strongly suggests that someone set the dials or aimed the dart, for it seems enormously improbable that such a coincidence could have happened by chance.

Although individual calculations of fine-tuning are only approximate and could be in error, the fact that the universe is fine-tuned for life is almost beyond question because of the large number of independent instances of apparent fine-tuning. As philosopher John Leslie has pointed out, "Clues heaped upon clues can constitute weighty evidence despite doubts about each element in the pile."[9] What is controversial, however, is the degree to which the fine-tuning provides evidence for the existence of God. As impressive as the argument from fine-tuning seems to be, atheists have raised several significant objections to it. Consequently, those who are aware of these objections, or have thought of them on their own, often will find the argument unconvincing. This is not only true of atheists, but also many theists. I have known, for instance, both a committed Christian Hollywood filmmaker and a committed Christian biochemist who remained unconvinced because of certain atheist objections to the argument. This is unfortunate, particularly since

the fine-tuning argument is probably the most powerful current argument for the existence of God. My goal in this chapter, therefore, is to make the fine-tuning argument as strong as possible. This will involve developing the argument in as objective and rigorous a way as I can, and then answering the major atheist objections to it. Before launching into this, however, I will need to make a preliminary distinction.

A Preliminary Distinction

To develop the fine-tuning argument rigorously, it is useful to distinguish between what I shall call the *atheistic single-universe hypothesis* and the *atheistic many-universes hypothesis*. According to the atheistic single-universe hypothesis, there is only one universe, and it is ultimately an inexplicable, "brute" fact that the universe exists and is fine-tuned. Many atheists, however, advocate another hypothesis, one which attempts to explain how the seemingly improbable fine-tuning of the universe could be the result of chance. We will call this hypothesis the *atheistic many-worlds hypothesis,* or the *atheistic many-universes hypothesis*. According to this hypothesis, there exists what could be imaginatively thought of as a "universe generator" that produces a very large or infinite number of universes, with each universe having a randomly selected set of initial conditions and values for the parameters of physics. Because this generator produces so many universes, just by chance it will eventually produce one that is fine-tuned for intelligent life to occur.

Plan of the Chapter

Below, we will use this distinction between the atheistic single-universe hypothesis and the atheistic many-universes hypothesis to present two separate arguments for theism based on the fine-tuning: one which argues that the fine-tuning provides strong reasons to prefer theism over the atheistic single-universe hypothesis and one which argues that we should prefer theism over the atheistic many-universes hypothesis. We will develop the argument against the atheistic single-universe hypothesis in section II below, referring to it as the core argument. Then we will answer objections to this *core* argument in section III, and finally develop the argument for preferring theism to the atheistic many-universes hypothesis in section IV. An appendix is also included that further elaborates and justifies one of the key premises of the core argument presented in section II.

II. CORE ARGUMENT RIGOROUSLY FORMULATED

General Principle of Reasoning Used

The Principle Explained   We will formulate the fine-tuning argument against the atheistic single-universe hypothesis in terms of what I will call the *prime principle of confirmation*. The prime principle of confirmation is a general principle of reasoning which tells us when some observation counts as evidence in favor of one hypothesis over another. *Simply put, the principle says that whenever we are considering two competing hypotheses, an observation counts as evidence in favor of the hypothesis under which the observation has the highest probability (or is the least improbable).* (Or, put slightly differently, the principle says that whenever we are considering two competing hypotheses, H_1 and H_2, an observation, O, counts as evidence in favor of H_1 over H_2 if O is more probable under H_1 than it is under H_2.) Moreover, the degree to which the evidence counts in favor of one hypothesis over another is proportional to the degree to which the observation is more probable under the one hypothesis than the other.[10] For example, the fine-tuning is much, much more probable under theism than under the atheistic single-universe hypothesis, so it counts as strong evidence for theism over this atheistic hypothesis. In the next major subsection, we will present a more formal and elaborated rendition of the fine-tuning argument in terms of the prime principle. First, however, let's look at a couple of illustrations of the principle and then present some support for it.

Additional Illustrations of the Principle   For our first illustration, suppose that I went hiking in the mountains, and found underneath a certain cliff a group of rocks arranged in a formation that clearly formed the pattern "Welcome to the mountains, Robin Collins." One hypothesis is that, by chance, the rocks just happened to be arranged in that pattern—ultimately, perhaps, because of certain initial conditions of the universe. Suppose the only viable alternative hypothesis is that my brother, who was in the mountains before me, arranged the rocks in this way. Most of us would immediately take the arrangements of rocks to be strong evidence in favor of the "brother" hypothesis over the "chance" hypothesis. Why? Because it strikes us as extremely *improbable* that the rocks would be arranged that way by chance, but *not improbable* at all that my brother would place them in that configuration. Thus, by the prime principle of confirmation we would conclude that the arrangement of rocks strongly supports the "brother" hypothesis over the chance hypothesis.

Or consider another case, that of finding the defendant's fingerprints on the murder weapon. Normally, we would take such a finding as strong evidence that the defendant was guilty. Why? Because we judge that it would be *unlikely* for these fingerprints to be on the murder weapon if the defendant was innocent, but *not unlikely* if the defendant was guilty. That is, we would go through the same sort of reasoning as in the above case.

Support for the Principle   Several things can be said in favor of the prime principle of confirmation. First, many philosophers think that this principle can be derived from what is known as the *probability calculus,* the set of mathematical rules that are typically assumed to govern probability. Second, there does not appear to be any case of recognizably good reasoning that violates this principle. Finally, the principle appears to have a wide range of applicability, undergirding much of our reasoning in science and everyday life, as the examples above illustrate. Indeed, some have even claimed that a slightly more general version of this principle undergirds all scientific reasoning. Because of all these reasons in favor of the principle, we can be very confident in it.

Further Development of Argument

To further develop the core version of the fine-tuning argument, we will summarize the argument by explicitly listing its two premises and its conclusion:

- *Premise 1.* The existence of the fine-tuning is not improbable under theism.

- *Premise 2.* The existence of the fine-tuning is very improbable under the atheistic single-universe hypothesis.

- *Conclusion*: From premises (1) and (2) and the prime principle of confirmation, it follows that the fine-tuning data provide strong evidence to favor the design hypothesis over the atheistic single-universe hypothesis.

At this point, we should pause to note two features of this argument. First, the argument does not say that the fine-tuning evidence proves that the universe was designed, or even that it is likely that the universe was designed. In order to justify these sorts of claims, we would have to look at the full range of evidence both for and against the design hypothesis, something we are not doing in this chapter. Rather, the argument merely concludes that the fine-tuning strongly *supports* theism *over* the atheistic single-universe hypothesis.

In this way, the evidence of the fine-tuning argument is much like fingerprints found on the gun: although they can provide strong evidence that the defendant committed the murder, one could not conclude merely from them alone that the defendant is guilty; one would also have to look at all the other evidence offered. Perhaps, for instance, ten reliable witnesses claimed to see the defendant at a party at the time of the shooting. In this case, the fingerprints would still count as significant evidence of guilt, but this evidence would be counterbalanced by the testimony of the witnesses. Similarly the evidence of fine-tuning strongly supports theism over the atheistic single-universe hypothesis, though it does not itself show that, everything considered, theism is the most plausible explanation of the world. Nonetheless, as I argue in the conclusion of this chapter, the evidence of fine-tuning provides a much stronger and more objective argument for theism (over the atheistic single-universe hypothesis) than the strongest atheistic argument does against theism.

The second feature of the argument we should note is that, given the truth of *the prime principle of confirmation*, the conclusion of the argument follows from the premises. Specifically, if the premises of the argument are true, then we are guaranteed that the conclusion is true: that is, the argument is what philosophers call *valid*. Thus, insofar as we can show that the premises of the argument are true, we will have shown that the conclusion is true. Our next task, therefore, is to attempt to show that the premises are true, or at least that we have strong reasons to believe them.

Support for the Premises

Support for Premise (1)   Premise (1) is easy to support and fairly uncontroversial. One major argument in support of it can be simply stated as follows: *since God is an all good being, and it is good for intelligent, conscious beings to exist, it is not surprising or improbable that God would create a world that could support intelligent life.* Thus, the fine-tuning is not improbable under theism, as premise (1) asserts.

Support for Premise (2)   Upon looking at the data, many people find it very obvious that the fine-tuning is highly improbable under the atheistic single-universe hypothesis. And it is easy to see why when we think of the fine-tuning in terms of the analogies offered earlier. In the dart board analogy, for example, the initial conditions of the universe and the fundamental parameters of physics are thought of as a dart board that fills the whole galaxy, and the conditions necessary for life to exist as a small one-foot-wide target. Accordingly, from this analogy it seems obvious that it would be highly improbable for the fine-tuning to occur under the atheistic single-universe hypothesis—that is, for the dart to hit the target by chance.

Typically, advocates of the fine-tuning argument are satisfied with resting the justification of premise (2), or something like it, on this sort of analogy. Many atheists and theists, however, question the legitimacy of this sort of analogy, and thus find the argument unconvincing. For these people, the appendix to this chapter offers a rigorous and objective justification of premise (2) using standard principles of probabilistic reasoning. Among other things, in the process of rigorously justifying premise (2), we effectively answer the common objection to the fine-tuning argument that because the universe is a unique, unrepeatable event, we cannot meaningfully assign a probability to its being fine-tuned.

III. SOME OBJECTIONS TO CORE VERSION

As powerful as the core version of the fine-tuning argument is, several major objections have been raised to it by both atheists and theists. In this section, we will consider these objections in turn.

Objection 1: More Fundamental Law Objection

One criticism of the fine-tuning argument is that, as far as we know, there could be a more fundamental law under which the parameters of physics *must* have the values they do. Thus, given such a law, it is not improbable that the known parameters of physics fall within the life-permitting range.

Besides being entirely speculative, the problem with postulating such a law is that it simply moves the improbability of the fine-tuning up one level, to that of the postulated physical law itself. Under this hypothesis, what is improbable is that of all the conceivable fundamental physical laws there could be, the universe just happens to have the one that constrains the parameters of physics in a life-permitting way. Thus, trying to explain the fine-tuning by postulating this sort of fundamental law is like trying to explain why the pattern of rocks below a cliff spell "Welcome to the mountains, Robin Collins" by postulating that an earthquake occurred and that all the rocks on the cliff face were arranged in just the right configuration to fall into the pattern in question. Clearly this explanation merely transfers the improbability up one level, since now it seems

enormously improbable that of all the possible configurations the rocks could be in on the cliff face, they are in the one which results in the pattern "Welcome to the mountains, Robin Collins."

A similar sort of response can be given to the claim that the fine-tuning is not improbable because it might be *logically necessary* for the parameters of physics to have life-permitting values. That is, according to this claim, the parameters of physics must have life-permitting values in the same way $2 + 2$ must equal 4, or the interior angles of a triangle must add up to 180 degrees in Euclidian geometry. Like the "more fundamental law" proposal above, however, this postulate simply transfers the improbability up one level: of all the laws and parameters of physics that conceivably could have been logically necessary, it seems highly improbable that it would be those that are life-permitting.[11]

Objection 2: Other Forms of Life Objection

Another objection people commonly raise to the fine-tuning argument is that as far as we know, other forms of life could exist even if the parameters of physics were different. So, it is claimed, the fine-tuning argument ends up presupposing that all forms of intelligent life must be like us. The answer to this objection is that most cases of fine-tuning do not make this presupposition. Consider, for instance, the case of the fine-tuning of the strong nuclear force. If it were slightly smaller, no atoms could exist other than hydrogen. Contrary to what one might see on *Star Trek*, an intelligent life-form cannot be composed merely of hydrogen gas: there is simply not enough stable complexity. So, in general the fine-tuning argument merely presupposes that intelligent life requires some degree of stable, reproducible organized complexity. This is certainly a very reasonable assumption.

Objection 3: Anthropic Principle Objection

According to the weak version of the so-called *anthropic principle,* if the laws of nature were not fine-tuned, we would not be here to comment on the fact. Some have argued, therefore, that the fine-tuning is not really *improbable or surprising* at all under atheism, but simply follows from the fact that we exist. The response to this objection is to simply restate the argument in terms of our existence: our existence as embodied, intelligent beings is extremely unlikely under the atheistic single-universe hypothesis (since our existence requires fine-tuning), but not improbable under theism. Then, we simply apply the prime principle of confirmation to draw the conclusion that *our existence* strongly confirms theism over the atheistic single-universe hypothesis.

To further illustrate this response, consider the following "firing squad" analogy. As John Leslie points out, if fifty sharpshooters all miss me, the response "if they had not missed me I wouldn't be here to consider the fact" is not adequate. Instead, I would naturally conclude that there was some reason why they all missed, such as that they never really intended to kill me. Why would I conclude this? Because my continued existence would be very improbable under the hypothesis that they missed me by chance, but not improbable under the hypothesis that there was some reason why they missed me. Thus, by the prime principle of confirmation, my continued existence strongly confirms the latter hypothesis.[12]

Objection 4: The "Who Designed God?" Objection

Perhaps the most common objection that atheists raise to the argument from design, of which the fine-tuning argument is one instance, is that postulating the existence of God does not solve the problem of design, but merely transfers it up one level. Atheist George Smith, for example, claims that

> If the universe is wonderfully designed, surely God is even more wonderfully designed. He must, therefore, have had a designer even more wonderful than He is. If *God* did not require a designer, then there is no reason why such a relatively less wonderful thing as the universe needed one.[13]

Or, as philosopher J. J. C. Smart states the objection:

> If we postulate God in addition to the created universe we increase the complexity of our hypothesis. We have all the complexity of the universe itself, and we have in addition the at least equal complexity of God. (The designer of an artifact must be at least as complex as the designed artifact).... *If the theist can show the atheist that postulating God actually reduces the complexity of one's total world view, then the atheist should be a theist.*[14]

The first response to the above atheist objection is to point out that the atheist claim that the designer of an artifact must be as complex as the artifact designed is certainly not obvious. But I do believe that their claim has some intuitive plausibility: for example, in the world we experience, organized complexity seems only to be produced by systems that already possess it, such as the human brain/mind, a factory, or an organism's biological parent.

The second, and better, response is to point out that, at most, the atheist objection only works against a version of the design argument that claims that all organized complexity needs an explanation, and that God is the best explanation of the organized complexity found in the world. The version of the argument I presented against the atheistic single-universe hypothesis, however, only required that the fine-tuning be more probable under theism than under the atheistic single-universe hypothesis. But this requirement is still met even if God exhibits tremendous internal complexity, far exceeding that of the universe. Thus, even if we were to grant the atheist assumption that the designer of an artifact must be as complex as the artifact, the fine-tuning would still give us strong reasons to prefer theism over the atheistic single-universe hypothesis.

To illustrate, consider the example of the "biosphere" on Mars presented at the beginning of this paper. As mentioned above, the existence of the biosphere would be much more probable under the hypothesis that intelligent life once visited Mars than under the chance hypothesis. Thus, by the prime principle of confirmation, the existence of such a "biosphere" would constitute strong evidence that intelligent, extraterrestrial life had once been on Mars, even though this alien life would most likely have to be much more complex than the "biosphere" itself.

The final response theists can give to this objection is to show that a supermind such as God would *not* require a high degree of unexplained organized complexity to create the universe. Although I have presented this response elsewhere, presenting it here is beyond the scope of this chapter.

IV. THE ATHEISTIC MANY-UNIVERSES HYPOTHESIS

The Atheistic Many-Universes Hypothesis Explained

In response to the theistic explanation of fine-tuning of the cosmos, many atheists have offered an alternative explanation, what I will call the atheistic many-universes hypothesis. (In the literature it is more commonly referred to as the *many-worlds hypothesis,* though I believe this name is somewhat misleading.) According to this hypothesis, there are a very large—perhaps infinite—number of universes, with the fundamental parameters of physics varying from universe to universe.[15] Of course, in the vast majority of these universes the parameters of physics would not have life-permitting values. Nonetheless, in a small proportion of universes they would, and consequently it is no longer improbable that universes such as ours exist that are fine-tuned for life to occur.

Advocates of this hypothesis offer various types of models for where these universes came from. We will present what are probably the two most popular and plausible, the so-called *vacuum fluctuation* models and the *oscillating big bang* models. According to the vacuum fluctuation models, our universe, along with these other universes, were generated by quantum fluctuations in a preexisting superspace.[16] Imaginatively, one can think of this preexisting superspace as an infinitely extending ocean full of soap, and each universe generated out of this superspace as a soap bubble which spontaneously forms on the ocean.

The other model, the oscillating big bang model, is a version of the big bang theory. According to the big bang theory, the universe came into existence in an "explosion" (that is, a "bang") somewhere between ten and fifteen billion years ago. According to the *oscillating* big bang theory, our universe will eventually collapse back in on itself (what is called the "big crunch") and then from that "big crunch" will arise another "big bang," forming a new universe, which will in turn itself collapse, and so on. According to those who use this model to attempt to explain the fine-tuning, during every cycle, the parameters of physics and the initial conditions of the universe are reset at random. Since this process of collapse, explosion, collapse, and explosion has been going on for all eternity, eventually a fine-tuned universe will occur, indeed infinitely many of them.

In the next section, we will list several reasons for rejecting the atheistic many-universes hypothesis.

Reasons for Rejecting the Atheistic Many-Universes Hypothesis

First Reason The first reason for rejecting the atheistic many-universes hypothesis, and preferring the theistic hypothesis, is the following general rule: *everything else being equal, we should prefer hypotheses for which we have independent evidence or that are natural extrapolations from what we already know.* Let's first illustrate and support this principle, and then apply it to the case of the fine-tuning.

Most of us take the existence of dinosaur bones to count as very strong evidence that dinosaurs existed in the past. But suppose a dinosaur skeptic claimed that she could explain the bones by postulating a "dinosaur-bone-producing-field" that simply materialized the bones out of thin air. Moreover, suppose further that, to avoid objections such as that there are no known physical laws that would allow for such a mechanism, the dinosaur skeptic simply postulated that we have not yet discovered these laws or detected these fields. Surely, none of us would let this skeptical hypothesis deter us from inferring the existence of dinosaurs. Why? Because although no one has directly observed dinosaurs, we do have experience of other animals leaving behind fossilized remains, and thus the dinosaur explanation is a *natural extrapolation* from our common experience. In contrast, to explain the dinosaur bones, the dinosaur skeptic has invented a set of physical laws, and a set of mechanisms that are *not* a natural extrapolation from anything we know or experience.

In the case of the fine-tuning, we already know that minds often produce fine-tuned devices, such as Swiss watches. Postulating God—a supermind—as the explanation of the fine-tuning, therefore, is a natural extrapolation from what we already observe minds to do. In contrast, it is difficult to see how the atheistic many-universes hypothesis could be considered a natural extrapolation from what we observe. Moreover, unlike the atheistic many-universes hypothesis, we have some experiential evidence for the existence of God, namely religious experience. Thus, by the above principle, we should prefer the theistic explanation of the fine-tuning over the atheistic many-universes explanation, everything else being equal.

Second Reason A second reason for rejecting the atheistic many-universes hypothesis is that the "many-universes generator" seems like it would need to be designed. For instance, in all current worked-out proposals for what this "universe generator" could be—such as the oscillating big bang and the vacuum fluctuation models explained above—the "generator" itself is governed by a complex set of physical laws that allow it to produce the universes. It stands to reason, therefore, that if these laws were slightly different the generator probably would not be able to produce any universes that could sustain life. After all, even my bread machine has to be made just right in order to work properly, and it only produces loaves of bread, not universes! Or consider a device as simple

as a mousetrap: it requires that all the parts, such as the spring and hammer, be arranged just right in order to function. It is doubtful, therefore, whether the atheistic many-universe theory can entirely eliminate the problem of design the atheist faces; rather, at least to some extent, it seems simply to move the problem of design up one level.[17]

Third Reason A third reason for rejecting the atheistic many-universes hypothesis is that the universe generator must not only select the parameters of physics at random, but must actually randomly create or select the very laws of physics themselves. This makes this hypothesis seem even more farfetched since it is difficult to see what possible physical mechanism could select or create laws.

The reason the "many-universes generator" must randomly select the laws of physics is that, just as the right values for the parameters of physics are needed for life to occur, the right set of laws is also needed. If, for instance, certain laws of physics were missing, life would be impossible. For example, without the law of inertia, which guarantees that particles do not shoot off at high speeds, life would probably not be possible.[18] Another example is the law of gravity: if masses did not attract each other, there would be no planets or stars, and once again it seems that life would be impossible. Yet another example is the *Pauli Exclusion Principle*, the principle of quantum mechanics that says that no two fermions—such as electrons or protons— can share the same quantum state. As prominent Princeton physicist Freeman Dyson points out,[19] without this principle all electrons would collapse into the nucleus and thus atoms would be impossible.

Fourth Reason The fourth reason for rejecting the atheistic many-universes hypothesis is that it cannot explain other features of the universe that seem to exhibit apparent design, whereas theism can. For example, many physicists, such as Albert Einstein, have observed that the basic laws of physics exhibit an extraordinary degree of beauty, elegance, harmony, and ingenuity. Nobel prize-winning physicist Steven Weinberg, for instance, devotes a whole chapter of his book *Dreams of a Final Theory*[20] to explaining how the criteria of beauty and elegance are commonly used to guide physicists in formulating the right laws. Indeed, one of the most prominent theoretical physicists of this century, Paul Dirac, went so far as to claim that "it is more important to have beauty in one's equations than to have them fit experiment."[21]

Now such beauty, elegance, and ingenuity make sense if the universe was designed by God. Under the atheistic many-universes hypothesis, however, there is no reason to expect the fundamental laws to be elegant or beautiful. As theoretical physicist Paul Davies writes, "If nature is so 'clever' as to exploit mechanisms that amaze us with their ingenuity, is that not persuasive evidence for the existence of intelligent design behind the universe? If the world's finest minds can unravel only with difficulty the deeper workings of nature, how could it be supposed that those workings are merely a mindless accident, a product of blind chance?"[22]

Final Reason   This brings us to the final reason for rejecting the atheistic many-universes hypothesis, which may be the most difficult to grasp: namely, neither the atheistic many-universes hypothesis (nor the atheistic single-universe hypothesis) can at present adequately account for the improbable initial arrangement of matter in the universe required by the second law of thermodynamics. To see this, note that according to the second law of thermodynamics, the entropy of the universe is constantly increasing. The standard way of understanding this entropy increase is to say that the universe is going from a state of order to disorder. We observe this entropy increase all the time around us: things, such as a child's bedroom, that start out highly organized tend to "decay" and become disorganized unless something or someone intervenes to stop it.

Now, for purposes of illustration, we could think of the universe as a scrabble-board that initially starts out in a highly ordered state in which all the letters are arranged to form words, but which keeps getting randomly shaken. Slowly, the board, like the universe, moves from a state of order to disorder. The problem for the atheist is to explain how the universe could have started out in a highly ordered state, since it is extraordinarily improbable for such states to occur by chance.[23] If, for example, one were to dump a bunch of letters at random on a scrabble-board, it would be very unlikely for most of them to form into words. At best, we would expect groups of letters to form into words in a few places on the board.

Now our question is, Could the atheistic many-universes hypothesis explain the high degree of initial order of our universe by claiming that given enough universes, eventually one will arise that is ordered and in which intelligent life occurs, and so it is no surprise that we find ourselves in an ordered universe? The problem with this explanation is that it is overwhelmingly more likely for local patches of order to form in one or two places than for the whole universe to be ordered, just as it is overwhelmingly more likely for a few letters on the scrabble-board randomly to form words than for all the letters throughout the board randomly to form words. Thus, the overwhelming majority of universes in which intelligent life occurs will be ones in which the intelligent life will be surrounded by a small patch of order necessary for its existence, but in which the rest of the universe is disordered. Consequently, even under the atheistic many-universes hypothesis, it would still be enormously improbable for intelligent beings to find themselves in a universe such as ours which is highly ordered throughout.[24]

Conclusion

Even though the above criticisms do not definitively refute the atheistic many-universes hypothesis, they do show that it has some severe disadvantages relative to theism. This means that if atheists adopt the atheistic many-universes hypothesis to defend their position, then atheism has become much less plausible than it used to be. Modifying a turn of phrase coined by philosopher Fred Dretske: these are inflationary times, and the cost of atheism has just gone up.

V. OVERALL CONCLUSION

In the above sections I showed there are good, objective reasons for claiming that the fine-tuning provides strong evidence for theism. I first presented an argument for thinking that the fine-tuning provides strong evidence for preferring theism over the atheistic single-universe hypothesis, and then presented a variety of different reasons for rejecting the atheistic many-universes hypothesis as an explanation of the fine-tuning. In order to help one appreciate the strength of the arguments presented, I would like to end by comparing the strength of the *core* version of the argument from the fine-tuning to what is widely regarded as the strongest atheist argument against theism, the argument from evil.[25]

Typically, the atheist argument against God based on evil takes a similar form to the core version of the fine-tuning argument. Essentially, the atheist argues that the existence of the kinds of evil we find in the world is very improbable under theism, but not improbable under atheism. Thus, by the prime principle of confirmation, they conclude that the existence of evil provides strong reasons for preferring atheism over theism.

What makes this argument weak in comparison to the core version of the fine-tuning argument is that, unlike in the case of the fine-tuning, the atheist does not have a significant objective basis for claiming that the existence of the kinds of evil we find in the world is highly improbable under theism. In fact, their judgment that it is improbable seems largely to rest on a mistake in reasoning. To see this, note that in order to show that it is improbable, atheists would have to show that it is *unlikely* that the types of evils we find in the world are necessary for any morally good, greater purpose, since if they are, then it is clearly not at all unlikely that an all good, all powerful being would create a world in which those evils are allowed to occur. But how could atheists show this without first surveying all possible morally good purposes such a being might have, something they have clearly not done? *Consequently, it seems, at most the atheist could argue that since no one has come up with any adequate purpose yet, it is unlikely that there is such a purpose.*

This argument, however, is very weak, as I will now show.

The first problem with this atheist argument is that it assumes that the various explanations people have offered for why an all good God would create evil—such as the free will theodicy—ultimately fail. But even if we grant that these theodicies fail, the argument is still very weak. To see why, consider an analogy. Suppose someone tells me that there is a rattlesnake in my garden, and I examine a portion of the garden and do not find the snake. I would only be justified in concluding that there was probably no snake in the garden if either: i) I had searched at least half the garden; or ii) I had good reason to believe that if the snake were in the garden, it would likely be in the portion of the garden that I examined. If, for instance, I were randomly to pick some small segment of the garden to search and did not find the snake, I would be unjustified in concluding from my search that there was probably no snake in the garden. Similarly, if I were blindfolded and did not have any idea of how large the garden was (e.g., whether it was ten square feet or several square miles), I would be unjustified in concluding that it was unlikely that there was a rattlesnake in the garden, even if I had searched for hours with my rattlesnake-detecting dogs. Why? Because I would not have any idea of what percentage of the garden I had searched.

As with the garden example, we have no idea of how large the realm is of possible greater purposes for evil that an all good, omnipotent being could have. Hence we do not know what proportion of this realm we have actually searched. Indeed, considering the finitude of our own minds, we have good reason to believe that we have so far only searched a small proportion, and we do not have significant reason to believe that all the purposes God might have for allowing evil would be in the proportion we searched. Thus, we have little objective basis for saying that the existence of the types of evil we find in the world is highly improbable under theism.

From the above discussion, therefore, it is clear that the relevant probability estimates in the case of the fine-tuning are much more secure than those estimates in the probabilistic version of the atheist's argument from evil, since unlike the latter, we can provide a fairly rigorous, objective basis for them based on actual calculations of the relative range of life-permitting values for the parameters of physics. (See the appendix to this chapter for a rigorous derivation of the probability of the fine-tuning under the atheistic single-universe hypothesis.) *Thus, I conclude, the core argument for preferring theism over the probabilistic version of the atheistic single-universe hypothesis is much stronger than the atheist argument from evil.*[26]

APPENDIX

In this appendix, I offer a rigorous support for premise (2) of the main argument: that is, the claim that the fine-tuning is very improbable under the atheistic single-universe hypothesis. Support for premise (2) will involve three major subsections. The first subsection will be devoted to explicating the fine-tuning of gravity since we will often use this to illustrate our arguments. Then, in our second subsection, we will show how the improbability of the fine-tuning under the atheistic single-universe hypothesis can be derived from a commonly used, objective principle of probabilistic reasoning called the *principle of indifference*. Finally, in our third subsection, we will explicate what it could mean to say that the fine-tuning is improbable given that the universe is a unique, unrepeatable event as assumed by the atheistic single-universe hypothesis. The appendix will in effect answer the common atheist objection that theists can neither *justify* the claim that the fine-tuning is improbable under the atheistic single-universe hypothesis, nor can they provide an account of what it could possibly *mean* to say that the fine-tuning is improbable.

i. The Example of Gravity

The force of gravity is determined by Newton's law $F = Gm_1m_2/r^2$. Here G is what is known as the *gravitational constant*, and is basically a number that determines the force of gravity in any given circumstance. For instance, the gravitational attraction between the moon and the earth is given by first multiplying the mass of the moon (m_1) times the mass of the earth (m_2), and then dividing by the distance between them squared (r^2). Finally, one multiplies this result by the number G to obtain the total force. Clearly the force is directly proportional to G: for example, if G were to double, the force between the moon and the earth would double.

In the previous section, we reported that some calculations indicate that the force of gravity must be fine-tuned to one part in 10^{40} in order for life to occur. What does such fine-tuning mean? To understand it, imagine a radio dial, going from 0 to $2G_0$, where G_0 represents the current value of the gravitational constant. Moreover, imagine the dial being broken up into 10^{40}—that is, ten thousand, billion, billion, billion, billion—evenly spaced tick marks. To claim that the strength of gravity must be fine-tuned to one part in 10^{40} is simply to claim that, in order for life to exist, the constant of gravity cannot vary by even one tick mark along the dial from its current value of G_0.

ii. The Principle of Indifference

In the following subsections, we will use the *principle of indifference* to justify the assertion that the fine-tuning is highly improbable under the atheistic single-universe hypothesis.

a. The Principle Stated Applied to cases in which there is a finite number of alternatives, the principle of indifference can be formulated as the claim that we should assign the same probability to what are called *equipossible alternatives*, where two or more alternatives are said to be equipossible if we have no reason to prefer one of the alternatives over any of the others. (In another version of the principle, alternatives that are relevantly symmetrical are considered equipossible and hence the ones that should be assigned equal probability.) For instance, in the case of a standard two-sided coin, we have no more reason to think that the coin will land on heads than that it will land on tails, and so we assign them each an equal probability. Since the total probability must add up to one, this means that the coin has a 0.5

chance of landing on heads and a 0.5 chance of landing on tails. Similarly, in the case of a standard six-sided die, we have no more reason to think that it will land on one number, say a 6, than any of the other numbers, such as a 4. Thus, the principle of indifference tells us to assign each possible way of landing an equal probability—namely ⅙.

The above explication of the principle applies only when there are a finite number of alternatives, for example six sides on a die. In the case of the fine-tuning, however, the alternatives are not finite but form a continuous magnitude. The value of G, for instance, conceivably could have been any number between 0 and infinity. Now, continuous magnitudes are usually thought of in terms of ranges, areas, or volumes depending on whether or not we are considering one, two, three, or more dimensions. For example, the amount of water in an 8 oz. glass could fall anywhere within the *range* 0 oz. to 8 oz., such as 6.012345645 oz. Or, the exact position that a dart hits a dart board can fall anywhere within the *area* of the dart board. With some qualifications to be discussed below, the principle of indifference becomes in the continuous case the principle that *when we have no reason to prefer any one value of a parameter over another, we should assign equal probabilities to equal ranges, areas, or volumes.* So, for instance, suppose one aimlessly throws a dart at a dart board. Assuming the dart hits the board, what is the probability it will hit within the bull's eye? Since the dart is thrown aimlessly, we have no more reason to believe it will hit one part of the dart board than any other part. The principle of indifference, therefore, tells us that the probability of its hitting the bull's eye is the same as the probability of hitting any other part of the dart board of equal area. This means that the probability of its hitting the bull's eye is simply the ratio of the area of the bull's eye to the rest of the dart board. So, for instance, if the bull's eye forms only 5 percent of the total area of the board, then the probability of its hitting the bull's eye will be 5 percent.

b. Application to Fine-Tuning In the case of the fine-tuning, we have no more reason to think that the parameters of physics will fall within the life-permitting range than within any other range, given the atheistic single-universe hypothesis. Thus according to the principle of indifference, equal ranges of these parameters should be assigned equal probabilities. As in the case of the dart board mentioned in the last section, this means that the probability of the parameters of physics falling within the life-permitting range under the atheistic single-universe hypothesis is simply the ratio of the range of life-permitting values (the "area of the bull's eye") to the total *relevant* range of possible values (the "relevant area of the dart board").

Now physicists can make rough estimates of the range of *life-permitting* values for the parameters of physics, as discussed above in the case of gravity, for instance. But what is the "total *relevant* range of possible values"? At first one might think that this range is infinite, since the values of the parameters could conceivably be anything. This, however, is not correct, for although the possible range of values could be infinite, for most of these values we have no way of estimating whether they are life-permitting or not. We do not truly know, for example, what would happen if gravity were 10^{60} times stronger than its current value: as far as we know, a new form of matter might come into existence that could sustain life. Thus, as far as we know, there could be other life-permitting ranges far removed from the actual values that the parameters have. Consequently, all we can say is that the life-permitting range is very, very small *relative* to the limited range of values for which we can make estimates, a range that we will here-after refer to as the "*illuminated*" range.

Fortunately, however, this limitation does not affect the overall argument. The reason is that, based on the principle of indifference, we can still say that it is very improbable for the values for the parameters of physics to have fallen in the life-permitting range *instead* of some other part of the "illuminated" range.[27] And this *improbability* is all that is actually needed for our main argument to work. To see this, consider an analogy. Suppose a dart landed on the bull's eye at the center of a huge dart board. Further, suppose that this bull's eye is surrounded by a very large empty, bull's-eye-free, area. Even if there were many other bull's eyes on the dart board, we would still take the fact that the dart landed on the bull's eye instead of some other part of the large empty area surrounding the bull's eye as strong evidence that it was aimed. Why? Because we would reason that *given that the dart landed in the empty area*, it was very improbable for it to land in the bull's eye by chance but not improbable if it were aimed. Thus, by the prime principle of confirmation, we could conclude that the dart landing on the bull's eye strongly confirms the hypothesis that it was aimed over the chance hypothesis.

c. The Principle Qualified Those who are familiar with the principle of indifference, and mathematics, will recognize that one important qualification needs to be made to the above account of how to apply the principle of indifference. (Those who are not mathematically adept might want to skip this and perhaps the next paragraph.) To understand the qualification, note that the ratio of ranges used in calculating the probability is dependent on how one parameterizes, or writes, the physical laws. For example, suppose for the sake of illustration that the range of life-permitting values for the gravitational constant is 0 to G_0, and the "illuminated" range of possible values for G is 0 to $2G_0$. Then, the ratio of life-permitting values to the range of "illuminated" possible values for the gravitational constant will be ½. Suppose, however, that one writes the law of gravity in the mathematically equivalent form of $F = \sqrt{U m_1 m_2 / r^2}$ instead of $F = G m_1 m_2 / r^2$, where $U = G^2$. (In this way of writing Newton's law, U becomes the new gravitational constant.) This means that $U_0 = G_0^2$, where U_0, *like* G_0, represents the actual value of U in our universe. Then, the range of life-permitting values would be 0 to U_0, and the "illuminated" range of possible values would be 0 to $4U_0$ on the U scale (which is equivalent to 0 to $2G_0$ on the G scale). Hence, calculating the ratio of life-permitting values using the U scale instead of the G scale yields a ratio of ¼ instead of ½. Indeed, for almost any ratio one chooses—such as one in which the life-permitting range is about

the same size as the "illuminated" range—there exist mathematically equivalent forms of Newton's law that will yield that ratio. So, why choose the standard way of writing Newton's law to calculate the ratio instead of one in which the fine-tuning is not improbable at all?

The answer to this question is to require that the proportion used in calculating the probability be between *real* physical ranges, areas, or volumes, not merely mathematical representations of them. That is, the proportion given by the scale used in one's representation must directly correspond to the proportions actually existing in physical reality. As an illustration, consider how we might calculate the probability that a meteorite will fall in New York state instead of somewhere else in the northern, contiguous United States. One way of doing this is to take a standard map of the northern, contiguous United States, measure the area covered by New York on the map (say 2 square inches) and divide it by the total area of the map (say 30 square inches). If we were to do this, we would get approximately the right answer because the proportions on a standard map directly correspond to the actual proportions of land areas in the United States.[28] On the other hand, suppose we had a map made by some lover of the east coast in which, because of the scale used, the east coast took up half the map. If we used the proportions of areas as represented by this map we would get the wrong answer since the scale used would not correspond to real proportions of land areas. Applied to the fine-tuning, this means that our calculations of these proportions must be done using parameters that directly correspond to physical quantities in order to yield valid probabilities. In the case of gravity, for instance, the gravitational constant G directly corresponds to the force between two unit masses a unit distance apart, whereas U does not. (Instead, U corresponds to the square of the force.) Thus, G is the correct parameter to use in calculating the probability.[29]

d. Support for Principle Finally, although the principle of indifference has been criticized on various grounds, several powerful reasons can be offered for its soundness if it is restricted in the ways explained in the last subsection. First, it has an extraordinarily wide range of applicability. As Roy Weatherford notes in his book, *Philosophical Foundations of Probability Theory*, "an astonishing number of extremely complex problems in probability theory have been solved, and usefully so, by calculations based entirely on the assumption of equiprobable alternatives [that is, the principle of indifference]."[30] Second, at least for the discrete case, the principle can be given a significant theoretical grounding in information theory, being derivable from Shannon's important and well-known measure of *information*, or *negative* entropy.[31] Finally, in certain everyday cases the principle of indifference seems the only justification we have for assigning probability. To illustrate, suppose that in the last ten minutes a factory produced the first fifty-sided die ever produced. Further suppose that every side of the die is (macroscopically) perfectly symmetrical with every other side, except for there being different numbers printed on each side. (The die we are imagining is like a fair six-sided die except that it has fifty sides instead of six.) Now, we all immediately know that upon being rolled the probability of the die coming up on any given side is one in fifty. Yet, we do not know this directly from experience with fifty-sided dice, since by hypothesis no one has yet rolled such dice to determine the relative frequency with which they come up on each side. Rather, it seems our only justification for assigning this probability is the principle of indifference: that is, given that every side of the die is relevantly macroscopically symmetrical with every other side, we have no reason to believe that the die will land on one side over any other side, and thus we assign them all an equal probability of one in fifty.[32]

iii. The Meaning of Probability

In the last section we used the principle of indifference to rigorously justify the claim that the fine-tuning is highly improbable under the atheistic single-universe hypothesis. We did not explain, however, what it could *mean* to say that it is improbable, especially given that the universe is a unique, unrepeatable event. To address this issue, we shall now show how the probability invoked in the fine-tuning argument can be straightforwardly understood either as what could be called *classical probability* or as what is known as *epistemic probability*.

Classical Probability The *classical conception of probability* defines probability in terms of the ratio of number of "favorable cases" to the total number of equipossible cases.[33] Thus, for instance, to say the probability of a die coming up "4" is one out of six is simply to say that the number of ways a die could come up "4" is one-sixth the number of equipossible ways it could come up. Extending this definition to the continuous case, classical probability can be defined in terms of the relevant ratio of ranges, areas, or volumes over which the principle of indifference applies. Thus, under this extended definition, to say that the probability of the parameters of physics falling into the life-permitting value is very improbable simply *means* that the ratio of life-permitting values to the range of possible values is very, very small. Finally, notice that this definition of probability implies the principle of indifference, and thus we can be certain that the principle of indifference holds for classical probability.

Epistemic Probability *Epistemic probability* is a widely recognized type of probability that applies to claims, statements, and hypotheses—that is, what philosophers call propositions.[34] (A proposition is any claim, assertion, statement, or hypothesis about the world.) Roughly, the epistemic probability of a proposition can be thought of as the degree of credence—that is, degree of confidence or belief—we rationally should have in the proposition. Put differently, epistemic probability is a measure of our rational degree of belief under a condition of ignorance concerning whether a proposition is true or false. For example, when one says that the special theory of relativity is probably true, one is making a statement of epistemic probability. After all, the theory is actually either true or false. But, we do not know for sure whether it is true or false, so we say it is probably true to indicate that we should put more confidence in its being true than in its being false. It is also commonly argued that the probability of a coin toss is best understood as a case of epistemic probability. Since the side the coin will land on is determined by the laws of physics, it is argued that our assignment of probability is simply a measure of our rational expectations concerning which side the coin will land on.

Besides epistemic probability sumpliciter, philosophers also speak of what is known as the *conditional* epistemic probability of one proposition on another. The conditional epistemic probability of a proposition *R* on another proposition *S*—written as $P(R/S)$—can be defined as the degree to which the proposition *S of itself* should rationally lead us to expect that *R* is true. For example, there is a high conditional probability that it will rain today on the hypothesis that the weatherman has predicted a 100 percent chance of rain, whereas there is a low conditional probability that it will rain today on the hypothesis that the weatherman has predicted only a 2 percent chance of rain. That is, the hypothesis that the weatherman has predicted a 100 percent chance of rain today should strongly lead us to expect that it will rain, whereas the hypothesis that the weatherman has predicted a 2 percent chance should lead us to expect that it will not rain. Under the epistemic conception of probability, therefore, the statement that *the fine-tuning of the Cosmos is very improbable under the atheistic single-universe hypothesis* makes perfect sense: it is to be understood as making a statement about the degree to which the atheistic single-universe hypothesis would or should, of *itself*, rationally lead us to expect the cosmic fine-tuning.[35]

Conclusion

The above discussion shows that we have at least two ways of understanding improbability invoked in our main argument: as classical probability or epistemic probability. This undercuts the common atheist objection that it is meaningless to speak of the probability of the fine-tuning under the atheistic single-universe hypothesis since under this hypothesis the universe is not a repeatable event.

NOTES

1. Freeman Dyson, *Disturbing the Universe* (New York: Harper and Row, 1979), 251.

2. Paul Davies, *The Cosmic Blueprint: New Discoveries in Nature's Creative Ability to Order the Universe* (New York: Simon and Schuster, 1988), 203.

3. Fred Hoyle, in *Religion and the Scientists* (1959); quoted in *The Anthropic Cosmological Principle*, ed. John Barrow and Frank Tipler (Oxford: Oxford University Press, 1986), 22.

4. See Paul Davies, *The Accidental Universe* (Cambridge: Cambridge University Press, 1982), 90–91. John Jefferson Davis, "The Design Argument, Cosmic 'Fine-tuning,' and the Anthropic Principle," *The International Journal of Philosophy of Religion* 22 (1987): 140.

5. John Leslie, *Universes* (New York: Routledge, 1989), 4, 35; *Anthropic Cosmological Principle*, 322.

6. Paul Davies, *Superforce: The Search for a Grand Unified Theory of Nature* (New York: Simon and Schuster, 1984), 242.

7. Leslie, *Universes*, 39–40.

8. John Leslie, "How to Draw Conclusions from a Fine-Tuned Cosmos," in *Physics, Philosophy and Theology: A Common Quest for Understanding*, ed. Robert Russell et al. (Vatican City State: Vatican Observatory Press, 1988), 299.

9. Leslie, "How to Draw Conclusions," 300.

10. For those familiar with the probability calculus, a precise statement of the degree to which evidence counts in favor of one hypothesis over another can be given in terms of the odds form of Bayes's Theorem: that is, $P(H_1/E)/P(H_2/E) = [P(H_1)/P(H_2)] \times [P(E/H_1)/(E/H_2)]$. The general version of the principle stated here, however, does not require the applicability or truth of Bayes's Theorem.

11. Those with some training in probability theory will want to note that the kind of probability invoked here is what philosophers call *epistemic probability*, which is a measure of the rational degree of belief we should have in a proposition (see appendix,

subsection iii). Since our rational degree of belief in a necessary truth can be less than 1, we can sensibly speak of it being improbable for a given law of nature to exist necessarily. For example, we can speak of an unproven mathematical hypothesis—such as Goldbach's conjecture that every even number greater than 6 is the sum of two odd primes—as being probably true or probably false given our current evidence, even though all mathematical hypotheses are either necessarily true or necessarily false.

12. Leslie, "How to Draw Conclusions," 304.

13. George Smith, "The Case Against God," reprinted in *An Anthology of Atheism and Rationalism*, ed. Gordon Stein (Buffalo: Prometheus Press, 1980), 56.

14. J. J. C. Smart, "Laws of Nature and Cosmic Coincidence," *The Philosophical Quarterly* 35 (July 1985): 275–76, italics added.

15. I define a "universe" as any region of space-time that is disconnected from other regions in such a way that the parameters of physics in that region could differ significantly from the other regions.

16. Quentin Smith, "World Ensemble Explanations," *Pacific Philosophical Quarterly* 67 (1986): 82.

17. Moreover, the advocate of the atheistic many-universes hypothesis could not avoid this problem by hypothesizing that the many universes always existed as "brute fact" without being produced by a universe generator. This would simply add to the problem: it would not only leave unexplained the fine-tuning or our own universe, but would leave unexplained the existence of these other universes.

18. Leslie, *Universes*, 59.

19. Dyson, *Disturbing the Universe*, 251.

20. Chapter 6, "Beautiful Theories."

21. Paul Dirac, "The Evolution of the Physicist's Picture of Nature," *Scientific American* (May 1963): 47.

22. Davies, *Superforce*, 235–36.

23. This connection between order and probability, and the second law of thermodynamics in general, is given a precise formulation in a branch of fundamental physics called *statistical mechanics*, according to which a state of high order represents a very improbable state, and a state of disorder represents a highly probable state.

24. See Lawrence Sklar, *Physics and Chance: Philosophical Issues in the Foundation of Statistical Mechanics* (Cambridge: Cambridge University Press, 1993), chapter 8, for a review of the nontheistic explanations for the ordered arrangement of the universe and the severe difficulties they face.

25. A more thorough discussion of the atheist argument from evil is presented in Daniel Howard-Snyder's chapter (pp. 76–115), and a discussion of other atheistic arguments is given in John O'Leary-Hawthorne's chapter (pp. 116–34).

26. This work was made possible in part by a Discovery Institute grant for the fiscal year 1997–1998.

27. In the language of probability theory, this sort of probability is known as a conditional probability. In the case of G, calculations indicate that this conditional probability of the fine-tuning would be less than 10^{-40} since the life-permitting range is less than 10^{-40} of the range 0 to $2G_0$, the latter range being certainly smaller than the total "illuminated" range for G.

28. I say "approximately right" because in this case the principle of indifference only applies to strips of land that are the same distance from the equator. The reason for this is that only strips of land equidistant from the equator are truly symmetrical with regard to the motion of the earth. Since the northern, contiguous United States are all about the same distance from the equator, equal land areas should be assigned approximately equal probabilities.

29. This solution will not always work since, as the well-known Bertrand Paradoxes illustrate (e.g., see Roy Weatherford, *Foundations of Probability Theory* [Boston: Routledge and Kegan Paul, 1982], 56), sometimes there are two equally good and conflicting parameters that directly correspond to a physical quantity and to which the principle of indifference applies. In these cases, at best we can say that the probability is somewhere between that given by the two conflicting parameters. This problem, however, typically does not seem to arise for most cases of fine-tuning. Also, it should be noted that the principle of indifference applies best to *classical* or *epistemic* probability, not other kinds of probability such as *relative frequency*. (See subsection iii below.)

30. Weatherford, *Probability Theory*, 35.

31. Sklar, *Physics and Chance*, 191; Bas van Fraassen, *Laws and Symmetry* (Oxford: Oxford University Press, 1989), 345.

32. Of course, one could claim that our experience with items such as coins and dice teaches us that whenever two alternatives are macroscopically symmetrical, we should assign them an equal probability, unless we have a particular reason not to. All this claim implies, however, is that we have experiential justification for the principle of indifference, and thus it does not take away from our main point that in certain practical situations we must rely on the principle of indifference to justify our assignment of probability.

33. See Weatherford, *Probability Theory*, ch. 2.

34. For an in-depth discussion of epistemic probability, see Richard Swinburne, *An Introduction to Confirmation Theory* (London: Methuen, 1973); Ian Hacking, *The Emergence of Probability: A Philosophical Study of Early Ideas About Probability, Induction and Statistical Inference* (Cambridge: Cambridge University Press, 1975); and Alvin Plantinga, *Warrant and Proper Function* (Oxford: Oxford University Press, 1993), chapters 8 and 9.

35. It should be noted here that this rational degree of expectation should not be confused with the degree to which one should expect the parameters of physics to fall within the life-permitting range if one believed the atheistic single-universe hypothesis. For even those who believe in this atheistic hypothesis should expect the parameters of physics to be life-permitting since this follows from the fact that we are alive. Rather, the conditional epistemic probability in this case is the degree to which the atheistic single-universe hypothesis *of itself* should lead us to expect parameters of physics to be life-permitting. This means that in assessing the conditional epistemic probability in this and other similar cases, one must exclude contributions to our expectations arising from other information we have, such as that we are alive. In the case at hand, one way of doing this is by means of the following sort of thought experiment. Imagine a disembodied being with mental capacities and a knowledge of physics comparable to that of the most intelligent physicists alive today, except that the being does not know whether the parameters of physics are within the life-permitting range. Further, suppose that this disembodied being believed in the atheistic single-universe hypothesis. Then, the degree that being should rationally expect the parameters of physics to be life-permitting will be equal to our conditional epistemic probability, since its expectation is solely a result of its belief in the atheistic single-universe hypothesis, not other factors such as its awareness of its own existence.

PART III

Evil and the Hiddenness of God

Is he willing to prevent evil, but not able? then is he impotent.
Is he able, but not willing? then is he malevolent. Is he both
able and willing? whence then is evil?
EPICURUS (341–270 B.C.E.)

Lord my God, who am I that You should forsake me? . . . I call,
I cling, I want—and there is no One to answer—no One on
Whom I can cling—no, No One.— Alone. . . . What are You
doing my God to one so small?
MOTHER TERESA (1910–1997)

IN PART II, WE EXAMINED several arguments in favor of God's existence. We turn now to the two most important arguments against belief in God. One is the problem of evil; the other—closely related to it—is the problem of divine hiddenness.

The problem of evil arises from the apparent tension between the divine attributes of omnipotence, omniscience, and omnibenevolence on the one hand and the existence of evil on the other. The Judeo-Christian tradition has affirmed each of the following propositions:

1. God is all-powerful.

2. God is all-knowing.

3. God is perfectly good.

4. Evil exists.

Generally, Western thought has distinguished between two types of evil: moral and natural. *Moral evil* covers all those bad things for which creatures are morally responsible. *Natural evil* includes those terrible events that occur in nature of their own accord, such as hurricanes, tornadoes, earthquakes, volcanic eruptions, natural diseases, and so on, that cause suffering to humans and animals. Evil of both kinds, obviously, is prevalent in our world. But if God is

228

perfectly good, it seems that God would not want evil to exist. Being omniscient, God must surely know what potentials for evil lurk in the world and what evils will arise apart from divine intervention. Being omnipotent, God could prevent any evil that God knows about and wants to prevent. So, then, why does our world contain so much evil? Indeed, why does it contain any evil at all? It seems that the existence of God logically precludes the existence of evil, and vice versa.

The problem of divine hiddenness is related to the problem of evil in that it focuses on what seems to be a particular and prevalent instance of evil—the hiddenness of God—and mounts an argument for the nonexistence of God on the basis of that. When people talk about the hiddenness of God, they usually have in mind at least this phenomenon: the evidence for God's existence and its distribution among human beings is such that it is possible for a reasonable person *not* to believe in God. The problem, in short, is as follows. As we have already seen, in the theistic traditions God is understood to be perfectly loving, perfectly powerful, and perfectly knowledgeable. Now, if God exists, a relationship with God is a great good—indeed, the highest good—for human beings; and if God is perfectly knowledgeable, God will know this fact. Furthermore, if God is perfectly loving, God will do whatever God can do to ensure that human beings can attain their highest good. But having a relationship with God requires believing in God. Thus, if God loves us, God will (if God is able) see to it that there is enough evidence for God's existence distributed widely enough throughout the world that *nobody* can reasonably fail to believe in God at any time. And, of course, if God is perfectly powerful, God is able to do this. But God has *not* done this—reasonable nonbelief occurs. Therefore, God does not exist.

Theists sometimes respond to these problems with what are known in the literature as defenses; other times they respond with an attempt at theodicy. A *theodicy* is a theory whose aim is to explain why God in fact permits evil; a *defense* is simply a demonstration of consistency—an effort to show that there is no formal contradiction between the existence of God on the one hand and the existence of evil or the phenomenon of divine hiddenness on the other. The difference is that one can offer a defense without affirming the details, and so without really offering a theory about why God permits evil. For example: You are told that the defendant's fingerprints were found on the gun, and security cameras in an outside room place him at the scene of the crime within five minutes of when the crime took place. If (as is unlikely) your goal is simply to show that the evidence is logically consistent with the defendant's innocence, you might say, "Well, for all we know, he walked in, saw the crime being committed, went over and handled the gun right afterward, and then departed without calling the police." You probably won't believe this story, and you might even go on to qualify it by saying something like, "Of course, I really doubt that that's what happened; but my point is just that it's *possible*." But that does not matter if your goal is simply to demonstrate consistency. This is analogous to a defense. If, on the other hand, you tried to offer a theory explaining the evidence in a way consistent with the defendant's innocence—perhaps, say, a story, complete with suspects, motives and opportunities, according to which the defendant was framed, and which you were proposing for us actually to believe—you would be giving something analogous to a theodicy.

One important defense of theism in response to the problem of evil is the free will defense, going back as far as St. Augustine (354–430 C.E.) and receiving modern treatment in the work of John Hick, Alvin Plantinga, and Richard Swinburne. The free will defense maintains that the existence of evil is consistent with the existence of an all powerful, perfectly loving, and knowledgeable God because (a) it is impossible even for an omnipotent being to create free creatures and *guarantee* that they will never do evil, and (b) for all we know, freedom might be a great enough good that God is justified in permitting evil in order to make room for freedom. A similar defense has been mounted in response to the problem of divine hiddenness.

Another response to both problems—sometimes set forth as a theodicy, other times set forth as a mere defense—cites the value of evil and divine hiddenness for "soul-making." This response trades on the familiar idea that character is built through suffering of various kinds. Indeed, suffering and other forms of evil appear to be necessary conditions for the manifestation of certain kinds of virtuous traits. One can manifest courage, for example, only in the face of danger; one can manifest compassion for the poor only if there are some poor to whom one can be compassionate; one can manifest perseverance in seeking after God only if God is to some extent difficult to find; and so on. Moreover, in human beings anyway, it appears that having opportunities to manifest such virtues is an important means of cultivating and developing them—so that one could not even *become* courageous or compassionate or persistent in seeking God unless there were danger, poverty, and divine hiddenness in the world. Then again, one might note that *God* managed to be good and virtuous before there was ever evil and suffering in the world; and so one might well wonder why God could not have created human beings with the same sort of goodness and virtue while at the same time locating us in a world free from evil.

Both of the responses just given argue, in effect, that there are *goods we know of*—freedom, or soul-making, for example—that might well justify God in permitting evil and divine hiddenness in our world. Atheists, however, often press the point that *no good we know of* seems adequate to justify horrendous evils like the holocaust, or the brutal mistreatment of innocent children. Given this, say the atheists, the existence of such evils counts as strong evidence against the existence of God. Even if the existence of evil or divine hiddenness is not absolutely inconsistent with God's existence, the fact that there are so many evils that seemingly cannot be justified by any known good at least renders very probable the hypothesis that God does not exist.

In response, many theists have adopted a strategy known as "skeptical theism"—skeptical because it expresses skepticism about the extent of our grasp of possible goods and evils and relations among them. According to the skeptical theist, it simply does not matter that no good we know of seems to be sufficient to justify permitting the evils that plague our world. For our understanding of good and evil and of the ways in which evils might lead to goods is miniscule in comparison with the understanding that would be possessed by an *omniscient* and *morally perfect* being. So, says the skeptical theist, our inability to see how any good might possibly justify God in permitting horrendous evil or widespread divine hiddenness is only to be expected given the small, self-centered brains with which we have to work.

There are, of course, other strategies and perspectives to be considered as well, many of which are captured in the readings that follow. We begin our treatment of the problems of evil and divine hiddenness in the first section with four important and widely discussed historical and literary treatments of the problem of evil. In the second section, we examine several contemporary formulations. Finally, in the third section, we look at responses.

III.A. HISTORICAL AND LITERARY PERSPECTIVES

Introduction

IN THE FIRST READING, "The Argument from Evil," David Hume argues through his persona Philo that the existence of God is called into doubt not just by the mere existence of evil, but by the enormous amount of evil in the world. It is arguable that there is actually more evil than good in the world, and it is hard to reconcile this fact with the existence of an all-powerful, omnibenevolent deity.

In the second reading, "Theodicy: A Defense of Theism," Gottfried Leibniz (1646–1716) argues that the fact of evil in no way refutes theism, and he answers the kinds of objections raised by Hume. He contends that God permitted evil to exist in order to bring about greater goods and that Adam's fall was a *felix culpa* ("blessed fault") because it led to the incarnation of the Son of God, raising humanity to an ultimately higher destiny. Leibniz's response to the problem of evil also includes the idea that, as the creation of a perfectly good God, our world must be the best of all possible worlds. As we saw in Part I.B, this idea raises interesting questions about divine freedom.

In the third reading—the famous "Rebellion" chapter from Dostoevsky's *The Brothers Karamazov*—we find a poignant response to the Leibnizian idea that God is justified in permitting evil in order to bring about greater goods. The troubled Ivan Karamazov angrily describes cases of horrendous suffering on the part of children and then challenges his religious brother Alyosha to say whether, if *he* were the architect of the universe, he could bring himself to permit such suffering in order to bring about global happiness. The expected answer is "No"; and that is precisely the answer that Alyosha sadly gives.

Finally, in the fourth selection, Ursula LeGuin, one of the most important fantasy and science-fiction writers of the twentieth century, tells the story of a fictional utopia, Omelas, where happiness is centrally founded upon the suffering of one small child. All in Omelas are aware of the child's suffering; some come to behold it. What happens when they do? Some come to terms with it. Others—following the path of Ivan Karamazov—become the ones who walk away from Omelas.

III.A.1

The Argument from Evil

DAVID HUME

A short biographical sketch of David Hume precedes selection II.C.2. In the present selection, Hume argues through his persona Philo that not merely the fact of evil, but the enormous amount of evil, makes it dubious that a deity exists. It is arguable that there is actually more evil than good in the world, so it is hard to see how one can reconcile the existence of evil with the existence of an all-powerful, omnibenevolent deity.

PART X

It is my opinion, I own, replied Demea, that each man feels, in a manner, the truth of religion within his own breast, and, from a consciousness of his imbecility and misery rather than from any reasoning, is led to seek protection from that Being on whom he and all nature is dependent. So anxious or so tedious are even the best scenes of life that futurity is still the object of all our hopes and fears. We incessantly look forward and endeavour, by prayers, adoration, and sacrifice, to appease those unknown powers whom we find, by experience, so able to afflict and oppress us. Wretched creatures that we are! What resource for us amidst the innumerable ills of life did not religion suggest some methods of atonement, and appease those terrors with which we are incessantly agitated and tormented?

I am indeed persuaded, said Philo, that the best and indeed the only method of bringing everyone to a due sense of religion is by just representations of the misery and wickedness of men. And for that purpose a talent of eloquence and strong imagery is more requisite than that of reasoning and argument. For is it necessary to prove what everyone feels within himself? It is only necessary to make us feel it, if possible, more intimately and sensibly.

The people, indeed, replied Demea, are sufficiently convinced of this great and melancholy truth. The miseries of life, the unhappiness of man, the general corruptions of our nature, the unsatisfactory enjoyment of pleasures, riches, honours—these phrases have become almost proverbial in all languages. And who can doubt of what all men declare from their own immediate feeling and experience?

In this point, said Philo, the learned are perfectly agreed with the vulgar; and in all letters, *sacred* and *profane*, the topic of human misery has been insisted on with the most pathetic eloquence that sorrow and melancholy could inspire. The poets, who speak from sentiment, without a system, and whose testimony has therefore the more authority, abound in images of this nature. From Homer down to Dr. Young, the whole inspired tribe have ever been sensible that no other representation of things would suit the feeling and observation of each individual.

As to authorities, replied Demea, you need not seek them. Look round this library of Cleanthes. I shall venture to affirm that, except authors of

Reprinted from David Hume, *Dialogues Concerning Natural Religion* (1979); London: Longmans Green, 1878.

particular sciences, such as chemistry or botany, who have no occasion to treat of human life, there is scarce one of those innumerable writers from whom the sense of human misery has not, in some passage or other, extorted a complaint and confession of it. At least, the chance is entirely on that side; and no one author has ever, so far as I can recollect, been so extravagant as to deny it.

There you must excuse me, said Philo: Leibniz has denied it, and is perhaps the first[1] who ventured upon so bold and paradoxical an opinion; at least, the first who made it essential to his philosophical system.

And by being the first, replied Demea, might he not have been sensible of his error? For is this a subject in which philosophers can propose to make discoveries especially in so late an age? And can any man hope by a simple denial (for the subject scarcely admits of reasoning) to bear down the united testimony of mankind, founded on sense and consciousness?

And why should man, added he, pretend to an exemption from the lot of all other animals? The whole earth, believe me, Philo, is cursed and polluted. A perpetual war is kindled amongst all living creatures. Necessity, hunger, want stimulate the strong and courageous; fear, anxiety, terror agitate the weak and infirm. The first entrance into life gives anguish to the new-born infant and to its wretched parent; weakness, impotence, distress attend each stage of that life, and it is, at last, finished in agony and horror.

Observe, too, says Philo, the curious artifices of nature in order to embitter the life of every living being. The stronger prey upon the weaker and keep them in perpetual terror and anxiety. The weaker, too, in their turn, often prey upon the stronger, and vex and molest them without relaxation. Consider that innumerable race of insects, which either are bred on the body of each animal or, flying about, infix their stings in him. These insects have others still less than themselves which torment them. And thus on each hand, before and behind, above and below, every animal is surrounded with enemies which incessantly seek his misery and destruction.

Man alone, said Demea, seems to be, in part, an exception to this rule. For by combination in society he can easily master lions, tigers, and bears, whose greater strength and agility naturally enable them to prey upon him.

On the contrary, it is here chiefly, cried Philo, that the uniform and equal maxims of nature are most apparent. Man, it is true, can, by combination, surmount all his real enemies and become master of the whole animal creation; but does he not immediately raise up to himself *imaginary* enemies, the demons of his fancy, who haunt him with superstitious terrors and blast every enjoyment of life? His pleasure, as he imagines, becomes in their eyes a crime; his food and repose give them umbrage and offence; his very sleep and dreams furnish new materials to anxious fear; and even death, his refuge from every other ill, presents only the dread of endless and innumerable woes. Nor does the wolf molest more the timid flock than superstition does the anxious breast of wretched mortals.

Besides, consider, Demea: This very society by which we surmount those wild beasts, our natural enemies, what new enemies does it not raise to us? What woe and misery does it not occasion? Man is the greatest enemy of man. Oppression, injustice, contempt, contumely, violence, sedition, war, calumny, treachery, fraud—by these they mutually torment each other, and they would soon dissolve that society which they had formed were it not for the dread of still greater ills which must attend their separation.

But though these external insults, said Demea, from animals, from men, from all the elements, which assault us form a frightful catalogue of woes, they are nothing in comparison of those which arise within ourselves, from the distempered condition of our mind and body. How many lie under the lingering torment of diseases? Hear the pathetic enumeration of the great poet.

> *Intestine stone and ulcer, colic-pangs,*
> *Demoniac frenzy, moping melancholy,*
> *And moon-struck madness, pining atrophy,*
> *Marasmus, and wide-wasting pestilence.*
> *Dire was the tossing, deep the groans: Despair*

Tended the sick, busiest from couch to couch.
And over them triumphant Death his dart
Shook: but delay'd to strike, though oft invok'd
With vows, as their chief good and final hope.[2]

The disorders of the mind, continued Demea, though more secret, are not perhaps less dismal and vexatious. Remorse, shame, anguish, rage, disappointment, anxiety, fear, dejection, despair—who has ever passed through life without cruel inroads from these tormentors? How many have scarcely ever felt any better sensations? Labour and poverty, so abhorred by everyone, are the certain lot of the far greater number; and those few privileged persons who enjoy ease and opulence never reach contentment or true felicity. All the goods of life united would not make a very happy man, but all the ills united would make a wretch indeed; and any one of them almost (and who can be free from every one?), nay, often the absence of one good (and who can possess all?) is sufficient to render life ineligible.

Were a stranger to drop on a sudden into this world, I would show him, as a specimen of its ills, an hospital full of diseases, a prison crowded with malefactors and debtors, a field of battle strewed with carcases, a fleet foundering in the ocean, a nation languishing under tyranny, famine, or pestilence. To turn the gay side of life to him and give him a notion of its pleasures—whither should I conduct him? To a ball, to an opera, to court? He might justly think that I was only showing him a diversity of distress and sorrow.

There is no evading such striking instances, said Philo, but by apologies which still further aggravate the charge. Why have all men, I ask, in all ages, complained incessantly of the miseries of life? . . . They have no just reason, says one: these complaints proceed only from their discontented, repining, anxious disposition. . . . And can there possibly, I reply, be a more certain foundation of misery than such a wretched temper?

But if they were really as unhappy as they pretend, says my antagonist, why do they remain in life? . . .

Not satisfied with life, afraid of death—

this is the secret chain, say I, that holds us. We are terrified, not bribed to the continuance of our existence.

It is only a false delicacy, he may insist, which a few refined spirits indulge, and which has spread these complaints among the whole race of mankind. . . . And what is this delicacy, I ask, which you blame? Is it anything but a greater sensibility to all the pleasures and pains of life? And if the man of a delicate, refined temper, by being so much more alive than the rest of the world, is only so much more unhappy, what judgment must we form in general of human life?

Let men remain at rest, says our adversary, and they will be easy. They are willing artificers of their own misery. . . . No! reply I: an anxious langour follows their repose; disappointment, vexation, trouble, their activity and ambition.

I can observe something like what you mention in some others, replied Cleanthes, but I confess I feel little or nothing of it in myself, and hope that it is not so common as you represent it.

If you feel not human misery yourself, cried Demea, I congratulate you on so happy a singularity. Others, seemingly the most prosperous, have not been ashamed to vent their complaints in the most melancholy strains. Let us attend to the great, the fortunate emperor, Charles V, when, tired with human grandeur, he resigned all his extensive dominions into the hands of his son. In the last harangue which he made on that memorable occasion, he publicly avowed *that the greatest prosperities which he had ever enjoyed had been mixed with so many adversities that he might truly say he had never enjoyed any satisfaction or contentment.* But did the retired life in which he sought for shelter afford him any greater happiness? If we may credit his son's account, his repentance commenced the very day of his resignation.

Cicero's fortune, from small beginnings, rose to the greatest lustre and renown; yet what pathetic complaints of the ills of life do his familiar letters, as well as philosophical discourses, contain? And suitably to his own experience, he introduces Cato, the great, the fortunate Cato protesting in his old age that had he a new life in his offer he would reject the present.

Ask yourself, ask any of your acquaintance, whether they would live over again the last ten or twenty years of their life. No! but the next twenty, they say, will be better:

And from the dregs of life, hope to receive
What the first sprightly running could not give.[3]

Thus, at last, they find (such is the greatness of human misery, it reconciles even contradictions) that they complain at once of the shortness of life and of its vanity and sorrow.

And is it possible, Cleanthes, said Philo, that after all these reflections, and infinitely more which might be suggested, you can still persevere in your anthropomorphism, and assert the moral attributes of the Deity, his justice, benevolence, mercy, and rectitude, to be of the same nature with these virtues in human creatures? His power, we allow, is infinite; whatever he wills is executed; but neither man nor any other animal is happy; therefore, he does not will their happiness. His wisdom is infinite; he is never mistaken in choosing the means to any end; but the course of nature tends not to human or animal felicity; therefore, it is not established for that purpose. Through the whole compass of human knowledge there are no inferences more certain and infallible than these. In what respect, then, do his benevolence and mercy resemble the benevolence and mercy of men?

Epicurus' old questions are yet unanswered.

Is he willing to prevent evil, but not able? then is he impotent. Is he able, but not willing? then is he malevolent. Is he both able and willing? whence then is evil?

You ascribe, Cleanthes, (and I believe justly) a purpose and intention to nature. But what, I beseech you, is the object of that curious artifice and machinery which she has displayed in all animals—the preservation alone of individuals, and propagation of the species? It seems enough for her purpose, if such a rank be barely upheld in the universe, without any care or concern for the happiness of the members that compose it. No resource for this purpose: no machinery in order merely to give pleasure or ease; no fund of pure joy and contentment; no indulgence without some want or

necessity accompanying it. At least, the few phenomena of this nature are overbalanced by opposite phenomena of still greater importance.

Our sense of music, harmony, and indeed beauty of all kinds, gives satisfaction, without being absolutely necessary to the preservation and propagation of the species. But what racking pains, on the other hand, arise from gouts, gravels, megrims, toothaches, rheumatisms, where the injury to the animal machinery is either small or incurable? Mirth, laughter, play, frolic seem gratuitous satisfactions which have no further tendency; spleen, melancholy, discontent, superstition are pains of the same nature. How then does the Divine benevolence display itself, in the sense of you anthropomorphites? None but we mystics, as you were pleased to call us, can account for this strange mixture of phenomena, by deriving it from attributes infinitely perfect but incomprehensible.

And have you, at last, said Cleanthes smiling, betrayed your intentions, Philo? Your long agreement with Demea did indeed a little surprise me, but I find you were all the while erecting a concealed battery against me. And I must confess that you have now fallen upon a subject worthy of your noble spirit of opposition and controversy. If you can make out the present point, and prove mankind to be unhappy or corrupted, there is an end at once of all religion. For to what purpose establish the natural attributes of the Deity, while the moral are still doubtful and uncertain?

You take umbrage very easily, replied Demea, at opinions the most innocent and the most generally received, even amongst the religious and devout themselves; and nothing can be more surprising than to find a topic like this—concerning the wickedness and misery of man—charged with no less than atheism and profaneness. Have not all pious divines and preachers who have indulged their rhetoric on so fertile a subject, have they not easily, I say, given a solution of any difficulties which may attend it? This world is but a point in comparison of the universe; this life but a moment in comparison of eternity. The present evil phenomena, therefore, are rectified in other regions, and in some future period of existence. And the eyes of men, being then opened to larger views of things, see the whole connection of general laws, and trace, with adoration, the benevolence and rectitude of the Deity through all the mazes and intricacies of his providence.

No! replied Cleanthes, no! These arbitrary suppositions can never be admitted, contrary to matter of fact, visible and uncontroverted. Whence can any cause be known but from its known effects? Whence can any hypothesis be proved but from the apparent phenomena? To establish one hypothesis upon another is building entirely in the air; and the utmost we ever attain by these conjectures and fictions is to ascertain the bare possibility of our opinion, but never can we, upon such terms, establish its reality.

The only method of supporting Divine benevolence—and it is what I willingly embrace—is to deny absolutely the misery and wickedness of man. Your representations are exaggerated; your melancholy views mostly fictitious; your inferences contrary to fact and experience. Health is more common than sickness; pleasure than pain; happiness than misery. And for one vexation which we meet with, we attain, upon computation, a hundred enjoyments.

Admitting your position, replied Philo, which yet is extremely doubtful, you must at the same time allow that, if pain be less frequent than pleasure, it is infinitely more violent and durable. One hour of it is often able to outweigh a day, a week, a month of our common insipid enjoyments; and how many days, weeks, and months are passed by several in the most acute torments? Pleasure, scarcely in one instance, is ever able to reach ecstasy and rapture; and in no one instance can it continue for any time at its highest pitch and altitude. The spirits evaporate, the nerves relax, the fabric is disordered, and the enjoyment quickly degenerates into fatigue and uneasiness. But pain often, good God, how often! rises to torture and agony; and the longer it continues, it becomes still more genuine agony and torture. Patience is exhausted, courage languishes, melancholy seizes us, and nothing terminates our misery but the removal of its cause or another event which is the sole cure of all evil, but which, from our natural folly, we regard with still greater horror and consternation.

But not to insist upon these topics, continued Philo, though most obvious, certain, and important, I must use the freedom to admonish you, Cleanthes, that you have put the controversy upon a most dangerous issue, and are unawares introducing a total scepticism into the most essential articles of natural and revealed theology. What! no method of fixing a just foundation for religion unless we allow the happiness of human life, and maintain a continued existence even in this world, with all our present pains, infirmities, vexations, and follies, to be eligible and desirable! But this is contrary to everyone's feeling and experience; it is contrary to an authority so established as nothing can subvert. No decisive proofs can ever be produced against this authority; nor is it possible for you to compute, estimate, and compare all the pains and all the pleasures in the lives of all men and of all animals; and thus, by your resting the whole system of religion on a point which, from its very nature, must forever be uncertain, you tacitly confess that that system is equally uncertain.

But allowing you what never will be believed, at least, what you never possibly can prove, that animal or, at least, human happiness in this life exceeds its misery, you have yet done nothing; for this is not, by any means, what we expect from infinite power, infinite wisdom, and infinite goodness. Why is there any misery at all in the world? Not by chance, surely. From some cause then. Is it from the intention of the Deity? But he is perfectly benevolent. Is it contrary to his intention? But he is almighty. Nothing can shake the solidity of this reasoning, so short, so clear, so decisive, except we assert that these subjects exceed all human capacity, and that our common measures of truth and falsehood are not applicable to them—a topic which I have all along insisted on, but which you have, from the beginning, rejected with scorn and indignation.

But I will be contented to retire still from this intrenchment, for I deny that you can ever force me in it. I will allow that pain or misery in man is *compatible* with infinite power and goodness in the Deity, even in your sense of these attributes: what are you advanced by all these concessions? A mere possible compatibility is not sufficient. You must prove these pure, unmixed, and uncontrollable attributes from the present mixed and confused phenomena, and from these alone. A hopeful undertaking! Were the phenomena ever so pure and unmixed, yet, being finite, they would be insufficient for that purpose. How much more, where they are also so jarring and discordant!

Here, Cleanthes, I find myself at ease in my argument. Here I triumph. Formerly, when we argued concerning the natural attributes of intelligence and design, I needed all my sceptical and metaphysical subtilty to elude your grasp. In many views of the universe and of its parts, particularly the latter, the beauty and fitness of final causes strike us with such irresistible force that all objections appear (what I believe they really are) mere cavils and sophisms; nor can we then imagine how it was ever possible for us to repose any weight on them. But there is no view of human life or of the condition of mankind from which, without the greatest violence, we can infer the moral attributes or learn that infinite benevolence, conjoined with infinite power and infinite wisdom, which we must discover by the eyes of faith alone. It is your turn now to tug the labouring oar, and to support your philosophical subtilties against the dictates of plain reason and experience.

NOTES

1. That sentiment had been maintained by Dr. King and some few others before Leibniz, though by none of so great fame as that German philosopher.

2. Milton: *Paradise Lost,* Bk. XI.
3. John Dryden, *Aureng-Zebe,* Act IV, sc. 1.

III.A.2

Theodicy: A Defense of Theism

GOTTFRIED LEIBNIZ

Gottfried Wilhelm Leibniz (1646–1716) was a German idealist who tried to set forth a thorough-going theodicy, a justification of the ways of God. In this selection he argues that the fact of evil in no way refutes theism, and he answers the kinds of objections raised by Hume. He contends that God permitted evil to exist in order to bring about greater good and that Adam's fall was a felix culpa *(a "blessed fault") because it led to the incarnation of the Son of God, raising humanity to an ultimately higher destiny. He argues that although God can foresee the future, humans are still free in that they act voluntarily.*

Reprinted from Gottfried Leibniz, The Theodicy: *Abridgement of the Argument Reduced to Syllogistic Form* (1710) in *The Philosophical Works of Leibnitz,* ed. & trans. by G. M. Duncan (New Haven: Tuttle, Morehouse, & Taylor, 1890).

Some intelligent persons have desired that this supplement be made [to the Theodicy], and I have the more readily yielded to their wishes as in this way I have an opportunity again to remove certain difficulties and to make some observations which were not sufficiently emphasized in the work itself.

I. Objection. Whoever does not choose the best is lacking in power, or in knowledge, or in goodness.

God did not choose the best in creating this world.

Therefore, God has been lacking in power, or in knowledge, or in goodness.

Answer. I deny the minor, that is, the second premise of this syllogism; and our opponent proves it by this.

Prosyllogism. Whoever makes things in which there is evil, which could have been made without any evil, or the making of which could have been omitted, does not choose the best.

God has made a world in which there is evil; a world, I say, which could have been made without any evil, or the making of which could have been omitted altogether.

Therefore, God has not chosen the best.

Answer. I grant the minor of this prosyllogism; for it must be confessed that there is evil in this world which God has made, and that it was possible to make a world without evil, or even not to create a world at all, for its creation has depended on the free will of God; but I deny the major, that is, the first of the two premises of the prosyllogism, and I might content myself with simply demanding its proof; but in order to make the matter clearer, I have wished to justify this denial by showing that the best plan is not always that which seeks to avoid evil, since it may happen that *the evil is accompanied by a greater good.* For example, a general of an army will prefer a great victory with a slight wound to a condition without wound and without victory. We have proved this more fully in the large work by making it clear, by instances taken from mathematics and elsewhere, that an imperfection in the part may be required for a greater perfection in the whole. In this I have followed the opinion of St. Augustine, who has said a hundred times, that God has permitted evil in order to bring about good, that is, a greater good; and that of Thomas Aquinas (in libr. II. sent. dist. 32, qu. I, art. 1), that the permitting of evil tends to the good of the universe. I have shown that the ancients called Adam's fall *felix culpa,* a happy sin, because it had been retrieved with immense advantage by the incarnation of the Son of God, who has given to the universe something nobler than anything that ever would have been among creatures except for it. For the sake of a clearer understanding, I have added, following many good authors, that it was in accordance with order and the general good that God allowed to certain creatures the opportunity of exercising their liberty, even when he foresaw that they would turn to evil, but which he could so well rectify; because it was not fitting that, in order to hinder sin, God should always act in an extraordinary manner. To overthrow this objection, therefore, it is sufficient to show that a world with evil might be better than a world without evil; but I have gone even farther, in the work, and have even proved that this universe must be in reality better than every other possible universe.

II. Objection. If there is more evil than good in intelligent creatures, then there is more evil than good in the whole work of God.

Now, there is more evil than good in intelligent creatures.

Therefore, there is more evil than good in the whole work of God.

Answer. I deny the major and the minor of this conditional syllogism. As to the major, I do not admit it at all, because this pretended deduction from a part to the whole, from intelligent creatures to all creatures, supposes tacitly and without proof that creatures destitute of reason cannot enter into comparison nor into account with those which possess it. But why may it not be that the surplus of good in the non-intelligent creatures which fill the world, compensates for, and even incomparably surpasses, the surplus of evil in the rational creatures? It is true that the value of the latter is greater; but, in compensation, the others are beyond comparison the more numerous, and it may be that the proportion of number and quantity surpasses that of value and of quality.

As to the minor, that is no more to be admitted; that is, it is not at all to be admitted that there is more evil than good in the intelligent creatures. There is no need even of granting that there is more evil than good in the human race, because it is possible, and in fact very probable, that the glory and the perfection of the blessed are incomparably greater than the misery and the imperfection of the damned, and that here the excellence of the total good in the smaller number exceeds the total evil in the greater number. The blessed approach the Divinity, by means of a Divine Mediator, as near as may suit these creatures, and make such progress in good as is impossible for the damned to make in evil, approach as nearly as they may to the nature of demons. God is infinite, and the devil is limited; the good may and does go to infinity, while evil has its bounds. It is therefore possible, and is credible, that in the comparison of the blessed and the damned, the contrary of that which I have said might happen in the comparison of intelligent and non-intelligent creatures, takes place; namely, it is possible that in the comparison of the happy and the unhappy, the proportion of degree exceeds that of number, and that in the comparison of intelligent and non-intelligent creatures, the proportion of number is greater than that of value. I have the right to suppose that a thing is possible so long as its impossibility is not proved; and indeed that which I have here advanced is more than a supposition.

But in the second place, if I should admit that there is more evil than good in the human race, I have still good grounds for not admitting that there is more evil than good in all intelligent creatures. For there is an inconceivable number of genii, and perhaps of other rational creatures. And an opponent could not prove that in all the City of God, composed as well of genii as of rational animals without number and of an infinity of kinds, evil exceeds good. And although in order to answer an objection, there is no need of proving that a thing is, when its mere possibility suffices; yet, in this work, I have not omitted to show that it is a consequence of the supreme perfection of the Sovereign of the universe, that the kingdom of God is the most perfect of all possible states or governments, and that consequently the little evil there is, is required for the consummation of the immense good which is found there.

III. *Objection.* If it is always impossible not to sin, it is always unjust to punish.

Now, it is always impossible not to sin; or, in other words, every sin is necessary.

Therefore, it is always unjust to punish.

The minor of this is proved thus:

1. *Prosyllogism.* All that is predetermined is necessary.
   Every event is predetermined.
   Therefore, every event (and consequently sin also) is necessary.

   Again this second minor is proved thus:

2. *Prosyllogism.* That which is future, that which is foreseen, that which is involved in the causes, is predetermined.
   Every event is such.
   Therefore, every event is predetermined.

Answer. I admit in a certain sense the conclusion of the second prosyllogism, which is the minor of the first; but I shall deny the major of the first prosyllogism, namely, that every thing predetermined is necessary; understanding by the *necessity* of sinning, for example, or by the impossibility of not sinning, or of not performing any action, the necessity with which we are here concerned, that is, that which is essential and absolute, and which destroys the morality of an action and the justice of punishments. For if anyone understood another necessity or impossibility, namely, a necessity which should be only moral, or which was only hypothetical (as will be explained shortly); it is clear that I should deny the major of the objection itself. I might content myself with this answer and demand the proof of the proposition denied; but I have again desired to explain my procedure in this work, in order to better elucidate the matter and to throw more light on the whole subject, by explaining the necessity which ought to be rejected and the determination which must take place. That *necessity* which is contrary to morality and which ought to be rejected, and which would render punishment unjust, is an insurmountable necessity which would make all opposition useless, even if we should wish with all our heart to avoid the necessary action, and should make all possible efforts to that end. Now, it is manifest that this is not applicable to voluntary actions, because we would not perform them if we did not choose to. Also their prevision and predetermination are not absolute, but presuppose the will: if it is certain that we shall perform them, it is not less certain that we shall choose to perform them. These voluntary actions and their consequences will not take place no matter what we do or whether we wish them or not; but, *through* that which we shall do and through that which we shall wish to do, which leads to them. And this is involved in prevision and in predetermination, and even constitutes their ground. And the necessity of such an event is called conditional or hypothetical, or the necessity of consequence, because it supposes the will, and the other *requisites*; whereas the necessity which destroys morality and renders punishment unjust and reward useless, exists in things which will be whatever we may do or whatever we may wish to do, and, in a word, is in that which is essential; and this is what is called an absolute necessity. Thus it is to no purpose, as regards what is absolutely necessary, to make prohibitions or commands, to propose penalties or prizes, to praise or to blame; it will be none the less. On the other hand, in voluntary actions and in that which depends upon them, precepts armed with power to punish and to recompense are very often of use and are included in the order of causes which make an action exist. And it is for this reason that not only cares and labors but also prayers are useful; God having had these prayers in view before he regulated things and having had that consideration for them which was proper. This is why the precept which says *ora et labora* (pray and work), holds altogether good; and not only those who (under the vain pretext of the necessity of events) pretend that the care which business demands may be neglected, but also those who reason against prayer, fall into what the ancients even then called the *lazy sophism*. Thus the predetermination of events by causes is just what contributes to morality instead of destroying it, and causes incline the will, without compelling it. This is why the

determination in question is not a necessitation—it is certain (to him who knows all) that the effect will follow this inclination; but this effect does not follow by a necessary consequence, that is, one the contrary of which implies contradiction. It is also by an internal inclination such as this that the will is determined, without there being any necessity. Suppose that one has the greatest passion in the world (a great thirst, for example), you will admit to me that the soul can find some reason for resisting it, if it were only that of showing its power. Thus, although one may never be in a perfect indifference of equilibrium and there may be always a preponderance of inclination for the side taken, it, nevertheless, never renders the resolution taken absolutely necessary.

IV. *Objection.* Whoever can prevent the sin of another and does not do so, but rather contributes to it although he is well informed of it, is accessory to it.

God can prevent the sin of intelligent creatures; but he does not do so, and rather contributes to it by his concurrence and by the opportunities which he brings about, although he has a perfect knowledge of it.

Hence, etc.

Answer. I deny the major of this syllogism. For it is possible that one could prevent sin, but ought not, because he could not do it without himself committing a sin, or (when God is in question) without performing an unreasonable action. Examples have been given and the application to God himself has been made. It is possible also that we contribute to evil and that sometimes we even open the road to it, in doing things which we are obliged to do; and, when we do our duty or (in speaking of God) when, after thorough consideration, we do that which reason demands, we are not responsible for the results, even when we foresee them. We do not desire these evils; but we are willing to permit them for the sake of a greater good which we cannot reasonably help preferring to other considerations. And this is a *consequent* will, which results from *antecedent* wills by which we will the good. I know that some persons, in speaking of the antecedent and consequent will of God, have understood by the *antecedent* that which wills that all men should be saved; and by the consequent, that which wills, in consequence of persistent sin, that some should be damned. But these are merely illustrations of a more general idea, and it may be said for the same reason that God, by his antecedent will, wills that men should not sin; and by his consequent or final and decreeing will (that which is always followed by its effect), he wills to permit them to sin, this permission being the result of superior reasons. And we have the right to say in general that the antecedent will of God tends to the production of good and the prevention of evil, each taken in itself and as if alone (*particulariter et secundum quid*, Thom. I, qu. 19, art. 6), according to the measure of the degree of each good and each evil; but that the divine consequent or final or total will tends toward the production of as many goods as may be put together, the combination of which becomes in this way determined, and includes also the permission of some evils and the exclusion of some goods, as the best possible plan for the universe demands. Arminius, in his *Antiperkinsus*, has very well explained that the will of God may be called consequent, not only in relation to the action of the creature considered beforehand in the divine understanding, but also in relation to other anterior divine acts of will. But this consideration of the passage cited from Thomas Aquinas, and that from Scotus (I. dist. 46, qu. XI), is enough to show that they make this distinction as I have done here. Nevertheless, if anyone objects to this use of terms let him substitute *deliberating* will, in place of antecedent, and final or decreeing will, in place of consequent. For I do not wish to dispute over words.

V. Objection.   Whoever produces all that is real in a thing, is its cause.

God produces all that is real in sin.

Hence, God is the cause of sin.

Answer. I might content myself with denying the major or the minor, since the term real admits of interpretations which would render these propositions false. But in order to explain more clearly, I will make a distinction. *Real* signifies either that which is positive only, or, it includes also privative beings: in the first case, I deny the major and admit

the minor; in the second case, I do the contrary. I might have limited myself to this, but I have chosen to proceed still farther and give the reason for this distinction. I have been very glad therefore to draw attention to the fact that every reality purely positive or absolute is a perfection; and that imperfection comes from limitation, that is, from the privative: for to limit is to refuse progress, or the greatest possible progress. Now God is the cause of all perfections and consequently of all realities considered as purely positive. But limitations or privations result from the original imperfection of creatures, which limits their receptivity. And it is with them as with a loaded vessel, which the river causes to move more or less slowly according to the weight which it carries: thus its speed depends upon the river, but the retardation which limits this speed comes from the load. Thus in the *Theodicy*, we have shown how the creature, in causing sin, is a defective cause; how errors and evil inclinations are born of privation; and how privation is accidentally efficient; and I have justified the opinion of St. Augustine (lib. I, ad Simpl. qu. 2) who explains, for example, how God makes the soul obdurate, not by giving it something evil, but because the effect of his good impression is limited by the soul's resistance and by the circumstances which contribute to this resistance, so that he does not give it all the good which would overcome its evil. *Nec* (inquit) *ab illo erogatur aliquid quo homo fit deterior, sed tantum quo fit melior non erogatur.* But if God had wished to do more, he would have had to make either other natures for creatures or other miracles to change their natures, things which the best plan could not admit. It is as if the current of the river must be more rapid than its fall admitted or that the boats should be loaded more lightly, if it were necessary to make them move more quickly. And the original limitation or imperfection of creatures requires that even the best plan of the universe could not receive more good, and could not be exempt from certain evils, which, however, are to result in a greater good. There are certain disorders in the parts which marvelously enhance the beauty of the whole; just as certain dissonances, when properly used, render harmony more beautiful. But this depends on what has already been said in answer to the first objection.

VI. Objection. Whoever punishes those who have done as well as it was in their power to do, is unjust.

God does so.

Hence, etc.

Answer. I deny the minor of this argument. And I believe that God always gives sufficient aid and grace to those who have a good will, that is, to those who do not reject this grace by new sin. Thus, I do not admit the damnation of infants who have died without baptism or outside of the church; nor the damnation of adults who have acted according to the light which God has given them. And I believe that if *any one has followed the light which has been given him,* he will undoubtedly receive greater light when he has need of it, as the late M. Hulseman, a profound and celebrated theologian at Leipzig, has somewhere remarked; and if such a man has failed to receive it during his lifetime he will at least receive it when at the point of death.

VII. Objection. Whoever gives only to some, and not to all, the means which produces in them effectively a good will and salutary final faith, has not sufficient goodness.

God does this.

Hence, etc.

Answer. I deny the major of this. It is true that God could overcome the greatest resistance of the human heart; and does it, too, sometimes, either by internal grace, or by external circumstances which have a great effect on souls; but he does not always do this. Whence comes this distinction? it may be asked, and why does his goodness seem limited? It is because, as I have already said in answering the first objection, it would not have been in order always to act in an extraordinary manner, and to reverse the connection of things. The reasons of this connection, by means of which one is placed in more favorable circumstances than another, are hidden in the depths of the wisdom of God; they depend upon the universal harmony. The best plan of the universe, which God could not fail to choose, made

it so. We judge from the event itself; since God has made it, it was not possible to do better. Far from being true that this conduct is contrary to goodness, it is supreme goodness which led him to it. This objection with its solution might have been drawn from what was said in regard to the first objection; but it seemed useful to touch upon it separately.

VIII. Objection. Whoever cannot fail to choose the best, is not free.

God cannot fail to choose the best.

Hence, God is not free.

Answer. I deny the major of this argument; it is rather true liberty, and the most perfect, to be able to use one's free will for the best, and to always exercise this power, without ever being turned aside either by external force or by internal passions, the first of which causes slavery of the body, the second, slavery of the soul. There is nothing less servile, and nothing more in accordance with the highest degree of freedom, than to be always led toward the good, and always by one's own inclination, without any constraint and without any displeasure. And to object therefore that God had need of external things, is only a sophism. He created them freely; but having proposed to himself an end, which is to exercise his goodness, wisdom has determined him to choose the means best fitted to attain this end. To call this a need, is to take that term in an unusual sense which frees it from all imperfection, just as when we speak of the wrath of God.

Seneca has somewhere said that God commanded but once but that he obeys always, because he obeys laws which he willed to prescribe to himself: *semel jussit, semper paret.* But he might better have said that God always commands and that he is always obeyed; for in willing, he always follows the inclination of his own nature, and all other things always follow his will. And as this will is always the same, it cannot be said that he obeys only that will which he formerly had. Nevertheless, although his will is always infallible and always tends toward the best, the evil, or the lesser good, which he rejects, does not cease to be possible in itself; otherwise the necessity of the good would be geometrical (so to speak), or metaphysical, and altogether absolute; the contingency of things would be destroyed, and there would be no choice. But this sort of necessity, which does not destroy the possibility of the contrary, has this name only by analogy; it becomes effective, not by the pure essence of things, but by that which is outside of them, above them, namely, by the will of God. This necessity is called moral, because, to the sage, *necessity* and *what ought to be* are equivalent things; and when it always has its effect, as it really has in the perfect sage, that is, in God, it may be said that it is a happy necessity. The nearer creatures approach to it, the nearer they approach to perfect happiness. Also this kind of necessity is not that which we try to avoid and which destroys morality, rewards and praise. For that which it brings, does not happen whatever we may do or will, but because we will it so. And a will to which it is natural to choose well, merits praise so much the more; also it carries its reward with it, which is sovereign happiness. And as this constitution of the divine nature gives entire satisfaction to him who possesses it, it is also the best and the most desirable for the creatures who are all dependent on God. If the will of God did not have for a rule the principle of the best, it would either tend toward evil, which would be the worst; or it would be in some way indifferent to good and to evil, and would be guided by chance: but a will which would allow itself always to act by chance, would not be worth more for the government of the universe than the fortuitous concourse of atoms, without there being any divinity therein. And even if God should abandon himself to chance only in some cases and in a certain way (as he would do, if he did not always work entirely for the best and if he were capable of preferring a lesser work to a greater, that is, an evil to a good, since that which prevents a greater good is an evil), he would be imperfect, as well as the object of his choice; he would not merit entire confidence; he would act without reason in such a case, and the government of the universe would be like certain games, equally divided between reason and chance. All this proves that this objection which is made against the choice of the best, perverts the notions of the free and of the necessary, and represents to us the best even as evil: which is either malicious or ridiculous.

III.A.3

Rebellion

FYODOR DOSTOEVSKY

Fyodor Dostoevsky (1821–1881) was one of the greatest and most influential Russian novelists. He is the author of Crime and Punishment, Notes from the Underground, The Gambler, *and* The Brothers Karamazov, *from which the present selection is taken. In this chapter, Ivan Karamazov challenges the idea that some greater good might justify the horrendous suffering of even one small child, much less the vast amounts of such suffering that our world has so far seen.*

"Rebellion," from *The Brothers Karamazov*, by Fyodor Dostoevsky. Trans. Constance Garnett. (New York: The MacMillan Company, 1922).

"I must make you one confession," Ivan began. "I could never understand how one can love one's neighbours. It's just one's neighbours, to my mind, that one can't love, though one might love those at a distance. I once read somewhere of John the Merciful, a saint, that when a hungry, frozen beggar came to him, he took him into his bed, held him in his arms, and began breathing into his mouth, which was putrid and loathsome from some awful disease. I am convinced that he did that from 'self-laceration,' from the self-laceration of falsity, for the sake of the charity imposed by duty, as a penance laid on him. For any one to love a man, he must be hidden, for as soon as he shows his face, love is gone."

"Father Zossima has talked of that more than once," observed Alyosha, "he, too, said that the face of a man often hinders many people not practised in love, from loving him. But yet there's a great deal of love in mankind, and almost Christ-like love. I know that myself, Ivan."

"Well, I know nothing of it so far, and can't understand it, and the innumerable mass of mankind are with me there. The question is, whether that's due to men's bad qualities or whether it's inherent in their nature. To my thinking, Christ-like love for men is a miracle impossible on earth. He was God. But we are not gods. Suppose I, for instance, suffer intensely. Another can never know how much I suffer, because he is another and not I. And what's more, a man is rarely ready to admit another's suffering (as though it were a distinction). Why won't he admit it, do you think? Because I smell unpleasant, because I have a stupid face, because I once trod on his foot. Besides there is suffering and suffering; degrading, humiliating suffering such as humbles me—hunger, for instance,—my benefactor will perhaps allow me; but when you come to higher suffering—for an idea, for instance—he will very rarely admit that, perhaps because my face strikes him as not at all what he fancies a man should have who suffers for an idea. And so he deprives me instantly of his favour, and not at all from badness of heart. Beggars, especially genteel beggars, ought never to show themselves, but to ask for charity through the newspapers. One can

love one's neighbours in the abstract, or even at a distance, but at close quarters it's almost impossible. If it were as on the stage, in the ballet, where if beggars come in, they wear silken rags and tattered lace and beg for alms dancing gracefully, then one might like looking at them. But even then we should not love them. But enough of that. I simply wanted to show you my point of view. I meant to speak of the suffering of mankind generally, but we had better confine ourselves to the sufferings of the children. That reduces the scope of my argument to a tenth of what it would be. Still we'd better keep to the children, though it does weaken my case. But, in the first place, children can be loved even at close quarters, even when they are dirty, even when they are ugly (I fancy, though, children never are ugly). The second reason why I won't speak of grown-up people is that, besides being disgusting and unworthy of love, they have a compensation—they've eaten the apple and know good and evil, and they have become 'like gods.' They go on eating it still. But the children haven't eaten anything, and are so far innocent. Are you fond of children, Alyosha? I know you are, and you will understand why I prefer to speak of them. If they, too, suffer horribly on earth, they must suffer for their fathers' sins, they must be punished for their fathers, who have eaten the apple; but that reasoning is of the other world and is incomprehensible for the heart of man here on earth. The innocent must not suffer for another's sins, and especially such innocents! You may be surprised at me, Alyosha, but I am awfully fond of children, too. And observe, cruel people, the violent, the rapacious, the Karamazovs are sometimes very fond of children. Children while they are quite little—up to seven, for instance—are so remote from grown-up people; they are different creatures, as it were, of a different species. I knew a criminal in prison who had, in the course of his career as a burglar, murdered whole families, including several children. But when he was in prison, he had a strange affection for them. He spent all his time at his window, watching the children playing in the prison yard. He trained one little boy to come up to his window and made great friends with him. . . .

You don't know why I am telling you all this, Alyosha? My head aches and I am sad."

"You speak with a strange air," observed Alyosha uneasily, "as though you were not quite yourself."

"By the way, a Bulgarian I met lately in Moscow," Ivan went on, seeming not to hear his brother's words, "told me about the crimes committed by Turks and Circassians in all parts of Bulgaria through fear of a general rising of the Slavs. They burn villages, murder, outrage women and children, they nail their prisoners by the ears to the fences, leave them so till morning, and in the morning they hang them—all sorts of things you can't imagine. People talk sometimes of bestial cruelty, but that's a great injustice and insult to the beasts; a beast can never be so cruel as a man, so artistically cruel. The tiger only tears and gnaws, that's all he can do. He would never think of nailing people by the ears, even if he were able to do it. These Turks took a pleasure in torturing children, too; cutting the unborn child from the mother's womb, and tossing babies up in the air and catching them on the points of their bayonets before their mother's eyes. Doing it before the mother's eyes was what gave zest to the amusement. Here is another scene that I thought very interesting. Imagine a trembling mother with her baby in her arms, a circle of invading Turks around her. They've planned a diversion; they pet the baby, laugh to make it laugh. They succeed, the baby laughs. At that moment a Turk points a pistol four inches from the baby's face. The baby laughs with glee, holds out its little hands to the pistol, and he pulls the trigger in the baby's face and blows out its brains. Artistic, wasn't it? By the way, Turks are particularly fond of sweet things, they say."

"Brother, what are you driving at?" asked Alyosha.

"I think if the devil doesn't exist, but man has created him, he has created him in his own image and likeness."

"Just as he did God, then?" observed Alyosha.

"'It's wonderful how you can turn words,' as Polonius says in *Hamlet,*" laughed Ivan. "You turn my words against me. Well, I am glad. Yours must be a fine God, if man created Him in His image and likeness. You asked just now what I was driving at. You see, I am fond of collecting certain facts, and, would you believe, I even copy anecdotes of a certain sort from newspapers and books, and I've already got a fine collection. The Turks, of course, have gone into it, but they are foreigners. I have specimens from home that are even better than the Turks. You know we prefer beating—rods and scourges—that's our national institution. Nailing ears is unthinkable for us, for we are, after all, Europeans. But the rod and the scourge we have always with us and they cannot be taken from us. Abroad now they scarcely do any beating. Manners are more humane, or laws have been passed, so that they don't dare to flog men now. But they make up for it in another way just as national as ours. And so national that it would be practically impossible among us, though I believe we are being inoculated with it, since the religious movement began in our aristocracy. I have a charming pamphlet, translated from the French, describing how, quite recently, five years ago, a murderer, Richard, was executed—a young man, I believe, of three and twenty, who repented and was converted to the Christian faith at the very scaffold. This Richard was an illegitimate child who was given as a child of six by his parents to some shepherds on the Swiss mountains. They brought him up to work for them. He grew up like a little wild beast among them. The shepherds taught him nothing, and scarcely fed or clothed him, but sent him out at age seven to herd the flock in cold and wet, and no one hesitated or scrupled to treat him so. Quite the contrary, they thought they had every right, for Richard had been given to them as a chattel, and they did not even see the necessity of feeding him. Richard himself describes how in those years, like the Prodigal Son in the Gospel, he longed to eat of the mash given to the pigs, which were fattened for sale. But they wouldn't even give him that, and beat him when he stole from the pigs. And that was how he spent all his childhood and his youth, till he grew up and was strong enough to go away and be a thief. The savage began to earn his living as a day labourer in Geneva. He drank what he earned, he lived like a brute, and finished by killing and robbing an old man. He was caught, tried, and condemned to death. They are not sentimentalists there. And in prison he was immediately surrounded by pastors, members of Christian brotherhoods, philanthropic ladies, and the like. They taught him to read and write in prison, and expounded the Gospel to him. They exhorted him, worked upon him, drummed at him incessantly, till at last he solemnly confessed his crime. He was converted. He wrote to the court himself that he was a monster, but that in the end God had vouchsafed him light and shown grace. All Geneva was in excitement about him—all philanthropic and religious Geneva. All the aristocratic and well-bred society of the town rushed to the prison, kissed Richard and embraced him; 'You are our brother, you have found grace.' And Richard does nothing but weep with emotion, 'Yes, I've found grace! All my youth and childhood I was glad of pigs' food, but now even I have found grace. I am dying in the Lord.' 'Yes, Richard, die in the Lord; you have shed blood and must die. Though it's not your fault that you knew not the Lord, when you coveted the pig's food and were beaten for stealing it (which was very wrong of you, for stealing is forbidden); but you've shed blood and you must die.' And on the last day, Richard, perfectly limp, did nothing but cry and repeat every minute: 'This is my happiest day. I am going to the Lord.' 'Yes,' cry the pastors and the judges and philanthropic ladies. 'This is the happiest day of your life, for you are going to the Lord!' They all walk or drive to the scaffold in procession behind the prison van. At the scaffold they call to Richard: 'Die, brother, die in the Lord, for even thou hast found grace!' And so, covered with his brothers' kisses, Richard is dragged on to the scaffold, and led to the guillotine. And they chopped off his head in brotherly fashion, because he had found grace. Yes, that's characteristic. That pamphlet is translated into Russian by some Russian philanthropists of aristocratic rank and evangelical aspirations, and has been distributed gratis for the enlightenment of the people. The case of Richard is interesting because it's national. Though to us it's absurd to cut off a man's head, because he has become our brother and has found grace, yet we have our own speciality, which is all but worse. Our

historical pastime is the direct satisfaction of inflicting pain. There are lines in Nekrassov describing how a peasant lashes a horse on the eyes, 'on its meek eyes,' every one must have seen it. It's peculiarly Russian. He describes how a feeble little nag has foundered under too heavy a load and cannot move. The peasant beats it, beats it savagely, beats it at last not knowing what he is doing in the intoxication of cruelty, thrashes it mercilessly over and over again. 'However weak you are, you must pull, if you die for it.' The nag strains, and then he begins lashing the poor defenseless creature on its weeping, on its 'meek eyes.' The frantic beast tugs and draws the load, trembling all over, gasping for breath, moving sideways, with a sort of unnatural spasmodic action—it's awful in Nekrassov. But that's only a horse, and God has given horses to be beaten. So the Tatars have taught us, and they left us the knout as a remembrance of it. But men, too, can be beaten. A well-educated, cultured gentleman and his wife beat their own child with a birch rod, a girl of seven. I have an exact account of it. The papa was glad that the birch was covered with twigs. 'It stings more,' said he, and so he began stinging his daughter. I know for a fact there are people who at every blow are worked up to sensuality, to literal sensuality, which increases progressively at every blow they inflict. They beat for a minute, for five minutes, for ten minutes, more often and more savagely. The child screams. At last the child cannot scream, it gasps, 'Daddy! daddy!' By some diabolical unseemly chance the case was brought into court. A counsel is engaged. The Russian people have long called a barrister 'a conscience for hire.' The counsel protests in his client's defense. 'It's such a simple thing,' he says, 'an everyday domestic event. A father corrects his child. To our shame be it said, it is brought into court.' The jury, convinced by him, give a favourable verdict. The public roars with delight that the torturer is acquitted. Ah, pity I wasn't there! I would have proposed to raise a subscription in his honor! . . . Charming pictures.

"But I've still better things about children. I've collected a great, great deal about Russian children, Alyosha. There was a little girl of five who was hated by her father and mother, 'most worthy and respectable people, of good education and breeding.' You see, I must repeat again, it is a peculiar characteristic of many people, this love of torturing children, and children only. To all other types of humanity these torturers behave mildly and benevolently, like cultivated and humane Europeans; but they are very fond of tormenting children, even fond of children themselves in that sense. It's just their defencelessness that tempts the tormentor, just the angelic confidence of the child who has no refuge and no appeal, that sets his vile blood on fire. In every man, of course, a demon lies hidden—the demon of rage, the demon of lustful heat at the screams of the tortured victim, the demon of lawlessness let off the chain, the demon of diseases that follow on vice, gout, kidney disease, and so on.

"This poor child of five was subjected to every possible torture by those cultivated parents. They beat her, thrashed her, kicked her for no reason till her body was one bruise. Then, they went to greater refinements of cruelty—shut her up all night in the cold and frost in a privy, and because she didn't ask to be taken up at night (as though a child of five sleeping its angelic, sound sleep could be trained to wake and ask), they smeared her face and filled her mouth with excrement, and it was her mother, her mother did this. And that mother could sleep, hearing the poor child's groans! Can you understand why a little creature, who can't even understand what's done to her, should beat her little aching heart with her tiny fist in the dark and the cold, and weep her meek unresentful tears to dear, kind God to protect her? Do you understand that, friend and brother, you pious and humble novice? Do you understand why this infamy must be and is permitted? Without it, I am told, man could not have existed on earth, for he could not have known good and evil. Why should he know that diabolical good and evil when it costs so much? Why, the whole world of knowledge is not worth that child's prayer to 'dear, kind God'! I say nothing of the sufferings of grown-up people, they have eaten the apple, damn them, and the devil take them all! But these little ones! I am making you suffer, Alyosha, you are not yourself. I'll leave off if you like."

"Never mind. I want to suffer too," muttered Alyosha.

"One picture, only one more, because it's so curious, so characteristic, and I have only just read it in some collection of Russian antiquities. I've forgotten the name. I must look it up. It was in the darkest days of serfdom at the beginning of the century, and long live the Liberator of the People! There was in those days a general of aristocratic connections, the owner of great estates, one of those men—somewhat exceptional, I believe, even then—who, retiring from the service into a life of leisure, are convinced that they've earned absolute power over the lives of their subjects. There were such men then. So our general, settled on his property of two thousand souls, lives in pomp, and domineers over his poor neighbors as though they were dependents and buffoons. He has kennels of hundreds of hounds and nearly a hundred dog-boys—all mounted, and in uniform. One day a serf boy, a little child of eight, threw a stone in play and hurt the paw of the general's favorite hound. 'Why is my favorite dog lame?' He is told that the boy threw a stone that hurt the dog's paw. 'So you did it.' The general looked the child up and down. 'Take him.' He was taken—taken from his mother and kept shut up all night. Early that morning the general comes out on horseback, with the hounds, his dependents, dog-boys, and huntsmen, all mounted around him in full hunting parade. The servants are summoned for their edification, and in front of them all stands the mother of the child. The child is brought from the lock-up. It's a gloomy cold, foggy autumn day, a capital day for hunting. The general orders the child to be undressed; the child is stripped naked. He shivers, numb with terror, not daring to cry.... 'Make him run,' commands the general. 'Run! run!' shout the dog-boys. The boy runs.... 'At him!' yells the general, and he sets the whole pack of hounds on the child. The hounds catch him, and tear him to pieces before his mother's eyes! ... I believe the general was afterwards declared incapable of administering his estates. Well—what did he deserve? To be shot? To be shot for the satisfaction of our moral feelings? Speak, Alyosha!"

"To be shot," murmured Alyosha, lifting his eyes to Ivan with a pale, twisted smile.

"Bravo!" cried Ivan delighted. "If even you say so ... You're a pretty monk! So there is a little devil sitting in your heart, Alyosha Karamazov!"

"What I said was absurd, but—"

"That's just the point that 'but'!" cried Ivan. "Let me tell you, novice, that the absurd is only too necessary on earth. The world stands on absurdities, and perhaps nothing would have come to pass in it without them. We know what we know!"

"What do you know?"

"I understand nothing," Ivan went on, as though in delirium. "I don't want to understand anything now. I want to stick to the fact. I made up my mind long ago not to understand. If I try to understand anything, I shall be false to the fact and I have determined to stick to the fact."

"Why are you trying me?" Alyosha cried, with sudden distress. "Will you say what you mean at last?"

"Of course, I will; that's what I've been leading up to. You are dear to me, I don't want to let you go, and I won't give you up to your Zossima."

Ivan for a minute was silent, his face became all at once very sad.

"Listen! I took the case of children only to make my case clearer. Of the other tears of humanity with which the earth is soaked from its crust to its centre, I will say nothing. I have narrowed my subject on purpose. I am a bug, and I recognize in all humility that I cannot understand why the world is arranged as it is. Men are themselves to blame, I suppose; they were given paradise, they wanted freedom, and stole fire from heaven, though they knew they would become unhappy, so there is no need to pity them. With my pitiful, earthly, Euclidean understanding, all I know is that there is suffering and that there are none guilty; that cause follows effect, simply and directly; that everything flows and finds its level—but that's only Euclidean nonsense, I know that, and I can't consent to live by it! What comfort is it to me that there are none guilty and that cause follows effect simply and directly, and that I know it—I must have

justice, or I will destroy myself. And not justice in some remote infinite time and space, but here on earth, and that I could see myself. I have believed in it. I want to see it, and if I am dead by then, let me rise again, for if it all happens without me, it will be too unfair. Surely I haven't suffered, simply that I, my crimes and my sufferings, may manure the soil of the future harmony for somebody else. I want to see with my own eyes the hind lie down with the lion and the victim rise up and embrace his murderer. I want to be there when every one suddenly understands what it has all been for. All the religions of the world are built on this longing, and I am a believer. But then there are the children, and what am I to do about them? That's a question I can't answer. For the hundredth time I repeat, there are numbers of questions, but I've only taken the children, because in their case what I mean is so unanswerably clear. Listen! If all must suffer to pay for the eternal harmony, what have children to do with it, tell me, please? It's beyond all comprehension why they should suffer, and why they should pay for the harmony. Why should they, too, furnish material to enrich the soil for the harmony of the future? I understand solidarity in sin among men. I understand solidarity in retribution, too; but there can be no such solidarity with children. And if it is really true that they must share responsibility for all their fathers' crimes, such a truth is not of this world and is beyond my comprehension. Some jester will say, perhaps, that the child would have grown up and have sinned, but you see he didn't grow up, he was torn to pieces by the dogs, at eight years old. Oh, Alyosha, I am not blaspheming! I understand, of course, what an upheaval of the universe it will be, when everything in heaven and earth blends in one hymn of praise and everything that lives and has lived cries aloud: 'Thou art just, O Lord, for Thy ways are revealed.' When the mother embraces the fiend who threw her child to the dogs, and all three cry aloud with tears, 'Thou art just, O Lord!' then, of course, the crown of knowledge will be reached and all will be made clear. But what pulls me up here is that I can't accept that harmony. And while I am on earth, I make haste to take my own measures. You see, Alyosha, perhaps it really may happen that if I live to that moment, or rise again to see it, I, too, perhaps, may cry aloud with the rest, looking at the mother embracing the child's torturer, 'Thou art just, O Lord!' but I don't want to cry aloud then. While there is still time, I hasten to protect myself and so I renounce the higher harmony altogether. It's not worth the tears of that one tortured child who beat itself on the breast with its little fist and prayed in its stinking outhouse, with its unexpiated tears to 'dear, kind God'! It's not worth it, because those tears are unatoned for. They must be atoned for, or there can be no harmony. But how? How are you going to atone for them? Is it possible? By their being avenged? But what do I care for avenging them? What do I care for a hell for oppressors? What good can hell do, since those children have already been tortured? And what becomes of harmony, if there is hell? I want to forgive. I want to embrace. I don't want more suffering. And if the sufferings of children go to swell the sum of sufferings which was necessary to pay for truth, then I protest that the truth is not worth such a price. I don't want the mother to embrace the oppressor who threw her son to the dogs! She dare not forgive him! Let her forgive him for herself, if she will, let her forgive the torturer for the immeasurable suffering of her mother's heart. But the sufferings of her tortured child she has no right to forgive; she dare not forgive the torturer, even if the child were to forgive him! And if that is so, if they dare not forgive, what becomes of harmony? Is there in the whole world a being who would have the right to forgive and could forgive? I don't want harmony. From love for humanity I don't want it. I would rather be left with the unavenged suffering. I would rather remain with my unavenged suffering and unsatisfied indignation, *even if I were wrong*. Besides, too high a price is asked for harmony; it's beyond our means to pay so much to enter on it. And so I hasten to give back my entrance ticket, and if I am an honest man I am bound to give it back as soon as possible. And that I am doing. It's not God that I don't accept, Alyosha, only I most respectfully return Him the ticket."

"That's rebellion," murmured Alyosha, looking down.

"Rebellion? I am sorry you call it that," said Ivan earnestly. "One can hardly live in rebellion, and I want to live. Tell me yourself, I challenge you—answer. Imagine that you are creating a fabric of human destiny with the object of making men happy in the end, giving them peace and rest at last, but that it was essential and inevitable to torture to death only one tiny creature—that little child beating its breast with its fist, for instance—and to found that edifice on its unavenged tears, would you consent to be the architect on those conditions? Tell me, and tell the truth."

"No, I wouldn't consent," said Alyosha softly.

"And can you admit the idea that men for whom you are building it would agree to accept their happiness on the foundation of the unexpiated blood of a little victim? And accepting it would remain happy forever?"

"No, I can't admit it. Brother," said Alyosha suddenly, with flashing eyes, "you said just now, is there a being in the whole world who would have the right to forgive and could forgive? But there is a Being and He can forgive everything, all and for all, because He gave His innocent blood for all and everything. You have forgotten Him, and on Him is built the edifice, and it is to Him they cry aloud, 'Thou art just, O Lord, for Thy ways are revealed!'"

"Ah! the One without sin and his blood! No, I have not forgotten Him; on the contrary I've been wondering all the time how it was you did not bring Him in before, for usually all arguments on your side put Him in the foreground. Do you know, Alyosha—don't laugh! I composed a poem about a year ago. If you can waste another ten minutes on me, I'll tell it to you."

"You wrote a poem?"

"Oh, no, I didn't write it," laughed Ivan, "and I've never written two lines of poetry in my life. But I composed up this poem in prose and I remembered it. I was carried away when I made it up. You will be my first reader—that is, listener. Why should an author forego even one listener?" smiled Ivan. "Shall I tell it to you?"

"I am all attention," said Alyosha. . . .

III.A.4

The Ones Who Walk Away from Omelas

URSULA K. LeGUIN

Ursula K. LeGuin (1929–) has written numerous works of poetry, realistic fiction, science fiction, fantasy, and children's fiction, many of which have been widely influential and have attained the status of contemporary classics. She is perhaps best known for her six Books of Earthsea *(1968–2001), as well as* The Left Hand of Darkness *(1969),* The Lathe of Heaven *(1971), and* The Dispossessed: An Ambiguous Utopia *(1974). In the present story, she tells the tale of a fictional utopia whose blessedness depends on the ongoing suffering of a lone child. We see the reactions of the inhabitants of Omelas as they discover the price of their happiness, and we are thus invited to reflect upon what goods, if any, might possibly justify the permission of suffering.*

With a clamor of bells that set the swallows soaring, the Festival of Summer came to the city Omelas, bright-towered by the sea. The rigging of the boats in harbor sparkled with flags. In the streets between houses with red roofs and painted walls, between old moss-grown gardens and under avenues of trees, past great parks and public buildings, processions moved. Some were decorous: old people in long stiff robes of mauve and grey, grave master workmen, quiet, merry women carrying their babies and chatting as they walked. In other streets the music beat faster, a shimmering of gong and tambourine, and the people went dancing, the procession was a dance. Children dodged in and out, their high calls rising like the swallows' crossing flights over the music and the singing. All the processions wound towards the north side of the city, where on the great water-meadow called the Green Fields boys and girls, naked in the bright air, with mud-stained feet and ankles and long, lithe arms, exercised their restive horses before the race. The horses wore no gear at all but a halter without bit.

Their manes were braided with streamers of silver, gold, and green. They flared their nostrils and pranced and boasted to one another; they were vastly excited, the horse being the only animal who has adopted our ceremonies as his own. Far off to the north and west the mountains stood up half encircling Omelas on her bay. The air of morning was so clear that the snow still crowning the Eighteen Peaks burned with white-gold fire across the miles of sunlit air, under the dark blue of the sky. There was just enough wind to make the banners that marked the racecourse snap and flutter now and then. In the silence of the broad green meadows one could hear the music winding through the city streets, farther and nearer and ever approaching, a cheerful faint sweetness of the air that from time to time trembled and gathered together and broke out into the great joyous clanging of the bells.

Joyous! How is one to tell about joy? How describe the citizens of Omelas?

They were not simple folk, you see, though they were happy. But we do not say the words of

Copyright © 1973, 2001 by Ursula K. Le Guin; first appeared in *New Dimensions 3*; from *The Wind's Twelve Quarters*; reprinted by permission of the Author and the Author's Agent, the Virginia Kidd Agency, Inc.

cheer much any more. All smiles have become archaic. Given a description such as this one tends to make certain assumptions. Given a description such as this one tends to look next for the King, mounted on a splendid stallion and surrounded by his noble knights, or perhaps in a golden litter borne by great-muscled slaves. But there was no king. They did not use swords, or keep slaves. They were not barbarians. I do not know the rules and laws of their society, but I suspect that they were singularly few. As they did without monarchy and slavery, so they also got on without the stock exchange, the advertisement, the secret police, and the bomb. Yet I repeat that these were not simple folk, not dulcet shepherds, noble savages, bland utopians. They were not less complex than us. The trouble is that we have a bad habit, encouraged by pedants and sophisticates, of considering happiness as something rather stupid. Only pain is intellectual, only evil interesting. This is the treason of the artist: a refusal to admit the banality of evil and the terrible boredom of pain. If you can't lick 'em, join 'em. If it hurts, repeat it. But to praise despair is to condemn delight, to embrace violence is to lose hold of everything else. We have almost lost hold; we can no longer describe a happy man, nor make any celebration of joy. How can I tell you about the people of Omelas? They were not naive and happy children—though their children were, in fact, happy. They were mature, intelligent, passionate adults whose lives were not wretched. O miracle! but I wish I could describe it better. I wish I could convince you. Omelas sounds in my words like a city in a fairy tale, long ago and far away, once upon a time. Perhaps it would be best if you imagined it as your own fancy bids, assuming it will rise to the occasion, for certainly I cannot suit you all. For instance, how about technology? I think that there would be no cars or helicopters in and above the streets; this follows from the fact that the people of Omelas are happy people. Happiness is based on a just discrimination of what is necessary, what is neither necessary nor destructive, and what is destructive. In the middle category, however—that of the unnecessary but undestructive, that of comfort, luxury, exuberance, etc.—they could perfectly well

have central heating, subway trains, washing machines, and all kinds of marvelous devices not yet invented here, floating light-sources, fuelless power, a cure for the common cold. Or they could have none of that; it doesn't matter. As you like it. I incline to think that people from towns up and down the coast have been coming in to Omelas during the last days before the Festival on very fast little trains and double-decked trams, and that the train station of Omelas is actually the handsomest building in town, though plainer than the magnificent Farmers' Market. But even granted trains, I fear that Omelas so far strikes some of you as goody-goody. Smiles, bells, parades, horses, bleh. If so, please add an orgy. If an orgy would help, don't hesitate. Let us not, however, have temples from which issue beautiful nude priests and priestesses already half in ecstasy and ready to copulate with any man or woman, lover or stranger, who desires union with the deep godhead of the blood, although that was my first idea. But really it would be better not to have any temples in Omelas—at least, not manned temples. Religion yes, clergy no. Surely the beautiful nudes can just wander about, offering themselves like divine soufflés to the hunger of the needy and the rapture of the flesh. Let them join the processions. Let tambourines be struck above the copulations, and the glory of desire be proclaimed upon the gongs, and (a not unimportant point) let the offspring of these delightful rituals be beloved and looked after by all. One thing I know there is none of in Omelas is guilt. But what else should there be? I thought at first there were not drugs, but that is puritanical. For those who like it, the faint insistent sweetness of *drooz* may perfume the ways of the city, *drooz* which first brings a great lightness and brilliance to the mind and limbs, and then after some hours a dreamy languor, and wonderful visions at last of the very arcana and inmost secrets of the Universe, as well as exciting the pleasure of sex beyond belief; and it is not habit-forming. For more modest tastes I think there ought to be beer. What else, what else belongs in the joyous city? The sense of victory, surely, the celebration of courage. But as we did without clergy, let us do without soldiers. The joy built upon successful slaughter is not the right kind of joy; it will not do; it is fearful and it is trivial. A boundless and generous contentment, a magnanimous triumph felt not against some outer enemy but in communion with the finest and fairest in the souls of all men everywhere and the splendor of the world's summer: this is what swells the hearts of the people of Omelas, and the victory they celebrate is that of life. I really don't think many of them need to take *drooz*.

Most of the procession have reached the Green Fields by now. A marvelous smell of cooking goes forth from the red and blue tents of the provisioners. The faces of small children are amiably sticky; in the benign grey beard of a man a couple of crumbs of rich pastry are entangled. The youths and girls have mounted their horses and are beginning to group around the starting line of the course. An old women, small, fat, and laughing, is passing out flowers from a basket, and tall young men [wear] her flowers in their shining hair. A child of nine or ten sits at the edge of the crowd, alone, playing on a wooden flute. People pause to listen, and they smile, but they do not speak to him, for he never ceases playing and never sees them, his dark eyes wholly rapt in the sweet, thin magic of the tune.

He finishes, and slowly lowers his hands holding the wooden flute.

As if that little private silence were the signal, all at once a trumpet sounds from the pavilion near the starting line: imperious, melancholy, piercing. The horses rear on their slender legs, and some of them neigh in answer. Sober-faced, the young riders stroke the horses' necks and soothe them, whispering, "Quiet, quiet, there my beauty, my hope...." They begin to form in rank along the starting line. The crowds along the racecourse are like a field of grass and flowers in the wind. The Festival of Summer has begun.

Do you believe? Do you accept the festival, the city, the joy? No? Then let me describe one more thing.

In a basement under one of the beautiful public buildings of Omelas, or perhaps in the cellar of one of its spacious private homes, there is a room. It has one locked door, and no window. A little light seeps in dustily between cracks in the boards, secondhand from a cobwebbed window somewhere across the cellar. In one corner of the little room a couple of mops, with stiff, clotted, foul-smelling heads stand near a rusty bucket. The floor is dirt, a little damp to the touch, as cellar dirt usually is. The room is about three paces long and two wide: a mere broom closet or disused tool room. In the room a child is sitting. It could be a boy or a girl. It looks about six, but actually is nearly ten. It is feeble-minded. Perhaps it was born defective, or perhaps it has become imbecile through fear, malnutrition, and neglect. It picks its nose and occasionally fumbles vaguely with its toes or genitals, as it sits hunched in the corner farthest from the bucket and the two mops. It is afraid of the mops. It finds them horrible. It shuts its eyes, but it knows the mops are still standing there; and the door is locked; and nobody will come. The door is always locked; and nobody ever comes, except that sometimes—the child has no understanding of time or interval—sometimes the door rattles terribly and opens, and a person, or several people, are there. One of them may come in and kick the child to make it stand up. The others never come close, but peer in at it with frightened, disgusted eyes. The food bowl and the water jug are hastily filled, the door is locked, the eyes disappear. The people at the door never say anything, but the child, who has not always lived in the tool room, and can remember sunlight and its mother's voice, sometimes speaks. "I will be good," it says. "Please let me out. I will be good!" They never answer. The child used to scream for help at night, and cry a good deal, but now it only makes a kind of whining, "eh-haa, eh-haa," and it speaks less and less often. It is so thin there are no calves to its legs; its belly protrudes; it lives on a half-bowl of corn meal and grease a day. It is naked. Its buttocks and thighs are a mass of festered sores, as it sits in its own excrement continually.

They all know it is there, all the people of Omelas. Some of them have come to see it, others are content merely to know it is there. They all know that it has to be there. Some of them understand why, and some do not, but they all understand that their happiness, the beauty of their city, the tenderness of their friendships, the health of their children, the wisdom of their scholars, the skill of their makers, even the abundance of their harvest and the kindly weathers of their skies, depend wholly on this child's abominable misery.

This is usually explained to children when they are between eight and twelve, whenever they seem capable of understanding; and most of those who come to see the child are young people, though often enough an adult comes, or comes back, to see the child. No matter how well the matter has been explained to them, these young spectators are always shocked and sickened at the sight. They feel disgust, which they had thought themselves superior to. They feel anger, outrage, impotence, despite all the explanations. They would like to do something for the child. But there is nothing they can do. If the child were brought up into the sunlight out of that vile place, if it were cleaned and fed and comforted, that would be a good thing indeed; but if it were done, in that day and hour all the prosperity and beauty and delight of Omelas would wither and be destroyed. Those are the terms. To exchange all the goodness and grace of every life in Omelas for that single, small improvement: to throw away the happiness of thousands for the chance of the happiness of one: that would be to let guilt within the walls indeed.

The terms are strict and absolute; there may not even be a kind word spoken to the child.

Often the young people go home in tears, or in a tearless rage, when they have seen the child and faced this terrible paradox. They may brood over it for weeks or years. But as time goes on they begin to realize that even if the child could be released, it would not get much good of its freedom: a little vague pleasure of warmth and food, no doubt, but little more. It is too degraded and imbecile to know any real joy. It has been afraid too long ever to be free of fear. Its habits are too uncouth for it to respond to humane treatment. Indeed, after so long it would probably be wretched without walls about it to protect it, and

darkness for its eyes, and its own excrement to sit in. Their tears at the bitter injustice dry when they begin to perceive the terrible justice of reality, and to accept it. Yet it is their tears and anger, the trying of their generosity and the acceptance of their helplessness, which are perhaps the true source of the splendor of their lives. Theirs is no vapid, irresponsible happiness. They know that they, like the child, are not free. They know compassion. It is the existence of the child, and their knowledge of its existence, that makes possible the nobility of their architecture, the poignancy of their music, the profundity of their science. It is because of the child that they are so gentle with children. They know that if the wretched one were not there sniveling in the dark, the other one, the flute-player, could make no joyful music as the young riders line up in their beauty for the race in the sunlight of the first morning of summer.

Now do you believe in them? Are they not more credible? But there is one more thing to tell, and this is quite incredible.

At times one of the adolescent girls or boys who go to see the child does not go home to weep or rage, does not, in fact, go home at all. Sometimes also a man or woman much older falls silent for a day or two, and then leaves home. These people go out into the street, and walk down the street alone. They keep walking, and walk straight out of the city of Omelas, through the beautiful gates. They keep walking across the farmlands of Omelas. Each one goes alone, youth or girl, man or woman. Night falls; the traveler must pass down village streets, between the houses with yellow-lit windows, and on out into the darkness of the fields. Each alone, they go west or north, towards the mountains. They go on. They leave Omelas, they walk ahead into the darkness, and they do not come back. The place they go towards is a place even less imaginable to most of us than the city of happiness. I cannot describe it at all. It is possible that it does not exist. But they seem to know where they are going, the ones who walk away from Omelas.

III.B. THE PROBLEMS OF EVIL AND DIVINE HIDDENNESS

Introduction

THE PREVIOUS FOUR SELECTIONS presented three (rather different) historical and literary formulations of the problem of evil and one of the most well-known historical replies. In the present section, we turn to contemporary philosophical formulations of the problems of evil and divine hiddenness.

We begin with J. L. Mackie's classic statement of the "logical problem of evil"—an argument for the conclusion that the existence of the God of the Judeo-Christian tradition is logically inconsistent with the existence of evil. A perfectly good being, Mackie contends, always eliminates evil as far as it can; and an omnipotent and omniscient being, he argues, can eliminate evil entirely. He considers the response that the value of creating a world with free creatures might justify God in permitting the existence of evil. But he argues that since it is not *impossible* for there to be a world in which free creatures always do what is right, God must have been able to create such a world. And so, since a world in which free creatures always do what is right is clearly better than one in which free creatures sometimes do what is wrong, the appeal to freedom fails to solve the problem.

Despite the intuitive appeal of Mackie's argument, most philosophers nowadays agree that the argument fails. As William Rowe puts it in one of the notes to our next selection:

> Some philosophers have contended that the existence of evil is logically inconsistent with the existence of the theistic God. No one, I think, has succeeded in establishing such an extravagant claim.

Rowe goes on to credit Alvin Plantinga for showing in a clear and compelling way why Mackie's argument fails. (Plantinga's argument is given in selection III.C.1.) Nevertheless, Rowe says,

> [t]here remains . . . what we may call the evidential form—as opposed to the logical form—of the problem of evil; the view that the variety and profusion of evil in our world although perhaps not logically inconsistent with the existence of the theistic God, provides, nevertheless, rational support for atheism.

It is the evidential form of the argument with which his article (selection III.B.2) is concerned.

As it is typically presented, the "evidential problem of evil" relies on the premise that a good God would permit evil only if it contributed to some greater good, together with the claim that many of the evils we in fact observe seem not to contribute to any greater good. This is roughly the argument defended by Rowe; but Paul Draper, in the third reading of this section, takes a different tack. According to Draper, the "pattern of both pain and pleasure" in the world constitutes evidence against theism and in favor of naturalism. (As he defines it, naturalism is the hypothesis that the universe is a closed system, and it entails that there are no supernatural beings—divine or otherwise.) In his view, the pattern of pain and pleasure that we in fact observe isn't what we would naturally expect if pain existed (say) to serve the purpose of punishing sinners, or of building moral character. Rather, it is systematically connected with reproductive success, which is what we would expect on the supposition that naturalism and evolutionary theory are both true. Thus, on his view, the fact that pain and pleasure are systematically connected with reproductive success, together with the truth of evolutionary theory, provides evidence in support of naturalism.

The fourth reading in this section, an excerpt from Grace M. Jantzen's *Becoming Divine*, issues an important feminist challenge to the traditional framing of the problem of evil. As we have seen, the problem of evil is standardly presented as an objection against *belief* in a particular *kind of deity*—the traditionally male-gendered "omni-everything" God of Western monotheism. Within the traditional framing, discussions of the problem of evil typically leave unquestioned the "valorization" of power and knowledge in the traditional conception of God; alternative ways of envisioning the divine are commonly ignored; and questions about where evil comes from and what can be done with it are, as a rule, left off the table. But, Jantzen argues, there is no methodological reason why matters ought to be so. There is no reason why the *intellectual* challenge posed to religious belief by the existence of evil ought to take center stage in philosophical discussions about God, religion, and evil rather than some of these other issues. Thus, she advocates for a reframing of the problem from what she takes to be a distinctively feminist perspective. On her view, the problem of evil viewed from a feminist perspective will be concerned not so much with the question of how a perfect deity can permit evil as with questions like "How are the resources of religion . . . used by those who inflict evil on others?" and "How are those resources used by those who resist?" Above all, she says, treating the problem from a feminist perspective would ask, "What does the face of the Other require of me, and how can I best respond for love of the world?" (The phrase "the face of the Other" is an allusion to the work of French philosopher Emmanuel Levinas [1906–1995], who uses that term in reference not to the outward appearance—the literal *face*—of another person but rather to the person as she is in her inmost, indefinable self. Levinas is particularly concerned with the ethical demands made upon us by the so-called face of the Other.[*])

In this section's final reading, we turn to the problem of divine hiddenness as formulated by J. L. Schellenberg. Schellenberg's *Divine Hiddenness and Human Reason* (1993) has largely set the agenda for discussions of the hiddenness of God over the past two decades. In the present article he offers a simplified account of his reasons for thinking that divine hiddenness justifies disbelief in God. As we saw in the general introduction to Part III, the problem in short is that one would expect an all powerful, all knowing, perfectly loving God to ensure that divine hiddenness does not occur—that evidence sufficient for belief in God is always widely available. And yet divine hiddenness does occur. Thus, Schellenberg concludes, we are justified in believing that God does not exist.

---

[*]For discussion, see R. Burggraeve, "Violence and the Vulnerable Face of the Other: The Vision of Emmanuel Levinas on Moral Evil and Our Responsibility," *Journal of Social Research* 30 (1999): 29–45.

III.B.1

Evil and Omnipotence

J. L. MACKIE

John L. Mackie (1917–1981) was born in Australia and taught at Oxford University until his death. He made important contributions to the fields of metaphysics, epistemology, ethics, and philosophy of religion. Among his works are The Cement of the Universe *(1974),* Ethics: Inventing Right and Wrong *(1977), and* The Miracle of Theism *(1982). In this essay, Mackie argues that the argument from evil demonstrates the incoherence of theism. If there is a God who is all-powerful and completely good, he will be able and willing to eliminate all evil in the world. But there is evil, so no God exists.*

The traditional arguments for the existence of God have been fairly thoroughly criticised by philosophers. But the theologian can, if he wishes, accept this criticism. He can admit that no rational proof of God's existence is possible. And he can still retain all that is essential to his position, by holding that God's existence is known in some other, non-rational way. I think, however, that a more telling criticism can be made by way of the traditional problem of evil. Here it can be shown, not that religious beliefs lack rational support, but that they are positively irrational, that the several parts of the essential theological doctrine are inconsistent with one another, so that the theologian can maintain his position as a whole only by a much more extreme rejection of reason than in the former case. He must now be prepared to believe, not merely what cannot be proved, but what can be *disproved* from other beliefs that he also holds.

The problem of evil, in the sense in which I shall be using the phrase, is a problem only for someone who believes that there is a God who is both omnipotent and wholly good. And it is a logical problem, the problem of clarifying and reconciling a number of beliefs: it is not a scientific problem that might be solved by further observations, or a practical problem that might be solved by a decision or an action. These points are obvious; I mention them only because they are sometimes ignored by theologians, who sometimes parry a statement of the problem with such remarks as "Well, can you solve the problem yourself?" or "This is a mystery which may be revealed to us later" or "Evil is something to be faced and overcome, not to be merely discussed."

In its simplest form the problem is this: God is omnipotent; God is wholly good; and yet evil exists. There seems to be some contradiction between these three propositions, so that if any two of them were true the third would be false. But at the same time all three are essential parts of most theological positions: the theologian, it seems, at once *must* adhere and *cannot consistently* adhere to all three. (The problem does not arise only for theists, but I shall discuss it in the form in which it presents itself for ordinary theism.)

However, the contradiction does not arise immediately; to show it we need some additional

From *Mind*, 64 (1955): 200–212. Reprinted by permission of Oxford University Press.

premises, or perhaps some quasi-logical rules connecting the terms "good, evil," and "omnipotent." These additional principles are that good is opposed to evil, in such a way that a good thing always eliminates evil as far as it can, and that there are no limits to what an omnipotent thing can do. From these it follows that a good omnipotent thing eliminates evil completely, and then the propositions that a good omnipotent thing exists, and that evil exists, are incompatible.

A. ADEQUATE SOLUTIONS

Now once the problem is fully stated it is clear that it can be solved, in the sense that the problem will not arise if one gives up at least one of the propositions that constitute it. If you are prepared to say that God is not wholly good, or not quite omnipotent, or that evil does not exist, or that good is not opposed to the kind of evil that exists, or that there are limits to what an omnipotent thing can do, then the problem of evil will not arise for you.

There are, then, quite a number of adequate solutions of the problem of evil, and some of these have been adopted, or almost adopted, by various thinkers. For example, a few have been prepared to deny God's omnipotence, and rather more have been prepared to keep the term "omnipotence" but severely to restrict its meaning, recording quite a number of things that an omnipotent being cannot do. Some have said that evil is an illusion, perhaps because they held that the whole world of temporal, changing things is an illusion, and that what we call evil belongs only to this world, or perhaps because they held that although temporal things are much as we see them, those that we call evil are not really evil. Some have said that what we call evil is merely the privation of good, that evil in a positive sense, evil that would really be opposed to good, does not exist. Many have agreed with Pope that disorder is harmony not understood, and that partial evil is universal good. Whether any of these views is true is, of course, another question. But each of them gives an adequate solution of the problem of evil in the sense that if you accept it this problem does not arise for you, though you may, of course, have *other* problems to face.

But often enough these adequate solutions are only *almost* adopted. The thinkers who restrict God's power, but keep the term "omnipotence," may reasonably be suspected of thinking, in other contexts, that his power is really unlimited. Those who say that evil is an illusion may also be thinking, inconsistently, that this illusion is itself an evil. Those who say that "evil" is merely privation of good may also be thinking, inconsistently, that privation of good is an evil. (The fallacy here is akin to some forms of the "naturalistic fallacy" in ethics, where some think, for example, that "good" is just what contributes to evolutionary progress, and that evolutionary progress is itself good.) If Pope meant what he said in the first line of his couplet, that "disorder" is only harmony not understood, the "partial evil" of the second line must, for consistency, mean "that which, taken in isolation, falsely appears to be evil," but it would more naturally mean "that which, in isolation, really is evil." The second line, in fact, hesitates between two views, that "partial evil" isn't really evil, since only the universal quality is real, and that "partial evil" is really an evil, but only a little one.

In addition, therefore, to adequate solutions, we must recognise unsatisfactorily inconsistent solutions, in which there is only a half-hearted or temporary rejection of one of the propositions which together constitute the problem. In these, one of the constituent propositions is explicitly rejected, but it is covertly re-asserted or assumed elsewhere in the system.

B. FALLACIOUS SOLUTIONS

Besides these half-hearted solutions, which explicitly reject but implicitly assert one of the constituent propositions, there are definitely fallacious solutions which explicitly maintain all the constituent propositions, but implicitly reject at least one of them in the course of the argument that explains away the problem of evil.

There are, in fact, many so-called solutions which purport to remove the contradiction without abandoning any of its constituent propositions. These must be fallacious as we can see from the very statement of the problem, but it is not so easy to see in each case precisely where the fallacy lies. I suggest that in all cases the fallacy has the general form suggested above: in order to solve the problem one (or perhaps more) of its constituent propositions is given up, but in such a way that it appears to have been retained, and can therefore be asserted without qualification in other contexts. Sometimes there is a further complication: the supposed solution moves to and fro between, say, two of the constituent propositions, at one point asserting the first of these but covertly abandoning the second, at another point asserting the second but covertly abandoning the first. These fallacious solutions often turn upon some equivocation with the words "good" and "evil," or upon some vagueness about the way in which good and evil are opposed to one another, or about how much is meant by "omnipotence." I propose to examine some of these so-called solutions, and to exhibit their fallacies in detail. Incidentally, I shall also be considering whether an adequate solution could be reached by a minor modification of one or more of the constituent propositions, which would, however, still satisfy all the essential requirements of ordinary theism.

(1) "Good cannot exist without evil" or "Evil is necessary as a counterpart to good."

It is sometimes suggested that evil is necessary as a counterpart to good, that if there were no evil there could be no good either, and that this solves the problem of evil. It is true that it points to an answer to the question "Why should there be evil?" But it does so only by qualifying some of the propositions that constitute the problem.

First, it sets a limit to what God can do, saying that God *cannot* create good without simultaneously creating evil, and this means either that God is not omnipotent or that there are *some* limits to what an omnipotent thing can do. It may be replied that these limits are always presupposed, that omnipotence has never meant the power to do what is

logically impossible, and on the present view the existence of good without evil would be a logical impossibility. This interpretation of omnipotence may, indeed, be accepted as a modification of our original account which does not reject anything that is essential to theism, and I shall in general assume it in the subsequent discussion. It is, perhaps, the most common theistic view, but I think that some theists at least have maintained that God can do what is logically impossible. Many theists, at any rate, have held that logic itself is created or laid down by God, that logic is the way in which God arbitrarily chooses to think. (This is, of course, parallel to the ethical view that morally right actions are those which God arbitrarily chooses to command, and the two views encounter similar difficulties.) And this account of logic is clearly inconsistent with the view that God is bound by logical necessities—unless it is possible for an omnipotent being to bind himself, an issue which we shall consider later, when we come to the Paradox of Omnipotence. This solution of the problem of evil cannot, therefore, be consistently adopted along with the view that logic is itself created by God.

But, secondly, this solution denies that evil is opposed to good in our original sense. If good and evil are counterparts, a good thing will not "eliminate evil as far as it can." Indeed, this view suggests that good and evil are not strictly qualities of things at all. Perhaps the suggestion is that good and evil are related in much the same way as great and small. Certainly, when the term "great" is used relatively as a condensation of "greater than so-and-so," and "small" is used correspondingly, greatness and smallness are counterparts and cannot exist without each other. But in this sense greatness is not a quality, not an intrinsic feature of anything; and it would be absurd to think of a movement in favour of greatness and against smallness in this sense. Such a movement would be self-defeating, since relative greatness can be promoted only by a simultaneous promotion of relative smallness. I feel sure that no theists would be content to regard God's goodness as analogous to this—as if what he supports were not the *good* but the *better*, and if he had the paradoxical aim that all things should be better than other things.

This point is obscured by the fact that "great" and "small" seem to have an absolute as well as a relative sense. I cannot discuss here whether there is absolute magnitude or not, but if there is, there could be an absolute sense for "great," it could mean of at least a certain size, and it would make sense to speak of all things getting bigger, of a universe that was expanding all over, and therefore it would make sense to speak of promoting greatness. But in *this* sense great and small are not logically necessary counterparts: either quality could exist without the other. There would be no logical impossibility in everything's being small or in everything's being great.

Neither in the absolute nor in the relative sense, then, of "great" and "small" do these terms provide an analogy of the sort that would be needed to support this solution of the problem of evil. In neither case are greatness and smallness *both* necessary counterparts *and* mutually opposed forces or possible objects for support and attack.

It may be replied that good and evil are necessary counterparts in the same way as any quality and its logical opposite: redness can occur, it is suggested, only if non-redness also occurs. But unless evil is merely the privation of good, they are not logical opposites, and some further argument would be needed to show that they are counterparts in the same way as genuine logical opposites. Let us assume that this could be given. There is still doubt of the correctness of the metaphysical principle that a quality must have a real opposite: I suggest that it is not really impossible that everything should be, say, red, that the truth is merely that if everything were red we should not notice redness, and so we should have no word "red"; we observe and give names to qualities only if they have real opposites. If so, the principle that a term must have an opposite would belong only to our language or to our thought, and would not be an ontological principle, and correspondingly, the rule that good cannot exist without evil would not state a logical necessity of a sort that God would just have to put up with. God might have made everything good, though *we* should not have noticed it if he had.

But, finally, even if we concede that this is an ontological principle, it will provide a solution for the problem of evil only if one is prepared to say, "Evil exists, but only just enough evil to serve as the counterpart of good." I doubt whether any theist will accept this. After all, the ontological requirement that non-redness should occur would be satisfied even if all the universe, except for a minute speck, were red, and, if there were a corresponding requirement for evil as a counterpart to good, a minute dose of evil would presumably do. But theists are not usually willing to say, in all contexts, that all the evil that occurs is a minute and necessary dose.

(2) "Evil is necessary as a means to good."

It is sometimes suggested that evil is necessary for good not as a counterpart but as a means. In its simple form this has little plausibility as a solution of the problem of evil, since it obviously implies a severe restriction of God's power. It would be a *causal* law that you cannot have a certain end without a certain means, so that if God has to introduce evil as a means to good, he must be subject to at least some causal laws. This certainly conflicts with what a theist normally means by omnipotence. This view of God as limited by causal laws also conflicts with the view that causal laws are themselves made by God, which is more widely held than the corresponding view about the laws of logic. This conflict would, indeed, be resolved if it were possible for an omnipotent being to bind himself, and this possibility has still to be considered. Unless a favourable answer can be given to this question, the suggestion that evil is necessary as a means to good solves the problem of evil only by denying one of its constituent propositions, either that God is omnipotent or that "omnipotent" means what it says.

(3) "The universe is better with some evil in it than it could be if there were no evil."

Much more important is a solution which at first seems to be a mere variant of the previous one, that evil may contribute to the goodness of a whole in which it is found, so that the universe as a whole is better as it is, with some evil in it, than it would be if there were no evil. This solution may be developed in either of two ways. It may be supported by an aesthetic analogy, by the fact that contrasts heighten beauty, that in a musical work, for example, there may occur discords which somehow add to the beauty of the work as a whole. Alternatively, it may be worked out in connection with the notion of progress, that the best possible organization of the universe will not be static, but progressive, that the gradual overcoming of evil by good is really a finer thing than would be the eternal unchallenged supremacy of good.

In either case, this solution usually starts from the assumption that the evil whose existence gives rise to the problem of evil is primarily what is called physical evil, that is to say, pain. In Hume's rather half-hearted presentation of the problem of evil, the evils that he stresses are pain and disease, and those who reply to him argue that the existence of pain and disease makes possible the existence of sympathy, benevolence, heroism, and the gradually successful struggle of doctors and reformers to overcome these evils. In fact, theists often seize the opportunity to accuse those who stress the problem of evil of taking a low, materialistic view of good and evil, equating these with pleasure and pain, and of ignoring the more spiritual goods which can arise in the struggle against evils.

But let us see exactly what is being done here. Let us call pain and misery "first order evil" or "evil (1)." What contrasts with this, namely, pleasure and happiness, will be called "first order good" or "good (1)." Distinct from this is "second order good" or "good (2)" which somehow emerges in a complex situation in which evil (1) is a necessary component—logically not merely causally, necessary. (Exactly *how* it emerges does not matter: in the crudest version of this solution good (2) is simply the heightening of happiness by the contrast with misery, in other versions it includes sympathy with suffering, heroism in facing danger, and the gradual decrease of first order evil and increase of first order good.) It is also being assumed that second order good is more important than first order good or evil, in particular that it more than outweighs the first order evil it involves.

Now this is a particularly subtle attempt to solve the problem of evil. It defends God's goodness and omnipotence on the ground that (on a sufficiently long view) this is the best of all logically possible worlds, because it includes the important second order goods, and yet it admits that real evils, namely first order evils, exist. But does it still hold that good and evil are opposed? Not, clearly, in the sense that we set out originally: good does not tend to eliminate evil in general. Instead, we have a modified, a more complex pattern. First order good (*e.g.* happiness) *contrasts with* first order evil (*e.g.* misery): these two are opposed in a fairly mechanical way; some second order goods (*e.g.* benevolence) try to maximize first order good and minimize first order evil; but God's goodness is not this, it is rather the will to maximize *second* order good. We might, therefore, call God's goodness an example of a third order goodness, or good (3). While this account is different from our original one, it might well be held to be an improvement on it, to give a more accurate description of the way in which good is opposed to evil, and to be consistent with the essential theist position.

There might, however, be several objections to this solution.

First, some might argue that such qualities as benevolence—and *a fortiori* the third order goodness which promotes benevolence—have a merely derivative value, that they are not higher sorts of good, but merely means to good (1), that is, to happiness, so that it would be absurd for God to keep misery in existence in order to make possible the virtues of benevolence, heroism, etc. The theist who adopts the present solution must, of course, deny this, but he can do so with some plausibility, so I should not press this objection.

Secondly, it follows from this solution that God is not in our sense benevolent or sympathetic: he is not concerned to minimize evil (1), but only to promote good (2); and this might be a disturbing conclusion for some theists.

But, thirdly, the fatal objection is this. Our analysis shows clearly the possibility of the existence of a *second* order evil, an evil (2) contrasting with good (2) as evil (1) contrasts with good (1). This would include malevolence, cruelty, callousness, cowardice, and states in which good

(1) is decreasing and evil (1) increasing. And just as good (2) is held to be the important kind of good, the kind that God is concerned to promote, so evil (2) will, by analogy, be the important kind of evil, the kind which God, if he were wholly good and omnipotent, would eliminate. And yet evil (2) plainly exists, and indeed most theists (in other contexts) stress its existence more than that of evil (1). We should, therefore, state the problem of evil in terms of second order evil, and against this form of the problem the present solution is useless.

An attempt might be made to use this solution again, at a higher level, to explain the occurrence of evil (2); indeed the next main solution that we shall examine does just this, with the help of some new notions. Without any fresh notions, such a solution would have little plausibility: for example, we could hardly say that the really important good was a good (3), such as the increase of benevolence in proportion to cruelty, which logically required for its occurrence the occurrence of some second order evil. But even if evil (2) could be explained in this way, it is fairly clear that there would be third order evils contrasting with this third order good: and we should be well on the way to an infinite regress, where the solution of a problem of evil, stated in terms of evil (*n*), indicated the existence of an evil (*n* + 1), and a further problem to be solved.

(4) "Evil is due to human free will."

Perhaps the most important proposed solution of the problem of evil is that evil is not to be ascribed to God at all, but to the independent actions of human beings, supposed to have been endowed by God with freedom of the will. This solution may be combined with the preceding one: first order evil (*e.g.* pain) may be justified as a logically necessary component in second order good (*e.g.* sympathy) while second order evil (*e.g.* cruelty) is not *justified*, but is so ascribed to human beings that God cannot be held responsible for it. This combination evades my third criticism of the preceding solution.

The free will solution also involves the preceding solution at a higher level. To explain why a wholly good God gave men free will although it would lead to some important evils, it must be argued that it is better on the whole that men should act freely, and sometimes err, than that they should be innocent automata, acting rightly in a wholly determined way. Freedom that is to say, is now treated as a third order good, and as being more valuable than second order goods (such as sympathy and heroism) would be if they were deterministically produced, and it is being assumed that second order evils, such as cruelty, are logically necessary accompaniments of freedom, just as pain is a logically necessary precondition of sympathy.

I think that this solution is unsatisfactory primarily because of the incoherence of the notion of freedom of the will: but I cannot discuss this topic adequately here, although some of my criticisms will touch upon it.

First I should query the assumption that second order evils are logically necessary accompaniments of freedom. I should ask this: if God has made men such that in their free choices they sometimes prefer what is good and sometimes what is evil, why could he not have made men such that they always freely choose the good? If there is no logical impossibility in a man's freely choosing the good on one, or on several, occasions, there cannot be a logical impossibility in his freely choosing the good on every occasion. God was not, then, faced with a choice between making innocent automata and making beings who, in acting freely, would sometimes go wrong: there was open to him the obviously better possibility of making beings who would act freely but always go right. Clearly, his failure to avail himself of this possibility is inconsistent with his being both omnipotent and wholly good.

If it is replied that this objection is absurd, that the making of some wrong choices is logically necessary for freedom, it would seem that "freedom" must here mean complete randomness or indeterminacy, including randomness with regard to the alternatives good and evil, in other words that men's choices and consequent actions can be "free" only if they are not determined by their characters. Only on this assumption can God escape the responsibility for men's actions; for if he made them as they are, but did not determine their wrong choices, this can only be because the wrong choices are not determined by men as they are. But then if freedom is randomness, how can it be a characteristic of *will*? And, still more, how can it be the most important good? What value or merit would there be in free choices if these were random actions which were not determined by the nature of the agent?

I conclude that to make this solution plausible two different senses of "freedom" must be confused, one sense which will justify the view that freedom is a third order good, more valuable than other goods would be without it, and another sense, sheer randomness, to prevent us from ascribing to God a decision to make men such that they sometimes go wrong when he might have made them such that they would always freely go right.

This criticism is sufficient to dispose of this solution. But besides this there is a fundamental difficulty in the notion of an omnipotent God creating men with free will, for if men's wills are really free this must mean that even God cannot control them, that is, that God is no longer omnipotent. It may be objected that God's gift of freedom to men does not mean that he *cannot* control their wills, but that he always *refrains* from controlling their wills. But why, we may ask, should God refrain from controlling evil wills? Why should he not leave men free to will rightly, but intervene when he sees them beginning to will wrongly? If God could do this, but does not, and if he is wholly good, the only explanation could be that even a wrong free act of will is not really evil, that its freedom is a value which outweighs its wrongness, so that there would be a loss of value if God took away the wrongness and the freedom together. But this is utterly opposed to what theists say about sin in other contexts. The present solution of the problem of evil, then, can be maintained only in the form that God has made men so free that he *cannot* control their wills.

This leads us to what I call the Paradox of Omnipotence: can an omnipotent being make things which he cannot subsequently control? Or, what is practically equivalent to this, can an omnipotent being make rules which then bind himself? (These are practically equivalent because any such

rules could be regarded as setting certain things beyond his control, and *vice versa*.) The second of these formulations is relevant to the suggestions that we have already met, that an omnipotent God creates the rules of logic or causal laws, and is then bound by them.

It is clear that this is a paradox: the questions cannot be answered satisfactorily either in the affirmative or in the negative. If we answer "Yes," it follows that if God actually makes things which he cannot control, or makes rules which bind himself, he is not omnipotent once he has made them: there are then things which he cannot do. But if we answer "No," we are immediately asserting that there are things which he cannot do, that is to say that he is already not omnipotent.

It cannot be replied that the question which sets this paradox is not a proper question. It would make perfectly good sense to say that a human mechanic has made a machine which he cannot control: if there is any difficulty about the question it lies in the notion of omnipotence itself.

This, incidentally, shows that although we have approached this paradox from the free will theory, it is equally a problem for a theological determinist. No one thinks that machines have free will, yet they may well be beyond the control of their makers. The determinist might reply that anyone who makes anything determines its ways of acting, and so determines its subsequent behaviour: even the human mechanic does this by his *choice* of materials and structure for his machine, though he does not know all about either of these: the mechanic thus determines, though he may not foresee, his machine's actions. And since God is omniscient, and since his creation of things is total, he both determines and foresees the ways in which his creatures will act. We may grant this, but it is beside the point. The question is not whether God *originally* determined the future actions of his creatures, but whether he can *subsequently* control their actions, or whether he was able in his original creation to put things beyond his subsequent control. Even on determinist principles the answers "Yes" and "No" are equally irreconcilable with God's omnipotence.

Before suggesting a solution of this paradox, I would point out that there is a parallel Paradox of Sovereignty. Can a legal sovereign make a law restricting its own future legislative power? For example, could the British parliament make a law forbidding any future parliament to socialise banking, and also forbidding the future repeal of this law itself? Or could the British parliament, which was legally sovereign in Australia in, say, 1899, pass a valid law, or series of laws, which made it no longer sovereign in 1933? Again, neither the affirmative nor the negative answer is really satisfactory. If we were to answer "Yes," we should be admitting the validity of a law which, if it were actually made, would mean that parliament was no longer sovereign. If we were to answer "No," we should be admitting that there is a law, not logically absurd, which parliament cannot validly make, that is, that parliament is not now a legal sovereign. This paradox can be solved in the following way. We should distinguish between first order laws, that is laws governing the actions of individuals and bodies other than the legislature, and second order laws, that is laws about laws, laws governing the actions of the legislature itself. Correspondingly, we should distinguish two orders of sovereignty, first order sovereignty (sovereignty (1)) which is unlimited authority to make first order laws, and second order sovereignty (sovereignty (2)) which is unlimited authority to make second order laws. If we say that parliament is sovereign we might mean that any parliament at any time has sovereignty (1), or we might mean that parliament has both sovereignty (1) and sovereignty (2) at present, but we cannot without contradiction mean both that the present parliament has sovereignty (2) and that every parliament at every time has sovereignty (1), for if the present parliament has sovereignty (2) it may use it to take away the sovereignty (1) of later parliaments. What the paradox shows is that we cannot ascribe to any continuing institution legal sovereignty in an inclusive sense.

The analogy between omnipotence and sovereignty shows that the paradox of omnipotence can be solved in a similar way. We must distinguish between first order omnipotence (omnipotence (1)),

that is unlimited power to act, and second order omnipotence (omnipotence (2)), that is unlimited power to determine what powers to act things shall have. Then we could consistently say that God all the time has omnipotence (1), but if so no beings at any time have powers to act independently of God. Or we could say that God at one time had omnipotence (2), and used it to assign independent powers to act to certain things, so that God thereafter did not have omnipotence (1). But what the paradox shows is that we cannot consistently ascribe to any continuing being omnipotence in an inclusive sense.

An alternative solution of this paradox would be simply to deny that God is a continuing being, that any times can be assigned to his actions at all. But on this assumption (which also has difficulties of its own) no meaning can be given to the assertion that God made men with wills so free that he could not control them. The paradox of omnipotence can be avoided by putting God outside time, but the free will solution of the problem of evil cannot be saved in this way, and equally it remains impossible to hold that an omnipotent God *binds himself* by causal or logical laws.

CONCLUSION

Of the proposed solutions of the problem of evil which we have examined, none has stood up to criticism. There may be other solutions which require examination, but this study strongly suggests that there is no valid solution of the problem which does not modify at least one of the constituent propositions in a way which would seriously affect the essential core of the theistic position.

Quite apart from the problem of evil, the paradox of omnipotence has shown that God's omnipotence must in any case be restricted in one way or another, that unqualified omnipotence cannot be ascribed to any being that continues through time. And if God and his actions are not in time, can omnipotence, or power of any sort, be meaningfully ascribed to him?

III.B.2

The Inductive Argument from Evil against the Existence of God

WILLIAM ROWE

A short biographical sketch of William Rowe appears before selection I.B.9. In the present selection, Rowe argues that an inductive or probabilistic version of the argument from evil justifies atheism. He concedes that deductive arguments against the existence of God on the basis of evil, such as J. L. Mackie uses (Reading III.B.1), do not succeed. Nevertheless, he says it is reasonable to believe that there is no God. In the last part of his essay, Rowe defines his position as "friendly atheism" because he admits that a theist may be justified in rejecting the probabilistic argument from evil.

This paper is concerned with three interrelated questions. The first is: Is there an argument for atheism based on the existence of evil that may rationally justify someone in being an atheist? To this first question I give an affirmative answer and try to support that answer by setting forth a strong argument for atheism based on the existence of evil.[1] The second question is: How can the theist best defend his position against the argument for atheism based on the existence of evil? In response to this question I try to describe what may be an adequate rational defense for theism against any argument for atheism based on the existence of evil. The final question is: What position should the informed atheist take concerning the rationality of theistic belief? Three different answers an atheist may give to this question serve to distinguish three varieties of atheism: unfriendly atheism, indifferent atheism, and friendly atheism. In the final part of the paper I discuss and defend the position of friendly atheism.

Before we consider the argument from evil, we need to distinguish a narrow and a broad sense of the terms "theist," "atheist," and "agnostic." By a "theist" in the narrow sense I mean someone who believes in the existence of an omnipotent, omniscient, eternal, supremely good being who created the world. By a "theist" in the broad sense I mean someone who believes in the existence of some sort of divine being or divine reality. To be a theist in the narrow sense is also to be a theist in the broad sense, but one may be a theist in the broad sense— as was Paul Tillich—without believing that there is a supremely good, omnipotent, omniscient, eternal being who created the world. Similar distinctions must be made between a narrow and a broad sense of the terms "atheist" and "agnostic." To be an atheist in the broad sense is to deny the existence of any sort of divine being or divine reality. Tillich was not an atheist in the broad sense. But he was an atheist in the narrow sense, for he denied that there exists a divine being that is all-knowing,

Reprinted from "The Problem of Evil and Some Varieties of Atheism," *American Philosophical Quarterly* 16 (1979) by permission. Footnotes edited.

all-powerful and perfectly good. In this paper I will be using the terms "theism," "theist," "atheism," "atheist," "agnosticism," and "agnostic" in the narrow sense, not in the broad sense.

I

In developing the argument for atheism based on the existence of evil, it will be useful to focus on some particular evil that our world contains in considerable abundance. Intense human and animal suffering, for example, occurs daily and in great plenitude in our world. Such intense suffering is a clear case of evil. Of course, if the intense suffering leads to some greater good, a good we could not have obtained without undergoing the suffering in question, we might conclude that the suffering is justified, but it remains an evil nevertheless. For we must not confuse the intense suffering in and of itself with the good things to which it sometimes leads or of which it may be a necessary part. Intense human or animal suffering is in itself bad, an evil, even though it may sometimes be justified by virtue of being a part of, or leading to, some good which is unobtainable without it. What is evil in itself may sometimes be good as a means because it leads to something that is good in itself. In such a case, while remaining an evil in itself, the intense human or animal suffering is, nevertheless, an evil which someone might be morally justified in permitting.

Taking human and animal suffering as a clear instance of evil which occurs with great frequency in our world, the argument for atheism based on evil can be stated as follows:

1. There exist instances of intense suffering which an omnipotent, omniscient being could have prevented without thereby losing some greater good or permitting some evil equally bad or worse.[2]

2. An omniscient, wholly good being would prevent the occurrence of any intense suffering it could, unless it could not do so without thereby losing some greater good or permitting some evil equally bad or worse.

3. There does not exist an omnipotent, omniscient, wholly good being.

What are we to say about this argument for atheism, an argument based on the profusion of one sort of evil in our world? The argument is valid; therefore, if we have rotational grounds for accepting its premises, to that extent we have rational grounds for accepting atheism. Do we, however, have rational grounds for accepting the premises of this argument?

Let's begin with the second premise. Let s_1 be an instance of intense human or animal suffering which an omniscient, wholly good being could prevent. We will also suppose that things are such that s_1 will occur unless prevented by the omniscient, wholly good (OG) being. We might be interested in determining what would be a sufficient condition of OG failing to prevent s_1. But, for our purpose here, we need only try to state a necessary condition for OG failing to prevent s_1. That condition, so it seems to me, is this:

Either

(i)   there is some greater good, G, such that G is obtainable by OG only if OG permits s_1,

or

(ii) there is some greater good, G, such that G is obtainable by OG only if OG permits either s_1 or some evil equally bad or worse,

or

(iii) s_1 is such that it is preventable by OG only if OG permits some evil equally bad or worse.

It is important to recognize that (iii) is not included in (i). For losing a good greater than s_1 is not the same as permitting an evil greater than s_1. And this because the *absence* of a good state of affairs need not itself be an evil state of affairs. It is also important to recognize that s_1 might be such that it is preventable by OG *without* losing G (so condition (i) is not satisfied) but also such that if OG did prevent it, G would be lost unless OG permitted some evil equal to or worse than s_1. If this were so, it does not seem correct to require that OG prevent s_1.

Thus, condition (ii) takes into account an important possibility not encompassed in condition (i).

Is it true that if an omniscient, wholly good being permits the occurrence of some intense suffering it could have prevented, then either (i) or (ii) or (iii) obtains? It seems to me that it is true. But if it is true then so is premise (2) of the argument for atheism. For that premise merely states in more compact form what we have suggested must be true if an omniscient, wholly good being fails to prevent some intense suffering it could prevent. Premise (2) says that an omniscient, wholly good being would prevent the occurrence of any intense suffering it could, unless it could not do so without thereby losing some greater good or permitting some evil equally bad or worse. This premise (or something not too distant from it) is, I think, held in common by many atheists and nontheists. Of course, there may be disagreement about whether something is good, and whether, if it is good, one would be morally justified in permitting some intense suffering to occur in order to obtain it. Someone might hold, for example, that no good is great enough to justify permitting an innocent child to suffer terribly. Again, someone might hold that the mere fact that a given good outweighs some suffering and would be lost if the suffering were prevented, is not a morally sufficient reason for permitting the suffering. But to hold either of these views is not to deny (2). For (2) claims only that *if* an omniscient, wholly good being permits intense suffering *then* either there is some greater good that would have been lost, or some equally bad or worse evil that would have occurred, had the intense suffering been prevented. (2) does not purport to describe what might be a *sufficient* condition for an omniscient, wholly good being to permit intense suffering, only what is a *necessary* condition. So stated, (2) seems to express a belief that accords with our basic moral principles, principles shared by both theists and nontheists. If we are to fault the argument for atheism, therefore, it seems we must find some fault with its first premise.

Suppose in some distant forest lightning strikes a dead tree, resulting in a forest fire. In the fire a fawn is trapped, horribly burned, and lies in terrible agony for several days before death relieves its suffering. So far as we can see, the fawn's intense suffering is pointless. For there does not appear to be any greater good such that the prevention of the fawn's suffering would require either the loss of that good or the occurrence of an evil equally bad or worse. Nor does there seem to be any equally bad or worse evil so connected to the fawn's suffering that it would have had to occur had the fawn's suffering been prevented. Could an omnipotent, omniscient being have prevented the fawn's apparently pointless suffering? The answer is obvious, as even the theist will insist. An omnipotent, omniscient being could have easily prevented the fawn from being horribly burned, or, given the burning, could have spared the fawn the intense suffering by quickly ending its life, rather than allowing the fawn to lie in terrible agony for several days. Since the fawn's intense suffering was preventable and, so far as we can see, pointless, doesn't it appear that premise (1) of the argument is true, that there do exist instances of intense suffering which an omnipotent, omniscient being could have prevented without thereby losing some greater good or permitting some evil equally bad or worse?

It must be acknowledged that the case of the fawn's apparently pointless suffering does not prove that (1) is true. For even though we cannot see how the fawn's suffering is required to obtain some greater good (or to prevent some equally bad or worse evil), it hardly follows that it is not so required. After all, we are often surprised by how things we thought to be unconnected turn out to be intimately connected. Perhaps, for all we know, there is some familiar good outweighing the fawn's suffering to which that suffering is connected in a way we do not see. Furthermore, there may well be unfamiliar goods, goods we haven't dreamed of, to which the fawn's suffering is inextricably connected. Indeed, it would seem to require something like omniscience on our part before we could lay claim to *knowing* that there is no greater good connected to the fawn's suffering in such a manner than an omnipotent, omniscient being could not have achieved that good without permitting that suffering or some evil equally bad or worse. So the case of the fawn's suffering surely does not enable us to *establish* the truth of (1).

The truth is that we are not in a position to prove that (1) is true. We cannot know with certainty that instances of suffering of the sort described in (1) do occur in our world. But it is one thing to *know* or *prove* that (1) is true and quite another thing to have *rational grounds* for believing (1) to be true. We are often in the position where in the light of our experience and knowledge it is rational to believe that a certain statement is true, even though we are not in a position to prove or to know with certainty that the statement is true. In the light of our past experience and knowledge it is, for example, very reasonable to believe that neither Goldwater nor McGovern will ever be elected President, but we are scarcely in the position of knowing with certainty that neither will ever be elected President. So, too, with (1), although we cannot know with certainty that it is true, it perhaps can be rationally supported, shown to be a rational belief.

Consider again the case of the fawn's suffering. Is it reasonable to believe that there is some greater good so intimately connected to that suffering that even an omnipotent, omniscient being could not have obtained that good without permitting that suffering or some evil at least as bad? It certainly does not appear reasonable to believe this. Nor does it seem reasonable to believe that there is some evil at least as bad as the fawn's suffering such that an omnipotent being simply could not have prevented it without permitting the fawn's suffering. But even if it should somehow be reasonable to believe either of these things of the fawn's suffering, we must then ask whether it is reasonable to believe either of these things of *all* the instances of seemingly pointless human and animal suffering that occur daily in our world. And surely the answer to this more general question must be no. It seems quite unlikely that all the instances of intense suffering occurring daily in our world are intimately related to the occurrence of greater goods or the prevention of evils at least as bad; and even more unlikely, should they somehow all be so related, that an omnipotent, omniscient being could not have achieved at least some of those goods (or prevented some of those evils) without permitting the instances of intense suffering that are supposedly related to them. In the light of our experience and knowledge of the variety and scale of human and animal suffering in our world, the idea that none of this suffering could have been prevented by an omnipotent being without thereby losing a greater good or permitting an evil at least as bad seems an extraordinary absurd idea, quite beyond our belief. It seems then that although we cannot prove that (1) is true, it is, nevertheless, altogether *reasonable* to believe that (1) is true, that (1) is a *rational* belief.

Returning now to our argument for atheism, we've seen that the second premise expresses a basic belief common to many theists and nontheists. We've also seen that our experience and knowledge of the variety and profusion of suffering in our world provides *rational support* for the first premise. Seeing that the conclusion, "There does not exist an omnipotent, omniscient, wholly good being" follows from these two premises, it does seem that we have *rational support* for atheism, that it is reasonable for us to believe that the theistic God does not exist.

II

Can theism be rationally defended against the argument for atheism we have just examined? If it can, how might the theist best respond to that argument? Since the argument from (1) and (2) to (3) is valid, and since the theist, no less than the nontheist, is more than likely committed to (2), it's clear that the theist can reject this atheistic argument only by rejecting its first premise, the premise that states that there are instances of intense suffering which an omnipotent, omniscient being could have prevented without thereby losing some greater good or permitting some evil equally bad or worse. How, then, can the theist best respond to this premise and the considerations advanced in its support?

There are basically three responses a theist can make. First, he might argue not that (1) is false or probably false, but only that the reasoning given in support of it is in some way *defective*. He may do this either by arguing that the reasons given in support of (1) are *in themselves* insufficient to justify accepting (1), or by arguing that there are other things we know which, when taken in conjunction with these reasons, do not justify us in accepting (1). I suppose some theists would be content with this rather modest response to the basic argument for atheism. But given the validity of the basic argument and the theist's likely acceptance of (2), he is thereby committed to the view that (1) is false, not just that we have no good reasons for accepting (1) as true. The second two responses are aimed at showing that it is reasonable to believe that (1) is false. Since the theist is committed to this view, I shall focus the discussion on these two attempts, attempts which we can distinguish as "the direct attack" and "the indirect attack."

By a direct attack, I mean an attempt to reject (1) by pointing out goods, for example, to which suffering may well be connected, goods which an omnipotent, omniscient being could not achieve without permitting suffering. It is doubtful, however, that the direct attack can succeed. The theist may point out that some suffering leads to moral and spiritual development impossible without suffering. But it's reasonably clear that suffering often occurs in a degree far beyond what is required for character development. The theist may say that some suffering results from free choices of human beings and might be preventable only by preventing some measure of human freedom. But, again, it's clear that much intense suffering occurs not as a result of human free choices. The general difficulty with this direct attack on premise (1) is twofold. First, it cannot succeed; for the theist does not know what greater goods might be served, or evils prevented, by each instance of intense human or animal suffering. Second, the theist's own religious tradition usually maintains that in this life it is not given to us to know God's purpose in allowing particular instances of suffering. Hence, the direct attack against premise (1) cannot succeed and violates basic beliefs associated with theism.

The best procedure for the theist to follow in rejecting premise (1) is the indirect procedure. This procedure I shall call "the G. E. Moore shift," so-called in honor of the twentieth century philosopher G. E. Moore, who used it to great effect in dealing with the arguments of the skeptics.

Skeptical philosophers such as David Hume have advanced ingenious arguments to prove that no one can know of the existence of any material object. The premises of their arguments employ plausible principles, principles which many philosophers have tried to reject directly, but only with questionable success. Moore's procedure was altogether different. Instead of arguing directly against the premises of the skeptic's arguments, he simply noted that the premises implied, for example, that he (Moore) did not know of the existence of a pencil. Moore then proceeded indirectly against the skeptic's premises by arguing:

> I do know that this pencil exists.
>
> If the skeptic's principles are correct I cannot know of the existence of this pencil.
> _____
>
> ∴ The skeptic's principles (at least one) must be incorrect.

Moore then noted that his argument is just as valid as the skeptic's, that both of their arguments contain the premise "If the skeptic's principles are correct Moore cannot know of the existence of this pencil," and concluded that the only way to choose between the two arguments (Moore's and the skeptic's) is by deciding which of the first premises it is more rational to believe—Moore's premise "I do know that this pencil exists" or the skeptic's premise asserting that his skeptical principles are correct. Moore concluded that his own first premise was the more rational of the two.

Before we see how the theist may apply the G. E. Moore shift to the basic argument of atheism, we should note the general strategy of the shift. We're given an argument: p, q, therefore, r. Instead of arguing directly against p, another argument is constructed not-r, q, therefore, not-p—which begins with the denial of the conclusion of the first argument, keeps its second premise, and ends with the denial of the first premise as its conclusion. Compare, for example, these two:

	I.		II.
	p		not-r
	q		q
	r		not-p

It is a truth of logic that if I is valid II must be valid as well. Since the arguments are the same so far as the second premise is concerned, any choice between them must concern their respective first premises. To argue against the first premise (p) by constructing the counter argument II is to employ the G. E. Moore shift.

Applying the G. E. Moore shift against the first premise of the basic argument for atheism, the theist can argue as follows:

not-3. There exists an omnipotent, omniscient, wholly good being.

2. An omniscient, wholly good being would prevent the occurrence of any intense suffering it could, unless it could not do so without thereby losing some greater good or permitting some evil equally bad or worse.

therefore,

not-1. It is not the case that there exist instances of intense suffering which an omnipotent, omniscient being could have prevented without thereby losing some greater good or permitting some evil equally bad or worse.

We now have two arguments: the basic argument for atheism from (1) and (2) to (3), and the theist's best response, the argument from (not-3) and (2) to (not-1). What the theist then says about (1) is that he has rational grounds for believing in the existence of the theistic God (not-3), accepts (2) as true, and sees that (not-1) follows from (not-3) and (2). He concludes, therefore, that he has rational grounds for rejecting (1). Having rational grounds for rejecting (1), the theist concludes that the basic argument for atheism is mistaken.

III

We've had a look at a forceful argument for atheism and what seems to be the theist's best response to that argument. If one is persuaded by the argument for atheism, as I find myself to be, how might one best view the position of the theist? Of course, he will view the theist as having a false belief, just as the theist will view the atheist as having a false belief. But what position should the atheist take concerning the *rationality* of the theist's belief? There are three major positions an atheist might take, positions which we may think of as some varieties of atheism. First, the atheist may believe that no one is rationally justified in believing that the theistic God exists. Let us call this position "unfriendly atheism." Second, the atheist may hold no belief concerning whether any theist is or isn't rationally justified in believing that the theistic God exists. Let us call this view "indifferent atheism." Finally, the atheist may believe that some theists are rationally justified in believing that the theistic God exists. This view we shall call "friendly atheism." In this final part of the paper I propose to discuss and defend the position of friendly atheism.

If no one can be rationally justified in believing a false proposition then friendly atheism is a paradoxical, if not incoherent position. But surely the truth of a belief is not a necessary condition of someone's being rationally justified in having that belief. So in holding that someone is rationally justified in believing that the theistic God exists, the friendly atheist is not committed to thinking that the theist has a true belief. What he is committed to is that the theist has rational grounds for his belief, a belief the atheist rejects and is convinced he is rationally justified in rejecting. But is this possible? Can someone, like our friendly atheist, hold a belief, be convinced that he is rationally justified in holding that belief, and yet believe that someone else is equally justified in believing the opposite? Surely this is possible. Suppose your friends see you off on a flight to Hawaii. Hours after take-off they learn that your plane has gone down at sea. After a twenty-four hour search, no survivors have been found. Under these circumstances they are rationally justified in believing that you have perished. But it is hardly rational for you to believe this, as you bob up and down in your life vest, wondering why the search planes have failed to spot you. Indeed, to amuse yourself while awaiting your fate, you might very well reflect on the fact that your friends are rationally justified in believing that you are now dead, a proposition you disbelieve and are rationally justified in disbelieving. So, too, perhaps an atheist may be rationally justified in his atheistic belief and yet hold that some theists are rationally justified in believing just the opposite of what he believes.

What sort of grounds might a theist have for believing that God exists? Well, he might endeavor to justify his belief by appealing to one or more of the traditional arguments: Ontological, Cosmological, Teleological, Moral, etc. Second, he might appeal to certain aspects of religious experience, perhaps even his own religious experience. Third, he might try to justify theism as a plausible theory in terms of which we can account for a variety of phenomena. Although an atheist must hold that the theistic God does not exist, can he not also believe, and be justified in so believing, that some of these "justifications of theism" do actually rationally justify some theists in their belief that there exists a supremely good, omnipotent, omniscient being? It seems to me that he can.

If we think of the long history of theistic belief and the special situations in which people are sometimes placed, it is perhaps as absurd to think that no one was ever rationally justified in believing that the theistic God exists as it is to think that no one was ever justified in believing that human beings would never walk on the moon. But in suggesting that friendly atheism is preferable to unfriendly atheism, I don't mean to rest the case on what some human beings might reasonably have believed in the eleventh or thirteenth century. The more interesting question is whether some people in modern society, people who are aware of the usual grounds for belief and disbelief and are acquainted to some degree with modern science, are yet rationally justified in accepting theism. Friendly

atheism is a significant position only if it answers this question in the affirmative.

It is not difficult for an atheist to be friendly when he has reason to believe that the theist could not reasonably be expected to be acquainted with the grounds for disbelief that he (the atheist) possesses. For then the atheist may take the view that some theists are rationally justified in holding to theism, but would not be so were they to be acquainted with the grounds for disbelief—those grounds being sufficient to tip the scale in favor of atheism when balanced against the reasons the theist has in support of his belief.

Friendly atheism becomes paradoxical, however, when the atheist contemplates believing that the theist has all the grounds for atheism that he, the atheist, has, and yet is rationally justified in maintaining his theistic belief. But even so excessively friendly a view as this perhaps can be held by the atheist if he also has some reason to think that the grounds for theism are not as telling as the theist is justified in taking them to be.

In this paper I've presented what I take to be a strong argument for atheism, pointed out what I think is the theist's best response to that argument, distinguished three positions an atheist might take concerning the rationality of theistic belief, and made some remarks in defense of the position called "friendly atheism." I'm aware that the central points of the paper are not likely to be warmly received by many philosophers. Philosophers who are atheists tend to be tough minded—holding that there are no good reasons for supposing that theism is true. And theists tend either to reject the view that the existence of evil provides rational grounds for atheism or to hold that religious belief has nothing to do with reason and evidence at all. But such is the way of philosophy.

NOTES

1. Some philosophers have contended that the existence of evil is *logically inconsistent* with the existence of the theistic God. No one, I think, has succeeded in establishing such an extravagant claim.

Indeed, granted incompatibilism, there is a fairly compelling argument for the view that the existence of evil is logically consistent with the existence of the theistic God. (For a lucid statement of this argument see Alvin Plantinga, *God, Freedom, and Evil* (New York, 1974), 29–59.) There remains, however, what we may call the *evidential* form—as opposed to the *logical* form—of the problem of evil; the view that the variety and profusion of evil in our world, although perhaps not logically inconsistent with the existence of the theistic God, provides, nevertheless, *rational support* for atheism. In this paper I shall be concerned solely with the evidential form of the problem, the form of the problem which, I think, presents a rather severe difficulty for theism. William L. Rowe, "The Problem of Evil and Some Varieties of Atheism," first published in *American Philosophical Quarterly*, 16 (1979), pp. 335–41. Used with permission.

2. If there is some good, G, greater than any evil, (1) will be false for the trivial reason that no matter what evil, E, we pick the conjunctive good state of affairs consisting of G and E will outweigh E and be such that an omnipotent being could not obtain it without permitting E. (See Alvin Plantinga, *God and Other Minds* [Ithaca, 1967], 167.) To avoid this objection we may insert "unreplaceable" into our premises (1) and (2) between "some" and "greater." If E isn't required for G, and G is better than G plus E, then the good conjunctive state of affairs composed of G and E would be replaceable by the greater good of G alone. For the sake of simplicity, however, I will ignore this complication both in the formulation and discussion of premises (1) and (2).

III.B.3

Evolution and the Problem of Evil

PAUL DRAPER

A short biographical sketch of Paul Draper appears before selection II.B.5. In the present article, Draper notes that traditionally the problem of evil has been, with few exceptions, the only atheological argument against the existence of God. He argues that the naturalistic account of evolution can provide a cogent alternative to theism and that by combining that with the problem of evil, one can begin to build a cumulative case against theism.

I. INTRODUCTION

Naturalism and theism are powerful and popular worldviews. They suggest very different conceptions of the nature of human beings, our relationship to the world, and our future. Though I hope that theism is true, I believe that it faces a number of evidential problems, problems that prevent my hope from becoming belief. In this paper I will examine two of those problems: evolution and evil. I will use certain known facts about the origin of complex life and the pattern of pain and pleasure in the world to construct a powerful *prima facie* case against theism.

By "theism" I mean the hypothesis[1] that God is the creator of the physical universe. I take the

This article appeared in print for the first time in the third edition of this book. Copyright © Paul Draper 1997.

word "God" to be a title that, by definition, can be borne only by a perfect supernatural person. To claim that God is a "person" is to claim that God performs actions and has beliefs and purposes. "Supernatural" persons are not natural—they are neither a part nor a product of the physical universe—and yet they can affect natural objects. A "perfect" person is, among other things, perfect in power (omnipotent), perfect in knowledge (omniscient), and perfect in moral goodness (morally perfect). While some have dismissed this conception of God as religiously insignificant, I am convinced that, for millions of Jews, Christians, and Muslims, factual belief in a perfect supernatural person is essential for making sense of their forms of worship. By "naturalism" I mean the hypothesis that the physical universe is a "closed system" in the sense that nothing that is neither a part nor a product of it can affect it. So naturalism entails the nonexistence of all supernatural beings, including the theistic God.

Arguments against theism can be divided into two main types. *Logical* arguments attempt to show that theism is either self-contradictory or logically inconsistent with some known fact. *Evidential* arguments attempt to show that certain known facts that are (at least so far as we can tell) consistent with theism nevertheless provide evidence against it.[2] The arguments in this paper will be evidential. I will show that certain known facts support the hypothesis of naturalism over the hypothesis of theism because we have considerably more reason to expect them to obtain on the assumption that naturalism is true than on the assumption that theism is true. This is a threat to theism because naturalism and theism are alternative hypotheses—they cannot both be true. Thus, if (after considering all of the evidence) naturalism turns out to be more probable than theism, then theism is probably false.

II. EVOLUTION

Ever since the publication of Darwin's *On the Origin of Species*, countless theologians, philosophers, and scientists have pointed out that evolution could be the means by which God has chosen to create

human beings and the rest of the living world. This is thought to show that, while the truth of evolution does refute the biblical story of creation as told in the book of Genesis, it in no way threatens the more general belief that the universe was created by God. In other words, it provides no reason to doubt theism. The plausibility of this argument is reflected by the fact that many scientists are both evolutionists and theists. Commenting on this fact, Stephen Jay Gould says:

> Unless at least half my colleagues are dunces, there can be—on the most raw and direct empirical grounds—no conflict between science and religion. I know hundreds of scientists who share a conviction about the fact of evolution, and teach it in the same way. Among these people I note an entire spectrum of religious attitudes—from devout daily prayer and worship to resolute atheism. Either there's no correlation between religious belief and confidence in evolution—or else half these people are fools.[3]

What Gould neglects to mention is that many well-educated people, including many of Gould's colleagues on the irreligious end of the spectrum, reject theism precisely because they believe in evolution. For example, William B. Provine, a leading historian of science, maintains that those who retain their religious beliefs while accepting evolution "have to check [their] brains at the church-house door."[4]

So who is correct? Is it compatibilists like Gould and the liberal preacher Henry Ward Beecher, who claimed in 1885 that evolution "will change theology, but only to bring out the simple temple of God in clearer and more beautiful lines and proportions"[5]? Or is it incompatibilists like Provine and the fundamentalist preacher William Jennings Bryan, who once defined "theistic evolution" as "an anesthetic which deadens the patient's pain while atheism removes his religion"[6]? My own position, as my introductory remarks suggest, lies somewhere between the view that theistic evolution is a happy marriage and the view that it must end in divorce. I agree with the compatibilists that theism and evolution are logically consistent. What I disagree with is the compatibilist's inference from no inconsistency to no conflict. For while consistency implies that the truth of evolution does not disprove theism—that there is no good *logical* argument from evolution against theism just as there is no good logical argument from evil against theism—it does not imply that the truth of evolution is no evidence at all against theism. My position is that evolution is evidence favoring naturalism over theism. There is, in other words, a good *evidential* argument from evolution against theism.

By "evolution," I mean the conjunction of two theses. The first, which I will call "the genealogical thesis," asserts that evolution did in fact occur—complex life did evolve from relatively simple life. Specifically, it is the view that all multicellular organisms and all (relatively) complex unicellular organisms on earth (both present and past) are the (more or less) gradually modified descendents of a small number of relatively simple unicellular organisms. The second thesis, which I will call "the genetic thesis," addresses the issue of how evolution occurred. It states that all evolutionary change in populations of complex organisms either is or is the result of trans-generational genetic change (or, to be more precise, trans-generational change in nucleic acids). It is important to distinguish this claim about the mechanisms by which evolution takes place from the much more specific claim that natural selection operating on random genetic mutation is the principal mechanism driving evolutionary change (or the principal mechanism driving the evolutionary change that results in increased complexity). Let's call this more specific claim "Darwinism" and its conjunction with evolution "Darwinian evolution."

Many evolutionary arguments against theism appeal to Darwinian evolution rather than just to evolution. I believe that such arguments overestimate the strength of the evidence for Darwinism. Darwinism may be highly probable on the assumption that naturalism is true. But it is far less probable on the assumption that theism is true, because on theism it is a real possibility that God has guided evolution by directly causing various genetic changes

to occur. Thus, any argument against theism that is based on the truth of Darwinism is at best question-begging. This is why my argument appeals only to evolution rather than to Darwinian evolution. It is my belief (which I won't defend here) that the evidence for evolution, unlike the evidence for Darwinian evolution, is overwhelming—so overwhelming that evolution can legitimately be taken as fact rather than mere theory for the purpose of arguing against theism.

The specific claim I wish to defend is the following:

> Antecedently, evolution is much more probable on the assumption that naturalism is true than on the assumption that theism is true.

By "antecedently" I mean "independent of the observations and testimony that together constitute the primary evidence upon which what we know about evolution, as well as the connection between pain and pleasure and reproductive success, is based." Thus, I intend to abstract from our information about selective breeding and other changes within populations of animals, as well as what we know about the geographical distribution of living things, homologies, the fossil record, genetic and biochemical evidence, imperfect adaptations, and vestigial organs. The additional abstraction concerning pain and pleasure is necessary because eventually I will combine my argument concerning evolution with an argument concerning the systematic connection between pain and pleasure and reproductive success. The claim will be made that evolution and this connection are, taken together, antecedently much more likely on naturalism than on theism. One last point. No other abstraction from what we know is intended. For example, I do not intend to abstract from our knowledge that complex life of various forms exists nor from our knowledge that this life has not always existed. It is an interesting and difficult question whether these facts are evidence favoring theism over naturalism, but that issue is beyond the scope of this paper.

Let "T," "N," and "E" stand for theism, naturalism and evolution, let "Pr(p)" stand for the antecedent probability of p being true, and let "Pr(p/q)" stand for the antecedent probability of p being true on the assumption that q is true. Finally, let ">!" stand for "is much greater than." The claim I wish to defend can now be restated as follows:

$$\text{Pr(E/N)} >! \text{Pr(E/T)}$$

My strategy for proving this claim requires one more symbol and one more definition. Let "S" stand for special creationism, by which I mean the statement that some relatively complex living things did not descend from relatively simple single-celled organisms but rather were independently created by a supernatural person. (The use of the word "independently" here signifies not just that the creation in question violates genealogical continuity, but also that it involves the direct intervention of the deity in the natural order.) Since evolution entails that special creationism is false, some basic theorems of the probability calculus give us:

$$\text{Pr(E/N)} >! \text{Pr(E/T) if and only if Pr(}\sim\text{S/N)} \times$$
$$\text{Pr(E/}\sim\text{S\&N)} >! \text{Pr(}\sim\text{S/T)} \times \text{Pr(E/}\sim\text{S\&T)}[7]$$

My strategy for establishing that Pr(E/N) >! Pr(E/T) will be to show both that Pr($\sim$S/N) >! Pr($\sim$S/T) and that Pr(E/$\sim$S&N) >! Pr(E/$\sim$S&T). In other words, I will show both that special creationism is antecedently much more likely to be false on naturalism than on theism and that, even on the assumption that special creationism is false, evolution is still antecedently at least as likely to be true on naturalism as it is on theism.

Since naturalism entails that no supernatural beings exist, it entails that special creationism is false. Thus, the falsity of special creationism is antecedently certain on naturalism: Pr($\sim$S/N) = 1. But on theism special creationism might, for all we know antecedently, be true: Pr($\sim$S/T) < 1. Thus, the falsity of special creationism is antecedently more probable on naturalism than on theism, which implies that the falsity of special creationism is some evidence favoring naturalism over theism— it raises the ratio of the probability of naturalism to the probability of theism. But how strong is this evidence? Is the falsity of special creationism *much* more probable on naturalism than on theism? I will

show that $\sim$S is at least twice as probable antecedently on naturalism as it is on theism, which implies that it at least doubles the ratio of the probability of naturalism to the probability of theism.[8] Since Pr($\sim$S/N) = 1, my task is to show that Pr($\sim$S/T) $\leq$ 1/2, which is to say that Pr(S/T) $\geq$ 1/2—that, independent of the evidence for evolution, special creationism is at least as likely as not on the assumption that theism is true. To defend this claim, I will first evaluate some antecedent reasons for believing that God, assuming he exists, did not create any complex living things independently. Then I will show that we have a very strong antecedent reason for believing that God, assuming he exists, did specially create.

At first glance, it seems that the evidence for evolution is the only strong reason theists have for believing that God is not a special creator (which is to say that we don't have any strong *antecedent* reasons for believing this). After all, for all we know antecedently, God might have chosen to create in a variety of different ways. For example, while he might have created life in a way consistent with genealogical continuity, he might also have created each species independently. Or he might have created certain basic types independently, allowing for evolutionary change, including change resulting in new species, within these types. Or he might have independently created only a few species or even only a single species, humans perhaps. Antecedently—that is, independent of the evidence for evolution—it appears we have no reason at all to think that an omnipotent, omniscient, and morally perfect creator would prefer evolution or any other "naturalistic" approach to one of these forms of special creation.

Some theists, however, are quite confident on purely *a priori* grounds that God is not a special creator. According to Diogenes Allen and Howard J. Van Till, for example, special creationism was implausible even before the evidence for evolution was discovered, because it is an implication of God's "rationality" or his status as creator rather than as "member of the universe" that God "creates a universe with members that are coherently connected."[9] This coherence precludes God's intervening in the natural order and hence precludes any sort of special creation, including the creation of those first simple life forms from which all subsequent life has evolved. Thus, according to these theists, the only sort of explanations of natural phenomena that theistic scientists should look for are ones that are consistent with naturalism. In short, these theists are committed methodological naturalists.

I don't find these arguments at all convincing. What possible justification could be given for thinking that if God were the immediate cause of a natural event that would reduce God's status from creator to "member of the universe"? Also, what does God's rationality have to do with this? Perhaps the idea is that, just as a perfectly rational car manufacturer would produce a car that never needed its gas tank filled or its air filter replaced, a perfectly rational creator would make a universe that ran on its own. But such a car would be preferable because filling up with gas or replacing parts has a cost in terms of time, energy, and so on. An omnipotent and omniscient creator wouldn't have such worries. In general, what counts as a rational or perfect or defective universe depends on the creator's goals. What goal or plan of God would be better served by a universe in which God never intervenes? Of course, human freedom may place limitations on the amount and type of God's interventions. But it doesn't rule out special creation. For all we know, God may have some goal that is furthered by the laws of nature we have, but those laws are such that they will not by themselves produce the sort of complex life God wants. If this were the case, then God would independently create that life. Surely such intervention in the course of nature would not conflict with God's status as creator or with his rationality. Nor would it imply that the universe is in some way defective or inferior to universes in which God never intervenes.

Another theist who holds that we have antecedent reasons for believing that God would not perform any special creative acts is the philosopher Ernan McMullin. In response to Alvin Plantinga's defense of special creationism, McMullin says that "from the theological and philosophical standpoints, such intervention is, if anything, antecedently *improbable*."[10] McMullin claims that "the eloquent texts of *Genesis, Job, Isaiah,* and *Psalms*" support his position, because "The Creator whose powers are gradually revealed in these texts is omnipotent and all-wise, far beyond the reach of human reckoning. His Providence extends to all His creatures; they are all part of His single plan, only a fragment of which we know, and that darkly."[11] But how this is supposed to support his position is never explained. It seems to do the opposite, since any claim to know that God would never intervene in the natural order will be difficult to justify if we are as much in the dark about God's plans as these texts suggest.[12]

Incidentally, I find it interesting that, when confronted with arguments against theism based on the idea that it is antecedently unlikely that God would permit heinous evil, theistic philosophers are quick to suggest that, since God is omniscient, humans are not in a position to make such a judgment. Yet, if we are to believe Allen and Van Till (McMullin has his doubts), then humans are in a position to judge that it is antecedently unlikely that God would create any life forms independently! Personally, I find the claim that the torturing of innocent children is antecedently improbable on theism vastly more plausible than the claim that special creationism is antecedently improbable on theism.

The problem with the theistic objections to special creationism considered so far is that they all involve *a priori* theological or philosophical speculation, the direction of which is influenced far too much by the conclusion desired.[13] Indeed, these attempts to make special creation seem incompatible with theism are no more objective and no more plausible than William B. Provine's attempt to make evolution seem incompatible with theism. While Allen, Van Till, and McMullin claim that God would never intervene in nature to create life, Provine claims that the idea of a God who "works through the laws of nature" is "worthless" and "equivalent to atheism."[14] How convenient!

A more serious attempt to show that special creationism is antecedently unlikely on theism is a posteriori in nature. We know by past experience that God, if he exists, has at least latent deistic tendencies. Teleology was, after all, eliminated from the physical sciences well before Darwin wrote *On the Origin of Species*. And even independent of the evidence for evolution there is considerable evidence that various biological processes work quite well without divine intervention. In general, even independent of the evidence on which evolution is based, the history of science is a history of success for naturalistic explanations and failure for supernaturalistic ones. Thus, we have a good antecedent *a posteriori* reason to believe that, assuming theism is true, God does not intervene in nature.

I believe that the past success of naturalistic science does provide some reason for theists to believe that God is not a special creator. But it is easy to overestimate the strength of this reason, especially for intellectual theists who must admit to living in a "post-mythological" era or else risk being held personally responsible for the plight of Galileo. But putting scientific propaganda aside, it is important to remember how little we actually know about the causal history of the universe! Were it not for the evidence for evolution, our sample of successful naturalistic explanations seems to me to be much too small to justify great confidence in the claim that, *assuming God exists*, God is not a special creator. Of course, it is worth mentioning that, if I am underestimating how successful the search for naturalistic explanations has been, then theists hardly escape unscathed. For if the search for such explanations has been so successful that any supernaturalistic explanation of a natural phenomenon is implausible even on the assumption that theism is true, then that would be powerful evidence against theism. For such extraordinary success would be antecedently much more likely on naturalism—which entails that all supernaturalistic explanations are false—than it would on theism.

More to the point, however, I believe theists have a very strong antecedent reason for believing that God did create at least some complex life independently. For the division between conscious and nonconscious life is enormously significant if theism is true. Theism implies an extreme metaphysical dualism—a mind existed prior to the physical world and was responsible for its existence. Thus, on the assumption that theism is true, it is antecedently likely that minds are fundamentally nonphysical entities and hence that conscious life is fundamentally different from nonconscious life. But this in turn makes it likely that conscious living things are not just the genetically modified descendents of nonconscious living things—that conscious life was created independently. And since special creationism is defined as the position that at least some complex life was created independently, it follows that, on the assumption that theism is true, it is antecedently likely that special creationism is true.

The dualism inherent in theism may explain why so many theists were drawn to the idea of special creationism before (and in many cases even after) the evidence for evolution was discovered. For this dualism supports a dualistic view of human nature—a view that must have made the idea that we are the effect of altering the nucleic acids of single-celled organisms seem ludicrous. Offspring don't have to be identical to their parents, but surely genetic change can't result in fundamental metaphysical lines being crossed! Thus, even if we know by past experience that God, assuming he exists, generally doesn't intervene in nature, the sort of metaphysics presupposed by theism makes it antecedently likely that God did intervene in the physical world in order to create a mental world within it. So it's hardly surprising that, before Darwin, many theists were special creationists. They had a good reason and we have a good *antecedent* reason to believe that God, assuming he or she exists, performed at least one special creative act. Thus, $\Pr(S/T) \geq 1/2$. And this implies that the falsity of special creationism is at least twice as probable antecedently on naturalism as it is on theism: $\Pr(\sim S/N) \geq 2 \times \Pr(\sim S/T)$.

Recall that, in order to show that $\Pr(E/N) >! \Pr(E/T)$, it is sufficient to show first that $\Pr(\sim S/N) >! \Pr(\sim S/T)$ and second that $\Pr(E/\sim S\&N) \geq \Pr(E/\sim S\&T)$. I have completed the first of these two tasks. Turning to the second, we are now assuming that special creationism is false and asking how likely evolution is on naturalism and on theism. Of course, naturalism entails that special creationism is false, so the denial of special creationism conjoined with naturalism (∼S&N) just is naturalism (N). I will call the denial of special creationism conjoined with theism (∼S&T) "regular theism." So my task is to show that evolution is antecedently at least as probable on naturalism as it is on regular theism.

It is important to recognize that the probabilities in question are to be assessed relative to the background knowledge that various complex life forms do exist. Thus, the issue is not whether complex life together with the evolutionary mechanisms that produce it are more surprising on theism or on naturalism. (Again, whether or not there is a good anthropic design argument supporting theism is beyond the scope of this paper.) Given that complex life exists, what makes evolution so likely on naturalism is the lack of plausible naturalistic alternatives to evolution. On naturalism, it is antecedently much more likely that all complex organisms descended from a small number of relatively simple organisms than that complex life descended from a large number of relatively simple single-celled organisms all of which arose independently from nonliving matter or that complex life arose directly from nonliving matter. Furthermore, given the genealogical thesis, it is antecedently likely on naturalism that all evolutionary change in complex life is or results from one basic sort of change like genetic change. On regular theism, alternatives to evolution are somewhat more likely, simply because there is less reason to assume that the complex must arise from the simple. When one starts with omnipotence and omniscience, so much is possible!

Even if the regular theist grants that these considerations favor naturalism, she might counter that it has never been proven that naturalistic evolution is biologically possible. Perhaps evolution could not have produced complex life without supernatural assistance. For example, it might be argued that, without some intelligent being guiding genetic change, such magnificent ordered systems as the human eye would never have evolved. The stronger the evidence for this, the lower the antecedent probability of evolution on naturalism. I do not believe, however, that the evidence for this is very

strong. Admittedly, no one can describe in detail exactly how the eye or any other complex organic system could have come about without supernatural assistance. And it's hard to see how anyone could prove that evolution could produce complex life in a naturalistic universe. But neither has anyone provided good reason for thinking that it couldn't either. (Some special creationists have tried, but their arguments are very weak.[15]) This is not to say that there are no real difficulties for naturalistic evolution. (For example, it's notoriously difficult to explain how sexual reproduction evolved.) It's just to say that no one has given a good reason to believe that naturalistic solutions to these problems will not be found. Indeed, the fact that plausible solutions have been found to some of these problems (e.g., the problem of altruistic behavior) gives the naturalist reason for optimism. So any advantage that the problems faced by naturalistic evolution give to regular theism is more than offset by the considerations favoring naturalism mentioned above. All things considered, then, the modest conclusion that evolution is at least as probable antecedently on naturalism as it is on regular theism is justified. Therefore, since the falsity of special creationism is antecedently much more probable on naturalism than on theism, it follows for the reasons explained earlier that evolution is antecedently much more probable on naturalism than on theism.

III. PAIN AND PLEASURE

It is true by definition that a morally perfect God would permit an instance of pain only if he or she had a morally sufficient reason to do so. (By "pain" I mean any suffering, physical or mental.) Thus, the "logical" problem of pain is the problem of whether or not God's being both omnipotent and omniscient is logically compatible with God's having a morally sufficient reason to permit all of the suffering in the world. No one has been able to demonstrate an incompatibility because not even an omnipotent being can do the logically impossible and it might, for all we know or can prove, be logically impossible to bring about certain important goods without at least risking the existence of the suffering we find in our world. So demonstrative logical arguments from pain have been unsuccessful. And nondemonstrative or probabilistic logical arguments from pain have been challenged on the grounds that they involve questionable inductive generalizations, questionable inferences from there being no *known* morally sufficient reasons for an omnipotent and omniscient being to permit certain instances of suffering to their probably being no such morally sufficient reasons. But these discussions of the logical problem of pain leave unsettled the issue of whether or not the suffering in our world is evidence against theism or evidence favoring naturalism over theism. In other words, the failure of logical arguments from evil, including probabilistic ones, does not preclude a successful evidential argument from evil.

I do not, however, wish to consider suffering in isolation. Instead, I will address the issue of whether the pattern of both pain and pleasure in the world is evidence favoring naturalism over theism. The more common strategy of focusing only on evil, indeed only on a few particularly heinous evils, has its advantages. I choose not to pursue this strategy because the theist might counter such an argument by pointing out a few particularly glorious goods and plausibly claiming that they are equally strong evidence favoring theism over naturalism. So my argument will be based on both pain and pleasure. There may, of course, be other intrinsic evils and intrinsic goods besides pain and pleasure, but the issue of whether or not there are, and whether or not, if there are, their existence is evidence against theism, will not be addressed in this paper.

There are many facts about pain and pleasure that might provide the resources for an evidential argument against theism. Because I wish to explore how our knowledge of evolution affects the problem of evil, I will focus on the fact that much of the pain and pleasure we find in the world is systematically connected (in a variety of often complex ways) to reproductive success. For example, it is no accident that we find a warm fire on a cold night pleasurable and lying naked in a snowbank painful. Maintaining a constant body temperature increases our chances of (temporary) survival and thereby increases our chances of reproducing. Of course, the connections are not all this obvious or this direct. For example, children enjoy playing, which promotes the development of various physical, social, and intellectual skills, which in turn increases children's chances of surviving and reproducing. Even less obviously and less directly, adults find play pleasurable (though typically not as much as children do), which may or may not promote reproductive success, but which results from our capacity to enjoy play as children, which, as we have seen, does promote reproductive success. I could give countless other examples, but the connection between pain and pleasure and reproductive success and the systematic nature of that connection is so striking that additional examples aren't really needed. Instead, I will now turn to the task of showing that, antecedently, this connection is much more probable on evolutionary naturalism than it is on evolutionary theism. I will offer a two-part argument for this position, and then reply to two objections.

The first part of my argument appeals to natural selection. I suggested earlier that Darwinism is much more likely to be true if evolutionary naturalism is true than if evolutionary theism is true. Allow me to explain why. Darwinism is likely on evolutionary naturalism both because it explains the increase in the complexity of life over time better than other naturalistic mechanisms and, most importantly for our purposes, it solves an explanatory problem for naturalism: the problem of explaining teleological or "means–end" order in organic systems. Since evolutionary theism can explain teleological order in terms of God's conscious purposes, it wouldn't be at all surprising on theism if the principal mechanisms driving evolution themselves displayed teleological order—if, for example, organisms had built-in mechanisms that would produce precisely those genetic changes needed to solve a problem arising because of some environmental change. (Such mechanisms would have made William Paley a happy evolutionist!) On naturalism, natural selection is just the sort of process one would expect to drive evolution: a simple "blind" process that can explain the extremely complex teleological order in the living world without itself displaying such order. Notice also that, contrary to popular belief, natural selection does not generally promote the good of individual animals. Variations that result in reproductive success will be favored, regardless of the other consequences—good or bad—of the variation. For example, if walking upright gave our distant ancestors a reproductive advantage (e.g., by allowing them to carry tools while they walked), then this trait was selected despite the foot, back, heart, and numerous other ailments that resulted from it. Further, natural selection requires competition for scarce resources and thus entails that many living things will not flourish. So the claim that natural selection is the principal mechanism driving evolutionary change is much more probable on evolutionary naturalism than on evolutionary theism.

Of course, if natural selection is the principal mechanism driving evolution, then it is likely on evolutionary naturalism that it played a significant role in the evolution of pain and pleasure and so it is likely on evolutionary naturalism that pain and pleasure will, like anything produced by natural selection, be systematically connected to reproductive success. Thus, the fact that natural selection is antecedently much more likely to have governed the evolution of pain and pleasure if evolutionary naturalism is true than if evolutionary theism is true supports my position that the systematic connection between reproductive success and the pain and pleasure we find in the world is antecedently much more likely on evolutionary naturalism than on evolutionary theism.

This position is further supported by our antecedent knowledge that many other parts of organic systems are systematically connected to reproductive success. This gives us much more reason to believe that pain and pleasure will also be so connected if we assume that evolutionary naturalism is true than if we assume that evolutionary theism is true. To see why, consider the inductive inference from a sample consisting of other physical and mental parts of organic systems that are systematically connected

to reproductive success to the conclusion that pain and pleasure are also systematically connected to reproductive success. Although a good number of parts of organic systems lack such a connection, this inference is potentially quite strong given the suitability of pain and pleasure for promoting reproductive success. But the assumption that evolutionary theism is true undermines this inference, while the assumption that evolutionary naturalism is true does not. To see why, notice that this inference is an inductive inference from a sample to another member of a population, and the strength of any such inference depends on how much reason one has to believe that this other member is relevantly different from the members of the sample. Now pain and pleasure are strikingly different from other parts of organic systems in one way: They have a specific sort of moral significance that other parts lack. (Other parts of organic systems may have moral significance, but not of the same sort.) But is this a relevant difference? We have much more reason to believe it is on the assumption that evolutionary theism is true than on the assumption that evolutionary naturalism is true. For the biological goal of reproductive success does not provide an omnipotent omniscient creator with a morally sufficient reason for permitting humans and animals to suffer in the ways they do or for limiting their pleasure to the sorts and amounts we find. Thus, on evolutionary theism, pain and pleasure would be systematically connected to the biological goal of reproductive success only if this goal and some unknown justifying moral goal happened to coincide in such a way that each could be simultaneously satisfied. Such a coincidence is (to say the least) antecedently far from certain. So on the assumption that evolutionary theism is true, the inference to the conclusion that pain and pleasure are systematically connected to reproductive success from the premise that other parts of organic systems are so connected is very weak. This inference is much stronger on the assumption that evolutionary naturalism is true because evolutionary naturalism entails nothing that would undermine the inference—on evolutionary naturalism the moral significance of pain and pleasure provides no antecedent reason at all to doubt that they will resemble other parts of organic systems by being systematically connected to reproductive success. Therefore, our antecedent knowledge that pain and pleasure have a certain sort of moral significance adds further support to my position that the systematic connection between pain and pleasure and reproductive success is antecedently much more probable on evolutionary naturalism than on evolutionary theism.

One might object that my argument ignores the many instances of pain and pleasure that are, so far as we can tell, disconnected from the biological goal of reproductive success. For example, some aesthetic pleasures seem to have at most a very remote connection to reproductive success. But neither the existence of such pain and pleasure, nor the fact that, in general, such pain and pleasure is more common in animals that are psychologically complex, is at all surprising on evolutionary naturalism. For the greater the complexity of a system, the more likely that some of its characteristics will be epiphenomenal. Also, much biologically gratuitous pain and pleasure is pathological—it results from the failure of an organic system to function properly. And the existence of this sort of pain and pleasure is also unsurprising on evolutionary naturalism. So on evolutionary naturalism, what we know about biologically gratuitous pain and pleasure is not surprising, while on evolutionary theism, the excess pleasure is perhaps to be expected, but this advantage is offset by the limited amount of such pleasure, by the existence of biologically gratuitous pain, and by the fact that a significant amount of biologically gratuitous pleasure and pain is pathological.

One might also object that theodicies undermine my argument; for theodicies make certain facts about pain antecedently more likely than they would otherwise be. The problem with existing theodicies, however, is that they explain certain facts at the price of making others even more mysterious. That is, they make certain facts more likely only by making others less likely. For example, if one of God's reasons for permitting pain is to punish sinners, then why do the innocent suffer as much as the guilty? Or, if we assume that God

wants to use pain to build moral character, then pain (and pleasure) that is demoralizing becomes even more surprising. If, instead of focusing on a few isolated cases, one looks at the overall pattern of pain and pleasure in the world, one cannot help but be struck by its apparent moral randomness. Pain and pleasure do not systematically promote justice or moral virtue. Nor are moral agents treated all that differently from nonmoral agents. Nonhuman animals suffer in many of the ways humans suffer (the more similar the animal, the more similar the suffering), despite the fact that such suffering cannot play a moral role in their lives, since they are not moral agents.

All of these facts, which might be summed up by saying that pain and pleasure do not systematically promote any discernible moral ends, are exactly what one would expect on evolutionary naturalism. For on evolutionary naturalism, the causes of good and evil are morally indifferent. Thus, on the assumption that evolutionary naturalism is true, it would be surprising in the extreme if pain and pleasure appeared to be anything but morally random. But a discernible moral pattern would be less surprising on theism even if, given the cognitive distance between humans and an omniscient being, it should not be expected. Notice that I am not claiming that the apparent moral randomness of pain and pleasure is antecedently unlikely on evolutionary theism. I'm just claiming that it is antecedently less likely on evolutionary theism than on evolutionary naturalism. And it seems to me that this is obvious. But that means that this apparent randomness adds to the evidence favoring evolutionary naturalism over evolutionary theism. It may not add a lot, but it certainly offsets any advantage evolutionary theism has as a result of the moral roles that pain and pleasure admittedly do play in human lives.

IV. CONCLUSION

I have argued both that evolution is antecedently much more probable on naturalism than on theism and that the systematic connection between pain, as well as pleasure, and reproductive success is antecedently much more probable on evolutionary naturalism than on evolutionary theism. This entails that the conjunction of evolution and the statement that pain and pleasure are systematically connected to reproductive success is antecedently very much more probable on naturalism than on theism. And since neither the truth nor falsity of naturalism or theism is certain, it follows that this conjunction substantially raises the ratio of the probability of naturalism to the probability of theism. Of course, if naturalism were far less plausible than theism (or if it were compatible with theism), then this sort of evidence would be worthless. But naturalism is a very serious alternative to theism. Neither evolution nor anything about pain and pleasure is built into it in an *ad hoc* way. (It is not as if I were claiming, for example, that *evolution* is antecedently more probable on *evolutionary* naturalism than on theism.) Also, naturalism doesn't deny the existence of all nonnatural beings—it only denies the existence of supernatural beings. And surely this is no less plausible than asserting the existence of a very specific sort of supernatural being. So naturalism is at least as plausible as theism.

Therefore, it follows from my arguments concerning evil and evolution that, other evidence held equal, naturalism is very much more probable than theism. And since naturalism and theism are alternative hypotheses—they cannot both be true—this implies that, other evidence held equal, it is highly likely that theism is false. So the evidence discussed in this paper provides a powerful *prima facie* case against theism. To put it another way, if one looks only at the evidence discussed here—evolution, the ability of natural selection to explain complex biological order without purpose, the systematic connection between pain and pleasure and reproductive success, and the apparent moral randomness of pain and pleasure—then Hume's words ring true: "The whole presents nothing but the idea of a blind nature, impregnated by a great vivifying principle, and pouring forth from her lap, without discernment or parental care, her maimed and abortive children."[16,17]

APPENDIX

My argument in this paper is based on the following two theorems of the probability calculus:

$$A : \frac{\Pr(N/E\&P)}{\Pr(T/E\&P)} = \frac{\Pr(N)}{\Pr(T)} \times \frac{\Pr(E\&P/N)}{\Pr(E\&P/T)}$$

$$B : \frac{\Pr(E\&P/N)}{\Pr(E\&P/T)} = \frac{\Pr(E/N)}{\Pr(E/T)} \times \frac{\Pr(P/E\&N)}{\Pr(P/E\&T)}$$

In using these two equations, I assume that neither naturalism nor theism is certainly true or certainly false.

$\Pr(N/E\&P)$ is the antecedent probability of naturalism given the conjunction of evolution and the statement (P) that pain and pleasure are systematically connected to reproductive success. In other words, it is the probability of naturalism, all things considered. (I assume here that the "given E&P" puts back everything of significance that the "antecedent" takes out.) Similarly, $\Pr(T/E\&P)$ is the probability of theism, all things considered. So the left side of equation A is the ratio of the probability of naturalism to the probability of theism. If this ratio is greater than 1, then naturalism is more probable than theism and hence theism is probably false.

Now consider the right side of equation A. The main purpose of my paper was to evaluate the second ratio here: The ratio of the antecedent probability of evolution conjoined with P given naturalism to the antecedent probability of this conjunction given theism. This ratio was evaluated using equation B. The first of the two ratios on the right side of B is the ratio of the antecedent probability of evolution given naturalism to the antecedent probability of evolution given theism. And the second is the ratio of the antecedent probability of P given evolutionary naturalism to the antecedent probability of P given evolutionary theism. I argued that each of these two ratios is much greater than 1. From this it follows (using equation B) that the ratio of $\Pr(E\&P/N)$ to $\Pr(E\&P/T)$ is very much greater than 1.

Now look at the first ratio on the right side of equation A. $\Pr(N)$ is the antecedent probability of naturalism. In other words, it is the probability of naturalism independent of our knowledge of E&P. And

Pr(T) is the probability of theism independent of our knowledge of E&P. So the first ratio on the right side of equation A depends on the plausibility of naturalism and theism as well as on other evidence (propositional or nonpropositional) for and against naturalism and theism (e.g., the existence of life on earth, the success of science, religious experiences, immorality, etc.). I argued very briefly that considerations of plausibility do not give us any reason to believe that this ratio is less than one. But I did not, of course, evaluate all of the other relevant evidence for and against theism and naturalism. So I did not come to any conclusion about this first ratio. This is why my case against theism is a *prima facie* one. I am entitled to conclude only that, other evidence held equal, the ratio on the left side of equation A is very much greater than 1. And this implies that, other evidence held equal, it is highly probable that theism is false.

The following summarizes my argument:

(1) Evolution is antecedently much more probable on the assumption that naturalism is true than on the assumption that theism is true [i.e., Pr(E/N) >! Pr(E/T)].

(2) The statement that pain and pleasure are systematically connected to reproductive success is antecedently much more probable on the assumption that evolutionary naturalism is true than on the assumption that evolutionary theism is true [i.e., Pr(P/E&N) >! Pr(P/E&T)].

(3) Therefore, evolution conjoined with this statement about pain and pleasure is antecedently very much more probable on the assumption that naturalism is true than on the assumption that theism is true [i.e., Pr(E&P/N) >!! Pr(E&P/T)]. (From 1 and 2)

(4) Naturalism is at least as plausible as theism [i.e., other evidence held equal, Pr(N) ≥ Pr(T)].

(5) Therefore, other evidence held equal, naturalism is very much more probable than theism [i.e., other evidence held equal, Pr(N/ E&P) >!! Pr(T/E&P)]. (From 3 and 4)

(6) Naturalism entails that theism is false.

(7) Therefore, other evidence held equal, it is highly probable that theism is false [i.e., other evidence held equal, Pr(T/E&P) <!! 1/2]. (From 5 and 6)

NOTES

1. By "hypothesis" I mean a statement that is neither certainly true nor certainly false.

2. It is worth noting that, although "probabilistic" arguments from evil are usually classified as evidential, many such arguments are logical—they attempt to show that theism is probably inconsistent with some known fact about evil.

3. "Darwinism Defined: The Difference Between Fact and Theory," *Discover*, Jan. 1987, p. 70. Quoted in James Rachels, *Created from Animals: The Moral Implications of Darwinism* (Oxford University Press, 1990), p. 100.

4. Quoted in Phillip E. Johnson, *Darwin on Trial* (InterVarsity Press, 1993), p. 126.

5. "The Two Revelations," in Gail Kennedy, *Evolution and Religion* (D. C. Heath and Company, 1957), p. 20. Also quoted on p. xiv.

6. Quoted in Kennedy, p. xiv.

7. Proof: Since E entails S, E is logically equivalent to ∼S&E. Thus, since it is a theorem of the probability calculus that logically equivalent statements are equally probable, it follows that Pr(E/N) >! Pr(E/T) if and only if Pr(∼S&E/N) >! Pr(∼S&E/T). But it is also a theorem of the probability calculus that Pr(p&q/r) = Pr(p/r) × Pr(q/p&r). Therefore, Pr(E/N) >! Pr(E/T) if and only if Pr(∼S/N) × Pr(E/∼S&N) >! × Pr(E/∼S&T).

8. Of course, whether this strong evidence is also significant depends on what the ratio of the probability of naturalism to the probability of theism is prior to considering the fact that special creationism is false. If it is extremely high or low, then the falsity of special creationism will not be significant evidence favoring naturalism. If, on the other hand, the other evidence is nearly balanced and both hypotheses are plausible, then this evidence will be significant. For example, if theism

starts out twice as probable as naturalism, then the two hypotheses will end up being equally probable.

9. Diogenes Allen, *Christian Belief in a Postmodern World* (Westminster: John Knox Press, 1989), p. 59. Quoted with approval in Howard J. Van Till, "When Faith and Reason Cooperate," *Christian Scholar's Review* 21.1 (1991), p. 43.

10. "Plantinga's Defense of Special Creation," *Christian Scholar's Review* 21.1 (1991), p. 74. Plantinga refers to McMullin's position as "semideism." McMullin complains that this terminology is loaded, yet he describes his own position as believing in "the integrity of the natural order." It would seem then that Christians have a dilemma. No good Christian wants to be called a "deist," but no good Christian would want to deny that God's creation has "integrity"!

11. Ibid., p. 75.

12. For additional criticisms of the positions of Van Till and McMullin, see Alvin Plantinga, "Evolution, Neutrality, and Antecedent Probability: A Reply to Van Till and McMullin," *Christian Scholar's Review* 21.1 (1991), pp. 80–109.

13. Cf. Plantinga, p. 100.

14. Review of "Trial and Error: The American Controversy over Creation and Evolution," *Academe* 73.1 (1987), 50–52. Quoted in McMullin, p. 58.

15. For an excellent defense of evolution against special creationist objections, see Philip Kitcher, *Abusing Science: The Case Against Creationism* (Cambridge, Massachusetts: The MIT Press, 1982).

16. *Dialogues Concerning Natural Religion*, ed. Norman Kemp Smith (Macmillan Publishing Co., 1947), p. 211.

17. I am grateful to Kai Draper, Daniel Howard Snyder, James Keller, George Mavrodes, Wes Morriston, William L. Rowe, Michael Tooley, and Stephen J. Wykstra for helpful comments on earlier versions of this paper.

III.B.4

Whose Problem Is the "Problem of Evil"?

GRACE M. JANTZEN

Grace M. Jantzen (1948–2006) was professor of religion, culture, and gender at the University of Manchester and was a leading feminist philosopher and theologian. Her most influential work lies at the intersection of French continental philosophy, feminist theology, and philosophy of religion; she has also made important contributions to the study of Western medieval mysticism. She is the author of numerous articles and several important books, including Julian of Norwich: Mystic and Theologian *(Paulist Press, 1987) and* Becoming Divine: Toward a Feminist Philosophy of Religion *(Indiana University Press, 1999). In this excerpt from* Becoming Divine, *she provides a feminist critique of the traditional framing of the problem of evil, arguing that not only have important alternative conceptions of God been neglected on both sides of the discussion, but important philosophical questions about the relationships between God, religion, and evil have been too long ignored. Note that her essay makes use of three terms*

From *Becoming Divine: Towards a Feminist Philosophy of Religion* by Grace M. Jantzen. (Indiana University Press, 1999). © 1999 by Grace Jantzen. Used with permission of Indiana University Press, Manchester University Press, and the estate of Grace Jantzen.

that may be unfamiliar to readers: (1) Natals is a term she uses for methodological reasons in place of the term mortals. Whereas mortals are "beings who die," natals are "beings who are born." She makes this distinction because she thinks philosophy of religion tends to be overly concerned with death and the afterlife, rather than with birth and this present life. (2) The term onto-theology refers to a way of doing theology that treats God as a being posited to explain phenomena in the world (e.g., the appearance of design), and that also presupposes that human reason is a reliable tool for arriving at clear and accurate knowledge of God. (3) The term the face of the Other was explained earlier, in the introduction to Part III.B.

The problem of evil is normally set out in traditional philosophy of religion as a conundrum for the orthodox believer who cannot avoid mutually incompatible beliefs: that God, being omnipotent and omniscient, could have created a world without evil if "he" chose (or could eradicate the evil in this world); that God, being wholly good, would choose to eradicate evil; and yet that evil exists (Peterson 1992: 3). This argument is then used by those who would discredit theism as a way of showing that such a God cannot exist (Mackie 1982). Those who wish to retain their belief in God, however, try to show how the apparently incompatible beliefs can be reconciled after all. One standard form of such a strategy is known as the "free-will defence," which aims to show that omnipotence requires only that God be able to do all logically possible things. However, it is not logically possible to create a world which is simultaneously free of evil and contains human beings with freedom of choice, and such freedom allegedly outweighs the evils of the world (Swinburne 1979: 200; Plantinga 1992). Another form is to argue that the world is a "veil of soul-making," in which evil and suffering are a necessary condition for moral progress, individual or collective (Hick 1968); or, less frequently in philosophical literature but still often found in popular writings, that what is apparently evil is not really so in the overall divine plan. The variations and combinations of these themes are then discussed with considerable vigour and ever-increasing intellectual sophistication, as also are the arguments against them (cf. Peterson 1992).

The discussion is clearly framed within the realist assumptions of onto-theology rather than from the perspective of a religious symbolic, let alone one which takes process, becoming divine, seriously. As has frequently been noted in the course of this book, it is the God of the west that is once again central to the philosophical discussion of the problem of evil: the conundrum does not arise unless the attributes of omnipotence, omniscience, and goodness are explicitly accepted as those of the God of the western onto-theological tradition. I have already discussed in several different ways the valorization of power and control which this account of God assumes and perpetuates, whether or not one believes that such a God exists: those same valorizations repeat themselves here. Even the term "theodicy," which is usually given to attempted resolutions of the problem of evil, means "to justify God"—that is, to show how a morally good omni-everything deity can be justified in permitting evil. The assumption throughout is that this is the only God worth talking about. But as we have seen, if we were to proceed by criteria of trustworthiness, thinking in terms of justice in the face of the natals and acting for love of the world, then such onto-theological assumptions are heavily problematized.

To be more specific, the outrageously unjust contextual values of the masculinist symbolic implicit in discussions of the problem of evil quickly show themselves when we ask what sorts of evils are suffered, and by whom; who inflicts them, and who benefits. What sort of flourishing is possible for natals in relation to these evils? Thus for example in "veil of soul-making" or "free-will" theodicies, where evil and suffering are held to be permitted for the overall moral progress or flourishing of humanity, it is important to ask whose face is the face of the Other. Are those who suffer the same as those who make progress? If so, then obviously the suffering has not been so great as to kill them or to incapacitate them for positive moral choices: those who are dead or mad or utterly demoralized cannot make moral progress. Yet much suffering kills or maddens. It does not lead to flourishing, even of this rarefied moral/spiritual variety. Are the lives of those who suffer to such acute degrees expendable for "our" moral progress? This point has of course often been raised, classically by Dostoevsky in *The Brothers Karamazov*, where Ivan protests that all the moral progress of the world stinks of corruption if it is bought at the price of the suffering of even one innocent victim.

Nevertheless, there is in many discussions of the "problem of evil" an implicit assumption that "they" suffer—in earthquakes, famines, wars, extermination camps—and that "we" learn from this suffering: "we" who are paradigmatically white, wealthy, highly privileged, and often male philosophers of religion. The obscenity of the idea that horrendous suffering for "them" is morally justified if it brings about the moral progress of "mankind"—read "us"—is matched by the iniquitous effect of this sort of discussion of the "problem of evil" in the first place. By making it an intellectual problem to be solved, concentration on the adequacy or inadequacy of the preferred solution can take up all the time and energy that could otherwise be devoted to doing something about the suffering itself. It is a classic case of the effect of prioritizing the onto-theological above the ethical, against which Levinas pitted himself.

The values of the symbolic which form the way in which the problem of evil is presented and discussed in fact exact a high moral cost in several respects. In the first place, as Ken Surin has eloquently shown in his book *Theology and the Problem of Evil* (1986), the assumption that the central significance of the problem of evil is its bearing on the God of the west, and on whether or not such a God could be justified in permitting the evil and suffering of the world, all too easily falls from an attempt to justify God into an implicit justification of the evil itself. After all, if evil is necessary in order to produce a greater good, such as "our" moral progress, then the urgency to eradicate evil is considerably undermined. Why should "we" be overly concerned to eliminate the political causes of homelessness or of the deprivation of people in materially deprived countries, if these forms of suffering contribute to

"our" development of generosity and compassion (to say nothing of "our" affluence)? If there are good reasons why a good and omnipotent God should permit evil, then surely that evil is permissible, and it would be futile for "us" to struggle against it.

Moreover, the discussion of whether God could be justified in permitting evil is regularly focused in such a way as to divert attention away from the question of where the evil comes from: who is it that is causing suffering, and to whom? Which natals, whose faces, present themselves? In traditional philosophy of religion the distinction is regularly made, of course, between natural and moral evil. Moral evil is what humans inflict on one another; natural evil is that which brings about suffering without any human agency being involved: disease, earthquake, and natural disaster are frequently cited examples, though with human interference in the natural world from genetics to the ozone layer, the line between natural and moral evil is ever thinner. However, in either case the "problem of evil" focuses on God rather than on human agency: why does God permit natural evils? Why does God permit human beings to do evil? Again, whatever the answers to these questions, and whether those evaluating the answers think them adequate or not, the focus of attention is diverted within this presentation away from what human beings are doing or might be doing to inflict or prevent evil, away from the earth and into the transcendent realm. It is a study in necrophilia.

Of course, it would be possible to object that while it is important to work against evil in every way we can, this is not the same thing as asking the philosophical question, and although the former task is incomparably more urgent than the latter, this does not mean that the latter is not important at all. Both are significant: there is no need to choose between them. Yet I suggest that while there is some plausibility in this response, it also masks important issues. The plausibility arises from the fact that it is indeed important, perhaps especially so at a time when the religious right is steadily gaining ground, for those attracted to belief in an omni-everything God to confront the question of whether that belief is actually compatible with the suffering of this world, and to explore the values implicit in the symbolic of such an onto-theological system. However, such an exploration could occur most helpfully in conjunction with actual engagement with evil and its causes. The face of the Other presents itself daily as people sleep rough, battered women seek refuge, and thousands are displaced by war and maimed by landmines. If we dare to face the Other, the intellectual questions will come thick and fast in such contexts, and the plausibility of answers will immediately be tested. There is much less scope for disengaged intellectual gymnastics, and much less patience with answers trotted out by privileged academics. It is, in short, more trustworthy to the flourishing of natals. When academics discussing the problem of evil begin to encourage the participants in that discussion to be actively involved in the struggle with suffering rather than defending themselves by saying that these are two separate issues, then their claim that active engagement and philosophical reflection are both important and should not be set up as false alternatives will be much more deserving of respect. As things stand, however, even the insistence that these are false alternatives slips readily into embracing the intellectual questions at the expense of active engagement, and thereby aligns itself with an expression of death rather than promoting the love of the world.

Moreover, if the response is that the problem of evil, or the development of a theodicy, just is the central philosophical question, then it is necessary to ask (again!) *why* this is so. Why is it not at least as important to ask who is committing evil, and against whom? If the reply is that these are, of course, important issues, but they do not belong to the philosophy of religion, then we are back again to the question of how the boundaries of the discipline are drawn up, and by whom. I have indicated more than once in this book that a study of the strategies of power and gender in the disciplining of religion is long overdue; and I hope to turn to it in another book. Here I can only repeat what I have already urged, namely that since religions concern themselves in large part with human propensity to evil and to good, surely it should be central to the philosophy of religion to take seriously questions about perpetrators and victims, and especially the ways in

which religion itself fosters or inhibits the infliction of evil and enables or impedes resistance to it. By any standards, western christendom, which has to a large extent been the religion of the dominant, has a great deal to answer for; and philosophers and theologians have been its intellectual servants. By refusing to engage with the question of the human distribution of evil and focusing instead on theodicy, it is possible to evade questions of domination and victimization while still appearing to "deal with" the problem of evil. It is parallel to the preoccupation noted in relation to the issues of morality and religion of being concerned only with one's own moral status rather than with its effects on others, keeping one's own hands clean though the rest of the world may go to hell; only here it is God's moral status that is being protected. What sort of symbolic of the divine does such a preoccupation bespeak?

From this perspective it is not surprising that the way the question is framed is not challenged by those on either side of the debate, and it is also apparent how a feminist critique can begin. Whether philosophers of religion believe that an adequate defence against the problem of evil can be developed or not, there is no large-scale demand among traditional philosophers of religion (exceptions like Ken Surin notwithstanding) that the whole issue be broadened to consider the human as well as the divine responsibility for suffering and how that responsibility is apportioned. What we find instead is a striking parallel to what we already noted in relation to the debates about the existence of God and about religion and morality: a collusion between those on both sides of the debate about how the question should be set out. As in the former cases there was substantial agreement about what sort of God was worth discussion, and any other concept of God was deemed unworthy of notice, so in this case there is agreement that debate centres on whether or not such a God could permit evil. Where the discussion of the problem of evil adds a further dimension is in the collusion of both sides to concentrate wholly on the issue of *divine* responsibility for evil and suffering and not investigate the human responsibility, and especially the unevenness of human responsibility between the powerful and the powerless. Nor is there willingness to consider the religious legitimation for that unevenness. Both sides proceed from a detached intellectual perspective, as privileged onlookers, rather than in solidarity with those in suffering. The technologies of dominance of largely privileged white male academics for the structuring of the philosophy of religion could hardly be clearer.

Process theologians with their emphasis on a God who suffers alongside the suffering of the world strike a somewhat different and welcome note here, since the obvious corollary of their position is the implication that solidarity with those who are suffering is of supreme importance. Yet in the works of such writers as Whitehead and Hartshorne, while there is obvious sensitivity and concern, there is little attention paid to actual suffering and how it comes about, who are the victims and who are the perpetrators. In this respect they are not different from other traditional philosophers of religion, in spite of the fact that they do tender a radically different concept of the divine, and thus are an exception to the general agreement that only the classical concept of God is worthy of discussion. Nevertheless, in their emphasis on divine becoming and their recognition that this divine becoming importantly includes involvement with the suffering of the world, there are implicit in their work aspects of a religious symbolic which can be appropriated for a feminist philosophy of religion.

From a feminist perspective, becoming divine is inseparable from solidarity with human suffering: a symbolic of the divine is a symbolic of outrage, imagination and desire, and compassionate action, not the detached and objective intellectual stance which traditional philosophers of religion assume and which they take also to be characteristic of God. A feminist approach to the "problem of evil" is first of all outrage and bewilderment at the suffering and evil itself: how *can* the world be like this? How *dare* some people make others suffer in the way that they do? What sort of divinity could we possibly be talking about if such suffering is allowed to continue? Now it is certainly true that some of the traditional discussion of the problem of evil does arise from the distress which philosophers of religion feel at the suffering and evil in the world. But whereas much of the traditional discussion of the problem seems to transform that distress into intellectual hot air, a feminist strategy intent on becoming divine would be to use the power of that anger in the work of love (Harrison 1985: 3), transforming outrage into solidarity and compassionate action for love of the world, recognizing and accepting the solidarity and compassion of one another also in our own suffering. Such action for love of the world obviously includes theory, but theory where imaginative insight has an important place. Rather than the development of theory becoming a diversion from action, theory is a reflection upon action, an effort to enable the action to be intelligent and creative rather than simply reactive. Whereas standard treatments of the problem of evil in the philosophy of religion set out the intellectual problems and use examples of actual suffering to illustrate their case, a feminist approach would be to start from engagement with suffering at some concrete level and see what sorts of theory such engagement requires or would find helpful. The struggle against suffering and injustice and towards flourishing takes precedence, beyond comparison, to the resolution of intellectual problems; and although it is important that the struggle is an intelligent one, there is no excuse for theory ever becoming a distraction from the struggle for justice itself. This is another way of putting the point of the previous chapter: onto-theology must not take precedence over response to the face of the Other.

This means that a feminist philosophy of religion will concentrate on the very questions which tend to be silenced by traditional accounts of the "problem of evil" and skated over too quickly even by process philosophers. The issue is not so much "how can a good God permit evil?" as it is "how are the resources of religion, particularly christendom, used by those who inflict evil on others? How are they used by those who resist?" And above all, "what does the face of the Other require of me, and how can I best respond for love of the world?" Posing the questions in this way means paying attention to who actually are the perpetrators of suffering, considering both the individuals and the structures within which they are embedded. It means also considering both how traditional theistic doctrines of power, mastery, and hierarchical patterns of domination feed into the ideologies propping up the structures of domination and reinforce racism, sexism, poverty, and homophobia. The question of what religion has to do with evil and suffering is thus posed in much more concrete ways, with a refusal to distract attention from the specific acts of evil that some specific human beings inflict on other specific human beings to a generalized and supernaturalized account, as though "evil" were some abstract monolithic entity which "God" permits or not.

And if the objection returns that these are different questions from those which are normally asked in the philosophy of religion, in fact that this is not properly philosophy of religion at all, then the response is that indeed they are different questions, and about time too. It has been the burden of this book that part of what is wrong with traditional philosophy of religion is precisely that such questions are not normally asked, which is why the philosophy of religion as it stands requires radical critique. That a feminist philosophy of religion which seeks a new symbolic and social order requires an altered demarcation of the boundaries of the philosophy of religion is not an objection, it is part of the point. Philosophy of religion more

intent on preserving the boundaries of the discipline than in engaging with issues of how particular religious beliefs perpetuate or alleviate suffering is in urgent need of exactly such radical revision, so that it can point the way, not towards a justification of the status quo, but towards becoming divine, towards the flourishing of natals.

REFERENCES

Mackie, J. L. 1982. *The Miracle of Theism: Arguments for and Against the Existence of God.* Oxford: Oxford University Press.

Peterson, Michael (ed.). 1992. *The Problem of Evil: Selected Readings.* Notre Dame, Ind.: University of Notre Dame Press.

Plantinga, Alvin. 1992. "Is Belief in God Properly Basic?" in R. Douglas Geivett and Brendan Sweetman (eds.), *Contemporary Perspectives in Religious Epistemology.* New York: Oxford University Press.

Surin, Kenneth. 1986. *Theology and the Problem of Evil.* Oxford: Blackwell.

Swinburne, Richard. 1979. *The Existence of God.* Oxford: Clarendon Press.

III.B.5

Divine Hiddenness Justifies Atheism

J. L. SCHELLENBERG

J. L. Schellenberg (1959–) is professor of philosophy at Mount Saint Vincent University in Canada. He has written numerous articles and books in the philosophy of religion, and is best known for his work on the hiddenness of God. In the present article, Schellenberg argues from the fact that divine hiddenness occurs to the conclusion that disbelief in God is justified.

Reprinted from *Contemporary Debates in Philosophy of Religion,* ed. Michael L. Peterson and Raymond VanArragon. (© Blackwell, 2004). Reproduced with permission of Blackwell Publishing Ltd.

Arguments from divine hiddenness often go unnoticed in the consideration of arguments for and against the existence of God—where by "God" is meant the *traditional* God: a separate but infinite consciousness, a personal and perfect creator of the universe. Perhaps the most interesting variety of this oversight occurs when people find themselves unable to settle the question of God's existence and therefore inclined toward agnosticism without noticing that these facts are *themselves* relevant to their quest and may support atheism. Of course, we need to be careful here. If by "God is hidden" you mean "There is an actually existing God who hides from us," it will be short work proving that divine hiddenness provides no basis for atheism. For how could a premise asserting the *actual existence* of God lead to the conclusion that God *does not exist?* But perhaps the careful reader will be able to see that it is also possible to take the language of hiddenness less literally—as referring simply to the absence of convincing evidence for the existence of God, or, more specifically, to the absence of some kind of positive experiential result in the search for God. That is how it will be taken here. I begin with an argument from analogy focused on the latter, more specific form of hiddenness. The possibility of broadening and strengthening this argument through a closer look at the concept of divine love is then considered. The first argument will here be called "the Analogy Argument"; its sibling, naturally, is called "the Conceptual Argument."

1 THE ANALOGY ARGUMENT

Imagine yourself in the following situation. You're a child playing hide-and-seek with your mother in the woods at the back of your house. You've been crouching for some time now behind a large oak tree, quite a fine hiding place but not undiscoverable—certainly not for someone as clever as your mother. However, she does not appear. The sun is setting, and it will soon be bedtime, but still no mother. Not only isn't she finding you, but, more disconcerting, you can't *hear* her anywhere: she's not beating the nearby bushes, making those exaggerated "looking for you" noises, and talking to you meanwhile as mothers playing this game usually do. Now imagine that you start *calling* for your mother. Coming out from behind the tree, you yell out her name, over and over again. "Mooooommmmm!" But no answer. You look everywhere: through the woods, in the house, down to the road. An hour passes, and you are growing hoarse from calling. Is she anywhere around? Would she fail to answer if she were around?

Now let's change the story a little. You're a child with amnesia—apparently because of a blow to the head (which of course you don't remember), your memory goes back only a few days—and you don't even know whether you *have* a mother. You see other children with their mothers and think it would sure be nice to have one. So you ask everyone you meet and look everywhere you can, but without forwarding your goal in the slightest. You take up the search anew each day, looking diligently, even though the strangers who took you in assure you that your mother must be dead. But to no avail. Is this what we should expect if you really have a mother and she is around, and aware of your search? When in the middle of the night you tentatively call out—"Mooooommmmm!"—would she not answer if she were really within earshot?

Let's change the story one more time. You're still a small child, and an amnesiac, but this time you're in the middle of a vast rain forest, dripping with dangers of various kinds. You've been stuck there for days, trying to figure out who you are and where you came from. You don't remember having a mother who accompanied you into this jungle, but in your moments of deepest pain and misery you call for her anyway: "MOOOOOMMMMM!" Over and over again. For days and days ... the last time when a jaguar comes at you out of nowhere ... but with no response. What should you think in this situation? In your dying moments, what should cross your mind? Would the thought that you have a mother who cares about you and hears your cry and *could* come to you but chooses *not* to even make it onto the list?

Now perhaps we could suppose, in each of these cases, that you *do* have a mother and that she *is* around, but that she simply *doesn't* care. We are inclined to think of mothers as almost by definition loving and caring, but just remember the mother of Hyde in *That 70s Show,* someone might say. Another possibility is that your mother has been prevented from doing what mothers tend naturally to do by factors external to her own desire and will: perhaps she fell into a deep well in the woods, or was kidnapped by that escaped convict who was spotted near town last week (from whose clutches you narrowly escaped, suffering only a memory-erasing blow to the head), or is fending off a crocodile even as you succumb to the jaguar. What we *can't* say is that a *loving* mother would in circumstances like these be hidden from her child *if she could help it.*

The first step in the Analogy Argument is the defense of this claim. As we might put it, our job is to find the proper filling for the blank at the end of the following sentence: "A loving mother would not be hidden from her child in circumstances like those mentioned if she could help it *because —.*" What we need here are propositions specifying the properties of love *in virtue of which* the claim appearing in front of the "because" is true. These would, I suggest, include the following: (1) A loving mother would consider each of her child's serious requests important and seek to provide a quick response. (2) A loving mother would wish to spare her child needless trauma, or, more positively, would wish to foster her child's physical and emotional well-being. (3) A loving mother would seek to avoid encouraging in her child false or misleading thoughts about herself or about their relationship. (4) A loving mother would want personal interaction with her child whenever possible, for the joy it brings as well as for its own sake. (5) A loving mother would *miss* her child if separated from her. It is clear that each of these propositions is true. It is also clear that, *if* they are true, the claim we are defending is true—that no loving mother who could help it would be hidden from her child in circumstances like those mentioned. We may therefore conclude that the latter claim *is* true.

The next step in the Analogy Argument involves pointing out that there are, in the actual world, circumstances of *divine* hiddenness very

similar to the circumstances we have highlighted in respect of our fictional mother and child. The relevant circumstances in our stories are those in which the mother is sought by the child but not found. Well, just so, God is (and has often been) hidden from many human beings: sought but not found. Some persons start out assured of the power and presence of God in their lives, and then *lose* all this—in the typical case because of reasoning that engenders doubt about the reliability of the support they have for theistic belief. And though they grieve what they have lost and seek to regain it, looking for God in all the old familiar places as well as in new, unfamiliar locales, they fail to do so: God seems simply absent, and their belief is gone. The situation of such individuals is relevantly similar to that of the child in the first story. Other persons don't start out in what they consider to be a relationship with God but, nonetheless, are, in their wanderings and in their attempts to determine where they belong, open to finding and being found by a divine parent; some of them seek long and hard for God, wishing to be related in love to God. But though they seek, they do not find. Their situation is relevantly similar to that of the second child. And many seekers, because of the inhospitable place this world can sometimes be, are at one time or another in a lot of *trouble,* and so have not only the usual and obvious reasons to seek to be united (or reunited) with a divine parent: they are also in serious need of divine help, calling out to God in conditions of great suffering and pain. But a divine answer to their calls is not forthcoming. What we see here is clearly relevantly similar to the situation of the third child.

Additional stories can be imagined, with features equally troubling from the perspective of motherly care, corresponding to other aspects of the form of divine hiddenness we are considering. We might have our first child, after many calls for her mother, hearing sounds in the woods that she is sure mark her mother's presence, but which turn out to come from nothing more than leaves rolling in the wind. This is like the experience of those who think they have detected traces of God in some happening or argument, only to have the former's theological significance undermined by convincing reinterpretation or the latter proved unsound. Our second child might come to be adopted by the strangers who take her in, and brought up in a manner that leaves her predisposed to be suspicious instead of trusting, calculatingly self-centered instead of generous and giving; or perhaps she comes to have experiences which cause her to deny the importance of personal relationship with a parent in the development of a child. This can be compared to what happens in the life of a seeker who, because of the influence of those who *do* answer her calls, is led to develop a character contrary to that which the God of traditional theism is said to desire for us, or whose search leads to religious experiences all right, but *nontheistic* ones. Clearly, the analogies between our fictional situations of parental hiddenness and the actual facts of divine hiddenness are very close.

So what can be done with these analogies? Well, the next step in the argument involves showing that what we have said about a mother's love applies to God as well. This is fairly easily done. For God, on the traditional theistic view we are challenging, is not only loving and caring, but *unsurpassably* loving and caring. Indeed, it seems that each of our propositions (1) to (5) above must specify a property that applies as much to God as to the mother. If God gives birth to the human race and is related to its members in a manner that is unimaginably close, caring, and loving, then surely: (1′) God would consider each serious request submitted by God's human children important and seek to provide a quick response; (2′) God would wish to spare human beings needless trauma or, more positively, would wish to foster their physical and emotional well-being; (3′) God would seek not to encourage in human beings false or misleading thoughts about God or about the divine-human relationship; (4′) God would want personal interaction with human beings whenever possible, for the joy it brings as well as for its own sake; and (5′) God would *miss* such personal interaction if it were absent.

Now perhaps someone will say that God might be totally different from ourselves, and thus unlike a human mother. But there are certain conceptual constraints that need to be respected here. Of course we don't mean that God should be conceptualized as physical and as biologically female. But situations of human interaction and discussions of human interaction, including interaction between mothers and their children, do represent the primary contexts in which such concepts as those of "closeness," "care," and "love" are used and acquire their meanings. What, then, could justify the supposition that God's closeness, caring, and loving would not be like those of the ideal mother, displayed in a manner appropriate to the divine nature (e.g., through religious experience instead of physical touching)? The question is rhetorical. Clearly what we have said about the best mother's love must in this way apply to God as well.

An important conclusion may now be reached quite easily. Let *P* be the conjunction of the various loving properties picked out by the original five propositions about a mother's love and the five propositions referring to God. We saw earlier that, in virtue of *P*, a loving mother who could help it would never be hidden from her child in the fictional circumstances we described. We also saw that the analogies between the latter circumstances and those of divine hiddenness are very close. But then we may infer that, very probably, *a God who could help it would never be hidden in those circumstances:* the operation of *P* would prevent this in the case of God, just as it would in the case of our fictional mother.

Thus far the Analogy Argument proper. Certain plausible additional moves may be made to bring us from this conclusion to atheism. In the case of the mother, we saw that there might be external actors that prevent her from responding to her child despite the presence of *P*—that she might be hidden and *not* able to help it. But if omnipotence means anything, it means that God couldn't *ever* be prevented from responding to the cries of God's human children. The disanalogy we see here, far from weakening the argument that starts out from the analogy, permits us to *complete* it. For it means that we may justifiably remove the little qualifier "who could help it" from our earlier conclusion and say simply that *God would never be hidden in the circumstances in question.* In other words, the Analogy Argument in conjunction with what we know about divine resourcefulness gives us a powerful reason to say that, if God exists, this form of divine hiddenness does not occur. But it *does* occur. Therefore, we have a powerful reason to believe that God does *not* exist.

2 IS THE ANALOGY ARGUMENT A SUCCESS?

Before getting too excited—or upset—about this argument, the reader should consider whether it can be defeated by counter-argument. It will, I think, be hard to question the claims we have made about how a loving mother would behave in our fictional scenarios. Most objections will quite naturally focus instead on questioning the closeness of the analogies we have drawn *between* those scenarios and the facts of divine hiddenness.

This can be done in various ways. One might argue, for example, that persons who seek God are not very much like *children*—the vulnerability and immaturity we attach to the latter and need to be able to transfer to the former if the argument is to succeed are in fact not transferable in this way. But this objection appears to assume that all who seek God in the relevant way are adult humans, and this is not at all obvious: actual children may (and do) seek God too, without in every case finding their search rewarded with positive results. More important, because of the evil we face and the evident frailty of our natures, even human grown-ups are not appropriately construed, theologically speaking, as mature adults. Theology has traditionally pictured us this way (while also referring to us as "God's children"), but a close look at the world suggests that a better picture would portray us as young and unformed, still needing a home—in particular, still in need of parental support and encouragement in the development of a character and self-esteem that can withstand the pressures toward fragmentation and despair that life presents and make the achievement of our full potential possible.

It might also be claimed that God is not appropriately thought of as mother—that in our application of human talk to the divine, non-motherly elements of human experience ought to predominate. Now it is clear that, traditionally, the notion of God as Father is much more common than that of God as Mother, but an appeal to "common practice" is always weak, especially when the practice in question has been (or can be) successfully challenged. Instead of getting into debates about feminism and patriarchy, though, let me simply point out that, whether presented under the label of "loving Father" or in some other way, such attributes as those of caring and closeness, compassion and empathy, are nonnegotiable in any theistic view that takes the moral perfection and worship-worthiness of God seriously. And these are the attributes at issue here. I have found it helpful to focus on the model of a mother because these attributes are still more closely linked in our experience and imagination with the notion of mother than with that of father. Indeed, the commonness in human experience of *distant* or *absent* fathers makes it possible for us to construe the connection between fatherhood and the attributes in question rather loosely. This fact, in conjunction with the tendency to think uncritically of God as Father, is, I think, a big part of the reason why so many are inclined to underestimate the force of arguments from divine hiddenness.

A third objection to our argument—a rather common sort—suggests that there is something presumptuous about *expecting* a response from God. God is not obligated to respond to our every whim; and if God responds, it will be in God's own way, not necessarily as we expect. Even if so-called seekers lack presumption, we ought still to consider that there may be some *other* human sin that prevents them from experiencing God. Perhaps God is hidden from us because of our *own* failings, instead of God's.

But the Analogy Argument, as you may have noticed, is not suggesting that God should satisfy our every *whim*, our every sudden, unreflective, unreasonable desire; only that God would respond to serious attempts to be united or reunited with God in a loving relationship. Observe how much more plausible the latter claim is than the former. The objection is here dealing with a caricature of our argument, not the real thing. As for presumption, the expectation of a seeker does not come in the form of a *demand*, but as anticipation or reasoned inference. Are we really to imagine seekers walking around demanding that God "show himself"? Some *philosophers* may do this, but these are usually individuals who have long since concluded that God does not exist and think the world is better off that way; it would be a mistake to confuse them with the earnest, hopeful seekers of our argument, or with those (perhaps the same individuals) who after careful reflection on all the available information conclude that it would be in the nature of God to be in some way revealed to anyone who calls upon God sincerely.

Turning now to the general reference to sin: this seems completely unsubstantiated—many who seek God seem in fact to be quite blameless in the relevant respects. It is important to notice here that beyond looking thoroughly and carefully for reason to believe in the existence of God and removing all observed impediments to success in the search, there is nothing the seeker *can do* to bring about belief. Belief as such is involuntary; it is something that happens to you when evidence adds up to a certain point, not something you can do directly (if you doubt this, just try to acquire right now, or to drop, as the case may be, the belief that God exists). Thus, if a search of the sort in question has been undertaken (as it often has), a nonbeliever cannot be "to blame" for not believing.

What about the possibility, also mentioned by the "sin" objection, that God *does* respond, and seekers simply miss the response, expecting something else—something other than what God has in mind? Well, what else might God have in mind? If the request is for the beginning or resumption of a loving relationship, and what is needed for this is, among other things, some measure of belief that there is someone there to relate *to,* what *could* count both as *loving* and as a *response* apart from some noticeable indication of God's presence? Certainly in the case of the unencumbered mother and her child, nothing apart from the mother actually coming to her child in a manner recognized by the child would qualify as a loving response. What

makes us think that something else would do in the case of God's immeasurably greater love? Perhaps it will be said that God, unlike the mother, is able to be present to us all the time without us noticing it and is, moreover, responsible for every single good thing we experience. This is indeed true, if God exists. But it still doesn't qualify as a *response* to the cry of those who seek God. And we need to recognize that the absence of love in one respect is not compensated for by *other* forms of love when what we're dealing with is not the love of a finite being but the perfect love of an unlimited God. Indeed, it's starting to look as though the relevant differences between God and ourselves make it *harder* to mount an "other response" objection, not easier.

But maybe we can press this notion of differences between ourselves and God a little further, in a different direction. Perhaps there is some *great good* for the seeker that depends on the continuation of her search, and thus prevents God from responding. Perhaps no loving human mother would ever have reason to consider continued separation from her child, in circumstances like those we have described, to be "for his own good," but God, the critic will say, is aware of so many more forms of goodness than we are, and has a design plan that spans incomprehensible distances in time and space. We are therefore not justified in concluding that God would do what the mother does, even if they share the loving properties we have discussed.

Now various possible goods we know of might be enumerated and discussed in response to this objection, but the objector would only reply by saying that the relevant goods may be *unknown* to us. Fortunately, there is a way around all this. First, let's notice that if the ultimate spiritual reality is a personal God, then all serious spiritual development must begin in personal relationship with God. And if God is infinitely deep and rich, then any such relationship must be multileveled and developmental—indeed, the development of it would surely be potentially unending. Third, such relationship with a perfect and infinitely rich personal reality would have to be the greatest good that any human being could experience, if God exists—certainly this is the claim of all theistic traditions. But then why this talk of some *other* good, for which God would *sacrifice* such relationship?

Perhaps it will be replied that God sacrifices only *some time* in the relationship, not the whole relationship, and that what is gained thereby may contribute to the *flourishing* of a *future* relationship with God. But it is hard to see how someone seeking God, desiring a loving personal relationship, could possibly be in a state such that experience of God or evidence of some other sort would inhibit or prevent the success of the relationship in the long term, as this point requires. Indeed, such individuals would seem to be in just the *right* position in this respect—a position emphasized as eminently desirable by theistic traditions. Certainly their state is no less appropriate to relationship with God than that of many who would be declared by those traditions to be enjoying it already.

Consider also, in this connection, the infinite *resourcefulness* of God. If God indeed possesses this attribute and is, moreover, unsurpassably deep and rich, then there must at any juncture be literally an *infinite number* of ways of developing in relationship with God, which omnipotence and omniscience could facilitate, despite obstacles to continuing relationship that might seem to present themselves. To say less than this, a theist must surely contradict what she believes about the greatness of God! Hence, even if we were *not* dealing with seekers, individuals optimally placed to benefit from God's presence, we would *still* lack reason to maintain the present objection.

One particular form that the exercise of God's resourcefulness might take may be highlighted here. Strange as it may seem, there is an important form of "hiddenness" that is quite compatible with—and indeed *requires*—a situation in which God is revealed to every seeker. To see this, suppose that God exists, and that our seeker finds reason to believe in God and responds by entering into a personal relationship with God ("conversing" with God in prayer, feeling God's presence, living her whole life in the context of divine-human communion). Suppose also that she subsequently lapses into some inappropriate state—say, arrogance or presumption. What can God do?

Well, there is still the possibility of a sort of divine withdrawal *within* the relationship. What I have in mind here is analogous to what has traditionally been called "the dark night of the soul"—a state in which there is evidence for God's existence on which the believer may rely, but in which God is not felt as directly present to her experience, and may indeed feel absent. While not removing the conditions of relationship, such a "withdrawal" would severely test the believer's faith, and, in particular, work against the sort of arrogance and presumption we have mentioned. Indeed, this form of hiddenness would seem capable of accomplishing much, perhaps all, of what theists sometimes say the *other* sort of hiddenness is designed to do! John Macquarrie, a Christian theologian, puts it nicely:

> As happens also in some of our deepest human relationships, the lover reveals himself enough to awaken the love of the beloved, yet veils himself enough to draw the beloved into an even deeper exploration of that love. In the love affair with God . . . there is an alternation of consolation and desolation and it is in this way that the finite being is constantly drawn beyond self into the depths of the divine.[1]

If this sort of hiddenness can produce the goods in question and is compatible with God having been revealed to the seeker, what possible reason could we have for insisting that God would leave the seeker in *doubt and nonbelief* in order to further those goods?

A final objection, significantly different from the rest, should briefly be mentioned. This is the claim that there are *other* reasons *for* belief in God which counterbalance or outweigh the reason *against* such belief that our argument represents. Our Analogy Argument, it should be emphasized, is broadly inductive, claiming only that its conclusion is very probable (i.e., much more probable than not). So it is always at least conceivable that the probability we assess for our conclusion on the basis of analogy may need to be adjusted when arguments *supporting* God's existence are taken into account. Someone, for example, who was deeply convinced of the soundness of a simple *deductive* argument for

God's existence (an argument with premises *entailing* the claim that God exists) and had only our Analogy Argument to consider on the side of atheism might well justifiably conclude, on the strength of her apparent proof of God's existence, that despite the closeness and persuasive force of the analogies, there must be *something* wrong with our argument and that God certainly exists, even if she can not put her finger on what the mistake in our reasoning is.

For how many will this sort of move function as a successful defeater? It is hard to say: everything depends on how the independent evidence is assessed, and whether it is properly assessed. Even if we had the space for an exhaustive discussion of other evidence (and of course we do not), it would be possible for others to justifiably disagree with our assessment of it, given facts of personality, experience, time, intelligence, opportunity, and so on that nonculpably incline them in another direction. But some general points can be made, that are not without interest or effect. Most readers, it must be said, are likely to be *without* such proofs of God as were earlier mentioned—indeed, that such proofs are in short supply is one of the circumstances that helps to generate the problem of divine hiddenness in the first place! Certainly, anyone who finds that the other evidence for and against God's existence leaves her thinking that theism and atheism are about equally probable should find the balance tipping toward atheism when this *new* evidence is considered. And it is interesting to note that even those who came to this discussion convinced of the truth of theism may find their epistemic situation changing because of the apparent force of our argument. This is because its apparent force may *affect*—and *negatively* affect—the confidence with which other arguments or experiences are taken to support theism, especially in cases where this other evidence has not previously been carefully examined. We should therefore not suppose that just anyone who comes to these discussions justified in theistic belief will leave that way.

That concludes our discussion of objections to the Analogy Argument. Nothing we have seen takes away from its initial persuasiveness (even the last defeater we discussed must concede this much). Indeed, we have encountered points in this discussion that add to its force. Does the divine hiddenness referred to in its premises therefore justify atheism? Does it justify *you, the reader,* in believing atheism? Well, it seems plausible and would be accepted by most philosophers that the following proposition refers to conditions necessary and sufficient for justification of the relevant sort.

> An individual S is epistemically justified in believing that *p* in response to evidence *e* if and only if (i) S does to some degree believe that *p* on *e,* (ii) has considered all available epistemic reasons for not believing that *p* on *e,* (iii) finds none to be a good reason, and (iv) has fulfilled all relevant epistemic duties in the course of her investigation.

Thinking of yourself as S, of *p* as atheism, of *e* as the form of divine hiddenness we have discussed, of the defeaters we have considered (including the defeater relying on independent evidence) and any others known to you as the available reasons for *not* believing atheism because of divine hiddenness, and of the relevant epistemic duties as including such things as care, thoroughness, and openness to the truth, you may, by reference to this standard, work out for *yourself* whether our argument justifies you in believing that God does not exist.

3 THE CONCEPTUAL ARGUMENT

The Analogy Argument is not the only argument from divine hiddenness. Indeed, in my previous work on this topic it is only alluded to, and another form of argumentation is utilized instead.[2] I wanted to develop the Analogy Argument here, and had thought to leave the other aside. But after proceeding, I realized that in developing the former argument, a natural basis for an abbreviated but still forceful presentation of the latter would be laid. So let us briefly consider the additional moves which the latter argument requires.

The Conceptual Argument takes further a theme already touched upon: namely, the proper understanding of the concept of divine love. In examining this concept, developing our understanding of it as we must, by reference to what is best in human love, we are led to endorse claims from which it follows that, if God exists, evidence sufficient to form belief in God is available to everyone capable of a personal relationship with God and not inclined to resist such evidence. As can be seen, this argument not only focuses more closely on the concept of divine love (while drawing information from what we know of human love, including a mother's love) but embraces a wider range of nonbelievers in its premises. In this new argument, the notion of divine hiddenness is, as it were, *expanded* to include events (or the absence of certain events) in the lives of people who, without being closed toward the traditional God, are for one reason or another not aware of any need to seek God. If a label is desired, we may call all those belonging to this new and broader category of non-believers *nonresisters*. Nonresisters might include, in addition to seekers, individuals-in the West whose upbringing has been completely secular. They certainly include the vast number of persons in both past and present living in parts of the world where the very *idea* of such a God is distant from human thought and imagination.

Now why should we suppose that the absence of evidence sufficient to form belief in God in the lives of nonresisters presents a problem for theism? Well, because reflection on the concept of divine love shows that a perfectly loving God would necessarily seek personal relationship with *all* individuals belonging to this type, and because such seeking entails the provision of evidence sufficient for belief in the existence of God. (As can be seen, here the emphasis is not on human seekers but on *God* as seeker.)

In defense of the first of these claims, we may point out that the seeking of a personal relationship is an essential part of the best human love. The best human lover encourages her beloved to draw from relationship with herself what he may need to flourish, but also quite naturally aspires to a kind of closeness between herself and her beloved: she reaches out to the one she loves immediately and spontaneously, and not only because of some prior calculation of advantages or disadvantages for either party. Something similar must apply to God's love for us: clearly an explicit divine-human relationship must do much to promote human flourishing, in which case God would seek it for that reason; and clearly God would also value personal relationship with human beings—creatures created in God's own image—for its own sake. No doubt God would not *force* such a loving relationship on anyone (the notion is logically contradictory and, in any case, contrary to love's respect for freedom), but surely a God who did not at least make such a relationship *available* to those who are *nonresisting* would not be perfectly loving.

This point sometimes has a hard time getting through. Due to a variety of social and religious factors, we seem to have got used to thinking of even God's love in a limited and limiting fashion, contrary to what all philosophical methods for working out an explication of the divine nature would indicate. But why suppose that if God exists there will be times when personal relationship with God will not be available to us? While a perfectly good and loving parent might occasionally stand to one side and let her child make the first move, and refuse to suffocate the child with her attentions, or even withdraw for a time to make a point, these are moments *within* the relationship, which *add* to its meaning. And while she might with deep sadness acknowledge that her child had completely cut himself off from the relationship, and not actively seek its resumption, it *would take* such resistance on the part of the child for the relationship to be put out of his immediate reach. What loving parent would ever willingly participate in bringing about such a state of affairs? And similar points apply to love as it occurs in the context of friendship and marriage relationships. So there seems no escaping this point: some form of personal relationship with God is always going to be available to nonresisters, if God is indeed loving.

A defense of our second claim—that for such relationship to be available, evidence sufficient for belief in God's existence would have to be similarly available—may now be added. The key point here is that it is logically impossible for you to hear God speaking to you or consciously to experience divine forgiveness and support or feel grateful to God or experience God's loving presence and respond thereto in love and obedience and worship or participate in any *other* element of a personal relationship with God while *not believing that there is a God*. Simply by looking at what it *means* to be in personal relationship with God, we can see that this is so. Since belief is involuntary, it follows that without evidence sufficient for belief in the existence of God, nonresisters are not in a position to relate personally to God. But where nonresisters are not in such a position, relationship with God has not been made available to them in the above sense. It follows that if relationship with God is to be made available to them, nonresisters must be provided with evidence sufficient for belief in God. This evidence, notice, would not need to be some thunderbolt from the sky or miracle or devastating theoretical proof. The quiet evidence of religious experience would do, and might also be most appropriate to the aims of any would-be divine relationship partner. But *some* such evidence must be available to nonresisters if they are to have the possibility of responding in love to God.

Taken in conjunction, the two points we have defended imply that if God exists, evidence sufficient for belief in God is *much more widely available than is in fact the case*. And from this it follows that God does *not* exist. Now this argument, like the other, has of course got to deal with objections. But as it turns out, the objections are pretty much the same ones, tailored to address the specifics of the new argument. And so are the replies. The reader is invited to go over the objections and replies again, this time with the Conceptual Argument in mind. She or he will see, I think, that the resources are there for a fully satisfying defense of the latter argument too. If so, we have not just the probable grounds of analogy but the more certain grounds of conceptual analysis for concluding that God does not exist.

4 CONSEQUENCES FOR THE PHILOSOPHY OF RELIGION

Suppose I am right and that the arguments we have discussed can be used to justify atheism. What should those who are convinced by them conclude with respect to God and religion? That neither matters, and that any reasonably intelligent inquirer will arrive at a place where concerns about such things no longer enter her head? That nature is all there is, and that we should limit our intellectual attention to the methods and results of the various sciences? Hardly. The perceptive reader will notice that our discussion has been restricted to the epistemic status of *traditional* theism. And anyone who thinks that traditional theism and naturalistic atheism are the only options worth exploring here has a woefully inadequate grasp of the range and diversity and complexity of religion. Indeed, there are intriguing religious possibilities that are only now beginning to receive the attention they deserve from Western philosophers. And as human beings continue to develop, intellectually and morally, as well as emotionally and socially, it may well be that new possibilities will come to light. The philosophy of religion is potentially far richer and far more wide-ranging in its explorations than it is at present. And so I conclude by suggesting that the hiddenness of the traditional God may ultimately only have the effect of allowing the *real* God—ultimate reality as it really is—to be more clearly revealed.

NOTES

1. John Macquarrie, *In Search of Deity* (London: SCM Press, 1984), p. 198.

2. See my *Divine Hiddenness and Human Reason* (Ithaca, NY: Cornell University Press, 1993). See also my "Response to Howard-Snyder" (and the paper to which it is a response), in *Canadian Journal of Philosophy,* 26/3 (1996), pp. 455–62, and my "What the Hiddenness of God Reveals: A Collaborative Discussion," in Daniel Howard-Snyder and Paul Moser (eds.), *Divine Hiddenness* (Cambridge: Cambridge University Press, 2001), pp. 33–61.

III.C. RESPONSES

Introduction

HAVING NOW CONSIDERED various different formulations of the problems of evil and divine hiddenness, we turn to responses.

In our first reading, Alvin Plantinga rebuts J. L. Mackie's defense of the "logical problem of evil." He argues that Mackie is wrong in thinking that the existence of evil is inconsistent with the existence of God, and he also argues that Mackie is wrong in thinking that every *possible* world is *creatable*. Unlike Leibniz, Plantinga is offering merely a defense rather than a theodicy. (See the general introduction to Part III for the distinction between "defense" and "theodicy.") Central to Plantinga's defense are the following three ideas: (a) a perfectly good being might have morally sufficient reason to permit evil, (b) the value of free will might provide such a morally sufficient reason if it is impossible for God to guarantee that a world containing free creatures would be free from evil, and (c) for all we know, it *is* impossible for God to guarantee that a world containing free creatures would be free from evil. In defense of (c), Plantinga sets forth the hypothesis of *transworld depravity*. Roughly, to suffer from transworld depravity is to be such that, no matter what total creative act God had performed, if God had created you and left you free, you would freely have done something wrong. According to Plantinga, for all we know everyone in the actual world suffers from transworld depravity. If that's so, then no matter what creative act God had performed, if he had created just those creatures who in fact exist, the world would have contained moral evil. Thus, though there are *possible* worlds in which everyone who actually exists freely does what is right, those worlds are not *creatable*. They are not creatable because, in effect, free creatures *cooperate* with God in determining what sort of world will exist; and (given the hypothesis of transworld depravity) no matter what God had done, his creatures would not have cooperated in such a way as to keep the world free from evil.

Our second reading, John Hick's "Evil and Soul-Making," provides an example of a theodicy that is based on the free will defense. Hick distinguishes between two different types of theodicy. The Augustinian theodicy starts with the idea that God created humans without sin and set them in a sinless paradise and goes on to maintain that humanity fell into sin through the misuse of free will. So we are to blame, not God, for the existence of suffering in the world. God's grace will save some of us, but others will perish everlastingly. In this division, God's goodness is manifested, for his mercy redeems some and his justice is served on the rest. On the other hand, the Irenaean theodicy, stemming from Irenaeus (120–202 C.E.), views Adam not as a free agent rebelling against God, but as more akin to a very small child. The fall is humanity's first faulty step in the direction of freedom. God is still working with humanity in order to bring it from undeveloped life (*bios*) to a state of self-realization in divine love, spiritual life (*zoe*). This life is viewed as the "vale of soul-making." Spiritual development requires obstacles and the opportunity to fail as well as to succeed. Hick declares that those who are opposed to the challenge that our freedom grants us are looking for a hedonistic paradise in which every desire is gratified and we are treated by God as pet animals rather than autonomous agents. On the other hand, those who accept the challenge of freedom consider themselves to be coworkers with God in bringing forth the kingdom of God.

As should be clear by now, the typical strategy in both defense and theodicy is to look for *greater goods* that might somehow justify God in permitting the evils of this world. The next four readings in this section each in their own way offer correctives to this trend.

In the third selection, Daniel Howard-Snyder defends the skeptical theist strategy for responding to the problem of evil (although he vehemently rejects that label for the position). The skeptical theist, as we have seen in the general introduction to Part III, maintains a kind of skepticism about human abilities to fathom the full range of possible goods and evils and relations among them. Because of this, she also maintains that there is no reason to think that we would be able to detect the goods that justify God in permitting the evils of this world even if there are such goods. Thus, the skeptical theist *as such* makes no effort to discover particular goods that might justify God in permitting various kinds of evil. However, opponents of the skeptical theist strategy commonly argue that the skeptical theist's views about the limits of human cognitive powers imply a much wider and unacceptable skepticism. If indeed the skeptical theist is right about how poorly we grasp the realm of value, then—so the objector argues—she has no good reason to accept many of the commonsense moral truths that we all wish to accept. The main goal of Howard-Snyder's paper is to provide a reply to this common and important objection.

In our fourth selection, Eleonore Stump notes that a great deal of human suffering comes from unfulfilled "desires of the heart"—desires that matter to us a great deal but whose satisfaction isn't strictly necessary for our flourishing as human beings. Traditional theodicies fail to accord sufficient value to this sort of suffering—as if it is rather easily outweighed, offset, or defeated by global goods (like the value of freedom) or by "replacement goods" (like a new family, to replace the old one that was lost in some catastrophe). To the extent that they do fail in this way, she argues, such theodicies are, at best, incomplete.

In a somewhat similar vein, Marilyn Adams argues that traditional responses to the problem of evil do not deal adequately with *horrendous evil*, where horrendous evil is (roughly) evil that we might intuitively regard as life-wrecking. The problem, she argues, is that, when it comes to accounting for horrendous evils, the standard responses to the problem of evil fail to accord these evils the weight they deserve, or they fail in other ways to respect our moral intuitions or our intuitions about value. She then goes on to sketch a way of responding to the problem of evil that does deal adequately with horrors. At the heart of her response is the idea that horrors in our lives are, or can be, defeated by a kind of intimacy and identification with God which is made possible by the incarnation.

In our sixth reading, Laura Waddell Ekstrom explores the idea that, far from constituting evidence *against* the existence of God (as the atheologians would have it), suffering may in fact be an avenue *to* knowledge of God. Finding affinities between her own (partial) theodicy and responses to the problem of evil offered by Eleonore Stump and Marilyn Adams, Ekstrom argues that some instances of suffering satisfy standard conceptions of religious experience (discussed more fully in Part IV of this volume) and serve as means of intimacy with God.

The final two readings in this section provide replies to the problem of divine hiddenness. In the seventh reading, Michael J. Murray offers a sustained critique of J. L. Schellenberg's argument for atheism from divine hiddenness. (The version of the argument that Murray engages is the one found in Schellenberg's *Divine Hiddenness and Human Reason* [1993].) Murray is particularly concerned to defend, against a critique offered by Schellenberg, the thesis that divine hiddenness is often a necessary condition for preserving free creatures' ability to fully undergo the process of soul-making. What Murray offers, then, is what we might call a "greater human goods" response to the problem: divine hiddenness is justified because it is required for (or at least often importantly contributes to) some outweighing human good. By contrast, in our eighth selection Michael Rea argues that perhaps divine hiddenness is justified even independently of whatever goods it might bring to human beings.

III.C.1

The Free Will Defense

ALVIN PLANTINGA

A brief biographical sketch of Alvin Plantinga appears before selection I.B.8. In the present selection, Plantinga argues that Mackie and other atheologians (those who argue against the existence of God) are mistaken in thinking that the existence of evil is inconsistent with the existence of a perfectly good and powerful God.

2. DOES THE THEIST CONTRADICT HIMSELF?

In a widely discussed piece entitled "Evil and Omnipotence" John Mackie makes this claim:

> I think, however, that a more telling criticism can be made by way of the traditional problem of evil. Here it can be shown, not

that religious beliefs lack rational support, but that they are positively irrational, that the several parts of the essential theological doctrine are *inconsistent* with one another. . . .[1]

Is Mackie right? Does the theist contradict himself? But we must ask a prior question: just what is being claimed here? That theistic belief contains an inconsistency or contradiction, of course. But what, exactly, is an inconsistency or contradiction? There

From *God, Freedom, and Evil* by Alvin Plantinga (Harper & Row, 1974). Reprinted by permission of the author. Footnotes edited.

are several kinds. An *explicit* contradiction is a *proposition* of a certain sort—a conjunctive proposition, one conjunct of which is the denial or negation of the other conjunct. For example:

> Paul is a good tennis player, and it's false that Paul is a good tennis player.

(People seldom assert explicit contradictions.) Is Mackie charging the theist with accepting such a contradiction? Presumably not; what he says is

> In its simplest form the problem is this: God is omnipotent; God is wholly good; yet evil exists. There seems to be some contradiction between these three propositions, so that if any two of them were true the third would be false. But at the same time all three are essential parts of most theological positions; the theologian, it seems, at once *must* adhere and *cannot consistently* adhere to all three.

According to Mackie, then, the theist accepts a group or set of three propositions; this set is inconsistent. Its members, of course, are

(1) God is omnipotent

(2) God is wholly good

and

(3) Evil exists.

Call this set *A*; the claim is that *A* is an inconsistent set. But what is it for a *set* to be inconsistent or contradictory? Following our definition of an explicit contradiction, we might say that a set of propositions is explicitly contradictory if one of the members is the denial or negation of another member. But then, of course, it is evident that the set we are discussing is not explicitly contradictory; the denials of (1), (2), and (3), respectively, are

(1′) God is not omnipotent (or it's false that God is omnipotent)

(2′) God is not wholly good

and

(3′) There is no evil

none of which is in set *A*.

Of course many sets are pretty clearly contradictory, in an important way, but not explicitly contradictory. For example, set *B*:

(4) If all men are mortal, then Socrates is mortal

(5) All men are mortal

(6) Socrates is not mortal.

This set is not explicitly contradictory; yet surely *some* significant sense of that term applies to it. What is important here is that by using only the rules of ordinary logic—the laws of propositional logic and quantification theory found in any introductory text on the subject—we can deduce an explicit contradiction from the set. Or to put it differently, we can use the laws of logic to deduce a proposition from the set, which proposition, when added to the set, yields a new set that is explicitly contradictory. For by using the law *modus ponens* (if *p,* then *q*; *p*; therefore *q*) we can deduce

(7) Socrates is mortal

from (4) and (5). The result of adding (7) to *B* is the set {(4), (5), (6), (7)}. This set, of course, is explicitly contradictory in that (6) is the denial of (7). We might say that any set which shares this characteristic with set *B* is *formally* contradictory. So a formally contradictory set is one from whose members an explicit contradiction can be deduced by the laws of logic. Is Mackie claiming that set *A* is formally contradictory?

If he is, he's wrong. No laws of logic permit us to deduce the denial of one of the propositions in *A* from the other members. Set *A* isn't formally contradictory either.

But there is still another way in which a set of propositions can be contradictory or inconsistent. Consider set *C*, whose members are

(8)   George is older than Paul

(9)   Paul is older than Nick

and

(10) George is not older than Nick.

This set is neither explicitly nor formally contradictory; we can't, just by using the laws of logic, deduce the denial of any of these propositions from the others. And yet there is a good sense in which it is inconsistent or contradictory. For clearly it is *not possible* that its three members all be true. It is *necessarily true* that

(11)   If George is older than Paul, and Paul is older than Nick, then George is older than Nick.

And if we add (11) to set *C*, we get a set that is formally contradictory; (8), (9), and (11) yield, by the laws of ordinary logic, the denial of (10).

I said that (11) is *necessarily true*; but what does *that* mean? Of course we might say that a proposition is necessarily true if it is impossible that it be false, or if its negation is not possibly true. This would be to explain necessity in terms of possibility. Chances are, however, that anyone who does not know what necessity is, will be equally at a loss about possibility; the explanation is not likely to be very successful. Perhaps all we can do by way of explanation is to give some examples and hope for the best. In the first place many propositions can be established by the laws of logic alone—for example,

(12)   If all men are mortal and Socrates is a man, then Socrates is mortal.

Such propositions are truths of logic; and all of them are necessary in the sense of question. But truths of arithmetic and mathematics generally are also necessarily true. Still further, there is a host of propositions that are neither truths of logic nor truths of mathematics but are nonetheless necessarily true; (11) would be an example, as well as

(13)   Nobody is taller than himself

(14)   Red is a color

(15)   No numbers are persons

(16)   No prime number is a prime minister

and

(17)   Bachelors are unmarried.

So here we have an important kind of necessity—let's call it "broadly logical necessity." Of course there is a correlative kind of *possibility*: a proposition *p* is possibly true (in the broadly logical sense) just in case its negation or denial is not

necessarily true (in that same broadly logical sense). This sense of necessity and possibility must be distinguished from another that we may call *causal* or *natural* necessity and possibility. Consider

(18)   Henry Kissinger has swum the Atlantic.

Although this proposition has an implausible ring, it is not necessarily false in the broadly logical sense (and its denial is not necessarily true in that sense). But there is a good sense in which it is impossible: it is *causally* or *naturally* impossible. Human beings, unlike dolphins, just don't have the physical equipment demanded for this feat. Unlike Superman, furthermore, the rest of us are incapable of leaping tall buildings at a single bound or (without auxiliary power of some kind) traveling faster than a speeding bullet. These things are *impossible* for us—but not *logically* impossible, even in the broad sense.

So there are several senses of necessity and possibility here. There are a number of propositions, furthermore, of which it's difficult to say whether they are or aren't possible in the broadly logical sense; some of these are subjects of philosophical controversy. Is it possible, for example, for a person never to be conscious during his entire existence? Is it possible for a (human) person to exist *disembodied*? If that's possible, is it possible that there be a person who *at no time at all* during his entire existence has a body? Is it possible to see without eyes? These are propositions about whose possibility in that broadly logical sense there is disagreement and dispute.

Now return to set *C*. . . . What is characteristic of it is the fact that the conjunction of its members—the proposition expressed by the result of putting "and's" between (8), (9), and (10)—is necessarily false. Or we might put it like this: what characterizes set *C* is the fact that we can get a formally contradictory set by adding a necessarily true proposition— namely (11). Suppose we say that a set is *implicitly contradictory* if it resembles *C* in this respect. That is, a set *S* of propositions is implicitly contradictory if there is a necessary proposition *p* such that the result of adding *p* to *S* is a formally contradictory set. Another way to put it: *S* is implicitly contradictory if there is some necessarily true proposition p such that by using just the laws of ordinary logic, we can deduce an explicit contradiction from p together with the members of S. And when Mackie says that set A is contradictory, we may properly take him, I think, as holding that it is implicitly contradictory in the explained sense. As he puts it:

> However, the contradiction does not arise immediately; to show it we need some additional premises, or perhaps some quasi-logical rules connecting the terms "good" and "evil" and "omnipotent." These additional principles are that good is opposed to evil, in such a way that a good thing always eliminates evil as far as it can, and that there are no limits to what an omnipotent thing can do. From these it follows that a good omnipotent thing eliminates evil completely, and then the propositions that a good omnipotent thing exists, and that evil exists, are incompatible.[2]

Here Mackie refers to "additional premises"; he also calls them "additional principles" and "quasi-logical rules"; he says we need them to show the contradiction. What he means, I think, is that to get a formally contradictory set we must add some more propositions to set A; and if we aim to show that set A is implicitly contradictory, these propositions must be necessary truths— "quasi-logical rules" as Mackie calls them. The two additional principles he suggests are

(19) A good thing always eliminates evil as far as it can

and

(20) There are no limits to what an omnipotent being can do.

And, of course, if Mackie means to show that set A is implicitly contradictory, then he must hold that (19) and (20) are not merely *true* but *necessarily true*.

But, are they? What about (20) first? What does it mean to say that a being is omnipotent? That he is *all-powerful*, or *almighty*, presumably. But are there no limits at all to the power of such a being? Could he create square circles, for example, or married bachelors? Most theologians and theistic philosophers who hold that God is omnipotent, do not hold that He can create round squares or bring it about that He both exists and does not exist. These theologians and philosophers may hold that there are no *nonlogical* limits to what an omnipotent being can do, but they concede that not even an omnipotent being can bring about logically impossible states of affairs or cause necessarily false propositions to be true. Some theists, on the other hand—Martin Luther and Descartes, perhaps— have apparently thought that God's power is unlimited even by the laws of logic. For these theists the question whether set A is contradictory will not be of much interest. As theists they believe (1) and (2), and they also, presumably, believe (3). But they remain undisturbed by the claim that (1), (2), and (3) are jointly inconsistent—because, as they say, God can do what is logically impossible. Hence He can bring it about that the members of set A are all true, even if that set is contradictory (concentrating very intensely upon this suggestion is likely to make you dizzy). So the theist who thinks that the power of God isn't *limited at all*, not even by the laws of logic, will be unimpressed by Mackie's argument and won't find any difficulty in the contradiction set A is alleged to contain. This view is not very popular, however, and for good reason; it is quite incoherent. What the theist typically means when he says that God is omnipotent is not that there are *no* limits to God's power, but at most that there are no nonlogical limits to what He can do; and given this qualification, it is perhaps initially plausible to suppose that (20) is necessarily true.

But what about (19), the proposition that every good thing eliminates every evil state of affairs that it can eliminate? Is that necessarily true? Is it true at all? Suppose, first of all, that your friend Paul unwisely goes for a drive on a wintry day and runs out of gas on a deserted road. The temperature dips to $-10°$, and a miserably cold wind comes up. You are sitting comfortably at home (twenty-five miles from Paul) roasting chestnuts in a roaring blaze.

Your car is in the garage; in the trunk there is the full five-gallon can of gasoline you always keep for emergencies. Paul's discomfort and danger are certainly an evil, and one which you could eliminate. You don't do so. But presumably you don't thereby forfeit your claim to being a "good thing"—you simply didn't know of Paul's plight. And so (19) does not appear to be necessary. It says that every good thing has a certain property—the property of eliminating every evil that it can. And if the case I described is possible—a good person's failing through ignorance to eliminate a certain evil he can eliminate—then (19) is by no means necessarily true.

But perhaps Mackie could sensibly claim that if you *didn't know* about Paul's plight, then in fact you were not, at the time in question, able to eliminate the evil in question; and perhaps he'd be right. In any event he could revise (19) to take into account the kind of case I mentioned:

(19a) Every good thing always eliminates every evil that *it knows about* and can eliminate.

{(1), (2), (3), (20), (19a)}, you'll notice is not a formally contradictory set—to get a formal contradiction we must add a proposition specifying that God *knows about* every evil state of affairs. But most theists do believe that God is omniscient or all-knowing; so if this new set—the set that results when we add to set *A* the proposition that God is omniscient—is implicitly contradictory then Mackie should be satisfied and the theist confounded. (And, henceforth, set *A* will be the old set *A* together with the proposition that God is omniscient.)

But is (19a) necessary? Hardly. Suppose you know that Paul is marooned as in the previous example, and you also know another friend is similarly marooned fifty miles in the opposite direction. Suppose, furthermore, that while you can rescue one or the other, you simply can't rescue both. Then each of the two evils is such that it is within your power to eliminate it; and you know about them both. But you can't eliminate *both*; and you don't forfeit your claim to being a good person by eliminating only one—it wasn't within your power

to do more. So the fact that you don't doesn't mean that you are not a good person. Therefore (19a) is false; it is not a necessary truth or even a truth that every good thing eliminates every evil it knows about and can eliminate.

We can see the same thing another way. You've been rock climbing. Still something of a novice, you've acquired a few cuts and bruises by inelegantly using your knees rather than your feet. One of these bruises is fairly painful. You mention it to a physician friend, who predicts the pain will leave of its own accord in a day or two. Meanwhile, he says, there's nothing he can do, short of amputating your leg above the knee, to remove the pain. Now the pain in your knee is an evil state of affairs. All else being equal, it would be better if you had no such pain. And it is within the power of your friend to eliminate this evil state of affairs. Does his failure to do so mean that he is not a good person? Of course not; for he could eliminate this evil state of affairs only by bringing about another, much worse evil. And so it is once again evident that (19a) is false. It is entirely possible that a good person fail to eliminate an evil state of affairs that he knows about and can eliminate. This would take place, if, as in the present example, he couldn't eliminate the evil without bringing about a *greater* evil.

A slightly different kind of case shows the same thing. A really impressive good state of affairs *G* will outweigh a trivial *E*—that is, the conjunctive state of affairs *G* and *E* is itself a good state of affairs. And surely a good person would not be obligated to eliminate a given evil if he could do so only by eliminating a good that outweighed it. Therefore (19a) is not necessarily true; it can't be used to show that set *A* is implicitly contradictory.

These difficulties might suggest another revision of (19); we might try

(19b) A good being eliminates every evil *E* that it knows about and that it can eliminate without either bringing about a greater evil or eliminating a good state of affairs that outweighs *E*.

Is this necessarily true? It takes care of the second of the two difficulties afflicting (19a) but leaves the first untouched. We can see this as follows. First, suppose we say that a being *properly eliminates* an evil state of affairs if it eliminates that evil without either eliminating an outweighing good or bringing about a greater evil. It is then obviously possible that a person find himself in a situation where he could properly eliminate an evil E and could also properly eliminate another evil E', but couldn't properly eliminate them *both*. You're rock climbing again, this time on the dreaded north face of the Grand Teton. You and your party come upon Curt and Bob, two mountaineers stranded 125 feet apart on the face. They untied to reach their cigarettes and then carelessly dropped the rope while lighting up. A violent, dangerous thunderstorm is approaching. You have time to rescue one of the stranded climbers and retreat before the storm hits; if you rescue both, however, you and your party and the two climbers will be caught on the face during the thunderstorm, which will very likely destroy your entire party. In this case you can eliminate one evil (Curt's being stranded on the face) without causing more evil or eliminating a greater good; and you are also able to properly eliminate the other evil (Bob's being thus stranded). But you can't properly eliminate them *both*. And so the fact that you don't rescue Curt, say, even though you could have, doesn't show that you aren't a good person. Here, then, each of the evils is such that you can properly eliminate it; but you can't properly eliminate them both, and hence can't be blamed for failing to eliminate one of them.

So neither (19a) nor (19b) is necessarily true. You may be tempted to reply that the sort of counterexamples offered—examples where someone is able to eliminate an evil A and also able to eliminate a different evil B, but unable to eliminate them both—are irrelevant to the case of a being who, like God, is both omnipotent and omniscient. That is, you may think that if an omnipotent and omniscient being is able to eliminate each of two evils, it follows that he can eliminate them *both*. Perhaps this is so; but it is not strictly to the point. The fact is the counterexamples show that (19a) and (19b) are not necessarily true and hence can't be used to show that set A is implicitly inconsistent.

What the reply does suggest is that perhaps the atheologian will have more success if he works the properties of omniscience and omnipotence into (19). Perhaps he could say something like

(19c) An omnipotent and omniscient good being eliminates every evil that it can properly eliminate.

And suppose, for purposes of argument, we concede the necessary truth of (19c). Will it serve Mackie's purposes? Not obviously. For we don't get a set that is formally contradictory by adding (20) and (19c) to set A. This set (call it A') contains the following six members:

(1)   God is omnipotent

(2)   God is wholly good

(2') God is omniscient

(3)   Evil exists

(19c) An omnipotent and omniscient good being eliminates every evil that it can properly eliminate

and

(20) There are no nonlogical limits to what an omnipotent being can do.

Now if A' were formally contradictory, then from any five of its members we could deduce the denial of the sixth by the laws of ordinary logic. That is, any five would *formally entail* the denial of the sixth. So if A' were formally inconsistent, the denial of (3) would be formally entailed by the remaining five. That is, (1), (2), (2'), (19c), and (20) would formally entail

(3') There is no evil.

But they don't; what they formally entail is not that there is no evil *at all* but only that

(3") There is no evil that God can properly eliminate.

So (19c) doesn't really help either—not because it is not necessarily true but because its addition [with (20)] to set A does not yield a formally contradictory set.

Obviously, what the atheologian must add to get a formally contradictory set is

(21)   If God is omniscient and omnipotent, then he can properly eliminate every evil state of affairs.

Suppose we agree that the set consisting in *A* plus (19c), (20), and (21) is formally contradictory. So if (19c), (20), and (21) are all necessarily true, then set *A* is implicitly contradictory. We've already conceded that (19c) and (20) are indeed necessary. So we must take a look at (21). Is this proposition necessarily true?

No. To see this let us ask the following question. Under what conditions would an omnipotent being be unable to eliminate a certain evil *E* without eliminating an outweighing good? Well, suppose that *E* is *included in* some good state of affairs that outweighs it. That is, suppose there is some good state of affairs *G* so related to *E* that it is impossible that *G* obtain or be actual and *E* fail to obtain. (Another way to put this: a state of affairs *S* includes *S'* if the conjunctive state of affairs *S but not S'* is impossible, or if it is necessary that *S'* obtains if *S* does.) Now suppose that some good state of affairs *G* includes an evil state of affairs *E* that it outweighs. Then not even an omnipotent being could eliminate *E* without eliminating *G*. But are there any cases where a good state of affairs includes, in this sense, an evil that it outweighs?[3] Indeed there are such states of affairs. To take an artificial example, let's suppose that *E* is Paul's suffering from a minor abrasion and *G* is your being deliriously happy. The conjunctive state of affairs, *G and E*—the state of affairs that obtains if and only if both *G* and *E* obtain—is then a good state of affairs: it is better, all else being equal, that you be intensely happy and Paul suffer a mildly annoying abrasion than that this state of affairs not obtain. So *G and E* is a good state of affairs. And clearly *G and E* includes *E*: obviously it is necessarily true that if you are deliriously happy and Paul is suffering from an abrasion, then Paul is suffering from an abrasion.

But perhaps you think this example trivial, tricky, slippery, and irrelevant. If so, take heart; other examples abound. Certain kinds of values, certain familiar kinds of good states of affairs, can't exist apart from evil of some sort. For example, there are people who display a sort of creative moral heroism in the face of suffering and adversity—a heroism that inspires others and creates a good situation out of a bad one. In a situation like this the evil, of course, remains evil; but the total state of affairs—someone's bearing pain magnificently, for example—may be good. If it is, then the good present must outweigh the evil; otherwise the total situation would not be *good*. But, of course, it is not possible that such a good state of affairs obtain unless some evil also obtain. It is a necessary truth that if someone bears pain magnificently, then someone is in pain.

The conclusion to be drawn, therefore, is that (21) is not necessarily true. And our discussion thus far shows at the very least that it is no easy matter to find necessarily true propositions that yield a formally contradictory set when added to set *A*.[4] One wonders, therefore, why the many atheologians who confidently assert that this set is contradictory make no attempt whatever to *show* that it is. For the most part they are content just to *assert* that there is a contradiction here. Even Mackie, who sees that some "additional premises" or "quasi-logical rules" are needed, makes scarcely a beginning towards finding some additional premises that are necessarily true and that together with the members of set *A* formally entail an explicit contradiction.

3. CAN WE SHOW THAT THERE IS NO INCONSISTENCY HERE?

To summarize our conclusions so far: although many atheologians claim that the theist is involved in contradiction when he asserts the members of set *A*, this set, obviously, is neither *explicitly nor formally* contradictory; the claim, presumably, must be that it is *implicitly* contradictory. To make good this claim the atheologian must find some necessarily true proposition *p* (it could be a conjunction of several propositions) such that the addition of *p* to set *A* yields a set that is formally contradictory. No atheologian has produced even a plausible candidate for this role, and it certainly is not easy to see what such a proposition might be. Now we might think we should simply declare set *A* implicitly consistent on the principle that a proposition (or set) is to be presumed consistent or possible until proven otherwise. This course, however, leads to trouble. The same principle would impel us to declare the atheologian's claim—that set *A* is inconsistent—possible or consistent. But the claim that a given set of propositions is implicitly contradictory, is itself either necessarily true or necessarily false; so if such a claim is *possible*, it is not necessarily false and is, therefore, true (in fact, necessarily true). If we followed the suggested principle, therefore, we should be obliged to declare set *A* implicitly consistent (since it hasn't been shown to be otherwise), but we should have to say the same thing about the atheologian's claim, since we haven't shown *that* claim to be inconsistent or impossible. The atheologian's claim, furthermore, is necessarily true if it is possible. Accordingly, if we accept the above principle, we shall have to declare set *A* both implicitly consistent and implicitly inconsistent. So all we can say at this point is that set *A* has not been shown to be implicitly inconsistent.

Can we go any further? One way to go on would be to try to *show* that set *A* is implicitly consistent or possible in the broadly logical sense. But what is involved in showing such a thing? Although there are various ways to approach this matter, they all resemble one another in an important respect. They all amount to this: to show that a set *S* is consistent you think of a *possible state of affairs* (it needn't *actually obtain*) which is such that if it were actual, then all of the members of *S* would be true. This procedure is sometimes called *giving a model of S*. For example, you might construct an axiom set and then show that it is consistent by giving a model of it; this is how it was shown that the denial of Euclid's parallel postulate is formally consistent with the rest of his postulates.

There are various special cases of this procedure to fit special circumstances. Suppose, for example, you have a pair of propositions *p* and *q* and wish to show them consistent. And suppose we

say that a proposition *p*1 entails a proposition *p*2 if it is impossible that *p*1 be true and *p*2 false—if the conjunctive proposition *p*1 and not *p*2 is necessarily false. Then one way to show that *p* is consistent with *q* is to find some proposition *r* whose conjunction with *p* is both possible, in the broadly logical sense, and entails *q*. A rude and unlettered behaviorist, for example, might hold that thinking is really nothing but movements of the larynx; he might go on to hold that

P   Jones did not move his larynx after April 30 is inconsistent (in the broadly logical sense) with

Q   Jones did some thinking during May.

By way of rebuttal, we might point out that *P* appears to be consistent with

R   While convalescing from an April 30 laryngotomy, Jones whiled away the idle hours by writing (in May) a splendid paper on Kant's *Critique of Pure Reason*.

So the conjunction of *P* and *R* appears to be consistent; but obviously it also entails *Q* (you can't write even a passable paper on Kant's *Critique of Pure Reason* without doing some thinking); so *P* and *Q* are consistent.

We can see that this is a special case of the procedure I mentioned above as follows. This proposition *R* is consistent with *P*; so the proposition *P and R* is possible, describes a possible state of affairs. But *P* and *R* entails *Q*; hence if *P and R* were true, *Q* would also be true, and hence both *P* and *Q* would be true. So this is really a case of producing a possible state of affairs such that, if it were actual, all the members of the set in question (in this case the pair set of *P* and *Q*) would be true.

How does this apply to the case before us? As follows, let us conjoin propositions (1), (2), and (2') and henceforth call the result (1):

(1) God is omniscient, omnipotent, and wholly good.

The problem, then, is to show that (1) and (3) (evil exists) are consistent. This could be done, as we've seen, by finding a proposition *r* that is consistent with (1) and such that (1) and (*r*) together entail (3). One proposition that might do the trick is

(22)   God creates a world containing evil and has a good reason for doing so.

If (22) is consistent with (1), then it follows that (1) and (3) (and hence set *A*) are consistent. Accordingly, one thing some theists have tried is to show that (22) and (1) are consistent.

One can attempt this in at least two ways. On the one hand, we could try to apply the same method again. Conceive of a possible state of affairs such that, if it obtained, an omnipotent, omniscient, and wholly good God would have a good reason for permitting evil. On the other, someone might try to specify *what God's reason is* for permitting evil and try to show, if it is not obvious, that it is a good reason. St. Augustine, for example, one of the greatest and most influential philosopher-theologians of the Christian Church, writes as follows:

> . . . some people see with perfect truth that a creature is better if, while possessing free will, it remains always fixed upon God and never sins; then, reflecting on men's sins, they are grieved, not because they continue to sin, but because they were created. They say: He should have made us such that we never willed to sin, but always to enjoy the unchangeable truth.
>
> They should not lament or be angry. God has not compelled men to sin just because He created them and gave them the power to choose between sinning and not sinning. There are angels who have never sinned and never will sin.
>
> Such is the generosity of God's goodness that He has not refrained from creating even that creature which He foreknew would not only sin, but remain in the will to sin. As a runaway horse is better than a stone which does not run away because it lacks self-movement and sense perception, so the creature is more excellent which sins by free will than that which does not sin only because it has no free will.[5]

In broadest terms Augustine claims that God could create a better, more perfect universe by permitting evil than He could by refusing to do so:

> Neither the sins nor the misery are necessary to the perfection of the universe, but souls as such are necessary, which have the power to sin if they so will, and become miserable if they sin. If misery persisted after their sins had been abolished, or if there were misery before there were sins, then it might be right to say that the order and government of the universe were at fault. Again, if there were sins but no consequent misery, that order is equally dishonored by lack of equity.[6]

Augustine tries to tell us *what God's reason is* for permitting evil. At bottom, he says, it's that God can create a more perfect universe by permitting evil. A really top-notch universe requires the existence of free, rational, and moral agents; and some of the free creatures He created went wrong. But the universe with the free creatures it contains and the evil they commit is better than it would have been had it contained neither the free creatures nor this evil. Such an attempt to specify God's reason for permitting evil is what I earlier called a *theodicy*; in the words of John Milton it is an attempt to "justify the ways of God to man," to show that God is just in permitting evil. Augustine's kind of theodicy might be called a Free Will Theodicy, since the idea of rational creatures with free will plays such a prominent role in it.

A theodicist, then, attempts to tell us why God permits evil. Quite distinct from a Free Will Theodicy is what I shall call a Free Will Defense. Here the aim is not to say what God's reason *is*, but at most what God's reason *might possibly be*. We could put the difference like this. The Free Will Theodicist and Free Will Defender are both trying to show that (1) is consistent with (22), and of course if so, then set *A* is consistent. The Free Will Theodicist tries to do this by finding some proposition *r* which in conjunction with (1) entails (22); he claims, furthermore, that this proposition is true, not just consistent with (1). He tries to tell us what God's reason for permitting evil *really is*. The Free Will Defender, on the other hand, though he also tries to find a proposition *r* that is consistent with (1) and in conjunction with it entails (22), does *not* claim to know or even believe that *r* is true. And here, of course, he is perfectly within his rights. His aim is to show that (1) is consistent with (22); all he need do then is find an *r* that is consistent with (1) and such that (1) and (*r*) entail (22); whether *r* is true is quite beside the point.

So there is a significant difference between a Free Will Theodicy and a Free Will Defense. The latter is sufficient (if successful) to show that set *A* is consistent; in a way a Free Will Theodicy goes beyond what is required. On the other hand, a theodicy would be much more satisfying, if possible to achieve. No doubt the theist would rather know what God's reason is for permitting evil than simply that it's possible that He has a good one. But in the present context (that of investigating the consistency of set *A*), the latter is all that's needed. Neither a defense or a theodicy, of course, gives any hint to what God's reason for some *specific* evil—the death or suffering of someone close to you, for example—might be. And there is still another function[7]—a sort of pastoral function—in the neighborhood that neither serves. Confronted with evil in his own life or suddenly coming to realize more clearly than before the *extent* and *magnitude* of evil, a believer in God may undergo a crisis of faith. He may be tempted to follow the advice of Job's "friends"; he may be tempted to "curse God and die." Neither a Free Will Defense nor a Free Will Theodicy is designed to be of much help or comfort to one suffering from such a storm in the soul (although in a specific case, of course, one or the other could prove useful). Neither is to be thought of first of all as a means of pastoral counseling. Probably neither will enable someone to find peace with himself and with God in the face of the evil the world contains. But then, of course, neither is intended for that purpose.

4. THE FREE WILL DEFENSE

In what follows I shall focus attention upon the Free Will Defense. I shall examine it more closely, state it more exactly, and consider objections to it;

and I shall argue that in the end it is successful. Earlier we saw that among good states of affairs there are some that not even God can bring about without bringing about evil: those goods, namely, that *entail* or *include* evil states of affairs. The Free Will Defense can be looked upon as an effort to show that there may be a very different kind of good that God can't bring about without permitting evil. These are good states of affairs that don't include evil; they do not entail the existence of any evil whatever; nonetheless God Himself can't bring them about without permitting evil.

So how does the Free Will Defense work? And what does the Free Will Defender mean when he says that people are or may be free? What is relevant to the Free Will Defense is the idea of *being free with respect to an action*. If a person is free with respect to a given action, then he is free to perform that action and free to refrain from performing it; no antecedent conditions and/or causal laws determine that he will perform the action, or that he won't. It is within his power, at the time in question, to take or perform the action and within his power to refrain from it. Freedom so conceived is not to be confused with unpredictability. You might be able to predict what you will do in a given situation even if you are free, in that situation, to do something else. If I know you well, I may be able to predict what action you will take in response to a certain set of conditions; it does not follow that you are not free with respect to that action. Secondly, I shall say that an action is *morally significant*, for a given person, if it would be wrong for him to perform the action but right to refrain or vice versa. Keeping a promise, for example, would ordinarily be morally significant for a person, as would refusing induction into the army. On the other hand, having Cheerios for breakfast (instead of Wheaties) would not normally be morally significant. Further, suppose we say that a person is *significantly free*, on a given occasion, if he is then free with respect to a morally significant action. And finally we must distinguish between *moral evil* and *natural evil*. The former is evil that results from free human activity; natural evil is any other kind of evil.[8]

Given these definitions and distinctions, we can make a preliminary statement of the Free Will Defense as follows. A world containing creatures who are significantly free (and freely perform more good than evil actions) is more valuable, all else being equal, than a world containing no free creatures at all. Now God can create free creatures, but He can't *cause* or *determine* them to do only what is right. For if He does so, then they aren't significantly free after all; they do not do what is right *freely*. To create creatures capable of *moral good*, therefore, He must create creatures capable of moral evil; and He can't give these creatures the freedom to perform evil and at the same time prevent them from doing so. As it turned out, sadly enough, some of the free creatures God created went wrong in the exercise of their freedom; this is the source of moral evil. The fact that free creatures sometimes go wrong, however, counts neither against God's omnipotence nor against His goodness; for He could have forestalled the occurrence of moral evil only by removing the possibility of moral good.

I said earlier that the Free Will Defender tries to find a proposition that is consistent with

(1) God is omniscient, omnipotent, and wholly good

and together with (1) entails that there is evil. According to the Free Will Defense, we must find this proposition somewhere in the above story. The heart of the Free Will Defense is the claim that it is *possible* that God could not have created a universe containing moral good (or as much moral good as this world contains) without creating one that also contained moral evil. And if so, then it is possible that God has a good reason for creating a world containing evil.

Now this defense has met with several kinds of objections. For example, some philosophers say that *causal determinism* and *freedom*, contrary to what we might have thought, are not really incompatible.[9] But if so, then God could have created free creatures who were free, and free to do what is wrong, but nevertheless were causally determined to do only what is right. Thus He could have created creatures who were free to do what was wrong, while nevertheless preventing them from ever performing any wrong actions— simply by seeing to it that they were causally determined to do only what is right. Of course this contradicts the Free Will Defense, according to which there is inconsistency in supposing that God determines free creatures to do only what is right. But is it really possible that all of a person's actions are causally determined while some of them are free? How could that be so? According to one version of the doctrine in question, to say that George acts freely on a given occasion is to say only this: *if George had chosen to do otherwise, he would have done otherwise.* Now George's action *A* is causally determined if some event *E*—some event beyond his control—has already occurred, where the state of affairs consisting in *E*'s occurrence conjoined with George's *refraining* from performing *A*, is a causally impossible state of affairs. Then one can consistently hold both that all of a man's actions are causally determined and that some of them are free in the above sense. For suppose that all of a man's actions are causally determined and that he *couldn't*, on any occasion, have made any choice or performed any action different from the ones he did make and perform. It could still be true that if he *had* chosen to do otherwise, he would have done otherwise. Granted, he couldn't have chosen to do otherwise; but this is consistent with saying that *if* he had, things would have gone differently.

This objection to the Free Will Defense seems utterly implausible. One might as well claim that being in jail doesn't really limit one's freedom on the grounds that if one were *not* in jail, he'd be free to come and go as he pleased. So I shall say no more about this objection here.[10]

A second objection is more formidable. In essence it goes like this. Surely it is possible to do only what is right, even if one is free to do wrong. It is *possible*, in that broadly logical sense, that there would be a world containing free creatures who always do what is right. There is certainly no *contradiction* or *inconsistency* in this idea. But God is omnipotent; his power has no nonlogical limitations. So if it's possible that there be a world containing creatures who are free to do what is wrong but never in fact do so, then it follows that an omnipotent God could create such a world. If so, however, the Free Will Defense must be mistaken in its insistence upon the possibility that God is omnipotent but unable to create a world containing moral good without permitting moral evil. J. L. Mackie ... states this objection:

> If God has made men such that in their free choices they sometimes prefer what is good and sometimes what is evil, why could he not have made men such that they always freely choose the good? If there is no logical impossibility in a man's freely choosing the good on one, or on several occasions, there cannot be a logical impossibility in his freely choosing the good on every occasion. God was not, then, faced with a choice between making innocent automata and making beings who, in acting freely, would sometimes go wrong; there was open to him the obviously better possibility of making beings who would act freely but always go right. Clearly, his failure to avail himself of this possibility is inconsistent with his being both omnipotent and wholly good.[11]

Now what, exactly, is Mackie's point here? This. According to the Free Will Defense, it is possible both that God is omnipotent and that He was unable to create a world containing moral good without creating one containing moral evil. But, replies Mackie, this limitation on His power to create is inconsistent with God's omnipotence. For surely it's *possible* that there be a world containing perfectly virtuous persons—persons who are significantly free but always do what is right. Surely there are *possible worlds* that contain moral good but no moral evil. But God, if He is omnipotent, can create any possible world He chooses. So it is *not* possible, contrary to the Free Will Defense, both that God is omnipotent and that He could create a world containing moral good only by creating one containing moral evil. If He is omnipotent, the only limitations of His power are *logical* limitations;

in which case there are no possible worlds He could not have created.

This is a subtle and important point. According to the great German philosopher G. W. Leibniz, *this* world, the actual world, must be the best of all possible worlds. His reasoning goes as follows. Before God created anything at all, He was confronted with an enormous range of choices; He could create or bring into actuality any of the myriads of different possible worlds. Being perfectly good, He must have chosen to create the best world He could; being omnipotent, He was able to create any possible world He pleased. He must, therefore, have chosen the best of all possible worlds; and hence *this* world, the one He did create, must be the best possible. Now Mackie, of course, agrees with Leibniz that God, if omnipotent, could have created any world He pleased and would have created the best world he could. But while Leibniz draws the conclusion that this world, despite appearances, must be the best possible, Mackie concludes instead that there is no omnipotent, wholly good God. For, he says, it is obvious enough that this present world is not the best of all possible worlds.

The Free Will Defender disagrees with both Leibniz and Mackie. In the first place, he might say, what is the reason for supposing that there is such a thing as the best of all possible worlds? No matter how marvelous a world is—containing no matter how many persons enjoying unalloyed bliss—isn't it possible that there be an even better world containing even more persons enjoying even more unalloyed bliss? But what is really characteristic and central to the Free Will Defense is the claim that God, though omnipotent, could not have actualized just any possible world He pleased.

5. WAS IT WITHIN GOD'S POWER TO CREATE ANY POSSIBLE WORLD HE PLEASED?

This is indeed the crucial question for the Free Will Defense. If we wish to discuss it with insight and authority, we shall have to look into the idea of *possible worlds*. And a sensible first question is this: what sort of thing is a possible world? The basic idea is that a possible world is *a way things could have been*; it is a *state of affairs* of some kind. Earlier we spoke of states of affairs, in particular of good and evil states of affairs. Suppose we look at this idea in more detail. What sort of thing is a state of affairs? The following would be examples:

Nixon's having won the 1972 election

7 + 5's being equal to 12

All men's being mortal

and

Gary, Indiana's, having a really nasty pollution problem.

These are *actual* states of affairs: states of affairs that do in fact obtain. And corresponding to each such actual state of affairs there is a true proposition—in the above cases, the corresponding propositions would be *Nixon won the 1972 presidential election, 7 + 5 is equal to 12, all men are mortal,* and *Gary, Indiana, has a really nasty pollution problem.* A proposition *p* corresponds to a state of affairs s_1, in this sense, if it is impossible that *p* be true and s_1 fail to obtain and impossible that s_1 obtain and *p* fail to be true.

But just as there are false propositions, so there are states of affairs that do *not* obtain or are *not* actual. *Kissinger's having swum the Atlantic* and *Hubert Horatio Humphrey's having run a mile in four minutes* would be examples. Some states of affairs that do not obtain are impossible: e.g., *Hubert's having drawn a square circle, 7 + 5's equal to 75,* and *Agnew's having a brother who was an only child.* The propositions corresponding to these states of affairs, of course, are necessarily false. So there are states of affairs that *obtain* or are *actual* and also states of affairs that don't obtain. Among the latter some are *impossible* and others are possible. And a possible world is a possible state of affairs. Of course not every possible state of affairs is a possible world; *Hubert's having run a mile in four minutes* is a possible state of affairs but not a possible world. No doubt it is an *element* of many possible worlds, but it isn't itself inclusive enough to be one. To be a possible world, a state of affairs must be very large—so large as to be *complete* or *maximal*.

To get at this idea of completeness we need a couple of definitions. As we have already seen . . . a state of affairs *A includes* a state of affairs *B* if it is not possible that *A* obtain and *B* not obtain or if the conjunctive state of affairs *A but not B*—the state of affairs that obtains if and only if *A* obtains and *B* does not—is not possible. For example, *Jim Whittaker's being the first American to climb Mt. Everest* includes *Jim Whittaker's being an American.* It also includes *Mt. Everest's being climbed, something's being climbed, no American's having climbed Everest before Whittaker did,* and the like. *Inclusion* among states of affairs is like *entailment* among propositions; and where a state of affairs *A* includes a state of affairs *B*, the proposition corresponding to *A* entails the one corresponding to *B*. Accordingly, *Jim Whittaker is the first American to climb Everest* entails *Mt. Everest has been climbed, something has been climbed,* and *no American climbed Everest before Whittaker did.* Now suppose we say further that a state of affairs *A precludes* a state of affairs *B* if it is not possible that *both* obtain, or if the conjunctive state of affairs *A and B* is impossible. Thus *Whittaker's being the first American to climb Mt. Everest* precludes *Luther Jerstad's being the first American to climb Everest,* as well as Whittaker's never having climbed any mountains. If *A* precludes *B,* than *A's* corresponding proposition entails the denial of the one corresponding to *B.* Still further, let's say that the *complement* of a state of affairs is the state of affairs that obtains just in case *A* does not obtain. [Or we might say that the complement (call it $\bar{A}$) of *A* is the state of affairs corresponding to the *denial* or *negation* of the proposition corresponding to *A.*] Given these definitions, we can say what it is for a state of affairs to be *complete*: *A* is a complete state of affairs if and only if for every state of affairs *B,* either *A includes B* or *A precludes B.* (We could express the same thing by saying that if *A* is a complete state of affairs, then for every state of affairs *B,* either *A* includes *B* or *A* includes $\bar{B}$, the complement of *B.*) And now we are able to say what a possible world is: a possible world is any possible state of affairs that is complete. If *A* is a possible world, then it says something about everything; every state of affairs *S* is either included in or precluded by it.

Corresponding to each possible world W, furthermore, there is a set of propositions that I'll call the book on W. A proposition is in the book on W just in case the state of affairs to which it corresponds is included in W. Or we might express it like this. Suppose we say that a proposition P *is true in a world W* if and only if P *would have been true if W had been actual*—if and only if, that is, it is not possible that W be actual and P be false. Then the book on W is the set of propositions true in W. Like possible worlds, books are *complete*; if B is a book, then for any proposition P, either P or the denial of P will be a member of B. A book is a *maximal consistent set* of propositions; it is so large that the addition of another proposition to it always yields an explicitly inconsistent set.

Of course, for each possible world there is exactly one book corresponding to it (that is, for a given world W there is just one book B such that each member of B is true in M; and for each book there is just one world to which it corresponds). So every world has its book.

It should be obvious that exactly one possible world is actual. At *least* one must be, since the set of true propositions is a maximal consistent set and hence a book. But then it corresponds to a possible world, and the possible world corresponding to this set of propositions (since it's the set of *true* propositions) will be actual. On the other hand there is at *most* one actual world. For suppose there were two: W and W'. These worlds cannot include all the very same states of affairs; if they did, they would be the very same world. So there must be at least one state of affairs S such that W includes S and W' does not. But a possible world is maximal; W', therefore, includes the complement $\bar{S}$ of S. So if both W and W' were actual, as we have supposed, then both S and $\bar{S}$ would be actual—which is impossible. So there can't be more than one possible world that is actual.

Leibniz pointed out that a proposition p is necessary if it is true in every possible world. We may add that p is possible if it is true in one world and impossible if true in none. Furthermore, p *entails* q if there is no possible world in which p is true and q is false, and p *is consistent with* q if there is at least one world in which both p and q are true.

A further feature of possible worlds is that people (and other things) exist in them. Each of us exists in the actual world, obviously; but a person also exists in many worlds distinct from the actual world. It would be a mistake, of course, to think of all of these worlds as somehow "going on" at the same time, with the same person reduplicated through these worlds and actually existing in a lot of different ways. This is not what is meant by saying that the same person exists in different possible worlds. What is meant, instead, is this: a person Paul exists in each of those possible worlds W which is such that, if W had been actual, Paul would have existed—actually existed. Suppose Paul had been an inch taller than he is, or a better tennis player. Then the world that does in fact obtain would not have been actual; some other world— W', let's say— would have obtained instead. If W' had been actual, Paul would have existed; so Paul exists in W'. (Of course there are still other possible worlds in which Paul does not exist—worlds, for example, in which there are no people at all.) Accordingly, when we say that Paul exists in a world W, what we mean is that Paul *would have* existed had W been actual. Or we could put it like this: Paul exists in each world W that includes the state of affairs consisting in Paul's existence. We can put this still more simply by saying that Paul exists in those worlds whose books contain the proposition *Paul exists*.

But isn't there a problem here? *Many* people are named "Paul": Paul the apostle, Paul J. Zwier, John Paul Jones, and many other famous Pauls. So who goes with "Paul exists"? Which Paul? The answer has to do with the fact that books contain *propositions*—not sentences. They contain the sort of thing sentences are used to express and assert. And the same sentence—"Aristotle is wise," for example—can be used to express many different propositions. When Plato used it, he asserted a proposition predicating wisdom of his famous pupil; when Jackie Onassis uses it, she asserts a proposition predicating wisdom of her wealthy husband. These are distinct propositions (we might even think they differ in truth value); but they are expressed by the same sentence. Normally (but not always) we don't have much trouble determining which of the several propositions expressed by a given sentence is relevant in the context at hand. So in this case a given person, Paul, exists in a world W if and only if W' book contains the proposition that says that *he*—that particular person—exists. The fact that the sentence we use to express this proposition can also be used to express *other* propositions is not relevant.

After this excursion into the nature of books and worlds we can return to our question. Could God have created just any world He chose? Before addressing the question, however, we must note that God does not, strictly speaking, *create* any possible worlds or states of affairs at all. What He creates are the heavens and the earth and all that they contain. But He has not created states of affairs. There are, for example, the state of affairs consisting in God's existence and the state of affairs consisting in His nonexistence. That is, there is such a thing as the state of affairs consisting in the existence of God, and there is also such a thing as the state of affairs consisting in the nonexistence of God, just as there are the two propositions *God exists* and *God does not exist*. The theist believes that the first state of affairs is actual and the first proposition true; the atheist believes that the second state of affairs is actual and the second proposition true. But, of course, both propositions *exist*, even though just one is true. Similarly, there are two states of affairs here, just one of which is actual. So both states of affairs *exist*, but only one *obtains*. And God has not created either one of them since there never was a time at which either did not exist. Nor has he created the state of affairs consisting in the earth's existence; there was a time when *the earth* did not exist, but none when the state of affairs consisting in the earth's existence didn't exist. Indeed, God did not bring into existence any states of affairs at all. What He did was to perform actions of a certain sort—creating the heavens and the earth, for example—which resulted in the *actuality* of certain states of affairs. God *actualizes* states of affairs. He actualizes the possible world that does in fact obtain; He does not create it. And while He has created Socrates, He did not create the state of affairs consisting in Socrates' existence.[12]

Bearing this in mind, let's finally return to our question. Is the atheologian right in holding that if God is omnipotent, then he could have actualized or created any possible world He pleased? Not obviously. First, we must ask ourselves whether God is a *necessary* or a *contingent* being. A necessary being is one that exists in every possible world—one that would have existed no matter which possible world had been actual; a contingent being exists only in some possible worlds. Now if God is not a necessary being (and many, perhaps most, theists think that He is not), then clearly enough there will be many possible worlds He could not have actualized—all those, for example, in which He does not exist. Clearly, God could not have created a world in which He doesn't even exist.

So, if God is a contingent being then there are many possible worlds beyond His power to create. But this is really irrelevant to our present concerns. For perhaps the atheologian can maintain his case if he revises his claim to avoid this difficulty; perhaps he will say something like this: if God is omnipotent, then He could have actualized any of these possible worlds *in which He exists*. So if He exists and is omnipotent, He could have actualized (contrary to the Free Will Defense) any of those possible worlds in which He exists and in which there exist free creatures who do no wrong. He could have actualized worlds containing moral good but no moral evil. Is this correct?

Let's begin with a trivial example. You and Paul have just returned from an Australian hunting expedition: your quarry was the elusive double-waffled cassowary. Paul captured an aardvark, mistaking it for a cassowary. The creature's disarming ways have won it a place in Paul's heart; he is deeply attached to it. Upon your return to the States you offer Paul $500 for his aardvark, only to be rudely turned down. Later you ask yourself, "What would he have done if I'd offered him $700?" Now what is it, exactly, that you are asking? What you're really asking in a way is whether, under a *specific set of conditions*, Paul would have sold it. These conditions include your having offered him $700 rather than $500 for the aardvark, everything else being as much as possible like the conditions that did in fact obtain. Let S' be this set of conditions or state of affairs. S' includes the state of affairs consisting in your offering Paul $700 (instead of the $500 you did offer him); of course it does not include his *accepting* your offer, and it does not include his *rejecting* it; for the rest, the conditions it includes are just like the ones that did obtain in the actual world. So, for example, S' includes Paul's being free to accept the offer and free to refrain; and if in fact the going rate for an aardvark was $650, then S' includes the state of affairs consisting in the going rate's being $650. So we might put your question by asking which of the following conditionals is true:

(23) If the state of affairs S' had obtained, Paul would have accepted the offer

(24) If the state of affairs S' had obtained, Paul would not have accepted the offer.

It seems clear that at least one of these conditionals is true, but naturally they can't both be; so exactly one is.

Now since S' includes neither Paul's accepting the offer nor his rejecting it, the antecedent of (23) and (24) does not entail the consequent of either. That is,

(25) S' *obtains* does not entail either

(26) Paul accepts the offer

or

(27) Paul does not accept the offer.

So there are possible worlds in which both (25) and (26) are true, and other possible worlds in which both (25) and (27) are true.

We are now in a position to grasp an important fact. Either (23) or (24) is in fact true; and either way there are possible worlds God could not have actualized. Suppose, first of all, that (23) is true. Then it was beyond the power of God to create a world in which (1) Paul is free to sell his aardvark and free to refrain, and in which the other states of affairs included in S' obtain, and (2) Paul does not sell. That is, it was beyond His power to create a world in which (25) and (27) are both true.

There is at least one possible world like this, but God, despite His omnipotence, could not have brought about its actuality. For let W be such a world. To actualize W, God must bring it about that Paul is free with respect to this action, and that the other states of affairs included in S' obtain. But (23), as we are supposing, is true; so if God had actualized S' and left Paul *free* with respect to this action, he would have sold: in which case W would not have been actual. If, on the other hand, God had *brought it about* that Paul didn't sell or had *caused him to* refrain from selling, then Paul would not have been free with respect to this action; then S' would not have been actual (since S' includes Paul's being free with respect to it), and W would not have been actual since W includes S'.

Of course if it is (24) rather than (23) that is true, then another class of worlds was beyond God's power to actualize—those, namely, in which S' obtains and Paul *sells* his aardvark. These are the worlds in which both (25) and (26) are true. But either (23) or (24) is true. Therefore, there are possible worlds God could not have actualized. If we consider whether or not God could have created a world in which, let's say, both (25) and (26) are true, we see that the answer depends upon a peculiar kind of fact; it depends upon what Paul would have freely chosen to do in a certain situation. So there are any number of possible worlds such that it is partly up to Paul whether God can create them.[13]

That was a past tense example. Perhaps it would be useful to consider a future tense case, since this might seem to correspond more closely to God's situation in choosing a possible world to actualize. At some time t in the near future Maurice will be free with respect to some insignificant action—having freeze-dried oatmeal for breakfast, let's say. That is, at time t Maurice will be free to have oatmeal but also free to take something else— shredded wheat, perhaps. Next, suppose we consider S', a state of affairs that is included in the actual world and includes Maurice's being free with respect to taking oatmeal at time t. That is, S' includes Maurice's being free at time t to take oatmeal and free to reject it. S' does not include

Maurice's taking oatmeal, however; nor does it include his rejecting it. For the rest S' is as much as possible like the actual world. In particular there are many conditions that do in fact hold at time t and are *relevant* to his choice—such conditions, for example, as the fact that he hasn't had oatmeal lately, that his wife will be annoyed if he rejects it, and the like; and S' includes each of these conditions. Now God no doubt knows what Maurice will do at time t, if S obtains; He knows which action Maurice would freely perform if S were to be actual. That is, God knows that one of the following conditionals is true:

(28) If S' were to obtain, Maurice will freely take the oatmeal

or

(29) If S' were to obtain, Maurice will freely reject it.

We may not know which of these is true, and Maurice himself may not know; but presumably God does.

So either God knows that (28) is true, or else He knows that (29) is. Let's suppose it is (28). Then there is a possible world that God, though omnipotent, cannot create. For consider a possible world W' that shares S' with the actual world (which for ease of reference I'll name "Kronos") and in which Maurice does not take oatmeal. (We know there is such a world, since S' does not include Maurice's taking the oatmeal.) S' obtains in W' just as it does in Kronos. Indeed, everything in W' is just as it is in Kronos up to time t. But whereas in Kronos Maurice takes oatmeal at time t, in W' he does not. Now W' is a perfectly possible world; but it is not within God's power to create it or bring about its actuality. For to do so He must actualize S'. But (28) is in fact true. So if God actualizes S' (as He must to create W') and leaves Maurice free with respect to the action in question, then he will take the oatmeal; and then, of course, W' will not be actual. If, on the other hand, God causes Maurice to *refrain* from taking the oatmeal, then he is not free to take it. That means, once again, that W' is not actual; for in W' Maurice is

free to take the oatmeal (even if he doesn't do so). So if (28) is true, then this world W' is one that God can't actualize, it is not within His power to actualize it even though He is omnipotent and it is a possible world.

Of course, if it is (29) that is true, we get a similar result; then too there are possible worlds that God can't actualize. These would be worlds which share S' with Kronos and in which Maurice *does* take oatmeal. But either (28) or (29) is true; so either way there is a possible world that God can't create. If we consider a world in which S' obtains and in which Maurice freely chooses oatmeal at time t, we see that whether or not it is within God's power to actualize it depends upon what Maurice would do if he were free in a certain situation. Accordingly, there are any number of possible worlds such that it is partly up to Maurice whether or not God can actualize them. It is, of course, up to God whether or not to create Maurice and also up to God whether or not to make him free with respect to the action of taking oatmeal at time t. (God could, if He chose, cause him to succumb to the dreaded *equine obsession*, a condition shared by some people and most horses, whose victims find it *psychologically impossible* to refuse oats or oat products.) But if He creates Maurice and creates him free with respect to this action, then whether or not he actually performs the action is up to Maurice—not God.[14]

Now we can return to the Free Will Defense and the problem of evil. The Free Will Defender, you recall, insists on the possibility that it is not within God's power to create a world containing moral good without creating one containing moral evil. His atheological opponent—Mackie, for example—agrees with Leibniz in insisting that *if* (as the theist holds) God is omnipotent, then it *follows* that He could have created any possible world He pleased. We now see that this contention—call it "Leibniz' Lapse"—is a mistake. The atheologian is right in holding that there are many possible worlds containing moral good but no moral evil; his mistake lies in endorsing Leibniz' Lapse. So one of his premises—that God, if omnipotent, could have actualized just any world He pleased—is false.

6. COULD GOD HAVE CREATED A WORLD CONTAINING MORAL GOOD BUT NO MORAL EVIL?

Now suppose we recapitulate the logic of the situation. The Free Will Defender claims that the following is possible:

(30)   God is omnipotent, and it was not within His power to create a world containing moral good but no moral evil.

By way of retort the atheologian insists that there are possible worlds containing moral good but no moral evil. He adds that an omnipotent being could have actualized any possible world he chose. So if God is omnipotent, it follows that He could have actualized a world containing moral good but no moral evil, hence (30), contrary to the Free Will Defender's claim, is not possible. What we have seen so far is that his second premise—Leibniz' Lapse—is false.

Of course, this does not settle the issue in the Free Will Defender's favor. Leibniz' Lapse (appropriately enough for a lapse) is false; but this doesn't show that (30) is possible. To show this latter we must demonstrate the possibility that among the worlds God could not have actualized are all the worlds containing moral good but no moral evil. How can we approach this question?

Instead of choosing oatmeal for breakfast or selling an aardvark, suppose we think about a morally significant action such as taking a bribe. Curley Smith, the mayor of Boston, is opposed to the proposed freeway route; it would require destruction of the Old North Church along with some other antiquated and structurally unsound buildings. L. B. Smedes, the director of highways, asks him whether he'd drop his opposition for $1 million. "Of course," he replies. "Would you do it for $2?" asks Smedes. "What do you take me for?" comes the indignant reply. "That's already established," smirks Smedes; "all that remains is to nail down your price." Smedes then offers him a bribe of $35,000; unwilling to break with the fine old traditions of Bay State politics, Curley accepts.

Smedes then spends a sleepless night wondering whether he could have bought Curley for $20,000.

Now suppose we assume that Curley was free with respect to the action of taking the bribe—free to take it and free to refuse. And suppose, furthermore, that he would have taken it. That is, let us suppose that

(31)   If Smedes had offered Curley a bribe of $20,000, he would have accepted it.

If (31) is true, then there is a state of affairs S' that (1) includes Curley's being offered a bribe of $20,000; (2) does not include either his accepting the bribe or his rejecting it; and (3) is otherwise as much as possible like the actual world. Just to make sure S' includes every relevant circumstance, let us suppose that it is a *maximal world segment*. That is, add to S' any state of affairs compatible with but not included in it, and the result will be an entire possible world. We could think of it roughly like this: S' is included in at least one world W in which Curley takes the bribe and in at least one world W' in which he rejects it. If S' is a maximal world segment, then S' is what remains of W when *Curley's taking the bribe* is deleted; it is also what remains of W' when *Curley's rejecting the bribe* is deleted. More exactly, if S' is a maximal world segment, then every possible state of affairs that includes S', but isn't included by S', is a possible world. So if (31) is true, then there is a maximal world segment S' that (1) includes Curley's being offered a bribe of $20,000; (2) does not include either his accepting the bribe or his rejecting it; (3) is otherwise as much as possible like the actual world—in particular, it includes Curley's being free with respect to the bribe; and (4) is such that if it were actual then Curley would have taken the bribe. That is

(32)   if S' were actual, *Curley would have accepted the bribe* is true.

Now, of course, there is at least one possible world W' in which S' is actual and Curley does not take the bribe. But God could not have created W'; to do so, he would have been obliged to actualize S', leaving Curley free with respect to the action of taking the bribe. But under these conditions Curley, as (32) assures us, would have accepted the bribe, so that the world thus created would not have been S'.

Curley, as we see, is not above a bit of Watergating. But there may be worse to come. Of course, there are possible worlds in which he is significantly free (i.e., free with respect to a morally significant action) and never does what is wrong. But the sad truth about Curley may be this. Consider W', any of these worlds: in W' Curley is significantly free, so in W' there are some actions that are morally significant for him and with respect to which he is free. But at least one of these actions—call it A—has the following peculiar property. There is a maximal world segment S' that obtains in W' and is such that (1) S' includes Curley's being free re A but neither his performing A nor his refraining from A; (2) S' is otherwise as much as possible like W' and (3) if S' had been actual, Curley would have gone wrong with respect to A.[15] (Notice that this third condition holds in fact, in the actual world; it does not hold in that world W'.)

This means, of course, that God could not have actualized W'. For to do so He'd have been obliged to bring it about that S' is actual; but then Curley would go wrong with respect to A. Since in W' he always does what is right, the world thus actualized would not be W'. On the other hand, if God *causes* Curley to go right with respect to A or *brings it about* that he does so, then Curley isn't free with respect to A; and so once more it isn't W' that is actual. Accordingly God cannot create W'. But W' was just any of the worlds in which Curley is significantly free but always does only what is right. It therefore follows that it was not within God's power to create a world in which Curley produces moral good but no moral evil. Every world God can actualize is such that if Curley is significantly free in it, he takes at least one wrong action.

Obviously Curley is in serious trouble. I shall call the malady from which he suffers transworld depravity. (I leave as homework the problem of comparing transworld depravity with what Calvinists call "total depravity.") By way of explicit definition:

(33)   A person P *suffers from transworld depravity* if and only if the following holds: for every world W such that P is significantly free in W and P does only what is right in W, there is

an action A and a maximal world segment S' such that

(1) S' includes A's being morally significant for P

(2) S' includes P's being free with respect to A

(3) S' is included in W and includes neither P's performing A nor P's refraining from performing A

and

(4)   If S' were actual, P would go wrong with respect to A.

(In thinking about this definition, remember that (4) is to be true in fact, in the actual world—not in that world W.)

What is important about the idea of transworld depravity is that if a person suffers from it, then it wasn't within God's power to actualize any world in which that person is significantly free but does no wrong—that is, a world in which he produces moral good but no moral evil.

We have been here considering a crucial contention of the Free Will Defender: the contention, namely, that

(30)   God is omnipotent, and it was not within His power to create a world containing moral good but no moral evil.

How is transworld depravity relevant to this? As follows. Obviously it is possible that there be persons who suffer from transworld depravity. More generally, it is possible that *everybody* suffers from it. And if this possibility were actual, then God, though omnipotent, could not have created any of the possible worlds containing just the persons who do in fact exist, and containing moral good but no moral evil. For to do so He'd have to create persons who were significantly free (otherwise there would be no moral good) but suffered from transworld depravity. Such persons go wrong with respect to at least one action in any world God could have actualized and in which they are free with respect to morally significant actions; so the price for creating a world in which they produce moral good is creating one in which they also produce moral evil.

NOTES

1. John Mackie, "Evil and Omnipotence," in *The Philosophy of Religion*, ed. Basil Mitchell (London Oxford University Press:, 1971), p. 92. [See previous reading.]

2. Ibid., p. 93. [*Philosophy of Religion: Selected Readings, Second Edition*, p. 224.]

3. More simply, the question is really just whether any good state of affairs includes an evil; a little reflection reveals that no good state of affairs can include an evil that it does not outweigh.

4. In Plantinga, *God and Other Minds* (Ithaca, N.Y.: Cornell University Press, 1967), chap. 5, I explore further the project of finding such propositions.

5. *The Problem of Free Choice,* Vol. 22 of *Ancient Christian Writers* (Westminster, Md.: The Newman Press, 1955), bk. 2, pp. 14–15.

6. Ibid., bk. 3, p. 9.

7. I am indebted to Henry Schuurman (in conversation) for helpful discussion of the difference between this pastoral function and those served by a theodicy or a defense.

8. This distinction is not very precise (how, exactly, are we to construe "results from"?), but perhaps it will serve our present purposes.

9. See, for example, A. Flew, "Divine Omnipotence and Human Freedom," in *New Essays in Philosophical Theology*, eds. A. Flew and A. MacIntyre (London SCM:, 1955), pp. 150–53.

10. For further discussion of it see Plantinga, *God and Other Minds*, pp. 132–35.

11. Mackie, in *The Philosophy of Religion*, pp. 100–101.

12. Strict accuracy demands, therefore, that we speak of God as actualizing rather than creating possible worlds. I shall continue to use both locutions, thus sacrificing accuracy to familiarity. For more about possible worlds see my book *The Nature of Necessity* (Oxford The Clarendon Press:, 1974), chaps. 4–8.

13. For a fuller statement of this argument see Plantinga, *The Nature of Necessity*, chap. 9, secs. 4–6.

14. For a more complete and more exact statement of this argument see Plantinga, *The Nature of Necessity*, chap. 9, secs. 4–6.

15. A person goes wrong with respect to an action if he either wrongfully performs it or wrongfully fails to perform it.

III.C.2

Evil and Soul-Making

JOHN HICK

John Hick (1922 – 2012) was for many years professor of theology at the University of Birmingham in England and, until his retirement, was professor of philosophy at Claremont Graduate School. His book Evil and the God of Love *(1966), from which this selection is taken, is considered one of the*

Pp. 253–261 from *Evil and the God of Love*, revised edition, by John Hick. Copyright © 1966, 1977 by John Hick. Used with permission. Footnotes edited.

most thorough treatises on the problem of evil. "Evil and Soul-Making" is an example of a theodicy argument that is based on the free will defense. Theodicies can be of two differing types depending on how they justify the ways of God in the face of evil. The Augustinian position is that God created humans without sin and set them in a sinless, paradisical world. However, humanity fell into sin through the misuse of free will. God's grace will save some of us, but others will perish everlastingly. The second type of theodicy stems from the thinking of Irenaeus. The Irenaean tradition views Adam not as a free agent rebelling against God but as more akin to a small child. The fall is humanity's first faulty step in the direction of freedom. God is still working with humanity in order to bring it from undeveloped life (bios) to a state of self-realization in divine love, spiritual life (zoe). This life is viewed as the "vale of soul-making." Hick favors this version and develops it in this reading.

Fortunately there is another and better way. As well as the "majority report" of the Augustinian tradition, which has dominated Western Christendom, both Catholic and Protestant, since the time of Augustine himself, there is the "minority report" of the Irenaean tradition. This latter is both older and newer than the other, for it goes back to St. Irenaeus and others of the early Hellenistic Fathers of the Church in the two centuries prior to St. Augustine, and it has flourished again in more developed forms during the last hundred years.

Instead of regarding man as having been created by God in a finished state, as a finitely perfect being fulfilling the divine intention for our human level of existence, and then falling disastrously away from this, the minority report sees man as still in process of creation. Irenaeus himself expressed the point in terms of the (exegetically dubious) distinction between the "image" and the "likeness" of God referred to in Genesis i.26: "Then God said, Let us make man in our image, after our likeness." His view was that man as a personal and moral being already exists in the image, but has not yet been formed into the finite likeness of God. By this "likeness" Irenaeus means something more than personal existence as such; he means a certain valuable quality of personal life which reflects finitely the divine life. This represents the perfecting of man, the fulfillment of God's purpose for humanity, the "bringing of many sons to glory," the creating of "children of God" who are "fellow heirs with Christ" of his glory.

And so man, created as a personal being in the image of God, is only the raw material for a further and more difficult stage of God's creative work. This is the leading of men as relatively free and autonomous persons, through their own dealings with life in the world in which He has placed them, towards that quality of personal existence that is the finite likeness of God. The features of this likeness are revealed in the person of Christ, and the process of man's creation into it is the work of the Holy Spirit. In St. Paul's words, "And we all, with unveiled faces, beholding the glory of the Lord, are being changed into his likeness (εἰκών) from one degree of glory to another; for this comes from the Lord who is the Spirit";[1] or again, "For God knew his own before ever they were, and also ordained that they should be shaped to the likeness (εἰκών) of his Son."[2] In Johannine terms, the movement from the image to the likeness is a transition from one level of existence, that of animal life (*Bios*), to another and higher level, that of eternal life (*Zoe*), which includes but transcends the first. And the fall of man was seen by Irenaeus as a failure within the second phase of this creative process, a failure that has multiplied the perils and complicated the route of the journey in which God is seeking to lead mankind.

In the light of modern anthropological knowledge some form of two-stage conception of the creation of man has become an almost unavoidable Christian tenet. At the very least we must acknowledge as two distinguishable stages the fashioning of *homo sapiens* as a product of the long evolutionary process, and his sudden or gradual spiritualization as a child of God. But we may well extend the first stage to include the development of man as a rational and responsible person capable of personal relationship with the personal Infinite who has created him. This first stage of the creative process was, to our anthropomorphic imaginations, easy for divine omnipotence. By an exercise of creative power God caused the physical universe to exist, and in the course of countless ages to bring forth within it organic life, and finally to produce out of organic life personal life; and when man had thus emerged out of the evolution of the forms of organic life, a creature had been made who has the possibility of existing in conscious fellowship with God. But the second stage of the creative process is of a different kind altogether. It cannot be performed by omnipotent power as such. For personal life is essentially free and self-directing. It cannot be perfected by divine fiat, but only through the uncompelled responses and willing co-operation of human individuals in their actions and reactions in the world in which God has placed them. Men may eventually become the perfected persons whom the New Testament calls "children of God," but they cannot be created ready-made as this.

The value-judgment that is implicitly being invoked here is that one who has attained to goodness by meeting and eventually mastering temptations, and thus by rightly making responsible choices in concrete situations, is good in a richer and more valuable sense than would be one created *ab initio* in a state either of innocence or of virtue. In the former case, which is that of the actual moral achievements of mankind, the individual's goodness has within it the strength of temptation overcome, a stability based upon an accumulation of right choices, and a positive and responsible character that comes from the investment of costly personal effort. I suggest, then, that it is an ethically reasonable judgment, even though in the nature of the case not one that is capable of demonstrative proof, that human goodness slowly built up through personal histories of moral effort has a value in the eyes of the Creator which justifies even the long travail of the soul-making process.

The picture with which we are working is thus developmental and teleological. Man is in process of becoming the perfected being whom God is seeking to create. However, this is not taking place—it is important to add—by a natural and inevitable evolution, but through a hazardous adventure in individual freedom. Because this is a pilgrimage within the life of each individual, rather than a racial

evolution, the progressive fulfillment of God's purpose does not entail any corresponding progressive improvement in the moral state of the world. There is no doubt a development in man's ethical situation from generation to generation through the building of individual choices into public institutions, but this involves an accumulation of evil as well as of good. It is thus probable that human life was lived on much the same moral plane two thousand years ago or four thousand years ago as it is today. But nevertheless during this period uncounted millions of souls have been through the experience of earthly life, and God's purpose has gradually moved towards its fulfillment within each one of them, rather than within a human aggregate composed of different units in different generations.

If, then, God's aim in making the world is "the bringing of many sons to glory," that aim will naturally determine the kind of world that He has created. Antitheistic writers almost invariably assume a conception of the divine purpose which is contrary to the Christian conception. They assume that the purpose of a loving God must be to create a hedonistic paradise; and therefore to the extent that the world is other than this, it proves to them that God is either not loving enough or not powerful enough to create such a world. They think of God's relation to the earth on the model of a human being building a cage for a pet animal to dwell in. If he is humane he will naturally make his pet's quarters as pleasant and healthful as he can. Any respect in which the cage falls short of the veterinarian's ideal, and contains possibilities of accident or disease, is evidence of either limited benevolence or limited means, or both. Those who use the problem of evil as an argument against belief in God almost invariably think of the world in this kind of way. David Hume, for example, speaks of an architect who is trying to plan a house that is to be as comfortable and convenient as possible. If we find that "the windows, doors, fires, passages, stairs, and the whole economy of the building were the source of noise, confusion, fatigue, darkness, and the extremes of heat and cold" we should have no hesitation in blaming the architect. It would be in vain for him to prove that if this or that defect were corrected greater ills would result: "still you would assert in general, that, if the architect had had skill and good intentions, he might have formed such a plan of the whole, and might have adjusted the parts in such a manner, as would have remedied all or most of these inconveniences."[3]

But if we are right in supposing that God's purpose for man is to lead him from human *Bios*, or the biological life of man, to that quality of *Zoe*, or the personal life of eternal worth, which we see in Christ, then the question that we have to ask is not, Is this the kind of world that an all-powerful and infinitely loving being would create as an environment for his human pets? or, Is the architecture of the world the most pleasant and convenient possible? The question that we have to ask is rather, Is this the kind of world that God might make as an environment in which moral beings may be fashioned, through their own free insights and responses, into "children of God"?

Such critics as Hume are confusing what heaven ought to be, as an environment for perfected finite beings, with what this world ought to be, as an environment for beings who are in process of becoming perfected. For if our general conception of God's purpose is correct the world is not intended to be a paradise, but rather the scene of a history in which human personality may be formed towards the pattern of Christ. Men are not to be thought of on the analogy of animal pets, whose life is to be made as agreeable as possible, but rather on the analogy of human children, who are to grow to adulthood in an environment whose primary and overriding purpose is not immediate pleasure but the realizing of the most valuable potentialities of human personality.

Needless to say, this characterization of God as the heavenly Father is not a merely random illustration but an analogy that lies at the heart of the Christian faith. Jesus treated the likeness between the attitude of God to man, and the attitude of human parents at their best towards their children, as providing the most adequate way for us to think about God. And so it is altogether relevant to a Christian understanding of this world to ask, How does the best parental love express itself in its influence upon the environment in which children are to grow up? I think it is clear that a parent who loves his children, and wants them to become the best human beings that they are capable of becoming, does not treat pleasure as the sole and supreme value. Certainly we seek pleasure for our children, and take great delight in obtaining it for them; but we do not desire for them unalloyed pleasure at the expense of their growth in such even greater values as moral integrity, unselfishness, compassion, courage, humour, reverence for the truth, and perhaps above all the capacity for love. We do not act on the premise that pleasure is the supreme end of life; and if the development of these other values sometimes clashes with the provision of pleasure, then we are willing to have our children miss a certain amount of this, rather than fail to come to possess and to be possessed by the finer and more precious qualities that are possible to the human personality. A child brought up on the principle that the only or the supreme value is pleasure would not be likely to become an ethically mature adult or an attractive or happy personality. And to most parents it seems more important to try to foster quality and strength of character in their children than to fill their lives at all times with the utmost possible degree of pleasure. If, then, there is any true analogy between God's purpose for his human creatures, and the purpose of loving and wise parents for their children, we have to recognize that the presence of pleasure and the absence of pain cannot be the supreme and overriding end for which the world exists. Rather, this world must be a place of soul-making. And its value is to be judged, not primarily by the quantity of pleasure and pain occurring in it at any particular moment, but by its fitness for its primary purpose, the purpose of soul-making.

In all this we have been speaking about the nature of the world considered simply as the God given environment of man's life. For it is mainly in this connection that the world has been regarded in Irenaean and in Protestant thought. But such a way of thinking involves a danger of anthropocentrism from which the Augustinian and Catholic tradition has generally been protected by its sense of the relative insignificance of man within the totality of the created universe. Man was dwarfed within the medieval worldview by the innumerable hosts of angels and archangels above him—unfallen rational natures which rejoice in the immediate presence of God, reflecting His glory in the untarnished mirror of their worship. However, this higher creation has in our modern world lost its hold upon the imagination. Its place has been taken, as the minimizer of men, by the immensities of outer space and by the material universe's unlimited complexity transcending our present knowledge. As the spiritual environment envisaged by Western man has shrunk, his physical horizons have correspondingly expanded. Where the human creature was formerly seen as an insignificant appendage to the angelic world, he is now seen as an equally insignificant organic excrescence, enjoying a fleeting moment of consciousness on the surface of one of the planets of a minor star. Thus the truth that was symbolized for former ages by the existence of the angelic hosts is today impressed upon us by the vastness of the physical universe, countering the egoism of our species by making us feel that this immense prodigality of existence can hardly all exist for the sake of man—though, on the other hand, the very realization that it is not all for the sake of man may itself be salutary and beneficial to man!

However, instead of opposing man and nature as rival objects of God's interest, we should perhaps rather stress man's solidarity as an embodied being with the whole natural order in which he is embedded. For man is organic to the world; all his acts and thoughts and imaginations are conditioned by space and time; and in abstraction from nature he would cease to be human. We may, then, say that the beauties and sublimities and powers, the microscopic intricacies and macroscopic vastnesses, the wonders and the terrors of the natural world and of the life that pulses through it, are willed and valued by their Maker in a creative act that embraces man together with nature. By means of matter and living flesh God both builds a path and weaves a veil between Himself and the creature made in His image. Nature thus has permanent significance; for God has set man in a creaturely environment, and the final fulfilment of our nature in relation to God will accordingly take the form of an embodied life within "a new heaven and a new earth." And as in the present age man moves slowly towards that fulfillment through the pilgrimage of his earthly life, so also "the whole creation" is "groaning in travail," waiting for the time when it will be "set free from its bondage to decay."

And yet however fully we thus acknowledge the permanent significance and value of the natural order, we must still insist upon man's special character as a personal creature made in the image of God; and our theodicy must still centre upon the soul-making process that we believe to be taking place within human life.

This, then, is the starting-point from which we propose to try to relate the realities of sin and suffering to the perfect love of an omnipotent Creator. And as will become increasingly apparent, a theodicy that starts in this way must be eschatological in its ultimate bearings. That is to say, instead of looking to the past for its clue to the mystery of evil, it looks to the future, and indeed to that ultimate future to which only faith can look. Given the conception of a divine intention working in and through human time towards a fulfilment that lies in its completeness beyond human time, our theodicy must find the meaning of evil in the part that it is made to play in the eventual outworking of that purpose; and must find the justification of the whole process in the magnitude of the good to which it leads. The good that outshines all ill is not a paradise long since lost but a kingdom which is yet to come in its full glory and permanence.

NOTES

1. II Corinthians iii. 18.

2. Romans viii. 29. Other New Testament passages expressing a view of man as undergoing a process of spiritual growth within God's purpose are: Ephesians ii. 21, iii. 16; Colossians ii. 19; I John iii. 2; II Corinthians iv. 16.

3. *Dialogues Concerning Natural Religion*, pt. xi. Kemp-Smith's ed. (Oxford: Clarendon Press, 1935), p. 251.

III.C.3

Epistemic Humility, Arguments from Evil, and Moral Skepticism

DANIEL HOWARD-SNYDER

Daniel Howard-Snyder (1959–) is professor of philosophy at Western Washington University and has written extensively in epistemology and the philosophy of religion. In this essay, he defends what is commonly (although, in his view, inappropriately) called the "skeptical theist" strategy for responding to the problem of evil. The skeptical theist maintains that we should be in doubt about whether the goods we know of constitute a representative sample of the goods there are. The skeptical theist offers this skeptical claim as a reason for doubting that we can infer that no good could possibly justify God in permitting some instance of evil from our inability to detect a good that might justify God in permitting that instance of evil. Howard-Snyder focuses in particular on replying to the objection that the skeptical theist's skepticism about our grasp of the realm of value leads to more widespread forms of moral skepticism.

Many arguments from evil at least tacitly rely on something like the following line of thought:

> *The Inference.* On sustained reflection, we don't see how any reason we know of would justify God in permitting all the evil in the world; therefore, there is no reason that would justify God.

The conclusion is frequently more nuanced: "it is very likely that there is no such reason" or "more likely than not" or "more likely than it otherwise would be." Some critics reject the premise: we do see how some reason would justify God. These are the theodicists. Others accept the premise but reject the conclusion: the evidence or non-evidential warrant for God's existence is much better than the evidence for no justifying reason. These are the natural theologians and Reformed epistemologists. Some critics, however, insist that *even if* the premise is true and *even if* there isn't better evidence

or non-evidential warrant for God's existence, we should not infer that there is no justifying reason. (Throughout the essay, keep the "even if"s in mind as definitive of agnosticism.) These are the agnostics about the Inference. In this essay I aim to assess an increasingly popular objection to agnosticism.

There are different versions of agnosticism about the Inference. The one I have in mind—henceforth *Agnosticism* with a capital *A*—affirms at least two theses:

> *Agnostic Thesis 1* (AT1). We should be in doubt about whether the Goods we know of constitute a representative sample of all the goods there are.

> *Agnostic Thesis 2* (AT2). We should be in doubt about whether each good we know of is such that the necessary conditions of its realization we know of are all there are.

Excerpted from 'Epistemic Humility, Arguments from Evil, and Moral Skepticism,' in *Oxford Studies in Philosophy of Religion*, vol. 2 (2009), edited by Jonathan Kvanvig. Used by permission of Oxford University Press.

(I will focus on AT1 although I will say a few words about AT2 shortly.) The Agnostic continues: since we should be in doubt about whether the goods we know of constitute a representative sample of all the goods there are, we should be in doubt about whether some good we don't know of figures in a reason that would justify God. But if we should be in doubt about that, then we should be in doubt about whether there is a reason that would justify God. And if we should be in doubt about that, we should not infer that there is no such reason, even if we don't see how any reason would justify God and even if there is no evidence and non-evidential warrant for God's existence.

The objection to Agnosticism that I aim to assess is the *Moral Skepticism Objection*, or the *Objection*, for short. There are different versions of the Objection. Here's a simple one. Let *Ashley's suffering* name the evil done to twelve-year-old Ashley Jones and what she suffered and lost in Stanwood, Washington, September 21, 1997, who while babysitting her neighbor's kids, was raped and bludgeoned to death by an escapee from a local juvenile detention center. Suppose we could have easily intervened to prevent Ashley's suffering without any cost to ourselves. In that case, it would be absurd to suppose that we should be in doubt about whether we should have intervened. *Obviously* we should have intervened. Agnosticism, however, implies otherwise. It tells us that since we should be in doubt about whether the goods we know of constitute a representative sample of all the goods there are, we should be in doubt about whether there is a reason that would justify God's nonintervention. But if that's right, then so is this: since we should be in doubt about whether the goods we know of constitute a representative sample of all the goods there are, we should also be in doubt about whether there is a reason that would justify *our* nonintervention, in which case we should be in doubt about whether *we* should have intervened. So Agnosticism implies that we should be in doubt about whether we should have intervened. But that's absurd. Obviously we should have. So Agnosticism is false.

It will prove useful to have before us the main thrust of this argument. I will call it the *simple version of the Objection*:

1. If Agnosticism is true, then we should be in doubt about whether we should have intervened to prevent Ashley's suffering.

2. We should not be in doubt about whether we should have intervened.

3. So, Agnosticism is false.

Here's the plan of the paper. In Section I, I clarify Agnosticism. In Sections II and III, I sketch a criticism of the simple version of the Objection. Absent qualification, it goes like this. Our assessment of the simple version of the Objection should reflect the epistemic implications of our moral theories or principles. There are two types of moral theory and principle: (i) those that posit right- and wrong-making features of an act that should leave us in doubt about its moral status and (ii) those that posit right- and wrong-making features of an act that should not leave us in doubt about its moral status. If we endorse an instance of the first type, then prior to our assessment of the simple version of the Objection we should already be in doubt about whether we should have intervened to prevent Ashley's suffering; in which case we should think that premise (2) is false. However, if we endorse an instance of the second type, then prior to our assessment of the simple version of the Objection we should deny that Agnosticism implies that we should be in doubt about whether we should have intervened; in which case we should think that premise (1) is false. Either way, the epistemic implications of our moral theories or principles imply that the simple version of the Objection is unsound. . . .

I. SOME PRELIMINARIES ABOUT AGNOSTICISM

Note, firstly, that Agnosticism is *not* a kind of theism. It is perfectly compatible with atheism. Thus, to call it "skeptical theism," as many people do, is to evince ineptitude at naming things.

Second, it is important to be clear about what the Agnostic means and does not mean when she says *we don't see* how any reason we know of would justify God in permitting all the evil in the world. She does not mean to comment on our visual capacities. Rather, she means that we don't understand or comprehend how any reason we know of would justify God. Furthermore, she does not mean that we don't see how any reason would justify God in permitting *any* of the evil in the world, nor does she mean that we don't see how any reason would *partially* justify God in permitting all of the evil in the world. She means that we don't see how any reason would *fully* justify God in permitting *all* of the evil in the world. Ashley's suffering is a case in point.

Sometimes the Agnostic will say "We don't see how any *good we know of* justifies God in permitting all the evil in the world." This is shorthand. What she means is, "We don't see how any *reason we know of that appeals to a good* justifies God in permitting all the evil in the world."I will frequently revert to the Agnostic's shorthand way of speaking. . . .

Fourth, it is important to be clear about what the Agnostic means and does not mean when she says that we should be in doubt about whether some good *we don't know of* would justify God in permitting all the evil in the world, including Ashley's suffering.

(a) I might know of something, in one sense, but not in another. I know of String Theory, in the sense that I know that it attempts to unite quantum mechanics and the theory of General Relativity, the most popular versions posit one-dimensional oscillating lines and eleven spatial dimensions, and so on. Anyone can know of String Theory in this sense by simply consulting an encyclopedia. But I don't know of String Theory in another sense, in the sense that would require me to have a substantive understanding of the mathematics of quantum mechanics, the theory of General Relativity, multi-dimensionality, and the like. Which sense does the Agnostic mean when she speaks of *goods we know of* and *goods we don't know of* (if there are any)? She means the second sense. When she speaks of goods we know of, she means goods we comprehend and understand in at least

somewhat of a substantive way; and when she speaks of goods we don't know of, she means goods we don't comprehend or understand (if there are any), not even in a somewhat substantive way.

(b) When the Agnostic says that we should be *in doubt* about whether some good we don't know of would justify God in permitting all the evil in the world she does not mean that we should *doubt that* there is such a good. To be in doubt about something is not to doubt that it is so. To doubt that something is so is to be (at least) more inclined to think it is false rather than true; to be in doubt about something is to be of two minds about it, ambivalent, undecided. I am in doubt about whether there is sentient extra-terrestrial life, whether the United States will be a world power in a thousand years, and whether the number of Douglas firs in Lake Padden State Park is odd. But I am not in the least bit inclined to think these things are false. Rather, given what information I have at my disposal, I don't know what to think about them. According to the Agnostic, the same goes for the Inference. Given the information she has at her disposal, she is in doubt about whether there is a reason that would justify God even though she can't see how any reason she knows of would do the trick. She thinks she is in no position to make such a judgment. She is in the dark. She confesses ignorance on the matter.

(c) When the Agnostic says that we *should* be in doubt about whether some good we don't know of would justify God in permitting all the evil in the world she means either that we have a duty to be in doubt about it, that it is wrong not to be in doubt, that we're irresponsible if we are not in doubt, or, alternatively, she means that it is fitting for us to be in doubt about it, being in doubt is the appropriate state of mind. Speaking for myself, although I do not reject the first way, I tend to think in terms of the second way. I tend to think of the Agnostic as saying that it is proper for us to be in doubt about whether some good we don't know of would justify God, proper in the sense that being in doubt about the matter exhibits a humility that befits the range of our cognitive powers whereas not being in doubt exhibits excessive self-confidence. (Hence the first phrase in the title of this paper.) . . .

(d) When the Agnostic speaks of a *good*, she means to refer to an abstract state of affairs which, if it were to obtain, would be good. She does not mean to refer to a concrete object or event. Goods are abstracta not concreta. (Cp. Bergmann and Rea [2005: 242]) Thus, when she says that we should be in doubt about whether some unknown *good* would justify God, she means that we should be in doubt about whether some unknown *abstract state of affairs the obtaining of which would be good* would justify God.

(e) The Agnostic assumes that states of affairs are necessary beings. They exist at every possible world. So every good state of affairs exists. However, not every good state of affairs obtains. Some good states of affairs do not obtain. For example, if no one has ever been free with respect to being the sort of person that they are, then the state of affairs of our sometimes being free with respect to the sorts of persons we are *exists* but it does *not obtain*. . . .

Fifth, we need to understand what the Agnostic means and does not mean when she says we should be in doubt about whether the goods we know of constitute a *representative sample* of all the goods there are (which is AT1).

(a) In general, a sample can be representative of a population with respect to one feature but not another. For example, the employees at Microsoft are representative of the human population with respect to planet of origin but not annual income, place of residence, or nationality, among other things. When the Agnostic says we should be in doubt about whether the goods we know of constitute a representative sample of all the goods there are she means that we should be in doubt about whether the goods we know of are representative of all the goods there are with respect to *being apt for justifying God's permission of all the evil in the world*. In what follows, I will typically leave the qualification made in this paragraph tacit.

(b) In general, a sample, S, is representative of a population, P, with respect to feature F, if and only if the frequency of members in S that are F is almost the same as the frequency of members in P that are F. Thus, when the Agnostic says that we should be in doubt about whether the goods we know of constitute a representative sample of all the goods there are with respect to being apt for justifying God's permission of all the evil in the world she means that we should be in doubt about whether the frequency of members of the goods we know of that are apt for justifying God's permission of all the evil in the world is almost the same as the frequency of members of the total population of goods that are apt for justifying God's permission of all the evil in the world.

Sixth, what reason do we have to think that we should be in doubt about whether the goods we know of constitute a representative sample of all the goods there are? Excellent question! The first thing to note about it is that it presupposes that we *need* good evidence to be in doubt about the matter for it to be the case that we should be in doubt. That's arguably false, however. To be in doubt about something is the stance from which we need good evidence to move, to believing it or believing its denial. We don't need good evidence to be in doubt for it to be the case that we should be in doubt. So, absent good evidence to believe that the goods we know of are representative of all the goods there are (or its denial), we should be in doubt about the matter.

Even if we don't need good evidence to be in doubt about something for it to be the case that we should be in doubt about it, we might nevertheless have good evidence to be in doubt about it. In this connection, the Agnostic argues that evidence to think that the goods we know of are representative of the total population is bad evidence and that more general considerations in favor of the Inference fail. Moreover, she argues, several considerations properly induce doubt about whether there are God-justifying goods outside our ken. (See e.g. Wykstra [1984 and 1996], Alston [1991 and 1996], Howard-Snyder [1996a], Bergmann [2001].) Since my aim in this essay is to assess a specific objection to Agnosticism and not to assess the general case for it, I will say no more about the latter.

Except this: If the goods we know of constitute a random sample of the total population of goods, then our sample is generated by a process that gives every member of the total population of goods an equal chance of being selected into our sample. (. . . or else there is a subclass, C, of the total population of goods, P, such that C is not S and C is representative of P with respect to being apt for justifying God, from which S is generated by a process that gives every member of C an equal chance of being selected into S. See Hawthorne [2004: n. 15]. This way for a sample to be random need not concern us here.) But if our sample is generated by a process that gives every member of the total population of goods an equal chance of being selected into our sample *but we lack the concepts needed to comprehend or understand every member of the total population of goods*, then we might have selected from the total population of goods a member that we in fact lack the concepts to comprehend or understand, in which case our sample might have included a good we know of but lack the concepts to understand or comprehend. But that's impossible. It is impossible that we know of a good but lack the concepts to comprehend or understand it. (For, as I said earlier, in the present context a good that we know of is one that "we comprehend and understand in at least somewhat of a substantive way.") So if our sample is generated by a process that gives every member of the total population of goods an equal chance of being selected into our sample, then we possess the concepts needed to comprehend or understand *every* member of the total population of goods. Thus, if the goods we know of constitute a random sample of the total population of goods, then

(i)   Each member of the total population of goods is such that we possess the concepts needed to comprehend or understand it. The Agnostic bids us to reflect on the fact that (i) is like some other

propositions in an epistemically relevant respect, for example

(ii)   Each member of the total population of empirically adequate physical theories is such that we possess the concepts needed to comprehend or understand it,

and

(iii)   Each member of the total population of ontologies of what we call "physical objects" is such that we have the concepts needed to comprehend or understand it.

We should be in doubt about (ii) and (iii) even if, unbeknownst to us, they are both true. It would be an extraordinary stroke of good epistemic luck if our evolutionary history to this point left us with every concept needed to comprehend and understand *every* physical theory and *every* ontology of physical objects. Similarly, says the Agnostic, and for the same reason, we should be in doubt about (i) even if, unbeknownst to us, it is true. Therefore, we have some good evidence to think that we should be in doubt about whether the goods we know of constitute a random sample of the total population of goods, and so we have some good evidence to think that we should be in doubt about whether the goods we know of constitute a representative sample of all the goods there are—which is exactly what AT1 says.

Finally, a word about AT2, the thesis that we should be in doubt about whether each good we know of is such that the necessary conditions of its realization we know of are all there are. As has been pointed out on occasion, we can *know of* a good without *seeing how* it would justify God in permitting horrific evil. This can happen in at least two ways. First, we might know of a good but fail to fully appreciate its goodness. Second, we might know of a good but fail to know of all the necessary conditions of its realization. (See Alston [1996: 315–6, 323–5], Howard-Snyder [1996a: 308 n. 13], and Bergmann [2001].) AT2 is about the second way.

What goods might be such that we know of them but fail to know of all the necessary conditions of their realization? Union with God is one candidate. It's hard to say whether or not created persons must be permitted to undergo horrific suffering in order to enter into the deepest union with God. To be sure, we have some idea of what it would require by way of understanding what union between human persons requires. But is our understanding of what union with God requires *complete*? Suppose we are in the following frame of mind: no aspect of God's nature that we know of is such that we think that by virtue of it, God cannot permit horrific suffering; moreover, for all we can tell, there are aspects of God's nature that we don't know of in virtue of which a created person can enter into the deepest union with God only if she is permitted to undergo horrific suffering. If we are in that frame of mind, then our understanding of what union with God required would be not only incomplete, it would be—much more importantly—incomplete in such a way that we should be in doubt about whether we know of all the necessary conditions of its realization. Are we in that frame of mind? I think I am. The Agnostic thinks you should be. If she's right, then we should be in doubt about whether union with God is such that the necessary conditions of its realization we know of are all there are. Thus, we should think AT2 is true.

So much for preliminaries. I now turn to my main task.

II. TAKING CONSEQUENCES VERY, *VERY* SERIOUSLY

Consider the following theory:

> *Objective Maximizing Act Consequentialism* (OMAC). An agent's act is permissible solely in virtue of the fact that its total consequences are no overall worse than those of any option open to him; otherwise, it is impermissible.

There are different concepts of consequence that might be plugged into OMAC and the resulting versions of OMAC will have different implications. Although I am not defending OMAC here, as will be apparent shortly I will assert that OMAC has certain epistemic implications. Whether I'm right or not will depend on what concept of consequence is deployed. So I have to say something about the matter.

Without trying to be precise, I have in mind a version of OMAC that most of my self-identifying maximizing consequentialist friends affirm. They say that what counts as a consequence of an act is *any* future event or fact causally downstream from the act. Some of them like a counterfactual condition on causation according to which A caused B only if B would not have occurred if A hadn't. In

that case, we can think of a chain of counterfactuals of the form *If A had not occurred then B would not have occurred* linking the act and the future event or fact. If you are happy with this concept of causal consequence, go with it. If not, go with whatever "link" you like *provided that* it has the implication that my maximizing friends want, namely, that what you do right now will have causal ramifications until the end of time and *all* of them are morally relevant. (Cp. Mason [2004: 317]: "consequentialism demands that we make decisions that have as their justification *the whole future*" [emphasis added]. Unless otherwise indicated explicitly or by context, in what follows all talk of consequences should be understood along these lines including talk of consequences in contexts other than OMAC.)

OMAC implies that the total consequences of intervening to prevent suffering and the total consequences of nonintervention make the difference as to whether we should intervene. If nonintervention in Ashley's case has overall better total consequences than intervention, then we should not intervene—even if the foreseeable consequences of intervention are vastly better than those of nonintervention. Now: since we are in no position to say what the unforeseeable consequences of intervention and nonintervention contain and the unforeseeable consequences swamp the foreseeable ones, we should be in doubt about whether the total consequences of intervention are overall worse than those of nonintervention. In that case, given OMAC, we should be in doubt about whether we should intervene to prevent Ashley's suffering. Thus, prior to assessing the simple version of the Objection, we should already be inclined to deny premise (2)—*if we endorse OMAC.*

In effect, I have just summarized the first step of the well-known Epistemic Objection to OMAC. Later steps connect that step with the denial of OMAC. I am not taking the later steps. I am only taking the first. Let me explain why I take the first step. What I have to say is not original.

The unforeseeable consequences of an act and its alternatives swamp the foreseeable consequences. Thus, what we can foresee is a minute fraction of the total consequences. Moreover, we are in the dark about what the unforeseeable consequences of an act and its alternatives contain. In an important article, James Lenman underscores how deeply darkness envelops us on this score by pointing out how much of our behavior has massive and inscrutable causal ramifications. (Lenman [2000]. I can't recommend this article strongly enough.) Killing and engendering, and refraining from killing and engendering, ramify in massive ways because they are directly identity-affecting actions. They directly "make a difference to the identities of future persons [that is, a difference to what people there will be] and these differences are apt to amplify exponentially down the generations." (Lenman [2000: 346].) Much of our other behavior is indirectly identity-affecting, as, for example, when a word harshly spoken, or eating raw garlic, or introducing your girlfriend to your best friend Ray makes a difference to who sleeps with whom tonight, or tomorrow morning, or next month. To illustrate the main point here, imagine Richard, a first-century bandit in southern Germany who, while raiding a small village, spares the life of a pregnant woman, Angie. (Lenman [2000: 344–6].) Angie, it turns out, is the great- great- ... (add 97 'great-'s) ... great-grandmother of Adolf Hitler. By permitting Angie to live, Richard played a role in the occurrence of the Holocaust. Moreover, anyone who refrained from killing any of the intermediate ancestors of Hitler before they engendered the relevant child, or assisted in introducing the parents of each generation, or refrained from introducing them to others, and so on, played a role as well. Which one of these people throughout the generations had an inkling that their behavior would contribute to such a horror?

Another source of massive causal ramification is causal systems that "are extremely sensitive to very small and localized variations or changes in their initial conditions." (Lenman [2000: 347].) Such sensitivity will underscore the skeptical implications of OMAC if such systems occur

> in even a small number of domains that have a significant influence on the human world. One such domain is perhaps the

> weather: differences in the weather make extremely widespread differences to the behavior of huge numbers of people. Such differences affect, for example, people's moods, the plans they make for any given day, and the way these plans evolve as the day goes on. For any significant difference in weather over a large populated area, some of these effects are certain to be identity-affecting. ([Lenman [2000: 348].)

Another such domain is financial markets:

> [T]hese are influenced by countless, often quite intrinsically insignificant, human actions, and probably—directly or indirectly—by a very high percentage of intrinsically more significant ones. And the effect of market movements on human life is again enormous and certainly often identity-affecting. (Lenman [2000: 348].)

As it was with Angie and Richard, so it is with Ashley and us. We are in the dark about the unforeseeable consequences of intervention and nonintervention; moreover, the foreseeable consequences are but a drop in the ocean of the total consequences, and all but that drop is inscrutable to us. So, *if we endorse OMAC*, then, when we turn to assess the simple version of the Objection, we should already be in doubt about whether we should prevent Ashley's suffering; that is, we should already be strongly inclined to deny premise (2).

OMAC posits right- and wrong-making features of an act which, given the limitations of our information and a sensible view about what is and is not of value, should leave us in doubt about its moral status. But perhaps appearances are deceiving. Perhaps there is a way friends of OMAC can avoid this skeptical implication. Let's look into the matter briefly.

A popular reply used to be that the consequences of our acts "approximate rapidly to zero like the furthermost ripples on a pond after a stone has been dropped in it." Or, ... "Consequences fizzle fast." (Smart and Williams [1973: 33]. See also Moore [1903: 153]).... To be sure, there are some concepts of a consequence according to which this is true. But, as I intimated above, those concepts are none of my concern here. I am concerned with a version of OMAC according to which, as I said, "what you do right now will have causal ramifications until the end of time and *all* of them are morally relevant." We all know objective maximizing consequentialists who take this line. And my point is simply this: no one privy to the facts to which Lenman calls our attention can retain the view that consequences *in that sense* fizzle fast. (Cp. Lenman [2000: 350–1].)

An appeal to expected value might be a more promising strategy. Suppose act *A* is an alternative action open to me. There are many possible outcomes, *O1, O2, O3, . . ., On*, each of which might obtain, for all I can tell, if I were to perform *A*. Each outcome has a value, *V(Oi)*. Moreover, for each outcome, *Oi*, there is a conditional probability of its obtaining given that I perform *A*: *P(Oi/A)*. The expected value of *A* is the sum, for all of these outcomes, of all of the products determined by *V(Oi) x P(Oi /A)*. Expected value can be put to use as follows. Although the foreseeable consequences of intervention and nonintervention in Ashley's case are a vanishingly small proportion of their total consequences, and although we are ignorant of their unforeseeable consequences, it does not follow from OMAC that we should be in doubt about whether we should intervene. For, despite our vast ignorance, we should not be in doubt about whether the expected value of intervention is greater than the expected value of nonintervention: we should think it is greater. Thus, says the friend of expected utility, we should not be in doubt about what we should do: we should intervene.

But *why* should we not be in doubt about whether the expected value of intervention is greater than the expected value of nonintervention? To answer that question, we need to answer two others. First, what general procedure should we follow to determine whether the expected value of an act is greater than the expected value of available alternative acts? Second, if we follow that procedure in Ashley's case, will it leave us in a position where we should not be in doubt about intervening?

In an important article, Fred Feldman contends that the nature of expected value itself recommends the following general procedure:

1. List all of the alternative actions available to us.

2. List all of the possible outcomes of the first alternative.

3. For each outcome of the first alternative, specify its value.

4. For each outcome of the first alternative, specify its probability on that alternative, given the information available to us.

5. For each outcome of the first alternative, multiply its value by its probability on that alternative.

6. Sum these products. This sum is the expected value of the first alternative.

7. Repeat steps 2–6 for each of the other alternatives. (Feldman [2006]; it's a must-read.)

Let's apply this procedure to Ashley's case.

Step 1 tells us to list the alternative actions available to us. What are they? At first blush, there are exactly two options: intervention and nonintervention. But that's a gross oversimplification. The fact is that there are a thousand (tens of thousands? millions? more?) ways in which we can intervene and many more ways in which we can fail to intervene. Each of them must be placed on our list. To the extent that we are in doubt about whether out list is complete, we should be in doubt about the results we arrive at.

Suppose we somehow identify a few of the most salient alternative actions. Step 2 tells us to list the possible outcomes of the first act on our list. Suppose the first act is firing a warning shot in the air to scare away the perpetrator. Recall that an outcome of an act is a total way the world might go if the act were performed. And note that the "might" in question is epistemic. We need to ask: how many total ways might the world go if we were to fire a warning shot, relative to the information at our disposal? There are millions of such ways, perhaps many, many more. We need to list each of them. To the extent that we should be in doubt about whether our list is complete, we should be in doubt about our results.

Suppose we somehow identify several of the most salient outcomes, say, a thousand of them. (To the extent that we lack a principled way to do this, more grounds for doubt arise.) The next two steps tell us that we need to assign numbers to those outcomes. Step 3 tells us to assign a number that represents the true value of each outcome. Step 4 tells us to assign a number that represents the probability of each outcome, given our firing a warning shot. (For each alternative act, the sum of the probabilities assigned to each outcome must equal exactly 1.) We haven't the foggiest idea what numbers to assign. We are awash in a sea of doubt.

Suppose we somehow assign the correct numbers. To arrive at the expected value of our first alternative action, we must multiply value and probability one thousand times, once for each outcome (step 5). Then we must add the products (step 6). By the time we finish this last step, Ashley's fate will have been long decided. Of course, even if, by some miracle, we arrive at this point in a second or two, we must now repeat the procedure for each of the salient alternative actions available to us, of which there are many (step 7). Our work has just begun. . . .

Perhaps friends of OMAC can avoid the epistemic fog surrounding expected utility by appealing to the Principle of Indifference which, for our purposes, can be put like this:

> *Indifference.* If we have no evidence favoring any of *n* mutually exclusive and jointly exhaustive possibilities, we should assign each a probability of 1/*n*.

Indifference might be put to use in Ashley's case as follows. It is virtually certain that she will be saved if we intervene and it is virtually certain that she will not be saved if we do not intervene. Those are the foreseeable consequences of intervention and nonintervention. We are in the dark about the unforeseeable consequences of intervention and nonintervention, however. For example, we have no evidence to suppose that the unforeseeable consequences of nonintervention will not be much better than the unforeseeable consequences of intervention. This fact

drives the Agnostic's worry. The corrective is to remember that, by the same token, we have no evidence to suppose that the unforeseeable consequences of intervention will not be much better than the unforeseeable consequences of nonintervention. Thus, says the friend of Indifference, since we have no evidence favoring one of these two mutually exclusive and jointly exhaustive possibilities, we should assign each a probability of 1/2, in which case they cancel each other out. So we are left with the foreseeable consequences. On that score, there is no doubt about what we should do—we should intervene.

I have three concerns about the appeal to Indifference here. First, we have no good reason to believe Indifference. Our grounds for believing it are either a priori or empirical. I haven't the space to consider all a priori grounds that have been offered. Here's the most recent attempt I know of:

> Let's say that possibilities n1 and n2 are *evidentially symmetrical* for you if and only if you have no more evidence to think that n1 is the case than you have to think that n2 is the case, or vice versa. Now, when two possibilities are evidentially symmetrical for you, you should assign a probability to them that adequately reflects your evidence for them. Thus,

> *Evidential Symmetry.* If n1 and n2 are evidentially symmetrical for you, then you should assign exactly the same probability to n1 that you assign to n2.

An obvious corollary of this principle is this:

> *Indifference.* If you have no evidence favoring any of *n* mutually exclusive and jointly exhaustive possibilities, then you should assign each a probability of 1/*n*. (I have gleaned this argument from White [forthcoming].)

What should we make of this argument?

I have two objections. First, . . . it is obvious that Indifference is *not* a corollary of Evidential Symmetry. For even if you should assign exactly the same probability to n1 that you assign to n2 when your evidence for them is symmetrical, it does not follow that you should assign $1/n$. You might well assign a vague or indeterminate probability, perhaps even the interval [0,1] in some circumstances, to each of them. In fact, this way of representing the probability of possibilities under complete ignorance is a much more accurate representation of that cognitive condition than is assigning a sharp probability to each of them. Second, suppose n1 and n2 are evidentially symmetrical for you. Does it follow that you should assign each of them a probability? Of course not. You should assign no probability at all. A fortiori, you should not assign exactly the same probability, contrary to Evidential Symmetry.

Perhaps we can do better with empirical grounds for Indifference, at least insofar as it applies to our present concern. Suppose we have empirical grounds to think that where we find cases of massive causal ramification in the human sphere, the total good and bad consequences tend to cancel each other out in the long run. I concur with James Lenman's assessment of this suggestion:

> There are no cases of massive causal ramification of the kind to which identity-affecting actions are liable where we have empirical data adequate to any such conclusion, for the simple reason that, even if such ramification were easy to trace (in fact it is quite impossible), there are no such cases in which we have good grounds to suppose the ramification has yet come close to running its course. (Lenman [2000: 354].)

But one might object. We have empirical grounds to think that

> P. All *observed* cases of massive causal ramification are such that the good and the bad consequences tend to cancel each other out.

In that case, what would be wrong with a straightforward enumerative induction to the conclusion that

> C. *All* cases of massive causal ramification, including future cases, are such that the

good and the bad consequences tend to cancel each other out?

With this conclusion in hand, we can reasonably ignore the unforeseeable consequences of intervention and nonintervention in Ashley's case and focus on the foreseeable consequences as a basis for reasonably believing we should intervene.

What's wrong with this inductive inference is that it is reasonable only if it is reasonable to suppose that the observed cases of massive causal ramification constitute a representative sample of the total population of massive causal ramifications. But is it reasonable to suppose this? If we had good reason to think that the observed cases were randomly selected from the total population, then we'd have good reason to suppose that they constitute a representative sample of the total population. But we *know* that's not the case: we know that the observed cases are *not* selected in such a way that gives every member of the total population of massive causal ramifications an equal chance of being in our sample. So why suppose they are representative of the total population? . . .

My second concern with the appeal to Indifference has to do with objections to Indifference itself. One is *Bertrand's Paradox*, a version of which is as follows. Imagine a factory that randomly produces square tiles of different lengths, ranging anywhere from 0 to 10 cm. What is the probability that the next tile to come out of the factory will have sides measuring 5 cm or less? The possible outcomes in this case correspond to all of the lengths from 0 cm to 10 cm—the next tile could have sides measuring 1 cm, or 4.5 cm, or 8 cm, or 9.87654321 cm, or. . . . There are many possibilities here but, on the face of it, half of these possibilities are ones in which the sides are 5 cm or less since 5 is halfway between 0 and 10. Since we have no evidence favoring any of these outcomes, Indifference tells us that each is equally likely, so *the probability that the next tile to come out of the factory will have sides measuring 5 cm or less is* 1/2. Here is a second question: What is the probability that the surface area of the next tile will be 25 cm^2 or less? Well, if all of the tiles are squares, and if the lengths range from 0 cm to 10 cm, then the surface areas will range from 0 cm² to 100 cm². The possible outcomes in this case correspond to all of the different surface areas—the next tile could have a surface area of 1 cm² or 26 cm² or 62 cm² or 99.999 cm². Again, there are many possibilities here but, on the face of it, a quarter of them are ones in which the surface area is 25 cm² or less, since 25 is a quarter of the way between 0 and 100. Since we have no evidence favoring any of these outcomes, Indifference tells us that each is equally likely, so *the probability that the next tile to come out of the factory will have a surface area of 25 cm² or less is 1/4.* Here is the problem: *The next tile to come out of the factory will have a surface area of 25 cm² or less if and only if that tile has a length of 5 cm or less.* So the probability that the surface area will be 25 cm² or less *just is* the probability that the length will be 5 cm or less. In other words, 1/4 = 1/2. Indifference leads to absurdity....

Bertrand's Paradox and other objections don't highlight the main problem with Indifference, namely that it codifies a way to get detailed information out of complete ignorance. Better that we assign vague or indeterminate probabilities, even the interval [0,1] if need be, or that we refrain from assigning any probabilities at all....

Perhaps friends of OMAC can ditch Indifference and argue as follows. Given the inscrutability of the distant future, in Ashley's case we have exactly as much reason to believe

A. The *unforeseeable* consequences of nonintervention outweigh the unforeseeable consequences of intervention

as we have to believe

B. The *unforeseeable* consequences of intervention outweigh the unforeseeable consequences of nonintervention.

Thus, we should—epistemically should—base our belief about what we should do on what reasons we have to believe

C. The foreseeable consequences of nonintervention outweigh the foreseeable consequences of intervention

and what reasons we have to believe

D. The foreseeable consequences of intervention outweigh the foreseeable consequences of nonintervention.

We have much more reason to believe (D) than we have to believe (C). Thus, we should *not* be in doubt about whether we should intervene given OMAC. Thus, OMAC is at home with premise (2) of the Moral Skepticism Objection.

On the face of it, this is a sensible line of thought. However, we can construct another argument for the opposite conclusion that, on the face of it, is equally sensible. Given that intervention and nonintervention have massive and inscrutable causal ramifications and given that the unforeseeable consequences swamp the foreseeable ones, in Ashley's case we have exactly as much reason to believe

E. The *total* consequences of nonintervention outweigh the total consequences of intervention

as we have to believe

F. The *total* consequences of intervention outweigh the total consequences of nonintervention.

Thus, we should—epistemically should—be in doubt about whether we should intervene given OMAC. So, OMAC is *not* at home with premise (2) of the Objection.

Which of the two arguments is more sensible? As expected, I give the nod to the second. Here's why. I grant that, given the inscrutability of the distant future, we have exactly as much reason to believe (A) as we do (B). But I deny that it follows that we should—epistemically should—base our belief about what we should do on what reasons we have to believe (C) and (D). For that follows only if we have *more* reason to believe (F) than we have to believe (E), despite the fact that intervention and nonintervention have massive and inscrutable causal ramifications and the unforeseeable consequences swamp the foreseeable ones. But given that intervention and nonintervention have massive and inscrutable causal ramifications and the unforeseeable consequences swamp the foreseeable ones, we do not have more reason to believe (F) than we have to believe (E). To suppose otherwise is like supposing that we have more reason to believe that the consequences of intervening to prevent the execution of Socrates outweigh the consequences of nonintervention than we have to believe that the consequences of not intervening to prevent the execution of Socrates outweigh the consequences of intervention. It is like supposing that we have more reason to believe that the consequences of intervening to prevent Brutus' assassination of Caesar outweigh the consequences of nonintervention than we have to believe that the consequences of not intervening to prevent the assassination of Caesar outweigh the consequences of intervention. We are in no position to suppose such things.

Much more might be said about all of these matters. Suffice to say, as I see things, OMAC posits right- and wrong-making features of an act that should leave us in doubt about its moral status.

OMAC is not alone on this score. Consider

> *Objective Rossianism* (OR). An agent's act is permissible solely in virtue of the fact that it has no less on balance prima facie rightness than any option open to him; otherwise it is impermissible. (In order to deal with conflicting *prima facie* duties, Ross said that our duty *simpliciter* is that which has "the greatest balance of *prima facie* rightness"; see [Ross 1930: 41].)

Suppose that, as Ross said, one prima facie duty, the duty of Beneficence, is the duty to better other people, e.g. to help them achieve a greater degree of virtue, intelligence, pleasure, etc., and another is the duty of Non Maleficence, the duty not to injure others. Now, for any act, whether it constitutes bettering or injuring others depends on its total consequences. (I injure the child whose leg is destroyed by a mine I planted fifty years earlier. You benefit me when the advice you gave me thirty years ago pays off.) So whether, on some particular occasion, intervening to prevent suffering has more on balance prima facie rightness than nonintervention depends on the total consequences of both.

Or consider the moral imperative

> *Requirement Ro.* Prevent suffering you can, unless *there is* better reason for you not to intervene.

Read Ro so that the total consequences of intervention and nonintervention might provide good reason not to intervene, even if we are ignorant of them. Then, whether or not on some particular occasion one's intervention violates Ro depends on the total consequences of intervention and nonintervention. Like OMAC, OR and Ro posit right- and wrong-making features of an act that should leave us in doubt about its moral status. Or so I have argued.

Let us say that any moral theory or principle that, like these three, posits right- and wrong-making features of an act that should leave us in doubt about its moral status is an instance of *Moral Inaccessibilism*, or *Inaccessibilism* for short. I contend that if we endorse an instance of Inaccessibilism, we should be in doubt about whether we should have intervened to prevent Ashley's suffering, i.e. we should reject premise (2) of the Moral Skepticism Objection.

III. TAKING CONSEQUENCES MUCH, *MUCH* LESS SERIOUSLY

Suppose we want to avoid the skeptical implications of Moral Inaccessibilism. In that case, we might convert OMAC into

> *Subjective Maximizing Act Consequentialism* (SMAC). An agent's act is permissible solely in virtue of the fact that she does not believe that its total consequences are overall worse than those of any option open to her; otherwise it is impermissible.

And we might convert OR into

> *Subjective Rossianism* (SR). An agent's act is permissible solely in virtue of the fact that she does not believe that it has less on balance prima facie rightness than that of any

option open to her; otherwise it is impermissible. (Ross himself moved from something OR-ish, in Ross [1930], to something SR-ish, in Ross [1939], due to what he deemed to be the undesirable epistemic implications of the former.)

And we might convert Requirement Ro into the moral imperative

> *Requirement Rs.* Intervene to prevent horrific evil you can prevent, unless you believe there is better reason for you not to intervene.

SMAC implies that even if the total consequences of our intervening to prevent Ashley's suffering are worse than the consequences of nonintervention, we should intervene, provided it is not the case that we believe that the total consequences of intervention are overall worse than those of nonintervention. Similarly, SR implies that even if the on balance *prima facie* rightness of intervention is less than that of nonintervention, we should intervene, provided it is not the case that we believe that the on balance *prima facie* rightness of intervention is less than that of nonintervention. And Rs implies that even if there is better reason not to intervene than there is to intervene, we should intervene, provided it is not the case that we believe that there is better reason not to intervene.

Notice that, on these views, the right- and wrong-making features of an act are typically accessible to us since our beliefs are typically accessible to us; consequently, we should not be in doubt about its moral status. Let's call any view that, like these three, posits right- and wrong-making features of an act that should not leave us in doubt about its moral status an instance of *Moral Accessibilism*, or *Accessibilism* for short.

Accessibilism is relevant to the Moral Skepticism Objection. For suppose we rightly endorse Requirement Rs. (The arguments to follow can be made with SMAC and SR, *mutatis mutandis*.) In that case, we should accept premise (2) of the objection. After all, it is not the case that we believe

that there is better reason for us not to intervene than to intervene, and so the presumption in favor of intervention that is expressed by Rs is not overridden. However, we should reject premise (1). For, given Rs, there is no tension between saying we should not be in doubt about whether we should intervene, on the one hand, and saying we should be in doubt about whether there is some reason we don't know of that would justify someone else's nonintervention, on the other hand. That's because, given Rs, the fact that we should not be in doubt about whether we should intervene is grounded in the twin fact that we should prevent suffering we can prevent and it is not the case that we believe that there is better reason for us not to intervene. The fact that we should not be in doubt about whether we should intervene is not grounded in what anyone else believes or fails to believe. So even if we should be in doubt about whether some reason we don't know of would justify *God's* nonintervention, it does not follow that we should be in doubt about whether *we* should intervene. Thus, premise (1) of the Objection is false *given Requirement Rs.* . . .

So far I have argued that if our moral theories or principles are instances of Inaccessibilism, then we should reject premise (2) of the Objection, but if they are instances of Accessibilism, then we should reject premise (1). More specifically, I have argued that if we endorse OMAC, OR, or Ro, then we should reject premise (2), but if we endorse SMAC, SR, or Rs, then we should reject premise (1). No doubt it will have occurred to some readers that the moral theories and principles on which I have focused are not plausible enough to decide the matter. . . .

So what moral principles might we endorse so that . . . the Moral Skepticism Objection . . . will have [some] bite? . . . Excellent question! Here's what I would find helpful.

Specify your favored theory of the right- and wrong-making features of an act, or specify a moral principle that you think governs the prevention of horrific evil. If it contains terms of art like "all things considered reason," as in "we have an all things considered reason to prevent Ashley's suffering," or "all things considered duty" and "grounded in virtue" as in "we have an all things considered duty—grounded in virtue—to prevent Ashley's suffering," and the like, give a helpful and informative account of what they mean. Then do two things.

First, explain how it is that, on your theory or principles, we should not be in doubt about whether we should intervene to prevent Ashley's suffering. When you give your explanation, be sure to take into account the fact that most of what we do is either directly or indirectly identity-affecting, and thus that most of what we do has massive causal ramifications. If you deny this fact, explain why. If you don't deny it, explain how it is that, despite this fact, we should not be in doubt about whether we should intervene, given your theory or principle. If your explanation appeals to expected value, indifference, intuition, virtue, duties, or the tea leaves in your kitchen sink, explain why objections to your explanation have no force.

Second, explain how it is that, given your theory or principles, Agnosticism implies that we should be in doubt about whether we should intervene to prevent Ashley's suffering. And whatever you say on that score, make it plain why it is that your own theory or principles aren't really driving the doubt and Agnosticism is just coming along for the ride.

I have considered only six theories or principles in this paper, none of which are up to these two tasks, by my lights. My *tentative* hypothesis is that your theory or principles won't be up to them either. But I may well be wrong about that. . . .

REFERENCES

Alston, William (1991), "The Inductive Argument from Evil and the Human Cognitive Condition," *Philosophical Perspectives* 5, 29–67: collected in Howard-Snyder (1996b), 97–125.

———, (1996), "Some (Temporarily) Final Thoughts on Evidential Arguments from Evil," in Howard-Snyder (1996b), 311–32.

Bergmann, Michael (2001), "Skeptical Theism and Rowe's New Evidential Argument from Evil," *Noûs* 35: 278–96.

———, (2009), "Skeptical Theism and the Problem of Evil," in Thomas Flint and Michael Rea (eds.), *The Oxford Handbook of Philosophical Theology* (New York: Oxford University Press).

———, and Rea, Michael (2005), "In Defense of Skeptical Theism: A Reply to Almeida and Oppy," *Australasian Journal of Philosophy* 83: 241–51.

Feldman, Fred (2006), "Actual Utility, the Objection from Impracticality, and the Move to Expected Utility," *Philosophical Studies* 129: 49–79.

Hawthorne, James (2004), "Inductive Logic," in Edward N. Zalta (ed.), *The Stanford Encyclopedia of Philosophy*.

Howard-Snyder, Daniel (1996a), "The Argument from Inscrutable Evil," in Howard-Snyder (1996b).

———, (1996b), (ed.), *The Evidential Argument from Evil* (Bloomington: Indiana University Press).

Lenman, James (2000), "Consequentialism and Cluelessness," *Philosophy and Public Affairs* 29: 342–70.

Mason, Elinor (2004), "Consequentialism and the Principle of Indifference," *Utilitas* 16: 316–21.

Moore, G. E. (1903), *Principia Ethica* (Cambridge: Cambridge University Press).

Ross, W. D. (1930), *The Right and the Good* (Oxford: Oxford University Press).

———, 1939. *Foundations of Ethics* (Oxford: Clarendon Press).

Smart, J. C. C., and Williams, Bernard (1973), *Utilitarianism: For and Against* (Cambridge: Cambridge University Press).

White, Roger (forthcoming), "Evidential Symmetry and Mushy Credence," *Oxford Studies in Epistemology*, MS.

Wykstra, Stephen (1984), "The Humean Obstacle to Evidential Arguments from Suffering: On Avoiding the Evils of 'Appearance'," *International Journal for the Philosophy of Religion*, 16: 73–94.

———, (1996), "Rowe's Noseeum Argument from Evil," in Howard-Snyder (1996b), 126–50.

III.C.4

The Problem of Evil and the Desires of the Heart

ELEONORE STUMP

Eleonore Stump (1947–) is professor of philosophy at St. Louis University. She has written exten-sively in the areas of medieval philosophy, metaphysics, and philosophy of religion. In this article, she argues that traditional theodicies often fail to accord proper importance to the suffering that results from unsatisfied "desires of the heart." She maintains that, to the extent that they fail in this way, such theodicies are, at best, incomplete.

I. INTRODUCTION

The problem of evil is raised by the existence of suffering in the world. Can one hold consistently both that the world has such suffering in it and that it is governed by an omniscient, omnipotent, per-fectly good God, as the major monotheisms claim? An affirmative answer to this question has often enough taken the form of a theodicy. A theodicy is an attempt to show that these claims are consistent by providing a morally sufficient reason for God to allow suffering. In the history of the discussions of the problem of evil, a great deal of effort has been expended on proposing and defending, or criticiz-ing and attacking, theodicies and the putative morally sufficient reasons which theodicies propose.

Generally, a putative morally sufficient reason for God to allow suffering is centred on a supposed benefit which could not be gotten without the suf-fering and which outweighs it. And the benefit is most commonly thought of as some intrinsically valuable thing supposed to be essential to general human flourishing, such as the significant use of free will or virtuous character, either for human beings in general or for the sufferer in particular.[1]

So, for example, in his insightful reflections on the sort of sufferings represented by the afflictions of Job, the impressive tenth-century Jewish thinker Saadiah Gaon says,

> Now He that subjects the soul to its trials is none other than the Master of the universe, who is, of course, acquainted with all its doings. This testing of the soul [that is, the suffering of Job] has been compared to the assaying by means of fire of [lumps of metal] that have been referred to as gold or silver. It is thereby that the true nature of their composition is clearly established. For the original gold and silver remain, while the alloys that have been mingled with them are partly burned and partly take flight... The pure, clear souls that have been refined are thereupon exalted and ennobled.[2]

The same approach is common in contemporary times. So, for example, John Hick has proposed a

Reprinted from *Oxford Studies in Philosophy of Religion*, vol. 1 (2008), pp. 196–215, edited by Jonathan Kvanvig. Used by permission of Oxford University Press.

soul-making theodicy, which justifies suffering as building the character of the sufferer and thereby contributing to the flourishing of the sufferer.[3] Or, to take a very different example which nonetheless makes the same point, Richard Swinburne has argued that suffering contributes to the flourishing of sufferers because, among other things, a person's suffering makes him useful to others, and being useful to others is an important constituent of human well-being in general.[4]

Those who have attacked theodicies such as these have tended to focus on the theodicist's claims about the connections between the putative benefit and the suffering. Opponents of theodicy have argued that the proposed benefit could have been obtained without the suffering, for example, or that the suffering is not a morally acceptable means to that (or any other) benefit. But these attacks on theodicy share an assumption with the attempted theodicies themselves. Both the attacks and the attempted theodicies suppose that a person's generic human flourishing would be sufficient to justify God in allowing that a person's suffering if only the suffering and the flourishing were connected in the right way. In this paper, I want to call this assumption into question.

I will argue that the sufferings of unwilling innocents cannot be justified only in terms of the intrinsically valuable things which make for general human flourishing (however that flourishing is understood). I will argue that even if such flourishing is connected in the appropriate ways to the suffering in a person's life, intrinsically valuable things essential to flourishing are not by themselves sufficient to constitute a morally sufficient reason for God to allow human suffering. That is because human beings can set their hearts on things which are not necessary for such flourishing, and they suffer when they lose or fail to get what they set their hearts on.[5] That suffering also needs to be addressed in consideration of the problem of evil.

II. THE DESIRES OF THE HEART

The suffering to which I want to call attention can be thought of in terms of what the Psalmist calls "the desires of the heart."[6] When the Psalmist says, "Delight yourself in the Lord, and he will give you the desires of your heart,"[7] we all have some idea what the Psalmist is promising. We are clear, for example, that some abstract theological good which a person does not care much about does not count as one of the desires of that person's heart. Suffering also arises when a human being fails to get a desire of her heart or has and then loses a desire of her heart.

I do not know how to make the notion of a desire of the heart precise; but, clearly, we do have some intuitive grasp of it, and we commonly use the expression or others related to it in ordinary discourse. We say, for example, that a person is heartsick because he has lost his heart's desire. He is filled with heartache because his heart's desire is kept from him. He loses heart, because something he had put his heart into is taken from him. It would have been different for him if he had wanted it only half-heartedly; but since it was what he had at heart, he is likely to be heartsore a long time over the loss of it, unless, of course, he has a change of heart about it—and so on, and on.

Perhaps we could say that a person's heart's desire is a particular kind of commitment on her part to something—a person or a project—which matters greatly to her but which need not be essential to her flourishing, in the sense that human flourishing for her may be possible without it. So, for example, Coretta Scott King's life arguably exemplifies flourishing, on any ordinary measure of human flourishing and yet her husband's assassination was undoubtedly heartbreaking for her. If there is such a thing as a web of belief, with some beliefs peripheral and others central to a person's set of beliefs, maybe there is also a web of desire. A desire of a person's heart is a desire which is at or near the centre of the web of desire for her. If she loses what she wants when her desire is at or near the centre of the web, then other things which she had wanted begin to lose their ability to attract her because what she had most centrally wanted is gone. The web of desire starts to fall apart when the centre does not hold, we might say. That is why the ordinary good things of life, like food and work, fail to draw a person who has lost the desires of her heart. She is heartbroken, we say, and that is why she has no heart for anything else now.

If things essential to general human flourishing are intrinsically valuable for all human beings, then those things which are the desires of the heart can be thought of as the things which have the value they do for a particular person primarily because she has set her heart on them, like the value a child has for its parents, the value they have *for her* is derivative from her love of them, not the other way around. A loving father, trying to deal gently with his small daughter's childish tantrums, finally said to her with exasperated adult feeling, "It isn't reasonable to cry about these things!" Presumably, the father means that the things for which his little daughter was weeping did not have much value on the scale which measures the intrinsic value of good things essential to human flourishing; and, no doubt, he was right in that assessment. But there is another scale by which to measure, too, and that is the scale which measures the value a thing has for a particular person because of the love she has for it. The second scale cannot be reduced to the first. Clearly, we care not just about general human flourishing and the intrinsically valuable things essential to it. We also care about those things which are the desires of our hearts, and we suffer when we are denied our heart's desires. I would say that it is not reasonable to say to a weeping child that it is not reasonable for her to weep about the loss of something she had her heart set on.

Suffering which stems from a loss of the heart's desires is often enough compatible with flourishing.[8] As far as that goes, for any particular historical person picked as an exemplar of a flourishing life, it is certainly arguable that, at some time in her life, that person will have lost or failed to get something on which she had fixed her heart. Think, for example, not only of Coretta Scott King but also of Sojourner Truth, who was sold away from her parents at the age of nine, or Harriet Tubman, who suffered permanent neurological damage from the beatings she sustained in adolescence. If any human lives manifest flourishing, the lives of these women certainly do. Each of them is an exemplar of a highly admirable, meaningful life. Yet each of these women undoubtedly experienced heartbreak.

In fact, stern-minded thinkers in varying cultures, including some Stoics, Buddhists, and many in the Christian tradition, have been fiercely committed to the position that human flourishing is independent of the vicissitudes of fortune. On their view, human flourishing ought to be understood in a way which makes it compatible even with such things as poverty, disease and disabilities, the death of loved ones, betrayal by intimate friends, estrangements from friends or family, and imprisonment. But it certainly seems as if each of these is sufficient to break the heart of a person who suffers them if the person is not antecedently in the grip of such a stern-minded attitude.

So, for example, in the history of the medieval Christian tradition, for example, human flourishing was commonly taken as a matter of a certain relationship with God, mediated by the indwelling of the Holy Spirit. On this view of flourishing, most of the evils human beings suffer are compatible with flourishing. That is because, as Christian confessional literature makes clear, a human person can feel that she is in such a relationship with God, even when she is afflicted with serious suffering of body or mind.

This sort of position is also common among the reflective in our own culture. In a moving passage reflecting on his long experience of caring for and living with the severely disabled, Jean Vanier says about the disabled and about himself, too,

> we can only accept ... [the] pain [in our lives] if we discover our true self beneath all the masks and realize that if we are broken, we are also more beautiful than we ever dared to suspect. When we realize our brokenness, we do not have to fall into depression ... Seeing our own brokenness and beauty allows us to recognize, hidden under the brokenness and self-centeredness of others, their beauty, their value, and their sacredness. This discovery is ... a blessed moment, a moment of grace, and a moment of enlightenment that comes in a meeting with the God of love, who reveals to us that we are beloved and so is everyone else.... We can start to live the pain of loss and accept anguish because a

new love and a new consciousness of self are being given to us.[9]

A particularly poignant example of such an attitude is given by John Hull in his memoir about his own blindness. After many pages of documenting the great suffering caused him by blindness, Hull summarizes his attitude towards his disability in this powerful passage:

> the thought keeps coming back to me . . . Could there be a strange way in which blindness is a dark, paradoxical gift? Does it offer a way of life, a purification, an economy? Is it really like a kind of painful purging through a death? . . . If blindness is a gift, it is not one that I would wish on anybody . . . [But in the midst of the experience of music in church] as the whole place and my mind were filled with that wonderful music, I found myself saying, "I accept the gift. I accept the gift." I was filled with a profound sense of worship. I felt that I was in the very presence of God, that the giver of the gift had drawn near to me to inspect his handiwork. . . . If I hardly dared approach him, he hardly dared approach me. . . . He had, as it were, thrown his cloak of darkness around me from a distance, but had now drawn near to seek a kind of reassurance from me that everything was all right, that he had not misjudged the situation, that he did not have to stay. "It's all right," I was saying to him, "There's no need to wait. Go on, you can go now; everything's fine."[10]

Everything *is* fine, in some sense having to do with relationship to God, and so with flourishing, on this understanding of flourishing. I have no wish to undermine the appealing attitude exemplified in this powerful text. And yet something more needs to be said. The problem is that suffering is not confined to things which undermine a person's flourishing and keep him from being *fine*, in this deep sense of "fine." What is bad about the evils human beings suffer is not just that they can undermine a

person's flourishing, but also that they can keep her from having the desires of her heart, when the desires of her heart are for something which is not essential for general human flourishing. Suffering arises also from the loss of the desires of one's heart; and, in considerations of the problem of evil and proposed theodicies, this suffering needs to be addressed as well. This suffering also needs to be justified.

III. THE STERN-MINDED ATTITUDE

Stated so baldly, this last claim looks less open to question than it really is. We do not ordinarily suppose that a parent's goodness is impugned if the parent refuses to provide for the child anything at all which the child happens to set its heart on. But, as regards the problem of evil, what is at issue is apparently analogous, namely, God's allowing some human being to fail to have the desires of her heart when those desires are focused on something not essential to her flourishing. Why, someone might ask, should we suppose that a good God must provide whatever goods not necessary for her flourishing a human person has fixed her heart on?

Now it is certainly true that there can be very problematic instances of heart's desires. A person could set his heart on very evil things, for example, or a person might set his heart in random ways on trivial things or on a set of mutually incompossible things. And no doubt, there are other examples as well. In cases such as these, reasonable people are unlikely to suppose that some explanation is needed for why a good God would fail to give a person the desires of his heart. Even if we exclude such cases, however, there remain many instances in which a person sets his heart, in humanly understandable and appropriate ways, on something which is not essential to his flourishing and whose value for him is derivative of his love for it.[11] Surely, in that restricted class of cases, some justification is needed for God's allowing a person to suffer heartbreak.

But even this weaker claim will strike some people as false. Some people will object, for example, that human flourishing is a very great good, sufficient to outweigh suffering. For those who think of human flourishing as a relationship to God, it can seem an infinite good or a good too great to be commensurable with other goods; and this good is possible even when many other goods are lost or denied.[12] If God provides *this* good for a human being, then, an objector might claim, that is or ought to be enough for her. A person who does not find this greatest of all goods good enough, an objector might say, is like a person who wins the lottery but who is nonetheless unhappy because she did not get exactly what she wanted for Christmas.

In the history of Christianity in particular, there have been stern-minded thinkers who would not accept the claim that the suffering caused by any loss of the heart's desires requires justification. In effect, this stern-minded attitude is unwilling to assign a positive value to anything which is not essential to general human flourishing. For this reason, the stern-minded approach is, at best, unwilling to accord any value to the desires of the heart and, at worst, eager to extirpate the desires themselves. Such an attitude is persistent in the history of Christian thought from the Patristic period onwards.

In its Patristic form, it can be seen vividly in a story which Cassian tells about a monk named "Patermutus." It is worth quoting at length the heartrendingly horrible story which Cassian recounts with so much oblivious admiration:

> Patermutus's constant perseverance [in his request to be admitted into the monastery finally] induced [the monks] to receive him along with his little son, who was about eight years old.... To test [Patermutus] the more, and see if he would be more moved by family affection and the love of his own brood than by the obedience and mortification of Christ, which every monk should prefer to his love, [the monks] deliberately neglected the child, dressed him in rags ... and even subjected [the child] to cuffs and slaps, which ... the father saw some of them inflict on the innocent for no reason, so that [the father]

never saw [his son] without [the son's] cheeks being marked by the signs of tears. Although he saw the child being treated like this day after day before his eyes, the father's feelings remained firm and unmoving, for the love of Christ.... The superior of the monastery ... decided to test [the father's] strength of mind still further: one day when he noticed the child weeping, he pretended to be enraged at [the child], and ordered the father to pick up [his son] and throw him in the Nile. The father, as if the command had been given him by our Lord, at once ran and snatched up his son and carried him in his own arms to the river bank to throw him in. The deed would have been done ... had not some of the brethren been stationed in advance to watch the riverbank carefully; as the child was thrown they caught him.... Thus they prevented the command, performed as it was by the father's obedience and devotion, from having any effect.[13]

Cassian plainly prizes Patermutus's actions and attitude; but surely most of us will find it chilling and reprehensible. For my part, I would say that one can only wonder why the monks bothered to catch the child, if the father's willingness to kill the child was so praiseworthy in their eyes. Can it be morally praiseworthy to will an act whose performance is morally prohibited?

An attitude similar to Cassian's but less appalling can still be found more than a millenium later in some texts (but not others) of the work of Teresa of Avila, to take just one example from among a host of thinkers who could have been selected. Writing to her sister nuns, Teresa says,

> Oh, how desirable is ... [the] union with God's will! Happy the soul that has reached it. Such a soul will live tranquilly in this life, and in the next as well. Nothing in earthly events afflicts it unless it finds itself in some danger of losing God ...: neither sickness, nor poverty, nor death.... For this soul sees

well that the Lord knows what He is doing better than ... [the soul] knows what it is desiring. ... But alas for us, how few there must be who reach [union with God's will!]. ... I tell you I am writing this with much pain upon seeing myself so far away [from union with God's will]—and all through my own fault. ... Don't think the matter lies in my being so conformed to the will of God that if my father or brother dies I don't feel it, or that if there are trials or sicknesses I suffer them happily.[14]

Not feeling it when one's father dies, not weeping with grief over his death, is, in Teresa's view, a good spiritual condition which she is not yet willing to attribute to herself. Teresa is here echoing a tradition which finds its prime medieval exemplar in Augustine's *Confessions*. Augustine says that, at the death of his mother, by a powerful command of his will, he kept himself from weeping at her funeral, only to disgrace himself in his own eyes later by weeping copiously in private.[15]

In the same text from which I just quoted, Teresa emphasizes the importance of love of neighbour; but it is hard to see how love of neighbour coheres with the stern-minded attitude manifested by Teresa and Augustine in the face of the death (real or imagined) of a beloved parent. As I have argued elsewhere, it is the nature of love to desire the good of the beloved and union with him.[16] But the desire for the good of the beloved is frustrated if the beloved gets sick or dies. Or, if the stern-minded attitude is unwilling to concede that point, then this much is incontrovertible even on the stern-minded attitude: the desire for union with the beloved is frustrated when the beloved dies and so is absent. One way or another, then, the desires of love are frustrated when the beloved dies.

Consequently, there is something bad and lamentable, something worth tears, something whose loss brings affliction with it, about the death of any person whom one loves—one's father, or even one's neighbour, whom one is bound to love too, as Teresa thinks.

Unmoved tranquillity at the death of another person is thus incompatible with love of that person. To the extent to which one loves another person, one cannot be unmoved at his death. And so love of neighbour is in fact incompatible with the stern-minded attitude.

The stance Teresa wishes she might take towards her father's death, as she imagines it, can be usefully contrasted with Bernard of Clairvaux's reaction to the death of his brother. Commenting on his grief at that death, Bernard says to his religious community, "You, my sons, know how deep my sorrow is, how galling a wound it leaves."[17] And, addressing himself, he says, "Flow on, flow on, my tears. ... Let my tears gush forth like fountains."[18] Reflecting on his own failure to repudiate his great sorrow over his brother's death, his failure, that is, to follow Augustine's model, Bernard says,

> It is but human and necessary that we respond to our friends with feeling, that we be happy in their company, disappointed in their absence. Social intercourse, especially between friends, cannot be purposeless: the reluctance to part and the yearning for each other when separated indicate how meaningful their mutual love must be when they are together.[19]

And Bernard is hardly the only figure in the Christian tradition who fails to accept and affirm Cassian's attitude. Aquinas is another.

There are isolated texts which might suggest to some readers that Aquinas himself is an adherent of Cassian's attitude. So, for example, in his commentary on Christ's line that he who loves his life will lose it, Aquinas reveals that he recognizes the concept of the desires of the heart; but, in this same passage, he also seems to suggest that such desires should be stamped out. He says,

> Everyone loves his own soul, but some love it *simpliciter* and some *secundum quid*. To love someone is to will the good for him; and so he who loves his soul wills the good for it. A person who wills for his soul

the good *simpliciter* also loves his soul *simpliciter*. But a person who wills some particular good for his soul loves his soul *secundum quid*. The goods for the soul *simpliciter* are those things by which the soul is good, namely, the highest good, which is God. And so he who wills for his soul the divine good, a spiritual good, loves his soul *simpliciter*. But he who wills for his soul earthly goods such as riches and honors, pleasures, and things of that sort, he loves his soul [only] *secundum quid* ... He who loves his soul *secundum quid* namely with regard to temporal goods, will lose it.[20]

And the implication seems to be that, for Aquinas, the person who does not want to lose his soul should extirpate from himself all desires for any good other than the highest good, which is, as Aquinas says, God.

But it is important to see that what is at issue for Aquinas in this passage is the desire for worldly things, that is for those goods, such as money or fame, which diminish when they are distributed. On Aquinas' scale of values, any good which diminishes when it is distributed is only a small good. When it comes to the desires of the heart for things which are earthly goods but great goods, such as the love of a particular person, Aquinas' attitude differs sharply from Cassian's. So, for example, in explaining why Christ told his disciples that he was going to the father in order to comfort them when they were sad at the prospect of being separated from him, Aquinas says,

> It is common among friends to be less sad over the absence of a friend when the friend is going to something which exalts him. That is why the Lord gives them this reason [for his leaving] in order to console them.[21]

Unlike Teresa's repudiation of grief at the prospect of losing her father, Aquinas is here, as in many other places, accepting the appropriateness of a person's grief at the loss of a loved person and validating the need for consolation for such grief.

So Aquinas is not to be ranked among the members of the stern-minded group, any more than Bernard is; and, of course, in other moods, when she is not self-consciously evaluating her own spiritual progress, Teresa herself sounds more like Bernard and Aquinas than like Cassian. As far as that goes, the Psalmist who authored Psalm 37 is not on Cassian's side. The Psalmist claims that God will give the desires of the heart to those who delight in the Lord; so the Psalmist is supposing that, for those who trust in God, God himself honours the desires of the heart. On this subject, then, the Christian tradition is of two minds. Not all its influential figures stand with Cassian; and, even among those who do, many are double-minded about it.

IV. A POSSIBLE CONFUSION

But, someone will surely object, isn't it a part of Christian doctrine that God allows the death of any person who dies? Does anyone die when God wills that that person live? So when a person dies, on Christian theology, isn't it the will of God that that person die? In what sense, then, could Teresa be united with God in will if she grieved over her father's death? How could she be united with God, as she explains she wants to be, if her will is frustrated in what God's will accepts or commands?

The position presupposed by the questions of this putative objector, in my view, rests on too simple an understanding of God's will and union with God's will.

To see why, assume that at death Teresa's father is united with God in heaven. Then the death which unites Teresa's father permanently with God has the opposite effect for Teresa: at least for the time being, it deprives Teresa of her father's presence and so keeps her from union with him, at least for the rest of Teresa's earthly life. For this reason, on the Christian doctrine Teresa accepts, love's desire for union with the beloved cannot be fulfilled in the same way for Teresa as for God. If Teresa's will is united with God's will in desiring union with a beloved person, then Teresa's will must also be frustrated at the very event, her father's dying, which fulfils God's will with respect to this desire.

Something analogous can be said about the other desire of love, for the good of the beloved. If Teresa desires the good of her father, she can only desire what her own mind sees as that good; but her mind's ability to see the good is obviously much smaller than God's. To the extent to which Teresa's will is united with God's will in desiring the good of the beloved, then Teresa will also desire for the beloved person things different from those desired by God, in virtue of Teresa's differing ability to see the good for the beloved person.

It is easy to become confused here because the phrase "the good" can be used either attributively or referentially.[22] In this context, "the good of the beloved" can be used either to refer to particular things which are conducive to the beloved's well-being; or it can be used opaquely, to refer to anything whatever, under the description *the good of the beloved*. A mother who is baffled by the quarrels among her adult children and clueless about how to bring about a just peace for them may say, despairingly, "I just want the good for everybody." She is then using the phrase "the good" attributively, with no idea of how to use it referentially.

If Teresa were tranquil over any affliction which happens to her father, because she thinks that in this tranquillity her will is united to God's will and that she is therefore willing the good for her father,[23] "the good" in this thought of hers is being used attributively, to designate *whatever* God thinks is good. But this cannot be the way "the good" is used in any thought of God's, without relativizing the good entirely to God's will. If we eschew such relativism, then it is not the case that anything God desires is good just because God desires it. And so it is also not true that God desires as the good of a beloved person *whatever* it is that God desires for her. When God desires the good for someone, then, God must desire it by desiring particular things as good for that person. Consequently, to say that God desires the good for a person is to use "the good" referentially.

For this reason, when, in an effort to will what God wills, Teresa desires *whatever* happens to her

father as the good for her father, she thereby actually *fails* to will what God wills. To be united with God in willing the good requires willing for the beloved particular things which are in fact the good for the beloved, and doing so requires recognizing those things which constitute that good.

At the death of Mao Tse-tung, one of the groups competing for power was called "the Whatever Faction," because the members of that group were committed to maintaining as true, and compulsory for all Chinese to believe, anything Mao said, whatever it was.[24] In trying to desire whatever happens as good because God wills it, a person is as it were trying to be part of a Whatever Faction for God. She is trying to maintain as good anything that happens, whatever it is, on the grounds that it is what God wills. By contrast, in his great lament over the death of his brother, Bernard of Clairvaux is willing to affirm both his passionate grief over the loss of his brother and his acceptance of God's allowing that death. Bernard says, "Shall I find fault with [God's] judgment because I wince from the pain?";[25] "I have no wish to repudiate the decrees of God, nor do I question that judgment by which each of us has received his due...."[26] Bernard grieves over this particular death as a bad thing, even while he accepts that God's allowing this bad thing is a good thing.

Understanding the subtle but important difference in attitude between Teresa and Bernard on this score helps to elucidate the otherwise peculiar part of the book of Job in which God rebukes Job's comforters because they did not say of God the thing which is right, unlike God's servant Job, who did. What the comforters had said was that God is justified in allowing Job's suffering. Job, on the other hand, had complained bitterly that his suffering is unjust and that God should not have allowed it to happen. How is it that, in the story, God affirms Job's position and repudiates that of the comforters? The answer lies in seeing that the comforters took Job's suffering to be good just because, in their view, Job's suffering was willed by God. In effect, then, the comforters were (and wanted to be) part of the Whatever Faction of God. Job, by contrast, was intransigent in his refusal to be partisan in this way. And so, on the apparently paradoxical view of the book of Job, in opposing God, Job is more allied with God's will than are the comforters, who were taking God's part. That is why when in the story God comes to adjudicate, he sides with Job, who had opposed him, and not with the comforters, who were trying to be his partisans.

The apparent paradox here can be resolved by the scholastic distinction between God's antecedent and consequent will. On this distinction, whatever happens in the world happens only because it is in accordance with God's will, but that will is God's *consequent* will. God's consequent will, however, is to be distinguished from his antecedent will; and many of the things which happen in the world are not in accordance with God's *antecedent* will. Roughly put, God's *antecedent* will is what God would have willed if things in the world had been up to God alone. God's *consequent* will is what God in fact will, given what he knows that his creatures will. God's consequent will is his will for the greatest good available in the circumstances which are generated through creaturely free will.

To try to be in accord with God's will by taking as acceptable, as unworthy of sorrow, everything that happens is to confuse the consequent will of God with the antecedent will. It is to accept as intrinsically good even those things which God wills as good only secundum quid, that is, as the best available in the circumstances. But God does not will as intrinsically good everything he wills; what he wills in his consequent will, what is the best available in the circumstances, might be only the lesser of evils, not the intrinsically good.

And so to accept as good whatever happens on the grounds that it is God's will is the wrong way to try to be united with God's will. One can desire as intrinsically good what one sees for oneself is good in the circumstances, or one can desire[27] as intrinsically good whatever happens, on the grounds that it is God's will. But only the former desire can be in accordance with God's will, given that God's consequent will is not the same as his antecedent will. For the same reasons, only the former desire is conductive to union with God. Although it appears paradoxical, then, the closest a human person may be able to come, in this life, to uniting her will with God's will may include her willing things (say, that a beloved person not die) which are opposed to God's (consequent) will.

It is also important to see in this connection that, in principle, there cannot be any competition between the love of God and the love of other persons. On the contrary, if one does not love one's neighbour, then one does not love God either. That is because to love God is to desire union with him; and union with God requires being united in will with him. But a person who does not love another, his father or brother, for example, cannot be united in will with a God who does love these people. So, in being tranquil and unmoved in the face of the death of a beloved father or mother, a person is not more united with God, or more in harmony with God's will, but less.

V. DENYING ONESELF

Something also needs to be said in this connection about the Christian doctrine mandating denial of the self. This much understanding of the two different ways in which one can try to will what God wills shows that there are also two correspondingly different interpretations of that doctrine.

Cassian and others who hold the stern-minded attitude manifest one such understanding. A person who shares Cassian's attitude will attempt to deny his self by, in effect, refusing to let his own mind and his own will exercise their characteristic functions. That is because a person who attempts to see as good whatever happens, on the grounds that whatever happens is willed by God, is trying to suppress, or trying to fail to acquire, his own understanding of the good. And a person who attempts to will as good whatever happens, on the same grounds, is trying to suppress the desires his own will forms, or trying not to acquire the desires his will would have formed if he were not in the grip of the stern-minded attitude. To attempt to deny the self in the stern-minded way is thus to try not to have a self at all. A woman who says sincerely to her father, "I want only what you want," and "whatever you think is good is good in my view, too," is a woman who is trying to be at one with her father by having no self of her own.

On the other hand, it is possible to let one's own faculties of intellect and will have their normal functioning and still deny oneself. This is a stance with which we are all familiar from our experiences of ordinary, daily life. Consider, for example, a mother with the stomach flu who creeps out of bed to care for her baby who also has the flu. When she leaves her bed to tend the baby, she is preferring to meet the baby's needs rather than her own. That is, she desires to stay in bed, but she also desires that the baby's needs take precedence over her own needs and desires. In her desire about the rank-ordering of desires, she does not cease to desire to stay in bed. She still has that desire; she just acts counter to it. This is to deny the self by first having a self to deny. Unlike the no-self position, this position is compatible with sorrow, and tears, for the things lost in the desires denied.

On reflection, it is clear that, contrary to first appearances, the no-self position is actually incompatible with the Christian injunction of self-denial. That is because one cannot crucify a self one does not have. To crucify one's self is to have desires and to be willing to act counter to them. An adherent to the Whatever Faction of God cannot deny his self, however, because he has constructed his desires in such a way that, whatever he wills, he does not will counter to his own desires. A person who is a partisan of the no-self position has a first-order desire for whatever it may be that is God's will, and he attempts to have no first-order desires which are in conflict with whatever it may be that is God's will. That is why (unlike the real Teresa, who was full of very human emotions) such a person would not weep if her father died. In theory, at any rate, whatever happens to her is in accordance with her first-order will and is therefore not a source of sorrow to her. In virtue of the fact that she has tried to extirpate from herself all desires except the one desire for whatever it may be that is God's will, such a person has no desires which are frustrated by whatever happens, as long as she herself remains committed to willing whatever God wills.[28]

The self-crucifying denier of the self, by contrast, has first-order desires for things his own intellect finds good, so that he is vulnerable to grief in the frustration of those desires. But he prefers his grief and frustration to the violation of God's will. In this sense, he also wills that God's will be done. His second-order desire is that God's desires take precedence over his own. When Christ says, "not my will but yours be done," he is not expressing the no-self position, because he is admitting that he has desires in conflict with God's desires. On the other hand, in virtue of preferring his pain to the violation of God's will, he is also willing that God's desires take precedence over his. This is the sense, then, in which he is willing that God's will be done.

VI. THE DESIRES OF THE HEART AND THE FLOURISHING OF A PERSON

So, for all these reasons, the stern-minded attitude is to be repudiated. Whatever its antiquity and ancestry, such influential thinkers as Bernard and Aquinas do not accept it. More importantly, it is an unpalatable position, even from the point of view of an ascetically minded Christianity. It underlies the repellent and lamentable mind-set exemplified in Cassian's story, and it is incompatible with the love of one's neighbour and consequently also with love of God. There are things worth desiring other than the intrinsically valuable things necessary for human flourishing, and the desires for these things should not be suppressed or stamped out. On the contrary, as Cassian's story makes plain, the attempt to extirpate any desires of the heart does not lead to human excellence, as Cassian thought it did, but to a kind of inhumanity willing to murder one's own child in the service of a confused and reprehensible attempt at self-denial.

There is an apparent paradox here, however. As I introduced the phrase, the desires of the heart are desires which are central to a person's web of desires but whose objects have the value they do for her because of her desire for them, not because of their connection to general human flourishing. On the face of it, then, losing the objects of such desires or giving up those desires themselves is compatible with general human flourishing for that person. But the rejection of the stern-minded attitude seems to imply that a person's flourishing requires that he have desires of the heart and that he strive to have what he desires. Consequently, it also seems to imply that it is essential to a person's flourishing that he have desires of the heart. But, then, if the desires of the heart are required for his flourishing, it seems that the objects of those desires are as well. And so it seems to follow, paradoxically, that it is essential to human flourishing that a person desire and seek to have things at least some of which are not necessary to human flourishing.

In recent work, Harry Frankfurt has argued that it is useful for a person to have final ends.[29] The central idea of his argument is the thought that a person with no final ends at all will have a life which lacks flourishing. And so final ends *are* useful as a means to an end, namely, human flourishing. The apparently paradoxical claim about the desires of the heart can be understood analogously. Human beings are constructed in such a way that they naturally set their hearts on things in addition to and different from intrinsically valuable things essential to general human flourishing. That is why confining a person's desires just to human flourishing has something inhuman about it. A person's flourishing therefore also requires that he care about and seek to have things besides those that are intrinsically valuable components of or means to human flourishing.[30] On Frankfurt's view, having a desire for something which is not a means to anything else is a means to a person's flourishing. On the view I have argued for here, having a desire for things which are not essential to flourishing and seeking to have those things is also necessary as a means to flourishing.

And so, although no particular thing valued as a desire of the heart is essential to a person's flourishing, human flourishing is not possible in the absence of the desires of the heart.

VII. CONCLUSION

For all these reasons, we can safely leave the objections of the stern-minded attitude to one side. It therefore remains the case that justification is also needed for suffering stemming from unfulfilled or frustrated desires of the heart. For this reason, theodicies which focus just on one or another variety of general human flourishing as the morally sufficient reason for God's allowing evil are, at best, incomplete. Even if we give a theodicy such as Hick's or Swinburne's everything it wants as regards the relation between suffering and flourishing, however flourishing is understood in their theodicies, there remains the problem of suffering stemming from the loss of the desires of one's heart.

Take the story of Job, for example. For the sake of argument, let it be the case, as Saadiah Gaon appears to hold in his excellent and impressive commentary, that Job's suffering is necessary to his ennobling and purification, morally acceptable as a means to these things, and outweighed by them, in the sense that (on some objective measure) Job's ennobling and purification are a greater good than his suffering is an evil. Even if this were entirely so, and even if it were right that ennobling and purification constituted consummate human flourishing, something more would be needed for theodicy in Job's case. Job might care about his children at least as much as about his own ennobling and purification; and he might be heartbroken at the loss of his children, even with the benefit to him of his ennobling and purification. Something also needs to be said about the moral justification for God's allowing such heartbreak.

Someone might object that if the benefit to Job really is connected to his suffering in the way I have just described, then nothing more is needed for theodicy, because the good given to Job through his suffering defeats the suffering. But this is to accord no value to the desires of Job's heart. It is, in effect, to say with regard to Job a much sterner version of what the loving but exasperated father said to his daughter: It is not reasonable to weep about these things. But, as I have been at pains to show, disregarding or downplaying the desires of the heart is itself unreasonable. Suffering is a function of what we care about, and we care not only about human flourishing; we care also about the things on which we have set our hearts. The suffering stemming from the loss of the heart's desires also needs to be redeemed. The benefit which outweighs the suffering for Job, as Saadiah Gaon sees it, outweighs that suffering only on the scale of values which measures the intrinsic worth of things essential to human flourishing in general. It does not outweigh it on the scale which measures things that have the value they do for a particular person only because he has set his heart on them.

That this is so helps to explain why so many people feel uneasy or disappointed at attempted solutions to the problem of evil which focus on some global good (for humanity in general—the significant use of free will, for example—as a morally sufficient reason for God to allow suffering. If a person's own flourishing is not sufficient to justify God in allowing her to be heartbroken, then, a fortiori, some component of or contribution to the flourishing of the human species considered as a whole cannot do so either.

And so the desires of the heart also need to be considered in connection with the problem of evil. For my part, I think it is possible to find a way to develop traditional theodicies to include satisfactory consideration of the problem posed by the desires of the heart;[31] but, clearly, that complicated and challenging task lies outside the scope of this paper.

REFERENCES

Adams, Marilyn, *Horrendous Evils and the Goodness of God* (Ithaca, NY: Cornell University Press, 1999).

Astell, Ann, *The Song of Songs in the Middle Ages* (Ithaca, NY: Cornell University Press, 1990).

Cassian, *The Monastic Institutes*, tr. Jerome Bertram (London: Saint Austin Press, 1999).

Frankfurt, Harry, "On the Usefulness of Final Ends," *Necessity, Volition, and Love* (Princeton, NJ: Princeton University Press, 1998).

Hick, John, *Evil and the God of Love* (New York: Harper and Row, 1966).

———, "God, Evil and Mystery," *Religious Studies* 3 (1968a): 539–46.

———, "The Problem of Evil in the First and Last Things," *Journal of Theological Studies* 19 (1968b): 591–602.

Hull, Jonathan, *Touching the Rock. An Experience of Blindness* (New York: Vintage Books, 1991).

MacFarquhar, Roderick, "The Succession to Mao and the End of Maoism," in *The Cambridge History of China*, vol. 15, *The People's Republic, pt.2: Revolutions within the Chinese Revolution: 1966–1982* (Cambridge: Cambridge University Press, 1991).

Saadiah Gaon, *The Book of Beliefs and Opinions*, tr. Samuel Rosenblatt (New Haven, CT: Yale University Press, 1948).

Stump, Eleonore, "Love, By All Accounts," Proceedings and Addresses of The American Philosophical Association, Vol. 80, No. 2, November 2006.

———, *Wandering in Darkness: Narrative and the Problem of Suffering* (Oxford: Oxford University Press, forthcoming).

Swinburne, Richard, *Providence and the Problem of Evil* (Oxford: Oxford University Press, 1998).

Teresa of Avila, *The Interior Castle* (Mahwah, NJ: Paulist Press, 1979).

Vanier, Jean, *Becoming Human* (Mahwah, NJ: Paulist Press, 1998).

NOTES

For helpful comments on earlier drafts of this paper or on its contents, I am grateful to Jeffrey Brower, Frank Burch Brown, John Foley, John Kavanaugh, Scott MacDonald, Michael Murray, Michael Rea, Theodore Vitali, and anonymous reviewers for *Oxford Studies in Philosophy of Religion*.

1. There is a large, contentious philosophical literature on the nature of human flourishing or well-being,

and it is not part of my purpose to try to engage that literature here. For my purposes in this paper, I will understand flourishing to consist in just those things necessary in a person's life for that person's life to be admirable and meaningful.

2. Saadiah Gaon 1948: 246–7.

3. Hick 1966. For Hick's defence of his solutions against objections, see, for example, Hick 1968a: 539–46, and Hick 1968b: 591–602.

4. See Swinburne 1998.

5. In Adams 1999, Marilyn Adams makes a distinction which is at least related to the distinction I am after here. She says, "the value of a person's life may be assessed from the inside (in relation to that person's own goals, ideals, and choices) and from the outside (in relation to the aims, tastes, values, and preferences of others). . . . My notion is that for a person's life to be a great good to him/her on the whole, the external point of view (even if it is God's) is not sufficient" (p. 145).

6. The expression "the desire of the heart" is also ambiguous. It can mean either a particular kind of desire or else the thing which is desired in that way. When we say, "the desire of his heart was to be a great musician," the expression refers to a desire; when we say, "In losing her, he lost the desire of his heart," the expression refers to the thing desired. I will not try to sort out this ambiguity here; I will simply trust to the context to disambiguate the expression.

7. Ps. 37:4–5.

8. Except for conceptions of flourishing which make flourishing identical to the satisfaction of desires, but equating flourishing just with desire satisfaction is problematic enough that it can be left to one side here.

9. Vanier 1998: 158–9.

10. Hull 1991: 205–6.

11. Elsewhere I consider the complication of cases in which an apparently appropriate heart's desire is such that its fulfilment would undermine the flourishing of the person who has it. So, for example, the great English poet John Milton apparently had a heart's desire to be an administrator in the Puritan government of his time; but his government work kept him from writing poetry. All his greatest poetry was written after the fail of the Puritan regime. There are also cases in which a person sets his heart

on what he himself takes to be essential to his flourishing, when in fact he is mistaken on this score. Viktor Klemperer supposed that his flourishing was dependent on his writing a great study of eighteenth-century French literature, and he describes his own sense of the blight of his life in consequence of his inability to write a great book in his stunningly excellent diaries, published now to rave reviews. For consideration of complicated cases such as these, see my *Wandering in Darkness: Narrative and the Problem of Suffering* (Oxford, forthcoming).

12. For a persuasive statement of a case for such a view, see Adams 1998.

13. Cassian 1999: 55–6.

14. Teresa of Avila 1979: 98, 99, 100.

15. *Confessions* IX.12.

16. Stump 2006.

17. Cited in Astell 1990: 126.

18. Cited in Astell 1990: 130.

19. Cited in Astell 1990: 133.

20. *Super Evangelium S. Ioannis Lectura,* John 12: 24–5, Lectio IV.7, 1643–1644.

21. *Super Evangelium S. Ioannis Lectura,* John 14: 27–31, Lectio VIII.l, 1966.

22. "The commander of the armed forces" is used referentially when it refers to the particular person who is the President; it is used attributively when it refers to anyone who holds the office of commander without reference to a particular person who in fact currently holds the office.

23. It is important to put the point in terms of what *happens* to her father, rather than in terms of any state or condition of her father, since there are certainly things her father might do which cause Teresa a grief she would approve of having.

24. The official formula was "Whatever policy Chairman Mao decided upon, we shall resolutely defend; whatever directives Chairman Mao issued, we shall steadfastly obey." See MacFarquhar 1991: 372

25. Cited in Astell 1990: 133.

26. Cited in Astell 1990: 130.

27. Or try to accept—a distinction manifested by Teresa's own description of herself.

28. The last clause is a necessary caveat because, presumably, even an adherent to the position would

be distressed at finding sin in himself (and maybe even at finding sin in others), since sin cannot be considered in accordance with God's will.

29. Frankfurt 1998.

30. In this respect, the desires of the heart are to human flourishing what accidents are to a primary substance. Any particular accident is not necessary to a substance,

but it is necessary to a substance that it have accidents. Analogously, no particular desire of the heart is necessary for a person's flourishing, but it is necessary for her flourishing that she have desires of the heart.

31. I argue for this claim in detail in my *Wandering in Darkness. Narrative and the Problem of Suffering* (Oxford, forthcoming).

III.C.5

Horrendous Evils and the Goodness of God

MARILYN McCORD ADAMS

Marilyn McCord Adams (1943–) is Honorary Professor at the Australian Catholic University. She has held positions in philosophy and theology at Oxford University, Yale University, and the University of California, Los Angeles, and has written extensively on topics at the intersection of these disciplines. In this article, Adams argues that standard responses to the problem of evil fall short in their ability to deal with "horrendous evil." She then argues that God could defeat such evils only by somehow "integrating participation in horrendous evils into a person's relationship with God."

1. INTRODUCTION

Over the past thirty years, analytic philosophers of religion have defined "the problem of evil" in terms of the prima-facie difficulty in consistently maintaining

(1) God exists, and is omnipotent, omniscient, and perfectly good

and

(2) Evil exists.

In a crisp and classic article, "Evil and Omnipotence,"[1] J. L. Mackie emphasized that the problem

is not that (1) and (2) are logically inconsistent by themselves, but that they together with quasi-logical rules formulating attribute-analyses—such as

(P1) A perfectly good being would always eliminate evil so far as it could,

and

(P2) There are *no limits* to what an omnipotent being can do—

constitute an inconsistent premiss-set. He added, of course, that the inconsistency might be removed by substituting alternative and perhaps more subtle analyses, but cautioned that such replacements of

First published in *Proceedings of the Aristotelian Society*, Supplementary Vol. 63 (1989), pp. 297–310, with revisions and additional notes from the revised version in *The Problem of Evil*, ed. Robert Merrihew Adams and Marilyn McCord Adams (Oxford University Press, 1990), © The Aristotelian Society 1989. Reprinted by permission of the Aristotelian Society and Oxford University Press.

(P1) and (P2) would save "ordinary theism" from his charge of positive irrationality, only if true to its "essential requirements."[2]

In an earlier paper, "Problems of Evil: More Advice to Christian Philosophers,"[3] I underscored Mackie's point and took it a step further. In debates about whether the argument from evil can establish the irrationality of religious belief, care must be taken, both by the atheologians who deploy it and by the believers who defend against it, to ensure that the operative attribute-analyses accurately reflect that religion's understanding of divine power and goodness. It does the atheologian no good to argue for the falsity of Christianity on the ground that the existence of an omnipotent, omniscient, pleasure-maximizer is incompossible with a world such as ours, because Christians never believed God was a pleasure-maximizer anyway. But equally, the truth of Christianity would be inadequately defended by the observation that an omnipotent, omniscient egoist could have created a world with suffering creatures, because Christians insist that God loves other (created) persons than Himself. The extension of "evil" in (2) is likewise important. Since Mackie and his successors are out to show that "the several parts of the *essential* theological doctrine are inconsistent with *one another*,"[4] they can accomplish their aim only if they circumscribe the extension of "evil" as their religious opponents do. By the same token, it is not enough for Christian philosophers to explain how the power, knowledge, and goodness of God could coexist with some evils or other; a full account must exhibit the compossibility of divine perfection with evils in the amounts and of the kinds found in the actual world (and evaluated as such by Christian standards).

The moral of my earlier story might be summarized thus: where the internal coherence of a system of religious beliefs is at stake, successful arguments for its inconsistency must draw on premises (explicitly, or implicitly) internal to that system or obviously acceptable to its adherents; likewise for successful rebuttals or explanations of consistency. The thrust of my argument is to push both sides of the debate towards more detailed attention to and subtle understanding of the religious system in question.

As a Christian philosopher, I want to focus in this paper on the problem for the truth of Christianity raised by what I shall call "horrendous" evils. Although our world is riddled with them, the biblical record punctuated by them, and one of them—namely, the passion of Christ; according to Christian belief, the judicial murder of God by the people of God—is memorialized by the Church on its most solemn holiday (Good Friday) and in its central sacrament (the Eucharist), the problem of horrendous evils is largely skirted by standard treatments for the good reason that they are intractable by them. After showing why, I will draw on other Christian materials to sketch ways of meeting this, the deepest of religious problems.

2. DEFINING THE CATEGORY

For present purposes, I define "horrendous evils" as "evils the participation in (the doing or suffering of) which gives one reason prima facie to doubt whether one's life could (given their inclusion in it) be a great good to one on the whole."[5] Such reasonable doubt arises because it is so difficult humanly to conceive how such evils could be overcome. Borrowing Chisholm's contrast between *balancing off* (which occurs when the opposing values of *mutually exclusive* parts of a whole partially or totally cancel each other out) and *defeat* (which cannot occur by the mere addition to the whole of a new part of opposing value, but involves some "organic unity" among the values of parts and wholes, as when the positive aesthetic value of a whole painting defeats the ugliness of a small colour patch),[6] horrendous evils seem prima facie, not only to balance off but to engulf the positive value of a participant's life. Nevertheless, that very horrendous proportion, by which they threaten to rob a person's life of positive meaning, cries out not only to be engulfed, but to be made meaningful through positive and decisive defeat.

I understand this criterion to be objective, but relative to individuals. The example of habitual complainers, who know to make the worst of a good situation, shows individuals not to be incorrigible experts on what ills would defeat the positive value of their lives. Nevertheless, nature and experience endow people with different strengths; one bears easily what crushes another. And a major consideration in determining whether an individual's life is/has been a great good to him/her on the whole, is invariably and appropriately how it has seemed to him/her.[7]

I offer the following list of paradigmatic horrors: the rape of a woman and axing off of her arms, psychophysical torture whose ultimate goal is the disintegration of personality, betrayal of one's deepest loyalties, cannibalizing one's own offspring, child abuse of the sort described by Ivan Karamazov, child pornography, parental incest, slow death by starvation, participation in the Nazi death camps, the explosion of nuclear bombs over populated areas, having to choose which of one's children shall live and which be executed by terrorists, being the accidental and/or unwitting agent of the disfigurement or death of those one loves best. I regard these as *paradigmatic*, because I believe most people would find in the doing or suffering of them prima-facie reason to doubt the positive meaning of their lives.[8] Christian belief counts the crucifixion of Christ another: on the one hand, death by crucifixion seemed to defeat Jesus' Messianic vocation; for according to Jewish law, death by hanging from a tree made its victim ritually accursed, definitively excluded from the compass of God's people, *a fortiori* disqualified from being the Messiah. On the other hand, it represented the defeat of its perpetrators' leadership vocations, as those who were to prepare the people of God for the Messiah's coming, killed and ritually accursed the true Messiah, according to later theological understanding, God Himself.

3. THE IMPOTENCE OF STANDARD SOLUTIONS

For better and worse, the by now standard strategies for "solving" the problem of evil are powerless in the face of horrendous evils.

3.1. Seeking the Reason-Why

In his model article "Hume on Evil,"[9] Pike takes up Mackie's challenge, arguing that (P1) fails to reflect ordinary moral intuitions (more to the point, I would add, Christian beliefs), and traces the abiding sense of trouble to the hunch that an omnipotent, omniscient being could have no reason compatible with perfect goodness for permitting (bringing about) evils, because all legitimate excuses arise from ignorance or weakness. Solutions to the problem of evil have thus been sought in the form of counter-examples to this latter claim, i.e. logically possible reasons-why that would excuse even an omnipotent, omniscient God! The putative logically possible reasons offered have tended to be *generic* and *global*: generic in so far as some *general* reason is sought to cover all sorts of evils; global in so far as they seize upon some feature of the world as a whole. For example, philosophers have alleged that the desire to make a world with one of the following properties—"the best of all possible worlds,"[10] "a world more perfect than which is impossible," "a world exhibiting a perfect balance of retributive justice,"[11] "a world with as favorable a balance of (created) moral good over moral evil as God can weakly actualize"[12]—would constitute a reason compatible with perfect goodness for God's creating a world with evils in the amounts and of the kinds found in the actual world. Moreover, such general reasons are presented as so powerful as to do away with any need to catalogue types of evils one by one, and examine God's reason for permitting each in particular. Plantinga explicitly hopes that the problem of horrendous evils can thus be solved without being squarely confronted.[13]

3.2. The Insufficiency of Global Defeat

A pair of distinctions is in order here: (i) between two dimensions of divine goodness in relation to creation—namely, "producer of global goods" and "goodness to" or "love of individual created persons"; and (ii) between the overbalance/defeat of evil by good on the global scale, and the overbalance/defeat of evil by good within the context of an individual person's life.[14] Correspondingly, we may separate two problems of evil parallel to the two sorts of goodness mentioned in (i).

In effect, generic and global approaches are directed to the first problem: they defend divine goodness along the first (global) dimension by suggesting logically possible strategies for the global defeat of evils. But establishing God's excellence as a producer of global goods does not automatically solve the second problem, especially in a world containing horrendous evils. For God cannot be said to be good or loving to any created persons the positive meaning of whose lives He allows to be engulfed in and/or defeated by evils—that is, individuals within whose lives horrendous evils remain undefeated. Yet, the only way unsupplemented global and generic approaches could have to explain the latter, would be by applying their general reasons-why to particular cases of horrendous suffering.

Unfortunately, such an exercise fails to give satisfaction. Suppose for the sake of argument that horrendous evil could be included in maximally perfect world orders; its being partially constitutive of such an order would assign it that generic and global positive meaning. But would knowledge of such a fact defeat for a mother the prima-facie reason provided by her cannibalism of her own infant to wish that she had never been born? Again, the aim of perfect retributive balance confers meaning on evils imposed. But would knowledge that the torturer was being tortured give the victim who broke down and turned traitor under pressure any more reason to think his/her life worth while? Would it not merely multiply reasons for the torturer to doubt that his/her life could turn out to be a good to him/her on the whole? Could the truck-driver who accidentally runs over his beloved child find consolation in the idea that this middle-known[15] but unintended side-effect was part of the price God accepted for a world with the best balance of moral good over moral evil he could get?

Not only does the application to horrors of such generic and global reasons for divine permission of evils fail to solve the second problem of evil; it makes it worse by adding *generic prima-facie* reasons to doubt whether human life would be a great good to individual human beings in possible worlds where such divine motives were operative. For, taken in isolation and made to bear the weight of the whole explanation, such reasons-why draw a picture of divine indifference or even hostility to the human plight. Would the fact that God permitted horrors because they were constitutive means to His end of global perfection, or that He tolerated them because He could obtain that global end anyway, make the participant's life more tolerable, more worth living for him/her? Given radical human vulnerability to horrendous evils, the ease with which humans participate in them, whether as victim or perpetrator, would not the thought that God visits horrors on anyone who caused them, simply because he/she deserves it, provide one more reason to expect human life to be a nightmare?

Those willing to split the two problems of evil apart might adopt a divide-and-conquer strategy, by simply denying divine goodness along the second dimension. For example, many Christians do not believe that God will ensure an overwhelmingly good life to each and every person He creates. Some say the decisive defeat of evil with good is promised only within the lives of the obedient, who enter by the narrow gate. Some speculate that the elect may be few. Many recognize that the sufferings of this present life are as nothing compared to the hell of eternal torment, designed to defeat goodness with horrors within the lives of the damned.

Such a road can be consistently travelled only at the heavy toll of admitting that human life in worlds such as ours is a bad bet. Imagine (adapting Rawls's device) persons in a pre-original position, considering possible worlds containing managers of differing power, wisdom, and character, and subjects of varying fates. The question they are to answer about each world is whether they would willingly enter it as a human being, from behind a veil of ignorance as to which position they would occupy. Reason would, I submit, dictate a negative verdict for worlds whose omniscient and omnipotent manager permits ante-mortem horrors that remain unde-feated within the context of the human participant's life; *a fortiori*, for worlds in which some or most humans suffer eternal torment.

3.3. Inaccessible Reasons

So far, I have argued that generic and global solu-tions are at best incomplete: however well their account of divine motivating reasons deals with the first problem of evil, the attempt to extend it to the second fails by making it worse. This verdict might seem prima facie tolerable to standard generic and global approaches and indicative of only a minor modification in their strategy: let the above-mentioned generic and global reasons cover divine permission of non-horrendous evils, and find other *reasons* compatible with perfect goodness *why* even an omnipotent, omniscient God would permit horrors.

In my judgement, such an approach is hope-less. As Plantinga[16] points out, where horrendous evils are concerned, not only do we not know God's *actual* reason for permitting them; we cannot even *conceive* of any plausible candidate sort of rea-son consistent with worthwhile lives for human participants in them.

4. THE HOW OF GOD'S VICTORY

Up to now, my discussion has given the reader cause to wonder whose side I am on anyway. For I have insisted, with rebels like Ivan Karamazov and John Stuart Mill, on spotlighting the problem hor-rendous evils pose. Yet, I have signalled my prefer-ence for a version of Christianity that insists on both dimensions of divine goodness, and maintains not only (*a*) that God will be good enough to cre-ated persons to make human life a good bet, but also (*b*) that each created person will have a life that is a great good to him/her on the whole. My cri-tique of standard approaches to the problem of evil thus seems to reinforce atheologian Mackie's ver-dict of "positive irrationality" for such a religious position.

4.1. Whys versus Hows

The inaccessibility of reasons-why seems especially decisive. For surely an all-wise and all-powerful God, who loved each created person enough (*a*) to defeat any experienced horrors within the context of the participant's life, and (*b*) to give each created person a life that is a great good to him/her on the whole, would not permit such persons to suffer horrors for no reason.[17] Does not our inability even to conceive of plausible candidate reasons suffice to make belief in such a God positively irrational in a world containing horrors? In my judgement, it does not.

To be sure, motivating reasons come in several varieties relative to our conceptual grasp: There are (i) reasons of the sort we can readily understand when we are informed of them (e.g. the mother who permits her child to undergo painful heart sur-gery because it is the only humanly possible way to save its life). Moreover, there are (ii) reasons we would be cognitively, emotionally, and spiritually equipped to grasp if only we had a larger memory or wider attention span (analogy: I may be able to memorize small town street plans; memorizing the road networks of the entire country is a task requir-ing more of the same, in the way that proving Gödel's theorem is not). Some generic and global approaches insinuate that divine permission of evils has motivating reasons of this sort. Finally, there are (iii) reasons that we are cognitively, emotionally, and/or spiritually too immature to fathom (the way a two-year-old child is incapable of understanding its mother's reasons for permitting the surgery). I agree with Plantinga that our ignorance of divine reasons for permitting horrendous evils is not of types (i) or (ii), but of type (iii).

Nevertheless, if there are varieties of ignorance, there are also varieties of reassurance.[18] The two-year-old heart patient is convinced of its mother's love, not by her cognitively inaccessible reasons, but by her intimate care and presence through its painful experience. The story of Job suggests some-thing similar is true with human participation in horrendous suffering: God does not give Job His reasons-why, and implies that Job isn't smart enough to grasp them; rather Job is lectured on the extent of divine power, and sees God's goodness face to face! Likewise, I suggest, to exhibit the logical compossibility of both dimensions of divine goodness with horrendous suffering, it is not necessary to find logically possible reasons *why* God might permit them. It is enough to show *how* God can be good enough to created persons despite their participation in horrors—by defeating them within the context of the individual's life and by giving that individual a life that is a great good to him/her on the whole.

4.2. What Sort of Valuables?

In my opinion, the reasonableness of Christianity can be maintained in the face of horrendous evils only by drawing on resources of religious value theory. For one way for God to be *good to* created persons is by relating them appropriately to relevant and great goods. But philosophical and religious theories differ importantly on what valuables they admit into their ontology. Some maintain that "what you see is what you get," but nevertheless admit a wide range of valuables, from sensory pleasures, the beauty of nature and cultural artefacts, the joys of creativity, to loving personal intimacy. Others posit a transcendent good (e.g. the Form of the Good in Platonism, or God, the Supremely Valuable Object, in Christianity). In the spirit of Ivan Karamazov, I am convinced that the depth of horrific evil cannot be accurately estimated without recognizing it to be incommensurate with any package of merely non-transcendent goods and so unable to be balanced off, much less defeated, thereby.

Where the *internal* coherence of Christianity is the issue, however, it is fair to appeal to its own store of valuables. From a Christian point of view God is a being a greater than which cannot be conceived, a good incommensurate with both created goods and temporal evils. Likewise, the good of beatific, face-to-face intimacy with God is simply incommensurate with any merely non-transcendent goods or ills a person might experience, Thus, the good of beatific face-to-face intimacy with

God would *engulf* (in a sense analogous to Chisholmian balancing off) even the horrendous evils humans experience in this present life here below, and overcome any prima-facie reasons the individual had to doubt whether his/her life would or could be worth living.

4.3. Personal Meaning, Horrors Defeated

Engulfing personal horrors within the context of the participant's life would vouchsafe to that individual a life that was a great good to him/her on the whole. I am still inclined to think it would guarantee that immeasurable divine goodness to any person thus benefited. But there is good theological reason for Christians to believe that God would go further, beyond engulfment to defeat. For it is the nature of persons to look for meaning, both in their lives and in the world. Divine respect for and commitment to created personhood would drive God to make all those sufferings which threaten to destroy the positive meaning of a person's life meaningful through positive defeat.[19]

How could God do it? So far as I can see, only by integrating participation in horrendous evils into a person's relationship with God. Possible dimensions of integration are charted by Christian soteriology. I pause here to sketch three:[20] (i) First, because God in Christ participated in horrendous evil through His passion and death, human experience of horrors can be a means of *identifying* with Christ, either through *sympathetic* identification (in which each person suffers his/her own pains, but their similarity enables each to know what it is like for the other) or through *mystical* identification (in which the created person is supposed literally to experience a share of Christ's pain[21]). (ii) Julian of Norwich's description of heavenly welcome suggests the possible defeat of horrendous evil through divine gratitude. According to Julian, before the elect have a chance to thank God for all He has done for them, God will say, "Thank you for all your suffering, the suffering of your youth." She says that the creature's experience of divine gratitude will bring such full and unending joy as could not be merited by the whole sea of human pain and suffering throughout the ages.[22] (iii) A third idea identifies temporal suffering itself with a vision into the inner life of God, and can be developed several ways. Perhaps, contrary to medieval theology, God is not impassible, but rather has matched capacities for joy and for suffering. Perhaps, as the Heidelberg catechism suggests, God responds to human sin and the sufferings of Christ with an agony beyond human conception.[23] Alternatively, the inner life of God may be, strictly speaking and in and of itself, beyond both joy and sorrow. But, just as (according to Rudolf Otto) humans experience divine presence now as *tremendum* (with deep dread and anxiety), now as *fascinans* (with ineffable attraction), so perhaps our deepest suffering as much as our highest joys may themselves be direct visions into the inner life of God, imperfect but somehow less obscure in proportion to their intensity. And if a face-to-face vision of God is a good for humans incommensurate with any non-transcendent goods or ills, so any vision of God (including horrendous suffering) would have a good aspect in so far as it is a vision of God (even if it has an evil aspect in so far as it is horrendous suffering). For the most part, horrors are not recognized as experiences of God (any more than the city slicker recognizes his visual image of a brown patch as a vision of Beulah the cow in the distance). But, Christian mysticism might claim, at least from the post-mortem perspective of the beatific vision, such sufferings will be seen for what they were, and retrospectively no one will wish away any intimate encounters with God from his/her life-history in this world. The created person's experience of the beatific vision together with his/her knowledge that intimate divine presence stretched back over his/her ante-mortem life and reached down into the depths of his/her worst suffering, would provide retrospective comfort independent of comprehension of the reasons-why akin to the two-year-old's assurance of its mother's love. Taking this third approach, Christians would not need to commit themselves about what in any event we do not know: namely, whether we will (like the two-year-old) ever grow up enough to understand the reasons why God permits our participation in

horrendous evils. For by contrast with the best of earthly mothers, such divine intimacy is an incommensurate good and would cancel out for the creature any need to know why.

5. CONCLUSION

The worst evils demand to be defeated by the best goods. Horrendous evils can be overcome only by the goodness of God. Relative to human nature, participation in horrendous evils and loving intimacy with God are alike disproportionate: for the former threatens to engulf the good in an individual human life with evil, while the latter guarantees the reverse engulfment of evil by good. Relative to one another, there is also disproportion, because the good that God *is*, and intimate relationship with Him, is incommensurate with created goods and evils alike. Because intimacy with God so outscales relations (good or bad) with any creatures, integration into the human person's relationship with God confers significant meaning and positive value even on horrendous suffering. This result coheres with basic Christian intuition: that the powers of darkness are stronger than humans, but they are no match for God!

Standard generic and global solutions have for the most part tried to operate within the territory common to believer and unbeliever, within the confines of religion-neutral value theory. Many discussions reflect the hope that substitute attribute-analyses, candidate reasons-why, and/or defeaters could issue out of values shared by believers and unbelievers alike. And some virtually make this a requirement on an adequate solution. Mackie knew better how to distinguish the many charges that may be levelled against religion. Just as philosophers may or may not find the existence of God plausible, so they may be variously attracted or repelled by Christian values of grace and redemptive sacrifice. But agreement on truth-value is not necessary to consensus on internal consistency. My contention has been that it is not only legitimate, but, given horrendous evils, necessary for Christians to dip into their richer store of valuables to exhibit the consistency of (1) and (2).[24] I would go one step further: assuming the pragmatic and/or moral (I would prefer to say, broadly speaking, religious) importance of believing that (one's own) human life is worth living, the ability of Christianity to exhibit how this could be so despite human vulnerability to horrendous evil, constitutes a pragmatic/moral/religious consideration in its favour, relative to value schemes that do not.

To me, the most troublesome weakness in what I have said lies in the area of conceptual under-development. The contention that God suffered in Christ or that one person can experience another's pain requires detailed analysis and articulation in metaphysics and philosophy of mind. I have shouldered some of this burden elsewhere,[25] but its full discharge is well beyond the scope of this paper.

NOTES

In the development of these ideas, I am indebted to the members of our Fall 1987 seminar on the problem of evil at UCLA—especially to Robert Merrihew Adams (its co-leader) and to Keith De Rose, William Fitzpatrick, and Houston Smit. I am also grateful to the Very Rcvd. Jon Hart Olson for many conversations in mystical theology.

1. J. L. Mackie, "Evil and Omnipotence," *Mind*, 64 (1955) [Chapter 1 in this collection]; repr. in Nelson Pike (ed.), *God and Evil* (Englewood Cliffs, NJ: Prentice-Hall, 1964), 46–60.

2. Ibid. 47 [pp. 26–7, 37 above].

3. Marilyn McCord Adams, "Problems of Evil: More Advice to Christian Philosophers," *Faith and Philosophy* (Apr. 1988), 121–43.

4. Mackie, "Evil and Omnipotence," pp. 46–7 [p. 25 above], (emphasis mine).

5. Stewart Sutherland (in his comment "Horrendous Evils and the Goodness of God—II," *Proceedings of the Aristotelian Society*, suppl. vol. 63 (1989), 311–23; esp. 311) takes my criterion to be somehow "first-person." This was not my intention. My definition may be made more explicit as follows: an evil *e* is horrendous if and only if participation in *e* by person *p* gives everyone prima-facie reason to doubt whether *p*'s life can, given *p*'s participation in *e*, be a great good to *p* on the whole.

6. Roderick Chisholm, "The Defeat of Good and Evil" [Chapter III in this collection].

7. Cf. Malcolm's astonishment at Wittgenstein's dying exclamation that he had had a wonderful life, *Ludwig Wittgenstein: A Memoir* (London: Oxford University Press, 1962), 100.

8. Once again, more explicitly, most people would agree that a person *p*'s doing or suffering of them constitutes prima-facic reason to doubt whether *p*'s life can be, given such participation, a great good to *p* on the whole.

9. "Hume on Evil," *Philosophical Review*, 72 (1963), 180–97 [Chapter II in this collection]; reprinted in Pike (ed.), *God and Evil*, p. 88 [pp. 40–1 above].

10. Following Leibniz, Pike draws on this feature as part of what I have called his Epistemic Defence ("Problems of Evil: More Advice to Christian Philosophers," pp. 124–5).

11. Augustine, *On Free Choice of Will*, iii. 93–102, implies that there is a maximum value for created worlds, and a plurality of worlds that meet it. All of these contain rational free creatures; evils are foreseen but unintended side-effects of their creation. No matter what they choose, however, God can order their choices into a maximally perfect universe by establishing an order of retributive justice.

12. Plantinga takes this line in numerous discussions, in the course of answering Mackie's objection to the Free Will Defence, that God should have made sinless free creatures. Plantinga insists that, given incompatibilist freedom in creatures, God cannot strongly actualize any world He wants. It is logically possible that a world with evils in the amounts and of the kinds found in this world is the best that He could do, Plantinga argues, given His aim of getting some moral goodness in the world.

13. Alvin Plantinga, "Self-Profile," in James E. Tomberlin and Peter van Inwagcn (eds.). *Profiles:*

Alvin Plantinga (Dordrecht, Boston, Mass., and Lancaster, Pa.: Reidel, 1985), 38.

14. I owe the second of these distinctions to a remark by Keith De Rose in our Fall 1987 seminar on the problem of evil at UCLA.

15. Middle knowledge, or knowledge of what is "in between" the actual and the possible, is the sort of knowledge of what a free creature *would do* in every situation in which that creature could possibly find himself. Following Luis de Molina and Francisco Suarez, Alvin Plantinga ascribes such knowledge to God, prior in the order of explanation to God's decision about which free creatures to actualize (in *The Nature of Necessity* (Oxford: Clarendon Press, 1974), pp. 164–93 [Chapter V in this collection]). Robert Merrihew Adams challenges this idea in his article "Middle Knowledge and the Problem of Evil," *American Philosophical Quarterly*, 14 (1977) [Chapter VI in this collection]; repr. in *The Virtue of Faith* (New York: Oxford University Press, 1987), 77–93.

16. Alvin Plantinga, "Self-Profile," pp. 34–5.

17. This point was made by William Fitzpatrick in our Fall 1987 seminar on the problem of evil at UCLA.

18. Contrary to what Sutherland suggests ("Horrendous Evils," pp. 314–15), so far as the compossibility problem is concerned, I intend no illicit shift from reason to emotion. My point is that intimacy with a loving other is a good, participation in which can defeat evils, and so provide everyone with reason to think a person's life can be a great good to his/her on the whole, despite his/her participation in evils.

19. Note, once again, contrary to what Sutherland suggests ("Horrendous Evils," pp. 321–3) "horrendous evil *e* is defeated" entails *none* of the following propositions: "*e* was not horrendous," "*e* was not unjust," "*e* was not so bad after all." Nor does my suggestion that even horrendous evils can be defeated by a great enough (because incommensurate and uncreated) good, in any way impugn the reliability of our moral intuitions about injustice, cold-bloodedness, or horror. The judgement that participation in *e* constitutes prima-facie reason to believe that *p*'s life is ruined, stands and remains a daunting measure of *e*'s horror.

20. In my paper "Redemptive Suffering: A Christian Solution to the Problem of Evil," in Robert Audi and William J. Wainwright (eds.). *Rationality, Religious Belief, and Moral Commitment: New Essays in Philosophy of Religion* (Cornell University Pres., 1986), 248–67, I sketch how horrendous suffering can be meaningful by being made a vehicle of divine redemption for victim, perpetrator, and onlooker, and thus an occasion of the victim's collaboration with God. In "Separation and Reversal in Luke-Acts," in Thomas Morris (ed.), *Philosophy and the Christian Faith* (Notre Dame, Ind.: Notre Dame University Press, 1988), 92–117, I attempted to chart the redemptive plot-line whereby horrendous sufferings are made meaningful by being woven into the divine redemptive plot. My considered opinion is that such collaboration would be too strenuous for the human condition were it not to be supplemented by a more explicit and beatific divine intimacy.

21. For example, Julian of Norwich tells us that she prayed for and received the latter (*Revelations of Divine Love*, ch. 17). Mother Theresa of Calcutta seems to construe Matthew 25: 31–46 to mean that the poorest and the least *are* Christ, and that their sufferings *are* Christ's (Malcolm Muggeridge, *Something Beautiful for God* [New York; Harper & Row, 1960], 72–5).

22. *Revelations of Divine Love*, ch. 14. I am grateful to Houston Smit for recognizing this scenario of Julian's as a case of Chisholmian defeat.

23. Cf. Plantinga, "Self-Profile," p. 36.

24. I develop this point at some length in "Problems of Evil: More Advice to Christian Philosophers," pp. 127–35.

25. For example in "The Metaphysics of the Incarnation in Some Fourteenth Century Franciscans," in William A. Frank and Girard J. Etzkorn (eds.), *Essays Honoring Allan B. Walter* (St. Bonaventure, NY: The Franciscan Institute, 1985), 21–57.

III.C.6

Suffering as Religious Experience

LAURA WADDELL EKSTROM

Laura Waddell Ekstrom (1966–) is professor of philosophy at the College of William and Mary, specializing primarily in ethics and agency theory. In this article, Ekstrom argues that some instances of suffering might reasonably be viewed as religious experiences that serve as a means of intimacy with God. Thus, whereas atheologians typically take suffering as evidence against the existence of God, Ekstrom argues that it might in fact be a route to knowledge of God.

INTRODUCTION

Works of literature, accounts of human history, and the events of everyday life confront us directly with the reality of pain and suffering. Some of us of a melancholy (some might say morbid) disposition are overcome with worry over this reality. Light-hearted neighbors and friends perplex us. How do they carry on so, trimming their yards and enjoying the weather, all the while maintaining faith in a perfect and provident Lord of the universe? Is it out of callousness, shallowness, blessedness, or wisdom? Have they any dark nights of the soul or anguish over the cries and shed blood of their fellow creatures? The worry leads some of us to academic study of the problem of evil. But our answers are incomplete and fail fully to satisfy. O God, where are you through the violent violation of a woman? Why tarry when a child falls feverish and is ripped from life too soon? Why still your hand through war, betrayal, and pain?

Yet through our own suffering, confusion and bitterness may take a startling turn. Job's heartrending cries of injustice against the Almighty become the breathtaking utterance, "My ears had heard of you but now my eyes have seen you."[1] In his suffering, Job reports, he has met God. God has shown himself, made himself known to the sufferer. The philosopher Nicholas Wolterstorff gives something of a similar account in his report of a vision of God. As we strain to discern an explanation for divine permission of suffering, "instead of hearing an answer," Wolterstorff writes, "we catch sight of God himself scraped and torn." He attests: "Through the prism of my tears I have seen a suffering God."[2] God is seen, God is known, in suffering.

The aim of this paper is to explore the idea of suffering as a kind of religious experience. It is argued by David Hume, William Rowe, and Paul Draper, among others, that pain and suffering constitute evidence against the existence of God.[3] But perhaps at least some such instances of pain and suffering are, rather, avenues to knowledge of God. Many individuals, Wolterstorff and Job among them, report that the times during which they have suffered the most deeply are the occasions of the most vivid of whatever glimpses they have been given into the character of God. The experiences are marked, that is, by intimacy with the divine. Is not precisely this the mark of (at least one

Reprinted from Peter van Inwagen, ed., *Christian Faith and the Problem of Evil* (Grand Rapids, MI: Wm. B. Eerdmans, 2009), pp. 95–110. Used by permission of Wm. B. Eerdmans.

important type of) religious experience? And is not suffering as a means to intimacy with God exactly what one would expect of a God who, on Christian scripture and tradition, took on human form and suffered along with and for the world?[4]

Understanding some instances of human suffering as means to intimacy with the divine makes available a line of partial theodicy distinct from the traditional soul-making, punishment, and free will theodicies. I call it the *divine intimacy theodicy*. The theodicy is suggested to an extent in the work of such contemporary philosophers as Marilyn Adams, Nicholas Wolterstorff, and Eleonore Stump, as well as in the writings of many Christian mystics of the medieval and later periods, including, for instance, Therese of Lisieux (1873–1897).[5] Why would the divine agent permit instances of evil? Perhaps a reply applicable to some instances of personal suffering is this: in order to provide occasions in which we can perceive God, understand him to some degree, know him, even meet him directly. In this essay I explore the plausibility of this line of thought.[6]

THE NATURE OF RELIGIOUS EXPERIENCE

Religious experience is variously characterized. Rudolf Otto (1869–1937) describes it as experience in which the soul is "held speechless, trembles inwardly to the farthest fiber of its being," as it faces something so forceful and overwhelming that one feels oneself to be "dust and ashes as against majesty." The experience is one of "fear and trembling" but also of "wonderfulness and rapture."[7] The Christian mystic Teresa of Avila (1515–1582) reports an experience in which the mystic is

> conscious of having been most delectably wounded.... [The soul] complains to its Spouse with words of love, and even cries aloud, being unable to help itself, for it realizes that he is present but will not manifest himself in such a way as to allow it to enjoy him, and this is a great grief, though a sweet and delectable one.... So powerful is the

effect of this upon the soul that it becomes consumed with desire, yet cannot think what to ask, so clearly conscious is it of the presence of God.[8]

John of the Cross (1542–1591) describes experience in which the understanding of the soul "is now moved and informed by . . . the supernatural light of God, and has been changed into the divine, for its understanding and that of God are now both one."[9]

One way of understanding religious experience is on analogy with sensory experience of the physical world. One might say that religious experience is experience of the divine by way of some perceptual faculties, perhaps including a special spiritual faculty or a *sensus divinitatus*. So as not to beg any questions concerning the veridicality of the experience, religious experience might be defined more cautiously as experience that the agent *takes to be* of the divine: experience perceived by the perceiver as acquaintance or intimacy with God. William Alston, for instance, understands religious experience as "(putative) direct awareness of God."[10]

I propose to understand the category of religious experience rather broadly. I consider the term "religious experience" to apply appropriately to at least the following three types of experience. First, a religious experience may be an experience in which it seems to one that one perceives God. Examples include a vision of divinity, a sense of God's presence during prayer or worship, and a feeling of God's nearness and comfort. Such experiences are regularly had by some theists. But an atheist may have them as well, as in Paul's experience on the road to Damascus.

Second, the category of religious experience includes experiences *like* those of God—experiences of the same sort as God's own experiences. In the Christian tradition, we could describe religious experience of the second sort as experience like that of one of the three persons comprising God. Or perhaps, so as not to beg any questions, we should describe the second type of religious experience as experience like what God would experience were God to exist with a nature as depicted by Christian scripture and tradition.

Third, an experience counts as a religious experience if it brings to consciousness the issue of God's nature and existence and makes vivid one's own attitude regarding this issue. Religious experiences of the third sort may include, for example, experience showing us ugly, horrifying or frightening aspects of the world; experience of our own capacity for evil; and experience of our frailty. Such experiences tend to bring to mind questions concerning the existence of God, as well as questions concerning the goodness, power, and knowledge of God. Religious experiences of the third type also include experiences carrying a sense of awe or wonder, such as witnessing the birth of a child or feeling moved by the beauty of a natural scene: the vista from a mountaintop or a seashore, for example.

Each of these types of experience has a legitimate claim to being religious in character. Consider an atheist who was raised in a religious family. She might sensibly describe her observations of pervasive poverty and disease during a visit to India as a *religious experience*: the experience raised vividly for her the problem of evil and occasioned her realization that she had become an atheist. A theist's sense of the majestic presence of God during worship is religious experience of a different (the first) sort: it is experience in which one is putatively aware of God. Further, insofar as it makes sense to describe experience like an eagle's (say, soaring above the rooftops) as *avian experience*, and insofar as it makes sense to describe experiences of running, jumping, and playing with toys *childhood experience*, so too there seems room for counting experiences similar to those of the divine being—if there is any—*religious experience*.

WHY COUNT SUFFERING AS RELIGIOUS EXPERIENCE?

Is it plausible to suppose that some instances of suffering qualify as religious experiences as characterized above? Testimonial evidence supports the claim that instances of suffering are sometimes instances of religious experience of the first type: experience in which it seems to the perceiver that he or she is aware of the presence of God. Consider, as one example, the divine vision recounted by Julian of Norwich in the midst of suffering a severe illness for which she had received last rites: "At once I saw the red blood trickling down under the garland, hot, fresh, and plentiful, just as it did at the time of his passion when the crown of thorns was pressed on to the blessed head of God-and-Man. . . . And I had a strong, deep, conviction that it was he himself,"[11] She reports of the divine being: "I saw that he is to us everything which is good and comforting for our help. He is our clothing, who wraps and enfolds us for love, embraces us and shelters us, surrounds us for his love."[12] Many individuals in sorrow and pain have reported a vision of the divine or a feeling of God's nearness and comfort in their distress.

It is likewise reasonable to consider some occasions of suffering as religious experiences of the third type: experiences that vividly raise fundamental religious questions and illuminate one's commitments regarding them. One's becoming the victim of a crime, for instance, or suffering a debilitating physical injury, commonly brings to one's mind the question of God's existence and nature. The experience of hardship is often a sort of testing experience in which one "shows one's true colors," demonstrating one's deepest commitments. Suffering is a religious experience of the third sort in driving us to seek God or in causing doubt, reinforcing unbelief, or in generating questions concerning God's nature and existence.

I would like to focus more attention on the notion that some instances of suffering qualify as religious experience of the second type: experiences *like* those of God.

Suppose that, as on traditional Christian doctrine, God created persons in order for them to love and to be intimate with him and to glorify him forever. Suppose that persons were once in a state of intimacy with God, but that we rebelled by choice, with the consequence that we suffer physical and emotional pain, as well as the spiritual pain of being out of harmony with the Creator. Suppose that God enacted a plan for reestablishing our harmony with him involving his taking on human form and suffering rejection, torture, and execution.

From the perspective of one who adopts this account, some human suffering may be viewed, in fact, as a kind of privilege, in that it allows us to share in some of the experiences of God and thus gives us a window into understanding his nature. Some instances of suffering are avenues for intimacy, oneness, with God. One cannot love what one does not know, and one means of knowing someone is to have experience like hers. Naturally we feel affinity toward and grow to understand and to cherish other persons with experiences similar to our own. These include educational, career, and family experiences, but also experiences of illness and adversity. A person whose experiences are quite different from one's own is difficult for one to come deeply to understand and fully to appreciate. Shared experiences facilitate dialogue in providing something in common about which to converse, and they make possible understanding that is beyond words, communicated perhaps with understanding looks or gestures. The parent of an ill newborn knows something about the other parents in the emergency room without their exchanging any words. Lovers become intimate through sharing experiences. Victims of a similar sort of oppression or injustice understand each other in a way that outsiders to their experience cannot.

For the Christian, then, instances of suffering can be occasions for identification with the person of Jesus Christ. Intimacy with Christ gained through suffering provides deeper appreciation of his passion.[13] I understand the notion of *identification with Christ* in a sympathetic rather than a mystical sense: the claim is not that the sufferer bears Christ's *actual* sufferings, as, first, it is unclear what the point of that bearing would be and, second, the mystical view would seem to require quite peculiar views concerning pain. Rather, I mean to suggest that the sufferer may sympathetically identify with Christ in sharing similar experience, as any other two persons identify with each other in the loose sense that they connect with, appreciate, or understand each other better when they share experiences of the same type or similar types.

Several objections immediately arise. The first is that this aspect of the theodicy is so thoroughgoingly

Christian. Since I accept the truth of orthodox Christian doctrine, this objection is from my perspective otiose. But to widen the appeal of the theodicy, we can set aside reference to the person of Christ and understand suffering as experience like that of God, like that of the divine being, if we join Wolterstorff and others in affirming, against tradition, that God is not impassible but is, rather, a God who suffers. Suppose, for instance, that God grieves over human sin. Then in feeling deep sorrow over the neglect and abuse of children, and in having regret and disapproval over the poverty and arrogance in our world, a person may have experience *like* God's and so may have a glimpse into the divine nature. An individual's own sorrow and suffering may, then, be a means to understanding and having intimacy with the divine being.

DIVINE PASSIBILITY

On the traditional conception of the divine nature, God is not affected by anything and so cannot suffer.[14] The doctrine of impassibility is defended primarily by appeal to philosophical considerations, including reflection on the natures of perfection, immutability, and transcendence. But the doctrine of divine impassibility has been recently criticized by a number of philosophers, including Alvin Plantinga, Charles Hartshore, Charles Taliaferro, Kelly James Clark, Nicholas Wolterstorff, and Richard Swinburne. Like Wolterstorff's avowal of a suffering God, Plantinga, for instance, affirms the existence of a God who "enters into and shares our suffering." Plantinga writes: "Some theologians claim that God cannot suffer. I believe they are wrong. God's capacity for suffering, I believe, is proportional to his greatness; it exceeds our capacity for suffering in the same measure as his capacity for knowledge exceeds ours."[15]

Of the considerations in favor of rejecting divine impassibility, the most salient from my perspective are the scriptural evidence and the natures of goodness and love. Many biblical passages depict God as experiencing emotions that entail suffering. Consider the following: "The LORD was grieved that he had made man on the earth, and his heart was filled with pain" (Gen. 6:6). "I have seen these people, the LORD said to Moses, and they are a stiff-necked people. Now leave me alone so that my anger may burn against them and that I may destroy them" (Exod. 32:9–10). The writer of Psalm 78 describes how the Israelites "grieved [God] ... they vexed the Holy One of Israel" (41–42) and speaks of God's "wrath, indignation and hostility" (49). Consider, as well: "Praise be to the Lord, to God our Savior, who daily bears our burdens" (Ps. 68:19).

Impassibilists dismiss such passages as mere anthropomorphism. Commenting on Genesis 6:6, for example, John Calvin writes:

> Since we cannot comprehend [God] as he is, it is necessary that, for our sake, he should, in a certain sense, transform himself.... Certainly God is not sorrowful or sad; but remains forever like himself in his celestial and happy repose; yet because it could not otherwise be known how great is God's hatred and detestation of sin, therefore the spirit accommodates himself to our capacity.... God was so offended by the atrocious wickedness of men, [he speaks] as if they had wounded his heart with mortal grief.[16]

According to Calvin, God permits biblical writers to use figures of speech about himself in accommodation to humanity's limited capacities of understanding. Given interpretive differences, the impassibility issue cannot be settled, of course, simply by citing biblical material. Nonetheless, a passibilist conception of God, it must be admitted, fits most naturally with the scriptural account of God's activities and involvement with human beings. The impassibilist must explain away or reinterpret numerous passages that, on their face, suggest that God is affected by and suffers over his creation.

On the traditional conception of the divine agent, God is not only omnipotent and omniscient, but also wholly good and perfectly loving. A number of philosophers, including Wolterstorff and Taliaferro, have registered their rejection of the Greek-influenced medieval conception of divine

love as non-suffering benevolence. The argument is that apathy, unperturbed emotional indifference to the plight of humanity, is incompatible with God's love of humanity.

Here is why the incompatibility claim seems right. Suppose that we understand love, rather uncontroversially, as consisting in or at least essentially involving concern for the well-being or flourishing of a beloved object. This understanding of love applies equally to love of a cause or of an ideal or of a person, but I am concerned particularly with love of persons. In his recent work on love, Harry Frankfurt adds that the lover's concern for the beloved is disinterested, in the sense that the good of the beloved is desired by the lover for its own sake rather than for the sake of promoting any other interests.[17] Frankfurt emphasizes that lovers are not merely concerned for the interests of their beloveds; further, they *identify* the interests of the beloveds as their own.[18] And he argues that if the lover "comes to believe that his beloved is not flourishing, then it is unavoidable that this causes him harm."[19] Lack of flourishing in the beloved, by the nature of love, causes harm in the lover.

Of course, it could be claimed that this account applies only to instances of human love and not to divine love. But the move appears *ad hoc*. If love of someone consists in or essentially involves concern for her well-being, then it involves valuing, or having concerned approval for, her flourishing and disvaluing, or having concerned disapproval for, her harm. To say that I love my daughter, yet that I experience no sorrow, grief, or passion of any kind at her pain or disgrace, stretches the concept of love beyond comprehensibility. Furthermore, since one can love something only insofar as one is acquainted with it, it would seem that God cannot love us fully without knowing us fully. But our being fully known requires acquaintance on the part of the knower with our suffering and with the evil in our world.[20] Thus, reflection on the nature of love supports the conception of a God who suffers.

Further support for the passibility of God comes from the consideration of the nature of goodness. A morally good being grieves over evil. In a recent book offering an extended defense of the traditional doctrine of divine impassibility,[21] Richard Creel argues in part that it serves no *purpose* to attribute suffering to God, as God may act out of love and justice without being sorrowful. But to the contrary, we question the goodness of an agent who acts correctly towards victims of crime or disease, yet wholly without sorrow or empathy for the persons served. Passibilism, Creel argues, makes God worthy of our pity rather than our worship. But a great moral character, one worthy of worship, shows itself great in part by its sorrow, what it sorrows over and to what degree. Noble sorrow at witnessing a tragic occurrence is a good. Hence it would seem that God's goodness and love include sorrow, as well as joy, over the world. This sorrow is arguably not a defect, but a strength or an asset, a part of being supremely good.

Taliaferro understands divine sorrow as "concerned disapproval." "God disapproves of our cruelty and malice," he writes, "God cares about our failures, and this concerned disapproval may rightly be counted as an instance of sorrow."[22] Consider, for instance, Miriam's rape. Taliaferro writes: "Part of what it means to be sorrowful here is that you do disapprove of it, the harming of someone who matters to you, and you disapprove of this profoundly. Any tenable notion of the goodness of the God of Christian theism must include the supposition that God exercises profound, concerned disapproval of creaturely ills."[23] It does seem reasonable to suppose that the God who is love, the God who is perfectly good, is deeply concerned for persons and suffers profound sorrow over their sins and afflictions. It is facile to presume oneself too sophisticated to go in for such supposed "sentimentalism." Proponents of the divine impassibility doctrine must defend it further against substantive religious and moral reasons for concluding that God suffers.

OBJECTIONS: PATHOLOGY, CRUELTY, AND INEFFICACY

In this section, I consider four central objections to a divine intimacy theodicy. The first, which I will address only briefly, comes from the direction of one unconvinced of the passibility of God. I have suggested that there is reason to think that God does suffer, provided by scripture and by reflection on the natures of goodness and love. But should the considerations in favor of the attribute of impassibility prove in the end more powerful, the divine intimacy theodicy is not thereby defeated. If suffering cannot be religious experience in the sense of being experience like that of God himself, it can qualify still as religious experience of the first and third sorts, and thus it can be justified as a means to intimacy with the divine. Furthermore, should traditional impassibilism survive recent attacks, Christian theism can yet make sense of suffering as experience shared with the person of Jesus Christ and so can count some occasions of suffering as avenues to intimacy with God through sympathetic identification with Christ.

A second and potentially more damaging objection is this: To view suffering as religious experience is evidence of a personality disturbance or psychological disorder. That is, it seems to indicate not right thinking but pathology that a person would glory in suffering or see spiritual dimensions to pain. The objection gains force from considering the physical conditions of the lives of some Christian mystics of the medieval and later periods who viewed suffering in such a manner. For instance, the Cistercian nun Beatrice of Nazareth (1200–1268), the author of *The Seven Manners of Love*, is reported to have deprived herself of food, worn uncomfortable garments, scourged herself, and slept on thorns.[24] Other religious figures may strike us as melodramatic and distressingly passive in their welcoming attitudes toward suffering. Consider the remarks of Therese of Lisieux concerning the onset of symptoms of the tuberculosis that took her life at the age of twenty-four:

Oh! how sweet this memory really is! After remaining at the Tomb until midnight, I returned to our cell, but I had scarcely laid my head upon the pillow when I felt something like a bubbling stream mounting to my lips. I didn't know what it was, but I thought that perhaps I was going to die and my soul was flooded with joy. However, as our lamp was extinguished, I told myself I would have to wait until the morning to be certain of my good fortune, for it seemed to me that it was blood I had coughed up. The morning was not long in coming; upon awakening, I thought immediately of the joyful thing that I had to learn, and so I went over to the window. I was able to see that I was not mistaken. Ah! my soul was filled with a great consolation; I was interiorly persuaded that Jesus, on the anniversary of his own death, wanted to have me hear his first call. It was like a sweet and distant murmur that announced the Bridegroom's arrival.[25]

Therese welcomes the blood in her cough as the answer to her prayer that God consume her with his love, that God carry her to him quickly, and that she be allowed to share in the suffering of Christ. She declares in her "Act of Oblation to Merciful Love":

I thank you, O my God! for all the graces you have granted me, especially the grace of making me pass through the crucible of suffering. It is with joy I shall contemplate you on the last day carrying the scepter of your cross. Since you deigned to give me a share in this very precious cross, I hope in heaven to resemble you and to see shining in my glorified body the sacred stigmata of your passion.[26]

In light of such passages, it may strike one as at best wishful thinking and, worse, indicative of a psychiatric condition, to believe that God is with one or is providing one intimacy with himself through suffering.

But of course those who report experience of supernatural phenomena are notoriously subject to the charge of being delusional. And certainly adopting the proposed partial theodicy need not lead one to self-mutilation or to other eccentric or damaging behaviors. The view under consideration is perfectly consistent with a mandate to *alleviate*

suffering so far as possible and with a mandate not to self-impose pain. Furthermore, which views indicate spiritual insight and which indicate a condition in need of medical or psychological treatment is a matter of opinion. As it stands, the objection from pathology amounts to no more than the claim that it seems to the objector that the proposed view is crazy or, in other words, false. Without any further positive reasons to doubt the sanity of the proponent of the divine intimacy theodicy, other than that she believes the view, the objection is dismissible.

The objector might respond by pointing to such factors as social isolation, inadequate sleep, poor nutrition, and lack of medical care in the lives of some religious mystics. These circumstances, it may be argued, indicate that the view of suffering as religious experience is pathological and not reasonable. Yet surely these considerations are inconclusive. Recall C. D. Broad's remark that a person "might need to be slightly 'cracked' in order to have some peep-holes into the super-sensible world."[27] Difficult living conditions might in fact facilitate spiritual insight. Furthermore, a charge of insanity against every adherent to a divine intimacy theodicy is grandiose.

A third objection is an objection from cruelty. Why would a loving God create such a cruel way of our getting to know him? Why would suffering as a *means* to knowing God be preferable to direct divine self-revelation? Since permitting suffering is a cruel way of fostering intimacy, the objection goes, the perfect being would not be justified in this permission and so the account of suffering as religious experience fails as a partial theodicy.

It is surely troubling to conceive of God as declaring to created beings in a tone of sinister delight, "Suffer, and then I will let you know me," as if enduring a crucible of suffering were a passkey. But this image inaccurately reflects the divine intimacy theodicy. A perfect being does not, of course, delight over suffering, but rather causes or allows it when it is necessary to bringing about a greater good or preventing a worse evil. And the suggestion I am exploring is that, perhaps, some occasions of suffering are necessary for certain individuals' coming to love of and intimacy with God. The objector may counter that some persons experience God in moments of great joy and beauty. Yet this may be true while it is also true that other persons' paths to God are paths through suffering. And it may be that the good thereby achieved could not be achieved in any other way: namely, the profound good of appreciation for and intimacy with a loving and suffering God.

The objector might be troubled with the question of why God would not simply show himself at all times, to everyone. Here the right line of response may be that for God to directly, constantly, and obviously manifest his presence would be coercive.[28] Perhaps God's remaining somewhat hidden protects our freedom, preserving our independence of thought and action. The rationale behind divine hiddenness may be something like this: I (the divine agent) will not intervene in the natural course of events to prevent your difficulties and your suffering, in part because perhaps then you will appreciate the ways in which I have loved and provided for you all along; perhaps you will freely come to recognize that acting wholly by your own lights is unsuccessful and that you need my help; perhaps you will be rid of some of your arrogance and will recognize your limitations. Suffering, that is, may be for some persons the most effective non-coercive means to achieving the end of love of and intimacy with God. Additionally, it may be that it is impossible fully to know God without personally experiencing suffering, because God himself suffers. If God is passible in emotion, then there is something that a person could not know about God if she did not suffer, one aspect of God's being that would remain entirely mysterious.

The fourth and final objection I will consider is this: a common reaction to suffering is not a sense of intimacy with the divine but rather confusion and rejection of God's existence. Suffering is easily interpreted as evidence that God does not exist or does not care about the sufferer. Hence, many cases of suffering, particularly those of non-theists, cannot plausibly be construed as religious experience.

In response, first, the divine intimacy theodicy is not designed to apply to all cases of suffering.

Second, from the fact that some persons reject the existence of God on the basis of suffering, it does not follow that some occasions of suffering do not provide an *opportunity* for intimacy with God. We can choose, it seems, the manner in which we respond to suffering, including which types of attitudes we adopt in the midst of it. The thesis at issue is not that meaning *is* always found in suffering by everyone who suffers, but rather that a certain kind of meaning *can* be found in suffering, through divine intimacy.

Suffering might be religious experience without the sufferer recognizing it as such. This claim seems unproblematic, since a person can have an experience of a certain type without ever recognizing it as an experience of that type. Consider the following examples. First, suppose that Keith thinks that he is devising a novel line of reasoning. But in fact he is remembering a conversation in which someone else recounted a certain line of thought. Keith is having a memory experience, but he does not, and need not ever, recognize it as such. Second, suppose that Sandra begins thinking about chance and providence. Although she need not ever recognize the experience as such, she may be having a telepathic experience of the thoughts of Peter, who is across the room. Third, imagine a husband who begins to have indigestion, headaches, and back pain during the pregnancy of his wife. He consults his doctor, who finds his symptoms mysterious. He is, perhaps, having an empathic experience without realizing it. The concept of a religious experience, unrecognized as such, appears cogent.

CONCLUSION

A full justificatory account of suffering may be unattainable for us. I have simply sketched here and begun to explore the suggestion that one justifying reason for certain instances of suffering is that those occasions constitute religious experiences. Some cases of suffering may be viewed as kinds of experience that can bring a person closer to God, such that the good either in or resulting from them is intimacy with the divine agent.

The account of suffering as religious experience may have use not only as a partial theodicy, but also as a method for the theist for dealing with the existential problem of evil. That is, one way of enduring unchangeable occasions of pain and suffering may be to adopt an attitude of acceptance and, oddly, enjoyment in identifying with God. Consider how this might work, in particular, for a Christian theist. One in the midst of dealing with a deep betrayal of loyalty, for instance, might call to mind the thought, "As I have been rejected, Christ was rejected even by his close friend, Peter," and take comfort in the sympathetic identification. Likewise, although perhaps Christ never experienced precisely the particular physical pain from which one suffers, the sufferer is in part able to appreciate something about the person of Christ that perhaps not all others fully can: the sacrifice of his passion.[29]

NOTES

1. Job 42:5.

2. Nicholas Wolterstorff, *Lament for a Son* (Grand Rapids: Eerdmans Publishing Co., 1987), pp. 80–81.

3. David Hume, *Dialogues Concerning Natural Religion*, ed. Richard Popkin (Indianapolis: Hackett, 1980); William Rowe, "The Problem of Evil and Some Varieties of Atheism," *American Philosophical Quarterly* 16 (1979): 335–41; Paul Draper, "Pain and Pleasure: An Evidential Problem for Theists," *Noûs* 23 (1989).

4. According to orthodox Christian tradition, the person of Jesus Christ suffered for us, yet God the Father is not capable of suffering.

5. Marilyn McCord Adams, "Redemptive Suffering: A Christian Solution to the Problem of Evil," *in Rationality, Religious Belief, and Moral Commitment*, ed. Robert Audi and William J. Wainwright (Ithaca, N.Y.: Cornell University Press, 1986), and "Horrendous Evils and the Goodness of God," *Proceedings of the Aristotelian Society*, supplementary vol. 63 (1989), pp. 297–310; Wolterstorff, *Lament for a Son*, and "Suffering Love," in *Philosophy and the Christian Faith*, ed. Thomas V. Morris (Notre Dame, Ind.: University of Notre Dame Press, 1988); Eleonore Stump, *Faith and the Problem of Evil: The Stob Lectures, 1998–99* (Grand Rapids: The Stob Lectures Endowment, 1999), and "The Mirror of Evil," in *God and the Philosophers*, ed. Thomas V. Morris (New York: Oxford University Press, 1994), pp. 235–47, and "The Problem of Evil," *Faith and Philosophy* 2:4 (1985): 392–418.

6. The divine intimacy theodicy most likely has some measure of plausibility only when applied to human suffering and not to the suffering of non-human animals. Nonetheless, the matter is open in the absence of conclusive information concerning the capacities of members of other species.

7. Rudolf Otto, *The Idea of the Holy* (London: Oxford University Press, 1936), pp. 17–26, 31–33.

8. *The Interior Castle*, trans. and ed. E. Allison Peers (Garden City, N.Y.: Doubleday Image, 1961), pp. 135–36.

9. *The Living Flame of Love*, trans. and ed. E. Allison Peers (Garden City, N.Y.: Doubleday Image, 1962), p. 78.

10. William Alston, *Perceiving God: The Epistemology of Religious Experience* (Ithaca, N.Y.: Cornell University Press, 1991), p. 35.

11. Julian of Norwich, *Revelations of Divine Love* (New York: Penguin Books, 1984), p. 66.

12. Julian of Norwich, Long Text 5, quoted in *Enduring Grace: Living Portraits of Seven Women Mystics* (New York: HarperCollins, 1993), p. 88.

13. Marilyn McCord Adams similarly suggests that instances of suffering, even horrendous ones, might be made *meaningful* by being integrated into the sufferer's relationship with God through identification with Christ, understood either as sympathetic identification (in which each person suffers her own pain, enabling her to understand something of Christ's suffering) or as mystical identification (in which the human sufferer literally experiences a share of Christ's pain). Alternately, Adams suggests, meaningfulness may derive from suffering serving as a vision into the inner life of God, either because God is not impassible, or because the sheer intensity of the experience gives

one a glimpse of what it is like to be beyond joy and sorrow. She proposes, as well, that sufferings might be made meaningful through defeat by divine gratitude which, when expressed by God in the afterlife, gives one full and unending joy. "Horrendous Evils and the Goodness of God," *Proceedings of the Aristotelian Society*, supplementary vol. 63 (1989), pp. 297–310; reprinted in *The Problem of Evil*, ed. Marilyn McCord Adams and Robert Merrihew Adams (New York: Oxford University Press, 1990), pp. 209–21.

14. The Westminster Confession of Faith (II.1) states: "There is but one . . . true God, who is infinite in being and perfection, a most pure spirit, invisible, without body, parts, or passions. . . ."

15. "Self-Profile," in *Alvin Plantinga*, ed. James E. Tomberlin and Peter van Inwagen (Dordrecht: D. Reidel, 1985), p. 36.

16. *Calvin's Commentaries*, vol. 1, trans, and ed. John Owen (Grand Rapids: Baker Book House, 1979), p. 249.

17. Harry Frankfurt, "On Caring," in *Necessity, Volition, and Love* (Cambridge: Cambridge University Press, 1999), p. 165.

18. Frankfurt, "On Caring," p. 168.

19. Frankfurt, "On Caring," p. 170.

20. Cf. Nicholas Wolterstorff, "Suffering Love," in *Philosophy and the Christian Faith*, ed. Thomas V. Morris (Notre Dame, Ind.: University of Notre Dame Press, 1988), p. 223.

21. Richard E. Creel, *Divine Impassibility* (Cambridge: Cambridge University Press, 1986).

22. Charles Taliaferro, "The Passibility of God," *Religious Studies*, vol. 25: 220.

23. Taliaferro, "Passibility," p. 220.

24. *Women Mystics in Medieval Europe*, ed. Emilie Zum Brunn and Georgette Epiney-Burgard, trans. Sheila Hughes (New York: Paragon House, 1989), p. 72.

25. *Story of a Soul: The Autobiography of St. Therese of Lisieux*, trans. John Clarke O.C.D. (Washington, D.C.: ICS Publications, 1996), pp. 210–11.

26. *Story of a Soul*, p. 277.

27. C. D. Broad, "Arguments for the Existence of God. II," *Journal of Theological Studies* 40 (1939): 164.

28. Michael J. Murray, "Coercion and the Hiddenness of God," *American Philosophical Quarterly* 30 (1993): 27–38.

29. I am grateful to Michael Murray and Kelly James Clark for comments on an earlier version of this essay.

III.C.7

Deus Absconditus

MICHAEL J. MURRAY

Michael J. Murray (1963–) is currently the Executive Vice President of the John Templeton Foundation. Previously he was professor of philosophy at Franklin and Marshall College. He works primarily in the fields of philosophy of religion and history of modern philosophy. In this article he offers

Reprinted from *Divine Hiddenness: New Essays*, ed. by Daniel Howard-Snyder and Paul K. Moser. Copyright © 2002 Cambridge University Press.

a critique of J. L. Schellenberg's argument from divine hiddenness to atheism, defending the conclusion that divine hiddenness is often necessary for allowing God's creatures to retain the freedom that is required for soul-making.

Awake, O Lord! Why do you sleep?
Rouse yourself! Do not reject us forever.
Why do you hide your face?

Psalm 44:23-4

It is no surprise to discover that few (if any) have found the existence of God to be an obvious fact about the world. At least this is so in the sense in which we normally use the word "obvious," as when we say that it is *obvious* that the World Trade Center weighs more than a deck of cards or that it is *obvious* that Van Gogh is a better painter than I. Despite St. Paul's claim that God's eternal power and divine nature "have been clearly seen, being understood from what has been made" (Romans 1:20), few (if any) think that such is as "clearly seen" as the book you now hold in your hand.

This fact has raised troubles of at least two sorts for the theist. First, it leads the theist to wonder why God postpones that time at which, according to Christian tradition, we will see God "face to face." Since, at that time, God *will* be as clearly seen as the book you now hold in your hand, what accounts for the delay? Why is there this period of the earthly life where God's reality is less than obvious? Second, the theist has to confront the fact that God's hiddenness seems to lead a number of people to reject God's existence outright and thus to be a contributing cause to what the traditional theist would regard as a great evil: unbelief. For some, the route to atheism is indeed found in the fact that there is, in the famous words of Bertrand Russell, "not enough evidence." But more recently, some have argued that the hiddenness of God provides positive, in fact decisive, evidence in favor of atheism. J. L. Schellenberg, in a recent work, argues that if the God of Western theism exists he would provide evidence of this fact sufficient to render reasonable unbelief impossible. Since, however, such evidence is not forthcoming, such a God does not exist.

Theists in the Judeo-Christian tradition have often argued that the hiddenness of God finds its explanation in the Fall and subsequent Curse. Sometimes the passage immediately following the one from St. Paul's epistle to the Romans cited above is taken as evidence that hiddenness should be explained in just this way, at least for the Christian, since Paul there goes on to claim that "For although they knew God, they neither glorified Him as God nor gave thanks to Him, but their thinking became futile and their foolish hearts were darkened" (Romans 1:21). Yet, while the Fall may play some part in explaining the hiddenness of God, the Judeo-Christian theist would be hard pressed to lay the full explanation for hiddenness here. The reason is simply that the Judeo-Christian Scriptures seem to teach that even prior to the Curse, there is a measure of divine hiddenness already. Even in Genesis 3, one finds that Adam and Eve think that they can somehow escape the presence of God by hiding from God in the garden (Genesis 3:8-10). Although it is Adam and Eve that do the hiding here, still the presence of God, while still obvious to them in a certain sense, is escapable in a way it seems not to be when one looks at descriptions of the beatified state as described, for example, in Revelation 22:1-5. In what follows I will offer an account of divine hiddenness that attempts to allay the two types of concerns raised above.

I. DIVINE HIDDENNESS AND "MORALLY SIGNIFICANT FREEDOM"

In an earlier essay I argued that at least one of the reasons that God must remain hidden is that failing to do so would lead to a loss of morally significant freedom on the part of creatures.[1] The reason, in brief, is that making us powerfully aware of the truth of God's existence would suffice to coerce (at least many of) us into behaving in accordance with God's moral commands. Such awareness can lead to this simply because God's presence would provide us with overpowering incentives which would make choosing the good ineluctable for us.

I will flesh out this account in some detail below, but before doing so, let's take notice of the overall strategy being pursued here. Theists have often argued that morally significant freedom is a good (indeed, a very good) thing. Thus, in creating the world, God would seek to establish conditions that would permit the existence of such freedom. A variety of such conditions are necessary, but among them is that there not be overwhelmingly powerful incentives present in the environment which consistently coerce or otherwise force creatures to follow a particular course of action.

Theists have, at least of late, lain a great deal of explanatory weight on the need to preserve creaturely freedom. Here I will attempt to lay the explanation of divine hiddenness there. Others have sought to lay the explanation for all (or at least much) of the evil that the world contains there as well. In such cases, the argument is roughly that morally significant freedom is an intrinsic good, and that though evil is a necessary consequence of allowing creatures to have freedom of such a sort, the intrinsic goodness of freedom outweighs evils liabilities.[2] The evil in question might not only be of the (moral) sort that we read about in the headlines of the newspaper, but of the (epistemic) sort in view in this essay, namely, the unbelief of great numbers of people due to the lack of evidence entailed by God's hiddenness.

But there is something odd about laying all this freight at freedom's doorstep; and it is an oddity that seems to be too little noticed by analytic Christian philosophers. We can begin to see what is odd by first noticing that it is not the intrinsic goodness of libertarian freedom *simpliciter* that is at issue here. For if it were, it seems that libertarian freedom simply could not do the work it has been given to do in these accounts. The reason for this is that there seems to be no reason why God could not create a world with libertarian free beings who are incapable of doing evil. If human minds were created in such a way that they were not, say, even capable of deliberating about evil courses of action, it might

still be the case that multiple courses of action would be open to them given the history of the world and the laws of nature. No doubt, this would restrict the kinds of behavior that such creatures could engage in (assuming that it must be possible for one to deliberate about a course of action for one to be able to freely choose it). But God surely restricts the sorts of activities we can choose to undertake in all sorts of ways by not only limiting the kinds of things we can think about (by, say, limiting the sorts of cognitive equipment we have), but even by limiting the kinds of things we are physically capable of accomplishing (by limiting the sorts of bodily equipment we have). It is hard to see why similar constraints could not simply preclude deliberation about evil courses of action, while stopping short of full blown determinism. If this is right, libertarian freedom *simpliciter* cannot explain or justify the existence of evil.

It is, then, libertarian freedom *to choose between good and evil courses of action* that is important here. And the theist might argue that this is just what was meant by "morally significant freedom" in the first place. Without the ability to choose freely between good and evil courses of action, freedom would have no moral significance and thus would not be an intrinsic good.[3] What is odd about this story, however, is just how rare this supposed intrinsic good is among rational beings on the Christian scheme of things. For if we consider the sorts of rational beings Christians admit to being aware of, it seems that only one type of being has freedom of this sort, and beings of this type possess it only for an infinitesimally small span of their existence. Traditional Christian theology holds that neither God, angels, nor demons have such freedom, and that of human beings, neither beatified nor damned have it either. Thus, freedom of this sort is found only among human beings during that narrow span of their existence spent in the earthly life.

All of this seems to argue that morally significant freedom of the sort described above might not be best regarded as the intrinsic good many have claimed it to be. If it is such a good, it would be odd, to say the least, that neither God, angels, nor the beatified possess it.

We might, however, look at the worth of morally significant freedom in creatures in another way. Reflecting on the rarity of such freedom as it is described above leads to the question: Why does God allow creatures to pass through this earthly phase of existence in the first place? Since all rational creatures will end up either perfected in the beatific vision, choosing good forever, or separated from God, choosing evil forever, why have them pass through this prior stage during which they stand poised between these two extremes?

When posed this way, I think an answer readily suggests itself, namely, that the function of this earthly life, a time during which we are capable of making free choices between morally good and evil courses of action, is to have the opportunity to develop morally significant characters. Developing characters which have moral significance requires that they be chosen and cultivated by their bearers. And this can only be done if creatures are first given the sort of morally significant freedom we have been discussing heretofore. Philosophers have taken to calling this sort of character development "soul-making," following the phrase coined by John Hick.[4] Thus, we might say that the function of the earthly life on this view is soul-making, and that a necessary condition for soul-making is morally significant libertarian freedom. Libertarian freedom alone simply will not do here since the point of character development is that one has the opportunity to choose to do *good* or *evil*, and by so choosing to become either a lover and imitator of God, or one who "worships and serves the creature rather than the creator."[5]

Thus, even if we have reason to doubt the *intrinsic* worth of morally significant freedom, there is good reason to think that it has significant *instrumental* value as a necessary condition for rational creatures engaging in soul-making. Of course, possessing the capacity for morally significant soul-making is not sufficient. In addition, external constraints on the agent must not preclude the possibility of the agent at least frequently being able to choose freely between good and evil courses of action. What I was claiming above is that among those conditions is the absence of circumstances which provide overwhelming incentives for creatures

to choose only good or only evil. For if the moral environment contained such incentives, the creature with the capacity to choose freely would be precluded from exercising that ability and thus blocked from engaging in the sort of soul-making that makes freedom (and the earthly life) valuable in the first place.

The result of all this is that God must remain hidden to a certain extent to prevent precluding incentives from being introduced. Here then we find an answer to the first concern regarding hiddenness. At least one reason why we do not see God face to face from the beginning is that to do so would be to lose the ability to develop morally significant characters. According to the Christian scriptures, God calls his creatures to be "imitators" of him.[6] But to do this in a way that yields moral significance requires that character be to some extent self-wrought.[7] And soul-making of this sort requires divine hiddenness, at least for a time.

As mentioned above, J. L. Schellenberg has offered an argument for atheism on the basis of divine hiddenness. Along the way, Schellenberg critiques a variety of accounts of hiddenness a theist might offer, including a soul-making account of the sort sketched above. In what follows I will develop this account in more detail against the background of and in response to this critique of Schellenberg's.

II. SCHELLENBERG'S CRITIQUE OF THE SOUL-MAKING RESPONSE

In his wonderfully provocative book, *Divine Hiddenness and Human Reason,* J. L. Schellenberg has presented an extended argument that the extent to which evidence for the existence God is not forthcoming, in conjunction with certain other plausible assumptions, entails the truth of atheism. This argument, which I will call "The Atheist Argument," is presented by Schellenberg as follows:

(1) If there is a God, he is perfectly loving.

(2) If a perfectly loving God exists, reasonable nonbelief does not occur.

(3) Reasonable nonbelief does occur.

(4) No perfectly loving God exists.

(5) There is no God.[8]

After an extended presentation and defense of the argument and its premises in the first half of the book, Schellenberg goes on, in the second half, to discuss various responses theists might lodge against its premises. Specifically, he focuses on theistic critiques of premise (2) since, he argues, only this premise of the argument is open to question. In this section I will examine Schellenberg's critique of the soul-making account and argue that his critique ultimately fails. As a result, the theist has plausible grounds for rejecting (2) and thus for rejecting The Atheist Argument.

Preliminary Considerations

Because Schellenberg recognizes that most theists will want to take issue with (2), he begins his survey of potential theistic responses by discussing what it is that the theist must show in order to defeat the premise. He contends that,

> (2) is false if and only if there is a state of affairs in the actual world which it would be logically impossible for God to bring about without permitting the occurrence of at least one instance of reasonable non-belief, for the sake of which God would be willing to sacrifice the good of belief and all it entails.[9]

As noted above, the second half of the book is devoted to explaining and critiquing various theistic attempts to provide accounts which attack (2) in just the way Schellenberg suggests. The first such attempt roughly mirrors the account described at the end of Section I. On this view, the state of affairs that God wants to actualize which logically requires him to permit some instances of reasonable unbelief consists of (i) creatures who have the capacity for acting freely and (ii) a world suitably constituted for the exercise of that freedom. On this view, if God were to make his existence evident to too great an extent, an extent that would

rule out reasonable non-belief, we would all become powerfully aware of the importance of not only believing in His existence but also obeying His will. Yet such a powerful awareness of God's existence and moral will would suffice to overwhelm the freedom of the creature in a way that would preclude further morally significant free actions by the creature. Because it would be utterly obvious to us that God, the one responsible for temporal happiness as well as eternal bliss or damnation, exists and wills that we act in certain ways, we would be compelled to believe and act accordingly. As a result, God must keep His existence veiled to a certain extent in order to insure that this sort of overwhelming does not occur.

To know whether or not such a claim is plausible, we first need to know whether God's revealing himself in the way Schellenberg thinks he would (and in fact *must* given the fact that God is a perfectly loving being) could lead to such a result.

It is noteworthy that Schellenberg has only argued that God's loving nature entails that God would make his *existence* known to creatures in such a way that reasonable unbelief is not possible. Schellenberg makes no claims about whether or not God's loving nature would also require that God make known the existence of other facts that might be necessary for human beings to be able to attain ultimate human fulfillment. In one sense, this minimalist strategy helps Schellenberg, since one might think that if God simply made his *existence* clearly known, there is no reason to think that this would introduce any incentives that might serve to derail human freedom. Bare knowledge that God exists simply doesn't seem to have any immediate practical import.

One might, of course, agree that God would make his existence plainly known, but might further argue that God's loving nature further entails that other facts would be made known as well. Many theists claim that ultimate human fulfillment requires not only belief in God, but a number of other beliefs about what it takes to be rightly related to God as well. If loving entails seeking the well-being of the beloved, God would surely seek to make the necessary information for human fulfillment available. As a result, I will assume for the moment (as I think all parties in the dispute must) that, all other things being equal, God's love would lead him to make us aware not merely of his bare existence, but also of all of the other truths needed to obtain our complete temporal and eternal happiness. Surely such a revelation would carry significant practical import. Nonetheless, for those who want to stick to Schellenberg's more minimalist strategy, I will return to address that view shortly.

III. THE SOUL-MAKING RESPONSE TO (2)

Given my more robust notion of what divine love entails, we can see why there might be good reason for God to remain hidden on the soul-making account. At the end of Section I I noted that introduction of powerful motives to choose either only good or only evil would preclude the possibility of soul-making. Instead, the environment needs to be such that there are, at least in a number of cases, incentives to choose to do good and incentives to choose to do evil, such that neither incentive induces desires that overwhelm all competing desires.

Yet surely a probabilifying demonstration or revelation of God's existence and plan for human well-being as described above would introduce just such incentives. If God were to reveal Himself and His will in the way required to eliminate reasonable nonbelief, any desire that we might have to believe or act in ways contrary to that which has been revealed would be overwhelmed. Our fear of punishment, or at least our fear of the prospect of missing out on a very great good, would compel us to believe the things that God has revealed and to act in accordance with them. But in doing this, God would have removed the ability for self-determination since there are no longer good and evil courses of action between which creatures could freely and deliberately choose. Thus we would all be compelled to choose in accordance with the divine will and would all thereby become conformed to the divine image.

However, a character wrought in this fashion would not be one for which we are responsible since it does not derive from morally significant choosing. It has instead been forced upon us. Richard Swinburne, defending a position regarding divine hiddenness summarizes these considerations in the following paragraph, also quoted by Schellenberg:

> The existence of God would be for [human beings] an item of evident common knowledge. Knowing that there was a God, men would know that their most secret thoughts and actions were known to God; and knowing that he was just, they would expect for their bad actions and thoughts whatever punishment was just.... In such a world men would have little temptation to do wrong—it would be the mark of both prudence and reason to do what was virtuous. Yet a man only has a genuine choice of destiny if he has reasons for pursuing either good or evil courses of action.[10]

Schellenberg emphasizes that on this view, desires for evil would not cease to exist were we to be given such a revelation, it is just that powerful new desires would be introduced, e.g., the desire to avoid punishment, with a strength that overwhelms contrary desires and renders them "inefficacious." He cites coercion as a similar case in which the introduction of a new desire renders all competing desires inefficacious. I may desire, says Schellenberg, to go to the university bookstore to buy a copy of a newly released book. Yet, if some crazy ideologue, bent on keeping scholars from being exposed to the ideas in the book, threatens me with serious physical harm if I go to the bookstore, I won't go. My desire to go is still present, but this desire has been overwhelmed by a newly introduced desire, the desire to avoid the serious physical harm.

Schellenberg thus summarizes the soul-making case against (2) of the Atheist Argument as follows:

(16) In the situation in question [that is, where God reveals himself in such powerful fashion

that reasonable unbelief is rendered impossible], persons would have strong prudential reasons for not doing wrong.

(17) Because of the strength of these reasons, it would require little in the way of an act of will to do what is right—there is little temptation to do wrong, contrary desires would be overcome.

(18) Where there is little temptation to do wrong, persons lack a genuine choice of destiny.

(19) Therefore, in the situation in question no one would have a choice of destiny.[11]

IV. INCENTIVES, COERCION, AND ''SOUL-MAKING''

The remainder of this chapter in Schellenberg's book is occupied with an assessment of (16) through (19). Here Schellenberg contends that there are good reasons to reject both (16) and (17). Before looking at his criticisms of these premises however, it will prove worthwhile to try to fill in a few more details in this argument. How exactly, one might wonder, would probabilifying knowledge of God's existence and will for human creatures influence our desires? What does it take for desires to be sufficiently strong to overwhelm competing desires? How does this overwhelming prevent our ability to engage in self-determination exactly? Answering these questions will help us both to understand the force of Schellenberg's critique of (16) and (17) and to see what, if anything, can be said in reply.

Recall that on the soul-making account the trouble that arises in a world in which God is not to some extent hidden is that incentives are introduced which serve to *coerce* otherwise free creatures, in ways which render them incapable of soul-making. Thus, if God were to make himself plainly evident to us in the ways described above, we would find ourselves confronted with what would amount to threats (if God were to reveal disobedience as subject to punishment) or offers (if God were to

reveal obedience as a source of temporal and eternal well-being) that would suffice to coerce human behavior.[12] In what follows I will speak generally about the ways in which God's revealing himself in perspicuous fashion can introduce "incentives" which can "overwhelm" competing desires. One can think of such incentives as consisting of either threats or offers, though I will frequently use examples drawn from cases of coercion via threats.

It should be obvious that not just any incentives will suffice to overwhelm our desires for contrary courses of action. The incentive must be sufficiently strong that it outweighs the desires I have for those things which are inconsistent with acting in accordance with it. Let's say that a desired course of action, A_1, renders competing desired courses of action, A_2-A_n, *ineligible* when A_1 is sufficiently compelling that it makes it impossible for me reasonably to choose A_2-A_n over A_1.[13] We can then say that an individual, P, is *coerced* to do some act, A, by a threat when a desire is induced by a threat, which desire is sufficiently compelling that it renders every other course of action except A ineligible for P.[14]

This next leads us to wonder what it is that makes desires induced by threats "sufficiently compelling." One might think that the only relevant variable is the *strength* of the threat, i.e., the degree to which the state of affairs that the threatener is promising to bring about (if the conditions of the threat are not met) is disutile for the threatened in comparison with the disutility of performing the act commanded by the threatener. Thus if a stranger threatens to call me a ninny if I fail to hand over my money to her, this threat would not compel me in the least since I am not a bit concerned about being called a name by this stranger and I would like to keep my money. On the other hand, if someone threatens to shoot me in the leg if I fail to give her my money, I would surely give her the money since I care a great deal about my bodily integrity, far more than keeping the few dollars I carry with me.

However, a moment's reflection should make it clear that threat strength alone does not determine whether or not a desire induced by a threat is sufficiently compelling to coerce me. To see why this is so, compare the following two cases. In the first case, a maximum security prison assigns one guard to each prisoner and gives the guards orders to shoot all who attempt to escape. Here the threat strength is very high. Thus, one can suppose that prisoners in such a situation would find all courses of action which include an attempted escape ineligible. In the second case, prisoners are again being watched by guards who have orders to shoot any who attempt to escape. However, in this case, there are only two guards on duty for the entire prison at anyone time, and they are perched high in a tower. While the threat strength is identical for prisoners in both prisons, it seems clear that prisoners in the latter case might find an escape attempt eligible. The reason for this difference, presumably, is that the prisoners in the second case might believe that the probability that the threat could be successfully carried out is quite low. The guards, the prisoner might reason, might be too busy watching other prisoners to notice an attempted escape, or they might miss when shooting from such a great distance. In any case, the prisoner's belief that the threat cannot be successfully carried out significantly mitigates the compelling force of the desire induced by the threat. Thus, in addition to threat strength, another factor, which I call *threat imminence,* is relevant. We can define threat imminence as the degree to which the threatened believes the consequences of the threat will be successfully carried out if the terms of the threat are not met.

But notice that there is more than one way that threats can be imminent or distant as I have characterized imminence. While the sort of imminence described above, which I will call *probabilistic imminence,* is one species of imminence, there are at least two others. First, there is *temporal imminence.* When the threatened understands that there will be a significant lapse between the time that he fails to meet the conditions of the threat and the time that the threat is carried out, the desire induced by the threat is less compelling than when the consequences will follow immediately upon the failure to meet the conditions. Thus, if someone was to threaten to give me a powerful shock that would

hospitalize me for two weeks if I failed to hand over my money immediately, this situation would be more compelling than one in which a threatener threatened to poke me with a delayed-reaction cattle prod which would cause me to receive the same shocking sensation fifty years hence, if I failed to hand over my money now. Even though the threat strength is the same, and even though I might have an equal degree of certainty that the threat will be carried out in both cases, I am less compelled by the threat in the latter case than I am in the former.

The final species of threat imminence is *epistemic imminence.* We might say that epistemic imminence is the degree to which the disutility of the threatened consequence is *epistemically forceful* to the threatened. To illustrate the role of epistemic imminence consider the fact that massive advertising campaigns against smoking, drug use, and drinking and driving have been successful in reducing the incidence of these behaviors. In all three cases, no one believes that the purpose of such advertisements is to convey information to the target audience that members of that audience do not already have. Instead, the goal is to make the disutility of engaging in that behavior more epistemically powerful. By repeatedly showing accident scenes strewn with dead or mangled bodies, people become more powerfully aware of how dangerous drinking and driving is.

Yet even these two factors, threat strength and threat imminence, are not sufficient to determine the degree to which threat-induced desires are compelling. This should be clear from the fact that two individuals, in circumstances where threat strength and threat imminence are identical for each, might feel differently about the eligibility of their alternatives. Two prisoners might find themselves under threats of identical strength and imminence and yet one might feel that an escape attempt is still eligible while another may not. One might simply feel that a probability of .5 that he will be shot is a risk too great to bear, whereas the other might think that the same probability makes for a "good bet." This factor, which I will call *threat-indifference,* is the third factor determining the strength of the compelling force of a threat. Some individuals are simply more threat-indifferent than others. Threat-indifference can be described in two ways. One might say that threat-indifference is the degree to which one finds pleasure in taking the risks posed by failing to abide by conditions of a threat. It might also be described as a sense of indifference to one's own well-being in the face of a threat. However we characterize this trait, it is surely relevant since something like it is needed to explain why, when two individuals are in the same circumstances, one is coerced while the other is not.

In sum, there are at least three factors which determine the degree to which a threat-induced desire is compelling: threat strength, threat imminence, and threat-indifference. The degree to which the desire compels me to act in accordance with the threat is directly proportional to the first two and inversely proportional to the third.

V. AN ASSESSMENT OF SCHELLENBERG'S CRITIQUE OF (16) AND (17)

With this in mind, let us return to Schellenberg's critique of (16) and (17) and see to what extent they are successful. Schellenberg raises two problems for (16) and I will treat each in turn. First, he charges that the only way in which probabilifying revelations of God's existence and moral will could provide strong prudential reasons for not doing wrong, is if the knowledge acquired as a result of this revelation were *certain*.

> The situation referred to [by Swinburne] is ... one in which humans know for *certain* that there is a God and in which whatever reasons humans take themselves to have for doing good actions they consider themselves *certainly* to have. A situation in which the evidence available is [merely] sufficient for belief ... is, however, not of this sort.... In any case, given evidence [merely] sufficient for belief instead of proof, one who is under the influence of

desires for what is "correctly believed to be evil" is likely to seize upon the margin of possible error: believing, but not certain of God's existence, or of punishment, she may well move, through self-deception, from the belief that God exists and will punish bad actions to [other beliefs which deny at least one of the two conjuncts].... If self-deception *is* still open to individuals, then clearly they are still in a position to yield to bad desires and so retain a genuine choice of destiny.[15]

Schellenberg holds here that unless we know with *certainty* that a threatener (God in this case) exists and will carry out the threat, we cannot be coerced, since it is always open to us to deceive ourselves about the truth of propositions we know less than certainly. As a result, it is false that these probabilifying revelations would suffice to provide the recipient of the revelation with strong prudential reasons for not doing evil (and correspondingly, with overwhelming incentives), since one can always reappropriate ones beliefs in such a way as to eliminate these strong prudential reasons.

But is this true? We might recast Schellenberg's point as the claim that probabilistic threat imminence must be maximal if a threat is to be sufficient to coerce. But clearly that is false. Consider a case in which someone comes up behind me late at night in Manhattan, sticks a small cylindrical object in my back, and demands that I hand over my money or be shot. I do not know with *certainty* that this threat can be carried out. There is some non-zero probability that, even if this mugger has a gun, he also has an overridingly strong aversion to shooting people. Furthermore, there is some non-zero probability that the cylinder I feel in my back is not a gun but a carrot. One might suppose there is even some non-zero probability that someone has surgically inserted a bullet-proof vest under my skin in my infancy that would, in this case, prevent me from being harmed by this mugger. And yet, while all of these things have some non-zero probability, none of these things matter in the least. Even if I thought there was only a .5 probability that the mugger would carry through on his threat, *I* would be coerced into handing over the money.

And something similar holds in the case under discussion here. Even if I do not know with certainty that God exists or that He will bring temporal and/or eternal punishments on me if I fail to believe or act in certain ways, I can still be coerced into acting or believing in those ways. This is not to deny that if probabilistic threat imminence falls below a certain point that I will not be coerced by the threat. Still, the sort of probabilifying revelation that critics of theism such as Schellenberg have in mind would insure that probabilistic threat imminence would remain above this threshold.

However, Schellenberg has one further problem with (16), a problem which also amounts to his only substantive critique of (17). He seems to think that even if the probabilistic imminence problem is soluble, there is an additional problem concerning temporal imminence that is not. The recipient of the clear and evident revelation will believe, he claims, that the punishments attending failure to believe or act in a certain way will be either temporal, eternal, or both. That is, the divine retribution may be meted out immediately, or it may be postponed to the after-life (in hell, say), or both. However, if punishments are *only* eternal, and, he claims, our experience surely teaches us that this, if anything, is the case,[16] we again find that threats of such punishment would fail to produce strong prudential reasons for not doing wrong, against (16). Furthermore, Schellenberg contends, in his only significant argument against (17), that even if such strong prudential reasons were to arise, they could easily be ignored or shoved willfully into the background of our deliberation. As a result, it is false that the desires to do evil would be overwhelmed:

> Human beings, it seems, might very well conceive of God as justly lenient in the moment of desire, and of punishment as, at worst, an afterlife affair, and hence find themselves in a situation of temptation [to engage in evil] after all.... As soon as punishment is pushed off into the future,

rendered less immediate and concrete, the force of any desires I may have to *avoid* punishment is reduced.... If punishment is seen as something in the future, its deterrent effect must be greatly reduced ... I suggest therefore, that it is only if an individual believes that God's policy of punishment implies that a failure to do good actions will in the *here and now* result in bodily harm or loss of life, that the motivating effect of his belief can plausibly be viewed as great.[17]

No doubt what Schellenberg is pointing to here is the role of temporal imminence in coercion. Greater temporal imminence translates into greater compelling force of the threat.

The adequacy of this criticism depends on how we answer two questions. First, is Schellenberg correct in his contention that the recipient of these probabilifying revelations would come to believe that the punishment for wrong-doing was ultimately to be meted out in eternity alone? If not, then his argument that one would not be coerced by such revelation due to the great temporal distance between performing the evil action and the punishment inflicted for it fails. Second, is it true that if punishment were to be meted out solely in eternity the temporal distance between performing the bad action and receiving the punishment would be great enough to mitigate the force of the threat and leave the creature free for soul-making? If so, then despite the fact that the "threat" will not be carried out until later, the creature will still be left with multiple eligible courses of action, and these will be sufficient to allow him or her to engage in soul-making.

It seems to me that the answer to the first question is certainly no and the answer to the second question is probably also no. Schellenberg argues that even if we were to believe, initially, that punishments for wrongdoing would be forthcoming immediately after an evil act is committed, experience would cure us of this error. Looking at others, or ourselves, it is obvious that there are a number of evils that we "get away with." And this may seem enough to make his point. But is it? Even if there are some evil acts for which we receive no temporal punishment (that we know of), all the theist must hold is that *on some occasions* we believe that evil-doing is met with temporal punishments. That alone can provide sufficient probabilistic imminence to yield coercion. Consider again the case of the mugger discussed above. Let's say that I know that during the recent rise in muggings, police have determined that only half of the muggers in fact have guns, guns which they inevitably use if the victim resists. The other half try to mug victims using mere water pistols. It does not at all seem implausible that this knowledge would make me any less coerced when a mugger approaches me and asks for my money. What this shows is that even if we agree with Schellenberg that experience shows us that negative temporal consequences do not *inevitably* follow our evil acts, our belief that such negative consequences *sometimes* follow evil acts can suffice for coercion.[18]

Furthermore, while it is admittedly true that reducing temporal imminence reduces the compelling force of a threat, it seems unlikely that pushing the threat of punishment for wrong-doing off into the afterlife in this case will suffice for mitigating its coercive force. The first reason for this is that, at least on the traditional Christian view, the punishment described in eternity is so great in magnitude and duration, viz., maximal and eternal, that the temporal distance suggested by the average human life span seems unlikely to mitigate the coercive force of the threat to any great degree. This reply gains even more force when one realizes that, while one's life span may be some seventy or so years, a given life might continue only for a few more minutes or hours. As a result, it is unreasonable to assume that the coercive force of the threat is mitigated by the fact that the punishment will not be realized for some number of years since, for all we know, it might be realized in the twinkling of an eye. We might liken the recipient of this probabilifying revelation to a victim of an extortion attempt who is told, "If you fail to carry out the plan, we will kill you. You never know when—maybe when you least expect it. But sometime, one of us will hunt you down and finish you off." The victim here might assume that it will take them a long time

to track him down and so he might refuse to comply. But since the recipient of this threat is unsure how long it will take for the threateners to find him, it is likely that a threat of this sort would nonetheless be coercive, and that is all we really need here. If many people, or even some people, would find a threat of this sort coercive, and the threat implied by the "clear and evident revelation" Schellenberg describes is of this sort, this seems to provide God with good reason for remaining hidden.[19]

At the end of Section II I noted that Schellenberg's official line of argument is that God's love entails that God would make his existence known to creatures. There I argued further that similar considerations should lead us to think that God's love equally entails that God would also reveal to creatures facts relevant to their achieving human flourishing, especially when those facts are accessible only via revelation. Let's call these two positions respectively the weaker and the stronger positions (weaker not being used pejoratively here, but merely to indicate that Schellenberg makes weaker claims concerning what God's love entails about what God would reveal about himself).

Note that while Schellenberg commits himself only to the weaker position, he is, as the discussion in this section makes clear, more than willing to dispute with those who hold the stronger view.[20] Throughout this section we have seen since not everyone will have this high degree of threat indifference, we should not expect revelations of high epistemic imminence to be the norm. This gives the theist good reason for denying that God would produce grand scale theophanies complete with parting clouds, lightening bolts and thunder claps, where God proclaims His existence, etc. to all of the worlds inhabitants. The variability of threat indifference across human beings just would not permit *this* sort of business. Still God might make His existence evident to everyone in more subtle ways, ways that mitigate the *epistemic imminence* of the threat involved and thus mitigate the coercive force of the attending threat.

There is, however, an important response available to the defender of the argument from hiddenness at this point.[21] At most, the argument

I give above shows that we should not expect grand public theophanies to be common. But that does not prevent God from making his existence known to creatures by way of private religious experience. In fact, a glance at the recent literature in philosophy of religion would lead one to think that this is the way religious believers in fact come into cognitive contact with God in the first place. Wouldn't it at least be reasonable to expect that God would make his existence as evident to each creature as it could be via religious experience, tailoring the epistemic imminence to the threat indifference of each creature so as not to coerce him or her? Nothing said above seems to preclude this. And yet, the defender of the argument from hiddenness could claim, this expectation is frustrated as well. For surely, each individual is not the recipient of this sort of religious experience.

This is an interesting and important response, one that deserves a more extensive treatment than I can give it here. A complete response would require a separate essay, I will only attempt to sketch an outline of a response here.[22]

To respond to the "private revelation" view in detail, we would first have to know a bit more about how its advocate understands religious experience. While much of this is contested territory, I propose that we regard religious experience, like sensory experience, as beginning with a perceiver coming to be in a state of directly perceiving some state of affairs, a state which provides the perceiver with *grounds* for coming to hold certain dispositional or occurrent beliefs. But being in possession of the grounds and forming beliefs on those grounds are two distinct perceptual moments. Even in ordinary cases of sensory experience, we are in possession of grounds which are sufficient to lead suitably disposed perceivers to form a variety of beliefs. The process of forming beliefs upon being in possession of certain perceptual grounds is one which is in turn dependent on other dispositions had by the perceiver. And there is little doubt that at least some of these dispositions are under the perceiver's direct or indirect voluntary control.

Thus I can train myself to form true beliefs about the species of plant I am perceiving by forming dispositions that lead me to have certain beliefs when I come to be in possession of certain grounds (these might be visual, tactile, or olfactory sensory grounds). In doing so I have indirect voluntary control over my belief-forming capacities. Likewise I can exercise direct voluntary control over belief-forming dispositions when I, for example, will myself to be more attentive to my surroundings. When I am told that I need to be careful of poisonous snakes in an area where I am hiking, I can voluntarily heighten my awareness, making me more apt to form beliefs about the presence of snakes than I would be if I were oblivious to the danger.

In the case of religious experience, God can provide the perceiver with certain religious experiential grounds, but whether those grounds will suffice to form true beliefs, or any beliefs at all, will depend in at least some measure on whether or not the perceiver has disposed himself to rightly forming beliefs on the basis of those grounds. It is a significant part of the Christian story of the Fall that one place where we would expect creatures to be especially self-deceived is with respect to whether or not one is properly disposed to form beliefs on the basis of religious experiential grounds. As a result, one should be especially wary when advocates of the "private revelation" view contend that it is obvious that not everyone is the recipient of clear religious experiences.

Schellenberg's final point is an attack on (18). This premise holds that "where there is little temptation to do wrong, persons lack a genuine choice of destiny." Schellenberg points out this is false since even in a world in which there is no temptation to do evil, one is still able to choose between merely doing the obligatory and doing the supererogatory. And this alone should be sufficient for soul-making.

Schellenberg argues here, as others have against this sort of theodicy, that evil is not in fact a necessary condition for soul-making. Is Schellenberg right that the distinction between obligatory and supererogatory acts pulls the rug out from under (18) and, by extension, we might assume, soul-making theodicies in general. I hold that it does not, at least for the Christian theist, because I am inclined to think that the Christian should not endorse the distinction between obligatory and supererogatory acts. One might reasonably hold that the ethical import of Christ's teaching had as a consequence that the supererogatory is, for the Christian, obligatory!

> But I tell you, do not resist an evil person. If someone strikes you on the right cheek, turn to him the other also. And if someone wants to sue you and take your tunic, let him have your cloak as well. If someone forces you to go one mile, go with him two miles.[23]

While this view has some strange consequences, there are not as many such consequences as one might think. However, further discussion or defense of this view would require a separate treatment.

VII. CONCLUSIONS

From this we can conclude that the argument set forth in (16) – (19) stands. Schellenberg's attacks on (16) through (18) seem to fail once we take into account those factors that determine the way in which incentives give rise to coercion. I have argued that the coercive force of a threat is determined by three factors: threat strength, threat imminence, and threat indifference. Further, threat imminence comes in three species, probabilistic, temporal, and epistemic. Schellenberg has set forth two serious challenges to the argument proposed by the soul-making account. First, he has argued that the probabilistic and temporal imminence of a threat attending a probabilifying revelation of

God's existence and moral will for His creatures would sufficiently mitigate the force of the induced desire that it allows freedom of a sort sufficient to engage in soul-making. I have argued that by looking at parallel cases of coercion we have good reason to deny this claim. Second, Schellenberg attempts to show that there are actual cases in which free creatures who believe they have been the recipients of probabilifying revelation are still free in the sense required for soul-making. I have argued that the theist should expect that there would be some such probabilifying revelations but that, given the wide variability of threat indifference across individuals, such revelations would be and are rare.

Notice then that this response to Schellenberg makes for a strong case that divine hiddenness is, in most cases, the only way to go if God hopes to preserve the ability of free creatures to engage in soul-making. On the traditional Christian view, at any rate, the strength of the threat for failure to believe and/or obey is fixed: There will be severe negative consequences—some temporal, others eternal. I have argued furthermore that probabilistic and temporal imminence cannot be attenuated in such a way as to eliminate the coerciveness of such a probabilifying revelation. Finally, a good case can be made that creaturely threat indifference also cannot be mitigated, by God anyway, since it appears to be a character trait that we, in some measure, freely cultivate. To fix this feature of our character would be to interfere in our self-determination in just the way this account argues God ought not. As a result, the only remaining factor that can be attenuated is epistemic imminence, i.e., divine hiddenness, and this, it seems, is what God has done.

NOTES

1. "Coercion and the Hiddenness of God," *American Philosophical Quarterly,* Vol. 30, Number 1, pp. 27–38.

2. Although such evil is necessary here only in the sense that there is no world God can actualize

which contains free creatures who do not go wrong (at least without a significant loss of overall goodness in the created world).

3. Nothing I have said here actually sustains such a strong conclusion. However, those theists who

propose libertarian freedom as an intrinsic good often cite its relation to moral good to ground its worth. Here I am arguing that there is no such intrinsic relation.

4. See his *Evil and the God of Love* (New York: Harper and Row, 1966 and 1977), pp. 255–61 and 318–36.

5. One might argue that this view on the purpose of the earthly life is summed up in the following passage from the second epistle of St. Peter: "Grace and peace be multiplied to you in the knowledge of God and of Jesus our Lord; seeing that His divine power has granted to us everything pertaining to life and godliness, through the true knowledge of Him who called us by His own glory and excellence. For by these He has granted to us His precious and magnificent promises, so that by them you may become partakers of the divine nature, having escaped the corruption that is in the world by lust. (11 Peter. 1::2–4)

6. Ephesians.5:1

7. Some Christian readers might fear that an account of this sort positively precludes the role of grace in salvation and sanctification, making it Pelagian *in excelsis.* I have responded to this charge in more detail in my "Heaven and Hell," in *Reason for the Hope Within,* Michael Murray (ed.) (Grand Rapids: William B. Eerdmans, 1998), pp. 298–9. But there is no reason on the view developed here for denying that grace is a necessary condition for soul-making. It cannot, however, be the case that such grace is intrinsically sufficient.

8. J. L. Schellenberg, *Divine Hiddenness and Human Reason* (Ithaca: Cornell University Press, 1993), p. 83.

9. Ibid., pp. 85–6.

10. Ibid., pp. 117–18.

11. Ibid., p. 121.

12. The question of whether or not offers can be coercive is widely disputed in the literature and cannot be addressed here. I have elsewhere argued that offers can be coercive, see, "Are Coerced Acts Free," David Dudrick and Michael Murray, *American Philosophical Quarterly,* Vol. 32, no. 2, p. 116.

13. One must, of course, define exactly what it means to be unable rationally to choose some course of action. I discuss this in detail in "Are Coerced Acts

Free?" pp. 116–19. Roughly, the idea is this. Each of us has a certain threshold such that if (i) a threat carries a grave enough consequence and (ii) the act required of the threatened by the threatener, P, is not, relative to the threat, sufficiently grave, then I am unable to deliberately choose to do anything other than P. So, for example, if one threatens to shoot me if I fail to touch my nose, I *cannot,* all other things being equal, choose to do other than touch my nose. Surely other factors might be added to the case that *would* make it possible for me to choose to do something other than touch my nose. For example, we might add that if I touch my nose I will suffer excruciating pain for eternity. Or we might add that I believe I have a bullet-proof vest on. But barring such additions to the case, I contend that *I* simply cannot choose to do other than touch my nose. To put it more strongly, no possible world continuous with a world segment up to that time, as described, contains me performing any free and deliberate action other than touching my nose.

14. The account of coercion here is vastly oversimplified. Unless a good deal is built into the notion of what counts as a threat, this definition will entail that I am coerced any time one course of action is vastly preferred by me over its competitors. Surely such an account fails to capture what is distinctive about coercion. A fully fleshed out account of coercion can be found in "Are Coerced Acts Free?" Op.cit.

15. *Divine Hiddenness and Human Reason,* pp. 121–4.

16. Schellenberg says this explicitly, "Even if the expectation of [temporal] punishment . . . were prevalent in some quarters at first, upon further experience and reflection the understanding of humans might be expected to mature and deepen . . . to the point where such views were universally rejected. Further, those who (unreasonably) expected severe punishment to follow each bad action would soon note that those who did not have this expectation, and so occasionally fell into temptation and did bad actions, were not immediately severely punished." *Divine Hiddenness and Human Reason,* p. 125.

17. Ibid., p. 124.

18. Of course, inevitable negative consequences alone are not sufficient for coercion. High threat strength,

probabilistic and epistemic imminence, and low threat-indifference must be present as well.

19. Schellenberg next presents a fallback position that the theist might retreat to in light of his criticisms discussed above. However, since I have argued these earlier criticisms fail, there seems little reason to discuss this weaker attempt to defend (16) and (17) which he proposes. His discussion of this fallback position is found at, Ibid., pp. 126–8.

20. Ibid., pp. 129–30.

21. In conversation, Schellenberg has indicated to me that he thinks this is the right response, and the one that gets to the heart of the argument from hiddenness. He also discusses this sort of position briefly at the close of section I in the essay in this volume.

22. I provide another response to this view in my "Coercion and the Hiddenness of God," section V.

23. Matthew 5:39-41.

III.C.8

Divine Hiddenness, Divine Silence

MICHAEL REA

Michael Rea (1968–) is professor of philosophy at the University of Notre Dame, and co-editor of the present volume. His research focuses primarily on metaphysics and philosophical theology. In this article, he explains why divine silence poses a serious intellectual obstacle to belief in God, and then goes on to consider ways of overcoming that obstacle. After considering several ways in which divine silence might actually be beneficial to human beings, he argues that perhaps silence is nothing more or less than God's preferred mode of interaction with creatures like us. Perhaps God simply desires communion *rather than overt communication with human beings, and perhaps God has provided ways for us to experience God's presence richly even amidst the silence.*

Several years ago, and a short while after her death, some of the private writings of Mother Teresa were published under the title *Come Be My Light*. The journal entries were shocking—not because they disclosed hidden sins or scandals, but because they revealed something far more troubling. They painted a picture of a woman celebrated for her faith and devotion to God but wracked by pain and doubt for lack of the felt presence of God in her life—a woman who sought God with tears and cried out for years for some small taste of the divine, for some tiny assurance in her soul of God's love and presence in her life, but, like so many of the rest of us, received nothing but silence in response. In one of the most poignant passages of the book, she writes:

> Lord, my God, who am I that You should forsake me? The child of your love—and now become as the most hated one— the one You have thrown away as

Published for the first time in the sixth edition of this volume. © 2010 by Michael Rea.

unwanted-unloved. I call, I cling, I want—and there is no One to answer—no One on Whom I can cling—no, No One.—Alone. The darkness is so dark ... The loneliness of the heart that wants love is unbearable.—Where is my faith?—even deep down, right in, there is nothing but emptiness & darkness.—My God—how painful is this unknown pain. It pains without ceasing ... I am told God loves me—and yet the reality of darkness & coldness & emptiness is so great that nothing touches my soul. ... The whole time smiling—Sisters & people pass such remarks.—They think my faith, trust & love are filling my very being & that the intimacy with God and union to His will must be absorbing my heart.—Could they but know—and how my cheerfulness is the cloak by which I cover the emptiness & misery.—What are You doing My God to one so small?[1]

What indeed? What are we to make of the silence of God?

Divine silence—or, as many think of it, divine hiddenness—is the source of one of the two most important and widely discussed objections to belief in God. It is also, I venture to say, one of the most important sources of doubt and spiritual distress for religious believers. Mother Teresa eventually reconciled herself to a certain extent with God's hiddenness, but (moving all the way to the other edge of the continuum) Friedrich Nietzsche saw it as just one more reason to sneer at religious belief. He writes:

A god who is all-knowing and all-powerful and who does not even make sure his creatures understand his intention—could that be a god of goodness? Who allows countless doubts and uncertainties to persist, for thousands of years, as though the salvation of mankind were unaffected by them, or who, on the other hand, holds out the prospect of frightful consequences if any mistake is made as to the nature of truth? Would he not be a cruel god if he possessed the truth and could behold mankind miserably tormenting itself over that truth?—But perhaps he is a god of goodness notwithstanding and merely *could* express himself more clearly! Did he perhaps lack the intelligence to do so? Or the eloquence? So much the worse! For then he was perhaps also in error as to that which he calls his "truth," and is himself not so very far from being the "poor deluded devil"![2]

It's pretty clear that Nietzsche thinks that the existence of an all good, all powerful God is outright incompatible with our experience of divine hiddenness. But why? In the next section of this article, I will try briefly to answer this question. That is, I will try briefly to get clear on exactly what the problem of divine hiddenness is supposed to be. (Only briefly, though, because I think we all have at least a basic grasp of what the worry is.) After that, I'll spend the remainder of the article discussing three strategies for dealing with the problem.

THE PROBLEM OF DIVINE HIDDENNESS

The problem of divine hiddenness starts with the supposition that *God exists*. There is no problem (for adults) about the hiddenness of Santa Claus, or of unicorns, or leprechauns, or the like. We simply don't believe in these sorts of things. The problem of divine hiddenness arises under the supposition—genuine, or "for the sake of argument"—that God exists. The problem gains traction because our concept of God is the concept of a being that we *ought* to encounter—*tangibly and vividly*, it would seem—at some point in our lives. Again, there is no real problem of the hiddenness of abstract objects. Nobody says, "Well, if there are such things, why don't they show themselves once in a while?" They're just not that sort of thing. God, however, is supposed to be the sort of being who *would* show up once in awhile. But almost none of us ever really see God, hear God, touch God, or encounter God in any other palpable way. Even those who say that God speaks to them in prayer don't usually mean that they hear voices—or have any other experience apart from the felt conviction that some particular idea they've had is, in some sense, "from the Lord." That, in a nutshell, is the problem.

Why do we think that we ought to encounter God? Simple: Our concept of God is the concept of a perfectly rational, perfectly wise being who loves us like a perfect parent. A being like that would want to have a relationship with us; and we all know that, in order to have a relationship with someone, you have to communicate with him or her. This is why the junior high approach to romance does not work. You know how this goes: Boy sees girl; boy likes girl; and . . . boy takes every possible measure to prevent this fact from becoming known to girl. If people never grew out of this sort of immaturity, the human race would die out. So it's a safe bet that a perfectly *rational* God wouldn't take this approach in trying to relate to us. So it stands to reason that God would show up in our lives once in a while.

More seriously: The theistic religions are in full agreement about the fact that it is *bad for us* to spend our lives without a relationship with God. We all know that, all else being equal, it is bad for a child to grow up without a father or a mother, or to believe—for *good* reasons or bad—that her father or mother doesn't love her. We all know that good parents go out of their way to talk to their children, to reassure them of their love, to be present in vivid and tangible ways—ways that the child can understand and benefit from at whatever stage of life she's at—and so on. Good parents don't lock themselves in a room day after day, waiting for their children to acquire the wherewithal to seek them out. Good parents don't expect that their children will discover their love for them simply by way of inference from the orderliness of the living room and the presence of fun toys in the basement. Good parents go out of their way to say, "I love you," and to hold their children and to comfort them when they're sad. How much more, then, should

we expect the same from a being who (we're told) loves us *like a perfect parent*? If my daughter were crying out for my presence in the way that Mother Teresa cried out for God's, I would move heaven and earth if I could to be there for her. If my son were in despair because he thought that he had irreparably disappointed me, I would hold his hand and tell him that that's not true. How could I not? And yet I'm selfish, imperfect, lacking in resources, and short on wisdom, only human. How much more then should we expect God to respond to such cries?

Of course, I don't mean to suggest that God would be bound to respond in some *very particular way* to us when we cry out for his presence. Nor, I should think, would God be bound to respond *every single time*. Good parents sometimes turn a deaf ear to their children's cries, and often for the child's good; they sometimes leave their children with babysitters (even when it's not strictly necessary), ignoring vehement protests; and so on. So what kind of encounter with God am I saying that we ought to expect?

Well, it's hard to say exactly. But you might think that, at a minimum we ought to expect at least one of the following to be the case:

- *Our evidence should be conclusive:* It shouldn't be the case that one can be fully aware of the available evidence of God's existence and at the same time rationally believe that God does not exist.

or

- *Experience of God's love and presence should be widely available:* It shouldn't be the case that, in general, people never (or only very rarely) have experiences that seem to be experiences of the love or presence of God.

And yet both of these things that seem like they *shouldn't* be the case *are* the case. It is exactly this that I have in mind when I say that God is *hidden* or *silent*, and when I say that we don't encounter God often in palpable ways: Our evidence is inconclusive; religious experience—of the interesting and unambiguous sort—is rare. And it's really hard to see any good reason why God might leave matters this way.

So it looks like we have only three options: (a) We identify some mistake in our reasoning thus far; (b) we find some believable, good reason why God might remain hidden; or (c) we concede that there is no God. There is really no other way forward.

If you're interested in identifying a mistake in the reasoning, it helps to have the premises of the argument carefully laid out and numbered. Like so:

1. Suppose that God exists—that is, suppose that there is a perfectly powerful, perfectly wise being who loves us like a perfect parent.

2. God is mostly hidden from people: Our evidence is inconclusive; religious experience of the interesting and unambiguous sort is rare.

3. There is no good reason for God to remain hidden.

4. If God is mostly hidden and there is no good reason for God to remain hidden, then one of the following is true:

   a. God exists but, like a **negligent father**, does not love us enough to make himself known.

   b. God exists but, like an **inept lover**, lacks the wisdom to appreciate the importance or proper way of revealing himself to us.

   c. God exists but is **too weak** to reveal himself in the ways that he should in order to secure his relational goals.

5. Premises (1)–(4) are inconsistent.

6. Therefore: God does not exist.

This will be our official statement of the problem of divine hiddenness.[3]

DEALING WITH THE PROBLEM

The advantage to articulating a problem in the way that I just have—with numbered premises and inferences signaled with "therefore's"—is that it gives us a pretty systematic way of addressing the problem. If premises (1–4) *really are inconsistent* (and

I think they are, since our concept of God rules out 4a–4c), then one of them is false. The trick then is to ask about each one, "Is this premise true or false? And if it is false, why is it false?" In the next few minutes, I'll suggest some reasons for thinking that premises (2) and (3) might be false. My own sympathies lie with those who reject premise (3). But I'll start with some thoughts about premise (2).

Conclusive Evidence?

In St. Paul's epistle to the Romans, Paul writes:

> The wrath of God is being revealed from heaven against all the godlessness and wickedness of men who suppress the truth by their wickedness, since what may be known about God is plain to them, because God has made it plain to them. For since the creation of the world God's invisible qualities—his eternal power and divine nature—have been clearly seen, being understood from what has been made, so that men are without excuse. For although they knew God, they neither glorified him as God nor gave thanks to him, but their thinking became futile and their foolish hearts were darkened.[4]

Does it sound like St. Paul would agree with the claim that God is mostly hidden? No. On Paul's view, as some people read it, there is no reasonable Non-belief: Non-belief is due to sin. Or, a bit more softly, what passes for non-belief is really a kind of self-deception. Being an atheist is sort of like being an alcoholic in denial: You want so badly not to see the truth that you suppress it and convince yourself that things are how you want them to be.

This is an offensive doctrine. But I think that it has to be taken seriously. Self-deception is a real phenomenon; and there is nothing at all implausible about the idea that people would prefer—indeed, would want very badly—for there to be no God. One of my colleagues once pointed out that most sensible people would recoil in horror upon hearing that a person of great power and influence had taken a special interest in them and had very definite, detailed, and not-easily-implemented views about how they ought to live their lives. Along the same lines, eminent philosopher Thomas Nagel, in a now famous chapter entitled "Naturalism and the Fear of Religion," writes:

> I want atheism to be true and am made uneasy by the fact that some of the most intelligent and well-informed people I know are religious believers. It is not just that I do not believe in God, and, naturally, hope that I'm right in my belief. It's that I hope there is no God! I do not want there to be a God; I do not want the universe to be like that. . . .
>
> My guess is that this cosmic authority problem is not a rare condition and that it is responsible for much of the scientism and reductionism of our time.[5]

So is it really so crazy to think—*on the supposition that there is a God, remember*—that many people would be in the grip of this kind of self-deception? No. To be sure, the view implies that a great many people—including many whom we regard as otherwise very wise and intelligent—suffer from a kind of deep-seated irrationality. But I don't think we should shrink from this sort of claim on principle. After all, atheists say that sort of thing about theists all the time.

Still, this is a hard doctrine, and it has some real problems as a general explanation of the phenomenon of divine hiddenness. Remember, even believers struggle with God's hiddenness. Many people seem to be utterly broken by divine silence in the midst of their own suffering or the suffering of others, or simply by the ongoing and unsatisfied longing for the presence of God. I've seen more than one friend break down in tears over this sort of thing. And remember Mother Teresa. Moreover, many people are atheists or agnostics despite years of what at least *seems* to them to be honest seeking after God. Is it possible that all of these people are radically self-deceived? Sure. But then we must ask why a compassionate God would allow such pervasive and destructive self-deception to go unchecked.

Every day drug, alcohol, and sex addicts, people with eating disorders and abusive personalities, and many others as well are made to face up to their own self-deception and admit to themselves and others what they very badly want to hide. Often— maybe mostly—they're made to do this by someone who simply confronts them vividly one way or another with the truth. Why wouldn't God do that for us? This question calls out for an answer as much as the original question of why God would remain hidden calls out for an answer. So denying that second premise seems to me to be just a way of relocating the problem—sort of like pushing around a bulge under the carpet instead of stomping it out entirely. And it seems that the only sensible answer is: God must have some very good reason.

Good Reason?

So now we come to the third premise: Maybe God does have a good reason for remaining hidden. But what could such a reason be? Here I want to consider two different *kinds* of response. One response says that he does it for *our* sake. Many philosophers think that, in general, God could be justified in permitting suffering of innocents only if the innocents themselves benefit.[6] The idea is that a perfectly loving being wouldn't make *me* suffer for the benefit of someone else. And even folks who think that God could allow some people to suffer for the benefit of others typically think that, at the very least, there would have to be some benefit to *human beings generally* in order for God to be justified in permitting the evils that come from his remaining hidden. The other sort of response denies this: God has reasons, but his reasons are his own and have nothing directly to do with benefiting us (which is why we often can't *see* any benefit to us in God's hiddenness). I'll take each in turn.

So first, what might be some of the ways in which *we* (humans generally) could benefit from divine hiddenness? Here I'll consider two suggestions.

First, one might think that hiddenness is necessary for preserving the *freedom and integrity* of our own responses to God.

Some folks suggest that if God were to show himself openly, we would effectively be coerced into submission. I have kids, and they each in their own ways sometimes try to manipulate and bully the other one. I want them to *freely* choose not to do this—which means I often don't appear in the doorway when I hear that the conditions for manipulation and bullying are growing ripe. If I appear in the doorway, they'll be on their guard; their freedom to grow will be, in a certain way, undermined.

That's one way of pitching the idea that divine hiddenness might help to preserve our freedom. But here's another: Suppose Bill Gates were to go back on the dating scene. Wouldn't it be natural for him to want to be with someone who would love him for himself rather than for his resources? Yet wouldn't it also be natural for him to worry that even the most virtuous of prospective dating partners would find it difficult to avoid having her judgment clouded by the prospect of living in unimaginable wealth? The worry wouldn't be that there would be anything coercive about his impressive circumstances; rather, it's that a certain kind of genuineness in a person's response to him is made vastly more difficult by those circumstances. But, of course, Bill Gates's impressiveness pales in comparison with God's; and, unlike Gates, God's resources and intrinsic nature are so incredibly impressive as to be not only overwhelmingly and unimaginably beautiful but also overwhelmingly and unimaginably *terrifying*. Viewed in this light, it is easy to suppose that God *must* hide from us if he wants to allow us to develop the right sort of non-self-interested love for him.

Note too that if this is God's motivation, divine hiddenness is as much for our benefit as God's. Which brings me to the second, but related, "benefit to us" strategy for understanding divine hiddenness. Perhaps God's hiddenness is good for our souls. Perhaps it helps to produce virtues in us that we wouldn't otherwise acquire. Maybe it teaches us to seek God, to hunger and thirst after him, to not take him for granted. Much in the scriptures suggests that this is what God wants for us. The psalmist writes, "As a deer longs for flowing streams, so my soul longs for you, O God," (Ps. 42:1, NRSV) and the idea seems clearly to be that we *all* should long after God in this way. Likewise, at one point in the Gospels Jesus gives thanks to God for hiding certain things from those who are not seeking him; and he admonishes us to ask, *seek*, and *knock* (Mt. 11:25; Mt. 7:7). God wants us to be seekers after him, and what better way to cultivate that disposition than to hide?

Or maybe divine hiddenness teaches us that God cannot be manipulated by us—that God is not at our beck and call. We cannot summon God by performing the right sorts of incantations; God is maximally free, maximally authoritative, and will be manipulated by no one. This too might be a lesson that is good for us to learn, and so it, too, might be among the purposes of divine hiddenness.

The Personality of God?

Or maybe . . . just maybe . . . although divine hiddenness often *does* have these salutary effects, and others, that still is not their point at all.

The last suggestion I'd like to consider is one that sees divine hiddenness not as something that God does to produce some great good for us, but rather as something that God engages in for his own reasons, independently of (though not in violation of) our good. Throughout this talk I have sometimes used the term divine *silence* to refer to the phenomenon of hiddenness. I think that that's a more fruitful way of thinking of God's mode of interaction with us. And what I want to suggest is that perhaps divine silence is nothing more or less than an expression of God's personality.

Remember our problem: We experience divine silence and, under the assumption that God exists, we ask, "*What's his problem? Doesn't he love me? Doesn't he care? Doesn't he understand that you have to talk to people to relate to them? What kind of father is he?*" The objections implied by these rhetorical questions are altogether natural, but they are flawed. They are flawed in just the same way in which complaints about the behavior of human persons are often flawed: They depend on a particular interpretation of behavior that can in fact be interpreted in a number of different ways, depending upon what assumptions we make about the person's beliefs, desires, motives, dispositions, and overall personality.

Someone from your school doesn't greet you in the hallway. Have you hurt her feelings? Does she think you're a fool and not want to be seen talking to you? Does she think so poorly of herself that she thinks *you* wouldn't want to be seen talking to her? Is she depressed and having a bad day? As a matter of fact, she's the class genius— beautiful mind sort of genius—and she's always off in her own world, introverted and totally preoccupied. Does that affect your interpretation of her behavior?

You're on a first date. After a while you notice that you've been doing almost all the talking. You start asking questions to draw her out, but her answers are brief, and the silences in between grow longer and longer. You spend the entire ride home without saying a word. Does she hate you? Does she find you boring? Have you offended her? Or is she just rude? As it happens, she just arrived in the United States and was raised with the view that if you *really* want to win a man over, you should be quiet and let him do all the talking. Does that information affect your interpretation?

My point? Interpreting silence requires a lot of information about what sort of person you're dealing with—about the person's cultural background, about what sorts of social norms he or she is likely to recognize and respect, about his or her views about what various kinds of behavior (both verbal and not) communicate to others, about his or her general "style" of interacting with other people, about what's going on in his or her life, and so on. But if this is what it takes to interpret the behavior of an ordinary human person, imagine how difficult it must be to interpret the behavior of an invisible and transcendent *divine* person.

Seen in this light, the suggestion that divine silence *in and of itself* somehow indicates disinterest or lack of love and concern on God's part is absurd. God is as alien and "wholly other" from us as it is possible for another person to be. So isn't it almost ridiculous to think that we would have any idea what divine silence would indicate? To assume that divine silence indicates a lack of concern for us involves quite a lot of unwarranted assumptions about the degree to which divine modes of interaction would likely resemble 21st-century human modes of interaction.

Granted, divine silence *would* indicate a lack of concern for rational creatures if we had good reason to think that God had provided no way for us to find him or to experience his presence in the midst of his silence. This would indicate a lack of concern because it would indicate that God is *trying* to prevent us from finding him, or at least doing nothing to help, and thus bringing about something that is both intrinsically very bad for us and totally beyond our control. But as far as I can tell, we don't have good reason for thinking that God has left us without *any* way of finding him or experiencing his presence.

I think that we have a tendency to assume that we can experience God's presence only if we tangibly *perceive* something—a voice, a vision, an ache in our stomachs or our heads, a tingly feeling of some sort. But experiencing the presence of a person sometimes involves none of this. Sometimes it is just a matter of the person *being* present, together with our believing that she is present and taking a certain attitude toward her presence. Consider: You're studying in the library. You look up and you see a reflection in the window: The girl you've been in love with all year but never had the courage to ask out has entered the library behind you. Without seeing you, she turns down the aisle of books adjacent to yours—just a single stack of shelves separates you—and takes up a seat. She's out of your view, but is there any doubt that you'll experience her presence? And you would, even apart from the initial glimpse that alerted you to her presence—all you'd need to experience it—to *genuinely experience it*—is the true conviction that she's right there on the other side of those books, together with a certain kind of attention and attitude toward that conviction.

In her book *A Wind in the Door*, Madeline L'Engle makes this point very nicely by way of the distinction between communication and communion:

> "Hey, Meg! [says Calvin] Communication implies sound. Communion doesn't." He sent her a brief image of walking silently through the woods, the two of them alone together, their feet almost noiseless on the rusty carpet of pine needles. They walked without speaking, without touching, and yet they were as close as it is possible for two human beings to be.... Mr. Jenkins had never had that kind of communion with another human being, a communion so rich and full that silence speaks more powerfully than words."[7]

And, of course, silent communion is not the only way to experience a person unseen. Think of times when you relay a story about an encounter with another person and, after a bit of effort, you falter and say, "Well, you just had to be there." What you communicate, I think, is that your words have failed at their goal—the goal of *putting us there, of mediating to us an experience of a person we don't see and maybe have never met.* Sometimes we do fail in that way, but often we succeed. When you say "You just had to be there," nobody ever says, "Well, of course! You *always* have to be there; you simply can't convey an experience like that in words!" *Stories about other persons can mediate their presence to us—they can give us a taste of what it is like to be in the presence of the person, sort of like memories give us a taste of what it is like to be in the presence of the remembered event, even when we 're not.* Again, though, it matters that we *believe* that the person reporting the events in question is reporting events involving *real persons.* When we do, we can be transported and get at least a bit of what it's like to be around the person we're being told about. And this, it seems, is what biblical narrative—and, to a certain extent, the liturgies of the church—can do for us when we approach them with eyes of faith.[8]

My claim, then, is that divine silence might just be an expression of God's preferred mode of interaction, and that we need not experience his silence as *absence*—especially if we see Biblical narratives and liturgies as things that in some sense mediate the presence of God to us, if we live out our lives in the conviction that God is ever present with us, and if we seek something more like *communion* with God rather than just communication.

The pressing question, however, is what to do with the fact that God's silence is *painful* for us. Many believers experience crippling doubt, overwhelming sadness, and ultimate loss of faith as a result of ongoing silence from their heavenly Father. On the assumption that God exists and that a loving relationship with God is a great good, it would appear that many people have been positively damaged by divine silence. Isn't it just this that leads us to take divine silence as evidence of God's lack of concern? Perhaps silence is just an expression of God's personality, but then, the objector might say, God's personality is just that of an unloving and inattentive parent.

The problem with this objection is that it completely ignores the fact that sometimes our being pained by another person's behavior is *our* problem rather than theirs—due to our own dysfunctional attitudes and ways of relating to others, our own epistemic or moral vices, our own immaturity, and the like. In such cases, it is our responsibility to find a way out of our suffering rather than the other person's responsibility to stop behaving in the ways that cause us pain. And maybe this is how it is with divine silence, too. Maybe our suffering in the face of divine silence is unreasonable, due more to our own immaturity or dysfunction than to any lack of kindness on God's part. Maybe it is a result of our own untrusting, uncharitable interpretations of divine silence, or an inappropriate refusal to accept God for who God is and to accept God's preferences about when and in what ways to communicate with us. And maybe there are ways of experiencing the world that are fully available to us, if only we would strive for maturity in the ways that we ought to, that would allow us to be content with or even to appreciate the silence of God in the midst of our joys and sufferings. Coping with divine silence, then, would just be a matter of finding these more positive ways of experiencing it.

It helps, in this vein, to be reminded of a fact about God and a fact about ordinary human relationships. The fact about God is that the most enigmatic, eccentric, and complicated people we might ever encounter in literature or in real life are, by comparison with God, utterly familiar and mundane. The fact about human relationships is that experiencing the silence of another person can, in the right context and seen in the right way, be an incredibly rich way of experiencing the *person*—all the more so with a person who is sufficiently beyond you in intellect, wisdom, and virtue. A wise and virtuous person who is utterly beyond you intellectually and silently leads you on a journey that might teach you a lot more about herself and about other things on your journey than she would if she tried to tell you all of the things that she wants to teach you. In such a case, objecting to the silence, interpreting it as an offence, or wishing that the person would just talk to you rather than make you figure things out for yourself might just be childish—an immature refusal to tolerate legitimate differences among persons and to be charitable in the way that you interpret another's behavior. And there is no reason to think that the person would owe it to you to cater to these objections—even if her decision to be silent was arrived at not for the sake of your greater good, but simply because *that's who she is, and that's how she prefers to communicate with people like you.*

You might be tempted to object that, on this view, God is like a father who neglects his children, leaving them bereft and unloved while he sits in stony silence thinking "I just gotta be me." But to object like this is to fail to take seriously the idea that God might have a genuine, robust personality and that it might be *deeply good* for God to live out his own personality. One odd feature of much contemporary philosophy of religion is that it seems to portray God as having a "personality" that is almost entirely empty, allowing his behavior to be almost exhaustively determined by facts about how it would be best *for others* for an omnipotent being to behave. But why should we think of God like this? God is supposed to be a person not only of unsurpassable love and goodness but of unsurpassable beauty. Could God really be *that* sort of person if he's nothing more than a cosmic, others-oriented, utility-maximizing machine? On that way of thinking, God—the being who is supposed to be a person *par excellence*—ends up having no real *self*. So, as I see it, silence of the sort we experience from God might just flow out of who God is, *and it might be deeply good for God to live out his personality.* If that's right, and if our suffering in the face of divine silence is indeed unreasonable, the result of immaturity or other dysfunctions that we can and should overcome anyway, then I see no reason why even perfect love would require God to desist from his preferred mode of interaction in order to alleviate our suffering.

On the view that I am developing, then, it is not true that divine silence serves no *greater good*. Rather, it serves the good that comes of the most perfect and beautiful person in the universe expressing himself in the way that he sees fit. This is good on its own terms, and it is justified if—as theists generally believe—God has provided ways (not our preferred ways, but ways nonetheless) of finding and experiencing his presence despite his silence. And if, as I have suggested, there are ways of experiencing divine silence that we would find non-burdensome or even beautiful, and if God's persisting in his silence provides opportunities for us to grow in maturity or in our ability to relate to others, then divine silence might even be good for us.[9]

NOTES

1. Mother Teresa, *Come Be My Light: The Private Writings of the Saint of Calcutta,* edited with commentary by Brian Kolodiejchuk, New York: Doubleday, 2007, pp. 186–87.

2. *Daybreak*, trans R. J. Holingdale, Cambridge: Cambridge University Press, 1982, pp. 89–90.

3. The most widely discussed articulation of the problem of divine hiddenness is J. L. Schellenberg's

Divine Hiddenness and Human Reason (Ithaca, NY: Cambridge University Press). *Divine Hiddenness: New Essays,* edited by Daniel Howard-Snyder and Paul K. Moser (Cambridge: Cambridge University Press, 2002) is another important volume which includes both further articulations of the problem as well as a variety of responses. All but the last of the responses that I present in the section entitled "Dealing with the Problem" are represented and defended in some detail in that volume. Finally, see also Ted Poston and Trent Dougherty, "Divine Hiddenness and the Nature of Belief," *Religious Studies* 43 (2007): 183–98, and my "Narrative, Liturgy, and the Hiddenness of God," pp. 76–96, in *Metaphysics and God: Essays in Honor of Eleonore Stump*, edited by Kevin Timpe (New York: Routledge, 2009).

4. Rom. 1:18–21; New Revised Standard Version Bible, copyright 1989, Division of Christian Education of the National Council of the Churches of Christ in the United States of America.

5. *The Last Word*, Oxford: Oxford University Press 2009; pp. 130–131.

6. See, e.g., Eleonore Stump, "The Problem of Evil," *Faith and Philosophy* 2 (1985): 393–423, and "Providence and the Problem of Evil," pp. 51–91 in *Christian Philosophy*, edited by Thomas P. Flint (Notre Dame, IN: University of Notre Dame Press, 1990). For critical discussion of this principle, along with references to other philosophers who endorse it, see Jeff Jordan, "Divine Love and Human Suffering," *International Journal for Philosophy of Religion* 56 (2004): 169–78.

7. *A Wind in the Door*, New York: Farrar, Straus, and Giroux, 1973, p. 171.

8. I develop this idea in more detail in "Narrative, Liturgy, and the Hiddenness of God." The idea takes inspiration from recent work by Eleonore Stump—especially her *Wandering in Darkness* (Oxford: Oxford University Press, 2010).

9. This essay has been given as a talk aimed at undergraduate and non-academic audiences on several occasions, most recently at Wake Forest University and Bethel College, South Bend. It was published for the first time in the sixth edition of this volume.

PART IV

Religion and Experience

THE HEART OF RELIGION is, for a vast number of believers across a wide range of traditions, experiential. Within every major religious tradition we find people bearing witness to their encounters with God, to the occurrence of miraculous signs and wonders, or to other experiences to which they attribute some distinctively religious significance. Religion is often sharply contrasted with science on the grounds that the latter is firmly rooted in empirical investigation whereas the former is not. But isn't this contrast rather puzzling in light of the fact that religion is so deeply experiential?

The nature of religious experience, and the relationship between religious doctrine and human experience generally is complex and fascinating. One important set of questions concerns the qualitative character of religious experience, and what (if anything) is revealed by mystical or other religious experiences. For example, are mystical experiences a mode of perceiving God? Or do they admit of purely naturalistic explanations? And if the latter, does this fact somehow show that they are evidentially worthless? These are the sorts of questions taken up in the first section of Part IV.

Another important set of questions concerns what we ought to think about the testimony that others bear to their (alleged) experiences of miraculous signs and wonders. What should we think, for example, of ancient reports that God parted the red sea? What should we think of contemporary reports that the local faith healer has cured somebody's cancer? Should we take such testimony seriously? *Can* we rationally take it seriously? These are challenging questions, several of which are explored in the second section.

Finally, a third set of questions focuses specifically on the relationship between religion and science. The sciences are set apart from other theoretical disciplines in no small part by the absolutely central role that experience plays in both theory-development and theory-assessment. But, as noted above, one cannot sensibly say that rootedness in experience is what separates science from religion; for religion is itself heavily reliant on experience. What, then, are the salient differences between the two realms? Are there differences in the way in which each relies on experience, or in the quality of the experiences that are relied upon, or in the attitudes that scientists or religious believers as such characteristically take toward various kinds of experiences? These are among the questions addressed by the readings in the third section of Part IV.

IV.A. MYSTICAL EXPERIENCE AND THE PERCEPTION OF GOD

Introduction

There was not a mere consciousness of something there, but fused in the central happiness of it, a startling awareness of some ineffable good. Not vague either; not like the emotional effect of some poem, or scene, or blossom, or music, but the sure knowledge of the close presence of a sort of mighty person, and after it went, the memory persisted as the one perception of reality. Everything else might be a dream, but not that.

(AN ANONYMOUS MYSTIC CITED BY WILLIAM JAMES IN *VARIETIES OF RELIGIOUS EXPERIENCE*, 1902.)

ENCOUNTERS WITH THE SUPERNATURAL, a transcendent dimension, the Wholly Other are at the base of every great religion. Abraham hears a Voice calling him to leave his family in Haran and venture out into a broad unknown, thus becoming the father of Israel. Abraham's grandson Jacob wrestles all night with an angel and is transformed, gaining the name *Israel*, "prince of God." While tending his father-in-law's flock, Moses has a vision of "I am that I am" (*Yahweh*) in the burning bush and is ordered to deliver Israel out of slavery into a land flowing with milk and honey. Isaiah has a vision of the Lord "high and exalted, and the skirt of his robe filled the temple" of heaven. In the New Testament, John, James, and Peter behold Jesus gloriously transformed on the Mount of Transfiguration and are themselves transformed by the experience. After the death of Jesus, Saul is traveling to Damascus to persecute Christians, when he is met by a blazing light and hears a Voice, asking him why he is persecuting the Lord. Changing his name to Paul, he becomes the leader of the Christian missionary movement. The Hindu experiences the *Atman* ("soul") as the *Brahman* ("God"), "That art Thou," or beholds the glories of Krishna. The Advaitian Hindu merges with the One, as a drop of water merges with the vast ocean. The Buddhist merges with Nirvana or beholds a vision of the Buddha. Allah reveals his holy word, the Qur'an, to Mohammed. Joan of Arc hears voices calling on her to save her people, and Joseph Smith has a vision of the Angel Moroni, calling him to do a new work for God.

What shall we make of religious experience? Is it a source of information, or justified belief, about God? Does it, in other words, have *evidential value*? Is it perhaps a mode of *perceiving* God? Or is it somehow to be dismissed, perhaps as a mere trick of the brain? These are some of the key questions that will occupy us in the present section.

We begin our study in this part with four descriptions of particular religious experiences from four different traditions: Jewish, Christian, Hindu, and Buddhist. It is important to note that, although the sorts of religious experiences reported in these excerpts are hardly isolated instances, religious experiences fall on a continuum of vividness and intensity, and experiences of a less vivid and intense sort than the "mystical" experiences reported here seem to be far more common. Many religious believers will report having had experiences like feeling overwhelmed by the love or forgiveness of God or feeling at one with nature or the cosmos. Experiences like these are much more ordinary, and it is as important to consider their evidential value as it is to consider the evidential value of mystical experiences like visions of Jesus or the experience of total loss of one's individuality.

Our second selection is an excerpt from William James's classic study *The Varieties of Religious Experience* (1902). In this selection, James describes mystical experience, which he considers to be the deepest kind of religious experience. It is something that transcends our ordinary, sensory experience and that cannot be described in terms of our normal concepts and language. It is "ineffable experience." The subject realizes that the experience "defies expression, that no adequate report of its content can be given in words," James writes. "It follows from this that its quality must be directly experienced; it cannot be imparted or transferred to others." And yet it contains a "noetic quality," a content. It purports to convey truth about the nature of reality, namely, that there is a unity of all things and that that unity is spiritual, not material. It is antinaturalistic, pantheistic, and optimistic. Further, mystical states are *transient*—that is, they cannot be sustained for long—and they are *passive*—that is, the mystic is acted upon by divine deliverance. We may prepare ourselves for the experience, but it is not something that we do; it is something that happens to us.

James is cautious about what can be deduced from mystical experience. Although he thinks that mystical states ought to be taken seriously by the individuals to whom they come, he denies that the rest of us are under any obligation to "accept their revelations uncritically." Nevertheless, he thinks that the mystical experiences of others can still have value for us by opening us up to the idea of alternative modes of experience and alternative ways of acquiring information about spiritual reality.

James's characterization of mysticism and mystical experience has been highly influential. However, in our third selection Grace M. Jantzen argues that James's characterization is misguided, arising more out of his own inaccurate preconceptions about mysticism than out of careful engagement with the writings of the mystics whose work he discusses. She defends this conclusion by examining two paradigm Christian mystics, Bernard of Clairvaux and Julian of Norwich. On her view, a study of these two mystics reveals not only that James has radically mischaracterized the nature of mystical experience, but that he has also misconceived "the essence and goal of the mystical pathway." She notes that if she is right and if her conclusions can be generalized to other mystics in the Christian tradition, then at least two important consequences follow: First, to the extent that subsequent philosophy of religious experience has been significantly shaped by James's characterizations, many of the key arguments in that literature concerning the nature and evidential value of mystical experience will have to be reconsidered. Second, she argues that

> if a study of paradigm mystics causes us thoroughly to reformulate how we are to understand the experience which mystics see as their goal, this leads to creative reformulation also of ideas of knowledge, selfhood, language, and other themes important in modern philosophy. . . .

This is an important consequence indeed.

In our fourth selection, provocatively titled "Perceiving God," William P. Alston defends the idea that religious experience might reasonably be construed as a form of perception. His basic idea is that, because of the ways in which religious experience is analogous to sensory experience, religious experience ought to be taken seriously as a source of justified belief about God. On his view, many of the reasons why people deny that religious experience is a source of evidence about spiritual reality would count equally as reasons to deny that sensory experience is a source of evidence about the external world. But, of course, few of us are willing to deny that sensory experience is a source of evidence. Thus, we should likewise be willing to grant that religious experience has evidential value.

One concern that people sometimes raise about the idea that religious experience has evidential value is that religious experience is typically private. If your friend says that she hears a pleasant tune, and you listen and say, "Yes, I hear it now too," there is no problem; but if you listen carefully and do not hear it, you (and your friend) might well wonder whether your friend is just imagining the sounds she thinks she hears. But the matter does not have to end there. You could try to bring in others to see if they hear the sound. You could also bring in scientific instruments—an audiometer, perhaps. But we can't really do the same with religious experience. You might have the sense of God forgiving you or of an angel speaking to you while your friend, in the same room with you, neither hears, nor sees, nor feels anything unusual. You might be praying and suddenly feel transported by grace and sense the unity of all reality while your friend sitting next to you simply wonders at the strange expression on your face and asks if something is wrong. Unlike in the case of perceptual experience, you cannot seek verification of your experience by bringing in other people, instruments, or other methods to "settle the matter."

According to Alston, the demand for some sort of external verification for our religious experiences is illegitimate because it amounts to holding religious experience to a higher standard than that to which we hold ordinary perceptual experience. In our fifth selection, however, Evan Fales defends a different perspective, arguing that religious experience can count as good evidence for religious belief only to the extent that it can be cross-checked, and that it cannot be cross-checked—or, at any rate, it cannot be cross-checked well enough to allow it to provide "serious support" for theistic religious beliefs.

Another concern that one might raise against the evidential value of religious experience is that there is some reason to think that many, if not all, religious experiences admit of fully naturalistic explanations. Our sixth reading in this section explores this concern. Experimental results in neuroscience have provided reason to think that the phenomenon of religious and mystical experience has a neuropsychological basis. Thus, some have concluded that religious experience has an entirely naturalistic explanation—one need not posit God or any other being of religious significance as the cause or explanation of such experience. It is an interesting question whether this fact undercuts the rationality of believing that religious experience puts us in touch with some genuine spiritual reality. After all, experience of the physical world also has a neuropsychological basis; but we do not doubt that sensory experience puts us in touch with the physical world. In this section's sixth selection, Jeff Jordan argues that the availability of naturalistic explanations for religious experiences would undercut the evidential value of those experiences. However, he says, there is no reason at present to think that all religious experiences admit of a fully naturalistic explanation.

IV.A.1

Selections of Mystical Experiences

AN OLD TESTAMENT SELECTION: THE CALL OF ISAIAH

In the year of King Uzziah's death I saw the Lord seated on a throne, high and exalted, and the skirt of his robe filled the temple. About him were attendant seraphim, and each had six wings; one pair covered his face and one pair his feet, and one pair was spread in flight. They were calling ceaselessly to one another,

> Holy, holy, holy is the Lord of Hosts:
> the whole earth is full of his glory.

And, as each one called, the threshold shook to its foundations, while the house was filled with smoke. Then I cried,

> Woe is me! I am lost,
> for I am a man of unclean lips

and I dwell among a people of unclean lips; yet with these eyes I have seen the King, the LORD of Hosts.

Then one of the seraphim flew to me carrying in his hand a glowing coal which he had taken from the altar with a pair of tongs. He touched my mouth with it and said,

> See, this has touched your lips;
> your iniquity is removed,
> and your sin is wiped away.

Then I heard the Lord saying, Whom shall I send? Who will go for me? And I answered, Here am I; send me. He said, Go and tell this people:

> You may listen and listen, but you will
>   not understand.
> You may look and look again, but you
>   will never know.
> This people's wits are dulled, their ears are
>   deafened and their eyes blinded, so that

they cannot see with their eyes nor listen with their ears nor understand with their wits, so that they may turn and be healed.

ISAIAH, Chapter 6, New English Bible.

THE CHRISTIAN MYSTIC, ST. TERESA OF ÁVILA

One day when I was at prayer . . . I saw Christ at my side—or, to put it better, I was conscious of Him, for I saw nothing with the eyes of the body or the eyes of the soul (the imagination). He seemed quite close to me and I saw that it was He. As I thought, He was speaking to me. Being completely ignorant that such visions were possible, I was very much afraid at first, and could do nothing but weep, though as soon as He spoke His first word of assurance to me, I regained my usual calm, and became cheerful and free from fear. All the time Jesus Christ seemed to be at my side, but as this was not an imaginary vision I could not see in what form. But I most clearly felt that He was all the time on my right, and was a witness of everything that I was doing . . . if I say that I do not see Him with the eyes of the body or the eyes of the soul, because this is no imaginary vision, how then can I know and affirm that he is beside me with greater certainty than if I saw Him? If one says that one is like a person in the dark who cannot see someone though he is beside him, or that one is like somebody who is blind, it is not right. There is some similarity here, but not much, because a person in the dark can perceive with the other senses, or hear his neighbor speak or move, or can touch him. Here this is not so, nor is there any feeling of darkness. On the contrary, He appears to the soul by a knowledge brighter than the sun. I do not mean that any sun is seen, or any brightness, but there is a light which, though unseen, illuminates the understanding.

J. M. Cohen, trans., *The Life of St. Teresa of Ávila,* London: Penguin, 1957.

A HINDU EXAMPLE

The Ego has disappeared. I have realized my identity with Brahman and so all my desires have melted away. I have arisen above my ignorance and my knowledge of this seeming universe. What is this joy I feel? Who shall measure it? I know nothing but joy, limitless, unbounded! The treasure I have found there cannot be described in words. The mind cannot conceive of it. My mind fell like a hailstone into that vast expanse of Brahman's ocean. Touching one drop of it, I melted away and became one with Brahman. Where is this universe? Who took it away? Has it merged into something else? A while ago, I beheld it—now it exists no longer. Is there anything apart or distinct from Brahman? Now, finally and clearly, I know that I am the Atman [the soul identified with Brahman], whose nature is eternal joy. I see nothing, I hear nothing, I know nothing that is separate from me.

Swami Prabhavandanda, trans., *Shankara's Crest-Jewel of Discrimination,* New York: Mentor Books, 1970.

A BUDDHIST MEDITATION

Of one who has entered the first trance the voice has ceased; of one who has entered the second trance reasoning and reflection have ceased; of one who has entered the third trance joy has ceased; of one who has entered the fourth trance the inspiration and expiration have ceased; of one who has entered the realm of the infinity of space the perception of form has ceased; of one who has entered the realm of the infinity of consciousness the perception of the realm of the infinity of space has ceased; of one who has entered the realm of nothingness the perception of the realm of the infinity of consciousness has ceased.

Samyutta-Nikaya, in Henry Clark Warren, ed., *Buddhism: In Translations,* New York: Atheneum, 1973.

IV.A.2

Mysticism

WILLIAM JAMES

William James (1842–1910), American philosopher and psychologist, was one of the most influential thinkers of his time. He taught at Harvard University and is considered, along with C. S. Peirce, to be one of the fathers of pragmatism. The Varieties of Religious Experience *(1902) is his classic study of religious experience. In this selection James describes mystical experience, which he considers to be the deepest kind of religious experience; it is something that transcends our ordinary, sensory experience and that cannot be described in terms of our normal concepts and language.*

Over and over again in these lectures I have raised points and left them open and unfinished until we should have come to the subject of Mysticism. Some of you, I fear, may have smiled as you noted my reiterated postponements. But now the hour has come when mysticism must be faced in good earnest, and those broken threads wound up together. One may say truly, I think, that personal religious experience has its root and centre in mystical states of consciousness; so for us, who in these lectures are treating personal experience as the exclusive subject of our study, such states of consciousness ought to form the vital chapter from which the other chapters get their light. Whether my treatment of mystical states will shed more light or darkness, I do not know, for my own constitution shuts me out from their enjoyment almost entirely, and I can speak of them only at second hand. But though forced to look upon the subject so externally, I will be as objective and receptive as I can; and I think I shall at least succeed in convincing you of the reality of the states in question, and of the paramount importance of their function.

First of all, then, I ask, What does the expression "mystical states of consciousness" mean? How do we part off mystical states from other states?

The words "mysticism" and "mystical" are often used as terms of mere reproach, to throw at any opinion which we regard as vague and vast and sentimental, and without a base in either facts or logic. For some writers a "mystic" is any person who believes in thought-transference, or spirit-return. Employed in this way the word has little value: there are too many less ambiguous synonyms. So, to keep it useful by restricting it, I will do what I did in the case of the word "religion," and simply propose to you four marks which, when an experience has them, may justify us in calling it mystical for the purpose of the present lectures. In this way we shall save verbal disputation, and the recriminations that generally go therewith.

1. Ineffability The handiest of the marks by which I classify a state of mind as mystical is negative. The subject of it immediately says that it defies expression, that no adequate report of its contents can be given in words. It follows from this that its

---

From William James, *The Varieties of Religious Experience* (Longman, Green & Co.: New York, 1902). Some footnotes deleted.

quality must be directly experienced; it cannot be imparted or transferred to others. In this peculiarity mystical states are more like states of feeling than like states of intellect. No one can make clear to another who has never had a certain feeling, in what the quality or worth of it consists. One must have musical ears to know the value of a symphony; one must have been in love one's self to understand a lover's state of mind. Lacking the heart or ear, we cannot interpret the musician or the lover justly, and are even likely to consider him weak-minded or absurd. The mystic finds that most of us accord to his experiences an equally incompetent treatment.

2. Noetic quality   Although so similar to states of feeling, mystical states seem to those who experience them to be also states of knowledge. They are states of insight into depths of truth unplumbed by the discursive intellect. They are illuminations, revelations, full of significance and importance, all inarticulate though they remain; and as a rule they carry with them a curious sense of authority for aftertime.

These two characters will entitle any state to be called mystical, in the sense in which I use the word. Two other qualities are less sharply marked, but are usually found. These are:—

3. Transiency   Mystical states cannot be sustained for long. Except in rare instances, half an hour, or at most an hour or two, seems to be the limit beyond which they fade into the light of common day. Often, when faded, their quality can but imperfectly be reproduced in memory; but when they recur it is recognized; and from one recurrence to another it is susceptible of continuous development in what is felt as inner richness and importance.

4. Passivity   Although the oncoming of mystical states may be facilitated by preliminary voluntary operations, as by fixing the attention, or going through certain bodily performances, or in other ways which manuals of mysticism prescribe; yet when the characteristic sort of consciousness once

has set in, the mystic feels as if his own will were in abeyance, and indeed sometimes as if he were grasped and held by a superior power. This latter peculiarity connects mystical states with certain definite phenomena of secondary or alternative personality, such as prophetic speech, automatic writing, or the mediumistic trance. When these latter conditions are well pronounced, however, there may be no recollection whatever of the phenomenon, and it may have no significance for the subject's usual inner life, to which, as it were, it makes a mere interruption. Mystical states, strictly so-called, are never merely interruptive. Some memory of their content always remains, and a profound sense of their importance. They modify the inner life of the subject between the times of their recurrence. Sharp divisions in this region are, however, difficult to make, and we find all sorts of gradations and mixtures.

These four characteristics are sufficient to mark out a group of states of consciousness peculiar enough to deserve a special name and to call for careful study. Let it then be called the mystical group.

Our next step should be to gain acquaintance with some typical examples. Professional mystics at the height of their development have often elaborately organized experiences and a philosophy based thereupon. But you remember what I said in my first lecture: phenomena are best understood when placed within their series, studied in their germ and in their over-ripe decay, and compared with their exaggerated and degenerated kindred. The range of mystical experience is very wide, much too wide for us to cover in the time at our disposal. Yet the method of serial study is so essential for interpretation that if we really wish to reach conclusions we must use it. I will begin, therefore, with phenomena which claim no special religious significance, and end with those of which the religious pretensions are extreme.

The simplest rudiment of mystical experience would seem to be that deepened sense of the significance of a maxim or formula which occasionally sweeps over one. "I've heard that said all my life," we exclaim, "but I never realized its full meaning until now." "When a fellow-monk," said Luther, "one day repeated the words of the Creed: 'I believe in the forgiveness of sins,' I saw the Scripture in an entirely new light; and straightway I felt as if I were born anew. It was as if I had found the door of paradise thrown wide open." This sense of deeper significance is not confined to rational propositions. Single words, and conjunctions of words, effects of light on land and sea, odors and musical sounds, all bring it when the mind is tuned aright. Most of us can remember the strangely moving power of passages in certain poems read when we were young, irrational doorways as they were through which the mystery of fact, the wildness and the pang of life, stole into our hearts and thrilled them. The words have now perhaps become mere polished surfaces for us; but lyric poetry and music are alive and significant only in proportion as they fetch these vague vistas of a life continuous with our own, beckoning and inviting, yet ever eluding our pursuit. We are alive or dead to the eternal inner message of the arts according as we have kept or lost this mystical susceptibility....

[...]

[An] incommunicableness of the transport is the keynote of all mysticism. Mystical truth exists for the individual who has the transport, but for no one else. In this, as I have said, it resembles the knowledge given to us in sensations more than that given by conceptual thought. Thought, with its remoteness and abstractness, has often enough in the history of philosophy been contrasted unfavorably with sensation. It is a commonplace of metaphysics that God's knowledge cannot be discursive but must be intuitive, that is, must be constructed more after the pattern of what in ourselves is called immediate feeling, than after that of proposition and judgment. But *our* immediate feelings have no content but what the five senses supply; and we have seen and shall see again that mystics may emphatically deny that the senses play any part in the very highest type of knowledge which their transports yield.

In the Christian church there have always been mystics. Although many of them have been viewed with suspicion, some have gained favor in the eyes of the authorities. The experiences of these have been treated as precedents, and a codified system of mystical theology has been based upon them, in which everything legitimate finds its place. The basis of the system is "orison" or meditation, the methodical elevation of the soul towards God. Through the practice of orison the higher levels of mystical experience may be attained. It is odd that Protestantism, especially evangelical Protestantism, should seemingly have abandoned everything methodical in this line. Apart from what prayer may lead to, Protestant mystical experience appears to have been almost exclusively sporadic. It has been left to our mind-curers to reintroduce methodical meditation into our religious life.

The first thing to be aimed at in orison is the mind's detachment from outer sensations for these interfere with its concentration upon ideal things. Such manuals as Saint Ignatius's *Spiritual Exercises* recommend the disciple to expel sensation by a graduated series of efforts to imagine holy scenes. The acme of this kind of discipline would be a semi-hallucinatory mono-ideism—an imaginary figure of Christ, for example, coming fully to occupy the mind. Sensorial images of this sort, whether literal or symbolic, play an enormous part in mysticism. But in certain cases imagery may fall away entirely, and in the very highest raptures it tends to do so. The state of consciousness becomes then insusceptible of any verbal description. Mystical teachers are unanimous as to this. Saint John of the Cross, for instance, one of the best of them, thus describes the condition called the "union of love," which, he says, is reached by "dark contemplation." In this the Deity compensates the soul, but in such a hidden way that the soul—

> finds no terms, no means, no comparison whereby to render the sublimity of the wisdom and the delicacy of the spiritual feeling with which she is filled.... We receive this mystical knowledge of God clothed in none of the kinds of images, in none of the sensible representations, which our mind makes use of in other circumstances. Accordingly in this knowledge,

since the senses and the imagination are not employed, we get neither form nor impression, nor can we give any account or furnish any likeness, although the mysterious and sweet-tasting wisdom comes home so clearly to the inmost parts of our soul. Fancy a man seeing a certain kind of thing for the first time in his life. He can understand it, use and enjoy it, but he cannot apply a name to it, nor communicate any idea of it, even though all the while it be a mere thing of sense. How much greater will be his powerlessness when it goes beyond the senses! This is the peculiarity of the divine language. The more infused, intimate, spiritual, and supersensible it is, the more does it exceed the senses, both inner and outer, and impose silence upon them.

... The soul then feels as if placed in a vast and profound solitude, to which no created thing has access, in an immense and boundless desert, desert the more delicious the more solitary it is. There, in this abyss of wisdom, the soul grows by what it drinks in from the wellsprings of the comprehension of love, ... and recognizes, however sublime and learned may be the terms we employ, how utterly vile, insignificant, and improper they are, when we seek to discourse of divine things by their means.

I cannot pretend to detail to you the sundry stages of the Christian mystical life. Our time would not suffice, for one thing; and moreover, I confess that the subdivisions and names which we find in the Catholic books seem to me to represent nothing objectively distinct. So many men, so many minds; I imagine that these experiences can be as infinitely varied as are the idiosyncrasies of individuals.

The cognitive aspects of them, their value in the way of revelation, is what we are directly concerned with, and it is easy to show by citation how strong an impression they leave of being revelations of new depths of truth. Saint Teresa is the expert of experts in describing such conditions, so I will turn immediately to what she says of one of the highest of them, the "orison of union."

In the orison of union (says Saint Teresa) the soul is fully awake as regards God, but wholly asleep as regards things of this world and in respect of herself. During the short time the union lasts, she is as it were deprived of every feeling, and even if she would, she could not think of any single thing. Thus she needs to employ no artifice in order to arrest the use of her understanding: it remains so stricken with inactivity that she neither knows what she loves, nor in what manner she loves, nor what she wills. In short, she is utterly dead to the things of the world and lives solely in God.... I do not even know whether in this state she has enough life left to breathe. It seems to me she has not; or at least that if she does breathe, she is unaware of it. Her intellect would fain understand something of what is going on within her, but it has so little force now that it can act in no way whatsoever. So a person who falls into a deep faint appears as if dead....

Thus does God, when he raises a soul to union with himself, suspend the natural action of all her faculties. She neither sees, hears, nor understands, so long as she is united with God. But this time is always short, and it seems even shorter than it is. God establishes himself in the interior of this soul in such a way, that when she returns to herself, it is wholly impossible for her to doubt that she has been in God, and God in her. This truth remains so strongly impressed on her that, even though many years should pass without the condition returning, she can neither forget the favor she received, nor doubt of its reality. If you, nevertheless, ask how it is possible that the soul can see and understand that she has been in God, since during the union she has neither sight nor understanding, I reply that she does not see it then, but that she sees it clearly later, after she has returned to herself, not by any vision, but by a certitude which abides with her and which God alone can give her. I knew a person who was ignorant of the truth that God's mode of being in everything must be either by presence, by power, or by essence, but who, after having received the grace of which I am speaking, believed this truth in the most unshakable manner. So much so that, having consulted a half-learned man who was as ignorant on this point as she had been before she was enlightened, when he replied that God is in us only by "grace," she disbelieved his reply, so sure she was of the true answer; and when she came to ask wiser doctors, they confirmed her in her belief, which much consoled her....

But how, you will repeat, can one have such certainty in respect to what one does not see? This question, I am powerless to answer. These are secrets of God's omnipotence which it does not appertain to me to penetrate. All that I know is that I tell the truth; and I shall never believe that any soul who does not possess this certainty has ever been really united to God.

The kinds of truth communicable in mystical ways, whether these be sensible or supersensible, are various. Some of them relate to this world—visions of the future, the reading of hearts, the sudden understanding of texts, the knowledge of distant events, for example; but the most important revelations are theological or metaphysical.

Saint Ignatius confessed one day to Father Laynez that a single hour of meditation at Manresa had taught him more truths about heavenly things than all the teachings of all the doctors put together could have taught him.... One day in orison, on the steps of the choir of the Dominican church, he saw in a distinct manner the plan of divine wisdom in the creation of the world. On another occasion, during a procession, his spirit was ravished in God, and it was given him to contemplate, in a form and images fitted to the weak understanding of a dweller on the earth, the deep mystery of the holy Trinity. This last vision flooded his heart with such sweetness, that the mere memory of it in after times made him shed abundant tears.

Similarly with Saint Teresa.

One day, being in orison (she writes), it was granted me to perceive in one instant how all things are seen and contained in God. I did not perceive them in their proper form, and nevertheless the view I had of them was of a sovereign clearness, and has remained vividly impressed upon my soul. It is one of the most signal of all the graces which the Lord has granted me.... The view was so subtle and delicate that the understanding cannot grasp it.

She goes on to tell how it was as if the Deity were an enormous and sovereignly limpid diamond, in which all our actions were contained in such a way their full sinfulness appeared evident as never before. On another day, she relates, while she was reciting the Athanasian Creed—

Our Lord made me comprehend in what way it is that one God can be in three persons. He made me see it so clearly that I remained as extremely surprised as I was comforted, ... and now, when I think of the holy Trinity, or hear It spoken of, I understand how the three adorable Persons form only one God and I experience an unspeakable happiness.

On still another occasion it was given to Saint Teresa to see and understand in what wise the Mother of God had been assumed into her place in Heaven.

The deliciousness of some of these states seems to be beyond anything known in ordinary consciousness. It evidently involves organic sensibilities, for it is spoken of as something too extreme to be borne, and as verging on bodily pain. But it is too subtle and piercing a delight for ordinary words to denote. God's touches, the wounds of his spear, references to ebriety and to nuptial union have to figure in the phraseology by which it is shadowed forth. Intellect and senses both swoon away in these highest states of ecstasy. "If our understanding comprehends," says Saint Teresa, "it is in a mode which remains unknown to it, and it can understand nothing of what it comprehends. For my own part, I do not believe that it does comprehend, because, as I said, it does not understand itself to do so. I confess that it is all a mystery in which I am lost." In the condition called *raptus* or ravishment by theologians, breathing and circulation are so depressed that it is a question among the doctors whether the soul be or be not temporarily dissevered from the body. One must read Saint Teresa's descriptions and the very exact distinctions which she makes, to persuade one's self that one is dealing, not with imaginary experiences, but with phenomena which, however rare, follow perfectly definite psychological types.

To the medical mind these ecstasies signify nothing but suggested and imitated hypnoid states, on an intellectual basis of superstition, and a corporeal one of degeneration and hysteria. Undoubtedly these pathological conditions have existed in many and possibly in all the cases, but that fact tells us nothing about the value for knowledge of the consciousness which they induce. To pass a spiritual judgment upon these states, we must not content ourselves with superficial medical talk, but inquire into their fruits for life.

Their fruits appear to have been various. Stupefaction, for one thing, seems not to have been altogether absent as a result. You may remember the helplessness in the kitchen and schoolroom of poor Margaret Mary Alacoque. Many other ecstatics would have perished but for the care taken of them by admiring followers. The "otherworldliness" encouraged by the mystical consciousness makes this over-abstraction from practical life peculiarly liable to befall mystics in whom the character is naturally passive and the intellect feeble; but in natively strong minds and characters we find quite opposite results. The great Spanish mystics, who carried the habit of ecstasy as far as it has often carried, appear for the most part to have shown indomitable spirit and energy, and all the more so for the trances in which they indulged.

Saint Ignatius was a mystic, but his mysticism made him assuredly one of the most powerfully practical human engines that ever lived. Saint John of the Cross, writing of the intuitions and "touches" by which God reaches the substance of the soul, tells us that—

> They enrich it marvelously. A single one of them may be sufficient to abolish at a stroke certain imperfections of which the soul during its whole life had vainly tried to rid itself, and to leave it adorned with virtues and loaded with supernatural gifts. A single one of these intoxicating consolations may reward it for all the labors undergone in its life—even were they numberless. Invested with an invincible courage, filled with an impassioned desire to suffer for its God, the soul then is seized with a strange torment—that of not being allowed to suffer enough.

Saint Teresa is as emphatic, and much more detailed. You may perhaps remember a passage I quoted from her in my first lecture. There are many similar pages in her autobiography. Where in literature is a more evidently veracious account of the formation of a new centre of spiritual energy, than is given in her description of the effects of certain ecstasies which in departing leave the soul upon a higher level of emotional excitement?

> Often, infirm and wrought upon with dreadful pains before the ecstasy, the soul emerges from it full of health and admirably disposed for action ... as if God had willed that the body itself, already obedient to the soul's desires, should share in

the soul's happiness.... The soul after such a favor is animated with a degree of courage so great that if at that moment its body should be torn to pieces for the cause of God, it would feel nothing but the liveliest comfort. Then it is that promises and heroic resolutions spring up in profusion in us, soaring desires, horror of the world, and the clear perception of our proper nothingness.... What empire is comparable to that of a soul who, from this sublime summit to which God has raised her, sees all the things of earth beneath her feet, and is captivated by no one of them? How ashamed she is of her former attachments! How amazed at her blindness! What lively pity she feels for those whom she recognizes still shrouded in the darkness! ... She groans at having ever been sensitive to points of honor, at the illusion that made her ever see as honor what the world calls by that name. Now she sees in this name nothing more than an immense lie of which the world remains a victim. She discovers, in the new light from above, that in genuine honor there is nothing spurious, that to be faithful to this honor is to give our respect to what deserves to be respected really, and to consider as nothing, or as less than nothing, whatsoever perishes and is not agreeable to God.... She laughs when she sees grave persons, persons of orison, caring for points of honor for which she now feels profoundest contempt. It is suitable to the dignity of their rank to act thus, they pretend, and it makes them more useful to others. But she knows that in despising the dignity of their rank for the pure love of God they would do more good in a single day than they would effect in ten years by preserving it.... She laughs at herself that there should ever have been a time in her life when she made any case of money, when she ever desired it.... Oh! if human beings might only agree together to regard it as so much useless mud, what harmony would then reign in the world! With what friendship we would all treat each other if our interest in honor and in money could but disappear from earth! For my own part, I feel as if it would be a remedy for all our ills.

Mystical conditions may, therefore, render the soul more energetic in the lines which their inspiration favors. But this could be reckoned an advantage only in case the inspiration were a true one. If the inspiration were erroneous, the energy would be all the more mistaken and misbegotten. So we stand once more before the problem of truth which confronted us at the end of the lectures on saintliness. You will remember that we turned to mysticism precisely to get some light on truth. Do mystical states establish the truth of those theological affections in which the saintly life has its root?

In spite of their repudiation of articulate self-description, mystical states in general assert a pretty distinct theoretic drift. It is possible to give the outcome of the majority of them in terms that point in definite philosophical directions. One of these directions is optimism, and the other is monism. We pass into mystical states from out of ordinary consciousness as from a less into a more, as from a smallness into a vastness, and at the same time as from an unrest to a rest. We feel them as reconciling, unifying states. They appeal to the yes-function more than to the no-function in us. In them the unlimited absorbs the limits and peacefully closes the account. Their very denial of every adjective you may propose as applicable to the ultimate truth—He, the Self, the Atman, is to be described by "No! no!": only, say the Upanishads—though it seems on the surface to be a no-function, is a denial made on behalf of a deeper yes. Whoso calls the Absolute anything in particular, or says that it is this, seems implicitly to shut it off from being *that*—it is as if he lessened it. So we deny the "this," negating the negation which it seems to us to imply, in the interests of the higher affirmative attitude by which we are possessed. The fountain-head of Christian mysticism is Dionysius the Areopagite.

He describes the absolute truth by negatives exclusively.

> The cause of all things is neither soul nor intellect; nor has it imagination, opinion, or reason, or intelligence; nor is it reason or intelligence; nor is it spoken or thought. It is neither number, nor order, nor magnitude, nor littleness, nor equality, nor inequality, nor similarity, nor dissimilarity. It neither stands, nor moves, nor rests. . . . It is neither essence, nor eternity, nor time. Even intellectual contact does not belong to it. It is neither science nor truth. It is not even royalty or wisdom; not one; not unity; not divinity or goodness; nor even spirit as we know it (etc., *ad libitum*).

But these qualifications are denied by Dionysius, not because the truth falls short of them, but because it so infinitely excels them. It is above them. It is *super*-lucent, *super*-splendent, *super*-essential, *super*-sublime, *super* everything that can be named. Like Hegel in his logic, mystics journey towards the positive pole of truth only by the "Methode der Absoluten Negativität."

Thus come the paradoxical expressions that so abound in mystical writings. As when Eckhart tells of the still desert of the Godhead, "where never was seen difference, neither Father, Son, nor Holy Ghost, where there is no one at home, yet where the spark of the soul is more at peace than in itself." As when Boehme writes of the Primal Love, that "it may fitly be compared to Nothing, for it is deeper than any Thing, and is as nothing with respect to all things, forasmuch as it is not comprehensible by any of them. And because it is nothing respectively, it is therefore free from all things, and is that only good, which a man cannot express or utter what it is, there being nothing to which it may be compared, to express it by." Or as when Angelus Silesius sings:—

> [God is pure Nothing. Neither Now
> nor Here affects Him.
> But the more you grasp him,
> the more He disappears"] (Ed. trans.)

To this dialectical use, by the intellect, of negation as a mode of passage towards a higher kind of affirmation, there is correlated the subtlest of moral counterparts in the sphere of the personal will. Since denial of the finite self and its wants, since asceticism of some sort, is found in religious experience to be the only doorway to the larger and more blessed life, this moral mystery intertwines and combines with the intellectual mystery in all mystical writings.

> Love (continues Boehme) [is Nothing, for] when thou art gone forth wholly from the Creature and from that which is visible, and art become Nothing to all that is Nature and Creature, then thou art in that eternal One, which is God himself, and then thou shalt feel within thee the highest virtue of Love. . . . The treasure of treasures for the soul is where she goeth out of the Somewhat into that Nothing out of which all things may be made. The soul here saith, *I have nothing*, for I am utterly stripped and naked; *I can do nothing*, for I have no manner of power, but am as water poured out; *I am nothing*, for all that I am is no more than an image of Being, and only God is to me I AM; and so, sitting down in my own Nothingness, I give glory to the eternal Being, and *will nothing* of myself, that so God may will all in me, being unto me my God and all things.

In Paul's language, I live, yet not I, but Christ liveth in me. Only when I become as nothing can God enter in and no difference between his life and mine remain outstanding.

This overcoming of all the usual barriers between the individual and the Absolute is the great mystic achievement. In mystic states we both become one with the Absolute and we become aware of our oneness. This is the everlasting and triumphant mystical tradition, hardly altered by differences of clime or creed. In Hinduism, in Neoplatonism, in Sufism, in Christian mysticism, in Whitmanism, we find the same recurring note, so that there is about mystical utterances an eternal unanimity which ought to make a critic stop and think, and which brings it about that the mystical classics have, as has been said, neither birthday nor native land. Perpetually telling of the unity of man with God, their speech antedates languages, and they do not grow old.

"That are Thou!" says the Upanishads, and the Vedantists add: "Not a part, nor a mode of That, but identically That, that absolute Spirit of the World." "As pure water poured into pure water remains the same, thus, O Gautama, is the Self of a thinker who knows. Water in water, fire in fire, ether in ether, no one can distinguish them: likewise a man whose mind has entered into the self." "Everyman," says the Sufi Gulshan-Raz, "whose heart is no longer shaken by any doubts, knows with certainty that there is no being save only One.... In his divine majesty the me, and we, the thou, are not found, for in the One there can be no distinction. Every being who is annulled and entirely separated from himself, hears resound outside of him this voice and this echo: *I am God*: he has an eternal way of existing, and is no longer subject to death." In the vision of God, says Plotinus, "what sees is not our reason, but something prior and superior to our reason—He who thus sees does not properly see, does not distinguish or imagine two things. He changes, he ceases to be himself, preserves nothing of himself. Absorbed in God, he makes but one with him, like a Centre of a circle coinciding with another centre." "Here," writes Suso, "the spirit dies, and yet is all alive in the marvels of the Godhead ... and is lost in the stillness of the glorious dazzling obscurity and of the naked simple unity. It is in this modeless *where* that the highest bliss is to be found." "Ich bin so gross als Gott," ["I am as great as God,"] sings Angelus Silesius again, "Er ist als ich so klein; Er kann nicht über mich, ich unter ihm nicht sein." ["He is as small as I. He cannot be above me, nor I under Him."] (Translations by Louis Pojman)

In mystical literature such self-contradictory phrases as "dazzling obscurity," "whispering silence," "teeming desert," are continually met with. They prove that not conceptual speech, but music rather, is the element through which we are best spoken to by mystical truth. Many mystical scriptures are indeed little more than musical compositions.

He who would hear the voice of Nada, "the Soundless Sound," and comprehend it, he has to learn the nature of Dhâranâ.... When to him-self his form appears unreal, as do on waking all the forms he sees in dreams; when he has ceased to hear the many, he may discern the ONE—the inner sound which kills the outer.... For then the soul will hear, and will remember. And then to the inner ear will speak THE VOICE OF THE SILENCE.... And now thy *Self* is lost in SELF, *thyself* unto THY-SELF, merged in that SELF from which thou first didst radiate.... Behold! thou hast become the Light, thou hast become the Sound, thou art thy Master and thy God. Thou art THYSELF the object of thy search: the VOICE unbroken, that resounds throughout eternities, exempt from change, from sin exempt, the seven sounds in one, the VOICE OF THE SILENCE. *Om tat Sat.*

These words, if they do not awaken laughter as you receive them, probably stir chords within you which music and language touch in common. Music gives us ontological messages which non-musical criticism is unable to contradict, though it may laugh at our foolishness in minding them. There is a verge of the mind which these things haunt; and whispers there-from mingle with the operations of our understanding, even as the waters of the infinite ocean send their waves to break among the pebbles that lie upon our shores.

> Here begins the sea that ends not till the
>   world's end. Where we stand,
> Could we know the next high sea-mark
>   set beyond these waves that gleam,
> We should know what never man hath
>   known, nor eye of man hath scanned.
> . . .
> Ah, but here man's heart leaps, yearning
>   towards the gloom with venturous glee,
> From the shore that hath no shore beyond
>   it, set in all the sea.

That doctrine, for example, that eternity is timeless, that our "immortality," if we live in the eternal, is not so much future as already now and here, which we find so often expressed today in certain philosophical circles, finds its support in a "hear, hear!" or an "amen," which floats up from that mysteriously deeper level. We recognize the passwords to the mystical region as we hear them, but we cannot use them ourselves; it alone has the keeping of "the password primeval."

I have now sketched with extreme brevity and insufficiency, but as fairly as I am able in the time allowed, the general traits of the mystic range of consciousness. *It is on the whole pantheistic and optimistic, or at least the opposite of pessimistic. It is antinaturalistic, and harmonizes best with twice-bornness and so-called other-worldly states of mind.*

My next task is to inquire whether we can invoke it as authoritative. Does it furnish any *warrant for the truth* of the twice-bornness and supernaturality and pantheism which it favors? I must give my answer to this question as concisely as I can.

In brief my answer is this—and I will divide it into three parts:—

1. Mystical states, when well developed, usually are, and have the right to be, absolutely authoritative over the individuals to whom they come.

2. No authority emanates from them which should make it a duty for those who stand outside of them to accept their revelations uncritically.

3. They break down the authority of the non-mystical or rationalistic consciousness, based upon the understanding and the senses alone. They show it to be only one kind of consciousness. They open out the possibility of other orders of truth, in which, so far as anything in us vitally responds to them, we may freely continue to have faith.

I will take up these points one by one.

1. As a matter of psychological fact, mystical states of a well-pronounced and emphatic sort are usually authoritative over those who have them. They have been "there," and know. It is vain for rationalism to grumble about this. If the mystical truth that comes to a man proves to be a force that he can live by, what mandate have we of the majority to order him to live in another way? We can throw him into a prison or a madhouse, but we cannot change his mind—we commonly attach it only the more stubbornly to its beliefs. It mocks our utmost efforts, as a matter of fact, and in point of logic it absolutely escapes our jurisdiction. Our own more "rational" beliefs are based on evidence exactly similar in nature to that which mystics quote for theirs. Our senses, namely, have assured us of certain states of fact; but mystical experiences are as direct perceptions of fact for those who have them as any sensations ever were for us. The records show that even though the five senses be in abeyance in them, they are absolutely sensational in their epistemological quality, if I may be pardoned the barbarous expression—that is, they are face to face presentations of what seems immediately to exist.

The mystic is, in short, *invulnerable*, and must be left, whether we relish it or not, in undisturbed enjoyment of his creed. Faith, says Tolstoy, is that by which men live. And faith-state and mystic state are practically convertible terms.

2. But I now proceed to add that mystics have no right to claim that we ought to accept the deliverance of their peculiar experiences, if we are ourselves outsiders and feel no private call thereto. The utmost they can ever ask of us in this life is to admit that they establish a presumption. They form a consensus and have an unequivocal outcome; and it would be odd, mystics might say, if such a unanimous type of experience should prove to be altogether wrong. At bottom, however, this would only be an appeal to numbers, like the appeal of rationalism the other way; and the appeal to numbers has no logical force. If we acknowledge it, it is for "suggestive," not for logical reasons: we follow the majority because to do so suits our life.

But even this presumption from the unanimity of mystics is far from being strong. In characterizing mystic states as pantheistic, optimistic, etc., I am afraid I over-simplified the truth. I did so for expository reasons, and to keep the closer to the classic mystical tradition. The classic religious mysticism, it now must be confessed, is only a "privileged case." It is an *extract*, kept true to type by the selection of the fittest specimens and their preservation in "schools." It is carved out from a much larger mass; and if we take the larger mass as seriously as religious mysticism has historically taken itself, we find that the supposed unanimity largely disappears. To begin with, even religious mysticism itself, the kind that accumulates traditions and makes schools, is much less unanimous than I have allowed. It has been both ascetic and antinomianly self-indulgent within the Christian church. It is dualistic in Sankhya, and monistic in Vedanta philosophy. I called it pantheistic; but the great Spanish mystics are anything but pantheists. They are with few exceptions non-metaphysical minds, for whom "the category of personality" is absolute. The "union" of man with God is for them much more like an occasional miracle than like an original identity. How different again, apart from the happiness common to all, is the mysticism of Walt Whitman, Edward Carpenter, Richard Jefferies, and other naturalistic pantheists, from the more distinctively Christian sort. The fact is that the mystical feeling of enlargement, union, and emancipation has no specific intellectual content whatever of its own. It is capable of forming matrimonial alliances with material furnished by the most diverse philosophies and theologies, provided only they can find a place in their framework for its peculiar emotional mood. We have no right, therefore, to invoke its prestige as distinctively in favor of any special belief, such as that in absolute idealism, or in the absolute monistic identity, or in the absolute goodness, of the world. It is only relatively in favor of all these things—it passes out of common human consciousness in the direction in which they lie.

So much for religious mysticism proper. But more remains to be told, for religious mysticism is only one half of mysticism. The other half has no accumulated traditions except those which the textbooks on insanity supply. Open any one of these and you will find abundant cases in which "mystical ideas" are cited as characteristic symptoms of enfeebled or deluded states of mind. In delusional insanity, paranoia, as they sometimes call it, we may have a *diabolical* mysticism, a sort of religious mysticism turned upside down. The same sense of ineffable importance in the smallest events, the same texts and words coming with new meanings, the same voices and visions and leadings and missions, the same controlling by extraneous powers; only this time the emotion is pessimistic: instead of consolations we have desolations; the meanings are dreadful; and the powers are enemies to life. It is evident from the point of view of their psychological mechanism, the classic mysticism and these lower mysticisms spring from the same mental level, from that great subliminal or transmarginal region of which science is beginning to admit the existence, but of which so little is really known. That region contains every kind of matter: "seraph and snake" abide there side by side. To come from thence is no infallible credential. What comes must be sifted and tested, and run the gauntlet of confrontation with the total context of experience, just like what comes from the outer world of sense. Its value must be ascertained by empirical methods, so long as we are not mystics ourselves.

Once more, then, I repeat that non-mystics are under no obligation to acknowledge in mystical states a superior authority conferred on them by their intrinsic nature.

3. Yet, I repeat once more, the existence of mystical states absolutely overthrows the pretension of non-mystical states to be the sole and ultimate dictators of what we may believe. As a rule, mystical states merely add a supersensuous meaning to the ordinary outward data of consciousness. They are excitements like the emotions of love or ambition, gifts to our spirit by means of which facts already objectively before us fall into a new expressiveness and make a new connection with our active life. They do not contradict these facts as such, or deny anything that our senses have immediately seized. It is the rationalistic critic rather who plays the part of denier in the controversy, and his denials have no strength, for there never can be a state of facts to which new meaning may not truthfully be added, provided the mind ascend to a more

enveloping point of view. It must always remain an open question whether mystical states may not possibly be such superior points of view, windows through which the mind looks out upon a more extensive and inclusive world. The difference of the views seen from the different mystical windows need not prevent us from entertaining this supposition. The wider world would in that case prove to have a mixed constitution like that of this world, that is all. It would have its celestial and its infernal regions, its tempting and its saving moments, its valid experiences and its counterfeit ones, just as our world has them; but it would be a wider world all the same. We should have to use its experiences by selecting and subordinating and substituting just as is our custom in this ordinary naturalistic world; we should be liable to error just as we are now; yet the counting in of that wider world of meanings, and the serious dealing with it, might, in spite of all the perplexity, be indispensable stages in our approach to the final fullness of the truth.

In this shape, I think, we have to leave the subject. Mystical states indeed wield no authority due simply to their being mystical states. But the higher ones among them point in directions to which the religious sentiments even of non-mystical men incline. They tell of the supremacy of the ideal, of vastness, of union, of safety, and of rest. They offer us *hypotheses*, hypotheses which we may voluntarily ignore, but which as thinkers we cannot possibly upset. The supernaturalism and optimism to which they would persuade us may, interpreted in one way or another, be after all the truest of insights into the meaning of this life.

"Oh, the little more, and how much it is; and the little less, and what worlds away!" It may be that possibility and permission of this sort are all that our religious consciousness requires to live on. In my last lecture I shall have to try to persuade you that this is the case. Meanwhile, however, I am sure that for many of my readers this diet is too slender. If supernaturalism and inner union with the divine are true, you think, then not so much permission, as compulsion to believe, ought to be found. Philosophy has always professed to prove religious truth by coercive argument; and the construction of philosophies of this kind has always been one favorite function of the religious life, if we use this term in the large historic sense. But religious philosophy is an enormous subject, and in my next lecture I can only give that brief glance at it which my limits will allow.

CONCLUSIONS ON RELIGIOUS EXPERIENCE

Let us agree, then, that Religion, occupying herself with personal destinies and keeping thus in contact with the only absolute realities which we know, must necessarily play an eternal part in human history. The next thing to decide is what she reveals about those destinies, or whether indeed she reveals anything distinct enough to be considered a general message to mankind. We have done as you see, with our preliminaries, and our final summing up can now begin. . . .

Both thought and feeling are determinants of conduct, and the same conduct may be determined either by feeling or by thought. When we survey the whole field of religion, we find a great variety in the thoughts that have prevailed there; but the feelings on the one hand and the conduct on the other are almost always the same, for Stoic, Christian, and Buddhist saints are practically indistinguishable in their lives. The theories which Religion generates, being thus variable, are secondary; and if you wish to grasp her essence, you must look to the feelings and the conduct as being the more constant elements. It is between these two elements that the short circuit exists on which she carries on her principal business, while the ideas and symbols and other institutions form loop-lines which may be perfections and improvements, and may even some day all be united into one harmonious system, but which are not to be regarded as organs with an indispensable function, necessary at all times for religious life to go on. This seems to me the first conclusion which we are entitled to draw from the phenomena we have passed in review.

The next step is to characterize the feelings. To what psychological order do they belong?

The resultant outcome of them is in any case what Kant calls "sthenic" affection, an excitement of the cheerful, expansive, "dynamogenic" order which, like any tonic, freshens our vital powers. In almost every lecture, but especially in the lectures on Conversion and on Saintliness, we have seen how this emotion overcomes temperamental melancholy and imparts endurance to the Subject, or a zest, or a meaning, or an enchantment and glory to the common objects of life. The name of "faith state," by which Professor Leuba designates it, is a good one. It is a biological as well as a psychological condition, and Tolstoy is absolutely accurate in classing faith among the forces *by which men live.* The total absence of it, anhedonia, means collapse.

The faith-state may hold a very minimum of intellectual content. We saw examples of this in those sudden raptures of the divine presence, or in such mystical seizures as Dr. Bucke described. It may be a mere vague enthusiasm, half spiritual, half vital, a courage, and a feeling that great and wondrous things are in the air.

When, however, a positive intellectual content is associated with a faith-state, it gets invincibly stamped in upon belief, and this explains the passionate loyalty of religious persons everywhere to the minutest details of their so widely differing creeds. Taking creeds and faith-state together, as forming "religions," and treating these as purely subjective phenomena, without regard to the question of their "truth," we are obliged, on account of their extraordinary influence upon action and endurance, to class them amongst the most important biological functions of mankind. Their stimulant and anaesthetic effect is so great that Professor Leuba, in a recent article, goes so far as to say that so long as men can use their God, they care very little who he is, or even whether he is at all. "The truth of the matter can be put," says Leuba, "in this way: *God is not known, he is not understood; he is used*—sometimes as meat-purveyor, sometimes as moral support, sometimes as friend, sometimes as an object of love. If he proves himself useful, the religious consciousness asks for no more than that. Does God really exist? How does he exist? What is he? are so many irrelevant questions. Not God, but life, more life, a larger, richer, more

satisfying life is, in the last analysis, the end of religion. The love of life, at any and every level of development, is the religious impulse."

At this purely subjective rating, therefore, Religion must be considered vindicated in a certain way from the attacks of her critics. It would seem that she cannot be a mere anachronism and survival, but must exert a permanent function, whether she be with or without intellectual content, and whether, if she have any, it be true or false.

We must next pass beyond the point of view of merely subjective utility, and make inquiry into the intellectual content itself.

First, is there, under all the discrepancies of the creeds, a common nucleus to which they bear their testimony unanimously?

And second, ought we to consider the testimony true?

I will take up the first question first, and answer it immediately in the affirmative. The warring gods and formulas of the various religions do indeed cancel each other, but there is a certain uniform deliverance in which religions all appear to meet. It consists of two parts:—

1. An uneasiness; and
2. Its solution.

1. The uneasiness, reduced to its simplest terms, is a sense that there is *something wrong about us* as we naturally stand.
2. The solution is a sense that *we are saved from the wrongness* by making proper connection with the higher powers.

In those more developed minds, which alone we are studying, the wrongness takes a moral character, and the salvation takes a mystical tinge. I think we shall keep well within the limits of what is common to all such minds if we formulate the essence of their religious experience in terms like these:—

The individual, so far as he suffers from his wrongness and criticizes it, is to that extent consciously beyond it, and in at least possible touch with something higher, if anything higher exist. Along with the wrong part there is thus a better part of him, even though it may be but a most helpless germ. With which part he should identify his real being is by no means obvious at this stage; but when stage 2 (the stage of solution or salvation) arrives, the man identifies his real being with the germinal higher part of himself; and does so in the following way. *He becomes conscious that this higher part is conterminous and continuous with a more of the same quality, which is operative in the universe outside of him, and which he can keep in working touch with, and in a fashion get on board of and save himself when all his lower being has gone to pieces in the wreck.*

It seems to me that all the phenomena are accurately describable in these very simple general terms. They allow for the divided self and the struggle; they involve the change of personal centre and the surrender of the lower self; they express the appearance of exteriority of the helping power and yet account for our sense of union with it; and they fully justify our feelings of security and joy. There is probably no autobiographic document, among all those which I have quoted, to which the description will not well apply. One need only add such specific details as will adapt it to various theologies and various personal temperaments, and one will then have the various experiences reconstructed in their individual forms.

So far, however, as this analysis goes, the experiences are only psychological phenomena. They possess, it is true, enormous biological worth. Spiritual strength really increases in the subject when he has them, a new life opens for him, and they seem to him a place of conflux where the forces of two universes meet; and yet this may be nothing but his subjective way of feeling things, a mood of his own fancy, in spite of the effects produced. I now turn to my second question: What is the objective "truth" of their content?

The part of the content concerning which the question of truth most pertinently arises is that "MORE of the same quality" with which our own higher self appears in the experience to come into harmonious working relation. Is such a "more" merely our own notion, or does it really exist? If so, in what shape does it exist? Does it act, as well as exist? And in what form should we conceive of that "union" with it of which religious geniuses are so convinced?

It is in answering these questions that the various theologies perform their theoretic work, and that their divergencies most come to light. They all agree that the "more" really exists; though some of them hold it to exist in the shape of a personal god or gods, while others are satisfied to conceive it as a stream of ideal tendency embedded in the eternal structure of the world. They all agree, moreover, that it acts as well as exists, and that something really is effected for the better when you throw your life into its hands. It is when they treat of the experience of "union" with it that their speculative differences appear most clearly. Over this point pantheism and theism, nature and second birth, works and grace and karma, immortality and reincarnation, rationalism and mysticism, carry on inveterate disputes.

At the end of my lecture on Philosophy I held out the notion that an impartial science of religions might sift out from the midst of their discrepancies a common body of doctrine which she might also formulate in terms to which physical science need not object. This, I said, she might adopt as her own reconciling hypothesis, and recommend it for general belief. I also said that in my last lecture I should have to try my own hand at framing such an hypothesis.

The time has now come for this attempt. Who says "hypothesis" renounces the ambition to be coercive in his arguments. The most I can do is, accordingly, to offer something that may fit the facts so easily that your scientific logic will find no plausible pretext for vetoing your impulse to welcome it as true.

The "more," as we called it, and the meaning of our "union" with it, form the nucleus of our inquiry. Into what definite description can these words be translated, and for what definite facts do they stand? It would never do for us to place ourselves offhand at the position of a particular theology, the Christian theology, for example, and proceed immediately to define the "more" as Jehovah, and the "union" as his imputation to us of the righteousness of Christ. That would be unfair to other religions, and from our present standpoint at least, would be an over-belief.

We must begin by using less particularized terms; and, since one of the duties of the science of religions is to keep religion in connection with the rest of science, we shall do well to seek first of all a way of describing the "more," which psychologists may also recognize as real. The *subconscious self* is nowadays a well-accredited psychological entity; and I believe that in it we have exactly the mediating term required. Apart from all religious considerations, there is actually and literally more life in our total soul than we are at any time aware of. The exploration of the transmarginal field has hardly yet been seriously undertaken, but what Mr. Myers said in 1892 in his essay on the Subliminal Consciousness is as true as when it was first written: "Each of us is in reality an abiding psychical entity far more extensive than he knows—an individuality which can never express itself completely through any corporeal manifestation. The Self manifests through the organism; but there is always some part of the Self unmanifested; and always, as it seems, some power of organic expression in abeyance or reserve." Much of the content of this larger background against which our conscious being stands out in relief is insignificant. Imperfect memories, silly jingles, inhibitive timidities, "dissolutive" phenomena of various sorts, as Myers calls them, enter into it for a large part. But in it many of the performances of genius seem also to have their origin; and in our study of conversion, of mystical experiences, and of prayer, we have seen how striking a part invasions from this region play in the religious life.

Let me then propose, as an hypothesis, that whatever it may be on its *further* side, the "more" with which in religious experience we feel ourselves connected is on its *hither* side the subconscious continuation of our conscious life. Starting thus with a recognized psychological fact as our basis, we seem to preserve a contact with "science" which the ordinary theologian lacks. At the same time the theologian's contention that the religious man is moved by an external power is vindicated, for it is one of the peculiarities of invasions from the subconscious region to take on objective appearances, and to suggest to the Subject an external control. In the religious life the control is felt as "higher"; but since on our hypothesis it is primarily the higher faculties of our own hidden mind which are controlling, the sense of union with the power beyond us is a sense of something, not merely apparently, but literally true.

This doorway into the subject seems to me the best one for a science of religions, for it mediates between a number of different points of view. Yet it is only a doorway, and difficulties present themselves as soon as we step through it, and ask how far our transmarginal consciousness carries us if we follow it on its remoter side. Here the over-beliefs begin: here mysticism and the conversion-rapture and Vedantism and transcendental idealism bring in their monistic interpretations and tell us that the finite self rejoins the absolute self, for it was always one with God and identical with the soul of the world. Here the prophets of all the different religions come with their visions, voices, raptures, and other openings, supposed by each to authenticate his own peculiar faith.

Those of us who are not personally favored with such specific revelations must stand outside of them altogether and, for the present at least, decide that, since they corroborate incompatible theological doctrines, they neutralize one another and leave no fixed result. If we follow any one of them, or if we follow philosophical theory and embrace monistic pantheism on non-mystical grounds, we do so in the exercise of our individual freedom, and build out our religion in the way most congruous with our personal susceptibilities. Among these susceptibilities intellectual ones play a decisive part. Although the religious question is primarily a question of life, of living or not living in the higher union which opens itself to us as a gift, yet the spiritual excitement in which the gift appears a real one will often fail to be aroused in an individual until certain particular intellectual beliefs or ideas which, as we say, come home to him, are touched. These ideas will thus be essential to that individual's religion;—which is as much as to say that over-beliefs in various directions are absolutely indispensable, and that we should treat them with tenderness and tolerance so long as they are not intolerant themselves. As I have elsewhere written, the most interesting and valuable things about a man are usually his over-beliefs.

Disregarding the over-beliefs, and confining ourselves to what is common and generic, we have in *the fact that the conscious person is continuous with a wider self through which saving experiences come*, a positive content of religious experience which, it seems to me, *is literally and objectively true as far as it goes.* If I now proceed to state my own hypothesis about the farther limits of this extension of our personality, I shall be offering my own over-belief—though I know it will appear a sorry under-belief to some of you—for which I can only bespeak the same indulgence which in a converse case I should accord to yours.

The further limits of our being plunge, it seems to me, into an altogether other dimension of existence from the sensible and merely "understandable" world. Name it the mystical region, or the supernatural region, whichever you choose. So far as our ideal impulses originate in this region (and most of them do originate in it, for we find them possessing us in a way for which we cannot articulately account), we belong to it in a more intimate sense than that in which we belong to the visible world, for we belong in the most intimate sense wherever our ideals belong. Yet the unseen region in question is not merely ideal, for it produces effects in this world. When we commune with it, work is actually done upon our finite personality, for we are turned into new men, and consequences in the way of conduct follow in the natural world upon our regenerative change. But that which produces effects within another reality must be termed a reality itself, so I feel as if we had no philosophic excuse for calling the unseen or mystical world unreal.

God is the natural appellation, for us Christians at least, for the supreme reality, so I will call this higher part of the universe by the name of God. We and God have business with each other; and in opening ourselves to his influence our deepest destiny is fulfilled. The universe, at those parts of it which our personal being constitutes, takes a turn genuinely for the worse or for the better in proportion as each one of us fulfills or evades God's demands. As far as this goes I probably have you with me, for I only translate into schematic language what I may call the instinctive belief of mankind: God is real since he produces real effects.

The real effects in question, so far as I have as yet admitted them, are exerted on the personal centres of energy of the various subjects, but the spontaneous faith of most of the subjects is that they embrace a wider sphere than this. Most religious men believe (or "know," if they be mystical) that not only they themselves, but the whole universe of beings to whom the God is present, are secure in his parental hands. There is a sense, a dimension, they are sure, in which we are *all* saved, in spite of the gates of hell and all adverse terrestrial appearances. God's existence is the guarantee of an ideal order that shall be permanently preserved. This world may indeed, as science assures us, some day burn up or freeze; but if it is part of his order, the old ideals are sure to be brought elsewhere to fruition, so that where God is, tragedy is only provisional and partial, and shipwreck and dissolution are not the absolutely final things. Only when this further step of faith concerning God is taken, and remote objective consequences are predicted, does religion, as it seems to me, get wholly free from the first immediate subjective experience, and bring a *real hypothesis* into play. A good hypothesis in science must have other properties than those of the phenomenon it is immediately invoked to explain, otherwise it is not prolific enough. God, meaning only what enters into the religious man's experience of union, falls short of being an hypothesis of this more useful order. He needs to enter into wider cosmic relations in order to justify the subject's absolute confidence and peace.

That the God with whom, starting from the hither side of our own extra-marginal self, we come at its remoter margin into commerce should be the absolute world-ruler, is of course a very considerable over-belief. Over-belief as it is, though, it is an article of almost every one's religion. Most of us pretend in some way to prop it up upon our philosophy, but the philosophy itself is really propped upon this faith. What is this but to say that Religion, in her fullest exercise of function, is not a mere illumination of facts already elsewhere given, not a mere passion, like love, which views things in a rosier light. It is indeed that, as we have seen abundantly. But it is something more, namely, a postulator of new *facts* as well. The world interpreted religiously is not the materialistic world over again, with an altered expression; it must have, over and above the altered expression, a *natural constitution* different at some point from that which a materialistic world would have. It must be such that different events can be expected in it, different conduct must be required.

This thoroughly "pragmatic" view of religion has usually been taken as a matter of course by common men. They have interpolated divine miracles into the field of nature, they have built a heaven out beyond the grave. It is only transcendentalist metaphysicians who think that, without adding any concrete details to Nature, or subtracting any, but by simply calling it the expression of absolute spirit, you make it more divine just as it stands. I believe the pragmatic way of taking religion to be the deeper way. It gives it body as well as soul, it makes it claim, as everything real must claim, some characteristic realm of fact as its very own. What the more characteristically divine facts are, apart from the actual inflow of energy in the faith-state and the prayer-state, I know not. But the over-belief on which I am ready to make my personal venture is that they exist. The whole drift of my education goes to persuade me that the world of our present consciousness is only one out of many worlds of consciousness that exist, and that those other worlds must contain experiences which have a meaning for our life also; and that although in the main their experiences and those of this world keep discrete, yet the two become continuous at certain points, and higher energies filter in. By being faithful in my poor measure to this over-belief, I seem to myself to keep more sane and true. I can, of course, put myself into the sectarian scientist's attitude, and imagine vividly that the world of sensations and of scientific laws and objects may be all. But whenever I do this, I hear that inward monitor of which W. K. Clifford once wrote, whispering the word "bosh!" Humbug is humbug, even though it bear the scientific name, and the total expression of human experience, as I view it objectively, invincibly urges me beyond the narrow "scientific" bounds. Assuredly, the real world is of a different temperament more intricately built than physical science allows. So my objective and my subjective conscience both hold me to the over-belief which I express. Who knows whether the faithfulness of individuals here below to their own poor over-beliefs may not actually help God in turn to be more effectively faithful to his own greater tasks? . . .

IV.A.3

Mysticism and Experience

GRACE M. JANTZEN

A brief biographical sketch of Grace M. Jantzen precedes selection III.B.4. In this article, she critically examines William James's conception of the nature and goals of mysticism and mystical experience, arguing that James's characterizations of these rest more on his own preconceptions than on careful engagement with the writings of mystics. She defends her conclusions through a study of two paradigm Christian mystics: Bernard of Clairvaux and Julian of Norwich.

From *Religious Studies* 25 (1989): 295–315. Copyright © 1989 Cambridge University Press. Reprinted with the permission of Cambridge University Press.

The definition of mysticism has shifted, in modern thinking, from a patristic emphasis on the objective content of experience to the modern emphasis on the subjective psychological states or feelings of the individual. Post Kantian Idealism and Romanticism was involved in this shift to a far larger extent than is usually recognized. An important conductor of the subjectivist view of mysticism to modern philosophers of religion was William James, even though in other respects he repudiated Romantic and especially Idealist categories of thought. In this article I wish first to explore William James' understanding of mysticism and religious experience, and then to measure that understanding against the accounts of two actual mystics, Bernard of Clairvaux and Julian of Norwich, who, for all their differences, may be taken as paradigms of the Christian mystical tradition. I shall argue that judging from these two cases, James' position is misguided and inadequate. Since James' account has been of enormous influence in subsequent thinking about mysticism, it follows that if his understanding of mysticism is inadequate, so is much of the work that rests upon it.

I. THE CONTRIBUTION OF WILLIAM JAMES

In 1901-2 James delivered a set of Gifford Lectures subsequently published as *The Varieties of Religious Experience* which continues to be reprinted in whole and in part. His clear and careful arguments are presented in a style congenial to philosophical thinking and temperament; as a result, much subsequent philosophizing about mysticism has based itself squarely on James' discussion of it.[1] While philosophers have regularly accepted James' account of the characteristics of mystical experience, however, they have less frequently recognized either how closely his account was tied to Romantic categories such as those articulated by Schelling and Schleiermacher, or how it fit into the rest of his philosophical programme. I suggest that both the strengths and the weaknesses of

James' discussion of mysticism emerge more clearly when it is seen in the wider context of his thought.

The Varieties of Religious Experience was written not long after his seminal two volume *Principles of Psychology,* and in some respects could plausibly be taken as a third volume of the same work. His approach in the *Principles of Psychology* was ground breaking in its emphasis on description of experiences and states of consciousness rather than restricting the account of experience by *a priori* metaphysical categories. All his life James was the enemy of *a priori* constructions, and stressed his conviction that theory must grow out of description rather than the other way around.[2]

Nevertheless, James also believed that there could be no such thing as neutral phenomenological description. All descriptions are inevitably conceptual; they take place within a context of human purposes and aims.[3] This means that assumptions are already embedded in descriptions.[4] Part of the business of philosophy is to bring to consciousness the assumptions implicit in description, measuring these against the facts and revising them in any instance where they distort the facts. Facts, for James, take precedence over theory, even though our theories and assumptions affect our selection of facts.

To this extent James set himself firmly in the empiricist tradition, against rationalist or idealist philosophical positions which he characterized as "tender-minded" contrasted with the "tough-minded" empirical respect for facts.[5] However, James' notion of experience is broader than that common in the British empirical tradition. Any and all sorts of human experience must be taken into account, not only the experiences of the senses which typically receive most attention in empirical writings. Psychic experiences and religious experiences in particular cannot be excluded: hence his treatment of them in *Principles of Psychology* and *Varieties of Religious Experience.*

James was very much aware of Kantian strictures on the limitation of knowledge to the phenomena of human experience. Nevertheless he held that Kant was mistaken in thinking that we could have no glimpse of a supernatural realm.

Just as our senses are able to perceive material things via ordinary consciousness, so perhaps the margins of our consciousness or our subconscious minds might be the point at which "higher spiritual agencies," if there are any, could directly touch us.[6] It was no doubt partly for this reason that James was particularly interested in the fringes of consciousness: psychic phenomena, hallucinations, the effects of nitrous oxide and intoxication, and intense or bizarre accounts of religious experience including trances, levitations, seizures, hallucinations, and the like. He was himself a religious believer, though hardly an orthodox Christian, and believed that "the evidence for God lies primarily in inner personal experiences."[7]

In this emphasis on the value of personal religious experience and his conception of its nature we can discern a strand in James' thought derived from the romantic tradition. James grew up in a unique household in which theological and philosophical issues were a regular part of meal time conversation. His father, Henry James Sr., was a Swedenborgian who spent much of his time and effort lecturing and writing books expressing his rather eccentric viewpoint, though without forcing it upon his sons. William James did not find his father's religious position satisfactory for himself, but he respected it deeply, particularly the inner experience that informed it, even if not the abstract accounts of it which the elder James produced.[8]

A wide circle of Henry James' friends made an impact on the family, among them Emerson and Carlyle, who have been described as "familiar divinities in the James household" with whom both father and son must settle their account.[9] Through Emerson and Carlyle, the James's made deeper acquaintance with romantic philosophy, both in the English version of Coleridge, and in the German tradition of Goethe, Schelling, Schiller, and others. Besides this acquaintance via his father, William James developed an intimate knowledge of romanticism in his own right. Part of his education took place in Europe where he was a regular visitor; he was fluent in German, and widely read in German philosophical literature.

Although he rejected monism and idealism, he took them very seriously in his lecturing and writing, treating them as the most significant conversation partners, and discussing in detail the views of Hegal and other German thinkers, along with French and English representatives of the view.[10]

Although James rejected rationalism and idealism in favour of empiricism and pragmatism, his empiricism was, as already noted, broad enough to include religious experience as a significant ingredient: we can see that at least part of the reason for this can be attributed to his background and upbringing. Thus when James considers religious experience, and particularly mysticism, his discussions can be seen to be influenced by both the empiricist and the romantic traditions. With the empiricists he insisted on facts and descriptions, seeking to look at actual cases and instances. But as he himself noted, there is no such thing as bare collection of facts; and description presupposes classification. The classificatory system which James used, particularly in his account of mystical experiences, was, whether consciously or not, imbued with the vocabulary and concepts of romanticism.

This can be documented from many of his writings. In his famous book *Pragmatism,* for instance, he discusses the attraction of monism to "mystical minds" and quotes Vivekananda on Vedantism which, he says, is "the mystical method" in which discipline rather than reason leads to the insight that at bottom all is One, "melted into oneness."

> In the passion of love we have the mystic germ of what might mean a total union of all sentient life. This mystical germ wakes up in us on hearing the monistic utterances, acknowledges their authority, and assigns to intellectual considerations a secondary place.[11]

James goes on to reject such monism; but what is of interest for our purposes is that even though he rejects the overall position, he accepts without question this conception of what mysticism is. In this passage we find all the romantic ingredients, familiar from a study of Schelling and Schleiermacher, of intense feeling, unity or "melting into oneness" of subject and object, and the secondary place of the intellect. Of course there are differences in German philosophy: romanticism, monism, and idealism cannot all be lumped together in a monolithic heap. There are also large differences in James' use of terms from that of romantic or idealist writers. For instance, for James, at least in this passage, the "mystical mind" indicates a particular philosophical temperament tending to monism rather than to pluralism; it is not, as in Schleiermacher, the universal essence of religion or the inner consciousness of everyone. Yet although we should not minimize these differences, what is striking is the extent to which the concept or working definition of mysticism is running along agreed lines, and is taken over by James without discussion or comment or even acknowledgement of debt.

These same strands are discernable in *The Varieties of Religious Experience*. On the one hand, James' approach is that of a psychologist exploring the phenomena of experience, concentrating on the subjective states involved in religious experience in general and on those states that he would regard as mystical in particular. He takes it as part of his brief to draw conclusions about the moral and religious significance and truth of the phenomena he explores, but, in line with his attitude in *Principles of Psychology,* these theoretical considerations are intended to rest on the descriptions and not the other way around.

Unlike many subsequent writers on mysticism who accepted James' characterization of mysticism without adopting his method, James himself did his best to anchor his philosophical discussion in the lives and writings of actual mystics. In *The Varieties of Religious Experience* he displays a breadth of acquaintance with primary sources, quoting liberally to illustrate his arguments: this was part of his avowed empiricist stance.

Nevertheless I suggest that James is a prime example of his own theory that description always takes place on the basis of prior assumptions, whether or not they are recognized; and further that in his case the assumptions were in large part derived from romantic categories. A revealing clue

to this is the unfortunate fact that in his citation of primary sources, relatively brief quotations are frequently made to stand on their own: James did not pay close enough attention to the contexts from which they were drawn, let alone to the historical and social conditions out of which they arose. When these are considered more carefully, we often find that James' interpretations are doubtful. To give only one example among many, James cites a passage from the Islamic mystic Al-Ghazali and one from John of the Cross to show that "the incommunicableness of the transport is the keynote of all mysticism":[12] whatever the views of Al-Ghazali, it is certain that this is a very superficial reading of John of the Cross, who has a carefully nuanced philosophy of language along Thomist lines, and who is able to move from the genre of erotic poetry to that of academic commentary to convey his meanings with precision. It is, however, exactly in line with the preconception that mystical experience is of its nature ineffable: a notion entirely compatible with Schleiermacher's account of mysticism.

From this and many other instances, it seems to me that part of the reason for James' inaccuracy and ignoring of the context was that although in principle James believed that theory should be dependent on description and not the other way around, in practice he never questioned the concept of mysticism he had absorbed from romantic thinkers. Because of this, his quotations from the mystics illustrate his preconceived categories, and do not after all constitute a fresh exploration of the experiences and teachings of actual mystics. In *The Varieties of Religious Experience* James claimed that mysticism had four main characteristics. The first and most important is ineffability: "no adequate report of its contents can be given in words,"[13] and therefore it cannot be transferred to others but can only be understood by personal experience. Second is its noetic quality, its sense of insight into deeply significant truth. Third is its transiency—its short duration; and fourth, the passivity of the mystic, who feels that he or she is in the power of something greater, while his or her own will is in abeyance.[14] Along with this goes the view, already mentioned, that mystical experience is a merging into unity or "melting into oneness" of the subject and the object.

As already mentioned, this understanding of mysticism has very close affinities to that developed by Schleiermacher and Schelling in a romantic response to Kantian critical philosophy. However, philosophers writing about mysticism after James regularly cite and accept his description of mysticism as a basis for their evaluation of it; but do not notice its provenance. Perhaps because of the empiricist strand in James' writing, and his liberal citation of sources, subsequent philosophers too readily take for granted that his description of mysticism is reliable, and, contrary to the spirit of James, do not investigate actual mystics for themselves.

This description is, however, highly questionable. In subsequent sections of this paper I wish to demonstrate that a study of two paradigm Christian mystics radically undermines the characterisation which contemporary philosophy inherited from romanticism via James; and that James' characteristics of mystical experience must be qualified out of recognition if they are to fit the facts. I shall further argue that the sorts of experiences which James thinks of as the essence and goal of the mystical pathway do not at all coincide with what these two mystics consider to be the essence and goal, either for themselves or for those whom they instruct.

If this is correct, and if, as I believe, it can be generalized to other mystics of the Christian tradition, then the discrepancy between the concept of mystical experience as held by thinkers following James and as held by the mystics themselves has several important consequences. First, if the idea of what constitutes mystical experience is fundamentally misconceived in much philosophical and theological writing on the subject, then it is to be expected that arguments based on this idea, such as arguments about the value of mystical experiences as evidence for the truth of religious claims, or arguments about whether there is a mystical core of religion, will be undermined radically (i.e. from the root), and will have to be reconsidered in the light of the new understanding of mystical experience which emerges. A second related consequence is

that if a study of paradigm mystics causes us thoroughly to reformulate how we are to understand the experience which mystics see as their goal, this leads to creative reformulation also of ideas of knowledge, selfhood, language, and other themes important in modern philosophy. The position that emerges is that the modern swing to subjectivization and away from the objective content of mystical experience cannot be sustained; and that this has major epistemological and ontological consequences reaching far beyond what is usually considered the phenomenon of mysticism.

Not only is it necessary to reexamine the characteristics of mystical experience, however, but the concept of experience itself as James presents it must be rethought; and it is this which will occupy our attention for the rest of this section.[15] The ambiguities in the concept of experience have often been noted, and to a certain extent James seems to be alive to them: indeed in one sense the whole point of his book is to draw attention to the variations in religious experience, as its title shows. For his purposes he defines religion as

> the feelings, acts and experiences of individual men in their solitude, so far as they apprehend themselves to stand in relation to whatever they may consider the divine.[16]

This definition could be challenged in a variety of ways, partly for its onesided emphasis on subjectivity, as already noted, but also in its privatization of religion, ignoring the development of religion in its social context; but that is not my present task. What I wish to take note of at present in this definition is that in it James includes "experience" in a wide range of senses. It incorporates special occasions in which a divine presence is sensed, it includes visions, voices, ecstasies, and other such phenomena, but it would also include a lifetime of "being towards God," living in a conscious relationship to God.

From subsequent chapters of his book in which James discusses the reality of the divine presence and its apprehension by people of varying temperaments it is clear that at least at times he wishes to include this wide sense of experience. He describes those with a "more habitual and so to speak chronic sense of God's presence,"[17] and says that this would be the self-description of "thousands of unpretending Christians." There are no trances here, no voices or visions or ecstasies; yet it would be a great mistake to say that there is no experience of God. James cites examples of those who "always knew" God loved them and prayed always to him, finding their whole life and being rooted in him.[18] He speaks of those with conscious "oneness of our life with God's life" which he sees as a regular interpretation of Christ's message.[19] He cites the practice of the presence of God, recollection, and contemplation as disciplined ways of life into which one can increasingly enter. All of this is experiential in the broad sense; it is anything but dry and abstract theory. Furthermore, this continuous relationship with God is arguably the heart and centre of Christianity, more important than abstract doctrine or ritual, which important though they are, exist to express and facilitate the personal relationship.

In spite of this occasional broader understanding of experience as a progressive opening out of all of life to God, on the whole James concentrates on a much narrower notion of experience, studying "the extremer expressions of the religious temperament."[20] He makes much of "moments of sentimental and mystical experiences":[21] seizures, ecstasies, visions, levitations, and the like. He argues that the essence of an experience must be judged from its intenser manifestations, even though these may be one-sided and exaggerated,[22] and therefore justifies his approach of studying the phenomena in the acutest possible form, even though that involves eccentricities and extremes.[23] Though he does not acknowledge it in this book, we can see in this practice James' reaction to Kant which we have already noted. If there are supernatural powers, and if these powers can in any way communicate with human beings, then such communication will take place, according to James, at the fringes of consciousness; hence it is these fringes which must come in for the closest attention.[24]

Accordingly, in the chapter which James devotes specifically to mysticism, the examples he gives are of particular states of consciousness: dream-like states, trances, an experience with chloroform, flashes of exaltation, experiences of ecstatic union. These, for James, are "mystical experiences," and it is to experiences of these sorts that he applies his famous characteristics of ineffability, noetic quality, passivity, and transiency. Subsequent philosophers have followed him not only in accepting these four characteristics, but more importantly in thinking of mysticism in terms of experiences in this narrower sense: voices, visions, ecstasies, and the like, to such an extent that in many people's minds phenomena of this sort are part of their conception of mysticism.

As I have already said, James himself was aware of a broader sense of mystical experience which need have nothing to do with these phenomena. However, because of his desire to circumvent Kantian strictures on the experience of the supernatural, he was drawn to these fringe experiences. He repeatedly moves across the ambiguities of the concept of experience, treating religious experience as central to religion, and therefore treating religious experiences in the narrow sense of visions and ecstasies as central. Once we have made the distinction between the broader and the narrower sense of experience, however, it is necessary to ask whether James was correct in this move. Granting for the sake of argument his premise that the essence of religion must be judged from its intenser manifestations, does it follow that it can best be studied from acute experiences in the narrow sense of the word, as James proceeds to do? Or might it be the case that these experiences are not essential to religion or even to mysticism, although experience in the broader sense is essential?

To come to a decision about this, it is necessary to examine actual mystics, not just by citing quotations out of context, but by considering their lives and teachings in some detail. For our purposes, therefore, we shall now investigate the two mystics who serve as paradigms for our investigation, to see what place experience (in both the broad and the narrow sense) played in their lives and writings.

II. BERNARD OF CLAIRVAUX

There can be no doubt that experience is central to the spirituality of Bernard of Clairvaux. According to his thinking, the whole aim of the Christian life is to come to union with God; and if this is the aim of the Christian life in general, all the more is it the aim of the Cistercian monk. The Cistercians adopted the Benedictine self-designation of a monastery as a "school for the service of the Lord," a service that was fundamentally one of love. Thus the motto of Clairvaux, the first of Bernard's new foundations, was "In schola Christi sumus": the main lesson to be learned was the lesson of how to live in charity.[25] This notion of charity, however, is not the watered down idea we have of it today, such that "living in charity" means little more than living in polite harmony. Charity (caritas) is, in its primary designation for Bernard, none other than God: God is love. In its secondary designation charity is the gift of God, identified with the gift of the Holy Spirit and the presence of the Spirit in the soul. To learn to live in charity, therefore, is nothing less than to learn to live in God, by virtue of God's Spirit of charity living in us and transforming us: this is the goal of the Christian life.

> Penetrated with charity, we become even in this world, in virtue of the gift, what God is in virtue of his nature. . . .[26]

Bernard's writings as well as his life are directed to an exploration of the dimensions of this life of love and how it can be developed. *The Twelve Steps of Humility and Pride,* for instance, is an often amusing discussion of how the individual comes to live in the truth of God's love through the development of humility, or descends away from truth to contempt of God and estrangement from God. His enormously influential treatise *On Loving God* has as its explicit theme the question "why and how God is to be loved,"[27] and moves through lower stages to the point where, by God's grace, God is to be loved for God's sake alone.

> When a feeling of this kind is experienced, the soul, drunk with divine love, forgetful of self, and seeming to be a broken vessel, goes completely into God, and cleaving to God becomes one spirit with him. . . .[28]

Bernard's eighty six sermons *On the Song of Songs* are an exploration of the ways of love between God and human beings, in which Bernard seeks the mystical meaning of the Scripture he contemplates. Early in the *Sermons,* when Bernard is about to expound upon the first verse of the *Song of Songs* ("Let him kiss me with the kisses of his mouth") he addresses his monks thus:

> Today the text we are to study is the book of our own experience. . . . Anyone who has received this mystical kiss from the mouth of Christ at least once, seeks again that intimate experience, and eagerly looks for its frequent renewal. . . .[29]

It is obvious from this that for Bernard experience is of central importance. Bernard has sometimes been contrasted with Augustine in the account he gives of love, making it an emotion rather than a desire, and therefore contrasting it with knowledge as a felt experience. Not that Bernard despises knowledge: even literary knowledge is important to him.[30] Yet of the two, love is fundamental, and most deeply engages the human psyche. It is love which can transform and fulfil us, rectifying the distortions of personality which have been twisted by sin and hurt, and bringing us to our true selves in union with God who is *caritas.*[31]

Fundamental as experience is for Bernard, however, it becomes apparent that we must reconsider whether the concept as used by James is adequate for an understanding of Bernard's meaning. There is no doubt that experience is essential to Bernard's mysticism, since it has union with God, not as an abstract concept but as a felt reality, as its goal. But what is the place in Bernard for the narrower sense of experiences, the visions and voices, levitations and ecstasies which James discusses? And what is their relation to the life-long experience of growth toward union with God which is the mystical pathway in Bernard's conception?

Some of the phenomena are not mentioned by Bernard at all: it would be totally at variance with the spirit of his writings to look for any stress on levitations or seizures or other such acute psychic phenomena. He does speak frequently of visions of God, however, as well as of hearing God's voice.[32] He cites Old Testament prophets like Jacob, Moses and Isaiah who saw God face to face, and mentions St Paul who was "rapt into Paradise, heard words that he could not explain, and saw his Lord Jesus Christ,"[33] though he says that even in such cases their experience of God was not "as he is but only in the form he thought fitting to assume."[34] The unqualified experience of God is reserved for life after death, and is spoken of by such terms as Paradise, union with God, and the Beatific Vision—all to some extent metaphors for a reality to which we can point but cannot in this life fully experience.

Far more important to Bernard than these external, quasi-sensory experiences of visual images or spoken words "is another form of divine contemplation, very different from the former because it takes place in the interior, when God himself is pleased to visit the soul that seeks him."[35] This is the deeply felt sense of the presence of God "not in bodily form but by inward infusion," of which Bernard says,

> It is beyond question that the vision is all the more delightful the more inward it is, and not external. It is the Word, who penetrates without sound; who is effective though not pronounced, who wins the affections without striking on the ears. His face, though without form, is the source of form, it does not dazzle the eyes of the body but gladdens the watchful heart; its pleasure is in the gift of love and not in the colour of the lover.[36]

Nor are these experiences always the same; they are varied according to the needs of the recipient. Sometimes the divine Word comes "like a physician with oil and ointments" healing hurts and correcting distortions; sometimes "he joins up as a traveller ... on the road" and by his presence makes hardship or drudgery easier to bear; or

perhaps he arrives like "a magnificent and powerful king" bringing courage in a time of stress or temptation. Bernard uses the imagery of the *Song of Songs,* and indeed of the Bible as a whole, to elucidate many such situations.[37] In each case the divine Word comes with love and helpfulness; but in each case the intense awareness of his presence is short-lived. The one who truly longs for God will find that "his heart's desire will be given to him, even while still a pilgrim on earth, though not in its fulness and only for a time, a short time."[38] The awareness fades, and though it may return again from time to time, for the most part this life must be lived by faith, not by continuous direct experience of God.

It might at first seem that this account fits neatly with James' characterization of mystical experiences as transient and passive; and in a sense that is true of Bernard's descriptions. However, there is much more involved in Bernard's understanding than James' characterization would lead us to expect. Note how Bernard describes the one who comes: God is the "divine Word." Furthermore, in each of the ways God comes, as physician, traveller on the road, king, and so on, the picture is drawn from one or another of the representations of Christ in the Gospels. What is happening here is that Bernard is speaking of encountering Christ by penetrating to the mystical meaning of Scripture, a particular type of Scriptural exegesis characteristic of patristic and medieval writing. He is finding the divine Word in the words of Scripture; seeing Christ as the deepest meaning of the Bible, and in meditation on that meaning, encountering Christ in his own soul. There is indeed a sense in which this is transient: even in a monastery one must move on to doing other things than meditating on the Scriptures; and even during the times of meditation one by no means always has the sense of the presence of Christ. There is also a sense in which it is passive: the ability to penetrate to the mystical meaning of the Scriptures, and the inner awareness of the presence of Christ, are alike the gift of God, as indeed are the Scriptures themselves. But this is far different from the notion we might have had from James that mystical experiences are odd psychic states that occur unexpectedly, catching one unawares, only to disappear again in a short time. Bernard is not interested in odd psychic states; he is concerned with opening one's heart to the deepest meaning of Scripture and thereby encountering Christ.

Bernard is quite clear that experiences of this sort, fleeting though they are, are to be sought and "ardently desired." External visions or voices, by contrast, are not to be sought, because such corporeal images could never be God, whose reality must be spiritual. As Gilson says,

> Bernard ... would not be content with anything in the nature of a mystic dream, or even a supernatural apparition, were it that of God himself. These, undoubtedly, would be graces of a very high order, which no one would be mad enough to despise, but it is not after these that Bernard would have us seek. The goal of his mystical ambition here below is a state of union with God which would not indeed be the beatific vision, for God does not reveal himself as he is, but one nevertheless in which he reveals something of what he is.[39]

Here is the crux of the matter. Experiences of God are not to be sought for their own sake, for their delightfulness, or out of intellectual curiosity. They are to be sought only and solely as the opening of the heart to God in communion with Christ through scripture and sacrament, which is the pathway of increasing union with God.

This raises the crucial question of what Bernard means by "union." According to Bernard union with God is not ontological merging, but is rather total harmony of intellect, will and emotion, so that the human being becomes "not indeed what he is, but such as he."[40] The full realization of this end is the beatific vision—the knowledge of God that beatifies, that is, makes blessed, whole, fulfilled. According to Bernard, this could not happen instantaneously. He accepts the Platonic principle that like can only be known by like: to see God in the beatific vision requires that we be made like God. As the words of Scripture put it, it is the pure in heart who will see God.[41]

Now, Bernard, in line with the Augustinian tradition in which he stands, does not believe that we can be made like God, pure in heart, in a moment of magical transformation, whether in a "mystical" experience in this life, or at the point of death. Rather, we are made like God gradually, through the long and arduous pathway of spiritual progress in which our hurt and twisted personalities which Bernard describes as curved in upon themselves in a grotesque distortion of what we were meant to be are gradually healed and opened to the *caritas* of God and neighbour as we proceed in gratitude, obedience, and humility, and we learn to live in the charity that is the gift of God and know the Charity that God is.

For example, we find that at the very beginning of his sermons on the *Song of Songs,* when he announces that he is going to preach a series of sermons on them, Bernard says

> Now ... by the grace of God you have understood quite well from the book of Ecclesiastes how to recognize and have done with the false promise of the world. And then the book of Proverbs—has not your life and your conduct been sufficiently amended and enlightened by the doctrine it inculcates?[42]

He makes it clear that unless this had been so, it would have been premature to teach them the wisdom of the *Song of Songs.*

Modern readers might pass this over as indicating no more, perhaps, than previous series of sermons which he had preached in his monastery. To his medieval listeners or readers, however, this comment would have been pregnant with allusion to a long tradition of what was involved in the spiritual journey. At least from the time of Origen in the third century, the *Song of Songs* had been considered the book which best described the summit or goal of spirituality, and its sexual imagery was taken, in its mystical meaning, as describing the union of Christ and the soul. Origen, however, and the tradition which followed him, held that there were preliminary steps. Origen expressed this in a three-fold way; though it would be mistaken to suppose that in his view these were rigidly successive. The first step was purification or purgation, the moral life without which spiritual insight was held to be impossible. The Biblical book of *Proverbs* was the book which best taught how this purgation should be developed. The second step was illumination or enlightenment, insight into truth and values, both natural and supernatural; the Biblical book of *Ecclesiastes* was used as a basis for this. Only after this could there be contemplation or union with God as described in the *Song of Songs*.[43]

Accordingly, when Bernard says that his sermons presuppose the enlightenment of the book of Ecclesiastes and the moral purification of the book of Proverbs, he is referring to the tradition of the three-stage spiritual journey; it is not a casual comment. The union with God of which he is about to speak, and which he sees as the goal of the Christian life, requires as its precondition purification and illumination. This is not to say that in Bernard, any more than in Origen or in the many intervening figures, these steps do not to some extent interpenetrate: none of these writers held that the process of purification is fully completed before any illumination can take place, for instance. However, they did hold that it would be folly to suppose that union with God, the summit of Christian experience, could occur unless one were also serious about purification and illumination, and indeed were making progress in these areas. Nor did they hold this to be arbitrary: they believed that there was a conceptual connection and progression involved, in such a way that it would be impossible to develop in enlightenment or illumination without purification; and likewise impossible to grow in union with God without enlightenment.

It is clear from all this that Bernard's account of experience involves rather more than James' discussion would have lead us to suppose. Bernard's mysticism is indeed profoundly experiential, in both the narrow and the broad sense; but contrary to James, it is the broad sense of experience, the gradual transformation of all of life in charity, through the lifelong journey of purification, enlightenment, and union, which is essential. Spiritual experiences in the narrow sense are of unequal value. Those

that are most "internal," that is, least like sensory perception, are much more likely to be of assistance in spiritual progress than those which are quasi-sensory, because the recipient is less likely to be side-tracked into concentrating on the manner and form of the experience, which is wholly subsidiary to the communication of the love and help of God as is appropriate to the particular situation of the recipient and paradigmatically received through scripture and sacrament. These internal experiences of divine love are therefore to be sought and treasured: one is to take time and effort in meditation on scripture and participation in the sacraments. Even they, however, are a means to an end, which is the full union of the soul with God, transformation into Charity.

Bernard would find alien and unacceptable James' focus on levitations, trances, quasi-sensory visions, and other such phenomena which James sees as "the intenser manifestations" of religious experience and from which he seeks to extract the essence of religion. Neither would he suppose that it is only on these fringes of consciousness that there could be any experience of God. Yet none of this would be because Bernard despises experience, but because his understanding of it is much richer than the concept of experience in James' writings; and indicates, as well, a vastly different anthropology and epistemology than that current in post-Enlightenment thought.

III. JULIAN OF NORWICH

To this rather negative view of mystical experiences in the narrow sense, however, Julian of Norwich is a counter-example. Smitten with a severe illness, she was given a crucifix to look upon during what were thought to be her dying moments. Recounting the experience, she says,

> And at this, suddenly I saw the red blood trickling down from under the crown, all hot, flowing freely and copiously, a living stream, just as it seemed to me that it was at the time when the crown of thorns was thrust down upon his head.[44]

After this came a series of visions, rich both in sensory detail and in teaching, as Christ speaks to Julian from the cross. Some of the visions relate directly to the passion of Christ which she finds herself witnessing. She tells, for instance, of how

> after this I saw, in bodily vision, in the face of the crucifix which hung before me, a part of Christ's passion: contempt, spitting to defoul his body, buffeting of his blessed face, and many woes and pains, more than I can tell; and his colour often changed, and all his blessed face was for a time caked with dry blood. This I saw bodily and sorrowfully and dimly; and I wanted more of the light of day, to have seen it more clearly.[45]

It appears from this passage that what Julian saw in the vision had such sensory reality to her that she supposed that if there were better natural light in the room she would see the contents of the vision more clearly.

Although all but the last of the visions took place while she was gazing at the crucifix which was held before her on her sick bed, not all of them were of Christ himself. It is perhaps not surprising, given the fourteenth-century context, that at one point she should see his mother.

> I saw her spiritually in her bodily likeness, a simple, humble maiden, young in years, of the stature which she had when she conceived. Also God showed me part of the wisdom and truth of her soul, and in this I understood the reverent contemplation with which she beheld her God, marvelling with great reverence that he was willing to be born of her who was a simple creature created by him.[46]

This vision was partly like ordinary sense perception: she sees Mary's "bodily likeness," her stature, and so on. Partly it is unlike sense perception: "God showed me part of the wisdom and truth of her soul."

Rather more unusual are the contents of some of the succeeding visions, still taking place while her

eyes are focussed on the crucifix. Once she finds herself led down to the bottom of the sea, where she saw "green hills and valleys, with the appearance of moss strewn with seaweed and gravel:"[47] from this she is taught about the safety that God's presence confers even in the unlikeliest of circumstances. Again, the vision is vivid in sensory detail. In one of the most famous of her visions,

> he showed me something small, no bigger than a hazelnut, lying in the palm of my hand, and I perceived that it was as round as any ball.[48]

This tiny thing is given to her to hold and to look at while she is taught about God's loving protection of all creation, fragile and vulnerable as it is; and from this, God's loving protection of her in her own personal vulnerability, most immediately in the illness from which she was suffering.

Julian makes a distinction similar to that found in Bernard between exterior and interior experiences. Julian calls them corporeal sight and spiritual sight or understanding, and the former would be more like sense data than the latter, and include things like touch, smell, and hearing as well as sight.[49] Whereas Bernard had emphasized the superiority of the interior experiences, however, Julian moves between them without indicating that one sort is more significant than the other; indeed she hardly could have done so in the way that Bernard did, since all Julian's experiences are based ultimately on the vivid sensory vision of Jesus bleeding on the cross. At one point she says that when a particular bodily vision ceased,

> the spiritual vision persisted in my understanding, and I waited with reverent fear, rejoicing in what I saw and wishing, as much as I dared, to see more, if that were God's will, or to see for a longer time what I already had seen.[50]

Far from reckoning the spiritual vision more valuable than the physical one, as Bernard had done, in this instance at least we find Julian wishing that the physical vision might return even while the spiritual vision continued.

Furthermore, Julian records that she had prayed for such a physical vision of Christ's passion long before these experiences occurred. She says that she had asked God for two things conditionally, and a third unconditionally. The two she had asked for conditionally were a physical illness to the point of death, "because I wanted to be purged by God's mercy, and afterwards live more to his glory because of that sickness;"[51] and secondly a vision of the passion of Christ,

> a bodily sight, in which I might have more knowledge of our Saviour's bodily pains, and of the compassion of our Lady and of all his true lovers who were living at that time and saw his pains, for I would have been one of them and suffered with them.[52]

The third, unconditional request was that she would receive three "wounds": true contrition, loving compassion, and longing with her will for God. These latter she asked for unconditionally and continually, because she held them to be at the heart of Christian life and growth in holiness. The bodily illness and the vision of the passion, however, she herself recognized to be highly unusual requests. In the context of her time, when identification with the suffering humanity of Jesus was much to the fore in devotional thought, desire for a participatory vision of the passion is not quite so odd as it might otherwise seem today. Similarly, the request for a severe illness can be at least partly understood as a desire both to achieve compassionate identification with the many who had suffered in the Black Death and other such disasters, and also as a way of preparing for one's own death, developing the deliberate awareness that this life has a terminus and must be lived accordingly.[53] Even so, Julian knew that these prayers were odd by any standards, and therefore asked that they be granted only if this was what God wanted for her. And then, she says, she forgot about them.

It was only when she became seriously ill and was on the point of death, with the attendant priest holding a crucifix before her eyes so that she could gaze on it while she expired, that she remembered that she had prayed for such an illness long before; and it occurred to her to renew her prayer for identification with the passion of Christ,

> that my body might be filled full of recollection and feeling of his blessed Passion ... for I wished that his pains might be my pains, with compassion which would lead to longing for God.[54]

It is clear that in this prayer she was thinking in terms of her continual and unconditional desire for contrition, compassion, and longing for God; and she says explicitly that at this point

> I never wanted any kind of bodily vision or any kind of revelation from God, but the compassion which I thought a loving soul could have for our Lord Jesus. ...[55]

Nevertheless, it was then that the visions began, and it is clear throughout Julian's discussion of them that she saw their significance in the context of this prayer.[56]

It is clear, therefore, that Julian considered the visions and the teaching that went with them to be wonderful gifts of God, so wonderful, indeed, that when she recovered from her illness she felt it incumbant upon her to write them down and share them with her fellow Christians, in spite of her felt inadequacies as "a woman, ignorant, weak and frail."[57] However, it is equally clear that the value of the visions did not, in Julian's mind, consist of ecstatic feelings or a sense of obliteration of personality, but rather in the way that they fostered in her and in her readers that which she supremely desired: contrition, compassion, and longing for God. It is for this reason also that she wishes to share them with her readers: not so that they might have exalted feelings, or think that they too should have visions, let alone that they should stand in wonder of her, but quite simply "that it should be to every man the same profit that I asked for myself."[58]

Julian is emphatic that the visions are not an end in themselves, but a means to greater love for God.

I am not good because of the revelations, but only if I love God better; and inasmuch as you love God better, it is more to you than to me.... For I am sure that there are many who never had revelations or visions, but only the common teaching of Holy Church, who love God better than I.... [59]

Though the visions were for her an important aid in growth in the love of God, therefore, she would entirely agree with Bernard that they were in no way central to religion, nor should they be thought of as essential. It is significant that although her whole book is taken up with trying to help her fellow Christians to deeper knowledge and love of God, she never offers any technique or method for obtaining a vision or revelation. She does not even make the slightest suggestion that they too should seek or even pray for one. In her view, that is not what counts.

What does count is the deep recognition of the love of God, and the response of human love to that divine love. For Julian, this is anything but an abstract theory. It is rooted in her depth of identification with the passion of Christ, an identification which she desires her readers to share, and which cannot, therefore, be necessarily connected with visions, though there is no doubt that in her own life there was a strong contingent connection.

We can see the relationship of the two in her life in several ways. In the first place, even while she was having the visions, Julian was not content to bask in a warm experiential glow, but seized the opportunity to ask God some hard questions about why God permitted evil and suffering. The discussion of what her questions were and how they were answered cannot be addressed here. What is important for our purposes is that far from giving herself up to trance or ecstasy, Julian kept her wits about her and treated the visions not as ends in themselves but as means to deepen her insight and understanding.

Secondly, it was this deepened insight that she most wanted to share. Julian meditated on the visions for twenty years before writing the Long Text, and it is demonstrable that during this time she acquired considerable knowledge of patristic and medieval theological writing which informed her subsequent account.[60] If she had thought of the visions as all that was important, she would hardly have bothered to do this, or indeed to write the Long Text at all, since the visions themselves are adequately presented in the Short Text. She used them, instead, as the basis for theological inquiry directly geared to the spiritual direction of her readers.[61]

We can see, therefore, that while the visions were of enormous personal importance to Julian, and her theological reflection never loses sight of them, their importance was of a different order than one would have expected from James' account of mysticism. They were in her view a wonderful gift, but it would be a tragic mistake to fasten on them rather than on their giver, or to think that by investigating the phenomena of the visions one was investigating what was of the essence of her religion. Like Bernard, Julian's religion was profoundly experiential in the broad sense; all of life was to be permeated and fulfilled with the joyful love of God. But she, no more than they, would accept James' account of experiences in the narrow sense as essential to her mysticism, nor would she suppose that by studying the phenomena of these "intenser manifestations" in themselves one would be any nearer to understanding the one thing needful, the integration of the whole life and personality in response to the love of God shown in the compassion of Christ.

She sums up her teaching as follows:

And from the time that it was revealed, I desired many times to know in what was our Lord's meaning. And fifteen years after and more, I was answered in spiritual understanding, and it was said: What, do you wish to know your Lord's meaning in this thing? Know it well, love was his meaning. Who reveals it to you? Love. What did he reveal to you? Love. Why does he reveal it to you? For love. Remain in this, and you will know more of the same. But you will never know different, without end. So I was taught that love was our Lord's meaning.[62]

IV. SUMMARY AND CONCLUSION

We are now in a position to sum up the findings of this study. We have seen that although the two mystics who serve as paradigms for our investigation disagree about the value of special experiences like visions and revelations, they are unanimous that these experiences are not the goal and centre of their religion. That goal is union with God. From this, two things have emerged clearly. The first is that union with God is experiential in the broad sense. It is not abstract theory or dogma, or ritual enacted for its own sake, nor is it simply a moral attitude, nor is it a combination of all three. Rather, it is that which lies beneath and beyond all these things, giving them life and significance. It is furthermore in part already known, and in part not yet known: union with God is both an experienced reality and a future hope; and the spiritual life is a life in which that union is steadily increasing.

The second thing that has emerged is that this union with God cannot be equated with intense experiences like voices and visions and subjective feelings of unity or ecstasy. At their best, these phenomena are a help toward the ongoing project of increasing union with God. At worst, if one becomes fixated upon them, they are an impediment. They are never an end in themselves, and they are never essential even as a means to union with God.

In so far as Bernard and Julian are representative of Christian mysticism, therefore, it would follow that James and those who follow him are fundamentally misguided in their approach to the study of mysticism. Experiences like voices and visions, though they undoubtedly occur, are not central to mysticism, judging by these two mystics, both of whom warn against fastening undue importance upon them. If they are right about this, then even if we agree with James that the essence of religion must be judged from its intenser manifestations, James is wrong to think that this means it must be judged by acute experiences in the narrow sense of the word as he proceeds to do. The fact that many subsequent philosophers have followed James in this mistake does not correct it.

It is of course James' prerogative to concentrate his study on "the extremer expressions of the religious temperament," as he puts it, and to consider the nature and significance of these phenomena. It would be ridiculous to deny that the mystical writings of Christianity as of other religions are full of accounts of all manner of phenomena: ecstasy, levitations, trances, visions, locutions, and many more. It is important to ask what their significance is, and whether they are products of healthy or sick minds or societies; nor should we assume that there is a blanket answer that will cover every case. The glance at two paradigms has already shown that their views differ about the nature and value of such experiences, even though they agree that they are not essential. These experiences must not be studied out of their social and historical context, furthermore, because as has already emerged, the context is often an indicator of the way in which intense experiences can be understood and evaluated. These phenomena do indeed call for psychological and sociological study and philosophical and theological evaluation. But it does not follow that studying and evaluating these is the same as studying or evaluating the essence of mysticism, even if one grants that that essence is experiential. We have seen that mystical experience is not reducible to a set of mystical experiences, no matter how intense they may be.

From this, important consequences follow. In the first place, if the focus of James' study of mysticism is misplaced, and if that focus ought to be on union with God rather than on intense psychic phenomena, then we will need to look closely at what mystics actually mean by the notion of union. Although James, because of his post-Kantian interest in the margins of consciousness as the possible place of interaction with a supernatural realm, focussed on experiences in the narrow sense, it might be that the experience of union as the four mystics discuss it should still be understood as Schleiermacher and Schelling described it, namely as an intense feeling or immediate consciousness of the Deity, in which there is complete merging of subject and object in a preconceptual unity. It would take another paper to show that this is as misguided as was James' fastening on acute psychic phenomena, and that it flows from an implicit acceptance of Kantian strictures which a study of the paradigm mystics helps us first to question and finally to reject.

Along with this, it becomes necessary to look at the characteristics which James accepted from romantic and idealist philosophers as descriptive of mystical experience: the merging of subject and object, ineffability, the noetic quality, transiency, and passivity. It would be enormously useful to measure these against actual mystics to see to what extent they do indeed characterize not simply non-essential psychic phenomena but the centre of the mystical experience of union with God. Of great importance in all this would be the question of language and the expressibility of mystical experience. I would argue that far from ineffability being the distinguishing feature of mystical experience, the mystics' use of language is a feature of their experience that provides the tool for our rejection of Kantian epistemology and stimulates a more adequate understanding of human personhood in community.

Also, the distinction between the broad and narrow senses of religious experience raises questions about the means of achieving the goal of mysticism. If it is taken that the goal is to have certain sorts of experiences of ecstasy or visions, then it would make sense to ask whether these experiences could not be achieved just as well by drugs as by the ascetical practices associated with Christian mysticism. If the goal is something quite different, however, then these ascetical practices and the traditional "threefold path" of purgation, illumination, and contemplation will need to be reconsidered. Again, it could be argued that doing so provides us with an alternative anthropology to those views current in post-Kantian philosophy, a

view of human personhood which correlates with an epistemology and ontology opposed to much post-Enlightenment thought and able to provide insight into contemporary problems, both philosophical and practical.

Arguing along these lines, it is clear that the question of the evidential value of mystical experience will again emerge. It may be, for instance, that visions and voices and other such phenomena can be discounted as evidence for the existence of God, but that mystical experience in the broad sense offers a much different perspective. Part of what should be considered is the presuppositions involved in what will count as evidence. Any such presuppositions are inevitably grounded in an epistemology and philosophy of language and reality: a study of the mystics brings these assumptions to light and enables us to reconsider them, and with them, the question of evidence.

Similarly with regard to the question of a mystical core of religion: if this core is sought in the similarities or dissimilarities between mystical experiences in the narrow sense, it may be that the investigation has taken place at altogether the wrong level and that we need to begin again, taking seriously what the mystics themselves say about what is essential as the basis for dialogue with mystics in other religious traditions. The whole idea of what would constitute such a core and how it could be discerned will need to be reconsidered.

These tasks cannot be undertaken in this paper. What I have tried to show is that a one-sided concentration on experiences in the narrow sense of that term has been a legacy of James to philosophical evaluation of mysticism; that a look at Bernard and Julian calls such a concentration into question; and that such questioning has wide implications for the philosophy of religion.

NOTES

1. See for example Anthony O'Hear, *Experience, Explanation and Faith* (Routledge and Kegan Paul, 1984), ch. 2; and J. L. Mackie, *The Miracle of Theism* (Oxford University Press, 1982), ch. 10, to name only two.

2. Cf. William James Earle, "James, William," in Paul Edwards (ed.)., *The Encyclopedia of Philosophy* (London and New York: Macmillan, 1967), vol. IV, pp. 240–9.

3. Cf. *Pragmatism: A New Name for Some Old Ways of Thinking* (New York and London: Longmans, Green and Co., 1907), pp. 231–2.

4. *Principles of Psychology* (New York, 1890), vol. I, p. 145.

5. *Pragmatism,* pp. 9–12; cf. *A Pluralistic Universe* (New York and London: Longmans, Green and Co., 1909), Lecture 1.

6. *Principles of Psychology,* vol. I, p. 162; cf. Graham Bird, *William James* (London and New York: Routledge and Kegan Paul, 1986), p. 176.

7. *Pragmatism,* p. 109.

8. See William James' "Introduction" in his (ed.), *The Literary Remains of the Late Henry James* (Boston, 1885).

9. Ralph Barton Perry, *The Thought and Character of William James,* 2 vols. (London and Boston: Oxford University Press, 1935), vol. I, p. 140.

10. Cf. *A Pluralistic Universe,* Lecture III; *Essays in Radical Empiricism* (London and New York: Longmans, Green and Co., 1912), pp. 276–7, etc.

11. *Pragmatism,* pp. 151–5.

12. *The Varieties of Religious Experience,* p. 391.

13. *Ibid.* p. 367.

14. *Ibid.* pp. 367–8.

15. For a recent treatment of this, see Nicholas Lash, *Easter in Ordinary: Reflections on Human Experience and the Knowledge of God* (London: SCM, 1988), pp. 18–104.

16. *Ibid.* p. 50.

17. *Ibid.* p. 85.

18. *Ibid.* p. 96.

19. *Ibid.* p. 117.

20. *Ibid.* p. 13.

21. *Ibid.* p. 37.

22. *Ibid.* p. 62.

23. *Ibid.* p. 67.

24. Another famous example of this approach is Aldous Huxley, *The Doors of Perception* (London: Chatto and Windus, 1954).

25. Etienne Gilson, *The Mystical Theology of St Bernard,* ch. 3.

26. Gilson, p. 24.

27. Bernard, *On Loving God,* ch. 1.

28. *Ibid.* x. 27.

29. *Sermons on the Song of Songs,* 3.1.1.

30. 37.2; cf. Jean Leclercq, *The Love of Learning and the Desire for God,* ch. 7.

31. Gilson, ch. 4.

32. *Sermons on the Song of Songs,* 31–33, etc.

33. *Ibid.* 33. IV. 6.

34. *Ibid.* 31. II. 4.

35. *Ibid.*

36. *Ibid.* 31. III. 6.

37. *Ibid.* 31. III. 7.

38. *Ibid.* 32. I. 2.

39. Gilson, p. 94; cf. *Sermons on the Song of Songs,* 3. I. I.

40. Gilson, p. 93.

41. Matt. 5.8.

42. *Sermons on the Song of Songs,* I. I. 2.

43. Cf. Origen, *The Prologue to the Commentary on the Song of Songs* (New York: Classics of Western Spirituality, Paulist Press and London: SPCK, 1979), pp. 231–6; see also the Introduction by Rowan A. Greer, pp. 17–28; Andrew Louth, *The Origins of the Christian Mystical Tradition,* ch. IV; Jean Daniélou, *Origen* (New York: Sheed and Ward, 1955), pp. 293–309; Joseph Wilson Trigg, *Origen: The Bible and Philosophy in the Third Century Church* (Atlanta, Georgia: John Knox Press, 1983), pp. 201–5.

44. Julian of Norwich, *Showings,* p. 129.

45. *Ibid.* p. 136.

46. *Ibid.* p. 131.

47. *Ibid.* p. 193.

48. *Ibid.* p. 130.

49. *Ibid.* pp. 130–5.

50. *Ibid.* p. 133, p. 190.

51. *Ibid.* p. 178.

52. *Ibid.* p. 178.

53. For a further explanation of these prayers in their context see my *Julian of Norwich, Mystic and Theologian* (London: SPCK, 1987), ch. 4.

54. *Ibid.* p. 180.

55. *Ibid.* p. 181.

56. *Julian of Norwich,* ch. 5.

57. *Ibid.* p. 135; cf. Simon Tugwell, "Julian of Norwich," in his *Ways of Imperfection* (Darton, Longman and Todd, 1984).

58. *Ibid.* p. 135.

59. *Ibid.* p. 191.

60. Cf. my *Julian of Norwich,* ch. 2.

61. Julia Gatta is importantly correct in her presentation of Julian's writing as intended for the spiritual direction of her readers, not merely as autobiography. See her *Three Spiritual Directors for our Time* (Cambridge, MA.: Cowley Publications, 1987).

62. *Ibid.* p. 342.

IV.A.4

Perceiving God

WILLIAM P. ALSTON

William P. Alston (1921–2009) was professor of philosophy at Syracuse University and one of the leading figures in the fields of epistemology and philosophy of religion throughout the latter half of the twentieth century. In this selection, he argues that religious experience plays a role with respect to beliefs about God that is analogous to the role played by sense perception with respect to beliefs about the external world. On his view, religious experience may be thought of as perception of God, and it is a source of justified belief about God.

I want to explore and defend the idea that the experience, or, as I shall say, the *perception,* of God plays an epistemic role with respect to beliefs about God importantly analogous to that played by sense perception with respect to beliefs about the physical world. The nature of that latter role is, of course, a matter of controversy, and I have no time here to go into those controversies. It is admitted, however, on (almost) all hands that sense perception provides us with knowledge (justified belief) about current states of affairs in the immediate environment of the perceiver and that knowledge of this sort is somehow required for any further knowledge of the physical world. The possibility I wish to explore is that what a person takes to be an experience of God can provide him/her with knowledge (justified beliefs) about what God is doing, or how God is "situated," vis-à-vis that subject at that moment. Thus, by experiencing the presence and activity of God, *S* can come to know (justifiably believe) that God is sustaining her in being, filling her with His love, strengthening her, or communicating a certain message to her. Let's call beliefs as to how God is currently related to the subject *M-beliefs* ("M" for manifestation); these are the "perceptual beliefs" of the theological sphere. I shall suppose that here too the "perceptual" knowledge one acquires from experience is crucial for whatever else we can learn about God, though I won't have time to

Reprinted from William P. Alston, "Perceiving God?", *The Journal of Philosophy* LXXXII (1986): 655–65. Used with permission.

explore and defend that part of the position; I will have my hands full defending the claim that M-beliefs are justified. I will just make two quick points about the role of M-beliefs in the larger scheme. First, just as with our knowledge of the physical world, the recognition of a crucial role for perceptual knowledge is compatible with a wide variety of views as to just how it figures in the total system and as to what else is involved. Second, an important difference between the two spheres is that in the theological sphere perceptual beliefs as to what God has "said" (communicated, revealed) to one or another person play a major role.

I have been speaking alternatively of perceptual *knowledge* and of the *justification* of perceptual beliefs. In this paper I shall concentrate on justification, leaving to one side whatever else is involved in knowledge. It will be my contention that (putative) experience of God is a source of justification for M-beliefs, somewhat in the way that sense experience is a source of justification for perceptual beliefs. Again, it is quite controversial what this latter way is. I shall be thinking of it in terms of a direct-realist construal of sense perception, according to which I can be justified in supposing that my dog is wagging his tail just because something is visually presenting itself to me as (looks like) my dog wagging his tail; that is, it looks to me in such a way that I am thereby justified in thereby supposing it to be my dog wagging his tail. Analogously I think of the "experience of God" as a matter of something's presenting itself to one's experience as God (doing so and so); so that here too the subject is justified in believing that God is present to her, or is doing so and so vis-à-vis her, just because that is the way in which the object is presented to her experience. (For the purposes of this paper let's focus on those cases in which this presentation is not via any *sensory* qualities or *sensorily* perceivable objects. The experience involved will be nonsensory in character.) It is because I think of the experience of God as having basically the same structure as the sense perception of physical objects that I feel entitled to speak of "perceiving God." But though

I construe the matter in direct-realist terms, most of what I have to say here will be relevant to a defense of the more general claim that the experiential justification of M-beliefs is importantly parallel to the experiential justification of perceptual beliefs about the physical environment, on any halfway plausible construal of the latter, at least on any halfway plausible realist construal.

I shall develop the position by way of responding to a number of objections. This procedure reflects my conviction that the very considerable incidence of putative perceptions of God creates a certain initial presumption that these experiences are what they seem to be and that something can thereby be learned about God.

Objection I. What reason do we have for supposing that anyone ever does really perceive God? In order for S to perceive God it would have to be the case that (1) God exists, and (2) God is related to S or to his experience in such a way as to be perceivable by him. Only after we have seen reason to accept all that will we take seriously any claim to perceive God.

Answer. It all depends on what you will take as a reason. What you have in mind, presumably, are reasons drawn from some source other than perceptions of God, e.g., metaphysical arguments for the existence and nature of God. But why do you think you are justified in that restriction? We don't proceed in this way with respect to sense perception. Although in determining whether a particular alleged perception was genuine we don't make use of the results of *that* perception, we do utilize what has been observed in many other cases. And what alternative is there? The conditions of veridical sense perception have to do with states of affairs and causal interactions in the physical world, matters to which we have no cognitive access that is not based on sense perception. In like fashion, if there is a divine reality why suppose that the conditions of veridically perceiving it could be ascertained without relying on perceptions of *it*? In requiring external validation in this case but not the other you are arbitrarily imposing a double standard.

Objection II. There are many contradictions in the body of M-beliefs. In particular, persons report communications from God that contradict other reported communications. How, then, can one claim that all M-beliefs are justified?

Answer. What is (should be) claimed is only *prima facie* justification. When a person believes that God is experientially present to him, that belief is justified *unless* the subject has sufficient reasons to suppose it to be false or to suppose that the experience is not, in these circumstances, sufficiently indicative of the truth of the belief. This is, of course, precisely the status of individual perceptual beliefs about the physical environment. When, seeming to see a lake, I believe there to be a lake in front of me, my belief is thereby justified unless I have sufficient reason to suppose it false or to suppose that, in these circumstances, the experience is not sufficiently indicative of the truth of the belief.

Objection III. It is rational to form beliefs about the physical environment on the basis of the way that environment appears to us in sense experience (call this practice of belief formation SP) because that is a generally reliable mode of belief formation. And it is reliable just because, in normal conditions, sense experience varies concomitantly with variations in what we take ourselves to be perceiving. But we have no reason to suppose any such regular covariation for putative perception of God. And hence we lack reason for regarding as rational the parallel practice of forming M-beliefs on the basis of what is taken to be a perception of God (call that practice RE).

Answer. This is another use of a double standard. How do we know that normal sense experience varies concomitantly with perceived objects? We don't know this a priori. Rather, we have strong empirical evidence for it. That is, by relying on sense perception for our data we have piled up evidence for the reliability of SP. Let's call the kind of circularity exhibited here *epistemic circularity*. It is involved whenever the premises in an argument for the reliability or rationality of a belief-forming practice have themselves been acquired by that practice.[1] If we allow epistemically circular

arguments, the reliability of RE can be supported in the same way. Among the things people have claimed to learn from RE is that God will enable people to experience His presence and activity from time to time in a veridical way. By relying on what one learns from the practice of RE, one can show that RE is a reliable belief-forming practice. On the other hand, if epistemically circular arguments are not countenanced, there can be no significant basis for a reliability claim in either case.

Objection IV. A claim to perceive X, and so to form reliable perceptual beliefs about X on the basis of this, presupposes that the experience involved is best explained by the activity of X, *inter alia*. But it seems that we can give adequate explanations of putative experiences of God in purely naturalistic terms, without bringing God into the explanation at all. Whereas we can't give adequate explanations of normal sense experience without bringing the experienced external objects into the explanation. Hence RE, but not SP, is discredited by these considerations.

Answer. I do not believe that much of a case can be made for the adequacy of any naturalistic explanation of experiences of God. But for present purposes I want to concentrate on the way in which this objection once more depends on a double standard. You will have no case at all for your claim unless you, question-beggingly, restrict yourself to sources of evidence that exclude RE. For from RE and systems built up on its output we learn that God is involved in the explanation of every fact whatever. But you would not proceed in that way with SP. If it is a question of determining the best explanation of sense experience you will, of course, make use of what you think you have learned from SP. Again, you have arbitrarily applied different standards to the two practices.

Here is another point. Suppose that one could give a purely psychological or physiological explanation of the experiences in question. That is quite compatible with God's figuring among their causes and, hence, coming into an ideally complete explanation. After all, it is presumably possible to give an adequate causal explanation of sense experience in terms of what goes on within the skull, but that is quite compatible with the external perceived objects' figuring further back along the causal chain.

Objection V. You have been accusing me of *arbitrarily* employing a double standard. But I maintain that RE differs from SP in ways that make different standards appropriate. SP is a pervasive and inescapable feature of our lives. Sense experience is insistent, omnipresent, vivid, and richly detailed. We use it as a source of information during all our waking hours. RE, by contrast, is not universally shared; and even for its devotees its practice is relatively infrequent. Moreover, its deliverances are, by comparison, meager, obscure, and uncertain. Thus when an output of RE does pop up, it is naturally greeted with more skepticism, and one properly demands more for its validation than in the case of so regular and central part of our lives as SP.

Answer. I don't want to deny either the existence or the importance of these differences. I want to deny only that they have the alleged bearing on the epistemic situation. Why should we suppose that a cognitive access enjoyed only by a part of the population is less likely to be reliable than one that is universally distributed? Why should we suppose that a source that yields less detailed and less fully understood beliefs is more suspect than a richer source? A priori it would seem just as likely that some aspects of reality are accessible only to persons that satisfy certain conditions not satisfied by all human beings as that some aspects are equally accessible to all. A priori it would seem just as likely that some aspects of reality are humanly graspable only in a fragmentary and opaque manner as that some aspects are graspable in a more nearly complete and pellucid fashion. Why view the one sort of cognitive claim with more suspicion than the other? I will agree that the spotty distribution of RE calls for explanation, as does the various cognitively unsatisfactory features of its output. But, for that matter, so does the universal distribution and cognitive richness of SP. And in both cases explanations are forthcoming, though in both cases the outputs of the practices are utilized in order to achieve those explanations. As for RE, the limited distribution may be explained by the fact

that many persons are not prepared to meet the moral and other "way of life" conditions that God has set for awareness of Himself. And the cognitively unsatisfactory features of the doxastic output are explained by the fact that God infinitely exceeds our cognitive powers.

Objection VI. When someone claims to see a spruce tree in a certain spot, the claim is checkable. Other people can take a look, photographs can be taken, the subject's condition can be diagnosed, and so on. But there are no comparable checks and tests available in RE. And how can we take seriously a claim to have perceived an objective state of affairs if there is, in principle, no intersubjective way of determining whether that claim is correct?

Answer. The answer to this objection is implicit in a point made earlier, viz., that putative experience of God yields only prima facie justification, justification (unqualifiedly) provided there are no sufficient overriding considerations. This notion has a significant application only where there is what we may call an *overrider system*, i.e., ways of determining whether the facts are such as to indicate a belief from the range in question to be false and ways of determining whether conditions are such that the basis of the belief is sufficiently indicative of its truth. SP does contain such a system. What about RE? Here we must confront a salient difference between the two spheres. If we consider the way in which a body of beliefs has been developed on the basis of SP we find pretty much the same system across all cultures. But our encounters with God have spawned a number of different religious communities with beliefs and practices of worship which are quite different, though with some considerable overlap. These differences carry with them differences in overrider systems. But it remains true that if we consider any particular religious community which exhibits a significant commonality in doctrine and worship it will feature a more or less definite overrider system. For concreteness let's think of what I will call the *mainline Christian community*. (From this point onward I will use the term "RE" for the practice of forming M-beliefs as it goes on in this community.) In that community a body of doctrine has developed concerning the nature of God, His purposes, and His interactions with mankind, including His appearances to us. If an M-belief contradicts this system that is a reason for deeming it false. Moreover there is a long and varied history of experiential encounters with God, embodied in written accounts as well as oral transmission. This provides bases for regarding particular experiences as more or less likely to be veridical, given the conditions, psychological or otherwise, in which they occurred, the character of the subject, and the effects in the life of the subject. Thus a socially established religious doxastic practice like RE will contain a rich system of overriders that provides resources for checking the acceptability of any particular M-belief.

But perhaps your point is rather that there are no *external* checks on a particular report, none that do not rely on other claims of the same sort. Let's agree that this is the case. But why suppose that to be any black mark against RE? Here is the double standard again. After all, particular claims within SP cannot be checked without relying on what we have learned from SP. Suppose I claim to see a fir tree in a certain spot. To check on this one would have to rely on other persons' perceptual reports as to what is at that spot, our general empirical knowledge of the likelihood of a fir tree in that locality, and so on. Apart from what we take ourselves to have learned from SP, we would have nothing to go on. One can hardly determine whether my report was accurate by intuiting self-evident truths or by consulting divine revelation. But if SP counts as having a system of checks even though this system involves relying on some outputs of the practice in order to put others to the test, why should RE be deemed to have no such system when its procedures exhibit the same structure? Once more you are, arbitrarily, setting quite different requirements for different practices.

Perhaps your point was that RE's system of checks is unlike SP's. In particular, the following difference can be discerned. Suppose I report seeing a morel at a certain spot in the forest. Now suppose that a number of qualified observers take a good look at that spot at that time and report that no

morel is to be seen. In that case my report would have been decisively disconfirmed. But nothing like that is possible in RE. We can't lay down any conditions (of a sort the satisfaction of which we can determine) under which a properly qualified person will experience the presence of God if God is "there" to be experienced. Hence a particular report cannot be decisively disconfirmed by the experience of others.

But what epistemic relevance does this difference have? Why should we suppose that RE is rendered dubious for lacking check ability of this sort? Let's consider what makes this kind of intersubjective test possible for SP. Clearly it is that we have discovered fairly firm regularities in the behavior of physical things, including human sense perception. Since there are stable regularities in the ways in which physical objects disclose themselves to our perception, we can be assured that if X exists at a certain time and place and if S satisfies appropriate conditions then S is sure to perceive X. But no such tight regularities are discoverable in God's appearances to our experience. We can say something about the way in which such matters as the distribution of attention and the moral and spiritual state of the subject are conducive to such appearances; but these most emphatically do not add up to the sort of lawlike connections we get with SP. Now what about this difference? Is it to the epistemic discredit of RE that it does not enable us to discover such regularities? Well, that all depends on what it would be reasonable to expect if RE does put us into effective cognitive contact with God. Given what we have learned about God and our relations to Him (from RE, supplemented by whatever other sources there be), should we expect to be able to discover such realities if God really exists? Clearly not. There are several important points here, but the most important is that it is contrary to God's plans for us to give us that much control, cognitive and practical. Hence it is quite understandable, if God exists and is as RE leads us to suppose, that we should not be able to ascertain the kinds of regularities that would make possible the kinds of intersubjective tests exhibited by SP. Hence, the epistemic status of RE is in no way diminished by its lack of such tests. Once more RE is subjected to an inappropriate standard. This time, however, it is not a double standard, but rather an inappropriate single standard. RE is being graded down for lacking positive features of other practices, where these features cannot reasonably be supposed to be generally necessary conditions of epistemic excellence, even for experiential practices. Thus my critic is exhibiting what we might term *epistemic chauvinism*, judging alien forms of life according to whether they conform to the home situation, a procedure as much to be deplored in the epistemic as in the political sphere.

Objection VII. How can it be rational to take RE as a source of justification when there are incompatible rivals that can lay claim to that status on exactly the same grounds? M-beliefs of different religious communities conflict to a considerable extent, particularly those concerning alleged divine messages, and the bodies of doctrine they support conflict even more. We get incompatible accounts of God's plans for us and requirements on us, of the conditions of salvation, and so on. This being the case, how can we pick out just one of these communal practices as yielding justified belief?

Answer. I take this to be by far the most serious difficulty with my position. I have chosen to concentrate on what I take to be less serious problems, partly because their consideration brings out better the main lineaments of the position, and partly because any serious treatment of this last problem would spill beyond the confines of this paper.[2] Here I shall have to content myself with making one basic point. We are not faced with the necessity of choosing only one such practice as yielding prima facie justified M-beliefs. The fact that there are incompatibilities between systems of religious beliefs, in M-beliefs and elsewhere, shows that not all M-beliefs can be true, but not that they cannot all be prima facie justified. After all, incompatible beliefs *within* a system can all be prima facie justified; that's the point of the prima facie qualification. When we are faced with a situation like

that, the hope is that the overrider system and other winnowing devices will weed out the inconsistencies. To be sure, intersystem winnowing devices are hazier and more meager than those which are available within a system; but consistency, consonance with other well-entrenched beliefs and doxastic practices, and general reasonability and plausibility give us something to go on. Moreover, it may be that some religious ways of life fulfill their own promises more fully than others. Of course, there is never any guarantee that a unique way of resolving incompatibilities will present itself, even with a system. But where there are established practices of forming beliefs on the basis of experience, I believe the rational course is to regard each such belief as thereby prima facie justified, hoping that future developments, perhaps unforeseeable at present, will resolve fundamental incompatibilities.

In conclusion I will make explicit the general epistemological orientation I have been presupposing in my defense of RE. I take our human situation to be such that we engage in a plurality of basic doxastic practices, each of which involves a distinctive sort of input to belief-forming "mechanisms," a distinctive range of belief contents (a "subject matter" and ways of conceiving it), and a set of functions that determine belief contents as a function of input features. Each practice is socially established: socially shared, inculcated, reinforced, and propagated. In addition to experiential practices, with which we have been concerned in this paper, there are, e.g., inferential practices, the input of which consists of beliefs, and the practice of forming memory beliefs. A doxastic practice is not restricted to the formation of first-level beliefs; it will also typically involve criteria and procedures of criticism of the beliefs thus formed; here we will find the "overrider systems" of which we were speaking earlier. In general, we learn these practices and engage in them long before we arrive at the stage of explicitly formulating their principles and subjecting them to critical reflection. Theory is deeply rooted in practice.

Nor, having arrived at the age of reason, can we turn our back on all that and take a fresh start, in the Cartesian spirit, choosing our epistemic procedures and criteria anew, on a purely "rational" basis.

Apart from reliance on doxastic tendencies with which we find ourselves, we literally have nothing to go on. Indeed, what Descartes did, as Thomas Reid trenchantly pointed out, was arbitrarily to pick one doxastic practice he found himself engaged in—accepting propositions that seem self-evident—and set that as a judge over all the others, with what results we are all too familiar. This is not to say that we must acquiesce in our pre-reflective doxastic tendencies in every respect. We can tidy things up, modify our established practices so as to make each more internally consistent and more consistent with the others. But, on the whole and for the most part, we have no choice but to continue to form beliefs in accordance with these practices and to take these ways of forming beliefs as paradigmatically conferring epistemic justification. And this is the way that epistemology has in fact gone, except for some arbitrary partiality. Of course it would be satisfying to economize our basic commitments by taking one or a few of these practices as basic and using them to validate the others; but we have made little progress in this enterprise over the centuries. It is not self-evident that sense perception is reliable, nor can we establish its reliability if we restrict ourselves to premises drawn from introspection; we cannot show that deductive reasoning is valid without using deductive reasoning to do so; and so on. We are endowed with strong tendencies to engage in a number of distinct doxastic practices, none of which can be warranted on the basis of others. It is clearly the better part of wisdom to recognize beliefs that emerge from these practices to be rational and justified, at least once they are properly sifted and refined.

In this paper I have undertaken to extend this account to doxastic practices that are not universally practiced. Except for that matter of distribution and the other peripheral matters mentioned in Objection V and except for being faced with actually existing rivals, a religious experiential doxastic practice like RE seems to me to be on all fours with SP and other universal practices. It too involves a distinctive range of inputs, a range of belief contents, and functions that map features of the former onto contents of the latter. It is socially established within a certain community. It involves higher-level procedures of correction and modification of its first-level beliefs. Though it *may* be acquired in a deliberate and self-conscious fashion, it is more typically acquired in a practical, prereflective form. Though it is obviously evitable in a way SP, e.g., is not, for many of its practitioners it is just about as firmly entrenched.

These similarities lead me to the conclusion that if, as it seems we must concede, a belief is prima facie justified by virtue of emerging from one of the universal basic practices, we should also concede the same status to the products of RE. I have sought to show that various plausible-sounding objections to this position depend on the use of a double standard or reflect arbitrary epistemic chauvinism. They involve subjecting RE to inappropriate standards. Once we appreciate these points, we can see the strength of the case for RE as one more epistemically autonomous practice of belief formation and source of justification.

NOTES

1. See my "Epistemic Circularity," Philosophy and Phenomenological Research, XLVII, 1 (September 1986): 1–30.

2. For an extended treatment of this issue, see my "Religious Experience and Religious Diversity," forthcoming in Christian Scholars' Review.

IV.A.5

Do Mystics See God?

EVAN FALES

Evan Fales (1943–) is professor of philosophy at the University of Iowa. He has written numerous articles in epistemology and the philosophy of religion. In this article he argues (against William Alston, among others) that (a) mystical experiences need to be cross-checked somehow if they are to count as evidence supporting belief in God, but (b) they cannot be cross-checked. Thus, on his view, it is not reasonable to treat such experiences as evidence in support of theism.

And [the Lord] said, Thou canst not see my face [panim]; *for there shall no man see my face and live*

—Exod. 33:20

And Jacob called the name of the place Peniel: for I have seen God face [panim] *to face, and my life is preserved*

—Gen. 32:30

There's more than one way to skin a cat.

1. A CAUTIONARY TALE

Theistic philosophers have perennially cited mystical experiences—experiences of God—as evidence for God's existence and for other truths about God. In recent years, the attractiveness of this line of thought has been reflected in its use by a significant number of philosophers.[1] But both philosophers and mystics agree that not all mystical experiences can be relied upon; many are the stuff of delusion.[2] So they have somehow to be checked out, their bona fides revealed. But can they be? I will be arguing that (a) they must indeed be cross-checked

to serve as good evidence; and that (b) they can't be—or not nearly well enough to permit pressing them into service as serious support for theism. The need for cross-checking, necessary in any case, is made acute by two facts: the extreme variability of mystical experiences and the doctrines they are recruited to support, and the fact that, especially in the face of this variability, mystical experiences are much more effectively explained naturalistically. Furthermore, our ability adequately to cross-check mystical experiences (hereafter, MEs), in a way that would reveal the hand of God, is crippled by the fact that theists offer no hypothesis concerning the causal mechanism by means of which God shows himself to mystics.

Let's begin with my third epigraph. This insightful, if grisly, bit of folk wisdom tells much of our story. Permit me to spell out the dolorous tale. I am greeted by the sight of poor Sylvester, a heap of flayed flesh upon the lawn. I set out to reconstruct the crime. With but the denuded corpse as evidence, the possibilities are multiple. So I must locate other clues. A bloodied knife nearby might have secrets to reveal: suppose the hemoglobin tests out feline. Even better, perhaps I can find an

From *Contemporary Debates in Philosophy of Religion*, edited by Michael L. Peterson and Raymond J. VanArragon © Blackwell 2004. Reproduced with permission of Blackwell Publishing Ltd.

eyewitness or two, discovering through further investigation that they are both sober and honest. I might find fingerprints on the knife. And so on.

In all this, I rely upon my senses to convey evidence of the deed. How is this managed? Why, through some causal sequence, a continuation of some of those sequences that converged upon the destruction of poor Sylvester, and that then diverged from there. Light waves bearing news of cat skin and flesh make their way from the *corpus delicti* to my "sensory surfaces," there to be processed in those still and possibly forever mysterious ways into cat-corpse-consciousness. Mysterious or not, what we do know is that cat and conscious episode are related as (partial) cause to (partial) effect. But for there being some suitable causal link between cat and experience, that experience, no matter its intrinsic characteristics, is not a perception of that cat.[3]

But if the intrinsic content of my experience can be caused in multiple ways (the presence of an actual cat-corpse being but one of these), then how shall I ascertain that my senses do not deceive? The short answer to this importunate and persistent problem, the problem of perception, is: I must cross-check. But we cannot explore the substance of this remark without making two antecedent observations. First, no amount of cross-checking can produce evidence that will satisfy the radical skeptic. I can decide to pinch myself to check that I'm not just dreaming of cats; but of course I might just be dreaming that I've pinched myself. Second, because of this, and because our project is to examine whether putative experiences of God must be cross-checked to carry evidential weight, not to respond to radical skepticism, we shall have to frame our discussion with some care. One could, of course, accept a counsel of despair: neither ordinary sense experience nor mystical experience can form the basis of justified beliefs about external matters. In that event, mystical theistic beliefs are in no worse shape, epistemically speaking, than ordinary perceptual beliefs. But that would be because neither set of beliefs could be in any worse shape, so far as justification goes. That sort of "pox on both your houses" skepticism is, however, not a very interesting position from the perspective of traditional debates

about the warrant for theism. The interesting question is: If we suppose ordinary perceptual beliefs (and we may throw in scientific theory for good measure) to be warrantable by appeal to sense experience, then why shouldn't theistic beliefs be similarly warrantable by appeal to perceptual experience, whether sensory or mystical?

Here, in a nutshell, is what I shall argue. The problem of perception derives largely from the general truth that any effect—hence a perceptual experience—can be caused in more ways than one. Our strategy for removing this ambiguity is cross-checking. Ultimately, cross-checking involves just collecting more data, which are subject to the same ambiguity. Our implicit reasoning is that the total amount of ambiguity can nevertheless be progressively reduced in this way. The means by which science draws a bead on postulated "unobservable" entities (like electrons) is not in principle or in practice different in kind; it is just more systematic and careful than the humdrum of everyday perceptual judgments. In everyday contexts, cross-checking is informal, and it is so automatic, continuous, and pervasive that, except under duress (e.g., as we try to catch out a magician), it is scarcely noticed. I propose to show how cross-checking works; to argue that it is a mandatory feature of any recruitment of perceptual experience to epistemic ends; and that, therefore, it is a requirement that must be met in theistic appeals to mystical experience as evidence for theism. Finally, I shall argue that this requirement has not, and probably cannot, be met. So, I shall conclude, mystical experience provides hardly any useful support for theism.

2. CROSS-CHECKING EXPLAINED

So, what is cross-checking? Why is it needed? And how does it work? Let "cross- checking" denote all those procedures and strategies we use to settle questions about the causes of something. These include, in particular, (1) using Mill's methods to pick out causally relevant antecedent conditions; (2) exploiting the fact that events have multiple effects, to "triangulate" the event in question, on the principle that qualitatively different causes will have *some* differences in their (potential) effects;[4] and (3) confirming the existence of causal mechanisms allegedly connecting a cause to its effects (when it is not a proximate cause). These strategies depend upon putting forward hypotheses and testing them by means of diagnostic experiments. I shall discuss mainly tests of type (3), but invoke strategy (2) when considering prophetic revelations as a test of MEs.

There are various ways in which cross-checking principles can be formally stated. One way to approach type-3 cross-checks is to consider the problem posed by Duhem's thesis. We have a hypothesis H (e.g., that the cat was skinned with a knife), on the basis of which we can, with the assistance of auxiliary hypothesis A, infer some observable effect E_0. In general, the occurrence of E_0 should confirm H, and its nonoccurrence disconfirm H. How that goes depends upon how strongly $H \& A$ probabilifies E_0 (or its negation), and how strongly it or its negation is probabilified by competing hypotheses-cum-auxiliaries.

But, as we know, even when E_0 fails to materialize and $H \& A$ is thereby disconfirmed, the opprobrium need not fall on H: the falsehood of A may be to blame. Here is where type-3 cross-checking comes in. It comes in two varieties. First, we can run further tests on H, pitting it against its rivals either in repeat performances of the first experiment or, often more tellingly, in different experiments which call upon different auxiliaries and predict different observations. Second, we can check A, now employing *it* as a hypothesis to be tested.[5] Thus, a defender of H in the face of *not-E_0* might insist that the relevant auxiliary is not A, but $A\star$, where $H \& A\star$ entails *not-E_0*. Now A and $A\star$ are competitors, and we can require an independent "crucial experiment"[6] in which they make conflicting predictions, E_1 and $E_1\star$. But of course, those predictions cannot be made without invoking further auxiliaries—call them A_1 and $A_1\star$. Clearly, if the experimental outcome is E_1, the defender of $A\star$ (and hence H) can protect $A\star$ by insisting upon modifying his $A_1\star$. And then we can play another round. Can this testing game go on forever, or will the regress eventually run the quarry (the truth-

value of H) to ground? One way to capture the radical skeptic's intuition is by arguing that the cycle of modifications to save the appearances can go on forever. (This is one form of the so-called underdetermination of theory by data.) The other side of the coin is that this way of formulating the problem of skepticism helps us see what sorts of minimal assumptions might head off an infinite regress, thereby making the evidential issue an interesting one. And this is just what we need to see when the observations in question are the mystic's experiences, and the hypothesis is theism.

I do not regard it as a settled question whether adjustment of auxiliaries in the face of recalcitrant data can go on forever. But even if after-the-fact revising can proceed indefinitely, there is a strong intuition that a system of beliefs which must constantly be revised as new evidence comes in loses plausibility in relation to one that does not. Let us make this anti-skeptical assumption. Evidence, in the face of which a hypothesis can be rescued only by revision of auxiliary assumptions, works to the disadvantage of that hypothesis—though perhaps not decisively so—in comparison with competitors which accommodate that evidence without revisions.[7]

An obvious objection to all this will be that, plausible as it may be as a rational reconstruction of scientific reasoning, it does not at all capture the process by which we acquire warranted perceptual beliefs. Perceptual knowledge seems much more direct than this, even to those who concede the obvious fact that it is causally mediated. So I now want to argue that this is an illusion, that in fact warrant accrues to perceptual beliefs only insofar as, rationally reconstructed, their acquisition, too, requires inference to the best explanation.

3. THE PERVASIVE NEED FOR CROSS-CHECKING

What, then, is it about cross-checking that establishes its essential and fundamental place as an epistemic method, even in the case of sense perception? This standing is a consequence of the fact that we are physical beings, situated within a spatiotemporal world in an environment with which we communicate via physical—that is, causal—processes. But the centrality of cross-checking is still more fundamental than this. It is demanded for knowledge of *any* causal process, in which causes are known *via* their effects. In particular, it is demanded in connection with any claim to have perceptual access to an extra-mental reality. It would be demanded, for example, if we were bodiless minds claiming perceptual contact with disembodied demons, evil or benign, with angels, or with a god. That is because the contact is perceptual, and because of the principle

> P: If S perceives (has a perceptual experience of) X, then X is a suitable cause of S's experience.

First, three comments about P; and then, more on the connection between (P) and cross-checking:

1. When I say that X is *a* cause of S's experience, I mean just that it plays a role as one of the causal antecedents of S's experience.

2. Strictly speaking, it is events or states of affairs that are causes. If X is a particular, then it is not X *per se,* but X's having some property or undergoing some change which constitutes the cause in question.

3. When I say that this is a *suitable* cause of S's experience, I mean that it must cause the experience in the right sort of way for the experience to count as perception *of X*. Obviously, not all of the causal conditions of my now perceiving this pen are conditions I now perceive (those conditions include my eyes and brain working properly, the pen being illuminated, and even God, if God caused the pen to exist and sustains me in existence). We cannot say *in general* what criteria distinguish the "right" sort of causal ancestry from the wrong sorts; but cross-checking has everything to do with how we justifiably identify the right items in particular cases.

Knowing what we are perceiving is a matter of knowing what is causing our experience in the right sort of way. But that is a matter of narrowing down the candidate causes of an experience so that—ideally—just one cause, situated in the right way, can explain our data. It is precisely here that cross-checking plays the crucial role, by enabling us to eliminate possible causes and to form a sufficiently precise conception of our environment and the causal processes that occur in it to "zero in" on the (or a) "suitable" cause.[8]

William Alston misses the mark when he insists that a demand for similar cross-checking of the claims of mystics amounts to a kind of epistemic imperialism.[9] He insists that each epistemic practice, including mystical practice, gets to dictate its own standards and cross-checking criteria. But, as we shall see, those invoked by mystics are characteristically vacuous. Obviously, the sorts of evidence relevant to checking a perceptual claim will depend upon its modality and content. But determining what makes something *count* as evidence and justification is dictated by the causal structure of perception and cannot be commandeered by epistemic practices, so-called.

Many philosophers will reject this conception of perception and perceptual knowledge. They do so partly for dialectical reasons—that is, because they believe that the road so paved leads straight to skeptical perdition. They do so, further, for broadly phenomenological reasons—that is, because we do not ordinarily make perceptual knowledge claims on the basis of anything more than having the right sort of experience. We don't indulge in any cross-checking or inference in judging, for example, that there is someone in the seat next to us.

But these objections are, in the present context, misdirected. The phenomenological objection ignores what we might call "subliminal information processing," both past and occurrent, and the vital role that cross-checking plays in this processing.[10] What sort of perceptual seemings a given environment can produce in one is a function not only of recent sensory stimulation, but of much else: of attention and motivational factors, of past experience and concepts thereby acquired, of expectations for which an inductive rationale could be supplied if required (but which ordinarily does not—and need not—enter into perceptual engagement with the world). We can look and just "see" that the refrigerator in the kitchen is white, in part because we have acquired an understanding of what refrigerators are and what they look like, readily expect such items to appear in kitchens, and know that white things look a certain way under the apparent conditions of illumination. An ability to "just see" directly that this refrigerator is white is a hard-won skill. Learning endows us with unconscious cognitive mechanisms that operate to apply concepts in forming a percept as if on the basis of various inductions.

Moreover, past learning and also the present cognitive processing incorporate cross-checking in fundamental ways. What our cognitive systems have learned is how "automatically" to make judgments that, were we rationally to reconstruct them, would involve *causal* reasoning to the best explanation for the multitude of sensory inputs with which we are provided. For example, the supposition that light travels in more or less straight lines, together with the hypotheses that there is a bulky, stationary, solid white object before us, and that we are in motion in a certain way relative to it, can help explain the sequence of our visual/tactile inputs. But any such reasoning (or unconscious surrogate for it) must invoke, implicitly, cross-checking. It is as if, for example, the various visual and tactile inputs serve to corroborate the judgment that there is a refrigerator, by eliminating alternative possibilities.

This kind of implicit cross-checking is absolutely pervasive; it comes to permeate all our perceptual "takings" as we mature and piece together our world.[11] This feature of sense-perceptual processes explains a fundamental phenomenological feature of perceptual judgments: namely, how we can directly take ourselves to be *en rapport* with our physical surroundings, even though no single bit of sensory information could form an adequate basis for such a judgment (or even, I would add, for the formation of the *concepts* required to envision a three-dimensional space inhabited by physical continuants). It explains how it is that we do this

without seeming to engage in any processes of inference from representations—of inference from effects to causes. That is why direct realist theories of perception can seem so plausible, even though in a *causal* sense, we are obviously *not* in direct contact with our physical surroundings.

4. SKEPTICISM BRACKETED

I have dwelt upon this point because I take it to be crucial to an assessment of the epistemic status of mystical experience, interpreted as perceptual contact with supernatural realities. But it also permits a response to the objection that conceding perception to involve an "indirect" (causal) contact with extramental reality, and perceptual judgment to require reasoning from effects to causes (or surrogates for that), gives the skeptic all he needs to undermine claims to have knowledge or justification.

Alston is particularly forceful and insightful in making this case with respect to sense perception (but of course it applies to mystical perception equally).[12] He argues that any attempt to justify a perceptual practice must fail on grounds of either unsoundness or circularity. Though Alston's argument is complex, we have seen why this result is to be expected and, consequently, can specify the way in which I believe the issue concerning mystical perception ought to be framed.

So as not to beg any questions, I shall adopt Alston's view that there are distinguishable belief-forming practices, including different perceptual practices.[13] Two such practices take as their inputs sense perception and mystical perception. If the possibility of mystical evidence for God is not automatically to be ruled out, we must find some way of deflecting skeptical objections as they apply to perceptual judgments generally. Seeing how this goes for sense perception will enable us to generalize to other perceptual practices, for the relevant similarities between them are more important than the differences. Alston, in spite of his insistence that each perceptual practice is beholden only to its own epistemic standards, recognizes this when he invokes, for all perceptual practices, what amounts to a kind of Principle of Credulity.[14] Alston takes it that, provided a perceptual practice meets certain conditions,[15] perceptual judgments formed in the normal ways provided for in that practice are prima facie justified. (They are only prima facie justified: every such practice must include what Alston calls an "overrider" system, and so a judgment can be overridden. Indeed, Alston's overrider systems reflect the importance of cross-checking, without properly recognizing its fundamentality.)

Any appeal to prima facie warrant—warrant occurring in the absence of even implicit or preconscious processes that could be rationally reconstructed in terms of inductive inference and cross-checking—is just the *wrong* way to bracket (radical) skepticism and frame our question. It is wrong because it short-circuits precisely the crucial justificatory procedures (or at least a crucial stage in their application), thereby begging, or at least certainly obscuring the bearing of, critical questions that the mystical theist must confront. They include the question whether cross-checking procedures must be, but are not, appropriately "built into," and cannot retrospectively be applied to, mystical experiences and the judgments they deliver. I shall argue that they are not, and that this flaw is fatal to mystical justifications of theism.

Cross-checking and cross-checkability must be integral parts of any perceptual epistemic practice because what a perceiver takes to be present on the basis of her experiences might not be what is in fact causally responsible for those experiences. Cross-checking "pins down" stages of the causal process, thereby eliminating alternative hypotheses as to how the input is produced.[16]

What goes for sense perception goes for mystical experience as well. Theists who invoke such experiences as evidence may help themselves to the same inductive principles that our sensory practices evidently presuppose—in particular, those that vindicate cross-checking. However, if, granting those principles, mystical experiences fail to supply significant evidence for theism, an appeal to them will be of little help to theists.

I have been insisting that what we need to frame the debate productively is *not* some principle of credulity, but more general and fundamental inductive principles that will not short-circuit the issues. But even if I were to *grant* some form of credulity principle,[17] it would avail the theist little. For the warrant it confers is only prima facie warrant, and, as it happens, there are good reasons to question that warrant in the mystical case. Since that is so, cross-checking can't be avoided, and its demands are made acute in proportion to the cogency of the cognitive challenges that mystical practices (MPs) confront.

5. CHRISTIAN MYSTICISM: CHALLENGES AND CHECKS

There are a number of such challenges, in the form of alternative explanations for mystical experiences (MEs). One of these, which I shall not pursue, comes from within many MPs. It is the possibility that an ME is demonically caused.[18] There are also naturalistic explanations. Here I shall mention two which complement one another and are jointly strong enough to outdistance any theistic explanation.[19] Fortunately (and *pace* Alston[20]), patterns of mystical encounter are so predictable and overtly manifested, in religious traditions ranging from Pentecostal worship to the ritual seances of Dinka and Tungus shamans, that it has been possible for anthropologists and psychologists to study the phenomenon in great detail in its natural settings.[21]

The first naturalistic explanation is due to the anthropologist I. M. Lewis, and derives from worldwide comparative studies which reveal certain general patterns among MPs.[22] In brief, Lewis shows that, at least where mystics "go public" and appeal to their experiences in the social arena, mysticism serves mundane interests either of the mystic him or herself, or of some group with which he or she identifies. Lewis discerns two types of mystics: socially marginalized mystics whose mysticism is a weapon in the struggle to achieve social justice for themselves and their group, and upwardly mobile mystics who use their mystical experiences as credentials to legitimate their claim on positions of social leadership. Lewis shows how the *descriptions* that mystics give of their experiences and the *behaviors* they exhibit prior to, during, and after mystical episodes serve these social ends in quite precise and predictable ways.

One of the great strengths of Lewis's theory is that it cuts across the entire spectrum of MPs, providing a unity of explanation that the theist cannot hope to match.[23] Lewis's theory has, however, a significant lacuna. It says little about how the occurrence of favorable social circumstances gets translated into the incidence of mystical phenomenology. Moreover, Lewis gives no very adequate explanation for the apparent frequency of MEs which remain private. Many people, it seems, have occasional mystical experiences, but almost never disclose them.

But it looks now as if these gaps can be closed by the second naturalistic approach, which has begun to indicate the details of the neurophysiological mechanisms by means of which mystical experience is mediated. Such experiences, it turns out, are associated with micro-seizures of the temporal lobes of the brain. When these seizures are severe, they result in temporal lobe epilepsy. But mild seizures, which can even be artificially induced during brain surgery, can result in powerful mystical experiences.[24] A substantial portion of the general population has a disposition to such mild seizures, and there is some circumstantial evidence that they can be provoked by techniques traditionally used to induce mystical trance states.[25]

A theist may wish to reply here that God may well have a hand in these mechanisms, indeed employ them as his means for appearing to his worshippers.[26] But this is implausible on a number of counts. For one thing, it is extraordinarily hard to explain why God would appear through the figure of Jesus to a Christian, as Allah to a Muslim, Brahman to a Hindu, the god Flesh to a Dinka, and as a variety of *loa* spirits to voodoo practitioners. And if a purely naturalistic explanation can be given for the nontheistic experiences, then why not also for the theistic ones?[27]

There are other problems. Suppose we take a naturalistic explanation of MEs and tack on the

hypothesis that God is involved in some way. This is a God-of-the-gaps strategy. Given the lacunae in our understanding of even simple physical processes—to say nothing of the neurophysiology of the brain—this strategy is one a theist can deploy with some ease.

Indeed, it incurs the danger of being too easy. A theist could invoke divine intervention to explain why the radiator of my car cracked overnight. Our natural explanation is full of holes: we may not know exactly how cold the engine got last night, nor exactly how strong the walls of the radiator were at the rupture point, nor how to apply the known laws of nature to such a complex system. So, in principle, all the theist need do is find some gap in the posited causal etiology, and tack on the hypothesis that here the finger of God helped the process along—no doubt, to punish my sins.

Why do we (most of us!) not credit such an "explanation"? First, of course, because a long history of experience teaches us that such gaps are often eventually filled by natural causes. But second, because the theistic explanation comes too cheaply: there are no constraints on when, how, and where God is likely to act, no attendant procedures for cross-checking or ferreting out the precise mode and locus of divine intervention, no positive suggestions about how the theistic account of theophysical interaction might be investigated, fleshed out, ramified—and virtually no concomitant predictive power. This theoretical poverty cripples cross-checking for divine influence.

Still, the presence of naturalistic competitors makes it imperative that we examine what sorts of cross-checking MP admits, and how successful such cross-checks have been. We run here into a number of obvious difficulties. Most prominent among them is the fact that mystical experiences are not public.[28] Moreover, the sorts of checks typically invoked, by Christian mystics at least, are either epistemically irrelevant or question begging, absent quite strong auxiliary assumptions.

It is not that mystics are unconcerned about the veridicality of MEs. On the contrary, they often display a lively concern with this and offer multiple tests. But let us look at some of these tests, using Teresa of Avila as a guide. Teresa exhibits a strong interest in the question of how veridical experiences are to be distinguished from those produced by what she calls "melancholy" and by Satan. (This interest is hardly surprising, given the regularity with which the Inquisition accused mystics—especially women—of nefarious motives, fraud, or demonic possession.) Teresa's list of tests includes: (1) the fruits of an experience—both in the actions and personality of the mystic and as producing an inner peace rather than a troubled state of mind, (2) the vividness of the memory of the experience, (3) conformity to Scripture, and (4) validation by the mystic's confessor.

It is not hard to see how these criteria might be designed to secure for the mystic immunity from Inquisitional prosecution, but not easy to see what epistemic force they could have.[29] Test 3 looks straightforwardly question begging, inasmuch as the authority of Scripture rests largely on the supposed authority of the revelations upon which it is based.[30] Tests 1, 2, and 4 have no epistemic force except on the assumption that only God, and neither Satan's best deceptive efforts nor natural causes, can produce experiences that are memorable, convincing to confessors, or have good fruits. But what independent evidence is there for that? What cross-checks for these claims can theists supply? On this, Teresa is silent.

The final—and in principle the best—hope for cross-checking MEs lies with successful prophecy. Perhaps a theistic account *does* after all yield checkable predictions in a way that bears directly upon the evidential force of MEs. For, often enough, one of the fruits of a mystical encounter with God has been the revelation of a prophecy. Not only that, but prophecy has figured as a central component of Christian mystical practice (CMP) and many other MPs, and of the apologetical strategies associated with them. This is because prophecies permit, when certain conditions are satisfied, type-2 cross-checks of a fairly powerful and peculiarly direct sort. When the *content* of a ME contains some message, putatively from God or some supernatural source assumed to be in the know, concerning future events, the claim of genuineness can in principle be checked; ordinarily, the prophesied events will be of such a sort that it is within the purview of ordinary sense perception to determine their occurrence or nonoccurrence.

Yet, Alston tries to downplay the prophetic dimensions of MP.[31] Why? After all, the plain fact is that prophecy is a major and central feature of the MPs of many religious traditions; moreover, putatively successful prophecy is regularly appealed to precisely by way of confirming the genuineness of the prophet, the veridicality of his or her ecstatic visions, and the uniquely truth-connected status of the tradition that claims him or her as its own. Ecstatics who develop prophetic practice into a vocation are familiar figures in religious traditions—witness the oracle at Delphi, the Hebrew prophets, John on Patmos, and Jesus of Nazareth. Nor is this an aspect only of ancient MPs, long since superseded (within Jewish and Christian MPs). Far from it, as anyone who considers the claims of contemporary televangelists can confirm.

Prophecy, therefore, is a feature intrinsic to CMP, a feature by means of which the truth-claims produced by that practice can be quite directly checked. However, no such check will be very informative unless certain conditions are satisfied. Briefly, these include:

1. The prophecy must be of some event not intrinsically likely (not, e.g., "wars and rumors of wars"—Mark 24:6).

2. The prophecy must not be self-fulfilling, or of events the prophet or his or her followers can themselves bring about.

3. The prophecy must demonstrably have been made prior to the events which count as its fulfillment.

4. The prophecy must be sufficiently specific and unambiguous to preclude *ex post facto* reinterpretation to fit any of a wide range of possible "fulfillments."

5. The fulfillment of the prophecy must be verified independently of the say-so of the prophet or his or her partisans or tradition.[32]

Here we have, at last, a cross-check which really *does* offer a test of mystical experience. The reasoning is straightforward: given 1–5, only the mystic's having received a message from a superhumanly prescient being (or, improbably, wild luck) can explain his or her prophetic success. (There are, to be sure, some added complications: for example, we must be careful to avoid the Jean Dixon fallacy. A clever prophet can issue hundreds of risky prophecies, in the hope of scoring a few memorable "hits," calculating that the "misses" will be forgotten. Our reasoning to the best explanation must take into account the prophet's entire track record.)

Now, just what is the record of Jewish and Christian MPs on this score? Rather than pursue this question at length, let me observe that I know of no recorded prophecy, either within the Jewish/Christian canon or outside it, that clearly satisfies criteria 1–5. (There are, however, a number of demonstrably *false* prophecies. Of these, perhaps the most decisive and poignant occurs at Matt. 16:27.[33])

Conclusion: Like any perceptual practice, CMP requires an elaborate system of cross-checks and cross-checking procedures. But, because of its theoretical poverty with respect to the causes of mystical experiences, no such system has been, or is likely to be, forthcoming. With respect to the one relatively strong cross-checking strategy that CMP has available (and has purported to use), its record is one of failure. Until these defects are remedied, mystical experience cannot hope to provide significant evidential support for theism.

NOTES

1. e.g., Alston, *Perceiving God;* William Wainwright, *Mysticism* (Madison: University of Wisconsin Press, 1981); Keith Yandell, *The Epistemology of Religious Experience* (New York: Cambridge University Press, 1993); Swinburne, *Existence of God,* rev. edn; Jerome I. Gellman, *Experience of God and the Rationality of Theistic Belief* (Ithaca, NY: Cornell University Press, 1997); Alvin Plantinga, "Reason and Belief in God," in Alvin Plantinga and Nicholas Wolterstorff (eds), *Faith and Rationality: Reason and Belief in God* (Notre Dame, Ind.: University of Notre Dame Press, 1983); Steven Payne, *John of the Cross and the Cognitive Value of Mysticism: An Analysis of Sanjuanist Teaching and its Philosophical Implications for Contemporary Discussions of Mystical Experience,* Synthese Historical Library (Dordrecht: Kluwer Academic Publishers, 1990); and Carolyn Franks-Davis, *The Evidential Force of Religious Experience* (Oxford: Clarendon Press, 1989).

2. Contrary to what is sometimes claimed, mystical beliefs are surely not self-certifying, no matter how much certainty mystical experience may generate in the mystic. On this point most philosophers—and mystics themselves—are agreed. The reason why testing is needed is, as I shall show, that mystical claims, when they are about an extra-subjective reality, aren't of the right *sort* to be self-certifying. It doesn't help the mystic's case, of course, if her mystical beliefs are contradicted by those of another mystic who displays equal certitude.

3. There are direct realists who deny that "*S* perceives *C*" entails any causal claim about *C*. That is not something that someone who rejects the direct realist's theory of perception need be concerned to deny. Nor, for present purposes, need I deny the view that, when I really do perceive a cat, I do so "directly," that is, not "in virtue of" perceiving something else more directly. So I shall here concede both these points. It suffices for my present purpose that we do not allow, where *C* is an "external" entity or state of affairs, that *S* perceives *C* unless *C* in *fact* plays a causal role in the production of *S*'s experience. I should say more: for external *C*, it is a metaphysical necessity that *C* be so involved in the production of *S*'s experience. The notion of externality can be sufficiently captured by saying that *C* is external to *S*'s experience just in case *C*'s existence doesn't entail the existence of *S*.

4. See Evan Fales, *Causation and Universals* (London: Routledge, 1990), ch. 8.

5. In practice, *A* will be a long conjunction of hypotheses which describe the antecedent conditions and the laws governing the causal mechanisms upon which the making of any measurement or observation depends. In the case of perception, *H* will articulate the causal pathways which mediate the transmission of sensory information. The component hypotheses of *A* will typically be independently (of each other) testable. For simplicity, I shall treat *A* as if it were a single hypothesis.

6. That is, one that does not make use of *H*.

7. Our goal is to vindicate the inverse-probability reasoning we use to infer causes from their effects as the best explanations of those effects. If we employ Bayes' theorem (or some qualitative analogue) for this purpose, we shall also need to assume some rough way to assign credences to competing hypotheses, antecedently to considering any of the empirical data. Let us assume this can be done. For present purposes, these anti-skeptical assumptions are enough to be getting on with.

8. There is often more than one. Even though I could not, ordinarily, be said to observe an image on my retina, I could be said, when watching a presidential press conference, alternatively to see either the TV or George W. Bush. An elementary particle physicist could rightly say both that she is observing tracks in a bubble chamber and that she is observing electrons.

9. See Alston, *Perceiving God,* pp. 209–22.

10. It also ignores the difference between our just perceptually *taking* there to be someone in the adjoining seat, perhaps in part because of the operation of hard-wired belief-forming mechanisms that operate "automatically," and our being *justified* in that belief.

11. In young infants these cognitive processes are observably in the process of formation.

12. See Alston, *Perceiving God,* ch. 3, and *idem. Reliability of Sense Perception.*

13. For details, see Alston. *Perceiving God,* ch. 4.

14. The term, and the principle itself, are due to Swinburne, though the idea can be traced back at least to Reid.

15. These conditions include being socially established, incorporating an overrider system, and being free of massive contradiction from within and from beliefs generated by other doxastic practices (see Alston, *Perceiving God,* ch. 4).

16. The trouble with this story is, as we saw, twofold. First, the only means we have for "pinning down" the facts about a given causal process are perceptual means; and if there is a skeptical question to be raised about the *original* process—the one generating the perceptual experience upon which a perceptual judgment is based—then entirely similar doubts will apply to the perceptual processes upon which cross-checking procedures depend. Second, our problem arises in the first place—and hence in the second place—because effects underdetermine their causes. (This is just a special case— undoubtedly the most central case—of the problem that theory is underdetermined by data: any given data can be explained by any number of incompatible theories.) It is to evade the skeptic here that we invoke the anti-skeptical principles.

17. Whether it be that adopted by Swinburne, *Existence of God,* Alston, *Perceiving God,* or Gellman, *Experience of God.*

18. I shall also largely ignore the major challenge which derives from the enormous variety and conflicting content of MEs worldwide. That is a severe problem in its own right.

19. So I argue with respect to Lewis's theory in Fales, "Scientific Explanations of Mystical Experience, Part I: The Case of St. Teresa," and "Scientific Explanations of Mystical Experience, Part II: The Challenge to Theism," *Religious Studies,* 32 (1996), pp. 143–63 and 297–313 respectively. This can now be supplemented with the neurophysiological findings.

20. Alston, *Perceiving God,* pp. 240-1.

21. I have the report (private communication) of a Christian mystic trained in neurophysiology who has been able to record her own brain waves, and those of a colleague, during trance, who confirms the temporal lobe finding (see below). For a more detailed summary of the evidence and references, see Fales, "Scientific Explanations," Parts I and II, and *idem,* "Can Science Explain Myslicism?" *Religious Studies,* 35 (1999). pp. 213–27.

22. I. M. Lewis, *Ecstatic Religion,* 2nd edn (London: Routledge, 1989).

23. See Fales, "Scientific Explanations of Mystical Experience, Part II."

24. The literature is substantial and growing. For a good bibliography, see Susan Blackmore, *Dying to Lice: Near-Death Experiences* (Buffalo, NY: Prometheus Books, 1993), especially the citations for ch. 10.

25. See William Sargant, *The Mind Possessed: A Physiology of Possession, Mysticism, and Faith Healing* (Philadelphia: J. E. Lippincotl, 1974).

26. Alston has suggested (his possibility on a number of occasions—e.g., in "Psychoanalytic Theory and Theistic Belief," in John Hick (ed.), *Faith and the Philosophers* (New York: St Martin's Press, 1964), and in *Perceiving God,* pp. 230–3.

27. This argument is fleshed out in Fales, "Scientific Explanations of Mysticism, Part II." It is, moreover, very unclear just how, in principle, God would be able to communicate with human beings. If this is to occur via divine influence upon a person's brain states, and those states are macroscopic physical states, then any divine intervention will involve local violations of the highly confirmed laws of conservation of momentum and energy. If, on the other hand, we suppose that God intervenes at the quantum level, acting as a kind of "hidden variable" in determining the outcomes of indeterministic processes, as Nancey Murphy has recently proposed, then we can avoid the violation of physical laws, but only at the price of making in principle unknowable (since hidden by quantum uncertainties) the presence of divine intervention. On these issues see the articles by Murphy and Tracy in Robert J. Russell, Nancey Murphy, and Arthur R. Peacocke (eds), *Chaos and Complexity: Scientific Perspectives on Divine Action* (Vatican City: Vatican Observatory Publications, 1995).

28. There are occasional reports of *sense*-perceptual supernatural apparitions witnessed by many—e.g., at Fatima and Zeitoun. Also, some mystics do report perceiving God via several sensory modalities—e.g., vision, hearing, and smell. I cannot pursue these matters here; and in any case, many theists—e.g., Alston and Wainwright—de-emphasize this sort of experience.

29. Indeed, most such tests aim at social acceptance within the religious community. These, and all the other tests of which I know, are such that passing them is largely under the control of the mystic or of her religious community. Thus, unlike proper cross-checks, they do not risk invalidation of the tested hypothesis by an uncooperative tester-independent world.

30. It is all too likely that the content of Teresa's experiences, as she describes them, is conditioned by her (and her superiors') prior acceptance of Scripture. And she gives no independent evidence that Scripture is authoritative. That authority could be independently confirmed by miracles and successful prophecy, however. Concerning the latter, see below.

31. See Alston, *Perceiving God,* pp. 222–5. Alston is there concerned with the general predictive power of CMP and does not mention religious prophecy specifically at all. On p. 291, he mentions in passing fulfillment of prophecy as a test, not of MEs, but of divine inspiration not associated with MEs. Yet on p. 298, he expresses skepticism concerning the record of Christian miracles generally.

32. It might be protested that this last condition reflects an improperly imperialistic imposition on CMP of criteria indigenous to SP. But to excuse CMP from this requirement on such grounds is to abandon good sense. First, the fulfilling events are typically ones which would be observed by ordinary sense perception; and second, as Hume correctly observed, the temptation to prevarication is too great here to rely upon the say-so of those whose interests are directly at stake. We have ample demonstration of the perennial creative reconstruction of the historical record by those who have a religious agenda; and the New Testament is certainly no exception.

33. Others occur at Josh. 4:7, Ezek. 26:14–21, and Isa. 60:1–62:12, esp. 62:8. Augustin Poulain, *The Graces of Interior Prayer: A Treatise on Mystical Theology,* 6th edn, tr. Leonora York Smith (Westminster, Vt.: Celtic Cross Books, 1978), ch. 21, reports with considerable embarrassment the false prophetic utterances of a number of mystics canonized by the Roman Catholic Church. As regards Matt. 16:27, see parallels at Mark 8:38–9:1 and Luke 9:26–7. John, writing later, discreetly omits this prophecy; see John 6 and 12:25, which in other respects parallel the Synoptic pericopes. It is clear that the parousia and final judgment are intended: cf. Matt. 25:31f and Rev. 20:11–21.

IV.A.6

Religious Experience and Naturalistic Explanations

JEFF JORDAN

Jeff Jordan (1959–) is professor of philosophy at the University of Delaware. His primary area of research is the philosophy of religion, and he is best known for his work on Pascal's Wager. In this article, Jordan argues that the evidential value of religious experiences is undercut by the availability of naturalistic explanations for them. However, he also notes that there is no reason at present to think that all religious experiences will admit of naturalistic explanation.

Would the discovery of an adequate naturalistic explanation of religious experiences diminish the evidential value of those experiences? Many prominent philosophers such as C.D. Broad, John Hick, Richard Swinburne and William Wainwright, among others, argue that a naturalistic explanation need not be detrimental to the evidential value of religious experiences at all.[1] These philosophers hold that a naturalistic explanation would be detrimental only if it were demonstrated that there is no God.

   Now the contention that, even if a naturalistic explanation were discovered, that alone would have no impact on the evidential value of religious experiences, in the absence of a good reason to think that God does not exist, is surprising. It is surprising because a naturalistic explanation of religious experience appears, at least *prima facie*, to threaten the evidential value of religious experience, since a naturalistic explanation would explain the occurrence of religious experiences via a list of purely natural (nonsupernatural) antecedents, with no need to include God among the causes. For instance, Freud saw religion as an illusory defence created by the human imagination against the dangers of nature. Such a reduction to purely natural causes leaves divine activity out of the picture. And if God is out of the picture, there seems to be no reason to consider these experiences as evidence of divine activity. It is the argument of this paper that not only is the contention of those philosophers mentioned above surprising, it is also wrong. In what follows, I argue that a naturalistic explanation, if considered adequate, would seriously diminish the evidential value of any argument from religious experience for theistic belief. While it is true that a naturalistic explanation, if considered adequate, would not prove that every religious experience is delusive, such an explanation would undermine any evidential value we would otherwise be inclined to grant those experiences.

I

Before asking whether a naturalistic explanation would undermine the evidential value of a religious experience, one must answer a prior question having to do with the relevance of examining an experience's causal origins with regard to its epistemic

Reprinted from Jeff Jordan, "Religious Experience and Naturalistic Explanations," *Sophia* 33 (1994): 58–73, with kind permission from Springer Science +Business Media B.V.

value. A long tradition championed by William James claims that it is the behavourial fruit which results from a given experience that is to be the criterion of epistemic value, and not the causal root of the experience.[2] The inquiry into the causes of an experience, according to this tradition, is irrelevant in an epistemic assessment of that purported religious experience.

But this Jamesian attitude neglects an important feature of any appeal to religious experience as evidence for the existence of God: the epistemic legitimacy of religious experience is said to derive largely from the similarities between it and sense experience. Religious experience, the claim goes, is as much a mode of perception as sense experience: either because of some general principle which subsumes both, or because of the large number of common features shared by the two modes of experience.[3] This epistemic parity provides a sort of perceptual authority to religious experience; it would also allow for the relevance of causal inquiry. Assessments of controversial sensory perceptual claims often involve causal inquiries. For example, S's claim to have seen a certain tree is vitiated by pointing out that the tree cannot be seen from S's viewpoint because of, say, a wall. The epistemic value of a given sense perception rests upon an assumed causal relationship: one's experience of X must have the presence of X as a relevant contributing cause if it is to be judged a veridical perception. Likewise, with religious experiences: S's claim to have experienced God can be considered veridical only if her experience of the presence of God was in fact caused by God being present.

Accepting the causal theory of perception as correct, then for all persons S and objects X, we can say that S's experience of X is a veridical perception only if:

A. (a) X is present to S; and (b) S's experience of X is caused by X in an appropriate way; and (c) S knows that it is X that she is perceiving.[4]

Condition (a), the "presence condition," entails that a perception is veridical only if the object of the perception exists, and is within the epistemic scope of the subject. So, for a person to see a particular tree, that tree must be within one's eyesight. Condition (b), the "causal condition," entails that the object of a veridical perception plays a relevant role in bringing about the experience. While it is true that the notions of causation and presence involved in (a) and (b) are vague and, as has been pointed out by Strawson and others, vary according to the mode of perception involved, they capture the important claim of the causal theory—if S's awareness of X is to be taken as a veridical perception, X must have been epistemically accessible to S and X must have played a relevant role in bringing about the experience of S.[5]

If a religious experience is to be taken as a sort of perception, both (a) and (b) must be met: God must be there for S to perceive, and God must play a relevant causal role in S's experience. An adequate naturalistic explanation of a purported religious experience would show (or at least tend to show) that one or the other of the two relevant conditions of (A) did not obtain.

II

Presumably a purported adequate naturalistic explanation of a religious experience would diminish the evidential value of that experience by denying it consideration as a legitimate mode of perception. Denying religious experience consideration as a legitimate mode of perception would be accomplished by showing—either conclusively or probabilistically—that one or the other of the necessary conditions for perception did not obtain for the religious experience in question. For example, a proponent of, say, the logical problem of evil might claim that the presence condition does not obtain when God is the object of that experience. This is so, according to the LPE proponent, because there is no God which could present himself to S.

It is often claimed that an attack on the presence condition requires a good argument—whether conclusive or probablistic—against the existence of God.[6] But it is not clear that such is required. For instance, two ways which might be cited as arguing against the epistemic accessibility of God without denying the existence of God, might be termed the "Kantian" and the "Barthian" ways respectively. The Kantian way would proceed along the line that God must be unknowable in order to leave room for faith and morality. Faith, if it is to be genuine, requires the hiddenness of God. The Barthian would make the characteristic Reformed claim that because of sin and moral turpitude, the human intellect, as well as the human will, is unreliable and cannot know the hidden God. Despite the complexity and obscurity of these two ways, it does seem clear enough that neither entails that God does not exist even though both do argue (or at least claim) that God is unknowable and so epistemically inaccessible.

On the other hand, short of a good argument for the nonexistence of God, an adequate naturalistic explanation of religious experience would be, at best, a good reason to hold that neither (a) nor (b) probably holds for religious experiences. A naturalistic explanation, *sans* an argument for the nonexistence of God, could not be a conclusive reason to think that neither (a) nor (b) holds for all religious experiences. Even if, up till now, all religious experiences thought to be veridical originated from purely physical causes, it does not follow that all experiences thought to be religious will originate from physical causes. If there is a God then it is possible that he may yet reveal himself; and so, it would be possible that there may yet be veridical religious experiences not subsumed under a naturalistic explanation. One further point is clear also: that an attack on the presence condition (utilizing either the Kantian or the Barthian way) would entail much supporting argumentation. The more promising target, it would seem then, would be not the presence condition of an apparent veridical perception; but rather, what we called the causal condition.

The causal condition requires that S has had a veridical perception of X only if X played a relevant causal role in bringing about the experience of S. That is, X must be a relevant causally necessary condition of S's experience of X. So to produce an experience of X without involving X as an appropriate causally necessary condition of that experience would demonstrate that the experience of X was not a veridical perception of X: that the causal condition did not obtain. One can show that the causal condition did not obtain by showing that the experience of X was due to something other than X. X was not, in other words, causally involved in bringing about one's apparent experience of X. Notice also, however, that an experience of X must have X as an *appropriate* causal condition.[7] For instance, if Teresa, through the use of an elaborate scheme of mirrors, causes John to have an experience of herself standing in front of him, that experience should be judged delusory because Teresa was not a causally necessary condition in an appropriate way. John did not see Teresa herself; he saw only a reflection, while Teresa, let us suppose, actually stood behind John manipulating the mirrors. John's experience is delusive because, even though Teresa is involved in the causal train leading up to it, the presence of Teresa was not a causal condition in an appropriate way: being behind John, Teresa could not have been causally involved in an appropriate way in John's visual experience. Teresa herself was beyond John's arc of vision and so a necessary feature of visual appropriateness was not met. John's experience is, at best, an indirect perception of Teresa.[8] One has not experienced the cup on the table, if the apparent cup is a hologram—even though the real cup may be a causally necessary condition in the production of the hologram and, consequently, of one's experience. So the causal condition can be impugned in either of two ways: (I) one may show that X had no causal input in an apparent experience of X; or (II) one may show that X had no relevant, no appropriate, causal input in the experience.

Suppose that we could produce, say with the use of a certain drug, experiences which were indistinguishable phenomenologically from those experiences traditionally taken to be religious experiences. That is, the ingestion of our hypothetical drug is sufficient to produce an apparent experience of God. The existence of a natural means of inducing an apparent religious experience would serve as evidence against the evidential value of any religious experience: the fact that religious experiences can be produced by purely natural causes would greatly diminish the probability that these experiences are veridical perceptions of their purported object. The existence of such a drug would constitute a plausible reason to think that (I) holds. Or again, suppose that it was discovered that religious experiences originated from some psychological abnormality present in all those and only those who have had such experiences. One might hold, as John Hick does, that "there may be a religious as well as a naturalistic interpretation of the psychological facts."[9] In other words, religious experiences could be overdetermined: they may admit of more than one sufficient causal condition at a time. But if one reasonably believed that religious experiences were due to some psychological state, then it would seem problematic to hold that these same experiences were a kind of perception of God. The attribution of God as a sufficient cause of the experiences may, in fact, be true: according to classical theism, God is a sufficient causal cause of all contingent things. But such an attribution seems wholly irrelevant as regards (A). God's causal input at this point, assuming for a moment that there is a God, does not seem to be the sort necessary for the satisfaction of (A). This sort of divine causation seems too general to constitute the sort required by (A). Even if God is a sufficient causal cause of all contingent things, such a drug-induced experience would be a good reason to think that (II) holds.

One possible objection to this would run as follows. Suppose we can produce a drug which generates delusive yet phenomenologically similar experiences of cups, say, or of persons. Does this by itself greatly diminish the probability that these experiences (experiences of real cups or of real persons) are veridical perceptions? Would the experience of such a drug serve as a good reason to think that (I) obtains vis-à-vis cup experiences or people experiences? It does not seem to; but then, why think so with regard to religious experiences?

One relevant difference between the cup/persons case and the religious case with regard to the "replication problem" involves the plausible, albeit defeasible, principle that:

> B. whenever there are distinct yet phenomenologically similar experiences M and N, it is likely that the causes of M and N are similar.[10]

A veridical perception of a cup or a person involves a physical cause—respectively the real cup or the person herself—just as the drug-generated replication involves a physical cause: namely, the drug itself. But in the case of religious experiences, the purported object of a veridical religious experience, God, is wholly unlike any physical cause. And this radical qualitative difference between the possible causes of religious experience seems to render (B) pernicious in the case of religious experiences. That is, (B) conjoined with the fact (if it is a fact) that there are, say, drug-induced experiences which replicate those experiences traditionally taken to be genuinely religious, seems to diminish greatly the probability that any religious experience is a veridical perception of God. No doubt this is not the full story of why a drug-generated replication is telling in the one case and not in the other. Nonetheless, it is enough to indicate that there is a relevant difference between the cases, and so, it is not surprising that the "replication problem" should impact the respective cases differently.

In the following sections we will examine two arguments—one having to do with the object of religious experience; the other, with the nature of religious experience—which support the contention that an adequate naturalistic explanation of religious experience would seriously diminish the cognitive worth of the experience.

III

In an influential essay published in 1939, C. D. Broad argued that a naturalistic explanation of religious experiences (specifically a psychological explanation) would not prove those experiences to be delusive.[11] Even if it were shown that religious experiences resulted from some psychological abnormality, one could not infer validly that religious experiences were delusive. This is so, Broad argued, because "one might need to be slightly 'cracked' in order to have some peep-holes into the supersensible world."[12] A certain psychological state might be a causally necessary condition for religious experiences to be veridical. According to Broad, then, the veridicality of religious experiences is compatible with a certain psychological state, even an abnormal psychological state, being the genetic origin of those experiences.

With regard to religious belief Broad's argument is sound; but with regard to the evidential value of religious experiences for theistic belief, Broad's argument could not provide support for a theistic use of psychologically generated experiences because of the following. Theists traditionally have claimed that God is sovereign by which is meant, at the least, that there are no causal determinates of the divine will independent of the divine nature. God is such a being that it is logically impossible that there be causally necessary conditions for the divine will. So to say that S experienced God is to say that God revealed himself to S—that the divine presence is a divine prerogative. God was experienced by S means according to classical theism that God actively manifested himself to S. It was up to God whether or not S would experience him. So, if we reasonably believed that religious experiences are causally due to a certain psychological state, then we would have a good reason to doubt the evidential value of those experiences with regard to the God of theism. Being sovereign, the God of theism, if he exists, is such as to have no causally necessary conditions of his will. Broad's claim, then, that it is possible that a certain psychological state be a causally necessary condition of veridicality is irrelevant. The discovery of such a natural origin of religious experiences would serve as a good reason to think that the causal condition did not obtain: the God of theism is sovereign with regard to causal determinates.

IV

Earlier it was noted that the criteria of appropriateness are relative to the mode of perception involved. We can now identify one such criterion for any theistic religious experience which is veridical:

> C. if there is a set of natural conditions which, when operative, bring about an experience which is phenomenologically indistinguishable from those experiences traditionally taken to be theistic experiences, then no experience which appears to be theistic can be taken as veridical perceptions.

According to (C), a theistic experience E should be considered veridical only if E lacks, as far as one can determine, a purely naturalistic explanation. If there was some naturalistic explanation N, such that whenever N was present, a theistic experience invariably occurred, we would have good reason to discount the evidential value of every theistic experience. It is not that the presence of N shows that every theistic experience is delusory. It is, rather, that N makes it appear likely that (II) holds for religious experiences. Some religious experiences may be veridical, but given that we know of a naturalistic way to produce those experiences, all religious experiences would lose any epistemic presumption that they would have enjoyed in the absence of a naturalistic explanation.

It may be objected that it is possible that God may will to reveal himself only to those who have satisfied certain conditions (such as, being virtuous, or being humble, or having a focused consciousness, or those who have fasted for a specified period). No doubt this is true, but it does not rescue Broad's argument. There is a real distinction between an intentional effort to fulfill certain objectives and being in certain mental states (one does not consciously will oneself to be neurotic, for instance). Broad's position, I take it, has to do with the latter and not the former. But those theists who claim that there are certain prerequisites, or at least facilitators, of religious experience are concerned with the former and not the latter. Broad's argument has to do with psychological states which are unintentional and which serve as necessary causal conditions of a revelation of God.[13] This, as has been argued, seems incompatible with theistic belief.

V

Both Richard Swinburne and William Wainwright argue that there could not be a naturalistic explanation which would impugn the causal condition of a religious experience.[14] According to these philosophers, the hypothetical drug of section III would not be sufficient to impugn the causal condition because if there is a God, then that being is involved in all causal processes. Any experience would have God among the causes: specifically, any religious experience will have God involved in its causal process by virtue of the fact that there are causal processes only because God sustains them.

Swinburne's argument can be formulated so:

1. According to classical theism God is both omnipresent and the sustainer of all causal processes. So,

2. if God exists, then any experience apparently of God will be a genuine experience of God (both the presence and the causal conditions will be satisfied). So,

3. in order to show that either the presence condition or the causal condition did not obtain, one would need a good argument against the existence of God. And,

4. such an argument is very unlikely.

Therefore,

5. a naturalistic explanation of religious experience would be detrimental to the evidential value of those experiences only if there is a good argument for the nonexistence of God.

There are two problems with this argument. The first has to do with the second premise: even a theist could not be comfortable with the truth of (2). Not all experiences of God, most theists would claim, turn out to be just that: genuine experiences

of God. Satan, St. Paul writes, can disguise himself as "an angel of light."[15] So if (2) were true, the theistically desirable distinction between genuine experiences and deceptive experiences would be lost.[16]

A second objection to the argument has to do with both the second and third premises and with the nature of perception itself. (A) entails that S's experience of X is veridical only if X played a relevant causal role in the production of S's experience. That is, X must be causally involved in an appropriate way. According to (1), if God exists, then he is a causally necessary condition in all causal processes. So, with our hypothetical drug, even though it alone seemed sufficient to induce a religious experience, it is possible that God was a causally necessary condition in the drug's efficacy. The drug was effective, according to this line of thought, only because God sustained the causal interactions; and therefore, his constant preservation was a causally necessary factor in the production of the experience. This notion of God as the necessary sustainer of all, found in (1), results from the doctrine of conservation.

There is no doubt that the doctrine of conservation is in fact a traditional belief of classical theism. Augustine wrote of it, "for the power and might of the creator, who rules and embraces all, makes every creature abide; and if this power ever ceased to govern creatures, their essences would pass away and all nature would perish."[17] Concerning the doctrine Thomas wrote that "the being of every creature depends on God, so that not for a moment could it subsist, but would fall into nothingness, were it not kept in being by the operation of the divine power."[18] And in the Third Meditation, Descartes utilized the doctrine in his causal proof for the existence of God. The import of the doctrine of conservation is the claim that the existence of every contingent being and event depends causally on the creative powers of God.[19] In other words:

> D. for any contingent thing X, X exists at a time t if and only if God brings about at t that X exists.

Now (D) not only entails that God is a causally necessary condition in all causal processes, but (D) also entails that God is a logically necessary condition in the existence of all contingent things.[20] Being preserved by God is an essential property of all contingent things because a thing could not remain what it is in the absence of God's constant conservation.

So the idea found in premise one of Swinburne's argument is right: if (D) is true (which is possible), then God is a causally necessary condition in all causal processes. But it is not clear that the possibility of (D) is at all relevant to whether (A) obtains or not. Remember (A) entails that X be an appropriate cause in the production of S's experience. So, by either showing that (I) or (II) holds, one can show that (A) does not obtain. While (D) precludes (I) from holding, it certainly seems irrelevant to whether (II) holds.

One feature of the appropriateness of theistic religious experience, as we have seen, is that all experiences of God, if genuine, are revelations on God's part. God intended to manifest himself to S, if S has had a veridical experience of God. God makes himself known. But not every apparent experience of God fulfills this feature of appropriateness. St. Teresa, for example, was constantly wary of taking a delusive experience as veridical, because not every apparent experience of God, she held, is a genuine experience of God. Some experiences are deceptive. In these spurious experiences, God did not, we might say, intend to reveal himself. According to (D), however, God is nonetheless a causally necessary condition in a delusive experience. Indeed, (D) entails that God would be a causally necessary condition in all experiences—whether he intended to reveal himself or not. Perhaps we can say with regard to (D) that God permits all contingent things—beings, experiences, events—to obtain. But he does not intend to reveal himself in all contingent things. To hold otherwise would extinguish the distinction that theists have traditionally wanted to hold between genuine experiences (those of God) and deceptive experiences (those of the devil).

With the distinction between God intending an experience and merely permitting an experience, we can see that both (2) and (3) are false: there is a real distinction between genuine and deceptive experiences of God even for the theist;

and one can show that the causal condition does not obtain independent of showing that there is no God. The latter is accomplished by showing that an experience of X is delusive because X was not a causally necessary condition in an appropriate way. This can be done even though X was, in fact, a causally necessary condition of the experience. The attempt by Wainwright and Swinburne to show that the causal condition of religious experience could not be impugned by, say, our hypothetical drug example fails. Even though (D) is possible, it is also irrelevant in the determination of whether the causal condition obtains in a given experience.

VI

A naturalistic explanation of religious experiences would, if considered adequate, seriously diminish the evidential value of those experiences. Such has been the argument of this paper. The loss of evidential value would come as a result of showing that the experiences were not appropriately connected to their purported object. The apparent object of the experience was just that: only an apparent and not a real contributing factor in a causally appropriate way. Just as a cup hologram does not constitute a veridical visual perception, neither does an experience purportedly of God that arises merely from physical causes.

Of course the question of whether there are naturalistic explanations of religious experiences is a completely different question from the one we have been considering. Certainly some historically influential thinkers, such as Feuerbach and Freud, have claimed that one can indeed provide an adequate naturalistic explanation of religious experience. But it is not controversial to note that such theories have not gained a wide acceptance. Perhaps, a cautious answer to this latest question is this: given our present state of knowledge, no one has yet provided a good reason to think that all religious experiences admit of a naturalistic explanation; and are, therefore, delusory.

NOTES

1. By religious experience I mean those experiences traditionally taken to be theistic experiences.

2. Actually we can identify two closely related but distinct traditions concerning the relevance of an inquiry into an experience's causal origins. The first tradition holds that an experience's fruits would identify the causal roots of that experience E. If E resulted in moral living, for instance, then, according to this tradition, E was produced by God. As Teresa of Avila put it, "when a location comes from the devil, it not only fails to leave behind good effects, but leaves bad ones" (*The Life of Teresa of Jesus*, trans. E.A. Pears (Garden City, NY: Image Books, 1960), p. 237. See also Jonathan Edwards, *A Treatise on Religious Affections* (Grand Rapids, MN: Baker, 1982), pp. 258–64).

   The second tradition, of which James was certainly a participant, held that all concern should be with the effects of E, and only indifference is shown to the causal origins of E. It does not matter, according to this second view, what the causal origin of a beneficial experience is. See *The Varieties of Religious Experience* (NY: Modern Library, 1936), pp. 16–22. W.T. Stace would also fit in this second tradition. See *Mysticism and Philosophy* (London: MacMillan, 1960), pp. 29–31.

3. Included among versions of the former sort are Richard Swinburne, *The Existence of God* (Oxford: Clarendon, 1978), pp. 254–71. And W.L. Alston, "Religious Experience as a Ground of Religious Belief," *Religious Experience and Religious Belief*, ed. J. Runzo and C.K. Ihara (NY: University Press of America, 1986), pp. 31–51. Of the latter sort, see Gary Gutting, *Religious Belief and Religious Scepticism* (Notre Dame, IN: University of Notre Dame Press, 1982), pp. 151–3. And William Wainwright, *Mysticism* (London: Harvester Press, 1981), pp. 100–1.

4. On the causal theory of perception see the classic essay by H.P. Grice, "The Causal Theory of Perception," *Proceedings of the Aristotelian Society* supplementary volume, 35 (1961): 121–54, and P.F. Strawson, "Causation in Perception," *Freedom and Resentment* (London: Methuen, 1974). pp. 66–84, and R.M. Chisholm, *Perceiving: A Philosophical Study* (Ithaca, NY: Cornell, 1957),

pp. 142–51. And see Robert Audi, *Belief, Justification and Knowledge* (Belmont, CA: Wadsworth, 1988), pp. 15–6.

5. So Strawson, op. cit., pp. 79–81. And Chisholm, op. cit., pp. 149–50.

6. See for example: Richard Swinburne, *The Existence of God*, p. 270; and see William Rowe, "Religious Experience and the Principle of Credulity," *International Journal for the Philosophy of Religion* 13 (1982): 88–9.

7. The criteria of appropriateness are relative to the mode of perception involved. A criterion of appropriateness for religious experience will be discussed in Section IV.

8. When the astronomer looks through the telescope at Mars, some philosophers would contend that she sees both Mars and the reflection of Mars. (So, George Mavrodes, *Belief in God*, [1970; rept., Washington, DC: University Press of America], pp. 58–70.) But given the noncontroversial distinction between an object p and an image of p, it seems more accurate to hold that the astronomer sees the image of Mars, and knowing (or at least believing) that her telescope is reliable and in good working order (it is not distorting the refracted light), she has then a good idea of what Mars looks like. Mavrodes's "rule of input alignment" is, therefore, if not false, metaphorical at best. See his *Belief in God*, p. 60.

9. *Philosophy of Religion* (Englewood Cliffs, NJ: Prentice-Hall, 1983), pp. 34–6. See also C.R. Brakenhielm, *Problems of Religious Experience* (Stockholm: Uppsala, 1985), pp. 95–101.

10. Principle (B) is, confessedly, much too imprecise. But the domain of "similar" must be construed as being broad enough to allow (B) to escape obvious falsehood; yet, narrow enough to escape vacuity.

11. *Religion, Philosophy and Psychical Research* (NY: Humanities Press, 1969), pp. 175–201.

12. Ibid., p. 198.

13. See *Religion, Philosophy and Psychical Research*, pp. 197–8.

14. So Swinburne, *The Existence of God*, pp. 269–71; and see Wainwright, "Natural Explanations and

Religious Experience," *Ratio* 15 (1973): 99–101; and Wainwright's *Philosophy of Religion* (Belmont, CA: Wadsworth, 1988), pp. 126–8. The arguments are similar, so we will look at Swinburne's version.

15. II Corinthians 11:14. See also George Mavrodes, "Real vs. Deceptive Mystical Experiences," *Mysticism and Philosophical Analysis*, ed. S.T. Katz (NY: Oxford U.P., 1978), pp. 235–58.

16. A version of this objection can be found in Michael P. Levine's "If there is a God, any Experience which seems to be of God, will be Genuine," *Religious Studies* 26/2 (1990): 207–18.

17. *The Literal Meaning of Genesis* IV. 12, trans. J.H. Taylor (NY: Newman Press, 1982), p. 117.

18. *Summa Theologica*, trans. A. Pegis (NY: Random House). IA IIae, q 104, al.

19. The act of conservation is usually seen as being identical with the act of creation. As Descartes put it "conservation and creation differ merely in respect of our mode of thinking and not in reality." (*Meditations*, trans. J. Veitch [La Salle, IL.: Open Court, 1950], pp. 58–9). This idea of "Continuous creation" is found also in Thomas (See St Ia Iiae, q 104, al.).

20. So Robert Oakes, "Perishability, the Actual World, and the Existence of God," *Religious Studies* 19 (1983), pp. 493–504.

IV.B. MIRACLES AND TESTIMONY

Introduction

WHAT ARE MIRACLES, and are they possible? Can we sensibly believe someone else's testimony that a miracle has occurred? These questions are intertwined. Some say that a miracle is a violation of the laws of nature, and that it is never reasonable to believe testimony that a law of nature has been violated. But, of course, each of these claims is controversial.

The idea that miracles are natural law violations has been disputed on the basis of the contention that in the Bible, which is the witness to the most significant alleged miracles in the Judeo-Christian tradition, there is no concept of nature as a closed system of law. For the biblical writers, says R. H. Fuller, miracles signify simply an "extraordinary coincidence of a beneficial nature."[1] This view is also endorsed by R. F. Holland in his article "The Miraculous," in which the following story is illustrative:

> A child riding his toy motor-car strays on to an unguarded railway crossing near his house and a wheel of his car gets stuck down the side of one of the rails. An express train is due to pass with the signals in its favour and a curve in the track makes it impossible for the driver to stop his train in time to avoid any obstruction he might encounter on the crossing. The mother coming out of the house to look for her child sees him on the crossing and hears the train approaching. She runs forward shouting and waving. The little boy remains seated in his car looking downward engrossed in the task of pedaling it free. The brakes of the train are applied and it comes to rest a few feet from the child. The mother thanks God for the miracle; which she never ceases to think of

---

[1] R. H. Fuller *Interpreting the Miracle* (London, 1968), 8.

as such, although, as she in due course learns, there was nothing supernatural about the manner in which the brakes of the train came to be applied. The driver had fainted, for a reason that had nothing to do with the presence of the child on the line, and the brakes were applied automatically as his hand ceased to exert pressure on the control lever. He fainted on this particular afternoon because his blood pressure had risen after an exceptionally heavy lunch during which he had quarreled with a colleague, and the change in blood pressure caused a clot of blood to be dislodged and circulate. He fainted at the time when he did on the afternoon in question because this was the time at which the coagulation in his blood stream reached the brain.[2]

Is this a miracle, or not? It is if we define miracles in Fuller's biblical sense. It is not if we define them as violations of laws of nature. We can certainly understand the woman's feeling on the matter, and perhaps in some mysterious way God had "allowed" nature to run its course so that the little boy would be saved. Perhaps we need not be overly exclusionary but say that if there is a God, each sense is valid: the *weaker* sense of an extraordinary coincidence and the *stronger* sense of a violation of the laws of nature. Philosophical discussion of miracles has tended to focus primarily on the stronger sense, that of a violation of the laws of nature by a divine force.

It is this stronger sense of the idea of miracle that is in play in our first selection, by David Hume, as well as in many of the subsequent discussions of his famous argument. In section 10 of his *An Enquiry Concerning Human Understanding*, Hume sets forth an argument for the conclusion that it is not rational to believe testimony that a miracle has occurred. The essay provoked a lively response in his own day, and it has continued to be the subject of vigorous dispute up to the present.

Hume begins his attack on belief in miracles by appealing to the biases of his Scottish Presbyterian readers. He tells of a marvelous proof that Dr. Tillotson has devised against the Roman Catholic doctrine of transubstantiation, the doctrine that the body and blood of Christ are present in Holy Communion. Tillotson argues that because the evidence of the senses is of the highest rank and because it is evident that it must diminish in passing through the original witnesses to their disciples, the doctrine of transubstantiation is always contrary to the rules of reasoning and opposed to our sense experience. Thus:

1. Our evidence for the truth of transubstantiation is weaker than the sensory evidence we have against it. (Even for the apostles this was the case, and their testimony must diminish in authority in passing from them to their disciples.)

2. We are never warranted in believing a proposition on the basis of weaker evidence when stronger evidence supports the denial of that proposition.

3. Therefore, we are not warranted in believing in transubstantiation. (Even if the doctrine of transubstantiation were clearly revealed in the Scriptures, it would be against the rule of reason to give our assent to it.)

---

[2]*American Philosophical Quarterly*, 2 (1965).

No doubt Hume's Protestant readers were delighted with such an attack on the doctrine of transubstantiation. But the mischievous Hume now turns the knife on his readers. A wise person always proportions one's belief to the evidence, he goes on. One has an enormous amount of evidence for the laws of nature, so that any testimony to the contrary is to be seriously doubted. Although miracles, as violations of the laws of nature, are not logically impossible, we are never justified in believing in one. The skeleton of the argument contained in the reading goes something like this:

1. One ought to proportion one's belief to the evidence.

2. Experience is generally better evidence than testimony (if for no other reason than that valid testimony is based on another's sense experience).

3. Therefore, when there is a conflict between experience and testimony, one ought to believe according to experience.

4. Miracles are contrary to experience. That is, experience testifies strongly to the fact that miracles never occur, laws of nature are never violated.

5. Therefore, we are never justified in believing in miracles, but we are justified in believing in the naturalness of all events.

Because we have enormous evidence in favor of the uniformity of nature, every miracle report must be weighed against that preponderance and be found wanting. Or, at any rate, it must be found wanting unless we have some reason for thinking that the falsehood of the testimony would itself be miraculous. Thus, as Hume writes:

> That no testimony is sufficient to establish a miracle, unless the
> testimony be of such a kind, that its falsehood would be more
> marvelous, than the fact, which it endeavors to establish; and even in
> that case there is a mutual destruction of argument, and the superior
> only gives us an assurance suitable to that degree of force, which
> remains, after deducting the inferior.

The best one can hope for, then, is a kind of agnostic standoff.

But what if we believe that we personally have beheld a miracle? Aren't we in that case justified in believing that a miracle has occurred? No, for given the principle that every time we pursue an event *far enough*, we discover it to have a natural cause, we are still not justified in believing the event to be a miracle. Rather we ought to look further until we discover the natural cause—unless, again, we have very good reason for thinking that the event's *having* a natural cause would somehow be miraculous.

Our second reading in this section is a contemporary defense of Hume's line of reasoning by the late J. L. Mackie of Oxford University, a man who loved Hume and exemplified his thought. Mackie argues that the evidence for miracles will never in practice be very great. The argument is epistemological, not ontological. That is, whereas miracles may be logically possible (and may indeed have occurred), we are never justified in believing in one. The concept of a miracle is a coherent one; but, Mackie argues, the *double* burden of showing both that the event took place *and* that it violated the laws of nature will be extremely hard to lift, for "whatever tends to show that it would have been a violation of natural law tends for that very reason to make it most unlikely that it actually happened." Correspondingly, the deniers of miracles have two strategies of defense. They may argue that the event took place but was not a violation of a law of nature (the event simply followed an unknown law of nature); or they can admit that if the event had happened, it would indeed have been a violation of a law of nature, but for that reason, "there is a very strong presumption against its having happened, which it is most unlikely that any testimony will be able to outweigh."

In our third reading, Peter van Inwagen attacks Hume's argument. Hume's argument, as we have seen, rests in part on the idea that miracles are the sorts of things that run significantly contrary to our experience. But, van Inwagen argues, it is hard to see what this idea really amounts to. Thus, he writes:

> It is very hard indeed to find a sense in which experience testifies in any direct or immediate sense that events of some sort never happen—or in which stories of events of some sort are contrary to experience. If direct, immediate experience testifies to anything (truly or falsely) its testimony seems to be essentially "positive": it testifies that events of certain sorts *do* happen.

Failing to find any other sense of "contrary to experience" that could drive Hume's argument, van Inwagen concludes that Hume's argument is a failure.

IV.B.1

Against Miracles

DAVID HUME

A short biographical sketch of David Hume precedes selection II.C.2. The following selection argues that we are virtually never justified in believing that a miracle has occurred.

Reprinted from David Hume, *An Enquiry Concerning Human Understanding* (Oxford: Oxford University Press, 1748). Footnotes edited.

PART I

There is, in Dr. Tillotson's writings, an argument against the *real presence*, which is as concise, and elegant, and strong as any argument can possibly be supposed against a doctrine, so little worthy of a serious refutation. It is acknowledged on all hands, says that learned prelate, that the authority, either of the scripture or of tradition, is founded merely in the testimony of the apostles, who were eyewitnesses to those miracles of our Saviour, by which he proved his divine mission. Our evidence, then, for the truth of the *Christian* religion is less than the evidence for the truth of our senses; because, even in the first authors of our religion, it was no greater; and it is evident it must diminish in passing from them to their disciples; nor can any one rest such confidence in their testimony, as in the immediate object of his senses. But a weaker evidence can never destroy a stronger; and therefore, were the doctrine of the real presence ever so clearly revealed in scripture, it were directly contrary to the rules of just reasoning to give our assent to it. It contradicts sense, though both the scripture and tradition, on which it is supposed to be built, carry not such evidence with them as sense; when they are considered merely as external evidences, and are not brought home to every one's breast, by the immediate operation of the Holy Spirit.

Nothing is so convenient as a decisive argument of this kind, which must at least *silence* the most arrogant bigotry and superstition, and free us from their impertinent solicitations. I flatter myself, that I have discovered an argument of a like nature, which, if just, will, with the wise and learned, be an everlasting check to all kinds of superstitious delusion, and consequently, will be useful as long as the world endures. For so long, I presume, will the accounts of miracles and prodigies be found in all history, sacred and profane.

Though experience be our only guide in reasoning concerning matters of fact; it must be acknowledged, that this guide is not altogether infallible, but in some cases is apt to lead us into errors. One, who in our climate, should expect better weather in any week of June than in one of December, would reason justly, and conformably to experience; but it is certain, that he may happen, in the event, to find himself mistaken. However, we may observe, that, in such a case, he would have no cause to complain of experience; because it commonly informs us beforehand of the uncertainty, by that contrariety of events, which we may learn from a diligent observation. All effects follow not with like certainty from their supposed causes. Some events are found, in all countries and all ages, to have been constantly conjoined together: Others are found to have been more variable, and sometimes to disappoint our expectations; so that, in our reasonings concerning matter of fact, there are all imaginable degrees of assurance, from the highest certainty to the lowest species of moral evidence.

A wise man, therefore, proportions his belief to the evidence. In such conclusions as are founded on an infallible experience, he expects the event with the last degree of assurance, and regards his past experience as a full *proof* of the future existence of that event. In other cases, he proceeds with more caution: He weighs the opposite experiments: He considers which side is supported by the greater number of experiments: to that side he inclines, with doubt and hesitation; and when at last he fixes his judgement, the evidence exceeds not what we properly call *probability*. All probability, then, supposes an opposition of experiments and observations, where the one side is found to overbalance the other, and to produce a degree of evidence, proportioned to the superiority. A hundred instances or experiments on one side, and fifty on another, afford a doubtful expectation of any event; though a hundred uniform experiments, with only one that is contradictory, reasonably beget a pretty strong degree of assurance. In all cases, we must balance the opposite experiments, where they are opposite, and deduct the smaller number from the greater, in order to know the exact force of the superior evidence.

To apply these principles to a particular instance; we may observe, that there is no species of reasoning more common, more useful, and even necessary to human life, than that which is derived from the testimony of men, and the reports of eyewitnesses and spectators. This species of reasoning, perhaps, one may deny to be founded on the relation of cause and effect. I shall not dispute about a word. It will be sufficient to observe that our assurance in any argument of this kind is derived from no other principle than our observation of the veracity of human testimony, and of the usual conformity of facts to the reports of witnesses. It being a general maxim, that no objects have any discoverable connexion together, and that all the inferences, which we can draw from one to another, are founded merely on our experience of their constant and regular conjunction; it is evident, that we ought not to make an exception to this maxim in favour of human testimony, whose connexion with any event seems, in itself, as little necessary as any other. Were not the memory tenacious to a certain degree; had not men commonly an inclination to truth and a principle of probity; were they not sensible to shame, when detected in a falsehood: Were not these, I say, discovered by *experience* to be qualities, inherent in human nature, we should never repose the least confidence in human testimony. A man delirious, or noted for falsehood and villany, has no manner of authority with us.

And as the evidence, derived from witnesses and human testimony, is founded on past experience, so it varies with the experience, and is regarded either as a *proof* or a *probability*, according to the conjunction between any particular kind of report and any kind of object has been found to be constant or variable. There are a number of circumstances to be taken into consideration in all judgements of this kind; and the ultimate standard, by which we determine all disputes, that may arise concerning them, is always derived from experience and observation. Where this experience is not entirely uniform on any side, it is attended with an unavoidable contrariety in our judgements, and with the same opposition and mutual destruction of argument as in every other kind of evidence. We frequently hesitate concerning the reports of others. We balance the opposite circumstances, which cause any doubt or uncertainty; and when we discover a superiority on any side, we incline to

it; but still with a diminution of assurance, in proportion to the force of its antagonist.

This contrariety of evidence, in the present case, may be derived from several different causes; from the opposition of contrary testimony; from the character or number of the witnesses; from the manner of their delivering their testimony; or from the union of all these circumstances. We entertain a suspicion concerning any matter of fact, when the witnesses contradict each other; when they are but few, or of a doubtful character; when they have an interest in what they affirm; when they deliver their testimony with hesitation, or on the contrary, with too violent asseverations. There are many other particulars of the same kind, which may diminish or destroy the force of any argument, derived from human testimony.

Suppose, for instance, that the fact, which the testimony endeavors to establish, partakes of the extraordinary and the marvelous; in that case, the evidence, resulting from the testimony, admits of a diminution, greater or less, in proportion as the fact is more or less unusual. The reason why we place any credit in witnesses and historians, is not derived from any *connexion*, which we perceive *a priori*, between testimony and reality, but because we are accustomed to find a conformity between them. But when the fact attested is such a one as has seldom fallen under our observation, here is a contest of two opposite experiences; of which the one destroys the other, as far as its force goes, and the superior can only operate on the mind by the force, which remains. The very same principle of experience, which gives us a certain degree of assurance in the testimony of witnesses, gives us also, in this case, another degree of assurance against the fact, which they endeavour to establish; from which contradiction there necessarily arises a counterpoise, and mutual destruction of belief and authority.

I should not believe such a story were it told me by Cato, was a proverbial saying in Rome, even during the lifetime of that philosophical patriot. The incredibility of a fact, it was allowed, might invalidate so great an authority.

The Indian prince, who refused to believe the first relations concerning the effects of frost, reasoned justly; and it naturally required very strong testimony to engage his assent to facts, that arose from a state of nature, with which he was unacquainted, and which bore so little analogy to those events, of which we had had constant and uniform experience. Though they were not contrary to his experience, they were not conformable to it.

But in order to increase the probability against the testimony of witnesses, let us suppose, that the fact, which they affirm, instead of being only marvelous, is really miraculous; and suppose also, that the testimony considered apart and in itself, amounts to an entire proof; in that case, there is proof against proof, of which the strongest must prevail, but still with a diminution of its force, in proportion to that of its antagonist.

A miracle is a violation of the laws of nature; and as a firm and unalterable experience has established these laws, the proof against a miracle, from the very nature of the fact, is as entire as any argument from experience can possibly be imagined. Why is it more than probable, that all men must die; that lead cannot, of itself, remain suspended in the air; that fire consumes wood, and is extinguished by water; unless it be, that these events are found agreeable to the laws of nature, and there is required a violation of these laws, or in other words, a miracle to prevent them? Nothing is esteemed a miracle, if it ever happen in the common course of nature. It is no miracle that a man, seemingly in good health, should die on a sudden: because such a kind of death, though more unusual than any other, has yet been frequently observed to happen. But it is a miracle, that a dead man should come to life; because that has never been observed in any age or country. There must, therefore, be a uniform experience against every miraculous event, otherwise the event would not merit that appellation. And as a uniform experience amounts to a proof, there is here a direct and full *proof,* from the nature of the fact, against the existence of any miracle; nor can such a proof be destroyed, or the miracle rendered credible, but by an opposite proof, which is superior.[1]

The plain consequence is (and it is a general maxim worthy of our attention), "That no testimony is sufficient to establish a miracle, unless the testimony be of such a kind, that its falsehood would be more miraculous, than the fact, which it endeavours to establish; and even in that case there is a mutual destruction of arguments, and the superior only gives us an assurance suitable to that degree of force, which remains, after deducting the inferior." When anyone tells me, that he saw a dead man restored to life, I immediately consider with myself, whether it be more probable, that this person should either deceive or be deceived, or that the fact, which he relates, should really have happened. I weigh the one miracle against the other; and according to the superiority, which I discover, I pronounce my decision, and always reject the greater miracle. If the falsehood of his testimony would be more miraculous, than the event which he relates; then, and not till then, can he pretend to command my belief or opinion.

PART II

In the foregoing reasoning we have supposed, that the testimony, upon which a miracle is founded, may possibly amount to an entire proof, and that the falsehood of that testimony would be a real prodigy: But it is easy to show, that we have been a great deal too liberal in our concession, and that there never was a miraculous event established on so full an evidence.

For *first,* there is not to be found, in all history, any miracle attested by a sufficient number of men, of such unquestioned good-sense, education, and learning, as to secure us against all delusion in themselves; of such undoubted integrity, as to place them beyond all suspicion of any design to deceive others; of such credit and reputation in the eyes of mankind, as to have a great deal to lose in case of their being detected in any falsehood; and at the same time, attesting facts performed in such a public manner and in so celebrated a part of the world, as to render the detection unavoidable. All which circumstances are requisite to give us a full assurance in the testimony of men.

Secondly. We may observe in human nature a principle which, if strictly examined, will be found to diminish extremely the assurance, which we might, from human testimony, have, in any kind of prodigy. The maxim, by which we commonly conduct ourselves in our reasonings, is, that the objects, of which we have no experience, resemble those, of which we have; that what we have found to be most usual is always most probable; and that where there is an opposition of arguments, we ought to give the preference to such as are founded on the greatest number of past observations. But though, in proceeding by this rule, we readily reject any fact which is unusual and incredible in an ordinary degree; yet in advancing farther, the mind observes not always the same rule; but when anything is affirmed utterly absurd and miraculous, it rather the more readily admits of such a fact, upon account of that very circumstance, which ought to destroy all its authority. The passion of *surprise* and *wonder*, arising from miracles, being an agreeable emotion, gives a sensible tendency towards the belief of those events, from which it is derived. And this goes so far, that even those who cannot enjoy this pleasure immediately, nor can believe those miraculous events, of which they are informed, yet love to partake of the satisfaction at second-hand or by rebound, and place a pride and delight in exciting the admiration of others.

With what greediness are the miraculous accounts of travellers received, their descriptions of sea and land monsters, their relations of wonderful adventures, strange men, and uncouth manners? But if the spirit of religion join itself to the love of wonder, there is an end of common sense; and human testimony, in these circumstances, loses all pretensions to authority. A religionist may be an enthusiast, and imagine he sees what has no reality: he may know his narrative to be false, and yet persevere in it, with the best intentions in the world, for the sake of promoting so holy a cause: or even where this delusion has not place, vanity, excited by so strong a temptation, operates on him more powerfully than on the rest of mankind in any other circumstances; and self-interest with equal force. His auditors may not have, and commonly have not, sufficient judgement to canvass his evidence: what judgement they have, they renounce

by principle, in these sublime and mysterious subjects: or if they were ever so willing to employ it, passion and a heated imagination disturb the regularity of its operations. Their credulity increases his impudence: and his impudence overpowers their credulity.

Eloquence, when at its highest pitch, leaves little room for reason or reflection; but addressing itself entirely to the fancy or the affections, captivates the willing hearers, and subdues their understanding. Happily, this pitch it seldom attains. But what a Tully or a Demosthenes could scarcely effect over a Roman or Athenian audience, every *Capuchin*, every itinerant or stationary teacher can perform over the generality of mankind, and in a higher degree, by touching such gross and vulgar passions.

The many instances of forged miracles, and prophecies, and supernatural events, which, in all ages, have either been detected by contrary evidence, or which detect themselves by their absurdity, prove sufficiently the strong propensity of mankind to the extraordinary and the marvellous, and ought reasonably to beget a suspicion against all relations of this kind. This is our natural way of thinking, even with regard to the most common and most credible events. For instance: There is no kind of report which rises so easily, and spreads so quickly, especially in country places and provincial towns, as those concerning marriages; insomuch that two young persons of equal condition never see each other twice, but the whole neighborhood immediately join them together. The pleasure of telling a piece of news so interesting, of propagating it, and of being the first reporters of it, spreads the intelligence. And this is so well known, that no man of sense gives attention to these reports, till he find them confirmed by some greater evidence. Do not the same passions, and others still stronger, incline the generality of mankind to believe and report, with the greatest vehemence and assurance, all religious miracles.

Thirdly. It forms a strong presumption against all supernatural and miraculous relations, that they are observed chiefly to abound among ignorant and barbarous nations; or if a civilized people has ever given admission to any of them, that people will be found to have received them from ignorant and barbarous ancestors, who transmitted them with that inviolable sanction and authority, which always attend received opinions. When we peruse the first histories of all nations, we are apt to imagine ourselves transported into some new world; where the whole frame of nature is disjointed, and every element performs its operations in a different manner, from what it does at present. Battles, revolutions, pestilence, famine and death, are never the effect of those natural causes, which we experience. Prodigies, omens, oracles, judgements, quite obscure the few natural events, that are intermingled with them. But as the former grow thinner every page, in proportion as we advance nearer the enlightened ages, we soon learn, that there is nothing mysterious or supernatural in the case, but that all proceeds from the usual propensity of mankind towards the marvellous, and that, though this inclination may at intervals receive a check from sense and learning, it can never be thoroughly extirpated from human nature.

It is strange, a judicious reader is apt to say, upon the perusal of these wonderful historians, *that such prodigious events never happen in our days.* But it is nothing strange, I hope, that men should lie in all ages. You must surely have seen instances enough of that frailty. You have yourself heard many such marvellous relations started, which, being treated with scorn by all the wise and judicious, have at last been abandoned even by the vulgar. Be assured, that those renowned lies, which have spread and flourished to such a monstrous height, arose from like beginnings; but being sown in a more proper soil, shot up at last into prodigies almost equal to those which they relate. . . .

I may add as a *fourth* reason, which diminishes the authority of prodigies, that there is no testimony for any, even those which have not been expressly detected, that is not opposed by an infinite number of witnesses; so that not only the miracle destroys the credit of testimony, but the testimony destroys itself. To make this the better understood, let us consider, that, in matters of religion, whatever is different is contrary; and that it is

impossible the religions of ancient Rome, of Turkey, of Siam, and of China should, all of them, be established on any solid foundation. Every miracle, therefore, pretended to have been wrought in any of these religions (and all of them abound in miracles), as its direct scope is to establish the particular system to which it is attributed; so has it the same force, though more indirectly, to overthrow every other system. In destroying a rival system, it likewise destroys the credit of those miracles, on which that system was established; so that all the prodigies of different religions are to be regarded as contrary facts, and the evidences of these prodigies, whether weak or strong, as opposite to each other. According to this method of reasoning, when we believe any miracle of Mahomet or his successors, we have for our warrant the testimony of a few barbarous Arabians: And on the other hand, we are to regard the authority of Titus Livius, Plutarch, Tacitus, and, in short, of all the authors and witnesses, Grecian, Chinese, and Roman Catholic, who have related any miracle in their particular religion; I say, we are to regard their testimony in the same light as if they had mentioned that Mahometan miracle, and had in express terms contradicted it, with the same certainty as they have for the miracle they relate. This argument may appear over subtile and refined; but is not in reality different from the reasoning of a judge, who supposes, that the credit of two witnesses, maintaining a crime against any one, is destroyed by the testimony of two others, who affirm him to have been two hundred leagues distant, at the same instant when the crime is said to have been committed. . . .

There is also a memorable story related by Cardinal de Retz, which may well deserve our consideration. When that intriguing politician fled into Spain, to avoid the persecution of his enemies, he passed through Saragossa, the capital of Arragon, where he was shown, in the cathedral, a man, who had served seven years as a doorkeeper, and was well known to every body in town, that had ever paid his devotions at that church. He had been seen, for so long a time, wanting a leg; but recovered that limb by the rubbing of holy oil upon the stump; and the cardinal assures us that he saw him with two legs. This miracle was vouched by all the canons of the church; and the whole company in town were appealed to for a confirmation of the fact; whom the cardinal found, by their zealous devotion, to be thorough believers of the miracle. Here the relater was also contemporary to the supposed prodigy, of an incredulous and libertine character, as well as of great genius; the miracle of so *singular* a nature as could scarcely admit of a counterfeit, and the witnesses very numerous, and all of them, in a manner, spectators of the fact, to which they gave their testimony. And what adds mightily to the force of the evidence, and may double our surprise on this occasion, is, that the cardinal himself, who relates the story, seems not to give any credit to it, and consequently cannot be suspected of any concurrence in the holy fraud. He considered justly, that it was not requisite, in order to reject a fact of this nature, to be able accurately to disprove the testimony, and to trace its falsehood, through all the circumstances of knavery and credulity which produced it. He knew, that, as this was commonly altogether impossible at any small distance of time and place; so was it extremely difficult, even where one was immediately present by reason of the bigotry, ignorance, cunning, and roguery of a great part of mankind. He therefore concluded, like a just reasoner, that such an evidence carried falsehood upon the very face of it, and that a miracle, supported by any human testimony, was more properly a subject of derision than of argument.

There surely never was a greater number of miracles ascribed to one person, than those, which were lately said to have been wrought in France upon the tomb of Abbe Paris, the famous Jansenist, with whose sanctity the people were so long deluded. The curing of the sick, giving hearing to the deaf, and sight to the blind, were everywhere talked of as the usual effects of that holy sepulchre. But what is more extraordinary; many of the miracles were immediately proved upon the spot, before judges of unquestioned integrity, attested by witnesses of credit and distinction, in a learned age, and on the most eminent theatre that is now in the world. Nor is this all: a relation of them was published and dispersed every where; nor were the *Jesuits*, though a learned body, supported by the civil magistrate, and determined enemies to those opinions, in whose favour the miracles were said to have been wrought, ever able distinctly to refute or detect them. Where shall we find such a number of circumstances, agreeing to the corroboration of one fact? And what have we to oppose to such a cloud of witnesses, but the absolute impossibility or miraculous nature of the events, which they relate? And this surely, in the eyes of all reasonable people, will alone be regarded as a sufficient refutation.

Is the consequence just, because some human testimony has the utmost force and authority in some cases, when it relates the battle of Philippi or Pharsalia for instance; that therefore all kinds of testimony must, in all cases, have equal force and authority? Suppose that the Caesarean and Pompeian factions had, each of them, claimed the victory in these battles, and that the historians of each party had uniformly ascribed the advantage to their own side; how could mankind, at this distance, have been able to determine between them? The contrariety is equally strong between the miracles related by Herodotus or Plutarch, and those delivered by Mariana, Bede, or any monkish historian.

The wise lend a very academic faith to every report which favours the passion of the reporter; whether it magnifies his country, his family, or himself, or in any other way strikes in with his natural inclinations and propensities. But what greater temptation than to appear a missionary, a prophet, an ambassador from heaven? Who would not encounter many dangers and difficulties, in order to attain so sublime a character? Or if, by the help of vanity and a heated imagination, a man has first made a convert of himself, and entered seriously into the delusion; who ever scruples to make use of pious frauds, in support of so holy and meritorious a cause?

The smallest spark may here kindle into the greatest flame; because the materials are always prepared for it. The *avidum genus auricularum*, the gazing populace, receive greedily, without examination, whatever sooths superstition, and promotes wonder.

How many stories of this nature have, in all ages, been detected and exploded in their infancy?

How many more have been celebrated for a time, and have afterwards sunk into neglect and oblivion? Where such reports, therefore, fly about, the solution of the phenomenon is obvious; and we judge in conformity to regular experience and observation, when we account for it by the known and natural principles of credulity and delusion. And shall we, rather than have a recourse to so natural a solution, allow of a miraculous violation of the most established laws of nature?

I need not mention the difficulty of detecting a falsehood in any private or even public history, at the place, where it is said to happen; much more when the scene is removed to ever so small a distance. Even a court of judicature, with all the authority, accuracy, and judgement, which they can employ, find themselves often at a loss to distinguish between truth and falsehood in the most recent actions. But the matter never comes to any issue, if trusted to the common method of altercations and debate and flying rumours; especially when men's passions have taken part on either side.

In the infancy of new religions, the wise and learned commonly esteem the matter too inconsiderable to deserve their attention or regard. And when afterwards they would willingly detect the cheat, in order to undeceive the deluded multitude, the season is now past, and the records and witnesses, which might clear up the matter, have perished beyond recovery.

No means of detection remain, but those which must be drawn from the very testimony itself of the reporters: and these, though always sufficient with the judicious and knowing, are commonly too fine to fall under the comprehension of the vulgar.

Upon the whole, then, it appears, that no testimony for any kind of miracle has ever amounted to a probability, much less to a proof; and that, even supposing it amounted to a proof, it would be opposed by another proof; derived from the very nature of the fact, which it would endeavour to establish. It is experience only, which gives authority to human testimony; and it is the same experience, which assures us of the laws of nature. When, therefore, these two kinds of experience are contrary, we have nothing to do but subtract the one from the other, and embrace an opinion, either on one side or the other, with that assurance which arises from the remainder. But according to the principle here explained, this subtraction, with regard to all popular religions, amounts to an entire annihilation; and therefore we may establish it as a maxim, that no human testimony can have such force as to prove a miracle, and make it a just foundation for any such system of religion.

I beg the limitations here made may be remarked, when I say, that a miracle can never be proved, so as to be the foundation of a system of religion. For I own, that otherwise, there may possibly be miracles, or violations of the usual course of nature, of such a kind as to admit of proof from human testimony; though, perhaps, it will be impossible to find any such in all the records of history. Thus, suppose, all authors, in all languages, agree, that, from the first of January 1600, there was a total darkness over the whole earth for eight days: suppose that the tradition of this extraordinary event is still strong and lively among the people: that all travellers, who return from foreign countries, bring us accounts of the same tradition, without the least variation or contradiction: it is evident, that our present philosophers, instead of doubting the fact, ought to receive it as certain, and ought to search for the causes whence it might be derived. The decay, corruption, and dissolution of nature, is an event rendered probable by so many analogies, that any phenomenon, which seems to have a tendency towards that catastrophe, comes within the reach of human testimony, if that testimony be very extensive and uniform.

But suppose, that all the historians who treat of England, should agree, that, on the first of January 1600, Queen Elizabeth died; that both before and after her death she was seen by her physicians and the whole court, as is usual with persons of her rank; that her successor was acknowledged and proclaimed by the parliament; and that, after being interred a month, she again appeared, resumed the throne, and governed England for three years: I must confess that I should be surprised at the concurrence of so many odd circumstances, but should not have the least inclination to believe so miraculous an event. I should not doubt of her pretended death, and of those other public circumstances that followed it: I should only assert it to have been pretended, and that it neither was, nor possibly could be real. You would in vain object to me the difficulty, and almost impossibility of deceiving the world in an affair of such consequence; the wisdom and solid judgement of that renowned queen; with the little or no advantage which she could reap from so poor an artifice: All this might astonish me; but I would still reply, that the knavery and folly of men are such common phenomena, that I should rather believe the most extraordinary events to arise from their concurrence, than admit of so signal a violation of the laws of nature.

But should this miracle be ascribed to any new system of religion; men, in all ages, have been so much imposed on by ridiculous stories of that kind, that this very circumstance would be a full proof of a cheat, and sufficient, with all men of sense, not only to make them reject the fact, but even reject it without farther examination. Though the Being to whom the miracle is ascribed, be, in this case, Almighty, it does not, upon that account, become a whit more probable; since it is impossible for us to know the attributes or actions of such a Being, otherwise than from the experience which we have of his productions, in the usual course of nature. This still reduces us to past observation, and obliges us to compare the instances of the violation of truth in the testimony of men, with those of the violation of the laws of nature by miracles, in order to judge which of them is most likely and probable. As the violations of truth are more common in the testimony concerning religious miracles, than in that concerning any other matter of fact; this must diminish very much the authority of the former testimony, and make us form a general resolution, never to lend any attention to it, with whatever specious pretence it may be covered.

Lord Bacon seems to have embraced the same principles of reasoning. "We ought," says he, "to make a collection or particular history of all monsters and prodigious births or productions, and in a word of every thing new, rare, and extraordinary in nature. But this must be done with the most severe scrutiny, lest we depart from truth. Above all, every relation must be considered as suspicious, which depends in any degree upon religion, as the prodigies of Livy: And no less so, every thing that is to be found in the writers of natural magic or alchemy, or such authors, who seem, all of them, to have an unconquerable appetite for falsehood and fable."

I am the better pleased with the method of reasoning here delivered, as I think it may serve to confound those dangerous friends or disguised enemies to the *Christian Religion*, who have undertaken to defend it by the principles of human reason. Our most holy religion is founded on *Faith*, not on reason; and it is a sure method of exposing it to put it to such a trial as it is, by no means, fitted to endure. To make this more evident, let us examine those miracles, related in scripture; and not to lose ourselves in too wide a field, let us confine ourselves to such as we find in the *Pentateuch*, which we shall examine, according to the principles of those pretended Christians, not as the word or testimony of God himself, but as the production of a mere human writer and historian. Here then we are first to consider a book, presented to us by a barbarous and ignorant people, written in an age when they were still more barbarous, and in all probability long after the facts which it relates, corroborated by no concurring testimony, and resembling those fabulous accounts, which every nation gives of its origin. Upon reading this book, we find it full of prodigies and miracles. It gives an account of a state of the world and of human nature entirely different from the present: Of our fall from that state: Of the age of man, extended to near a thousand years: Of the destruction of the world by a deluge: Of the arbitrary choice of one people, as the favorites of heaven; and that people the countrymen of the author: Of their deliverance from bondage by prodigies the most astonishing imaginable: I desire any one to lay his hand upon his heart, and after a serious consideration declare, whether he thinks that the falsehood of such a book, supported by such a testimony, would be more extraordinary and miraculous than all the miracles it relates; which is, however, necessary to make it be received, according to the measures of probability above established.

What we have said of miracles may be applied, without any variation, to prophecies; and indeed, all prophecies are real miracles, and as such only, can be admitted as proofs of any revelation. If it did not exceed the capacity of human nature to foretell future events, it would be absurd to employ any prophecy as an argument for a divine mission or authority from heaven. So that, upon the whole, we may conclude, that the *Christian Religion* not only was at first attended with miracles, but even at this day cannot be believed by any reasonable person without one. Mere reason is insufficient to convince us of its veracity: And whoever is moved by *Faith* to assent to it, is conscious of a continued miracle in his own person, which subverts all the principles of his understanding, and gives him a determination to believe what is most contrary to custom and experience.

NOTE

1. Sometimes an event may not, *in itself*, seem to be contrary to the laws of nature, and yet, if it were real, it might, by reason of some circumstances, be denominated a miracle; because, in *fact* it is contrary to these laws. Thus if a person, claiming a divine authority, should command a sick person to be well, a healthful man to fall down dead, the clouds to pour rain, the winds to blow, in short, should order many natural events, which immediately follow upon his command; these might justly be esteemed miracles, because they are really, in this case, contrary to the laws of nature. For if any suspicion remain, that the event and command concurred by accident, there is no miracle and no transgression of the laws of nature. If this suspicion be removed, there is evidently a miracle, and a transgression of these laws; because nothing can be more contrary to nature than that the voice or command of a man should have such an influence. A miracle may be accurately defined, a *transgression of a law of nature by a particular volition of the Deity, or by the interposition of some invisible agent.* A miracle may either be discoverable by men or not. This alters not its nature and essence. The raising of a house or ship into the air is a visible miracle. The raising of a feather, when the wind wants ever so little of a force requisite for that purpose, is as real a miracle, though not so sensible with regard to us.

IV.B.2

Miracles and Testimony

J. L. MACKIE

A biographical sketch of J. L. Mackie appears before selection III.B.1. In this article he argues that the evidence for miracles will never in practice be very great.

Reprinted from *The Miracle of Theism* by J. L. Mackie (1982) by permission of Oxford University Press. Copyright © 1982 by John Mackie. Used by permission of Oxford University Press.

(A) INTRODUCTION

Traditional theism, as defined in the Introduction [to *The Miracle of Theism*], does not explicitly include any contrast between the natural and the supernatural. Yet there is a familiar, if vague and undeveloped, notion of the natural world in contrast with which the theistic doctrines stand out as asserting a supernatural reality. The question whether and how there can be evidence for what, if real, would be supernatural is therefore one of central significance. Besides, explicit assertions about supernatural occurrences, about miracles or divine interventions which have disrupted the natural course of events, are common in nearly all religions: alleged miracles are often cited to validate religious claims. Christianity, for example, has its share of these. In the life of Christ we have the virgin birth, the turning of water into wine, Christ's walking on the water, his healing of the sick, his raising of Lazarus from the dead, and, of course, the resurrection. The Roman Catholic church will not recognize anyone as a saint unless it is convinced that at least two miracles have been performed by the supposed saint, either in his or her life or after death.

The usual purpose of stories about miracles is to establish the authority of the particular figures who perform them or are associated with them, but of course these stories, with their intended interpretation, presuppose such more general religious doctrines as that of the existence of a god. We can, therefore, recognize, as one of the supports of traditional theism, an argument from miracles: that is, an argument whose main premise is that such and such remarkable events have occurred, and whose conclusion is that a god of the traditional sort both exists and intervenes, from time to time, in the ordinary world. . . .

[Here follows a brief exposition of Hume's essay "Of Miracles."]

(B) HUME'S ARGUMENT— DISCUSSION

What Hume has been expounding are the principles for the rational acceptance of testimony, the rules that ought to govern our believing or not believing what we are told. But the rules that govern people's actual acceptance of testimony are very different. We are fairly good at detecting dishonesty, insincerity, and lack of conviction, and we readily reject what we are told by someone who betrays these defects. But we are strongly inclined simply to accept, without question, statements that are obviously assured and sincere. As Hume would say, a firm association of ideas links someone else's saying, with honest conviction, that *p*, and its being the case that *p*, and we pass automatically from the perception of the one to belief in the other. Or, as he might also have said, there is an intellectual sympathy by which we tend automatically to share what we find to be someone else's belief, analogous to sympathy in the original sense, the tendency to share what we see to be someone else's feelings. And in general this is a useful tendency. People's beliefs about ordinary matters are right, or nearly right, more often than they are wildly wrong, so that intellectual sympathy enables fairly correct information to be passed on more smoothly than it could be if we were habitually cautious and constantly checked testimony against the principles for its rational acceptance. But what is thus generally useful can sometimes be misleading, and miracle reports are a special case where we need to restrain our instinctive acceptance of honest statements, and go back to the basic rational principles which determine whether a statement is really reliable or not. Even where we are cautious, and hesitate to accept what we are told—for example by a witness in a legal case—we often do not go beyond the question "How intrinsically reliable is this witness?", or, in detail, "Does he seem to be honest? Does he have a motive for misleading us? Is he the sort of person who might tell plausible lies? Or is he the sort of person who, in the circumstances, might have made a mistake?" If we are satisfied on all these scores, we are inclined to believe what the witness says, without weighing very seriously the question "How intrinsically improbable is what he has told us?" But, as Hume insists, this further question is highly relevant. His general approach to the problem of when to accept testimony is certainly sound.

Hume's case against miracles is an epistemological argument: it does not try to show that miracles never do happen or never could happen, but only that we never have good reasons for believing that they have happened. It must be clearly distinguished from the suggestion that the very concept of a miracle is incoherent. That suggestion might be spelled out as follows. A miracle is, by definition, a violation of a law of nature, and a law of nature is, by definition, a regularity—or the statement of a regularity—about what happens, about the way the world works; consequently, if some event actually occurs, no regularity which its occurrence infringes (or, no regularity-statement which it falsifies) can really be a law of nature; so this event, however unusual or surprising, cannot after all be a miracle. The two definitions together entail that whatever happens is not a miracle, that is, that miracles never happen. This, be it noted, is not Hume's argument. If it were correct, it would make Hume's argument unnecessary. Before we discuss Hume's case, then, we should consider whether there is a coherent concept of a miracle which would not thus rule out the occurrence of miracles *a priori*.

If miracles are to serve their traditional function of giving spectacular support to religious claims—whether general theistic claims, or the authority of some specific religion or some particular sect or individual teacher—the concept must not be so weakened that anything at all unusual or remarkable counts as a miracle. We must keep in the definition the notion of a violation of natural law. But then, if it is to be even possible that a miracle should occur, we must modify the definition given above of a law of nature. What we want to do is to contrast the order of nature with a possible divine or supernatural intervention. The laws of nature, we must say, describe the ways in which the world—including, of course, human beings—works when left to itself, when not interfered with. A miracle occurs when the world is not left to itself, when something distinct from the natural order as a whole intrudes into it.

This notion of ways in which the world works is coherent and by no means obscure. We

know how to discover causal laws, relying on a principle of the uniformity of the course of nature—essentially the assumption that there are some laws to be found—in conjunction with suitable observations and experiments, typically varieties of controlled experiment whose underlying logic is that of Mill's "method of difference." Within the laws so established, we can further mark off basic laws of working from derived laws which hold only in a particular context or contingently upon the way in which something is put together. It will be a derived law that a particular clock, or clocks of a particular sort, run at such a speed, and this will hold only in certain conditions of temperature, and so on; but this law will be derived from more basic ones which describe the regular behaviour of certain kinds of material, in view of the way in which the clock is put together, and these more basic laws of materials may in turn be derived from yet more basic laws about sub-atomic particles, in view of the ways in which those materials are made up of such particles. In so far as we advance towards a knowledge of such a system of basic and derived laws, we are acquiring an understanding of ways in which the world works. As well as what we should ordinarily call causal laws, which typically concern interactions, there are similar laws with regard to the ways in which certain kinds of things simply persist through time, and certain sorts of continuous process just go on. These too, and in particular the more basic laws of these sorts, help to constitute the ways in which the world works. Thus there are several kinds of basic "laws of working." For our present purpose, however, it is not essential that we should even be approaching an understanding of how the world works; it is enough that we have the concept of such basic laws of working, that we know in principle what it would be to discover them. Once we have this concept, we have moved beyond the definition of laws of nature merely as (statements of) what always happens. We can see how, using this concept and using the assumption that there are some such basic laws of working to be found, we can hope to determine what the actual laws of working are by reference to a restricted range of experiments and observations. This opens up the possibility that we might determine that something *is* a basic law of working of natural objects, and yet also, independently, find that it was occasionally violated. An occasional violation does not in itself necessarily overthrow the independently established conclusion that this is a law of working.

Equally, there is no obscurity in the notion of intervention. Even in the natural world we have a clear understanding of how there can be for a time a closed system, in which everything that happens results from factors within that system in accordance with its laws of working, but how then something may intrude from outside it, bringing about changes that the system would not have produced of its own accord, so that things go on after this intrusion differently from how they would have gone on if the system had remained closed. All we need do, then, is to regard the whole natural world as being, for most of the time, such a closed system; we can then think of a supernatural intervention as something that intrudes into that system from outside the natural world as a whole.

If the laws by which the natural world works are deterministic, then the notion of a violation of them is quite clear-cut: such a violation would be an event which, given that the world was a closed system working in accordance with these laws, and given some actual earlier complete state of the world, simply could not have happened at all. Its occurrence would then be clear proof that either the supposed laws were not the real laws of working, or the earlier state was not as it was supposed to have been, or else the system was not closed after all. But if the basic laws of working are statistical or probabilistic, the notion of a violation of them is less precise. If something happens which, given those statistical laws and some earlier complete state of the world, is extremely improbable—in the sense of physical probability: that is, something such that there is a strong propensity or tendency for it not to happen—we still cannot say firmly that the laws have been violated: laws of this sort explicitly allow that what is

extremely improbable may occasionally come about. Indeed it is highly probable (both physically and epistemically) that some events, each of which is very improbable, will occur at rare intervals. If tosses of a coin were governed by a statistical law that gave a 50 per cent propensity to heads at each toss, a continuous run of ten heads would be a highly improbable occurrence; but it would be highly probable that there would be some such runs in a sequence of a million tosses. Nevertheless, we can still use the contrast between the way of working of the natural world as a whole, considered as a normally closed system, and an intervention or intrusion into it. This contrast does not disappear or become unintelligible merely because we lack decisive tests for its application. We can still define a miracle as an event which would not have happened in the course of nature, and which came about only through a supernatural intrusion. The difficulty is merely that we cannot now say with certainty, simply by reference to the relevant laws and some antecedent situation, that a certain event would not have happened in the course of nature, and therefore must be such an intrusion. But we may still be able to say that it is very probable—this is now an epistemic probability—that it would not have happened naturally, and so is likely to be such an intrusion. For if the laws made it physically improbable that it would come about, this tends to make it epistemically improbable that it did come about through those laws, if there is any other way in which it could have come about and which is not equally improbable or more improbable. In practice the difficulty mentioned is not much of an extra difficulty. For even where we believe there to be deterministic laws and an earlier situation which together would have made an occurrence actually impossible in the course of nature, it is from our point of view at best epistemically very probable, not certain, that those are the laws and that that was the relevant antecedent situation.

Consequently, whether the laws of nature are deterministic or statistical, we can give a coherent definition of a miracle as a supernatural intrusion into the normally closed system that works in accordance with those laws, and in either case we can identify conceivable occurrences, and alleged occurrences, which if they were to occur, or have occurred, could be believed with high probability, though not known with certainty, to satisfy that definition.

However, the full concept of a miracle requires that the intrusion should be purposive, that it should fulfil the intention of a god or other supernatural being. This connection cannot be sustained by any ordinary causal theory; it presupposes a power to fulfil intentions directly, without physical means, which is highly dubious; so this requirement for a miracle will be particularly hard to confirm. On the other hand it is worth noting that successful prophecy could be regarded as a form of miracle for which there could in principle be good evidence. If someone is reliably recorded as having prophesied at t_1 an event at t_2 which could not be predicted at t_1 on any natural grounds, and the event occurs at t_2, then at any later time t_3 we can assess the evidence for the claims both that the prophecy was made at t_1 and that its accuracy cannot be explained either causally (for example, on the ground that it brought about its own fulfilment) or as accidental, and hence that it was probably miraculous.

There is, then, a coherent concept of miracles. Their possibility is not ruled out a priori, by definition. So we must consider whether Hume's argument shows that we never have good reason for believing that any have occurred.

Hume's general principle for the evaluation of testimony, that we have to weigh the unlikelihood of the event reported against the unlikelihood that the witness is mistaken or dishonest, is substantially correct. It is a corollary of the still more general principle of accepting whatever hypothesis gives the best overall explanation of all the available and relevant evidence. But some riders are necessary. First, the likelihood or unlikelihood, the epistemic probability or improbability, is always relative to some body of information, and may change if additional information comes in. Consequently, any specific decision in accordance with Hume's principle must be provisional.

Secondly, it is one thing to decide which of the rival hypotheses in the field at any time should be provisionally accepted in the light of the evidence then available; but it is quite another to estimate the weight of this evidence, to say how well supported this favoured hypothesis is, and whether it is likely that its claims will be undermined either by additional information or by the suggesting of further alternative hypotheses. What is clearly the best-supported view of some matter at the moment may still be very insecure, and quite likely to be overthrown by some further considerations. For example, if a public opinion poll is the only evidence we have about the result of a coming election, this evidence may point, perhaps decisively, to one result rather than another; yet if the poll has reached only a small sample of the electorate, or if it was taken some time before the voting day, it will not be very reliable. There is a dimension of reliability over and above that of epistemic probability relative to the available evidence. Thirdly, Hume's description of what gives support to a prediction, or in general to a judgement about an unobserved case that would fall under some generalization, is very unsatisfactory. He seems to say that if *all* so far observed As have been Bs, then this amounts to a "proof" that some unobserved A will be (or is, or was) a B, whereas if some observed As have been Bs, but some have not, there is only a "probability" that an unobserved A will be a B (pp. 110–12). This mixes up the reasoning to a generalization with the reasoning *from* a generalization to a particular case. It is true that the premises "All As are Bs" and "This is an A" constitute a proof of the conclusion "This is a B," whereas the premises "x per cent of As are Bs" and "This is an A" yield—if there is no other relevant information—a probability of x per cent that this is a B: they *probabilify* the conclusion to this degree, or, as we can say, the probability of the conclusion "This is a B" relative to that evidence is x per cent. But the inductive argument from the observation "All so far observed As have been Bs" to the generalization "All As are Bs" is far from secure, and it would be most misleading to call this a proof, and therefore misleading also to describe as a proof the whole line of inference from "All so far observed *A*s have been *B*s" to the conclusion "This as yet unobserved *A* is a *B*." Similarly, the inductive argument from "*x* per cent of observed *A*s have been *B*s" to the statistical generalization "*x* per cent of *A*s are *B*s" is far from secure, so that we cannot say that "*x* per cent of observed *A*s have been *B*s" even probabilifies to the degree *x* per cent the conclusion "This as yet unobserved *A* is a *B*." A good deal of other information and background knowledge is needed, in either case, before the generalization, whether universal or statistical, is at all well supported, and hence before the stage is properly set for either proof or probabilification about an as yet unobserved *A*. It is harder than Hume allows here to arrive at well-supported generalizations of either sort about how the world works.

These various qualifications together entail that what has been widely and reasonably thought to be a law of nature may not be one, perhaps in ways that are highly relevant to some supposed miracles. Our present understanding of psychosomatic illness, for example, shows that it is not contrary to the laws of nature that someone who for years has seemed, to himself as well as to others, to be paralysed should rapidly regain the use of his limbs. On the other hand, we can still be pretty confident that it is contrary to the laws of nature that a human being whose heart has stopped beating for forty-eight hours in ordinary circumstances—that is, without any special life-support systems—should come back to life, or that what is literally water should without addition or replacement turn into what is literally good-quality wine.

However, any problems there may be about establishing laws of nature are neutral between the parties to the present debate, Hume's followers and those who believe in miracles; for both these parties need the notion of a well-established law of nature. The miracle advocate needs it in order to be able to say that the alleged occurrence is a miracle, a violation of natural law by supernatural intervention, no less than Hume needs it for his

argument against believing that this event has actually taken place.

It is therefore not enough for the defender of a miracle to cast doubt (as he well might) on the certainty of our knowledge of the law of nature that seems to have been violated. For he must himself say that this *is* a law of nature: otherwise the reported event will not be miraculous. That is, he must in effect *concede* to Hume that the antecedent improbability of this event is as high as it could be, hence that, apart from the testimony, we have the strongest possible grounds for believing that the alleged event did not occur. This event must, by the miracle advocate's own admission, be contrary to a genuine, not merely a supposed, law of nature, and therefore maximally improbable. It is this maximal improbability that the weight of the testimony would have to overcome.

One further improvement is needed in Hume's theory of testimony. It is well known that the agreement of two (or more) *independent* witnesses constitutes very powerful evidence. Two independent witnesses are more than twice as good as each of them on his own. The reason for this is plain. If just one witness says that *p*, one explanation of this would be that it was the case that *p* and that he has observed this, remembered it, and is now making an honest report; but there are many alternative explanations, for example that he observed something else which he mistook for its being that *p*, or is misremembering what he observed, or is telling a lie. But if two witnesses who can be shown to be quite independent of one another both say that *p*, while again one explanation is that each of them has observed this and remembered it and is reporting honestly, the alternative explanations are not now so easy. They face the question "How has there come about this *agreement* in their reports, if it was not the case that *p*? How have the witnesses managed to misobserve to the same effect, or to misremember in the same way, or to hit upon the same lie?" It is difficult for even a single liar to keep on telling a *consistent* false story; it is much harder for two or more liars to do so. Of course if there is any collusion between the witnesses, or if either has been influenced, directly or indirectly, by the other, or if both stories have a common source, this question is easily answered. That is why the independence of the witnesses is so important. This principle of the improbability of coincident error has two vital bearings upon the problem of miracles. On the one hand, it means that a certain sort of testimony can be more powerful evidence than Hume's discussion would suggest. On the other, it means that where we seem to have a plurality of reports, it is essential to check carefully whether they really are independent of one another; the difficulty of meeting this requirement would be an important supplement to the points made in Part II of Hume's essay. Not only in remote and barbarous times, but also in recent ones, we are usually justified in suspecting that what look like distinct reports of a remarkable occurrence arise from different strands of a single tradition between which there has already been communication.

We can now put together the various parts of our argument. Where there is some plausible testimony about the occurrence of what would appear to be a miracle, those who accept this as a miracle have the double burden of showing both that the event took place and that it violated the laws of nature. But it will be very hard to sustain this double burden. For whatever tends to show that it would have been a violation of natural law tends for that very reason to make it most unlikely that it actually happened. Correspondingly, those who deny the occurrence of a miracle have two alternative lines of defense. One is to say that the event may have occurred, but in accordance with the laws of nature. Perhaps there were unknown circumstances that made it possible; or perhaps what were thought to be the relevant laws of nature are not strictly laws; there may be as yet unknown kinds of natural causation through which this event might have come about. The other is to say that this event would indeed have violated natural law, but that for this very reason there is a very strong presumption against its having happened, which it is most unlikely that any testimony will be able to outweigh. Usually one of these defenses will be stronger than the other. For many supposedly miraculous cures, the former will be quite a likely sort of explanation, but for such feats as the bringing back to life of those who are really dead the latter will be more likely. But the *fork*, the disjunction of these two sorts of explanation, is as a whole a very powerful reply to any claim that a miracle has been performed.

However, we should distinguish two different contexts in which an alleged miracle might be discussed. One possible context would be where the parties in debate already both accept some general theistic doctrines, and the point at issue is whether a miracle has occurred which would enhance the authority of a specific sect or teacher. In this context supernatural intervention, though *prima facie* unlikely on any particular occasion, is, generally speaking, on the cards: it is not altogether outside the range of reasonable expectation for these parties. Since they agree that there is an omnipotent deity, or at any rate one or more powerful supernatural beings, they cannot find it absurd to suppose that such a being will occasionally interfere with the course of nature, and this *may* be one of these occasions. For example, if one were already a theist and a Christian, it would not be unreasonable to weigh seriously the evidence of alleged miracles as some indication whether the Jansenists or the Jesuits enjoyed more of the favour of the Almighty. But it is a very different matter if the context is that of fundamental debate about the truth of theism itself. Here one party to the debate is initially at least agnostic, and does not yet concede that there is a supernatural power at all. From this point of view the intrinsic improbability of a genuine miracle, as defined above, is very great, and one or other of the alternative explanations in our fork will always be much more likely—that is, either that the alleged event is not miraculous, or that it did not occur, that the testimony is faulty in some way.

This entails that it is pretty well impossible that reported miracles should provide a worthwhile argument for theism addressed to those who are initially inclined to atheism or even to agnosticism. Such reports can form no significant part of what, following Aquinas, we might call a *Summa contra Gentiles*, or what, following Descartes, we could describe as being addressed to infidels. Not only are such reports unable to carry any rational conviction on their own, but also they are unable even to contribute independently to the kind of accumulation or battery of arguments referred to in the Introduction. To this extent Hume is right, despite the inaccuracies we have found in his statement of the case.

One further point may be worth making. Occurrences are sometimes claimed to be literally, and not merely metaphorically, miracles, that is, to be genuine supernatural interventions into the natural order, which are not even *prima facie* violations of natural law, but at most rather unusual and unexpected, but very welcome. Thus the combination of weather conditions which facilitated the escape of the British army from Dunkirk in 1940, making the Luftwaffe less than usually effective but making it easy for ships of all sizes to cross the Channel, is sometimes called a miracle. However, even if we accepted theism, and could plausibly assume that a benevolent deity would have favoured the British rather than the Germans in 1940, this explanation would still be far less probable than that which treats it as a mere meteorological coincidence: such weather conditions can occur in the ordinary course of events. Here, even in the context of a debate among those who already accept theistic doctrines, the interpretation of the event as a miracle is much weaker than the rival natural explanation. *A fortiori*, instances of this sort are utterly without force in the context of fundamental debate about theism itself.

There is, however, a possibility which Hume's argument seems to ignore—though, as we shall see, he did not completely ignore it. The argument has been directed against the acceptance of miracles on testimony; but what, it may be objected, if one is not reduced to reliance on testimony, but has observed a miracle for oneself? Surprisingly, perhaps, this possibility does not make very much difference. The first of the above-mentioned lines of defence is still available;

maybe the unexpected event that one has oneself observed did indeed occur, but in accordance with the laws of nature. Either the relevant circumstances or the operative laws were not what one has supposed them to be. But at least a part of the other line of defence is also available. Though one is not now relying literally on another witness or other witnesses, we speak not inappropriately of the evidence of our senses, and what one takes to be an observation of one's own is open to questions of the same sort as is the report of some other person. I may have misobserved what took place, as anyone knows who has even been fooled by a conjurer or "magician," and, though this is somewhat less likely, I may be misremembering or deceiving myself after an interval of time. And of course the corroboration of one or more independent witnesses would bring in again the testimony of others which it was the point of this objection to do without. Nevertheless, anyone who is fortunate enough to have carefully observed and carefully recorded, for himself, an apparently miraculous occurrence is no doubt rationally justified in taking it very seriously; but even here it will be in order to entertain the possibility of an alternative natural explanation.

As I said, Hume does not completely ignore this possibility. The Christian religion, he says, cannot at this day be believed by any reasonable person without a miracle. "Mere reason is insufficient to convince us of its veracity: And whoever is moved by *Faith* to assent to it, is conscious of a continued miracle in his own person, which subverts all the principles of his understanding ..." (p. 131). But of course this is only a joke. What the believer is conscious of in his own person, though it may be a mode of thinking that goes against "custom and experience," and so is contrary to the ordinary rational principles of the understanding is not, as an occurrence, a violation of natural law. Rather it is all too easy to explain immediately by the automatic communication of beliefs between persons and the familiar psychological processes of wish fulfillment, and ultimately by what Hume himself was later to call "the natural history of religion."

IV.B.3

Of "Of Miracles"

PETER VAN INWAGEN

Peter van Inwagen (1942–) is professor of philosophy at the University of Notre Dame and is one of the leading figures in contemporary metaphysics and philosophy of religion. In this article, he attacks Hume's argument against miracles. Hume's argument rests in part on the idea that miracles are the sorts of things that run significantly contrary to our experience. But, according to van Inwagen, there is no clear sense in which experience rules out events of any particular sort. Failing to find any other sense of "contrary to experience" that could drive Hume's argument, van Inwagen concludes that the argument is a failure.

In the first and briefer part of this essay, my concerns are ontological. I shall explain what a miracle *is* (or would be if there were any). In the second part, my concerns are epistemological: I shall discuss and attempt to refute Hume's argument for the conclusion that it is unreasonable to believe any historical report that would count as a report of a miracle.

THE ONTOLOGY OF MIRACLES

The account of "miracles" that I shall present here is a summary of the account I presented in "The Place of Chance in a World Sustained by God."[1] (It is, I believe, entirely consistent with Hume's "official" definition of "miracle": "a transgression of a law of nature by a particular volition of the Deity, or by the interposition of some invisible agent." And, I believe, it will not weaken Hume's argument for the conclusion that it would be unreasonable to accept any report of an alleged "miracle" if, in evaluating his argument, we

understand the word in the sense I supply in the present section.)

Let us suppose that the physical world is made up of certain fundamental building blocks or units, certain tiny physical things without proper parts. I shall call them elementary particles. Elementary particles are sorted into kinds by their causal powers (e.g., rest, mass, and charge). It will simplify my account of miracles if I make the assumption (false, of course, at least in our present state of knowledge) that there is only one type of elementary particle. Each particle is continuously sustained in existence by God: At each instant, he supplies it with existence and the causal powers it then has. The motions over the interval t_1-t_2 of the particles that compose the world are determined (insofar as they are determined) entirely by their distribution at t_1 and the causal powers they have at each instant in t_1-t_2. (Here we make a second simplifying assumption: that the propagation of causal influence is instantaneous.)

God always, *or almost always*, supplies each particle with the same causal powers. But he may, *very*

From *The Possibility of Resurrection and Other Essays in Christian Apologetics* (Boulder, CO: Westview Press, 1998). Copyright © Peter van Inwagen 1998. Used with permission.

rarely, supply *just a few* particles—"just a few" in comparison with the number of all the particles there are—with different causal powers from the powers they normally have. If he momentarily supplies some of the particles in a certain small region of space with powers different from their normal powers, the particles in that region will follow trajectories different from the trajectories they would have followed if he had continued to supply them with their normal powers. Here is a preliminary definition of "miracle": The early stages of any such "divergence" constitute a miracle. (The later stages of a divergence will be classified as "consequences of a miracle" and not "parts of a miracle.")

Now a qualification and refinement of this definition. A proposition will be called a law of nature in a possible world x if it is a contingent proposition that is true in every world y in which particles *always* have the causal powers that they *always or almost always* have in x. If some particles in the world x do sometimes have "unusual" powers, some of the propositions that are laws in x may be false propositions in x. (If x is a deterministic world, this must be so.) If a proposition p is both a law of nature in x and false in x, it will be said to be violated in x; it will be violated by the behavior of those particles that (owing to their or their neighbors' unusual causal powers) follow trajectories inconsistent with the truth of p.

If a world is indeterministic, some events that are miracles according to our preliminary definition may not involve violations of laws. If the laws of a world allow A to be followed either by B or by C, and if God temporarily changes the causal powers of certain particles in such a way as to determine that A be followed by B, the consequent occurrence of B will be a miracle by our preliminary definition but will not be a violation of the laws of the world in which it occurs. In "The Place of Chance in a World Sustained by God," my topic was Providence, and it suited my purposes to have a definition of "miracle" that had this feature. In the present essay, however, I wish to conform my usage (more or less) to Hume's. I shall, therefore, understand "miracle" to imply "violation of the laws of nature." God performs a miracle, then, if he momentarily supplies certain particles with unusual causal powers and the consequent divergence of the trajectories of those (and no doubt some other) particles from the courses they would have followed is a violation of the laws of nature. (Of course, a violation of one law will in most cases be a violation of many, since if two propositions are laws, so is their conjunction.) The miracle is the early stages of the divergence.

HUME'S ARGUMENT

In this section, I shall present and attempt to refute the central argument of "Of Miracles."[2] More exactly, the argument I shall present and attempt to refute is my own reconstruction of the central argument of "Of Miracles." I believe that there are, in Hume's presentation of his argument, certain infelicities that arise from his imprecise use of terminology, and my reconstruction is designed to remove them. To subject one's reconstruction of a philosopher's argument to criticisms of one's own devising is a somewhat dubious procedure, and it is dubious on two grounds: First, one's "improvements" may be ones that the author of the original argument would reject, and, worse, they may introduce defects into the argument that were not present in the original. I think, however, that the points I shall make against the reconstructed argument would apply to the original even if Hume would have emphatically rejected my modifications of his argument and even if these modifications introduced errors that were not present in the original.

What, exactly, is the conclusion of the central argument of "Of Miracles"? It is a commonplace that Hume's conclusion is not ontological: He does not claim to show that there are no miracles. His conclusion is epistemological. But it is not that one should not believe that there are miracles. It is not so general as that. It has to do with the attitude one should take toward any (supposed, putative) report of a miracle one might encounter. It is something like this: If one hears a report of a miracle, one should not believe it (or one should believe it only in very special circumstances, circumstances so special that no one has in fact ever been in them). But this formulation of Hume's conclusion raises two important questions. First, what counts as a "report of a miracle"? Secondly, does "one should not believe it" mean "one should reject it" or "one should refrain from accepting it"—or perhaps some third thing?

Let us say that a report of a miracle (or a miracle-report) is any narrative, presented as historical or factual, such that (a) it does not follow logically from that narrative that a miracle has occurred, and (b) if the narrative were true, the only reasonable conclusion would be that at least one of the events it recounted was a miracle.[3] The following story

Jill was about to cross Sixth Avenue in New York when, all in an instant, she was miraculously translated to Sydney,

does not satisfy the terms of this definition, since it follows logically from the story that a miracle has occurred.[4] Here, by way of contrast, are two stories that—whatever other features they may have—do not logically entail that a miracle has occurred:

Jill was about to cross Sixth Avenue in New York when, without any sensation of motion, she suddenly found herself in Sydney.[5]

And when he got into the boat his disciples followed him. And behold there arose a great storm on the sea, so that the boat was being swamped by the waves; but he was asleep. And they went and woke him, saying, "Save us, Lord, for we are perishing." And he said to them, "Why are you afraid, O men of little faith?" Then he rose and he rebuked the wind and the sea, and there was a great calm. And the men marveled, saying, "What manner of man is this that even the wind and the wave obey him?" (Matt. 8:23–27).[6]

Whether either of these two stories satisfies condition (b) in our definition of "miracle-report"—and

thereby qualifies as a miracle-report—is an epistemological question: Given that the story was true, would the only reasonable conclusion be that one of the events recounted in the story was a miracle?[7] It would be possible to argue, some no doubt have argued, that one should never believe of any story (unless it logically entails the occurrence of a miracle) that if that story is true, some of the events it recounts were miracles. One should rather believe (the argument might continue) that if the story is true, there is *some* explanation of the events it relates that is consistent with the laws of nature and this explanation is the correct explanation. (It is not hard to provide gestures at such explanations. Take the story of the stilling of the storm. This story could be embedded in a logically consistent science fiction novel according to which Christianity was "founded" by extraterrestrial beings as an adjunct to a project involving the manipulation of human history; it might be that, in the novel, all the "miracles" related in the New Testament actually happened—at least as far as appearances went—but were the products of an advanced technology rather than true miracles.)

I shall not attempt to answer the (intrinsically very interesting) question whether there in fact are any stories that satisfy the terms of the above definition of "miracle-report," for the cogency of Hume's argument does not depend on what the right answer to this question is. His conclusion is that one should react in a certain way to any miracle-report one encounters, and his reasoning can be evaluated independently of the question whether anyone ever does encounter any miracle-reports.

But what *does* Hume say about how one should react to a miracle-report? Is his position simply that one should *not* believe the report, or is it that one should *disbelieve* (not believe *and* believe the denial of) the report—or is it some third thing? I do not think that Hume is clear or entirely consistent about the matter, but I believe that the best way to state his conclusion is this: One should *dismiss* any miracle-report one encounters. The concept of dismissal may be spelled out as follows: One dismisses a report—an allegedly historical narrative—if one either disbelieves it or (does not believe it and) assigns it a very low probability.[8] (How low? Well, let's say very low—a probability of the sort that we describe in ordinary speech by phrases like "of insignificant probability" and "no real possibility.")

We shall need one more definition before we turn to Hume's argument for this conclusion. Let us say that a proposition is a *contravention of one's experience* (for short, a contravention) if the truth of that proposition is contrary to one's experience.[9] ("Contravention"—this may be true of "miracle-report" as well—is obviously a person-and-time-relative concept: A proposition may be a contravention of one person's experience and not of another's—or a proposition may be a contravention of a person's experience at one time and not at another. I shall, however, generally speak of contraventions and miracle-reports *sans phrase* and leave it to the reader to fill in the necessary qualifications about person-and-time relativity. And I shall speak of various propositions as "contrary to experience" without bothering to specify whose experience they are contrary to.) Contraventions, moreover, come in "sizes": p is a larger or greater contravention than q if, although q is contrary to experience, p is "even more contrary to experience" than q.[10] (At this point it should be evident, if it was not already, that I am presenting a reconstruction of Hume's argument, for Hume speaks of "greater" and "lesser" *miracles*, and he employs no term that corresponds to my "contravention.") If I tell my friends that on a recent trip from Boston to Los Angeles my 1973 Cadillac averaged sixty miles to the gallon, what I tell them will no doubt be a contravention. If Calvin tells his mother that the jammy handprints on the new sofa were put there not by himself but by an evil Calvin doppelgänger constructed by beings from Arcturus, that will also be a contravention, and perhaps there is some intuitive sense in which it is a larger contravention than the one I have asserted. An *historical narrative* will be called a contravention if its propositional content is a contravention.

I will now present Hume's argument, or my reconstruction of it. The argument has three premises, two epistemological premises and one "historical" premise. The first epistemological premise is:

E1. Any miracle-report must necessarily be a contravention and, in fact, a very *large* contravention.[11] (If a story is a miracle-report for some audience, it will also be a contravention for that audience. If a story is not a contravention, it will not qualify as a miracle-report. Suppose, for example, that we hear the story of Jill's sudden translation from New York to Sydney. It may or may not be reasonable for us to classify this as a miracle-report, but if the proposition that people sometimes find themselves suddenly on the other side of the earth is not contrary to experience, a necessary condition for classifying the story as a miracle-report will be absent. There are, moreover, stories that are contraventions but not large enough contraventions to qualify as miracle-reports. If I am told that Sally, who was hitherto entirely ignorant of French, spoke perfect French after spending three months in France, that story would be a contravention but no doubt not one that is large enough to qualify as a miracle-report. And how large a contravention must a miracle report be? One way to answer this question would be to specify some story that is a large enough contravention by just about anyone's reckoning to be a miracle-report and say, "At least as large as that." I think that the following story will do for this purpose: Let us suppose that we have heard a report of a shaman in Peru who has, it is alleged, restored several incontestably long-dead people to life. Suppose we are willing to agree that this story is "more contrary to experience" than the story of Sally's remarkably quick mastery of French. Then, according to the criterion I have proposed, the story of Sally is not a large enough contravention to be a miracle-report.

We should note that it does not follow from the proposed criterion that just any story that is as large a contravention as the "shaman" story *is* a miracle-report. Indeed, it does not follow from anything we have said that the "shaman" story itself is a miracle-report. And if someone maintained that Calvin's story of the origin of the jammy handprints was as large a contravention as the "shaman" story, despite the fact that Calvin's story was not a miracle-report and the "shaman" story was, that person would have said nothing inconsistent with the proposed criterion. Let us say that any contravention that is at least as large as the "shaman" story is *very large*.)

The second epistemological premise requires a little stage-setting. Let us say that two narratives are (historically) independent if neither is derived from the other. Two narratives will be said to support each other if they are independent and "tell the same story"—(purport to) describe events that are the same or at least very similar. ("Similarity" is to include the elements "cast of characters" and "place and time.") Hume's second epistemological premise is

E2. One should dismiss any very large contravention one encounters unless one knows that one of the following two conditions holds:

(a) if the very large contravention is unhistorical—if it is not a reasonably accurate description of events that actually happened—its existence is itself a contravention and a larger contravention than its truth would be

(b) it is one of two or more mutually supporting narratives such that if they are unhistorical, their (collective) existence is a contravention and a larger contravention than their truth (i.e., the truth of their common propositional content) would be.

(Suppose that X tells me that Jimmy Carter is a tool of malign extraterrestrial beings. And suppose no one else has told me that. X's statement is a very large contravention[12] and should therefore be dismissed—unless X's telling me falsely that Carter is a tool of malign extraterrestrial beings is a contravention and a larger contravention than his being a tool of malign extraterrestrial beings would be. Or suppose that shortly after X has told me that Carter is a tool of malign extraterrestrial beings, Y tells me the same thing. And suppose I am somehow satisfied that X's statement and Y's statement are historically independent. I should dismiss what they have told me—unless the existence of two independent false allegations that Carter is a tool of malign extraterrestrial beings is a contravention and a larger

contravention than his being a tool of malign extraterrestrial beings would be.)

Here, finally, is Hume's "historical" premise:

H. Although it may be possible to imagine a miracle-report that satisfies one or the other of the conditions set out in E2, no miracle-report known to history satisfies either; indeed, all known narratives that anyone might be inclined to classify as miracle-reports (such as the Gospel story of the stilling of the storm) fall far short of satisfying either of them.

I will make a few remarks about E2 and H and then proceed to argue against E1. I shall, in discussing Hume's views, write as if he were familiar with the vocabulary and distinctions of the present essay. I believe that this anachronism could be eliminated from my argument, although only at the cost of a great deal of circumlocution.

Hume wrote in an era when photography and sound recordings had not yet been invented—in an era when almost the only evidence as to what had occurred in the past was human testimony. No doubt if he were writing today, he would want to emend E2 to take account of "nontestimonial" evidence about the past. But any such emendation of E2 would affect no point of principle, and the question of its proper formulation need not detain us.

It is evident that Hume believed that clause (a) in E2 could not possibly be satisfied, for (such is human credulity and epistemic frailty) the proposition that a given person has made a false statement about the past could not possibly be a "very large" contravention. Hume's position was, therefore, that the only possibility of a case in which a very large contravention should not be dismissed would be of this sort: It was one of two or more historically independent contraventions with essentially the same propositional content. It is, however, unclear whether Hume thought that even a very large number of mutually supporting false statements about the past could constitute a "very large" contravention. In introducing the important "eight-day darkness" example ("Thus, suppose, all authors, in all languages, agree, that, from the first of January 1600, there was a total darkness over the whole earth for eight days...."), he says,

"For I own, that otherwise [i.e., if we imagine testimony much more extensive and uniform than the testimony to the supposed miracles foundational to Christianity and its rivals], there may possibly be miracles, or violations of the usual course of nature, of such a kind as to admit of proof from human testimony, though, perhaps, it will be impossible to find any such in all the records of history." Although Hume uses the word "miracle" here, he goes on to say that although philosophers of his own day, if they had available to them the testimony he imagines, ought to grant the historicity of the eight-day darkness (in fact, they should "receive it as certain"), they should proceed to "search for the causes whence it might be derived"—and hence they should presumably *not* regard the darkness as a miracle as the term is "accurately defined" ("A transgression of a law of nature by a particular volition of the Deity, or by the interposition of some invisible agent") but only in the loose and much weaker sense he has supplied: as a violation of the usual course of nature. He then argues that various (unspecified) analogies with known events suggest that a universal eight-day darkness "comes within the reach of human testimony, if that testimony be very extensive and uniform." And this statement implies that other imaginable events might not come within the reach of any testimony, however extensive and uniform. This argument is immediately followed by an example of such an imaginable event: the death and "resurrection" of Elizabeth I. It seems likely, therefore, that Hume would maintain that no imaginable human testimony could be such that its falsity would be what we are calling a very large contravention. And from this and our two epistemological premises, it follows that any imaginable miracle-report should be dismissed.

Even if I have not interpreted Hume correctly, however, even if, in his view, there are imaginable miracle-reports that should not be *dismissed*, it does not follow from this that any imaginable miracle-report should be *accepted*. (I do not believe that the story of King Alfred and the cakes is false—that is, I do not assent to the proposition that the story of King Alfred and the cakes is false. And I do not think that the probability of this story's being true is so low as to be insignificant. I therefore do not *dis-miss* the story of Alfred and the cakes. But I certainly do not assent to the proposition that the story is *true*—and, in fact, I think it's very unlikely to be true.) And I think that it would certainly be Hume's position that none should be: Whether or not every imaginable miracle-report should be dismissed, no imaginable miracle-report should be accepted. No imaginable miracle-report should be accepted because a miracle-report, no matter what testimony might support it, is a very large contravention, and no testimonial evidence in favor of a very large contravention could be so good as to make it worthy of belief—even if it were possible for there to be testimonial evidence good enough to lead the judicious reasoner not to dismiss it. (In the most favorable possible case, there would be, as Hume says, "a mutual destruction of arguments.") And, of course, if we leave the realm of the merely imaginable and turn to the actual and historical, it is clear—this is the import of our "historical" premise—that Hume believes that all actual miracle-reports should be dismissed.[13]

Is Hume's argument, as I have reconstructed it, cogent? I think not. My defense of this judgment begins with an examination of E1, the premise that any miracle-report must be a very large contravention. That is, for any story about the past one might hear, one should refuse to make the following judgment about it:

> If that story is true, then some of the events it relates involve violations of the laws of nature,

unless one is also willing to make the following judgment:

> That story is contrary to my experience—and *as* contrary to my experience as the "shaman" story.

In order to evaluate this premise, we must turn to a question we have so far glossed over. What is it for a story to be "contrary to one's experience"? Hume generally writes as if the following were true: A story is contrary to one's experience if that story involves something's having the property F and the property G and one has observed many things having the property F and has observed that all of them had the complement of G. For example, on this account, a story about a man's returning from the dead is contrary to my experience owing simply to the fact that I have known of a very large number of people who have died and all of them have the property "not having returned from the dead." But this account of what it is for a story to be contrary to one's experience is useless for Hume's purposes, since it will classify far too many stories as contrary to one's experience. Suppose for example, that I know of many visits that Tom has made to his mother over the past ten years; it is all but inevitable that if I hear a detailed account of his latest visit to her, this account will ascribe to this visit some property that all of the others lacked. And this will be true even if we do not "count" the *date* of the latest visit as a relevant property. It may, for example, be that the story I have been told of his latest visit includes the information that he arrived on her doorstep at 3:21 P.M. and that the comprehensive diary I have for some reason kept of his earlier visits reveals that on all the other occasions on which he has visited her he arrived at some other time. No doubt we could play a lengthy game of "counterexample and revision" with the above account of what it is for a story to be contrary to experience. But I do not know of any way of "improving" this account that will enable it to avoid consequences like the following: The first reports of someone's making a solo flight across the Atlantic or running a four-minute mile or reaching the summit of Mount Everest were contrary to the experience of those who heard them.

But might Hume not reply that these consequences are acceptable? Might he not argue that such reports would indeed be a *bit* contrary to the experience of those who heard them? Might he not go on to say, "But it would be *more* contrary to the experience of those who heard them if all the reports of these events were false, and that is why it was proper for those who heard the reports to believe them"? Perhaps so. But how, then, are we to understand the relevant notion of *degree* of contrariety? If I hear on Monday that Lindbergh has flown across the Atlantic without a copilot and on Tuesday that a rival has flown across the Atlantic

without an aircraft, on what basis am I to judge that the second story is more contrary to my experience (is a larger contravention) than the first? My experience tells me that all previous transatlantic flights have involved an aircraft of some sort, but it also tells me that all previous transatlantic flights have involved two or more pilots. There simply do not seem to be any materials in the "property-complement" account of a story's being contrary to experience from which to construct an account of the concept of one story's being "more contrary to experience" than another is.

Let us consider an actual example (at least I believe it to be actual, although, unfortunately, I no longer remember where I heard or read it) of someone's applying the "property-complement" account of this concept. Thomas Jefferson was once told that in a museum in Cambridge (Massachusetts) there was exhibited a stone that had fallen from the sky. Jefferson declined to believe this story on the ground that although he had never known a stone to fall from the sky, he had often known a Yankee parson—the staff of Harvard College in those days comprised Congregational ministers—to prevaricate. (He had observed the sky on many occasions, and on each of those occasions, it had the property "not being the source of a falling stone"; he had observed many Yankee parsons making assertions, and on many of these occasions, the assertions had the property "being a lie." He concluded that stones falling from the sky were contrary to his experience and lying Yankee parsons were not.) Now even if Jefferson's statement about his experience of the New England clergy was something of an exaggeration, he was no doubt telling the truth when he said he had never known a stone to fall from the sky. But there were many, many things he had "never known" that he wouldn't have been disinclined to believe reports of, even reports from Yankee parsons. If he thought the story unlikely on the basis of his experience, it cannot have been simply because such a thing had never happened in his experience. If the story was indeed "contrary to his experience," it cannot have been simply because events of the type related in the story were not included in the totality of his experience to date. This observation might lead us to conclude that the "property-complement" account of an event's being contrary to experience must be replaced by some other account.

Was there *any* sense in which the story Jefferson was told was contrary to his experience? Well, suppose that Jefferson had fallen asleep like Rip van Winkle and had slept till the existence and nature of meteors was common knowledge. Suppose that, on awakening, he was given an encyclopedia article on the subject to read and had afterward received the testimony of several eminent (Virginian) astronomers that what the article said was true. Would he have been in a position to complain that his eighteenth-century experience was misleading—that it had somehow "told" him that stones never fell from the sky when stones in fact sometimes *do* fall from the sky? Certainly not. No doubt Descartes was wrong in holding that the testimony of experience was never false, but it does not seem to have testified falsely to Jefferson on this point. Experience may have testified to some persons at some points in history that the earth is at the center of the universe or that maggots are spontaneously generated in dung, but it had never testified to anyone that stones do not fall from the sky (or, for most people, that they do—not "directly," not otherwise than via the testimony of other people; for most people, "direct" experience has had nothing to say about whether stones fall from the sky). Although experience may have testified that if stones ever fall from the sky, their doing so is a very uncommon event, it has not testified that stones never fall from the sky.

It is very hard indeed to find a sense in which experience testifies in any direct or immediate sense that events of some sort never happen—or in which stories of events of some sort are contrary to experience. If direct, immediate experience testifies to anything (truly or falsely) its testimony seems to be essentially "positive": It testifies that events of certain sorts *do* happen. One might of course point out that it is *reasonable* to *believe* of events of various sorts that events of those sorts never happen, and that the reasonableness of such beliefs must ultimately be based on experience. Having made this

observation, one might propose an account of what it is for a story to be "contrary to experience" that is based on what it is reasonable to believe. It would go something like this: A story is contrary to one's experience if that story involves the occurrence of events of sorts such that given one's experience at the time one hears the story, it is reasonable for one to believe that events of those sorts never happen—or perhaps that it is highly improbable that such events ever happen (or, more simply, a story is contrary to one's experience if, given one's experience at the time one hears the story, it is reasonable for one to believe that the story is false or is highly improbable). And one might go on to spell out the concept "more contrary to one's experience" in terms of its being more unreasonable to believe one proposition than another. (One might say that p is more contrary to one's experience than q just in the case that although what it is reasonable to believe, on the basis of one's experience, is that p and q are both false, one should also believe that if one or the other of them is, after all, true, it is q. Thus, or so I would judge, Calvin's story about the handprints on the sofa is "more contrary to experience" than my story about the mileage my Cadillac got, and the "shaman" story is "more contrary to experience" than the story of Sally's quick mastery of French.)

I think, however, that it is reasonably clear that this is not what Hume means by "contrary to experience" and "more contrary to experience." Whatever he means by these phrases and the related phrases he uses, he means something much more concrete, much more immediate than this. For Hume, if one judges that a story of a man's rising from the dead is "contrary to one's experience," the experience that the story is contrary to is one's experience of the dead's staying dead, not the totality of one's experience of the world to date. But at least in my view, what it is now *reasonable for me to believe* about men's rising from the dead must be based on pretty nearly the whole of my experience to date (e.g., those experiences that are relevant to the truth or falsity of the principles of thermodynamics and the truth or falsity of judgments about the historical reliability of the New Testament and the authority of the Church). In any case, if this is what "contrary to experience" and "more contrary to experience" mean, there seems to me to be no very compelling reason for anyone to accept E1.

It may be reasonable to believe that if the Matthean story of the stilling of the storm is historical, then a miracle, a violation of the laws of nature, occurred. I certainly think that this would be the reasonable conclusion to draw from the truth of the story. But I do not think that this story is, by the terms of the definition we are considering, at least as contrary to experience as the "shaman" story is. In fact, I think that the Matthean story is *true* (and, of course, I think I am being reasonable in thinking that it is true), and I think that anyone who heard and believed the "shaman" story and whose experience of the world was otherwise like mine would be very unreasonable indeed. I am not trying to convince you, the reader, that these epistemological judgments are correct. I am saying only that nowhere in "Of Miracles" do I find any reason to suppose they are not correct. Hume's argument, after all, is of this general form: *Because certain propositions are contrary to experience—*

very contrary to experience—it is unreasonable to accept them. And it is, to say the least, very hard to see how an argument of this form could be cogent if "contrary to experience" *means* "unreasonable to believe."

I can think of no other plausible sense that can be given to the phrase "contrary to experience." I conclude, provisionally, that Hume's argument is a failure, owing to the fact that there is no sense that can be given to "contrary to experience" such that E1 is compelling when "contrary to experience" is interpreted in that sense. It should be noted that I do not claim to have shown that anyone is ever justified in believing a miracle-report. Indeed, I do not even claim to have addressed this question. It is perfectly consistent with everything I have said to suppose that anyone who believed any story that could conceivably count as a miracle-report (such as the Matthean story of the stilling of the storm) would be wholly unreasonable. I claim to have shown only that the argument of "Of Miracles" (as I understand the argument) does not establish either this conclusion or any other negative conclusion about the reasonableness of accepting miracle-reports.

NOTES

1. Included in Thomas V. Morris, ed., *Divine and Human Action: Essays in the Metaphysics of Theism* (Ithaca, N.Y.: Cornell University Press, 1988), pp. 211–235. Reprinted in Peter van Inwagen, *God, Knowledge, and Mystery: Essays in Philosophical Theology* (Ithaca, N.Y.: Cornell University Press, 1995), pp. 42–65.

2. "Of Miracles" is section X of *An Enquiry Concerning Human Understanding.* There are numerous editions of the *Enquiry.* I have used the Open Court edition (La Salle, Ill.: 1907 and 1966), which, according to the publisher's preface is "an unannotated reprint . . . made from the second volume of the posthumous edition of 1777." No editor is given on the title page, but the preface notes that the editing was done by one Thomas J. McCormack. Because there are numerous editions

of the *Enquiry* (and, of course, "Of Miracles" appears in whole or in part in scores of anthologies) and because "Of Miracles" is very short, I have not provided page citations for the very few direct quotations I have made.

3. The idea behind (b) is as follows. If two people consider the narrative, and one of them says, "If that story is true, at least one of the events it recounts was a miracle," and the other says, "Even if that story is true in every detail, there is some purely natural explanation for every event it recounts," the first speaker is being reasonable and the second unreasonable. Note that if the second speaker is indeed unreasonable, he nevertheless does not contradict himself, since by (a) it does not follow logically from the story that a miracle has occurred.

4. The purpose of clause (a) of the definition is to rule out of consideration as "miracle-reports" narratives that would satisfy clause (b) *only* because the narrative logically entailed that a miracle had occurred. Here are two examples of such narratives: "Last week Sally witnessed a miracle" and "A feather rose when the resultant of all the natural forces acting on it fell short by an insensible amount of the force requisite for that purpose."

5. It does not follow from our definition of "miracle-report" that if a miracle-report is true, the people whose deeds and experiences are related in that report should believe that they have witnessed or been involved in a miracle. Consider the story of Jill's translation to Sydney (the second version, the version in which the translation is not described as miraculous). Suppose that we who hear the story should conclude that if the story is true, it recounts a miracle. (It follows from this supposition that the story is a miracle-report.) And suppose that the story *is* true. It does not follow that *Jill* should conclude from her experience that a miracle has happened. We know that if the story is true, Jill was translated instantaneously to Sydney. But it is not evident that Jill knows (or that she will presently come to know) that she has been translated instantaneously to Sydney—or even that it would be reasonable for her to believe that she has been. Perhaps she should believe that she is still in New York but dreaming or mad or that she was never in New York in the first place.

6. To continue the theme of the previous note: It may or may not be true that we should believe that if the events related in this story really happened, at least one of them was a miracle. But if this is what we should believe, it does not follow that if these events really happened, those who witnessed them should have regarded at least one of them as a miracle. For one thing, it is extremely doubtful whether anyone in the first century A.D. possessed the concept expressed by the modern word "miracle."

7. It will simplify the statement of our argument if in applying this definition we assume that "miracle" and "violation of a law of nature" are interchangeable. The equation of "miracle" and "violation" would be objectionable if my purpose were to defend the thesis that it was sometimes reasonable to believe that a miracle

had occurred. This would be objectionable because it might be reasonable to believe that an event of type X had occurred and reasonable to believe that the occurrence of an event of type X required the violation of a law of nature, but *not* reasonable to believe that the "transgression of a law of nature" required by the occurrence of X was a consequence of a "particular volition of the Deity." My purpose, however, is to show that Hume's argument does not establish its conclusion, and not that this conclusion is false. And Hume's conclusion is (roughly) that it is unreasonable to believe any report of an event that would require a violation of a law—*whatever* the reason for that violation might be.

8. In my view, the two disjuncts of the definiens are independent: One can disbelieve something without assigning it a low probability (if in no other way, by assigning it no probability at all), and one can assign something a low probability without disbelieving it. A lot of people will want to say that these contentions represent a confused picture of the relation between belief and probability (I am thinking primarily of those who think that belief comes in degrees and that probabilities are measures of these degrees, a conception of the nature of belief and its relation to probability that I reject), but since nothing of substance in this essay turns on the thesis that the two disjuncts of the definiens are independent, I shall not defend it.

9. We shall later discuss the possible meanings of the phrase "contrary to one's experience." For the moment, let us simply assume that we understand this phrase.

10. As we did with the phrase "contrary to experience," let us for the present simply assume that we understand the phrase "even more contrary to experience." We shall later try to decide what it might mean.

11. As our examples show, not all contraventions are miracle-reports. Hume calls the stories that we are calling miracle-reports "miraculous." Contraventions that do not qualify as miraculous he calls "extraordinary" or "prodigies" or "marvelous."

12. Or so I shall assume for the sake of the example. Anyone who would deny this—that is, anyone who would regard the shaman story as a greater

contravention than Carter's being a tool of malign extraterrestrial beings—may change the example.

13. Even the "memorable story related by Cardinal de Retz" and the accounts of those miracles "which were lately said to have been wrought in France upon the tomb of Abbe Paris. . . ." "And what have we [Hume asks after telling these two stories] to oppose to such a cloud of witnesses, but the absolute impossibility or miraculous nature of the events, which they relate." It is, incidentally, very hard to reconcile Hume's description of the testimony recorded in these two stories with a statement he had made a few pages before:

> For . . . there is not to be found in all history, any miracle attested by a sufficient number of men, of such unquestioned good-sense,

education, and learning, as to secure us against all delusion in themselves; of such undoubted integrity, as to place them beyond all suspicion of any design to deceive others; of such credit and reputation in the eyes of mankind, as to have a great deal to lose in case of their being detected in any falsehood; and at the same time, attesting facts performed in such a public manner and in so celebrated a part of the world, as to render the detection unavoidable. . . .

I suspect that what Hume means is that we cannot imagine evidence that would establish the persons who have reported some event as so reliable that it is logically impossible for that evidence to exist and those persons to have given a false report.

IV.C. SCIENCE AND RELIGION

Introduction

WHAT IS THE RELATIONSHIP between science and religion? Many think that the relationship is one of conflict: Scientific theories, and the modern scientific worldview, contradict the claims of religion. Others, however, think that the relationship must necessarily be one of concord. All truth is God's truth, some are inclined to say; thus, to the extent that science is (as it seems to be) a way of discovering the truth about the world, it cannot possibly come into conflict with religious truth (whatever the religious truth might happen to be).

The (alleged) tension between science and religion is interesting and important for at least three interconnected reasons. First, scientific and religious beliefs both make a big difference in how we live our lives and in how we interact with others. Medical, environmental, and mechanical disasters, new vaccines, better telecommunication equipment, and so on are all caused at least in part by people's beliefs in the domain covered by science. People have been persecuted, tortured, and killed as a result of other people's religious beliefs. People have also benefited from mind-boggling generosity as a result of such beliefs; and, according to many religious believers, one's very eternal destiny depends critically on one's own personal religious beliefs. Second, the methods of science have established an impressive and publicly measurable track record of success as a way of investigating their domain. No method of forming religious belief can make the same claim. Third, taken as a whole, the fields of theology and religion are a lot like philosophy: a mess of disagreement on matters big and small, with arguments typically founded on little more than what seems "obviously to be true" or on what seems to have been "revealed by God (or the gods)." So it is deeply worrisome when science and religion appear to conflict because that seems to suggest that a lot of people (either religious believers of a particular sort or else the scientific establishment) are forming and propagating false beliefs on topics that matter quite a lot. Consider, in this vein, W. K. Clifford's attitude (expressed in selection V.B.2) toward people like the negligent ship owner, who quite literally put the lives of others in jeopardy because of their sloppy belief-forming habits. Neither religion nor science is to be treated lightly, and any apparent conflict between them is rightly very disturbing. For this reason, questions about the relationship between science and religion are receiving a lot of attention in the scientific, philosophical, and theological literature, and also in the popular media.

In his 1989–1990 Gifford Lectures, Ian Barbour proposed what has become a widely influential taxonomy of four ways in which science and religion might be thought to relate to one another (two of which we have already mentioned):

1. *Conflict:* Science and religion investigate common questions, but their theories contradict one another and so compete with one another for our acceptance.

2. *Independence:* Science and religion are separate disciplines addressing distinct, nonoverlapping subjects.

3. *Dialogue:* Science and religion share some common methods and presuppositions and can fruitfully employ one another's concepts in developing their respective theories.

4. *Integration:* Science and religion are partners in a common quest for a comprehensive understanding of the world, and the theories and results of science can be brought to bear in fruitful ways on the development of theories in theology, and vice versa.

There has been much discussion about whether this fourfold classification is adequate to capture all of the different ways in which science might be thought to relate to religion. (Some have proposed eight- or ninefold classification schemes.) For our purposes, however, it is perhaps more useful to collapse Barbour's taxonomy into just two options: independence and overlap. Some people think that science and religion investigate a common subject matter. Those who do will see at least the possibility for conflict, but they might also hope for a more fruitful sort of interaction—what Barbour might call dialogue or integration. Others think that science and religion investigate wholly different questions. On this view, any apparent conflict is simply the result of misunderstanding the nature and limits of science, the nature and bounds of religion, or both.

We begin with a selection in which Richard Dawkins forcefully articulates an antireligious version of the idea that science and religion overlap in their subject matter but are irremediably in conflict with one another. On Dawkins's view, both science and religion aim at telling us true stories about things like the origin of life, but one of the main differences is that science pursues this aim in a rational and objective way whereas religion does not. The main vice of religion, Dawkins says, is *faith*, and this, he thinks, is a vice that science wholly avoids. Thus, when the theories of science and religion conflict—as they inevitably do, on his view—the scientific theories are always to be preferred precisely because they, unlike religious theories, are grounded in evidence rather than faith. There are a lot of questions that one might want to raise about Dawkins's essay, but two rather important ones seem to be these: (a) Is it really true that there is no faith at all involved in believing a scientific theory, or that believing on faith is at odds with or fundamentally distinct from believing on the basis of evidence? and (b) Why is "rational moral *philosophy*" (which Dawkins recommends at the end of his essay as a better alternative to religion) any better off evidentially speaking than religion? (Part V.A. of this volume, which explores the nature of faith in some detail, will shed some further light on the first of these questions.)

Whereas Dawkins regards religion ultimately as a virulent influence in the world—he characterizes it as a "brain virus"—Stephen Jay Gould regards it as valuable and important as long as it stays within the bounds of its proper *magisterium* (teaching authority). In our second reading in this section, Gould articulates his view that science and religion constitute nonoverlapping realms of teaching authority. Broadly speaking, the proper domain of science is matters of fact, the proper domain of religion is matters of value, and as long as each confines its claims to subjects falling within its proper domain, both will make valuable contributions to human life and human understanding, and there will not even be the appearance of conflict between the two.

Gould, an important and influential paleontologist, speaks as a representative of the magisterium of science, and he cites Pope John Paul II as a representative of the magisterium of religion who shares his view that science and religion do not overlap. However, we have included as our third reading in this section excerpts from two essays by Pope John Paul II that together seem to provide an excellent contrast both to Dawkins's suggestion that conflict is inevitable (religion being, by and large, just bad science) and to Gould's suggestion that the two modes of inquiry concern themselves with wholly nonoverlapping domains. In the first essay, "Lessons from the Galileo Case," John Paul II urges the view that there can be no *true conflict* between science and religion because both are simply different branches of inquiry cooperating in the task of discovering the total truth about the world. To whatever extent there seems to be conflict, then, either science has erred in its reflections upon the relevant empirical data or else religion has gone astray in its understanding of the meaning of divine revelation. However, we can and sometimes do find points of apparent conflict. Thus, for example, in his "Message on Evolution to the Pontifical Academy of Sciences," he notes that certain ways of developing evolutionary theory will contradict Catholic doctrines about the soul and about original sin. In those cases, he argues, Catholic doctrine is to be preferred. But here, too, caution on both sides is required: The church should look carefully to see whether its understanding of divine revelation has been articulated in the most perspicuous manner or whether the apparent conflict might be avoided by a clearer statement of the relevant doctrines. And one must also be careful to distinguish between those aspects of scientific theory that are virtually undeniable in light of the empirical data and those aspects that, in one way or another, represent rationally contestable extrapolations from the data.

IV.C.1

Is Science a Religion?

RICHARD DAWKINS

Richard Dawkins (1941–) is professor of biology at Oxford University and the author of several important books, including The Selfish Gene *(1976),* The Blind Watchmaker *(1986), and* The God Delusion *(2006). He argues that science is a far more defensible process than religion for securing truth.*

It is fashionable to wax apocalyptic about the threat to humanity posed by the AIDS virus, "mad cow" disease, and many others, but I think a case can be made that *faith* is one of the world's great evils, comparable to the smallpox virus but harder to eradicate.

Faith, being belief that isn't based on evidence, is the principle vice of any religion. And who, looking at Northern Ireland or the Middle East, can be confident that the brain virus of faith is not exceedingly dangerous? One of the stories told to young Muslim suicide bombers is that martyrdom is the quickest way to heaven—and not just heaven but a special part of heaven where they will receive their special reward of 72 virgin brides. It occurs to me that our best hope may be to provide a kind of "spiritual arms control": send in specially trained theologians to deescalate the going rate in virgins.

Given the dangers of faith—and considering the accomplishments of reason and observation in the activity called science—I find it ironic that, whenever I lecture publicly, there always seems to be someone who comes forward and says, "Of course, your science is just a religion like ours. Fundamentally, science just comes down to faith, doesn't it?"

Well, science is not religion and it doesn't just come down to faith. Although it has many of religion's virtues, it has none of its vices. Science is based upon verifiable evidence. Religious faith not only lacks evidence, its independence from evidence is its pride and joy, shouted from the rooftops. Why else would Christians wax critical of doubting Thomas? The other apostles are held up to us as exemplars of virtue because faith was enough for them. Doubting Thomas, on the other hand, required evidence. Perhaps he should be the patron saint of scientists.

One reason I receive the comment about science being a religion is because I believe in the fact of evolution. I even believe in it with passionate conviction. To some, this may superficially look like faith. But the evidence that makes me believe in evolution is not only overwhelmingly strong; it is freely available to anyone who takes the trouble to read up on it. Anyone can study the same evidence that I have and presumably come to the same conclusion. But if you have a belief that is based solely on faith, I can't examine your reasons. You can retreat behind the private wall of faith where I can't reach you.

Now in practice, of course, individual scientists do sometimes slip back into the vice of faith, and a

Transcript of a speech delivered to the American Humanist Association, accepting the award of 1996 Humanist of the Year.

few may believe so single-mindedly in a favorite theory that they occasionally falsify evidence. However, the fact that this sometimes happens doesn't alter the principle that, when they do so, they do it with shame and not with pride. The method of science is so designed that it usually finds them out in the end.

Science is actually one of the most moral, one of the most honest disciplines around—because science would completely collapse if it weren't for a scrupulous adherence to honesty in the reporting of evidence. (As James Randi has pointed out, this is one reason why scientists are so often fooled by paranormal tricksters and why the debunking role is better played by professional conjurors; scientists just don't anticipate deliberate dishonesty as well.) There are other professions (no need to mention lawyers specifically) in which falsifying evidence or at least twisting it is precisely what people are paid for and get brownie points for doing.

Science, then, is free of the main vice of religion, which is faith. But, as I pointed out, science does have some of religion's virtues. Religion may aspire to provide its followers with various benefits—among them explanation, consolation, and uplift. Science, too, has something to offer in these areas.

Humans have a great hunger for explanation. It may be one of the main reasons why humanity so universally has religion, since religions do aspire to provide explanations. We come to our individual consciousness in a mysterious universe and long to understand it. Most religions offer a cosmology and a biology, a theory of life, a theory of origins, and reasons for existence. In doing so, they demonstrate that religion is, in a sense, science; it's just bad science. Don't fall for the argument that religion and science operate on separate dimensions and are concerned with quite separate sorts of questions. Religions have historically always attempted to answer the questions that properly belong to science. Thus religions should not be allowed now to retreat from the ground upon which they have traditionally attempted to fight. They do offer both a cosmology and a biology; however, in both cases it is false.

Consolation is harder for science to provide. Unlike religion, science cannot offer the bereaved a glorious reunion with their loved ones in the hereafter. Those wronged on this earth cannot, on a scientific view, anticipate a sweet comeuppance for their tormentors in a life to come. It could be argued that, if the idea of an afterlife is an illusion (as I believe it is), the consolation it offers is hollow. But that's not necessarily so; a false belief can be just as comforting as a true one, provided the believer never discovers its falsity. But if consolation comes that cheap, science can weigh in with other cheap palliatives, such as pain-killing drugs, whose comfort may or may not be illusory, but they do work.

Uplift, however, is where science really comes into its own. All the great religions have a place for awe, for ecstatic transport at the wonder and beauty of creation. And it's exactly this feeling of spine-shivering, breath-catching awe—almost worship—this flooding of the chest with ecstatic wonder, that modern science can provide. And it does so beyond the wildest dreams of saints and mystics. The fact that the supernatural has no place in our explanations, in our understanding of so much about the universe and life, doesn't diminish the awe. Quite the contrary. The merest glance through a microscope at the brain of an ant or through a telescope at a long-ago galaxy of a billion worlds is enough to render poky and parochial the very psalms of praise.

Now, as I say, when it is put to me that science or some particular part of science, like evolutionary theory, is just a religion like any other, I usually deny it with indignation. But I've begun to wonder whether perhaps that's the wrong tactic. Perhaps the right tactic is to accept the charge gratefully and demand equal time for science in religious education classes. And the more I think about it, the more I realize that an excellent case could be made for this. So I want to talk a little bit about religious education and the place that science might play in it.

I do feel very strongly about the way children are brought up. I'm not entirely familiar with the way things are in the United States, and what I say may have more relevance to the United Kingdom, where there is state-obliged, legally enforced religious instruction for all children. That's unconstitutional in the United States, but I presume that children are nevertheless given religious instruction in whatever particular religion their parents deem suitable.

Which brings me to my point about mental child abuse. In a 1995 issue of the *Independent*, one of London's leading newspapers, there was a photograph of a rather sweet and touching scene. It was Christmas time, and the picture showed three children dressed up as the three wise men for a nativity play. The accompanying story described one child as a Muslim, one as a Hindu, and one as a Christian. The supposedly sweet and touching point of the story was that they were all taking part in this nativity play.

What is not sweet and touching is that these children were all four years old. How can you possibly describe a child of four as a Muslim or a Christian or a Hindu or a Jew? Would you talk about a four-year-old economic monetarist? Would you talk about a four-year-old neoisolationist or a four-year-old liberal Republican? There are opinions about the cosmos and the world that children, once grown, will presumably be in a position to evaluate for themselves. Religion is the one field in our culture about which it is absolutely accepted, without question—without even noticing how bizarre it is—that parents have a total and absolute say in what their children are going to be, how their children are going to be raised, what opinions their children are going to have about the cosmos, about life, about existence. Do you see what I mean about mental child abuse?

Looking now at the various things that religious education might be expected to accomplish, one of its aims could be to encourage children to reflect upon the deep questions of existence, to invite them to rise above the humdrum preoccupations of ordinary life and think *sub specie aeternitatis*.

Science can offer a vision of life and the universe which, as I've already remarked, for humbling poetic inspiration far outclasses any of the mutually contradictory faiths and disappointingly recent traditions of the world's religions.

For example, how could any child in a religious education class fail to be inspired if we could get across to them some inkling of the age of the universe? Suppose that, at the moment of Christ's death, the news of it had started traveling at the maximum possible speed around the universe outwards from the earth? How far would the terrible tidings have traveled by now? Following the theory of special relativity, the answer is that the news could not, under any circumstances whatever, have reached more than one-fiftieth of the way across one galaxy—not one-thousandth of the way to our nearest neighboring galaxy in the 100-million-galaxy strong universe. The universe at large couldn't possibly be anything other than indifferent to Christ, his birth, his passion, and his death. Even such momentous news as the origin of life on earth could have traveled only across our little local cluster of galaxies. Yet so ancient was that event on our earthly time-scale that, if you span its age with your open arms, the whole of human history, the whole of human culture, would fall in the dust from your fingertip at a single stroke of a nail file.

The argument from design, an important part of the history of religion, wouldn't be ignored in my religious education classes, needless to say. The children would look at the spellbinding wonders of the living kingdoms and would consider Darwinism alongside the creationist alternatives and make up their own minds. I think the children would have no difficulty in making up their minds the right way if presented with the evidence. What worries me is not the question of equal time but that, as far as I can see, children in the United Kingdom and the United States are essentially given *no* time with evolution yet are taught creationism (whether at school, in church, or at home).

It would also be interesting to teach more than one theory of creation. The dominant one in this culture happens to be the Jewish creation myth, which is taken over from the Babylonian creation myth. There are, of course, lots and lots of others, and perhaps they should all be given equal time (except that wouldn't leave much time for studying anything else). I understand that there are Hindus who believe that the world was created in a cosmic butter churn and Nigerian peoples who believe that the world was created by God from the excrement of ants. Surely these stories have as much right to equal time as the Judeo-Christian myth of Adam and Eve.

So much for Genesis; now let's move on to the prophets. Halley's Comet will return without fail in the year 2062. Biblical or Delphic prophecies don't begin to aspire to such accuracy; astrologers and Nostradamians dare not commit themselves to factual prognostications but, rather, disguise their charlatanry in a smokescreen of vagueness. When comets have appeared in the past, they've often been taken as portents of disaster. Astrology has played an important part in various religious traditions, including Hinduism. The three wise men I mentioned earlier were said to have been led to the cradle of Jesus by a star. We might ask the children by what physical route do they imagine the alleged stellar influence on human affairs could travel.

Incidentally, there was a shocking program on the BBC radio around Christmas 1995 featuring an astronomer, a bishop, and a journalist who were sent off on an assignment to retrace the steps of the three wise men. Well, you could understand the participation of the bishop and the journalist (who happened to be a religious writer), but the astronomer was a supposedly respectable astronomy writer, and yet she went along with this! All along the route, she talked about the portents of when Saturn and Jupiter were in the ascendant up Uranus or whatever it was. She doesn't actually believe in astrology, but one of the problems is that our culture has been taught to become tolerant of it, even vaguely amused by it—so much so that even scientific people who don't believe in astrology sort of think it's a bit of harmless fun. I take astrology very seriously indeed: I think it's deeply pernicious because it undermines rationality, and I should like to see campaigns against it.

When the religious education class turns to ethics, I don't think science actually has a lot to say, and I would replace it with rational moral philosophy. Do the children think there are absolute standards of right and wrong? And if so, where do they come from? Can you make up good working principles of right and wrong, like "do as you would be done by" and "the greatest good for the greatest number" (whatever that is supposed to mean)? It's a rewarding question, whatever your personal morality, to ask as an evolutionist where morals come from; by what route has the human brain gained its tendency to have ethics and morals, a feeling of right and wrong?

Should we value human life above all other life? Is there a rigid wall to be built around the species *Homo sapiens*, or should we talk about whether there are other species which are entitled to our humanistic sympathies? Should we, for example, follow the right-to-life lobby, which is wholly preoccupied with *human* life, and value the life of a human fetus with the faculties of a worm over the life of a thinking and feeling chimpanzee? What is the basis of this fence we erect around *Homo sapiens*—even around a small piece of fetal tissue? (Not a very sound evolutionary idea when you think about it.) When, in our evolutionary descent from our common ancestor with chimpanzees, did the fence suddenly rear itself up?

Well, moving on, then, from morals to last things, to eschatology, we know from the second law of thermodynamics that all complexity, all life, all laughter, all sorrow, is hell-bent on leveling itself out into cold nothingness in the end. They—and we—can never be more than temporary, local buckings of the great universal slide into the abyss of uniformity.

We know that the universe is expanding and will probably expand forever, although it's possible it may contract again. We know that, whatever happens to the universe, the sun will engulf the earth in about 60 million centuries from now.

Time itself began at a certain moment, and time may end at a certain moment—or it may not. Time may come locally to an end in miniature crunches called black holes. The laws of the universe seem to be true all over the universe. Why is this? Might the laws change in these crunches? To be really speculative, time could begin again with new laws of physics, new physical constants. And it has even been suggested that there could be many universes, each one isolated so completely that, for it, the others don't exist. Then again, there might be a Darwinian selection among universes.

So science could give a good account of itself in religious education. But it wouldn't be enough. I believe that some familiarity with the King James versions of the Bible is important for anyone wanting to understand the allusions that appear in English literature. Together with the Book of Common Prayer, the Bible gets 58 pages in the *Oxford Dictionary of Quotations*. Only Shakespeare has more. I do think that not having any kind of biblical education is unfortunate if children want to read English literature and understand the provenance of phrases like "through a glass darkly," "all flesh is as grass," "the race is not to the swift," "crying in the wilderness," "reaping the whirlwind," "amid the alien corn," "Eyeless in Gaza," "Job's comforters," and "the widow's mite."

I want to return now to the charge that science is just a faith. The more extreme version of this charge—and one that I often encounter as both a scientist and a rationalist—is an accusation of zealotry and bigotry in scientists themselves as great as that found in religious people. Sometimes there may be a little bit of justice in this accusation; but as zealous bigots, we scientists are mere amateurs at the game. We're content to *argue* with those who disagree with us. We don't kill them.

But I would want to deny even the lesser charge of purely verbal zealotry. There is a very, very important difference between feeling strongly, even passionately, about something because we have thought about and examined the evidence for it on the one hand, and feeling strongly about something because it has been internally revealed to us, or internally revealed to somebody else in history and subsequently hallowed by tradition. There's all the difference in the world between a belief that one is prepared to defend by quoting evidence and logic and a belief that is supported by nothing more than tradition, authority, or revelation.

IV.C.2

Nonoverlapping Magisteria

STEPHEN JAY GOULD

Stephen Jay Gould (1941–2002) was a leading figure in paleontology, evolutionary biology, and the history of science, and was the author of several important books, both popular and scholarly, on these subjects. He taught at Harvard University and also worked at the American Museum of Natural History. In this essay, he argues that science and religion constitute nonoverlapping magisteria— separate domains of teaching authority that are concerned with wholly different subjects of inquiry.

Originally published in *Natural History* (1997, March). Used with permission.

Incongruous places often inspire anomalous stories. In early 1984, I spent several nights at the Vatican housed in a hotel built for itinerant priests. While pondering over such puzzling issues as the intended function of the bidets in each bathroom, and hungering for something other than plum jam on my breakfast rolls (why did the basket only contain hundreds of identical plum packets and not a one of, say, strawberry?), I encountered yet another among the innumerable issues of contrasting cultures that can make life so interesting. Our crowd (present in Rome for a meeting on nuclear winter sponsored by the Pontifical Academy of Sciences) shared the hotel with a group of French and Italian Jesuit priests who were also professional scientists.

At lunch, the priests called me over to their table to pose a problem that had been troubling them. What, they wanted to know, was going on in America with all this talk about "scientific creationism"? One asked me: "Is evolution really in some kind of trouble; and if so, what could such trouble be? I have always been taught that no doctrinal conflict exists between evolution and Catholic faith, and the evidence for evolution seems both entirely satisfactory and utterly overwhelming. Have I missed something?"

A lively pastiche of French, Italian, and English conversation then ensued for half an hour or so, but the priests all seemed reassured by my general answer: Evolution has encountered no intellectual trouble; no new arguments have been offered. Creationism is a homegrown phenomenon of American sociocultural history—a splinter movement (unfortunately rather more of a beam these days) of Protestant fundamentalists who believe that every word of the Bible must be literally true, whatever such a claim might mean. We all left satisfied, but I certainly felt bemused by the anomaly of my role as a Jewish agnostic, trying to reassure a group of Catholic priests that evolution remained both true and entirely consistent with religious belief.

Another story in the same mold: I am often asked whether I ever encounter creationism as a live issue among my Harvard undergraduate students. I reply that only once, in nearly thirty years of teaching, did I experience such an incident. A very sincere and serious freshman student came to my office hours with the following question that had clearly been troubling him deeply: "I am a devout Christian and have never had any reason to doubt evolution, an idea that seems both exciting and particularly well documented. But my roommate, a proselytizing Evangelical, has been insisting with enormous vigor that I cannot be both a real Christian and an evolutionist. So tell me, can a person believe both in God and evolution?" Again, I gulped hard, did my intellectual duty, and reassured him that evolution was both true and entirely compatible with Christian belief—a position I hold sincerely, but still an odd situation for a Jewish agnostic.

These two stories illustrate a cardinal point, frequently unrecognized but absolutely central to any understanding of the status and impact of the politically potent, fundamentalist doctrine known by its self-proclaimed oxymoron as "scientific creationism"—the claim that the Bible is literally true, that all organisms were created during six days of twenty-four hours, that the earth is only a few thousand years old, and that evolution must therefore be false. Creationism does not pit science against religion (as my opening stories indicate), for no such conflict exists. Creationism does not raise any unsettled intellectual issues about the nature of biology or the history of life. Creationism is a local and parochial movement, powerful only in the United States among Western nations, and prevalent only among the few sectors of American Protestantism that choose to read the Bible as an inerrant document, literally true in every jot and tittle.

I do not doubt that one could find an occasional nun who would prefer to teach creationism in her parochial school biology class, or an occasional orthodox rabbi who does the same in his yeshiva, but creationism based on biblical literalism makes little sense in either Catholicism or Judaism, for neither religion maintains any extensive tradition for reading the Bible as literal truth rather than illuminating literature, based partly on metaphor and allegory (essential components of all good writing) and demanding interpretation for proper understanding. Most Protestant groups, of course, take the same position—the fundamentalist fringe notwithstanding.

The position that I have just outlined by personal stories and general statements represents the standard attitude of all major Western religions (and of Western science) today. (I cannot, through ignorance, speak of Eastern religions, although I suspect that the same position would prevail in most cases.) The lack of conflict between science and religion arises from a lack of overlap between their respective domains of professional expertise—science in the empirical constitution of the universe, and religion in the search for proper ethical values and the spiritual meaning of our lives. The attainment of wisdom in a full life requires extensive attention to both domains—for a great book tells us that the truth can make us free and that we will live in optimal harmony with our fellows when we learn to do justly, love mercy, and walk humbly.

In the context of this standard position, I was enormously puzzled by a statement issued by Pope John Paul II on October 22, 1996, to the Pontifical Academy of Sciences, the same body that had sponsored my earlier trip to the Vatican. In this document, entitled "Truth Cannot Contradict Truth," the pope defended both the evidence for evolution and the consistency of the theory with Catholic religious doctrine. Newspapers throughout the world responded with front-page headlines, as in the *New York Times* for October 25: "Pope Bolsters Church's Support for Scientific View of Evolution."

Now I know about "slow news days," and I do admit that nothing else was strongly competing for headlines at that particular moment. (The *Times* could muster nothing more exciting for a lead story than Ross Perot's refusal to take Bob Dole's advice and quit the presidential race.) Still, I couldn't help feeling immensely puzzled by all the attention paid to the pope's statement (while being wryly pleased, of course, for we need all the good press we can get, especially from respected outside sources). The Catholic Church had never opposed evolution and had no reason to do so. Why had the pope issued

such a statement at all? And why had the press responded with an orgy of worldwide, front-page coverage?

I could only conclude at first, and wrongly as I soon learned, that journalists throughout the world must deeply misunderstand the relationship between science and religion, and must therefore be elevating a minor papal comment to unwarranted notice. Perhaps most people really do think that a war exists between science and religion, and that (to cite a particularly newsworthy case) evolution must be intrinsically opposed to Christianity. In such a context, a papal admission of evolution's legitimate status might be regarded as major news indeed—a sort of modern equivalent for a story that never happened, but would have made the biggest journalistic splash of 1640: Pope Urban VIII releases his most famous prisoner from house arrest and humbly apologizes, "Sorry, Signor Galileo ... the sun, er, is central."

But I then discovered that the prominent coverage of papal satisfaction with evolution had not been an error of non-Catholic Anglophone journalists. The Vatican itself had issued the statement as a major news release. And Italian newspapers had featured, if anything, even bigger headlines and longer stories. The conservative *Il Giornale*, for example, shouted from its masthead: "Pope Says We May Descend from Monkeys."

Clearly, I was out to lunch. Something novel or surprising must lurk within the papal statement, but what could it be?—especially given the accuracy of my primary impression (as I later verified) that the Catholic Church values scientific study, views science as no threat to religion in general or Catholic doctrine in particular, and has long accepted both the legitimacy of evolution as a field of study and the potential harmony of evolutionary conclusions with Catholic faith.

As a former constituent of Tip O'Neill's, I certainly know that "all politics is local"—and that the Vatican undoubtedly has its own internal reasons, quite opaque to me, for announcing papal support of evolution in a major statement. Still, I knew that I was missing some important key, and I felt frustrated. I then remembered the primary rule of intellectual life: when puzzled, it never hurts to read the primary documents—a rather simple and self-evident principle that has, nonetheless, completely disappeared from large sectors of the American experience.

I knew that Pope Pius XII (not one of my favorite figures in twentieth-century history, to say the least) had made the primary statement in a 1950 encyclical entitled *Humani Generis*. I knew the main thrust of his message: Catholics could believe whatever science determined about the evolution of the human body, so long as they accepted that, at some time of his choosing, God had infused the soul into such a creature. I also knew that I had no problem with this statement, for whatever my private beliefs about souls, science cannot touch such a subject and therefore cannot be threatened by any theological position on such a legitimately and intrinsically religious issue. Pope Pius XII, in other words, had properly acknowledged and respected the separate domains of science and theology. Thus, I found myself in total agreement with *Humani Generis*—but I had never read the document in full (not much of an impediment to stating an opinion these days).

I quickly got the relevant writings from, of all places, the Internet. (The pope is prominently on-line, but a Luddite like me is not. So I got a computer-literate associate to dredge up the documents. I do love the fracture of stereotypes implied by finding religion so hep and a scientist so square.) Having now read in full both Pope Pius's *Humani Generis* of 1950 and Pope John Paul's proclamation of October 1996, I finally understand why the recent statement seems so new, revealing, and worthy of all those headlines. And the message could not be more welcome for evolutionists and friends of both science and religion.

The text of *Humani Generis* focuses on the magisterium (or teaching authority) of the Church—a word derived not from any concept of majesty or awe but from the different notion of teaching, for *magister* is Latin for "teacher." We may, I think, adopt this word and concept to express the central point of this essay and the principled resolution of supposed "conflict" or "warfare" between science and religion. No such conflict should exist because each subject has a legitimate magisterium, or domain of teaching authority—and these magisteria do not overlap (the principle that I would like to designate as NOMA, or "nonoverlapping magisteria"). The net of science covers the empirical universe: what is it made of (fact) and why does it work this way (theory). The net of religion extends over questions of moral meaning and value. These two magisteria do not overlap, nor do they encompass all inquiry (consider, for starters, the magisterium of art and the meaning of beauty). To cite the arch clichés, we get the age of rocks, and religion retains the rock of ages; we study how the heavens go, and they determine how to go to heaven.

This resolution might remain all neat and clean if the nonoverlapping magisteria (NOMA) of science and religion were separated by an extensive no man's land. But, in fact, the two magisteria bump right up against each other, interdigitating in wondrously complex ways along their joint border. Many of our deepest questions call upon aspects of both for different parts of a full answer—and the sorting of legitimate domains can become quite complex and difficult. To cite just two broad questions involving both evolutionary facts and moral arguments: Since evolution made us the only earthly creatures with advanced consciousness, what responsibilities are so entailed for our relations with other species? What do our genealogical ties with other organisms imply about the meaning of human life?

Pius XII's *Humani Generis* is a highly traditionalist document by a deeply conservative man forced to face all the "isms" and cynicisms that rode the wake of World War II and informed the struggle to rebuild human decency from the ashes of the Holocaust. The encyclical, subtitled "Concerning some false opinions which threaten to undermine the foundations of Catholic doctrine," begins with a statement of embattlement:

> Disagreement and error among men on moral and religious matters have always been a cause of profound sorrow to all

good men, but above all to the true and loyal sons of the Church, especially today, when we see the principles of Christian culture being attacked on all sides.

Pius lashes out, in turn, at various external enemies of the Church: pantheism, existentialism, dialectical materialism, historicism, and of course and preeminently, communism. He then notes with sadness that some well-meaning folks within the Church have fallen into a dangerous relativism—"a theological pacifism and egalitarianism, in which all points of view become equally valid"—in order to include people of wavering faith who yearn for the embrace of Christian religion but do not wish to accept the particularly Catholic magisterium.

What is this world coming to when these noxious novelties can so discombobulate a revealed and established order? Speaking as a conservative's conservative, Pius laments:

> Novelties of this kind have already borne their deadly fruit in almost all branches of theology. . . . Some question whether angels are personal beings, and whether matter and spirit differ essentially. . . . Some even say that the doctrine of Transubstantiation, based on an antiquated philosophic notion of substance, should be so modified that the Real Presence of Christ in the Holy Eucharist be reduced to a kind of symbolism.

Pius first mentions evolution to decry a misuse by overextension often promulgated by zealous supporters of the anathematized "isms":

> Some imprudently and indiscreetly hold that evolution . . . explains the origin of all things. . . . Communists gladly subscribe to this opinion so that, when the souls of men have been deprived of every idea of a personal God, they may the more efficaciously defend and propagate their dialectical materialism.

Pius's major statement on evolution occurs near the end of the encyclical in paragraphs 35 through 37.

He accepts the standard model of NOMA and begins by acknowledging that evolution lies in a difficult area where the domains press hard against each other. "It remains for US now to speak about those questions which, although they pertain to the positive sciences, are nevertheless more or less connected with the truths of the Christian faith."[1]

Pius then writes the well-known words that permit Catholics to entertain the evolution of the human body (a factual issue under the magisterium of science), so long as they accept the divine Creation and infusion of the soul (a theological notion under the magisterium of religion).

> The Teaching Authority of the Church does not forbid that, in conformity with the present state of human sciences and sacred theology, research and discussions, on the part of men experienced in both fields, take place with regard to the doctrine of evolution, in as far as it inquires into the origin of the human body as coming from pre-existent and living matter—for the Catholic faith obliges us to hold that souls are immediately created by God.

I had, up to here, found nothing surprising in *Humani Generis*, and nothing to relieve my puzzlement about the novelty of Pope John Paul's recent statement. But I read further and realized that Pope Pius had said more about evolution, something I had never seen quoted, and that made John Paul's statement most interesting indeed. In short, Pius forcefully proclaimed that while evolution may be legitimate in principle, the theory, in fact, had not been proven and might well be entirely wrong. One gets the strong impression, moreover, that Pius was rooting pretty hard for a verdict of falsity.

Continuing directly from the last quotation, Pius advises us about the proper study of evolution:

> However, this must be done in such a way that the reasons for both opinions, that is, those favorable and those unfavorable to evolution, be weighed and judged with the necessary seriousness, moderation and measure. . . . Some, however, rashly

transgress this liberty of discussion, when they act as if the origin of the human body from pre-existing and living matter were already completely certain and proved by the facts which have been discovered up to now and by reasoning on those facts, and as if there were nothing in the sources of divine revelation which demands the greatest moderation and caution in this question.

To summarize, Pius generally accepts the NOMA principle of nonoverlapping magisteria in permitting Catholics to entertain the hypothesis of evolution for the human body so long as they accept the divine infusion of the soul. But he then offers some (holy) fatherly advice to scientists about the status of evolution as a scientific concept: the idea is not yet proven, and you all need to be especially cautious because evolution raises many troubling issues right on the border of my magisterium. One may read this second theme in two different ways: either as a gratuitous incursion into a different magisterium or as a helpful perspective from an intelligent and concerned outsider. As a man of good will, and in the interest of conciliation, I am happy to embrace the latter reading.

In any case, this rarely quoted second claim (that evolution remains both unproven and a bit dangerous)—and not the familiar first argument for the NOMA principle (that Catholics may accept the evolution of the body so long as they embrace the creation of the soul)—defines the novelty and the interest of John Paul's recent statement.

John Paul begins by summarizing Pius's older encyclical of 1950, and particularly by reaffirming the NOMA principle—nothing new here, and no cause for extended publicity:

> In his encyclical "Humani Generis" (1950), my predecessor Pius XII had already stated that there was no opposition between evolution and the doctrine of the faith about man and his vocation.

To emphasize the power of NOMA, John Paul poses a potential problem and a sound resolution: How can we reconcile science's claim for physical continuity in human evolution with Catholicism's insistence that the soul must enter at a moment of divine infusion:

> With man, then, we find ourselves in the presence of an ontological difference, an ontological leap, one could say. However, does not the posing of such ontological discontinuity run counter to that physical continuity which seems to be the main thread of research into evolution in the field of physics and chemistry? Consideration of the method used in the various branches of knowledge makes it possible to reconcile two points of view which would seem irreconcilable. The sciences of observation describe and measure the multiple manifestations of life with increasing precision and correlate them with the time line. The moment of transition to the spiritual cannot be the object of this kind of observation.

The novelty and news value of John Paul's statement lies, rather, in his profound revision of Pius's second and rarely quoted claim that evolution, while conceivable in principle and reconcilable with religion, can cite little persuasive evidence, and may well be false. John Paul states—and I can only say amen, and thanks for noticing—that the half century between Pius's surveying the ruins of World War II and his own pontificate heralding the dawn of a new millennium has witnessed such a growth of data, and such a refinement of theory, that evolution can no longer be doubted by people of good will:

> Pius XII added . . . that this opinion [evolution] should not be adopted as though it were a certain, proven doctrine. . . . Today, almost half a century after the publication of the encyclical, new knowledge has led to the recognition of more than one hypothesis in the theory of evolution. It is indeed remarkable that this theory has been progressively accepted by researchers, following a series of discoveries in various fields of knowledge. The convergence, neither sought nor fabricated, of the results

of work that was conducted independently is in itself a significant argument in favor of the theory.

In conclusion, Pius had grudgingly admitted evolution as a legitimate hypothesis that he regarded as only tentatively supported and potentially (as I suspect he hoped) untrue. John Paul, nearly fifty years later, reaffirms the legitimacy of evolution under the NOMA principle—no news here—but then adds that additional data and theory have placed the factuality of evolution beyond reasonable doubt. Sincere Christians must now accept evolution not merely as a plausible possibility but also as an effectively proven fact. In other words, official Catholic opinion on evolution has moved from "say it ain't so, but we can deal with it if we have to" (Pius's grudging view of 1950) to John Paul's entirely welcoming "it has been proven true; we always celebrate nature's factuality, and we look forward to interesting discussions of theological implications." I happily endorse this turn of events as gospel—literally *good news*. I may represent the magisterium of science, but I welcome the support of a primary leader from the other major magisterium of our complex lives. And I recall the wisdom of King Solomon: "As cold waters to a thirsty soul, so is good news from a far country" (Prov. 25:25).

Just as religion must bear the cross of its hardliners, I have some scientific colleagues, including a few prominent enough to wield influence by their writings, who view this rapprochement of the separate magisteria with dismay. To colleagues like me—agnostic scientists who welcome and celebrate the rapprochement, especially the pope's latest statement—they say: "C'mon, be honest; you know that religion is addlepated, superstitious, old-fashioned b.s.; you're only making those welcoming noises because religion is so powerful, and we need to be diplomatic in order to assure public support and funding for science." I do not think that this attitude is common among scientists, but such a position fills me with dismay—and I therefore end this essay with a personal statement about religion, as a testimony to what I regard as a virtual consensus among thoughtful scientists (who support the NOMA principle as firmly as the pope does).

I am not, personally, a believer or a religious man in any sense of institutional commitment or practice. But I have enormous respect for religion, and the subject has always fascinated me, beyond almost all others (with a few exceptions, like evolution, paleontology, and baseball). Much of this fascination lies in the historical paradox that throughout Western history organized religion has fostered both the most unspeakable horrors and the most heart-rending examples of human goodness in the face of personal danger. (The evil, I believe, lies in the occasional confluence of religion with secular power. The Catholic Church has sponsored its share of horrors, from Inquisitions to liquidations—but only because this institution held such secular power during so much of Western history. When my folks held similar power more briefly in Old Testament times, they committed just as many atrocities with many of the same rationales.)

I believe, with all my heart, in a respectful, even loving concordat between our magisteria— the NOMA solution. NOMA represents a principled position on moral and intellectual grounds, not a mere diplomatic stance. NOMA also cuts both ways. If religion can no longer dictate the nature of factual conclusions properly under the magisterium of science, then scientists cannot claim higher insight into moral truth from any superior knowledge of the world's empirical constitution. This mutual humility has important practical consequences in a world of such diverse passions.

Religion is too important to too many people for any dismissal or denigration of the comfort still sought by many folks from theology. I may, for example, privately suspect that papal insistence on divine infusion of the soul represents a sop to our fears, a device for maintaining a belief in human superiority within an evolutionary world offering no privileged position to any creature. But I also know that souls represent a subject outside the magisterium of science. My world cannot prove or disprove such a notion, and the concept of souls cannot threaten or impact my domain. Moreover, while I cannot personally accept the Catholic view of souls, I surely honor the metaphorical value of such a concept both for grounding moral discussion and for expressing what we most value about human potentiality: our decency, care, and all the ethical and intellectual struggles that the evolution of consciousness imposed upon us.

As a moral position (and therefore not as a deduction from my knowledge of nature's factuality), I prefer the "cold bath" theory that nature can be truly "cruel" and "indifferent"—in the utterly inappropriate terms of our ethical discourse—because nature was not constructed as our eventual abode, didn't know we were coming (we are, after all, interlopers of the latest geological microsecond), and doesn't give a damn about us (speaking metaphorically). I regard such a position as liberating, not depressing, because we then become free to conduct moral discourse—and nothing could be more important—in our own terms, spared from the delusion that we might read moral truth passively from nature's factuality.

But I recognize that such a position frightens many people, and that a more spiritual view of nature retains broad appeal (acknowledging the factuality of evolution and other phenomena, but still seeking some intrinsic meaning in human terms, and from the magisterium of religion). I do appreciate, for example, the struggles of a man who wrote to the *New York Times* on November 3, 1996, to state both his pain and his endorsement of John Paul's statement:

> Pope John Paul II's acceptance of evolution touches the doubt in my heart. The problem of pain and suffering in a world created by a God who is all love and light is hard enough to bear, even if one is a creationist. But at least a creationist can say that the original creation, coming from the hand of God was good, harmonious, innocent and gentle. What can one say about evolution, even a spiritual theory of evolution? Pain and suffering, mindless cruelty and terror are its means of creation. Evolution's engine is the grinding of predatory teeth upon the screaming, living flesh and bones of prey.... If evolution be true, my faith has rougher seas to sail.

I don't agree with this man, but we could have a wonderful argument. I would push the "cold bath" theory; he would (presumably) advocate the theme of inherent spiritual meaning in nature, however opaque the signal. But we would both be enlightened and filled with better understanding of these deep and ultimately unanswerable issues. Here, I believe, lies the greatest strength and necessity of NOMA, the nonoverlapping magisteria of science and religion. NOMA permits—indeed enjoins—the prospect of respectful discourse, of constant input from both magisteria toward the common goal of wisdom. If human beings are anything special, we are the creatures that must ponder and talk. Pope John Paul II would surely point out to me that his magisterium has always recognized this distinction, for *in principio erat verbum*—"In the beginning was the Word."

Postscript

Carl Sagan organized and attended the Vatican meeting that introduces this essay; he also shared my concern for fruitful cooperation between the different but vital realms of science and religion. Carl was also one of my dearest friends. I learned of his untimely death on the same day that I read the proofs for this essay. I could only recall Nehru's observations on Gandhi's death—that the light had gone out, and darkness reigned everywhere. But I then contemplated what Carl had done in his short sixty-two years and remembered John Dryden's ode for Henry Purcell, a great musician who died even younger: "He long ere this bad tuned the jarring spheres, and left no bell below."

The days I spent with Carl in Rome were the best of our friendship. We delighted in walking around the Eternal City, feasting on its history and architecture—and its food! Carl took special delight in the anonymity that he still enjoyed in a nation that had not yet aired Cosmos, the greatest media work in popular science of all time.

I dedicate this essay to his memory. Carl also shared my personal suspicion about the nonexistence of souls—but I cannot think of a better reason for hoping we are wrong than the prospect of spending eternity roaming the cosmos in friendship and conversation with this wonderful soul.

NOTE

1. Interestingly, the main thrust of these paragraphs does not address evolution in general but lies in refuting a doctrine that Pius calls "polygenism," or the notion of human ancestry from multiple parents—for he regards such an idea as incompatible with the doctrine of original sin, "which proceeds from a sin actually committed by an individual Adam and which, through generation, is passed on to all and is in everyone as his own." In this one instance, Pius may be transgressing the NOMA principle—but I cannot judge, for I do not understand the details of Catholic theology and therefore do not know how symbolically such a statement may be read. If Pius is arguing that we cannot entertain a theory about derivation of all modern humans from an ancestral population rather than through an ancestral individual (a potential fact) because such an idea would question the doctrine of original sin (a theological construct), then I would declare him out of line for letting the magisterium of religion dictate a conclusion within the magisterium of science.

IV.C.3

Faith and Science: Lessons from the Galileo Case and Message on Evolution

POPE JOHN PAUL II

Pope John Paul II, originally Karol Józef Wojtyla (1920–2005), served as Pope of the Roman Catholic Church from 1978 until his death in 2005. The present selection consists of two of his more important addresses on the relationship between faith and science: Lessons from the Galileo Case *(1992)* and Message on Evolution to the Pontifical Academy of Sciences *(1996). In these essays, he argues that although there can be no true conflict between religion and science, apparent conflicts sometimes do arise. When that happens, we must take care to be sure that divine revelation has been properly interpreted and understood, but we must also distinguish between those aspects of scientific theory that report the observed data and those aspects that, in one way or another, go beyond the data.*

From *L'Osservatore Romano*, "Weekly Edition in English," 4 Nov. 1992, and *L'Osservatore Romano*, "Weekly Edition in English," 30 October 1996. Copyright © 1992 and 1996 Catholic Information Network (CIN). Notes renumbered.

FAITH CAN NEVER CONFLICT WITH REASON

[. . .]

5. A twofold question is at the heart of the debate of which Galileo was the centre. The first is of the epistemological order and concerns biblical hermeneutics. In this regard, two points must again be raised. In the first place, like most of his adversaries, Galileo made no distinction between the scientific approach to natural phenomena and a reflection on nature, of the philosophical order, which that approach generally calls for. That is why he rejected the suggestion made to him to present the Copernican system as a hypothesis, inasmuch as it had not been confirmed by irrefutable proof. Such therefore, was an exigency of the experimental method of which he was the inspired founder.

Secondly, the geocentric representation of the world was commonly admitted in the culture of the time as fully agreeing with the teaching of the Bible of which certain expressions, taken literally seemed to affirm geocentrism. The problem posed by theologians of that age was, therefore, that of the compatibility between heliocentrism and Scripture.

Thus the new science, with its methods and the freedom of research which they implied, obliged theologians to examine their own criteria of scriptural interpretation. Most of them did not know how to do so.

Paradoxically, Galileo, a sincere believer, showed himself to be more perceptive in this regard than the theologians who opposed him. "If Scripture cannot err," he wrote to Benedetto Castelli, "certain of its interpreters and commentators can and do so in many ways."[1] We also know of his letter to Christine de Lorraine (1615) which is like a short treatise on biblical hermeneutics.[2]

6. From this we can now draw our first conclusion. The birth of a new way of approaching the study of natural phenomena demands a clarification on the part of all disciplines of knowledge. It obliges them to define more clearly their own field, their approach, their methods, as well as the precise import of their conclusions. In other words, this new way requires each discipline to become more rigorously aware of its own nature.

The upset caused by the Copernican system thus demanded epistemological reflection on the biblical sciences, an effort which later would produce abundant fruit in modern exegetical works and which has found sanction and a new stimulus in the Dogmatic Constitution *Dei Verbum* of the Second Vatican Council.

7. The crisis that I have just recalled is not the only factor to have had repercussions on biblical interpretation. Here we are concerned with the second aspect of the problem, its pastoral dimension.

By virtue of her own mission, the Church has the duty to be attentive to the pastoral consequences of her teaching. Before all else, let it be clear that this teaching must correspond to the truth. But it is a question of knowing how to judge a new scientific datum when it seems to contradict the truths of faith. The pastoral judgement which the Copernican theory required was difficult to make, in so far as geocentrism seemed to be a part of scriptural teaching itself. It would have been necessary all at once to overcome habits of thought and to devise a way of teaching capable of enlightening the people of God. Let us say, in a general way, that the pastor ought to show a genuine boldness, avoiding the double trap of a hesitant attitude and of hasty judgement, both of which can cause considerable harm.

8. Another crisis, similar to the one we are speaking of, can be mentioned here. In the last century and at the beginning of our own, advances in the historical sciences made it possible to acquire a new understanding of the Bible and of the biblical world. The rationalist context in which these data were most often presented seemed to make them dangerous to the Christian faith. Certain people, in their concern to defend the faith, thought it necessary to reject firmly-based historical conclusions. That was a hasty and unhappy decision. The work of a pioneer like Fr. Lagrange was able to make the necessary discernment on the basis of dependable criteria.

It is necessary to repeat here what I said above. It is a duty for theologians to keep themselves regularly informed of scientific advances in order to examine if such be necessary, whether or not there are reasons for taking them into account in their reflection or for introducing changes in their teaching.

9. If contemporary culture is marked by a tendency to scientism, the cultural horizon of Galileo's age was uniform and carried the imprint of a particular philosophical formation. The unitary character of culture, which in itself is positive and desirable even in our own day, was one of the reasons for Galileo's condemnation. The majority of theologians did not recognize the formal distinction between Sacred Scripture and its interpretation, and this led them unduly to transpose into the realm of the doctrine of the faith a question which in fact pertained to scientific investigation.

In fact, as Cardinal Poupard has recalled, Robert Bellarmine, who had seen what was truly at stake in the debate personally felt that, in the face of possible scientific proofs that the earth orbited round the sun, one should "interpret with great circumspection" every biblical passage which seems to affirm that the earth is immobile and "say that we do not understand, rather than affirm that what has been demonstrated is false."[3] Before Bellarmine, this same wisdom and same respect for the divine Word guided St Augustine when he wrote: "If it happens that the authority of Sacred Scripture is set in opposition to clear and certain reasoning, this must mean that the person who interprets Scripture does not understand it correctly. It is not the meaning of Scripture which is opposed to the truth but the meaning which he has wanted to give to it. That which is opposed to Scripture is not what is in Scripture but what he has placed there himself, believing that this is what Scripture meant."[4] A century ago, Pope Leo XIII echoed this advice in his Encyclical *Providentis-simus Deus*: "Truth cannot contradict truth and we may be sure that some mistake has been made either in the interpretation of the sacred words, or in the polemical discussion itself."[5]

Cardinal Poupard has also reminded us that the sentence of 1633 was not irreformable, and that the debate which had not ceased to evolve thereafter, was closed in 1820 with the imprimatur given to the work of Canon Settele.[6]

10. From the beginning of the Age of Enlightenment down to our own day, the Galileo case has been a sort of "myth," in which the image fabricated out of the events was quite far removed from reality. In this perspective, the Galileo case was the symbol of the Church's supposed rejection of scientific progress, or of "dogmatic" obscurantism opposed to the free search for truth. This myth has played a considerable cultural role. It has helped to anchor a number of scientists of good faith in the idea that there was an incompatibility between the spirit of science and its rules of research on the one hand and the Christian faith on the other. A tragic mutual incomprehension has been interpreted as the reflection of a fundamental opposition between science and faith. The clarifications furnished by recent historical studies enable us to state that this sad misunderstanding now belongs to the past.

11. From the Galileo affair we can learn a lesson which remains valid in relation to similar situations which occur today and which may occur in the future.

In Galileo's time, to depict the world as lacking an absolute physical reference point was, so to speak, inconceivable. And since the cosmos, as it was then known, was contained within the solar system alone, this reference point could only be situated in the earth or in the sun. Today, after Einstein and within the perspective of contemporary cosmology neither of these two reference points has the importance they once had. This observation, it goes without saying, is not directed against the validity of Galileo's position in the debate; it is only meant to show that often, beyond two partial and contrasting perceptions, there exists a wider perception which includes them and goes beyond both of them.

12. Another lesson which we can draw is that the different branches of knowledge call for different methods. Thanks to his intuition as a brilliant physicist and by relying on different arguments, Galileo, who practically invented the experimental method, understood why only the sun could

function as the centre of the world, as it was then known, that is to say, as a planetary system. The error of the theologians of the time, when they maintained the centrality of the earth, was to think that our understanding of the physical world's structure was, in some way, imposed by the literal sense of Sacred Scripture. Let us recall the celebrated saying attributed to Baronius "Spiritui Sancto mentem fuisse nos docere quomodo ad coelum eatur, non quomodo coelum gradiatur." In fact, the Bible does not concern itself with the details of the physical world, the understanding of which is the competence of human experience and reasoning. There exist two realms of knowledge, one which has its source in Revelation and one which reason can discover by its own power. To the latter belong especially the experimental sciences and philosophy. The distinction between the two realms of knowledge ought not to be understood as opposition. The two realms are not altogether foreign to each other, they have points of contact. The methodologies proper to each make it possible to bring out different aspects of reality. . . .

MAGISTERIUM IS CONCERNED WITH QUESTION OF EVOLUTION FOR IT INVOLVES CONCEPTION OF MAN

Science at the Dawn of the Third Millennium

[. . .]

3. Before offering a few more specific reflections on the theme of the origin of life and evolution, I would remind you that the magisterium of the Church has already made some pronouncements on these matters, within her own proper sphere of competence. I will cite two such interventions here.

In his encyclical *Humani Generis* (1950), my predecessor Pius XII has already affirmed that there is no conflict between evolution and the doctrine

of the faith regarding man and his vocation, provided that we do not lose sight of certain fixed points.

For my part, when I received the participants in the plenary assembly of your Academy on October 31, 1992, I used the occasion—and the example of Galileo—to draw attention to the necessity of using a rigorous hermeneutical approach in seeking a concrete interpretation of the inspired texts. It is important to set proper limits to the understanding of Scripture, excluding any unseasonable interpretations which would make it mean something which it is not intended to mean. In order to mark out the limits of their own proper fields, theologians and those working on the exegesis of the Scripture need to be well informed regarding the results of the latest scientific research.

Evolution and the Church's Magisterium

4. Taking into account the scientific research of the era, and also the proper requirements of theology, the encyclical *Humani Generis* treated the doctrine of "evolutionism" as a serious hypothesis, worthy of investigation and serious study, alongside the opposite hypothesis. Pius XII added two methodological conditions for this study: one could not adopt this opinion as if it were a certain and demonstrable doctrine, and one could not totally set aside the teaching Revelation on the relevant questions. He also set out the conditions on which this opinion would be compatible with the Christian faith—a point to which I shall return.

Today, more than a half-century after the appearance of that encyclical, some new findings lead us toward the recognition of evolution as more than an hypothesis. In fact it is remarkable that this theory has had progressively greater influence on the spirit of researchers, following a series of discoveries in different scholarly disciplines. The convergence in the results of these independent studies—which was neither planned nor sought—constitutes in itself a significant argument in favor of the theory.

What is the significance of a theory such as this one? To open this question is to enter into the field of epistemology. A theory is a meta-scientific elaboration, which is distinct from, but in harmony with, the results of observation. With the help of such a theory a group of data and independent facts can be related to one another and interpreted in one comprehensive explanation. The theory proves its validity by the measure to which it can be verified. It is constantly being tested against the facts; when it can no longer explain these facts, it shows its limits and its lack of usefulness, and it must be revised.

Moreover, the elaboration of a theory such as that of evolution, while obedient to the need for consistency with the observed data, must also involve importing some ideas from the philosophy of nature.

And to tell the truth, rather than speaking about the theory of evolution, it is more accurate to speak of the theories of evolution. The use of the plural is required here—in part because of the diversity of explanations regarding the mechanism of evolution, and in part because of the diversity of philosophies involved. There are materialist and reductionist theories, as well as spiritualist theories. Here the final judgment is within the competence of philosophy and, beyond that, of theology.

5. The magisterium of the Church takes a direct interest in the question of evolution, because it touches on the conception of man, whom Revelation tells us is created in the image and likeness of God. The conciliar constitution *Gaudium et Spes* has given us a magnificent exposition of this doctrine, which is one of the essential elements of Christian thought. The Council recalled that "man is the only creature on earth that God wanted for its own sake." In other words, the human person cannot be subordinated as a means to an end, or as an instrument of either the species or the society; he has a value of his own. He is a person. By this intelligence and his will, he is capable of entering into relationship, of communion, of solidarity, of the gift of himself to others like himself. St. Thomas observed that man's resemblance to God resides especially in his speculative intellect, because his relationship with the object of his knowledge is like God's relationship with his creation. (*Summa*

Theologica I–II, q 3, a 5, ad 1) But even beyond that, man is called to enter into a loving relationship with God himself, a relationship which will find its full expression at the end of time, in eternity. Within the mystery of the risen Christ the full grandeur of this vocation is revealed to us. (*Gaudium et Spes*, 22) It is by virtue of his eternal soul that the whole person, including his body, possesses such great dignity. Pius XII underlined the essential point: if the origin of the human body comes through living matter which existed previously, the spiritual soul is created directly by God ("animas enim a Deo immediate creari catholica fides non retimere iubet"). (*Humani Generis*)

As a result, the theories of evolution which, because of the philosophies which inspire them, regard the spirit either as emerging from the forces of living matter, or as a simple epiphenomenon of that matter, are incompatible with the truth about man. They are therefore unable to serve as the basis for the dignity of the human person.

6. With man, we find ourselves facing a different ontological order—an ontological leap, we could say. But in posing such a great ontological discontinuity, are we not breaking up the physical continuity which seems to be the main line of research about evolution in the fields of physics and chemistry? An appreciation for the different methods used in different fields of scholarship allows us to bring together two points of view which at first might seem irreconcilable. The sciences of observation describe and measure, with ever greater precision, the many manifestations of life, and write them down along the time-line. The moment of passage into the spiritual realm is not something that can be observed in this way— although we can nevertheless discern, through experimental research, a series of very valuable signs of what is specifically human life. But the experience of metaphysical knowledge, of self-consciousness and self-awareness, of moral conscience, of liberty, or of aesthetic and religious experience—these must be analyzed through philosophical reflection, while theology seeks to clarify the ultimate meaning of the Creator's designs. . . .

NOTES

1. Letter of 21 November 1613, in *Edizione nazionale delle Opere de Galileo Galilei*, dir. A. Favaro, edition of 1968, vol. V. p. 282.

2. Letter to Christine de Lorraine, 1615, in *Edizione nazionale delle Opere de Galileo Galilei*, dir. A Favaro, edition of 1968, vol. V, pp. 307–348.

3. Letter to Fr A. Foscarini, 12 April 1615, cf. *Edizione nazionale delle Opere de Galileo Galilei*, dir. A. Favaro, edition of 1968, vol. XII, p. 172.

4. Saint Augustine, *Espitula* 143, n. 7 PL 33, col. 588.

5. Leonis XIII Pont. Max. Acta, vol. XIII (1894), p. 361.

6. Cf. Pontificia Academia Scientiarum Copernico, Galilei e la Chiesa. Fine della controversia (1820). Gli atti del Sant'Ufficio, a cura di W. Brandmuller e E. J. Griepl, Firenze, Olschki, 1992.

Faith and Reason

ONE OF THE MOST IMPORTANT and widely discussed issues in the philosophy of religion is the relationship of faith to reason. Is religious faith rational? If so, is that because religious faith is somehow supported by evidence? Or might our religious beliefs be rendered rational in some other way? These are among the central questions in the debate over faith and reason.

We begin in Part V.A. with an examination of the nature of faith. Richard Dawkins has famously characterized faith as "belief that isn't based on evidence" (see selection IV.C.1 in this volume). According to the Christian scriptures, faith is "the assurance of things hoped for, the conviction of things not seen" (Hebrews 11:1, NRSV translation). Both characterizations might seem to suggest that faith is more akin to wishful thinking, or a stubborn refusal to subject one's beliefs to serious scrutiny. Both characterizations also suggest that faith is a propositional attitude—an attitude like belief or hope that one takes toward propositions, for example, *that God exists*, or *that there is a blessed afterlife*—rather than a form of personal trust or a mere disposition to act. Furthermore, both characterizations suggest that the propositional attitude involved in faith is *belief*, rather than, say, mere hope. Finally, the connection with "what we hope for" that is highlighted in the quotation from the Epistle to the Hebrews suggests that faith is essentially an attitude taken toward something one regards as *positive*. (Could one really be said to have *faith* that some horrible event was about to occur?) All of these suggestions are controversial, however; and they are explored in the essays that comprise the first section of this part.

In Part V.B., we turn to the question whether it is appropriate to hold religious beliefs, or to engage in religious practices, simply because we find it in our best interests to do so. According to Blaise Pascal, even if we do not yet have *evidence* for believing in God, we do have strong pragmatic, or practical, reason to believe in God. Though this by itself does not necessarily render belief in God rational, Pascal does think it gives us good reason to live as if there is a God and to try to cultivate belief in God. But is he right? Many are inclined to think that cultivating a belief simply because it is in our best interests to hold it is positively irrational. Indeed, some would say it is morally repugnant. Cultivating beliefs on important matters for reasons of self-interest rather than as a result of hard-nosed objective inquiry might seem grossly irresponsible; and when acting on those beliefs has serious consequences for others (as is often the case with religious belief) such irresponsibility might also seem terribly immoral. Just imagine how you would feel if you discovered that many of your surgeon's beliefs about surgery were cultivated not as a result of reading medical journals but rather because she discovered that she would feel better if she thought that it was sensible to follow this or that surgical procedure.

Finally, in the third section of this part we explore the question of how, if at all, religious belief might come to be epistemically justified. (Epistemic justification and rationality pertain to what is rationally permissible or fitting in light of one's evidence given the goal of forming true beliefs rather than false ones.) Many suppose that in order for our religious beliefs to be justified, we would need to have *arguments* to support them. Suppose you have the experience of seeming to see a boat on a lake; and suppose that, on the basis of this experience, you form the belief that there is a boat on a lake in front of you. In this case, you have no argument for your belief. Your only evidence is experiential. You have not inferred that there is a boat on a lake in front of you from anything else you believe; you have simply formed it on the basis of an experience. But, of course, we do not at all think that *this* fact renders your belief unjustified. In fact, we think that most of our perceptual beliefs are prime examples of justified belief. Might the same be the case for religious belief? Might religious belief be rationally grounded in experience? If not, then what would it take for religious belief to be justified? These and related questions are taken up in Part V.C.

V.A. THE NATURE OF FAITH

Introduction

IN "THE SENTIMENT OF RATIONALITY" (1879), William James defines "faith" as follows:

> Faith means belief in something concerning which doubt is still
> theoretically possible: and as the test of belief is willingness to act, one
> may say that faith is the readiness to act in a cause the prosperous issue of
> which is not certified to us in advance.

Unlike Richard Dawkins, James defines faith in a way that does not preclude the idea that what is believed on faith might also be believed at least partly on the basis of evidence. For, after all, much of what we believe on the basis of evidence is, nevertheless, "something concerning which doubt is still theoretically possible." This conception is closer to the various understandings of faith that one more commonly finds in (for example) the monotheistic religious traditions. Although many in those traditions will still object that James's conception seems to preclude the sort of "assurance" and "conviction" that often accompanies religious faith and that is spoken of in the New Testament Epistle to the Hebrews (quoted in the general introduction to Part V).

Note, too, that in the quotation from James, there are two ideas about faith resting side by side. One idea treats faith as a kind of belief, a propositional attitude. The other treats faith as a disposition to act that, in principle, might be independent of what one believes. Although James combines the ideas in this passage, it is an interesting question whether we ought to do so. Philosophical discussions of the nature of faith, including those in the present section, have tended to focus greater attention on the notion that faith involves propositional attitudes; but some also try to do justice to the connections between faith and dispositions to act, personal trust in others, and so on.

In the first reading in this section, Richard Swinburne explores three different conceptions of faith, which he refers to as *Thomistic, Lutheran,* and *Pragmatist.* The Thomistic conception of faith, so-called because Swinburne attributes it to St. Thomas Aquinas, maintains that faith is belief without knowledge—indeed, belief that lies somewhere in between mere opinion and knowledge. According to the Lutheran conception, faith is belief plus trust; and according to the Pragmatist conception, faith is a form of trust, manifest in a tendency to *act as if* certain doctrines are true. All three conceptions leave open the possibility that faith might be supported by evidence. Moreover, despite initial appearances, all three conceptions are ones according to which faith involves some sort of belief. On the first two conceptions, belief is an explicit component in faith; but, Swinburne argues, even on the third conception *some* sort of belief is required—in particular, belief that acting as if particular religious doctrines are true is an effective means to reaching one's goals.

In our second reading, Lara Buchak explores the connections between faith and rationality. Although her main goal is to answer the question whether faith can be rational, we have included her paper in this section on the *nature of faith* because she devotes considerable attention to that topic. In particular, she examines the way in which faith requires going *beyond* one's evidence; and she seeks to develop an account of faith that will cover both religious faith as well as faith in more mundane matters. She concludes that having propositional faith—having faith *that* something is the case—crucially involves terminating one's search for further evidence on the topic. This is, of course, different from believing wholly in the absence of evidence; but it does provide content to the idea that having faith involves believing in a way that somehow goes beyond one's evidence.

Our third selection, an essay by Daniel Howard-Snyder, also seeks to develop an account of propositional faith. Whereas Buchak is primarily concerned with the relationship between faith and evidence, and with questions about the rationality of faith, Howard-Snyder is primarily concerned to provide a full account of the nature of faith that contrasts with what he calls "the Common View"—that propositional faith requires propositional belief. Howard-Snyder mounts an argument for the conclusion that, in fact, propositional faith does not require anything so strong as belief. Rather, faith is consistent with weaker attitudes than belief and, indeed, is even consistent with some measure of doubt.

In the fourth essay, "Faith, Hope, and Doubt," Louis Pojman examines the relationship between belief and faith and argues that religious faith can exist and flourish in the absence of belief. One may not be able to believe in God because of an insufficiency of evidence, but one may still live committed to a theistic worldview, in hope. Pojman argues that this is an authentic religious position, too often neglected in the literature.

V.A.1

The Nature of Faith

RICHARD SWINBURNE

A short biographical sketch of Richard Swinburne precedes selection II.C.3. In this selection, Swinburne presents three different accounts of the nature of faith: the Thomistic account, according to which faith is belief that falls short of knowledge; the Lutheran account, according to which faith is belief plus trust; and the Pragmatist account, according to which faith involves a kind of trust made manifest in acting as if *certain doctrines are true. On all three conceptions, faith involves some kind of belief; but on the third conception, it involves only the "weak" kind of belief that acting as if particular religious doctrines are true is likely to be an effective means of achieving one's goals.*

[In earlier parts of] this book [i.e., *Faith and Reason*] I have been concerned with propositional belief. I have analysed what it is to have a belief that so-and-so is the case, when it matters what we believe, and what we can do to improve our beliefs; and so I have analysed when belief is "rational" in various senses of "rational." I claimed that it matters greatly that one should have a true belief about whether there is a God, what He is like and what He has done; and about whether and how we can attain a deep and permanent well-being which I am calling salvation. However, the virtue which the Christian religion commends is not propositional belief but the virtue called in English "faith." What is faith, and what is its relation to belief? The faith which the Christian religion commends is basically faith in a person or persons, God (or Christ) characterized as possessing certain properties and having done certain actions; and secondarily in some of the deeds which He has done, and the good things which He has provided and promised. Thus, in the

Nicene Creed, the person who pledges his allegiance before being baptized or in the course of worship affirms (in Greek) πιστύω εἰς ("I believe in" or "I have faith in") "... one God, Father Almighty, maker of Heaven and Earth ...; and in one Lord Jesus Christ ... and in the Holy Spirit, the Lord, the Giver of Life ...; one Holy Catholic and apostolic Church ... the resurrection of the dead. ..." But there have been different views in the Christian tradition as to what this "belief in" or "faith in" amounts to. In this chapter I shall spell these views out and show their relation to each other. We shall find that, despite appearances, advocates of the different views are not necessarily commending very different conduct or affirming very different doctrines from each other.

THE THOMIST VIEW OF FAITH

First, then, there is what I shall call the Thomist view of faith. It is a view which is found in St Thomas

Faith and Reason, 2nd edition, by Swinburne (2005), pp. 137–159. By permission of Oxford University Press.

Aquinas and has been held by many Protestants and many outside Christianity, and by many Christians long before Aquinas. Indeed, it is by far the most widespread and natural view of the nature of religious faith. This is the view that, with one addition and two qualifications, to have faith in God is simply to have a belief-that, to believe that God exists. Although to speak strictly, the object of faith is the "first truth," God himself, to have that faith it is alone necessary that you believe a proposition, that God exists.[1] The person of religious faith is the person who has the theoretical conviction that there is a God.[2]

The addition which Aquinas adds to this simple doctrine is that to have faith in God, you have to believe not merely that there is a God, but certain other propositions as well. The existence of God could be demonstrated by natural theology, and so made known (nota); but—to speak strictly—it was a preamble of faith. More central to faith were the other propositions about what God is like and what acts He has done, and you have to believe these latter propositions on the ground that God has revealed them. The belief which is affirmed in the Nicene Creed in God as having done certain things (e.g. as "maker of Heaven and Earth") is the belief that God did these things (e.g. "made Heaven and Earth"); the belief in the good things which God has promised and provided (e.g. "the resurrection of the dead") is the belief that they are or will be (e.g. "there will be a resurrection of the dead"). Aquinas writes that "the things of faith surpass human understanding, and so man becomes aware of them only because God reveals them. To some, the prophets and apostles, for example, this revelation comes from God immediately; to others, the things of faith are announced by God's sending preachers of the faith."[3] The First Vatican Council also taught that this revelation is to be believed "on the authority of God himself who reveals it."[4] . . .

The first qualification on this view that faith is belief is that the belief that is involved is a belief which does not amount to scientific knowledge (scientia). Aquinas, like others, quotes the definition given by Hugh of St Victor that "faith (fides) is a form of mental certitude about absent realities that is greater than opinion (opinio) and less than scientific knowledge (scientia)."[5] Indeed, every Christian writer who has written about faith has said something similar. But this agreement on words conceals a very significant disagreement, of which some of the various writers seem not fully aware and which was not the subject of very much discussion. For Aquinas, the difference between faith and scientific knowledge (scientia) was that scientia involved not merely strong belief that something true was indeed true, but also understanding of what made it true. You had scientific knowledge that if you drop a ball it will fall to the ground, or that $2 + 2 = 4$ if you understood the principles of physics or mathematics, which principles Aquinas thought to be in some sense necessary. But you had no scientific knowledge of isolated contingent matters of fact—this was the realm of opinio, though sometimes very well justified opinio—for example, that it is a sunny day or that I am now in Oxford. Now, Aquinas generally holds that faith is as strong a belief as the belief involved in scientific knowledge, differing from such knowledge only in that we do not understand what makes its object true: "The act of believing is firmly attached to one alternative [that the belief is true rather than not] and in this respect the believer is in the same state of mind as one who has scientific knowledge and understanding."[6] Even the existence of God, he normally[7] holds, cannot be an object of scientia,[8] since only God can understand why there has to be a God.

Despite his more usual insistence that the belief of faith has to be as strong as the belief involved in scientific knowledge, Aquinas does, at times, also allow that faith can be a matter of degree, so that for some who have faith there is still doubt.[9] And he allows that there can be greater faith in one person than in another, even in respect of being "more certain" in one person than another. "Greatness or smallness in faith is a fact."[10]

The Thomist view of faith as a matter of having certain beliefs looks an odd view, because the Christian religion (like some other religions) normally regards faith as a virtue, something for having which the person of faith deserves praise and/or will be rewarded with salvation. Yet the Thomist person of faith may be a complete scoundrel, one who does his best to defy God. That leads to the second qualification on the Thomist view of faith as belief. For Aquinas, faith is not, as such, meritorious. Indeed, he explicitly allows that devils (who have enough true beliefs about God) have faith. In support of his view, he quotes the Letter of St James: "You believe that God is one; you do well. Even the demons believe—and shudder."[11] and he interprets the claim about their belief as a claim about their faith. However, although the devils have faith, there are, on the Thomist view, two things lacking to them, which they would need to have if their faith was to be meritorious. The first thing which the faith of the devils lack, in Aquinas's view, is that it does not come into being in the right way. It is not meritorious faith, because it is not a voluntary faith. Aquinas writes that "the devils' faith is, so to speak, forced from them by the evidence of signs. That they believe, then, is in no way to the credit of their wills." For the devils "the signs of faith are so evident that they are forced to believe."[12] By contrast, Aquinas holds that humans can choose whether or not to have faith—the signs are not for us so evident that we have to believe; and so, if we do believe, it is to our credit that we do. However, I argued in Chapter 1 [of *Faith and Reason*] that all belief, as such, is an involuntary matter. We cannot help having the beliefs that we do at the time at which we have them. All that we can do is to set ourselves to submit them to impartial investigation or change them in less reputable ways over a period. I argued in Chapter 3 [of *Faith and Reason*] that only in very unusual cases can it be good to try to acquire a belief specified in advance of investigation; but that, for those of us for whom it is neither overwhelmingly obvious that there is a God or overwhelmingly obvious that there is no God, it is normally obligatory to investigate the issue. Hence, if we are to maintain that Thomist faith is a voluntary matter, we must maintain that the voluntariness of it is a matter of its resulting from adequate investigation. (Those few to whom the existence of God is overwhelmingly obvious will be in the same position as the devils, and for them Thomist faith will not be meritorious in this respect.) Aquinas does, however, seem to write as though, at any rate normally, the merit of faith resulted from one's choosing there and then to follow the dictates of reason; yet this, I have argued, cannot be. He is, however, aware elsewhere … that a mistaken conscience can be the result of negligence; and so he must allow that lack of faith can result from negligence, and, hence, that there is merit in faith resulting from adequate investigation.

The second and more substantial reason why, in Aquinas's view, the faith of devils is not meritorious is that it is not "formed by love";[13] that is, it not joined to the firm purpose of doing those actions which love for God (properly understood) involves—worship of God, feeding the starving, visiting the sick, and converting the irreligious. The Council of Trent put the point in similar terms.[14] It was not, I think, insisting that actual good works were needed for the meritorious faith which conduces to salvation, for someone might acquire perfect love and then die before he had any opportunity to do any, but only complete readiness to do good works.

So, although Thomist faith by itself is a very intellectual thing, a faith of the head and not the heart, a faith which may be held without any natural fruit in Christian living, the meritorious faith which the Thomist commends, the saving faith which puts the person of faith on the way to salvation, involves the whole person. It remains to be seen just how different is this view of faith from other Christian views of faith.

THE LUTHERAN VIEW OF FAITH

The second view of faith which I shall consider is the view that faith involves *both* theoretical beliefs-that (Thomist faith) *and* a trust in the Living God. The person of faith, on this view, does not merely believe that there is a God (and believe certain propositions about him), he trusts Him and commits himself to Him. The "believe in" of the Creed is to be read as affirming a belief that there is a God who has the properties stated, and has provided the good things stated (e.g. "the resurrection of the dead") and also a trust in God who has these properties and has provided these good things.

I shall call this second view of faith the Lutheran view of faith; for Luther stressed this aspect of faith as trust[15] to such an extent that the Council of Trent was moved to declare: "If anyone shall say that justifying faith is nothing else but trust in the divine mercy, which pardons our sins for Christ's sake, or that it is by such trust alone that we are justified, let him be anathema."[16] Later Lutheran theologians distinguished three parts of faith (*fides*): knowledge (*notitia*), assent (*assensus*), and trust (*fiducia*), and declared that the first two were subordinate to the trust. Trust is, on this view, the central element in faith.[17] The *notitia* is, presumably, roughly the Thomist belief-that; and the *assensus* is public confession of faith which Aquinas thought as a normal, and sometimes necessary, expression of a faith formed by love.[18] A similar threefold division of the parts of faith occurs in the opening chapters of Barth's *Dogmatics in Outline* where, after an introductory chapter, there are three chapters on faith entitled "Faith as Trust," "Faith as Knowledge," and "Faith as Confession."[19]

However, this notion of trust in God needs careful examination. To start with, what is it to put one's trust in an ordinary person? To trust someone is to act on the assumption that she will do for you what she knows that you want or need, when the evidence gives some reason for supposing that she may not and where there will be bad consequences if the assumption is false. Thus, I may trust a friend by lending a valuable to her when she has previously proved careless with valuables. I act on the assumption that she will do what she knows that I want (namely, treat the valuable with care), where the evidence gives some reason for supposing that she will not, and where there are bad consequences (namely, the valuable gets damaged) if she does not. An escaping British prisoner of war may have trusted some German by telling him of his identity and asking for help to get out of Germany. Here again, he acts on the assumption that the German will do for him what he knows that he wants (namely, provide help), when many Germans are ill-disposed towards escaping British prisoners and

likely to surrender them to the police. Or, again, a patient who trusts a doctor to cure him acts on the assumption that the doctor will do for the patient what he knows that he needs him to do, where there is some possibility that he may not (because attempts to cure are not always successful), and where things will get worse unless the doctor is successful. . . . [T]o act on the assumption that p is to do those actions which you would do if you believed that p. To act on the assumption that p is to use p as a premiss in your practical inferences, whether or not you believe p.

But why *should* you act on the assumption that p if, in fact, you do not believe p? Because you have the purpose to achieve X (e.g. get out of Germany, or be cured of disease); and you are more likely to achieve X by doing action A than by doing any alternative action, and action A will achieve X only if p is true. If your purpose to achieve X is strong enough (is far stronger than your other purposes) then you will still do A even if you believe that p is not very probable. . . . [T]he belief that in fact guides you is the belief that there is at least a small, but not negligible, probability that p. But we can describe you as acting on the assumption that p, because you would do the same action if you believed strongly that p. Within limits, the degree of p's probability does not make any difference to your action. So a simplified description of what you are doing is "acting on the assumption" that p. We saw that to trust someone is to act on the assumption that he will do for you what he knows that you want or need, where the evidence gives some reason for supposing that he may not, and there are bad consequences if the assumption proves false. This, it now follows, is to do those actions which you would do if you believed the stated assumption strongly, where, in fact, the evidence gives some reason for doubting the assumption (and there are bad consequences if it is false). The prisoner of war may not, on balance, believe that the German will help him; but he believes that there is some probability that the German will help, and he does the action which he would do if he believed that the German would help.

So much for trusting an ordinary person. What about trusting God? We have seen that, on the

Lutheran view, trusting God is something additional to believing that He exists and to believing propositions about Him. It is presumably to act on the assumption that He will do for us what He knows that we want or need, when the evidence gives some reason for supposing that He may not and where there will be bad consequences if the assumption is false. Yet one who believes that God exists and believes the propositions of the Christian creeds about Him already believes that God will do for us what He knows that we want or need; that follows immediately from the goodness of God, and so the person of Thomist faith will also believe this. Luther wrote: "Let no one be content with believing that God is able, or has power to do great things: we must also believe that he will do them and that he delights to do them. Nor indeed is it enough to think that God will do great things with other people, but not with you."[20] Belief in such things as "One Holy Catholic and apostolic Church" and "The life of the world to come," which the Nicene Creed affirms, is, then, presumably to be construed as believing that God has provided one Holy Catholic and apostolic Church and a life for humans in a future world; and acting on the assumption that God will do for the believer by means of these things what he wants or needs when there is some reason for supposing that He will not, in which case bad consequences would follow.

The trouble with the Lutheran account of faith, as I have expounded it so far, is that it has in common with the Thomist account the feature that the perfect scoundrel may yet be a person of faith. For what you do when you act on an assumption depends on what your purposes are. One who acts on the assumption that there is money in a till and who has the purpose of stealing will break open the till; one who acts on the same assumption and who has the purpose of protecting the money will lock the room carefully. A person may act on the assumption that God will do for him what he wants or needs, with purposes good or evil. Acting on that assumption, he may try to conquer the world, believing that God will help him in his task. Shall we call such a person a person of faith? Does he

not trust God? Or the antinomian whom St Paul attacks for suggesting that people should "continue in sin in order that grace may abound"?[21] Does he not trust God, to care for him abundantly well?

The Lutheran, like Aquinas, may be prepared to allow that the scoundrel can be a person of faith. But historically Lutherans have wanted to claim, against Aquinas and with Luther, that faith alone suffices for salvation (although, for them, there is no merit involved in having this faith). If the Lutheran also claims this, he might seem committed to the view that the would-be world conqueror and the antinomian are exhibiting the sort of trust which alone a person has to exhibit in order to obtain from God (unmerited) salvation. If he wishes, as he surely does, to deny that they exhibit such trust, he will have to put some further restriction on the concept of faith. He will have to say that those who act on the assumption that God will do for them what they need or want, have faith only if their purposes are good ones.[22] The good purposes will derive for the Lutheran as for the Thomist from the basic purpose of doing those actions which the believer would do if he was moved by the love of God. Many of these purposes will be good ones, I would hold (though Luther might not have held), whether or not there is a God. For example, it is good to feed the starving or educate one's children whether or not there is a God. But these purposes are also purposes which the love of God ought properly to bring about. But some of the other purposes on which, the Lutheran will hold, the person of faith should act (purposes which the love of God would lead him to have) will be ones which will only have a point if there is a God (who will provide for us what we want or need). There is no point in worshipping God if there is no God, or asking His forgiveness if He is too hard-hearted to give it. There is no point in seeking an after-life in Heaven for ourselves or for others whom we seek to convert if God will not provide it. So, unless it is absolutely certain that there is a God who will provide for us what we want or need, pursuing these good purposes inevitably involves trusting God, acting on the assumption that He will provide for us what we want or need. Hence—so long as the Thomist is prepared to allow some doubt about whether there is a God who will provide for us, and the Lutheran is prepared to say that that is not ruled out by his further view of faith as knowledge (*notitia*)— Thomist faith with the right purposes (that is faith formed by love) will entail and be entailed by Lutheran faith.

It is beginning to look as if the Reformation controversy about whether faith alone would secure salvation would seem no real controversy about matters of substance, only a dispute resulting from a confusion about the meaning of words. The Lutheran and Catholic could agree that love is needed on top of Thomist faith, while admitting that Lutheran faith (since it included love) was sufficient for salvation. The parties only quarrelled, on this view, because they misunderstood each other's use of the word "faith." In so far as one thinks that the Reformation controversy was not merely a result of verbal confusion, one must think of the Reformers as insisting on points implicit in the Catholic position, but not always made explicit—as denying that one's works need to be successful (i.e. that one's attempts to bring about good should succeed), or that one needs to have been trying to do many or even any good works (one might die before one had the opportunity). What is needed for salvation (in addition to beliefs) is a basically good character, that is, a mind full of good purposes arising from the love of God set to bring about good results as opportunity arises, to guide the beliefs on which one acts. Failure to attempt to do good works in appropriate circumstances shows, however, the lack of such good purposes. Luther himself was conscious of the close tie between faith and good works. In one passage, he writes as though the tie were a logical one. In the preface to his commentary on the Letter to the Romans, he writes that faith "cannot do other than good at all times. It never waits to ask whether there is some good to do. Rather, before the question is raised, it has done the deed and keeps on doing it. A man not active in this way is a man without faith."[23] Elsewhere, however, he seems to write as though the tie were less strict, perhaps merely contingent.

"Faith without good works does not last," he wrote in his "Sermon on Three Sides of the Good Life,"[24] implying that, for a time, one could exist without the other.

THE PRAGMATIST VIEW OF FAITH

While Lutheran faith involves both belief-that and trust, Luther stresses that the trust is the important thing. Is a third form of faith possible, where one can have the trust without the belief-that? I think that it is and that many recent writers who stress the irrelevance to faith of "belief-that" have been feeling their way towards such a form of faith. I shall call this view of faith the Pragmatist view.

As we have seen, one can act on assumptions which one does not believe. To do this is to do those actions which you would do if you did believe. In particular, you can act on the assumption not merely that God, whom you believe to exist, will do for you what you need or want, but also on the assumption that there is such a God (and that He has the properties which Christians or others have ascribed to Him). One can do this by doing those actions which one would do if one believed these things. In Chapter 1 [of *Faith and Reason*] I quoted Pascal, who responded to someone who said "But I can't believe" by giving him a recipe for how to acquire belief. The recipe was that the person should act as if he believed, do the actions which believers do, "taking holy water, having masses said," etc. and that would produce belief. Although Pascal did not hold that acting-as-if was the essence of faith, he saw it as a step on the road to acquiring it. But it is natural to develop this third view of faith according to which the belief-that is irrelevant, the acting-as-if is what matters. After all, belief is an involuntary state. Plausibly, if someone does those actions which a believer would do and for which he is to be esteemed, then that person should be esteemed whether or not he has the belief.

I suggested above that trusting God should be regarded not just as acting on assumptions; but doing so where one has good purposes. Those who have wanted to define faith in terms of trust alone would, I think, also wish such a restriction to be included in the understanding of trust. So, on the Pragmatist view, a person has Christian faith if he acts on the assumption that there is a God who has the properties which Christians ascribe to him and seeks to do those good actions which the love of God (if there is a God) would lead him to do. He will, therefore, worship God; do those actions which are such that he believes that if there is a God, God has commanded them; and seek to live in a way and to get others to live in a way which would lead God, if there is a God, to give them eternal life with the Beatific Vision of Himself. He does these actions because he believes it so worthwhile to attain the goals which they will attain if there is a God, much more worthwhile than to attain more mundane goals, that it is worth doing them in the hope that they will attain those goals. The person of Pragmatist faith will thus do the same things as the person with Lutheran faith will do. He will, for example, worship and pray and live a good life partly in the hope to find a better life in the world to come. He prays for his brethren, not necessarily because he believes that there is a God who hears his prayers, but because there is a chance that there is a God who will hear those prayers and help his brethren. He worships not necessarily because he believes that there is a God who deserves worship, but because it is very important to express gratitude for existence if there is a God to whom to be grateful, and there is some chance that there is.

I have called this view of faith the "Pragmatist view," because in "The Will to Believe" William James[25] commends a faith which is a matter of acting-as-if some hypothesis were true. This, he claims, is a rational thing to do when faced with some "momentous" option, if only by so doing can we gain some good which would otherwise be unattainable. Religion offers a "vital good" now, and an eternal well-being hereafter. But to gain these goods we must decide to act as if the religious hypothesis were true. To delay "is as if a man should hesitate indefinitely to ask a certain woman to marry him because he was not perfectly sure that she would prove an angel after he brought her home. Would he not cut himself off from that particular angel-possibility as decisively as if he went and married some one else?" Unfortunately, James confuses things by calling this "acting-as-if" "believing" and so sees himself as endorsing Pascal. That he was not doing, because Pascal had the more normal understanding of belief, which I have analysed in Chapter 1 [of *Faith and Reason*]. Though Kierkegaard is in most ways a very different sort of philosopher from James, the Pragmatist view is also that of Kierkegaard; and Kierkegaard bears much of the responsibility for the many traces of this view in modern theology. "The leap of faith" which Kierkegaard commends is a matter of acting-as-if with "the passion of the infinite."[26] He commends Socrates for having the right sort of faith in immortality because "he stakes his whole life" on this. "When Socrates believed that God is, he held fast the objective uncertainty with the entire passion of inwardness, and faith is precisely in this contradiction, in this risk." "Without risk, no faith. Faith is the contradiction between the infinite passion of inwardness and the objective uncertainty."

The person of Pragmatist Christian faith need not believe that there is a God (in the sense of believing that it is more probable than not that there is a God), but he does need another belief of a kind which I called in Chapter 1 [of *Faith and Reason*] a weak belief, in the efficacy of his actions to obtain his goal—a belief that it is at least as probable that he will attain the goals he seeks by doing certain actions (e.g. those which the love of God, if there is a God, would lead him to do) as by doing any other actions, and more probable that he will attain these goals by doing these actions than by doing some other actions (e.g. nothing at all). He will need, therefore, to have such beliefs as that he is more likely to honour God by participating in Christian worship than by doing nothing; and more likely to get to Heaven by feeding the starving than by taking heroin. He may believe that there is more than one way which he can pursue equally likely to attain his goals, but he will need to believe that some ways are less likely to attain those goals. But no-one is going to hold such means-ends beliefs except in virtue of holding theoretical beliefs from which they follow—e.g. that it is at least as probable that any God is as the Christian Creed depicts him as that he is as any other creed depicts him. For if the believer believes that the Islamic Creed is more likely to be true than the Christian Creed, he will have the means-end belief that he is more likely to honour God by participating in Islamic worship. And the believer needs the theoretical belief that there is some probability that there is a God and so that he will obtain his goal; otherwise he cannot be doing certain actions in order to obtain his goal of honouring God. Hence, Pragmatist faith does not differ from Lutheran faith by Pragmatist faith not involving any belief-that, but (it might seem) simply in that it involves less in the way of belief-that than does Lutheran faith. To express the apparent difference in terms of the common ultimate goal of doing those actions which the love of God would lead you to do—on the Pragmatist view, you do not need believe that there is a God and that, in consequence, you will show love for Him if you do certain actions, only that there may be a God and that you are more likely to show love for Him if you do certain actions rather than others. That Pragmatist faith involves a belief about the relative probability of credal beliefs was recognized, in effect, by James when he wrote that we have to choose between living options (that is, between the different ways to achieve our goals commended by what we believe to be the more probable world-views): and he commented that for his audience belief "in the Mahdi . . . refuses to scintillate with any credibility at all."[27] But I am not aware that Kierkegaard recognized the need for such beliefs.

So it looks at this stage as if the Thomist and Lutheran views of the faith which conduces to salvation (that is Thomist "formed faith" and Lutheran "faith") are essentially the same, while the Pragmatist view differs from these in that it does not require belief that there is a God and that He has certain properties and has done certain things, only a weaker belief. On all these views, the person who has the virtue of faith (that is, "formed faith" in the Thomist sense) seeks to do those actions which the love of God would lead him to do. Whether, however, there is this ultimate difference

between the three views depends on how the Thomist and Lutheran understandings of belief are spelled out, as we shall see shortly.

DIFFERENCES WITHIN THE THOMIST AND LUTHERAN VIEWS

There are two important differences between ways in which the Thomist and Lutheran views can be spelled out. The first difference which is seldom—if ever—noticed by those who write on this subject concerns what is the contrast which is being made when the person of faith affirms a belief that some creed is true. Is the creed as a whole being contrasted with its negation, or with more specific alternatives; or are merely the individual items of the creed being contrasted with their negations or various more specific alternatives?

. . . [T]o believe a proposition is to believe it more probable than any alternative. So what the belief amounts to depends on what are the alternatives. The normal alternative to a proposition is its negation. To believe that p is to believe that p is more probable than not-p. But the alternatives to a proposition may be narrower than the negation. In that case to believe that p is to believe that p is more probable than each of these alternatives q, r, s, etc., but not necessarily more probable than their disjunction. It follows from this that there are different things which believing a creed such as the Nicene Creed might amount to. First, it might be a matter of believing each item of the Creed to be more probable than its negation. Thus, understanding "I believe *in* one God, Father Almighty, maker of Heaven and Earth and of all things visible and invisible" as "I believe that there is one God who is Father Almighty, Maker of Heaven and Earth and of all things visible and invisible," we may, in turn, understand this as "I believe that it is more probable that there is a God who is Father Almighty, Maker of Heaven and Earth, and of all things visible and invisible, than that there is not." And so on, for each item of the Creed. This interpretation makes it crucial just how one divides up the Creed into items.

For. . .it does not follow from *p* being more probable than not-*p*, and *q* being more probable than not-*q*, that (*p* and *q*) is more probable than not-(*p* and *q*). Although it is to some extent clear how the Nicene Creed is to be divided up into items (for example, belief in "God, Father Almighty" is belief in a different item from belief in "One Holy Catholic and Apostolic Church"), it is by no means always obvious exactly where the line is to be drawn between different items. Is belief in "one God, Father Almighty, Maker of Heaven and Earth" belief in one item or belief in two or three separate items?

Secondly, believing a creed such as the Nicene Creed might be a matter of believing each item of the Creed to be more probable than each of a number of specific heretical or non-Christian alternatives. Someone affirming his belief in "the resurrection of the body" may be claiming that it is more probable that humans rise embodied than that (as some other religions claimed) they have an everlasting new life in a disembodied state. In affirming his belief that Christ was "begotten, not made," someone may only be affirming a belief that it is more probable that the pre-Incarnate Christ was brought into being out of nothing than that he was made from pre-existent matter. And so on. This view has the difficulty of the previous view about how the Creed is to be cut up into items, and the further difficulty of how we are to know what are the alternatives to each item. The historical circumstances of the formulation of the Creed provide guidance on the latter issue, and indeed on the former one, too. By studying the reasons which led a Church Council to put a certain clause in the Creed, we can see what it was designed to deny. But it remains the case that, on either of these views, there is very considerable uncertainty as to what believing a creed amounts to.

The third and fourth interpretations of what believing a creed amounts to avoid the problem of how the creed is to be cut up into items, by supposing that to believe a creed is to believe the whole creed (the conjunction of all its items, however individuated) to be more probable than any alternative. On the third interpretation, the only alternative with which a creed is being contrasted is its negation. To believe the creed is to believe that the conjunction of propositions which form it is more probable than the negation of that conjunction. This is a very high demand indeed. Most of us who believe each of many complex historical or scientific claims also believe that we have made some error somewhere, although we do not know where. On the fourth interpretation, a creed is being contrasted with each of a number of specific heretical or non-Christian alternatives. Some of these will differ from the creed in question in only one item (on some way of cutting up the creed into items); one who believes the creed (*p*, *q*, and *r*) may believe it to be more probable than (*p*, *q*, and not-*r*). Of these four interpretations of what believing a creed amounts to, clearly the third is the strongest, and the second and fourth are the weakest. (Which of these is weaker than the other will depend on the creed in question, and what are the alternatives to it.)[28]

The second difference within the Thomist and Lutheran views concerns how strong the contrast between alternatives has to be. The belief may be the minimum belief that the probability of one proposition (or the whole creed) is greater than that of another, or the stronger belief that the probability of one proposition (or the whole creed) is quite a lot greater than that of the other. We have already noted a certain ambivalence within Aquinas's own thought about how deep this conviction involved in faith needs to be.

Now, if we interpret the belief required on the Thomist and Lutheran accounts in the fourth way as a belief that the creed as a whole is more probable than various alternatives, and insist on no more than the minimum belief that the probability of the creed exceed that of its rivals, there is then, in principle, virtually no difference from Pragmatist faith, which—as we have seen—amounts to a belief that one creed is more probable than others. (I write "virtually," because the Pragmatist may believe that his creed—the Christian Creed—is as probable as some other creed—e.g. the Judaic Creed—so long as he believes that it is more probable than some other creed—e.g. the Islamic Creed. This difference is, however, too small to deserve further attention.) I write "in principle" because everything depends on how the alternatives to a creed are picked out.

FAITH IN EARLIER CHRISTIAN THOUGHT

The response required to the preaching of the Gospel by St Peter at Pentecost was simply that his hearers should "repent, and be baptised."[29] But very soon the response required before baptism was described as "believe in the Lord Jesus"[30] (πίστευσον) and Christians were described as "believers"[31] (πεπιστευκότες). What sort of belief is involved here is unclear; it may be either credal belief of some kind or trust in God involving acting on assumptions, or maybe both. The long sermon on faith in the *Letter to the Hebrews* 11 seems to contain an understanding of faith both as belief-that and as action on-the-assumption-that. On the one hand, "whoever would approach [God] must believe that he exists and that he rewards those who seek him." But, on the other hand, "faith is the assurance of things hoped for, the conviction of things not seen";[32] and more generally as I read that chapter, the faith of many heroes of the Old Testament is seen by the writer as a matter of their doing actions in hope rather than belief. In the *Letter to the Romans* Paul describes Abraham, his paradigm of a person of faith, as "hoping against hope" that God's promise to him that he would become "the father of many nations" would be fulfilled.[33] And there are other New Testament passages which imply that faith may be accompanied by a certain amount of uncertainty or hesitation. There is the remark of the father who, having asked Jesus to cure his epileptic son, responded to Jesus's comment "All things can be done for the one who believes," with the words "I believe; help my unbelief!."[34] His limited faith was rewarded. And there is Paul's remark, "we walk by faith, not by sight."[35]

The same ambiguity seems to arise when we come to the early Christian theologians. Two major writers who wrote at a little length about faith were Clement of Alexandria and Cyril of Jerusalem.[36] For Clement, faith is firm conviction: "He who believes the divine scriptures with sure judgement, receives in the voice of God who bestowed the scripture an incorrigible demonstration." And so "who is so impious as to disbelieve God and to demand proofs from God as from humans?"[37] Cyril of Jerusalem, on the other hand, after making the point that all human institutions (such as marriage) require faith, illustrates the notion of faith by the faith of seafarers "who commit themselves to hopes that are not certainties (ἀδήλοις)."[38] Faith is a matter of putting one's trust in things that are not certain.

I do not think that the early Church had any clear doctrine of the kind of belief required in the faith expected of Christians—what kind of contrast with which other propositions was involved in that belief, and how strong the belief needed to be. It had not needed to face these issues as a doctrinal problem. However, although it would need much historical research to substantiate my conjecture, I suggest that implicitly in earlier centuries people tended to assume that Christianity was being contrasted with various other religions and philosophical systems; and that, in expressing belief in Christianity, you were expressing a belief that the Christian system as a whole was more probable than each of those other systems. Those, like Augustine, who agonized over religious allegiance in the first centuries AD, were concerned with a choice between Christianity, Judaism, Mithraism, Manichaeism, Epicureanism, Stoicism, etc. Their concern in making a choice was with which was most likely to be true; and so, among religions which offered salvation, which was most likely to provide it. There was not in those days a vast pool of "agnostics" who owed allegiance to no system. Yet if in order to believe a system you had to believe each item of its creed to be more probable than its negation—let alone believe the whole creed to be more probable than its negation, then since you might expect most people to think that no system had all its items each more probable than its negation (although they would think that systems differed among each other in probability), you might expect most people to believe no one system and to belong to a vast agnostic pool. I am also inclined to think that, in earlier days, all that was (implicitly) required of the candidate for baptism was a belief that the Christian system was marginally more probable than each of its alternatives, not very much more probable than them—so long, of course, as the belief was joined to a total commitment to action. The ever-present inveighing against Christians who are hesitant is to be read more often as inveighing against lack of commitment rather than lack of conviction.

In the early Middle Ages Abelard seems to have noted the uncertainty involved in faith. He described faith as an "estimate" (aestimatio) of things not apparent; and regarded hope as a species of faith, differing from other kinds of faith by being concerned with good things and with the future.[39] Bernard inveighed against Abelard's account of faith—it was no "estimate" but a certainty—"if faith were something that fluctuates, our hope would be empty."[40] I do not find in the discussion in Hugh of S. Victor, which contains the definition cited by Aquinas, the same understanding as in Aquinas of what being "greater than opinion, and less than scientific knowledge" amounts to. Hugh writes that faith concerns what we "hope for" and so it does not involve "sight." He describes "believers" as those who "approve" one view as opposed to the alternative view "so far as to assume it in what they assert."[41] That seems nothing like Aquinas's account, and is a further reason for holding that the belief-element in the faith required of Christians in patristic and early medieval times need not involve total conviction.

In later centuries there seems to be a change. The post-Renaissance centuries saw the emergence and steady growth, among intellectuals to start with and then more widely, of a vast pool of "agnostics." Of course, there was more than one reason for the growth of agnosticism, but many of these agnostics must have felt that one religion was more probable than others, and yet they still felt themselves unqualified for entry to it. We hear the great cry of "I would like to believe, but unfortunately I cannot." Clearly, people supposed that there were stronger conditions for belief than those which, I have claimed, existed in

early centuries. It was, I suspect, partly as a reaction to this situation that the Pragmatist view of faith was developed. But, as we have seen, all three views of faith can be spelled out in very different ways according to how the belief involved in them is understood, and on some understandings the Thomist and Lutheran views collapse into the Pragmatist view. However, although the historian may read an implicit understanding of what faith is assumed to involve in various centuries, to my knowledge neither the Catholic Church, nor the Orthodox Church, nor—I suspect—any large mainstream Protestant Church has ever made any dogmatic pronouncements about the kind of belief which is involved in faith. In due course, I shall consider on more aprioristic grounds what kind of belief is needed in order to pursue the goals of religion, and what kind of belief a Church ought to demand of its adherents.

Before ending this chapter, I must mention one minor matter. All the kinds of faith which I have discussed involve attitudes towards, behaviour in the light of, *propositions*. They are not necessarily always so phrased, but my claim is that talk about believing in God or trusting God can, without loss of meaning, be analysed in one of these ways. However, a view of faith developed within twentieth-century Protestant theology which Hick calls "non-propositional." On this view, faith "conceived in this way as a voluntary recognition of God's activity in human history, consists in seeing, apperceiving, or interpreting events in a special way."[42] The person of faith "sees" the world as God's creation, sees not merely the defeat of Nazi Germany in the Second World War but the hand of God in guiding the Allied forces to victory. But this view of faith seems easily expressible in propositional terms. Is not to experience X as Y in this kind of case simply to experience X and in so doing automatically and naturally to *believe* that X is Y? The person of faith is one who sees the world and so doing automatically and naturally *believes that* the world is God's creation; does not merely see the defeat of Nazi Germany but in so doing automatically and naturally *believes that* God has brought it about. The "non-propositional" aspect of this Protestant view of faith is simply a matter of the way in which it is expressed.[43] There is nothing essentially non-propositional about it.

The three views which I have described in this chapter are all views about the kind of faith required of a Christian; but there can be a similar range of views about the kind of faith required for the practice of some other religion. Is it just a matter of believing that certain things are true, or merely acting on the assumption that certain things are true—with good purposes (perhaps ones somewhat different from the Christian good purpose of doing the actions which love of God would lead one to do)?[44] We shall be in a better position to answer that when we have considered more fully what is the purpose of pursuing a religion; what are the goals which it is good that someone should try to achieve by pursuing a religious way. . . .

NOTES

1. Aquinas adds that "the only reason for formulating propositions is that through them we may have knowledge of things," *Summa Theologiae,* 2a. 2ae. 1.2. ad.2.

2. This equation of faith and belief was encouraged by the fact that, while one could make a distinction in Greek and Latin between "believing that" so-and-so is the case and "believing in" or having "faith in" some person, it was made by what followed the one available verb (πιστέω, credo). There was only one noun available in each language to denote the two states (πίστις, fides).

3. Ibid., 2a. 2ae. 6.1.

4. H. Denzinger, *Enchiridion Symbolorum* (Herder, 1963), 3008.

5. De Sacramentis 1.10.2.

6. *Summa Theologiae* 2a. 2ae. 2.1.

7. Aquinas is not totally consistent on this point. In *Summa Theologiae* 2a. 2ae. 1.5. ad.3 he seems to allow the claim of the objector that the existence of God can be an object of *scientia.* He is thus operating here with a wider understanding of *scientia,* according to which we can have *scientia* of anything demonstrable from evident non-revealed truths.

8. Aquinas allows that theology can be a science (*scientia*) in a derivative sense that it develops the consequences of first principles revealed by God; see *Summa Theologiae* 1a. 1.2.

9. *Summa Theologiae* 2a. 2ae. 4.8. ad 1 accepts the claim of the objector that faith may at times admit of doubt.

10. *Summa Theologiae* 2a. 2ae. 5.4.

11. James: 2: 19.

12. *Summa Theologiae,* 2a. 2ae. 5. 2 ad.3.

13. *Summa Theologiae,* 2a. 2ae. 4.3, 4, and 5. I translate *caritas* as "love." Aquinas writes elsewhere (2a. 2ae. 23.1) that "love is a sort of friendship of man towards God." Thinking of faith as involving a voluntary element. Aquinas writes that "in the case of a voluntary act the form is in some way that end to which the action is directed." (2a. 2ae. 4.3).

14. Denzinger 1559 and 1561.

15. See his "The Freedom of a Christian," § 11, in *Reformation Writings of Martin Luther,* trans. B. L. Woolf, Vol. 1 (Lutterworth Press, 1952). The Lutheran view is found in the *Book of Homilies,* commended in the Thirty-nine Articles of the Church of England (1562): "A quick and living faith is not only the common belief of the articles of our faith, but it is also a true trust and confidence of the mercy of God through our Lord Jesus Christ, and a steadfast hope of good things to be received at God's hands." (Sermon of Faith, Part I)

16. Denzinger 1562.

17. In his *Faith and Belief* (Princeton University Press, 1979), ch. 6, and *Belief and History* (University of Virginia Press, 1977), ch. 2, W. Cantwell-Smith argues that, until the seventeenth century, the English word "believe" meant "trust." The quotation from the *Book of Homilies* in n. 15 casts some doubt on this, but Cantwell-Smith has accumulated many quotations to illustrate his view.

18. *Summa Theologiae* 2a. 2ae. 3.

19. Karl Barth, *Dogmatics in Outline* (SCM Press, 1949).

20. M. Luther, *Magnificat,* in *Reformation Writings of Martin Luther,* Vol. 2 (Lutter-worth Press, 1956), 199.

21. Letter to the Romans 6: 1.

22. Calvin claimed that faith can "in no way be separated from a devout disposition" and he attacked "the Schools" for distinguishing between "formed" and "unformed" faith and supposing that "people who are touched by no fear of God, no sense of piety, nevertheless believe what is necessary to know for salvation" (J. Calvin, *Institutes of the Christian Religion,* III. 2; trans. F. L. Battles (Westminster Press, 1960, Vol. 1, 553 and 551.)

23. *Reformation Writings of Martin Luther,* Vol. 2, 288–9.

24. Ibid., Vol. 2, 124.

25. "The Will to Believe," in William James, *The Will to Believe and Other Essays in Popular Philosophy,* first publ. 1897 (Dover Publications, 1956). See esp. 25–6, 30–1 and 29, n. 1. I read James's assertion that religion says that "the best things are the more eternal things" when coupled with his long quotation from Fitz James Stephen at the end of his essay as affirming the doctrine that the religious person will attain a life after death.

26. See, e.g., S. Kierkegaard, *Concluding Unscientific Postscript,* Vol. 1, trans. H. V. Hong and E. H. Hong (Princeton University Press, 1992), see 201, 210, 204.

27. *The Will to Believe,* 2. The Mahdi was a would-be Islamic Messiah, powerfully influential in the Sudan in the 1880s, who led a revolt against British rule.

28. My account in the first edition of [*Faith and Reason*] of the different ways in which believing a creed could be construed was loose in not making a sharp distinction between the second and fourth interpretations. I am grateful to Stephen Maitzen for pointing this out-see section 2 of his article "Swinburne on Credal belief," *International Journal for the Philosophy of Religion,* 1991, 29, 143–57.

29. Acts 2: 38.

30. Acts 16: 31.

31. Acts 15: 5, 18: 27, 19: 18.

32. Hebrews 11: 1 and 11: 6.

33. Romans 4: 18.

34. Mark 9: 24.

35. II Corinthians 5: 7.

36. Clement of Alexandria, *Stomateis,* Bk 2; Cyril of Jerusalem, *Catechetical Lectures* Book 5.

37. *Stromateis* 2.2 and 5.1.

38. *Catechetical Lectures* 5.3. In ch. 5 of his *Faith and Belief,* W. Cantwell-Smith argues at length that in this book Cyril holds that the commitment (expressed by the word πισςεύω) involved in the creeds used at baptisms involves doing an action (putting trust) rather than expressing a passive conviction.

39. *Epitome Theologiae Christianae,* 1.1 (PL 178, 1695).

40. *Contra Quaedam Capitula Errorum Abelardi,* ch. 4. (PL 182, 1061).

41. Hugh distinguishes five attitudes towards a view or proposition. One may deny it, doubt it, "opine" it, believe it, or know it. Opining is a matter of thinking the view more probable (*magis probabile*) than the alternative; believing goes beyond that and actually involves asserting it. Believers "sic alteram partem approbant, ut eius approbationem etiam in assertionem assumant."

42. John Hick, *Philosophy of Religion,* 3rd edn. (Prentice Hall, 1983), 69.

43. The same may be said about Cantwell-Smith's attacks on propositional accounts of belief. See his bold claim: "No one ... has ever believed a proposition"—*Faith and Belief,* 146. For Aquinas's reply to an objection that faith is not concerned with propositions (*Summa Theologiae* 2a. 2ae. 1.2 obj. 2), see my n. 1 above.

44. In his *The Concept of Faith* (Cornell University Press, 1994), 200–41, W. L. Sessions analysed a Hindu conception and two different Buddhist conceptions of notions which have been translated into English as "faith." All of these notions seem to involve some belief (though on the Son Buddhist account, it is belief in one's own power and nature) and at least two of them seem to involve commitment to a way of life.

V.A.2

Can It Be Rational to Have Faith?

LARA BUCHAK

Lara Buchak (1981–) is professor of philosophy at the University of California at Berkeley. She works primarily in the fields of epistemology and the philosophy of religion. In this essay, she explores the relationship between faith and rationality, developing an account of the nature of faith according to which having faith involves terminating one's search for further evidence pertaining to the object of one's faith.

I. INTRODUCTION

My concern in this paper is the relationship between faith and rationality. I seek to develop a unified account of statements of faith concerning mundane matters and those concerning religious faith. To do so, I consider the sense in which faith requires going beyond the evidence, and argue that faith requires terminating the search for further evidence. Having established this, I turn to the question of whether it can still be rational to have faith; arguing that, contrary to common assumptions, there need be no conflict between faith and rationality. We shall see that whether faith can be practically rational depends both on whether there are extrinsic costs associated with postponing the decision to have faith and the extent to which potential counter evidence would be conclusive.

II. PRELIMINARIES

I begin with the idea that faith statements in religious contexts and in more mundane contexts express the same attitude and so share some typical characteristics. By "faith statements" I simply mean statements involving the term "faith." The following are representative examples:

I have faith in your abilities.	*He has faith that his spouse won't cheat on him.*
I have faith in you.	*He has faith that you won't reveal his secret.*
She acted on faith.	*She has faith that her car will start.*
It was an act of faith.	*I have faith that God exists.*
I have faith in God's goodness.	*I have faith in God.*

These statements share three important features: they involve a relationship between the agent and a particular proposition, between the agent and a particular (actual or potential) action, and between the proposition and the evidence the agent currently possesses.

The first thing to notice is that faith statements typically involve a proposition to which the actor involved acquiesces. This is obvious in the case of

Reprinted with modifications from Lara Buchak, "Can it be Rational to Have Faith?", Chapter 12 of *Probability in the Philosophy of Religion*, Oxford University Press (2012), 225–247. Used by permission of Oxford University Press. This paper has been edited by the author to simplify and make accessible the primary mathematical results.

"faith that" statements: when a person has faith that *p*, he acquiesces to *p*.[1] It is also clear in the case of those statements that can be easily translated into "faith that" statements: for example, the statement *I have faith in your abilities* is equivalent to *I have faith that you will be able to do such-and-such*. It is less obvious in the case of those statements claiming that an individual has faith in a person; however, upon further inspection, having faith in a person does typically require acquiescing to particular propositions about that person. For example, having faith in a person might involve acquiescing to the claim that the person will do the right thing or will succeed at a task, and having faith in God might involve acquiescing to (at least) the claims that God exists and that God is good. By the same token, performing an act of faith or acting on faith seems to involve acquiescing to a proposition, and which proposition one acquiesces to will be set by the context. For example, if setting down one's own weapons is an act of faith, then this is because setting down one's own weapons involves acquiescing to the claim that the other person will then set down his.

The second thing to notice about faith statements is that the truth or falsity of the proposition(s) involved is ordinarily a matter of importance to the actor. For example, it does not seem apt to state that I have faith that the Nile is the longest river in Egypt, because I do not care whether or not this is true. We do not attribute faith to a person unless the truth or falsity of the proposition involved makes a difference to that person. I might consider whether to have faith *that my spouse won't cheat on me* or *that my car will start* precisely because it makes a difference to me whether or not these things are true.

Along the same lines, having faith typically involves an action: a person's having faith in something should make a difference to her behaviour. However, this needn't be an actual action. It would be enough for faith that if a person were put in a particular situation, she would then manifest the relevant behaviour (assuming that there are no forces that would stop her). Faith is thus linked to a *disposition* to act.

This brings us to the next point about the relationship between faith and behaviour: it seems that one can have faith in a particular proposition relative to one action but not to another. For example, I might have faith that my car will start when I only need to drive to work but lack that faith when I am relied upon to carry a life-saving organ to the hospital (as evidenced by the fact that I may double-check my engine or arrange for a backup mode of transportation in the latter case but not the former). A person might have faith in God when it comes to giving weekly donations to the poor but lack faith in God when it comes to allowing himself to be martyred.

There are two ways in which we might interpret the fact that one might have faith when it comes to the performance of some actions but not others: we might say that faith is context-dependent, or we might say that faith comes in degrees. There is something to be said in favour of each of these approaches. However, whether one has faith that *X*, expressed by a particular act *A*, will be determinate on either approach, and since this will be our basic unit of analysis in this paper, we needn't choose between them.

The next thing to bring into the picture is the relationship between the agent who has faith that *X* (expressed by some act *A*) and the evidence he has for *X*. We make assertions of faith only when the outcome of the proposition involved is uncertain or when the evidence we have is inconclusive. For example, when a friend is worried about the outcome of an exam, we might reassure her by saying "I have faith that you passed"; however, once she shows us that she got an A we would no longer say this. Clearly, this is not because we are less willing to acquiesce to the claim that she passed, but because we now know for certain that she did. For similar reasons, it seems odd to claim to have faith in logical truths.

These considerations suggest that a person cannot have faith in propositions of which he is antecedently certain or for which he has conclusive evidence.[2] Are there further restrictions on which propositions a person can have faith in? I don't believe so. Indeed, a person may have no evidence at all for the proposition he has faith in, or even may have evidence that tells *against* the proposition. For example, we could imagine someone saying "Although she's spilled all the secrets I've told her so far, I have faith that this time will be different," or "I don't think there's any evidence that God exists, but I have faith that he does." Therefore, that a person has faith that X implies nothing about his evidence for X, aside from its inconclusiveness. Statements in which the actor has faith despite no or contrary evidence do seem correctly described as cases of faith, even though they are not cases in which we are inclined to think that the actor is *wise* to have faith; rather, we think his faith is misplaced. We will later see that we can do justice to the distinction between well-placed faith and misplaced faith.

My final preliminary observation is that having faith seems to involve going *beyond* the evidence in some way. The bulk of my argument will be devoted to spelling out in what way one must go beyond the evidence in order to count as having faith. I postpone discussion of this to the next section.

We can now begin to give a formal analysis of faith. As we've seen, the term "faith" appears in many different grammatical constructions: you might have faith in a *person*, you might have faith in a *proposition*, you might perform an *act of faith*, or you might *act on faith*. We require an account that makes sense of all of these uses of the term. I've already pointed out that faith typically involves a *proposition* as well as an *action* to which the truth or falsity of the proposition makes a difference. I propose, then, to make *faith that X, expressed by A* the basic unit of analysis, where X is a proposition and A is an act, and define the other constructions in terms of this one.

It is important that our analysis express the relationship between the proposition and the act. I have explained that a person can have faith that X only if he cares whether X is true or false, and presumably this is because the act of faith constitutes taking a risk on X. What is it for an act to constitute taking a risk on a proposition? We can say that doing A constitutes an individual's taking a

risk on X just in case there is some alternative available act B such that A is preferred to B on the supposition that X holds and B is preferred to A on the supposition that $\sim X$ holds. For example, telling my friend a secret constitutes taking a risk that she will keep it because on the supposition that she will keep it, I would rather tell her, but on the supposition that she won't keep it, I would rather not tell her. Whether an act constitutes a risk on X will of course be relative to the individual performing the act. So, as a first pass, we might say:

> A person has faith that X, expressed by A, only if that person performs act A and performing A constitutes taking a risk on X.

This is not yet the whole story, but it does allow us to go a step further and identify what it is to have faith in a person, and to perform an act of faith:

> A person P has faith in another person Q if and only if there is some act A and some proposition(s) X that express(es) a positive judgment about Q such that P has faith that X, expressed by A.[3]

So, Bob might have faith in Mary because he has faith that Mary won't reveal a secret he tells her, expressed by the act of telling her his secret. Paul might have faith in God because he has faith that God exists and that God is good, expressed by the act of praying. Again, faith only requires a disposition to choose particular acts, and these acts need not be actually available.

We can now take the next step and identify what it is to perform an act of faith, or to act on faith:

> A person performs an act of faith (or acts on faith) if and only if he performs some act A such that there is a proposition X in which he has faith, expressed by A.

With these preliminaries in place, the rest of this paper will elaborate what else faith that X, expressed by A, requires and under what circumstances it is rational to have such faith.

III. GOING BEYOND THE EVIDENCE: THREE VIEWS

Before outlining my own view I consider three initially promising ways to make sense of the requirement that faith goes *beyond* the evidence. I conclude that each of these attempts fails to reveal a genuine requirement of faith.

First, however, let me briefly say something about the philosophical framework in which I am working. One way to talk about belief states is as "on" or "off": you either believe something or you fail to believe it (this could be because you actively disbelieve it or because you withhold judgment from it). But notice that of the many things you believe, you are more confident of some than others; furthermore, of the many things you fail to believe, you take some to nonetheless be more likely than others. As evidence of these facts, we could ask you how much you are willing to bet on various propositions: in general, you will be willing to bet more (accept lower odds) on the ones in which you are more confident. To capture these facts, many philosophers have found it helpful to talk about belief states in a "graded" way: beliefs come in degrees (sometimes called "credences" or "subjective probabilities") between 0 and 1, and degrees of belief should behave like probabilities. For example, if you assign a degree of belief 0.7 to the claim that the Giants will win the World Series ($p(\text{GIANTS}) = 0.7$), then you should assign degree of belief 0.3 to the claim that the Giants won't win the World Series. As we will see later, degrees of belief underlie a formal theory of rational decision-making, but for now we can just notice that choosing an action is like taking a bet whose outcome is determined by the state of the world. For example, when one assigns $p(\text{RAIN}) = 0.6$ and $p(\text{NOT-RAIN}) = 0.4$, and one leaves the house without one's umbrella, one is taking a bet that involves a 60% chance of getting wet and a 40% chance of staying dry.

With this framework in mind, let us consider some attempts to analyse the way in which faith goes beyond the evidence. The first analysis claims that faith in X requires believing X to a higher degree than one thinks the evidence warrants.[4] More precisely, for an agent to have faith that X, he must think that the evidence warrants believing X to some degree, say, r, but he nonetheless believes X to degree q, where q is greater than r. More particularly, one might think that faith requires believing X to degree 1 (being certain or fully confident that X), even though one thinks that the evidence warrants a definite credence less than this.

On this analysis, having faith involves being entrenched in a kind of partial belief version of Moore's paradox: one thinks something like *X is likely to degree r, but I believe X to degree q*. Ignoring the issue of whether this could ever be rational—since we don't want to prejudge the issue by assuming there must be cases of rational faith—there are two problems with taking this to be a requirement of faith. First, it seems hard to imagine someone actually having faith in this sense and, especially, recognizing that he has faith in this sense. Yet having faith seems to be a common occurrence, one that does not involve psychological tricks or self-deception. Second, because it is unclear that one can reliably or stably have faith in this sense, or even take steps to set oneself up to have faith in this sense, it does not seem to be the kind of thing that ethics would require. And yet, religious ethics and the ethics of friendship do seem to require faith in certain cases.

The second analysis is more initially plausible. According to this, for the person who thinks that the evidence warrants believing X to degree r, faith requires *acting as if* he has degree of belief q—that is, performing the actions that he would perform if he had degree of belief q—where *q is greater than r*. For example, one would take the bets that would be rational to take if one had degree of belief r. Thus, one can maintain a degree of belief in r—and so avoid epistemic inconsistency—while still behaving, as regards the likelihood of X, in a way that goes beyond the evidence. Again, more particularly, we might think that faith requires acting as if you have credence 1, that is, using $p(X) = 1$ when making decisions. This would amount to acting as if one is certain that X: not considering or caring about states of the world in which $\sim X$ holds when making decisions.

I admit that this analysis has some plausibility. However, I again think that there are problems concerning both the phenomenology and ethics of faith.

The phenomenological worry is that, on this analysis, faith requires simultaneously keeping track of two things: one's actual credences, and the "faith-adjusted" credences that one employs in decision making. However, the phenomenology of faith doesn't seem to involve a lot of mental accounting. Yet perhaps this is not a serious problem, because the defender of this view could argue that since faith is relative to particular acts, one only needs to consider one's faith-adjusted credences when making the relevant decision.

There are two more serious problems arising from the fact that although religious ethics and the ethics of friendship endorse faith in many situations, they wouldn't endorse certain demands that this analysis suggests. First, consider what this analysis recommends that a faithful person do when asked whether he believes that X. Since this is an action, presumably the faithful person ought, if he ought to have faith, to figure out what to do using his faith-adjusted credences, not his actual ones. So he ought to claim to believe X more strongly than he does; that is, he ought to lie. But those that endorse faith often strongly denounce lying.

The second problem is brought to the fore when we consider the particular view that faith requires acting as if $p(X) = 1$. On this view, the faithful person ought to take any bet that is favourable on the condition that X obtains, regardless of the stakes. So, if asked to bet \$1m on a gamble that pays 1 penny if X obtains, the person with faith in X ought to say yes: after all, he can disregard the possibility of $\sim X$ for the purposes of decision making. I'm extremely doubtful that religious ethics would endorse the claim that the truly faithful ought to risk \$1m for a mere penny if God exists, especially since they recognize that the evidence isn't conclusive.[5]

So we can dismiss the first two analyses which held that in order for a person to count as having faith that X, he must treat his credence in X as higher than it in fact is, either by actually raising it or by acting as if it were higher. Perhaps these analyses have gone astray because they took for granted an inadequate account of when faith enters into one's belief formation process. They both assume that one examines all of the evidence dispassionately, forms a belief, and then decides whether to adjust this belief in light of faith. But perhaps the relationship between faith and belief formation is more complex than this assumption recognizes. Instead, faith might require taking evidence into account in a particular way—a way that favours X or gives the truth of X the benefit of the doubt, so to speak. Following this line of thought, a third analysis of faith holds that faith requires setting one's degree of belief to $p(X) = 1$ prior to examining the evidence. On this view, one interprets evidence, not with an eye towards finding out whether or not X holds, but in light of the assumption that X does hold. On this view, we might say that faith goes *before* the evidence, not beyond it.

Note that this third analysis is different from the "special cases" of the first two analyses. On those analyses, the faithful individual sets $p(X) = 1$ (either in his beliefs or for his actions) even though he believes that the evidence warrants something less. On the present analysis the agent doesn't have an opinion about what the evidence warrants that is separate from the question of whether he has faith. So let's say that I have faith that my friend won't reveal a secret I told him, and I overhear a third party complaining that my friend is a gossip. On the first analysis, I consider this to be evidence against the claim that my friend will keep my secret, but I nonetheless ignore it and continue to have a high degree of belief in the claim. On the second analysis, I consider this to be evidence against the claim, and I lower my degree of belief in the claim, but I nonetheless continue to act as if I have a high degree of belief (I carry on as if no one knows my secret, and I continue to confide in this friend). On the analysis we are now considering, I don't consider this to be evidence against the claim, precisely because I have faith in the claim. Indeed, there will be no possible evidence that tells against X.

This third analysis has a number of advantages. For one, it sheds light on the fact that there seems to be no good answer to the question of how a rational person ought to set his credences before encountering any evidence. On this view, the reason that there is no good answer is that epistemic rationality stops just short of this question and faith takes over: one can't avoid having faith in something, because one can't avoid setting one's initial credences.[6] This vindicates William James' claim that one's non-rational or "passional" nature must determine what to believe when reason alone doesn't dictate an answer, and that the passional nature generally comes into play in figuring out how to interpret evidence (see James 1896). It also supports an insight of Søren Kierkegaard's pseudonymous Johannes Climacus that reason alone cannot produce faith; instead, faith requires an act of will (see Kierkegaard 1846). Roughly, Climacus argues that one can never get to religious faith by engaging in objective inquiry because religious faith requires total commitment to particular historical claims. Objective inquiry can never yield certainty in these matters: it always leaves room for doubt. On Robert Adam's interpretation of Kierkegaard, total commitment to a belief requires a commitment not to revise it in the future (see Adams 1976). Thus, it requires setting $p(X) = 1$ and interpreting any new evidence in light of this.

However, despite its attractiveness, this view is incorrect because it is vulnerable to similar phenomenological and ethical objections to the ones discussed above. Adams himself raises the ethical objection: "It has commonly been thought to be an important part of religious ethics that one ought to be humble, teachable, open to correction, new inspiration, and growth of insight, even (and perhaps especially) in important religious beliefs" (Adams 1976: 233). We might add that the ethics involved in friendship similarly do not seem to require that we remain determined not to abandon our belief in a friend's trustworthiness come what may.

The phenomenological objection can be brought out by considering that anyone who is acting on faith typically feels like she is taking a risk of some sort. The act A that you are performing on faith (that X) is supposed to be better than some alternative if X holds and worse than that alternative if X does not hold. But if one is certain that X holds, then doing A is not a risk at all. On the contrary, A is simply an act that, from your point of view, will undoubtedly turn out well. It is like the act of taking a bet on which you win $100 if water is H_2O and lose $100 if it is not. One might reply that from an objective standpoint, doing A is a risk—because setting one's initial credences is risky in some sense. But even if that is the case, the view still fails to explain the phenomenology of acts of faith, since they feel risky even from an internal perspective. What is distinctive about taking a leap of faith, so to speak, is that you are fully aware that it might turn out badly—even if you think that it is unlikely that it will.

An additional objection to this third analysis is that it cannot distinguish between cases of well-placed faith and cases of misplaced faith. Recall the above example of the person who knows that her friend has spilled all of her secrets so far but who has faith that he will not spill future secrets. We likely regard this as a case of misplaced faith. At any rate, when we compare this person to the person whose friend has never spilled a secret and who has faith that he will not spill future secrets, we think that this second person's faith has a lot more in its favour. But we cannot make sense of this on the present view, since rationality has no conclusions about which initial credences are laudable and since faith enters the picture before any evidence is interpreted.

So, although this third analysis was initially promising, it does not ultimately succeed. On my view, whether someone has faith is not determinable from the credences he brings to the table before examining evidence: a person who starts out sceptical, but who then amasses evidence in favour of X, could indeed end up choosing to have faith that X (consider the conversion of St Paul). Furthermore, a person who begins by assuming that X must be true doesn't thereby count as having faith that X: credulity and faith come apart. So do credence and faith, as we will see in the next section.

IV. FAITH AND EXAMINING FURTHER EVIDENCE

There is something to Kierkegaard's idea that one can never arrive at faith by engaging in empirical inquiry—that faith instead requires an act of will. However, this is not because faith requires a kind of certainty that empirical inquiry cannot provide, nor because faith must precede inquiry. Instead, it is because engaging in an inquiry itself *constitutes* a lack of faith. That is, faith requires not engaging in an inquiry whose only purpose is to figure out the truth of the proposition one purportedly has faith in. So the sense in which faith in X requires some response to the evidence aside from that normally warranted by epistemic norms is that it requires a decision to stop searching for additional evidence and to perform the act one would perform on the supposition that X.

Consider an example. If a man has faith that his spouse isn't cheating, this seems to rule out his hiring a private investigator, opening her mail, or even striking up a conversation with her boss to check that she really was working late last night—that is, it rules out conducting an inquiry to verify that his spouse isn't cheating. If he does any of these things, then she can rightfully complain that he didn't have faith in her, *even if* she realizes that, given his evidence, he should not assign degree of belief 1 to her constancy. Similarly, if I have faith that my friend will keep a secret, this seems to rule out asking a third party whether he thinks that friend is trustworthy. To use a religious example, when so-called "doubting" Thomas asks to put his hand in Jesus' side to verify that he has been resurrected in the flesh, this is supposed to indicate that he lacks faith.

We can say something even stronger: faith seems to require not looking for further evidence even if one knows that the evidence is *readily available*. For example, consider a case in which a man simply stumbles across an envelope which he knows contains evidence that will either vindicate his wife's constancy or suggest that she has been cheating. He seems to display a lack of faith in her constancy if he opens it and to display faith in her constancy if he does not. And this seems true even if the evidence has been acquired in a scrupulous way: we might imagine the wife herself presents the envelope to the man, as a test of his faith.[7]

So we now have the following first pass at a full analysis of faith:

> A person has faith that X, expressed by A, if and only if that person performs act A, and performing A constitutes taking a risk on X; *and the person refrains from gathering further evidence to determine the truth or falsity of X, or would refrain, if further evidence were available.*

This formulation has an unfortunate upshot, though: it implies that anyone who has faith that X, expressed by some act A, must decline evidence in the matter of X even if he wants the evidence for purposes other than deciding between the available acts. For example, consider the Christian apologist who has faith that Jesus was resurrected (expressed by, say, the action of going to church every week) but who combs through the historical evidence surrounding Jesus' resurrection in the hopes of finding evidence to convince someone who does not believe. Or consider the person who intends to open the private investigator's envelope publicly precisely to show that he has faith in his spouse's constancy.[8] On the current analysis, neither of these acts can be acts of faith: indeed, performing them entails that the agent does not have faith in the proposition in question.

The reason that we would say that the apologist has faith in the resurrection even though he continues to look for evidence is that he doesn't consider his decision to attend church dependent on the outcome of his investigation. Indeed, if he had no desire to convince other people, he would not look for evidence. Similarly, the reason we know that the husband has faith in his spouse, expressed by, say, the action of remaining constant himself, is that his constancy doesn't depend on the contents of the envelope, even though it does depend on his (current) beliefs about whether his spouse is cheating. So what these examples show is that the claim that the faithful person does not look for evidence at all is too strong. Instead, the faithful person does not look for evidence *for the purposes of deciding whether to do A.* Thus, if he does look for evidence, he considers this search irrelevant to his decision to do A.

A precise way to spell out that the act doesn't depend on the evidence is that the faithful agent is willing to commit to A before viewing any additional evidence in the matter of X; indeed, he wants to commit to A. In preference terms, he prefers to commit to A before viewing any additional evidence rather than to first view additional evidence and then decide whether to do A. This covers both the case of the person who looks for no additional evidence and the person who does look for evidence, but not in order to decide whether to do A.

We can now formulate my final analysis:

A person has faith that X, expressed by A, if and only if that person performs act A, and performing A constitutes taking a risk on X; and the person prefers {to commit to A before he examines additional evidence} rather than {to postpone his decision about A until he examines additional evidence}.[9]

As mentioned above, my analysis vindicates part of Kierkegaard's insight that faith does require total commitment, and that looking for evidence reveals that one is not totally committed. But what one must commit to is an *act*, not a belief: specifically, one must commit to performing an act regardless of what the evidence reveals. My analysis also vindicates the idea that faith requires an act of will—on my account one consciously chooses not to look for more evidence (even though doing so might be tempting!)—which is difficult to explain if faith requires a certain degree of belief and belief is not directly under one's volitional control.

One upshot of my analysis is that it is possible for two people to have the same evidence, have the same probability function, value the possible outcomes in the same way, and perform the same

act, and yet one of these acts displays faith while the other doesn't. So, for example, assume Ann and Erin have the same evidence about Dan's secret-keeping ability; that both have p(Dan will keep a secret) = 0.9; and that both have the same utility functions (that is, the stakes are the same for both of them). Now assume that each has a choice whether to ask a third party what he thinks about Dan's secret-keeping ability before deciding whether to tell Dan her secret. Ann decides to simply tell her secret; Erin decides to ask the third party, and then ends up telling her secret to Dan on the advice of this third party. Here, Ann displays faith that Dan will keep a secret (expressed by the act of revealing her own secret), whereas Erin does not display faith, even though she also performs this act. So the same act in the same circumstances can be done with or without faith.

The argument so far has told us nothing about the circumstances, if indeed there are any, in which faith can be rational. I now turn to this question. First I briefly explain the distinction between epistemic rationality and practical rationality, beginning with the former.

V. EPISTEMIC AND PRACTICAL RATIONALITY

I will assume a broadly evidentialist conception of epistemic rationality: one should proportion one's beliefs to one's evidence. One should not, for example, simply believe what one likes or believe what would make one happy. More generally, one should not take non-truth-conducive reasons as reasons for belief. I will also make some fairly standard assumptions about degrees of belief: degrees of belief obey the probability calculus; one updates one's beliefs by conditionalizing on new evidence; and two people can (rationally) have different degrees of belief in a proposition if and only if they have different evidence that bears on that proposition, or they believe the same evidence bears on that proposition differently, or they have different initial degrees of belief. An important upshot of these assumptions is that a rational person can only change his degrees of belief in response to evidence—and, in fact, *must* update them in response to new evidence, at least in matters he cares enough about to form beliefs.

Epistemic rationality concerns believing what the evidence suggests. Practical rationality, on the other hand, concerns selecting the means to achieve one's ends.

An informal way to characterize practical rationality is that it consists in taking the means to one's ends. And just as philosophers use a formal theory (probability theory) to characterize epistemic rationality more precisely, so too do they use a formal theory to characterize instrumental rationality more precisely: decision theory. Recall the earlier point that an action is essentially a gamble in which the state of the world determines which outcome you get. We already know that we can represent the likelihood you assign to various states—and thus the likelihood that an act will lead to each particular outcome—by a degree of belief function. According to decision theory, we can also represent how much you value particular outcomes by a "utility" function.[10] On the standard view, subjective expected utility (EU) theory, rational agents maximize expected utility: they prefer the act with the highest mathematical expectation of utility, relative to their utility and credence functions. Here "mathematical expectation" just means a weighted average: the value of each outcome is weighted by the likelihood of getting that outcome, and the resultant values are summed. So, for example, if p(RAIN) = 0.6 and p(NOT-RAIN) = 0.4, and if u(getting wet) = −3 and u(staying dry) = 2, then EU(don't bring umbrella) = 0.6(−3) + 0.4(2) = −1. If EU(bring umbrella) = u(carrying around an umbrella) > −1, then a rational decision-maker will bring her umbrella.

In my view, EU theory is too restrictive. However, since this is the widely accepted view, and since I agree that expected utility maximizers *are* practically rational (I merely hold that there are other ways to be rational as well), I will postpone discussion of an alternative view to section IX.

Before turning to the question of whether faith can be rational, it is worth clearing up a worry: that the definitions of rationality that I've adopted might not be strong enough. On the present definition of epistemic rationality, one may adopt any degrees of belief, including any degrees of belief concerning the relationship between particular hypotheses and particular pieces of evidence, as long as one's degrees of belief cohere with *each other*. For example, a person may rationally believe he has been abducted by aliens, as long as he also believes that the evidence he has supports this to the degree that he believes it. A similar point holds about preferences in the case of practical rationality. Both epistemic rationality and practical rationality, as I define them here, are notions of *consistency*: the only restriction on degrees of belief is that they are consistent with one another, and the only restriction on preferences is that they are consistent with one another, given one's degrees of belief in each possible state of the world. However, there is another notion of rationality, which rules out believing one has been abducted by aliens and rules out certain preferences, which we might call *reasonableness*.

I cannot fully respond to this worry in depth here. But it is important that the consistency notion of rationality and the reasonableness notion come apart quite readily. Consistency restrictions are structural: they rule out particular patterns of belief or desire, regardless of the content of these attitudes. On the other hand, reasonableness restrictions are substantial: they rule out particular beliefs or desires, regardless of which other beliefs or desires one has. Therefore, we can talk about what they require separately, and this project is about the requirements of rationality in the consistency sense. Or, since this sense of rationality exhausts the subjective sense of rationality, this project addresses the question of whether it can ever be rational *given the agent's own attitudes* to have faith. If we want to answer the further question of whether it is reasonable to have faith—that is, of whether a person has objective reasons to have faith—we can address this separately. Indeed, nothing in my argument relies on the content of the propositions believed or desired. Hence the question of whether faith is reasonable can be answered by asking whether there are any contents for which it is reasonable to have the patterns of belief and desire presented in my examples.

Finally, I want to be clear that I am not assuming here that there are any benefits to believing false propositions, or to holding certain beliefs regardless of whether they are true. In my analysis, I assume that knowing the truth in the matter of X is always beneficial to the agent who is making a decision based on X: it allows her to choose the action that in fact turns out better for her.

VI. PRACTICAL RATIONALITY AND EVIDENCE-GATHERING

It should be clear that on the first two analyses of faith, considered in section III, above, faith is irrational. On the first analysis, which requires the agent's credences to be higher than those the evidence suggests, faith is epistemically irrational, and on the second analysis, which requires the agent to act as if his beliefs are different than they are (that is, to take something other than his credences as "what he believes" for the purposes of decision making), faith is practically irrational, however we spell out practical rationality. On the third analysis, faith is always rational, provided one has consistent credences and preferences (though one can't, for example, have faith in two contradictory propositions).

On my analysis faith can also be epistemically rational: that one has faith in X implies nothing about one's degrees of belief or the consistency thereof.[11] Therefore, one can clearly meet the requirements of epistemic rationality, as I've stated them, while having faith—whether one has faith is completely separate from whether one is epistemically rational because it is separate from whether one has appropriately evaluated the evidence one has.[12]

But can faith also be practically rational? Faith requires two actions: choosing A rather than the alternatives and not looking for further evidence for the purposes of this choice (or committing to A before seeing further evidence rather than seeing

further evidence before deciding). Therefore, faith can only be practically rational if both of these actions are practically rational. Assessing the rationality of the first action is fairly straightforward: choosing A rather than the alternatives is rational just in case A has a higher expected utility than the alternatives, given the agent's credences. So the first (fairly obvious) restriction on when faith is rational is this: one's credence in X must be sufficiently high as to make A the practically rational act.

What about the second action? Can it be rational to commit to A rather than seeing more evidence before deciding? To address this question, it will help to have a canonical example of the kinds of situations in which the question of faith arises. Again, these situations involve an agent performing an act A in a situation in which the status of some proposition X is in question, and in which there is an alternative B such that he prefers A to B on the supposition that X, and B to A on the supposition that $\sim X$. Let us simplify by assuming that A and B are the only two alternatives, and that B is such that its value does not depend on X, that is, the outcome of B is not affected by whether X holds.[13] To put some concrete utility values in place:

$$u(A\&X) = 10 \qquad u(B\&X) = 1$$
$$u(A\&\sim X) = 0 \quad u(B\&\sim X) = 1$$

We could generalize by assuming there is a high value, a middle value, and a low value such that $u(A\&X) = H$, $u(B\&X) = u(B\&\sim X) = M$, $u(A\&\sim X) = L$, and $H > M > L$. In other words: A performed when X holds yields the best outcome, A performed when $\sim X$ holds yields the worst outcome, and B performed either way yields an intermediate outcome.

Here are some examples of decisions that might include the relevant values. Consider an individual who is deciding whether to become a monk and does not have conclusive evidence that God exists. If God exists, then becoming a monk is very good—the individual will experience all the goods of the religious life. But if God does not exist, then becoming a monk will result in the agent living a life that is ultimately wasted. On the other hand, failing to become a monk is fine, but not great, either way, if we assume that from a religious point of view becoming a monk is supererogatory and that the individual lives roughly the same life as a non-monk whether or not God exists. To take another example, consider an individual who is deciding whether to use his van to transport 10 critically injured patients to the hospital rather than using his car to transport 1 and who does not have conclusive evidence that his van works (but he has, say, near-conclusive evidence that his car works, or a backup plan in case it doesn't). Or consider an individual who is deciding whether to reveal a secret to someone else, and who does not have conclusive evidence that the friend will keep it; or an individual who is deciding whether to marry a particular person, and does not have conclusive evidence that this person will make a good spouse. In each case, performing the act could turn out very well or poorly, whereas not performing the act is the same either way.[14] We could think of the act as an opportunity for something great—but a risky opportunity—that one might take or pass up.

Let us assume that given the individual's current credences and utility function, A has a higher expected utility than B, and so A is practically rational given the individual's current information. Now we want to know whether practical rationality requires that the individual gather more information before she makes her decision. There is a theorem that bears directly on this question: I. J. Good (1967) showed that gathering additional evidence (in Good's terminology, making a new observation) and then using it to update one's beliefs before making a decision always has a higher expected utility than making a decision without doing so, provided the following two conditions are met:

(1) It is not the case that the agent will perform the same act regardless of the evidence she receives.

(2) Gathering additional evidence is cost-free.

If condition (2) holds but, contrary to (1), the agent will perform the same act regardless of the evidence, then gathering the evidence will have the *same* expected utility as not doing so.[15] In other words, if these two conditions are met, and if rational individuals must choose the act that maximizes expected utility, then it is always rationally permissible to make a new observation and use it, and it is rationally *required* that one do so if some piece of evidence that might result from doing so will lead one to do B instead of A.

VII. COMMITMENT AND INTERPERSONAL COST

We can now consider under which circumstances, if any, one is rationally permitted, or rationally required, to have faith. In this section and the next I spell out when it is rational to refrain from examining additional evidence for the purposes of the choice at hand. I assume throughout that the other conditions for the rationality of faith have been met: that the agent's credences are coherent and are such that doing A rather than B maximizes expected utility. I also assume, as Good does, that for each "experiment" (or bit of searching) the agent is considering performing, the agent can assign credences to the experiment yielding each possible result, and can say how he ought to update his credences given each possible result. For example, if the individual from our above example is considering the "experiment" of turning on the weather channel to see whether the weatherman predicts rain, he may assign credence 0.65 to the weatherman predicting rain and credence 0.35 to the weatherman predicting no rain; and he may think that if the weatherman does predict rain, he ought to raise his credence in the hypothesis that it will rain to 0.9, and if the weatherman does not predict rain, he ought to lower his credence to 0.05.[16] Furthermore, I assume that after seeing the results of the experiment, the individual will update his credence in RAIN and NOT-RAIN accordingly and choose the action that maximizes expected utility given his updated credences.

As we saw in the previous section, one case in which it would be rationally permissible not to examine additional evidence is the case in which the agent will do the same thing no matter which result obtains. According to expected utility theory, doing so will be rational just in case no matter what the results of the experiment, A still maximizes expected utility given his updated credences. In less technical terms, this will hold when none of the observations the individual is considering would tell against X conclusively enough to make him perform B instead of A.

However, in these cases the agent will never *strictly* prefer not examining the evidence; instead, he will be indifferent to whether he examines the evidence or not (provided, again, that doing so is cost-free). So if we think that faith requires a strict preference against examining additional evidence—and I myself am not sure which stance to take—then pointing to situations in which the agent will do the same regardless of the evidence will not help us.

We can measure the value of an experiment by considering the difference between the expected utility of {performing the experiment and then choosing an act} and the expected utility of {choosing an act without further evidence}. If the former number minus the latter number is positive, rationality requires one to perform the experiment, and if it is negative, rationality requires one not to perform the experiment (if this number is 0, the agent will be neutral about performing the experiment, as in the case just discussed). We can examine which factors contribute positively to this value and which contribute negatively: these will roughly be the pros and cons associated with performing the experiment, and so we can precisely characterize in what situations the cons outweigh the pros. The most important positive factor is associated with the possibility that ~X holds and the evidence one gets leads one to do B instead of A. (For example, the third party says your friend is a gossip and so you don't tell her your secret, and your friend is in fact a gossip—you have benefitted by getting a payoff of 1 rather than 0, because you have refrained from telling your secret, rather than told

your secret and have it revealed.) Another positive factor is associated with the possibility that X holds and the evidence one gets makes one more certain that A is the right choice. (For example, the third party confirms that your friend is not a gossip, and your friend is in fact not a gossip.) However, this factor will make less of an overall difference in most of the situations we are considering, since if one's credence in X is already high, additional confirmation will not make a substantial difference.

There are also factors which negatively impact the value of an experiment. As Good notes, it can be rational to eschew additional evidence if that evidence is costly. If the experiment has some monetary or cognitive cost that is measurable in utility and that does not depend on which action the agent chooses, the result of the experiment, or the state of the world, then the cost remains the same under all eventualities, and it is a simple matter to calculate it.

However, the costs of gathering evidence needn't be monetary or cognitive. Indeed, there are two types of (non-monetary) costs that seem particularly relevant to situations involving faith: interpersonal costs and the costs of postponing a decision. We need to examine each of these, to see whether and when they can make faith rational.

The first kind of cost comes up primarily in contexts in which one has faith in another person. In these cases, lacking faith might in itself cause harm to the relationship. For example, one's spouse or friend might be upset if one doesn't have faith in her, or one might miss out on certain goods that mutual faith is a prerequisite for (a feeling of connection or security, perhaps). In the religious case, it might be that one's relationship with God will be lacking if one does not have faith and will be lacking *for that fact*. We might think of these costs as intrinsic costs to lacking faith.

Before concluding that these costs can play a role in rationalizing faith, though, we should consider *why* it should be upsetting to someone that another person lacks faith in them. I suspect that the most common reason is that a lack of faith *indicates* that the agent is not as he ought to be with respect to his beliefs and desires regarding the other person, for example, a husband assigns low credence to the possibility that his wife is constant even though she's given him evidence through her actions and character that should be sufficient for a high credence, or he assigns a low utility to continuing the marriage with her. But these aren't complaints against the husband's lack of faith per se. In one case, it is a complaint that he is being irrational in a particularly hurtful way. In the other, it is a complaint that he has the wrong values given their relationship. So there is no "additional" cost to lacking faith, beyond the costs of these actions.

I tentatively conclude that the intrinsic cost of lacking faith *might* be a way in which evidence could be costly for a rational agent, but that this position would need to be further supported.

VIII. THE COSTS OF POSTPONEMENT

The second kind of cost that might be associated with gathering evidence is the cost of postponing the decision. In the most extreme case, looking for further evidence amounts to losing the option of doing A. For example, it might be that one's friend is only available to listen to one's secret today, so if one does not reveal it, one will lose that option forever. Or it might be that one is deciding whether to get married and one's potential spouse has given one an ultimatum. Or it might be that one needs to choose a vehicle to drive critically injured patients to the hospital, and any delay will result in their certain death. In these cases, the overall value of gathering further evidence will be negative: it will be the difference between the expected value (on one's current credences) of doing A and that of doing B, since deciding to gather further evidence is equivalent to deciding to do B.[17]

In a less extreme version, A might be an action that provides more good to the decision-maker the earlier he chooses it (in the event that X holds), so the utility of choosing A tomorrow might be slightly lower than the utility of choosing A today. If we imagine that the agent always prefers a day of marriage with a faithful spouse to a day of bachelorhood, or that in the event that God does exist, the agent prefers a day spent as a monk to a day spent as an ordinary citizen, then each day of postponing the decision is costly.

For decisions where postponement is costly but does not prevent the agent from eventually choosing A, under what conditions do these costs outweigh the benefit of gathering additional evidence? To answer this question, let us assume that the only cost associated with postponing the decision occurs in the event that one eventually does A and that X obtains. Then let us fix the cost of postponing the decision while one does a particular experiment as c: specifically, c is the difference between doing A when X obtains without gathering more evidence (or while committing to A regardless of the evidence) and doing A when X obtains after gathering more evidence.

We can now say something about when the value of performing the experiment is apt to be negative. It will be lower when c is higher; that is, when the costs of doing the experiment in the circumstances in which it is costly are higher. It will also be lower when M (the value of the "middling" act B) is lower, and H and L (the value of A if X obtains and if ∼X obtains, respectively) are higher; that is, when there is less of a risk involved in doing A. Next, it will be lower to the extent that one of the following situations is likely to result (that is, to the extent that these situations are probable, given the evidence). Both situations are situations in which X in fact holds. The first is when X in fact holds and the experiment yields some result that will make it rational for the individual to do A. In this situation, performing the experiment hurt the individual because he paid a cost c that he otherwise would not have paid. (For example, the third party says your friend is trustworthy and so you stick with your original plan of sharing your secret, but you incur the cost of the time it took to listen to the third party—perhaps by the time you ask the third party, the friend is no longer available today.)

The second situation is when X in fact holds but the experiment yields some result that makes it no longer rational for the individual to do A. This is a situation in which the evidence is "misleading" in the sense that it leads to the rational performance of an action that in fact has a lower payoff than its alternative. (For example, the third party says your friend is a gossip, and so you don't reveal your secret, but your friend is in fact trustworthy—here you get a payoff of 1 rather than 10, because you have refrained from telling your secret rather than telling it to a trustworthy friend.)[18] Both of these situations are more likely the higher the credence one already assigns to X. The second of these situations is more likely to the extent that evidence against X is *non-conclusive*: to the extent that it will lower one's credence enough to make it rational to do B instead of A, but not enough to *guarantee* that B is in fact the better choice.

The overall expected utility of gathering evidence depends on how likely each of the "beneficial" situations is (the situation in which you get evidence that steers you away from your original choice when that would have in fact been the wrong choice, and, to a lesser extent, the situation in which you get evidence that confirms your original choice when that is in fact the right choice) as compared to how likely each of the "detrimental" situations is (the situation in which you get evidence that doesn't alter your choice but is costly, and the situation in which you get misleading evidence that steers you away from what would have in fact been the right choice). Holding fixed H, M, and L, in situations in which gathering the evidence proves costly in the event that X obtains and the agent does A, refraining from gathering further evidence is more likely to be rationally required (1) when this cost is high; (2) when one already has a high credence in X; or (3) when the experiment is likely to result in *misleading* evidence against X, that is, evidence that makes one "miss out" on the possibility of doing A when X in fact holds. This third possibility holds to the extent that the potential evidence that could tell against X does not tell conclusively against X.

The fact that costs associated with postponing a decision can make faith rational vindicates an observation made by William James, though he did not express it in these terms. James argued that when a decision about what to believe is momentous—in that it involves a once-in-a-lifetime opportunity, for example—then it must be made by the will, and that postponing the decision is a decision in itself. He used this observation to argue that it is rationally permissible to choose to believe in God even when one does not have conclusive evidence for God's existence. I don't think that it is rationally permissible to *believe* that God exists when one does not have conclusive evidence, if this means setting one's credences differently from what one has evidence for (though I'm not saying that this is what James is suggesting). However, I do think that it is sometimes rationally permissible (and indeed, sometimes rationally required!) to *have faith* in God—as evidenced by doing some particular religious act without looking for further evidence—in circumstances in which postponing the decision to act is costly, provided one has the appropriate credences, and provided these are the correct credences to have given one's evidence.

The upshot of this discussion is that, if we accept expected utility theory as the correct theory of practical rationality, then faith can be rational—depending, of course, on one's credences and the situation in which one finds oneself. We have seen three important results in this regard. First, if we think that faith requires only a weak preference for not gathering additional evidence—that is, if you count as having faith when you are indifferent between making the decision on current evidence and postponing the decision—then faith is rationally permissible, but not rationally required, in cases in which no piece of evidence that one could potentially gather would alter the agent's decision about what to do. This will hold when no piece of evidence will tell conclusively enough against X such that doing A will no longer maximize expected utility. However, if we think that faith requires a strict preference for no additional evidence—that is, you must strictly prefer making the decision on current evidence—then faith will not be rationally permissible in these circumstances.[19]

Second, faith (under both the strict and weak reading of preference) will be rationally required in circumstances in which there is an interpersonal cost to looking for more evidence; that is, in which lacking faith is intrinsically worse than having faith. However, it is unclear whether such circumstances obtain. In my opinion, the right explanation for the fact that there are relational goods one can't get unless one has faith isn't that faith is in itself valuable, but rather that there are some goods that one can't get if one is more suspicious of another person than the evidence warrants, or if one hesitates to act on a matter involving the relationship.

Third, and most crucially, faith (under both readings) is rationally required in circumstances in which the costs of delaying the decision are high enough to outweigh the benefit of additional evidence. Holding fixed the costs of delay, whether these costs outweigh the benefits depends both on one's credence in the proposition one has faith in and on the character of the potential evidence one might encounter: in particular, faith is more apt to be rational if potential evidence against X will be inconclusive.

IX. RISK AVERSION AND THE POSSIBILITY OF MISLEADING EVIDENCE

There are two reasons to think that our results so far are incomplete. First, one might think that faith requires more than a choice not to gather additional evidence—or more than a choice to commit to an action before the evidence comes in. It requires a choice to not gather additional evidence *even when this evidence is cost-free.* For example, we may think that the person who examines the private investigator's envelope even when there are no "postponement costs" lacks faith. Second, one might think that expected utility maximization is too strong a criterion of rationality, and that one can be practically rational without being an expected utility maximizer.

While I am sympathetic to the general aim of decision theory, and hold that expected utility theory is largely correct in its analysis of practical rationality, I nonetheless think that expected utility theory employs too narrow a criterion of rationality and should therefore be modified.[20] In my view, expected utility theory dictates a too-narrow way in which risk-considerations can play a role in an individual's choices. It dictates that rational individuals cannot, for example, care proportionally more about what happens in the worst-case scenario than the best, or vice versa. But most people do pay special attention to these features of their decisions. Moreover, rather than being an example of human irrationality, I think this tendency can be rational.

Above, I explained that decision theory formalizes means-ends reasoning: utility corresponds to how much an individual values particular outcomes, while credence corresponds to the likelihood with which the individual thinks some particular act will realize one of these outcomes. But even once we know an individual's credence and utility function, there is an additional question of how to move from considerations about how a choice will turn out under various circumstances to an overall evaluation of that choice. For example, how should one trade off a small chance of something great against a high chance of something fairly good? We need to know the relative priority the individual places on the worst-case and best-case scenario (and all the scenarios in between). We might think of this additional factor, the individual's risk-attitude, as corresponding to how he structures the potential realization of some of his aims. What is at issue here is, roughly speaking, the following: when an individual is making a single decision, ought he to care only about how a decision would turn out on average if it were to be repeated, or can he place some weight on "global" features of a decision like how spread out the utility values are?[21] In an earlier paper, I demonstrated that individuals who care proportionally more about what happens in the worse-case scenario will sometimes rationally reject cost-free evidence (see Buchak 2010). In particular, in scenarios like those outlined in the previous section, it will be rationally required for these individuals to commit to an action A before looking at additional evidence rather than to look at additional evidence and then decide. This will be the case in situations with the following properties, familiar from the previous section: (1) the individual already has a high credence in X (that is, $p(X)$ is antecedently high); and (2) the experiment is likely to result in *misleading* evidence against X (again, evidence that makes him "miss out" on the possibility of doing A when X in fact holds) because potential evidence that tells against X will not be conclusive. This is the case because if an individual already has a high credence that X, more evidence in favour of X won't be very helpful; and while evidence against X could be helpful if $\sim X$ holds, it will be harmful if X holds—and to the extent that evidence against X is inconclusive these two situations will be closer in likelihood.

In short, agents who care about global features of decisions are concerned with a particular risk involved in looking for additional evidence: the risk of coming across evidence that makes it rational to refrain from doing A even though X in fact holds. In other words, they are concerned, and rationally so, about the risk of getting evidence that is misleading. I already mentioned that the possibility of misleading evidence will make it rational for the EU maximizer to reject costly evidence. However, on the more permissive decision theory, the risk of misleading evidence makes faith rational even in cases in which there is no cost to looking for evidence. If one accepts the more permissive decision theory, then faith is rational in more cases than it is on standard decision theory, and precisely in cases in which the risks of getting misleading evidence outweigh the benefits of getting non-misleading evidence.

X. CONCLUSION

We have seen that whether faith that X, expressed by A, is rational depends on two important factors: (1) whether one has a high enough (rational) credence in X, and (2) the character of the available evidence. Specifically, faith in X is rational only if the available evidence is such that no potential piece of evidence would tell conclusively enough against X.

There are two interesting practical upshots of this conclusion. First, notice that in a standard class of cases, when one has a high degree of belief in a proposition, the odds of any particular experiment being such that it could drastically lower one's degree of belief decreases the larger the collection of evidence the agent already has.[22] So, in a rough-and-ready way, we might say that faith that X (expressed by some particular act A) is practically rational to the extent that the individual's degree of belief in X is already based on a large body of evidence. Second, whether faith is rational depends on the kind of situation we find ourselves in. Faith will be rational to the extent that potential counterevidence wouldn't be very conclusive with respect to the position in question, or to the extent that our decisions usually do have postponement costs. We won't be able to vindicate the claim that faith is rational regardless of the circumstances. But we can explain why having faith is rational in certain circumstances, perhaps circumstances some of us find ourselves in some of the time. Individuals who lack faith because they insist on gathering all of the available evidence before making a decision stand to miss out on opportunities that could greatly benefit them.

WORKS CITED

Adams, R. (1976) "Kierkegaard's Arguments against Objective Reasoning in Religion," *The Monist*, 60, 2: 228–243.

Buchak, L. (2010) "Instrumental Rationality, Epistemic Rationality, and Evidence-gathering," *Philosophical Perspectives*, 24, 1: 85–120.

Buchak, L. (2012) "Can it be Rational to Have Faith?", Chapter 12 of *Probability in the Philosophy of Religion*, Oxford University Press, 225–247.

Buchak, L. (2013) *Risk and Rationality*, Oxford University Press.

Dreier, J. (1996) "Rational Preference: Decision Theory as a Theory of Practical Rationality" *Theory and Decision*, 40: 249–276.

Good, I. J. (1967) "On the Principle of Total Evidence," *British Journal for the Philosophy of Science*, 17, 4: 319–321.

James, W. (1896) *The Will to Believe: And other Essays in Popular Philosophy*. London: Longmans, Green & Co.

Joyce, J. (2005) "How Probabilities Reflect Evidence," *Philosophical Perspectives*, 19: 153–178.

Kierkegaard, S. (1846) *Concluding Unscientific Postscript*. Translated by D. F. Swenson. Princeton, N.J.: Princeton University Press, 1941.

Rothschild, M. and J. Stiglitz (1970) "Increasing Risk: I. A Definition," *Journal of Economic Theory* 2, 3: 225–243.

NOTES

1. I speak of acquiescing to a proposition rather than believing it because I am not sure that if I have faith in something, I thereby believe it. While it sounds infelicitous to say "I believe that ∼X but I have faith that X," there may not be anything wrong with saying "I don't know whether X—I have no idea whether I believe that X or not—but I have faith that X." So as not to prejudge that issue, I make a weaker claim: that having faith involves taking the proposition to be true, that is, "going along with it," but not necessarily adopting an attitude we might describe as belief.

2. Although the following worry arises from the possibility of over-determination. I might have faith in my friend, and therefore have faith that my friend hasn't transformed me into a brain in a vat for his own merriment (this example is due to an anonymous referee), and yet I might be antecedently certain that I'm not a brain in a vat (on the basis of philosophical arguments, perhaps). Or I might have complete faith in a friend's testimony, and thus have faith in anything he says; however, it might be that he sometimes says things of which I am already certain. What should we say in these cases? One possible response is to say that a friend's testimony simply can't produce faith in propositions of which I am already certain. After all, we may think it sounds strange to say *I am independently convinced that I can't be a brain in a vat, and I also have faith that you haven't envatted me.* Another possibility is to claim that these statements, to the extent that we can imagine circumstances in

which they could be uttered felicitously, are really modal in character: the actor is claiming that if she wasn't independently convinced that she wasn't a brain in a vat, she would have faith that you haven't envatted her.

3. Notice that the judgment must be positive from the point of view of the agent, in the sense that the agent has a preference for A on the supposition that X, otherwise the account would be subject to the following counterexample: we think that if a person prefers that his friend refrain from smoking, even though he thinks his friend is inclined to smoke, he can't appropriately be said to have faith that she will smoke.

4. In some of the analyses under review here the act does not figure into the proposal. Therefore, for readability, I will say "faith that X" or "faith in X" when I really mean "faith that X expressed by A, for some particular A."

5. Perhaps the defender of the second analysis could claim that his view doesn't entail an affirmative answer because betting itself, when the payoffs are so frivolous, has an inherent disutility. But it is not clear that he can respond in this way to the case in which the "payoffs" are goods of real value, e.g., in the gamble that results in a million lives lost if God doesn't exist and one life improved mildly if God does exist.

6. Technically, one could avoid having complete faith in anything, since one could avoid setting p(X) = 1 for all X. However, if we think that degrees of faith

correspond to setting lower initial credences, then one would have some degree of faith in many things.

7. Indeed, my account can easily explain why presenting him with the envelope could be a test of faith: it is a test to see whether he will choose to acquire further evidence.

8. Thanks to Sherrilyn Roush for this example.

9. I formulate this condition in terms of preference because the theory of practical rationality that forms the basis of the discussion in the rest of this paper concerns preferences rather than choices. I note, however, that if the reader finds it more natural to formulate this condition in terms of a disposition to choose to commit to A, rather than formulating it in terms of a preference to commit to A, that is acceptable. (In any case, preference is strongly linked to a disposition to choose.)

10. On the debate between realism and functionalism about the utility function, see J. Dreier (1996).

11. Technically, it implies that $p(X) \neq 1$, but if $p(X) = 1$ then X is not an appropriate object of faith, so this is not a restriction on one's credences, but on what can count as an object of faith.

12. Even if epistemic rationality requires that one look for further evidence, it will not conflict with faith on my definition, since having faith doesn't forbid one from looking for evidence; it only dictates that one must commit to an act before seeing more evidence to postponing the decision.

13. We can represent this by stating that the individual is indifferent between $B\&X$ and $B\&\sim X$. What if X is something that the agent strongly prefers to be true, so that $A\&X$ and $B\&X$ both have a high utility? One might think, for example, that faith in God is typically like this, since the agent often prefers worlds in which God exists to worlds in which God does not exist, regardless of the agent's choices. As it turns out, the assumption that the agent is indifferent between $B\&X$ and $B\&\sim X$ is not crucial to the results discussed here: see Buchak (2012) for details.

14. One might argue that the act couldn't be the same either way, since, e.g., passing up the possibility of a faithful spouse (or an opportunity to save 10 lives) is worse than passing up the possibility of an unfaithful spouse (or an opportunity not to save any

lives). I think the question of how decision theory should handle these nuances is an interesting one, but for now, I will just assume that facts about what might have happened do not make a difference to the agent's utility function—or at least that they make a negligible difference.

15. For a further discussion of Good's setup and his result, see Buchak (2010) and Buchak (2012).

16. Note that these numbers need to satisfy the constraints that $p(\text{RAIN}) = p(\text{RAIN} | \text{PREDICT})p(\text{PREDICT}) + p(\text{RAIN} | \text{NOT-PREDICT})p(\text{NOT-PREDICT})$ and $p(\text{NOT-RAIN}) = p(\text{NOT-RAIN} | \text{PREDICT})p(\text{PREDICT}) + p(\text{NOT-RAIN} | \text{NOT-PREDICT})p(\text{NOT-PREDICT})$. The credences above do satisfy these constraints, with rounding.

17. Recall the supposition that one's credence before gathering evidence is high enough to make A the rational choice.

18. See Buchak (2012) for specific mathematical results.

19. Perhaps we could argue that faith is rational in these circumstances by stipulating that every experiment has some cost? However, when we consider that faith requires not just a (strict) preference for avoiding evidence in the matter of X when deciding whether to do A or B, but more precisely a (strict) preference for committing to a decision before seeing the evidence, we realize that we would have to stipulate that not committing before performing the experiment always has a cost, and this is less plausible.

20. See L. Buchak (2013).

21. I say "roughly speaking" because on certain interpretations of what utility amounts to, this will be a controversial way of putting things. But the exact formulation is not important to the point here, which is that there are some ways of evaluating gambles that expected utility theory cannot capture, that appear to stem from individuals caring proportionately more about certain possible outcomes of a gamble and less about others, and that (I argue elsewhere) are rational.

22. As James Joyce avers, it is "usually the case that the greater volume of data a person has for a hypothesis the more resilient her credence tends to be across a wide range of additional data" (2005: 161).

V.A.3

Propositional Faith: What It Is and What It Is Not

DANIEL HOWARD-SNYDER

A short biographical sketch of Daniel Howard-Snyder precedes selection III.C.3. In this article, Howard-Snyder aims to develop an account of propositional faith that contrasts with what he calls the "Common View," according to which faith requires belief. He concludes that having faith that p *(where* p *is a proposition, like the proposition* that God exists*) is consistent with taking attitudes toward* p *that fall short of belief and is, indeed, consistent with being to some extent in doubt about* p.

Super Bowl XLV. It's Super Bowl Sunday, 2011. Pittsburgh's down to Green Bay, 21–3; it's near the end of the second quarter. I'm taking in the game at my favorite dive, working on some nachos and a super-sized margarita. I'm a partisan of neither team. I just want to see a good game. The guy sitting next to me, however, is a loyal Pittsburgh fan, as indicated by the grim look on his face. The Packers have possession; they're moving steadily toward Steelers territory, again. During a break in the action, I strike up a conversation:

ME: I was hoping the game would be close. Oh well ... another Super Bowl blowout. I think I'll head home at halftime.

FAN: Be patient; be patient. The Steelers'll win.

ME: You can't be serious. No team has ever overcome more than a 9-point deficit to win a Super Bowl. And look at the Packer's position: Pittsburgh's 47 with a first down.

FAN: I *am* serious. I have faith that they'll win.

ME: What? You *believe* they're going to win?

FAN: No, I *don't* believe they'll win; I said I have *faith* that they will.

My topic is faith. More accurately, my topic is propositional faith. What is propositional faith? At a first approximation, we might answer that it is the psychological attitude picked out by standard uses of the English locution "S has faith that p," where p takes declarative sentences as instances, as in "He has faith that they'll win." Although correct, this answer is not nearly as informative as we might like. Many people say that there is a more informative answer. They say that, at the very least, propositional faith requires propositional belief. More precisely, they say that faith that p requires belief that p or that it must be partly constituted by belief that p. This view is common enough; call it *the Common View.*

I have two main aims in this paper: (i) to exhibit the falsity of the Common View and the paucity of reasons for it, and (ii) to sketch a more accurate and comprehensive account of what propositional faith is.

From *American Philosophical Quarterly.* Copyright 2013 by the Board of Trustees of the University of Illinois. Used with permission of the University of Illinois Press.

1. CLEARING THE BRUSH, SETTING THE STAGE

There are many things labeled "faith" that are clearly not propositional faith. To avoid error and to circumscribe my topic, I begin by clearing them away.

In *The Epistle of Jude*, the author exhorts readers to "earnestly contend for *the faith*," that is, the propositions constitutive of the basic Christian story and ethic.[1] Propositional faith is not those propositions, or any others. It is an attitude that has a proposition as its object, or a state of affairs. Occasionally, one hears that faith is a process. For example, according to Alvin Plantinga, "the term 'faith'... denote[s] the whole tripartite process" of coming to believe the gospel as a result of the Holy Spirit's instigating such belief upon encountering the gospel.[2] Propositional faith is not this process, or any other. Nor is it an adventure or journey, as when people sometimes speak of their "journey of faith." Like propositional fear and propositional hope, propositional faith is a propositional attitude.

Sometimes people speak of believing or taking something *on faith*. I believe on faith that Half-Mile's Pacific Crest Trail maps are accurate; Mark takes it on faith that devotion to Amitābha will result in enlightenment. That is, we believe or take these things on testimony or authority.[3] Propositional faith is not to be identified with believing or taking something on testimony or authority. Frances has faith that her pubescent sons will live long and fulfilling lives but she does not believe or take it on testimony or authority.

According to Martin Luther, faith is "confidence and *knowledge* of God's grace."[4] John Calvin concurs: faith is "a firm and sure *knowledge* of the divine favor toward us."[5] The *Catholic Encyclopedia* says faith is a "kind of *knowledge*."[6] Propositional faith, however, is not to be identified with knowledge. Hud can have faith that the President will lead us to victory without knowing she will. Knowledge is factive, propositional faith is not. (I leave it open whether faith is compatible with knowledge.)

According to Thomas Aquinas, says Eleonore Stump, faith is "assent [to a proposition] generated by the will's acting on the intellect," held "with certainty, without any hesitation or hanging back."[7] This is not propositional faith, for four reasons. First, if propositional faith is assent, then, since assent is a mental act and not even partly constituted by belief, propositional faith cannot be partly constituted by belief—but it can be. Second, if propositional faith is assent, then, since assent lasts about as long as a handshake, propositional faith is a fleeting affair—but it typically is not. Third, although propositional faith might have an act of will in its causal genesis, it need not. Fourth, propositional faith does not require "certainty, without any hesitation or hanging back." A wife might have faith that her marriage will survive a crisis while harboring doubts about it. Indeed, propositional faith is precisely that attitude in virtue of which she might possess the inner stability and impetus that enables her to contribute to the realization of that state of affairs, despite her lack of certainty. Moreover, her faith might well involve some "hesitation or hanging back." We must take care not to identify what we might regard as an ideal instance of propositional faith—say, one that exhibits "certainty, without any hesitation or hanging back"—with a real instance of it. The real need not be the ideal.

We sometimes say things of the form "S has faith in x," where x takes as instances the name of a person or some other entity. So said, faith *in* something is relative to some domains but not others. I have faith in my hiking sticks—as stabilizers, not bear deterrents. I have faith in my wife—as a friend, wife, and lover, not a horticulturalist. Some people say that propositional faith cannot be the attitude picked out by uses of "faith in x" since one can have faith *that* x is thus-and-so even if x does not exist, but one can no more have faith *in* x when x does not exist than one can jump in a lake when there are no lakes. Faith in x implies the existence of x; faith that x is thus-and-so does not.[8] I suspect these people are wrong. Just as faith-that is nonfactive, so faith-in lacks existential import. But even if they're right, we can still ask whether propositional faith is the attitude one would have if x existed and one had faith in x. Although, in that case, it might seem natural to identify faith in something, as thus-and-so, with faith that it is thus-and-so, faith *in* something requires more: entrusting one's welfare to it in some way. But one can have faith that something is thus-and-so without entrusting one's welfare to it in any way, as when I have faith that Emily will survive breast cancer but I do not entrust my well-being to her or her survival.

Propositional faith is not a proposition, state of affairs, process, or journey; it's an attitude, an attitude that is not to be identified with knowledge or assent; it need not be based on authority or testimony, and it need not involve certainty, eagerness, generation by an act of will, or entrusting one's welfare to someone. However, to say what something is not is not to say what it is. So our question remains: what is propositional faith? (Unless I indicate otherwise, I will hereafter use "faith" to mean propositional faith, faith *that*.)

To set the stage for assessing the Common View's answer, a word on belief and doubt are in order. What I have to say will be contentious and unconscionably brief.

Belief is something mental, specifically a mental state, not a mental occurrence like an act of mental assent or a process of deliberation. More specifically still, it is a dispositional state that manifests itself under certain conditions like those in the partial dispositional profile William Alston provides:

1. If S believes that p, then if someone asks S whether p, S will tend to respond affirmatively.

2. If S believes that p, then, if S considers whether it is the case that p, S will tend to feel it to be the case that p.

3. If S believes that p, then, if S takes q to follow from p, S will tend to believe q.

4. If S believes that p, then, if S engages in practical or theoretical reasoning, S will tend to use p as a premise when appropriate.

5. If S believes that p, then, if S learns that not-p, S will tend to be surprised.

6. If S believes that p, then, given S's goals, aversions, and other cognitive stances, S will tend to act in appropriate ways.[9]

Note that the consequent in each embedded conditional involves a tendency to a certain manifestation. That's because whether any such manifestation is forthcoming will depend on whether any psychological or other obstacles are present. Note also the term "feel" in (2). By it, Alston does *not* mean a sensation or emotion. Rather, he means to "convey the idea that [the manifestation in question] possesses a kind of *immediacy*, that it is something one *experiences* rather than something that one *thinks out*, that it is a matter of being *struck by* (a sense of) how things are rather than deciding how things are."[10] Others, he observes, call it "consciously [or occurrently] believing p."[11] Moreover, I cannot just by an act of will stop believing something I now believe, nor can I just by an act of will begin to believe something I do not now believe. Belief is not under our direct voluntary control. Finally, folk psychology is right: there really are beliefs. Of course, there is much to be said in favor of trading in belief for graded confidence or credence, as many Bayesians do. So it would be wise to put what I have to say in terms of both views. To do that, however, would complicate the discussion too much. Therefore, with apologies, I'll stick with the folk psychological characterization of the relevant terrain.

As for doubt, we must distinguish *having doubts* about whether p from *being in doubt* about whether p, and both of them from *doubting* that p. For one to *have doubts* about whether p—note the 's'—is for one to have what appear to one to be grounds to believe not-p and, as a result, for one to be at least somewhat inclined to disbelieve p. For one to be *in* doubt about whether p is for one neither to believe nor disbelieve p as a result of one's grounds for p seeming to be roughly on a par with one's grounds for not-p. One can have doubts without being in doubt, and one can be in doubt without having doubts. Having doubts and being in doubt are not to be identified with doubting that. If one *doubts* that something is so, one is at least strongly inclined to disbelieve it; having doubts and being in doubt lack that implication.

These remarks must suffice to indicate how I will be thinking of belief and doubt. I should add, though, that while some things I have to say in what follows depend on my characterizations of belief and doubt, others do not. Notably, the structure of faith on offer by the end of the essay, and the basic thrust of the rationale for it, might be wed to other characterizations of belief and doubt.

2. THE COMMON VIEW

According to the Common View, faith that p requires belief that p, or it must be partially constituted by belief that p. I suspect that the Common View is mistaken. Before I explain why, it will prove useful to understand why belief that p is not sufficient for faith that p. There are at least two reasons, both of which shed light on what faith it is.

First, one can believe something and not be *for* its truth, but one cannot have faith that something is so and not be for its truth. Alston illustrates the point well: "[if someone] is said to have faith that democracy will eventually be established everywhere, that implies . . . that [she] looks on this prospect with favor."[12] Robert Adams concurs: "[t]o have faith is always to be *for* that in which one has faith. It is perfectly consistent to say you believe that Bill Clinton will win but you are still planning to vote for George Bush; but a genuine Bush supporter could hardly have faith that Clinton will win."[13] And Robert Audi too: "if I do not have a favorable attitude toward something's happening, I cannot have faith that it will."[14] This is why we do not have faith that terrorism will occur frequently in the 21st century, although we believe it will. To be for the truth of a proposition minimally requires considering its truth to be good or desirable, and we do not consider the truth of that proposition to be good or worthy of desire.[15] (I'll have more to say about the being-for-it requirement later.)

Second, one can believe something even though one has no tendency at all to feel disappointment upon learning that it's not so, but one cannot have faith that something is so without at least some tendency to feel disappointment upon learning that it's not so. That's because one can have faith that something is so only if one cares that

it is so; and one can care that something is so only if one has some tendency to feel disappointment upon learning that it's not so.

One might object: you can care that p without having any tendency to feel disappointment upon learning not-p. The farmer cares that the drought will continue but she has no tendency to feel disappointment upon learning that it won't. In reply, we must distinguish caring *that* from caring *about*. One can care about whether p even though one has no tendency to feel disappointment upon learning it's not so, since caring about is compatible with negative valence toward its truth. Caring that p, however, requires positive valence toward its truth. So although the farmer cares *about* whether the drought will continue, she does not care *that* it will continue given her negative valence toward its continuing. If you find this distinction specious, substitute "one can care-with-positive-valence that p only if one has some tendency to feel disappointment upon learning that it's not so" for the premise and adjust the argument here and elsewhere when relevant.[16]

Belief is not sufficient for faith. One has faith that p only if one cares that p and one is for p's truth, at least in the sense that one considers p's truth to be good or desirable.

Of course, even if belief that p is insufficient for faith that p, it might nevertheless be necessary. This is the Common View. Four considerations jointly tell against it.

First, suppose we were talking about the sour economy and our retirement plans and I said, "I am in doubt about whether I'll recover my losses, but I still have faith that I will." Or suppose I confided in you, my friend, "I don't know what to believe, whether she'll stay with me or not, but I have faith that she'll stay." Or imagine that I disclosed to you in a heart-to-heart exchange, "I can't tell whether what I've got to go on favors the existence of God, but I have faith that God exists nonetheless." You wouldn't be perplexed, bewildered, or suspicious at all about what I said; at least you need not be. What I said wasn't weird, or infelicitous; there's nothing here that cries out for explanation. That's because, given the standard uses of "faith that" and "being in doubt about whether" in contemporary English, being in doubt about something *need not be* at odds with having faith that it is so. But in that case, our concept of propositional faith allows one to have faith that p without belief that p. For, unlike faith that p, belief that p *is* at odds with being in doubt about it, not least because if one is in doubt one will lack tendencies that one has if one believes, e.g. a tendency to assert p upon being asked whether p.[17]

Second, one can have faith that p but lack a tendency to be surprised upon learning it's not so; disappointment, yes, but not surprise. However, one cannot believe p while lacking a tendency to be surprised upon learning it's not so. Thus, one can have faith that p without belief that p.

Third, one can have faith that p even if one does not believe *p* but rather merely believes *p is likely*, or *p is twice as likely as not*, and so on. For example, Harvey might know that his colon cancer will get the best of him before the season's end; nevertheless, he might yet have faith that he will face death with grace and courage even if he only believes that he will probably succeed. In this respect, faith is like propositional hope and propositional fear: it allows probabilistic beliefs to stand in for the cognitive stance it requires.

A question naturally arises at this point: if faith that p does not require believing p, is it compatible with *dis*believing p? I think not. For if you disbelieve p, you will have tendencies to behavior, feeling, and so on that are at odds with faith that p. For example, if I disbelieve that my marriage will last, I'll tend to say it won't when asked, I'll tend to feel it to be the case that it won't when I consider the matter, I'll tend to use the proposition that it won't as a premise in my practical reasoning, and I'll tend to do things appropriate to its not lasting, e.g. withdraw from intimacy, look for another place to live, and the like.

The incongruity of faith and disbelief suggests that faith requires a more *positive* cognitive stance toward its object precisely because the dispositional profiles of negative stances like disbelief are incongruent with faith. This opens the door to stances distinct from belief to stand in for the positive

cognitive stance faith requires, provided that their dispositional profiles are congruent with faith. Are there any such stances?

One might think so; after all, notice the plethora of folk psychological terms for positive cognitive stances: "acceptance," "acknowledgement," "affirmation," "assent," "assumption," "belief," "confidence," "conviction," "credence," etc. Although it would be hasty to suppose that each term stands for a different stance, it would be equally hasty to suppose that every term stands for the same stance. Interestingly, many philosophers think some of them stand for different stances. For example, many think that belief differs from acceptance, although they disagree over the difference. This isn't the place to enter that dispute. Instead, I'll make my point on the assumption that there is a difference and that Alston's account of it is near enough true to serve my purpose.[18]

According to Alston, belief differs from acceptance in three ways. (i) Belief is a dispositional mental state while acceptance is a mental act. One finds oneself with a belief, whereas to accept p is "to adopt" or "take on" a positive attitude toward p. (ii) Belief is not under our direct voluntary control while acceptance is. (iii) The *act* of acceptance normally engenders a dispositional *state* much like belief, a state also labeled "acceptance," unfortunately. This state differs from belief. Recall Alston's partial dispositional profile of belief, items (1)–(6) on page 544 above. Contrasting belief and the state of acceptance with reference to that list, he writes:

> Belief will involve more confident, unhesitating manifestations of these sorts than acceptance will. But in the main, the story on these components—specifically (1), (3), (4), (5), and (6)—will be the same for acceptance. (In (3), substitute "tend to accept" for "tend to believe.") By far the largest difference is the absence of (2). The complex dispositional state engendered by accepting p will definitely *not* include a tendency to feel that p if the question of whether p arises.[19]

By way of illustration, Alston describes a field general who must dispose his forces for battle with information insufficient to believe any of several competing views about how he might best do so. What does he do? He adopts the view that seems most likely to succeed, takes a stand on its truth, and acts on that basis. In short, he accepts it, which engenders dispositions to appropriate troop dispersal, and the like.[20] Alston describes his stance on libertarian freedom similarly. He doesn't believe we have it; he takes objections much too seriously for that. Rather he adopts it, regards it as true, and draws inferences from it in his theoretical and practical reasoning.[21]

So, according to Alston, the state of acceptance differs from belief in two ways: its manifestations will tend to be less confident and more hesitating than those of belief and its dispositional profile lacks a tendency to feel that p if the question of whether p arises.

Despite these differences, the profile of the state of acceptance is congruent with faith since, first of all, one instance of faith can be weaker than another because it is less confident and more hesitating—weak faith is faith nonetheless. Secondly, any concern due to the lack of a tendency to feel that p comes from the thought that faith requires a disposition to take a stand on the truth of its object and only belief suffices for that. But one can be disposed to take a stand on the truth of a proposition in many ways, one of which is to have a tendency to assert it when asked whether it's so. One need not have in addition a tendency to feel that it's so. So, acceptance suffices for the positive cognitive stance faith requires.

We have, then, a fourth reason to think that the Common View is mistaken: acceptance is not belief, and it can stand in for the positive cognitive stance faith requires.

3. REASONS FOR THE COMMON VIEW

The difference between acceptance and belief also provides a basis for assessing reasons for the Common View.

In "Moral Faith," Robert Adams focuses on a sort of faith typified by faith that a terminally ill friend's life is still worth living. It is characteristic of such faith, he says, that one recognize "the possibility of error," that one "recognize that [one] could be tragically mistaken, mistaken in a way characteristic of false beliefs." He continues,

> We do give and entertain reasons for and against items of moral faith.... And the structure of giving and entertaining reasons for them is at least very similar to the structure of reasoning about other sorts of belief. In thinking about items of moral faith, one uses logic, one aims at consistency and at coherence with one's beliefs on other subjects, and one is responsive to one's sense of "plausibility," as we sometimes put it. All of that is grounds for classifying moral faith as a sort of belief.[22]

Reply. I don't see it. I don't see why "[a]ll of that is grounds for classifying moral faith as a sort of belief." Our acceptances can be in error or mistaken. Moreover, in thinking about what one has accepted, one can reflect on its plausibility, use logic, and aim for consistency and coherence with other items on which one takes a stance. But acceptance is not belief. Hence, Adams's basis for classifying faith as a sort of belief does not support that classification.

Here are four more reasons for the Common View found in the literature.[23]

1. If you have faith that p, you will tend to assert p when asked whether p (absent contravening influences). But you have that tendency only if you believe p. Thus, you have faith that p only if you believe p.

Reply: I will argue later that a certain mental state whose dispositional profile lacks a tendency to assert p can stand in for the positive cognitive stance required by faith. If I'm right, then one can have faith that p and yet have no such tendency. But even if I'm wrong, faith that p does not require belief that p. For one need not believe p in order to have a tendency to assert p. One might accept p instead.

2. If you have faith that p, then you are disposed to believe p; and, since a disposition to believe p *just is* believing p, you have faith that p only if you believe p.

Reply: First, suppose the first premise is right that faith that p implies a disposition to believe something. Why can't it be a mere disposition to believe that *p is likely*, or *twice as likely as not*, and the like? Second, the first premise is false: accepting p can stand in for the positive cognitive stance required by faith and, since you can accept p without believing p, you can have faith that p without being disposed to believe p. Third, the second premise is false: one can be disposed to believe p without believing p. For example, on some occasion I might be disposed to believe that I'm talking too loudly—imagine me talking excitedly with you about faith in a quiet cafe—but it does not follow that at that time I believe that I am talking too loudly. Indeed, if you brought it to my attention, I might say sheepishly, and truly, "Oops, sorry; I didn't realize I was blathering so loudly. Thanks for letting me know. I'll pipe down."[24]

One might insist that, even if faith that p in general does not imply believing p, religious faith does. The next two reasons take this tack. Although I am concerned with propositional faith *per se*, assessing these reasons will prove instructive.

3. If you have religious faith that p, then you are totally committed in a practical way to p's truth and to what you see follows from it—even to the point of making fundamental sacrifices. But you can't be totally committed in a practical way unless you believe p and what you see follows from it. Therefore, you have religious faith that p only if you believe p.

Reply: First, religious faith that p does not require a total practical commitment to p's truth. Maybe at its best it does, but it does not as such. We must not mistake what is required by an ideal instance of a kind for what is required by a real instance. Second, religious faith that p at its best might not require a total practical commitment to p's truth, at least in some situations. Suppose that Mark, a Buddhist, has some doubts about whether devotion to Amitābha will result in enlightenment, but he still has faith that it will. In that case, if he were to dig in his heels and believe it anyway, he'd exhibit intellectual vice, pigheadedness or close-mindedness perhaps. In the circumstances in which he finds himself, he would be an overall better person if he adopted some other cognitive stance that is more at home with his doubts and yet also at home with his faith, in which case a degree of practical commitment more consonant with that stance and doubts would be, all else being equal, more virtuous *for him in his particular situation*, a degree of practical commitment short of being "total."

4. Authentic religious faith involves a longing for God as the "all-dominating longing" of one's life, one's "master passion." Belief-less religious faith would involve no such thing. It would at best involve a "longing to know whether or not God exists." Religious faith that p, therefore, requires belief that p.

Reply: First, authentic religious faith need not involve a longing for God that constitutes one's master passion, one's all-dominating longing. Perhaps at its best it does, but it need not as such. Again: we must not mistake the ideal for the real. Second, a longing for God central to one's life can be wed to acceptance; as such, a faith without belief can involve a longing for God suitable to be one's master passion.

Another argument for the Common View goes like this. The Common View is aptly named. After all, people do commonly think that the psychological attitude they pick out when they say things of the form "S has faith that p" requires belief that p. Just ask them! Likewise, they commonly intend to pick out something that involves belief that p when they use such talk. Furthermore, a vast rule-governed way of using faith-that talk has grown up around this thought and intention, a way of speaking that spans centuries and cultures. In that case, the way in which people commonly use "faith that p" *must* pick out something that requires belief that p, if it picks out anything at all. Therefore, faith that p requires belief that p.[25]

Reply. Suppose that by "belief" the proponent of the argument means what I earlier said belief was: an involuntary mental state with a partial dispositional profile indicated by (1)–(6) on page 544 above. In that case, it is dubious whether people commonly think that faith requires belief. For, first of all, people do not commonly think that the attitude they pick out with "belief" is an involuntary mental state. Second, people do not commonly think that the attitude they pick out when they use faith-that talk has the dispositional profile indicated by (1)–(6). The profile of acceptance would be good enough.

But now suppose that by "belief" the proponent of the argument does not mean what I said belief was but rather what some scholarly account says it is.[26] In that case, the same premise would be false for the same reasons, given the appropriate changes. For on virtually every scholarly account, belief is involuntary; and on every scholarly account, belief has necessary features not commonly thought to be necessary for the attitude people intend to pick out with their faith-that talk.

Finally, suppose that by "belief" the proponent of the argument means what I expect most people commonly have in mind when they use the term, something they'd report as belief, assent, acceptance, judgment, affirmation, decision, assumption, confidence, credence, etc. for a long list of items that fall under the rubric of "positive cognitive stance." In that case, the conclusion of the argument is that faith that p requires a positive cognitive stance toward p. With this conclusion I am in complete agreement.

Despite the frequency with which one encounters the Common View, there is little to be said for it, so far as I can see.

4. FAITH AND DESIRE

One can have faith that something is so only if one is for it, at least in the sense that one considers its truth to be good or desirable. The being-for-it requirement of faith requires more, however.

For consider this. You have faith that p only if you consider p's truth to be good or desirable, but you cannot do that unless you want it to be the case that p; so you have faith that p only if you want it to be the case that p. To be sure, you might have conflicting desires; indeed, you might only want it a little bit. Nevertheless, unless you want p to be the case, you cannot have faith that p.

Many will deny the premise that you cannot consider p's truth to be good or desirable unless you want it to be the case that p. This is an ancient dispute, one that I will sidestep. For, even if you *can* consider p's truth to be good or desirable without wanting it to be the case that p, three other considerations remain for thinking that faith that p requires at least something in the neighborhood of desire for the truth of p.

First: one has faith that p only if one cares that p, but one cares that p only if one has some desire for p to be true. After all, if I have no desire that you finish your novel or that our friendship continues, I am indifferent to these things, I don't care that they are so. Therefore, one has faith that p only if one has some desire for p to be true.

We might resist. Imagine a meth addict who has no desire whatsoever *to stop* but who, upon coming to recognize how much better his life might be if he were to stop, *wants to* want to stop. In that case, if he's disposed to do something about changing his first-order desire and his behavior, say, by seeking therapy, then, even if he has so far failed, he is not indifferent to stopping, he cares at least somewhat that he stops.[27]

Notice that the first- and second-order desire cases share something in common: having a desire in virtue of which one cares that p. Might one have a desire in virtue of which one cares that p without having a first- or higher-order desire for p's truth? Maybe. Imagine a young mother battling a recurrence of breast cancer; she has no first- or higher-order desire to live due to the depression-inducing side-effects of the treatment. Nevertheless, she cares that she survives since she considers her survival desirable for the sake of her children and she longs for them to flourish. She wants what her detestable life can bring, their flourishing; but she has no desire to live, first- or higher-order. If this is possible, one can have faith that something is so while having no first- or higher-order desire for its truth. Nevertheless, one must have a desire in virtue of which one cares that it is so. This is what faith requires.

Here's a second argument. Like other complex propositional attitudes, e.g. fear and hope, faith motivates behavior. In the case of fear, this is indicated by the fact that all you need to know to understand why the hiker is beating the grass as she walks through the meadow is that she fears that rattlesnakes lie nearby. In the case of hope, it's indicated by the fact that all you need to know to understand why the climber is waving toward the sky is that he hopes that he'll catch the eye of the search-and-rescue pilot. Fear and hope have built into them what it takes to motivate behavior; that's why they explain it. The same goes for faith. All you need to know to understand why Yehuda continues to study Torah despite his doubts is that he has faith that the basic Jewish story is true. All you need to know to understand why a couple seeks marital counseling is that they have faith that they can work things out. Like fear and hope, faith motivates behavior; that's why it explains it. But cognition alone cannot motivate behavior; desire is required. Like propositional fear and hope, therefore, propositional faith has desire built into it.

Third: One can have faith that something is so only if one has a tendency to feel disappointment upon learning that it's false. But if one has a tendency to feel disappointment upon learning that it's false, then one cares that it's so. However, if one cares that it's so, one desires its truth, or at least has a desire in virtue of which one cares that it's so. So one can have faith that something is so only if one has a desire in virtue of which one cares that it's so.

If any of these considerations is on target, then, even if one can have faith that p without desire for the truth of p, one cannot have faith that p without a desire in virtue of which one cares that p. As we've just seen, different sorts of desires might satisfy that description; so let's gather them all under the rubric of a *positive conative orientation* and say that faith that p requires a positive conative orientation toward the truth of p.

5. FAITH AND DOUBT

Belief and acceptance are distinct; nevertheless, each can stand in for the positive cognitive stance faith requires. However, each is at odds with being in doubt; if one believes or accepts something, one will have tendencies that one will lack if one is in doubt about it, e.g. a tendency to assert it when asked whether it is so. Therefore, since faith need not be at odds with being in doubt, something else can stand in for the positive cognitive stance faith requires. What might it be?

To begin to see one answer to our question, consider the following three very short stories.

Northbound. It's May 6, 2010. I'm at the southern terminus of the Pacific Crest Trail, the Mexican border with California. After some goodbyes, I start to walk to Canada, 2,655 miles north. A lot can go wrong in 2,655 miles. Most nights, after two dozen up-and-down miles in the sun, I'm beat. Now, nearly four weeks and 500 miles later, I'm terribly homesick. Do I believe I *won't* make it to Canada? Not at all. I feel stronger every day; trail camaraderie is pleasurable, as is meeting demanding daily goals; and the beauty of the high desert in Spring is astounding. Moreover, my family is planning a rendezvous. Besides, what better way to express gratitude at midlife than a walk from Mexico to Canada? So then, do I believe I *will* make it? Not at all. A lot can go wrong in 2,155 miles. Indeed, given what I've got to go on, I can't even hazard a guess as to how likely it is that I will make it. Nevertheless, each morning I picture Monument 78 at the Canadian border just north of Hart's Pass with me standing next to it smiling, and I head north on the assumption that, come September, that picture will be reality.

Captain Morgan. On the trail, there's a saying about the relationship between a sleeping trailside rattlesnake and a group of hikers passing by: the first wakes it up, the second pisses it off, and the third gets bit. I was the third. Fortunately for me, this unseen rattler, coiled deep in the sand under some scrub, did not bite me. Captain Morgan was not so fortunate. It's dusk and four paces behind me he speaks of his new right hip and shoulder, replacements for the ones he lost to a roadside bomb in Iraq nine months earlier. He tells me how he aims to continue his recovery on his walk to Canada, when—all of a sudden—he stops and says matter-of-factly, "It bit me. It didn't even rattle," pointing to a 40-inch Mojave Green, silent and still. We inspect his wound. I dial 911; no reception. Twenty minutes later, at Tyler Horse Creek, he's calm with no symptoms. Rattlesnakes control envenomation, sometimes delivering 'dry bites' to animals too large to eat; moreover, a snake's timing can be off so that it releases its venom before sinking its fangs. Maybe Captain got lucky. The next morning he says he feels fine, so the other hikers congregated at the creek move on. I stay. Thirty minutes later, he heaves up his breakfast and continues to wretch every two minutes or so; he quickly becomes weak and feverish, breathing with difficulty; signs of delirium appear.[28] He needs help . . . fast. But which way should he go? Should he backtrack 24 miles to Highway 138, or forge ahead 24 miles to Highway 58? Our maps give us no reason to prefer either route. Three miles ahead, there's a two-mile side-trail to a trailhead; might we find a vehicle to hotwire at midweek? Five miles back there's a dirt road into the hills; might it lead to a home? Maybe he should stay put at the creek, the only sure source of water in this 48-mile stretch; perhaps a hiker with a working phone will arrive and we can call in an airlift. Time is short; he needs to decide. He rules out staying put and decides that moving ahead is slightly better than going back. So he stumbles forward on the assumption that help lies ahead.

Eliotwright. In an insightful autobiographical essay, William Wainwright characterizes his stance toward God as one filtered through a "congenital skepticism" that renders it difficult for him "to embrace *any* controversial [proposition] without *some* hesitation."[29] Nevertheless, he writes, "classical theistic metaphysics" has come to seem "more reasonable to me, on the whole, than its alternatives" and it "survives criticism at least as well as, and probably better than, its competitors."[30] Moreover, sensitive to what he describes as the frailty of "human effort, thought, and ideals when confronted

by what [Paul] Tillich called the threat of death, meaninglessness, and sin," he has long been attracted to what the Christian story has to say about these matters. In light of these and other considerations, he says that "even if Christian theism isn't more probable than not, it is still reasonable to embrace it" since, by his lights, it best addresses the whole of human experience and the evidence favors it over its competitors.[31] He concludes the essay with this paragraph:

> My attitude is in many ways similar to T.S. Eliot's. Eliot appears to have combined a deeply serious faith with both irony and skepticism. (When asked why he accepted Christianity, he said he did so because it was the least false of the options open to him.). . . I do not regard my stance as exemplary. If Christianity (or indeed any form of traditional theism) is true, a faith free from doubt is surely better. I suspect, however, that my religious life may be fairly representative of the lives of many intelligent, educated, and sincere Christians in the latter part of the twentieth century.[32]

In personal correspondence, Wainwright indicates that he himself thinks Christianity is more likely than not. Eliot, however, is a different story. He thinks Christianity is "the least false" of the credible options, which suggests that by his lights it is more likely than each of them but less likely than their disjunction. Imagine, then, someone with Wainwright's evaluative, conative, and behavioral orientation to Christianity but with Eliot's cognitive stance. Call him *Eliotwright*.

Five observations about our protagonists are relevant to our concerns.

First, it seems apt to say that each of them has faith. I have faith that I will make it to Canada; Captain Morgan has faith that help lies ahead; Eliotwright has faith that the basic Christian story is true.

Second, we neither believe nor accept these things. I have no tendency to feel it to be the case that I'll make it to Canada. Captain Morgan not only lacks that tendency, he lacks any tendency to assert that help lies ahead, and he lacks any tendency to be surprised upon learning that it doesn't. We can easily imagine that the same goes for Eliotwright.

Third, each of us is in doubt about the object of his faith. I think that what I've got to go on puts me in no position to say whether I'll make it to Canada, not even very roughly how likely it is. Captain Morgan thinks staying put has the least going for it, and that moving forward is slightly better than backtracking. Eliotwright thinks Christianity is the least false of the credible options, which suggests the he deems his evidence for Christianity to be no better than the evidence for their disjunction.

Fourth, despite our lack of belief and acceptance and despite our doubt, each of us acts on a certain assumption. I act on the assumption that I will make it to Canada. Captain acts on the assumption that help lies ahead. Eliotwright acts on the assumption that the basic Christian story is true. Take note: *there really is something that each of us acts on*; it's called an *assumption*.

Fifth, in virtue of our assumptions, each of us tends to behave in expectable ways. I assume I will make it to Canada, and so I pick up camp each morning and head north, whittling away at the six million steps between borders, scheduling resupplies, dreaming of family rendezvouses along the way, and so on. Captain Morgan assumes help lies ahead, and so he rises from his knees, slings his pack onto his back, and staggers forward. Eliotwright assumes the basic Christian story is true, and so he makes confession, gives thanks, kneels to receive the Body of Christ, and so on.

It seems, therefore, that we have found something distinct from belief and acceptance, something that is at home with being in doubt, something that can stand in for the positive cognitive stance faith requires: assuming.

6. FAITH AND ASSUMING

What, exactly, is assuming? This is a very difficult question. Unlike belief and acceptance, assuming has received little attention. Still, perhaps half a dozen observations might not fall too far from the truth.

First, we use "assume" in different ways. We sometimes use it with reference to things we believe or accept; and we sometimes use it with reference to things we disbelieve and reject. But, as with our protagonists, we sometimes use it with reference to things we neither believe nor accept, and things we neither disbelieve nor reject; things we are in doubt about. I mean to employ that use of the word.

Second observation: we must not identify assuming with acting as if. One can act as if p while disbelieving p, but one cannot assume p while disbelieving p. For when one assumes p, one has not settled on not-p; but when one disbelieves p, one has settled on not-p, even though one might dissemble and act as if p.

Third, perhaps the relation between acting as if and assuming—or, more accurately, perhaps the relation between *a disposition* to act as if and assuming—is that of genus to species. If it is, then acting as if need not involve pretense. For although some species of acting as if might require pretense, e.g. acting as if you're a frog while playing charades, the assumings of our protagonists involve no pretense. I am not pretending I will make it to Canada; Captain Morgan is not pretending that help lies ahead; and Eliotwright is not pretending that Christianity is true.

Fourth observation: since assuming of the sort at issue is at home with being in doubt, its dispositional profile will differ from those of belief and acceptance. In particular, if S assumes p, she will *lack* a tendency to feel it to be the case that p upon considering whether p; she will *lack* a tendency to assert that p when asked whether p, unless it is clear to her that she will not be misunderstood for expressing a more positive cognitive stance; and she will *lack* a tendency to be surprised upon learning not-p.

Fifth, despite these differences, assuming functions similarly to belief and acceptance in reasoning and other behavior. Specifically, if one assumes p, then, if one takes q to follow from p, one will tend to assume q. And if one assumes p, then, if one engages in practical or theoretical reasoning, one will tend to use p as a premise when appropriate.

And, in general, if one assumes p, then, given one's goals, aversions, and other cognitive stances, one will tend to act in appropriate ways.

Finally, although the dispositional profile of assuming differs from that of acceptance, it is nonetheless congruent with propositional faith. Three considerations jointly suggest this.

(i)   Like the profiles of believing p and accepting p but unlike the profile of disbelieving p, the profile of assuming p lacks the tendencies to feel *not-p* is the case upon considering p, to affirm or assert *not-p* when asked whether p, and to be surprised upon learning *p*. In these respects, the profile of assuming p is congruent with faith that p.

(ii)   One can be in doubt about something and still have faith that it's so. But one can be in doubt about something only if one lacks a tendency to be surprised upon learning it's not so and one lacks a tendency to assert it (absent some special motive to assert it, e.g. to deceive someone). Thus, one can have faith while lacking both of these tendencies, in which case the difference between the profiles of acceptance and assuming do not render assuming incongruent with faith.

(iii) Although the profile of assuming lacks these two tendencies, it includes other tendencies that constitute a disposition to take a stand on the truth of what is assumed. For just as when one accepts p, when one assumes p, one will tend to use p as a premise in practical and theoretical reasoning when appropriate and one will, more generally, tend to act in ways befitting one's goals, aversions, and other mental states. This is why we expect that, when Eliotwright assumes the basic Christian story, he will have a tendency to infer that, in the end, all will be well, that he should confess his sins, and so on; this is why we expect that, when Captain Morgan assumes that help lies ahead and he wants to get help, he will walk forward. By performing these actions rather than others,

they manifest their disposition to take a stand on the truth of their assumptions, albeit a weaker stand than that of acceptance (or belief).

7. PROPOSITIONAL FAITH: WHAT IT IS

An account of propositional faith emerges from the foregoing reflections. Faith that p is a complex propositional attitude consisting of (i) a positive evaluation of p, i.e. considering p to be good or worthy of desire, (ii) a positive conative orientation toward p, and (iii) a positive cognitive stance toward p. Although nothing can be faith without these constituents, different items can stand in for each. To clarify the proposal, consider *Diagram 1*:

A positive evaluation of p	
A positive conative orientation toward p	
A positive cognitive stance toward p	

Each box to the left is filled to convey the idea that nothing is propositional faith unless it answers to those descriptions. Each box to the right is empty to convey the idea that different things can answer to those descriptions. Nothing that fills in an empty box is a necessary constituent of faith; rather, some filling in or other that answers the description to its left is required.

Belief that p can stand in for the positive cognitive stance, and desire for p's truth can stand in for the positive conative orientation. Hence *Diagram 2*:

A positive evaluation of p	Considering p's truth to be good or desirable
A positive conative orientation toward p	Wanting p to be the case
A positive cognitive stance toward p	Believing p

Acceptance and a second-order desire can stand in as well. Hence *Diagram 3*:

A positive evaluation of p	Considering p's truth to be good or desirable
A positive conative orientation toward p	Wanting it to be the case that one wants p
A positive cognitive stance toward p	Accepting p

I have argued that assuming can stand in too, which is displayed in *Diagram 4*:

A positive evaluation of p	Considering p's truth to be good or desirable
A positive conative orientation toward p	Wanting p to be the case
A positive cognitive stance toward p	Assuming that p

Although it has gone unmentioned, a variety of positive cognitive stances can stand in for "considering" p to be good or desirable, the positive evaluation of p. And there may be other items that can stand in for the required constituents of faith.

8. THE OBAMA OBJECTION

Suppose you believe that Barack Obama will win the election; moreover, you think that his winning would be a good thing, and you want him to win. If the account of propositional faith on offer is complete, then you have faith that Obama will win. The problem is that you don't. The account, therefore, is incomplete.

What's missing is resilience in the face of new contrary evidence. What if unemployment increased? What if it came out that Obama pulled a lewinsky? What if his popularity ratings took a dive? Let your imagination rip! In the face of increasing counter-evidence, would you still think it a good thing that he won? "Of course," you say. Would you still want him to? "Absolutely," you reply. "After all, the economy is Bush's fault and

adultery isn't relevant to presidential leadership; moreover, consider the alternative." The crucial question, though, is this: would you still *believe* that he'll win? "Yes!," you say. Then you have faith that he will. Nothing counts as faith unless one's cognitive stance—in this case, your belief—is resistant to what one regards as contrary evidence.

This line of thought is mistaken. For although I agree that what's missing is resilience in the face of what one regards as new contrary evidence, it is a mistake to understand that resilience *solely* in terms of the resistance of one's cognitive stance to what one regards as new counter-evidence. That's one way the resilience faith requires can be instantiated, but it is not the only way; nor is it necessary. For the resilience of one's faith can be manifested instead by one's being disposed to behave in certain ways upon discovering new counter-evidence.

To illustrate the point, consider a variation on the Obama story. As before, you believe he'll win the election, you think his winning is a good thing, and you want him to win. And, as before, if you were to discover new counter-evidence to his winning, you would still think his winning is a good thing and still want him to win. Unlike before, however, suppose that your cognitive stance, your belief that he'll win, is *not* resistant to new counter-evidence. If you were to recognize new evidence that led you to think that the election was going to be close, you would not dig in your cognitive heels and believe all the same; rather, you would properly adjust, perhaps going from belief to weak belief, or belief to belief that it's only slightly more likely than not, or belief to mere assuming, or what have you. Even so, you might yet have faith that he'll win. For it might be that, in relevant counterfactual situations like the one we are imagining, despite properly adjusting your positive cognitive stance, you would remain resolved—as you presently are, let's suppose—to spend an evening each week talking with undecided voters, to tithe your earnings to his campaign, and so on. Alternatively, it might be that you would resolve to make investments and plans that would most likely pay off only if Obama won, and the like. And there are plenty of other options as well. The point is that if you have faith that he'll win, new counter-evidence would not take the wind out of your sails; it would not deter you; it would not discourage you into inaction; it would not dishearten you. If something like *that* constitutes your present dispositional profile, then you have faith that Obama will win. You satisfy faith's demand for some measure of resilience and tenacity in the face of counter-evidence even though your cognitive stance is properly responsive to new counter-evidence.[33]

9. "BY DEFINITION, FAITH IS BELIEF IN THE ABSENCE OF EVIDENCE"

En route to pooh-poohing faith in *The Harvard Crimson*, linguist Steven Pinker writes that faith is "believing something *without good reasons to do so*."[34] Similarly, philosopher Alex Rosenberg began a recent debate ostensibly on the question of whether faith in God is reasonable by declaring that reasonable faith in God wasn't even possible since "by definition, faith is *belief in the absence of evidence*."[35] Not to be outdone by his fellow brights, biologist-rock-star Richard Dawkins goes one step further: "[f]aith is belief in spite of, *even perhaps because of*, the lack of evidence."[36] But no one goes as far as Mark Twain: faith is "believing what *you know ain't so*"![37] Let's set aside the excesses of Dawkins and Twain and focus on Pinker and Rosenberg, according to whom one can have faith that something is so only if one has no good reason to believe it, no evidence at all. (I don't mean to suggest that only secularists take this line. They're just the shrillest.)

Of course, if the Pinker-Rosenberg line is right, then it is absolutely impossible for one to have faith that something is so while one has *some* good reason for believing it, *some* evidence for it. But surely one can. Maria can have faith that her new venture, Prairie Road Farm, will succeed even though she has some good reason for believing it, e.g. an accurate estimation of her resolve and her partner's support in the endeavor.[38] Christian can

have faith that he will find another with whom he can be close despite the fact that he has some evidence in the form of couples not so different from himself who are close.

The Pinker-Rosenberg account can be moderated into something more plausible: one can have faith that something is so only if one has *insufficient* reason for believing it, *insufficient* evidence. This moderate line is more plausible; nevertheless, it is implausible. For if it is correct, then it is absolutely impossible for one to have faith that something is so while one has sufficient reason or evidence to believe it. But surely one can. Suppose I care that your marriage flourishes but you confide that certain difficulties persist; I naturally express concern. You may well assure me that things are not so far gone that either you or your partner intend to split up but rather that you both anticipate happy results from the therapy you've begun. Your word is sufficient evidence for my faith that your marriage will survive despite the fact that it might also be sufficient evidence for me to believe the same. A child worried sick about her father's prostate cancer asks his oncologist whether he will live. He tells her that her father's prognosis is very favorable, so favorable that she should plan for him to walk her down the aisle some day if she wishes. Thus assured, she may well have faith that there will be such a day despite the fact that she has evidence sufficient for belief. Faith does not require insufficient evidence for belief.

I have deeper misgivings. First, Pinker and Rosenberg *identify* faith with believing something on insufficient reason or evidence; if they're right, one can have faith that p without either considering p's truth to be good or desirable or caring that p— but one cannot. Second, if they're right, faith *requires* belief—but it does not. For although one can have faith that p when one is in doubt about whether p, one cannot believe p in that case; moreover, although one can have faith that p when one lacks a tendency to be surprised upon learning not-p, one cannot believe p in that condition; furthermore, although one can have faith that p when one merely believes *p is likely*, or *p is twice as likely as not*, or *p is much more likely than its credible contraries*, one cannot believe that p while that is the case; finally, although one can have faith that p when one merely accepts p, or merely assents to p, or (belief-less-ly) assumes p, one cannot believe p in that condition.

Third, Pinker, Rosenberg and company imply that faith is *necessarily* evidentially subpar. Every other complex propositional attitude can fit one's total evidence, e.g. Dennis's hope that, while lost in the wilderness southeast of Lake Ann near Mt. Shuksan, Whatcom County Search and Rescue will find him, and his fear that they won't. So why do they single out faith as *necessarily* evidentially subpar, as *requiring* insufficient reasons and evidence?

Four reasons, I conjecture, but one of them isn't very nice to say and so I will mention only three. First, Pinker, Rosenberg, *et al* think of faith only with religious content, and every instance of it is evidentially subpar, by their lights. Second, they mistake the false "nothing is faith unless it is evidentially sub*par*" for the true "nothing is faith unless it is evidentially sub*optimal*," a natural error. Third, they rightly discern that nothing counts as faith unless it is resilient to new counter-evidence, but they take a narrow view of the ways in which such resilience can be realized. If my conjecture is correct, Pinker, Rosenberg and company would do well to reflect on instances of secular faith, recognize the import of the subpar-suboptimal distinction, and expand their view of the ways in which the resilience required by faith can be realized.

10. CONCLUSION

According to the account on offer here, faith that p is a complex propositional attitude consisting of (i) a positive evaluation of p, (ii) a positive conative orientation toward p, (iii) a positive cognitive stance toward p, and (iv) resilience to new counter-evidence to p. Importantly, assuming—assuming of the sort displayed above—can stand in for the positive cognitive stance faith requires. Since assuming is at home with being in doubt, being in doubt is no impediment to faith. Doubt is not faith's enemy; rather, the enemies of faith are misevaluation, indifference or hostility, and faintheartedness.

Naturally, many questions remain about the account on offer. For example, I characterized belief and acceptance in a particular way, the way in which Alston did. What might faith look like given different characterizations, or given their elimination altogether in exchange for graded confidence? In addition, there are more objections to consider. For example, haven't I simply confused faith and hope? Or, having packed so much into faith *that*, is there any room for faith *in*? Furthermore, alternative accounts of faith similarly at odds with the Common View have begun to sprout up. Why prefer the one on offer here? Finally, implications of theoretical and practical significance have gone unmentioned. For example, what does the account on offer imply for how we should go about evaluating the overall rationality or propriety of faith? What does it imply for our understanding of the virtue of faith? What does it imply for the age-old "problem of faith and reason" in the philosophy of religion? I aim to address these questions, objections, alternatives, and implications elsewhere.[39] Here, however, I must rest content with a first pass at saying what propositional faith is and what it is not.[40]

NOTES

1. Jude 1:3, KJV, emphasis added; cf. Acts 6:7, Philippians 1:27.

2. Plantinga, *Warranted Christian Belief* (New York: Oxford University Press, 2000), 252. Plantinga says that this isn't the only thing that "faith" denotes.

3. John Locke: faith is "assent to a proposition . . . upon the credit of the proposer . . .," *Essay Concerning Human Understanding*, IV, xviii, 2. *Catholic Encyclopedia*: faith "rests on grave authority," online at http://www.catholic.org/encyclopedia/view.php?id=4554.

4. "An Introduction to St. Paul's Letter to the Romans," in Luther's German Bible of 1522; online at: http://www.iclnet.org/pub/resources/text/wittenberg/luther/luther-faith.txt, emphasis mine.

5. *The Institutes of Christian Religion*, Book III, chapter 2, section 7; online at http://www.vor.org/rbdisk/html/institutes/3_02.htm, emphasis mine.

6. Online at http://www.newadvent.org/cathen/05752c.htm.

7. Eleonore Stump, *Aquinas* (New York: Routledge, 2003), 363; cp. *Summa Theologica* IIaIIae.1.4 and IIaIIae.4.8. *Catholic Encyclopedia*: "doubt cannot coexist with faith . . . in regard to any given subject; faith and doubt are mutually exclusive" (entry on doubt), online at http://www.newadvent.org/cathen/05141a.htm. According to Hebrews 11:1, "Now faith is being sure of what we hope for and certain of what we do not see" (NIV). The translation is inaccurate. See Rik Peels, "Doxastic Doubt, Fiducial Doubt, and Christian Faith," *Neue Zeitschrift für Systematische Theologie und Religionsphilosophie* 49.2 (June 2007), 183–98, for a more accurate translation and discussion of other biblical texts thought to suggest that faith implies certainty.

8. See, e.g., W. Lad Sessions, *The Concept of Faith* (Ithaca NY: Cornell University Press, 1994), 29–30.

9. "Belief, Acceptance, and Religious Faith," eds. Jeff Jordan and Daniel Howard-Snyder, *Faith, Freedom, and Rationality* (Lanham MD: Rowman & Littlefield, 1996), 4, slightly altered for readability.

10. *Ibid.*, 3–4.

11. *Ibid.*, 241, n4.

12. Alston 1996, 12.

13. Robert Adams, "Moral Faith," *Journal of Philosophy* (1995), 88–89.

14. Robert Audi, "Belief, Acceptance, and Faith," *International Journal for Philosophy of Religion* 63 (2008), 97.

15. Cf. J. L. Schellenberg, *Prolegomena to a Philosophy of Religion* (Ithaca: Cornell University Press, 2005), 128ff.

16. Thanks to Gerald Marsh here.

17. Cf. Lara Buchak, "Can it be Rational to Have Faith," in eds. Jake Chandler and Victoria S. Harrison, *Probability in the Philosophy of Religion*

18. See Alston 1996 and William Alston, "Audi on Nondoxastic Faith," in eds. Mark Timmons, John Greco, and Alfred Mele, *Rationality and the Good: Critical Essays on the Ethics and Epistemology of Robert Audi* (New York: Oxford University Press, 2007), 123–39.

19. Alston 1996, 9, slightly altered for readability.

20. Alston 2007.

21. Alston 1996, 10.

22. Adams 1995, 84–85.

23. The first two are stated and rejected in Robert Audi, "Faith, Belief, and Rationality," *Philosophical Perspectives* (1991), 213–39; the last two are affirmed by Gary Gutting, *Religious Belief and Religious Skepticism* (South Bend IN: University of Notre Dame Press, 1982), 105ff.

24. See Audi (1982) and (1994).

25. Thanks to Frances Howard-Snyder here.

26. For the sorts of accounts I have in mind *in philosophy*, see the items listed by Eric Schwitzgebel in the bibliography of "Belief," *The Stanford Encyclopedia of Philosophy*.

27. Thanks to John Schellenberg and Terence Cuneo here.

28. Wikipedia: "*C. scutulatus* is widely regarded as producing one of the most toxic snake venoms in the New World. . . . In people bitten by Venom A Mojave rattlesnakes (those outside the relatively small Venom B area in south-central Arizona), the onset of serious signs and symptoms can be delayed, sometimes leading to an initial underestimation of the severity of the bite. Significant envenomation . . . can produce vision abnormalities and difficulty swallowing and speaking. In severe cases, skeletal muscle weakness can lead to difficulty breathing and even respiratory failure."

29. William J. Wainwright, "Skepticism, Romanticism, and Faith," in Thomas V. Morris (ed), *God and the Philosophers* (New York: Oxford University Press, 1994), 78.

30. *Ibid.*, 78.

31. *Ibid.*, 80.

32. *Ibid.*, 87.

(New York: Oxford University Press, 2012), 225–248; manuscript, page 2, note 1.

33. Thanks to Kenny Boyce, Frances Howard-Snyder and, especially, Wes Morriston here.

34. "Less Faith, More Reason," October 27, 2006, my emphasis; online at: http://www.thecrimson.com/article/2006/10/27/less-faith-more-reason-there-is/.

35. "Is Faith in God Reasonable? Debate: Alex Rosenberg vs William Lane Craig," Purdue University, February 1, 2013, my emphasis. For his own part, Craig never addressed the question of the debate, preferring instead to address the question of whether *belief* that God exists is reasonable. It's a sad day when even a Christian apologist can't tell the difference between faith in God and belief that God exists.

36. Online at http://www.brainyquote.com/quotes/authors/r/richard_dawkins.html, my emphasis.

37. Online at http://quotationsbook.com/quote/14040/, my emphasis.

38. http://www.facebook.com/PrairieRoadFarm; www.prairieroadfarm.com

39. I begin some of this work in "Schellenberg on Propositional Faith," *Religious Studies* (2013).

40. Thanks go to the late William Alston, Robert Audi, Nathan Ballantyne, Kenny Boyce, Lara Buchak, Doug Bunnell, Andrew Chignell, Andrew Cortens, Tom Crisp, Terence Cuneo, Jeanine Diller, Brett Dison, Andrew Dole, The Forge, Andre Gallois, Allan Hazlett, Frances Howard-Snyder, Mark Heller, Hud Hudson, Jon Kvanvig, Steve Layman, Christian Lee, Gerald Marsh, Captain Morgan (who survived), Wes Morriston, Anthony Nault, Rik Peels, Ted Poston, Joshua Rasmussen, Michael Rea, Alex Rivera, Blake Roeber, John Schellenberg, Tom Senor, Joshua Spencer, Steve Steward, Nancy Taylor, William Wainwright, Peter van Inwagen, Mark Webb, Dennis Whitcomb, Ed Wierenga, two anonymous referees for this journal, and the southernmost 631.4 miles of the Pacific Crest Trail, on whose terrain this paper was born during a leave funded by Western Washington University in May 2010, for which I am also thankful.

V.A.4

Faith, Hope, and Doubt

LOUIS P. POJMAN

Louis Pojman (1935–2005), the original editor of this anthology, was professor of philosophy at the United States Military Academy, West Point, New York. In this selection, Pojman examines the relationship between belief and faith and argues that belief is not necessary for religious faith. One may not be able to believe in God because of an insufficiency of evidence, but one may still live in hope, committed to a theistic worldview.

Many religious people have a problem because they doubt various credal statements contained in their religions. Propositional beliefs are often looked upon as necessary, though not sufficient, conditions for salvation. This doubt causes great anxiety and raises the question of the importance of belief in religion and in

Reprinted from *Philosophy of Religion*, McGraw-Hill Publishing Co. 2001. Copyright © 1999, Louis P. Pojman.

life in general. It is a question that has been neglected in the philosophy of religion and theology. In this paper I shall explore the question of the importance of belief as a religious attitude and suggest that there is at least one other attitude which may be adequate for religious faith, even in the absence of belief—that attitude being hope. I shall develop a concept of *faith as hope* as an alternative to the usual notion that makes a propositional belief that God exists a necessary condition for faith, as Plantinga implies in the following quotation. For simplicity's sake I shall concentrate on the most important proposition in Western religious creeds, which states that God exists (defined broadly as a benevolent, supreme Being, who is responsible for the creation of the universe), but the analysis could be applied *mutatis mutandis* to many other important propositions in religion (e.g., the Incarnation and the doctrine of the Trinity).

> It is worth noting, by way of conclusion, that the mature believer, the mature theist, does not typically accept belief in God tentatively, or hypothetically, or until something better comes along. Nor, I think, does he accept it as a conclusion from other things he believes; he accepts it as basic, as a part of the foundations of his noetic structure. The mature theist commits himself to belief in God: this means that he accepts belief in God as basic (Alvin Plantinga, "Is Belief in God Rational?").

> Entombed in a secure prison, thinking our situation quite hopeless, we may find unutterable joy in the information that there is, after all, the slimmest possibility of escape. Hope provides comfort, and hope does not always require probability. But we must believe that what we hope for is at least possible (Gretchen Weirob in John Perry's *A Dialogue on Personal Identity and Immortality*).

INTRODUCTION

Traditionally, orthodox Christianity has claimed (1) that faith in God and Christ entails belief that God exists and that Christ is God incarnate and (2) that

without faith we are damned to eternal hell. Thus doubt is an unacceptable propositional attitude. I argue that this thesis is misguided. One may doubt—that is, lack propositional belief—and yet have faith in God and Christ.

Let me preface my remarks with a confession. I am a religious doubter. Doubt has haunted my life as long as I can remember. My mother was a devout Roman Catholic and my father an equally convinced rationalistic atheist. From an early age metaphysical tension produced in me a sense of wonder about religion. In the process of seeking a solution to this conflict, at the age of seven I became a Protestant. But doubts continued to haunt me. I recall coming home from my high school biology class, where we had studied naturalistic evolution, and weeping over the Bible, trying to reconcile evolution with the creation account in Genesis 1 through 3. Finally, when I was about 15, I went to a minister and confessed my doubts about God and Christianity. He listened carefully and said the situation was grave indeed. My eternal soul was at stake. Thus I must will myself to believe the message of Christianity. He quoted Romans 14:23: "He that doubteth is damned ... for whatsoever is not of faith is sin." I was thrown into paroxysms of despair, for the attempt to get myself to believe that God exists or that Christ is perfect God and perfect man failed. Yet, I wanted to believe with all my heart, and some days I would find myself believing—only to wake up the next day with doubts. Hence, this preoccupation with faith and doubt. Hence, this paper.

I. IS BELIEF A NECESSARY CONDITION FOR SALVATION?

According to traditional Christianity, belief is a necessary condition for salvation. Paul says in Romans 10:10, "If you confess with your lips that Jesus is Lord and believe in your heart that God raised him from the dead, you will be saved." In Hebrews 11 we are told that he who would please God must believe that He exists and is a rewarder of them that seek Him. The Athanasian Creed, an official doctrine of orthodox Christianity, states that salvation requires that one believe not only that God exists but also that God is triune and that Christ is perfect God and perfect man.[1] Most theologians and philosophers hold, at the least, that Christian faith requires propositional belief.[2] You can be judged and condemned according to your beliefs. As Romans 14:23 states, "He that doubteth is damned."

The basic argument goes Like this:

1. Faith in God through Christ is a necessary and sufficient condition for eternal salvation.

2. Belief that God exists is a necessary condition for faith.

3. Therefore belief is a necessary condition for salvation.

4. Therefore, doubt—the absence of belief—is an unacceptable attitude for salvation. No doubter will be saved.

Let us begin with some definitions:

1. **Belief**—an involuntary assenting of the mind to a proposition (a "yessing" to a proposition), a feeling of conviction about p—a *nonvolitional event.*

Consider the following belief line, defined in terms of subjective probability, the degree to which I think the proposition is probable. Let "S" stand for the believer or *subject,* "B" for *believe,* and "p" for the *proposition* in question. Then we can roughly locate our beliefs on the Belief Line. Greater than 0.5 equals various degrees of positive belief that p. Less than 0.5 equals various degrees of unbelief (or belief that the complement, "not-p" is true). 0.5 equals agnosticism or suspension of judgment.

Belief Line

0 ———————	0.5 ———————————	1
SB not-p	Not-*SBp* & Not-*SB* not-p	*SBp*

2. **Acceptance**—deciding to include p in the set of propositions that you are willing to act on in certain contexts—*a volitional act.*

For example, in a *legal* context—say a jury, where there is insufficient evidence to convict an accused criminal—I may believe the subject is guilty but accept the proposition that he is not because the high standards of criminal justice have not been met; or in a *scientific* context—say, in testing the hypothesis that a formula will lead to the development of cold fusion—I may not believe the hypothesis I am testing is true but accept it for purposes of the experiment. Acceptance is different from belief in that we have some direct control over our acceptances, whereas we don't over our beliefs. We may or may not believe our acceptances and we may or may not accept our beliefs.

3. **Faith**—a commitment to something X (e.g., a person, hypothesis, religion, or worldview).

Faith is a *deep* kind of acceptance. An acceptance can be tentative. For example, when I make a marriage vow, I will to be faithful until death to my beloved, whether or not I believe that I will succeed. If my marriage vow were merely an acceptance, I suppose, it would be "I promise to be faithful to you for at least three years or until I lose interest in you." Faith involves commitment to its object. Under normal circumstances, it involves trusting and obeying the object of faith or doing what has the best chance of bringing its goals to fulfillment. It is a *volitional act.*

We may note at this point that the New Testament word *pistis* can be translated as either belief or faith. The distinction is discernible only by the context.

II. PHENOMENOLOGY OF BELIEF

First we must understand what is involved in direct volitionalism (the act of acquiring a belief directly by willing to have it). The following features seem to be necessary and jointly sufficient conditions for a minimally interesting thesis of volitionalism:

1. The acquisition is a basic act. That is, some of our beliefs are obtained by acts of will directly upon being willed. Believing itself need not be an action. It may be dispositional. The volitionalist need not assert that all belief

acquisitions occur via the fiat of the will, only that some of them do.

2. The acquisition must be done in full consciousness of what one is doing. The paradigm cases of acts of will are those in which the agent deliberates over two courses of action and decides on one of them. However, acts of will may take place with greater or lesser awareness. Here our notion of will is ambiguous between two meanings: "desiring" and "deciding." Sometimes by "act of will" we mean simply a desire that manifests itself in action, such as my being hungry and finding myself going to the refrigerator or tired and finding myself heading for bed. We are not always aware of our desires or intentions. There is a difference between this type of willing and the sort where we are fully aware of a decision to perform an act. If we obtain beliefs via the will in the weaker sense of desiring, of which we are only dimly aware, how can we ever be sure that it was really an act of will that caused the belief directly rather than the will simply being an accompaniment of the belief? That is, there is a difference between willing to believe and believing willingly. The latter case is not an instance of acquiring a belief by fiat of the will; only the former is. In order for the volitionalist to make his case, he must assert that the acts of will that produce beliefs are decisions of which he is fully aware.

3. The belief must be acquired independently of evidential considerations. That is, the evidence is not what is decisive in forming the belief. Perhaps the belief may be influenced by evidence (testimony, memory, inductive experience, and the like), so that the leap of faith cannot occur at just any time over any proposition, but only over propositions that have some evidence in their favor, though still inadequately supported by that evidence. They have an initial subjective probability of—or just under—0.5. According to Descartes, we ought to withhold belief in such situations where the evidence is exactly equal, whereas with

Kierkegaard religious and existential considerations may justify leaps of believing even when the evidence is weighted against the proposition in question. William James prescribes such leaps only when the option is forced, living, and momentous. It may not be possible to volit* in the way Kierkegaard prescribes without a miracle of grace, as he suggests, but the volitionalist would have to assert that volitional belief goes beyond all evidence at one's disposal and hence the believer must acquire the belief through an act of choice that goes beyond evidential considerations. It is as though we place our volitional finger on the mental scales of evidence assessment, tipping the scale one way or the other.

In sum, then, a volit must be an act of will whereby I acquire a belief directly upon willing to have the belief, and it is an act made in full consciousness and independently of evidential considerations. The act of acquiring a belief may itself not be a belief but a way of moving from mere entertainment of a proposition to the disposition of having the belief. There is much to be said in favor of volitionalism. It seems to extend the scope of human freedom to an important domain, and it seems to fit our experience of believing where we are conscious of having made a choice. The teacher who sees that the evidence against a pupil's honesty is great and yet decides to trust him, believing that somehow he is innocent in spite of the evidence, and the theist who believes in God in spite of insufficient evidence, seem to be everyday examples confirming our inclination toward a volitional account of belief formation. We suspect, at times, that many of our beliefs, while not formed through *fully conscious* volits, have been formed through *half-aware* desires, for on introspection we note that past beliefs have been acquired in ways that could not have taken the evidence seriously into consideration. Volitionalism seems a good

---

***Volit**: (v.) to acquire a belief by choosing to have it or (n.) a belief acquired by exercising one's will. Voliting: obtaining beliefs by choosing to have them.

explanatory theory to account for a great deal of our cognitive experience.

Nonetheless, there are considerations which may make us question whether, upon reflection, volitionalism is the correct account of our situation. I will argue that choosing is not the natural way in which we acquire beliefs, and that whereas it may not be logically *impossible* that some people volit, it seems psychologically odd and even conceptually incoherent.

1. Beliefs-Are-Not-Chosen Argument against Volitionalism

Beliefs are not chosen but occur involuntarily as responses to states of affairs in the world. Beliefs are, to use Frank Ramsey's metaphor, mappings in the mind by which we steer our lives. As such, the states of affairs that beliefs represent exist independently of the mind; they exist independently of whether we want them to exist. Insofar as beliefs presume to represent the way the world is, and hence serve as effective guides to action, the will seems superfluous. Believing seems more like seeing than looking, falling than jumping, catching a cold than catching a ball, getting drunk than taking a drink, blushing than smiling, getting a headache than giving one to someone else. Indeed, this involuntary, passive aspect seems true on introspection of most propositional attitudes: anger, envy, fearing, suspecting, and doubting—although not necessarily of imagining or entertaining a proposition, where an active element may often be present.

When a person acquires a belief, the world forces itself upon him. Consider perceptual beliefs. If I am in a normal physiological condition and open my eyes, I cannot help but see certain things—for example, this piece of white paper in front of me. It seems intuitively obvious that I don't have to choose to have a belief that I see this piece of white paper before I believe I see it. Here "seeing is believing." This is not to deny a certain active element in perception. I can explore my environment—focus on certain features and turn from others. I can direct my perceptual mechanism, but once I do this the perceptions I obtain come of themselves whether or not I will to have them. I may even have an aversion to white paper and not want to have such a perception, but I cannot help having it. Likewise, if I am in a normal physiological state and someone nearby turns on loud music, I hear it. I cannot help believing that I hear it. Belief is forced on me.[3]

2. Logic-of-Belief Argument against Volitionalism

The notion of volitional believing involves a conceptual confusion; it is broadly speaking a logical mistake. There is something incoherent in stating that one can obtain or sustain a belief in full consciousness *simply* by a basic act of the will—that is, purposefully disregarding the evidence connection. This strategy does not altogether rule out the possibility of voliting when one is less than fully conscious (although one is not truly voliting if one is not fully conscious), but it asserts that when full consciousness enters, the "belief" will wither from one's noetic structure. One cannot believe in full consciousness "that p and I believe that p for other than truth considerations." If you understand that to believe that p is to believe that p is true and that *wishing never makes it so*, then there is simply no epistemic reason for believing p. Suppose I say that I believe I have $1,000,000 in my checking account, and suppose that when you point out to me that there is no reason to believe this, I respond, "I know that there is not the slightest reason to suppose that there is $1,000,000 in my checking account, but I believe it anyway, simply because I want to." If you were convinced that I was not joking, you would probably conclude that I was insane or didn't know what I was talking about.

If I said that I somehow find myself believing that I have $1,000,000 but don't know why, you might suppose that there is a memory trace of my having deposited $1,000,000 into my account or evidence to that effect in the guise of an intuition that caused my belief. But if I denied that and said— "No, I don't have any memory trace of depositing of $1,000,000 in my account; in fact, I'm sure that I never deposited $1,000,000 in the account; I just find it good to believe that it's there, so I have chosen to believe it,"—you would be stumped.

The point is that because beliefs are just about the way the world is and are made true (or false) depending on the way the world is, it is a confusion to believe that any given belief is true simply on the basis of its being willed. As soon as the believer—assuming that he understands these basic concepts—discovers the basis of his belief as being caused by the will alone, he must drop the belief. In this regard, saying "I believe that *p*, but I believe it only because I want to believe it," has the same incoherence attached to it as G. E. Moore's paradoxical, "I believe *p* but it is false that *p*." Structurally, neither is a strictly logical contradiction, but both show an incoherence that might be broadly called contradictory.

If this reasoning is sound, then we cannot be judged for our beliefs because beliefs are not actions. That is, if *ought* implies *can*, and we cannot acquire beliefs directly by choosing them, we cannot be judged according to our beliefs. Of course, we can be judged by our actions and by how well we have investigated the evidence and paid attention to the arguments on the various sides of the issue. That leads to the matter of the ethics of belief.

III. THE ETHICS OF BELIEF

Of course we can obtain beliefs indirectly by willing to have them. I can desire to believe that I am innocent of an unjust act against my neighbor—say directing my drain pipes to drain onto his property. I can bring to mind all the nasty things my neighbor may have done and use autosuggestion to convince myself that I am justified in redirecting may drain pipes toward his property, thus bringing about the desired belief. This manipulation of the mind is immoral. At the least, there is a strong case against indirect volitionalism.

W. K. Clifford has given a classic absolutist injunction against voliting: "It is wrong always, everywhere and for anyone to believe anything on insufficient evidence." This may have the sound of

too "robustious pathos in the voice" as James notes, but it may sound hyperbolic only because we have not taken truth seriously enough. Nevertheless, I defend the principle of an ethic of belief only as a *prima facie* moral principle—one which can be over-ridden by other moral principles—but which has strong presumptive force.[4]

Why do we want true justified beliefs—beliefs based on the best evidence available?

We want true justified beliefs because beliefs make up our road map of life; they guide our desires. If I believe that I can fly and jump out of the top of the Empire State Building to take a short cut to Columbia University, I'm likely to be disappointed. If I want to live a long life and believe that living on alcohol and poison ivy will enable me to do so, I will not attain my desire.

The importance of having well-justified beliefs is connected with truth-seeking in general. We believe that these two concepts are closely related, so the best way to assure ourselves of having true beliefs is to seek to develop one's belief-forming mechanisms in such ways as to become good judges of various types of evidence, attaining the best possible justification of our beliefs. The value of having the best possible justified beliefs can be defended on both deontological grounds with regard to the individual and on teleological or utilitarian grounds with regard to society as a whole. The deontological argument is connected with our notion of autonomy. To be an autonomous person is to have at one's disposal a high degree of warranted beliefs upon which to base one's actions. There is a tendency to lower one's freedom of choice as one lowers the repertoire of well-justified beliefs regarding a plan of action, and because it is a generally accepted moral principle that it is wrong to lessen one's autonomy or personhood, it is wrong to lessen the degree of justification of one's beliefs on important matters. Hence, there is a general presumption against beliefs by *willing* to have them. Cognitive voliting is a sort of lying or cheating in that it enjoins believing against what has the best guarantee of being the truth. When a friend or doctor lies to a terminally ill patient about her condition, the patient is deprived of the best evidence available for making decisions about her limited future. She is being treated less than fully autonomously. Whereas a form of paternalism may sometimes be justified, there is always a presumption against it and in favor of truth-telling. We even say that the patient has a *right* to know what the evidence points to. Cognitive voliting is a sort of lying to oneself, which, as such, decreases one's own freedom and personhood. It is a type of doxastic suicide that may be justified only in extreme circumstances. If there is something intrinsically wrong about lying (making it *prima facie* wrong), then there is something intrinsically wrong with cognitive voliting, either directly or indirectly. Whether it be Pascal, William James, John Henry Newman, or Søren Kierkegaard, all prescriptive volitionalists (consciously or not) seem to undervalue the principle of truthfulness and its relationship to personal autonomy.

The utilitarian, or teleological, argument against cognitive voliting is fairly straightforward. General truthfulness is a *desideratum* without which society cannot function. Without it language itself would not be possible because it depends on faithful use of words and sentences to stand for appropriately similar objects and states of affairs. Communication depends on a general adherence to accurate reporting. More specifically, it is very important that a society have true beliefs with regard to important issues so that actions that are based on beliefs have a firm basis.

The doctor who cheated her way through medical school and who, as a consequence, lacks appropriate beliefs about certain symptoms may endanger a patient's health. A politician who fails to take into consideration the amount of pollutants being discharged into the air or water by large corporations that support his candidacy may endanger the health and even the lives of his constituents. Even the passer-by who gives wrong information to a stranger who asks for directions may seriously inconvenience the stranger. Here Clifford's point about believing against the evidence is well taken, despite its all-too-robustious tone: the shipowner who failed to make necessary repairs on his vessel and "chose" to believe that the ship was seaworthy is guilty of the deaths of the passengers. "He had no right to believe on such evidence as was before him." It is because beliefs

are action-guiding maps by which we steer and, as such, tend to cause actions, that society has a keen interest in our having the best justified beliefs possible regarding important matters.

Some people object to my model of the verific person, the truth-seeker, as being neutral on the matter of religion. They point out that the issue is too important to permit neutrality as an appropriate attitude. Let me clear this up by making a distinction between *neutrality* and *impartiality*. The verific person is not neutral but impartial. For a proper model of the verific person—one seeking to proportion his or her beliefs to the strength of the evidence—consider the referee in an Army vs. Notre Dame football game. The veterans of foreign wars and Army alumni will tend to be biased toward Army, considering close calls against "their" team by the referee as clear instances of poor officiating—even of injustice. Roman Catholics throughout the nation will tend to be biased toward Notre Dame, seeing close calls against "their" team by the referee as clear instances of poor officiating—even of injustice. The neutral person is the atheist pacifist in the crowd—the one who doesn't care who wins the game. But the impartial person is the referee who, knowing that his wife has just bet their family fortune on the underdog, Notre Dame, still manages to call a fair game. He is able to separate his concerns about his financial security from his ability to discern the right calls in appropriate situations. The verific person is one who can be trusted to reach sound judgments where others are driven by bias, prejudice, and self-interest.

If we have a moral duty not to volit but to seek the truth impartially and passionately, then we ought not to obtain religious beliefs by willing to have them; instead we should follow the best evidence we can get.

IV. HOPE AS THE PROPER RELIGIOUS PROPOSITIONAL ATTITUDE FOR DOUBTERS

For those who find it impossible to believe directly that God exists and who follow an ethic of belief acquisition (voliting), hope may be a sufficient substitute for belief. I can hope that God exists without believing that He does.

Let us first analyze the concept of hope in order to determine whether it is a viable option. Consider some examples of hope.

1. Ryan hopes that he will get an A in his philosophy course.

2. Mary hopes that Tom will marry her.

3. Susan hopes that Happy Dancer will win the Kentucky Derby next week.

4. Steve hopes that the Cubs won their game yesterday.

5. Although Bill desires a cigarette, he hopes he will not give in to his desire.

6. Christy hopes her saying "no" to Ron's proposal of marriage is the right decision.

If we look closely at these examples of hoping, we can pick out salient features of the concept. First of all, hope involves *belief in the possibility* that a state of affairs obtains or can obtain. We cannot hope for what we believe to be impossible. If Ryan hopes to get an A in philosophy, he must believe that it is possible to do so, and if Mary hopes that Tom will marry her, she must deem it possible. The *Oxford English Dictionary* defines *hope* as an "expectation of something desired," but this seems too strong. Expectation implies belief that something will occur, whereas we may hope even when we do not expect the object to obtain, as when Mary hopes that Tom will marry her or when Steve hopes the languishing Cubs won their game against the awesome Atlanta Braves. Susan may hope that Happy Dancer will win the race even though she doesn't expect that to happen. Thus belief that the object of desire will obtain does not seem necessary for hope. It is enough that the hoper believe that the proposition in question is possible, though not necessarily probable (it has a subjective probability of greater than 0 but not necessarily greater than 0.5).

Second, hope precludes certainty. Mary is not certain that Tom will marry her, and Susan is not certain that Happy Dancer will win the race. There must

be an apparent possibility that the state of affairs will not obtain. We would think it odd to say, "Steve knows that the Cubs won the game yesterday, for he was there, but he still hopes that the Cubs won the game." As Paul wrote in Romans 8:24, "For hope that is seen is not hope: for what a man sees, why does he yet hope for?" Hope entails uncertainty, a subjective probability index of greater than 0 but less than 1.

Third, hope entails desire (or a pro-attitude) for the state of affairs in question to obtain or for the proposition to be true. In all of the preceding examples a propositional content can be seen as the object of desire. The states of affairs envisaged evoke a pro-attitude. The subject wants some proposition *p* to be true. It matters not whether the state of affairs is past (case 4) or present (cases 5 and 6) or future (cases 1 through 3), although it generally turns out, because of the role hope plays in goal orientation, that the state of affairs will be a future situation.

Fourth, the desire involved in hoping must be motivational—greater than mere *wishing*. I may wish to live forever, but if I don't think it is sufficiently probable or possible, it will not serve as a spring for action. I can wish, but not hope, for what I believe to be impossible—as when I wish I were twenty-years-old again. If I hope for some state of affairs to occur, under appropriate circumstances I will do what I can to bring it about—as Ryan will study hard to earn his A in philosophy. Bill's hope that he will not give in to his first-order desire for a cigarette will lead him to strive to reject the weed now being offered to him.

In this regard, hoping involves a willingness to run some risk because of the positive valuation of the object in question. Consider case 3 (Susan hopes Happy Dancer will win the Kentucky Derby). For this to be the case, Susan must be disposed to act in some way as to manifest trust in Happy Dancer. She may bet on the horse without believing he will win the race, and the degree to which she hopes Happy Dancer will win the race may be reflected in how much she is willing to bet.

Fifth, hoping—unlike believing—is typically under our direct control. I may decide to hope that the Cubs will win, but it doesn't make sense to decide to believe that they will win. I hear that my enemy is suffering and find myself hoping that he will suffer great harm. Then I reflect that this *schadenfreude* is a loathsome attitude and decide to change it (to hoping he will suffer only as he deserves!). I may or may not be able to give up a hope, but, unlike a belief, normally I am able to alter the degree to which I hope for something. I may find that I am hoping too strongly that I will get an A—I notice that I am preoccupied with it to the point of distraction—and decide to invest less hope in that goal. It seems that the degree of hope has something to do with cost-benefit analysis about the pay-off involved in obtaining a goal. The greater the combination of the (perceived) probability of *p* obtaining and the value to me of its obtaining, the more likely I am to hope for *p*. So reflection on the cost-benefits of *p* will affect hope. Still, I can exercise some voluntary control over my hopes in a way that I can't over beliefs.

Sixth, hoping—like wanting—is evaluative in a way that believing is not. We may have morally unacceptable hopes, but not morally unacceptable beliefs. Consider the difference between:

  i. "I believe that we are heading toward World War III in which nuclear weapons will destroy the world."

and

  ii. "I hope that we are heading toward World War III in which nuclear weapons will destroy the world."

Beliefs may be formed through a culpable lack of attention and thus have a moral dimension, but a belief itself cannot be judged moral or immoral. This is applicable to beliefs about racial or gender differences. Sometimes being a "racist" or a "sexist" is defined by holding that people of different races or genders have different native cognitive abilities. The inference is then made that because racism and sexism are immoral, anyone holding these beliefs is immoral. Such beliefs may be false, but unless the believer has obtained the belief through immoral activities, there is nothing immoral in having such beliefs, as such. So either racism and sexism should be defined differently (as immoral actions) or the

charge of immorality should be dropped (if it is simply the cognitive feature that is in question).

Finally, we must make a distinction between ordinary hope (such as hoping you will receive a high grade) and deep hope. Consider Susan's situation as she hopes that Happy Dancer will win. She may believe that horse has only a 1-in-10 chance of winning the Kentucky Derby, but she may judge this to be significantly better than the official odds of 100-to-1 against him. Suppose that she has only $10 but wants desperately to enter a professional program that costs $1,000. She has no hope of getting the money elsewhere, and if she bets on Happy Dancer and wins, she will get the required amount. Because she believes that the real odds are better than the official odds and that winning will enable her to get into the professional program, she bets her $10 on the horse. She commits herself to Happy Dancer although she never *believes* that he will win. We might call such cases where one is disposed to risk something significant on the possibility of the proposition's being true *deep* or *profound* hope. When the risk involves something of enormous value, we might call it *desperate* hope.

We conclude, then, that *hoping is distinguished from believing* in that it may involve a strong volitional or affective aspect in a way that believing does not and that, as such, it is subject to moral assessment in a way that believing is not. Hoping is desiderative, but it is more inclined to action than mere wishing. Hope may be ordinary or profound.

Let us apply this distinction to religious faith. Can hope serve as a *type of faith* in a religion like Christianity without the belief that the object of faith exists? Let me tell a story to help focus our discussion.

Suppose that when Moses decides to launch a pre-emptive strike against the Amalekites in obedience to the command of Yahweh (in the book of Exodus in the Hebrew Bible), his brother Aaron doubts whether such a pre-emptive strike is morally right, let alone the command of God. Aaron is inclined to make a treaty with the neighboring tribe. He doubts whether Yahweh has revealed such a command to Moses, doubts whether God appeared to Moses in the burning bush, and wonders whether

Moses is hallucinating. When Moses points out that God annihilated the Egyptian pharaoh's army, Aaron is inclined to see that deed as merely the army's getting caught in a flash flood. When Moses offers the fact that a cloud pillar leads them by day and that a pillar of fire leads them by night, Aaron entertains the supposition that the clouds are natural phenomena and the appearance of "fire" is simply the effect of the rays of the setting sun on the distant sands. Aaron is agnostic about both the existence of Yahweh and His "revelation" to Moses. Although he cannot bring himself to overcome his doubts, he opts for the better story. He decides to accept the proposition that Yahweh exists and has revealed himself to Moses, and so he lives according to this hypothesis as an experimental faith. He assists Moses in every way in carrying out the campaign. He proclaims the need for his people to fight against the enemy, helps hold up Moses's arms during the battle, and urges the warriors on to victory in the name of God.

True, Aaron may not act out of spontaneous abandon as Moses does. On the other hand, his scrupulous doubt may help him to notice problems and evidence that might otherwise be neglected and to which the true believer may be impervious. This awareness may signal danger that may be avoided, thus saving the tribe from disaster. Doubt may have as many virtues as belief, although they may be different.

Moses is the true believer, whereas Aaron— the doubter—lives in hope, *profound* hope. He believes that it would be a good thing if Moses's convictions are true and that it is possible that they are true, and so he decides to throw in his lot with his brother, living as if God exists and has revealed his plans to Moses.

The point may be put more simply. Suppose you are fleeing a murderous gang of desperados— perhaps members of the Mafia—who are bent on your annihilation. You come to the edge of a cliff that overlooks a yawning gorge. You find a rope spanning the gorge—tied to a tree on the cliff on the opposite side—and a man who announces that he is a tight-rope walker and can carry you over the gorge on the rope. He doesn't look as if he can do it, so you wonder whether he is insane or simply overconfident. He takes a few steps on the rope to assure you that he can balance himself. You agree that it's possible that he can navigate the rope across the gorge, but you have grave doubts about whether he can carry you. But your options are limited. Soon your pursuers will be upon you. You must decide. Whereas you still don't believe that the "tight-rope walker" can save you, you decide to trust him. You place your faith in his ability, climb on his back, close your eyes (so as not to look down into the yawning gorge), and do your best to relax and obey his commands in adjusting your body as he steps onto the rope. You have a profound, even *desperate*, hope that he will be successful.

This is how I see religious hope functioning in the midst of doubt. The verific person recognizes the tragedy of existence, that unless there is a God and life after death, the meaning of life is less than glorious, but if there is a God and life after death, the meaning of that life is glorious. There is just enough evidence to whet his or her appetite, to inspire hope, a decision to live according to theism or Christianity as an experimental hypothesis, but not enough evidence to cause belief. So keeping his or her mind open, the hoper opts for the better story, gets on the back of what may be the Divine Tight-Rope Walker, and commits to the pilgrimage. Perhaps the analogy is imperfect, for it may be possible to get off the tight-rope walker's back in actual existence and to get back to the cliff. Perhaps the Mafia men make a wrong turn or take their time searching for you. Still, the alternative to the tight-rope walker is not exactly welcoming: death and the extinction of all life in a solar system that will one day be extinguished. We may still learn to enjoy the fruits of finite love and resign ourselves to a final, cold fate. As Russell wrote:

> Brief and powerless is man's life; on him and all his race the slow, sure doom falls pitiless and dark. Blind to good and evil, reckless of destruction, omnipotent matter rolls on its relentless way; for man, condemned today to lose his dearest, tomorrow himself to pass through the gate of darkness, it remains only to cherish, ere yet the blow fall, the lofty thoughts that ennoble his little day; disdaining the

coward terrors of the slave of Fate, to worship at the shrine that his own hands have built; undismayed by the empire of chance, to preserve a mind free from the wanton tyranny that rules his outward life; proudly defiant of the irresistible forces that tolerate, for a moment, his knowledge and his condemnation, to sustain alone, a weary but unyielding Atlas, the world that his own ideals have fashioned despite the trampling march of unconscious power.[5]

But if there is some evidence for something better, something eternal, someone benevolent who rules the universe and will redeem the world from evil and despair, isn't it worth betting on that worldview? Shouldn't we, at least, consider getting on the back of the tight-rope walker and letting him carry us across the gorge?

CONCLUSION

1. What's so great about belief? Note that the Epistle of James tells us that belief is insufficient for salvation, for "the devils believe and also tremble" (James 2:19). Note too that the verse quoted by the minister to me as a 15-year-old (Romans 14:23) was taken out of context. The passage reads: "For meat destroy not the work of God. All things are pure; but it is evil for that man who eateth with offense. It is good neither to eat flesh, nor to drink wine, nor any thing whereby thy brother stumbleth, or is offended, or is made weak. Hast thou faith? Have it to thyself before God. Happy is he that condemneth not himself in that thing which he alloweth. And he that doubteth is damned if he eats, because he eateth not of faith, for whatsoever is not of faith is sin." The passage is not about one's eternal salvation but about eating meat previously offered to idols. Paul is saying, "Let your conscience be your guide here. If your conscience condemns you—if you have doubts about this act—then refrain!"

2. Can we be judged (condemned) for our beliefs? No, not for our beliefs, as such, for they are not things we choose, so we're not (directly) responsible for them; we can be judged only according to what we have responsibly done (ought implies can).

    a. We can be judged only for things over which we have control.

    b. We only have control over our actions.

    c. Beliefs are not actions.

    d. Therefore we cannot be judged for our beliefs, but only for our actions.

    Although we have some *indirect* control over acquiring beliefs, we ought not violate the ethics of belief and force ourselves to believe more than the evidence warrants.

3. We can be judged by how faithful we have been to the light we have, to how well we have lived, including how well we have impartially sought the truth. We may adopt theism and/or Christianity as experimental faith, living by hope in God, yet keeping our minds open to new evidence that may confirm or disconfirm our decision.

    If this argument is sound, the people who truly have faith in God are those who live with moral integrity within their lights—some unbelievers will be in heaven and some religious, true believers, who never doubted, will be absent. My supposition is that they will be in purgatory. What is purgatory? It is a large philosophy department where people who compromised the truth and the good will be taught to think critically and morally, according to the ethics of belief. The faculty, God's servants in truth-seeking, will be David Hume, John Stuart Mill, Voltaire, Immanuel Kant, and Bertrand Russell.

NOTES

1. Whoever desires to be saved must above all things hold the Catholic faith. Unless a man keeps it in its entirety, inviolate, he will assuredly perish eternally. Now this is the Catholic faith, that we worship one God in Trinity and Trinity in unity without either confusing the persons or dividing the substance. . . . So he who desires to be saved should think thus of the Trinity.

   It is necessary, however, to eternal salvation that he should also faithfully believe in the Incarnation of our Lord Jesus Christ. Now the right faith is that we should believe and confess that our Lord Jesus Christ, the Son of God, is equally both God and man.

   This is the Catholic faith. Unless a man believes it faithfully and steadfastly, he will not be able to be saved. (Athanasian Creed).

2. Most theologians and Christian philosophers hold that belief is a necessary condition for faith. For example, Alvin Plantinga writes, "The mature theist does not typically accept belief in God tentatively or hypothetically or until something better comes along. Nor, I think, does he accept it as a conclusion from other things he believes; he accepts it as basic, as a part of the foundations of his noetic structure. The mature theist commits himself to belief in God: this means that he accepts belief in God as basic." ("Is Belief in God Rational" in *Rationality and Religious Belief*, ed. C. F. Delaney, Notre Dame University Press, 1979, p. 27).

3. Much more needs to be said than can be said here. I have developed a fuller argument against direct volitionalism in my book *What Can We Know?* (Wadsworth Publishing Co., 2001).

4. Many philosophers have criticized Clifford's advice as being self-referentially incoherent. It doesn't have sufficient evidence for itself. But, suitably modified, I think this problem can be overcome. We can give reasons why we ought generally to try to believe according to the evidence, and if these reasons are sound, then we do have sufficient evidence for accepting the principle. See W. K. Clifford, Reading V.B.2 in this book.

5. Bertrand Russell, "A Free Man's Worship," pp. 104–116 in his *Why I Am Not A Christian and Other Essays on Religion and Related Subjects*, edited by Paul Edwards (Simon & Schuster, 1967).

V.B. PRAGMATIC JUSTIFICATION OF RELIGIOUS BELIEF

Introduction

THIS SECTION CONTAINS readings that deal with the practical reasonableness of religious belief. Even if we cannot find good evidence for religious beliefs, would it perhaps be in our interest to get ourselves to believe in these propositions anyway? And would such believing be morally permissible? In the first reading, "The Wager," the renowned French physicist and mathematician Blaise Pascal (1623–1662) argues that if we do a cost–benefit analysis of the matter, we find that it is eminently reasonable to take steps to put ourselves in a position to believe that God exists—and this regardless of whether we have good evidence for that belief.

The argument goes something like this: Regarding the proposition "God exists," reason is neutral. It can neither prove nor disprove the proposition. But we must wager. That is, we must live as if God exists or as if he does not exist—where living as if God exists involves acting as if theistic doctrines (and, for Pascal,

TABLE 5.1

	God exists	God does not exist
Bet that God exists	A. Infinite gain with minimal finite loss	B. Overall finite loss in terms of sacrifice of earthly goods
Bet that God does not exist	C. Infinite loss with finite gain	D. Overall finite gain

specifically Christian doctrines) are true. Living as if God exists does not guarantee that belief will follow; but, on Pascal's view, it makes belief more likely. And since the benefits associated with belief promise to be infinite (and the loss equally infinite if we bet against God's existence and turn out to be wrong), we might set forth the possibilities shown in Table 5.1. There is some sacrifice of earthly pleasures involved in betting on God. But the fact is, no matter how enormous the *finite* gain associated with betting against God's existence, the mere possibility of *infinite* gain associated with betting in favor of God's existence will always make the latter preferable to the former. In short, we have a clear self-interested reason for betting on God.

Pascal is commonly understood as suggesting that we ought to *believe* in God (as opposed to simply living as if God exists in the hope or expectation that evidentially grounded belief will follow) because it is in our interests to do so. In the second reading, "The Ethics of Belief," the British philosopher W. K. Clifford (1845–1879) assembles reason's roadblocks to such pragmatic justifications for religious belief. Clifford argues that there is an ethics to belief that makes it immoral to believe something without sufficient evidence. Pragmatic justifications are not justifications at all but counterfeits of genuine justifications, which must always be based on evidence.

Clifford illustrates his thesis with the example of a ship owner who sends an emigrant ship to sea. He knows that the ship is old and not well built but fails to have the ship inspected. Dismissing from his mind all doubts about the vessel's seaworthiness, the owner trusts in Providence to care for his ship. He acquires a sincere and comfortable conviction in this way and collects his insurance money without a trace of guilt after the ship sinks and all the passengers drown. Clifford comments that although the ship owner sincerely believed that all was well with the ship, his sincerity in no way exculpates him because "he had no right to believe on such evidence as was before him." One has an obligation to get oneself in a position in which one will believe propositions only on sufficient evidence.

Some may object that the ship owner simply had an obligation to *act* in a certain way (viz., inspect the ship), not to *believe* in a certain way. Granted, the ship owner does have an obligation to inspect the ship; but the objection overlooks the function of believing in guiding action. "No man holding a strong belief on one side of a question, or even wishing to hold a belief on one side, can investigate it with such fairness and completeness as if he were really in doubt and unbiased; so that the existence of a belief not founded on fair inquiry unfits a man for the performance of this necessary duty." The general conclusion is that it is always wrong for anyone to believe anything on insufficient evidence.

The classic response to Clifford's ethics of belief is William James's "The Will to Believe" (1896), the last reading in this section. James argues that life would be greatly impoverished if we confined our beliefs to such a Scrooge-like epistemology as Clifford proposes. In everyday life, where the evidence for important propositions is often unclear, we must live by faith or cease to act at all. Although we may not make leaps of faith just anywhere, sometimes practical considerations force us to make decisions about propositions that do not have their truth value written on their faces. Thus, in "The Will to Believe" James argues on behalf of the rationality of believing, even with insufficient evidence, certain kinds of hypotheses—namely, those where the choice between the hypothesis and its denial is *live, momentous*, and *unavoidable*. For, he argues, to withhold belief on such momentous matters until sufficient evidence is forthcoming may, in the end, be too costly.

There is a good illustration of James's point in a different essay, "The Sentiment of Rationality," from which we quoted in the introduction to Part V.A. A mountain climber in the Alps finds himself in a position from which he can escape only by means of an enormous leap. If he tries to calculate the evidence, believing only on sufficient evidence, he will be paralyzed by emotions of fear and mistrust and hence will be lost. Without evidence that he is capable of performing this feat successfully, the climber would be better off getting himself to believe that he can and will make the leap. "In this case ... the part of wisdom clearly is to believe what one desires; for the belief is one of the indispensable preliminary conditions of the realization of its object. *There are then cases where faith creates its own verification.*" James claims that religion may be such an optional hypothesis for many people, and in this case one has the right to believe the better story rather than the worse. To do so, one must will to believe what the evidence alone is inadequate to support.

There are two questions, one descriptive and the other normative, that are important to consider in connection with the essays in this section. The first is whether it is possible to believe propositions at will. In what sense can we get ourselves to believe propositions that the evidence does not force upon us. Surely we cannot believe that the world is flat or that two plus two equals five simply by willing to do so, but which propositions (if any) are subject to volitional influences? Is it, then, psychologically impossible to believe something simply because it is in our interests to do so? Does it involve self-deception? If we know that the primary cause for our belief in a religious proposition is our desire to believe, can we rationally continue to believe that proposition?

The second question involves the ethics of belief, stressed by Clifford. Supposing that we can get ourselves to believe or disbelieve propositions for self-interested reasons, is this morally permissible? What are the arguments for and against integrity of belief? Note too that Pascal, unlike James, does not seem to suppose that we have *direct* voluntary control over our beliefs. Pascal's advice, again, is to *cultivate* belief—to *act* as if you believe (e.g., by going to church, participating in Mass, taking holy water) in the hope and expectation that belief will naturally follow. James, on the other hand, seems to be defending the rationality of acquiring beliefs simply by fiat of the will.

V.B.1

The Wager

BLAISE PASCAL

Blaise Pascal (1623–1662) was a renowned French physicist and mathematician. In 1654, at the age of 31, Pascal had an intense religious experience that completely changed his life. After this experience, he devoted himself to prayer and the study of Scripture, abandoned his mathematical and scientific endeavors, and set himself to the task of writing a defense of the Christian faith. The book was never finished, but this selection is taken from Pascal's notes, compiled under the title Pensées. *Here he argues that if we do a cost–benefit analysis of the matter, we find that it is eminently reasonable to take steps to put ourselves in a position to believe that God exists, regardless of whether we now have good evidence for that belief.*

Infinite—nothing.—Our soul is cast into a body, where it finds number, time, dimension. Thereupon it reasons, and calls this nature, necessity, and can believe nothing else.

Unity joined to infinity adds nothing to it, no more than one foot to an infinite measure. The finite is annihilated in the presence of the infinite, and becomes a pure nothing. So our spirit before God, so our justice before divine justice. There is not so great disproportion between our justice and that of God, as between unity and infinity.

The justice of God must be vast like His compassion. Now, justice to the outcast is less vast, and ought less to offend our feelings than mercy towards the elect.

We know that there is an infinite, and are ignorant of its nature. As we know it to be false that numbers are finite, it is therefore true that there is an infinity in number. But we do not know what it is. It is false that it is even, it is false that it is odd; for the addition of a unit can make no change in its nature. Yet it is a number, and every number is odd or even (this is certainly true of every finite number). So we may well know that there is a God without knowing what He is. Is there not one substantial truth, seeing there are so many things which are not the truth itself?

We know then the existence and nature of the finite, because we also are finite and have extension. We know the existence of the infinite, and are ignorant of its nature, because it has extension like us, but not limits like us. But we know neither the existence nor the nature of God, because He has neither extension nor limits.

But by faith we know His existence; in glory we shall know His nature. Now, I have already shown that we may well know the existence of a thing, without knowing its nature.

Let us now speak according to natural lights.

If there is a God, He is infinitely incomprehensible, since, having neither parts nor limits, He has no affinity to us. We are then incapable of knowing either what He is or if He is. This being so, who will dare to undertake the decision of the question? Not we, who have no affinity to Him.

Who then will blame Christians for not being able to give a reason for their belief, since they profess a religion for which they cannot give a reason?

Reprinted from Blaise Pascal, *Thoughts*, translated by W. F. Trotter (New York: Collier & Son, 1910).

They declare, in expounding it to the world, that it is a foolishness, *stultitiam*; and then you complain that they do not prove it! If they proved it, they would not keep their words; it is in lacking proofs, that they are not lacking in sense. "Yes, but although this excuses those who offer it as such, and takes away from them the blame of putting it forward without reason, it does not excuse those who receive it." Let us then examine this point, and say, "God is, or He is not." But to which side shall we incline? Reason can decide nothing here. There is an infinite chasm which separates us. A game is being played at the extremity of this infinite distance where heads or tails will turn up. What will you wager? According to reason, you can do neither the one thing nor the other, according to reason, you can defend neither of the propositions.

Do not then reprove for error those who have made a choice; for you know nothing about it. "No, but I blame them for having made, not this choice, but a choice; for again both he who chooses heads and he who chooses tails are equally at fault, they are both in the wrong. The true course is not to wager at all."

—Yes; but you must wager. It is not optional. You are embarked. Which will you choose then; let us see. Since you must choose, let us see which interests you least. You have two things to lose, the true and the good; and two things to stake, your reason and your will, your knowledge and your happiness; and your nature has two things to shun, error and misery. Your reason is no more shocked in choosing one rather than the other, since you must of necessity choose. This is one point settled. But your happiness? Let us weigh the gain and the loss in wagering that God is. Let us estimate these two chances. If you gain, you gain all; if you lose, you lose nothing. Wager them without hesitation that He is.—"That is very fine. Yes, I must wager; but I may perhaps wager too much."—Let us see.

Since there is an equal risk of gain and of loss, if you had only to gain two lives, instead of one, you might still wager. But if there were three lives to gain, you would have to play (since you are under the necessity of playing), and you would be imprudent, when you are forced to play, not to chance your life to gain three at a game where there is an equal risk of loss and gain. But there is an eternity of life and happiness. And this being so, if there were an infinity of chances, of which one only would be for you, you would still be right in wagering one to win two, and you would act stupidly, being obliged to play, by refusing to stake one life against three at a game in which out of an infinity of an infinitely happy life to gain. But there is here an infinity of an infinitely happy life to gain a chance of gain against a finite number of chances of loss, and what you stake is infinite. It is all divided; wherever the infinite is and there is not an infinity of chances of loss against that of gain, there is no time to hesitate, you must give all. And thus, when one is forced to play, he must renounce reason to preserve his life, rather than risk it for infinite gain, as likely to happen as the loss of nothingness.

For it is no use to say it is uncertain if we will gain, and it is certain that we risk, and that the infinite distance between the *certainty* of what is staked and the *uncertainty* of what will be gained, equals the finite good which is certainly staked against the uncertain infinite. It is not so, as every player stakes a certainty to gain an uncertainty, and yet he stakes a finite certainty to gain a finite uncertainty, without transgressing against reason. There is not an infinite distance between the certainty staked and the uncertainty of the gain; that is untrue. In truth, there is an infinity between the certainty of gain and the certainty of loss. But the uncertainty of the gain is proportioned to the certainty of the stake according to the proportion of the chances of gain and loss. Hence it comes that, if there are as many risks on one side as on the other, the course is to play even; and then the certainty of the stake is equal to the uncertainty of the gain, so far is it from the fact that there is an infinite distance between them. And so our proposition is of infinite force, when there is the finite to stake in a game where there are equal risks of gain and loss, and the infinite to gain. This is demonstrable; and if men are capable of any truths, this is one.

V.B.2

The Ethics of Belief

W. K. CLIFFORD

W. K. Clifford (1845–1879) was a British philosopher and mathematician. The selection that follows is perhaps his best known and most widely discussed philosophical essay. Clifford argues that there is an ethics to belief that makes it always wrong for anyone to believe anything on insufficient evidence. Pragmatic justifications are not justifications at all but counterfeits of genuine justifications, which must always be based on evidence.

A shipowner was about to send to sea an emigrant ship. He knew that she was old, and not over-well built at the first; that she had seen many seas and climes, and often had needed repairs. Doubts had been suggested to him that possibly she was not seaworthy. These doubts preyed upon his mind and made him unhappy; he thought that perhaps he ought to have her thoroughly overhauled and refitted, even though this should put him to great expense. Before the ship sailed, however, he succeeded in overcoming these melancholy reflections. He said to himself that she had gone safely through so many voyages and weathered so many storms that it was idle to suppose she would not come safely home from this trip also. He would put his trust in Providence, which could hardly fail to protect all these unhappy families that were leaving their fatherland to seek for better times elsewhere. He would dismiss from his mind all ungenerous suspicions about the honesty of builders and contractors. In such ways he acquired a sincere and comfortable conviction that his vessel was thoroughly safe and seaworthy; he watched her departure with a light heart, and benevolent wishes for the success of the exiles in their strange new home that was to be; and he got his insurance money when she went down in midocean and told no tales.

What shall we say of him? Surely this, that he was verily guilty of the death of those men. It is admitted that he did sincerely believe in the soundness of his ship; but the sincerity of his conviction can in no wise help him, because he had no right to believe on such evidence as was before him. He had acquired his belief not by honestly earning it in patient investigation, but by stifling his doubts. And although in the end he may have felt so sure about it that he could not think otherwise, yet inasmuch as he had knowingly and willingly worked himself into that frame of mind, he must be held responsible for it.

Let us alter the case a little, and suppose that the ship was not unsound after all; that she made her voyage safely, and many others after it. Will that diminish the guilt of her owner? Not one jot. When an action is once done, it is right or wrong forever; no accidental failure of its good or evil fruits can possibly alter that. The man would not have been innocent, he would only have been not found out. The question of right or wrong has to do with the origin of his belief, not the matter of it; not what it was, but how he got it; not whether it

Reprinted from W. K. Clifford, *Lecturers and Essays* (London: Macmillan, 1879).

turned out to be true or false, but whether he had a right to believe on such evidence as was before him.

There was once an island in which some of the inhabitants professed a religion teaching neither the doctrine of original sin nor that of eternal punishment. A suspicion got abroad that the professors of this religion had made use of unfair means to get their doctrines taught to children. They were accused of wresting the laws of their country in such a way as to remove children from the care of their natural and legal guardians; and even of stealing them away and keeping them concealed from their friends and relations. A certain number of men formed themselves into a society for the purpose of agitating the public about this matter. They published grave accusations against individual citizens of the highest position and character, and did all in their power to injure those citizens in the exercise of their professions. So great was the noise they made, that a Commission was appointed to investigate the facts; but after the Commission had carefully inquired into all the evidence that could be got, it appeared that the accused were innocent. Not only had they been accused on insufficient evidence, but the evidence of their innocence was such as the agitators might easily have obtained, if they had attempted a fair inquiry. After these disclosures the inhabitants of that country looked upon the members of the agitating society, not only as persons whose judgment was to be distrusted, but also as no longer to be counted honorable men. For although they had sincerely and conscientiously believed in the charges they had made, yet they had no right to believe on such evidence as was before them. Their sincere convictions, instead of being honestly earned by patient inquiring, were stolen by listening to the voice of prejudice and passion.

Let us vary this case also, and suppose, other things remaining as before, that a still more accurate investigation proved the accused to have been really guilty. Would this make any difference in the guilt of the accusers? Clearly not; the question is not whether their belief was true or false, but whether they entertained it on wrong grounds.

They would no doubt say, "Now you see that we were right after all; next time perhaps you will believe us." And they might be believed, but they would not thereby become honorable men. They would not be innocent, they would only be not found out. Every one of them, if he chose to examine himself *in foro conscientiae*, would know that he had acquired and nourished a belief, when he had no right to believe on such evidence as was before him; and therein he would know that he had done a wrong thing.

It may be said, however, that in both of these supposed cases it is not the belief which is judged to be wrong, but the action following upon it. The shipowner might say, "I am perfectly certain that my ship is sound, but still I feel it my duty to have her examined, before trusting the lives of so many people to her." And it might be said to the agitator, "However convinced you were of the justice of your cause and the truth of your convictions, you ought not to have made a public attack upon any man's character until you had examined the evidence on both sides with the utmost patience and care."

In the first place, let us admit that, so far as it goes, this view of the case is right and necessary; right, because even when a man's belief is so fixed that he cannot think otherwise, he still has a choice in regard to the action suggested by it, and so cannot escape the duty of investigating on the ground of the strength of his convictions; and necessary, because those who are not yet capable of controlling their feelings and thoughts must have a plain rule dealing with overt acts.

But this being premised as necessary, it becomes clear that it is not sufficient, and that our previous judgment is required to supplement it. For it is not possible so to sever the belief from the action it suggests as to condemn the one without condemning the other. No man holding a strong belief on one side of a question, or even wishing to hold a belief on one side, can investigate it with such fairness and completeness as if he were really in doubt and unbiased; so that the existence of a belief not founded on fair inquiry unfits a man for the performance of this necessary duty.

Nor is that truly a belief at all which has not some influence upon the actions of him who holds it. He who truly believes that which prompts him to an action has looked upon the action to lust after it, he has committed it already in his heart. If a belief is not realized immediately in open deeds, it is stored up for the guidance of the future. It goes to make a part of that aggregate of beliefs which is the link between sensation and action at every moment of all our lives, and which is so organized and compacted together that no part of it can be isolated from the rest, but every new addition modifies the structure of the whole. No real belief, however trifling and fragmentary it may seem, is ever truly insignificant; it prepares us to receive more of its like, confirms those which resembled it before, and weakens others; and so gradually it lays a stealthy train in our inmost thoughts, which may some day explode into overt action, and leave its stamp upon our character forever.

And no one man's belief is in any case a private matter which concerns himself alone. Our lives are guided by that general conception of the course of things which has been created by society for social purposes. Our words, our phrases, our forms and processes and modes of thought are common property, fashioned and perfected from age to age; an heirloom which every succeeding generation inherits as a precious deposit and a sacred trust to be handed on to the next one, not unchanged but enlarged and purified, with some clear marks of its proper handiwork. Into this, for good or ill, is woven every belief of every man who has speech of his fellows. An awful privilege, and an awful responsibility, that we should help to create the world in which posterity will live.

In the two supposed cases which have been considered, it has been judged wrong to believe on insufficient evidence, or to nourish belief by suppressing doubts and avoiding investigation. The reason of this judgment is not far to seek: it is that in both these cases the belief held by one man was of great importance to other men. But for as much as no belief held by one man, however seemingly trivial the belief, and however obscure the believer, is ever actually insignificant or without its effect on the fate of mankind, we have no choice but to extend our judgment to all cases of belief whatever. Belief, that sacred faculty which prompts the decisions of our will, and knits into harmonious working all the compacted energies of our being, is ours not for ourselves, but for humanity. It is rightly used on truths which have been established by long experience and waiting toil, and which have stood in the fierce light of free and fearless questioning. Then it helps to bind men together, and to strengthen and direct their common action. It is desecrated when given to unproved and unquestioned statements, for the solace and private pleasure of the believer; to add a tinsel splendor to the plain straight road of our life and display a bright mirage beyond it; or even to drown the common sorrows of our kind by a self-deception which allows them not only to cast down, but also to degrade us. Whoso would deserve well of his fellows in this matter will guard the purity of his belief with a very fanaticism of jealous care, lest at any time it should rest on an unworthy object, and catch a stain which can never be wiped away.

It is not only the leader of men, statesman, philosopher or poet, that owes this bounden duty to mankind. Every rustic who delivers in the village alehouse his slow, infrequent sentences, may help to kill or keep alive the fatal superstitions which clog his race. Every hard-worked wife of an artisan may transmit to her children beliefs which shall knit society together, or rend it in pieces. No simplicity of mind, no obscurity of station, can escape the universal duty of questioning all that we believe.

It is true that this duty is a hard one, and the doubt which comes out of it is often a very bitter thing. It leaves us bare and powerless where we thought that we were safe and strong. To know all about anything is to know how to deal with it under all circumstances. We feel much happier and more secure when we think we know precisely what to do, no matter what happens, than when we have lost our way and do not know where to turn. And if we have supposed ourselves to know all about anything, and to be capable of doing what is fit in regard to it, we naturally do not like to find that we are really ignorant and powerless, that we have to begin again at the beginning, and try to learn what the thing is and how it is to be dealt with—if indeed anything can be learned about it. It is the sense of power attached to a sense of knowledge that makes men desirous of believing, and afraid of doubting.

This sense of power is the highest and best of pleasures when the belief on which it is founded is a true belief, and has been fairly earned by investigation. For then we may justly feel that it is common property, and holds good for others as well as for ourselves. Then we may be glad, not that I have learned secrets by which I am safer and stronger, but that we men have got mastery over more of the world; and we shall be strong, not for ourselves, but in the name of Man and in his strength. But if the belief has been accepted on insufficient evidence, the pleasure is a stolen one. Not only does it deceive ourselves by giving us a sense of power which we do not really possess, but it is sinful, because it is stolen in defiance of our duty to mankind. That duty is to guard ourselves from such beliefs as from a pestilence, which may shortly master our own body and then spread to the rest of the town. What would be thought of one who, for the sake of a sweet fruit, should deliberately run the risk of bringing a plague upon his family and his neighbors?

And, as in other such cases, it is not the risk only which has to be considered; for a bad action is always bad at the time when it is done, no matter what happens afterwards. Every time we let ourselves believe for unworthy reasons, we weaken our powers of self-control, of doubting, of judicially and fairly weighing evidence. We all suffer severely enough from the maintenance and support of false beliefs and the fatally wrong actions which they lead to, and the evil born when one such belief is entertained is great and wide. But a greater and wider evil arises when the credulous character is maintained and supported, when a habit of believing for unworthy reasons is fostered and made permanent. If I steal money from any person, there may be no harm done by the mere transfer of possession; he may not feel the loss, or it may prevent him from using the money badly. But I cannot help doing this great wrong towards Man, that I make myself dishonest. What hurts society is

not that it should lose its property, but that it should become a den of thieves; for then it must cease to be society. This is why we ought not to do evil that good may come; for at any rate this great evil has come, that we have done evil and are made wicked thereby. In like manner, if I let myself believe anything on insufficient evidence, there may be no great harm done by the mere belief; it may be true after all, or I may never have occasion to exhibit it in outward acts. But I cannot help doing this great wrong toward Man, that I make myself credulous. The danger to society is not merely that it should believe wrong things, though that is great enough; but that it should become credulous, and lose the habit of testing things and inquiring into them; for then it must sink back into savagery.

The harm which is done by credulity in a man is not confined to the fostering of a credulous character in others, and consequent support of false beliefs. Habitual want of care about what I believe leads to habitual want of care in others about the truth of what is told to me. Men speak the truth to one another when each reveres the truth in his own mind and in the other's mind; but how shall my friend revere the truth in my mind when I myself am careless about it, when I believe things because I want to believe them, and because they are comforting and pleasant? Will he not learn to cry, "Peace," to me, when there is no peace? By such a course I shall surround myself with a thick atmosphere of falsehood and fraud, and in that must live. It may matter little to me, in my closed castle of sweet illusions and darling lies; but it matters much to Man that I have made my neighbors ready to deceive. The credulous man is father to the liar and the cheat; he lives in the bosom of this his family, and it is no marvel if he should become even as they are. So closely are our duties knit together, that whoso shall keep the whole law, and yet offend in one point, he is guilty of all.

To sum up: it is wrong always, everywhere and for anyone, to believe anything upon insufficient evidence.

If a man, holding a belief which he was taught in childhood or persuaded of afterwards, keeps down and pushes away any doubts which arise about it in his mind, purposely avoids the reading of books and the company of men that call in question or discuss it, and regards as impious those questions which cannot easily be asked without disturbing it—the life of that man is one long sin against mankind.

If this judgment seems harsh when applied to those simple souls who have never known better, who have been brought up from the cradle with a horror of doubt, and taught that their eternal welfare depends on what they believe, then it leads to the very serious question, Who hath made Israel to sin? . . .

Inquiry into the evidence of a doctrine is not to be made once for all, and then taken as finally settled. It is never lawful to stifle a doubt; for either it can be honestly answered by means of the inquiry already made, or else it proves that the inquiry was not complete.

"But," says one, "I am a busy man; I have no time for the long course of study which would be necessary to make me in any degree a competent judge of certain questions, or even able to understand the nature of the arguments." Then he should have no time to believe. . . .

V.B.3

The Will to Believe

WILLIAM JAMES

William James (1842–1910) was a philosopher and psychologist, the elder brother of novelist Henry James, and one of the central figures in the American pragmatist school of philosophy. Among his more important works are The Varieties of Religious Experience *(1902),* Pragmatism *(1907), and* The Meaning of Truth *(1909). In this essay James argues, against W. K. Clifford, that sometimes practical considerations force us to make decisions on propositions for which we do not yet and, indeed, may never have sufficient evidence.*

I

Let us give the name of hypothesis to anything that may be proposed to our belief; and just as the electricians speak of live and dead wires, let us speak of any hypothesis as either *live* or *dead*. A live hypothesis is one which appeals as a real possibility to him to whom it is proposed. If I ask you to believe in the Mahdi, the notion makes no electric connection with your nature—it refuses to scintillate with

any credibility at all. As an hypothesis it is completely dead. To an Arab, however (even if he be not one of the Mahdi's followers), the hypothesis is among the mind's possibilities: It is alive. This shows that deadness and liveness in an hypothesis are not intrinsic properties, but relations to the individual thinker. They are measured by his willingness to act. The maximum of liveness in an hypothesis means willingness to act irrevocably. Practically, that means belief; but there is some

Reprinted from William James, *The Will to Believe* (New York: Longmans Green & Co., 1897).

believing tendency wherever there is willingness to act at all.

Next, let us call the decision between two hypotheses an option. Options may be of several kinds. They maybe first, *living* or *dead*; secondly, *forced* or *avoidable*; thirdly, *momentous* or *trivial*; and for our purposes we may call an option a *genuine* option when it is of a forced, living, and momentous kind.

1. A living option is one in which both hypotheses are live ones. If I say to you: "Be a theosophist or be a Mohammedan," it is probably a dead option, because for you neither hypothesis is likely to be alive. But if I say: "Be an agnostic or be a Christian," it is otherwise: trained as you are, each hypothesis makes some appeal, however small, to your belief.

2. Next, if I say to you: "Choose between going out with your umbrella or without it," I do not offer you a genuine option, for it is not forced. You can easily avoid it by not going out at all. Similarly, if I say, "Either love me or hate me," "Either call my theory true or call it false," your option is avoidable. You may remain indifferent to me, neither loving nor hating, and you may decline to offer any judgment as to my theory. But if I say, "Either accept this truth or go without it," I put on you a forced option, for there is no standing place outside of the alternative. Every dilemma based on a complete logical disjunction, with no possibility of not choosing, is an option of this forced kind.

3. Finally, if I were Dr. Nansen and proposed to you to join my North Pole expedition, your option would be momentous; for this would probably be your similar opportunity, and your choice now would either exclude you from the North Pole sort of immortality altogether or put at least the chance of it into your hands. He who refuses to embrace a unique opportunity loses the prize as surely as if he tried and failed. Per contra, the option is trivial when the opportunity is not unique, when the stake is insignificant, or when the decision is reversible if it later proves unwise. Such trivial options abound in the scientific life. A chemist finds an hypothesis live enough to spend a year in its verification: he believes in it to that extent. But if his experiments prove inconclusive either way, he is quit for his loss of time, no vital harm being done.

It will facilitate our discussion if we keep all these distinctions well in mind.

II

The next matter to consider is the actual psychology of human opinion. When we look at certain facts, it seems as if our passional and volitional nature lay at the root of all our convictions. When we look at others, it seems as if they could do nothing when the intellect had once said its say. Let us take the latter facts up first.

Does it not seem preposterous on the very face of it to talk of our opinions being modifiable at will? Can our will either help or hinder our intellect in its perceptions of truth? Can we, by just willing it, believe that Abraham Lincoln's existence is a myth, and that the portraits of him in *McClure's Magazine* are all of some one else? Can we, by any effort of our will, or by any strength of wish that it were true, believe ourselves well and about when we are roaring with rheumatism in bed, or feel certain that the sum of the two one-dollar bills in our pocket must be a hundred dollars? We can say any of these things, but we are absolutely impotent to believe them; and of just such things is the whole fabric of the truths that we do believe in made up—matters of fact, immediate or remote, as Hume said, and relations between ideas, which are either there or not there for us if we see them so, and which if not there cannot be put there by any action of our own.

In Pascal's *Thoughts* there is a celebrated passage known in literature as Pascal's Wager. In it he tries to force us into Christianity by reasoning as if our concern with truth resembled our concern with the stakes in a game of chance. Translated freely his words are these: You must either believe or not believe that God is—which will you do? Your human reason cannot say. A game is going on between you and the nature of things which at the day of judgment will bring out either heads or tails. Weigh what your gains and your losses would be if you should stake all you have on heads, or God's existence: if you win in such case you gain eternal beatitude; if you lose, you lose nothing at all. If there were an infinity of chances and only one for God in this wager, still you ought to stake your all on God; for though you surely risk a finite loss by this procedure, any finite loss is reasonable, even a certain one is reasonable, if there is but the possibility of infinite gain. Go then, and take holy water, and have masses said: belief will come and stupefy your scruples. ... Why should you not? At bottom, what have you to lose?

You probably feel that when religious faith expresses itself thus, in the language of the gaming-table, it is put to its last trumps. Surely Pascal's own personal belief in masses and holy water had far other springs; and this celebrated page of his is but an argument for others, a last desperate snatch at a weapon against the hardness of the unbelieving heart. We feel that a faith in masses and holy water adopted wilfully after such a mechanical calculation would lack the inner soul of faith's reality; and if we were ourselves in the place of the Deity, we should probably take particular pleasure in cutting off believers of this pattern from their infinite reward. It is evident that unless there be some pre-existing tendency to believe in masses and holy water, the option offered to the will by Pascal is not a living option. Certainly no Turk ever took to masses and holy water on its account and even to us Protestants these means of salvation seem such foregone impossibilities that Pascal's logic, invoked for them specifically, leaves us unmoved. As well might the Mahdi write to us saying, "I am the Expected One whom God has created in his effulgence. You shall be infinitely happy if you confess me; otherwise you shall be cut off from the light of the sun. Weigh, then, your infinite gain if I am genuine against your finite sacrifice if I am not!" His logic would be that of Pascal; but he would

vainly use it on us, for the hypothesis he offers us is dead. No tendency to act on it exists in us to any degree.

The talk of believing by our volition seems, then from one point of view, simply silly. From another point of view it is worse than silly, it is vile. When one turns to the magnificent edifice of the physical sciences, and sees how it was reared; what thousands of disinterested moral lives of men lie buried in its mere foundations; what patience and postponement, what choking down of preference, what submission to the icy laws of outer fact are wrought into its very stones and mortar; how absolutely impersonal it stands in its vast augustness— then how besotted and contemptible seems every little sentimentalist who comes blowing his voluntary smoke-wreaths, and pretending to decide things from out of his private dream! Can we wonder if those bred in the rugged and manly school of science should feel like spewing such subjectivism out of their mouths? The whole system of loyalties which grow up in the schools of science go dead against its toleration; so that it is only natural that those who have caught the scientific fever should pass over to the opposite extreme, and write sometimes as if the incorruptibly truthful intellect ought positively to prefer bitterness and unacceptableness to the heart in its cup.

It fortifies my soul to know
That though I perish, truth is so

sings Clough, while Huxley exclaims: "My only consolation lies in the reflection that, however bad our posterity may become, so far as they hold by the plain rule of not pretending to believe what they have no reason to believe, because it may be to their advantage so to pretend [the word "pretend" is surely here redundant], they will not have reached the lowest depths of immorality." And that delicious *enfant terrible* Clifford writes: "Belief is desecrated when given to unproved and unquestioned statements for the solace and private pleasure of the believer. ... Whoso would deserve well of his fellows in this matter will guard the purity of his belief with a very fanaticism of jealous care, lest at any time it should rest on an unworthy object, and catch a stain which can never be wiped away. . . . If [a] belief has been accepted on insufficient evidence [even though the belief be true, as Clifford on the same page explains] the pleasure is a stolen one. . . . It is sinful because it is stolen in defiance of our duty to mankind. That duty is to guard ourselves from such beliefs as from a pestilence which may shortly master our own body and then spread to the rest of the town. . . . It is wrong always, everywhere, and for every one, to believe anything upon insufficient evidence."

III

All this strikes one as healthy, even when expressed, as by Clifford, with somewhat too much of robustious pathos in the voice. Free will and simple wishing do seem, in the matter of our credences, to be only fifth wheels to the coach. Yet if any one should thereupon assume that intellectual insight is what remains after wish and will and sentimental preference have taken wing, or that pure reason is what then settles our opinions, he would fly quite as directly in the teeth of the facts.

It is only our already dead hypotheses that our willing nature is unable to bring to life again. But what has made them dead for us is for the most part a previous action of our willing nature of an antagonistic kind. When I say "willing nature," I do not mean only such deliberate volitions as may have set up habits of belief that we cannot now escape from—I mean all such factors of belief as fear and hope, prejudice and passion, imitation and partisanship, the circumpressure of our caste and set. As a matter of fact we find ourselves believing, we hardly know how or why. Mr. Balfour gives the name of "authority" to all those influences, born of the intellectual climate, that make hypotheses possible or impossible for us, alive or dead. Here in this room, we all of us believe in molecules and the conservation of energy, in democracy and necessary progress, in Protestant Christianity and the duty of fighting for "the doctrine of the immortal Monroe," all for no reasons worthy of the name. We see into these matters with no more inner clearness,

and probably with much less, than any disbeliever in them might possess. His unconventionality would probably have some grounds to show for its conclusions; but for us, not insight, but the *prestige* of the opinions, is what makes the spark shoot from them and light up our sleeping magazines of faith. Our reason is quite satisfied, in nine hundred and ninety-nine cases out of every thousand of us, if it can find a few arguments that will do to recite in case our credulity is criticized by some one else. Our faith is faith in some one else's faith, and in the greatest matters this is the most the case. Our belief in truth itself, for instance, that there is a truth, and that our minds and it are made for each other,— what is it but a passionate affirmation of desire, in which our social system backs us up? We want to have a truth; we want to believe that our experiments and studies and discussions must put us in a continually better and better position towards it; and on this line we agree to fight out our thinking lives. But if a pyrrhonistic sceptic asks *us how we know* all this, can our logic find a reply? No! certainly it cannot. It is just one volition against another,—we willing to go in for life upon a trust or assumption which he, for his part, does not care to make.

As a rule we disbelieve all facts and theories for which we have no use. Clifford's cosmic emotions find no use for Christian feelings. Huxley belabors the bishops because there is no use for sacerdotalism in his scheme of life. Newman, on the contrary, goes over to Romanism, and finds all sorts of reasons good for staying there, because a priestly system is for him an organic need and delight. Why do so few "scientists" even look at the evidence for telepathy, so called? Because they think, as a leading biologist, now dead, once said to me, that even if such a thing were true, scientists ought to band together to keep it suppressed and concealed. It would undo the uniformity of Nature and all sorts of other things without which scientists cannot carry on their pursuits. But if this very man had been shown something which as a scientist he might *do* with telepathy, he might not only have examined the evidence, but even have found it good enough.

This very law which the logicians would impose upon us—if I may give the name of logicians to those who would rule out our willing nature here—is based on nothing but their own natural wish to exclude all elements for which they, in their professional quality of logicians, can find no use.

Evidently, then, our non-intellectual nature does influence our convictions. There are passional tendencies and volitions which run before and others which come after belief, and it is only the latter that are too late for the fair; and they are not too late when the previous passional work has been already in their own direction. Pascal's argument, instead of being powerless, then seems a regular clincher, and is the last stroke needed to make our faith in masses and holy water complete. The state of things is evidently far from simple; and pure insight and logic, whatever they might do ideally, are not the only things that really do produce our creeds.

IV

Our next duty, having recognized this mixed up state of affairs, is to ask whether it be simply reprehensible and pathological, or whether, on the contrary, we must treat it as a normal element in making up our minds. The thesis I defend is, briefly stated, this: *Our passional nature not only lawfully may, but must, decide an option between propositions, whenever it is a genuine option that cannot by its nature be decided on intellectual grounds; for to say, under such circumstances, "Do not decide, but leave the question open," is itself a passional decision—just like deciding yes or no—and is attended with the same risk of losing the truth....*

VII

One more point, small but important, and our preliminaries are done. There are two ways of looking at our duty in the matter of opinion—ways entirely different, and yet ways about whose difference the theory of knowledge seems hitherto to have shown very little concern. *We must know the truth; and we must avoid error*—these are our first and great commandments as would-be knowers; but they are not two ways of stating an identical commandment, they are two separable laws. Although it may indeed happen that when we believe the truth A, we escape as an incidental consequence from believing the falsehood B, it hardly ever happens that by merely disbelieving B we necessarily believe A. We may in escaping B fall into believing other falsehoods, C or D, just as bad as B; or we may escape B by not believing anything at all, not even A.

Believe truth! Shun error!—these, we see, are two materially different laws; and by choosing between them we may end by coloring differently our whole intellectual life. We may regard the chase for truth as paramount, and the avoidance of error as secondary; or we may, on the other hand, treat the avoidance of error as more imperative, and let truth take its chance. Clifford, in the instructive passage which I have quoted, exhorts us to the latter course. Believe nothing, he tells us, keep your mind in suspense forever, rather than by closing it on insufficient evidence incur the awful risk of believing lies. You, on the other hand, may think that the risk of being in error is a very small matter when compared with the blessings of real knowledge, and be ready to be duped many times in your investigation rather than postpone indefinitely the chance of guessing true. I myself find it impossible to go with Clifford. We must remember that these feelings of our duty about either truth or error are in any case only expressions of our passional life. Biologically considered, our minds are as ready to grind out falsehood as veracity, and he who says, "Better go without belief forever than believe a lie!" merely shows his own preponderant private horror of becoming a dupe. He may be critical of many of his desires and fears, but this fear he slavishly obeys. He cannot imagine any one questioning its binding force. For my own part, I have also a horror of being duped; but I can believe that worse things than being duped may happen to a man in this world; so Clifford's exhortation has to my ears a thoroughly fantastic sound. It is like a general informing his soldiers that it is better to keep out of battle forever than to risk a single wound. Not so are victories either over enemies or over nature gained. Our errors are surely not such awfully solemn things. In a world where we are so certain to incur them in spite of all our caution, a certain lightness of heart seems healthier than this excessive nervousness on their behalf. At any rate, it seems the fittest thing for the empiricist philosopher.

VIII

And now, after all this introduction, let us go straight at our question. I have said, and now repeat it, that not only as a matter of fact do we find our passional nature influencing us in our opinions, but that there are some options between opinions in which this influence must be regarded both as an inevitable and as a lawful determinant of our choice.

I fear here that some of you my hearers will begin to scent danger, and lend an inhospitable ear. Two first steps of passion you have indeed had to admit as necessary—we must think so as to avoid dupery, and we must think so as to gain truth; but the surest path to those ideal consummations, you will probably consider, is from now onwards to take no further passional step.

Well, of course, I agree as far as the facts will allow. Wherever the option between losing truth and gaining it is not momentous, we can throw the chance of *gaining truth* away, and at any rate save ourselves from any chance of *believing falsehood*, by not making up our minds at all till objective evidence has come. In scientific questions, this is almost always the case; and even in human affairs in general, the need of acting is seldom so urgent that a false belief to act on is better than no belief at all. Law courts, indeed, have to decide on the best evidence attainable for the moment, because a judge's duty is to make law as well as to ascertain it, and (as a learned judge once said to me) few cases are worth spending much time over: the great thing is

to have them decided on *any* acceptable principle, and got out of the way. But in our dealings with objective nature we obviously are recorders, not makers, of the truth; and decisions for the mere sake of deciding promptly and getting on to the next business would be wholly out of place. Throughout the breadth of physical nature facts are what they are quite independently of us, and seldom is there any such hurry about them that the risks of being duped by believing a premature theory need be faced. The questions here are always trivial options, the hypotheses are hardly living (at any rate not living for us spectators), the choice between believing truth or falsehood is seldom forced. The attitude of sceptical balance is therefore the absolutely wise one if we would escape mistakes. What difference, indeed, does it make to most of us whether we have or have not a theory of the Röntgen rays, whether we believe or not in mind-stuff, or have a conviction about the causality of conscious states? It makes no difference. Such options are not forced on us. On every account it is better not to make them, but still keep weighing reasons *pro et contra* with an indifferent hand.

I speak, of course, here of the purely judging mind. For purposes of discovery such indifference is to be less highly recommended, and science would be far less advanced than she is if the passionate desires of individuals to get their own faiths confirmed had been kept out of the game. See for example the sagacity which Spencer and Weismann now display. On the other hand, if you want an absolute duffer in an investigation, you must, after all, take the man who has no interest whatever in its results: he is the warranted incapable, the positive fool. The most useful investigator, because the most sensitive observer, is always he whose eager interest in one side of the question is balanced by an equally keen nervousness lest he become deceived.[1] Science has organized this nervousness into a regular *technique*, her so-called method of verification; and she has fallen so deeply in love with the method that one may even say she has ceased to care for truth by itself at all. It is only truth as technically verified that interests her. The truth of truths might come in merely affirmative form, and she would decline to touch it. Such truth as that, she might repeat with Clifford, would be stolen in defiance of her duty to mankind. Human passions, however, are stronger than technical rules. *"Le coeur a ses raisons,"* as Pascal says, *"que la raison ne connait pas"*;[2] and however indifferent to all but the bare rules of the game the umpire, the abstract intellect, may be, the concrete players who furnish him the materials to judge of are usually, each one of them, in love with some pet "live hypothesis" of his own. Let us agree, however, that wherever there is no forced option, the dispassionately judicial intellect with no pet hypothesis, saving us, as it does, from dupery at any rate, ought to be our ideal.

The question next arises: Are there not somewhere forced options in our speculative questions, and can we (as men who may be interested at least as much in positively gaining truth as in merely escaping dupery) always wait with impunity till the coercive evidence shall have arrived? It seems *a priori* improbable that the truth should be so nicely adjusted to our needs and powers as that. In the great boarding-house of nature, the cakes and the butter and the syrup seldom come out so even and leave the plates so clean. Indeed, we should view them with scientific suspicion if they did.

IX

Moral questions immediately present themselves as questions whose solution cannot wait for sensible proof. A moral question is a question not of what sensibly exists, but of what is good, or would be good if it did exist. Science can tell us what exists; but to compare the *worths*, both of what exists and of what does not exist, we must consult not science, but what Pascal calls our heart. . . .

Turn now from these wide questions of good to a certain class of questions of fact, questions concerning personal relations, states of mind between one man and another. *Do you like me or not?*—for example. Whether you do or not depends, in countless instances, on whether I meet you halfway, am willing to assume that you must like me, and show you trust and expectation. The previous faith on my part in your liking's existence is in such cases what makes your liking come. But if I stand aloof, and refuse to budge an inch until I have objective evidence, until you shall have done something apt, as the absolutists say, *ad extorquendum assensum meum,* ten to one your liking never comes. How many women's hearts are vanquished by the mere sanguine insistence of some man that they must love him! He will not consent to the hypothesis that they cannot. The desire for a certain kind of truth here brings about that special truth's existence; and so it is in innumerable cases of other sorts. . . . *And where faith in a fact can help create the fact*, that would be an insane logic which should say that faith running ahead of scientific evidence is the "lowest kind of immorality" into which a thinking being can fall. Yet such is the logic by which our scientific absolutists pretend to regulate our lives!

X

In truths dependent on our personal action, then faith based on desire is certainly a lawful and possibly an indispensable thing.

But now, it will be said, these are all childish human cases, and have nothing to do with great cosmical matters, like the question of religious faith. Let us then pass on to that. Religions differ so much in their accidents that in discussing the religious question we must make it very generic and broad. What then do we now mean by the religious hypothesis? Science says things are; morality says some things are better than other things; and religion says essentially two things.

First, she says that the best things are the more eternal things, the overlapping things, the things in the universe that throw the last stone, so to speak and say the final word. "Perfection is eternal"— this phrase of Charles Secrétan seems a good way of putting this first affirmation of religion, an affirmation which obviously cannot yet be verified scientifically at all.

The second affirmation of religion is that we are better off even now if we believe her first affirmation to be true.

Now, let us consider what the logical elements of this situation are *in case the religious hypothesis in both its branches be really true.* (Of course, we must admit that possibility at the outset. If we are to discuss the question at all, it must involve a living option. If for any of you religion be a hypothesis that cannot, by any living possibility, be true, then you need go no farther. I speak to the "saving remnant" alone.) So proceeding, we see, first, that religion offers itself as a *momentous* option. We are supposed to gain, even now, by our belief, and to lose by our non-belief, a certain vital good. Secondly religion is a *forced* option, so far as that good goes. We cannot escape the issue by remaining sceptical and waiting for more light, because, although we do avoid error in that way *if religion be untrue,* we lose the good, *if it be true,* just as certainly as if we positively chose to disbelieve. It is as if a man should hesitate indefinitely to ask a certain woman to marry him because he was not perfectly sure that she would prove an angel after he brought her home. Would he not cut himself off from that particular angel-possibility as decisively as if he went and married some one else? Scepticism, then, is not avoidance of option; it is option of a certain particular kind of risk. *Better risk loss of truth than chance of error*—that is your faith-vetoer's exact position. He is actively playing his stake as much as the believer is; he is backing the field against the religious hypothesis, just as the believer is backing the religious hypothesis against the field. To preach scepticism to us as a duty until "sufficient evidence" for religion to be found is tantamount therefore to telling us, when in presence of the religious hypothesis, that to yield to our fear of its being error is wiser and better than to yield to our hope that it may be true. It is not intellect against all passions, then; it is only intellect with one passion laying down its law. And by what, forsooth, is the supreme wisdom of this passion warranted? Dupery for dupery, what proof is there that dupery through hope is so much worse than dupery through fear? I, for one, can see no proof; and I simply refuse

obedience to the scientist's command to imitate his kind of option, in a case where my own stake is important enough to give me the right to choose my own form of risk. If religion be true and the evidence for it be still insufficient, I do not wish, by putting your extinguisher upon my nature (which feels to me as if it had after all some business in this matter), to forfeit my sole chance in life of getting upon the winning side—that chance depending, of course, on my willingness to run the risk of acting as if my passional need of taking the world religiously might be prophetic and right.

All this is on the supposition that it really may be prophetic and right, and that, even to us who are discussing the matter, religion is a live hypothesis which may be true. Now, to most of us religion comes in a still further way that makes a veto on our active faith even more illogical. The more perfect and more eternal aspect of the universe is represented in our religions as having personal form. The universe is no longer a mere *It* to us, but a *Thou,* if we are religious; and any relation that may be possible from person to person might be possible here. For instance, although in one sense we are passive portions of the universe, in another we show a curious autonomy, as if we were small active centers on our own account. We feel, too, as if the appeal of religion to us were made to our own active goodwill, as if evidence might be forever withheld from us unless we met the hypothesis halfway to take a trivial illusion; just as a man who in a company of gentlemen made no advances, asked a warrant for every concession, and believed no one's word without proof, would cut himself off by such churlishness from all the social rewards that a more trusting spirit would earn—so here, one who should shut himself up in snarling logicality and try to make the gods extort his recognition willy-nilly, or not get it at all, might cut himself off forever from his only opportunity of making the gods' acquaintance. This feeling, forced on us we know not whence that by obstinately believing that there are gods (although not to do so would be so easy both for our logic and our life) we are doing the universe the deepest service we can, seems part of the living essence of the religious hypothesis.

If the hypothesis were true in all its parts, including this one, then pure intellectualism, with its veto on our making willing advances, would be an absurdity; and some participation of our sympathetic nature would be logically required. I therefore, for one, cannot see my way to accepting the agnostic rules for truth-seeking, or wilfully agree to keep my willing nature out of the game. I cannot do so for this plain reason, that *a rule of thinking which would absolutely prevent me from acknowledging certain kinds of truth if those kinds of truth were really there, would be an irrational rule.* That for me is the long and short of the formal logic of the situation, no matter what the kinds of truth might materially be.

I confess I do not see how this logic can be escaped. But sad experience makes me fear that some of you may still shrink from radically saying with me, *in abstracto,* that we have the right to believe at our own risk any hypothesis that is live enough to tempt our will. I suspect, however, that if this is so, it is because you have got away from the abstract logical point of view altogether, and are thinking (perhaps without realizing it) of some particular religious hypothesis which for you is dead. The freedom to "believe what we will" you apply to the case of some patent superstition; and the faith you think of is the faith defined by the schoolboy when he said, "Faith is when you believe something that you know ain't true." I can only repeat that this is misapprehension. *In concreto,* the freedom to believe can only cover living options which the intellect of the individual cannot by itself resolve; and living options never seem absurdities to him who has them to consider. When I look at the religious question as it really puts itself to concrete men, and when I think of all the possibilities which both practically and theoretically it involves, then this command that we shall put a stopper on our heart, instincts, and courage, and *wait*—acting of course meanwhile more or less as if religion were not true[3]—till doomsday, or till such time as our intellect and senses working together may have raked in evidence enough—this command, I say, seems to me the queerest idol ever manufactured in the philosophic cave. Were we scholastic absolutists, there might be more excuse. If we had an infallible intellect with its objective certitudes, we might feel ourselves disloyal to such a perfect organ or knowledge in not trusting to it exclusively, in not waiting for its releasing word. But if we are empiricists, if we believe that no bell in us tolls to let us know for certain when truth is in our grasp, then it seems a piece of idle fantasticality to preach so solemnly our duty of waiting for the bell. Indeed we may wait if we will—I hope you do not think that I am denying that—but if we do so, we do so at our peril as much as if we believed. In either case we act, taking our life in our hands. No one of us ought to issue vetoes to the other, nor should we bandy words of abuse. We ought, on the contrary, delicately and profoundly to respect one another's mental freedom: then only shall we bring about the intellectual republic; then only shall we have that spirit of inner tolerance without which all our outer tolerance is soulless, and which is empiricism's glory; then only shall we live and let live, in speculative as well as in practical things.

I began by a reference to Fitz-James Stephen; let me end by a quotation from him. "What do you think of yourself? What do you think of the world? ... These are questions with which all must deal as it seems good to them. They are riddles of the Sphinx, and in some way or other we must deal with them. ... In all important transactions of life we have to take a leap in the dark. ... If we decide to leave the riddles unanswered, that is a choice; if we waver in our answer, that, too, is a choice: but whatever choice we make, we make it at our peril. If a man chooses to turn his back altogether on God and the future no one can prevent him; no one can show beyond reasonable doubt that he is mistaken. If a man thinks otherwise and acts as he thinks, I do not see that any one can prove that he is mistaken. Each must act as he thinks best; and if he is wrong, so much the worse for him. We stand on a mountain pass in the midst of whirling snow and blinding mist, through which we get glimpses now and then of paths which may be deceptive. If we stand still we shall be frozen to death. If we take the wrong road we shall be dashed to pieces. We do not certainly know whether there is any right one. What must we do? 'Be strong and of a good courage.' Act for the best, hope for the best, and take what comes. ... If death ends all, we cannot meet death better."

NOTES

1. Compare Wilfrid Ward's Essay "The Wish to Believe," in his *Witnesses to the Unseen* (Macmillan & Co., 1893).

2. "The heart has its reasons which reason does not know."

3. Since belief is measured by action, he who forbids us to believe religion to be true, necessarily also forbids us to act as we should if we did believe it to be true. The whole defence of religious faith hinges upon action. If the action required or inspired by the religious hypothesis is in no way different from that dictated by the naturalistic hypothesis, then religious faith is a pure superfluity, better pruned away, and controversy about its legitimacy is a piece of idle trifling, unworthy of serious minds. I myself believe, of course, that the religious hypothesis gives to the world an expression which specifically determines our reactions, and makes them in a large part unlike what they might be on a purely naturalistic scheme of belief.

V.C. RATIONALITY AND JUSTIFIED RELIGIOUS BELIEF

Introduction

THE PREVIOUS SECTION FOCUSED on the *practical* rationality of religious belief. Now, in this section, we turn to issues about the *epistemic* status of religious belief. To talk about the epistemic status of a belief is just to talk about whether the belief has whatever it takes (besides *truth*) to count as knowledge. If, for example, you believe that aliens from outer space have landed in New Mexico for no reason other than the fact that your favorite comic book series is premised on that claim, your belief has rather low, or poor, epistemic status—and this regardless of whether the belief is true. Believing things just because one's favorite comic book series is premised upon them is not a good way of forming beliefs if one is interested in maximizing one's true beliefs about the world. In other words, forming beliefs in that way is epistemically irrational. On the other hand, if you believe that aliens have landed in New Mexico because CNN, MSNBC, the BBC, and a variety of other respectable news outlets are all presently doing "Breaking News" reports on the occurrence, your belief will have quite a bit more by way of positive epistemic status, or epistemic rationality. For purposes here, we are concerned with two main questions about the epistemic status of religious belief: (1) whether religious beliefs can be epistemically rational even if they are not based on arguments, and (2) whether one might still have religious *faith* even in the absence of religious *belief*. Both are questions about the relation between evidence, religious belief, and faith. The first asks what sort of evidence (if any) is needed in order to make religious belief rational. The second asks whether faith is possible for those whose evidential situation leaves them unable to believe.

In the first reading, "Rational Theistic Belief without Proof," John Hick discusses the relevance of the proofs or arguments for theistic beliefs that we studied in Part II. He argues that the proofs are largely irrelevant to religion. They are neither sufficient nor necessary for the religious life. Not only do the so-called proofs for the existence of God fail to accomplish what they set out to do, but even if they did demonstrate what they purported to demonstrate, this would at best only force our notional assent. They would not bring about the deep devotion and sense of worship necessary for a full religious life. Furthermore, they are not necessary because believers have something *better*—an intense, coercive, indubitable experience—which convinces them of the reality of the being in question. For believers, God is not a hypothesis brought in ex machina to explain the world, but a living presence, closer to them than the air they breathe.

Hick develops a notion of religious experience as analogous to our experience of an external world. Neither the existence of an external world nor the existence of an external religious reality can be proven, but belief in each is a natural response to our experience. The main difference between the two kinds of experiences is that virtually everyone has external-world experiences, but only a relatively small minority of humankind have noticeable religious experiences. Should this undermine the argument from religious experience? Not necessarily, for it may be the case that the few have access to a higher reality. They cannot easily be dismissed as insane or simply hallucinating, for the "general intelligence and exceptionally high moral quality of the great religious figures clashes with any analysis of their experience in terms of abnormal psychology." At the end of his article Hick applies his thesis about the sense of the presence of God to the problem of the plurality of religions. He suggests that there is a convergence of religious experience, indicating the existence of a common higher reality.

In our next reading, Antony Flew defends the view that debate about the existence of God should start with a "presumption of atheism." As Flew uses the term, an "atheist" is anyone who is not a theist, and the *presumption of atheism* is akin to the presumption of innocence in a criminal trial: It is the procedural idea that one should not move from the "presumed" position unless sufficient proof has been given. One might think that proof is not needed if one agrees with Hick that religious belief can be justified on the basis of experience rather than argument. But, Flew argues, even if one can (in principle) be justified in believing in God on the basis of experience, this does not remove the burden of proof: One must still provide an argument for the claim that "having religious experience really is a kind of perceiving, and hence a sort of being in a position to know about its putative object." Absent an argument for that claim, he thinks, it is "impossible to vindicate [one's] claims to be harbouring rational beliefs."

One might look to the work of William Alston on perceiving God (selection IV.A.4) for a reply to Flew. Along similar lines, one might look to what has come to be called "Reformed epistemology." Reformed epistemology—so called because it traces its roots through the Protestant Reformed tradition to John Calvin—maintains (with both Alston and Hick) that religious beliefs, like the belief that God exists, can be rationally held on the basis of experience and in the absence of argument. The main difference between Reformed epistemology as such and the sorts of views defended by Alston and Hick is that Reformed epistemologists are concerned with a wider range of experiences than the ones that might plausibly count as perceptual experiences of God.

The foremost contemporary developer and defender of Reformed epistemology is Alvin Plantinga; and the two most important sources for the view are his "Reason and Belief in God" and the magisterial conclusion to his *Warrant* trilogy: *Warranted Christian Belief.* Doing justice to the view in the short space that we have here, however, requires either a patchwork quilt of excerpts from these and perhaps other works by Plantinga or a summary essay written with the aim of providing an accessible overview. We have gone the latter route, with a specially commissioned essay by Michael Bergmann. In our third selection, "Rational Religious Belief without Arguments," Bergmann presents the essentials of Reformed epistemology, along with replies to some of the most important objections. Along the way, he considers the question whether religious believers are indeed under a burden to defend with arguments the claim that their experiences are genuinely experiences *of God.* Drawing on an analogy with sense perception, Bergmann argues (contrary to Flew) that they are not.

In our fourth reading in this section, Linda Zagzebski provides an alternative model for thinking about the rationality of religious belief. The preceding essays approach the topic in a way that assumes that *individual beliefs* are the appropriate objects of epistemic evaluation. That is, it is first and foremost individual beliefs rather than the persons holding the beliefs that are evaluated as rational or irrational, justified or unjustified, and so on. This approach to epistemic evaluation mirrors the common approach to moral evaluation, wherein we assess particular *acts* as good or bad, right or wrong, and so on rather than focusing on evaluating *agents* with regard to their progress toward virtue. Zagzebski advocates a virtue-based approach to morality, and highlights several advantages that such an approach has over traditional act-based theories. She then argues that these advantages carry over to the epistemic realm, and especially so when one takes a virtue-based approach to the epistemology of religious belief.

V.C.1

Rational Theistic Belief without Proof

JOHN HICK

A short biographical sketch of John Hick precedes selection III.C.2. In this article, Hick argues that the so-called proofs for the existence of God are largely irrelevant for religion. Religious belief, he argues, can be rationally grounded in religious experience.

Reprinted from John Hick, *Arguments for the Existence of God* (Macmillan: London and Basingstoke, 1971) by permission of the author. Footnotes edited.

(A) THE RELIGIOUS REJECTION OF THE THEISTIC ARGUMENTS

We have seen that the major theistic arguments are all open to serious philosophical objections. Indeed we have in each case concluded, in agreement with the majority of contemporary philosophers, that these arguments fail to do what they profess to do. Neither those which undertake strictly to demonstrate the existence of an absolute Being, nor those which profess to show divine existence to be probable, are able to fulfil their promise. We have seen that it is impossible to demonstrate the reality of God by *a priori* reasoning, since such reasoning is confined to the realm of concepts; impossible to demonstrate it by *a posteriori* reasoning, since this would have to include a premise begging the very question at issue; and impossible to establish it as in a greater or lesser degree probable, since the notion of probability lacks any clear meaning in this context. A philosopher unacquainted with modern developments in theology might well assume that theologians would, *ex officio*, be supporters of the theistic proofs and would regard as a fatal blow this conclusion that there can be neither a strict demonstration of God's existence nor a valid probability argument for it. In fact however such an assumption would be true only of certain theological schools. It is true of the more traditional Roman Catholic theology, of sections of conservative Protestantism, and of most of those Protestant apologists who continue to work within the tradition of nineteenth-century idealism. It has never been true, on the other hand, of Jewish religious thought; and it is not true of that central stream of contemporary Protestant theology which has been influenced by the "neo-orthodox" movement, the revival of Reformation studies and the "existentialism" of Kierkegaard and his successors; or of the most significant contemporary Roman Catholic thinkers, who are on this issue (as on so many others) in advance of the official teaching of the magisterium. Accordingly we have now to take note of this theological rejection of the theistic proofs, ranging from a complete lack of concern for them

to a positive repudiation of them as being religiously irrelevant or even harmful. There are several different considerations to be evaluated.

1. It has often been pointed out that for the man of faith, as he is depicted in the Bible, no theistic proofs are necessary. Philosophers in the rationalist tradition, holding that to know means to be able to prove, have been shocked to find that in the Bible, which is supposed to be the basis of Western religion, no attempt whatever is made to demonstrate the existence of God. Instead of professing to establish the divine reality by philosophical reasoning the Bible throughout takes this for granted. Indeed to the biblical writers it would have seemed absurd to try to establish by logical argumentation that God exists. For they were convinced that they were already having to do with him and he with them in all the affairs of their lives. They did not think of God as an inferred entity but as an experienced reality. Many of the biblical writers were (sometimes, though doubtless not all times) as vividly conscious of being in God's presence as they were of living in a material world. It is impossible to read their pages without realising that to them God was not a proposition completing a syllogism, or an idea adopted by the mind, but the supreme experiential reality. It would be as sensible for a husband to desire a philosophical proof of the existence of the wife and family who contribute so much of the meaning and value of his life as for the man of faith to seek for a proof of the existence of the God within whose purpose he believes that he lives and moves and has his being.

As Cook Wilson wrote:

> If we think of the existence of our friends; it is the "direct knowledge" which we want: merely inferential knowledge seems a poor affair. To most men it would be as surprising as unwelcome to hear it could not be directly known whether there were such existences as their friends, and that it was only a matter of (probable) empirical argument and inference from facts which are directly known. And even if we convince ourselves on reflection that this is

really the case, our actions prove that we have a confidence in the existence of our friends which can't be derived from an empirical argument (which can never be certain) for a man will risk his life for his friend. We don't want merely inferred friends. Could we possibly be satisfied with an inferred God?

In other words the man of faith has no need of theistic proofs; for he has something which for him is much better. However it does not follow from this that there may not be others who do need a theistic proof, nor does it follow that there are in fact no such proofs. All that has been said about the irrelevance of proofs to the life of faith may well be true, and yet it might still be the case that there are valid arguments capable of establishing the existence of God to those who stand outside the life of faith.

2. It has also often been pointed out that the God whose existence each of the traditional theistic proofs professes to establish is only an abstraction from and a pale shadow of the living God who is the putative object of biblical faith. A First Cause of the Universe might or might not be a deity to whom an unqualified devotion, love and trust would be appropriate; Aquinas's *Et hoc omnes intelligunt Deum* ("and this all understand to be God") is not the last step in a logical argument but merely an exercise of the custom of overlooking a gap in the argument at this point. A Necessary Being, and indeed a being who is metaphysically absolute in every respect—omnipotent, omniscient, eternal, uncreated—might be morally good or evil. As H. D. Aitken has remarked, "Logically, there is no reason why an almighty and omniscient being might not be a perfect stinker." A divine Designer of the world whose nature is read off from the appearances of nature might, as Hume showed, be finite or infinite, perfect or imperfect, omniscient or fallible, and might indeed be not one being but a veritable pantheon. It is only by going beyond what is proved, or claimed to have been proved, and identifying the First Cause, Necessary Being, or Mind behind Nature with the God of biblical faith that these proofs could ever properly impel to worship. By themselves and without supplementation of content and infusion of emotional life from religious traditions and experiences transcending the proofs themselves they would never lead to the life of faith.

The ontological argument on the other hand is in this respect in a different category. If it succeeds it establishes the reality of a being so perfect in every way that no more perfect can be conceived. Clearly if such a being is not worthy of worship none ever could be. It would therefore seem that, unlike the other proofs, the ontological argument, if it were logically sound, would present the relatively few persons who are capable of appreciating such abstract reasoning with a rational ground for worship. On the other hand, however, whilst this is the argument that would accomplish most if it succeeded it is also the argument which is most absolutely incapable of succeeding; for it is, as we have seen, inextricably involved in the fallacy of professing to deduce existence from a concept.

3. It is argued by some religious writers that a logical demonstration of the existence of God would be a form of coercion and would as such be incompatible with God's evident intention to treat his human creatures as free and responsible persons. A great deal of twentieth-century theology emphasises that God as the infinite personal reality, having made man as person in his own image, always treats men as persons, respecting their relative freedom and autonomy. He does not override the human mind by revealing himself in overwhelming majesty and power, but always approaches us in ways that leave room for an uncompelled response of human faith. Even God's own entry into our earthly history, it is said, was in an "incognito" that could be penetrated only by the eyes of faith. As Pascal put it, "willing to appear openly to those who seek him with all their heart and to be hidden from those who flee from him with all their heart, he so regulates the knowledge of himself that he has given indications of himself which are visible to those who seek him and not to those who do not seek him. There is enough light for those to see who only desire to see, and enough obscurity for

those who have a contrary disposition." God's self-revealing actions are accordingly always so mediated through the events of our temporal experience that men only become aware of the divine presence by interpreting and responding to these events in the way which we call religious faith. For if God were to disclose himself to us in the coercive manner in which our physical environment obtrudes itself we should be dwarfed to nothingness by the infinite power thus irresistibly breaking open the privacy of our souls. Further, we should be spiritually blinded by God's perfect holiness and paralysed by his infinite energy; "for human kind cannot bear very much reality." Such a direct, unmediated confrontation breaking in upon us and shattering the frail autonomy of our finite nature would leave no ground for a free human response of trust, self-commitment and obedience. There could be no call for a man to venture upon a dawning consciousness of God's reality and thus to receive this consciousness as an authentic part of his own personal existence precisely because it has not been injected into him or clamped upon him by magisterial exercise of divine omnipotence.

The basic principle invoked here is that for the sake of creating a personal relationship of love and trust with his human creatures God does not force an awareness of himself upon them. And (according to the view which we are considering) it is only a further application of the same principle to add that a logically compelling demonstration of God's existence would likewise frustrate this purpose. For men—or at least those of them who are capable of following the proof—could then be forced to know that God is real. Thus Alasdair MacIntyre, when a Christian apologist, wrote: "For if we could produce logically cogent arguments we should produce the kind of certitude that leaves no room for decision; where proof is in place, decision is not. We do not decide to accept Euclid's conclusions; we merely look to the rigour of his arguments. If the existence of God were demonstrable we should be as bereft of the possibility of making a free decision to love God as we should be if every utterance of doubt or unbelief was answered by thunderbolts from heaven." This is the "religious coercion" objection to the theistic proofs.

To what extent is it a sound objection? We may accept the theological doctrine that for God to force men to know him by the coercion of logic would be incompatible with his purpose of winning the voluntary response and worship of free moral beings. But the question still remains whether the theistic proofs could ever do this. Could a verbal proof of divine existence compel a consciousness of God comparable in coerciveness with a direct manifestation of his divine majesty and power? Could anyone be moved and shaken in their whole being by the demonstration of a proposition, as men have been by a numinous experience of overpowering impressiveness? Would the things that have just been said about an overwhelming display of divine glory really apply to verbal demonstrations—that infinite power would be irresistibly breaking in upon the privacy of our souls and that we should be blinded by God's perfect holiness and paralysed by his infinite energy? Indeed could a form of words, culminating in the proposition that "God exists," ever have power by itself to produce more than what Newman calls a notional assent in our minds?

It is of course true that the effect of purely rational considerations such as those which are brought to bear in the theistic proofs are much greater in some minds than in others. The more rational the mind the more considerable is the effect to be expected. In many persons—indeed taking mankind as a whole, in the great majority—the effect of a theistic proof, even when no logical flaw is found in it, would be virtually nil! But in more sophisticated minds the effect must be greater, and it is at least theoretically possible that there are minds so rational that purely logical considerations can move them as effectively as the evidence of their senses. It is therefore conceivable that someone who is initially agnostic might be presented with a philosophical proof of divine existence—say the ontological argument, with its definition of God as that than which no more perfect can be conceived—and might as a result be led to worship the being whose reality has thus been demonstrated to him. This seems to be possible; but I believe that even in such a case there must, in addition to an intelligent appreciation of the argument, be a distinctively religious response to the idea of God which the argument presents. Some propensity to respond to unlimited perfection as holy and as rightly claiming a response of unqualified worship and devotion must operate, over and above the purely intellectual capacity for logical calculation. For we can conceive of a purely or merely logical mind, a kind of human calculating machine, which is at the same time devoid of the capacity for numinous feeling and worshipping response. Such a being might infer that God exists but be no more existentially interested in this conclusion than many people are in, say, the fact that the Shasta Dam is 602 feet high. It therefore seems that when the acceptance of a theistic proof leads to worship, a religious reaction occurs which turns what would otherwise be a purely abstract conclusion into an immensely significant and moving fact. In Newman's terminology, when a notional assent to the proposition that God exists becomes a real assent, equivalent to an actual living belief and faith in God, there has been a free human response to an idea which could instead have been rejected by being held at the notional level. In other words, a verbal proof of God's existence cannot by itself break down our human freedom; it can only lead to a notional assent which has little or no positive religious value or substance.

I conclude, then, that the theological objections to the theistic proofs are considerably less strong than the philosophical ones; and that theologians who reject natural theology would therefore do well to do so primarily on philosophical rather than on theological grounds. These philosophical reasons are, as we have seen, very strong; and we therefore now have to consider whether, in the absence of any theistic proofs, it can nevertheless be rational to believe in the existence of God.

(B) CAN THERE BE RATIONAL THEISTIC BELIEF WITHOUT PROOFS?

During the period dominated by the traditional theistic arguments the existence of God was often treated by philosophers as something to be discovered through reasoning. It was seen as the conclusion of an inference; and the question of the rationality of the belief was equated with that of the soundness of the inference. But from a religious point of view, as we have already seen, there has always been something very odd about this approach. The situation which it envisages is that of people standing outside the realm of faith, for whom the apologist is trying to build a bridge of rational inference to carry them over the frontier into that realm. But of course this is not the way in which religious faith has originally or typically or normally come about. When the cosmological, ontological, teleological and moral arguments were developed, theistic belief was already a functioning part of an immemorially established and developing form of human life. The claims of religion are claims made by individuals and communities on the basis of their experience—and experience which is none the less their own for occurring within an inherited framework of ideas. We are not dealing with a merely conceivable metaphysical hypothesis which someone has speculatively invented but which hardly anyone seriously believes. We are concerned, rather, with convictions born out of experience and reflection and living within actual communities of faith and practice. Historically, then, the philosophical proofs of God have normally entered in to support and confirm but not to create belief. Accordingly the proper philosophical approach would seem to be a probing of the actual foundations and structure of a living and operative belief rather than of theoretical and nonoperative arguments subsequently formulated for holding those beliefs. The question is not whether it is possible to prove, starting from zero, that God exists; the question is whether the religious man, given the distinctively religious form of human existence in which he participates, is properly entitled as a rational person to believe what he does believe?

At this point we must consider what we mean by a rational belief. If by a belief we mean a proposition believed, then what we are to be concerned with here are not rational beliefs but rational believings. Propositions can be well-formed or ill-formed, and they can be true or false, but they cannot be rational or irrational. It is *people* who are rational or irrational, and derivatively their states and their actions, including their acts and states of believing. Further, apart from the believing of analytic propositions, which are true by definition and are therefore rationally believed by anyone who understands them, the rationality of acts (or states) of believing has to be assessed separately in each case. For it is a function of the relation between the proposition believed and the evidence on the basis of which the believer believes it. It might conceivably be rational for Mr. *X* to believe *p* but not rational for Mr. *Y* to believe *p*, because in relation to the data available to Mr. *X p* is worthy of belief but not in relation to the data available to Mr. *Y*. Thus the question of the rationality of belief in the reality of God is the question of the rationality of a particular person's believing given the data that he is using; or that of the believing of a class of people who share the same body of data. Or putting the same point the other way round, any assessing of the belief-worthiness of the proposition that God exists must be an assessing of it in relation to particular ranges of data.

Now there is one area of data or evidence which is normally available to those who believe in God, and that provides a very important part of the ground of their believing, but which is normally not available to and therefore not taken into account by those who do not so believe; and this is religious experience. It seems that the religious man is in part basing his believing upon certain data of religious experience which the non-religious man is not using because he does not have them. Thus our question resolves itself into one about the theist's right, given his distinctively religious experience, to be certain that God exists. It is the question of the rationality or irrationality, the well-groundedness or ill-groundedness, of the religious man's claim to know God. The theist cannot hope to prove that God exists; but despite this it may nevertheless be possible for him to show it to be wholly reasonable for him to believe that God exists.

What is at issue here is not whether it is rational for someone else, who does not participate in the distinctively religious mode of experience, to believe in God on the basis of the religious man's reports. I am not proposing any kind of "argument from religious experience" by which God is inferred as the cause of the special experiences described by mystics and other religious persons. It is not the non-religious man's theoretical use of someone else's reported religious experience that is to be considered, but the religious man's own practical use of it. The question is whether he is acting rationally in trusting his own experience and in proceeding to live on the basis of it.

In order to investigate this question we must consider what counts as rational belief in an analogous case. The analogy that I propose is that between the religious person's claim to be conscious of God and any man's claim to be conscious of the physical world as an environment, existing independently of himself, of which he must take account.

In each instance a realm of putatively cognitive experience is taken to be veridical and is acted upon as such, even though its veridical character cannot be logically demonstrated. So far as sense experience is concerned this has emerged both from the failure of Descartes' attempt to provide a theoretical guarantee that our senses relate us to a real material environment, and from the success of Hume's attempt to show that our normal non-solipsist belief in an objective world of enduring objects around us in space is neither a product of, nor justifiable by, philosophical reasoning but is what has been called in some expositions of Hume's thought (though the term does not seem to have been used by Hume himself) a natural belief. It is a belief which naturally and indeed inevitably arises in the normal human mind in response to normal human perceptual experience. It is a belief on the basis of which we live and the rejection of which, in favour of a serious adoption of the solipsist alternative, would so disorient our relationship to other persons within a common material environment that we should be accounted insane. Our insanity would consist in the fact that we should no longer regard other people as independent centres of consciousness, with their own purposes and wills, with whom interpersonal relationships are possible. We should instead be living in a one-person world.

It is thus a basic truth in, or a presupposition of, our language that it is rational or sane to believe in the reality of the external world that we inhabit in common with other people, and irrational or insane not to do so.

What are the features of our sense experience in virtue of which we all take this view? They would seem to be twofold: the givenness or the involuntary character of this form of cognitive experience, and the fact that we can and do act successfully in terms of our belief in an external world. That is to say, being built and circumstanced as we are we cannot help initially believing as we do, and our belief is not contradicted, but on the contrary continuously confirmed, by our continuing experience. These characteristics jointly constitute a sufficient reason to trust and live on the basis of our perceptual experience in the absence of any positive reason to distrust it; and our inability to exclude the theoretical possibility of our experience as a whole being purely subjective does not constitute such a reason. This seems to be the principle on which, implicitly, we proceed. And it is, by definition, rational to proceed in this way. That is to say, this is the way in which all human beings do proceed and have proceeded, apart from a very small minority who have for that very reason been labelled by the majority as insane. This habitual acceptance of our perceptual experience is thus, we may say, part of our operative concept of human rationality.

We can therefore now ask whether a like principle may be invoked on behalf of a parallel response to religious experience. "Religious experience" is of course a highly elastic concept. Let us restrict attention, for our present purpose, to the theistic "sense of the presence of God," the putative awareness of a transcendent divine Mind within whose field of consciousness we exist and with whom therefore we stand in a relationship of mutual awareness. This sense of "living in the

divine presence" does not take the form of a direct vision of God, but of experiencing events in history and in our own personal life as the medium of God's dealings with us. Thus religious differs from non-religious experience, not as the awareness of a different world, but as a different way of experiencing the same world. Events which can be experienced as having a purely natural significance are experienced by the religious mind as having also and at the same time religious significance and as mediating the presence and activity of God.

It is possible to study this type of religious experience either in its strongest instances, in the primary and seminal religious figures, or in its much weaker instances in ordinary adherents of the traditions originated by the great exemplars of faith. Since we are interested in the question of the claims which religious experience justifies it is appropriate to look at that experience in its strongest and purest forms. A description of this will accordingly apply only very partially to the ordinary rank-and-file believer either of today or in the past.

If then we consider the sense of living in the divine presence as this was expressed by, for example, Jesus of Nazareth, or by St. Paul, St. Francis, St. Anselm or the great prophets of the Old Testament, we find that their "awareness of God" was so vivid that he was as indubitable a factor in their experience as was their physical environment. They could no more help believing in the reality of God than in the reality of the material world and of their human neighbours. Many of the pages of the Bible resound with the sense of God's presence as a building might reverberate from the tread of some gigantic being walking through it. God was known to the prophets and apostles as a dynamic will interacting with their own wills; a sheerly given personal reality, as inescapably to be reckoned with as destructive storm and life-giving sunshine, the fixed contours of the land, or the hatred of their enemies and the friendship of their neighbours.

Our question concerns, then, one whose "experience of God" has this compelling quality, so that he is no more inclined to doubt its veridical character than to doubt the evidence of his senses.

Is it rational for him to take the former, as it is certainly rational for him to take the latter, as reliably cognitive of an aspect of his total environment and thus as knowledge in terms of which to act? Are the two features noted above in our sense experience—its givenness, or involuntary character, and the fact that we can successfully act in terms of it—also found here? It seems that they are. The sense of the presence of God reported by the great religious figures has a similar involuntary and compelling quality; and as they proceed to live on the basis of it they are sustained and confirmed by their further experiences in the conviction that they are living in relation, not to illusion, but to reality. It therefore seems prima facie, that the religious man is entitled to trust his religious experience and to proceed to conduct his life in terms of it.

The analogy operating within this argument is between our normal acceptance of our sense experiences as perception of an objective external world, and a corresponding acceptance of the religious experience of "living in God's presence" as the awareness of a divine reality external to our own minds. In each case there is a solipsist alternative in which one can affirm *solus ipse* to the exclusion of the transcendent—in the one case denying a physical environment transcending our own private consciousness and in the other case denying a divine Mind transcending our own private consciousness. It should be noted that this analogy is not grounded in the perception of particular material objects and does not turn upon the contrast between veridical and illusory sense perceptions, but is grounded in our awareness of an objective external world as such and turns upon the contrast between this and a theoretically possible solipsist interpretation of the same stream of conscious experience.

(C) RELIGIOUS AND PERCEPTUAL BELIEF

Having thus set forth the analogy fairly boldly and starkly I now want to qualify it by exploring various differences between religious and sensory experience. The resulting picture will be more complex than the first rough outline presented so far; and yet its force as supporting the rationality of theistic faith will not, I think, in the end have been undermined.

The most obvious difference is that everyone has and cannot help having sense experiences, whereas not everyone has religious experiences, at any rate of the very vivid and distinct kind to which we have been referring. As bodily beings existing in a material environment, we cannot help interacting consciously with that environment. That is to say, we cannot help "having" a stream of sense experiences; and we cannot help accepting this as the perception of a material world around us in space. When we open our eyes in daylight we cannot but receive the visual experiences that come to us; and likewise with the other senses. And the world which we thus perceive is not plastic to our wishes but presents itself to us as it is, whether we like it or not. Needless to say, our senses do not coerce us in any sense of the word "coerce" that implies unwillingness on our part, as when a policeman coerces an unwilling suspect to accompany him to the police station. Sense experience is coercive in the sense that we cannot when sane believe that our material environment is not broadly as we perceive it to be, and that if we did momentarily persuade ourselves that what we experience is not there we should quickly be penalised by the environment and indeed, if we persisted, destroyed by it.

In contrast to this we are not obliged to interact consciously with a spiritual environment. Indeed it is a commonplace of much contemporary theology that God does not force an awareness of himself upon mankind but leaves us free to know him by an uncompelled response of faith. And yet once a man has allowed himself freely to become conscious of God—it is important to note—that experience is, at its top levels of intensity, coercive. It creates the situation of the person who *cannot help* believing in the reality of God. The apostle, prophet or saint may be so vividly aware of God that he can no more doubt the veracity of his religious awareness than of his sense experience.

During the periods when he is living consciously in the presence of God, when God is to him the divine Thou, the question whether God exists simply does not arise. Our cognitive freedom in relation to God is not to be found at this point but at the prior stage of our coming to be aware of him. The individual's own free receptivity and responsiveness plays an essential part in his dawning consciousness of God; but once he *has* become conscious of God that consciousness can possess a coercive and indubitable quality.

It is a consequence of this situation that whereas everyone perceives and cannot help perceiving the physical world, by no means everyone experiences the presence of God. Indeed only rather few people experience religiously in the vivid and coercive way reported by the great biblical figures. And this fact immediately suggests a sceptical question. Since those who enjoy a compelling religious experience form such a small minority of mankind, ought we not to suspect that they are suffering from a delusion comparable with that of the paranoiac who hears threatening voices from the walls or the alcoholic who sees green snakes?

This is of course a possible judgment to make. But this judgment should not be made *a priori*, in the absence of specific grounds such as we have in the other cases mentioned. And it would in fact be difficult to point to adequate evidence to support this hypothesis. On the contrary the general intelligence and exceptionally high moral quality of the great religious figures clashes with any analysis of their experience in terms of abnormal psychology. Such analyses are not indicated, as is the parallel view of paranoiacs and alcoholics, by evidence of general disorientation to reality or of incapacity to live a productive and satisfying life. On the contrary, Jesus of Nazareth, for example, has been regarded by hundreds of millions of people as the fulfilment of the ideal possibilities of human nature. A more reasonable negative position would therefore seem to be the agnostic one that whilst it is proper for the religious man himself, given his distinctive mode of experience, to believe firmly in the reality of God, one does not oneself share that experience and therefore has no ground upon which to hold that belief. Theism is then not positively denied, but is on the other hand consciously and deliberately not affirmed. This agnostic position must be accepted by the theist as a proper one. For if it is reasonable for one man, on the basis of his distinctively religious experience, to affirm the reality of God it must also be reasonable for another man, in the absence of any such experience, not to affirm the reality of God.

The next question that must be raised is the closely connected one of the relation between rational belief and truth. I suggested earlier that, strictly, one should speak of rational believings rather than of rational beliefs. But nevertheless it is sometimes convenient to use the latter phrase, which we may then understand as follows. By a rational belief we shall mean a belief which it is rational for the one who holds it to hold, given the data available to him. Clearly such beliefs are not necessarily or always true. It is sometimes rational for an individual to have, on the basis of incomplete data, a belief which is in fact false. For example, it was once rational for people to believe that the sun revolves round the earth; for it was apparently perceived to do so, and the additional theoretical and observational data were not yet available from which it has since been inferred that it is the earth which revolves round the sun. If, then, a belief may be rational and yet false, may not the religious man's belief be of this kind? May it not be that when the data of religious experience are supplemented in the believer's mind by further data provided by the sciences of psychology or sociology, it ceases to be rational for him to believe in God? Might it not then be rational for him instead to believe that his "experience of the presence of God" is to be understood as an effect of a buried infancy memory of his father as a benevolent higher power; or of the pressure upon him of the human social organism of which he is a cell; or in accordance with some other naturalistic theory of the nature of religion?

Certainly this is possible. Indeed we must say, more generally, that all our beliefs, other than our acceptance of logically self-certifying propositions, are in principle open to revision or retraction in the light of new data. It is always conceivable that something which it is now rational for us to believe, it may one day not be rational for us to believe. But the difference which this general principle properly makes to our present believing varies from a maximum in relation to beliefs involving a considerable theoretical element, such as the higher-level hypotheses of the sciences, to a minimum in relation to perceptual beliefs, such as the belief that I now see a sheet of paper before me. And I have argued that so far as the great primary religious figures are concerned, belief in the reality of God is closer to the latter in that it is analogous to belief in the reality of the perceived material world. It is not an explanatory hypothesis, logically comparable with those developed in the sciences, but a perceptual belief. God was not, for Amos or Jeremiah or Jesus of Nazareth, an inferred entity but an experienced personal presence. If this is so, it is appropriate that the religious man's belief in the reality of God should be no more provisional than his belief in the reality of the physical world. The situation is in each case that given the experience which he has and which is part of him, he cannot help accepting as "there" such aspects of his environment as he experiences. He cannot help believing either in the reality of the material world which he is conscious of inhabiting, or of the personal divine presence which is overwhelmingly evident to him and to which his mode of living is a free response. And I have been suggesting that it is as reasonable for him to hold and to act upon the one belief as the other.

V.C.2

The Presumption of Atheism

ANTONY FLEW

Antony Flew (1923–2010) was one of the most well known and influential atheistic philosophers of religion of the twentieth century. He was a professor of philosophy at the University of Keele, among other places, and was co-editor of the 1963 volume New Essays in Philosophical Theology, *which is widely credited as marking the revival of philosophy of religion in the latter half of the twentieth century. In 2004, he stirred up controversy with the book* There Is a God: How the World's Most Notorious Atheist Changed His Mind. *In the present essay, he argues that dispute over God's existence should start from a "presumption of atheism" (akin to the "presumption of innocence" that is the starting point of criminal trials). In other words, the "burden of proof" lies on the theist.*

Flew, Antony, "The Presumption of Atheism," *Canadian Journal of Philosophy*, 2 (1972), pp. 29–46. Used by permission of University of Calgary Press. Some footnotes deleted.

A. INTRODUCTORY

At the beginning of Book X of his last work *The Laws* Plato turns his attention from violent and outrageous actions in general to the particular case of undisciplined and presumptuous behaviour in matters of religion: "We have already stated summarily what the punishment should be for temple-robbing, whether by open force or secretly. But the punishments for the various sorts of insolence in speech or action with regard to the gods, which a man can show in word or deed, have to be proclaimed after we have provided an exordium. Let this be it: 'No one believing, as the laws prescribe, in the existence of the gods has ever yet performed an impious action willingly, or uttered a lawless word. Anyone acting in such a way is in one of three conditions: either, first, he does not believe the proposition aforesaid; or, second, he believes that though the gods exist they have no concern about men; or, third, he believes that they can easily be won over by the bribery of prayer and sacrifice'" (§ 885B).[1]

So Plato in this notorious treatment of heresy might be said to be rebuking the presumption of atheism. The word "presumption" would then be employed as a synonym for "presumptuousness." But, interesting though the questions here raised by Plato are, the word has in my title a different interpretation. The presumption of atheism which I want to discuss is not a form of presumptuousness; indeed it might be regarded as an expression of the very opposite, a modest teachability. My presumption of atheism is closely analogous to the presumption of innocence in the English Law; a comparison which we shall later find it illuminating to develop. What I want to examine in this paper is the contention that the debate about the existence of God should properly begin from a presumption of atheism, that the onus of proof must lie on the theist.

The word "atheism," however, has in this contention to be construed unusually. Whereas nowadays the usual meaning of "atheist" in English is "someone who asserts that there is no such being as God," I want the word to be understood here much less positively. I want the originally Greek prefix "a" to be read in the same way in "atheist" as it customarily is read in such other Greco-English words as "amoral," "atypical," and "asymmetrical." In this interpretation an atheist becomes: not someone who positively asserts the non-existence of God; but someone who is simply not a theist. Let us, for future ready reference, introduce the labels "positive atheism" for the former doctrine and "negative atheism" for the latter.

The introduction of this new sense of the word "atheism" may appear to be a piece of perverse Humpty-Dumptyism,[2] going arbitrarily against established common usage. "Whyever," it could be asked, "don't you make it not the presumption of atheism but the presumption of agnosticism?" But this pardonably petulant reaction fails to appreciate just how completely noncommittal I intend my negative atheist to be. For in this context the agnostic—and it was, of course, in this context that Thomas Henry Huxley first introduced the term[3]—is by the same criterion of established common usage someone who, having entertained the existence of God as at least a theoretical possibility, now claims not to know either that there is or that there is not such a being. To be in this ordinary sense an agnostic you have already to have conceded that there is, and that you have, a legitimate concept of God; such that, whether or not this concept does in fact have application, it theoretically could. But the atheist in my peculiar interpretation, unlike the atheist in the usual sense, has not as yet and as such conceded even this.

This point is important, though the question whether the word "agnosticism" can bear the meaning which I want now to give to the word "atheism" is not. What the protagonist of the presumption of atheism, in my sense, wants to show is: that the debate about the existence of God ought be conducted in a particular way; and that the issue should be seen in a certain perspective. His thesis about the onus of proof involves that it is up to the theist: first, to introduce and to defend his proposed concept of God; and, second, to provide sufficient reason for believing that this concept of his does in fact have an application. It is the first of these two stages which needs perhaps to be emphasized even more strongly than the second. Where the question of existence concerns, for instance, a Loch Ness Monster or an Abominable Snowman this stage may perhaps reasonably be deemed to be more or less complete before the argument begins. But in the controversy about the existence of God this is certainly not so: not only for the quite familiar reason that the word "God" is used—or misused—in more than one way; but also, and much more interestingly, because it cannot be taken for granted that even the would-be mainstream theist is operating with a legitimate concept which theoretically could have an application to an actual being.

This last suggestion is not really as new-fangled and factitious as it is sometimes thought to be. But its pedigree has been made a little hard to trace. For the fact is that, traditionally, issues which should be seen as concerning the legitimacy or otherwise of a proposed or supposed concept have by philosophical theologians been discussed: either as surely disposable difficulties in reconciling one particular feature of the Divine nature with another; or else as aspects of an equally surely soluble general problem of saying something about the infinite Creator in language intelligible to his finite creatures. These traditional and still almost universally accepted forms of presentation are fundamentally prejudicial. For they assume: that there is a Divine being, with an actual nature the features of which we can investigate; and that there is an infinite Creator, whose existence—whatever difficulties we finite creatures may have in asserting anything else about Him—we may take for granted.

The general reason why this presumption of atheism matters is that its acceptance must put the whole question of the existence of God into an entirely fresh perspective. Most immediately relevant here is that in this fresh perspective problems which really are conceptual are seen as conceptual problems; and problems which have tended to be regarded as advanced and, so to speak, optional extras now discover themselves as both elementary and indispensable. The theist who wants to build a systematic and thorough apologetic finds that he is required to begin absolutely from the beginning;

and this absolute beginning is to ensure that the word "God" is provided with a meaning such that it is theoretically possible for an actual being to be so described.

Although I shall later be arguing that the presumption of atheism is neutral as between all parties to the main dispute, in as much as to accept it as determining a procedural framework is not to make any substantive assumptions, I must give fair warning now that I do nevertheless believe that in its fresh perspective the whole enterprise of theism appears even more difficult and precarious than it did before. In part this is a corollary of what I have just been suggesting; that certain difficulties and objections, which may previously have seemed peripheral or even factitious, are made to stand out as fundamental and unavoidable. But it is also in part, as we shall be seeing soon, a consequence of the emphasis which it places on the imperative need to produce some sort of sufficient reason to justify theist belief.

B. THE PRESUMPTION OF ATHEISM AND THE PRESUMPTION OF INNOCENCE

1. One thing which helps to conceal this need is a confusion about the possible varieties of proof, and this confusion is one which can be resolved with the help of the first of a series of comparisons between my proposed presumption of atheism and the legal presumption of innocence. It is frequently said nowadays, even by professing Roman Catholics, that everyone knows that it is impossible to prove the existence of God. The first objection to this putative truism is, as my reference to Roman Catholics should have suggested, that it is not true. For it is an essential dogma of Roman Catholicism, defined as such by the First Vatican Council, that "the one and true God our creator and lord can be known for certain through the creation by the natural light of human reason."[4] So even if this dogma is, as I myself believe, false, it is certainly not known to be false by those many Roman Catholics

who remain, despite all the disturbances consequent upon the Second Vatican Council, committed to the complete traditional faith.

To this a sophisticated objector might reply that the definition of the First Vatican Council speaks of knowing for certain rather than of proving or demonstrating; adding perhaps, if he was very sophisticated indeed, that the word "demonstrari" in an earlier draft was eventually replaced by the expression "*certo cognosci.*" But though this is, I am told,[5] correct it is certainly not enough to vindicate the conventional wisdom. For the word "proof" is not ordinarily restricted in its application to demonstratively valid arguments; arguments, that is, in which the conclusion cannot be denied without thereby contradicting the premises. So it is too flattering to suggest that most of those who make this facile claim, that everyone knows that it is impossible to prove the existence of God, are intending only the strictly limited assertion that one special sort of proof is impossible.

The truth, and the danger, is that wherever there is any awareness of such a limited and specialized interpretation, there will be a quick and illegitimate move to the much wider general conclusion that it is impossible and, furthermore, unnecessary to provide any sufficient reason for believing. It is, therefore, worth underlining that when the presumption of atheism is explained as insisting that the onus of proof must be on the theist, the word "proof" is being used in the ordinary wide sense in which it can embrace any and every variety of sufficient reason. It is, of course, in this and only this sense that the word is interpreted when the presumption of innocence is explained as laying the onus of proof on the prosecution.

2. A second element of positive analogy between these two presumptions is that both are defeasible; and that they are, consequently, not to be identified with assumptions. The presumption of innocence indicates where the court should start and how it must proceed. Yet the prosecution is still able, more often than not, to bring forward what is in the end accepted as sufficient reason to warrant the verdict "Guilty"; which appropriate sufficient reason is properly characterized as a proof

of guilt. The defeasible presumption of innocence is thus in this majority of cases in fact defeated; whereas, were the indefeasible innocence of all accused persons an assumption of any legal system, there could not be within that system any provision for any verdict other than "Not Guilty." To the extent that it is, for instance, an assumption of the English Common Law that every citizen is cognizant of all that the law requires of him, that law cannot admit the fact that this assumption is, as in fact it is, false.

The presumption of atheism is similarly defeasible. It lays it down that thorough and systematic inquiry must start from a position of negative atheism, and that the burden of proof lies on the theist proposition. Yet this is not at all the same thing as demanding that the debate should proceed on a positive atheist assumption, which must preclude a theist conclusion. Counsel for theism no more betrays his client by accepting the framework determined by this presumption than counsel for the prosecution betrays the state by conceding the legal presumption of innocence. The latter is perhaps in his heart unshakeably convinced of the guilt of the defendant. Yet he must, and with complete consistency and perfect sincerity may, insist that the proceedings of the court should respect the presumption of innocence. The former is even more likely to be persuaded of the soundness of his brief. Yet he too can with a good conscience allow that a thorough and complete apologetic must start from, meet, and go on to defeat, the presumption of atheism.

Put as I have just been putting it the crucial distinction between a defeasible presumption and a categorical assumption will, no doubt, seem quite obvious. But I know from experience that many do find it difficult to grasp, at least in its application to the present highly controversial case. Theists fear that if once they allow this procedural presumption they will have sold the pass to the atheist enemy. Most especially when the proponent of this procedure happens to be a known opponent of theism, the theist is inclined to mistake it that the procedure itself prejudicially assumes an atheist conclusion. But this, as the comparison with the legal presumption of innocence surely makes clear, is wrong. Such presumptions are procedural and not substantive; they assume no conclusion, either positive or negative.

3. However, and here we come to a third element in the positive analogy, to say that such presumptions are in themselves procedural and not substantive is not to say that the higher-order questions of whether to follow this presumption or that are trifling and merely formal rather than material and substantial. These higher-order questions are not questions which can be dismissed cynically as "issues of principle as opposed to issues of substance." It can matter a lot which presumption is adopted. Notoriously there is a world of difference between legal systems which follow the presumption of innocence, and those which do not. And, as I began to indicate at the end of Part A, to adopt the presumption of atheism does put the whole argument into a distinctive perspective.

4. Next, as a fourth element in the positive analogy, it is a paradoxical consequence of the fact that these presumptions are procedural and not substantive that particular defeats do not constitute any sort of reason, much less a sufficient reason, for a general surrender. The fact that George Joseph Smith was in his trial proved guilty of many murders defeats the original presumption of his innocence. But this particular defeat has no tendency at all to show that even in this particular case the court should not have proceeded on this presumption. Still less does it tend to establish that the legal system as a whole was at fault in incorporating this presumption as a general principle. It is the same with the presumption of atheism. Suppose that someone is able to prove the existence of God. This achievement must, similarly, defeat our presumption. But it does not thereby show that the original contention about the onus of proof was mistaken.

One may, therefore, as a mnemonic think of the word "defeasible" (= defeatable) as implying precisely this capacity to survive defeat. A substantive generalization—such as, for instance, the assertion that all persons accused of murder are in fact innocent—is falsified decisively by the production

of even one authentic counter-example. That is part of what is meant by the Baconian slogan: "Magis est vis instantiae negativae."[6] But a defeasible presumption is not shown to have been the wrong one to have made by being in a particular case in fact defeated. What does show the presumption of atheism to be the right one to make is what we have now to investigate.

C. THE CASE FOR THE PRESUMPTION OF ATHEISM

1. An obvious first move is to appeal to the old legal axiom: "Ei incumbit probatio qui dicit, non qui negat." Literally and unsympathetically translated this becomes: "The onus of proof lies on the man who affirms, not on the man who denies." To this the objection is almost equally obvious. Given just a very little verbal ingenuity, contrary motions can be rendered alternatively in equally positive forms: either, "That this house affirms the existence of God"; or, "That this house takes its stand for positive atheism." So interpreted, therefore, our axiom provides no determinate guidance.[7]

Suppose, however, that we take the hint already offered in the previous paragraph. A less literal but more sympathetic translation would be: "The onus of proof lies on the proposition, not on the opposition." The point of the change is to bring out that this maxim was offered in a legal context, and that our courts are institutions of debate. An axiom providing no determinate guidance outside that framework may nevertheless be fundamental for the effective conduct of orderly and decisive debate. Here the outcome is supposed to be decided on the merits of what is said within the debate itself, and of that alone. So no opposition can set about demolishing the proposition case until and unless that proposition has first provided them with a case for demolition.

Of course our maxim even when thus sympathetically interpreted still offers no direction on which contending parties ought to be made to undertake which roles. Granting that courts are to operate as debating institutions, and granting that this maxim is fundamental to debate, we have to appeal to some further premise principle before we become licensed to infer that the prosecution must propose and the defence oppose. This further principle is, once again, the familiar presumption of innocence. Were we, while retaining the conception of a court as an institution for reaching decisions by way of formalized debate, to embrace the opposite presumption, the presumption of guilt, we should need to adopt the opposite arrangements. In these the defence would first propose that the accused is after all innocent, and the prosecution would then respond by struggling to disintegrate the case proposed.

2. The first move examined cannot, therefore, be by itself sufficient. To have considered it does nevertheless help to show that to accept such a presumption is to adopt a policy. And policies have to be assessed by reference to the aims of those for whom they are suggested. If for you it is more important that no guilty person should ever be acquitted than that no innocent person should ever be convicted, then for you a presumption of guilt must be the rational policy. For you, with your preference structure, a presumption of innocence becomes simply irrational. To adopt this policy would be to adopt means calculated to frustrate your own chosen ends; which is, surely paradigmatically irrational. Take, as an actual illustration, the controlling elite of a ruling Leninist party, which must as such refuse to recognize any individual rights if these conflict with the claims of the party, and which in fact treats all those suspected of actual or potential opposition much as if they were already known "counter-revolutionaries," "enemies of socialism," "friends of the United States," "advocates of free elections," and all other like things bad. I can, and do, fault this policy and its agents on many counts. Yet I cannot say that for them, once granted their scale of values, it is irrational.

What then are the aims by reference to which an atheist presumption might be justified? One key word in the answer, if not the key word, must be "knowledge." The context for which such a policy is proposed is that of enquiry about the existence of God; and the object of the exercise is, presumably, to discover whether it is possible to establish that the word "God" does in fact have application. Now to establish must here be either to show that you know or to come to know. But knowledge is crucially different from mere true belief. All knowledge involves true belief; not all true belief constitutes knowledge. To have a true belief is simply and solely to believe that something is so, and to be in fact right. But someone may believe that this or that is so, and his belief may in fact be true, without its thereby and necessarily constituting knowledge. If a true belief is to achieve this more elevated status, then the believer has to be properly warranted so to believe. He must, that is, be in a position to know.

Obviously there is enormous scope for disagreement in particular cases: both about what is required in order to be in a position to know; and about whether these requirements have actually been satisfied. But the crucial distinction between believing truly and knowing is recognized as universally as the prior and equally vital distinction between believing and believing what is in fact true. If, for instance, there is a question whether a colleague performed some discreditable action, then all of us, though we have perhaps to admit that we cannot help believing that he did, are rightly scrupulous not to assert that this is known unless we have grounds sufficient to warrant the bolder claim. It is, therefore, not only incongruous but also scandalous in matters of life and death, and even of eternal life and death, to maintain that you know either on no grounds at all, or on grounds of a kind which on other and comparatively minor issues you yourself would insist to be inadequate.

It is by reference to this inescapable demand for grounds that the presumption of atheism is justified. If it is to be established that there is a God, then we have to have good grounds for believing that this is indeed so. Until and unless some such grounds are produced we have literally no reason at all for believing; and in that situation the only reasonable posture must be that of either the negative atheist or the agnostic. So the onus of proof has to rest on the proposition. It must be up to them: first, to give whatever sense they choose to the word "God," meeting any objection that so defined it would relate only to an incoherent pseudo-concept; and, second, to bring forward sufficient reasons to warrant their claim that, in their present sense of the word "God," there is a God. The same applies, with appropriate alterations, if what is to be made out is, not that atheism is known to be true, but only—more modestly—that it can be seen to be at least more or less probable.

D. OBJECTIONS TO THE PRESUMPTION OF ATHEISM

1. Once the nature of this presumption is understood, the supporting case is short and simple. One reason why it may appear unacceptable is a confusion of contexts. In a theist or post-theist society it comes more easily to ask why a man is not a theist than why he is. Provided that the question is to be construed biographically this is no doubt methodologically inoffensive. But our concern here is not all with biographical questions of why people came to hold whatever opinions they do hold. Rather it is with the need for opinions to be suitably grounded if they are to be rated as items of knowledge, or even of probable belief. The issue is: not what does or does not need to be explained biographically; but where the burden of theological proof should rest.

2. A more sophisticated objection of fundamentally the same sort would urge that our whole discussion has been too artificial and too general, and that any man's enquiries have to begin from wherever he happens to be. "We cannot begin," C. S. Peirce wrote, "with complete doubt. We must begin with all the prejudices which we actually have.... These prejudices are not to be dispelled by a maxim...."[8] With particular present reference Professor John Hick has urged: "The right question is whether it is rational for the religious man himself, given that his religious experience is coherent, persistent, and compelling, to affirm the reality of God. What is in question is not

the rationality of an inference from certain psychological events to God as their cause; for the religious man no more infers the existence of God than we infer the existence of the visible world around us. What is in question is the rationality of the one who has the religious experiences. If we regard him as a rational person we must acknowledge that he is rational in believing what, given his experiences, he cannot help believing."[9]

To the general point drawn from Peirce the answer comes from further reading of Peirce himself. He was in the paper from which I quoted arguing against the Cartesian programme of simultaneous, systematic, and (almost) universal doubt. Peirce did not want to suggest that it is impossible or wrong to subject any of our beliefs to critical scrutiny. In the same paragraph he continues: "A person may, it is true, find reason to doubt what he began by believing; but in that case he doubts because he has a positive reason for it, and not on account of the Cartesian maxim." One positive reason for being especially leery towards religious opinions is that these vary so very much from society to society; being, it seems, mainly determined, in Descartes' phrase, "by custom and example."[10]

To Hick it has at once to be conceded: that it is one thing to say that a belief is unfounded or well-founded; and quite another to say that it is irrational or rational for some particular person, in his particular time and circumstances, and with his particular experience and lack of experience, to hold or to reject that belief. Granted that his usually reliable Intelligence were sure that the enemy tank brigade was in the town, it was entirely reasonable for the General also to believe this. But the enemy tanks had in fact pulled back. Yet it was still unexceptionally sensible for the General on his part to refuse to expose his flank to those tanks which were in fact not there. This genuine and important distinction cannot, however, save the day for Hick.

In the first place, to show that someone may reasonably hold a particular belief, and even that he may properly claim that he knows it to be true, is at best still not to show that that belief is indeed well-grounded, much less that it constitutes an item of his knowledge.

Nor, second, is to accept the presumption of atheism as a methodological framework, as such: either to deprive anyone of his right "to affirm the reality of God"; or to require that to be respectable every conviction should first have been reached through the following of an ideally correct procedure. To insist on the correctness of this presumption as an initial presumption is to make a claim which is itself procedural rather than substantive; and the context for which this particular procedure is being recommended is that of justification rather than of discovery.

Once these fundamentals are appreciated those for whom Hick is acting as spokesman should at first feel quite content. For on his account they consider that they have the very best of grounds for their beliefs. They regard their "coherent, consistent, and compelling" religious experience as analogous to perception; and the man who can see something with his own eyes and feel it in his own hands is in a perfect position to know that it exists. His position is indeed so perfect that, as Hick says, it is wrong to speak here of evidence and inference. If he saw his wife in the act of intercourse with a lover then he no longer needs to infer her infidelity from bits and pieces of evidence. He has now what is better than inference; although for the rest of us, who missed this display, his testimony still constitutes an important part of the evidence in the case. The idiomatic expression "the evidence of my own eyes" derives its paradoxical piquancy from the fact that to see for oneself is better than to have evidence.

All this is true. Certainly too anyone who thinks that he can as it were see God must reject the suggestion that in so doing he infers "from certain psychological events to God as their cause." For to accept this account would be to call down upon his head all the insoluble difficulties which fall to the lot of all those who maintain that what we see, and all we ever really and directly see, is visual sense-data. And, furthermore, it is useful to be reminded that when we insist that knowledge as opposed to mere belief has to be adequately warranted, this grounding may be a matter either of having sufficient evidence or of being in a position

to know directly and without evidence. So far, therefore it might seem that Hick's objection was completely at cross-purposes; and that anyway his protégés have no need to appeal to the distinction between actual knowledge and what one may rationally and properly claim to know.

Wait a minute. The passage of Hick which has been under discussion was part of an attempt to show that criticism of the Argument from Religious Experience is irrelevant to such claims to as it were see God. But on the contrary: what such criticism usually challenges is just the vital assumption that having religious experience really is a kind of perceiving, and hence a sort of being in a position to know about its putative object. So this challenge provides just exactly that positive reason, which Peirce demanded, for doubting what, according to Hick, "one who has the religious experiences ... cannot help believing." If therefore he persists in so believing without even attempting to overcome this criticism, then it becomes impossible to vindicate his claims to be harbouring rational beliefs; much less items of authentic knowledge.

3. A third objection, of a different kind, starts from the assumption, mentioned in section B(1) earlier, that any programme to prove the existence of God is fundamentally misconceived; that this enterprise is on all fours with projects to square the circle or to construct a perpetual motion machine. The suggestion then is that the territory which reason cannot inhabit may nevertheless be freely colonized by faith:

"The world was all before them, where to choose."[11]

Ultimately perhaps it is impossible to establish the existence of God, or even to show that it is more or less probable. But, if so, this is not the correct moral: the rational man does not thereby become in this area free to believe, or not to believe, just as his fancy takes him. Faith, surely, should not be a leap in the dark but a leap towards the light. Arbitrarily to plump for some particular conviction, and then stubbornly to cleave to it, would be—to borrow the term which St. Thomas employed in discussing natural reason, faith, and revelation[12]—frivolous. If your venture of faith is not to be arbitrary, irrational, and frivolous, you must have presentable reasons: first for making any such commitment in this area, an area in which by hypothesis the available grounds are insufficient to warrant any firm conclusion; and second for opting for one particular possibility rather than any of the other available alternatives. To most such offerings of reasons the presumption of atheism remains relevant. For though, again by the hypothesis, these cannot aspire to prove their conclusions they will usually embrace some estimation of their probability. If the onus of proof lies on the man who hopes definitively to establish the existence of God, it must also by the same token rest on the person who plans to make out only that this conclusion is more or less probable.

I put in the qualifications "most" and "usually" in order to allow for apologetic in the tradition of Pascal's Wager.[13] Pascal makes no attempt in this most famous argument to show that his Roman Catholicism is true or probably true. The reasons which he suggests for making the recommended bet on his particular faith are reasons in the sense of motives rather than reasons in our previous sense of grounds. Conceding, if only for the sake of the present argument, that we can have no knowledge here, Pascal tries to justify as prudent a policy of systematic self-persuasion, rather than to provide grounds for thinking that the beliefs recommended are actually true.

Another instructive feature of Pascal's argument is his unwarranted assumption that there are only two betting options, neither of which, on the assumption of total ignorance, can be awarded any measure of positive probability. Granted all this it then appears compulsively reasonable to wager one's life on the alternative which promises and threatens so inordinately much. But the number of theoretically possible world-systems is infinite, and the subset of those making similar promises and threats is also infinite. The immediate relevance of this to us is that it will not do, without further reason given, to set up as the two mutually exclusive and together exhaustive alternatives (one sort of) theism and (the corresponding sort of) positive atheism; and then to suggest that, since neither

position can be definitely established, everyone is entitled simply to take their pick. The objection that this way of constructing the book leaves out a third, agnostic, opinion is familiar; and it is one which Pascal himself tried to meet by arguing that to refuse to decide is in effect to decide against religion. The objection based on the point that the number of theoretically possible Hell-threatening and Heaven-promising world-systems is infinite, is quite different and against the Wager as he himself sets it up decisive. The point is that on the given assumption of total ignorance, combined with our present recognition of the infinite range of alternative theoretical possibilities; to bet on any one of the, so to speak, positive options, none of which can by the hypothesis be awarded any measure of positive probability, must be in the last degree arbitrary and capricious.

E. THE FIVE WAYS AS AN ATTEMPT TO DEFEAT THE PRESUMPTION OF ATHEISM

I have tried, in the first four sections, to explain what I mean by "the presumption of atheism," to bring out by comparison with the presumption of innocence in law what such a presumption does and does not involve, to deploy a case for adopting my presumption of atheism, and to indicate the lines on which two sorts of objection may be met. Now, finally, I want to point out that St. Thomas Aquinas presented the Five Ways in his *Summa Theologica* as an attempt to defeat just such a presumption. My hope in this is, both to draw attention to something which seems generally to be overlooked, and by so doing to summon a massive authority in support of a thesis which many apparently find scandalous.

These most famous arguments were offered there originally, without any inhibition or equivocation, as proofs, period: "I reply that we must say that God can be proved in five ways"; and the previous second Article, raising the question "Whether the existence of God can be demonstrated?," gives the categorical affirmative answer that "the existence of God ... can be demonstrated."[14] Attention usually and understandably concentrates on the main body of the third Article, which is the part where Aquinas gives his five supposed proofs. But, as so often, it is rewarding to read the entire Article, and especially the second of the two Objections to which these are presented as a reply: "Furthermore, what can be accounted for by fewer principles is not the product of more. But it seems that everything which can be observed in the world can be accounted for by other principles, on the assumption of the non-existence of God. Thus natural effects are explained by natural causes, while contrived effects are referred to human reason and will. So there is no need to postulate the existence of God."[15]

The Five Ways are thus at least in one aspect an attempt to defeat this presumption of (an Aristotelian) atheist naturalism, by showing that the things "which can be observed in the world" cannot "be accounted for ... on the assumption of the nonexistence of God," and hence that there is "need to postulate the existence of God."[16] One must never forget that Aquinas composed his own Objections, and hence that it was he who introduced into his formulation here the idea of (this Aristotelian) scientific naturalism. No such idea is integral to the presumption of atheism as that has been construed in the present paper. When the addition is made the presumption can perhaps be labelled "Stratonician." (Strato was the next but one in succession to Aristotle as head of the Lyceum, and was regarded by Bayle and Hume as the archetypal ancient spokesman for an atheist scientific naturalism.)

By suggesting, a century before Ockham, an appeal to an Ockhamist principle of postulational economy Aquinas also indicates a reason for adopting such a presumption. The fact that the Saint cannot be suspect of wanting to reach atheist conclusions can now be made to serve as a spectacular illustration of a point laboured in Part B, above, that to adopt such a presumption is not to make an assumption. And the fact, which has been put forward as an objection to this reading of Aquinas,

that "Thomas himself was never in the position of a Stratonician, nor did he live in a milieu in which Stratonicians were plentiful,"[17] is simply irrelevant. For the thesis that the onus of proof lies upon the theist is entirely independent of these biographical and sociological facts.

What is perhaps slightly awkward for present purposes is the formulation of the first Objection: "It seems that God does not exist. For if of two contrary things one were to exist without limit the other would be totally eliminated. But what is meant by this word 'God' is something good without limit. So if God were to have existed no evil would have been encountered. But evil is encountered in the world. Therefore, God does not exist."

It would from my point of view have been better had this first Objection referred to possible difficulties and incoherencies in the meaning proposed for the word "God." Unfortunately it does not, although Aquinas is elsewhere acutely aware of such problems. The changes required, however, are, though important, not extensive. Certainly, the Objection as actually given is presented as one of the God hypothesis falsified by familiar fact. Yet a particular variety of the same general point could be represented as the detection of an incoherence, not in the proposed concept of God as such, but between that concept and another element in the theoretical structure in which it is normally involved.

The incoherence—or perhaps on this occasion I should say only the ostensible incoherence—is between the idea of creation, as necessarily involving complete, continual and absolute dependence of creature upon Creator, and the idea that creatures may nevertheless be sufficiently autonomous for their faults not to be also and indeed primarily His fault. The former idea, the idea of creation, is so essential that it provides the traditional criterion for distinguishing theism from deism. The latter is no less central to the three great theist systems of Judaism, Christianity, and Islam, since all three equally insist that creatures of the immaculate Creator are corrupted by sin. So where Aquinas put as his first Objection a statement of the traditional

Problem of Evil, conceived as a problem of squaring the God hypothesis with certain undisputed facts, a redactor fully seized of the presumption of atheism as expounded in the present paper would refer instead to the ostensible incoherence, within the system itself, between the concept of creation by a flawless Creator and the notion of His creatures flawed by their sins.

NOTES

1. This and all later translations from the Greek and Latin are by me.

2. See Chapter VI of Lewis Carroll's *Through the Looking Glass*:

   "But 'glory' doesn't mean 'a nice knock-down argument,'" Alice objected.

   "When I use a word," Humpty Dumpty said in rather a scornful tone, "it means just what I choose it to mean—neither more nor less."

   "The question is," said Alice, "whether you can make words mean so many different things."

   "The question is," said Humpty Dumpty, "which is to be master—that's all."

3. See the essay 'Agnosticism', and also that on "Agnosticism and Christianity," in Volume V of his *Collected Essays* (MacMillan: London, 1894). I may perhaps also refer to my own article on "Agnosticism" for the 1972 revision of the *Encyclopaedia Britannica*.

4. H. Denzingerd (Ed.) *Enchiridion Symbolorum* (Twenty-ninth Revised Edition, Herder: Freiburg im Breisgau, 1953), section 1806.

5. By Professor P. T. Geach of Leeds.

6. "The force of the negative instance is greater." For, whereas a single positive, supporting instance can do only a very little to confirm an universal generalization, one negative, contrary example would be sufficient decisively to falsify that generalization.

7. See the paper "Presumptions" by my former colleague Patrick Day in the *Proceedings of the XIVth International Congress of Philosophy* (Vienna, 1968), Vol. V, at p. 140. I am pleased that it was I who first suggested to him an exploration of this unfrequented philosophical territory.

8. In "Some Consequences of Four Incapacities" at pp. 156–157 of Volume V of the *Collected Papers* (Harvard University Press; Cambridge (Mass.), 1934).

9. In his review of *God and Philosophy* in *Theology Today* 1967, pp. 86–87. He makes his point not against the general presumption but against one particular application.

10. *Discourse on the Method*, Part II. It occurs almost immediately after his observation: "I took into account also the very different character which a person brought up from infancy in France or Germany exhibits, from that which . . . he would have possessed had he lived among the Chinese or with savages."

11. *Paradise Lost*, Bk. XII, line 646.

12. *Summa contra Gentiles*, Bk. I, Ch. VI. The whole passage, in which Aquinas gives his reasons for believing that the Christian candidate does, and that of Mohammed does not, constitute an authentic revelation of God, should be compared with some defence of the now widely popular *assumption* that the contents of a religious faith must be without evidential warrant.

    Professor A. C. Macintyre, for instance, while he was still himself a Christian argued with great vigour for the Barthian thesis that "Belief cannot argue with unbelief: it can only preach to it." Thus, in his paper on 'The Logical Status of Religious Belief' in *Metaphysical Beliefs* (Student Christian Movement press: London, 1957), Macintyre urged: ". . . suppose religion could be provided with a method of proof . . . since the Christian faith sees true religion only in a free decision made in faith and love, the religion would by this vindication be destroyed, For all possibility of free choice would have been done away. Any objective justification of belief would have the same effect . . . faith too would have been eliminated" (p. 209).

Now, first, in so far as this account is correct any commitment to a system of religious belief has to be made altogether without evidencing reasons. Macintyre himself concludes with a quotation from John Donne to illustrate the "confessional voice" of faith, commenting: "The man who speaks like this is beyond argument" (p. 211). But this, we must insist, would be nothing to be proud off. It is certainly no compliment, even if it were a faithful representation, to portray the true believer as necessarily irrational and a bigot. Furthermore, second, it is not the case that where sufficient evidence is available there can be no room for choice. Men can, and constantly do, choose to deceive themselves about the most well-evidenced, inconvenient truths. Also no recognition of any facts, however clear, is by itself sufficient to guarantee one allegiance and to preclude its opposite. MacIntyre needs to extend his reading of the Christian poets to the greatest of them all. For the hero of Milton's *Paradise Lost* had the most enviably full and direct knowledge of God. Yet Lucifer, if any creature could, chose freely to rebel.

13. *Pensées*, section 233 in the Brunschvicg arrangement. For a discussion of Pascal's argument see Chapter VI, section 7 of my *An Introduction to Western Philosophy* (Thames & Hudson, and Bobbs-Merrill: London and New York, 1971).

14. It is worth stressing this point, since nowadays it is frequently denied. Thus L. C. Velecky in an article in *Philosophy* 1968 asserts: "He did not prove here the existence of God, nor indeed, did he prove it anywhere else, for a very good reason. According to Thomas, God's existence is unknowable and, hence, cannot be proved" (p. 226). The quotations from Aquinas given in my text ought to be decisive. Yet there seems to be quite a school of devout interpretation which waives aside what the Saint straightforwardly said as almost irrelevant to the question of what he really meant.

15. I, Q2 A3.

16. In this perspective it becomes easier to see why Aquinas makes so much use of Aristotelian scientific ideas in his arguments. That they are in fact much more dependent on these now largely obsolete ideas is usefully emphasized in Anthony Kenny's *The Five Ways* (Routledge and Kegan Paul, and Schocken Books: London and New York, 1969). But Kenny does not bring out that they were deployed against a presumption of atheist naturalism.

17. Velecky *loc. cit.*, pp. 225–226.

V.C.3

Rational Religious Belief without Arguments

MICHAEL BERGMANN

Michael Bergmann (1964–) is professor of philosophy at Purdue University and works primarily in the fields of epistemology and philosophy of religion. In this chapter, Bergmann explains and defends the view (held by Alvin Plantinga and other so-called Reformed epistemologists) that religious beliefs—like the belief that God exists—can be rational even if they are not based on arguments.

This essay was published for the first time in the 6th edition of this anthology.

There have been many different attempts, by philosophers and others, to show that religious belief of various kinds is irrational. And there have been at least as many attempts by religious people to defend the rationality of their beliefs. Perhaps the most common religious belief to be attacked and defended in this way is belief in God—an omniscient, omnipotent, immaterial, eternal, perfectly good, wholly loving person on whom everything else depends. It will be convenient to focus our attention on belief in God, though much of our discussion will be relevant to other religious beliefs as well. Believers in God (theists) have for centuries now offered a variety of arguments for God's existence: they've argued that there must be a first cause (an uncaused cause) of the existence of things; they've argued that there must be a designer to account for the apparent design found in the natural world; they've argued that we can't make sense of morality without appealing to the existence of God; they've even argued that simply by reflecting on the concept of God we can see that God exists because such reflection reveals that God is the sort of being that *must* exist. The goal of these arguments is, at least in part, to show that belief in God is rational. Reliance on these sorts of arguments is supposed by many to be what *makes* belief in God rational. In fact, it is commonly thought that belief in God *couldn't* be rational unless it is held on the basis of such arguments. But is that last thought right? Could a person's belief in God be rational even if it is not held on the basis of any of these alleged theistic proofs? Could there be rational religious belief without arguments?

For the past few decades, a prominent position within the philosophy of religion literature is that belief in God *can* be rational even if it isn't based on any arguments. This position is often called "Reformed Epistemology" to signify its roots in the writings of John Calvin (1509–1564), the great Protestant theologian and the main source of the Reformed tradition within Christendom. But one can find developments of the same idea in the writings of earlier figures such as Aquinas, Augustine, and even the apostle Paul. The central thesis of Reformed Epistemology is simply that religious belief, including belief in God, can be rational (sensible, reasonable, justified) even if it is not inferred from any other beliefs—even if it is not held on the basis of any argument at all. In what follows, I will explain this view in greater detail and then consider and respond to a number of objections to it.

I. UNDERSTANDING REFORMED EPISTEMOLOGY

A. A Little Background in Epistemology

In order to understand Reformed Epistemology, it will be helpful to begin with a little background in epistemology, which is the study of knowledge and rational belief. Epistemologists typically aren't concerned with religious belief in particular. Their concern is more general. They are trying to understand the nature of knowledge and rationality as these concepts apply to any belief whatsoever, regardless of the belief's topic or the means by which it was produced.

Let's begin by highlighting two distinctions. The first, which we've already been employing, is the distinction between rational and irrational beliefs. This is an *evaluative* distinction insofar as rational beliefs are, by definition, epistemically *better* than irrational beliefs. The second distinction is between basic beliefs and nonbasic beliefs. A basic belief is a belief that is not based on or inferred from another belief. A nonbasic belief is a belief that *is* based on or inferred from another belief. This is a *psychological* distinction, not an evaluative one. It has to do with how the beliefs are formed. Let's consider some examples of basic and nonbasic beliefs. Suppose you're visiting your doctor after being in a minor car accident and she is trying to determine the extent of your injuries. She gently presses on various parts of your back and neck, asking if it hurts when she does so. At one point you feel a very sharp pain and you tell her that it hurts. You tell her that because you *believe* that it hurts. That belief isn't inferred from other beliefs you have. (You don't first believe that you flinched when she pressed that spot and then infer that, because you flinch only when you're in pain, you must be in pain now). Instead, that belief is an automatic noninferential response to the feeling of pain you experience; it is based on that experience, even though it isn't based on another belief. Because it is not based on another belief of yours, it is a basic (or noninferential) belief. Nonbasic (or inferential) beliefs are different. Suppose you want to figure out in your head what 9×53 equals. To do this, you typically will come first to believe that $9 \times 50 = 450$, that $9 \times 3 = 27$, and that $450 + 27 = 477$. Then you infer from those beliefs the further belief that $9 \times 53 = 477$. Since that last belief is inferred from other beliefs, it is a nonbasic belief.

An important question that has been of interest to philosophers as early as Aristotle (384–322 BCE) is whether any basic beliefs are rational. It's natural to think that for a belief to be rational, you must have a reason for holding it, where your reason is another belief of yours. But to hold a belief for a reason is to base it on or infer it from that other belief that is your reason. These considerations might incline a person to endorse *Inferentialism*, the view that a belief can be rational only if it's inferred from another belief. But there is a powerful and influential objection to Inferentialism, first proposed by Aristotle (*Posterior Analytics*, Book I, Chapters 2–3). This objection starts by noting that it's implausible to think that a belief can be rational in virtue of being inferred from an *irrational belief*. Hence, Inferentialism implies that a belief is rational only if it's inferred from another *rational* belief. But according to Inferentialism, for that second belief to be rational, it too must be inferred from another belief—which also must be rational. And so on. Thus, Inferentialism implies that in order for a belief to be rational, you must either base it on an infinite chain of reasoning or else reason in a circle. But it's obvious that reasoning in a circle cannot make a belief rational. And none of us is able to carry out an infinite chain of reasoning. (And even if we could, an infinite chain of reasoning cannot, by itself, make a belief rational without some original rationality to be transferred along the chain.) The upshot is that if Inferentialism is true, then it's impossible to have rational beliefs. Given that most

philosophers think that it isn't impossible to have rational beliefs, it's widely believed that Inferentialism is false: basic beliefs can be, and often are, rational. These rational basic beliefs are often called "properly basic beliefs."

Not just any basic belief is *properly* basic (i.e., both rational and noninferential). The reckless gambler who is having a run of terrible luck in the casino and who believes on a whim, not on the basis of any other beliefs, that his luck is about to improve, is thereby forming an irrational basic belief. Unlike your basic belief that you're in pain (when the doctor presses on your neck), the gambler's basic belief is not *properly* basic. So although some basic beliefs are properly basic, not all of them are. Which of our basic beliefs *are* properly basic? The answer to this question has to do with which belief-forming abilities we have. We humans have the ability to tell, without inference, that we're in pain. But we don't have the ability to tell, without inference, that our gambling luck is about to improve. We also have the ability to tell, without inference, what our own thoughts are. But we don't have the ability to tell, without inference, what others are thinking. Likewise, we have the ability to tell just by looking, without inference from other beliefs, that there's a book on the table in front of us. But we don't have the ability to tell in complete darkness, without inference, that there's a pillar six feet in front of us (though if we had the echolocation abilities that bats have, we could reasonably form such basic beliefs in the darkness). So which beliefs can be properly basic for us depends on which noninferential belief-forming abilities we have.

Which noninferential belief-forming abilities do we have? Which of our basic beliefs can be rational? There is wide agreement that we can tell noninferentially via introspection what we're thinking and feeling. In addition, there's wide agreement that we can tell noninferentially via rational intuition that one thing is logically implied by another, though this ability is limited for most people to very simple logical implications. (For example, we can tell noninferentially via rational intuition that if Jack and Jill are at the party then it logically follows that Jack is at the party.) Suppose that those were the only sorts of properly basic beliefs we had and that the only way for us to have rational beliefs in addition to beliefs of those kinds would be to draw inferences from them. The famous philosopher René Descartes (1596–1650) began with only those sorts of basic belief—i.e., those formed via introspection and rational intuition—and tried from there to see what he could learn by inference. He thought that in that way, starting from those meager foundations, he could prove that God exists and that there is a physical world surrounding us. Most philosophers think that he failed in this attempt and that the problem had a lot to do with the fact that he allowed so few beliefs to count as properly basic. Today, most epistemologists think that in addition to the ability to form noninferential beliefs via introspection and rational intuition, we also have the ability to form noninferential beliefs via perception and memory. When, upon glancing at a nearby basketball, I believe there's a ball in front of me, I don't do this via inference: I don't first notice that it visually appears to me as if there's a ball there and that such appearances are good indicators that there is a ball there and from this infer that there's a ball in front of me. I can just tell noninferentially via perception that there's a ball in front of me. Likewise, I can tell noninferentially via memory that I had orange juice at breakfast. I don't infer this from the fact that there's a glass on the kitchen counter that looks as if it contained orange juice a few hours ago and that no one else in the house likes orange juice. Thus, it's very common for epistemologists to think we have the ability to form noninferential beliefs via perception, memory, introspection, and rational intuition. Because we have these abilities, the beliefs so produced are properly basic (i.e., noninferentially rational). And from these starting points, we can make inferences via good reasoning to the many other beliefs we hold; these other beliefs are then inferentially rational.

It's important to emphasize that although these properly basic beliefs aren't inferred from other beliefs, it doesn't follow that they are groundless or that we hold them without any evidence. Take for example the belief that you are in pain. It's true you don't infer that from other beliefs. But it's not groundless. Instead, it's based on your experience of pain. It's that experience, not another belief, which is the ground of your belief that you're in pain—that experience is your evidence for that belief. Other introspective beliefs are also based on experiences (such as the belief that you're happy or sad, which is based on your experience of feeling happy or sad).[1] Likewise, although perceptual beliefs aren't inferred from other beliefs, they aren't lacking in grounds or evidence. My belief that there's a ball in front of me is based on my visual experience at the moment (not on the belief that I'm having such a visual experience—I typically don't form such beliefs about my visual experience). That visual experience is my evidence—it is the ground of that visual belief. In the case of beliefs formed via memory or rational intuition, it's more difficult to say what they are based on. According to one common way of thinking about memory beliefs, they are based on memory seemings. It seems to me—in a remembering sort of way—that I had orange juice for breakfast. On the basis of that seeming (that memory seeming) I hold the memory belief that I had orange juice for breakfast. Similarly, beliefs in simple logical truths, formed via rational intuition are based on rational intuitions. I can just *see* (intellectually) that one thing logically follows from another. This "seeing" is a sort of insight, a rational intuition; it's an experience of something's seeming to me a certain way—it's an experience of its seeming obvious to me that this thing logically follows from that thing. And my belief that the one thing follows from the other is based on this rational intuition. Both the memory seeming and the rational intuition are experiences. They aren't themselves beliefs. So beliefs based on them still count as basic.

The resulting picture, widely endorsed by contemporary epistemologists, is the following. Some beliefs are rational and some are not. Those that are rational are either basic or not. The rational beliefs that aren't basic are inferred from other rational beliefs. These inference chains are ultimately traced back to properly basic beliefs—i.e., rational beliefs that aren't based on any other beliefs. What makes a basic belief rational has to do with which noninferential belief-forming abilities we have. At the very least, we humans seem to have the ability to form beliefs via perception, memory, rational intuition, and introspection. And the beliefs produced by these noninferential belief-forming abilities are based not on other beliefs but on experiences of various kinds—perceptual experiences, memory seemings, rational intuitions, and introspectable experiences such as pain, pleasure, happiness, sadness, etc.

There is one further "background epistemology" question that often gets discussed by philosophers and which will be relevant to our discussion of religious belief. The question is this: can a belief be properly basic for a person who has never thought at all about the epistemology of such beliefs in anything like the way we just have? For example, can a sad child be rational in remembering that his mother left the room a moment ago even if the child has no idea that that belief is based on a memory seeming? The answer, it seems, is "yes." One can be rational in forming noninferential beliefs via memory even if one has never thought about how memory works or what memory beliefs are based on or whether memory beliefs are basic or nonbasic.

However, given that rationality seems to rule out haphazard or careless belief formation, some might be tempted by a contrary view that we can call "Confirmationalism," which requires for a belief's rationality that we confirm that it was produced in the right way:

> *Confirmationalism:* In order for a belief to be rational, the person holding it needs a further belief that the first belief has an adequate basis.

So, for example, Confirmationalism would say that I can't be rational in my memory belief that I was in Florida last year unless I have an additional belief that that memory belief of mine has an adequate basis. Of course that second belief—required to confirm the adequacy of the first belief's basis—must itself be rational. But according to

Confirmationalism, that second belief (like any other belief) is rational only if the person holding it has yet another belief that the second belief has an adequate basis. And that third belief must be rational too, which will require a fourth belief confirming the adequacy of its basis. And so on. Thus, Confirmationalism implies that in order for a simple belief—such as the belief that *there is a ball in front of me*—to be rational, I need to have an infinite number of other beliefs, each of which is about the previous belief having an adequate basis. (Because each belief is about the previous belief, this chain of beliefs will not circle back on itself.) But people aren't able to have an infinite number of extra beliefs for each of the simple beliefs they hold. Given Confirmationalism, this implies that people aren't able to have any rational beliefs. For this reason, most epistemologists reject Confirmationalism.[2]

B. Reformed Epistemology

Let us turn now to the task of trying to gain a better understanding of Reformed Epistemology, the view that belief in God can be rational even if it is not inferred from any other beliefs. Our background reflections in epistemology will benefit us as our discussion proceeds.

A helpful way to begin our more careful examination of Reformed Epistemology is to consider the context in which it was introduced into the contemporary philosophy of religion literature. A prominent twentieth-century objection to the rationality of belief in God runs as follows:

The Evidentialist Objection

1. *The Evidentialist Thesis*: Belief in God is rational only if it is inferred from other rational beliefs via good arguments.

2. But there aren't any good arguments for God's existence.

3. Therefore, belief in God is irrational.

The reason this objection is called "The Evidentialist Objection" is that it relies on the Evidentialist Thesis as its first premise.[3] According to that premise, theistic belief is rational only if it is based on good evidence in the form of good theistic arguments. The proponent of this objection to theism will, of course, endorse the Evidentialist Thesis but will not believe in God. Let's call such a proponent a "Nontheistic Evidentialist." For most of the twentieth century, the most common response to this argument, by those who wanted to defend theistic belief, was the response given by Theistic Evidentialists. Like Nontheistic Evidentialists, they accept the first premise, the Evidentialist Thesis. But they reject the second premise. They think there *are* good arguments for God's existence. And they spend a lot of time devising such arguments and defending those arguments against objections. It was in just this context of disagreement (between Theistic Evidentialists and Nontheistic Evidentialists over whether there are good theistic arguments) that a second theistic response to the Evidentialist Objection was offered, this time by Reformed Epistemologists. They turned their sights on the first premise, the Evidentialist Thesis itself. Their claim was that belief in God—like the belief that I had orange juice for breakfast or the belief that there's a ball in front of me—can be properly basic. (As for the second premise, some Reformed Epistemologists join Nontheistic Evidentialists in accepting it; others join Theistic Evidentialists in rejecting it. But all Reformed Epistemologists reject the first premise; and that is what they tend to focus on in responding to the Evidentialist Objection.)

Given that Reformed Epistemologists think belief in God is properly basic (and in light of our background excursion into epistemology in the previous section), you would expect Reformed Epistemologists to also think that we have a noninferential belief-forming ability enabling us to tell, without inference, that God exists. And that's just what we find in their writings. Alvin Plantinga, perhaps the most prominent of contemporary Reformed Epistemologists, suggests that we have a "sense of divinity" enabling us to form properly basic beliefs about God. And just as noninferential beliefs formed via perception and memory are not groundless but instead based on experience, so also properly basic beliefs about God are, according to the Reformed Epistemologist, not groundless but

based on experience. Plantinga gives some examples of the sort of experiential grounds on which noninferential beliefs about God are based:

> [T]here is in us a disposition to believe propositions of the sort *this flower was created by God* or *this vast and intricate universe was created by God* when we contemplate the flower or behold the starry heavens or think about the vast reaches of the universe.... Upon reading the Bible, one may be impressed with a deep sense that God is speaking to him. Upon having done what I know is cheap, or wrong, or wicked I may feel guilty in God's sight and form the belief *God disapproves of what I've done.* Upon confession and repentance, I may feel forgiven, forming the belief *God forgives me for what I've done.* A person in grave danger may turn to God asking for his protection and help; and of course he or she then forms the belief that God is indeed able to hear and help if he sees fit. When life is sweet and satisfying, a spontaneous sense of gratitude may well up within the soul; someone in this condition may thank and praise the Lord for his goodness, and will of course form the accompanying belief that indeed the Lord is to be thanked and praised.[4]

The proposal here is that experiences of awe, guilt, forgiveness, fear, and gratitude can operate as grounds for beliefs about God. The beliefs so formed aren't usually of the form "God exists." They're more often of the form "God does this" or "God has done that" or "God is able to do such and such." In this way, they're like our more ordinary beliefs about the world around us. We typically don't form beliefs like "that lake exists." Instead, we think "that lake is cold" or "that lake is beautiful" or some such thing. But it's a short step from the belief about the lake (or God) to the further belief that the lake (or God) exists.[5]

It's important to emphasize (because it's so common for people to mistakenly think otherwise) that Reformed Epistemologists hold that ordinary unsophisticated religious believers who know nothing of the epistemological views discussed in this paper can have properly basic belief in God. As I already noted, most epistemologists (whether religious or not) think that a child's memory-produced belief that his mother left the room a few moments ago is rational even if the child can give no account of what that memory belief is based on or why it is rational. What matters for the rationality of that memory belief is that the child *has* the ability to form beliefs using his memory, not whether the child can give an account of the epistemology of memory beliefs. Likewise, Reformed Epistemologists say that what matters for properly basic belief in God is that the believer *has* the ability to form beliefs via the sense of divinity, not that the person can give an account of the epistemology of noninferential theistic beliefs. So a belief in God can be rational even if the person holding it doesn't have the further belief that her belief in God has an adequate basis via the sense of divinity. Some objectors will insist that your belief via this alleged sense of divinity won't be rational without a further belief, based on good reasons, that the experiences on which you base your belief in God provide an adequate basis for such a belief. In response, the Reformed Epistemologist will point out that this complaint seems to rely on an appeal to Confirmationalism discussed above—a principle which most philosophers reject, and for good reason.

Here is a simple way to think of the Reformed Epistemologist's position: *belief in God is more like belief in other people than it is like belief in electrons*. We are able to form properly basic beliefs that there are people around us because, by using our vision, we can tell noninferentially that there are people nearby. But we aren't able to tell noninferentially, just by looking, that there are electrons nearby. We don't have that sort of ability. Instead, humans arrived at the belief in electrons via inference: we inferred their existence because it provided the best explanation of all the experimental evidence collected by scientists. According to the Evidentialist Thesis, belief in God—like belief in electrons—is rational only if we infer it as the best explanation of the available evidence (in the case of belief in God,

the evidence in question is what gets cited in the premises of theistic arguments). But according to the Reformed Epistemologist, belief in God is more like belief in other people.[6] We don't first notice that it visually appears to us as if there are other people and then conclude that the best explanation of these visual appearances is that there really are other people that are the causes of these visual appearances. Rather, we just have the visual experiences and believe on the basis of them, without inference, that there are people around us. Likewise, the Reformed Epistemologist thinks that for many people, belief in God is not an inferred explanatory hypothesis but a noninferential response to experience. It's worth noting that it wouldn't be surprising for a loving God who wants all people to believe in him to give us the ability to believe in him noninferentially through a sense of divinity. That way of believing in God seems to be easier and less affected by differences in intelligence than inferential belief-formation, which requires an expertise (that isn't widely shared) in formulating and evaluating arguments.

As I signaled at the beginning of this essay, the Reformed Epistemologist's views don't apply only to the belief that God exists. Other religious beliefs as well can be rational in a similar way—beliefs in specific doctrines of this or that religion. There are a number of accounts of how these other religious beliefs are formed.[7] But ultimately it comes down to something very much like the views described above concerning properly basic belief in God.

II. OBJECTIONS TO REFORMED EPISTEMOLOGY

Let's turn now to some objections to Reformed Epistemology and consider what sorts of response are available.

Objection 1: Religious Interpretation of Experiential Evidence Needs Defense. The Reformed Epistemologist says that beliefs about God are based on experiences such as feeling forgiven after confession and repentance.

On the basis of such an experience a person believes "God forgives me for what I've done." But this is to *interpret* the experience within a particular theological framework—it's to impose one interpretation among many possible ones on a raw experience consisting of a feeling of being forgiven replacing a feeling of guilt. In order for the belief about God's forgiveness to be rational, one needs some reason for favoring that particular theological interpretation over some other nontheistic interpretation of that same raw experience.

Consider a parallel complaint lodged against perceptual beliefs: "When you believe, on the basis of visual experience, that there is a chair and a desk nearby, you are imposing one interpretation among many possible interpretations on the raw experience consisting of a visual appearance that seems to be of a chair and desk nearby. You've adopted the "standard" interpretation according to which there really is a chair and a desk nearby causing you to have that visual appearance. But perhaps you are dreaming. Or perhaps you are the victim of an experiment in which computers are connected to your brain causing you to have that visual appearance. You aren't rational in believing there really is a chair and desk nearby unless you first have a reason for favoring the standard interpretation over the dreaming interpretation and the computer–simulation interpretation."

How have epistemologists responded to this parallel complaint about perception? One common response is to note the following things. First, if this complaint were legitimate, then most people wouldn't be rational in their beliefs about the world around them since most people simply don't have any reasons they could produce for favoring the standard interpretation of perceptual experience. Second, epistemologists have worked very hard for centuries trying to come up with good reasons for preferring the standard interpretation of perceptual experience to its rivals and have yet to come up with an argument acknowledged to be convincing. Because of this failure, it is widely believed that there is no good argument for preferring the standard

interpretation of perceptual experience that doesn't itself rely on perceptual experience to tell us about the world around us.[8] Third, it seems that, in looking around us and forming visual beliefs about our environment, we don't first have a visual experience and then consider various ways to interpret it, ultimately selecting the standard interpretation. Instead, the world seems to present itself to us in visual experience as if the standard interpretation is true—the standard interpretation comes along unbidden with the visual experience. In light of all this, many epistemologists conclude that our perceptual beliefs are rational not because we've got a good reason for preferring the standard interpretation of our perceptual experience but because the rational response to having such experiences is to form beliefs, without inference, in accord with the standard interpretation.

The Reformed Epistemologist will say similar things about belief in God based on things such as an experience of feeling forgiven.[9] Many who believe, on the basis of such an experience, that God has forgiven them don't have any arguments available for favoring a theistic interpretation of that experience over a nontheistic one. Moreover, in many cases, they don't first have the experience and then consider various ways of interpreting it, ultimately selecting the theistic interpretation. Instead, that theistic interpretation comes along unbidden with that experience of feeling forgiven. And just as the rational response to perceptual experience is to form noninferential beliefs in the objects one takes oneself to see nearby, so also (says the Reformed Epistemologist) the rational response to the experience of feeling forgiven is to believe, without inference, that God is as one takes God to be on the basis of that experience.

Objection 2: The Great Pumpkin Objection. The Reformed Epistemologist's strategy for defending the rationality of religious belief is seriously problematic because the same strategy could be used to defend any bizarre belief you like, including Linus's belief (in the Charlie Brown comics) that the gift-delivering Great Pumpkin rises each Halloween over the most sincere pumpkin patch. When challenged to give reasons for their belief, Great Pumpkinites could simply point out that their belief is properly basic so they don't need to give any arguments for it. The fact that this strategy can be used to defend such a bizarre view reveals the bankruptcy of the strategy. But it seems that the Reformed Epistemologist, in endorsing this sort of strategy for defending the rationality of her belief in God, cannot offer any principled objection to this same strategy used by others in defense of silly views like belief in the Great Pumpkin.

Here too we can consider a parallel complaint, this time against those who think introspective beliefs are rational. Suppose you tell me that you're feeling a little hungry and I ask you what your argument is for that claim. You tell me that you don't need an argument in order to be rational in believing that claim; you have the ability to tell, just by thinking about it, what sorts of feelings you are having. In response I say "Oh really? Well, with that sort of reasoning, you could have no objection to a person who claimed to be a mind-reader with the special ability to tell, just by thinking about it, what those around her are thinking and feeling." Notice what I would be suggesting by that response. I'd be suggesting that because you claim to be able to tell *one* thing without argument (namely, what sorts of feelings you're having), you can have no objection to a person who claims to be able to tell *another* thing without argument (namely, what those around her are thinking and feeling). But that suggestion of mine would be silly. It's perfectly sensible to say there are some things people can tell without argument and other things they can't tell without argument.

Reformed Epistemologists respond to the Great Pumpkin Objection in a similar manner. They think there are some things people can tell without argument and other things people can't tell without argument. They think people can tell without argument that God exists but they can't tell without argument that the Great Pumpkin exists. There is

nothing remarkable about the suggestion that people have abilities to tell some things, but not others, without inference. We already know that people can tell, just by looking and without inference, that there are people around them; but they can't tell just by looking and without inference that there are electrons. People can also tell, just by thinking about it and without inference, what thoughts they are having; but they can't in the same way tell, without inference, what thoughts others are having. They can, without inference, remember what happened in the recent past; but they can't in the same way tell, without inference, what is going to happen in the future. The Reformed Epistemologist's claim—that we have the ability to tell noninferentially that God exists but we don't have any such ability with respect to the Great Pumpkin—is just another claim of this sort. The "strategy" of claiming to have an ability to know something noninferentially can be employed in defending the rationality of a belief even by those who think there are many things we don't have the ability to know noninferentially. So Reformed Epistemologists aren't committed to approving of others who use the same sort of strategy to defend all sorts of silly views.

Objection 3: Why Doesn't Everyone Believe in God? The previous two responses have compared basic belief in God to properly basic perceptual beliefs or properly basic introspective beliefs. But this ignores a very important difference between basic belief in God, on the one hand, and basic perceptual and introspective beliefs, on the other: pretty much everybody forms basic beliefs about their surroundings via perception and basic beliefs about their thoughts and feelings via introspection; but there are many people who don't believe in God at all. That's an important difference. If we have the ability to tell, without inference, that God exists, why are there so many people who don't believe in God?

The first thing to note here is that belief in some sort of deity is very widespread throughout human history, across many different cultures.[10] This of course doesn't prove that it's true. But it's important to keep in mind that it's not as if only a small minority of the world's population believes in God. Nevertheless, there are many people who don't seem to have any belief in God, and this is strikingly different from what we see when we compare basic belief in God with basic perceptual belief in the world around us or introspective belief in our mental states. What does the Reformed Epistemologist have to say about this?

The natural thing to say is that the *sense of divinity* isn't working equally well in all people. It is either damaged or hindered in its operation in many people and this has been so for a long time. It would be as if all humans had their vision damaged or otherwise hindered from normal operation and this condition of humanity lasted for many centuries. If that were to happen, some humans wouldn't be able to see at all and others would have only distorted or unclear vision. It might then happen that some who could see better than others would believe that the moon existed, but those who were blind or couldn't see as well, might not believe that the moon existed. Of course this analogy breaks down after a while.[11] But the main point of it, according to Reformed Epistemologists, is just that the sense of divinity is more damaged in some people than it is in others, and this explains why some people don't have properly basic belief in God whereas others do.[12]

Objection 4: Sinfulness Doesn't Explain Atheism. In responding to the last objection, Reformed Epistemologists say that the sense of divinity is more damaged in some people than in others. But what is it that causes this damage? A common suggestion by some Reformed Epistemologists is that "sinfulness" is the cause of this damage. But that's both insulting and implausible. It's easy to give examples of nontheists and theists where the nontheists are, morally speaking, much better behaved than the theists.

It's true that many in the Reformed tradition say that operational deficiencies in the sense of divinity

are caused by sinfulness. And it's also clear that some morally well-behaved people are nontheists and that some theists behave terribly (the Bible itself points to fallen angels as well as to many humans in giving examples of badly behaved theists). So how can anyone take seriously the suggestion that sinfulness explains why many people don't believe in God?

What follows is one possible way to make sense of the suggestion that sinfulness can explain lack of belief in God. (Notice that the goal here isn't to prove the truth of the explanation of unbelief in terms of sinfulness or of this particular way of making sense of it. Rather, it's to show how explaining unbelief by pointing to sinfulness can be consistent with the observation that nontheists often seem to be better behaved than theists.) We first need to distinguish inherited sinfulness from willful sinfulness. Ever since humans fell into sin, the result (according to Christians, including those in the Reformed tradition) has been that *all* of their descendents have been born with an inherited tendency to selfishness and pride.[13] This inherited tendency seems to come in various degrees. Because it is inherited, this tendency is not something we've chosen. Nor did we choose how severe it is in our own case.[14] In addition to inherited sinfulness, which we don't choose, there is also willful sinfulness. This occurs when we freely choose to act in a way that is contrary to our conscience. We are responsible for our willful sinfulness even though we aren't responsible for our inherited sinfulness. The explanation I want to consider for why not all people believe in God appeals, in part, to both inherited sinfulness and willful sinfulness.

There are really two things that need explaining: how sinfulness can keep people from believing in God and why, despite that first explanation, there isn't a tight correlation between one's belief status (as theist or nontheist) and one's moral status (as well-behaved or badly behaved). As for the first explanation, there are two ways sinfulness can hinder belief in God: it can hinder it in a way for which the unbeliever is *not* to blame; and it can hinder it in a way for which the unbeliever *is* to blame. Let's consider how it might hinder it in ways for which the unbeliever is not to blame. For starters, the inherited tendency to selfishness and pride damages the sense of divinity in all people so that it doesn't work as it was originally intended.[15] It's as if all of us have blurred vision when it comes to detecting God noninferentially. And because our inherited sinfulness comes in varying degrees, the damage it causes to the sense of divinity also comes in varying degrees. On top of that, due to both the inherited and willful sinfulness of those in our family and our larger society, our upbringing can cause further damage or hindrance to the operation of the sense of divinity in us. Here too, the resulting damage will come in varying degrees, depending on what has happened in our family and society, on what damage was caused by our own inherited sinfulness, and on how those two kinds of damage interact. All of these sin-caused effects on our sense of divinity hinder belief in God in a way for which the unbeliever is *not* to blame.

But, in addition to the above-mentioned things that affect what we might think of as our unchosen "starting point," there are other things that hinder belief in God. These other things affect how we progress from our starting point either further from or closer to belief in God. One contributor here could be willful sinfulness. By choosing to go against my conscience, I can perhaps further contribute to the damage to my sense of divinity. This is a case in which I am partially to blame for the way in which sin hinders my belief in God. But there are other possible contributors as well. God may choose to give experiential evidence for theistic belief to some people and not to others—evidence on which a properly basic belief in God can be based without inference.[16] (This might involve giving experiences to a person that the person wouldn't otherwise have had. Or it might involve correcting damage to the sense of divinity so that the person treats as evidence for belief about God experiences that the person wouldn't otherwise have treated in that way.) God's decision to give or delay giving such evidence might be based on the willful sinfulness of the person in question. But it

might be based on other things as well. Perhaps God thinks the person isn't yet ready to respond correctly to such evidence. Or perhaps God has a reason for wanting this person to progress further morally than others before coming to believe in God. And there may be other good reasons God has for delay in giving evidence, reasons that we don't know of.

In light of the above explanation for how sinfulness can hinder belief in God, we can see why it might be that there isn't a tight correlation between one's theistic-belief status and one's moral-behavior status. For, as we've just noted, though unbelief may be due to sinfulness in the ways described, God might give or delay giving evidence for properly basic belief in God on the basis of considerations that aren't correlated with how well-behaved the person is. And we aren't well placed to discern why there is unbelief in a particular case.

Moreover, appearances can be deceiving when we consider the moral goodness of those around us. It's natural to think that if God existed and were just and fair, he would judge people based on how well they did with the moral resources they were given. Consider two people, one of whom is given the opportunities of a naturally pleasant and cooperative personality and excellent moral training in her home and society while the other naturally has a more irritable and stubborn personality and is raised in a terrible home environment and influenced by a morally depraved society. It's easy to see how it might turn out that the person with the less fortunate background *might* be judged by God to have done much better, morally speaking, with what she was given than the more fortunate person; and this could be so even though the more fortunate person appears in many ways to behave better than the one with the less fortunate background. The point here is just that we really aren't able to tell how people are to be judged unless we can look into their hearts and backgrounds to see how well they are doing with what they were given, something we are rarely, if ever, able to do with much accuracy. This point is reinforced when we consider that motives matter tremendously. A person may perform many seemingly kind and generous actions but be doing them from motives of selfishness and pride. Again, it seems that if God existed and were to judge us fairly, he would take that into account. Because we can't always tell how good people are (in terms of their motives or how well they've done with what they've been given), we aren't well placed to draw conclusions about how belief in God is in fact correlated with goodness in people. There might be more of a correlation there than meets the eye. But even if there isn't (and Reformed Epistemologists certainly aren't committed to thinking there is), there are the other considerations noted above explaining why there needn't be any such correlation even if sinfulness (both inherited and willful) does go some way toward explaining why people don't believe in God.

Objection 5: Religious Disagreement as a Reason for Doubt. In addition to the problem of people who don't believe in God, there's the problem of people who do believe in God but hold very different views about God. If each of them is relying on the sense of divinity and yet getting such different beliefs as a result, doesn't that give a person good reason to mistrust this alleged belief-forming ability in herself, especially given that many don't seem to have it at all? This problem is especially disconcerting when we consider that intelligent, thoughtful people who are sincerely seeking the truth discuss their disagreements about theism at length, explaining their evidence to each other, and yet continue to disagree.

There are three points to make in response to this objection.[17] The first has to do with the principle on which the objection seems to be based. The principle focuses on disagreement with someone who is intellectually virtuous (let's say a person is intellectually virtuous when he or she is intelligent, thoughtful, and sincerely seeking the truth). The basic idea seems to be that when someone who is

intellectually virtuous disagrees with you, especially if you recognize that this person is about as intellectually virtuous as you are, then you thereby have a good reason to give up your belief. We can call this principle on which this objection seems to rely "the Withholding Principle." It can be formulated as follows:

Withholding Principle: If an intellectually virtuous person (whom you realize is about as intellectually virtuous as you are) disagrees with you on a controversial topic even after each of you has tried your best to disclose all your relevant evidence to the other (where this evidence falls short of being a knockdown proof that every intelligent thoughtful truth-seeker would accept), then to be rational each of you should give up your contentious belief on this topic and, instead, withhold judgment on the matter.

The problem is that intelligent, thoughtful truth-seekers disagree about the Withholding Principle itself. Some think you should withhold judgment whenever you're in the circumstances described in the principle; but others think that's not so. Moreover, those who endorse the Withholding Principle don't have a knockdown proof for the principle, one that every intelligent, thoughtful truth-seeker would accept. The result is that if the principle is true, then rationality requires you to reject it—since you can't *prove* the principle's truth to intelligent, thoughtful truth-seekers who think it's false. And that means that the principle is self-undermining, saying about itself that it's irrational to accept it.

A second thing worth pointing out is that the Reformed Epistemologist can distinguish internal rationality from external rationality, conceding the former but not the latter to those who disagree about religious matters. This distinction highlights the fact that there are two stages in the formation of noninferential beliefs based on experiential evidence rather than on arguments. The first stage is where the person comes to have the experiential evidence; the second stage is where the person bases the noninferential belief in question on that experiential evidence. The belief so based is *internally rational* if it is an appropriate (reasonable, sensible) response for a person to have to that sort of experiential evidence. One way to put this point is to say that, in the formation of an internally rational belief, all is going well *downstream* from (i.e., in response to) the experience on which it is based. The belief is *externally* rational if, in addition to being internally rational, it's also the case that all is going well *upstream* from that experience—that is to say, the experiential evidence arises in the right way in the person who has it and is not due, for example, to any sort of cognitive malfunction. With this distinction in hand, the Reformed Epistemologist can point out that those who disagree with her may well be internally rational even if they aren't externally rational. Thus, for example, a Jewish theist who denies the divinity of Christ and who endorses the Reformed Epistemologist approach[18] can say (i) the Christian is internally rational in believing, on the basis of her experiential evidence in support of the doctrine, that *Jesus is God incarnate* and (ii) the atheist who lacks any experiential evidence in support of belief in God is internally rational in believing there is no God. But the Jewish believer can go on to add that the Christian is externally *irrational* because it is only due to some sort of cognitive malfunction that the Christian has that experiential evidence supporting the doctrine that Jesus is God incarnate; likewise, the Jewish believer can say that the atheist is externally irrational in believing there is no God because it is only due to some sort of cognitive malfunction (affecting the sense of divinity) that the atheist lacks any experiential evidence in support of belief in God.[19] In this way, those who endorse the Reformed Epistemologist approach can recognize that there is a sense in which the intelligent, thoughtful truth-seekers who disagree with them may be rational—they may be internally rational. But the Reformed Epistemologist can also explain why her beliefs are epistemically better than the religious beliefs of those who disagree—her own beliefs are externally rational whereas the beliefs of those who disagree with her are externally irrational.

The third point to make is that there seem to be examples where it is entirely appropriate to say—of intelligent, thoughtful truth-seekers whose views you disagree with but can't prove wrong—that their contrary views are externally irrational and mistaken whereas yours are externally rational and correct. Consider a case of moral disagreement about how to evaluate the following very disturbing behavior of Jack's. Jack takes pleasure in torturing and killing children, and he has found a way to do this without getting caught. I assume that you think this behavior of Jack's is morally wrong (extremely so). But you have a friend—who, like you, is an intelligent, thoughtful truth-seeker—who disagrees. She is a moral nihilist, someone who thinks it's false that Jack's behavior is morally wrong because there are no moral facts and nothing is morally wrong—or morally right. Like you, this friend is utterly disgusted by Jack's behavior and very strongly wishes that Jack wouldn't engage in it. But, unlike you, your friend doesn't think it is morally wrong. Now suppose you and your friend try to share with each other all your evidence for your opposing views. You point to your properly basic belief (based on some sort of intuitive seeming[20]) that actions of the sort Jack performs are morally wrong, which shows that moral nihilism is false. Your friend points to her properly basic belief (also based on some sort of intuitive seeming) in a key premise used to support her belief in moral nihilism—a view implying that Jack's behavior is neither morally wrong nor morally right. Unfortunately, even after you each try your best to share your relevant evidence, the disagreement persists. Does rationality require that, upon learning of this persistent disagreement with your friend, you should give up your belief that Jack's behavior is wrong? No. Instead of being moved to doubt the reliability of our own beliefs on this topic, we are sensibly moved to feel badly for the friend who disagrees with us and to be glad that we are fortunate enough not to lack the moral insight we have or to have the misleading moral views that our moral nihilist friend has.

Moreover, you can acknowledge that your moral nihilist friend may be *internally* rational in thinking Jack's behavior isn't wrong. After all, your friend has strong experiential evidence (i.e., *her* intuitive seemings) in support of that noninferential belief in the premise supporting moral nihilism. And your friend doesn't have the additional evidence you have which would outweigh this—namely, stronger experiential evidence (i.e., *your* intuitive seemings) in support of the view that Jack's behavior is wrong. You can concede that the right response to the evidence your friend has may be to believe in moral nihilism; so all may be going well downstream from your friend's experiential evidence. But you will insist that your friend isn't externally rational because something has gone wrong upstream from her experiential evidence. The very fact that moral nihilism seems intuitively more plausible to your friend than the claim that Jack's behavior is morally wrong shows that your friend is suffering from some sort of cognitive malfunction or problem, despite your friend's intelligence, thoughtfulness, and sincere interest in discovering the truth.[21]

The Reformed Epistemologist can, therefore, insist that, in the above scenario, it is appropriate for you to think Jack's behavior is wrong despite the fact that your intelligent, thoughtful, and truth-seeking friend continues to disagree with you about this, even after you share all your evidence. Moreover, it seems sensible for you to think that your friend is mistaken and externally irrational in her moral nihilist view that Jack's behavior is not wrong, though you could allow that that view of hers may be internally rational. And the Reformed Epistemologist can then point out that something similar is going on in the case of religious disagreement. Those who disagree with her religious beliefs might be *internally* rational in their beliefs in a different religion or against all religions. But the beliefs of those who disagree with her are both mistaken and *externally* irrational, despite the fact that they are held by intelligent, thoughtful truth-seekers. The point here is most definitely *not* that there is any connection between rejecting moral nihilism and endorsing a religious view. Rather, the point is that *if*—in the case of your belief that Jack's behavior is wrong—you

can sensibly think your friend is mistaken and externally irrational despite the fact that she's also an internally rational, intelligent, thoughtful truth-seeker, *then* there is, in principle, no bar to your sensibly thinking something similar of a friend in the case of a religious disagreement. In addition, the fact that you and your friend are both relying on intuitive seemings in arriving at your opposing views about the morality of Jack's behavior doesn't show that you rationally ought to give up all views you have that are based on intuitive seemings. Likewise, the fact that you and someone else differ in your views about God even though you both rely on the sense of divinity doesn't show that you rationally ought to give up all your views based on the sense of divinity.

Of course, it's true that the nontheist will be inclined to think that her nontheistic beliefs are externally rational and that it's the *theist* that is externally irrational. But why think this should be a problem for the theist? After all, your moral nihilist friend will be inclined to think that she is externally rational and that *you* are externally irrational in thinking Jack's behavior is morally wrong. Should the fact that the moral nihilist views you this way lead you to give up your view that you, not her, are the one that is holding the externally rational belief on this matter? It seems not. Even if your moral nihilist friend thinks that of you, it seems perfectly reasonable for you to continue holding your belief and thinking that you are externally rational in doing so.[22] In the same way, even if the nontheist will be inclined to view the theist as externally irrational, it doesn't follow that the theist should give up her view that she, and not the nontheist, is externally rational.

CONCLUSION

We've considered in this paper the Reformed Epistemologist's position that belief in God can be rational even if it is not based on any argument. We've tried to understand what her view is—the sense in which she thinks belief in God is more like belief in other people than like belief in electrons. And we've considered several challenging objections to the Reformed Epistemologist's proposal. There is a lot more that could be said in explaining and trying to make plausible the Reformed Epistemologist's position, especially as it applies to religious beliefs other than belief in God. And more should also be said in response to the above objections and to others besides.[23] Nevertheless, I hope what has been said here helps the reader to appreciate why many people take this sort of view seriously.[24]

NOTES

1. What about your introspective beliefs about what you're thinking? What are they based on? They're based on your experience of having those thoughts. They aren't inferred from other beliefs of yours.

2. Confirmationalism is similar to Inferentialism; in fact, it seems to be one version of Inferentialism.

3. Notice, by the way, that the Evidentialist Thesis is different from Inferentialism. The latter says that *no* belief can be rational unless it is inferred from other rational beliefs; the former says merely that *belief in God* cannot be rational unless it is inferred from other beliefs.

4. Plantinga (1983:80).

5. For this reason, Plantinga suggests (1983:81–82) that it is beliefs about what God does or is like, not the belief that God exists, that are properly basic. But for simplicity's sake, I'll speak as if he and others think belief in God is properly basic.

6. Interestingly, current research in the cognitive science of religion has arrived at a similar conclusion in its attempts to explain the origins of religious belief (which is widespread across times and cultures). One common theme in this research is that belief in God is a natural and instinctive reaction to a variety of stimuli; it is not the result of inferences or arguments. See Clark and Barrett (2010) for a summary of this research and a discussion of how it compares to the views of Reformed Epistemologists.

7. See Plantinga (2000) for one prominent example.

8. See Alston (1993) where this point is defended at length.

9. See, for example, Alston (1983).

10. For an extended explanation, from the perspective of cognitive science, of why this is so, see Barrett (2004).

11. Some might think that the analogy breaks down because vision can be cross-checked with other perceptual faculties such as sense of touch whereas we can't cross-check the sense of divinity in that same way. But see Alston (1991, ch. 5) for a discussion of how something like the sense of divinity might be subject to cross-checking.

12. Additional explanations for differences between properly basic religious belief and properly basic perceptual belief are given in Alston (1983) and Alston (1991).

13. Must one believe in a literal reading of early Genesis to believe that there was a time that humans fell into sin? And doesn't that literal reading conflict with the well-established theory of evolution? A literal reading of early Genesis does seem to conflict with evolutionary theory. But many religious people who accept the teachings of the Bible as authoritative think that (i) early Genesis is not best interpreted in that literal way, (ii) evolutionary theory is true, and (iii) one thing we can learn from early Genesis is that humanity fell into sin in some way or other, even if not in the precise way described there. For a discussion of how inherited sinfulness can be combined with an evolutionary account of human origin, see Collins (2003).

14. Is it fair for Gold to let the immoral choices of our ancestors cause us to have this inherited tendency? This is just an instance of the more general question: is it fair for God to let the wrong choices of some people negatively affect the lives of others?

It's not implausible to think that, so long as God has some justifying reason for doing so (one that treats those negatively affected with love and respect), it is fair for God to do that.

15. How does selfishness and pride cause damage to the sense of divinity? This might happen in any number of ways: perhaps selfishness and pride make one less inclined to believe in a being to whom they owe worship and service; or perhaps the sense of divinity works by way of divine blessing that is withheld from those who are selfish and proud; or perhaps the damage to the sense of divinity caused by selfishness and pride comes about in some other way.

16. Recall that, although basic beliefs are ones that are not inferred from other beliefs, they might still be based on evidence of some kind.

17. These three points are developed at greater length in a different context in Bergmann (2009).

18. To endorse the Reformed Epistemologist approach is *not* to endorse the teachings of the Reformed tradition within Christendom or any other distinctively Christian doctrines. Rather, it's to say that belief in God (or other religious beliefs) can be properly basic.

19. This example is not meant to suggest that Jewish believers must or often do explain Christian and atheistic belief in this way. The point is just to give an illustration of how one *could* explain the beliefs of those with whom one disagrees on religious matters. Moreover, in explaining that Christian and atheistic belief involve cognitive malfunction, the Jewish believer needn't think the Christian and the atheist are insane or brain-damaged. Instead, the Jewish believer would just be saying that the sense of divinity isn't working property in the Christian or in the atheist.

20. An intuitive seeming that p is true is an experience of it seeming intuitively to you that p is true.

21. Again, the point isn't that your friend is insane or brain-damaged but just that the process by which her moral intuitions are formed is not working properly.

22. But won't the same hold for your moral nihilist friend? Won't the fact that you view her as externally irrational fail to show that she should give up her view that she, not you, is the one that is externally rational? That may be right. But if that's right, which of you *really is* externally rational? Presumably it could only be the one whose views on this matter are correct. Which one of you is that? Unfortunately, that's a matter of dispute. But you (and many others) will sensibly think that your view (that Jack's behavior is morally wrong) is both true and externally rational. Questions parallel to those raised here can be raised in the case of disagreement over theistic belief and parallel answers can be given.

23. The main places to look for further discussion of these topics are Alston (1991) and Plantinga (2000).

24. Thanks to Jeffrey Brower and Michael Rea for helpful comments on earlier drafts of this paper.

REFERENCES

Alston, William, "Christian Experience and Christian Belief" pp. 103–34 in *Faith and Rationality*, eds. Alvin Plantinga and Nicholas Wolterstorff (Notre Dame: University of Notre Dame Press, 1983).

Alston, William, *Perceiving God* (Ithaca: Cornell University Press, 1991).

Alston, William, *The Reliability of Sense Perception* (Ithaca: Cornell University Press, 1993).

Barrett, Justin. *Why Would Anyone Believe in God?* (Lanham, MD: AltaMira Press, 2004).

Bergmann, Michael, "Rational Disagreement after Full Disclosure," *Episteme* 6(2009): 336–53.

Clark, Kelly James and Justin Barrett. "Reformed Epistemology and the Cognitive Science of Religion." *Faith and Philosophy* 27 (2010): 174–89.

Collins, Robin. "Evolution and Original Sin" pp. 469–501 in *Perspectives on an Evolving Creation*, ed. Keith B. Miller 2006 (Grand Rapids: Eerdmans Publishing Company, 2003).

Plantinga, Alvin, "Reason and Belief in God" pp. 16–93 in *Faith and Rationality*, eds. Alvin Plantinga and Nicholas Wolterstorff (Notre Dame: University of Notre Dame Press, 1983).

Plantinga, Alvin, *Warranted Christian Belief* (New York: Oxford University Press, 2000).

V.C.4

Intellectual Virtue in Religious Epistemology

LINDA ZAGZEBSKI

Linda Zagzebski (1946–) is professor of philosophy at the University of Oklahoma. She is the author of numerous articles and several books in epistemology, ethics, and the philosophy of religion, including Virtues of the Mind *(1996) and* Divine Motivation Theory *(2004). She is perhaps best known for her work in the area of virtue epistemology. In this essay, Zagzebski highlights several advantages that virtue-based ethical theories enjoy over theories that understand morality in terms of the consequences or dutifulness of particular acts. She then argues that epistemological theories that focus primarily on the* intellectual virtues *enjoy similar advantages over theories that focus simply on evaluating* individual beliefs *as justified or unjustified, rational or irrational, warranted or unwarranted. She argues furthermore that the advantages of virtue-based approaches are especially attractive within the context of religious epistemology.*

1. INTRODUCTION

Some thirty-five years ago Roderick Chisholm observed that "many of the characteristics which philosophers and others have thought peculiar to ethical statements also hold of epistemic statements."[1] Since then we have seen epistemologists routinely referring to epistemic *duty*, to epistemic *responsibility*, to the fact that we *ought* to form beliefs in one way rather than another, to epistemic *norms* and *values*, and more recently to intellectual *virtue*. The use of these moral concepts in epistemic discourse is not superfluous, but is central to the attempt to explicate the normative aspects of epistemic states, a goal that has justifiably become one of the central concerns of contemporary epistemology. It is generally acknowledged, then, that moral concepts are important to epistemological inquiry. What is not often acknowledged, however, is that when epistemologists borrow moral concepts, they implicitly borrow the theoretical background of those concepts. An awareness of the differences in function of concepts in different types of moral theory can illuminate their use in epistemology. If there are problems with the moral theory epistemologists use as their normative model, these problems may adversely affect the epistemological project. On the other hand, any advantages of a particular approach to moral evaluation may also prove advantageous to epistemic evaluation.

In this paper I call attention to the fact that virtually all contemporary theories in epistemology take an act-based moral theory as their normative model, even those that promote the concept of intellectual virtue. Contemporary epistemological theories are belief-based, just as most contemporary ethical theories are act-based. Next I argue that a virtue-based epistemological theory has certain advantages over a

Reprinted by permission of Open Court Publishing Company, a division of Carus Publishing Company, Chicago, IL, from pp. 171 - 188 in *Faith in Theory and Practice: Essays on Justifying Religious Belief*, edited by Elizabeth S. Radcliffe and Carol J. White, Copyright Open Court 1993.

belief-based theory which parallel some of the advantages of a virtue-based ethical theory over an act-based ethical theory. I then consider the principal recent objections to virtue ethics and argue that these objections either do not apply or do not jeopardize the virtue approach to epistemology. I conclude with reasons why this approach should be of particular interest to religious epistemology.

2. CONTEMPORARY EPISTEMOLOGICAL THEORIES AND THEIR NORMATIVE MODELS

Contemporary discussions of justification and knowledge almost always focus on particular instances of beliefs, just as most modern ethical theory until recently has focused on the morality of particular acts. The epistemologist assumes that the normative concepts of interest to their inquiry are properties of beliefs in one of two senses of "belief": either they are properties of the psychological states of believing, or they are properties of the propositional objects of such states. The dispute between foundationalists and coherentists and between externalists and internalists are disputes about the nature of such properties.

The epistemic analogue of the concept of a right act is that of a justified belief. To be justified is a way of being right. Alternatively, epistemologists may speak of a warranted or well-founded belief. In these cases also it is the epistemic analogue of a right act. Just as the right act is usually the primary concept for moral philosophers, the justified (warranted, well-founded) belief is the primary concept for epistemologists. Roderick Firth expresses the position which is almost universal among contemporary epistemologists: "The ultimate task of a theory of knowledge is to answer the question, 'What is knowledge?' But to do this it is first necessary to answer the question, 'Under what conditions is a belief warranted?'"[2] What Firth calls "the unavoidable first step" is generally the major part of the theory. It is not surprising that the answer to this question often involves the concept of epistemic duty and the application of epistemic rules, both of which are closely associated with the deontological concept of right. Alternatively, the answer may involve the idea of a reliable process for the obtaining of the good of truth, the epistemic analogue of the consequentialist concept of right.

Contemporary epistemology, then, is belief-based and it is no surprise that the type of moral theory from which moral concepts are borrowed is almost always an act-based theory. In those cases in which the theory identifies justification or the normative element in knowledge with epistemic duty, the theory is clearly and usually consciously deontological. In those cases in which justification or the normative element in knowledge is identified with reliability in the obtaining of truth, the theory is consequentialist, though generally only implicitly so. An interesting variant is the theory of Ernest Sosa, who identifies justification with intellectual virtue. Sosa argues that the concept of intellectual virtue can be used to bypass the dispute between foundationalists and coherentists on proper cognitive structure.[3] But Sosa does not adapt his concept of virtue from a virtue theory of morality; rather, his model of a moral theory is act-based, and his definition of virtue consequentialist: "An intellectual virtue is a quality bound to help maximize one's surplus of truth over error."[4] Sosa does not distinguish between intellectual virtues and faculties, and his examples of intellectual virtues are nothing like virtues in the Aristotelian sense. While Sosa is welcomely sensitive to the importance of the social conditions for believing in his understanding of intellectual virtue, he does not attempt to benefit from the history of the concept of virtue. In any case, he makes no attempt to integrate intellectual virtue into the broader context of a subject's psychic structure, as that has been done by many philosophers for the moral virtues.

John Greco and Jonathan Kvanvig also define an intellectual virtue in such a way that reliabilism is a form of virtue epistemology, and Greco gives as examples of intellectual virtues such faculties as sight, hearing, introspection, and memory.[5] Kvanvig's primary examples of virtue epistemology are the theories of Armstrong, Goldman, and Nozick, all of which are forms of reliabilism.[6] None of these theories attempts to analyze intellectual virtue as a *virtue,* nor do they look to moral philosophers for help in understanding the nature of virtue. Even when Kvanvig traces the roots of virtue epistemology to Aristotle, it is to Aristotle's epistemology that he briefly turns, not Aristotle's theory of virtue. Kvanvig's subsequent rejection of what *he* calls the virtue approach, then, has no bearing on the project I am proposing here, nor do the objections offered by Greco.

Two theories which come closer to the one I wish to promote are those of Lorraine Code and James Montmarquet. In *Epistemic Responsibility* Code gives a provocative account of intellectual virtue, stressing a "socialized" approach to epistemology, pointing out the connections between epistemology and moral theory, and exhibiting a sensitivity to the epistemological importance of other aspects of human nature than the purely cognitive.[7] Code justly credits Sosa with the insight that epistemology ought to give more weight to the knowing subject, her environment, and epistemic community, but argues that Sosa's reliabilism does not go far enough in that direction. Code urges a move to what she calls a "responsibilist epistemology":

> I call my position "responsibilism" in contradistinction to Sosa's proposed "reliabilism," at least when *human* knowledge is under discussion. I do so because the concept "responsibility" can allow emphasis upon the active nature of knowers/believers, whereas the concept "reliability" cannot. In my view, a knower/believer has an important degree of choice with regard to modes of cognitive structuring, and is accountable for these choices; whereas a "reliable" knower could simply be an accurate, and relatively passive, recorder of experience. One speaks of a "reliable" computer, not a "responsible" one.[8]

Although this suggestion is promising, Code looks only at consequentialist and deontological ethics for analogies with epistemology rather than at a virtue theory.[9] And even that much she does not pursue very far, saying, "Despite the analogy I argue for ... between epistemological and ethical reasoning, they are not amenable to adequate discussion under the rubric of any of the traditional approaches to ethics, nor under any reasonable amalgam thereof."[10] Code's account supports the rejection of the atomistic approach to epistemology, also argued in the later book by Kvanvig, but she neither makes such a rejection explicitly, nor does she see the problem in using act-based moral theory as the analogue for epistemic theory when such a rejection is made. She seems, then, to identify with Sosa's theory more than she should, given the insights she develops in her book.

Montmarquet gives a very interesting defense of the claim that epistemology ought to focus on the epistemic virtues in a sense of virtue that is at least similar to the moral virtues.[11] He says:

> I characterize the epistemic virtues as traits of epistemic character which, if they are not epistemic conscientiousness itself, are desired by the epistemically conscientious person in virtue of their apparent truth-conduciveness under a very wide variety of ordinary, uncontrived circumstances. Partly for this reason, they possess the kind of entrenchment Aristotle describes the moral virtues as having.[12]

The most important classes of such virtues, as described by Montmarquet, are the virtues of impartiality and the virtues of intellectual courage. The former include such qualities as openness to the ideas of others, the willingness to exchange ideas with and learn from them, the lack of jealousy and personal bias towards other people's ideas, and the lively sense of one's own fallibility. The latter include the willingness to conceive and to examine alternatives to popularly held beliefs, perseverance in the face of opposition from others, and the Popperian willingness to examine, and even actively seek out, evidence that would refute one's own hypotheses. Montmarquet considers these virtues to be complementary because they concern opposite sides of the balanced intellectual personality: the inner-directed virtues of a person of intellectual integrity and the other-directed virtues necessary to sustain an intellectual community.

Montmarquet's approach is roughly, though somewhat vaguely, Aristotelian, but like the others, his epistemology is belief-based. Montmarquet links the concept of epistemic virtue to justification; he claims that the idea of virtuously formed belief forms an important partial account of the concept of epistemic justification. He does not link epistemic virtue with reliability, explaining virtue in terms of a certain motive, namely, the desire for truth. Montmarquet's account is insightful, but it seems to me that once we give up the atomistic approach in favor of a virtue approach, there is no reason to link intellectual virtue and justification. The latter is a property of a belief, while the former is a property of a person.

3. SOME ADVANTAGES OF VIRTUE-BASED THEORIES

Until recently contemporary moral theories were almost exclusively act-based, with more and more subtle forms of consequentialism vying with more and more subtle deontological theories for the allegiance of philosophers. Lately there has been a resurgence of interest in virtue theories, as well as some strong and well-known attacks on contemporary act-based theories, although curiously, the latter is not always associated with the former.[13] The mark of a virtue theory of morality is that the primary object of evaluation is persons rather than acts. To describe a good person is to describe that person's virtues, and these theories maintain that a virtue is not reducible to the performance of acts independently identified as right nor to a disposition to perform such acts. Furthermore, a virtue is not reducible to a disposition to perform acts which can be independently identified descriptively. There is both more and less to a moral virtue than a disposition to act in a specified way. There is more because a virtue also includes being disposed

to have characteristic feelings, desires, motives, and attitudes. There is less because a virtuous person does not invariably act in a way that can be fully captured by any set of independent criteria; morally right action is not strictly rule-governed.[14] This means that virtues and vices are conceptually prior to right and wrong acts and cannot be adequately defined in the manner favored by act-based theories. The approach to ethics I have just described would not be agreeable to all adherents of virtue theories. Nonetheless, it is clearly conceptually opposed to both consequentialist and deontological styles of ethics. As far as I know, no one has proposed an epistemological theory which is closely modeled on such a theory. Considering the fact that contemporary epistemology has reached an impasse on the important question of the nature of the normative aspect of knowing and other epistemic states, it is worth investigating such an approach.

Let us now consider some of the principal advantages of a virtue-based ethics.

One of the first major attempts in recent philosophy to call attention to the advantages of focusing ethics on virtues rather than acts was Elizabeth Anscombe's important paper "Modern Moral Philosophy," which appeared in 1958.[15] In this paper Anscombe argues that the principal notions of modern moral discourse, namely, *right, wrong,* and moral *duty,* lack content. On the other hand, concepts such as *just, chaste, courageous,* and *truthful* are substantively rich. Furthermore, she argues, *right, wrong,* and *duty* are legal concepts which make no sense without a lawgiver and judge. Traditionally, such a legal authority was God. In the absence of an ethic grounded in theism, however, legalistic ethics makes no sense. It would be far better to return to an Aristotelian virtue ethics which contains neither a blanket concept of wrong, nor a concept of duty.

In the same year that Anscombe made her appeal for a return to the virtues, Bernard Mayo wrote that the virtues are more natural categories for making moral judgments than are principles.[16] Virtue categories allow for nuances of judgment that principles can handle only with grave difficulty. Consider, for example, the virtue of truth-telling. Mayo says:

> Telling the truth, for Aristotle, is not, as it was for Kant, fulfilling an obligation; again it is quality of character, or, rather, a whole range of qualities of character, some of which may actually be defects, such as tactlessness, boastfulness, and so on—a point which can be brought out, in terms of principles, only with the greatest complexity and artificiality, but quite simply and naturally in terms of character.[17]

While moral philosophers have not widely accepted Anscombe's position that the concepts favored by legalistic, act-based ethics are incoherent or unnatural in the absence of a divine lawgiver, it is hard to find fault with the claim that virtue concepts have the advantage of greater richness. In fact, the distinction between "thin" and "thick" moral concepts is now well known.[18]

A second set of considerations favoring a virtue approach to ethics is that now fewer philosophers are convinced that morality is strictly rule-governed. With the exception of act- utilitarianism, act-based theorists have been faced with the problem that more and more complex sets of rules are necessary to capture the particularity of moral decision-making. Philosophers such as Martha Nussbaum have argued for a more particularist approach, using literature as the basis for proposing a model that does not begin with the rule or principle, but with the insight into the particular case.[19] While particularists are not necessarily virtue theorists,[20] dissatisfaction with attempts to force the making of a moral judgment into a strictly rule-governed model is one of the motivations for contemporary virtue ethics.

A third reason favoring the focus of morality on virtues rather than acts and principles is that some virtues do not seem to be reducible to specifiable acts or act-dispositions. Gregory Trianosky, for example, has argued that higher-order moral virtues cannot be analyzed in terms of relations to acts. He points out that it is a virtue to have well-ordered feelings. A person with such a virtue has positive higher-order feelings towards her own emotions. Similarly, it is a virtue to be morally integrated, to have a positive higher-order evaluation of one's own moral commitments. These are virtues that cannot be analyzed in terms of some relation to right action.[21] Furthermore, while Trianosky does not say so explicitly, such higher-order virtues are connected to the virtue of integrity since integrity in one of its senses is the virtue of having a morally unified self, and it is difficult to see how such a virtue can be explicated in terms of dispositions to perform acts of a specified kind.

The resurgence of interest in virtue ethics in recent philosophy is obviously not due solely to the three sets of considerations to which I have just alluded. Nonetheless, these reasons are important and are generating serious discussion in the literature. I call attention to these three sets of reasons in particular because all of them have analogues in the evaluation of cognitive activity. In fact, some of them are even stronger in the epistemic case than in the moral case.

I have said that contemporary epistemology is belief-based, just as modern ethics is act-based. Epistemic states are evaluated in terms of properties of beliefs or belief-dispositions, just as moral evaluations are given in terms of properties of acts or act-dispositions. Epistemic states which are evaluated positively are called "justified," just as acts evaluated positively are called "right." Some epistemologists go farther with the act-based moral analogy and speak of epistemic duty.

Now if Anscombe is right that legalistic moral language makes no sense without a divine lawgiver, such language in epistemology is even more peculiar. We can at least find practical reasons for continuing to judge acts and render verdicts in the moral case, but it is hard to see the point of such a conceptual system in the evaluation of beliefs and cognitive activities. What purpose is served by declaring that Jones has violated her epistemic duty in believing in UFOs? Is she to be declared epistemically guilty? What follows from *that*?

As was said above, however, the stronger point is not Anscombe's claim about the need for a divine lawgiver, but the claim that the concepts of right, wrong, and duty lack content. This is clearly applicable to the case of epistemic evaluation. The concept of justified is even more artificial and lacking in content than the concept of right. Ordinary people will speak of what is right and wrong, but never of what is justified or unjustified. This is not to say that ordinary people lack the idea of evaluation in the cognitive area. It is simply that they direct their evaluations to persons themselves and call them narrow-minded, careless, intellectually cowardly or rash, prejudiced, rigid, obtuse. People are accused of jumping to conclusions, ignoring relevant facts, relying on untrustworthy authority, lacking insight, being unable to "see the forest for the trees," and so on. Of course, the beliefs formed as the result of such defects are evaluated negatively, but the lack of a blanket term for this negative evaluation in ordinary discourse suggests that the content is given by the concepts just named. All of these terms are names for either intellectual vices or for categories of acts exhibiting intellectual vice. It is possible, of course, that all of these defects involve using improper procedures; the point is that there does not seem to be any single property of epistemic impropriety or wrongness which can be explicated in a way that is not excessively complex and unnatural. A virtue approach to epistemic evaluation, then, has the same advantage of naturalness and richness of content possessed by a virtue approach to moral evaluation.

The second set of reasons for preferring a virtue approach in ethics also applies to epistemology. There is no reason to think that being in an epistemically positive state is any more rule-governed than being in a morally positive state. Insight, for example, is an intellectual virtue that is not rule-governed, but differs significantly in the form it takes from one person to another and from one area of knowledge to another. Insight is necessary for another virtue, trust, which has an intellectual as well as a moral form. One cannot know who or what is trustworthy by following a specified procedure, even in principle. Not only does one need insight into the character of others to have trust in its virtuous form, but trust also involves certain affective qualities that are not describable in procedural terms. In addition, such intellectual virtues as adaptability of intellect, the ability to recognize the salient facts, sensitivity to detail, the ability to think

up explanations of complex sets of data, as well as such virtues as intellectual care, perseverance, and discretion are not strictly rule-governed. In each case, the virtue involves an aspect of knowing-how that is learned by imitation and practice. If those philosophers who advise a more particularist approach to moral evaluation are right, it is reasonable to think the same point applies to epistemic evaluation. An interesting consequence is that the recent turn to literature for help in understanding the right way to act might also help us in understanding the right way to think and to form beliefs.

Consider next the epistemic analogue of the third objection to act-based theories. The type of higher-order moral virtue identified by Trianosky has a cognitive parallel. It is an intellectual virtue to be cognitively integrated, just as it is a moral virtue to be morally integrated. A person who is cognitively integrated has positive higher-order attitudes towards her own intellectual character and the quality of the beliefs and level of understanding that such a character produces. When belief-based theorists, such as William Alston, attempt to identify this desirable quality, they say that it is not only epistemically valuable to *[be]* justified in one's beliefs, it is epistemically valuable to be justified in believing one's beliefs are justified. But this way of approaching this virtue is inadequate because the quality in question is not a property of a single belief, not even a belief about all of one's beliefs. To have a good intellectual character, it is not sufficient to simply pile up justified beliefs and judge that they are justified. A person who is cognitively integrated has epistemic values that determine such things as the proportion of one's time spent gathering evidence or the epistemic worth of one belief over another. Cognitive integration is partially constitutive of intellectual integrity, the virtue of having an intellect with an identity. Therefore, at least some intellectual virtues cannot be analyzed in terms of a relation to good (justified, warranted) beliefs. The virtue of intellectual integrity requires a virtue approach to epistemic evaluation.

Besides the three advantages I have mentioned, several epistemologists have recently criticized contemporary epistemic theories on grounds that would make a virtue approach more promising. A common objection is that contemporary epistemology is too atomistic and insufficiently social. We already noted this objection in the work of Sosa and Kvanvig. The complaint here is that it is a mistake to attempt to evaluate beliefs singly since a belief cannot be separated from other beliefs of the same person or from beliefs of other persons. Furthermore, evidence suggests that beliefs cannot be separated from non-cognitive psychic states such as feelings, desires, and motivations. Elsewhere I have argued that there are intimate connections between cognitive and feelings states and, concomitantly, between intellectual and moral virtues.[22] Such connections make a belief-based approach to evaluating epistemic states awkward at best. Virtues, however, are naturally understood as connected with desires and motivations, even in the case of intellectual virtues.

4. OBJECTIONS TO VIRTUE THEORY

Along with the new interest in virtue theory in recent philosophy, there have been objections to the aretaic approach by those who favor an act-based theory. It is illuminating to see how little these objections threaten a virtue approach in epistemology. Perhaps the most serious objection to virtue ethics is that it is imperative to have concepts of rights and duties in order to single out a certain class of acts which are intolerable.[23] Aristotelian virtue ethics may seem soft precisely because it lacks such a category. Regardless of the strength of this objection to virtue ethics, however, it is irrelevant to the virtue approach to epistemology since no one speaks of violating other people's epistemic rights, and those who find the idea of epistemic duties illuminating do not imply anything close to the several kind of moral judgment which accompanies such talk in ethics. While it may sometimes be helpful to speak of a duty to weigh evidence or to proportion one's belief to the evidence, no one claims that such a way of speaking is the only one capable of expressing the idea that one should conduct oneself cognitively in certain ways.

A second common objection to virtue ethics is that it is too vague to be of much use in making moral decisions in difficult cases, say, a decision concerning abortion or euthanasia. This also does not have an analogue in an objection to the virtue approach to evaluating epistemic states and cognitive activities. Rarely, if ever, do we think of a single cognitive act as having the level of significance often given to moral decisions. The fact that an account of intellectual virtue will leave unspecified the precise manner in which a particular cognizer should proceed is something we can live with. Vagueness is never welcome, of course, but its presence is not as threatening in the epistemic case as in the moral case.

A third objection to virtue ethics is that our society is so pluralistic that we cannot hope for agreement on the virtues which a moral person aims to acquire. This objection also does not seriously jeopardize the virtue approach in epistemology since there is little disagreement that the qualities I have called intellectual virtues are in fact virtues. Almost everyone admires intellectual care, perseverance, discretion, open-mindedness, fair-mindedness, insight, sensitivity to detail, thoroughness, the ability to understand the whole picture, and so on. Of course, there are disagreements about how these virtues operate in the particular case, but that is to be expected. The objection as it applies to the moral virtues goes far beyond the application to particulars. The problem there is said to reside in the identity of the virtues themselves. Again, I cannot say how great this problem is for virtue ethics, but it is unlikely to pose a serious problem for virtue epistemology.

5. VIRTUE THEORY IN RELIGIOUS EPISTEMOLOGY

The approach to epistemology I advocate ought to be particularly pleasing to the epistemologist of religion. Religious practice unifies the self in a way that mere beliefs do not, and so religious people have an appreciation for the importance of integrity. Religions are forms of life, not just coherent (or not so coherent) systems of beliefs, and it is important that this not be ignored when religious beliefs are evaluated. It does violence to the reality of religion to evaluate religious beliefs individually, in isolation from the character of the believer and the community with which the believer identifies. This is not to say that religious belief can get by with lower standards of rationality or justification than other sorts of belief. It simply means that religious belief calls attention to features that most of our beliefs have anyway but which are sometimes overlooked. One such feature is their connection with non-cognitive states of the person. This not only means that sets of beliefs must be evaluated as a whole, but that there is no autonomous whole to evaluate independently of non-belief states. Virtue theory has gone the farthest in explaining both this connection between beliefs and other states of a person's psyche, and the connection between the cognitive processes of an individual and that of a community. Virtue theory is therefore a promising alternative to a belief-based theory for an understanding of the normative aspect of religious belief.

How would we proceed with such an approach? In the first place, the emphasis would not be on isolating individual beliefs, such as "There is a God" or "Jesus rose from the dead," in an attempt to identify features of the belief that can then be tested against some criterion for justification or warrant. Instead, it would be appropriate to consider the kind of intellectual character to which we all should aspire, and then we would ask whether people with such a character in the requisite circumstances have such beliefs. The Christian emphasis on living a life in imitation of saintly persons would extend to imitating the cognitive activities of persons of intellectual virtue. Some qualities of intellectual character may turn out to be causally connected with qualities of moral character, in which case, moral properties would be relevant to *epistemic* evaluation, and conversely.

The virtue approach promises a richer analysis of the normative element in epistemic states than that given by the well-known approach of Alvin Plantinga.[24] Plantinga defines the normative element of knowledge—what he calls "warrant"—as that quality which a belief has when it is formed by faculties

functioning properly in the appropriate environment, according to a design plan aimed at truth. It is interesting that in ancient Greek philosophy a virtue is a quality that permits a creature to perform properly those functions specific to its nature. Those qualities of a person which permit the proper functioning of faculties designed for the obtaining of truth would therefore be what I call virtues. If so, my virtue approach and Plantinga's proper-functioning approach should yield the same results. The difference is that Plantinga does not link his account of warrant with a tradition that guides us in explicating the content of the character of persons with properly functioning faculties. The virtue tradition does provide such guidance with a long history of investigation on the nature of virtue and the connection between a virtue and human ends. The study of this tradition, I believe, yields an understanding of intellectual virtue that is more internalist and voluntarist than Plantinga's, as well as more social.[25] In any case, since Plantinga says very little about what proper functioning actually amounts to, this approach provides a much richer and more detailed content.

I suggested above that perhaps the particularist interest in investigating literature for its moral insight should be extended to investigating literature for insight into good cognitive behavior as well. Religious epistemologists might find helpful models of the nature of rational religiosity in the study of narratives with religious themes. Theologians are more familiar with this method than are philosophers, but philosophers are well suited to investigate the connections among virtues, feelings, beliefs, and cognitive activity in a well-ordered psyche. As far as I know, the use of literature by philosophers has been limited to the area of moral philosophy. I suggest that epistemologists, including religious epistemologists ought to turn to it as well.

The implication of adopting a virtue-centered approach to analyzing the normative aspects of belief-forming and other cognitive behavior is that one should give up the current focus on justification as the key normative concept in epistemology. The primary focus of inquiry simply should not be a belief, and that means that no property of a belief can be the primary normative property in epistemology. Replacing justification by the concept of warrant will not solve the underlying deficiencies of the belief-based approach either, since warrant also is a property of a belief.

Recently there has been a lot of interest in philosophy in finding new models of rationality. Considering how poorly religious belief fared under the restricted model of rationality favored since Descartes, religious epistemologists have a special interest in finding such models. I hope that an approach centered on the virtues will prove a rich source for such investigations.

NOTES

1. Roderick Chisholm, *Perceiving: A Philosophical Study* (Ithaca, N.Y.: Cornell University Press, 1969), p. 4.

2. Roderick Firth, "Are Epistemic Concepts Reducible to Ethical Concepts?" in Alvin I. Goldman and Jaegwon Kim, eds., *Values and Morals: Essays in Honor of William K. Frankena, Charles Stevenson, and Richard Brandt* (Boston: D. Reidel, 1978), p. 216.

3. Ernest Sosa, "The Raft and the Pyramid," *Journal of Philosophy* 75 (October 1978): 509–23.

4. Ernest Sosa, "Knowledge and Intellectual Virtue," *The Monist* 68 (April 1985): 226–45.

5. John Greco, "Virtue Epistemology," in Jonathan Dancy and Ernest Sosa, eds., *A Companion to Epistemology* (Cambridge, Mass.: Basil Blackwell, 1992).

6. Jonathan Kvanvig, *The Intellectual Virtues and the Life of the Mind: On the Place of the Virtues in Epistemology* (Lanham, Md.: Rowman & Littlefield, 1992).

7. Lorraine Code, *Epistemic Responsibility* (Hanover, N.H.: University Press of New England, 1987).

8. Ibid., pp. 50–51.

9. Ibid., pp. 40–42.

10. Ibid., p. 68.

11. James A. Montmarquet, "Epistemic Virtue," *Mind* 95 (1986): 482–97.

12. Ibid., p. 484.

13. A good example of this is Susan Wolf's paper, "Moral Saints," *Journal of Philosophy* 79 (1982): 419–39. Wolf's provocative and convincing attack on both utilitarian and Kantian theories is not accompanied by a call to bring back classical Aristotelianism. In fact, she explicitly denies that our conception of the moral will permit this move.

14. Several philosophers have argued recently that virtues cannot be tied to act-descriptions, e.g., James Wallace, *Virtues and Vices* (Ithaca, N.Y.: Cornell University Press, 1978). Gregory Trianosky says that primary and secondary actional virtues are conceptually or causally tied to right action respectively, but what he calls spiritual virtues are not so tied in "Virtue, Action, and the Good Life: Towards a Theory of the Virtues," *Pacific Philosophical Quarterly* 68 (June 1987): 124–47.

15. Elizabeth Anscombe, "Modern Moral Philosophy," *Philosophy* 33 (January 1958): 1–19.

16. Bernard Mayo, *Ethics and the Moral Life* (London: Macmillan, 1958); excerpt reprinted in Louis Pojman, *Ethical Theory* (Belmont, Calif.: Wadsworth, 1989), pp. 302–4.

17. Ibid., p. 302.

18. Bernard Williams makes this distinction throughout *Ethics and the Limits of Philosophy* (Cambridge, Mass.: Harvard University Press, 1985). Williams's examples of thick ethical concepts include *courage, treachery, brutality,* and *gratitude.* Clearly not only virtues are "thick," but virtues are among the paradigm examples. Allan Gibbard also uses this distinction in *Wise Choices, Apt Feelings* (Cambridge, Mass.: Harvard University Press, 1990).

19. Martha Nussbaum takes this position in numerous places. See especially *Love's Knowledge* (New York: Oxford University Press, 1990).

20. W. D. Ross is an example of a particularist, act-based theorist.

21. Trianosky, "Virtue, Action, and the Good Life."

22. "Theology and Epistemic Virtue," in Stephen T. Davis, ed., *Philosophy and the Future of Christian Theology* (New York: Macmillan, 1993). I am presently working on a theory of the intellectual

virtues as forms of moral virtue in a book to be called *Virtues of the Mind*.

23. Robert Louden, "Some Vices of Virtue Ethics," *American Philosophical Quarterly* 21 (1984): 227–36.

24. Plantinga's fullest and most recent presentation of his theory appears in *Warrant and Proper Function* (New York: Oxford University Press, 1992).

25. My criticisms of Plantinga's approach for its externalism, non-voluntarism, and individualism appear in "Religious Knowledge and the Virtues of the Mind," in my edited collection, *Rational Faith: Catholic Responses to Reformed Epistemology* (Notre Dame, Ind.: University of Notre Dame Press, 1993).

PART VI

Religious Pluralism

IS THERE ONLY ONE WAY to God? If God exists, why isn't God's presence more widely accessible, being made manifest at all times and places, to all nations and individuals? Or has God been revealed widely after all, but through different faiths, different symbols, and different interpretations of the divine? Are all religions simply different paths to the same ultimate reality?

In recent decades, the question of religious pluralism has become a burning issue among theologians and philosophers of religion. On the one side are the *pluralists*, those who hold that all religions, or at least all major religions, are different paths to the same God, or ultimate reality. On the other side are the *exclusivists*, who argue that there is only one way to God. Pluralist philosophers like John Hick (see our first reading in this section) believe that the major religions—Judaism, Christianity, Hinduism, Buddhism, and Islam—are different paths to the same ultimate reality. The Buddhist parable of the six blind men is sometimes used to illustrate this point:

> Once upon a time a group of religious seekers from different traditions came together and began to discuss the nature of God. Offering quite different answers, they began quarreling among themselves as to who was right and who wrong. Finally, when no hope for a reconciliation was in sight, they called in the Buddha and asked him to tell them who was right. The Buddha proceeded to tell the following story.
>
> There was once a king who asked his servants to bring him all the blind people in a town and an elephant. Six blind men and an elephant were soon set before him. The king instructed the blind men to feel the animal and describe the elephant. "An elephant is like a large waterpot," said the first who touched the elephant's head. "Your Majesty, he's wrong," said the second, as he touched an ear. "An elephant is like a fan." "No," insisted a third, "an elephant is like a snake," as he held his trunk. "On the contrary, you're all mistaken," said a fourth, as he held the tusks, "An elephant is like two prongs of a plow." The fifth man demurred and said, "It is quite clear that an elephant is like a pillar," as

he grasped the animal's rear leg. "You're all mistaken," insisted the sixth. "An elephant is a long snake," and he held up the tail. Then they all began to shout at each other about their convictions of the nature of an elephant.

After telling the story the Buddha commented, "How can you be so sure of what you cannot see. We are all like blind people in this world. We cannot see God. Each of you may be partly right, yet none completely so."

The religious pluralist calls on us to give up our claims to exclusivity and accept the thesis that many paths lead to God and to salvation or liberation. As Lord Krishna says in the Bhagavad Gita, "In whatever way men approach me, I am gracious to them; men everywhere follow my path."

On the other side of the debate are exclusivists. They believe that only one way leads to God or salvation. Whereas Hinduism, reflected in the words of Lord Krishna (above), has tended to be pluralistic, Christianity and Islam have tended toward exclusivity. In the Gospel of John, Jesus says, "I am the way, the truth, and the life. No one comes to the Father but by me." And Peter says in the Book of Acts, "Nor is there salvation in any other, for there is no other name under heaven given among men, whereby we must be saved." The inspiration of the missionary movement within Christianity and Islam has been to bring salvation to those who would otherwise be lost.

Christians and Muslims have historically rejected pluralism. If Christ or Mohammed is the unique way to God, the other creeds must be erroneous because they deny these claims. Since Muslims and Christians believe that they have good reasons for their beliefs, why should they give them up? Why should they give up their claims to exclusivity?

One consideration given by the pluralists is that it is an empirical fact that people generally adhere to the religion of their geographical location, of their native culture. Thus, Indians are likely to be Hindus, Tibetans Buddhists, Israelis Jews, Arabs Muslims, and Europeans and Americans Christians. If we recognize the accidentality of our religious preference, shouldn't we give up the claim to exclusivity?

The exclusivist responds that one might give up a claim to religious *certainty* as he or she recognizes that other traditions have different beliefs. But if reconsideration of relevant evidence leaves one still believing that one's original religious views are more likely than the alternatives to be correct, then one might well be perfectly reasonable in continuing to hold those beliefs and in continuing to think that one's own religious tradition offers the only path to salvation. The fact that one's religious beliefs are partly a result of where one lives does not by itself show that exclusivist claims are false. At best, the exclusivist will say, it shows that sociological factors have some role to play in determining how easy it is for one to happen upon the truth.

In our readings, John Hick defends the pluralist position and Alvin Plantinga defends religious exclusivism. Plantinga argues that religious exclusivism is not (or need not be) morally or epistemically improper and that a certain exclusivism is present no matter what we believe. For example, suppose the pluralist believes that all the major religions are equally good paths to God. Many others disagree; but the pluralist persists in thinking that they are mistaken. Thus, the pluralist is an exclusivist with regard to her belief that all of the major religions are equally good paths to God. Believing anything implies that those who believe the contrary of what you believe are wrong. So virtually all of us fall into exclusivism with respect to some belief or other.

David Basinger, in the third reading, attempts to reconcile Hick's religious pluralism with Plantinga's exclusivism. Basinger argues that, properly understood, the two positions are compatible, both offering valid insights on the diversity of religious phenomena.

In our fourth and final reading, the Dalai Lama reflects on the Buddhist perspective on world religions, indicating some areas of unity within diversity.

VI.1

Religious Pluralism and Ultimate Reality

JOHN HICK

Biographical remarks about John Hick precede selection III.C.2. In this essay from his groundbreaking work God and the Universe of Faiths, *Hick sets forth the thesis that God historically revealed God-self through various individuals in various situations where geographic isolation prevented a common revelation to all humanity. Each major religion has a different interpretation of the same ultimate reality, to the same salvation. Now the time has come to engage in interreligious dialogue so that we may discover our common bonds and realize that other religious people participate in ultimate reality as validly as we do within our religion, "for all these exist in time, as ways through time to eternity."*

Let me begin by proposing a working definition of religion as an understanding of the universe, together with an appropriate way of living within it, which involves reference beyond the natural world to God or gods or to the Absolute or to a transcendent order or process. Such a definition includes such theistic faiths as Judaism, Christianity, Islam, Sikhism; the theistic Hinduism of the Bhagavad Gītā; the semi-theistic faith of Mahayana Buddhism and the non-theistic faiths of Theravada Buddhism and non-theistic Hinduism. It does not however include purely naturalistic systems of belief,

Reprinted from John Hick, *God and the Universe of Faiths,* published 1988 (Palgrave MacMillan). Reproduced with permission of Palgrave MacMillan. Notes deleted.

such as communism and humanism, immensely important though these are today as alternatives to religious life.

When we look back into the past we find that religion has been a virtually universal dimension of human life—so much so that man has been defined as the religious animal. For he has displayed an innate tendency to experience his environment as being religiously as well as naturally significant, and to feel required to live in it as such. To quote the anthropologist, Raymond Firth, "religion is universal in human societies." "In every human community on earth today," says Wilfred Cantwell Smith, "there exists something that we, as sophisticated observers, may term religion, or a religion. And we are able to see it in each case as the latest development in a continuous tradition that goes back, we can now affirm, for at least one hundred thousand years." In the life of primitive man this religious tendency is expressed in a belief in sacred objects endowed with *mana*, and in a multitude of natural and ancestral spirits needing to be carefully propitiated. The divine was here crudely apprehended as a plurality of quasianimal forces which could to some extent be controlled by ritualistic and magical procedures. This represents the simplest beginning of man's awareness of the transcendent in the infancy of the human race—an infancy which is also to some extent still available for study in the life of primitive tribes today.

The development of religion and religions begins to emerge into the light of recorded history as the third millennium B.C. moves towards the period around 2000 B.C. There are two main regions of the earth in which civilisation seems first to have arisen and in which religions first took a shape that is at least dimly discernible to us as we peer back through the mists of time—these being Mesopotamia in the Near East and the Indus valley of northern India. In Mesopotamia men lived in nomadic shepherd tribes, each worshipping its own god. Then the tribes gradually coalesced into nation states, the former tribal gods becoming ranked in hierarchies (some however being lost by amalgamation in the process) dominated by great national deities such as Marduk of Babylon, the Sumerian Ishtar, Amon of Thebes, Jahweh of Israel, the Greek Zeus, and so on. Further east in the Indus valley there was likewise a wealth of gods and goddesses, though apparently not so much tribal or national in character as expressive of the basic forces of nature, above all fertility. The many deities of the Near East and of India expressed man's awareness of the divine at the dawn of documentary history, some four thousand years ago. It is perhaps worth stressing that the picture was by no means a wholly pleasant one. The tribal and national gods were often martial and cruel, sometimes requiring human sacrifices. And although rather little is known about the very early, pre-Aryan Indian deities, it is certain that later Indian deities have vividly symbolised the cruel and destructive as well as the beneficent aspects of nature.

These early developments in the two cradles of civilisation, Mesopotamia and the Indus valley, can be described as the growth of natural religion, prior to any special intrusions of divine revelation or illumination. Primitive spirit-worship expressed man's fears of unknown forces; his reverence for nature deities expressed his sense of dependence upon realities greater than himself; and his tribal gods expressed the unity and continuity of his group over against other groups. One can in fact discern all sorts of causal connections between the forms which early religion took and the material circumstances of man's life, indicating the large part played by the human element within the history of religion. For example, Trevor Ling points out that life in ancient India (apart from the Punjab immediately prior to the Aryan invasions) was agricultural and was organised in small village units; and suggests that "among agricultural peoples, aware of the fertile earth which brings forth from itself and nourishes its progeny upon its broad bosom, it is the mother-principle which seems important." Accordingly God the Mother, and a variety of more specialised female deities, have always held a prominent place in Indian religious thought and mythology. This contrasts with the characteristically male expression of deity in the Semitic religions, which had their origins among nomadic, pastoral, herd-keeping peoples in the Near East.

The divine was known to the desert-dwelling herdsmen who founded the Israelite tradition as God the King and Father; and this conception has continued both in later Judaism and in Christianity, and was renewed out of the desert experience of Mohammed in the Islamic religion. Such regional variations in our human ways of conceiving the divine have persisted through time into the developed world faiths that we know today. The typical western conception of God is still predominantly in terms of the male principle of power and authority; and in the typical Indian conceptions of deity the female principle still plays a distinctly larger part than in the west.

Here then was the natural condition of man's religious life: religion without revelation. But sometime around 800 B.C. there began what has been called the golden age of religious creativity. This consisted in a remarkable series of revelatory experiences occurring during the next five hundred or so years in different parts of the world, experiences which deepened and purified men's conception of the ultimate, and which religious faith can only attribute to the pressure of the divine Spirit upon the human spirit. First came the early Jewish prophets, Amos, Hosea and first Isaiah, declaring that they had heard the Word of the Lord claiming their obedience and demanding a new level of righteousness and justice in the life of Israel. Then in Persia the great prophet Zoroaster appeared; China produced Lao-tzu and then Confucius; in India the Upanishads were written, and Gotama the Buddha lived, and Mahavira, the founder of the Jain religion and, probably about the end of this period, the writing of the Bhagavad Gītā, and Greece produced Pythagoras and then, ending this golden age, Socrates and Plato. Then after the gap of some three hundred years came Jesus of Nazareth and the emergence of Christianity; and after another gap the prophet Mohammed and the rise of Islam.

The suggestion that we must consider is that these were all moments of divine revelation. But let us ask, in order to test this thought, whether we should not expect God to make his revelation in a single mighty act, rather than to produce a number of different, and therefore presumably partial, revelations at different times and places? I think that in seeing the answer to this question we receive an important clue to the place of the religions of the world in the divine purpose. For when we remember the facts of history and geography we realise that in the period we are speaking of, between two and three thousand years ago, it was not possible for God to reveal himself through any human mediation to all mankind. A world-wide revelation might be possible today, thanks to the inventions of printing, and even more of radio, TV and communication satellites. But in the technology of the ancient world this was not possible. Although on a time scale of centuries and millennia there has been a slow diffusion and interaction of cultures, particularly within the vast Euro-Asian land mass, yet the more striking fact for our present purpose is the fragmented character of the ancient world. Communications between the different groups of humanity was then so limited and slow that for all practical purposes men inhabited different worlds. For the most part people in Europe, in India, in Arabia, in Africa, in China were unaware of the others' existence. And as the world was fragmented, so was its religious life. If there was to be a revelation of the divine reality to mankind it had to be a pluriform revelation, a series of revealing experiences occurring independently within the different streams of human history. And since religion and culture were one, the great creative moments of revelation and illumination have influenced the development of the various cultures, giving them the coherence and impetus to expand into larger units, thus creating the vast, many-sided historical entities which we call the world religions.

Each of these religio-cultural complexes has expanded until it touched the boundaries of another such complex spreading out from another centre. Thus each major occasion of divine revelation has slowly transformed the primitive and national religions within the sphere of its influence into what we now know as the world faiths. The early Dravidian and Aryan polytheisms of India were drawn through the religious experience and thought of the Brahmins into what the west calls

Hinduism. The national and mystery cults of the Mediterranean world and then of northern Europe were drawn by influences stemming from the life and teaching of Christ into what has become Christianity. The early polytheism of the Arab peoples has been transformed under the influence of Mohammed and his message into Islam. Great areas of Southeast Asia, of China, Tibet and Japan were drawn into the spreading Buddhist movement. None of these expansions from different centres of revelation has of course been simple and uncontested, and a number of alternatives which proved less durable have perished or been absorbed in the process—for example, Mithraism has disappeared altogether; and Zoroastrianism, whilst it greatly influenced the development of the Judaic-Christian tradition, and has to that extent been absorbed, only survives directly today on a small scale in Parseeism.

Seen in this historical context these movements of faith—the Judaic-Christian, the Buddhist, the Hindu, the Muslim—are not essentially rivals. They began at different times and in different places, and each expanded outwards into the surrounding world of primitive natural religion until most of the world was drawn up into one or other of the great revealed faiths. And once this global pattern had become established it has ever since remained fairly stable. It is true that the process of establishment involved conflict in the case of Islam's entry into India and the virtual expulsion of Buddhism from India in the medieval period, and in the case of Islam's advance into Europe and then its retreat at the end of the medieval period. But since the frontiers of the different world faiths became more or less fixed there has been little penetration of one faith into societies moulded by another. The most successful missionary efforts of the great faiths continue to this day to be "downwards" into the remaining world of relatively primitive religions rather than "sideways" into territories dominated by another world faith. For example, as between Christianity and Islam there has been little more than rather rare individual conversions; but both faiths have successful missions in Africa. Again, the Christian population of the Indian subcontinent,

after more than two centuries of missionary effort, is only about 2.7 percent; but on the other hand the Christian missions in the South Pacific are fairly successful. Thus the general picture, so far as the great world religions is concerned, is that each has gone through an early period of geographical expansion, converting a region of the world from its more primitive religious state, and has thereafter continued in a comparatively settled condition within more or less stable boundaries.

Now it is of course possible to see this entire development from the primitive forms of religion up to and including the great world faiths as the history of man's most persistent illusion, growing from crude fantasies into sophisticated metaphysical speculations. But from the standpoint of religious faith the only reasonable hypothesis is that this historical picture represents a movement of divine self-revelation to mankind. This hypothesis offers a general answer to the question of the relation between the different world religions and of the truths which they embody. It suggests to us that the same divine reality has always been self-revealingly active towards mankind, and that the differences of human response are related to different human circumstances. These circumstances—ethnic, geographical, climatic, economic, sociological, historical—have produced the existing differentiations of human culture, and within each main cultural region the response to the divine has taken its own characteristic forms. In each case the post-primitive response has been initiated by some spiritually outstanding individual or succession of individuals, developing in the course of time into one of the great religio-cultural phenomena which we call the world religions. Thus Islam embodies the main response of the Arabic peoples to the divine reality; Hinduism, the main (though not the only) response of the peoples of India; Buddhism, the main response of the peoples of South-east Asia and parts of northern Asia; Christianity, the main response of the European peoples, both within Europe itself and in their emigrations to the Americas and Australasia.

Thus it is, I think, intelligible historically why the revelation of the divine reality to man, and the disclosure of the divine will for human life, had to occur separately within the different streams of human life. We can see how these revelations took different forms related to the different mentalities of the peoples to whom they came and developed within these different cultures into the vast and many-sided historical phenomena of the world religions.

But let us now ask whether this is intelligible theologically. What about the conflicting truth claims of the different faiths? Is the divine nature personal or non-personal; does deity become incarnate in the world; are human beings born again and again on earth; is the Bible, or the Koran, or the Bhagavad Gītā the Word of God? If what Christianity says in answer to these questions is true, must not what Hinduism says be to a large extent false? If what Buddhism says is true, must not what Islam says be largely false?

Let us begin with the recognition, which is made in all the main religious traditions, that the ultimate divine reality is infinite and as such transcends the grasp of the human mind. God, to use our Christian term, is infinite. He is not a thing, a part of the universe, existing alongside other things; nor is he a being falling under a certain kind. And therefore he cannot be defined or encompassed by human thought. We cannot draw boundaries around his nature and say that he is this and no more. If we could fully define God, describing his inner being and his outer limits, this would not be God. The God whom our minds can penetrate and whom our thoughts can circumnavigate is merely a finite and partial image of God.

From this it follows that the different encounters with the transcendent within the different religious traditions may all be encounters with the one infinite reality; though with partially different and overlapping aspects of that reality. This is a very familiar thought in Indian religious literature. We read, for example, in the ancient Rig-Vedas, dating back to perhaps as much as a thousand years before Christ:

> They call it Indra, Mitra, Varuna, and Agni
> And also heavenly, beautiful Garutman:
> The real is one, though sages name it
> variously.

We might translate this thought into the terms of the faiths represented today in Britain:

> They call it Jahweh, Allah, Krishna, Param
> Atma,
> And also holy, blessed Trinity:
> The real is one, though sages name it
> differently.

And in the Bhagavad Gītā the Lord Krishna, the personal God of love, says, "However men approach me, even so do I accept them: for, on all sides, whatever path they may choose is mine."

Again, there is the parable of the blind men and the elephant, said to have been told by the Buddha. An elephant was brought to a group of blind men who had never encountered such an animal before. One felt a leg and reported that an elephant is a great living pillar. Another felt the trunk and reported that an elephant is a great snake. Another felt the tusk and reported that an elephant is like a sharp ploughshare. And so on. And then they all quarrelled together, each claiming that his own account was the truth and therefore all the others false. In fact of course they were all true, but each referring only to one aspect of the total reality and all expressed in very imperfect analogies.

Now the possibility, indeed the probability, that we have seriously to consider is that many different accounts of the divine reality may be true, though all expressed in imperfect human analogies, but that none is "the truth, the whole truth, and nothing but the truth." May it not be that the different concepts of God, as Jahweh, Allah, Krishna, Param Atma, Holy Trinity, and so on; and likewise the different concepts of the hidden structure of reality, as the eternal emanation of Brahman or as an immense cosmic process culminating in Nirvana, are all images of the divine, each expressing some aspect or range of aspects and yet none by itself fully and exhaustively corresponding to the infinite nature of the ultimate reality?

Two immediate qualifications however to this hypothesis. First, the idea that we are considering is not that any and every conception of God or of the transcendent is valid, still less all equally valid; but that every conception of the divine which has come out of a great revelatory religious experience and has been tested through a long tradition of worship, and has sustained human faith over centuries of time and in millions of lives, is likely to represent a genuine encounter with the divine reality. And second, the parable of the blind men and the elephant is of course only a parable and like most parables it is designed to make one point and must not be pressed as an analogy at other points. The suggestion is not that the different encounters with the divine which lie at the basis of the great religious traditions are responses to different *parts* of the divine. They are rather encounters from different historical and cultural standpoints with the same infinite divine reality and as such they lead to differently focused awareness of the reality. The indications of this are most evident in worship and prayer. What is said about God in the theological treatises of the different faiths is indeed often widely different. But it is in prayer that a belief in God comes alive and does its main work. And when we turn from abstract theology to the living stuff of worship we meet again and again the overlap and confluence of faiths.

Here, for example, is a Muslim prayer at the feast of Ramadan:

Praise be to God, Lord of creation, Source of all livelihood, who orders the morning, Lord of majesty and honour, of grace and beneficence. He who is so far that he may not be seen and so near that he witnesses the secret things. Blessed be he and for ever exalted.

And here is a Sikh creed used at the morning prayer:

There is but one God. He is all that is.
He is the Creator of all things and He is all pervasive.
He is without fear and without enmity.
He is timeless, unborn and self-existent.
   He is the Enlightener
And can be realised by grace of Himself alone. He was in the beginning; He was in all ages.

The True One is, was, O Nanak, and shall for ever be.

And here again is a verse from the Koran:

To God belongs the praise. Lord of the heavens and Lord of the earth, the Lord of all being. His is the dominion in the heavens and in the earth: he is the Almighty, the All-wise.

Turning now to the Hindu idea of the many incarnations of God, here is a verse from the Rāmāyana:

Seers and sages, saints and hermits, fix on Him their reverent gaze,
And in faint and trembling accents, holy scripture hymns His praise.
He the omnipresent spirit, lord of heaven and earth and hell,
To redeem His people, freely has vouchsafed with men to dwell.

And from the rich literature of devotional song here is a Bhakti hymn of the Vaishnavite branch of Hinduism:

Now all my days with joy I'll fill, full to the brim
With all my heart to Vitthal cling, and only Him.
He will sweep utterly away all dole and care;
And all in sunder shall I rend illusion's snare.
O altogether dear is He, and He alone,
For all my burden He will take to be His own.
Lo, all the sorrow of the world will straight way cease,
And all unending now shall be the reign of peace.

And a Muslim mystical verse:

Love came a guest
Within my breast,
My soul was spread,
Love banqueted.

And finally another Hindu (Vaishnavite) devotional hymn:

> O save me, save me, Mightiest, Save me
>   and set me free.
> O let the love that fills my breast Cling to
>   thee lovingly.
> Grant me to taste how sweet thou art;
>   Grant me but this, I pray.
> And never shall my love depart Or turn
>   from thee away.
> Then I thy name shall magnify And tell
>   thy praise abroad,
> For very love and gladness I Shall dance
>   before my God.

Such prayers and hymns as these must express, surely, diverse encounters with the same divine reality. These encounters have taken place within different human cultures by people of different ways of thought and feeling, with different histories and different frameworks of philosophical thought, and have developed into different systems of theology embodied in different religious structures and organisations. These resulting large-scale religio-cultural phenomena are what we call the religions of the world. But must there not lie behind them the same infinite divine reality, and may not our divisions into Christian, Hindu, Muslim, Jew, and so on, and all that goes with them, accordingly represent secondary, human, historical developments?

There is a further problem, however, which now arises. I have been speaking so far of the ultimate reality in a variety of terms—the Father, Son and Spirit of Christianity, the Jahweh of Judaism, the Allah of Islam, and so on—but always thus far in theistic terms, as a personal God under one name or another. But what of the non-theistic religions? What of the non-theistic Hinduism according to which the ultimate reality, Brahman, is not He but It; and what about Buddhism, which in one form is agnostic concerning the existence of God even though in another form it has come to worship the Buddha himself? Can these non-theistic faiths be seen as encounters with the same divine reality that is encountered in theistic religion?

Speaking very tentatively, I think it is possible that the sense of the divine as non-personal may indeed reflect an aspect of the same infinite reality that is encountered as personal in theistic religious experience. The question can be pursued both as a matter of pure theology and in relation to religious experience. Theologically, the Hindu distinction between Nirguna Brahman and Saguna Brahman is important and should be adopted into western religious thought. Detaching the distinction, then from its Hindu context we may say that Nirguna God is the eternal self-existent divine reality, beyond the scope of all human categories, including personality; and Saguna God is God in relation to his creation and with the attributes which express this relationship, such as personality, omnipotence, goodness, love and omniscience. Thus the one ultimate reality is both Nirguna and non-personal, and Saguna and personal, in a duality which is in principle acceptable to human understanding. When we turn to men's religious awareness of God we are speaking of Saguna God, God in relation to man. And here the larger traditions of both east and west report a dual experience of the divine as personal and as other than personal. It will be a sufficient reminder of the strand of personal relationship with the divine in Hinduism to mention Iswaru, the personal God who represents the Absolute as known and worshipped by finite persons. It should also be remembered that the characterisation of Brahman as *satcitananda*, absolute being, consciousness and bliss, is not far from the conception of infinitely transcendent personal life. Thus there is both the thought and the experience of the personal divine within Hinduism. But there is likewise the thought and the experience of God as other than personal within Christianity. Rudolph Otto describes this strand in the mysticism of Meister Eckhart. He says:

> The divine, which on the one hand is conceived in symbols taken from the social sphere, as Lord, King, Father, Judge—a person in relation to persons—is on the other hand denoted in dynamic symbols as the power of life, as light and life, as spirit ebbing

and flowing, as truth, knowledge, essential justice and holiness, a glowing fire that penetrates and pervades. It is characterized as the principle of a renewed, supernatural Life, mediating and giving itself, breaking forth in the living man as his nova vita, as the content of his life and being. What is here insisted upon is not so much an immanent God, as an "experienced" God, known as an inward principle of the power of new being and life. Eckhart knows this *deuteros theos* besides the personal God . . .

Let me now try to draw the threads together and to project them into the future. I have been suggesting that Christianity is a way of salvation which, beginning some two thousand years ago, has become the principal way of salvation in three continents. The other great faiths are likewise of salvation, providing the principal path to the divine reality for other large sections of humanity. I have also suggested that the idea that Jesus proclaimed himself as God incarnate, and as the sole point of saving contact between God and man, is without adequate historical foundation and represents a doctrine developed by the church. We should therefore not infer, from the christian experience of redemption through Christ, that salvation cannot be experienced in any other way. The alternative possibility is that the ultimate divine reality—in our christian terms, God—has always been pressing in upon the human spirit, but in ways which leave men free to open or close themselves to the divine presence. Human life has developed along characteristically different lines in the main areas of civilisation, and these differences have naturally entered into the ways in which men have apprehended and responded to God. For the great religious figures through whose experience divine revelation has come have each been conditioned by a particular history and culture. One can hardly imagine Gotama the Buddha except in the setting of the India of his time, or Jesus the Christ except against the background of Old Testament Judaism, or Mohammed except in the setting of Arabia. And human history and culture have likewise shaped

the development of the webs of religious creeds, practices and organisations which we know as the great world faiths.

It is thus possible to consider the hypothesis that they are all, at their experiential roots, in contact with the same ultimate reality, but that their differing experiences of that reality, interacting over the centuries with the different thought-forms of different cultures, have led to increasing differentiation and contrasting elaboration—so that Hinduism, for example, is a very different phenomenon from Christianity, and very different ways of conceiving and experiencing the divine occur within them.

However, now that the religious traditions are consciously interacting with each other in the "one world" of today, in mutual observation and dialogue, it is possible that their future developments may be on gradually converging courses. For during the next few centuries they will no doubt continue to change, and it may be that they will grow closer together, and even that one day such names as "Christianity," "Buddhism," "Islam," "Hinduism," will no longer describe the then current configurations of men's religious experience and belief. I am not here thinking of the extinction of human religiousness in a universal wave of secularisation. This is of course a possible future; and indeed many think it the most likely future to come about. But if man is an indelibly religious animal he will always, even in his secular cultures, experience a sense of the transcendent by which he will be both troubled and uplifted. The future I am thinking of is accordingly one in which what we now call the different religions will constitute the past history of different emphases and variations within a global religious life. I do not mean that all men everywhere will be overtly religious, any more than they are today. I mean rather that the discoveries now taking place by men of different faiths of central common ground, hitherto largely concealed by the variety of cultural forms in which it was expressed, may eventually render obsolete the sense of belonging to rival ideological communities. Not that all religious men will think alike, or worship in the same way or experience the divine identically. On the contrary, so long as there is a rich variety of human cultures—and let us hope there will always be this—we should expect there to be correspondingly different forms of religious cult, ritual and organisation, conceptualised in different theological doctrines. And so long as there is a wide spectrum of human psychological types—and again let us hope that there will always be this—we should expect there to be correspondingly different emphases between, for example, the sense of the divine as just and as merciful, between *karma* and *bhakti*; or between worship as formal and communal and worship as free and personal. Thus we may expect the different world faiths to continue as religiocultural phenomena, though phenomena which are increasingly influencing one another's development. The relation between them will then perhaps be somewhat like that now obtaining between the different denominations of Christianity in Europe or the United States. That is to say, there will in most countries be a dominant religious tradition, with other traditions present in varying strengths, but with considerable awareness on all hands of what they have in common; with some degree of osmosis of membership through their institutional walls; with a large degree of practical cooperation; and even conceivably with some interchange of ministry.

Beyond this the ultimate unity of faiths will be an eschatological unity in which each is both fulfilled and transcended—fulfilled in so far as it is true, transcended in so far as it is less than the whole truth. And indeed even such fulfilling must be a transcending; for the function of a religion is to bring us to a right relationship with the ultimate divine reality, to awareness of our true nature and our place in the Whole, into the presence of God. In the eternal life there is no longer any place for religions; the pilgrim has no need of a way after he has finally arrived. In St. John's vision of the heavenly city at the end of our christian scriptures it is said that there is no temple—no christian church or chapel, no jewish synagogue, no hindu or buddhist temple, no muslim mosque, no sikh gurdwara.... For all these exist in time, as ways through time to eternity.

VI.2

A Defense of Religious Exclusivism

ALVIN PLANTINGA

Biographical remarks about Alvin Plantinga appear before selection I.B.8. In this selection, Plantinga argues for three theses: (1) The religious exclusivist is not necessarily guilty of any moral wrongdoing; (2) the religious exclusivist is not necessarily guilty of any epistemic fault; and (3) some exclusivism in our beliefs is inevitable. If a person truly believes her creed, it may be wrong to expect her to treat all religions as equally good ways to God, or even as ways to God at all. Nevertheless, Plantinga agrees that the knowledge of other religions is something to be sought, and that this may sensibly lessen our assurance in our own belief.

This essay appeared in print for the first time in an earlier edition of this text. Used with permission. Endnotes edited.

When I was a graduate student at Yale, the philosophy department prided itself on diversity, and it was indeed diverse. There were idealists, pragmatists, phenomenologists, existentialists, Whiteheadians, historians of philosophy, a token positivist, and what could only be described as observers of the passing intellectual scene. In some ways, this was indeed something to take pride in; a student could behold and encounter real, live representatives of many of the main traditions in philosophy. However, it also had an unintended and unhappy side effect. If anyone raised a philosophical question inside, but particularly outside, of class, the typical response would be to catalog some of the various different answers the world has seen: There is the Aristotelian answer, the existentialist answer, the Cartesian answer, Heidegger's answer, perhaps the Buddhist answer, and so on. But the question "What is the truth about this matter?" was often greeted with disdain as unduly naive. There are all these different answers, all endorsed by people of great intellectual power and great dedication to philosophy; for every argument *for* one of these positions, there is another *against* it; would it not be excessively naive, or perhaps arbitrary, to suppose that one of these is in fact true, the others being false? Or, if even there really is a truth of the matter, so that one of them is true and conflicting ones false, wouldn't it be merely arbitrary, in the face of this embarrassment of riches, to *endorse* one of them as the truth, consigning the others to falsehood? How could you possibly know which was true?

A similar attitude is sometimes urged with respect to the impressive variety of religions the world displays. There are theistic religions but also at least some nontheistic religions (or perhaps nontheistic strands) among the enormous variety of religions going under the names Hinduism and Buddhism; among the theistic religions, there are strands of Hinduism and Buddhism and American Indian religion as well as Islam, Judaism, and Christianity; and all differ significantly from each other. Isn't it somehow arbitrary, or irrational, or unjustified, or unwarranted, or even oppressive and imperialistic to endorse one of these as opposed to all the others? According to Jean Bodin, "each is

refuted by all";[1] must we not agree? It is in this neighborhood that the so-called problem of pluralism arises. Of course, many concerns and problems can come under this rubric; the specific problem I mean to discuss can be thought of as follows. To put it in an internal and personal way, I find myself with religious beliefs, and religious beliefs that I realize aren't shared by nearly everyone else. For example, I believe both

(1) The world was created by God, an almighty, all-knowing, and perfectly good personal being (one that holds beliefs; has aims, plans, and intentions; and can act to accomplish these aims).

(2) Human beings require salvation, and God has provided a unique way of salvation through the incarnation, life, sacrificial death, and resurrection of his divine son.

Now there are many who do not believe these things. First, there are those who agree with me on (1) but not (2): They are non-Christian theistic religions. Second, there are those who don't accept either (1) or (2) but nonetheless do believe that there is something beyond the natural world, a something such that human well-being and salvation depend upon standing in a right relation to it. Third, in the West and since the Enlightenment, anyway, there are people—*naturalists*, we may call them—who don't believe any of these three things. And my problem is this: When I become really aware of these other ways of looking at the world, these other ways of responding religiously to the world, what must or should I do? What is the right sort of attitude to take? What sort of impact should this awareness have on the beliefs I hold and the strength with which I hold them? My question is this: How should I think about the great religious diversity the world in fact displays? Can I sensibly remain an adherent of just one of these religions, rejecting the others? And here I am thinking specifically of *beliefs*. Of course, there is a great deal more to any religion or religious practice than just belief, and I don't for a moment mean to deny it. But belief is a crucially important part of most religions;

it is a crucially important part of *my* religion; and the question I mean to ask here is, What does the awareness of religious diversity mean or should mean for my religious beliefs?

Some speak here of a *new* awareness of religious diversity and speak of this new awareness as constituting (for us in the West) a crisis, a revolution, an intellectual development of the same magnitude as the Copernican revolution of the sixteenth century and the alleged discovery of evolution and our animal origins in the nineteenth.[2] No doubt there is at least some truth to this. Of course, the fact is all along many Western Christians and Jews have known that there are other religions and that not nearly everyone shares *their* religion. The ancient Israelites—some of the prophets, say—were clearly aware of Canaanite religion; and the apostle Paul said that he preached "Christ crucified, a stumbling block to Jews and folly to the Greeks" (1 Corinthians 1:23). Other early Christians, the Christian martyrs, say, must have suspected that not everyone believed as they did; and the church fathers, in offering defenses of Christianity, were certainly apprised of this fact. Thomas Aquinas, again, was clearly aware of those to whom he addressed the *Summa Contra Gentiles*; and the fact that there are non-Christian religions would have come as no surprise to the Jesuit missionaries of the sixteenth and seventeenth centuries or to the Methodist missionaries of the nineteenth. To come to more recent times, when I was a child, *The Banner*, the official publication of my church, contained a small column for children; it was written by "Uncle Dick" who exhorted us to save our nickels and send them to our Indian cousins at the Navaho mission in New Mexico. Both we and our elders knew that the Navahos had or had had a religion different from Christianity, and part of the point of sending the nickels was to try to rectify that situation.

Still, in recent years, probably more of us Christian Westerners have become aware of the world's religious diversity; we have probably learned more about people of other religious persuasions, and we have come to see that they display what looks like real piety, devoutness, and spirituality. What is new,

perhaps, is a more widespread sympathy for other religions, a tendency to see them as more valuable, as containing more by way of truth, and a new feeling of solidarity with their practitioners.

Now there are several possible reactions to awareness of religious diversity. One is to continue to believe—what you have all along believed; you learn about this diversity but continue to believe that is, take to be true—such propositions as (1) and (2) above, consequently taking to be false any beliefs, religious or otherwise, that are incompatible with (1) and (2). Following current practice, I will call this *exclusivism*; the exclusivist holds that the tenets or some of the tenets of *one* religion—Christianity, let's say—are in fact true; he adds, naturally enough, that any propositions, including other religious beliefs, that are incompatible with those tenets are false. And there is a fairly widespread apprehension that there is something seriously wrong with exclusivism. It is irrational, or egotistical and unjustified,[3] or intellectually arrogant,[4] or elitist,[5] or a manifestation of harmful pride,[6] or even oppressive and imperialistic.[7] The claim is that exclusivism as such is or involves a vice of some sort: It is wrong or deplorable. It is this claim I want to examine. I propose to argue that exclusivism need not involve either epistemic or moral failure and that, furthermore, something like it is wholly unavoidable, given our human condition.

These objections, of course, are not to the *truth* of (1) or (2) or any other proposition someone might accept in this exclusivist way (although objections of that sort are also put forward); they are instead directed to the *propriety or rightness* of exclusivism. There are initially two different kinds of indictments of exclusivism: broadly moral, or ethical, indictments and other broadly intellectual, or epistemic, indictments. These overlap in interesting ways as we will see below. But initially, anyway, we can take some of the complaints about exclusivism as *intellectual* criticisms: It is *irrational* or *unjustified* to think in an exclusivistic way. The other large body of complaint is moral: There is something *morally* suspect about exclusivism—it is arbitrary, or intellectually arrogant, or imperialistic. As Joseph Runzo suggests, exclusivism is "neither tolerable nor any longer intellectually honest in the context of our contemporary knowledge of other faiths."[8] I want to consider both kinds of claims or criticisms; I propose to argue that the exclusivist as such is not necessarily guilty of any of these charges.

MORAL OBJECTIONS TO EXCLUSIVISM

I turn to the moral complaints: that the exclusivist is intellectually arrogant, or egotistical or self-servingly arbitrary, or dishonest, or imperialistic, or oppressive. But first, I provide three qualifications. An exclusivist, like anyone else, will probably be guilty of some or of all of these things to at least some degree, perhaps particularly the first two. The question, however, is whether she is guilty of these things just by virtue of being an exclusivist. Second, I will use the term *exclusivism* in such a way that you don't count as an exclusivist unless you are rather fully aware of other faiths, have had their existence and their claims called to your attention with some force and perhaps fairly frequently, and have to some degree reflected on the problem of pluralism, asking yourself such questions as whether it is or could be really true that the Lord has revealed Himself and His programs to us Christians, say, in a way in which He hasn't revealed Himself to those of other faiths. Thus, my grandmother, for example, would not have counted as an exclusivist. She had, of course, *heard* of the heathen, as she called them, but the idea that perhaps Christians could learn from them, and learn from them with respect to religious matters, had not so much as entered her head; and the fact that it *hadn't* entered her head, I take it, was not a matter of moral dereliction on her part. This same would go for a Buddhist or Hindu peasant. These people are not, I think, properly charged with arrogance or other moral flaws in believing as they do.

Third, suppose I am an exclusivist with respect to (1), for example, but nonculpably believe, like Aquinas, say, that I have a knock-down, drag-out argument, a demonstration or conclusive proof of the proposition that there is such a person as God; and suppose I think further (and nonculpably) that if those who don't believe (1) were to be apprised of this argument (and had the ability and training necessary to grasp it and were to think about the argument fairly and reflectively), *they* too would come to believe (1)? Then I could hardly be charged with these moral faults. My condition would be like that of Gödel, let's say, upon having recognized that he had a proof for the incompleteness of arithmetic. True, many of his colleagues and peers didn't believe that arithmetic was incomplete, and some believed that it was complete; but presumably Gödel wasn't arbitrary or egotistical in believing that arithmetic is in fact incomplete. Furthermore, he would not have been at fault had he nonculpably but *mistakenly* believed that he had found such a proof. Accordingly, I will use the term *exclusivist* in such a way that you don't count as an exclusivist if you nonculpably think you know of a demonstration or conclusive argument for the beliefs with respect to which you are an exclusivist, or even if you nonculpably think you know of an argument that would convince all or most intelligent and honest people of the truth of that proposition. So an exclusivist, as I use the term, not only believes something like (1) or (2) and thinks false any proposition incompatible with it; she also meets a further condition C that is hard to state precisely and in detail (and in fact any attempt to do so would involve a long and presently irrelevant discussion of *ceteris paribus* clauses). Suffice it to say that C includes (a) being rather fully aware of other religions, (b) knowing that there is much that at the least looks like genuine piety and devoutness in them, and (c) believing that you know of no arguments that would necessarily convince all or most honest and intelligent dissenters.

Given these qualifications then, why should we think that an exclusivist is properly charged with these moral faults? I will deal first and most briefly with charges of oppression and imperialism: I think we must say that they are on the face of it wholly implausible. I daresay there are some among you who reject some of the things I believe; I do not believe that you are thereby oppressing me, even if you do not believe you have an argument that would convince me. It is conceivable that exclusivism might in some way *contribute* to oppression, but it isn't in itself oppressive.

The more important moral charge is that there is a sort of self-serving arbitrariness, an arrogance or egotism, in accepting such propositions as (1) or (2) under condition *C*; exclusivism is guilty of some serious moral fault or flaw. According to Wilfred Cantwell Smith, "... except at the cost of insensitivity or delinquency, it is morally not possible actually to go out into the world and say to devout, intelligent, fellow human beings: '... we believe that we know God and we are right; you believe that you know God, and you are totally wrong.'"[9]

So what can the exclusivist have to say for himself? Well, it must be conceded immediately that if he believes (1) or (2), then he must also believe that those who believe something incompatible with them are mistaken and believe what is false. That's no more than simple logic. Furthermore, he must also believe that those who do not believe as he does—those who believe neither (1) nor (2), whether or not they believe their negations—*fail* to believe something that is deep and important and that he *does* believe. He must therefore see himself as *privileged* with respect to those others—those others of both kinds. There is something of great value, he must think, that *he* has and *they* lack. They are ignorant of something—something of great importance—of which he has knowledge. But does this make him properly subject to the above censure?

I think the answer must be no. Or if the answer is yes, then I think we have here a genuine moral dilemma; for in our earthly life here below, as my Sunday School teacher used to say, there is no real alternative; there is no reflective attitude that is not open to the same strictures. These charges of arrogance are a philosophical tar baby: Get close enough to them to use them against the exclusivist and you are likely to find them stuck fast to yourself. How so? Well, as an exclusivist, I realize that I can't convince others that they should believe as I do, but I nonetheless continue to believe as I do. The charge is that I am, as a result, arrogant or egotistical, arbitrarily preferring my way of doing things to other ways.[10] But what are my alternatives with respect to a proposition like (1)? There seem to be three choices. I can continue to hold it; I can withhold it, in Roderick Chisholm's sense, believing neither it nor its denial, and I can accept its denial. Consider the third way, a way taken by those pluralists who, like John Hick, hold that such propositions as (1) and (2) and their colleagues from other faiths are literally false, although in some way still valid responses to the Real. This seems to me to be no advance at all with respect to the arrogance or egotism problem; this is not a way out. For if I do this, I will then be in the very same condition as I am now: I will believe many propositions others don't believe and will be in condition *C* with respect to those propositions. For I will then believe the denials of (1) and (2) (as well as the denials of many other propositions explicitly accepted by those of other faiths). Many others, of course, do not believe the denials of (1) and (2) and in fact believe (1) and (2). Further, I will not know of any arguments that can be counted on to persuade those who do believe (1) or (2) (or propositions accepted by the adherents of other religions). I am therefore in the condition of believing propositions that many others do not believe and furthermore am in condition *C*. If, in the case of those who believe (1) and (2), that is sufficient for intellectual arrogance or egotism, the same goes for those who believe their denials.

So consider the second option: I can instead *withhold* the proposition in question. I can say to myself: "The right course here, given that I can't or couldn't convince these others of what I believe, is to believe neither these propositions nor their denials." The pluralist objector to exclusivism can say that the right course, under condition *C*, is to abstain from believing the offending proposition and also abstain from believing its denial; call him, therefore, "the abstemious pluralist." But does he thus really avoid the condition that, on the part of the exclusivist, leads to the charges of egotism and arrogance in this way? Think, for a moment, about disagreement. Disagreement, fundamentally, is a matter of adopting conflicting propositional attitudes with respect to a given proposition. In the simplest and most familiar case, I disagree with you if there is some proposition p such that I believe p and you believe $-p$. But that's just the simplest case; there are also others. The one that is presently of interest is this: I believe p and you withhold it, fail to believe it. Call the first kind of disagreement "contradicting"; call the second "dissenting."

My claim is that if contradicting others (under the condition C spelled out above) is arrogant and egotistical, so is dissenting (under that same condition). Suppose you believe some proposition p but I don't; perhaps you believe that it is wrong to discriminate against people simply on the grounds of race, but I, recognizing that there are many people who disagree with you, do not believe this proposition. I don't disbelieve it either, of course, but in the circumstances I think the right thing to do is to abstain from belief. Then am I not implicitly condemning your attitude, your *believing* the proposition, as somehow improper—naive, perhaps, or unjustified, or in some other way less than optimal? I am implicitly saying that my attitude is the superior one; I think my course of action here is the right one and yours somehow wrong, inadequate, improper, in the circumstances at best second-rate. Of course, I realize that there is no question, here, of *showing* you that your attitude is wrong or improper or naive; so am I not guilty of intellectual arrogance? Of a sort of egotism, thinking I know better than you, arrogating to myself a privileged status with respect to you? The problem for the exclusivist was that she was obliged to think she possessed a truth missed by many others; the problem for the abstemious pluralist is that he is obliged to think that he possesses a virtue others don't or acts rightly where others don't. If, in condition C, one is arrogant by way of believing a proposition others don't, isn't one equally, under those reflective conditions, arrogant by way of withholding a proposition others don't?

Perhaps you will respond by saying that the abstemious pluralist gets into trouble, falls into arrogance, by way of implicitly saying or believing that his way of proceeding is better or wiser than other ways pursued by other people; and perhaps he can

escape by abstaining from *that* view as well. Can't he escape the problem by refraining from believing that racial bigotry is wrong and also refraining from holding the view that it is *better*, under the conditions that obtain, to withhold that proposition than to assert and believe it? Well, yes he can; then he has no *reason* for his abstention; he doesn't believe that abstention is better or more appropriate; he simply does abstain. Does this get him off the egotistical hook? Perhaps. But then he can't, in consistency, also hold that there is something wrong with *not* abstaining, with coming right out and *believing* that bigotry is wrong; he loses his objection to the exclusivist. Accordingly, this way out is not available for the abstemious pluralist who accuses the exclusivist of arrogance and egotism.

Indeed, I think we can show that the abstemious pluralist who brings charges of intellectual arrogance against exclusivism is hoist with his own petard, holds a position that in a certain way is self-referentially inconsistent in the circumstances. For he believes

(3) If S knows that others don't believe p and that he is in condition C with respect to p, then S should not believe p.

This or something like it is the ground of the charges he brings against the exclusivist. But the abstemious pluralist realizes that many do not accept (3); and I suppose he also realizes that it is unlikely that he can find arguments for (3) that will convince them; hence, he knows that condition obtains. Given his acceptance of (3), therefore, the right course for him is to abstain from believing (3). Under the conditions that do in fact obtain— namely, his knowledge that others don't accept it and that condition C obtains—he can't properly accept it.

I am therefore inclined to think that one can't, in the circumstances, properly hold (3) or any other proposition that will do the job. One can't find here some principle on the basis of which to hold that the exclusivist is doing the wrong thing, suffers from some moral fault—that is, one can't find such a principle that doesn't, as we might put it, fall victim to itself.

So the abstemious pluralist is hoist with his own petard; but even apart from this dialectical argument (which in any event some will think unduly cute), aren't the charges unconvincing and implausible? I must concede that there are a variety of ways in which I can be and have been intellectually arrogant and egotistic; I have certainly fallen into this vice in the past and no doubt am not free of it now. But am I really arrogant and egotistic just by virtue of believing what I know others don't believe, where I can't show them that I am right? Suppose I think the matter over, consider the objections as carefully as I can, realize that I am finite and furthermore a sinner, certainly no better than those with whom I disagree; but suppose it still seems clear to me that the proposition in question is true. Can I really be behaving immorally in continuing to believe it? I am dead sure that it is wrong to try to advance my career by telling lies about my colleagues; I realize there are those who disagree; I also realize that in all likelihood there is no way I can find to show them that they are wrong; nonetheless I think they are wrong. If I think this after careful reflection, if I consider the claims of those who disagree as sympathetically as I can, if I try my level best to ascertain the truth here, and it *still* seems to me sleazy, wrong, and despicable to lie about my colleagues to advance my career, could I really be doing what is immoral by continuing to believe as before? I can't see how. If, after careful reflection and thought, you find yourself convinced that the right propositional attitude to take to (1) and (2) in the face of the facts of religious pluralism is abstention from belief, how could you properly be taxed with egotism, either for so believing or for so abstaining? Even if you knew others did not agree with you?

EPISTEMIC OBJECTIONS TO EXCLUSIVISM

I turn now to *epistemic* objections to exclusivism. There are many different specifically epistemic virtues and a corresponding plethora of epistemic vices.

The ones with which the exclusivist is most frequently charged, however, are *irrationality* and *lack of justification* in holding his exclusivist beliefs. The claim is that as an exclusivist he holds unjustified beliefs and/or irrational beliefs. Better, *he* is unjustified or irrational in holding these beliefs. I will therefore consider those two claims, and I will argue that the exclusivist views need not be either unjustified or irrational. I will then turn to the question whether his beliefs could have *warrant*—that property, whatever precisely it is, that distinguishes knowledge from mere true belief—and whether they could have enough warrant for knowledge.

Justification

The pluralist objector sometimes claims that to hold exclusivist views, in condition *C*, is *unjustified*—*epistemically* unjustified. Is this true? And what does he mean when he makes this claim? As even a brief glance at the contemporary epistemological literature will show, justification is a protean and multifarious notion. There are, I think, substantially two possibilities as to what he means. The central core of the notion, its beating heart, the paradigmatic center to which most of the myriad contemporary variations are related by way of analogical extension and family resemblance, is the notion of *being within one's intellectual rights*, having violated no intellectual or cognitive duties or obligations in the formation and sustenance of the belief in question. This is the palimpsest, going back to Rene Descartes and especially John Locke, that underlies the multitudinous battery of contemporary inscriptions. There is no space to argue that point here; but chances are, when the pluralist objector to exclusivism claims that the latter is unjustified, it is some notion lying in this neighborhood that he has in mind. (Here we should note the very close connection between the moral objections to exclusivism and the objection that exclusivism is epistemically unjustified.)

The duties involved, naturally enough, would be specifically *epistemic* duties: perhaps a duty to proportion degree of belief to (propositional) evidence from what is *certain*, that is, self-evident or incorrigible, as with Locke, or perhaps to try one's best to get into and stay in the right relation to the truth, as with Chisholm, the leading contemporary champion of the justificationist tradition with respect to knowledge. But at present there is widespread (and as I see it, correct) agreement that there is no duty of the Lockean kind. Perhaps there is one of the Chisholmian kind; but isn't the exclusivist conforming to that duty if, after the sort of careful, indeed prayerful consideration I mentioned in the response to the moral objection, it still seems to him strongly that (1), say, is true and he accordingly still believes it? It is therefore very hard to see that the exclusivist is necessarily unjustified in this way.

The second possibility for understanding the charge—the charge that exclusivism is epistemically unjustified—has to do with the oft-repeated claim that exclusivism is intellectually *arbitrary*. Perhaps the idea is that there is an intellectual duty to treat similar cases similarly; the exclusivist violates this duty by arbitrarily choosing to believe (for the moment going along with the fiction that we *choose* beliefs of this sort) (1) and (2) in the face of the plurality of conflicting religious beliefs the world presents. But suppose there is such a duty. Clearly you do not violate it if you nonculpably think the beliefs in question are not on a par. And as an exclusivist, I *do* think (nonculpably, I hope) that they are not on a par: I think (1) and (2) *true* and those incompatible with either of them *false*.

The rejoinder, of course, will be that it is not alethic parity (their having the same truth value) that is at issue: it is *epistemic* parity that counts. What kind of epistemic parity? What would be relevant, here, I should think, would be *internal* or internalist epistemic parity: parity with respect to what is internally available to the believer. What is internally available to the believer includes, for example, detectable relationships between the belief in question and other beliefs you hold; so internal parity would include parity of propositional evidence. What is internally available to the believer also includes the *phenomenology* that goes with the beliefs in question: the *sensuous* phenomenology but also the nonsensuous phenomenology involved, for example, in the belief's just having the feel of being *right*. But once

more, then, (1) and (2) are not on an internal par, for the exclusivist, with beliefs that are incompatible with them. (1) and (2), after all, seem to me to be true; they have for me the phenomenology that accompanies that seeming. The same cannot be said for propositions incompatible with them. If, furthermore, John Calvin is right in thinking that there is such a thing as the *Sensus Divinitatis* and the Internal Testimony of the Holy Spirit, then perhaps (1) and (2) are produced in me by those belief-producing processes and have for me the phenomenology that goes with them; the same is not true for propositions incompatible with them.

But then the next rejoinder: Isn't it probably true that those who reject (1) and (2) in favor of other beliefs have propositional evidence for their beliefs that is on a par with mine for my beliefs? And isn't it also probably true that the same or similar phenomenology accompanies their beliefs as accompanies mine? So that those beliefs really are epistemically and internally on a par with (1) and (2), and the exclusivist is still treating like cases differently? I don't think so; I think there really are arguments available for (1), at least, that are not available for its competitors. And as for similar phenomenology, this is not easy to say; it is not easy to look into the breast of another; the secrets of the human heart are hard to fathom; it is hard indeed to discover this sort of thing even with respect to someone you know really well. I am prepared, however, to stipulate both sorts of parity. Let's agree for purposes of argument that these beliefs are on an epistemic par in the sense that those of a different religious tradition have the same sort of internally available markers—evidence, phenomenology and the like—for their beliefs as I have for (1) and (2). What follows?

Return to the case of moral belief. King David took Bathsheba, made her pregnant, and then, after the failure of various stratagems to get her husband Uriah to think the baby was his, arranged for him to be killed. The prophet Nathan came to David and told him a story about a rich man and a poor man. The rich man had many flocks and herds; the poor man had only a single ewe lamb, which grew up with his children, "ate at his table, drank from his cup, lay in his bosom, and was like a daughter to him." The rich man had unexpected guests. Rather than slaughter one of his own sheep, he took the poor man's single ewe lamb, slaughtered it, and served it to his guests. David exploded in anger: "The man who did this deserves to die!" Then, in one of the most riveting passages in all the Bible, Nathan turns to David and declares, "You are that man!" And then David sees what he has done.

My interest here is in David's reaction to the story. I agree with David: Such injustice is utterly and despicably wrong; there are really no words for it. I believe that such an action is wrong, and I believe that the proposition that it *isn't* wrong— either because really *nothing* is wrong, or because even if some things are wrong, *this* isn't—is false. As a matter of fact, there isn't a lot I believe more strongly. I recognize, however, that there are those who disagree with me; and once more, I doubt that I could find an argument to show them that I am right and they wrong. Further, for all I know, their conflicting beliefs have for them the same internally available epistemic markers, the same phenomenology, as mine have for me. Am I then being arbitrary, treating similar cases differently in continuing to hold, as I do, that in fact that kind of behavior *is* dreadfully wrong? I don't think so. Am I wrong in thinking racial bigotry despicable, even though I know that there are others who disagree, and even if I think they have the same internal markers for their beliefs as I have for mine? I don't think so. I believe in serious actualism, the view that no objects have properties in worlds in which they do not exist, not even nonexistence. Others do not believe this, and perhaps the internal markers of their dissenting views have for them the same quality as my views have for me. Am I being arbitrary in continuing to think as I do? I can't see how.

And the reason here is this: in each of these cases, the believer in question doesn't really think the beliefs in question *are* on a relevant epistemic par. She may agree that she and those who dissent are equally convinced of the truth of their belief and even that they are internally on a par, that the internally available markers are similar, or relevantly similar. But she must still think that there is an important epistemic difference, she thinks that somehow the other person has *made a mistake,* or *has a blind spot,* or hasn't been wholly attentive, or hasn't received some grace she has, or is in some way epistemically less fortunate. And, of course, the pluralist critic is in no better case. He thinks the thing to do when there is internal epistemic parity is to withhold judgment; he knows that there are others who don't think so, and for all he knows that belief has internal parity with his; if he continues in that belief, therefore, he will be in the same condition as the exclusivist; and if he doesn't continue in this belief, he no longer has an objection to the exclusivist.

But couldn't I be wrong? Of course I could! But I don't avoid that risk by withholding all religious (or philosophical or moral) beliefs; I can go wrong that way as well as any other, treating all religions, or all philosophical thoughts, or all moral views as on a par. Again, there is no safe haven here, no way to avoid risk. In particular, you won't reach a safe haven by trying to take the same attitude toward all the historically available patterns of belief and withholding; for in so doing, you adopt a particular pattern of belief and withholding, one incompatible with some adopted by others. "You pays your money and you takes your choice," realizing that you, like anyone else, can be desperately wrong. But what else can you do? You don't really have an alternative. And how can you do better than believe and withhold according to what, after serious and responsible consideration, seems to you to be the right pattern of belief and withholding?

Irrationality

I therefore can't see how it can be sensibly maintained that the exclusivist is unjustified in his exclusivist views; but perhaps, as is sometimes claimed, he or his view is *irrational*. Irrationality, however, is many things to many people; so there is a prior question: What is it to be irrational? More exactly, precisely what quality is it that the objector is attributing to the exclusivist (in condition *C*) when the former says the latter's exclusivist beliefs are irrational? Since the charge is never developed at all fully, it isn't easy to say. So suppose we simply consider the main varieties of irrationality (or, if you prefer, the main senses of "irrational") and ask whether any of them attach to the exclusivist just by virtue of being an exclusivist. I believe there are substantially five varieties of rationality, five distinct but analogically connected senses of the term *rational*; fortunately not all of them require detailed consideration.

Aristotelian Rationality   This is the sense in which man is a rational animal, one that has *ratio*, one that can look before and after, can hold beliefs, make inferences and is capable of knowledge. This is perhaps the basic sense, the one of which the others are analogical extensions. It is also, presumably irrelevant in the present context; at any rate I hope the objector does not mean to hold that an exclusivist will by that token no longer be a rational animal.

The Deliverances of Reason   To be rational in the Aristotelian sense is to possess reason: the power of thinking, believing, inferring, reasoning, knowing. Aristotelian rationality is thus *generic*. But there is an important more specific sense lurking in the neighborhood; this is the sense that goes with reason taken more narrowly, as the source of a priori knowledge and belief. An important use of *rational* analogically connected with the first has to do with reason taken in this more narrow way. It is by reason thus construed that we know *self-evident* beliefs—beliefs so obvious that you can't so much as grasp them without seeing that they couldn't be false. These will be among the *deliverances of reason*. Of course there are other beliefs—$38 \times 39 = 1482$, for example—that are not self-evident but are a consequence of self-evident beliefs by way of arguments that are self-evidently valid; these too are among the deliverances of reason. So say that the deliverances of reason is the set of those propositions that are self-evident for us human beings, closed under self-evident consequence. This yields another sense of rationality: a belief is *rational* if it is among the deliverances of reason and *irrational* if it is contrary to the deliverances of reason. (A belief

can therefore be neither rational nor irrational, in this sense.) This sense of *rational* is an analogical extension of the fundamental sense, but it is itself extended by analogy to still other senses. Thus, we can broaden the category of reason to include memory, experience, induction, probability, and whatever else goes into science; this is the sense of the term when reason is sometimes contrasted with faith. And we can also soften the requirement for self-evidence, recognizing both that self-evidence or a priori warrant is a matter of degree and that there are many propositions that have a priori warrant, but are not such that no one who understands them can fail to believe them.[11]

Is the exclusivist irrational in *these* senses? I think not; at any rate, the question whether he is isn't the question at issue. His exclusivist beliefs are irrational in these senses only if there is a good argument from the deliverances of reason (taken broadly) to the denials of what he believes. I do not believe that there are any such arguments. Presumably, the same goes for the pluralist objector: at any rate, his objection is not that (1) and (2) are demonstrably false or even that there are good arguments against them from the deliverances of reason; his objection is instead that there is something wrong or subpar with believing them in condition *C*. This sense too, then, is irrelevant to our present concerns.

The Deontological Sense   This sense of the term has to do with intellectual *requirement*, or *duty*, or *obligation*; a person's belief is irrational in this sense if in forming or holding it she violates such a duty. This is the sense of *irrational* in which according to many contemporary evidentialist objectors to theistic belief, those who believe in God without propositional evidence are irrational. Irrationality in this sense is a matter of failing to conform to intellectual or epistemic duties; the analogical connection with the first, Aristotelian sense is that these duties are thought to be among the deliverances of reason (and hence among the deliverances of the power by virtue of which human beings are rational in the Aristotelian sense). But we have already considered whether the exclusivist is flouting duties; we need say no more about the matter here. As we say, the exclusivist is not necessarily irrational in this sense either.

Zweckrationalität   A common and very important notion of rationality is *means-end rationality*—what our continental cousins, following Max Weber, sometimes call *Zweckrationalität*, the sort of rationality displayed by your actions if they are well calculated to achieve your goals. (Again, the analogical connection with the first sense is clear: The calculation in question requires the power by virtue of which we are rational in Aristotle's sense.) Clearly, there is a whole constellation of notions lurking in the nearby bushes: What would *in fact* contribute to your goals? What you *take* it would contribute to your goals? What you *would* take it would contribute to your goals if you were sufficiently acute, or knew enough, or weren't distracted by lust, greed, pride, ambition, and the like? What you would take it would contribute to your goals if you weren't thus distracted and were also to reflect sufficiently? and so on. This notion of rationality has assumed enormous importance in the last 150 years or so. (Among its laurels, for example, is the complete domination of the development of the discipline of economics.) Rationality thus construed is a matter of knowing how to get what you want; it is the cunning of reason. Is the exclusivist properly charged with irrationality in this sense? Does his believing in the way he does interfere with his attaining some of his goals, or is it a markedly inferior way of attaining those goals?

An initial *caveat*: It isn't clear that this notion of rationality applies to belief at all. It isn't clear that in *believing* something, I am acting to achieve some goal. If believing is an action at all, it is very far from being the paradigmatic kind of action taken to achieve some end; we don't have a choice as to whether to have beliefs, and we don't have a lot of choice with respect to which beliefs we have. But suppose we set this *caveat* aside and stipulate for purposes of argument that we have sufficient control over our beliefs for them to qualify as actions. Would the exclusivist's beliefs then be irrational in this sense? Well, that depends upon what his goals

are; if among his goals for religious belief is, for example, not believing anything not believed by someone else, then indeed it would be. But, of course, he needn't have that goal. If I do have an end or goal in holding such beliefs as (1) and (2), it would presumably be that of believing the truth on this exceedingly important matter or perhaps that of trying to get in touch as adequately as possible with God, or more broadly with the deepest reality. And if (1) and (2) are *true*, believing them will be a way of doing exactly that. It is only if they are *not* true, then, that believing them could sensibly be thought to be irrational in this means–ends sense. Because the objector does not propose to take as a premise the proposition that (1) and (2) are false—he holds only that there is some flaw involved in *believing* them—this also is presumably not what he means.

Rationality as Sanity and Proper Function
One in the grip of pathological confusion, or flight of ideas, or certain kinds of agnosia, or the manic phase of manic-depressive psychosis will often be said to be irrational; the episode may pass, after which he has regained rationality. Here *rationality* means absence of dysfunction, disorder, impairment, or pathology with respect to rational faculties. So this variety of rationality is again analogically related to Aristotelian rationality; a person is rational in this sense when no malfunction obstructs her use of the faculties by virtue of the possession of which she is rational in the Aristotelian sense. Rationality as sanity does not require possession of particularly exalted rational faculties; it requires only normality (in the nonstatistical sense) or health, or proper function. This use of the term, naturally enough, is prominent in psychiatric discussions—Oliver Sacks's male patient who mistook his wife for a hat, for example, was thus irrational. This fifth and final sense of rationality is itself a family of analogically related senses. The fundamental sense here is that of sanity and proper function, but there are other closely related senses. Thus, we may say that a belief (in certain circumstances) is irrational, not because no sane person would hold it, but because no person who was sane

and had also undergone a certain course of education would hold it or because no person who was sane and furthermore was as intelligent as we and our friends would hold it; alternatively and more briefly, the idea is not merely that no one who was functioning properly in those circumstances would hold it, but rather no one who was functioning *optimally*, as well or nearly as well as human beings ordinarily do (leaving aside the occasional great genius) would hold it. And this sense of rationality leads directly to the notion of *warrant*; I turn now to that notion; in treating it, we will also treat *ambulando*—this fifth kind of irrationality.

Warrant

So we come to the third version of the epistemic objection: that at any rate the exclusivist doesn't have warrant, or anyway *much* warrant (enough warrant for knowledge) for his exclusivistic views. Many pluralists—for example, Hick, Runzo, and Cantwell Smith—unite in declaring that, at any rate, the exclusivist certainly can't *know* that his exclusivistic views are true. But is this really true? I will argue briefly that it is not. At any rate, from the perspective of each of the major contemporary accounts of knowledge, it may very well be that the exclusivist knows (1) or (2) or both. First, consider the two main internalistic accounts of knowledge: the justified true belief accounts and the coherentist accounts. As I have already argued, it seems clear that a theist, a believer in (1) could certainly be *justified* (in the primary sense) in believing as she does: she could be flouting no intellectual or cognitive duties or obligations. But then on the most straightforward justified true belief account of knowledge, she can also *know* that it is true—if, that is, it *can* be true. More exactly, what must be possible is that both the exclusivist is justified in believing (1) and/or (2) and they be true. Presumably, the pluralist does not mean to dispute this possibility.

For concreteness, consider the account of justification given by the classical foundationalist Chisholm. On this view, a belief has warrant for me to the extent that accepting it is apt for the fulfillment of my epistemic duty, which (roughly speaking) is

that of trying to get and remain in the right relation to the truth. But if after the most careful, thorough, open, and prayerful consideration, it still seems to me—perhaps more strongly than ever—that (1) and (2) are true, then clearly accepting them has great aptness for the fulfillment of that duty.

A similarly brief argument can be given with respect to *coherentism*, the view that what constitutes warrant is coherence with some body of belief. We must distinguish two varieties of coherentism. On the one hand, it might be held that what is required is coherence with some or all of the other beliefs I actually hold; on the other, that what is required is coherence with my *verific* noetic structure (Keith Lehrer's term): the set of beliefs that remains when all the false ones are deleted or replaced by their contradictories. But surely a coherent set of beliefs could include both (1) and (2) together with the beliefs involved in being in condition *C*, what would be required, perhaps, would be that the set of beliefs contain some explanation of why it is that others do not believe as I do. And if (1) and (2) are true, then surely (and a fortiori) there can be coherent verific noetic structures that include them. Hence, neither of these versions of coherentism rule out the possibility that the exclusivist in condition *C* could know (1) and/or (2).

And now consider the main externalist accounts. The most popular externalist account at present would be one or another version of *reliabilism*. And there is an oft-repeated pluralistic argument that seems to be designed to appeal to reliabilist intuitions. The conclusion of this argument is not always clear, but here is its premise, in Hick's words:

> For it is evident that in some ninety-nine percent of cases the religion which an individual professes and to which he or she adheres depends upon the accidents of birth. Someone born to Buddhist parents in Thailand is very likely to be a Buddhist, someone born to Muslim parents in Saudi Arabia to be a Muslim, someone born to Christian parents in Mexico to be a Christian, and so on.

As a matter of sociological fact, this may be right. Furthermore, it can certainly produce a sense of intellectual vertigo. But what is one to do with this fact, if fact it is, and what follows from it? Does it follow, for example, that I ought not to accept the religious views that I have been brought up to accept, or the ones that I find myself inclined to accept, or the ones that seem to me to be true? Or that the belief-producing processes that have produced those beliefs in me are unreliable? Surely not. Furthermore, self-referential problems once more loom; this argument is another philosophical tar baby.

For suppose we concede that if I had been born of Muslim parents in Morocco rather than Christian parents in Michigan, my beliefs would have been quite different. (For one thing, I probably wouldn't believe that I was born in Michigan.) The same goes for the pluralist. Pluralism isn't and hasn't been widely popular in the world at large; if the pluralist had been born in Madagascar, or medieval France, he probably wouldn't have been a pluralist. Does it follow that he shouldn't be a pluralist or that his pluralist beliefs are produced in him by an unreliable belief-producing process? I doubt it. Suppose I hold the following, or something similar:

(4) If S's religious or philosophical beliefs are such that if S had been born elsewhere and else when, she wouldn't have held them, then those beliefs are produced by unreliable belief producing mechanisms and hence have no warrant.

Once more I will be hoist with my own petard. For in all probability, someone born in Mexico to Christian parents wouldn't believe (4) itself. No matter what philosophical and religious beliefs we hold and withhold (so it seems), there are places and times such that if we have been born there and then, then we would not have displayed the pattern of holding and withholding of religious and philosophical beliefs we *do* display. As I said, this can indeed be vertiginous; but what can we make of it? What can we infer from it about what has warrant and how we should conduct our intellectual lives?

That's not easy to say. Can we infer *anything at all* about what has warrant or how we should conduct our intellectual lives? Not obviously.

To return to reliabilism then: For simplicity, let's take the version of reliabilism according to which S knows p if the belief that p is produced in S by a reliable belief producing mechanism or process. I don't have the space here to go into this matter in sufficient detail, but it seems pretty clear that if (1) and (2) are true, then it *could* be that the beliefs that (1) and (2) be produced in me by a reliable belief-producing process. For either we are thinking of *concrete* belief-producing processes, like your memory or John's powers of a priori reasoning (tokens as opposed to types), or else we are thinking of types of belief-producing processes (type reliabilism). The problem with the latter is that there are an enormous number of *different* types of belief-producing processes for any given belief, some of which are reliable and some of which are not; the problem (and a horrifying problem it is) is to say which of these is the type the reliability of which determines whether the belief in question has warrant. So the first (token reliabilism) is a better way of stating reliabilism. But then clearly enough if (1) or (2) are true, they could be produced in me by a reliable belief-producing process. Calvin's *Sensus Divinitatis*, for example, could be working in the exclusivist in such a way as to reliably produce the belief that (1) is true; Calvin's Internal Testimony of the Holy Spirit could do the same for (2). If (1) and (2) are true, therefore, then from a reliabilist perspective there is no reason whatever to think that the exclusivist might not know that they are true.

There is another brand of externalism which seems to me to be closer to the truth than reliabilism; call it (*faute de mieux*) "proper functionalism." This view can be stated to a first approximation as follows: S knows p if (1) the belief that p is produced in S by cognitive faculties that are functioning properly (working as they ought to work, suffering from no dysfunction), (2) the cognitive environment in which p is produced is appropriate for those faculties, (3) the purpose of the module of the epistemic faculties producing the belief in question is to produce true beliefs (alternatively, the module of the design plan governing the production of p is aimed at the production of true beliefs), and (4) the objective probability of a belief's being true, given that it is produced under those conditions, is high. All of this needs explanation, of course; for present purposes, perhaps, we can collapse the account into the first condition. But then clearly it could be, if (1) and (2) are true, that they are produced in me by cognitive faculties functioning properly under condition C. For suppose (1) is true. Then it is surely possible that God has created us human beings with something like Calvin's *Sensus Divinitatis*, a belief-producing process that in a wide variety of circumstances functions properly to produce (1) or some very similar belief. Furthermore it is also possible that in response to the human condition of sin and misery, God has provided for us human beings a means of salvation, which he has revealed in the Bible. Still further, perhaps he has arranged for us to come to believe what he means to teach there by way of the operation of something like the Internal Testimony of the Holy Spirit of which Calvin speaks. So on this view, too, if (1) and (2) are true, it is certainly possible that the exclusivist know that they are. We can be sure that the exclusivist's views are irrational in this sense, then, only if they are false; but the pluralist objector does not mean to claim that they are false; this version of the objection, therefore, also fails. The exclusivist isn't necessarily irrational, and indeed might *know* that (1) and (2) are true, if indeed they *are* true.

All this seems right. But don't the realities of religious pluralism count for anything at all? Is there nothing at all to the claims of the pluralists? Could that really be right? Of course not. For many or most exclusivists, I think, an awareness of the enormous variety of human religious response functions as a *defeater* for such beliefs as (1) and (2)—an *undercutting defeater*, as opposed to a rebutting defeater. It calls into question, to some degree or other, the sources of one's belief in (1) or (2). It doesn't or needn't do so by way of an *argument*; and indeed

there isn't a very powerful argument from the proposition that many apparently devout people around the world dissent from (1) and (2) to the conclusion that (1) and (2) are false. Instead, it works more directly; it directly reduces the level of confidence or degree of belief in the proposition in question. From a Christian perspective, this situation of religious pluralism and our awareness of it is itself a manifestation of our miserable human condition; and it may deprive us of some of the comfort and peace the Lord has promised his followers. It can also deprive the exclusivist of the *knowledge* that (1) and (2) *are* true, if even they are true and he *believes* that they are. Because degree of warrant depends in part on degree of belief, it is possible, though not necessary, that knowledge of the facts of religious pluralism should reduce an exclusivist's degree of belief and hence of warrant for (1) and (2) in such a way as to deprive him of knowledge of (1) and (2). He might be such that if he *hadn't* known the facts of pluralism, then he would have known (1) and (2), but now that he *does* know those facts, he doesn't know (1) and (2). In this way, he may come to know less by knowing more.

Things *could* go this way with the exclusivist. On the other hand, they *needn't* go this way. Consider once more the moral parallel. Perhaps you have always believed it deeply wrong for a counselor to use his position of trust to seduce a client. Perhaps you discover that others disagree; they think it more like a minor peccadillo, like running a red light when there's no traffic; and you realize that possibly these people have the same internal markers for their beliefs that you have for yours. You think the matter over more fully, imaginatively recreate and rehearse such situations, become more aware of just what is involved in such a situation (the breach of trust, the breaking of implied promises, the injustice and unfairness, the nasty irony of a situation in which someone comes to a counselor seeking help but receives only hurt), and come to believe even more fully that such an action is wrong—and indeed to have more warrant for that belief. But something similar can happen in the case of religious beliefs. A fresh or heightened awareness of the facts of religious pluralism could bring about a reappraisal of one's religious life, a reawakening, a new or renewed and deepened grasp and apprehension of (1) and (2). From Calvin's perspective, it could serve as an occasion for a renewed and more powerful working of the belief-producing processes by which we come to apprehend (1) and (2). In that way, knowledge of the facts of pluralism could initially serve as a defeater, but in the long run have precisely the opposite effect.

NOTES

1. *Colloquium Heptaplomeres de Rerum Sublimium Arcanis Abditis*, written by 1593 but first published in 1857. English translation by Marion Kuntz (Princeton, N.J.: Princeton Univ. Press, 1975), p. 256.

2. Joseph Runzo: "Today, the impressive piety and evident rationality of the belief systems of other religious traditions, inescapably confronts Christians with a crisis and a potential revolution." "God, Commitment, and Other Faiths: Pluralism vs. Relativism," *Faith and Philosophy* 5, no. 4 (October 1988): 343f

3. Gary Gutting: "Applying these considerations to religious belief, we seem led to the conclusion that, because believers have many epistemic peers who do not share their belief in God..., they have no right to maintain their belief without a justification. If they do so, they are guilty of epistemological egoism." *Religious Belief and Religious Skepticism* (Notre Dame, Ind.: Univ. of Notre Dame Press, 1982), p. 90 (but see the following pages for an important qualification).

4. Wilfred Cantwell Smith: "Here my submission is that on this front the traditional doctrinal position of the Church has in fact militated against its traditional moral position, and has in fact encouraged Christians to approach other men immorally. Christ has taught us humility, but we have approached them with arrogance.... This charge of arrogance is a serious one." *Religious Diversity* (New York: Harper & Row, 1976), p. 13.

5. Runzo: "Ethically, Religious Exclusivism has the morally repugnant result of making those who have privileged knowledge, or who are intellectually astute, a religious elite, while penalizing those who happen to have no access to the putatively correct religious view, or who are incapable of advanced understanding." Op. cit., p. 348.

6. John Hick: "But natural pride, despite its positive contribution to human life, becomes harmful when it is elevated to the level of dogma and is built into the belief system of a religious community. This happens when its sense of its own validity and worth is expressed in doctrines implying an exclusive or a decisively superior access to the truth or the power to save." "Religious Pluralism and Absolute Claims," *Religious Pluralism* (Notre Dame, Ind.: Univ. of Notre Dame Press, 1984), p. 197.

7. John Cobb: "I agree with the liberal theists that even in Pannenberg's case, the quest for an absolute as a basis for understanding reflects the long tradition of Christian imperialism and triumphalism rather than the pluralistic spirit." "The Meaning of Pluralism or Christian Self-Understanding," *Religious Pluralism*, ed. Leroy Rouner (Notre Dame, Ind.: Univ. of Notre Dame Press, 1984), p. 171.

8. "God, Commitment, and Other Faiths: Pluralism vs. Relativism," *Faith and Philosophy* 5, no. 4 (October 1988):357.

9. Smith, op. cit., p. 14.

10. John Hick: "... the only reason for treating one's tradition differently from others is the very human but not very cogent reason that it is one's own!" *An Interpretation of Religion*, loc. cit.

11. *An Interpretation of Religion* (New Haven, Conn.: Yale Univ. Press, 1989), p. 2.

VI.3

Hick's Religious Pluralism and "Reformed Epistemology"—A Middle Ground

DAVID BASINGER

David Basinger is professor of philosophy at Roberts Wesleyan College in Rochester, New York, and is the author of several works in the philosophy of religion. His goal in this article is to analyze comparatively the influential argument for religious pluralism offered by John Hick and the argument for religious exclusivism (sectarianism) that can be generated by proponents of what has come to be labeled "Reformed epistemology." He argues that while Hick and the Reformed exclusivist appear to be giving us incompatible responses to the same question about the true nature of "religious" reality, they are actually responding to related but distinct questions, each of which must be considered by those desiring to give a religious explanation for the phenomenon of religious diversity. Moreover, he concludes that the insights of neither ought to be emphasized at the expense of the other.

No one denies that the basic tenets of many religious perspectives are, if taken literally, quite incompatible. The salvific claims of some forms of Judeo-Christian thought, for example, condemn the proponents of all other perspectives to hell, while the incompatible salvific claims of some forms of Islamic thought do the same.

Such incompatibility is normally explained in one of three basic ways. The nontheist argues that all religious claims are false, the product perhaps of wish fulfillment. The religious pluralist argues that the basic claims of at least all of the major world religions are more or less accurate descriptions of the same reality. Finally, the religious exclusivist argues that the tenets of only one religion (or some limited number of religions) are to any significant degree accurate descriptions of reality.

The purpose of this discussion is to analyze comparatively the influential argument for religious pluralism offered by John Hick and the argument for religious exclusivism which can be (and perhaps has been) generated by proponents of what has come to be labeled "Reformed Epistemology." I shall argue that while Hick and the Reformed epistemologist appear to be giving us incompatible responses to the same question about the true nature of "religious" reality, they are actually responding to related, but distinct questions, each of which must be considered by those desiring to give a religious explanation for the phenomenon of religious diversity. Moreover, I shall conclude that the insights offered by both Hick and the Reformed epistemologist are of value and, accordingly, that those of neither ought to be emphasized at the expense of the other.

JOHN HICK'S THEOLOGICAL PLURALISM

Hick's contention is not that different religions make no conflicting truth claims. In fact, he

Reprinted from *Faith and Philosophy* 5 (1988): 421–32, by permission. Endnotes deleted.

believes that "the differences of belief between (and within) the traditions are legion," and has often in great detail discussed them. His basic claim, rather, is that such differences are best seen as "different ways of conceiving and experiencing the one ultimate divine Reality."

However, if the various religions are really "responses to a single ultimate transcendent Reality," how then do we account for such significant differences? The best explanation, we are told, is the assumption that "the limitless divine reality has been thought and experienced by different human mentalities forming and formed by different intellectual frameworks and devotional techniques." Or, as Hick has stated the point elsewhere, the best explanation is the assumption that the correspondingly different ways of responding to divine reality "owe their differences to the modes of thinking, perceiving and feeling which have developed within the different patterns of human existence embodied in the various cultures of the earth." Each "constitutes a valid context of salvation/liberation; but none constitutes the one and only such context."

But why accept such a pluralistic explanation? Why not hold, rather, that there is no higher Reality beyond us and thus that all religious claims are false—i.e., why not opt for naturalism? Or why not adopt the exclusivistic contention that the religious claims of only one perspective are true?

Hick does not reject naturalism because he sees it to be an untenable position. It is certainly *possible*, he tells us, that the "entire realm of [religious] experience is delusory or hallucinatory, simply a human projection, and not in any way or degree a result of the presence of a greater divine reality." In fact, since the "universe of which we are part is religiously ambiguous," it is not even *unreasonable* or *implausible* "to interpret any aspect of it, including our religious experience, in non-religious as well as religious ways."

However, he is quick to add, "it is perfectly reasonable and sane for us to trust our experience"—including our religious experience—"as generally cognitive of reality except when we have some reason to doubt it." Moreover, "the mere theo-

retical possibility that any or all [religious experience] may be illusory does not count as a reason to doubt it." Nor is religious experience overturned by the fact that the great religious figures of the past, including Jesus, held a number of beliefs which we today reject as arising from the now outmoded science of their day, or by the fact that some people find "it impossible to accept that the profound dimension of pain and suffering is the measure of the cost of creation through creaturely freedom."

He acknowledges that those who have "no positive ground for religious belief within their own experience" often do see such factors as "insuperable barriers" to religious belief. But given the ambiguous nature of the evidence, he argues, it cannot be demonstrated that all rational people must see it this way. That is, belief in a supernatural realm can't be shown to be any less plausible than disbelief. Accordingly, he concludes, "those who actually participate in this field of religious experience are fully entitled, as sane and rational persons, to take the risk of trusting their own experience together with that of their tradition, and of proceeding to live and to believe on the basis of it, rather than taking the alternative risk of distrusting it and so—for the time being at least—turning their backs on God."

But why choose pluralism as the best religious hypothesis? Why does Hick believe we ought not be exclusivists? It is not because he sees exclusivism as incoherent. It is certainly possible, he grants, that "one particular 'Ptolemaic' religious vision does correspond uniquely with how things are." Nor does Hick claim to have some privileged "cosmic vantage point from which [he can] observe both the divine reality in itself and the different partial human awarenesses of that reality." But when we individually consider the evidence in the case, he argues, the result is less ambiguous. When "we start from the phenomenological fact of the various forms of religious experience, and we seek an hypothesis which will make sense of this realm of phenomena" from a religious point of view, "the theory that most naturally suggests itself postulates a divine Reality which is itself limitless, exceeding the scope of human conceptuality and language, but which is humanly thought and experienced in various conditioned and limited ways."

What is this evidence which makes the pluralistic hypothesis so "considerably more probable" than exclusivism? For one thing, Hick informs us, a credible religious hypothesis must account for the fact, "evident to ordinary people (even though not always taken into account by theologians) that in the great majority of cases—say 98 to 99 percent—the religion in which a person believes and to which he adheres depends upon where he was born." Moreover, a credible hypothesis must account for the fact that within all of the major religious traditions, "basically the same salvific process is taking place, namely the transformation of human existence from self-centeredness to Reality-centeredness." And while pluralism "illuminates" these otherwise baffling facts, the strict exclusivist's view "has come to seem increasingly implausible and unrealistic."

But even more importantly, he maintains, a credible religious hypothesis must account for the fact, of which "we have become irreversibly aware in the present century, as the result of anthropological, sociological and psychological studies and the work of philosophy of language, that there is no one universal and invariable" pattern for interpreting human experience, but rather a range of significantly different patterns or conceptual schemes "which have developed within the major cultural streams." And when considered in light of this, Hick concludes, a "pluralistic theory becomes inevitable."

THE REFORMED OBJECTION

There are two basic ways in which Hick's pluralistic position can be critiqued. One "appropriate critical response," according to Hick himself, "would be to offer a better [religious] hypothesis." That is, one way to challenge Hick is to claim that the evidence he cites is better explained by some form of exclusivism.

But there is another, potentially more powerful type of objection, one which finds its roots in the currently popular "Reformed Epistemology" being championed by philosophers such as Alvin Plantinga. I will first briefly outline Plantinga's latest version of this epistemological approach and then discuss its impact on Hick's position.

According to Plantinga, it has been widely held since the Enlightenment that if theistic beliefs—e.g., religious hypotheses—are to be considered rational, they must be based on propositional evidence. It is not enough for the theist just to refute objections to any such belief. The theist "must also have something like an argument for the belief, or some positive reason to think that the belief is true." But this is incorrect, Plantinga maintains. There are beliefs which acquire their warrant propositionally—i.e., have warrant conferred on them by an evidential line of reasoning from other beliefs. And for such beliefs, it may well be true that proponents need something like an argument for their veridicality.

However, there are also, he tells us, *basic* beliefs which are not based on propositional evidence and, thus, do not require propositional warrant. In fact, *if* such beliefs can be affirmed "without either violating an epistemic duty or displaying some kind of noetic defect," they can be considered *properly* basic. And, according to Plantinga, many theistic beliefs can be properly basic: "Under widely realized conditions it is perfectly rational, reasonable, intellectually respectable and acceptable to believe [certain theistic tenets] without believing [them] on the basis of [propositional] evidence."

But what are such conditions? Under what conditions can a belief have positive epistemic status if it is not conferred by other propositions whose epistemic status is not in question? The answer, Plantinga informs us, lies in an analysis of belief formation.

[We have] cognitive faculties designed to enable us to achieve true beliefs with respect to a wide variety of propositions—propositions about our immediate environment, about our interior lives, about the thoughts and experiences of other persons, about our universe at large, about right and wrong, about the whole realm of *abstracta*—numbers, properties, propositions, states of affairs, possible worlds and their like, about modality—what is necessary and possible—and about [ourselves]. These faculties work in such a way that under the appropriate circumstances we form the appropriate belief. More exactly, the appropriate belief is *formed in us*; in the typical case we do not *decide* to hold or form the belief in question, but simply find ourselves with it. Upon considering an instance of *modus ponens*, I find myself believing its corresponding conditional; upon being appeared to in the familiar way, I find myself holding the belief that there is a large tree before me; upon being asked what I had for breakfast, I reflect for a moment and find myself with the belief that what I had was eggs on toast. In these and other cases I do not *decide* what to believe; I don't total up the evidence (I'm being appeared to redly; on most occasions when thus appeared to I am in the presence of something red, so most probably in this case I am) and make a decision as to what seems best supported; I simply find myself believing.

And from a theistic point of view, Plantinga continues, the same is true in the religious realm. Just as it is true that when our senses or memory are functioning properly, "appropriate belief is formed in us," so it is that God has created us with faculties which will, "when they are working the way they were designed to work by the being who designed and created us and them," produce true theistic beliefs. Moreover, if these faculties are functioning properly, a basic belief thus formed has "positive epistemic status to the degree [the individual in question finds herself] inclined to accept it."

What, though, of the alleged counter-evidence to such theistic beliefs? What, for example, of all the arguments the conclusion of which is that God does not exist? Can they all be dismissed as irrelevant? Not immediately, answers Plantinga. We must seriously consider potential defeaters of our basic beliefs. With respect to the belief that God exists, for example, we must seriously consider the claim that religious belief is mere wish fulfillment and the claim that God's existence is incompatible with (or at least improbable given) the amount of evil in the world.

But to undercut such defeaters, he continues, we need not engage in positive apologetics: produce propositional evidence for our beliefs. We need only engage in negative apologetics: refute such arguments. Moreover, it is Plantinga's conviction that such defeaters do normally exist. "The non-propositional warrant enjoyed by [a person's] belief in God, for example, [seems] itself sufficient to turn back the challenge offered by some alleged defeaters"—e.g., the claim that theistic belief is mere wish fulfillment. And other defeaters such as the "problem of evil," he tells us, can be undercut by identifying validity or soundness problems or even by appealing to the fact that "experts think it unsound or that the experts are evenly divided as to its soundness."

Do Plantinga or other proponents of this Reformed epistemology maintain that their exclusivistic religious hypotheses are properly basic and can thus be "defended" in the manner just outlined? I am not *certain* that they do. However, when Plantinga, for example, claims that "God exists" is for most adult theists properly basic, he appears to have in mind a classical Christian conception of the divine—i.e., a being who is the triune, omnipotent, omniscient, perfectly good, *ex nihilo* creator of the universe. In fact, given his recent claim that "the internal testimony of the Holy Spirit . . . is a source of reliable and perfectly acceptable beliefs about what is communicated [by God] in Scripture," and the manner in which most who make such a claim view the truth claims of the other world religions, it would appear that Plantinga's "basic" conception of God is quite exclusive.

However, even if no Reformed epistemologist actually does affirm an exclusivistic hypothesis she claims is properly basic, it is obvious that the Reformed analysis of belief justification can be used to critique Hick's line of reasoning. Hick claims that an objective inductive assessment of the relevant evidence makes his pluralistic thesis a more plausible religious explanation than any of the competing exclusivistic hypotheses. But a Reformed exclusivist could easily argue that this approach to the issue is misguided. My affirmation of an exclusivistic Christian perspective, such an argument might begin, is not evidential in nature. It is, rather, simply a belief I have found formed in me, much like the belief that I am seeing a tree in front of me or the belief that killing innocent children is wrong.

Now, of course, I must seriously consider the allegedly formidable defeaters with which pluralists such as Hick have presented me. I must consider the fact, for example, that the exclusive beliefs simply formed in most people are not similar to mine, but rather tend to mirror those beliefs found in the cultures in which such people have been raised. But I do not agree with Hick that this fact is best explained by a pluralistic hypothesis. I attribute this phenomenon to other factors such as the epistemic blindness with which most of humanity has been plagued since the fall.

Moreover, to defend my position—to maintain justifiably (rationally) that I am right and Hick is wrong—I need not, as Hick seems to suggest, produce objective "proof" that his hypothesis is weaker than mine. That is, I need not produce "evidence" that would lead most rational people to agree with me. That would be to involve myself in Classical Foundationalism, which is increasingly being recognized as a bankrupt epistemological methodology. All I need do is undercut Hick's defeaters—i.e., show that his challenge does not require me to abandon my exclusivity thesis. And this I can easily do. For Hick has not demonstrated that my thesis is self-contradictory. And it is extremely doubtful that there exists any other non-question-begging criterion for plausibility by which he could even attempt to demonstrate that my thesis is less plausible (less probable) than his.

Hick, of course, believes firmly that his hypothesis makes the most sense. But why should

this bother me? By his own admission, many individuals firmly believe that, given the amount of seemingly gratuitous evil in the world, God's non-existence is by far most plausible. Yet this does not keep him from affirming theism. He simply reserves the right to see things differently and continues to believe. And there is no reason why I cannot do the same.

Moreover, even if what others believed were relevant, by Hick's own admission, the majority of theists doubt that his thesis is true. Or, at the very least, I could rightly maintain that "the experts are evenly divided as to its soundness." Thus, given the criteria for defeater assessment which we Reformed exclusivists affirm, Hick's defeaters are clearly undercut. And, accordingly, I remain perfectly justified in continuing to hold that my exclusivity thesis is correct and, therefore, that all incompatible competing hypotheses are false.

A MIDDLE GROUND

It is tempting to see Hick and the Reformed exclusivist as espousing incompatible approaches to the question of religious diversity. If Hick is correct—if the issue is primarily evidential in nature—then the Reformed exclusivist is misguided and vice versa. But this, I believe, is an inaccurate assessment of the situation. There are two equally important, but distinct, questions which arise in this context, and Hick and the Reformed exclusivist, it seems to me, each *primarily* address only one.

The Reformed exclusivist is primarily interested in the following question:

Q1. Under what conditions is an individual within her epistemic rights (is she rational) in affirming one of the many mutually exclusive religious diversity hypotheses?

In response, as we have seen, the Reformed exclusivist argues (or at least could argue) that a person need not grant that her religious hypothesis (belief) requires propositional (evidential) warrant. She is within her epistemic rights in maintaining that it is a *basic* belief. And if she does so, then to preserve rationality, she is not required to "prove" in some objective manner that her hypothesis is most plausible. She is fulfilling all epistemic requirements solely by defending her hypothesis against claims that it is less plausible than competitors.

It seems to me that the Reformed exclusivist is basically right on this point. I do believe, for reasons mentioned later in this essay, that attempts by any knowledgeable exclusivist to define her hypothesis will ultimately require her to enter the realm of positive apologetics—i.e., will require her to engage in a comparative analysis of her exclusivistic beliefs. But I wholeheartedly agree with the Reformed exclusivist's contention that to preserve rationality, she need not actually demonstrate that her hypothesis is most plausible. She need ultimately only defend herself against the claim that a thoughtful assessment of the matter makes the affirmation of some incompatible perspective—i.e., pluralism or some incompatible exclusivistic perspective— the only rational option. And this, I believe, she can clearly do.

What this means, of course, is that if Hick is actually arguing that pluralism is the only rational option, then I think he is wrong. And his claim that pluralism "is considerably more probable" than exclusivism does, it must be granted, make it appear as if he believes pluralism to be the only hypothesis a knowledgeable theist can justifiably affirm.

But Hick never actually calls his opponents irrational in this context. That is, while Hick clearly believes that sincere, knowledgeable exclusivists are *wrong*, he has never to my knowledge claimed that they are guilty of violating the basic epistemic rules governing rational belief. Accordingly, it seems best to assume that Q1—a concern with what can be rationally affirmed—is not Hick's primary interest in this context.

But what then is it with which Hick is concerned? As we have seen, Q1 is defensive in nature. It asks for identification of conditions under which we can justifiably continue to affirm a belief we *already* hold. But *why* hold the specific religious beliefs we desire to defend? Why, specifically, choose to defend religious pluralism rather than

exclusivism or vice versa? Or, to state this question of "belief origin" more formally:

Q2. Given that an individual can be within her epistemic rights (can be rational) in affirming either exclusivism or pluralism, upon what basis should her actual choice be made?

This is the type of question in which I believe Hick is primarily interested.

Now, it might be tempting for a Reformed exclusivist to contend that she is exempt from the consideration of Q2. As I see it, she might begin, this question is based on the assumption that individuals consciously choose their religious belief systems. But the exclusivistic hypothesis which I affirm was not the result of a conscious attempt to choose the most plausible option. I have simply discovered this exclusivistic hypothesis formed in me in much the same fashion I find my visual and moral beliefs just formed in me. And thus Hick's question is simply irrelevant to my position.

But such a response will not do. There is no reason to deny that Reformed exclusivists do have, let's say, a Calvinistic religious hypothesis just formed in them. However, although almost everyone in every culture does in the appropriate context have similar "tree-beliefs" just formed in them, there is no such unanimity within the religious realm. As Hick rightly points out, the religious belief that the overwhelming majority of people in any given culture find just formed in them is the dominant hypothesis of that culture or subculture. Moreover, the dominant religious hypotheses in most of these cultures are exclusivistic—i.e., incompatible with one another.

Accordingly, it seems to me that Hick can rightly be interpreted as offering the following challenge to the knowledgeable Reformed exclusivist (the exclusivist aware of pervasive religious diversity): I will grant that your exclusivistic beliefs were not originally the product of conscious deliberation. But given that most sincere theists initially go through a type of religious belief-forming process similar to yours and yet usually find formed in themselves the dominant exclusivistic hypotheses of their own culture, upon what basis can you justifiably continue to claim that the hypothesis you affirm has some special status just because you found it formed in you? Or, to state the question somewhat differently, Hick's analysis of religious diversity challenges knowledgeable Reformed exclusivists to ask themselves why they now believe that their religious belief-forming mechanisms are functioning properly while the analogous mechanisms in all others are faulty.

Some Reformed exclusivists, as we have seen, have a ready response. Because of "the fall," they maintain, most individuals suffer from religious epistemic blindness—i.e., do not possess properly functioning religious belief-forming mechanisms. Only our mechanisms are trustworthy. However, every exclusivistic religious tradition can—and many do—make such claims. Hence, an analogous Hickian question again faces knowledgeable Reformed exclusivists: Why do you believe that only those religious belief-forming mechanisms which produce exclusivistic beliefs compatible with yours do not suffer from epistemic blindness?

Reformed exclusivists cannot at this point argue that they have found this belief just formed in them for it is *now* the reliability of the belief-forming mechanism, itself, which is being questioned. Nor, since they are anti-foundationalists, can Reformed exclusivists argue that the evidence demonstrates conclusively that their religious position is correct. So upon what then can they base their crucial belief that their belief-forming mechanisms *alone* produce true beliefs?

They must, it seems to me, ultimately fall back on the contention that their belief-forming mechanisms can alone be trusted because that set of beliefs thus generated appears to them to form the most plausible religious explanatory hypothesis available. But to respond in this fashion brings them into basic methodological agreement with Hick's position on Q2. That is, it appears that knowledgeable Reformed exclusivists must ultimately maintain with Hick that when attempting to discover which of the many self-consistent hypotheses that *can* rationally be affirmed is the one that *ought* to be affirmed, a person must finally decide which hypothesis she believes best explains the phenomena.

Or, to state this important point differently yet, what Hick's analysis of religious diversity demonstrates, I believe, is that even for those knowledgeable Reformed exclusivists who claim to find their religious perspectives just formed in them, a conscious choice among competing religious hypotheses is ultimately called for.

This is not to say, it must again be emphasized, that such Reformed exclusivists must attempt to "prove" their choice is best. But, given the culturally relative nature of religious belief-forming mechanisms, a simple appeal to such a mechanism seems inadequate as a basis for such exclusivists to continue to affirm their perspective. It seems rather that knowledgeable exclusivists must ultimately make a conscious decision whether to retain the religious hypothesis that has been formed in them or choose another. And it further appears that they should feel some prima facie obligation to consider the available options—consciously consider the nature of the various religious hypotheses formed in people—before doing so.

Now, of course, to agree that such a comparative analysis should be undertaken is not to say that Hick's pluralistic hypothesis, is, in fact, the most plausible alternative. I agree with the Reformed exclusivist that "plausibility" is a very subjective concept. Thus, I doubt that the serious consideration of the competing explanatory hypotheses for religious phenomena, even by knowledgeable open-minded individuals, will produce consensus.

However, I do not see this as in any sense diminishing the importance of engaging in the type of comparative analysis suggested. For even if such comparative assessment will not lead to consensus, it will produce two significant benefits. First, only by such assessment, I feel, can a person acquire "ownership" of her religious hypothesis. That is, only by such an assessment can she insure herself that her belief is not solely the product of environmental conditioning. Second, such an assessment should lead all concerned to be more tolerant of those with whom they ultimately disagree. And in an age where radical religious exclusivism again threatens world peace, I believe such tolerance to be of inestimable value.

This does not mean, let me again emphasize in closing, that the consideration of Q1—the consideration of the conditions under which a religious hypothesis can be rationally affirmed—is unimportant or even less important than the consideration of Q2. It is crucial that we recognize who must actually shoulder the "burden of proof" in this context. And we need to thank Reformed exclusivists for helping us think more clearly about this matter. But I fear that a preoccupation with Q1 can keep us from seeing the importance of Q2—the consideration of the basis upon which we choose the hypothesis to be defended—and the comparative assessments of hypotheses to which such consideration leads us. And we need to thank pluralists such as Hick for drawing our attention to this fact.

VI.4

Buddhism, Christianity, and the Prospects for World Religion

DALAI LAMA

Dalai Lama, originally Tenzin Gyatso (1935–), the spiritual and temporal head of Tibet, was born in China. In 1937 he was designated the fourteenth Dalai Lama, but his right to rule was delayed until 1950. An ardent advocate of nonviolent liberation, he was awarded the Nobel Prize for Peace in 1989. In this selection he responds to questions from José Ignacio Cabezon on the possibility of a religious integration of Buddhism and Christianity. The Dalai Lama (referred to as "His Holiness") doesn't think such an integration is possible, for there are unique features in these religions that cannot be compromised without loss of identity. But he argues that all the major religions have much in common. They aim at the same goal of permanent happiness, and all encourage moral integrity. These common concerns should enable people of all faiths to find common ground in building a better world of peace and justice.

Question: Do you see any possibility of an integration of Christianity and Buddhism in the West? An overall religion for Western society?

His Holiness: It depends upon what you mean by integration. If you mean by this the possibility of the integration of Buddhism and Christianity within a society, where they co-exist side by side, then I would answer affirmatively. If, however, your view of integration envisions all of society following some sort of composite religion which is neither pure Buddhism nor pure Christianity, then I would have to consider this form of integration implausible.

It is, of course, quite possible for a country to be predominantly Christian, and yet that some of the people of that country choose to follow

Reprinted from *The Bodhgaya Interviews*, ed. Jose Ignacio Cabezon (Snow Lion Publications, 1988) by permission.

Buddhism. I think it is quite possible that a person who is basically a Christian, who accepts the idea of a God, who believes in God, could at the same time incorporate certain Buddhist ideas and techniques into his/her practice. The teachings of love, compassion, and kindness are present in Christianity and also in Buddhism. Particularly in the Bodhisattva vehicle there are many techniques which focus on developing compassion, kindness, etc. These are things which can be practiced at the same time by Christians and by Buddhists. While remaining committed to Christianity it is quite conceivable that a person may choose to undergo training in meditation, concentration, and onepointedness of mind, that, while remaining a Christian, one may choose to practice Buddhist ideas. This is another possible and very viable kind of integration.

Question: Is there any conflict between the Buddhist teachings and the idea of a creator God who exists independently from us?

His Holiness: If we view the world's religions from the widest possible viewpoint, and examine their ultimate goal, we find that all of the major world religions, whether Christianity or Islam, Hinduism or Buddhism, are directed to the achievement of permanent human happiness. They are all directed toward that goal. All religions emphasize the fact that the true follower must be honest and gentle, in other words, that a truly religious person must always strive to be a better human being. To this end, the different world's religions teach different doctrines which will help transform the person. In this regard, all religions are the same, there is no conflict. This is something we must emphasize. We must consider the question of religious diversity from *this* viewpoint. And when we do, we find no conflict.

Now from the philosophical point of view, the theory that God is the creator, is almighty and permanent, is in contradiction to the Buddhist teachings. From this point of view there is disagreement. For Buddhists, the universe has no first cause and hence no creator, nor can there be such a thing as a permanent, primordially pure being. So, of course, doctrinally, there is conflict. The views are opposite to one another. But if we consider the purpose of these different philosophies, then we see that they are the same. This is my belief.

Different kinds of food have different tastes: one may be very hot, one may be very sour, and one very sweet. They are opposite tastes, they conflict. But whether a dish is concocted to taste sweet, sour or hot, it is nonetheless made in this way so as to taste good. Some people prefer very spicy hot foods with a lot of chili peppers. Many Indians and Tibetans have a liking for such dishes. Others are very fond of bland tasting foods. It is a wonderful thing to have variety. It is an expression of individuality; it is a personal thing.

Likewise, the variety of the different world religious philosophies is a very useful and beautiful thing. For certain people, the idea of God as creator and of everything depending on his will is beneficial and soothing, and so for that person such a doctrine is worthwhile. For someone else, the idea that there is no creator, that ultimately, one is oneself the creator—in that everything depends upon oneself—is more appropriate. For certain people, it may be a more effective method of spiritual growth, it may be more beneficial. For such persons, this idea is better and for the other type of person, the other idea is more suitable. You see, there is no conflict, no problem. This is my belief.

Now conflicting doctrines are something which is not unknown even within Buddhism itself. The Mādhyamikas and Cittamātrins, two Buddhist philosophical subschools, accept the theory of emptiness. The Vaibhāṣikas and Sautrāntikas, two others, accept another theory, the theory of selflessness, which, strictly speaking, is not the same as the doctrine of emptiness as posited by the two higher schools. So there exists this difference, some schools accepting the emptiness of phenomena and others not. There also exists a difference as regards the way in which the two upper schools explain the doctrine of emptiness. For the Cittamātrins, emptiness is set forth in terms of the non-duality of subject and object. The Mādhyamikas, however, repudiate the notion that emptiness is tantamount to idealism, the claim that everything is of the nature of mind. So you see, even within Buddhism, the Mādhyamikas and Cittamātrins schools are in conflict. The Mādhyamikas are again divided into Prāsaṅgikas and Svātantrikas, and between these two sub-schools there is also conflict. The latter accept that things exist by virtue of an inherent characteristic, while the former do not.

So you see, conflict in the philosophical field is nothing to be surprised at. It exists within Buddhism itself. . . .

Question: I would like to know the role that consciousness plays in the process of reincarnation.

His Holiness: In general, there are different levels of consciousness. The more rough or gross levels of consciousness are very heavily dependent upon the physical or material sphere. Since one's own physical aggregate (the body) changes from birth to birth, so too do these gross levels of consciousness. The more subtle the level of consciousness, however, the more independent of the physical sphere and hence the more likely that it will remain from one life to the next. But in general, whether more subtle or more gross, all levels of consciousness are of the same nature.

Question: It is generally said that teachers of other religions, no matter how great, cannot attain liberation without turning to the Buddhist path. Now suppose there is a great teacher, say he is a Śaivite, and suppose he upholds very strict discipline and is totally dedicated to other people all of the time, always giving of himself. Is this person, simply because he follows Śiva, incapable of attaining liberation, and if so, what can be done to help him?

His Holiness: During the Buddha's own time, there were many non-Buddhist teachers whom the Buddha could not help, for whom he could do nothing. So he just let them be.

The Buddha Śākyamuni was an extraordinary being, he was the manifestation (*nirmānakāya*), the physical appearance, of an already enlightened being. But while some people recognized him as a Buddha, others regarded him as a black magician with strange and evil powers. So, you see, even the Buddha Śākyamuni himself was not accepted as an enlightened being by all of his contemporaries. Different human beings have different mental predispositions, and there are cases when even the Buddha himself could not do much to overcome these—there was a limit.

Now today, the followers of Śiva have their own religious practices and they reap some benefit from engaging in their own forms of worship. Through this, their life will gradually change. Now my own position on this question is that Śivaji's followers should practice according to their own beliefs and traditions, Christians must genuinely and sincerely follow what they believe, and so forth. That is sufficient.

Question: But they will not attain liberation!

His Holiness: We Buddhists ourselves will not be liberated at once. In our own case, it will take time. Gradually we will be able to reach *mokṣa* or *nirvāna*, but the majority of Buddhists will not achieve this within their own lifetimes. So there's no hurry. If Buddhists themselves have to wait, perhaps many lifetimes, for their goal, why should we expect that it be different for non-Buddhists? So, you see, nothing much can be done.

Suppose, for example, you try to convert someone from another religion to the Buddhist religion, and you argue with them trying to convince them of the inferiority of their position. And suppose you do not succeed, suppose they do not become Buddhist. On the one hand, you have failed in your task, and on the other hand, you may have weakened the trust they have in their own religion, so that they may come to doubt their own faith. What have you accomplished by all this? It is of no use. When we come into contact with the followers of different religions, we should not argue. Instead, we should advise them to follow their own beliefs as sincerely and as truthfully as possible. For if they do so, they will no doubt reap certain benefit. Of this there is no doubt. Even in the immediate future they will be able to achieve more happiness and more satisfaction. Do you agree?

This is the way I usually act in such matters, it is my belief. When I meet the followers of different religions, I always praise them, for it is enough, it is sufficient, that they are following the moral teachings that are emphasized in every religion. It is enough, as I mentioned earlier, that they are trying to become better human beings. This in itself is very good and worthy of praise.

Question: But is it only the Buddha who can be the ultimate source of refuge?

His Holiness: Here, you see, it is necessary to examine what is meant by liberation or salvation. Liberation in which "a mind that understands the sphere of reality annihilates all defilements in the sphere of reality" is a state that only Buddhists can accomplish. This kind of *mokṣa* or *nirvāna* is only explained in the Buddhist scriptures, and is achieved only through Buddhist practice. According to certain religions, however, salvation is a place, a beautiful paradise, like a peaceful valley. To attain such a state as this, to achieve such a state of *mokṣa*, does not require the practice of emptiness, the understanding of reality. In Buddhism itself, we believe that through the accumulation of merit one can obtain rebirth in heavenly paradises like *Tuṣita....*

Question: Could you please give us some brief advice which we can take with us into our daily lives?

His Holiness: I don't know, I don't really have that much to say—I'll simply say this. We are all human beings, and from this point of view we are the same. We all want happiness, and we do not want suffering. If we consider this point, we will find that there are no differences between people of different faiths, races, color or cultures. We all have this common wish for happiness.

Actually, we Buddhists are supposed to save all sentient beings, but practically speaking, this may be too broad a notion for most people. In any case, we must at least think in terms of helping all

human beings. This is very important. Even if we cannot think in terms of sentient beings inhabiting different worlds, we should nonetheless think in terms of the human beings on our own planet. To do this is to take a practical approach to the problem. It is necessary to help others, not only in our prayers, but in our daily lives. If we find we cannot help another, the least we can do is to desist from harming them. We must not cheat others or lie to them. We must be honest human beings, sincere human beings.

On a very practical level, such attitudes are things which we need. Whether one is a believer, a religious person, or not, is another matter. Simply as an inhabitant of the world, as a member of the human family, we need this kind of attitude. It is through such an attitude that real and lasting world peace and harmony can be achieved. Through harmony, friendship, and respecting one another, we can solve many problems. Through such means, it is possible to overcome problems in the right way, without difficulties.

This is what I believe, and wherever I go, whether it be to a communist country like the Soviet Union or Mongolia, or to a capitalist and democratic country like the United States and the countries of Western Europe, I express this same message. This is my advice, my suggestion. It is what I feel. I myself practice this as much as I can. If you find you agree with me, and you find some value in what I have said, then it has been worthwhile.

You see, sometimes religious persons, people who are genuinely engaged in the practice of religion, withdraw from the sphere of human activity. In my opinion, this is not good. It is not right. But I should qualify this. In certain cases, when a person genuinely wishes to engage in intensive meditation, for example when someone wishes to attain *śamatha*, then it is alright to seek isolation for certain limited periods of time. But such cases are by far the exception, and the vast majority of us must work out a genuine religious practice within the context of human society.

In Buddhism, both learning and practice are extremely important and they must go hand in hand. Without knowledge, just to rely on faith, faith and more faith is good but not sufficient. So the intellectual part must definitely be present. At the same time, strictly intellectual development without faith and practice, is also of no use. It is necessary to combine knowledge born from study with sincere practice in our daily lives. These two must go together. . . .

Question: The Christian notion of God is that He is omniscient, all-compassionate, all-powerful, and the creator. The Buddhist notion of Buddha is the same, except that He is not the Creator. To what extent does the Buddha exist apart from our minds, as the Christians believe their God to?

His Holiness: There are two ways of interpreting this question. The general question is whether the Buddha is a separate thing from mind. Now in one sense, this could be asking whether or not the Buddha is a phenomenon imputed or labelled by mind, and of course all phenomena in this sense must be said to be labelled by name and conceptual thought. The Buddha is not a separate phenomenon from mind because our minds impute or label Him by means of words and conceptual thought.

In another sense, the question could be asking about the relationship of buddhahood to our own minds, and in this sense we must say that buddhahood, or the state of a buddha, is the object to be attained by us. Buddhahood is the resultant object of refuge. Our minds are related to buddhahood (they are not separate from buddhahood) in the sense that this is something that we will gradually attain by the systematic purification of our minds. Hence, by purifying our minds step by step, we will eventually attain the state of buddhahood. And that buddha which we will eventually become is of the same continuity as ourselves. But that buddha which we will become is different, for example, from Śākyamuni Buddha. They are two distinct persons. We cannot attain Śākyamuni Buddha's enlightenment, because that is His own individual thing.

If instead the question is referring to whether or not our minds are separate from the state of buddhahood, and if we take buddhahood to refer to the essential purity of the mind, then of course this is something which we possess even now. Even today, our minds have the nature of essential purity. This is something called the "buddha nature." The very nature of the mind, the mere quality of knowledge and clarity without being affected by conceptual thoughts, that too we may call "buddha nature." To be exact, it is the innermost clear light mind which is called the "buddha nature."

Question: When creating merit, one must acknowledge that Christians create merit as well as Buddhists, so that the whole source of merit cannot reside solely in the object, i.e., Buddha or God, to which one is making offerings. This leads me to think that the source of merit is in our own minds. Could you please comment on this?

His Holiness: The main thing is motivation, but probably there is some difference in regard to the object to which one makes offering and so forth. The pure motivation must, however, be based on reasoning, that is, it must be verified by valid cognition; it must be unmistaken. But no doubt that the main point is the motivation.

For example, when we generate great compassion we take as our object sentient beings. But it is not due to anything on the side of sentient beings, on the part of sentient beings, that great compassion is special. It is not due to any blessing from sentient beings that great compassion is special. Nonetheless, when we meditate in this way on great compassion and we generate it from our hearts, we know that there is a tremendous amount of benefit that results from this. This is not, however, due to anything from the side of sentient beings, from the object of the great compassion. It is simply by thinking of the kindness of sentient beings and so forth that we generate great compassion and that benefit comes, but not due to the blessing of (or anything inherent in) sentient beings themselves. So strictly from the point of view of motivation, from one's own motivation, a great amount of benefit can result, isn't it so?

Likewise, when we take the Buddha as our object, if our motivation is that of great faith, of very strong faith, and we make offerings and so forth, then again, great benefit can result from this. Although a suitable object is necessary, that is, an object which, for example, has limitless good qualities, nonetheless the principal thing is our motivation, i.e., the strong faith. Still there is probably some difference as regards the kind of object to which one is making these offerings.

From one point of view, were sentient beings not to exist, then we could not take them as our object, and great compassion could not arise. So from this perspective, the object is, once again, very important. If suffering sentient beings did not exist, compassion could never arise. So from that point of view, the object, sentient beings, is a special one. . . .

Question: To what do you attribute the growing fascination in the West, especially in America, with Eastern religions. I include many, many cults and practices which are becoming extremely strong in America. To what do you attribute, in this particular age, the reasons for this fascination, and would you encourage people who are dissatisfied with their own Western way of life, having been brought up in the Mosaic religions (Christianity, Judaism and Islam), dissatisfied with their lack of spiritual refreshment, would you encourage them to search further in their own religions or to look into Buddhism as an alternative?

His Holiness: That's a tricky question. Of course, from the Buddhist viewpoint, we are all human beings and we all have every right to investigate either one's own religion or another religion. This is our right. I think that on the whole a comparative study of different religious traditions is useful.

I generally believe that every major religion has the potential for giving any human being good advice; there is no question that this is so. But we must always keep in mind that different individuals have different mental predispositions. This means that for some individuals one religious system or philosophy will be more suitable than another. The only way one can come to a proper conclusion as to what is most suitable for *oneself* is through comparative study. Hence, we look and study, and we find a teaching that is most suitable to our own taste. This, you see, is my feeling.

I cannot advise everyone to practice Buddhism. That I cannot do. Certainly, for some people the Buddhist religion or ideology is most suitable, most effective. But that does not mean it is suitable for *all*.

PART VII

Death and Immortality

Of all the many forms which natural religion has assumed none
probably has exerted so deep and far-reaching an influence on
human life as the belief in immortality and the worship of the
dead; hence [a discussion] of this momentous creed and of the
practical consequences which have been deduced from it can
hardly fail to be at once instructive and impressive, whether we
regard the record with complacency as a noble testimony to the
aspiring genius of man, who claims to outlive the sun and the
stars, or whether we view it with pity as a melancholy
monument of fruitless labour and barren ingenuity expended
in prying into that great mystery of which fools profess their
knowledge and wise men confess their ignorance.

SIR JAMES FRAZIER,
THE BELIEF IN IMMORTALITY, VOL. 1
(LONDON: MACMILLAN, 1913), VII–VIII.

IS THERE LIFE AFTER DEATH? Few questions have troubled humans as
deeply as this one. Is this finite, short existence of three score and ten years all that
we have? Or is there reason to hope for a blessed postmortem existence where
love, justice, and peace, which we now experience in only fragmented ways, will
unfold in all their fullness and enable human existence to find fulfillment? Are we
merely mortal or blessedly immortal?

Anthropological studies reveal a widespread and ancient sense of immortality.
Prehistoric societies buried their dead with food so that the deceased would not
be hungry in the next life. Most cultures and religions have some version of a
belief in another life, whether it be in the form of a resurrected body, a transmi-
grated soul, reincarnation, or an ancestral spirit present with the tribe.

Let us begin by understanding what we mean by immortality. Being immortal is not simply a matter of living on through our works or in the memories of
our loved ones. Rather, for our purposes, immortality involves freedom

from death. To be immortal is to be the sort of being who will never undergo the permanent cessation of one's conscious existence.

For most people, death is the ultimate tragedy. It is the paramount evil, for it deprives us of all that we know and love on earth. Our fear of death is profound; we have a passionate longing to live again and to be with our loved ones. And yet there is not a shred of direct empirical evidence that we shall live again. As far as we can tell scientifically, mental function is tied to brain function, so that when the latter comes permanently to an end, the former does as well. Some claim to have experienced the afterlife, but there are naturalistic explanations for such experiences and, in any case, their veridicality cannot be confirmed by empirical means.

Many have thought, however, that philosophical argument can shed light on the question of immortality. In the Western tradition three views have dominated: one denying life after death and two affirming it. The negative view, going back to the ancient Greek atomist philosophers Democritus and Leucippus, holds that we are identical with our bodies (including our brains), so that when the body dies, the self does as well. We may call this view materialist monism, because it does not allow for the possibility of a soul or spiritual self that can live without the body.

The positive views divide into dualist and monist theories of life after death. The dualist views separate the body from the soul or self of the agent and affirm that it is the soul or self that lives forever. This view was held by the pre-Socratic philosopher Pythagoras (570–500 B.C.E.) and is developed by Plato (427–347 B.C.E.). In modern philosophy it is represented by René Descartes (1596–1650). It is sometimes referred to as the Platonic-Cartesian view of immortality. These philosophers argue that we are essentially spiritual or mental beings and that our bodies are either unreal or not part of our essential selves. Death is merely the separation of our souls from our bodies, a sort of spiritual liberation.

Many in the dualist tradition maintain that the (typical) soul will be reincarnated several, perhaps many, times before attaining the final goal of permanent separation from the body. On this view—found in various strands of Pythagoreanism, Platonism, Buddhism, and Hinduism—embodiment is an undesirable state, and only those who lead the right sort of lifestyle have any hope of freeing themselves from the cycle of reincarnation. By contrast, Christian dualists deny reincarnation and maintain instead that the ultimate destination for the soul (after becoming disembodied at death) is to be re-embodied in one's *resurrected* earthly body. The difference between reincarnation and resurrection is just the difference between getting a brand new body (reincarnation) after death and getting one and the same body (resurrection). This is not to say, of course, that our bodies in the afterlife will have exactly the same properties—flaws, limitations, and so on—as our present earthly bodies. Indeed, according to the Christian tradition anyway, quite the opposite is the case: Our resurrected bodies will be greatly improved, or glorified. But the point is that the body you have in the afterlife will be the *same* body that you have now, despite its differences—much like your body after a successful diet or workout regimen is the same body you had before, albeit healthier, stronger, and in other respects better.

Although the Christian tradition has been predominantly dualistic, many Christians endorse a monistic view of immortality. This is the second of the two positive views on immortality just mentioned. On this view, either there is no soul or else the soul is not the sort of thing that can properly be said to "live" apart from the body. Either way, then, the afterlife can never be a disembodied life. Our hope for an afterlife is nothing other than a hope for our own resurrection—for the reconstitution or re-creation or miraculous resuscitation of our present earthly bodies (albeit, again, in an improved or glorified form).

We begin this section with a selection from Plato defending the view that the soul can exist apart from the body. Although Plato has many arguments for this thesis, one of the most famous is found in the *Phaedo* and is included in our first reading. One section is worth quoting in full:

> When the soul employs the body in any inquiry, and makes use of sight, or hearing, or any other sense—for inquiry with the body must signify inquiry with the senses—she is dragged away by the body to the things which are impermanent, changing, and the soul wanders about blindly, and becomes confused and dizzy, like a drunken man, from dealing with things that are changing. . . . [But] when the soul investigates any question by herself, she goes away to the pure and eternal, and immortal and unchangeable, to which she is intrinsically related, and so she comes to be ever with it, as soon as she is by herself, and can be so; and then she rests from her wandering and dwells with it unchangingly, for she is related to what is unchanging. And is not this state of the soul called wisdom?[*]

The argument may be reconstructed as follows:

1. If a person's soul while in the body is capable of any activity independently of the body, then it can perform that activity in separation from the body (i.e., after death, surviving death).

2. In pure or metaphysical thinking (i.e., in contemplating the forms and their interrelationships), a person's soul performs an activity independently of the body. No observation is necessary for this investigation.

3. Therefore, a person's soul can engage in pure or metaphysical thinking in separation from the body. That is, it can and must survive death.

This is a positive argument for the existence of the soul. Unfortunately, the second premise is dubious, for it could be the case that the mind's activity is dependent on the brain. And it is precisely this latter claim that is defended by Bertrand Russell in the second reading in this section. According to Russell, there is no reason at all to believe in the immortality of the soul because all of the best empirical evidence points to the conclusion that a person's mental life comes to an end with the death of her brain.

In our third reading, Jeffrey Olen focuses on questions about criteria of identity. He examines two views on the matter: the "memory criterion" and the "bodily criterion." According to the memory criterion, person A is the same person as person B if and only if A and B have the right sort of overlap in their memories and the right sort of continuity between their memories and other psychological states. For example, if B exists later than A and is the same person as A, then B

Phaedo, 79 c–d, trans. Louis Pojman.

should remember a lot of what A remembers; furthermore, B should remember at least some of what A takes to be "present experience." There should also be some continuity among their goals, beliefs, desires, and other mental states. (This is not to deny that goals, beliefs, and desires change over time. But the idea is that if B exists, say, a mere ten seconds later than A, and if B has beliefs, desires, goals, and memories virtually *none* of which overlap with A's, then B just is not the same person as A.) Olen favors the memory—or, psychological continuity—criterion, and he argues furthermore in favor of the possibility of life after death. On his view, the mind is like computer software: Just as the same software can be transferred to different hardware, so too a mind can be transferred to a different brain (or other supporting medium). But to say that the mind can be transferred to a different medium is just to say that the mind can *change bodies*; and if it can change bodies, he contends, then the mind can survive the death of the body.

In our fourth reading, Lynne Rudder Baker examines the prospects for developing a satisfying doctrine of resurrection. She discusses some of the conceptual problems posed by the doctrine of resurrection, as well as the way in which different theories about personal identity over time give rise to different views about what resurrection consists in. She then defends her own favored view: the "constitution" view of human persons and their resurrection. On her view, human persons are material substances (so, not immaterial souls) that are constituted by but not identical to human bodies. The relationship between a person and her body is the same relation as that between a bronze statue and the piece of bronze that constitutes it. Resurrecting a human person is, then, just a matter of getting *a* body (though not necessarily the same body) to re-constitute the human person. (Note, then, that she apparently rejects the conceptual distinction between resurrection and reincarnation mentioned earlier in this introduction.)

Finally, we close this section with an essay on the Hindu view of life, death, and reincarnation by Prasannatma Das.

VII.1

Immortality of the Soul

PLATO

Plato (c. 427–347 B.C.E.) lived in Athens, was a student of Socrates, and is almost universally recognized as one of the most important philosophers who ever lived. Indeed, it has been remarked that

Reprinted from *Alcibiades I* and the *Phaedo*, translated by William Jowett (New York: Charles Scribner's Sons, 1889).

the entire history of Western philosophy is but a footnote to Plato. The excerpts that comprise the following selection concern Plato's views about the soul. According to Plato, human beings are composed of two substances: body and soul. Of these, the true self is the soul, which lives on after the death of the body. All of Plato's writings are in the form of dialogues. In the first dialogue (from Alcibiades I) Socrates argues with Alcibiades about the true self. The second dialogue (from the Phaedo) takes place in prison, where Socrates awaits his execution. He is offered a way of escape but rejects it, arguing that it would be immoral to flee such a fate at this time and that he is certain of a better life after death.

FROM ALCIBIADES I

SOC. And is self-knowledge an easy thing, and was he to be lightly esteemed who inscribed the text on the temple at Delphi? Or is self-knowledge a difficult thing, which few are able to attain?

AL. At times, I fancy, Socrates, that anybody can know himself; at other times, the task appears to be very difficult.

SOC. But whether easy or difficult, Alcibiades, still there is no other way; knowing what we are, we shall know how to take care of ourselves, and if we are ignorant we shall not know.

AL. That is true.

SOC. Well, then, let us see in what way the self-existent can be discovered by us; that will give us a chance to discover our own existence, which without that we can never know.

AL. You say truly.

SOC. Come, now, I beseech you, tell me with whom you are conversing?—with whom but with me?

AL. Yes.

SOC. As I am with you?

AL. Yes.

SOC. That is to say, I, Socrates, am talking?

AL. Yes.

SOC. And I in talking use words?

AL. Certainly.

SOC. And talking and using words are, as you would say, the same?

AL. Very true.

SOC. And the user is not the same as the thing which he uses?

AL. What do you mean?

SOC. I will explain: the shoemaker, for example, uses a square tool, and a circular tool, and other tools for cutting?

AL. Yes.

SOC. But the tool is not the same as the cutter and user of the tool?

AL. Of course not.

SOC. And in the same way the instrument of the harper is to be distinguished from the harper himself?

AL. He is.

SOC. Now the question which I asked was whether you conceive the user to be always different from that which he uses?

AL. I do.

SOC. Then what shall we say of the shoemaker? Does he cut with his tools only or with his hands?

AL. With his hands as well.

SOC. He uses his hands too?

AL. Yes.

SOC. And does he use his eyes in cutting leather?

AL. He does.

SOC. And we admit that the user is not the same with the things which he uses?

AL. Yes.

SOC. Then the shoemaker and the harper are to be distinguished from the hands and feet which they use?

AL. That is clear.

SOC. And does not a man use the whole body?

AL. Certainly.

SOC. And that which uses is different from that which is used?

AL. True.

SOC. Then a man is not the same as his own body?

AL. That is the inference.

SOC. What is he, then?

AL. I cannot say.

SOC. Nay, you can say that he is the user of the body.

AL. Yes.

SOC. And the user of the body is the soul?

AL. Yes, the soul.

SOC. And the soul rules?

AL. Yes.

SOC. Let me make an assertion which will, I think, be universally admitted.

AL. What is that?

SOC. That man is one of three things.

AL. What are they?

SOC. Soul, body, or the union of the two.

AL. Certainly.

SOC. But did we not say that the actual ruling principle of the body is man?

AL. Yes, we did.

SOC. And does the body rule over itself?

AL. Certainly not.

SOC. It is subject, as we were saying?

AL. Yes.

SOC. Then that is not what we are seeking?

AL. It would seem not.

SOC. But may we say that the union of the two rules over the body, and consequently that this is man?

AL. Very likely.

SOC. The most unlikely of all things: for if one of the members is subject, the two united cannot possibly rule.

AL. True.

SOC. But since neither the body, nor the union of the two, is man, either man has no real existence, or the soul is man?

AL. Just so.

SOC. Would you have a more precise proof that the soul is man?

AL. No; I think that the proof is sufficient.

SOC. If the proof, although not quite precise, is fair, that is enough for us; more precise proof will be supplied when we have discovered that which we were led to omit, from a fear that the inquiry would be too much protracted.

AL. What was that?

SOC. What I meant, when I said that absolute existence must be first considered; but now, instead of absolute existence, we have been considering the nature of individual existence, and that may be sufficient; for surely there is nothing belonging to us which has more absolute existence than the soul?

AL. There is nothing.

SOC. Then we may truly conceive that you and I are conversing with one another, soul to soul?

AL. Very true.

SOC. And that is just what I was saying—that I, Socrates, am not arguing or talking with the face of Alcibiades, but with the real Alcibiades; and that is with his soul.

AL. True. . . .

FROM THE PHAEDO

SOCRATES: What again shall we say of the actual acquirement of knowledge?—is the body, if invited to share in the inquiry, a hinderer or a helper? I mean to say, have sight and hearing any truth in them? Are they not, as the poets are always telling us, inaccurate witnesses? and yet, if even they are inaccurate and indistinct, what is to be said of the other senses?—for you will allow that they are the best of them?

Certainly, he replied.

Then when does the soul attain truth?—for in attempting to consider anything in company with the body she is obviously deceived.

Yes, that is true.

Then must not existence be revealed to her in thought, if at all?

Yes.

And thought is best when the mind is gathered into herself and none of these things trouble her—neither sounds nor sights nor pain nor any pleasure,—when she has as little as possible to do with the body, and has no bodily sense or feeling, but is aspiring after being?

That is true.

And in this the philosopher dishonors the body; his soul runs away from the body and desires to be alone and by herself?

That is true.

Well, but there is another thing, Simmias: Is there or is there not an absolute justice?

Assuredly there is.

And an absolute beauty and absolute good?

Of course.

But did you ever behold any of them with your eyes?

Certainly not.

Or did you ever reach them with any other bodily sense? (and I speak not of these alone, but of absolute greatness, and health, and strength, and of the essence or true nature of everything). Has the reality of them ever been perceived by you through the bodily organs? or rather, is not the nearest approach to the knowledge of their several natures made by him who so orders his intellectual vision as to have the most exact conception of the essence of that which he considers?

Certainly.

And he attains to the knowledge of them in their highest purity who goes to each of them with the mind alone, not allowing when in the act of thought the intrusion or introduction of sight or any other sense in the company of reason, but with the very light of the mind in her clearness penetrates into the very light of truth in each; he has got rid, as far as he can, of eyes and ears and of the whole body, which he conceives of only as a

disturbing element, hindering the soul from the acquisition of knowledge when in company with her—is not this the sort of man who, if ever man did, is likely to attain the knowledge of existence?

There is admirable truth in that, Socrates, replied Simmias.

And when they consider all this, must not true philosophers make a reflection, of which they will speak to one another in such words as these: We have found, they will say, a path of speculation which seems to bring us and the argument to the conclusion, that while we are in the body, and while the soul is mingled with this mass of evil our desire will not be satisfied, and our desire is of the truth. For the body is a source of endless trouble to us by reason of the mere requirement of food; and also is liable to diseases which overtake and impede us in the search after truth: and by filling us so full of loves, and lusts, and fears, and fancies, and idols, and every sort of folly, prevents our ever having, as people say, so much as a thought. From whence come wars, and fightings, and factions? whence but from the body and the lusts of the body? For wars are occasioned by the love of money, and money has to be acquired for the sake and in the service of the body; and in consequence of all these things the time which ought to be given to philosophy is lost. Moreover, if there is time and an inclination toward philosophy, yet the body introduces a turmoil and confusion and fear into the course of speculation, and hinders us from seeing the truth; and all experience shows that if we would have pure knowledge of anything we must be quit of the body, and the soul in herself must behold all things in themselves: then I suppose that we shall attain that which we desire, and of which we say that we are lovers, and that is wisdom; not while we live, but after death, as the argument shows; for if while in company with the body, the soul cannot have pure knowledge, one of two things seems to follow—either knowledge is not to be attained at all, or, if at all, after death. For then, and not till then, the soul will be in herself alone and without the body. In this present life, I reckon that we make the nearest approach to knowledge when we have the least possible concern or interest in the body, and are not saturated with the bodily nature, but remain pure until the hour when God himself is pleased to release us. And then the foolishness of the body will be cleared away and we shall be pure and hold converse with other pure souls, and know of ourselves the clear light everywhere; and this is surely the light of truth. For no impure thing is allowed to approach the pure. These are the sort of words, Simmias, which the true lovers of wisdom cannot help saying to one another, and thinking. You will agree with me in that?

Certainly, Socrates.

But if this is true, O my friend, then there is great hope that, going whither I go, I shall there be satisfied with that which has been the chief concern of you and me in our past lives. And now that the hour of departure is appointed to me, this is the hope with which I depart, and not I only, but every man who believes that he has his mind purified.

Certainly, replied Simmias.

And what is purification but the separation of the soul from the body, as I was saying before; the habit of the soul gathering and collecting herself into herself, out of all the courses of the body; the dwelling in her own place alone, as in another life, so also in this, as far as she can; the release of the soul from the chains of the body?

Very true, he said.

And what is that which is termed death, but this very separation and release of the soul from the body? To be sure, he said.

And the true philosophers, and they only, study and are eager to release the soul. Is not the separation and release of the soul from the body their especial study?

That is true.

And as I was saying at first, there would be a ridiculous contradiction in men studying to live as nearly as they can in a state of death, and yet repining when death comes.

Certainly.

Then Simmias, as the true philosophers are ever studying death, to them, of all men, death is the least terrible. Look at the matter in this way: how inconsistent of them to have been always

enemies of the body, and wanting to have the soul alone, and when this is granted to them, to be trembling and repining; instead of rejoicing at their departing to that place where, when they arrive, they hope to gain that which in life they loved (and this was wisdom), and at the same time to be rid of the company of their enemy. Many a man has been willing to go to the world below in the hope of seeing there an earthly love, or wife, or son, and conversing with them. And will he who is a true lover of wisdom, and is persuaded in like manner that only in the world below he can worthily enjoy her, still repine at death? Will he not depart with joy? Surely, he will, my friend, if he be a true philosopher. For he will have a firm conviction that there only, and nowhere else, he can find wisdom in her purity. And if this be true, he would be very absurd, as I was saying, if he were to fear death.

SOCRATES: And were we not saying long ago that the soul when using the body as an instrument of perception, that is to say, when using the sense of sight or hearing or some other sense (for the meaning of perceiving through the body is perceiving through the senses),—were we not saying that the soul too is then dragged by the body into the region of the changeable, and wanders and is confused; the world spins round her, and she is like a drunkard when under their influence?

Very true.

But when returning into herself she reflects; then she passes into the realm of purity, and eternity, and immortality, and unchangeableness, which are her kindred, and with them she ever lives, when she is by herself and is not let or hindered; then she ceases from her erring ways, and being in communion with the unchanging is unchanging. And this state of the soul is called wisdom?

That is well and truly said, Socrates, he replied.

And to which class is the soul more nearly alike and akin, as far as may be inferred from this argument, as well as from the preceding one?

I think, Socrates, that, in the opinion of every one who follows the argument, the soul will be infinitely more like the unchangeable,—even the most stupid person will not deny that.

And the body is more like the changing?

Yes.

Yet once more consider the matter in this light: When the soul and the body are united, then nature orders the soul to rule and govern, and the body to obey and serve. Now which of these two functions is akin to the divine? and which to the mortal? Does not the divine appear to you to be that which naturally orders and rules, and the mortal that which is subject and servant?

True.

And which does the soul resemble?

The soul resembles the divine, and the body the mortal,—there can be no doubt of that, Socrates.

VII.2

The Finality of Death

BERTRAND RUSSELL

Bertrand Russell (1872–1970), once a student and tutor at Cambridge University, was one of the most significant philosophers and social critics of the twentieth century. In this short essay, Russell outlines some of the major objections to the idea of life after death. He argues that it is not reasonable to believe that our personality and memories will survive the destruction of our bodies. He claims that the inclination to believe in immortality comes from emotional factors, notably the fear of death.

Before we can profitably discuss whether we shall continue to exist after death, it is well to be clear as to the sense in which a man is the same person as he was yesterday. Philosophers used to think that there were definite substances, the soul and the body, that each lasted on from day to day, that a soul, once created, continued to exist throughout all future time, whereas a body ceased temporarily from death till the resurrection of the body.

The part of this doctrine which concerns the present life is pretty certainly false. The matter of the body is continually changing by processes of nutriment and wastage. Even if it were not, atoms in physics are no longer supposed to have continuous existence; there is no sense in saying: this is the same atom as the one that existed a few minutes ago. The continuity of a human body is a matter of appearance and behavior, not of substance.

Reprinted with the permission of Simon & Schuster, Inc. from Bertrand Russell, *Why I Am Not a Christian* (London: George Allen & Unwin, 1957), pp. 88–93. Copyright 1957 by George Allen & Unwin. Ltd; copyright renewed ©1985. Reproduced by permission of Taylor and Francis Book UK.

The same thing applies to the mind. We think and feel and act, but there is not, in addition to thoughts and feelings and actions, a bare entity, the mind or the soul, which does or suffers these occurrences. The mental continuity of a person is a continuity of habit and memory: there was yesterday one person whose feelings I can remember, and that person I regard as myself of yesterday; but, in fact, myself of yesterday was only certain mental occurrences which are now remembered and are regarded as part of the person who now recollects them. All that constitutes a person is a series of experiences connected by memory and by certain similarities of the sort we call habit.

If, therefore, we are to believe that a person survives death, we must believe that the memories and habits which constitute the person will continue to be exhibited in a new set of occurrences.

No one can prove that this will not happen. But it is easy to see that it is very unlikely. Our memories and habits are bound up with the structure of the brain, in much the same way in which a river is connected with the riverbed. The water in the river is always changing, but it keeps to the same course because previous rains have worn a channel. In like manner, previous events have worn a channel in the brain, and our thoughts flow along this channel. This is the cause of memory and mental habits. But the brain, as a structure, is dissolved at death, and memory therefore may be expected to be also dissolved. There is no more reason to think otherwise than to expect a river to persist in its old course after an earthquake has raised a mountain where a valley used to be.

All memory, and therefore (one may say) all minds, depend upon a property which is very noticeable in certain kinds of material structures but exists little if at all in other kinds. This is the property of forming habits as a result of frequent similar occurrences. For example: a bright light makes the pupils of the eyes contract; and if you repeatedly flash a light in a man's eyes and beat a gong at the same time, the gong alone will, in the end, cause his pupils to contract. This is a fact about the brain and nervous system—that is to say, about a certain material structure. It will be found that exactly similar facts explain our response to language and our use of it, our memories and the emotions they arouse, our moral or immoral habits of behavior, and indeed everything that constitutes our mental personality, except the part determined by heredity. The part determined by heredity is handed on to our posterity but cannot, in the individual, survive the disintegration of the body. Thus both the hereditary and the acquired parts of a personality are, so far as our experience goes, bound up with the characteristics of certain bodily structures. We all know that memory may be obliterated by an injury to the brain, that a virtuous person may be rendered vicious by encephalitis lethargica, and, that a clever child can be turned into an idiot by lack of iodine. In view of such familiar facts, it seems scarcely probable that the mind survives the total destruction of brain structure which occurs at death.

It is not rational arguments but emotions that cause belief in a future life.

The most important of these emotions is fear of death, which is instinctive and biologically useful. If we genuinely and wholeheartedly believed in the future life, we should cease completely to fear death. The effects would be curious, and probably such as most of us would deplore. But our human and subhuman ancestors have fought and exterminated their enemies throughout many geological ages and have profited by courage; it is therefore an advantage to the victors in the struggle for life to be able, on occasion, to overcome the natural fear of death. Among animals and savages, instinctive pugnacity suffices for this purpose; but at a certain stage of development, as the Mohammedans first proved, belief in Paradise has considerable military value as reinforcing natural pugnacity. We should therefore admit that militarists are wise in encouraging the belief in immortality, always supposing that this belief does not become so profound as to produce indifference to the affairs of the world.

Another emotion which encourages the belief in survival is admiration of the excellence of man.

As the Bishop of Birmingham says, "His mind is a far finer instrument than anything that had appeared earlier—he knows right and wrong. He can build Westminster Abbey. He can make an airplane. He can calculate the distance of the sun.... Shall, then, man at death perish utterly? Does that incomparable instrument, his mind, vanish when life ceases?"

The Bishop proceeds to argue that "the universe has been shaped and is governed by an intelligent purpose," and that it would have been unintelligent, having made man, to let him perish.

To this argument there are many answers. In the first place, it has been found, in the scientific investigation of nature, that the intrusion of moral or aesthetic values has always been an obstacle to discovery. It used to be thought that the heavenly bodies must move in circles because the circle is the most perfect curve, that species must be immutable because God would only create what was perfect and what therefore stood in no need of improvement, that it was useless to combat epidemics except by repentance because they were sent as a punishment for sin, and so on. It has been found, however, that, so far as we can discover, nature is indifferent to our values and can only be understood by ignoring our notions of good and bad. The Universe may have a purpose, but nothing that we know suggests that, if so, this purpose has any similarity to ours.

Nor is there in this anything surprising. Dr. Barnes tells us that man "knows right and wrong." But, in fact, as anthropology shows, men's views of right and wrong have varied to such an extent that no single item has been permanent. We cannot say, therefore, that man knows right and wrong, but only that some men do. Which men? Nietzsche argued in favor of an ethic profoundly different from Christ's, and some powerful governments have accepted his teaching. If knowledge of right and wrong is to be an argument for immortality, we must first settle whether to believe Christ or Nietzsche, and then argue that

Christians are immortal, but Hitler and Mussolini are not, or vice versa. The decision will obviously be made on the battlefield, not in the study. Those who have the best poison gas will have the ethic of the future and will therefore be the immortal ones.

Our feelings and beliefs on the subject of good and evil are, like everything else about us, natural facts, developed in the struggle for existence and not having any divine or supernatural origin. In one of Aesop's fables, a lion is shown pictures of huntsmen catching lions and remarks that, if he had painted them, they would have shown lions catching huntsmen. Man, says Dr. Barnes, is a fine fellow because he can make airplanes. A little while ago there was a popular song about the cleverness of flies in walking upside down on the ceiling, with the chorus: "Could Lloyd George do it? Could Mr. Baldwin do it? Could Ramsay Mac do it? Why, no." On this basis a very telling argument could be constructed by a theologically-minded fly, which no doubt the other flies would find most convincing.

Moreover, it is only when we think abstractly that we have such a high opinion of man. Of men in the concrete, most of us think the vast majority very bad. Civilized states spend more than half their revenue on killing each other's citizens. Consider the long history of the activities inspired by moral fervor: human sacrifices, persecutions of heretics, witch-hunts, pogroms leading up to wholesale extermination by poison gases, which one at least of Dr. Barnes's episcopal colleagues must be supposed to favor, since he holds pacifism to be un-Christian. Are these abominations, and the ethical doctrines by which they are prompted, really evidence of an intelligent Creator? And can we really wish that the men who practiced them should live forever? The world in which we live can be understood as a result of muddle and accident; but if it is the outcome of deliberate purpose, the purpose must have been that of a fiend. For my part, I find accident a less painful and more plausible hypothesis.

VII.3

Personal Identity and Life after Death

JEFFREY OLEN

Jeffrey Olen (1946–) is a writer–philosopher who for many years taught philosophy at the University of Wisconsin at Stevens Point. In this essay he discusses the criteria of personal identity in order to determine what would have to survive our death if we were to be able to say that it is truly we who survive. Through some intriguing thought experiments, Olen builds a case for the possibility of survival. Olen has a functionalist view of personhood, believing that "the human brain is analogous to a computer." On this view, a given brain state is also a given mental state because it performs the appropriate function in the appropriate "program." Olen argues that just as different computers can run the same program, so too different brains (or other media) can "run" the same mind. So we can change bodies and therefore survive the death of our own body just as long as our personalities and memories are preserved intact.

It is Sunday night. After a long night of hard drinking, John Badger puts on his pajamas, lowers the heat in his Wisconsin home to fifty-five degrees and climbs into bed beneath two heavy blankets. Meanwhile, in Florida, Joe Everglade kisses his wife goodnight and goes to sleep.

The next morning, two very confused men wake up. One wakes up in Wisconsin, wondering where he is and why he is wearing pajamas, lying under two heavy blankets, yet shivering from the cold. He looks out the window and sees nothing but pine trees and snow. The room is totally unfamiliar. Where is his wife? How did he get to this cold, strange place? Why does he have such a terrible hangover? He tries to spring out of bed with his usual verve but feels an unaccustomed aching in his joints. Arthritis? He wanders unsurely through the house until he finds the bathroom. What he sees in the mirror causes him to spin around in sudden fear. But there is nobody behind him. Then the

fear intensifies as he realizes that it was his reflection that had stared back at him. But it was the reflection of a man thirty years older than himself, with coarser features and a weather-beaten face.

In Florida, a man awakens with a young woman's arm around him. When she too awakens, she snuggles against him and wishes him good morning. "Who are you?" he asks. "What am I doing in your bed?" She just laughs, then tells him that he will have to hurry if he is going to get in his ten miles of jogging. From the bathroom she asks him about his coming day. None of the names or places she mentions connect with anything he can remember. He climbs out of bed, marveling at the ease with which he does so, and looks first out the window and then into the mirror over the dresser. The sun and swimming pool confound him. The handsome young man's reflection terrifies him.

Then the phone rings. The woman answers it. It is the man from Wisconsin. "What happened last

From *Persons and Their World: An Introduction to Philosophy*, by Jeffrey Olen. Copyright Jeffrey Olen. Reprinted by permission of the author.

night, Mary? How did I get here? How did I get to look this way?"

"Who is this?" she asks.

"Don't you recognize my voice, Mary?" But he knew that the voice was not his own. "It's Joe."

"Joe who?"

"Your husband."

She hangs up, believing it to be a crank call. When she returns to the bedroom, the man in her husband's robe asks how he got there from Wisconsin, and why he looks as he does.

PERSONAL IDENTITY

What happened in the above story? Who woke up in Joe Everglade's bed? Who woke up in John Badger's? Which one is Mary's husband? Has Badger awakened with Everglade's memories and Everglade with Badger's? Or have Badger and Everglade somehow switched bodies? How are we to decide? What considerations are relevant?

To ask such questions is to raise the problem of *personal identity*. It is to ask what makes a person the same person he was the day before. It is to ask how we determine that we are dealing with the same person that we have dealt with in the past. It is to ask what constitutes personal identity over time. It is also to ask what we mean by the same person. And to answer this question, we must ask what we mean by the word "person."

Persons

In the previous chapter, we asked what a human being is. We asked what human beings are made of, what the nature of the human mind is, and whether human beings are part of nature or distinct from it.

To ask what a *person* is, however, is to ask a different question. Although we often use the terms "person" and "human being" interchangeably, they do not mean the same thing. If we do use them interchangeably, it is only because all the persons we know of are human beings, and because, as far as we know, whenever we are confronted with the same human being we are confronted with the same person.

But the notion of a human being is a *biological* notion. To identify something as a human being is to identify it as a member of *Homo sapiens*, a particular species of animal. It is a type of organism defined by certain physical characteristics.

The notion of a person, on the other hand, is not a biological one. Suppose, for instance, that we find life on another planet, and that this life is remarkably like our own. The creatures we discover communicate through a language as rich as our own, act according to moral principles, have a legal system, and engage in science and art. Suppose also that despite these cultural similarities, this form of life is biologically different from human life. In that case, these creatures would be persons, but not humans. Think, for example, of the alien in *E. T.* Since he is biologically different from us, he is not human. He is, however, a person.

What, then, is a person? Although philosophers disagree on this point, the following features are relatively noncontroversial.

First, a person is an intelligent, rational creature. Second, it is a creature capable of a peculiar sort of consciousness—self-consciousness. Third, it not only has beliefs, desires, and so forth, but it has beliefs about its beliefs, desires, and so forth. Fourth, it is a creature to which we ascribe moral responsibility. Persons are responsible for their actions in a way that other things are not. They are subject to moral praise and moral blame. Fifth, a person is a creature that we treat in certain ways. To treat something as a person is to treat it as a member of our own moral community. It is to grant it certain rights, both moral and legal. Sixth, a person is a creature capable of reciprocity. It is capable of treating us as members of the same moral community. Finally, a person is capable of verbal communication. It can communicate by means of a *language*, not just by barks, howls, and tail-wagging.

Since, as far as we know, only human beings meet the above conditions, only human beings are considered to be persons. But once we recognize that to be a person is not precisely the same thing that it is to be a human being, we also recognize that other creatures, such as the alien in *E. T.*, is also a person. We also recognize that perhaps not all human beings are persons—human fetuses, for example, as some have argued. Certainly, in the American South before the end of the Civil War, slaves were not considered to be persons. We might also mention a remark of D'Artagnan, in Richard Lester's film version of *The Three Musketeers*. Posing as a French nobleman, he attempted to cross the English Channel with a companion. When a French official remarked that his pass was only for one person, D'Artagnan replied that he was only one person—his companion was a servant.

Moreover, once we recognize the distinction between human beings and persons, certain questions arise. Can one human being embody more than one person, either at the same time or successive times? In the example we introduced at the beginning of this chapter, has Badger's body become Everglade's and Everglade's Badger's? Can the person survive the death of the human being? Is there personal survival after the death of the body?

Concerning identity through time in general, two issues must be distinguished. First, we want to know how we can *tell* that something is the same thing we encountered previously. That is, we want to know what the *criteria* are for establishing identity through time. Second, we want to know what *makes* something the same thing it was previously. That is, we want to know what *constitutes* identity through time.

Although these issues are related, they are not the same, as the following example illustrates. We can *tell* that someone has a case of the flu by checking for certain symptoms, such as fever, lack of energy, and sore muscles. But having these symptoms does not *constitute* having a case of the flu. It is the presence of a flu virus—not the symptoms—that makes an illness a case of the flu.

We commonly use two criteria for establishing personal identity. The first is the *bodily criterion*, the second the *memory criterion*. How do we apply them?

We apply the bodily criterion in two ways. First, we go by physical resemblance. If I meet someone on the street who looks, walks, and sounds just like Mary, I assume that it is Mary. Since the body I see resembles Mary's body exactly, I assume that the person I see is Mary. But that

method can sometimes fail us, as in the case of identical twins. In such cases, we can apply the bodily criterion in another way. If I can discover that there is a continuous line from one place and time to another that connects Mary's body to the body I now see, I can assume that I now see Mary. Suppose, for example, that Mary and I went to the beach together, and have been together all afternoon. In that case, I can say that the person I am now with is the person I began the day with.

There are, however, times when the bodily criterion is not available. If Mary and Jane are identical twins, and I run across one of them on the street, I may have to ask who it is. That is, I may have to rely on Mary's memory of who she is. And, if I want to make sure that I am not being fooled, I may ask a few questions. If Mary remembers things that I believe only Mary can remember, and if she remembers them as happening to *her*, and not to somebody else, then I can safely say that it really is Mary.

Generally, the bodily criterion and the memory criterion do not conflict, so we use whichever is more convenient. But what happens if they do conflict? That is what happened in our imagined story. According to the bodily criterion, each person awoke in his own bed, but with the memories of someone else. According to the memory criterion, each person awoke in the other's bed with the body of someone else. Which criterion should we take as decisive? Which is fundamental, the memory criterion or the bodily criterion?

The Constitution of Personal Identity

To ask the above questions is to ask what *constitutes* personal identity. What is it that makes me the same person I was yesterday? What makes the author of this book the same person as the baby born to Sam and Belle Olen in 1946? Answers to these questions will allow us to say which criterion is fundamental.

Perhaps the most widely discussed answer to our question comes from John Locke (1632–1704), whose discussion of the topic set the stage for all future discussions. According to Locke, the bodily criterion cannot be fundamental. Since the concept of a person is most importantly the concept of a conscious being who can be held morally and legally responsible for past actions, it is *continuity of consciousness* that constitutes personal identity. The bodily criterion is fundamental for establishing sameness of *animal*, but not sameness of *person*.

Suppose, for instance, that John Badger had been a professional thief. If the person who awoke in Badger's bed could never remember any of Badger's life as his own, but had only Everglade's memories and personality traits, while the man who awoke in Everglade's bed remembered all of Badger's crimes as his own, would we be justified in jailing the man who awoke in Badger's bed while letting the man who awoke in Everglade's go free? Locke would say no. The person who awoke in Badger's bed was not Badger.

If we agree that it is sameness of consciousness that constitutes personal identity, we must then ask what constitutes sameness of consciousness. Some philosophers have felt that it is sameness of *mind*, where the mind is thought of as a continuing non-physical substance. Although Locke did not deny that minds are nonphysical, he did not believe that sameness of nonphysical substance is the same thing as sameness of consciousness. If we can conceive of persons switching *physical* bodies, we can also conceive of persons switching *non*physical ones.

Then what does Locke take to be crucial for personal identity? *Memory.* It is my memory of the events of Jeffrey Olen's life as happening to me that makes me the person those events happened to. It is my memory of his experiences as *mine* that makes them mine.

Although Locke's answer seems at first glance a reasonable one, many philosophers have considered it inadequate. One reason for rejecting Locke's answer is that we don't remember everything that happened to us. If I don't remember anything that happened to me during a certain period, does that mean that whoever existed "in" my body then was not me? Hardly.

Another reason for rejecting Locke's answer is that memory is not always accurate. We often sincerely claim to remember things that never happened. There is a difference, then, between *genuine*

memory and *apparent* memory. What marks this difference is the *truth* of the memory claim. If what I claim to remember is not true, it cannot be a case of genuine memory.

But that means that memory cannot constitute personal identity. If I claim to remember certain experiences as being my experiences, that does not make them mine, because my claim may be a case of apparent memory. If it is a case of genuine memory, that is because it is true that the remembered experiences are mine. But the memory does not *make* them mine. Rather, the fact that they are mine makes it a case of genuine memory. So Locke has the situation backward. But if memory does not constitute personal identity, what does?

Some philosophers have claimed that, regardless of Locke's views, it *must* be sameness of mind, where the mind is thought of as a continuing nonphysical entity. This entity can be thought of as the self. It is what makes us who we are. As long as the same self continues to exist, the same person continues to exist. The major problem with this answer is that it assumes the truth of mind-body dualism, a position we found good reason to reject in the previous chapter. But apart from that, there is another problem.

In one of the most famous passages in the history of philosophy, David Hume (1711–1776) argued that there is no such self—for reasons that have nothing to do with the rejection of dualism. No matter how hard we try, Hume said, we cannot discover such a self. Turning inward and examining our own consciousness, we find only individual experiences—thoughts, recollections, images, and the like. Try as we might, we cannot find a continuing self. In that case, we are justified in believing only that there are *experiences*—not that there is a continuing *experiencer*. Put another way, we have no reason to believe that there is anything persisting through time that underlies or unifies these experiences. There are just the experiences themselves.

But if we accept this view, and still require a continuing nonphysical entity for personal identity, we are forced to the conclusion that there is no such thing as personal identity. We are left, that is, with the position that the idea of a person existing through time is a mere fiction, however useful in daily life.

And that is the position that Hume took. Instead of persons, he said, there are merely "bundles of ideas."

Thus, the view that personal identity requires sameness of mind can easily lead to the view that there is no personal identity. Since this conclusion seems manifestly false, we shall have to look elsewhere? But where?

The Primacy of the Bodily Criterion

If neither memory nor sameness of mind constitutes personal identity, perhaps we should accept the view that sameness of *body* does. Perhaps it is really the bodily criterion that is fundamental.

If we reflect on the problem faced by Locke's theory because of the distinction between genuine and apparent memory, it is tempting to accept the primacy of the bodily criterion. Once again, a sincere memory claim may be either genuine memory or apparent memory. How can we tell whether the claim that a previous experience was mine is genuine memory? By determining whether I was in the right place in the right time to have it. And how can we determine that? By the bodily criterion. If my *body* was there, then I was there. But that means that the memory criterion must rest on the bodily criterion. Also, accepting the primacy of the bodily criterion gets us around Hume's problem. The self that persists through and has the experiences I call mine is my physical body.

This answer also has the advantage of being in keeping with materialism, a view accepted in the previous chapter. If human beings are purely physical, then persons must also be purely physical, whatever differences there may be between the notion of a person and the notion of a human being. But if persons are purely physical, what makes me the same person I was yesterday is no different in kind from what makes my typewriter the same typewriter it was yesterday. In both cases, we are dealing with a physical object existing through time. In the latter case, as long as we have the same physical materials (allowing for change of ribbon, change of keys, and the like) arranged in the same way, we have the same typewriter. So it is with persons. As long as we have the same physical

materials (allowing for such changes as the replacement of cells) arranged in the same way, we have the same person.

Although this answer is a tempting one, it is not entirely satisfactory. Suppose that we could manage a brain transplant from one body to another. If we switched two brains, so that all the memories and personality traits of the persons involved were also switched, wouldn't we conclude that the persons, as well as their brains, had switched bodies? When such operations are performed in science-fiction stories, they are described this way.

But this possibility does not defeat the view that the bodily criterion is fundamental. It just forces us to hold that the bodily criterion must be applied to the brain, rather than the entire body. Personal identity then becomes a matter of brain identity. Same brain, same person. Unfortunately, even with this change, our answer does not seem satisfactory. Locke still seems somehow right. Let us see why.

Badger and Everglade Reconsidered

Returning to our tale of Badger and Everglade, we find that some troubling questions remain. If Mrs. Everglade continues to live with the man who awoke in her bed, might she not be committing adultery? Shouldn't she take in the man who awoke in Badger's bed? And, once again assuming that Badger was a professional thief, would justice really be served by jailing the man who awoke in his bed? However we answer these questions, one thing is certain—the two men would always feel that they had switched bodies. So, probably, would the people who knew them. Furthermore, whenever we read science-fiction stories describing such matters, we invariably accept them as stories of switched bodies. But if we accept the bodily criterion as fundamental, we are accepting the impossible, and the two men in our story, Mrs. Everglade, and their friends are mistaken in their beliefs. How, then, are we to answer our questions?

If we are unsure, it is because such questions become very tricky at this point. Their trickiness seems to rest on two points. First, cases like the Badger-Everglade case do not happen in this world.

Although we are prepared to accept them in science-fiction tales, we are totally unprepared to deal with them in real life.

Second, and this is a related point, we need some way of *explaining* such extraordinary occurrences. Unless we know how the memories of Badger and Everglade came to be reversed, we will be unable to decide the answers to our questions. In the movies, it is assumed that some nonphysical substance travels from one body to another, or that there has been a brain transplant of some sort. On these assumptions, we are of course willing to describe what happens as a change of body. This description seems to follow naturally from such explanations.

What explains what happened to Badger and Everglade? We can rule out change of nonphysical substance, because of what was said in the previous chapter and earlier in this chapter. If we explain what happened as the product of a brain switch, then the bodily criterion applied to the brain allows us to say that Badger and Everglade did awaken in each other's bed, and that Mrs. Everglade would be committing adultery should she live with the man who awoke in her bed.

Are there any other possible explanations? One that comes readily to mind is hypnotism. Suppose, then, that someone had hypnotized Badger and Everglade into believing that each was the other person. In that case, we should not say that there had been a body switch. Badger and Everglade awoke in their own beds, and a wave of the hypnotist's hand could demonstrate that to everyone concerned. Their memory claims are not genuine memories, but apparent ones.

But suppose it was not a case of hypnotism? What then? At this point, many people are stumped. What else could it be? The strong temptation is to say nothing. Without a brain transplant or hypnotism or something of the sort, the case is impossible.

Suppose that we accept this conclusion. If we do, we may say the following: The memory criterion and the bodily criterion cannot really conflict. If the memories are genuine, and not apparent, then whenever I remember certain experiences as

being mine, it is possible to establish that the same brain is involved in the original experiences and the memory of them. Consequently, the memory criterion and the bodily criterion are equally fundamental. The memory criterion is fundamental in the sense that consciousness determines what part of the body is central to personal identity. Because sameness of consciousness requires sameness of brain, we ultimately must apply the bodily criterion to the brain. But the bodily criterion is also fundamental, because we assume that some physical object—the brain—must remain the same if the person is to remain the same.

The Memory Criterion Revisited

Although the answer given above is a tidy one, it may still seem unsatisfactory. Perhaps it is a cheap trick just to dismiss the Badger-Everglade case as mere fantasy and then ignore it. After all, if we can meaningfully describe such cases in books and films, don't we have to pay some attention to them? As long as we can imagine situations in which two persons can switch bodies without a brain transplant, don't we need a theory of personal identity to cover them?

Philosophers are divided on this point. Some think that a theory of personal identity has to account only for what can happen in this world, while others think it must account for whatever can happen in any conceivable world. Then again, some do not believe that there is any conceivable world in which two persons could change bodies without a brain switch, while there are others who are not sure that such things are impossible in the actual world.

Without trying to decide the matter, I can make the following suggestion for those who demand a theory of personal identity that does not rely on the assumption that genuine memory is tied to a particular brain.

In the previous chapter, I concluded that functionalism is the theory of mind most likely to be true. To have a mind, I said, is to embody a psychology. I also said that we don't merely move our bodies, but write poetry, caress the cheek of someone we love, and perform all sorts of human actions. I might have expressed this point by saying that we are not just human beings, but persons as well. What makes a human being a person? We are persons because we embody a psychology.

If that is true, then it may also be true that we are the persons we are because of the psychologies we embody. If it is a psychology that makes a human being a person, then it is a particular psychology that makes a particular human being a particular person. Sameness of psychology constitutes sameness of person. In that case, we can agree with this much of Locke's theory—it is continuity of consciousness that constitutes personal identity. But what is continuity of consciousness, if not memory?

An answer to this question is provided by the contemporary British philosopher Anthony Quinton. At any moment, we can isolate a number of mental states belonging to the same momentary consciousness. Right now, for instance, I am simultaneously aware of the sound and sight and feel of my typewriter, plus the feel and taste of my pipe, plus a variety of other things. Such *momentary* consciousnesses belong to a continuous series. Each one is linked to the one before it and the one following it by certain similarities and recollections. This series is my own *continuity* of consciousness, my own *stream* of consciousness. It is this stream of consciousness that makes me the same person I was yesterday.

If we accept Quinton's theory, we can then say that the memory criterion, not the bodily criterion, is fundamental. We can also say that, even if in this world continuity of consciousness requires sameness of brain, we can conceive of worlds in which it does not. To show this, let us offer another possible explanation of the Badger-Everglade situation.

Suppose a mad computer scientist has discovered a way to reprogram human beings. Suppose that he has found a way to make us the embodiment of any psychology he likes. Suppose further that he decided to experiment on Badger and Everglade, giving Badger Everglade's psychology and Everglade Badger's and that is why the events of our story occurred. With this explanation and the considerations of the previous paragraphs, we can conclude that Badger and Everglade did change bodies. By performing his experiment, the mad scientist has made it possible for a continuing stream of consciousness to pass from one body to another. He has, in effect, performed a body transplant. . . .

Should we accept Quinton's theory? There seems to be no good reason not to. In fact, there are at least two good reasons for accepting it. First, it seems consistent with a functionalist theory of the mind. Second, it allows us to make sense of science-fiction stories while we continue to believe that in the real world to be the same person we were yesterday is to have the same brain.

LIFE AFTER DEATH

Is it possible for the person to survive the death of the body? Is there a sense in which we can continue to live after our bodies have died? Can there be a personal life after death?

According to one popular conception of life after death, at the death of the body the soul leaves the body and travels to a realm known as heaven. Of course, this story must be taken as metaphorical. Does the soul literally leave the body? How? Out of the mouth? Ears? And how does it get to heaven? By turning left at Mars? Moreover, if the soul remains disembodied, how can it perceive anything? What does it use as sense organs? And if all souls remain disembodied, how can one soul recognize another? What is there to recognize?

As these questions might suggest, much of this popular story trades on a confusion. The soul is thought of as a translucent physical substance much like Casper the ghost, through which other objects can pass as they do through air or water. But if the soul is *really* nonphysical, it can be nothing like that.

If this story is not to be taken literally, is there some version of it that we can admit as a possibility? Is there also the possibility of personal survival through reincarnation as it is often understood—the re-embodiment of the person without memory of the former embodiment?

Materialism and the Disembodied Soul

So far, we have considered both the mind and the body as they relate to personal identity. Have we neglected the soul? It may seem that we have, but philosophers who discuss the mind-body question and personal identity generally use the terms "mind" and "soul" interchangeably. Is the practice legitimate, or is it a confusion?

The practice seems to be thoroughly legitimate. If the soul is thought to be the crucial element of the person, it is difficult to see how it could be anything but the mind. If it is our character traits, personality, thoughts, likes and dislikes, memories, and continuity of experience that make us the persons we are, then they must belong to the soul. If they are taken to be crucial for one's personal identity, then it seems impossible to separate them from one's soul.

Moreover, people who accept some version of the popular conception of life after death noted above believe in certain continuities between earthly experiences and heavenly ones. In heaven, it is believed, we remember our earthly lives, we recognize friends and relatives, our personalities are like our earthly personalities, and we are judged by God for our actions on earth. But if we believe any of this, we must also believe that the soul cannot be separated from the mind.

If that is the case, it is difficult to accept the continued existence of a disembodied soul. Once we accept some form of materialism, we seem compelled to believe that the soul must be embodied. Does that rule out the possibility of any version of the popular story being true?

Some philosophers think that it does. Suppose, for instance, that the mind-brain identity theory is true. In that case, when the brain dies, so does the mind. Since the mind is the repository of memory and personality traits, it is identical with the soul. So when the brain dies, so does the soul.

This is a powerful argument, and it has convinced a number of people. On the other hand, it has also kept a number of people from accepting materialism of any sort. If it is felt that materialism and life after death are incompatible, and if one is firmly committed to the belief in life after death, then it is natural for one to reject materialism.

Is there a way of reconciling materialism and life after death? I think so.

Although it seems necessary that persons must be embodied, it does not seem necessary that the same person must be embodied by the same body. In our discussion of personal identity, we allowed that Badger and Everglade might have changed bodies, depending on our explanation of the story. Let us try a similar story.

Mary Brown is old and sick. She knows she will die within a couple of weeks. One morning she does die. At the same time, in some other world, a woman wakes up believing herself to be Mary. She looks around to find herself in a totally unfamiliar place. Someone is sitting next to her. This other woman looks exactly like Mary's mother, who died years earlier, and believes herself to be Mary's mother. Certainly, she knows everything about Mary that Mary's mother would know.

Before the woman believing herself to be Mary can speak, she notices some surprising things about herself. She no longer feels old or sick. Her pains are gone, and her mind is as sharp as ever. When she asks where she is, she is told heaven. She is also told that her husband, father, and numerous old friends are waiting to see her. All of them are indistinguishable from the persons they claim to be. Meanwhile, back on earth, Mary Brown is pronounced dead. Is this woman in "heaven" really Mary Brown? How could we possibly explain the phenomenon?

Suppose we put the story in a religious context. Earlier, we saw that one possible explanation of the Badger-Everglade case is that some mad computer scientist had reprogrammed the two so that each embodied the psychology of the other. Suppose we replace the mad scientist with God, and say that God had kept a body in heaven for the purpose of embodying Mary's psychology when she died, and that the person believing herself to be Mary is the new embodiment of Mary's psychology. Would this count as a genuine case of life after death?

If we accept the Badger-Everglade story, appropriately explained, as a case of two persons switching bodies, there seems no reason to deny that Mary has continued to live "in" another body. But even if we are unsure of the Badger-Everglade case, we can approach Mary Brown's this way. What is it that we want to survive after death? Isn't it our memories, our consciousness of self, our personalities, our relations with others? What does it matter whether there is some nonphysical substance that survives? If that substance has no memories of a prior life, does not recognize the soul of others who were important in that earlier life, what comfort could such a continuing existence bring? In what sense would it be the survival of the *person*? How would it be significantly different from the return of the lifeless body to the soil?

If we assume that our story is a genuine case of personal survival of the death of the body, we may wonder about another point. Is it compatible with Christian belief? According to John Hick, a contemporary British philosopher who imagined a similar story, the answer is yes. In I Corinthians 15, Paul writes of the resurrection of the body—not of the physical body, but of some spiritual body. Although one can think of this spiritual body as a translucent ghost-like body that leaves the physical body at death, Hick offers another interpretation.

The human being, Hick says, becomes extinct at death. It is only through God's intervention that the spiritual body comes into existence. By the resurrection of this spiritual body, we are to understand a *recreation* or *reconstitution* of the person's body in heaven. But that is precisely what happened in our story.

Thus, a materialist view of the nature of human beings is not incompatible with the Christian view of life after death. Nor, for that matter, is it incompatible with the belief that the spiritual body is nonphysical. If we can make sense of the claim that there might be such things as nonphysical bodies, then there is no reason why a nonphysical body could not embody a psychology. Remember—according to functionalism, an abstract description such as a psychology is independent of any physical description. Just as we can play chess using almost anything as chess pieces, so can a psychology be embodied by almost anything, assuming that it is complex enough. So if there can be nonphysical bodies, there can be nonphysical persons. Of course, nothing said so far assures us that the Christian story—or any other story of life after death—is true. That is another matter. . . .

Reincarnation

Much of what has been said so far does, however, rule out the possibility of reincarnation as commonly understood. If human beings are purely physical, then there is no nonphysical substance that is the person that can be reincarnated in another earthly body. Moreover, even if there were such a substance, it is difficult to see how its continued existence in another body could count as the reincarnation of a particular person, *if* there is no other continuity between the old life and the new one. Once again, personal survival requires some continuity of consciousness. It is not sameness of *stuff* that constitutes personal identity, but sameness of consciousness. This requirement is often overlooked by believers in reincarnation.

But suppose that there is some continuity of consciousness in reincarnation. Suppose that memories and the rest do continue in the next incarnation, but that they are not easily accessible. Suppose, that is, that the slate is not wiped completely clean, but that what is written on it is hard to recover. In that case, the passage of the soul into a new incarnation would count as personal survival *if* there were such a soul to begin with.

Assuming, again, that there is not, what can we say about the possibility of reincarnation? To conceive of such a possibility, we must conceive of some very complicated reprogramming by God or some mad scientist or whatever. I shall leave it to you to come up with such a story, but I shall say this much. There does not seem to be any good reason to think that any such story is remotely plausible, least of all true.

The Final Word?

In this chapter we looked at two closely related questions: What constitutes personal identity? And is it possible for a person to survive the death of her own body?

The answer to the second question depended on the first. If we had concluded that the basis of personal identity is sameness of body, then we would have been forced to conclude that life after death is impossible. And there did seem to be good reason to come to these conclusions. How, we asked, could we assure that any memory claim is a case of genuine memory? Our answer was this. In the cases likely to confront us in our daily lives, we must establish some physical continuity between the person who had the original experience and the person who claims to remember it.

But the problem with this answer is that it is too limited. Because we can imagine cases like the Everglade-Badger example, and because our science-fiction tales and religious traditions offer stories of personal continuity without bodily continuity, we can say the following. Regardless of what happens in our daily lives, our concept of a person is a concept of something that does not seem tied to a particular body. Rather, our concept of a person seems to be tied to a particular stream of consciousness. If there is one continuing stream of consciousness over time, then there is one continuing person. Our question, then, was whether we can give a coherent account of continuity of consciousness from one body to another.

The answer was yes. Using the computer analogy of the functionalist, we can explain such continuity in terms of programming. If it is possible to "program" another brain to have the same psychology as the brain I now have, then it is possible for me to change bodies. And if it is possible for me to change bodies, then it is also possible for me to survive the death of my body.

VII.4

Death and the Afterlife

LYNNE RUDDER BAKER

Lynne Rudder Baker (1944–) is professor of philosophy at the University of Massachusetts Amherst. She has written extensively in metaphysics and philosophy of religion, and is perhaps best known for her work on the metaphysics of material objects and on the "first person perspective". In the present article, she applies some of that work to making sense of the Christian doctrine of resurrection. After discussing some of the conceptual problems posed by resurrection and a variety of rival views about what it might consist in, she then goes on to defend her own "constitution" theory of human persons and their resurrection.

Reprinted from *The Oxford Handbook for the Philosophy of Religion*, edited by William J. Wainwright (2005), pp. 366–91. © 2004 by Oxford University Press, Inc. By permission of Oxford University Press, USA.

1.

Death comes to all creatures, but human beings are unique in realizing that they will die. Hence, they are unique in being able to consider the possibility of life after death. Ideas of an afterlife of one sort or another have been promulgated by all manner of cultures and religions. For ancient peoples, the afterlife was a realm of vastly diminished existence populated by shades, ghostly counterparts of bodies. Ancient Indians and Egyptians before 2000 postulated a judgment after death. The Greeks had Hades; the Hebrews had Sheol. Far from being a matter of wish fulfillment, an afterlife, as pictured by ancient cultures, was not particularly desirable, just inevitable (Hick 1994, 55–60).

There are many conceptions of an afterlife. To say that there is an afterlife (of any kind) is to say that biological death is not the permanent end of a human being's existence: At least some people continue to exist and to have experiences after death. The idea of reincarnation is shared by a number of religions, including Hindu, Jaina, and Buddhist. According to the idea of reincarnation, one is born over and over, and the circumstances of one's life, even what sort of being one is, depend on one's actions in the preceding life. Among philosophers, Plato had a view of reincarnation. Plato developed the idea of the immortality of the soul in the *Phaedo*. According to Plato, a person is an immaterial soul, temporarily imprisoned by a body. Death is liberation from the prison of the body, but after an interval of disembodied existence, the soul is again imprisoned and is born again into this world. On Plato's view, all this occurs in the natural course of things.

1a. Christian Doctrine

All the great monotheistic religions—Judaism, Christianity, and Islam—recognize doctrines of an afterlife. I focus on doctrines of resurrection of the dead, which are common to them, and in particular on Christian doctrines.

Christian doctrines have two sources. The first source is Second-Temple Judaism, which contributed the idea of resurrection of the body. (The New Testament mentions that the Pharisees believed in bodily resurrections, but that the Sadducees did not believe in an afterlife. Jesus endorsed the former, which was fixed as Christian doctrine by his own bodily resurrection.) The second source was Greek philosophy, which contributed the idea of the immortality of the soul (Cullman 1973).

To the early Church fathers, belief in the immortality of the soul was connected with belief in resurrection of the body. The belief that Jesus rose from the dead was the belief that his soul survived death of the body and was "reinvested with his risen body" (Wolfson 1956-57, 8). The belief in a general resurrection was the belief that surviving souls, at the end of time, would be "reinvested" with risen bodies. During the interval between death and the general resurrection, a soul would have a life without a body, but a person's final state would be embodied in some sense. In this general picture, belief in resurrection includes belief in immortal souls and belief in postmortem bodies (of some sort).

The Christian doctrine of an afterlife is pieced together out of hints and metaphors in Scripture. Jesus' resurrection is the paradigm case. According to Christian doctrine, Jesus was the Son of God, who was crucified, died, and was buried. On the third day he rose from the dead and ascended into Heaven. Although Jesus' resurrection is the ground of the Christian doctrine of resurrection, many questions are left open. Perhaps the most explicit, but still sketchy and metaphorical, account of an afterlife in the New Testament is in I Corinthians 15, with its "seed" metaphor. Our bodies are said to be sown in corruption and raised in incorruption; sown in dishonor, raised in glory; sown in weakness, raised in power; sown a natural body, raised a "spiritual" body. But this passage is notoriously open to several interpretations. What is a "spiritual body"? Is it made of the same flesh-and-blood particles as the premortem body? Of the same kind of particles if not exactly the same ones? Of some entirely different kind of stuff? There is no unanimity.

There are two kinds of leading metaphors to guide answers to these questions: on the one hand, the seed metaphor, just mentioned (I Corinthians 15), or the metaphor of tents or garments that we take on as a covering in incorruption (II Corinthians 5); and on the other hand, the statue metaphor that Augustine preferred. According to the seed metaphor, developed by Origen, the body is dynamic and always in flux. Just as the body is transformed in life, so too it is transformed in death. The resurrected body will be radically changed, and will not be made of the same material as the premortem body (Bynum 1995, 63ff). Augustine, by contrast, insisted on the reanimation of the same bodily material, which would be reassembled from dust and previous bones (Bynum 1995, 95). Thomas Aquinas rejected both metaphors for understanding the nature of the body that is to be resurrected. His concern was more with the integrity of the body than with the identity of material particles. The resurrected body will contain the same fragments and organs, if not the identical particles (Bynum 1995, 265). However, Aquinas sometimes suggested that there would be material continuity of the body in the resurrection.

The various Christian views of resurrection have at least these characteristics in common. First, *embodiment*: resurrection requires some kind of bodily life after death. Postmortem bodies are different from premortem bodies in that they are said to be spiritual, incorruptible, glorified. Even if there is an "intermediate state" between death and a general resurrection, in which the soul exists unembodied, those who live after death will ultimately be embodied, according to Christian doctrine. Second, *identity*: the very same person who exists on earth is to exist in an afterlife. Individuals exist after death, not in some undifferentiated state merged with the universe, or with an Eternal Mind, or anything else. Not only is there to be individual existence in the Resurrection, but the very same individuals are to exist both now and after death. "Survival" in some weaker sense of, say, psychological similarity is not enough. The relation between a person here and now and a person in an afterlife must be identity. Third, *miracle*: life after death, according to Christian doctrine, is a gift from God. Christian doctrine thus contrasts with the Greek idea of immortality as a natural property of the soul. The idea of miracle is built into the Christian doctrine of life after death from the beginning.

There are many questions to be answered about the doctrine of resurrection. For example, is there immediate resurrection at the instant of death, or is there a temporary mode of existence (an intermediate state) before a general resurrection at the end of time (Cooper 1989)? There is no general agreement. But whatever the details of the conception of an afterlife, a particular *philosophical* question arises: In virtue of what is a person in an afterlife identical to a certain person in a premortem state? A similar question arises for traditions of reincarnation: In virtue of what is a person of one generation the same person as a person who lived previously? The philosophical issue in any conception of an individual afterlife is the question of personal identity. To have life after death is to have postmortem experiences linked to each other and to premortem experiences in a way that preserves personal identity (Price 1964, 369).

1b. The Problem of Personal Identity

There are at least two philosophical problems of personal identity. The synchronic problem is solved by answering this question: In virtue of what is something a person, at some given time? The diachronic problem is solved by answering this question: In virtue of what is a person at one time identical to a person at another time? The problem of personal identity as it is raised by the idea of an afterlife is a diachronic problem: Under what conditions are persons at t1 and at t2 the same person? People change dramatically over time, physically and mentally. A woman of 50 is very unlike a girl of 10 physically, even if the woman of 50 is the same person who, forty years earlier, had been the girl of 10. They do not even have any matter in common. A girl of 10 has different memories, attitudes, personality from a woman of 50—even if the woman of 50 is the same person, considered forty years later, as the girl of 10. In virtue of what is the woman of 50 identical to the girl of 10 considered forty years later?

The needed criterion of personal identity is not epistemological. It does not say how an observer can tell that the woman of 50 is the girl at 10 considered forty years later. Rather, the criterion of personal identity is metaphysical. It says what makes it the case that the woman of 50 is the same person as the girl of 10, whether anyone recognizes the identity or not.

This question of a criterion of personal identity extends to the conception of an afterlife. The question How is survival of bodily death even possible? requires a theory of personal identity. In virtue of what is a person in an afterlife (in heaven, purgatory, or hell, say) the same person as a person who lived a certain life at a certain time on earth and died in bed at the age of 90, say? We can divide potential answers to this question into categories, according to what they take personal identity to depend on: an immaterial substance (such as a soul); a physical substance (such as a human body or brain); a composite of an immaterial substance and a physical substance; or some kind of mental or psychological continuity (such as memory). In addition, my own view is that personal identity depends on a mental property—an essential property in virtue of which a person is a person (having a first-person perspective) and in virtue of which a person is the person she is (having that very first-person perspective). Although to be a person is to be an entity with mental properties essentially, on my view, sameness of person does not require mental continuity over time.

2.

Four traditional positions on personal identity yield four views on the resurrection. In virtue of what is a postmortem person the same premortem person who walked the earth? The four answers are that the premortem person and the postmortem person (1) have the same soul, or (2) are the same soul-body composite, or (3) have the same body, or (4) are connected by memory.

2a. Sameness of Soul

The idea of an incorporeal soul is the idea of a nonphysical part of a human being, a nonphysical part

that thinks and wills. The early Christian Church considered three theories of the soul: (1) souls as custom-made: God creates especially for each new child a new soul at birth (creationalism); (2) souls as ready-made: God has a stock of souls from eternity and allocates them as needed (preexistentialism); (3) souls as second-hand: God created only one soul (the soul of Adam), which is passed down to his descendants (traducianism). All the traditional theories of the soul (custom-made, ready-made, traducian) describe the soul as being in a body as in a garment, or as in a temple, or as in a house. That is, they all allow that souls can exist apart from bodies. (Wolfson 1956-57, 21–2). Even Thomas Aquinas, who rejects these metaphors, takes the soul to be capable of the vision of God in a (temporary) disembodied state (Bynum 1995, 266).

These theories of the soul allow for a conception of an afterlife as populated with incorporeal souls. Experience without a biological organism has seemed to many to be conceivable. One might have visual, auditory, olfactory, sensual images—images of bodies, including one's own. The images would be mental images, acquired in premortem life, and the postmortem person's experiences would be like dreams. The images would be governed by peculiar causal laws—psychological, not physical. For example, a "wish to go to Oxford might be immediately followed by the occurrence of a vivid and detailed set of Oxford-like images; even though, at the moment before, one's images had resembled Piccadilly Circus or the palace of the Dalai Lama in Tibet" (Price 1964, 370). These images would constitute a world—"the next world"—where everything still had shape, color, size, and so on, but had different causal properties.

The postmortem world, although similar to a dream world, need not be solipsistic. One postmortem person could have a telepathic apparition of another person, who "announces himself" in a way that is recognizably similar on different occasions. Thus, an image-world need not be altogether private. It "would be the joint product of a group of telepathetically interacting minds and public to all of them" (Price 1964, 373, 377). There may be various postmortem image-worlds in which people communicate telepathically with each other.

The image-worlds would be constructed from a person's desires and memories and telepathic interactions. The postmortem worlds are "wish-fulfillment" worlds, but of one's genuine wishes. If repression is a biological phenomenon, then repressed desires and memories would be revealed. In that case, in the next world, one's mental conflicts would be out in the open, and the fulfillment of one's wishes may be horrifying. One's guilt feelings may produce images of punishments, which would be a kind of appropriate purgatory for each person. The kind of world one would experience after death would depend on the kind of person one was.

Where, one may wonder, is this "next world"? The question of its spatial relation to the physical world has no meaning. The images that make up the next world are in a space of their own, but, like dream images, they bear no spatial relations to our world. If you dream of a tree, its branches are spatially related to its trunk; you can ask how tall the dreamed-of tree is, but not how far it is from the mattress (Price 1964, 373). "Passing" from this world to the next is not a physical passage. It is more like passing from waking experience to dreaming.

Richard Swinburne (1997) has developed a contemporary view of the soul as the immaterial seat of mental life, or conscious experience. Mental events like believings, desirings, purposings, sensing, though not themselves brain events, interact with brain events. Although Swinburne believes in evolution in biology, and sometimes speaks of souls as having evolved (182), the evolution of souls requires God's hand. On Swinburne's view, the human soul does not develop naturally from genetic material, but each soul is created by God and linked to the body (199).

Although souls are in this world linked to brains, there is no contradiction, according to Swinburne, in the soul's continuing to exist without a body. Indeed, the soul is the necessary core of a person which must continue if a person is to continue (1997, 146). Because, on Swinburne's view, no natural laws govern what happens to souls after death, there would be no violation of natural law if God were to give to souls life after death, with or without a new body. Swinburne solves the problem of personal identity for this world and the next by appeal to immaterial souls.

Recently, scientific philosophers have suggested materialistic conceptions of the soul. For example, the soul is software to the hardware of the brain; if persons are identified with souls (software), they can be "re-embodied, perhaps in a quite different medium" (MacKay 1987, 724–25). Another materialistic view of the soul conceives of the soul as an "information-bearing pattern, carried at any instant by the matter of my animated body." At death, God will remember the pattern and "its instantiation will be recreated by him" at the resurrection (Polkinghorne 1996, 163).

2b. Sameness of Soul-Body Composite

Thomas Aquinas took over Aristotle's framework for understanding human beings, modifying it as little as possible to accommodate Christian doctrine. On Aristotle's view, all living things had souls: plants had nutritive souls, nonhuman animals had sensitive souls, and human animals ("men") had rational souls. The soul was not separable from the body. A human being was a substance: formed matter. The body supplied the matter, the soul the form. No more could a rational soul exist apart from the body whose form it was than could the shape of a particular axe exist apart from that axe. The soul is the form of the body. So, Aristotle had no place for an afterlife.

Following Aristotle, Aquinas agreed that the soul is the form of the body, but, building on Aristotle's concession that the "agent intellect" is separable (1941, *De Anima* 3.5, 430a17), Aquinas held that the soul is a substantial form that could "subsist" on its own. Aquinas assumed that there is a general resurrection at the end of time, before which those who have died are in an "intermediate state." The human being—the substance, the individual—does not exist as such during the intermediate state. What continues through the intermediate state is only the rational soul, which "subsists" until reunited with the body, at which time the human being is fully recovered. The disembodied soul can neither sense nor feel; it is only the part of the person that thinks and wills. While the soul is disembodied, the soul is *not* the person who died. It is merely a remnant of the person, awaiting reunion with the person's body. It is only when the soul is reunited with the body (the same body) that the person resumes life.

So Aquinas's view of a human person is rather of a composite of body and soul. He does not equate personal identity over time with identity of soul. However, Aquinas's conception of the afterlife does require separability of souls from bodies, albeit temporary, and continued existence of souls after death. So, it is reasonable to include Aquinas's view both with the theories of survival of souls and with the theories of bodily resurrection.

2c. Sameness of Body

The Christian doctrine of resurrection of the body suggests that personal identity, at least in part, consists of bodily identity. If personal identity consists in bodily identity, even in part, then reincarnation is ruled out, as is Price's (1964) conception of an afterlife. Reincarnation requires that the same person have different bodies, and Price's conception of an afterlife was of a disembodied consciousness.

For millennia "resurrection of the body" has been taken to mean that the very same body that died would come back to life. Although I Corinthians 15 plainly asserts that the resurrected body is an incorruptible "spiritual" (or "glorified") body, the spiritual body was to be reconstituted from the dust and bones of the original premortem body. The body may undergo radical change, but it is to persist in its postmortem state as the same body. The earliest Christians supposed the body to be the person; later Christians (such as Aquinas) took the body to be an essential part of the person, along with the soul. Either way—whether personal identity is bodily identity or personal identity just entails bodily identity—if a person is to be resurrected, the person's body, the same body, must exist in the afterlife.

There are at least two ways that this story may be filled out, depending on how the idea of "same body" is taken. The first way of understanding "same body," shared by most of the Church fathers, is in terms of same constituent particles. Suppose that Jane is to be resurrected. At the general resurrection, God finds the particles that had composed Jane's body, say, and reassembles them exactly as they had been before Jane's death, thereby restoring Jane's body. If personal identity is bodily identity, then God thereby restores Jane, that is, brings her back to life. The same body, in both its premortem and postmortem phases, has the same particles.

The second way of understanding "same body" appeals to a natural way to understand identity of human bodies over time. Unlike inanimate objects, human bodies undergo a complete change of cells every few years. Not a single one of Sam's cells today was one of his cells ten years ago; yet Sam has not changed bodies. So, perhaps identity of body should not consist of identity of constituent cells, or even of identity of some small percentage of constituent cells. The natural thing to say is that identity of body consists of spatiotemporal continuity of ever-changing constituent cells. Perhaps in the resurrection God slowly replaces the atoms that had composed Jane's organic cells by glorified and incorruptible elements, and He carries out the replacement in a way that preserves spatiotemporal continuity of the body. If that is possible, and if identity of bodies consists in spatiotemporal continuity, then a premortem body could be the same body as a postmortem body even though the premortem body is corruptible and the postmortem body is incorruptible.

2d. The Memory Criterion

The memory criterion is that sameness of person is determined by psychological continuity, not by continuity of substance, material or immaterial. The originator of the memory criterion was John Locke, who was explicitly motivated in part by a desire to make sense of the idea of resurrection. Locke took identity of a person over time to be identity of consciousness over time—regardless of identity of substance (1924, II, xxvii). Locke's idea allows for the possibility that a single consciousness could unite several substances into a single person and for the possibility that a single consciousness could even exist over temporal gaps. Such an approach is clearly congenial to the idea of resurrection.

Suppose we say that A and B are the same person if and only if A can remember what B did, or B can remember what A did. What it means to say that A can remember what B did is that what B did caused, in the right way, A's memory of what B did. What secures sameness of person are causal connections of a certain sort among mental states. It is difficult to spell out just the right kind of causal connection, but "of a certain sort" is supposed to rule out cases like the one where B cuts the grass and tells C what she had done; then B gets amnesia, and C reports back to B that B had cut the grass. C's telling B that B had cut the grass causes B to have a mental state of thinking that she had cut the grass, and B's apparent memory of cutting the grass is ultimately caused by B's having cut the grass. But B's apparent memory is not a real memory, because B's mental state of thinking that she had cut the grass was caused by her cutting the grass, but it was not caused in the right way. The causal chain between B's cutting the grass and her apparent memory went through C. B would not have had the apparent memory of cutting the grass if C had not told B that she had cut the grass.

So, it seems that we have a criterion for sameness of resurrected person and earthly person that does not require sameness of body or sameness of soul: if a resurrected person has Jones's memories (i.e., mental states of what Jones did, caused in the right way), then that resurrected person is Jones.

3.

All the traditional views of personal identity just canvassed have been targets of criticism. Some of the criticisms that follow are well-known; others, as far as I know, are novel.

3a. Sameness of Soul

There are familiar arguments in the secular literature from the seventeenth century on about the problem of understanding how immaterial minds can interact with material bodies. These arguments apply equally to the conception of the soul as an immaterial substance that can exist unembodied.

Another important criticism of the idea of a disembodied soul, however, concerns the question of individuating souls at a time: the synchronic problem. In virtue of what is there one soul or two? If souls are embodied, the bodies individuate. There is one soul per body. But if souls are separated from bodies—existing on their own, apart from bodies—then there is apparently no difference between there being one soul with some thoughts and two souls with half as many thoughts. If there is no difference between there being one soul and two, then there are no souls. So, it seems that the concept of a soul is incoherent.

As we saw in 2b, Aquinas has a response to this problem of distinguishing between one and two unembodied immaterial souls at a single time. Each separated soul had an affinity to the body with which it had been united in premortem life. Even when Smith's soul is disembodied, what makes Smith's soul *Smith's* soul—and not Brown's soul, say—is that Smith's soul has a tendency and potential to be reunited with Smith's body, and not with Brown's body. (But see 3b.) This reply is not available to proponents of immaterial souls, such as Plato or Descartes, who take a human person to be identical to a soul.

Even if we could individuate souls at a time, and thus at a single time distinguish one soul from two souls, there would still be a problem of individuating a soul over time: the diachronic problem. To see this, consider: either souls are subject to change or they are not. Suppose first that souls are not subject to change. In that case, they cannot be the locus of religious life. Religious life consists in part of phenomena like religious conversion and "amendment of life." If souls are immune to change, they can hardly participate in religious conversion or amendment of life. Souls must be subject to change if they are to play their roles in religious life.

So, suppose that souls are subject to change. In that case, the same difficulty that arises for the identity of a person over time also arises for the identity of a soul over time. Just as we asked, *In virtue of what is person 1 at t1 the same person as person 2 at t2?* we can ask, *In virtue of what is disembodied soul 1 at t1 the same soul as disembodied soul 2 at t2?* Consider Augustine before and after his conversion—at t1 and t2, respectively. In virtue of what was the soul at t1 the same soul as the soul at t2? The only answer that I can think of is that the soul at t1 and the soul at t2 were both Augustine's soul. But, of course, that answer is untenable inasmuch as it presupposes sameness of person over time, and sameness of person over time is what we need a criterion of sameness of soul over time to account for. So, it seems that the identity of a person over time cannot be the identity of a soul over time.

The materialistic conceptions of the soul (MacKay 1987; Polkinghorne 1996) do not seem to fare any better. They would seem to succumb to the duplication problem that afflicts the memory criterion (see 3d). But if the Matthews argument (see 3d) rehabilitates the memory criterion, an analogue of that argument could save these materialistic conceptions of the soul.

3b. Sameness of Soul-Body Composite

Aquinas's contribution was to give an account of what happens between death and resurrection in terms of the subsistence of the rational soul. Aquinas's view has the advantage over the substance dualists like Plato and Descartes in that it gives a reason why resurrection should be bodily resurrection: the body is important to make a complete substance.

On the other hand, Aquinas's account buys these advantages at a cost. His account commits him to a new ontological category of being: the rational soul as a subsisting entity that is not a substance. It is not really an individual, but a kind of individual manqué. We can say very little about this new kind of entity except that it fills the bill. It would be desirable to make sense of a Christian doctrine of resurrection without appealing to a new and strange kind of entity, and in section 4, there will be an attempt to do so.

More important, however, is a problem internal to Aquinas's thought. There is a tension in Aquinas, with respect to ontological priority, between his conception of the human being as a composite of soul (form) and body (matter), and his conception of the soul as itself a substantial form that accounts for the identity of a human being through an unembodied period. On the one hand, Aquinas says that the soul without a body is only a fragment, not a human being. So, the human being seems to have ontological priority. On the other hand, he says that the soul is a substantial form that carries our identity and can enjoy the beatific vision on its own; the body is just an expression of its glory. So, the soul alone seems to have ontological priority. The tension arises between whether the human being (the body-soul composite, either part of which is incomplete without the other) or the substantial soul has ontological priority.

The reason this tension threatens the Thomistic view is that Aquinas holds that disembodied souls are individuated by the bodies that they long for and desire reunion with. But if the soul is the substantial form that accounts for the identity of the resurrected person, and if the body is merely matter (potency) of which the soul is the form, then the body of the resurrected human being that rises—*whatever* its matter—will be that human being's body, by definition. As Bynum put it, "God can make the body of Peter out of the dust that was once the body of Paul" (1995, 260). If this is the case, souls cannot be individuated at a time by their yearning for a certain body—because the identity of the body (whose body it is) will depend on the identity of the soul. It is difficult to see how Aquinas can combine the Aristotelian view that matter individuates with his view that the soul is a substantial form that can "subsist"—and experience God—apart from a body.

3c. Sameness of Body

During much of Christian history, the idea of the resurrection of the body was of a literal, material resurrection. The resurrected body was considered to be the same body as the earthly body in the sense that it is composed of (at least some of) the same particles as the earthly body. At the resurrection, it was held, God will reassemble and reanimate the same particles that composed the person's earthly body, and in that way personal identity would be secured in the afterlife.

There are some well-known difficulties with taking the resurrection body to require reassembly of the premortem body. For example, in the early years of Christian martyrdom, there was concern about cannibalism: the problem becomes acute if, say, a hungry soldier eats a captive, who himself has eaten a civilian. So, the soldier's body is composed in part of the captive's, which in turn is composed of the civilian's. The same cells may be parts of three earthly bodies, and there seems to be no principled way for God to decide which parts belong to which postmortem bodies. In light of God's omnipotence and omniscience, however, I doubt that this objection is insurmountable.

Three further difficulties raise more serious logical concerns. Suppose that Jane's body was utterly destroyed, and the atoms that had composed it were spread throughout the universe. Gathering the atoms and reassembling them in their exact premortem positions relative to each other would *not* bring Jane's body back into existence. To see this, consider an analogy. Suppose that one of Augustine's manuscripts had been entirely burned up, and that later God miraculously reassembled the atoms in the manuscript. The reassembled atoms would be a perfect duplicate of the manuscript, but they do not compose the very manuscript that had been destroyed. The reassembled atoms have their positions as a result of God's activity, not of Augustine's. The duplicate manuscript is related to the original manuscript as a duplicate tower of blocks is related to your child's original tower that you accidentally knocked over and then put the blocks back in their original positions. The tower that you built is

not the same one that your child built; the manuscript that God produced is not the same one that Augustine produced (van Inwagen 1992).

The situation with respect to God's reassembling the atoms of a body that had been totally destroyed is similar to God's reassembling the atoms in Augustine's manuscript. If a corpse had not decayed too badly, God could "start it up" again. But if the body had been cremated or had been entirely destroyed, there is no way that *it* could be reconstituted. The most that is metaphysically possible is that God could create a duplicate body out of the same atoms that had composed the original body. The same body that had been destroyed—the same person on the bodily criterion—could not exist again. Not even an omnipotent and omniscient God could bring that very body back into existence. So, the "reassembly" view cannot contribute to an account of the resurrection. But because the preceding argument depends on metaphysical intuitions about bodily identity, perhaps this second argument is not insurmountable either.

There is a third argument, also from van Inwagen (1992), that seems to be logically conclusive against the view that resurrection involves reassembly of a premortem person's atoms. None of the atoms that were part of me in 1960 are part of me now. Therefore, God could gather up all the atoms that were part of me in 1960 and put them in exactly the same relative positions they had in 1960. He could do this without destroying me now. Then, if the reassembly view were correct, God could confront me now with myself as I was in 1960. As van Inwagen points out, each of us could truly say to the other, "I am you." But that is conceptually impossible. Therefore, the reassembly view is wrong.

I should point out that these considerations do not make van Inwagen a skeptic about bodily resurrection. God could accomplish bodily resurrection in some other way, for example, by replacing a person's body with a duplicate right before death or cremation, and the duplicate is what is cremated or buried. This shows that it is logically possible that bodily resurrection, where the resurrected body is the same one as the premortem body, be accomplished by an omnipotent being—even if we lack the conceptual resources to see how. The present point, however, is that resurrected bodies are not produced by God's reassembling the atoms of premortem bodies.

Putting aside van Inwagen's arguments, the final difficulty for bodily resurrection comes from reflection on the following question: How can an earthly body that is subject to decay or destruction by fire be the same body as an incorruptible glorified body? I suggested that if identity of bodies consists of spatiotemporal continuity, and if God could replace the organic cells of a body by incorruptible and glorified cells in a way that preserved spatiotemporal continuity, then a premortem body could be the same body as a postmortem body even though the premortem body is corruptible and the postmortem body is incorruptible.

However, I doubt that one and the same body (or one and the same anything else) can be corruptible during part of its existence and incorruptible during another part of its existence. The reason for my doubt is that being corruptible and being incorruptible concern the persistence conditions of a thing, and a thing has its persistence conditions essentially. To say that a thing is corruptible is to say that there are a range of conditions under which it would go out of existence; to say that a thing is incorruptible is to say that there are no such conditions. It is logically impossible—or at least it seems so—that a single thing is such that there are conditions at one time under which it could go out of existence, and that there are no such conditions at another time under which it could go out of existence. This difficulty could be overcome by not requiring that the (incorruptible) resurrected body be the very same body as the (corruptible) earthly body; see section 4.

3d. The Memory Criterion

Many philosophers find psychological continuity an attractive criterion of personal identity, but there are well-known, and potentially devastating, problems with it. The major problem is called "the duplication problem." The problem is that,

however "in the right way" is spelled out for the causal connections between mental states of Jones now and a future person, two future persons can have mental states caused by Jones's mental states now in the right way. It is logically possible that Jones's memories be transferred to two future persons in exactly the same "right way" (whatever that is). In that case, the memory criterion would hold, per impossibile, that two future persons are Jones. Whatever causal connections hold between the mental states of Jones now and person B in the future could also hold between the mental states of Jones now and a different person C in the future. But it is logically impossible that Jones be both B and C.

To put this point another way: there is an important constraint on any criterion of personal identity. Identity is a one-one relation, and no person can be identical with two distinct future persons. So, any criterion of personal identity that can be satisfied both by person A at t1 and person B at t2 and by person A at t1 and person C at t2 entails that B = C. So, if B is a different person from C, a criterion that allows that A is identical to both is logically untenable. However, if sameness of memories sufficed for sameness of person, one person could become two: A's memories could be transferred to B and C, where B ≠ C, in such a way that B's and C's memories are continuous with A's memories in exactly the same way ("the right way"). It would follow on the memory criterion that A = B and A = C. But since B ≠ C, this is a contradiction. Hence, the memory criterion does not work (Williams 1973a).

The problem of duplication seems insurmountable for the memory criterion. Philosophers have responded to the problem of duplication with rather desperate measures; for example, Jones is the same person as a future person, as long as there are no duplicates. If there are two future persons at t2 related to Jones at t1 in the same way, then Jones is neither. Jones just does not survive until t2; at t2, there are two replicas of Jones, but Jones herself is no longer there. But if only one future person at t2 is related to Jones at t1 in exactly that way, then, according to this response to the duplication problem, Jones is that person at t2. Thus, Jones can be made not to survive by duplication. This sort of move seems to many a most unsatisfying way to think of personal identity.

There may be another way, at least if we allow religious assumptions, to salvage the memory criterion. A religious philosopher may respond to the duplication argument by saying that God would not bring it about (or let it be brought about) that both B and C have A's memories. Thus, God in His goodness would prevent duplication (Locke 1924, II, xxvii, 13). But the memory criterion would still be vulnerable to the charge that, even if God would not allow both B and C to have A's memories, memory would not be a metaphysically sufficient criterion for personal identity. It would still be metaphysically possible for two people, B and C, to have all A's memories, that is, for each to have memories continuous with A's.

However, there is an argument using religious premises that rehabilitates the memory criterion by showing that it is metaphysically impossible for God to bring it about that B and C both have all A's memories. Because this way was suggested to me by Gareth B. Matthews, call it "the Matthews argument." The premises of this argument are explicitly religious. They appeal to God's necessary attributes—namely, that God is essentially just—and to the notion of a judgment after death. If God is essentially just and God judges everyone, and A is a person who deserves punishment, then it would be metaphysically impossible for B and C to have A's memories.

The reason it would be metaphysically impossible for B and C to have A's memories is this: A deserves punishment. God is essentially just and judges everyone. Suppose that B and C both had A's memories (caused in the right way). Whom does God punish? If God punished B but not C, or C but not B, then God would not be essentially just: B and C are related to A in exactly the same way; it is impossible to be just and to judge B and C differently. On the other hand, if God punished both B and C, then there would be twice the punishment that A deserved, and again God would not be essentially just. Either way, supposing that B and C both had A's memories (caused in the right way) violates God's essential justice in judgment. Because God is essentially just, if A deserves punishment, it is metaphysically impossible for God to bring it about that B and C both have A's memories.

If everyone deserves punishment except Christ, then this argument shows that it is metaphysically impossible for God to transfer A's memories to two distinct nondivine people. It is metaphysically impossible for God to transfer Christ's memories to two distinct nondivine people since Christ is divine. The Matthews argument relies on heavy theological assumptions, but it does rescue the memory criterion from the duplication problem.

4.

There is yet another view of human persons, which is compatible with the doctrine of resurrection. Suppose that human persons are purely material substances—constituted by human bodies, but not identical to the bodies that constitute them (Baker 2000). On this view, "the constitution view," something is a person in virtue of having a first-person perspective, and a person is a *human* person in virtue of being constituted by a human body. (I do not distinguish between human organisms and human bodies; the body that constitutes me now is identical to a human organism.) The relation between a person and her body is the same relation that a statue bears to the piece of bronze (say) that makes it up: constitution. So, there are two theoretical ideas—the notion of constitution and the notion of a first-person perspective—that need explication. I'll discuss each of these ideas briefly.

4a. The First-Person Perspective

A first-person perspective is the ability to conceive of oneself as oneself. This is not just the ability to use the first-person pronoun; rather, it requires that one can *conceive of* oneself as the referent of the first-person pronoun independently of any name or description of oneself. In English, this ability is manifested in the use of a first-person pronoun embedded in a clause introduced by a psychological or linguistic verb in a first-person sentence. For example, "I wish that I were a movie star," or "I said that I would do it" or "I wonder how I'll die" all illustrate a first-person perspective. If I wonder how I will die, or I promise that I'll stick with you, then I am thinking of myself as myself; I am not thinking of myself in any third-person way (e.g., not as Lynne Baker, nor as the person who is thinking, nor as her, nor as the only person in the room) at all. Even if I had total amnesia and didn't know my name or anything at all about my past, I could still think of myself as myself. Anything that can wonder how it will die ipso facto has a first-person perspective and thus is a person. In short, any being whatever with the ability to think of itself as itself—whether a divine being, an artificially manufactured being (such as a computer), a human clone, a Martian, anything that has a first-person perspective—is a person.

A being may be conscious without having a first-person perspective. Nonhuman primates and other higher animals are conscious, and they have psychological states such as believing, fearing, and desiring. They have points of view (e.g., "danger in that direction"), but they cannot conceive of themselves as the subjects of such thoughts. They cannot *conceive of* themselves from the first person. (We have every reason to think that they do not wonder how they will die.) So, having psychological states such as beliefs and desires and having a point of view are necessary but not sufficient conditions for being a person. A sufficient condition for being a person—whether human, divine, ape, or silicon-based—is having a first-person perspective. What makes something a person is not the "stuff" it is made of. It does not matter whether something is made of organic material or silicon or, in the case of God, no material stuff at all. If a being has a first-person perspective, it is a person.

Person is an ontological kind whose defining characteristic is a capacity for a first-person perspective. A first-person perspective is the basis of all self-consciousness. It makes possible an inner life, a life of thoughts that one realizes are one's own. The appearance of first-person perspectives in a world makes an ontological difference in that world: a world populated with beings with inner lives is ontologically richer than a world populated with no beings with inner lives. But what is ontologically distinctive about being a person—namely, the capacity for a first-person perspective—does not have to be secured by an immaterial substance like a soul.

4b. Constitution

What distinguishes human persons from other logically possible persons (God, Martians, perhaps computers) is that human persons are constituted by human bodies (i.e., human animals), rather than, say, by Martian green-slime bodies.

Constitution is a very general relation that we are all familiar with (though probably not under that label). A river at any moment is constituted by an aggregate of water molecules. But the river is not identical to the aggregate of water molecules that constitutes it at that moment. Because one and the same river, call it R, is constituted by different aggregates of molecules at different times, the river is not identical to any of the aggregates of water molecules that make it up. So, assuming here the classical conception of identity, according to which if a = b, then necessarily, a = b, constitution is not identity.

Another way to see that constitution is not identity is to notice that even if an aggregate of molecules, A1, actually constitutes R at t1, R might have been constituted by a different aggregate of molecules, A2, at t1. So, constitution is a relation that is in some ways similar to identity, but is not actually identity. If the relation between a person and her body is constitution, then a person is not identical to her body. The relation is more like the relation between a statue and the piece of bronze that makes it up, or between the river and the aggregates of molecules.

The answer to the question What most fundamentally is x? is what I call "x's primary kind." Each thing has its primary-kind property essentially. If x constitutes y, then x and y are of different primary kinds. If x constitutes y, then what "the thing" is is determined by y's primary kind. For example, if a human body constitutes a person, then what there is is a person-constituted-by-a-human-body. So you—a person constituted by a human body—are most fundamentally a person. Person is your primary kind. If parts of your body were replaced by bionic parts until you were no longer human, you would still be a person. You are a person as long as you exist. If you ceased to have a first-person perspective, then you would cease to exist—even if your body was still there.

Whether we are talking about rivers, statues, human persons, or any other constituted thing, the basic idea is this: when certain things of certain kinds (aggregates of water molecules, pieces of marble, human organisms) are in certain circumstances (different ones for different kinds of things), then new entities of different kinds come into existence. The circumstances in which a piece of marble comes to constitute a statue have to do with an artist's intentions, the conventions of the art world, and so on. The circumstances in which a human organism comes to constitute a human person have to do with the development of a (narrowly defined capacity for a) first-person perspective. In each case, new things of new kinds, with new sorts of causal powers, come into being. Because constitution is the vehicle, so to speak, by which things of new kinds come into existence in the natural world, it is obvious that constitution is not identity. Indeed, this conception is relentlessly antireductive.

Although not identity, constitution is a relation of real unity. If x constitutes y at a time, then x and y are not separate things. A person and her body have lots of properties in common: the property of having toenails and the property of being responsible for certain of her actions. But notice: the person has the property of having toenails only because she is constituted by something that could have had toenails even if it had constituted nothing. And her body is responsible for her actions only because it constitutes something that would have been responsible no matter what constituted it.

So, I'll say that the person has the property of having toenails derivatively, and her body has the property of being responsible for certain of her actions derivatively; the body has the property of having toenails nonderivatively, and the person has the property of being responsible for certain of her actions nonderivatively. If x constitutes y, then some of x's properties have their source (so to speak) in y, and some of y's properties have their source in x. The unity of the object x-constituted-by-y is shown by the fact that x and y borrow properties from each other. The idea of having properties derivatively accounts for the otherwise strange fact that if x constitutes y at t, x and y share so many properties even though $x \neq y$

To summarize the general discussion of the idea of constitution: constitution is a very general relation throughout the natural order. Although it is a relation of real unity, it is short of identity. (Identity is necessary; constitution is contingent. Identity is symmetrical; constitution is asymmetrical.) Constitution is a relation that accounts for the appearance of genuinely new kinds of things with new kinds of causal powers. If F and G are primary kinds and Fs constitute Gs, then an inventory of the contents of the world that includes Fs but leaves out Gs is incomplete. Gs are not reducible to Fs.

4c. Human Persons

A *human* person at time t is a person (i.e., a being with a first-person perspective) that is constituted by a human body at t and was constituted by a human body at the beginning of her existence. (I say "was constituted by a human body at the beginning of her existence" to avoid problems raised by the Incarnation. The orthodox Christian view is that the eternal Second Person of the Trinity was identical with the temporal human Jesus of Nazareth, and that that Being was both fully divine and fully human. How this could be so is ultimately a mystery that requires special treatment far beyond the scope of this chapter.)

According to the constitution view, an ordinary human person is a material object in the same way that a statue or a carburetor is a material object. A statue is constituted by, say, a piece of marble, but it is not identical to the piece of marble that constitutes it. The piece of marble could exist in a world in which it was the only occupant, but no statue could. Nothing that is a statue could exist in a world without artists or institutions of art. A human person is constituted by an organism, a member of the species *Homo sapiens,* but is not identical to the organism that constitutes her. The human organism could exist in a world in which no psychological properties whatever were exemplified, but no person could. Nothing that is a person could exist in a world without first-person perspectives. A human organism that develops a first-person perspective comes to constitute a new thing: a person.

Just as different statues are constituted by different kinds of things (pieces of marble, pieces of bronze, etc.), so too different persons are (or may be) constituted by different kinds of things (human organisms, pieces of plastic, Martian matter, or, in the case of God, nothing at all). What makes something a person (no matter what it is "made of") is a first-person perspective; what makes something a piece of sculpture (no matter what it is "made of") is its relation to an art world. A person could start out as a human person and have organic parts replaced by synthetic parts until she was no longer constituted by a *human* body. If the person whose organic parts were replaced by synthetic parts retained her first-person perspective—no matter what was doing the replacing—then she would still exist and still be a person, even with a synthetic body. If she ceased to be a person (i.e., ceased to have a first-person perspective), however, she would cease to exist altogether. To put it more technically, a person's persistence conditions are determined by the property of being a person (i.e., of having a first-person perspective): a human person could cease to be organic without ceasing to exist. (She might have a resurrected body or a bionic body.) But she could not cease to be a person without ceasing to exist.

On the constitution view, then, a human person and the animal that constitutes her differ in persistence conditions without there being any actual physical intrinsic difference between them. The persistence conditions of animals—all animals, human or not—are biological; and the persistence conditions of persons—all persons, human or not—are not biological.

4d. Resurrection on the Constitution View

The constitution view can solve some outstanding conceptual problems about the doctrine of resurrection. The two elements of the constitution view needed to show how resurrection is metaphysically possible are these: (1) human persons are essentially embodied, and (2) human persons essentially have first-person perspectives.

1. Essential embodiment: although human persons cannot exist without some body or other (a body that can support a first-person perspective), they can exist without the bodies that they actually have. We can speak of human persons in the resurrection, where, though still embodied, they do not have human bodies with human organs and DNA. The same persons who had been constituted by earthly bodies can come to be constituted by resurrected bodies. The bodies on earth and in heaven are not the same, but the persons are.

2. Essential first-person perspectives: if a person's first-person perspective were extinguished, the person would go out of existence. What makes a person the individual that she is is her first-person perspective. So, what must persist in the resurrection is the person's first-person perspective—not her soul (there are no souls), and not her body (she may have a new body in the resurrection).

What is needed is a criterion for sameness of first-person perspective over time. In virtue of what does a resurrected person have the same first-person perspective as a certain earthly person who was born in 1800? Although I think that the constitution view solves the synchronic problem of identity noncircularly (Baker 2000), I think that, on anyone's view, there is no informative noncircular answer to the question: In virtue of what do person PI at t1 and person P2 at t2 have the same first-person perspective over time? It is just a primitive, unanalyzable fact that some future person is I, but there is a fact of the matter nonetheless.

The constitution view is compatible with the three features of the Christian doctrine of resurrection mentioned at the outset: embodiment, identity, miracle. In the first place, the constitution view shows why resurrection should be bodily: human persons are essentially embodied, and hence could not exist unembodied. The first-person perspective is an essential property of a person constituted by a body of some kind. A nondivine first-person perspective cannot exist on its own, disembodied. So, the question Why is resurrection bodily? cannot arise. On the interpretation of the doctrine of resurrection according to which a human person exists in some intermediate state between her death and a general resurrection in the future, the constitution view would postulate an intermediate body. (Alternatively, the constitution view is compatible with there being a temporal gap in the person's existence). Because the constitution view does not require that there be the same body for the same person, the problems found with the traditional theories of body are avoided.

In the second place, on the constitution view, it is possible that a future person with a resurrected body is identical to Smith now, and there is a fact of the matter about which, if any, such future person is Smith. To see that there is a fact of the matter about which resurrected person is Smith, we must proceed to the third feature of the doctrine of resurrection.

In the third place, resurrection is a miracle, a gift from God. The constitution view can use this feature to show that there is a fact of the matter about which resurrected person is, say, Smith. The question is this: Which of the resurrected people is Smith? Because the constitution view holds that Smith might have had a different body from the one that he had on earth, he may be constituted by a different (glorified) body in heaven. So, "Smith is the person with body 1" is contingently true if true at all.

Now, according to the traditional doctrine of Providence, God has two kinds of knowledge: free knowledge and natural knowledge. God's free knowledge is knowledge of contingent truths, and His natural knowledge is knowledge of logical and metaphysical necessities. (I'm disregarding the possibility of middle knowledge here.) Again, according to the traditional doctrine of Providence, the obtaining of any contingent state of affairs depends on God's free decree. Whether the person with resurrected body 1, or body 2, or some other body is Smith is a contingent state of affairs. Therefore, which if any of these states of affairs obtains depends on God's free decree. No immaterial soul is needed for there to be a fact of the matter as to whether Smith is the person with resurrected body 1. All that is needed is God's free decree that brings about one contingent state of affairs rather than another. If God decrees that the person with body 1 have Smith's first-person perspective, then Smith is the person with body 1 (Davis 1993, 119–21). So, there is a fact of the matter as to which, if any, of the persons in the Resurrection is Smith, even if we creatures cannot know it. On the Christian idea of Providence, it is well within God's power to bring it about that a certain resurrected person is identical to Smith.

Notice that this use of the doctrine of God's Providence provides for the metaphysical impossibility of Smith's being identical to both the person with body 1 and the person with body 2. For it is part of God's natural knowledge that it is metaphysically impossible for one person to be identical to two persons. And according to the traditional notion of God's power, what is metaphysically impossible is not within God's power to bring about. So, the constitution view excludes the duplication problem.

4e. Advantages of the Constitution View

The constitution view can offer those who believe in immaterial souls (immaterialists) almost everything that they want—without the burden of making sense of how there can be immaterial souls in the natural world. For example, human persons can survive change of body; truths about persons are not exhausted by truths about bodies; persons have causal powers that their bodies would not have if they did not constitute persons; there is a fact of the matter about which, if any, future person is I; persons are not identical to bodies.

The constitution view also has advantages, at least for Christians, over its major materialistic competitor: animalism. (Animalism is the view that a human person is identical to a human organism.) On the constitution view, being a person is not just a contingent property of things that are fundamentally nonpersonal (animals).

On the animalist view, our having first-person perspectives (or any mental states at all) is irrelevant to the kind of being that we are. But the Christian story cannot get off the ground without presuppositions about first-person perspectives. On the human side, without first-person perspectives, there would be no sinners and no penitents. Because a person's repentance requires that she realize that she herself has offended, nothing lacking a first-person perspective could possibly repent. On the divine side: Christ's atonement required that he suffer, and an important aspect of his suffering was his anticipation of his death (e.g., the agony in the Garden of Gethsemane); and his anticipation of his death would have been impossible without a first-person perspective. This part of Christ's mission specifically required a first-person perspective. What is important about us (and Christ) according to the Christian story is that we have first-person perspectives. Given how important the first-person perspective is to the Christian story, Christians have good reason to take our having first-person perspectives to be central to the kind of being that we are.

The second reason for a Christian to endorse the constitution view over animalism is that the constitution view allows that a person's resurrection body may be nonidentical with her earthly biological body. According to the constitution view, it is logically possible that a person have different bodies at different times; whether anyone ever changes bodies or not, the logical possibility is built into the constitution view. By contrast, on the animalist view, a person just is—is identical to—an organism. Whatever happens to the organism happens to the person. On an animalist view, it is logically impossible for you to survive the destruction of your body. So, on an animalist view, if Smith, say, is resurrected, then the organism that was Smith on

earth must persist in heaven. The resurrection body must be that very organism. In that case, any animalist view compatible with Christian resurrection will have implausible features about the persistence conditions for organisms.

Let me elaborate. If, as on the animalist view, a person's postmortem body were identical to her premortem body, then we would have new questions about the persistence conditions for bodies. Non-Christian animalists understand our persistence conditions in terms of continued biological functioning. But Christian animalists who believe in resurrection cannot construe our persistence conditions biologically unless they think that resurrected persons are maintained by digestion, respiration, and so on as earthly persons are. Because postmortem bodies are incorruptible, it seems unlikely that they are maintained by biological processes (like digestion, etc.) as ours are. But if biological processes are irrelevant to the persistence conditions of *resurrected* persons, and if, as animalism has it, biological processes are essential to *our* persistence conditions, then it does not even seem logically possible for a resurrected person to be identical to any of us. Something whose persistence conditions are biological cannot be identical to something whose persistence conditions are not biological.

To put it another way, a Christian animalist who believes in resurrection must hold that earthly bodies, which are corruptible, are identical to resurrection bodies, which are incorruptible. Because I think that biological organisms are essentially corruptible, I do not believe that a resurrection body, which is incorruptible, could be identical to a biological organism. Even if I'm wrong about the essential corruptibility of organisms, however, the fact remains that on Christian animalism, the persistence conditions for organisms would be beyond the purview of biology. A Christian animalist who believed in resurrection would have to allow that organisms can undergo physically impossible changes without ceasing to exist. For example, organisms would disappear at one place (on earth at the place where the death certificate says that they died) and reappear at some other place.

Moreover, death would have to be conceived of in a very unusual way by an animalist who is a Christian: on a Christian animalist view, a person/organism does not really die. For example, God snatches the body away immediately before death and replaces it with a simulacrum that dies (van Inwagen 1992). Alternatively, God makes organisms disappear at one place (on earth at the place where the death certificate says that they died) and reappear at some other place (Zimmerman 1999). In either case, Christian animalists who believed in resurrection would have to suppose that organisms routinely undergo physically impossible changes without ceasing to exist. Platonists would say that the body dies, but the soul never dies; it lives straight on through the body's death. Christian animalists would have to say something even stranger: the body of a resurrected person does not die either, if by "die" we mean cease functioning permanently. Death for human persons who will be resurrected, on this view, would just be an illusion. I do not think that that conception of death comports well with the story of the Crucifixion, which suggests that death is horrendous and not at all illusory.

So, there are several reasons why a Christian should prefer the constitution view to animalism. To make animalism compatible with the doctrine of resurrection, the Christian animalist would have to make two unpalatable moves: she would have to conceive of persistence conditions for organisms as at least partly nonbiological, and she would have to reconceive the death of a human person in a way that did not involve demise of the organism to which the person is allegedly identical.

Perhaps even more important is the fact that, according to animalism, the property of being a person or of having a first-person perspective is just a contingent and temporary property of essentially nonpersonal beings: animalism severs what is most distinctive about us from what we most fundamentally are. On the animalist view, persons qua persons have no ontological significance. I think that these are all good reasons for a Christian to prefer the constitution view to animalism.

5.

The doctrine of resurrection has not received as much philosophical attention as some other aspects of Christian theology (e.g., the problem of evil and the traditional arguments for the existence of God), but views on personal identity suggest intriguing possibilities for identifying conditions under which a premortem person can be identical to a postmortem person. Only if a premortem and postmortem person can be one and the same individual is resurrection even a logical possibility.

REFERENCES

Aquinas, Thomas. 1945. *Summa Theologica* I. Questions 75–89. New York: Random House.

Aristotle. 1941. *De Anima.* In *The Basic Works of Aristotle,* ed. Richard McKeon. New York: Random House.

Baker, Lynne Rudder. 2000. *Persons and Bodies: A Constitution View.* Cambridge, England: Cambridge University Press.

Bynum, Caroline Walker. 1995. *The Resurrection of the Body in Western Christianity.* New York: Columbia University Press.

Cooper, John W. 1989. *Body, Soul and Life Everlasting: Biblical Anthropology and the Monism-Dualism Debate.* Grand Rapids, Mich.: Eerdmans.

Cullman, Oscar. 1973. "Immortality of the Soul or Resurrection of the Dead?" In *Immortality,* ed. Terence Penelhum, 53–85. Belmont: Wadsworth.

Davis, Stephen T. 1993. *Risen Indeed: Making Sense of the Resurrection.* Grand Rapids, Mich.: Eerdmans.

Hick, John. 1994. *Death and Eternal Life.* Louisville, Ky.: Westminster/John Knox.

Locke, John. 1924. *An Essay Concerning Human Understanding,* ed. A. S. Pringle-Pattison. Oxford: Clarendon Press.

MacKay, D. M. 1987. "Brain Science and the Soul." In *The Oxford Companion to the Mind,* ed. Richard L. Gregory, 723–25. Oxford: Oxford University Press.

Polkinghorne, John. 1996. *The Faith of a Physicist: Reflections of a Bottom-up Thinker.* Minneapolis: Fortress Press.

Price, H. H. 1964. "Personal Survival and the Idea of Another World." In *Classical and Contemporary Readings in the Philosophy of Religion,* ed. John Hick, 364–386. Englewood Cliffs, N.J.: Prentice-Hall.

Swinburne, Richard. 1997. *The Evolution of the Soul.* Oxford: Oxford University Press.

van Inwagen, Peter. 1992. "The Possibility of Resurrection." In *Immortality,* ed. Paul Edwards, 242–6. New York: Macmillan. Reprinted from the *International Journal for Philosophy of Religion* 9 (1978).

van Inwagen, Peter. 1995. "Dualism and Materialism: Athens and Jerusalem?" *Faith and Philosophy* 12: 475–88.

Williams, Bernard. 1973. "Bodily Continuity and Personal Identity." In *Problems of the Self,* 19–25. Cambridge, England: Cambridge University Press.

Wolfson, Harry A. 1956–57. "Immortality and Resurrection in the Philosophy of the Church Fathers." *Harvard Divinity School Bulletin* 22: 5–40.

Zimmerman, Dean. 1999. "The Compatibility of Materialism and Survival: The 'Falling Elevator' Model." *Faith and Philosophy* 16: 194–212.

VII.5

A Hindu Theory of Life, Death, and Reincarnation

PRASANNATMA DAS

When he wrote this article, Prasannatma Das as a young Hindu philosopher studying at the Krishna Temple in Vrindavan, India. In this essay he describes the basic Hindu view of karma—the doctrine that says the way we live in this life will determine our initial state in the next life—and reincarnation—the notion that the same person lives in a different body in future lives based on the idea of karma. Prasannatma Das appeals to the Bhagavad Gita, the most sacred of Hindu scriptures, for his exposition. Lord Krishna, the main speaker in that work, is viewed by Hindus as an avatar (manifestation) of God. As with most major religions, there are many versions of Hinduism. This is one important Hindu version of the meaning of life and death, but not the only one. The term cosmogonal in the quotation from Thoreau refers to the origin of the world.

A HINDU VIEW OF LIFE AND DEATH

In a previous age, there lived a wise king named Yudhisthira. Having been banished by an evil cousin, he and his four brothers were wandering in a forest. One day the youngest brother went to get water from a nearby lake. When, after a time, he did not come back, the next brother went. He did

not come back either. Twice more this happened until finally Yudhisthira himself went. He came to the lake and was about to drink from it when suddenly a voice boomed forth, "Do not drink this water. I am the owner of this lake, and if you drink this water, you shall die like your brothers have before you!" Yudhisthira then saw the lifeless bodies of his brothers lying nearby. The voice continued. "You may drink of this water only on the condition that you answer my questions. If you

This essay was commissioned for the first edition of *Life & Death,* ed. Louis Pojman (Jones & Bartlett, 1993) and is reprinted here by permission of the author. All references are to the Bhagavad Gita, translated by A. C. Bhaktivedanta Swami Prabhupada (Los Angeles: The Bhaktivedanta Book Trust, 1983).

answer them correctly, you and your brothers shall live. If you fail, then you too shall die."

The voice then presented a series of questions to the king, all of which he answered perfectly. One of these questions was, "Of all the amazing things in this world, what is the most amazing?" The king replied, "The most amazing thing is that although everyone sees his parents dying, and everything around him dying, still we live as though we will live forever. This is truly amazing."

It is indeed amazing that even in the face of inevitable death, few perceive the urgency of our predicament; however, in every culture and tradition there have been those thoughtful souls who have done so. Within the Hindu tradition many such seekers have found the teachings of Lord Krishna as presented in the *Bhagavad Gita* to be a source of knowledge and inspiration. Appearing as an episode in the great epic of ancient India, the *Mahabharata,* the *Bhagavad Gita* is one of the most profound theological dialogues known to man. Henry David Thoreau once said, "In the morning I bathe my intellect in the stupendous and cosmogonal philosophy of the *Bhagavad Gita*, in comparison with which our modern world and its literature seem puny and trivial."

The first message of Lord Krishna's teaching in the *Bhagavad Gita* is that we are not these bodies. The body is constantly changing; we once had the body of a small baby, then that of a child, of an adult, of an old person, and eventually the body will return to the dust from whence it came. Yet when we look in the mirror we think that this body is what we are.

But what are we really? Krishna explains that we are the eternal soul within the body and what we call death is merely the soul leaving one body and going elsewhere:

> Never was there a time when I did not exist, nor you, nor all these kings; nor in the future shall any of these cease to be.
>
> As the embodied soul continuously passes, in this body, from boyhood to youth to old age, the soul similarly passes into another body at the time of death.

A sober person is not bewildered by such a change.

> For the soul there is neither birth nor death at any time. He has not come into being, does not come into being, and will not come into being. He is unborn, eternal, ever-existing, and primeval. He is not slain when the body is slain.
>
> As a person puts on new garments, giving up old and useless ones, the soul similarly accepts new material bodies, giving up old and useless ones. (2.12–13, 20, 22)

Krishna is explaining that we are not these bodies; we are the soul inside. I am not a twenty-year-old college student about to fail his philosophy course, but rather I am an eternal spirit-soul who, out of ignorance of his true nature, now identifies himself with the temporary forms of this world. When I enter a new body, I remain the same person.

For example, imagine a candle over which a series of filters are placed; the light appears to be changing according to the color of the filter obscuring it—blue, green, etc. But the original source of the light, the flame, is not changing, only the covering is. In the same way, the soul does not change, only the covering, the body, changes.

Sometimes at night we look up at the sky and see that the clouds are luminous. From the glowing of the clouds we can understand that because the moon is behind them, the clouds themselves appear to be luminous. Similarly when examining this body we can infer the existence of the soul by its symptom consciousness, which pervades the body and gives it the appearance of being alive.

Another basic teaching of the *Bhagavad Gita* is the law of karma, which states that for every action there is a corresponding reaction, or "whatever goes around, comes around." Our situation in this life was caused by the activities and desires of our previous lives. Similarly our future existence—our body, education, amount of wealth, happiness and distress, etc., will be determined by how we live now. If we harm others then we must suffer in return, and if we do good then we correspondingly enjoy. Moreover, we are given a body which suits our consciousness. If, like an animal, a human spends his life eating, sleeping, mating, and defending, ignoring his higher capacities, then he may be placed into the body of an animal. At the time of death the consciousness we have cultivated during our life will carry us, the soul, to our next body. "Whatever state of being one remembers when he quits his body, that state he will attain without fail." (8.6)

The goal is not to come back to this world at all but to attain the supreme destination:

> From the highest planet in the material world down to the lowest, all are places of misery wherein repeated birth and death take place. But one who attains to My abode . . . never takes birth again. (8.16)

Death is perceived according to the quality of one's existence. The ignorant see death as something to be feared. They have material desires, and death will defeat them. Those who are seeking wisdom understand death as an impetus to live correctly, as a time when their knowledge will be put to test. The most amazing thing in this world is that although everyone knows they are going to die, they still act as though they will live forever. Imagine a person who has received an eviction notice—he must vacate his apartment in two weeks. If he promptly prepared for this, and found another place to go, he would not be in anxiety. Unfortunately, even though our eviction notice was given at the time of birth, very few take heed.

Krishna states:

> What is night for all living beings is the time of awakening for the self-controlled, and the time of awakening for all beings is the night for the introspective sage. (2.69)

There are different types of activities which have different values. There are pious activities which lead to taking birth in a situation of relative enjoyment, there are impious activities which lead to suffering and ignorance, and there are spiritual activities which lead one to God. Such spiritual activities are called *yoga*. (*Yoga* does not mean Indian gymnastics but actually refers to the process of reuniting one's self with God.)

This yoga, or real religious life, is not just a passive activity, but is an active cultivation. If a farmer wants to harvest crops, he must begin working early in the season; plowing the fields, planting seeds, watering, weeding, etc. The fruits of his labor will manifest themselves at harvest time. Similarly, one who desires to attain to perfection must engage in a cultivation of the soul which will yield the harvest of spiritual perfection. When death comes, he will taste the fruit of his endeavor.

In this world there is nothing so sublime and pure as transcendental knowledge. Such knowledge is the mature fruit of all mysticism. One who has become accomplished in the practice of devotional service enjoys this knowledge within himself in due course of time. "That is the way of the spiritual and godly life, after attaining which a person is not bewildered. If one is in this situation even at the hour of death, one can enter into the kingdom of God." (4.38; 2.72)

Death will come. No situation in this world is permanent. All changes. Whether a table, a car, a human body, a civilization, or a mountain, everything comes into being, remains for some time, and then finally dwindles and disappears. What of this world can survive the passage of time? As Krishna says, "One who has been born is sure to die." (2.27) Of this there is no doubt.

Yet many people do not see the urgency of our situation. "Yes, I know one day I shall have to die; but for now let me eat, drink, have fun, and get a big bank balance," they think. Dedicated to the pursuit of the temporary phenomena of this world, living a life of vanity, they die like ignorant animals without higher knowledge. They and their fantasies are put to ruin. Their valuable human form of life with its great potential of knowledge and self-realization is wasted.

On the other hand, a thoughtful person understands the reality of this world, and, like a student who knows he must pass a test before he can graduate, prepares himself. This process of preparation begins with inquiry. Who am I? When this body is finished, what happens to me? Why do I exist?

How can I be happy? By nature the eternal soul is full of happiness and knowledge. But now that eternal, blissful, fully cognizant being is something like a fish out of water. The lost creature will not be happy until it is placed back into the water. Giving the fish a new car or expensive jewelry will not rectify its problem; it will not become happy in this way. So too, no degree of rearranging this material world will solve our problems; we will not be satisfied until we are back in the spiritual world. Thus a wise person is not interested in attaining any of the tempting but temporary offerings of this world, knowing that they have a beginning and an end. As the founder of Christianity pointed out, "Seek ye first the kingdom of God, and all these things will be added unto you" (Luke 12.31). Therefore, "The yogis,* abandoning attachment, act . . . only for the sake of purification." (5.11).

The sage is not interested in attaining temporary things like fame, adoration or distinction.

> An intelligent person does not take part in the sources of misery, which are done to contact with the material senses . . . such pleasures have a beginning and an end, and so the wise man does not delight in them. (5.22)

He does not mind leaving this world because he is not attached to it. Rather he is interested in things with real value. Krishna lists some qualities which a thoughtful person might cultivate:

> Humility; pridelessness; non-violence; tolerance; simplicity approaching a bona fide spiritual master; cleanliness; steadiness; self-control; the perception of the evil of birth, death, old age, and disease; detachment; freedom from entanglement with children, wife, home and the rest; even-mindedness amid

pleasant and unpleasant events; constant and unalloyed devotion to Me; aspiring to live in a solitary place; detachment from the general mass of people; accepting the importance of self-realization; and philosophical search for the Absolute Truth. . . . (13.8–12)

A yogi has no desire to fulfill in this world. Thus he is not attached to it. Thus he does not mind leaving it. Thus he has no fear of death.

Since he has no personal desire in this world and has faith in God, he welcomes death in the same way that the kitten welcomes the jaws of the mother cat, whereas they are feared by the mouse. Krishna states:

> To those who are constantly devoted to serving Me with love, I give the understanding by which they can come back to Me.
>
> To show them special mercy, I, dwelling in their hearts, destroy with the shining lamp of knowledge the darkness born of ignorance. (10.10–11)

For those of us who are not enlightened beings, the fact that we must die can serve as an impetus to reach that higher transcendental state; what have we to lose? If we are wrong in our hopes, and death does indeed end all, then have we lost anything by our effort? And if our hopes are correct, then certainly we have all to gain.

A faithful man who is dedicated to transcendental knowledge and who subdues his senses is eligible to achieve such knowledge, and having achieved it he quickly attains the supreme spiritual peace.

When one is enlightened with the knowledge by which [ignorance] is destroyed, then his knowledge reveals everything, as the sun lights up everything in the daytime. (4.39, 5.16)

---

*Yogis are holy men. ED.

Bibliography

General

Anderson, Pamela, and Beverly Clack. *Feminist Philosophy of Religion: Critical Readings.* London: Routledge, 2004.

Craig, William Lane, and J. P. Moreland. *Philosophical Foundations for a Christian Worldview.* Downers Grove, IL: InterVarsity Press, 2003.

Davies, Brian. *Philosophy of Religion: A Guide and Anthology.* New York: Oxford University Press, 2000.

Flint, Thomas, and Michael Rea. *The Oxford Handbook of Philosophical Theology.* Oxford, Eng.: Oxford University Press, 2008.

Harrison, Jonathan. *God, Freedom and Immortality.* Aldershot, Eng.: Ashgate Publishing Co., 1999.

Jantzen, Grace. *Becoming Divine: Toward a Feminist Philosophy of Religion.* Bloomington, IN: Indiana University Press, 1999.

Martin, Michael. *Atheism.* Philadelphia, PA: Temple University Press, 1990.

Murray, Michael. *Reason for the Hope Within.* Grand Rapids, MI: Eerdmans, 1998.

Murray, Michael, and Michael Rea. *Introduction to Philosophy of Religion.* Cambridge, Eng.: Cambridge University Press, 2008.

Pojman, Louis. *Philosophy of Religion.* New York: McGraw-Hill, 2000.

Rea, Michael, ed. *Oxford Readings in Philosophical Theology,* 2 vols. Oxford, Eng.: Oxford University Press, 2009.

Rowe, William. *Philosophy of Religion: An Introduction.* Belmont, CA: Wadsworth, 1978.

Wainwright, William J. *Philosophy of Religion.* Belmont, CA: Wadsworth, 1998.

___. *The Oxford Handbook of Philosophy of Religion.* Oxford, Eng.: Oxford University Press, 2005.

Part I: The Concept of God

Concepts of God and the Ultimate

Hartshorne, Charles. *The Divine Reality.* New Haven, CT: Yale University Press, 1948.

Hick, John. *An Interpretation of Religion: Human Responses to the Transcendent,* 2d. New Haven, CT: Yale University Press, 1989.

Johnston, Mark. *Saving God: Religion after Idolatry.* Princeton, NJ: Princeton University Press, 2009.

Miller, David. *The New Polytheism.* New York: Harper & Row Publishers, 1974.

Morris, Thomas V. *Our Idea of God.* Notre Dame, IN: University of Notre Dame Press, 1991.

Pinnock, Clark, et al. *The Openness of God: A Biblical Challenge to the Traditional Understanding of God.* Downers Grove, IL: InterVarsity Press, 1994.

Tessier, Linda J., ed. *Concepts of the Ultimate.* New York: St. Martin's Press, 1989.

Classical Theistic Attributes

Davis, Stephen T. *Logic and the Nature of God.* Grand Rapids, MI: Eerdmans, 1983.

Fischer, John M., ed. *God, Foreknowledge, and Freedom.* Palo Alto, CA: Stanford University Press, 1989.

Geach, Peter. *Providence and Evil.* Cambridge, MA: Cambridge University Press, 1977.

Hoffman, Joshua, and Gary Rosenkrantz. *Divine Attributes.* New York: Wiley-Blackwell, 2002.

Kenny, Anthony, ed. *Aquinas: A Collection of Critical Essays.* New York: Doubleday, 1969.

Kretzmann, Norman. "Ominiscience and Immutability." *Journal of Philosophy* 63(1966):409–21.

Pike, Nelson. *God and Time.* Ithaca, NY: Cornell University Press, 1970.

Stump, Eleonore, and Norman Kretzmann. "Eternity." *Journal of Philosophy* 78(August 1981):429–58.

Swinburne, Richard. *The Coherence of Theism,* rev. ed. Oxford, Eng.: Oxford University Press, 1993.

Wierenga, Edward R. *The Nature of God: An Inquiry into Divine Attributes.* Ithaca, NY: Cornell University Press, 1989.

Wolterstorff, Nicholas. "God Everlasting." In *God and the Good,* eds. C. Orlebeke and L. Smedes. Grand Rapids, MI: Eerdmans, 1975.

Part II: Traditional Arguments for the Existence of God

Hick, John. *Arguments for the Existence of God.* London: Macmillan, 1971.

Mackie, J. L. *The Miracle of Theism.* Oxford, Eng.: Oxford University Press, 1982.

Swinburne, Richard. *The Existence of God,* 2nd ed. Oxford, Eng.: Oxford University Press, 2004.

The Ontological Argument

Hartshorne, Charles. *The Logic of Perfection.* LaSalle, IL: Open Court, 1962.

___. *Anselm's Discovery.* LaSalle, IL: Open Court, 1965.

Oppy, Graham. *Ontological Arguments and Belief in God.* New York: Cambridge University Press, 1995.

Plantinga, Alvin, ed. *The Ontological Argument from St. Anselm to Contemporary Philosophers.* Garden City, NY: Doubleday, 1965.

The Cosmological Argument

Craig, William Lane. *The Cosmological Argument from Plato to Leibniz.* New York: Barnes & Noble, 1980.

___. *The Kalām Cosmological Argument.* New York: Harper & Row, 1980.

Gale, Richard. *On the Nature and Existence of God.* Cambridge, Eng.: Cambridge University Press, 1992.

Moreland, J. P., and Kai Nielsen, eds. *Does God Exist?: The Great Debate.* Nashville, TN: Thomas Nelson, 1990.

Rowe, William. *The Cosmological Argument.* Princeton, NJ: Princeton University Press, 1971.

The Teleological Argument

Barr, Stephen. *Modern Physics and Ancient Faith.* Notre Dame, IN: University of Notre Dame Press, 2003.

Manson, Neil. *God and Design.* New York: Routledge & Kegan Paul, 2003.

Salmon, Wesley. "Religion and Science: A New Look at Hume's Dialogue." *Philosophical Studies* 33(1978):145.

Swinburne, Richard. "The Argument from Design." *Philosophy* 43(1968):199–212.

___. "The Argument from Design—A Defence." *Religious Studies* 8(1972):193–205.

Part III: Evil and the Hiddenness of God

Overview

Adams, Marilyn McCord., and Robert Merrihew Adams, eds. *The Problem of Evil.* Oxford, Eng.: Oxford University Press, 1990.

Gale, Richard. *On the Nature and Existence of God.* Cambridge, Eng.: Cambridge University Press, 1991.

Howard-Snyder, Daniel, and Paul Moser. *Divine Hiddenness: New Essays.* Bloomington, IN: Indiana University Press, 2001.

Lewis, C. S. *The Problem of Pain.* London: Geoffrey Bles, 1940. Clearly and cogently written.

Peterson, Michael, ed. *The Problem of Evil.* Notre Dame, IN: University of Notre Dame Press, 1992.

The Problems of Evil and Divine Hiddenness

Draper, Paul. "Pain and Pleasure: An Evidential Problem for Theists," *Nous* 23(1989).

Hick, John. *Evil and the God of Love.* London: Macmillan, 1966. A classic defense of theodicy.

Howard-Snyder, Daniel, ed. *The Evidential Argument from Evil.* Bloomington, IN: Indiana University Press, 1996.

___. *The Miracle of Theism*. Oxford, Eng.: Oxford University Press, 1982, chap. 9.

McCloskey, H. J. "God and Evil." *The Philosophical Quarterly* 10(1960):97–114.

Schellenberg, J. L. *Divine Hiddenness and Human Reason*. Ithaca, NY: Cornell University Press. 1993.

Responses

Adams, Marilyn McCord. *Horrendous Evils and the Goodness of God*. Ithaca, NY: Cornell University Press, 1999.

Moser, Paul. *The Elusive God*. Cambridge: Cambridge University Press, 2009.

Murray, Michael. *Nature Red Tooth and Claw: Theism and the Problem of Animal Suffering*. New York: Oxford University Press, 2008.

Pike, Nelson. "Human on Evil." *The Philosophical Review* 72(1963):180–97.

Plantinga, Alvin. *God, Freedom and Evil*. New York: Harper & Row, 1974.

Plantinga, Alvin. *The Nature of Necessity*. Oxford, Eng.: Clarendon Press, 1974, chap. 9.

Stump, Eleonore. *Wandering in Darkness: Narrative and the Problem of Suffering*. Oxford, Eng.: Oxford University Press, 2010.

Van Inwagen, Peter. *The Problem of Evil*. Oxford, Eng.: Oxford University Press, 2006.

Van Inwagen, Peter, ed. *Christian Faith and the Problem of Evil*. Grand Rapids, MI: Wm. B. Eerdmans, 2004.

Wainwright, William J. "God and the Necessity of Physical Evils." *Sophia* 11(1972):16–9.

Wykstra, Stephen J. "The Humean Obstacle to Evidential Arguments from Suffering: On Avoiding the Evils of 'Appearance.'" *International Journal of Philosophy of Religion* 16(1984).

Part IV: Religion and Experience
Mystical Experience and the Perception of God

Alston, William. *Perceiving God*. Ithaca, NY: Cornell University Press, 1991.

Freud, Sigmund. *The Future of an Illusion*. New York: Norton, 1961.

Gale, Richard. "Mysticism and Philosophy." *Journal of Philosophy* 57(1960). (Republished in *Contemporary Philosophy of Religion*, eds. Steven M. Cahn and David Shatz. Oxford, Eng.: Oxford University Press, 1982.)

___. *On the Nature and Existence of God*. Cambridge, MA: Cambridge University Press, 1991.

Gavrilyuk, Paul, and Sarah Coakley, eds. *The Spiritual Senses*. New York: Cambridge University Press, 2012.

James, William. *Varieties of Religious Experience*. New York: Modern Library, 1902. This marvelous treatise is the definitive work on the subject.

Jantzen, Grace. *Julian of Norwich: Mystic and Theologian*. New York: Paulist Press, 1968.

Martin, C. B. "A Religious Way of Knowing." *Mind* 61(1952). A watershed article. (Reprinted and expanded in his book *Religious Belief*. Ithaca, NY: Cornell University Press, 1959, chap. 5.)

Mavrodes, George. *Belief in God*. New York: Random House, 1970, chap. 3.

Otto, Rudolf. *The Idea of the Holy*, trans. J. W. Harvey. Oxford, Eng.: Oxford University Press, 1923. A classic study of religious experience.

Stace, Walter T., ed. *The Teaching of the Mystics*. New York: New American Library, 1960.

Wainwright, William. "Mysticism and Sense Perception." *Religious Studies* 9(1973).

___. *Mysticism*. Madison, WI: University of Wisconsin Press, 1981.

Miracles and Testimony

Broad, C. D. "Hume's Theory of the Credibility of Miracles." *Proceedings of the Aristotelian Society* 17(1916–17).

Flew, Antony. "Miracles." In *Encyclopedia of Philosophy*, ed. Paul Edwards. New York: Macmillan, 1966.

Holland, R. F. "The Miraculous." *American Philosophical Quarterly* 2(1965):43–51.

Lewis, C. S. *Miracles*. New York: Macmillan, 1947.

Nowell-Smith, Patrick. "Miracles." In *New Essays in Philosophical Theology*, eds. Antony Flew and Alasdair Macintyre. London: Macmillan, 1955.

Rowe, William. *Philosophy of Religion*. Belmont, CA: Wadsworth, 1978, chap. 9.

Smart, Ninian. *Philosophers and Religious Truth*. London: SCM, 1964, chap. 2.

Swinburne, Richard. *The Concept of Miracle*. London: Macmillan, 1970.

Religion and Science

Barbour, Ian. *Religion and Science*. San Francisco, CA: Harper San Francisco, 1997.

___. *When Science Meets Religion*. San Francisco, CA: Harper San Francisco, 2000.

Murphy, Nancy. *Theology in the Age of Scientific Reasoning*. Ithaca, NY: Cornell University Press, 1990.

Polkinghorne, John. *Belief in God in an Age of Science*. New Haven, CT: Yale University Press, 1998.

Part V: Faith and Rationality

The Nature of Faith

Plantinga, Alvin, and Nicholas Wolterstorff, eds. *Faith and Rationality*. Notre Dame, IN: University of Notre Dame Press, 1983.

Swinburne, Richard. *Faith and Reason*. Oxford, Eng: Clarendon Press, 1981.

Pragmatic Justification of Religious Belief

Jordan, Jeff, ed. *Gambling on God: Essays on Pascal's Wager*. Lanham, MD: Rowman & Littlefield, 1994.

Pojman, Louis. *Religious Belief and the Will*. London: Routledge & Kegan Paul, 1986.

Rationality and Justified Religious Belief

Davis, Stephen. *Faith, Skepticism and Evidence*. Lewisburg, PA: Bucknell University Press, 1978.

Delaney, C. F., ed. *Rationality and Religious Belief*. Notre Dame, IN: University of Notre Dame Press, 1978.

Mavrodes, George. *Belief in God*. New York: Random House, 1970. A clear presentation of religious epistemology.

Mitchell, Basil. *The Justification of Religious Belief*. London: Macmillan, 1973.

Peterson, Michael, William Hasker, Bruce Reichenbach, and David Basinger. *Reason and Religious Belief*. New York: Oxford University Press, 1991.

Plantinga, Alvin. *Warranted Christian Belief*. Oxford, Eng.: Oxford University Press, 2000.

Part VI: Religious Pluralism

Dean, Thomas, ed. *Religious Pluralism and Truth: Essays on Cross-Cultural Philosophy of Religion*. Albany, NY: SUNY Press, 1995.

Heim, S. Mark. *Salvations: Truth and Difference in Religion*. Maryknoll, NY: Orbis, 1993.

Hick, John. *God and the Universe of Faiths*. London: Macmillan, 1973.

___. *An Interpretation of Religion: Human Responses to the Transcendent*. New Haven, CT: Yale University Press, 1989.

___. Advisory ed. *Religious Pluralism*. A special issue of *Faith and Philosophy* 5:4 (October 1988).

Hick, John, and Paul Knitter, eds. *The Myth of Christian Uniqueness: Towards a Pluralistic Theology of Religions*. Maryknoll, NY: Orbis, 1987.

Ogden, Schubert. *Is There Only One True Religion or Are There Many?* Dallas, TX: SMU Press, 1992.

___. *Doing Theology Today*. Valley Forge, PA: Trinity Press, 1996.

Senor, Thomas, ed. *The Rationality of Belief and the Plurality of Faith*. Ithaca, NY: Cornell University Press, 1996.

Smith, Wilfred Cantwell. *Towards a World Theology*. Philadelphia, PA: Westminster, 1981.

Yandell, Keith. "Religious Experience and Rational Appraisal." *Religious Studies* 8 (June 1974).

Part VII: Death and Immortality

Ducasse, C. J. *A Critical Examination of the Belief in Life after Death*. Springfield, IL: Thomas, 1961.

Edwards, Paul, ed. *Immortality*. New York: Macmillan, 1992.

Flew, Antony. "Immortality." In *Encyclopedia of Philosophy*, ed. Paul Edwards. New York: Free Press, 1965.

Geach, Peter. *God and the Soul*. London: Routledge & Kegan Paul, 1969.

Johnson, Raynor. *The Imprisoned Splendor*. London: Hodder and Stoughton, 1953.

Moody, Raymond. *Life after Life*. New York: Bantam Books, 1976.

Penelhum, Terrence. *Survival and Disembodied Existence*. London: Routledge & Kegan Paul, 1970.

Perry, John. *Personal Identity and Immortality*. Indianapolis, IN: Hackett, 1979.

Purtill, Richard. *Thinking about Religion*. Englewood Cliffs, NJ: Prentice Hall, 1978, chaps. 9 and 10.

Quinton, Anthony. "The Soul." *Journal of Philosophy* 59(1962):393–409.